The World's Top 30 Multinational Companies

1. General Electric (United States)

2. Vodafone Group PLC (United Kingdom)

3. General Motors (United States)

4. BP PLC (United Kingdom)

5. Royal Dutch/Shell Group (UK, Netherlands)

6. ExxonMobil (United States)

7. Toyota Motor Corporation (Japan)

8. Ford Motor (United States)

9. Total (France)

10. Eléctricité de France (France)

11. France Télécom (France)

12. Volkswagen (Germany)

13. RWE Group (Germany)

14. Chevron Corp. (United States)

15. E.ON (Germany)

*Ranked by 2005 foreign assets, according to United Nations Conference on Trade and Development (UNCTAD)
www.unctad.org

16. Suez (France)

17. Deutsche Telekom AG (Germany)

18. Siemens AG (Germany)

19. Honda Motor Company Limited (Japan)

20. Hutchison Whampoa (Hong Kong, China)

21. Procter & Gamble (United States)

22. Sanofi-Aventis (France)

23. ConocoPhillips (United States)

24. BMW AG (Germany)

25. Nissan Motor Company Limited (Japan)

26. Daimler Chrysler (United States, Germany)

27. Nestlé SA (Switzerland)

28. Pfizer Inc. (United States)

29. ENI (Italy)

30. IBM (United States)

International Financial Management

The Prentice Hall Series in Finance

Alexander/Sharpe/Bailey
Fundamentals of Investments

Andersen
Global Derivatives: A Strategic Risk Management Perspective

Bear/Moldonado-Bear
Free Markets, Finance, Ethics, and Law

Berk/DeMarzo
Corporate Finance*

Berk/DeMarzo
Corporate Finance: The Core*

Bierman/Smidt
The Capital Budgeting Decision: Economic Analysis of Investment Projects

Bodie/Merton/Cleeton
Financial Economics

Click/Coval
The Theory and Practice of International Financial Management

Copeland/Weston/Shastri
Financial Theory and Corporate Policy

Cornwall/Vang/Hartman
Entrepreneurial Financial Management

Cox/Rubinstein
Options Markets

Dorfman
Introduction to Risk Management and Insurance

Dietrich
Financial Services and Financial Institutions: Value Creation in Theory and Practice

Dufey/Giddy
Cases in International Finance

Eakins
Finance (a.learn eBook)

Eiteman/Stonehill/Moffett
Multinational Business Finance

Emery/Finnerty/Stowe
Corporate Financial Management

Fabozzi
Bond Markets, Analysis and Strategies

Fabozzi/Modigliani
Capital Markets: Institutions and Instruments

Fabozzi/Modigliani/Jones/Ferri
Foundations of Financial Markets and Institutions

Finkler
Financial Management for Public, Health, and Not-for-Profit Organizations

Francis/Ibbotson
Investments: A Global Perspective

Fraser/Ormiston
Understanding Financial Statements

Geisst
Investment Banking in the Financial System

Gitman
Principles of Managerial Finance*

Gitman
Principles of Managerial Finance— Brief Edition*

Gitman/Joehnk
Fundamentals of Investing*

Gitman/Madura
Introduction to Finance

Guthrie/Lemon
Mathematics of Interest Rates and Finance

Haugen
The Inefficient Stock Market: What Pays Off and Why

Haugen
Modern Investment Theory

Haugen
The New Finance: Overreaction, Complexity, and Uniqueness

Holden
Excel Modeling and Estimation in the Fundamentals of Corporate Finance

Holden
Excel Modeling and Estimation in the Fundamentals of Investments

Holden
Excel Modeling and Estimation in Investments

Holden
Excel Modeling and Estimation in Corporate Finance

Hughes/MacDonald
International Banking: Text and Cases

Hull
Fundamentals of Futures and Options Markets

Hull
Options, Futures, and Other Derivatives

Hull
Risk Management and Financial Institutions

Keown
Personal Finance: Turning Money into Wealth

Keown/Martin/Petty/Scott
Financial Management: Principles and Applications

Keown/Martin/Petty/Scott
Foundations of Finance: The Logic and Practice of Financial Management

Kim/Nofsinger
Corporate Governance

Levy/Post
Investments

May/May/Andrew
Effective Writing: A Handbook for Finance People

Madura
Personal Finance

Marthinsen
Risk Takers: Uses and Abuses of Financial Derivations

McDonald
Derivatives Markers

McDonald
Fundamentals of Derivatives Markets

Megginson
Corporate Finance Theory

Melvin
International Money and Finance

Mishkin/Eakins
Financial Markets and Institutions

Moffett
Cases in International Finance

Moffett/Stonehill/Eiteman
Fundamentals of Multinational Finance

Nofsinger
Psychology of Investing

Ogden/Jen/O'Connor
Advanced Corporate Finance

Pennacchi
Theory of Asset Pricing

Rejda
Principles of Risk Management and Insurance

Schoenebeck
Interpreting and Analyzing Financial Statements

Scott/ Martin/ Petty/Keown/Thatcher
Cases in Finance

Seiler
Performing Financial Studies: A Methodological Cookbook

Shapiro
Capital Budgeting and Investment Analysis

Sharpe/Alexander/Bailey
Investments

Solnik/McLeavey
Global Investments

Stretcher/Michael
Cases in Financial Management

Titman/Martin
Valuation: The Art and Science of Corporate Investment Decisions

Trivoli
Personal Portfolio Management: Fundamentals and Strategies

Van Horne
Financial Management and Policy

Van Horne
Financial Market Rates and Flows

Van Horne/Wachowicz
Fundamentals of Financial Management

Vaughn
Financial Planning for the Entrepreneur

Weston/Mitchel/Mulherin
Takeovers, Restructuring, and Corporate Governance

Winger/Frasca
Personal Finance

* denotes  titles   Log onto www.myfinancelab.com to learn more

International Financial Management

Geert Bekaert

Columbia University and the National Bureau of Economic Research

Robert J. Hodrick

Columbia University and the National Bureau of Economic Research

Pearson Education International

Executive Editor: Donna Battista
Editorial Director: Sally Yagan
Editor in Chief: Denise Clinton
Product Development Manager: Ashley Santora
Assistant Editor: Mary Kate Murray
Senior Marketing Manager: Andrew Watts
Marketing Assistant: Ian Gold
Permissions Project Manager: Charles Morris
Senior Managing Editor: Judy Leale
Production Project Manager: Kelly Warsak
Senior Operations Specialist: Arnold Vila
Operations Specialist: Michelle Klein
Cover Designer: Margaret Kenselaar
Cover Photo: Getty Images
Manager, Cover Visual Research & Permissions: Karen Sanatar
Composition: GGS Book Services
Full-Service Project Management: Heidi Allgair/GGS Book Services
Printer/Binder: Edwards Brothers
Cover Printer: Coral Graphics
Typeface: 10/12 Times

Credits and acknowledgments borrowed from other sources and reproduced, with permission, in this textbook appear on appropriate page within text.

If you purchased this book within the United States or Canada you should be aware that it has been wrongfully imported without the approval of the Publisher or the Author.

Pearson Education Ltd., London
Pearson Education Singapore, Pte. Ltd
Pearson Education, Canada, Inc.
Pearson Education–Japan
Pearson Education Australia PTY, Limited

Pearson Education North Asia, Ltd., Hong Kong
Pearson Educación de Mexico, S.A. de C.V.
Pearson Education Malaysia, Pte. Ltd
Pearson Education Upper Saddle River, New Jersey

10 9 8 7 6 5 4 3 2 1
ISBN-13: 978-0-13-605490-0
ISBN-10: 0-13-605490-0

To my world of women, Emma, Britt, Laura and Ann
— Geert

To my wife, Laurie, and my children, Reid and Courtney,
with love — Bob

BRIEF CONTENTS

CONTENTS

PART II   INTERNATIONAL PARITY CONDITIONS AND EXCHANGE RATE DETERMINATION   178

PART V   MANAGING ONGOING OPERATIONS   650

PREFACE

When we were graduate students, we chose to study international finance because we wanted to understand issues such as how exchange rates are determined and how people manage the risks that fluctuations in exchange rates create. We also recognized that the economic forces that people now call *globalization* were trends that would only increase in importance over time. We like to think that we made a good call on our careers because, without a doubt, globalization of business is now a fact. Our goal with this book is to equip future global business leaders with the tools they need to understand the issues, to make sound international financial decisions, and to manage the myriad risks that their businesses face in a competitive global environment.

Over the years, the markets for goods and services as well as capital and labor have become increasingly open to the forces of international competition. All business schools have consequently "internationalized" their curriculums. Nevertheless, our combined 47 years of teaching experience indicates that most students will not be ready for the real world, with its global complications, unless they know the material in this book. They will not really understand how fluctuations in exchange rates create risks and rewards for multinational corporations and investment banks, and they will not understand how those risks can be managed. They will not really understand how to determine the value of an overseas project or the nature of country risk. The purpose of this book is to prepare students to deal with these and other real-world issues.

THIS BOOK'S APPROACH: MAKING BETTER DECISIONS BY BLENDING THEORY AND PRACTICE WITH REAL-WORLD DATA ANALYSIS

International Financial Management blends theory, the analysis of data, examples, and practical case situations to allow students to truly understand not only what to do when confronted with an international financial decision but why that decision is the correct one. When we explore international financial markets, we do so with an eye on risk management. We thereby incorporate practical considerations into what other textbooks take as background theory or institutional detail. For example, when we introduce the forward market, we show how forward contracts are used to hedge currency risk. When we discuss fluctuations in real exchange rates, we first quantify the variability of real exchange rates and then demonstrate how to evaluate the performance of a foreign subsidiary in this real-world environment.

Multinational companies face a daunting array of risks, but they also have a wide variety of financial instruments available to manage them. In this book, we detail the sources of risks that arise in international financial markets and how these risks can be managed. For example, a basic risk of international trade involves the fact that goods are being shipped out of the country. How does an exporter make sure that he is paid? We do not stop at identifying the risks and showing how to manage them; we also reflect on why a firm should manage them and how that management affects the firm's value. We do this by developing the valuation methodologies needed to determine the value of any foreign project—from the establishment of a foreign subsidiary to the takeover of a foreign company. Because we have a well-defined valuation methodology, we present international financial management using a modern, theoretically correct approach, building on the newest insights from international corporate finance. How international risk management affects the value of a firm falls out naturally from our framework. We also provide considerable detail about the institutional aspects of international financial markets for debt and equity. For example, we show how firms can obtain international equity financing, but we also discuss theories and empirical work on the costs and benefits of these decisions.

PEDAGOGY FOR STUDENTS

This book necessarily combines theory and business practice. We provide plenty of real-world examples and case studies, and at the same time, we stress fundamental concepts, principles, and analytical theories that are bound to be more resilient to the constantly changing challenges of operating in a competitive global marketplace.

To help students develop an in-depth and enduring knowledge of international financial management, *International Financial Management* incorporates the following features:

- **Real data analysis:** We incorporate the analysis of data in each relevant chapter to allow students to learn how well or poorly the current theories are supported by the data.
- **Extended cases:** Where relevant, we introduce and solve intricate cases that illustrate the application of theory. These case solutions can serve as templates for future analyses.
- *Point–Counterpoint* **features:** We reinforce the subtleties of many international financial management issues by presenting a *Point–Counterpoint* feature for each chapter. Many textbooks provide short, easy answers to difficult questions. That approach is fine when there is general agreement about an issue, but many situations are more subtle and intricate than standard books may lead the reader to believe. The *Point–Counterpoint* features are designed to raise issues that are contentious and that are often not fully resolved or well understood by the academic and practitioner communities. Each *Point–Counterpoint* feature ends by summarizing the state-of-the-art thinking on the issue.
- **Boxes:** We provide boxes to serve two purposes. First, they may contain concrete historical or current illustrations of important concepts introduced during the chapter. Second, they explore and illustrate basic finance concepts that are used in the chapter.
- **Appendixes:** We have included some mathematical and statistical material in appendixes to various chapters in an effort to make the book self-contained. We intend the book to be accessible to students with limited financial backgrounds.
- **End-of-chapter questions and problems:** At the end of each chapter we have provided a set of interesting questions and problems that are designed to help students ensure that they have mastered the chapter material.
- **Bibliographies:** Each chapter contains a bibliography of further reading that contains not only citations to the books and articles mentioned in the text but also some additional readings that interested students can explore.

MATERIALS FOR INSTRUCTORS

At the Instructor Resource Center, located at www.prenhall.com/irc, instructors can download a variety of print, digital, and presentation resources available for this textbook, including the following:

Solutions Manual
Test Bank
TestGen EQ
PowerPoint slides

Printed versions of the Solutions Manual (ISBN: 0-13-186047-X) and Test Bank (ISBN: 0-13-606862-6) are available from Prentice Hall.

Solutions Manual—Prepared by the authors, Geert Bekaert and Robert Hodrick. The Solutions Manual contains fully worked out solutions for all the end-of-chapter problems.

Test Bank—Prepared by Dr. Joseph Greco of California State University, Fullerton. The Test Bank for each chapter will contain approximately 25 multiple choice questions with fully worked out solutions, 5 short answer questions with answers, and 2 essays with answers. The question difficulty levels of each chapter will be approximately 60% easy, 30% moderate, and 10% difficult.

TestGen—The computerized TestGen package allows instructors to customize, save, and generate classroom tests. The test program permits instructors to edit, add, or delete questions from the test banks; edit existing graphics and create new graphics; analyze test results; and organize a database of test and student results. This software allows for extensive flexibility and ease of use. It provides many options for organizing and displaying tests, along with search and sort features. The software and the test banks can be downloaded from the Instructor's Resource Center (www.prenhall.com/bekaert).

PowerPoint slides—Prepared by Dr. Joseph Greco of California State University, Fullerton. The PowerPoint slides provide the instructor with individual lecture outlines to accompany the text. The slides include many of the figures and tables from the text. These lecture notes can be used as is or professors can easily modify them to reflect specific presentation needs.

FOR STUDENTS

This book's companion website, www.prenhall.com/bekaert, contains valuable resources for both students and professors.

ACKNOWLEDGMENTS

We are indebted to many people who provided us with insight and guidance as we wrote this book. Their careful review of the manuscript improved the final product immensely. These people include:

Michael Adler, Columbia University; Torben Andersen, Northwestern University; Rahul Bhargava, University of Nevada, Reno; Lloyd Blenman, University of North Carolina–Charlotte; Gordon Bodnar, Johns Hopkins University; John Bonie, North Park University; William Callahan, Northeastern State University; Murillo Campello, University of Illinois–Urbana/Champaign; Haiyang Chen, William Paterson University; David Cleeton, Oberlin College; Mitchell Conover, University of Richmond; Barbara Craig, Oberlin College; Drew Dahl, Utah State University; John Doukas, Old Dominion

University; Paul Duda, Canyon College; Robert Duvic, University of Texas; Gloria Edwards, San Jose State University; Larry Fauver, University of Miami; Demetrios Giannaros, University of Hartford; Ian Giddy, New York University; Harold Green, Ohio State University; Gary Griepentrog, University of Wisconsin–Oshkosh; Andrea Heuson, University of Miami; Mary Hines, Butler University; Abigail Hornstein, Wesleyan University; Kurt Jesswein, Murray State University; S. Kyle Jones, Sam Houston State University; James Jordan-Wagner, Eastern Illinois University; Ivan Katchanovski, University of Toronto; Brent Lekvin, Michigan Technological University; Karen Lewis, University of Pennsylvania; Bob Lynch, Webster University; D. K. Malhotra, Philadelphia University; Speros Margetis, University of Tampa; Paul McGrath, Purdue University; Galina Ovtcharova, University of Notre Dame; Mark Perry, University of Michigan, Flint; Thomas Sanders, University of Miami; William Shaniel, University of West Georgia; Joseph Steinman, University of North Florida; Jerry Stevens, University of Richmond; Aysar Sussan, Canyon College; Peggy Swanson, University of Texas, Arlington; Andrew Szakmary, University of Richmond; Kishore Tandon, Baruch College; Phillip Uhlmann, Bentley College; David Vanderlinden, University of Southern Maine; and Anu Vuorikoski, San Jose State University.

We would also like to acknowledge, with thanks, other individuals who made this text possible. Without the help of the many professionals at Prentice Hall, this book would not be a reality. We are especially indebted to our acquisitions editors, Leah Jewel and Valery Ashton, who got the project started; P. J. Boardman, who was instrumental in keeping the project going; and Donna Battista, who has gotten the book published with the help of our project manager, Mary Kate Murray.

Over the years, we have benefited from the comments of three terrific development editors: Rebecca Kohn, Jane Tufts, and Amy Ray. We thank them for their efforts to make the book more readable.

Our heartfelt thanks also go out to the many students who helped compile data and exhibits for the book, and to our administrative assistants, who painstakingly helped type the manuscript. Former students who worked as research assistants include Christian Capuano, Amadeo DaSilva, Jason Eisenstadt, Carlos Finger, Chang Ha, Wassim Hammoude, Adam Honig, Nick Parks, Andreas Stathopoulos, Ching-Yu Yao, and Xiaozheng Wang. Our administrative assistants at the Columbia Business School were Jessica Brucas, Leticia Jerman, Esther Jones, Clara Magram, Catherine O'Connor, and Glendaly Santos.

YOUR FEEDBACK

We would appreciate hearing from you! Let us know what you think about this textbook by writing to college_marketing@prenhall.com. Please include "Feedback about Bekaert and Hodrick" in the subject line.

If you have questions related to this product, please contact our customer service department online, at http://247.prenhall.com.

Geert Bekaert
Columbia University

Robert J. Hodrick
Columbia University

About the Authors

Geert Bekaert is the Leon G. Cooperman Professor of Finance and Economics at Columbia Business School and a Research Associate at the National Bureau of Economic Research. He received his Ph.D. from Northwestern University's Economics Department. Before joining Columbia, where he teaches courses on investments and wealth management. Bekaert was a tenured Associate Professor of Finance at the Graduate School of Business, Stanford University. His research focus is international finance, with particular emphasis on foreign exchange market efficiency and global equity market valuation. In addition, Geert is a Managing Member and the Director of Research of Pani Bekaert Pluim, LLC., a private investment company specializing in global markets and a consultant for Financial Engines, a private firm providing personalized investment advice to individual investors. Geert lives in New York and Belgium and enjoys playing basketball, squash, and listening to weird alternative music.

Robert J. Hodrick is the Nomura Professor of International Finance at Columbia Business School and a Research Associate of the National Bureau of Economic Research. He received his Ph.D. from the University of Chicago and has taught at Carnegie-Mellon University and J.L. Kellogg Graduate School of Management before joining the faculty at Columbia Business School. Professor Hodrick currently teaches both fundamental and advanced courses in international finance. His expertise is in the valuation of financial assets. His current research explores the empirical implications of theoretical pricing models that generate time-varying risk premiums in the markets for bonds, equities, and foreign currencies. Bob lives in Scarsdale, New York, and enjoys long bike rides.

Chapter 1

Globalization and the Multinational Corporation

1.1 INTRODUCTION

The world economy is becoming increasingly globalized. Look around you, and you will see students from many different countries. The pen you use to take notes may have been made in China, the chips in your laptop computer may have come from Korea, and its software could have been developed by Indian engineers. We hope that during your study break, you savor some Italian espresso, although the "Italian" coffee beans that were roasted in Italy were likely grown in Indonesia or Brazil. The concept of **globalization** refers to the increasing connectivity and integration of countries and corporations and the people within them in terms of their economic, political, and social activities.

Because of globalization, multinational corporations are dominating the corporate landscape. A **multinational corporation (MNC)** is a company that produces and sells goods or services in more than one nation. A prototypical example is the Coca-Cola Company, which operates in more than 200 countries.

It is also likely that a multinational corporation is producing your favorite brew. For example, InBev is a publicly traded company headquartered in Belgium, which until recently was a family-controlled firm with origins dating back to 1366. Over time, the local Belgian firm grew into a large multinational corporation called Interbrew, with famous brands such as Stella Artois and Leffe. In 2004, Interbrew and Companhia de Bebidas das Américas (AmBev), from Brazil, merged to create InBev, which is now the world's largest brewer by volume. In 2004, InBev sold 202 million hectoliters (hl) of beer and 31.5 million hl of soft drinks.

The link between a large European company and a large company from an emerging economy is no coincidence. One of the major trends in recent years has been the strong growth of Brazil, Russia, India, and China (sometimes referred to as BRIC). Today, BRIC accounts for two-fifths of the gross domestic product (GDP) of all emerging countries. The integration of these emerging economies into the global economy was forcefully illustrated in 2006, with the creation of the world's largest steel company. Mittal Steel, an Indian company, took over the European steel producer Arcelor, which was created by an earlier merger of steel companies in France, Belgium, Luxembourg, and Spain. The fact that Arcelor's management at first opposed the takeover shows that globalization does not necessarily proceed smoothly.

The international scope of business has created many new opportunities for firms, but it also poses many challenges. This book provides a guide to financial management in an increasingly globalized world, and in particular, to the financial management problems that multinational firms face. In this introductory chapter, we first reflect generally on the globalization phenomenon. We then discuss multinational firms in more detail, including their effects on the economy and society at large. We also survey the different important players in this globalizing world, ranging from international banks to international institutions and institutional investors. We end with a quick preview of the book.

1.2 GLOBALIZATION AND THE GROWTH OF INTERNATIONAL TRADE AND CAPITAL FLOWS

Globalization affects all aspects of society, but from an economic perspective, two main trends define globalization: One is occurring in the markets for goods and services, and the other is occurring in financial markets. First, countries continue to expand their trade with one another. Second, countries continue to reduce their barriers to capital flows. This has led to the globalization of financial markets and the spectacular growth in cross-border capital flows. We discuss each in turn.

The Growth of International Trade

Trade Liberalization

As any international economics textbook will tell you, the writings of David Ricardo in the nineteenth century taught us that countries gain from trade if each nation specializes in the production of those goods in which it has a **comparative advantage**. Even if one country is more productive at producing a given item than other countries, it should still focus its production on those goods in which it is relatively most efficient at producing, and doing so will make all trading partners better off.[1] There also appears to be a link in the data between trade and growth: More open countries tend to grow faster.[2]

Unfortunately, protectionist tendencies have long kept the world relatively closed, with many countries restricting international trade through tariffs on imports, non-tariff barriers such as subsidies to local producers, quotas on imported products, onerous regulations applying to imported products, and so forth. In a recent study, economists Romain Wacziarg and Karen Horn Welch (2003) pinpointed when various countries liberalized their trade regimes—in other words, when the countries became open to trade. They looked at a variety of criteria, including the extent of the countries' tariffs and non-tariff barriers, and state control on major export sectors. Exhibit 1.1 shows the fraction of countries that were open to trade from 1970 onward. Around 1970, about 60% of countries were open to trade, but since 1985, the trade openness measure has really started to climb toward 1. This is primarily due to the fall of the Iron Curtain in 1990 and to trade liberalizations occurring in many developing countries.

Exhibit 1.2 presents the actual dates of trade liberalization for all the countries that Wacziarg and Welch (2003) considered. As you can see in Exhibit 1.2, only a few countries, such as the United Kingdom and the United States, have a tradition of openness to international trade. The liberalization dates are not necessarily driven by country-specific policies. Many European countries liberalized in 1959 or 1960, after the creation of the **European Economic Community (EEC)**, which set out to establish free trade among a number of European countries (as described later in this chapter). This fits into a wider effort to encourage free trade in a multilateral context that started after World War II.

---

[1]This law of comparative advantage will show up again when we discuss the foreign currency swap market in Chapter 21. The Point–Counterpoint of Chapter 21 lays out an economic example that you can read independently if you want a refresher on the issue.

[2]Frequently cited articles on this issue include Jeffrey Frankel and David Romer (1999) and Jeffrey Sachs and Andrew Warner (1995). While there is some debate (see Dani Rodrik and Francisco Rodriguez, 1999, for a dissenting opinion), more recent work (see, for example, Francisco Alcalá and Antonio Ciccone, 2004) continues to confirm the positive effect of trade on growth. A number of articles have also shown directly that trade liberalization, the policy decision to open a country to foreign trade, has led to higher growth and productivity (see Geert Bekaert, Campbell Harvey, and Christian Lundblad, 2007; David Greenway, Wyn Morgan, and Peter Wright, 2002; and Romain Wacziarg, 2001).

Exhibit 1.1 Trade and Financial Openness

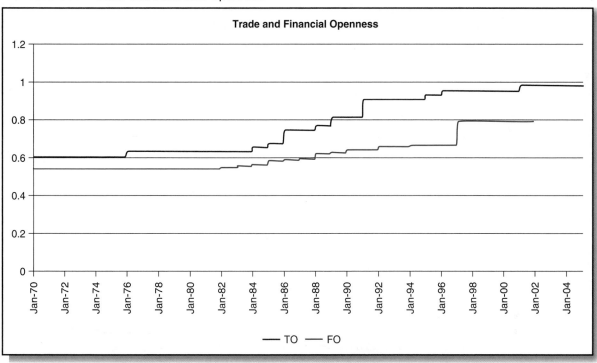

Notes: The TO (trade openness) line represents the fraction of countries that have liberalized trade according to the definition in Wacziarg and Welch (2003). The FO (financial openness) line represents the average degree of capital market openness across a large number of developing and developed countries, compiled by Quinn and Toyoda (2004).

International Efforts to Promote Free Trade

After World War II, the **General Agreement on Tariffs and Trade (GATT)**, signed in 1947, was designed to encourage free trade between member states by regulating and reducing tariffs on traded goods and by providing a common mechanism for resolving trade disputes. GATT signatories occasionally negotiated new trade agreements, called "rounds," that all countries would enter into. In general, each agreement bound members to reduce certain tariffs.

The Tokyo round in 1979 also reduced non-tariff barriers to trade, and the Uruguay round, begun in 1986, established the **World Trade Organization (WTO)** in 1995 to replace the GATT Treaty (as discussed later in this chapter). GATT succeeded in lowering trade barriers in a multilateral, worldwide way, but a number of important regional trade agreements have slashed trade barriers even more in particular regions. The best known of these regional agreements are the **European Union (EU)** in Europe; The **North America Free Trade Agreement (NAFTA)** between Canada, the United States, and Mexico; and the **Association of Southeast Asian Nations (ASEAN)**, whose signatories include Brunei Darussalam, Cambodia, Indonesia, Laos, Malaysia, Myanmar, Philippines, Singapore, Thailand, and Vietnam.

Recent Developments

The idea that economies should be open to trade got a further boost in 1980, when Western governments started to deregulate their economies and privatize government firms. After the fall of the Iron Curtain in 1990, eastern European countries were finally able to trade more with the rest of the world, and at the same time, emerging economies everywhere liberalized their trade policies. Advances in information and computer technology made the world seem like a smaller place. They also increased the relative share of services in economic output and made increasing the international tradability of services a new focus of international trade policy.

Exhibit 1.2 Trade Liberalization Dates by Country

Country	Date	Country	Date	Country	Date
Albania	1992	Greece	1959	Norway	Always
Algeria	n/a	Guatemala	1988	Pakistan	2001
Angola	n/a	Guinea	1986	Panama	1996
Argentina	1991	Guinea-Bissau	1987	Papua New Guinea	n/a
Armenia	1995	Guyana	1988	Paraguay	1989
Australia	1964	Haiti	n/a	Peru	1991
Austria	1960	Honduras	1991	Philippines	1988
Azerbaijan	1995	Hong Kong, China	Always	Poland	1990
Bangladesh	1996	Hungary	1990	Portugal	Always
Barbados	1966	Iceland	n/a	Romania	1992
Belarus	n/a	India	n/a	Russian Federation	n/a
Belgium	1959	Indonesia	1970	Rwanda	n/a
Benin	1990	Iran, Islamic Rep.	n/a	Senegal	n/a
Bolivia	1985	Iraq	n/a	Sierra Leone	2001
Botswana	1979	Ireland	1966	Singapore	1965
Brazil	1991	Israel	1985	Slovak Republic	1991
Bulgaria	1991	Italy	1959	Slovenia	1991
Burkina Faso	1998	Jamaica	1989	Somalia	n/a
Burundi	1999	Japan	1964	South Africa	1991
Cameroon	1993	Jordan	1965	Spain	1959
Canada	1952	Kazakhstan	n/a	Sri Lanka	1991
Cape Verde	1991	Kenya	1993	Swaziland	n/a
Central African Republic	n/a	Korea, Rep.	1968	Sweden	1960
Chad	n/a	Kyrgyz Republic	1994	Switzerland	Always
Chile	1976	Latvia	1993	Syrian Arab Republic	n/a
China	n/a	Lesotho	n/a	Taiwan, China	1963
Colombia	1986	Liberia	n/a	Tajikistan	1996
Congo, Dem. Rep.	n/a	Lithuania	1993	Tanzania	1995
Congo, Rep.	n/a	Luxembourg	1959	Thailand	Always
Costa Rica	1986	Macedonia, FYR	1994	Togo	n/a
Cote d'Ivoire	1994	Madagascar	1996	Trinidad and Tobago	1992
Croatia	n/a	Malawi	n/a	Tunisia	1989
Cyprus	1960	Malaysia	1963	Turkey	1989
Czech Republic	1991	Mali	1988	Turkmenistan	n/a
Denmark	1959	Malta	n/a	Uganda	1988
Dominican Republic	1992	Mauritania	1995	Ukraine	n/a
Ecuador	1991	Mauritius	1968	United Kingdom	Always
Egypt, Arab Rep.	1995	Mexico	1986	United States	Always
El Salvador	1989	Moldova	1994	Uruguay	1990
Estonia	n/a	Morocco	1984	Uzbekistan	n/a
Ethiopia	1996	Mozambique	1995	Venezuela	1996
Finland	1960	Myanmar	n/a	Yemen, Rep.	Always
France	1959	Nepal	1991	Yugoslavia, FR	2001
Gabon	n/a	The Netherlands	1959	(Serbia/Montenegro)	
The Gambia	1985	New Zealand	1986	Zambia	1993
Georgia	1996	Nicaragua	1991	Zimbabwe	n/a
Germany	1959	Niger	1994		
Ghana	1985	Nigeria	n/a		

Note: The data are taken from Wacziarg and Welsh, 2003. Copyright © 2003. Reprinted by permission of the authors.

These developments also made outsourcing an increasingly important phenomenon. **Outsourcing** is the shifting of non-strategic functions—such as payroll, information technology (IT), maintenance, facilities management, and logistics—to specialist firms to reduce costs. Today, outsourcing IT work to low-cost countries, such as India, has become increasingly commonplace.

During the latest GATT trade round, the Doha round, which began in November 2001, trade in services was put on the agenda. In addition, the Doha round focused on agriculture, industrial goods, and updated custom codes. However, the trade talks have been going far from smoothly, and there have been no concrete results so far. The process toward free trade among countries therefore remains incomplete.

The Growth in Trade

The evolution toward trade openness has dramatically increased trade flows between countries. One measure of the size of the trade sector is the sum of exports and imports in a given year divided by a measure of output, such as **gross domestic product (GDP)**. Exhibit 1.3 presents this relative size of the trade sector for a number of countries over a number of years. In Panel A, the data for large, developed countries reveal a significant increase in trade to GDP ratios between 1970 and 1985. If we compare 1985 with 2005, with the exception of the United Kingdom, the trade sector has continued to increase, although the increase is minimal for Japan. Of the countries listed, Germany is the most open, with its trade sector comprising 61% of GDP in 2005, whereas the U.S. trade sector now exceeds 20% of its GDP.

In Panel B, large, developing countries such as Brazil and India also have seen the relative size of their trade sectors increase, and their ratios of trade to GDP were around 25% in 2005. China's trade sector nearly doubled between 1985 and 2000, and it increased by another 50% between 2000 and 2005. This increase mirrors the major trade reforms that took place in China during the 1980s and 1990s, including China's accession to the WTO in 2001. The accession, in turn, led to a steady decrease in tariffs on imports. Because of its large size and increased openness, China has recently become a major player in the world economy.

As you can see from Exhibit 1.3, although the global trend is toward freer trade, some countries are clearly more open than others. Many factors affect why, how much, and with whom countries trade. For example, countries that border on oceans tend to trade more than inland countries. You might be surprised to learn that very large countries tend to trade relatively less than smaller countries. This is obvious from the numbers for the U.S. relative to most other countries; and, indeed, China is a relative outlier. Small open countries such as Belgium and Singapore (see Panel C of Exhibit 1.3) have trade-to-GDP ratios well over 150% and 250%, respectively.

How Multinational Corporations Are Affecting Free Trade

The phenomenal growth of MNCs after World War II has also boosted international trade. In 2003, there were 64,000 international companies with 870,000 subsidiaries, whereas even in the early 1990s, there were only 37,000 companies with 175,000 subsidiaries. According to the **United Nations Conference on Trade and Development (UNCTAD)**, 60% of international trade in 2003 occurred within multinational companies (that is, firms trading with themselves).

In MNCs, capital, labor, management skills, and technology are all transferred to other countries to produce abroad rather than export from a domestic factory. Although some products may be destined for the local market, some products are also exported to other markets. Sometimes the components of different goods are produced in different countries, depending on their relative advantages in terms of costs and technological ability. A classic example is the Barbie doll. The raw materials for dolls come from Taiwan and Japan, their assembly takes place in the Philippines, Indonesia, and China (due to the low labor costs), and the design and the final coat of paint come from the United States, which still has an edge in design and marketing.

The Globalization of Financial Markets

The globalization of financial markets and the profound changes they have undergone since 1980 have also dramatically changed how MNCs can manage their various business risks, improved their access to foreign capital, and enhanced their ability to reduce financing costs. We provide a short overview of the major developments.

Trends in Financial Openness

After World War II, most countries had controls or restrictions in place that prevented the free flow of capital across borders. However, in the 1980s, many developed countries began liberalizing their capital markets. For example, Japan started to liberalize in 1984; in Europe, the

Exhibit 1.3   The Growth in International Trade

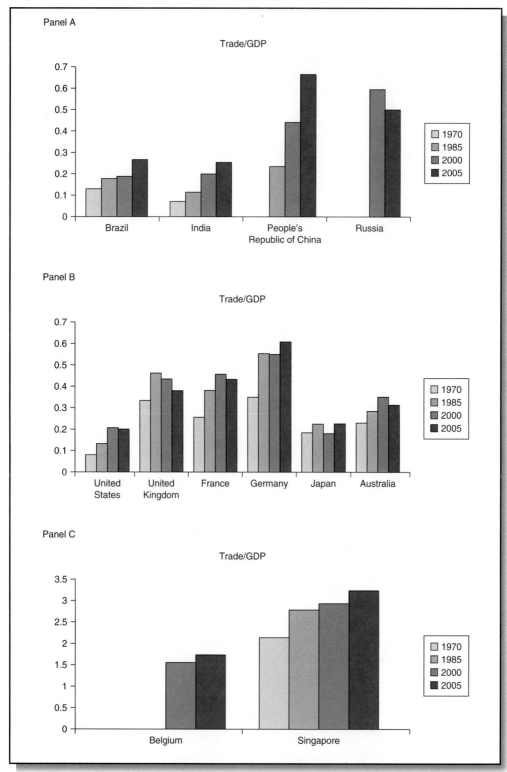

Note: The data represent the sum of exports and imports divided by GDP, a measure of total output. The import and export data are from the IMF as reported by Global Insight. The GDP data are from international financial statistics produced by the IMF.

AMB: Betting on Global Trade

AMB, which owns and develops industrial real estate, is a **real estate investment trust (REIT)** that trades on the New York Stock Exchange. You might think that real estate is not an easily exchangeable asset. Consequently, you might think that AMB has little to do with international business. But in fact, the fortunes of AMB totally depend on continuing globalization.

You see, AMB develops, acquires, and operates distribution facilities in locations tied to global trade, such as international airports, seaports, and major highway systems. AMB has investments in 11 countries, ranging around the world from Spain to Brazil to China. With the increase in international trade and the need to minimize inventories, companies have realized that distribution efficiency has become a key to their success. AMB therefore targets properties that are built for the efficient movement of goods and are strategically located in the world's global distribution markets. Although the value of the property depends to a certain degree on local factors, as is the case for any piece of real estate, AMB's business is primarily a bet on the globalization process. In short, investors are betting on the increasing demand for such strategically located distribution facilities. By investing in AMB, investors are betting on the continued growth of international trade and are also buying a diversified portfolio of real estate around the world.

movement toward the Single Market forced many countries to abolish their capital controls, with France abolishing capital controls in 1986, Italy in 1988, and Belgium in 1990.

At the end of the 1980s, and during most of the 1990s, many developing countries embarked on a financial liberalization process, relaxing restrictions on foreign ownership of their assets and taking other measures to develop their capital markets, often in tandem with macroeconomic and trade reforms. These developments created new markets and a new asset class in which to invest: emerging markets. We discuss these markets in more detail in Chapter 12.

Exhibit 1.1 shows how financial openness has evolved over time since 1970. A country is financially open if it allows foreigners to invest in its capital markets and allows its citizens to invest abroad. To gauge the free flow of capital across borders, we use an estimate of the degree of capital market openness constructed by Dennis Quinn and Maria Toyoda (2004). A fully open market is scored as a 1; in contrast, a fully closed market is scored as a 0. We average this measure over a large number of developing and developed countries in Exhibit 1.1. As you can see, until 1982, the average measure was about 0.55. It then slowly rose and reached 0.80 in early 2000. Clearly, financial openness has not yet evolved as far as trade openness.

Note that it is not necessarily the case that countries whose capital markets are open to foreign investors enjoy large inflows of foreign capital. Foreign investors may be put off by a country's poor supervision of financial markets, by poor corporate governance of local firms (as discussed in more detail later in this chapter), or by an inefficient stock market. Conversely, countries that want to keep their foreign capital markets closed must realize that the regulations they pass in an attempt to do so are often ineffective. For example, London's Big Bang in 1986 automated the London Stock Exchange, slashed transaction costs, and allowed foreigners to participate in the trading. As a result, the volumes traded of both British and foreign stocks soared. In contrast, the effective openness of developing countries has grown less spectacularly over time than that of developed countries.

One way to assess how open countries are to capital inflows and outflows is to examine their foreign assets and liabilities.[3] Philip Lane and Gian Maria Milesi-Ferretti (2006) examined the ratio of a country's foreign assets plus its foreign liabilities to its GDP for a number of industrial, emerging, and developing countries. In 1970, this financial ratio for industrial countries was slightly less than 50%. By 1985, the ratio was 100%, whereas in 2004, the ratio was over 300%. In developing countries, it was only slightly above 150% in 2004.

---

[3]See Chapter 4 for a discussion of the relationship between flows of capital that are recorded in a country's balance of payments and the balance sheet position of the country's foreign assets and liabilities.

The New Financial Landscape

The deregulatory zeal of governments worldwide happened against the background of and perhaps as a reaction to a vastly different financial landscape that had begun to emerge in the 1980s. Most importantly, backed by advances in financial and computer technology, the markets for financial derivatives exploded. A **derivative security** is an investment from which the payoff over time is *derived* from the performance of underlying assets (such as commodities, equities, or bonds), interest rates, exchange rates, or indices (such as a stock market index, a consumer price index [CPI], or an index of weather conditions). The main types of derivatives are futures, forwards, options, and swaps. These derivatives are traded over the counter (that is, on a bilateral basis among financial institutions or between financial institutions and their clients) and on organized exchanges. Chapters 20 and 21 discuss some of these derivative contracts in more detail.

In the 1980s, the old and venerable U.S.-based derivative exchanges got competition from a bunch of upstarts—LIFFE in London (1981), Matif in France (1986), and DTB (Deutsche Teminborse) in 1989—that grew phenomenally quickly. Trading volumes for financial contracts traded over-the-counter also experienced exponential growth.

These and other developments, such as **securitization** (that is, the repackaging of "pools" of loans or other receivables to create a new financial instrument that can be sold to investors), increased the complexity in the financial intermediation business. Soon, the good old 3–5–3 days (take money in at 3%, lend it out at 5%, and go home at 3 P.M.) were gone for good. However, these developments also dramatically improved the ability of banks and corporations to manage risk. For example, corporations with earnings denominated in foreign currencies could now easily hedge their risks using sophisticated derivatives contracts. Similarly, companies could now easily tap foreign investors for capital with bond issues denominated in different currencies, while using the derivative markets to convert the loans back to their domestic currency if they desired to do so.

The new financial landscape also made it increasingly difficult for governments to regulate their domestic capital markets without smart financiers finding loopholes around the rules. For example, a major impetus to the growth of the swap market was regulatory arbitrage, where financial institutions exploited country-specific regulations or taxes to lower the cost of funding for multinational companies. In Chapter 11, we give some concrete examples of such regulatory arbitrage.

The derivatives revolution of the 1970s and 1980s experienced something of a backlash in the 1990s, when a number of companies, including Showa Shell of Japan, Metallgesellschaft of Germany, and Procter & Gamble in the United States, among others, sustained huge losses on derivative contracts. But the crown jewel in this chain of events was the collapse of Barings Bank, the oldest British bank, which had funded the Napoleonic Wars and was the personal bank for the queen. Barings collapsed when one rogue trader, Nick Leeson, lost $1.4 billion on the derivatives exchanges of Singapore and Osaka in Japan in 1995. While Leeson's activities were fraudulent, and he spent time in Singapore's prison system, these events shook up the financial world, and voices keen on regulating the freewheeling financial derivative markets became louder.

1.3 MULTINATIONAL CORPORATIONS

A **multinational corporation (MNC)** is a firm that does business in two or more foreign countries. A multinational company consists of a parent company in the firm's originating country and the operating subsidiaries, branches, and affiliates it controls both at home and abroad. The United Nations refers to such firms as *transnational corporations* to emphasize the fact that the operation and ownership of these enterprises is spread throughout the world.

Exhibit 1.4 lists the largest multinational corporations in 2004, ranked by the dollar value of their foreign assets in each of 19 countries. General Electric (GE) was the largest MNC by this

Exhibit 1.4 World's Top Nonfinancial Transnational Corporations by Foreign Assets

Ranking by Foreign Assets	Corporation	Home Economy	Industry	Assets Foreign	Assets Total	Sales Foreign	Sales Total	Employees Foreign	Employees Total	No. of Affiliates Foreign	No. of Affiliates Total
1	General Electric	United States	Electrical and electronic equipment	449	751	57	153	142	307	787	1157
2	Vodafone Group	United Kingdom	Telecommunications	248	259	53	62	46	57	70	198
7	Royal Dutch/Shell Group	Netherlands/UK	Petroleum expl./ ref./distr.	130	193	170	265	96	114	328	814
8	Toyota Motor Corp.	Japan	Motor vehicles	123	234	103	171	95	266	129	341
9	Total	France	Petroleum expl./ref./distr.	99	114	123	152	62	111	410	576
11	Volkswagen AG	Germany	Motor vehicles	84	173	80	110	165	343	147	228
17	Hutchinson Whampoa	Hong Kong, China	Diversified	68	84	17	23	151	180	94	103
19	Nestle	Switzerland	Food and beverages	65	77	69	70	240	247	460	487
27	ENI	Italy	Petroleum expl./ref./distr.	50	99	48	90	30	71	162	222
33	Telefonica	Spain	Telecommunications	43	86	15	38	78	174	62	279
59	Petronas	Malaysia	Petroleum expl./ref./distr.	23	63	11	36	4	34	167	234
61	Volvo	Sweden	Motor vehicles	22	34	27	29	53	81	244	307
72	Nokia	Finland	Telecommunications	19	31	36	36	31	54	125	131
73	Singtel	Singapore	Telecommunications	19	21	5	7	9	19	99	104
86	Samsung	Rep. of Korea	Electrical and electronic equipment	15	67	56	72	21	62	75	87
88	CRH Plc	Ireland	Lumber and building products	15	16	15	16	58	60	484	573
90	Statoil Asa	Norway	Petroleum expl./ref./distr.	15	41	9	45	11	24	60	135
94	CITIC Group	China	Diversified	14	85	2	6	16	93	14	59
99	Nortel Networks	Canada	Telecommunications	14	17	9	10	25	34	58	64

Notes: The data are taken from *The World Investment Report 2005*, Annex Table A.1.9, p. 299. Copyright © 2006. Reprinted by permission of the United Nations Conference on Trade and Development. Assets and sales are in billions of U.S. dollars. Employees are in thousands.

measure, with $449 billion in foreign assets. Exhibit 1.4 also indicates that GE had 787 foreign affiliates employing 142,000 people. The petroleum exploration, refining, and distributing industry and the telecommunications industry had five representatives among these companies.

Nestlé of Switzerland was the most international of these companies, with the largest ratio of foreign assets to total assets (84.4%) and the largest ratio of foreign sales to total sales (98.6%). The largest Chinese company was state-owned CITIC Group (formerly China International Trust and Investment Corporation), which oversees the government's foreign investments and some domestic ones, as well. CITIC Group's assets include financial institutions (more than 80% of its assets), industrial concerns (satellite telecommunications, energy, and manufacturing), and service companies (construction and advertising).

One way to think about the size of large MNCs is to compare their value added (the difference between the value of their final sales and the value of their material inputs) to the GDPs of countries. According to a 2002 UNCTAD study, which lists both countries and multinational companies according to their value-added wealth, 29 of the world's 100 largest economic entities are transnational or multinational companies. Exxon (prior to its merger with Mobil to form ExxonMobil) was the largest multinational by that measure, in 45th place, with $63 billion in value-added wealth, which placed it on a par with the economies of Chile and Pakistan. The GDP of Nigeria, in 57th place, fell just between the value added at DaimlerChrysler and General Electric.

How Multinational Corporations Enter Foreign Markets

Many MNCs initially start out simply as exporting or importing firms. Later, however, an MNC often gives local firms abroad the right to manufacture the company's products or provide its services in return for **royalties**. MNCs don't have to invest a lot of money to expand internationally by **licensing** their products to foreign firms—that is, by giving the firms the right to produce the products in exchange for a fee. However, it can be difficult for licensing firms to maintain their product quality standards when they do so. **Franchising** involves somewhat more involvement. Here the firm provides a specialized sales or service strategy, offers support at various levels, and may even initially invest in the franchise in exchange for periodic fees. McDonald's is almost surely the best-known franchising firm. A **joint venture** is a company that is jointly owned and operated by two or more firms. This is another way of penetrating foreign markets. Joint ventures are often used in the automotive industry; the joint venture forged between France's Renault and Japan's Nissan in 1999 is a particularly successful example.

Still other MNCs enter foreign markets by setting up local production and distribution facilities abroad. They often do so by acquiring or merging with foreign companies or by simply establishing new operations in the countries (in what are called *greenfield investments*). It is this latter category that constitutes the bulk of **foreign direct investment (FDI)**, which we discuss in more detail later in this chapter.

Today, there is much talk about the globally integrated corporation. As IBM CEO Samuel Palmisano put it in a 2006 speech, such a firm shapes its strategy, management, and operations as a single global entity. True to form, Mr. Palmisano's speech took place not at its corporate headquarters in Armonk, New York, but in Bangalore, India, where IBM now has more than 50,000 employees.

The Goals of an MNC

The premise of this book is that the appropriate goal of the management of any corporation is to maximize shareholder wealth. Therefore, a multinational corporation should also maximize shareholder wealth. This is the tradition in what are often called the "Anglo-American" countries, including Australia, Canada, the United Kingdom, and especially the United States.

The management of a corporation maximizes shareholder wealth by making investments in projects whose returns are sufficiently large to compensate its shareholders, through dividends and capital gains, for the risk involved in the projects.

Chapter 13 is devoted to how shareholders derive the appropriate expected rates of return on equities, which we argue corporations should take as given in their assessments of the cost of capital. Corporations add value when they can invest in projects or activities that return more than the cost of capital. Doing otherwise destroys value.

The Investment Time Horizon

The appropriate time horizon for management to consider is the long term. When deciding if an investment today maximizes shareholder value, the current value of all its future benefits must be compared to the cost of the investment. It is sometimes argued that shareholder maximization leads management to be too short-term focused on meeting the quarterly expectations of stock analysts, and it is certainly possible for management to mislead the markets in the short run, as the U.S. accounting scandals discussed shortly aptly demonstrate. Yet we believe that markets are pretty efficient at finding and aggregating information. Thus, good management should not be willing to trade off an increase in the stock price today for a major fall in the stock price shortly thereafter. Rather, it is the job of management to inform the markets about the costs and future profitability of the firm's investments.

The Stakeholder Alternative

Shareholder wealth maximization is not what is traditionally practiced by large European or Asian firms. Firms in those areas tend to lump shareholder interests together with those of other "stakeholders," including management, labor, governments (both local and national), banks and other creditors, and suppliers. Because management must juggle these various interests, its objectives are less clear in the stakeholder model than in the shareholder model.

Agency Theory and Corporate Governance

In a modern corporation, stockholders hire managers, and managers make decisions about production and marketing. How can the ultimate owners of the assets motivate the managers to act in the owners' interest? The economic field of **agency theory** (see, for instance, Jensen and Meckling, 1976) explores the problems that arise from the separation of ownership and control and devises ways to resolve them. A manager of a firm, in particular the chief executive officer (CEO), is viewed as an agent who contracts with various principals—most importantly the firm's shareholders but also the firm's creditors, suppliers, clients, and employees. The principals must design contracts that motivate the agent to perform actions and make decisions that are in the best interests of the principals.

Unfortunately, the world is too complicated for investors to write a contract that specifies all the actions that managers will take in the future. Yet the managers will surely acquire important information that the shareholders do not have and thus retain a great deal of discretion about which actions to take in response to such "private" information.

The legal and financial structure that controls the relationship between a company's shareholders and its management is called **corporate governance**. It is its role to establish the framework within which the managers operate and to mitigate the principal–agent problem. The importance of poor corporate governance was forcefully illustrated in a series of recent corporate scandals.

Corporate Scandals

One of the most spectacular cases of corporate fraud involved the Enron Corporation of Houston, Texas. By late 2001, the company, which was founded in 1985, had transformed itself from a regional gas pipeline operator into the largest buyer and seller of natural gas and electricity in the United States, as well as a major trader in numerous other commodities. The Enron bankruptcy was a disaster for many of the company's 21,000 employees not only because they lost their jobs but also because many had invested substantial amounts of their retirement savings in Enron stock. The market price of an Enron share fell from a high of $90 in August 2000 to zero in 2006, as creditors eventually liquidated the company.

A criminal investigation begun in 2001 soon revealed that Enron's meteoric rise in value was fed mostly by institutionalized, systematic, creative accounting fraud. Moreover, Enron's top executives—such as its founder, Kenneth Lay; its CEO, Jeffrey Skilling; and its CFO, Andrew Fastow—were found to be busily selling their stock positions while telling investors everything was fine. All three were found guilty of fraud and conspiracy. Kenneth Lay died before he could be sentenced, and Skilling and Fastow received prison sentences. The CEOs of Worldcom, a telecommunications firm, and Tyco, a sprawling conglomerate, also received prison sentences at around the same time for corporate misdeeds.

In addition, the Enron scandal led to the demise of Arthur Andersen, which was one of the "Big Five" accounting firms at the time. Arthur Andersen, as Enron's auditor, was convicted of obstruction of justice for shredding documents related to its audits of Enron. In 2002, Arthur Andersen voluntarily gave up its license to do certified public accounting.

Lest you think that only managers of large U.S. companies are capable of fraud, consider the case of Parmalat, an Italian dairy and food-processing company founded in 1961 by Calisto Tanzi. Parmalat is the global leader in the production of ultra high temperature (UHT) milk. The UHT process sterilizes food in 1 to 2 seconds by exposing it to temperatures exceeding 135° C, and such milk can be kept on the shelf, unrefrigerated, for between 6 and 9 months.

In 2003, accounting irregularities were uncovered in Parmalat's books, and it became apparent that €3.95 billion of assets were missing from the accounts of Bonlat, a Parmalat subsidiary in the Cayman Islands. The finding flung Parmalat into bankruptcy, and Tanzi was arrested. Under questioning by the Italian authorities, Tanzi eventually admitted to illegally diverting funds from Parmalat into other ventures he controlled. He is currently in prison in Milan, Italy.

Corporate Governance Around the World

It is clear from the corporate scandals described here that management does not always act in the interest of shareholders. Yet most corporations function quite well and without fraud and corruption. This section examines how shareholders deal with management not only to try to prevent outright illegal activities but to align the interests of management with those of shareholders.

Multinationals must worry about more than "in-house" corporate governance. Whether they acquire an existing foreign firm, set up a joint venture, or simply adopt a licensing agreement may depend on the corporate governance practices in that country. Corporate governance differences across countries and firms affect a firm's valuation and may lead firms to cross-list shares in stock markets with a legal environment that fosters good corporate governance, or MNCs may improve their own corporate governance standards to attract international investors.

In their review of corporate governance and control, the economists Marco Becht, Patrick Bolton, and Ailsa Röell (2005) examine five ways of overcoming agency problems. The pros and cons of the different approaches are discussed in the following sections and are presented in condensed form in Exhibit 1.5.

An Independent Board of Directors

In the Anglo-American model, the board of directors is considered to have the most important role in corporate governance. It is the responsibility of the board of directors to help management develop a strategy and to approve its major investments. The board controls the management's activities by appointing and compensating the management with the goal of making the organization accountable to its owners and the authorities.

Exhibit 1.5 Methods of Overcoming Agency Problems Due to the Separation of Ownership and Control

Method	Pros	Cons
1. Independent board of directors	Protection of minority shareholders' interests. Increased risk sharing.	Often not sufficiently independent of management and therefore ineffective.
2. Partial concentration of ownership and control in the hands of a large shareholder	A large shareholder has the self-interest to monitor management's activities to prevent abuses.	Possible collusion between management and large shareholder against smaller shareholders. Reduced liquidity in the stock.
3. Executive compensation with options or bonuses related to performance.	Provides a direct incentive to maximize stock price.	Rewards management for good luck. Subject to manipulation and possible short-term focus to allow management to get rich.
4. Clearly defined fiduciary duties for CEOs with class-action law suits.	Provides a complementary disciplining device.	Increases legal costs and enriches lawyers at the expense of stockholders.
5. Hostile takeovers and proxy contests.	Directly disciplines bad management.	Provides an incentive for raiders to expropriate wealth from creditors and employees.

How well the board of directors does its job depends on whether the directors are truly independent of the management. If the board is dominated by the friends and golfing partners of the CEO, the board may not be able to appropriately represent the interests of shareholders. If the board is not independent, international expansion of the activities of the firm could be a manifestation of empire building; why else would you need a corporate jet?

While the Anglo-American model of corporate governance embraces the independent board of directors, things are different in Europe. In Germany, for example, the *Aufsichtsrat*, or supervisory board, of a large corporation has 20 members. Shareholders elect 10 members, and the other 10 members are employee representatives. The Supervisory Board oversees and appoints the members of the *Vorstand*, or management board, which must approve major business decisions.

Concentrated Ownership

The most common method of overcoming the agency problem in developed countries outside of the United Kingdom and the United States is through concentrated ownership in which a block of stock is held by either a wealthy investor or a financial intermediary, which might be a bank, a holding company, or a pension fund. A positive aspects of this approach is that a large shareholder clearly has a vested interest in monitoring management and has the power to implement changes in management. There are two negative aspects of this approach. First, it is possible that the large shareholder and the management may collude to expropriate wealth from the smaller shareholders. Second, the stock may be more difficult to trade on the stock market if a substantial block of shares is withdrawn from the market but still available to be sold should the large shareholder want to sell.

Executive Compensation

An important aspect in aligning the interests of an agent and a principal is how the agent is compensated. The compensation committee of the board of directors has the responsibility to design appropriate executive compensation that overcomes shareholder/management conflicts. Here, ownership of stock by the management and grants of stock options should encourage the management to think like the shareholders.

Positive aspects of this method include the obvious fact that people respond to incentives, and the economics of the problem indicate the need to pay for performance. Unfortunately, it is often difficult to ascertain whether the actions of the management increased the stock price or whether the management was simply lucky. An increase in the price of oil raises the value of the large firms that extract oil and sit on large reserves, and consequently oil price increases lead to big paydays for managers whose decisions had nothing to do with the increase in the oil price.

Shareholder Activism and Litigation

Poor corporate performance eventually leads to unhappy shareholders. If the performance isn't too bad, the shareholders may just bide their time and allow management to improve performance. Alternatively, the unhappy shareholders may sell their shares to someone who is more optimistic about the firm's prospects. Disgruntled shareholders also may try to use the legal system to sue the board of directors for failure to perform their fiduciary duty. Clearly defining the fiduciary responsibilities of the CEO raises the threat of litigation and keeps managers from expropriating shareholder value, thus providing a complementary method of aligning management's actions with shareholders' interests.

If shareholders disagree with the management's strategy or its implementation, they may actively try to change the management or vote for different directors. For example, in 2004, billionaire investor Kirk Kerkorian bought 9.9% of General Motors shares, and one of his employees was granted a seat on the GM board of directors. Kerkorian hoped that he could persuade GM to merge with Renault and Nissan. Talks collapsed in November 2006, and Kerkorian sold a substantial amount of his shares, causing GM's share price to fall 4.1%.

Hostile Takeovers

Ultimately, management is disciplined by the market for hostile takeovers. In a hostile takeover, the candidate acquiring company, the "raider," bids for a majority of the voting rights of the "target" company and, if successful, uses the acquired voting power to replace the CEO and redirect the strategy of the target.

Such takeovers are common in the United States, the United Kingdom, and France, but they are very rare in Germany. Nevertheless, in 2000, Vodafone of the United Kingdom completed a $199 billion cross-border hostile takeover of the German company Mannesmann, in the largest-ever European takeover. Such takeover activity has now even spread to the Italian banking industry, as the Illustration Box "Raiding Italy" notes. Hostile takeovers are also rare in Japan because of the presence of keiretsu, an arrangement in which a group of firms is linked, usually with a prominent bank, through cross-shareholding agreements.

The Sarbanes-Oxley Act

In response to the corporate scandals described here, the U.S. Congress passed legislation to attempt to improve the practice of corporate governance in the United States. The Sarbanes-Oxley Act of 2002, commonly called SOX, is a federal law that covers issues such as auditor independence, corporate governance, and enhanced financial disclosure. The following are some of the most important features of the act:

1. Establishment of the Public Company Accounting Oversight Board, which is charged with overseeing, regulating, inspecting, and disciplining accounting firms in their roles as auditors of public companies.
2. The requirement that public companies and their internal auditors evaluate and disclose the effectiveness of their internal controls as they relate to financial reporting.
3. The requirement that CEOs and CFOs of publicly traded companies certify their financial reports.
4. The requirement that the audit committee of the board of directors, which oversees the relationship between the corporation and its auditor, be composed of independent directors.
5. Prohibition against companies making loans to corporate directors.

One problem with the Sarbanes-Oxley Act is its insistence that only independent directors serve on the audit committee, which conflicts with European and Asian traditions. As noted previously, the German supervisory board has employee representatives, who are clearly not independent.

The issue is really one of getting the right form for corporate governance. While the Sarbanes-Oxley Act may further improve corporate governance in the United States, the

Raiding Italy

On September 14, 2005, the board of directors of Banca Popolare Italiana (B.P.I.) accepted the offer of the Dutch bank ABN Amro to acquire B.P.I.'s 29.5% stake in Antonveneta, Italy's ninth-largest bank, for about €2.5 billion ($3.1 billion). This is nothing special, you may think. Isn't the EU actively trying to promote a single European market in financial services to improve the efficiency of the banking system? Think again. The takeover took a full 7 months to accomplish, and it represents the first cross-border bank takeover in Italy. In fact, Spain's Banco Bilbao Vizcaya Argentario failed to take over Italy's Banca Nazionale del Lavoro earlier in 2005.

Worse, none other than Antonio Fazio, the governor of Italy's central bank (the Banca d'Italia), allegedly tried to help B.P.I.'s barely legal maneuvers to maintain control over Antonveneta, but his phone conversations with B.P.I.'s chief, Giampiero Fiorani, were intercepted by the financial police in July. The incident damaged the reputations of Fazio and the Banca d'Italia and sullied Italy's image as a safe place to do business. Mr. Fazio stubbornly did not think he did anything inappropriate, and it took a new minister of finance, Mr. Tremonti, to force Mr. Fazio out. Politics and economics will always remain strange bedfellows.

United States was already considered the country with the best corporate governance. Moreover, implementing the new requirements is expensive, and it is likely one of the factors behind the decision of many international companies not to list their stock on the U.S. stock market but in European countries with less onerous regulations. (See also Chapter 13.)

What the Data Show

Differences across countries in corporate governance are examined in a series of influential and controversial articles by the economists Rafael La Porta, Florencio Lopez-de-Silanes, Andrei Shleifer, and Rob Vishny (LLSV; 1997, 1998, 2000a, 2000b). The LLSV articles show that measures of investor protection across countries correlate very strongly with a classification of legal systems based on the idea of "legal origin"—the primary distinction being between English common law countries, such as Canada, the United Kingdom, and the United States; French civil law countries, such as Belgium, France, and Italy; German civil law countries, such as Austria, Germany, and Switzerland; and Scandinavian civil law countries, such as Denmark, Finland, and Sweden. The English common law countries provide more investor protections than the civil law countries.

LLSV show that legal origin correlates very well with concentration of ownership, the size of the stock market, and the level of dividend payments. For example, in civil law countries with low ownership protection, corporate ownership is much more concentrated than in the English common law countries. LLSV also show that countries with greater legal protection of investor rights have more firms listed on public stock markets, larger corporate valuations, and greater economic growth.

China provides an important counterexample to the findings on the importance of legal systems in promoting the growth of financial systems and the overall economy. The economists Franklin Allen, Jun Qian, and Meijun Qian (2005) note that neither China's legal system nor its financial system is particularly well developed, yet China has experienced extraordinary real growth. While China retains a large state-controlled sector, it is the private sector that has been the engine of growth. This suggests that alternative financing channels and corporate governance mechanisms, possibly based on reputation considerations, promote the growth of the private sector.

Multinational Corporations and Foreign Direct Investment

Foreign direct investment (FDI) has existed since Sumerian merchants stationed men abroad in 2500 B.C. to receive, store, and sell their goods, but it is fair to say that the main growth in FDI came after World War II. FDI occurs when a company from one country makes a significant investment that leads to at least a 10% ownership interest in a (new or existing) firm in another country.

FDI by the Numbers

Exhibit 1.6 shows that between 1980 and 2000, FDI flows increased more than 20-fold. FDI flows were over $1 trillion in 2000 and then fell back a bit. The outstanding stock of FDI is estimated to be worth around $9 trillion.[4]

While the growth in FDI in developing economies was faster than in developed economies, FDI remains primarily an activity between developed countries. This is especially

Exhibit 1.6 Foreign Direct Investment

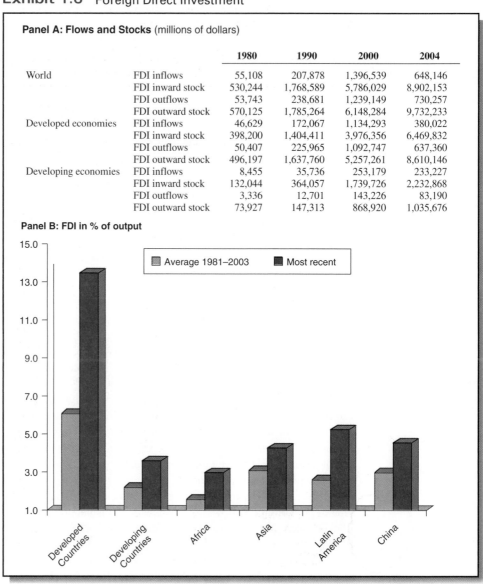

Panel A: Flows and Stocks (millions of dollars)

		1980	1990	2000	2004
World	FDI inflows	55,108	207,878	1,396,539	648,146
	FDI inward stock	530,244	1,768,589	5,786,029	8,902,153
	FDI outflows	53,743	238,681	1,239,149	730,257
	FDI outward stock	570,125	1,785,264	6,148,284	9,732,233
Developed economies	FDI inflows	46,629	172,067	1,134,293	380,022
	FDI inward stock	398,200	1,404,411	3,976,356	6,469,832
	FDI outflows	50,407	225,965	1,092,747	637,360
	FDI outward stock	496,197	1,637,760	5,257,261	8,610,146
Developing economies	FDI inflows	8,455	35,736	253,179	233,227
	FDI inward stock	132,044	364,057	1,739,726	2,232,868
	FDI outflows	3,336	12,701	143,226	83,190
	FDI outward stock	73,927	147,313	868,920	1,035,676

Panel B: FDI in % of output

Notes: The FDI data in Panel A are compiled from *The UNCTAD Handbook of Statistics 2005* (www.unctad.org/en/docs/tdstat30p6_enfr.pdf<http://www.unctad.org/en/docs/tdstat30p6_enfr.pdf>). Table 6.2, p. 33–34, and The World Investment Report 2005, Annex Table B.1, p. 303, and Annex Table B.2, p. 308. The data in Panel B are the sum of inflows and outflows of FDI recorded in the balance of payment's financial account. The graph is based on Bekaert, Harvey, and Lundblad (2006b). Copyright © 2006. Reprinted by permission of the United Nations Conference on Trade and Development. "Most recent" represents an average over 2000–2003.

---

[4]Note that inflows and outflows (and the value of the stock of FDI) should theoretically be the same, but international capital flows involve tricky measurement and valuation issues, so reported numbers do not always match.

clear from Panel B of the Exhibit 1.6, where we scale FDI relative to the size of the economy by dividing by GDP. We show the numbers not only for developed countries but also for developing countries in Africa, Asia, and Latin America. Over the whole period, FDI flows represent less than 2.5% of GDP for the developing countries, whereas they are around 6% of GDP for developed countries.

In the early twenty-first century, FDI flows doubled in size relative to GDP, with higher relative growth in Latin America than in Asia. Although the popular press has made much of China's ability to absorb large quantities of foreign capital through FDI, the figures reveal that China's total FDI flows are rather moderate and are, on average, at about the same level as those of other developing countries in Asia.

Exhibit 1.7 Cross-Border Mergers and Acquisitions by Buyer and Seller, 1990–2004 (in millions of dollars)

	1990		2000		2004	
World	150,576		1,143,816		380,598	
	By Buyer	**By Seller**	**By Buyer**	**By Seller**	**By Buyer**	**By Seller**
Developed Countries	143,070	134,465	1,088,961	1,070,911	339,799	315,851
Europe	92,567	67,596	854,058	625,499	176,095	185,809
Denmark	767	496	4,590	9,122	4,703	5,893
France	21,828	8,183	168,710	35,018	14,994	20,132
Germany	6,795	6,220	58,671	246,990	18,613	35,868
Ireland	730	595	5,675	5,246	3,554	2,878
Italy	5,314	2,165	16,932	18,877	5,167	10,953
Netherlands	5,619	1,484	52,430	33,656	9,130	13,321
Spain	4,087	3,832	39,443	22,248	32,492	7,143
Sweden	12,572	4,489	21,559	13,112	5,906	10,916
United Kingdom	25,873	29,102	382,422	180,029	47,307	58,107
Norway	1,380	668	7,376	10,613	3,080	1,603
Switzerland	4,503	4,569	43,228	13,334	5,564	4,776
North America	30,766	60,427	198,915	401,429	144,068	101,574
Canada	3,139	5,731	39,646	77,079	34,047	19,635
United States	27,627	54,697	159,269	324,350	110,022	81,939
Others	19,736	6,442	35,988	43,983	19,636	28,467
Australia	3,806	2,545	10,856	21,699	10,492	15,128
Japan	14,048	148	20,858	15,541	3,787	8,875
New Zealand	1,854	3,704	1,913	4,397	1,354	4,292
Developing Countries	7,181	16,052	48,475	70,503	39,809	54,700
Argentina	10	6,274	675	5,273	103	285
Bermuda	483	1,296	11,492	3,596	1,883	1,580
Brazil	0	217	429	23,013	9,124	6,639
Chile	0	434	507	2,929	95	1,720
China	60	8	470	2,247	1,125	6,768
Hong Kong, China	1,198	2,620	5,768	4,793	2,963	3,936
India	0	5	910	1,219	863	1,760
Indonesia	49	0	1,445	819	491	1,269
Korea, Republic of	33	0	1,712	6,448	409	5,638
Malaysia	144	86	761	441	816	638
Mexico	680	2,326	4,231	3,965	1,973	6,403
Russia	0	59	225	758	949	4,062
Saudi Arabia	0	0	1,550	2	78	0
Singapore	438	1,143	8,847	1,532	11,638	1,190
South Africa	146	0	6,393	1,171	2,320	1,935
Taiwan	1,385	11	1,138	644	710	398
Thailand	18	70	5	2,569	185	1,236
Turkey	0	113	48	182	108	132

Source: The data are from the UNCTAD, cross-border M&A database (http://stats.unctad.org/FDI/TableViewer/tableView.aspx?ReportId=901). Copyright © 2004. Reprinted by permission of the United Nations Conference on Trade and Development.

Note: The data cover deals involving the acquisition of an equity stake of more than 10 per cent.

International Mergers and Acquisitions

An FDI can be viewed as an international acquisition and is therefore part of the important area of international mergers and acquisitions (M&A). In an international merger or acquisition, a corporation in one country merges with or acquires a corporation in another country. To develop an understanding of the magnitude of such cross-border activity, Exhibit 1.7 presents data on cross-border mergers and acquisitions that is taken from UNCTAD's database, broken down by country of purchaser on the left side and by country of seller on the right side.

Exhibit 1.7 shows that $381 billion of cross-border M&A occurred in 2004. This was substantially above the $151 billion in 1990 but substantially below the $1,144 billion of 2000. Exhibit 1.7 clearly indicates that most M&A activity remains primarily a developed country phenomenon. Of the $381 billion of M&A activity in 2004, purchasers in developed countries accounted for $340 billion, while sellers in developed countries accounted for $316 billion. The United States, United Kingdom, and Canada are the largest acquirers, but the United States and United Kingdom also are the largest sellers.

Determining the appropriate amount a firm should pay for a cross-border acquisition is clearly a skill that will be increasingly important for financial managers in the future. In Chapter 15, we will discuss in more detail how this can be done.

1.4 OTHER IMPORTANT INTERNATIONAL PLAYERS

In the course of its international business activities, an MNC may need financing from an internationally active bank, use economic information provided by an international organization, operate within a regulatory framework set by local governments or international institutions, and need to deal with investor relations in several countries. We provide a brief survey of these other important players in international finance.

International Banks

Where multinational companies go, their banks will follow in order to provide banking services. The globalization of the world economy has gone hand in hand with an internationalization of the banking sector. For example, Citibank, part of the Citigroup financial services company, now operates in virtually every country in the world, and it has a very long tradition of foreign activity, having established offices in Europe and Asia in 1902. Cross-border mergers have also created a few top global asset management firms. For example, Barclays Global Investors (BGI), based in San Francisco and one of the world's largest asset managers, with over $1.5 trillion under management, has a particularly international background. In the 1980s, Wells Fargo Bank in California was one of the leaders in the development of *index funds*, investment vehicles that track existing stock indices without trying to outperform the market. In 1989, Wells Fargo and Nikko Securities, a leading Japanese broker, merged their asset management activities to form a major global investment manager called Wells Fargo Nikko Advisors. In 1995, Barclays, a major British bank, bought that firm and created BGI.

The emergence of more consolidated financial institutions at the global level is a recent phenomenon. One reason is that banks were often protected from foreign takeovers, either through explicit regulation or through political maneuvering, because they are considered to be important and strategic components of the economy. The story of ABN-AMRO trying to take over Antonveneta is a nice illustration of this second case. It was the Uruguay round in the context of GATT that paved the way for the deregulation of the financial services sector. Chapter 11 presents a fuller discussion of these issues.

International Institutions

The International Monetary Fund

The **International Monetary Fund (IMF)** is an international organization of 184 member countries, based in Washington, DC, which was conceived at a United Nations conference convened in Bretton Woods, New Hampshire, in July 1944. The 45 governments represented at that conference sought to build a framework for economic cooperation that would avoid a repetition of the disastrous economic policies that had contributed to the Great Depression of the 1930s. The main goal of the IMF is to ensure the stability of the international monetary and financial system—the system of international payments and exchange rates among national currencies that enables trade to take place between countries, to help resolve crises when they occur, and to promote growth and alleviate poverty. To meet these objectives, the IMF offers *surveillance* and *technical assistance*. Surveillance is the regular dialogue and policy advice that the IMF offers to each of its members. On a regular basis, usually once each year, the IMF conducts in-depth appraisals of each member country's economic situation and suggests sound economic policies.

Technical assistance and training are offered—mostly free of charge—to help member countries strengthen their capacity to design and implement effective policies, including fiscal policy, monetary and exchange rate policies, banking and financial system supervision and regulation, and statistics.

Economic crises often occur when countries borrow excessively from foreign lenders and subsequently experience difficulties financing their balance of payments. We discuss the balance of payments in detail in Chapter 4. The IMF is set up to offer temporary financial assistance to give member countries the breathing room they need to correct balance-of-payment problems. A policy program supported by IMF financing is designed by the national authorities in close cooperation with the IMF, and continued financial support is conditional on effective implementation of this program. This is known as IMF conditionality. The IMF charges market interest rates for these loans. In addition, the IMF is also actively working to reduce poverty in countries around the globe, independently and in collaboration with the World Bank and other organizations. Here, loans are provided at below-market rates.

The IMF's main resources are provided by its member countries, primarily through the payment of quotas, which broadly reflect each country's economic size.

The World Bank

The **World Bank** was created with the IMF in 1944, as the **International Bank for Reconstruction and Development (IBRD)** to facilitate postwar reconstruction and development. Since that time, IBRD's focus has shifted toward poverty reduction, and in 1960, the **International Development Association (IDA)** was established as an integral part of the World Bank. Whereas the IBRD focuses on middle-income countries, the IDA focuses on the poorest countries in the world. Together they provide low-interest loans, interest-free credits, and grants to developing countries for investments in education, health, infrastructure, communications, and other activities.

The World Bank also provides advisory services to developing countries and is actively involved with efforts to reduce and cancel the international debt of the poorest countries. Ken Rogoff, an economist at Harvard University and former chief economist at the IMF, described the World Bank as a complex hybrid of a long-term development bank, an aid agency, and a technical assistance outsourcing center.

Because the contributions from its 184 member countries are relatively modest, the World Bank is also an important borrower in international capital markets. It then lends these funds to developing countries at a small markup.

The World Bank has a number of closely associated sister development organizations that are part of the World Bank Group. The best known is the **International Finance Corporation (IFC)**. The IFC is a global investor and advisor that is committed to promoting private-sector development in developing countries. One of its priorities is the development of domestic financial markets through institution building and the use of innovative financial products.

Multilateral Development Banks

Multilateral Development Banks (MDBs) are generally institutions that provide financial support and professional advice for economic and social development activities in developing countries. The term typically refers to the World Bank Group and four regional development banks: the African Development Bank, the Asian Development Bank, the European Bank for Reconstruction and Development, and the Inter-American Development Bank. These banks have a broad membership that includes both borrowing developing countries and developed donor countries, and their membership is not limited to countries from the region of the regional development bank. While each bank has its own independent legal and operational status, the similar mandates and a considerable number of joint owners lead to a high level of cooperation among MDBs.

The MDBs provide financing for development in three ways. First, they provide long-term loans at market interest rates. To fund these loans, the MDBs borrow on the international capital markets and re-lend to borrowing governments in developing countries. Second, the MDBs offer very long-term loans (often termed *credits*) with interest rates set well below market rates. These credits are funded through direct contributions of governments in donor countries. Finally, grants are sometimes offered mostly for technical assistance, advisory services, or project preparation.

The World Trade Organization (WTO)

In 1995, the GATT members created the WTO, headquartered in Geneva, Switzerland, which had 150 member countries as of 2007. Whereas GATT was a set of rules agreed upon by participating nations, the WTO is an institutional body. The WTO expanded its scope from traded goods to trade within the service sector and intellectual property rights. Various WTO agreements set the legal ground rules for international commerce to hopefully ensure that the multilateral trading system operates smoothly. They are negotiated and signed by a large majority of the world's trading nations, and the agreements are ratified in the parliaments of the member countries.

If there is a trade dispute between countries, the WTO's dispute settlement process helps interpret the agreements and commitments, and it ensures that countries' trade policies conform to them. In the past decade, for example, Europe and the United States have bickered over international trade rules regarding steel and bananas and have needed WTO rulings to end the conflicts.

The Organization for Economic Cooperation and Development (OECD)

In 1961, the **Organization for Economic Cooperation and Development (OECD)** replaced the Organization for European Economic Co-operation (OEEC), which was set up in 1948 with support from the United States and Canada to coordinate the Marshall Plan, which disbursed funds from the United States to Europe for its reconstruction after World War II. Based in Paris, the OECD is a group of 30 relatively rich member countries that provide a setting to examine, devise, and coordinate policies that foster sustainable economic growth and employment, rising standards of living, and financial stability in member countries and beyond. Analysis by the OECD staff and representatives of the member countries in specialized committees may culminate in formal agreements or treaties between member countries. Negotiations at the OECD on taxation and transfer pricing, for example, have paved the way for bilateral tax treaties around the world.

The OECD is renowned for its high-quality databases on economic and social data. Among its publications, its country reviews and surveys are a must-read for policymakers and provide useful information for businesses. The OECD is funded by national contributions from its 30 member countries.

The Bank for International Settlements (BIS)

The **Bank for International Settlements (BIS)**, established in 1930, is an international organization that fosters international monetary and financial cooperation and serves as a bank for central banks. Its head office is in Basel, Switzerland. Promoting monetary and financial stability is one key objective of the BIS. Bimonthly meetings of the governors and other senior officials of the BIS member central banks to discuss monetary and financial matters are instrumental in pursuing this goal. The BIS has standing committees located in Basel to support central banks, and authorities in charge of financial stability more generally, by providing background analysis and policy recommendations. Perhaps the best known is the Basel Committee on Banking Supervision. This committee has developed into a standard-setting body on all aspects of banking supervision, including the Basel II regulatory capital framework, which now regulates the amount of capital that international banks must hold. We discuss this in detail in Chapter 11.

The European Union (EU)

The member states of the European Union set out to create a common market in which goods, services, people, and capital can move around freely and to achieve some degree of economic and political integration. They have developed common policies in a very wide range of fields—from agriculture to culture, from consumer affairs to competition, and from the environment and energy to transport and trade. Now consisting of 27 members, the EU grew out of the post–World War II desire to prevent such killing and destruction as occurred during that war from ever happening again. In the early years, the cooperation was between six countries (Belgium, West Germany, Luxembourg, France, Italy, and the Netherlands) and was mainly about trade and the economy. The EC eventually turned into the EU with the 1992 Treaty of Maastricht. The treaty introduced new forms of cooperation between the member state governments—for example, on defense and in the area of justice and home affairs.

The EU has grown in size with successive waves of country accessions. Denmark, Ireland, and the United Kingdom joined the EC in 1973, followed by Greece in 1981 and Spain and Portugal in 1986. In 1995, Austria, Finland, and Sweden joined what was by that time the EU. The EU welcomed 10 new countries in 2004: Cyprus, the Czech Republic, Estonia, Hungary, Latvia, Lithuania, Malta, Poland, Slovakia, and Slovenia.

While all the original goals of the EU have not yet been completely fulfilled, its importance for everyday life in Europe is undeniable. The Single Market was formally completed at the end of 1992, though there is still work to be done in some areas (for example, creating a genuinely single market in financial services).

During the 1990s, it became increasingly easy for people to move around in Europe, as passport and customs checks were abolished at most of the EU's internal borders. One consequence is greater mobility for EU citizens and businesspeople.

In 1992, the EU decided to go for **economic and monetary union (EMU)**, involving the introduction of a single European currency managed by a European central bank. The single currency, the euro, became a reality on January 1, 2002, when euro notes and coins replaced national currencies in 12 of the 15 countries of the EU (Belgium, Germany, Greece, Spain, France, Ireland, Italy, Luxembourg, the Netherlands, Austria, Portugal, and Finland). We discuss how exchange rate policies evolved within the EU in more detail in Chapter 5.

The EU also negotiates major trade and aid agreements with other countries and is developing a common foreign and security policy. Decision power within the EU rests with the European Commission, a collection of bureaucrats, the Council of Ministers (for example, ministers of finance of the member states who get together regarding financial decisions), and the European Parliament (which is chosen through direct elections).

Governments

Governments are very important players in international financial management as they set the regulatory environment in which multinationals operate. In Chapter 14, we describe how corporations ought to take into account political risk—the risk that government decisions may adversely affect the cash flows of international firms in the country. Governments (central banks in particular) also affect important asset prices, such as interest rates, which constitute the main component of a firm's cost of debt. In Chapter 5, we discuss how central banks influence the value of exchange rates, which is, of course, one of the most critical asset prices for an international financial manager.

Institutional and Individual Investors

Individual Investors

You may wonder what role individual investors play in a book about international financial management of companies. For one thing, as the company's shareholders, they represent the ultimate owners of the company, and we argued earlier that the management should act in the interest of the ultimate investors.

More importantly, though, when the equity of a company is publicly traded on a stock market, individual and institutional investors determine the price of the stock and implicitly determine its expected rate of return. As we will explain in Chapter 13, in doing so, they also determine the cost of equity capital to the company. The company must understand this cost of capital, which, in turn, affects how the company values projects and thus how much investment the company undertakes. Chapters 15 and 16 explore international project valuation using the tools of modern corporate finance.

Institutional Investors

An **institutional investor** is an organization that invests a large pool of money on behalf of individual investors or another organization. Examples of institutional investors include banks, insurance companies, retirement funds, mutual funds, and university endowments. Institutional investors, together with individual investors, help determine the prices of stocks and corporate bonds and therefore also determine the costs of equity and debt for the companies in which they invest.

As noted previously, institutional investors often own relatively large portions of the shares of particular companies and are consequently well positioned to try to exert control on management. The 1980s and 1990s displayed a slow trend of institutionalization, with more savings channeled through institutional investors, which were more sophisticated and more interested in the international diversification of their portfolios.

Hedge Funds and Private Equity Firms

In recent years, much of investors' money has flowed to **hedge funds**. Like mutual funds, hedge funds pool investors' money and invest those funds in financial instruments in an effort to make a positive return. Many hedge funds seek to profit in all kinds of markets by pursuing leveraging and other speculative investment practices that may increase the risk of investment loss. The number of such funds has grown exponentially, particularly in the United States and Europe. Whereas mutual funds are strictly regulated—in the United States they fall under the Investment Act of 1940—hedge funds operate under exemptions to the law. Theoretically, this limits their investors to people who are sophisticated and affluent. For example, hedge fund investors must have a minimum amount of marketable wealth to qualify. Because of their light regulation, hedge funds can invest in just about anything and may make extensive use of derivatives. They also charge fees as a function of performance, whereas mutual funds charge fees as a percentage of assets under management. As the hedge fund industry continues to grow, hedge funds may become more and more important in determining asset prices.

Operating under a structure similar to that of hedge funds are **private equity firms**. These firms raise money from rich individual investors and institutional investors and invest in a number of individual companies. These companies can be private (that is, not traded on a stock market), but larger private equity firms, such as Kohlberg Kravis Roberts & Co. and The Blackstone Group also invest in companies listed on public exchanges and take them private (that is, de-list from the exchange). Private equity firms typically control the management of the companies they invest in, often bringing in new management teams that focus on making the overall company more valuable. Private equity firms are increasingly involved in international acquisitions and may own genuine MNCs. Hedge funds and private equity firms are often very actively looking for firms with poor corporate governance as potential targets for their value-enhancing activities.

1.5 GLOBALIZATION AND THE MULTINATIONAL FIRM: BENEFACTOR OR MENACE?

Over the past few decades, the world economy has witnessed enormous momentum toward trade and capital liberalization, deregulation, and the privatization of state-owned companies. The multinationalization of business is proceeding at a rapid pace. Yet, toward the end of the 1990s and the beginning of the current century, several events and developments threatened the trend toward increasing globalization. These events include the recent problems experienced by multilateral trade liberalization, the currency and banking crises many countries experienced at the end of the 1990s, derivatives and corporate scandals that put capitalism more generally in a negative light, and the rise of the so-called anti-globalist movement.

In this section, we reflect on the possibility that these events may lead to a slowing or halting of the globalization process. This is a critical question that every international financial manager should ponder regularly. Managing financial risks in an integrated world economy is very different from managing risk in a world where governments fully assert their sovereignty, hamper international trade, and limit international capital flows. While nobody can foresee the future, it is our opinion that if societal trends are generally welfare enhancing, they will likely continue. Much ink has flowed on this topic, and the effects of trade liberalization (economic integration) and capital market liberalization (financial integration) on economic welfare are controversial. We turn to the rapidly growing academic literature on the real effects of globalization and foreign direct investment to find some hopefully objective clues as to whether recent events really have the potential to undermine globalization.

A Rocky Road to Free Trade

Several recent developments have slowed the trend toward more trade openness. First, unilateral trade liberalization in the developing world has slowed down considerably. There seems to be more emphasis on preferential trade agreements in particular regions, but these may challenge the viability of multilateral trade rules. Second, recent efforts to open the European services markets to increased competition in the context of the European Union fell short of initial ambitions. Third, the multinational trade talks in the Doha round have all but collapsed after very rocky proceedings. Violent demonstrations by opponents of free trade have interrupted several meetings, and the various countries have had difficulty even setting the agenda. The WTO clearly faces an identity crisis following the suspension of the Doha round of trade negotiation in 2006, after countries failed to reach agreement about reducing farming subsidies and lowering import taxes.

The sudden increase in economic protectionism seems dangerous, as we have argued that trade openness seems to unambiguously create economic growth. Here, we review two critiques of the trade liberalization process that have some merit. They do not call for less trade openness but for a different emphasis and process toward trade openness.

Trade Openness and Economic Risk

Countries should not only care about their long-term level of economic growth but also about the variability of growth. If a global economy exposes countries to additional risks and causes deeper recessions than a closed economy would face, many policymakers and their citizens may prefer the calmer waters of steady growth in a relatively closed economy. Harvard economist Dani Rodrik, among others, has argued that trade openness increases external risk because open economies are more buffeted by international shocks (changes in commodity prices, exchange rates, foreign business cycles, and so forth). These shocks may create volatile swings in the fortunes of internationally oriented businesses, with adverse implications for the job security of the people employed in these companies (see Rodrik, 1998).

Such increases in real variability call for government transfers to mitigate external risk: Social Security, unemployment benefits, job training, and so on. Indeed, small European countries, such as those in Scandinavia, have simultaneously opened their economies and developed very extensive welfare states to protect their citizens against the economic insecurities generated by globalization. However, the social safety nets in most developing countries are anemic. This argument suggests that unbridled trade openness without the existence of government welfare programs may be ill advised.

Fairer Trade Openness?

Within the EU, the Common Agricultural Policy protects farmers through subsidies and other measures. In the 1980s, enormous dairy subsidies led to such overproduction of butter and milk that increasingly drastic measures had to be taken to get rid of the "butter mountain" and "milk lake." This unfortunately also included disposing of vast quantities of butter on the world market at low prices. While the introduction of production quotas has reduced this problem, it has not gone away completely. In the United States, growers of corn, wheat, cotton, soybeans, and rice receive more than 90% of all farm subsidies; Japan is notorious for the protection of its rice farmers.

Clearly, developed countries have maintained protectionist measures and subsidies in the agricultural sector. Yet, it is in that sector that the comparative advantage of developing countries is likely largest. The Columbia University Nobel Prize–winning economist Joseph Stiglitz, in his 2002 book *Globalization and Its Discontents*, has railed against such inequalities in the movement toward trade openness. Other examples include the Uruguay round opening up markets for financial services (benefiting developed countries with large international banks) but not for maritime and construction services (benefiting developing countries). As often happens, what is desirable at an economic level is not always achievable politically. For example, while the agricultural sector has shrunk considerably in most developed countries, its political power remains disproportionately large.

Do International Capital Flows Cause Havoc?

In the 1990s, a number of emerging markets that had previously opened up their capital markets to foreign investment experienced significant currency and banking crises. First, Mexico was hit in 1994, and then Southeast Asia in 1997 and Russia in 1998. These crises caused real economic pain, with output falling and unemployment rising dramatically in their wake. The crises also resulted in a reversal of capital flows, and many developing countries are now exporting capital to rather than importing capital from developed countries. We discuss these issues further in Chapter 4. Many blamed the crises on foreigners—either foreign investors or international organizations such as the IMF. The crises also intensified the political and economic debate about the benefits and costs of financial globalization. Are these criticisms well founded? Let's examine the theoretical benefits and costs of financial globalization and what the record to date shows.

Benefits of Financial Openness

In theory, the economic benefits of financial globalization are undeniable. With free capital markets, the international capital market channels savings to its most productive uses, wherever they may be. International financial markets allow residents of different countries to pool various risks, achieving more effective insurance than purely domestic arrangements would allow. A country suffering a temporary recession, a natural disaster, or simply a lack of capital can borrow abroad. Because risks are shared, the cost of funding may decrease, leading firms to invest more and in higher-yielding, riskier projects. This in turn should increase growth.

Costs of Financial Globalization

Of course, foreign capital need not be efficiently invested. One view holds that in the aftermath of crises, foreign capital led to a consumption binge, unrealistically high asset prices, and low interest rates, which in turn fueled construction and real estate booms. These phenomena were greatly helped by weak banking sectors in the capital receiving countries which failed to stop excessive borrowing using inflated assets as collateral. A boom–bust cycle resulted. Fickle foreign capital can leave at the first hint of trouble, and financial volatility can easily turn into real volatility when businesses go broke and banks collapse. This view suggests that liberalization dramatically increased financial-sector vulnerability in many countries and increased real volatility.

Financial globalization may also mean a loss of fiscal autonomy as it is difficult to tax internationally footloose capital relative to less mobile factors of production, notably labor. Analogously, MNCs can also shift "profits" across countries and make it more difficult for tax offices to collect taxes.

Nevertheless, in a globalizing world where multinational corporations account for much economic activity, the effectiveness of capital controls likely decreases. Desai, Foley, and Hines (2004) show that multinational corporations employ "internal capital markets" (between the affiliates of the MNC) to circumvent capital controls. They also demonstrate that MNCs in countries with capital controls shift profits to other countries and invest less than in other, similar countries. Consequently, imposing capital controls can have potentially severe economic costs and lead to reduced tax revenues.

What the Data Show

Because a large number of emerging economies have liberalized at different times, we can examine the data and see what has happened in countries that liberalized relative to countries that did not. While such exercises are never definitive, they at least give us a better overall picture of the evidence than some well-chosen case studies. Recent work by Bekaert, Harvey, and Lundblad (2005) demonstrates that countries with open equity markets grow 1% faster per year than countries with closed markets and that countries with open capital accounts also grow faster than countries with severe capital controls. Although not everyone agrees with these findings, they do appear to be robust. It is generally accepted that countries with better financial development (a stronger banking sector, for instance) and better institutions (higher-quality governments) are more likely to experience growth benefits after opening up their capital markets than countries with weak development and poor institutions.

The evidence on real volatility is more mixed (see Bekaert, Harvey, and Lundblad, 2006a; and Kose, Prasad, and Terrones, 2003). Liberalizing countries on average appear to experience a small decrease in real volatility, but the institutional background of the countries is very important. Countries with a highly (less) developed banking sector or high- (low-) quality government institutions experience decreases (increases) in real volatility. The assertion that globalization has gone too far for emerging economies is consequentially not supported by empirical analysis. Nevertheless, the crises that have occurred suggest that financial integration is best accompanied with vigorous reforms of the domestic financial sector and local institutions.

Interestingly, MNCs can provide a buffer during an economic crisis. When emerging markets suffer a currency crisis, it often goes hand in hand with severe economic disruption and recession. While the currency depreciation should improve the international competitiveness of local firms, imperfect capital markets often make it difficult for local companies to avail themselves of these opportunities. Desai, Foley, and Forbes (2004) show that multinational affiliates are both better able to capitalize on these competitiveness effects and better able to circumvent the financing difficulties that local firms face. In doing so, multinational affiliates expand activity precisely when local firms are handicapped. They can do so because they can sell products within the multinational network (to the U.S. parent, for example) and obtain intra-firm borrowing and equity infusions. In short, the enhanced access to global product and capital markets of multinational firms allows them to buffer crisis economies from the severity of economic shocks.

The Anti-globalist Movement and MNCs

Recent trade rounds have not only had to cope with political squabbling between countries but also with a powerful anti-globalist movement that has organized demonstrations around trade talk centers, which have often turned violent. The anti-globalist movement is particularly important as it has identified the multinational corporations as one of the main "villains" of the globalization phenomenon.

What Are Anti-globalists?

Anti-globalization is an umbrella term that encompasses a number of separate social movements, united in their opposition to the globalization of corporate economic activity and the free trade with developing nations that results from such activity. Members of the anti-globalist movement generally believe that laissez-faire capitalism on a global scale is detrimental to poor countries and to disadvantaged people in rich countries.[5]

Apart from multinationals, much of the critique is aimed at global financial institutions such as the World Bank, the IMF, and the WTO. Especially under attack is the so-called Washington consensus model of development, which, as promoted by international financial institutions (especially the IMF), is interpreted as requiring macroeconomic austerity, privatization, and a relatively laissez-faire approach to economic management. It is believed that these policies exacerbate unemployment and poverty. While there are serious criticisms of IMF-supported policies, the point should be made that seeing a doctor near a patient does not mean the doctor made the patient sick. The doctor was called because the patient was sick. Too often, unsustainable policies in the developing countries are the root of the problem.

Many anti-globalists are part of so-called nongovernmental organizations (NGOs), which advocate global human rights, protection of the environment, poverty alleviation, fair trade, and so on. The movement's largest and most visible mode of organizing remains mass demonstrations against international meetings. An anti-globalist protest against the 1999 WTO meetings in Seattle, Washington, turned violent, and more than 600 protesters were arrested and dozens of people were injured. Anti-globalists also destroyed the windows of storefronts of businesses owned or franchised by targeted corporations such as Nike and Starbucks. At the Genoa, Italy, Group of Eight (G8) Summit in 2001, a young Genoa citizen died and several demonstrators were hospitalized.

---

[5]*No Logo*, the book by the Canadian journalist Naomi Klein, which criticized the production practices of multinational corporations and the omnipresence of brand-driven marketing in popular culture, has become a manifesto of the movement.

Why Do Anti-globalists Dislike Multinationals so Much?

One worry is that multinational activities will harm the environment. This can happen because governments keen on FDI degrade environmental standards (the race-to-the-bottom effect) or because heavily polluting industries relocate to countries with lower standards, in particular to developing countries (the pollution-haven effect). The evidence to date is inconclusive. A second critique is the "sweatshop" argument: People in developing nations slave away for MNCs at low wages and for excruciating long hours under horrific conditions.

Finally, globalization is seen as a threat to employment in the home countries. The internationalization of the labor market brought about both by financial and economic globalization is arguably the most contentious issue in the societal debate about the effects of globalization.

First, there was the idea that international trade would suck blue-collar manufacturing jobs to lower-cost countries. For example, when Ross Perot ran for president in the United States in 1992, he opposed NAFTA, arguing that voters should listen for the "giant sucking sound" of American jobs heading south to Mexico should NAFTA be ratified.

More recently, the outsourcing phenomenon is seen as threatening white-collar jobs. Because telecom charges have tumbled worldwide, workers in far-flung locations are easily and inexpensively connected to customers in the developed world. Moreover, it is no longer just basic data processing and call centers that are being outsourced to lower-wage countries but also software programming, medical diagnostics, engineering design, law, accounting, finance, and even business consulting. These services can now be delivered electronically from anywhere in the world, exposing skilled white-collar workers to increased competition.

The Economic Effects of FDI and Multinational Activity

Setting aside nationalistic pride and anti-globalist slogans, scholars have studied the economic effects of FDI quite thoroughly, and some firm conclusions can be drawn.[6]

The bleak view that FDI simply leads to unemployment in the company's home country and depressed wages and exploited workers in the host country does not hold up to close scrutiny.

Let's start with the effects on the home country. There is no denying that job losses occur when production facilities are shifted abroad or certain tasks are outsourced. However, FDI is a two-way street. Foreign companies investing in the home country create jobs. For example, studies indicate that over the past 30 years, the jobs and output created by foreign-owned affiliates offset the losses suffered by the U.S. manufacturing sector.

Moreover, Mihir Desai, Fritz Foley, and James Hines, Jr. (2005a) show that U.S. firms investing abroad also increase their domestic investment and domestic employment. Hence, a company's investment abroad could end up protecting jobs at home by strengthening the parent company, for example, by shielding it from the damaging effects of currency fluctuations and trade-inhibiting tax policies in the home country. Recent studies (see, for example, Amiti and Wei, 2005) also suggest that outsourcing so far has not led to net job losses because globalizing firms also create many jobs.

Let's turn to the effects of FDI on host countries. While it is likely that some working conditions may be less than ideal (definitely compared to what workers are used to in developed countries), the preponderance of the evidence suggests that MNCs pay higher wages than local firms. Unfortunately, there is only sparse evidence of those higher wages having a "spillover" effect on the wages local companies pay.

Proponents of FDI argue that its main advantages are an improvement in allocative efficiency (employing capital where it is most productive) and technology transfer and productivity spillovers. Foreign direct investors presumably have access to productive knowledge that is otherwise not available to producers in the host country: technological know-how, marketing and managing skills, export contacts, coordinated relationships with suppliers and

---

[6]Most of what is written here builds on the review article by Robert Lipsey (2002). Other articles include Linda Goldberg (2004), focusing on the financial services sector, and Brian Aitken and Ann Harrison (1999), which is a nice example of a careful empirical study with detailed data for one country (Venezuela).

customers, and reputation. FDI may consequently help close the "idea gap" between developing and developed countries. Yet the empirical evidence on FDI-induced improvements in productivity is somewhat inconclusive to date.[7] Nevertheless, there is general agreement that FDI has boosted economic growth in host countries, with one authoritative study suggesting that the growth effects are only significant when the host countries boast a sufficiently educated population (see Borenzstein, De Gregorio, and Lee, 1998).

Pondering the economic effects of FDI for host countries is important because many countries offer incentives (outright subsidies or reduced taxes) to attract FDI, and host countries must make sure the benefits from FDI justify the costs.

Some Final Thoughts on Globalization

Can globalization withstand all the challenges already discussed? These problems got worse in the beginning of the twenty-first century. The terrorist attacks of September 11, 2001, at New York City's World Trade Center and at the Pentagon in Washington, DC, ushered in a new era of geopolitical tension that may increase the pressures for governments to increase oversight and re-regulate.

The risk that the globalization process may be halted is now real. Jeffrey Garten (2003) suggests that the leaders of multinational companies are today the only natural champions of an increasingly open world economy. Their agenda needs to include vigorous pressure on governments to move ahead with trade negotiations and a push toward better mechanisms to ensure global financial stability.

We believe globalization is the only way forward, yet the arguments of the critics should not be ignored. There does seem to be some evidence that, on average, workers in developed countries have not benefited from globalization and that the benefits of globalization in developing countries have not as of yet brought widespread welfare enhancements.[8] It is possible that this is because of the incompleteness of the process; it is equally possible that governments must intervene to help better spread the newly created wealth. For example, whereas it was generally believed that the IT revolution increased the relative value of skilled workers relative to nonskilled ones, it is now becoming clear that globalization also contributes to this trend. With the vast labor forces of India and China gradually becoming integrated into the world's labor force, this massive increase in labor relative to capital is likely to have affected their relative return. High returns to capital typically mean that the rich get richer. At the same time, the skill level in emerging markets is rising so that even some skilled labor in the Western world will feel the brunt. Because globalization destroys some jobs and creates others, it is natural that it creates uncertainty and that trade-displaced workers feel left behind by the benefits. This should put pressure on governments to help as much as possible those displaced by globalization, for example, by effective retraining and employment policies. If the average worker does not feel better off due to the globalization process, resentment will rise. Similarly, developing countries must ensure that the benefits of openness are shared widely. And the dialogue between developing countries and developed countries should change. A fair globalization should probably involve developed countries opening their markets more to these products in which developing countries can be highly competitive (such as agricultural products). 1987 Nobel Peace Prize Laureate and former president of Costa Rica, Oskar Arias Sánchez, said it best: "We [the developing countries] don't want your [the developed countries'] handouts; we want the right to sell our products in the world markets."

---

[7]Lee Branstetter (2005) uses citations of patents to demonstrate that Japanese FDI in the United States increases the flow of knowledge spillovers both from the Japanese investing firms to American companies and vice versa. However, Bruce Aitken and Ann Harrison (1999) find that the net gains from foreign investment are small as FDI improves the productivity of the foreign-owned plant but negatively affects the productivity of domestically owned plants.
[8]The evidence in Mittali Das and Sanket Mohapatra (2003) suggests that the lowest income classes benefit from liberalization, but it is possible that the results do not extend to other forms of liberalizations in countries not included in the study.

The field of international management addresses financial decisions facing corporate managers regarding trade and investment across national borders. While practical examples and case studies are useful study guides, we stress fundamental concepts, principles, and analytical theories that are bound to be more resilient to the constantly changing challenges of operating in a competitive global market place.

The fundamental idea of this book is to present international financial management in a modern, theoretically correct approach that incorporates analysis of data and thus allows the student to learn how well or poorly the current theories are supported by the data. Throughout the book, we emphasize the sources of risks that arise in international financial markets and how these risks can be managed. This book is unique in its proposed treatment of international markets and instruments as well as standard issues in international corporate finance.

This book is divided into six parts:

- Part I: Introduction to Foreign Exchange Markets and Risks
- Part II: International Parity Conditions and Exchange Rate Determination
- Part III: International Capital Markets
- Part IV: International Corporate Finance
- Part V: Managing Ongoing Operations
- Part VI: Foreign Currency Derivatives

Part I: Introduction to Foreign Exchange Markets and Risks

Part I examines the spot foreign exchange market in Chapter 2, the forward foreign exchange market in Chapter 3, the balance of payments in Chapter 4, and alternative exchange rate systems in Chapter 5. By the time you have finished these chapters, you will understand the nature of transactions foreign exchange risk and how it can be managed, and you will have an understanding of the links between the balance of payments and the demands and supplies of currencies that flow through the foreign exchange market. The fact that different countries choose different exchange rate systems implies that risks of loss due to fluctuations in exchange rates and the ability to manage these risks differ across countries.

Part II: International Parity Conditions and Exchange Rate Determination

Part II examines the relationships between interest rates and exchange rates, and prices and exchange rates. Chapter 6 explains the foremost building block of international finance: the theory of interest rate parity. This crucial concept explains why differences in interest rates across countries are neither an opportunity for investors to make money nor an opportunity for corporations to lower their borrowing costs. Chapter 7 discusses speculation and risk in the foreign exchange market. We examine the issue of whether the uncertainty of future exchange rates affects the expected profitability from investing abroad. Chapter 8 examines the concept of purchasing power parity, which describes the relationship between the prices of goods in different countries and the exchange rate. It also discusses the links between inflation rates and rates of change of exchange rates. We will show that purchasing power parity works quite poorly in contrast to interest rate parity. Chapter 9 then discusses management issues that arise in such an environment. The competitive pricing of products in different countries and the evaluation of foreign subsidiaries are examined in some depth. With all the building blocks out of the way, Chapter 10 explains how economists think about exchange rate determination and explores alternative methods that are used to forecast future exchange rates.

Part III: International Capital Markets

Part III surveys the international capital markets. The international bond market is examined in Chapter 11. Multinational corporations that want to issue debt have a variety of issues to consider. Foremost among these is the currency of the debt, and other issues include the maturity of the debt, the type of interest rate payments that are promised and when the principal will be repaid, and who to use as a marketing agent for the debt. The international equity markets are explored in Chapter 12. A key consideration for firms is the cost of capital. Only projects whose rate of return exceeds the firm's cost of capital are viable, and Chapter 13 explains how international investors determine the expected return on equity and thus set the costs of capital for corporations. Chapter 14 explores the ideas of political risk and country risk. The history of direct foreign investment by multinational corporations is replete with instances in which the MNC has lost either part or all of the value of an investment because of a political decision in the host country. Evaluating and managing these risks are particularly important skills to have as the forces of globalization induce even more overseas investments.

Part IV: International Corporate Finance

Part IV contains a blueprint for how to evaluate the viability of international projects. Chapter 15 lays the foundation with an extensive analysis of international capital budgeting using the adjusted net present value (ANPV) framework. The value of a project is decomposed into parts that are attributable to the cash flows that would accrue to the firm if it were all-equity financed, parts that are attributable to how the project is financed including interest tax shields, and parts that are attributable to growth options. Chapter 16 continues, with some additional more advanced issues in international capital budgeting. Foreign projects can be valued, as in Chapter 15, by discounting expected foreign currency cash flows. They can also be valued by discounting expected domestic currency cash flows. Chapter 16 explains how these two approaches are related. It also explores interest tax shields on foreign currency borrowing in more detail. Although risk management issues arise throughout the book, Chapter 17 uses the ANPV framework to show how risk management can add value to a multinational corporation.

Part V: Managing Ongoing Operations

Part V considers two basic topics that are part of the toolkit of any international financial manager. Chapter 18 examines how firms finance international trade. Because shipping goods across countries involves both time and a change of legal jurisdiction, multinational corporations and the international banks that service them have developed a variety of vehicles to make sure that exporters get paid by the importers and the importers actually receive the goods. Managing working capital is the topic of Chapter 19. With operations in many countries, the management of a multinational corporation's short-term assets and liabilities is a complex task. The fall in communication costs that was one of the spurs to increased globalization has increased the ability of the MNC to manage its assets and liabilities more efficiently. When one subsidiary of an MNC sells goods to another, transfer prices are involved. Chapter 19 also explores how transfer pricing is used to shift income around the world while recognizing that the MNC operates within a particular legal environment that constrains its ability to evade taxes.

Part VI: Foreign Currency Derivatives

Part VI introduces foreign currency options in Chapter 20 and interest rate and foreign currency swaps in Chapter 21. These derivative instruments are incredibly useful in managing foreign exchange risks. Option strategies can be described as purchasing insurance in the sense that you pay up front to protect yourself against bad events, but you participate in the profitability if the bad event doesn't occur. Interest rate swaps allow a financial manager to change a firm's debt from fixed interest rate payments to floating interest rate payments, while currency swaps allow the financial manager to change the currency of denomination of the debt.

A Final Introduction

We still have one introduction to make. Throughout the book, two brothers, Ante and Freedy Handel, will be discussing various international financial management problems and important controversial issues in international finance in the *Point–Counterpoint* feature. These brothers, who are enrolled in an international finance class, certainly don't share a common viewpoint. Ante typically rails against free trade and free markets as he believes financial markets are less than efficient. He consequently thinks that prices do not necessarily correctly reflect information about a firm's prospects. Freedy believes more in the power of the capitalist system to allocate resources efficiently, and he consequently believes that financial markets by and large get things right.[9]

The *Point–Counterpoint* feature is designed to explore areas of controversy and is consistent with the philosophy of this book. Many textbooks often provide short, easy answers to difficult questions. That approach is fine when there is general agreement about an issue, but often the situation is more subtle and intricate than standard books may make you believe. The *Point–Counterpoint* feature is designed to raise issues that are contentious and that are often not fully resolved or well understood by the academic and practitioner communities. Luckily, the two brothers have a very sober thinking cousin, Suttle Trooth, who moderates their discussions and reflects state-of-the-art thinking on the issues. Here, we start the brothers off discussing a recent takeover attempt of a U.S. oil company by a Chinese company.

POINT–COUNTERPOINT

China Goes Global and Gets Rebuffed

It's early August, and Ante and Freedy Handel enjoy their vacation, relaxing at home. Ante, comfortably lounging in a splendid sofa designed and produced in Milan, Italy, looks up from his newspaper and barks to Freedy: "Hey, that Chinese company withdrew its bid on Unocal. Our Congressional Representatives finally got something right because we don't want the Chinese government owning our strategic assets." Freedy, savoring a refreshing Leffe, sounded baffled. "I have not heard of this case, can I see the paper? I thought foreign direct investment is good for the world economy as it places the control of assets into the hands of the people that value them the most."

Ante gives the article to Freedy, who grows increasingly agitated as he reads. Here are the facts. On April 4, 2005, directors of Unocal, the twelfth-largest U.S. oil company, accepted a $16.5 billion offer to be bought by Chevron, the second-largest U.S. oil company. However, on June 22, 2005, the Chinese National Offshore Oil Corporation (CNOOC), the third-largest Chinese oil company and a company smaller than Unocal, made an $18.5 billion counteroffer to purchase Unocal. In mid-July 2005, Chevron increased its bid to $17.3 billion, still below CNOOC's bid. However, CNOOC's offer was facing unprecedented political opposition in Washington. For example, in a letter to the Treasury Department, 41 politicians, both Republicans and Democrats, raised concerns that a Chinese takeover of Unocal could compromise national security. Many other high-ranking U.S. government officials also expressed doubts about the desirability of CNOOC's purchase of Unocal. The situation was resolved August 2, 2005, when CNOOC withdrew its bid, thus allowing Chevron to complete the takeover.

---

[9]For the language buffs, *handel* is Dutch for "trade" or "commerce." In German, it means "trade" or "transaction," but *händel suchen* also means "making trouble" or "quarreling," and the brothers do a lot of that.

"See!" blurts Ante. "Clearly, the Chinese want to grab strategic U.S. oil assets, and that simply is a threat to U.S. national security." Freedy gasps, "Mercantilism is dead, Ante. You have got to be joking. Unocal is a small player. It only produces 0.8% of total U.S. crude oil production. Most of what you buy is international anyway. Where do you think your sofa is from?"

"Wait a minute, wise guy," Ante retorts. "Read the article! Unocal is a significant provider of natural gas to Southeast Asia (the Philippines, Bangladesh, and Thailand), where 70% of its oil and gas reserves are located. It is also a primary investor in the Baku-Tbilisi-Ceyhan (BTC) Pipeline, which carries oil from the Caspian to the Mediterranean. If China acquired a share through CNOOC, it would gain a foothold in a region of utmost strategic importance to the United States."

At that point, Suttle Trooth strolls in, sporting a cool red iPod Nano. "Hey, guys, have you heard that new killer CD by Radiohead?" Noting Ante and Freedy's agitated faces, he quickly gets the picture. "Boy, you really are quarreling again."

Ante and Freedy show the article to Suttle, both smirking confidently and thinking that Suttle will prove them right. "Aha." Suttle sighs, "What else is new? The American public and its politicians were up in arms in the 1970s when the Saudis recycled their petrodollars buying into U.S. industries, and again in the 1980s when Japan embarked on a buying spree of American assets including a real estate icon like Rockefeller Center in New York. The Americans just do not like foreigners getting their hands on important, 'symbolic,' American assets. Nevertheless, it remains bad economics. The results on the economic effects of FDI for host countries are rather unanimously positive. Freedy is hence correct that much of the economic protectionism that goes on is simply bad politics catering to some latent xenophobic feelings that exist everywhere. I also do not believe the strategic value of Unocal is large or that a Chinese takeover of a relatively small American oil and gas firm is a risk to U.S. national security. However, there is one thing about the takeover that is a bit unfair. Look at what the article says about the financing of the deal."

Suttle continues, "CNOOC planned to pay for Unocal by using substantial loans ($7 billion) from its parent company (also called CNOOC), $6 billion from a major Chinese government-owned bank (Industrial and Commercial Bank of China), and only $3 billion from its financial advisers (JPMorgan and Goldman Sachs). The problem is that the $7 billion loan from the government-owned parent company would require interest payments at 3.6% (lower than U.S. government Treasury bonds yield), and the loan from the government-owned bank was interest free. While these rates are certainly 'off-market,' the fact of the matter is that governments routinely subsidize firms all around the world, and such subsidies are quite valuable to those who can obtain them. Overall, though, I think this situation was much ado about nothing. China's tremendous economic growth requires tons of energy, and the country simply must be assertive in securing oil and gas supplies from the Middle East, Central Asia, South America, and Africa, regions that provide the U.S. with a large share of its own imported oil, as well. Oil and natural gas are commodities that are traded on world markets. I just hope China doesn't find a way to retaliate against the U.S. after being rebuffed this blatantly. After all, CNOOC's bid should have won." Freedy smiles while Ante sinks a bit deeper in the Italian sofa.

1.7 SUMMARY

This chapter introduces the globalization phenomenon and the resulting dominance of the corporate landscape by multinational corporations. The main points and concepts of the chapter are as follows:

1. Globalization refers to the increasing connectivity and integration of countries and corporations and the people within them in terms of their economic, political, and social activities. A multinational

corporation is a company that produces and sells goods or services in more than one country.

2. Globalization proceeded through a process of trade and financial liberalization. Trade liberalizations happened through countries reducing trade barriers unilaterally, within regional arrangements such as the European Union, and through multilateral action within the context of GATT. The abolition of capital controls, occurring first in many developed countries in the 1980s and then in many emerging markets in the 1990s, led to increasingly globalized financial markets.

3. Financial markets also became more sophisticated, especially because of a derivatives revolution occurring in the 1970s and 1980s. A derivative security is an investment from which the payoff is derived from the performance of underlying assets or asset prices, such as exchange rates. Derivatives make it easy to hedge various business risks, including the risks of changes in the value of the exchange rate.

4. Multinationals enter foreign markets through exports and imports, licensing arrangements (where they earn royalties from companies that manufacture and distribute their products abroad), franchising (where the MNC is more involved but still receives periodic fees), joint ventures, or simply local production and distribution facilities. Globally integrated firms with strategy, management, and operations all streamlined in one global entity are also appearing.

5. In the Anglo-American countries such as the United States, the goal of an MNC is to maximize shareholder wealth, whereas in many other countries, the interests of other stakeholders (such as labor, governments, creditors, and suppliers) are also taken into account. Modern corporate finance holds that shareholder wealth maximization is the goal of each corporation.

6. Agency theory explores the problems that arise because the owners of the firm do not typically manage the firm, and it devises ways to resolve these problems.

7. Corporate governance is the legal and financial structure that controls the relationship between the company's owners and its management. Recent corporate scandals at Enron, Tyco, Worldcom, Parmalat, and many other companies demonstrate that corporate governance can be rather poor, even in developed countries.

8. Corporate governance can be enhanced at the firm level by an independent board of directors, concentrated share ownership (although this has drawbacks), executive compensation that motivates management to act in the interest of the shareholders, shareholder activism and litigation, and ultimately (the threat of) hostile takeovers.

9. The Sarbanes-Oxley Act of 2002 attempts to improve corporate governance in the United States, but many domestic and international companies view it as costly to implement.

10. Foreign direct investment occurs when a company from one country makes an investment in a new or existing firm in another country that leads to an ownership interest of at least 10%. FDI flows across countries have increased manifold over the last decades.

11. Important international organizations that provide financing to countries include the IMF, the World Bank and various multilateral development banks.

12. The WTO sets the legal ground rules for international trade, whereas the BIS is the central bank for the central banks and promotes monetary and financial stability.

13. The EU unites 27 European countries in a common market with common policies for a wide range of fields—essentially free mobility of capital and people, and, for a subset of countries, a common currency and monetary policy.

14. Both trade liberalization and financial globalization seem to have beneficial economic effects; yet the process toward globalization is less than smooth and has many critics. One criticism is that globalization increases "real risk"—that is, that it increases the chance that economies will suffer recessions and temporary slumps in employment.

15. The anti-globalist movement encompasses a number of social movements that are opposed to globalization because it is supposedly detrimental to poor countries and disadvantaged people in rich countries. However, the academic evidence strongly suggests that FDI typically has genuinely positive effects, both in target and in host countries. Yet globalization may destroy jobs and leaves some people worse off; it is not clear yet how its macroeconomic benefits have distributed throughout society at large.

16. The field of international financial management addresses financial decisions facing corporate managers regarding trade and investment across national borders.

BIBLIOGRAPHY

Aitken, Brian J., and Ann E. Harrison, 1999, "Do domestic firms benefit from direct foreign investment? Evidence from Venezuela," *American Economic Review 89,* pp. 605–618.

Alcalá, Francisco, and Antonio Ciccone, May 2004, "Trade and Productivity," *Quarterly Journal of Economics* 119, pp. 613–646.

Allen, Franklin, Jun Qian, and Meijun Qian, 2005, "Law, Finance, and Economic Growth in China," *Journal of Financial Economics* 77, pp. 57–116.

Amiti, Mary, and Shang-Jin Wei, 2005, "Fear of Service Outsourcing: Is It Justified?", *Economic Policy* 42, p. 307.

Auer, Peter, 2006, *Offshoring and the Internationalization of Employment: A Challenge for a Fair Globalization?* Geneva: International Institute for Labor Studies.

Baxter, Marianne, and Michael A. Kouparitsas, 2006, "What Determines Bilateral Trade Flows?" National Bureau of Economic Research working paper.

Becht, Marco, Patrick Bolton, and Ailsa Röell, 2005, "Corporate Governance and Control," European Corporate Governance Institute working paper.

Bekaert, Geert, and Campbell R. Harvey, 2003, "Emerging Markets Finance," *Journal of Empirical Finance* 10, pp. 3–55.

Bekaert, Geert, Campbell R. Harvey, and Christian Lundblad, 2005, "Does financial liberalization spur growth?" *Journal of Financial Economics* 77, pp. 3–55.

_____, 2006a, "Growth, Volatility and Financial Liberalization," *Journal of International Money and Finance* 25, pp. 370–403.

_____, 2006b, "Financial Openness and the Chinese Growth Experience," working paper.

_____, 2007, "International Risk Sharing, Openness and Growth?" working paper.

Borenzstein, Eduardo, José De Gregorio, and Jong-Wha Lee, 1998, "How Does Foreign Direct Investment Affect Economic Growth?" *Journal of International Economics* 45, pp. 115–135.

Branstetter, Lee, 2005, "Is Foreign Direct Investment a Channel of Knowledge Spillovers? Evidence from Japan's FDI in the United States," Columbia University working paper.

Claessens, Stijn, Simeon Djankov, and Larry H.P. Lang, 2000, "The Separation of Ownership and Control in East Asian Corporations," *Journal of Financial Economics* 58, pp. 81–112.

Das, Mittali, and Sanket Mohapatra, 2003, "Income Inequality: The Aftermath of Stock Market Liberalization in Emerging Markets," *Journal of Empirical Finance* 10, pp. 217–248.

Desai, Mihir, C. Fritz Foley, and Kristin Forbes, 2004, "Shelters from the Storm: Multinational Linkages During Currency Crisis," working paper.

Desai, Mihir, C. Fritz Foley, and James Hines, Jr., 2004, "Chains of Ownership, Regional Tax Competition, and Foreign Direct Investment," NBER working paper no. 9224.

_____, 2005a, "Capital Controls, Liberalizations and Foreign Direct Investment," Harvard Business School working paper.

_____, 2005b, "Foreign Direct Investment and Domestic Economic Activity," working paper.

Frankel, Jeffrey A., and David Romer, 1999, "Does Trade Cause Growth?" *American Economic Review* 89, pp. 379–399.

Garten, Jeffrey, January 2003, "A New Year; A New Agenda," *The Economist,* pp. 54–56.

Goldberg, Linda, 2004, "Financial-Sector Foreign Direct Investment and Host Countries: New and Old Lessons," Federal Reserve Bank of New York staff report.

Greenaway, David, Wyn Morgan, and Peter Wright, 2002, "Trade Liberalization and Growth in Developing Countries," *Journal of Development Economics* 67, pp. 229–244.

"IBM and Globalization," *The Economist,* April 7, 2007, pp. 67–69.

Jensen, Michael, and William Meckling, 1976, "The Theory of Firm-Managerial Behavior, Agency Costs and Ownership Structure," *Journal of Financial Economics* 3, pp. 305–360.

Klein, Naomi, 2000, *No Logo: Taking Aim at the Brand Bullies,* Canada: Knopf.

Kogut, Bruce, and Gordon Walker, 2001, "The Small World of Germany and the Durability of National Networks," *American Sociological Review,* pp. 317–335.

Kose, M. Ayhan, Eswar S. Prasad, and Marco E. Terrones, 2003, International Monetary Fund staff paper.

La Porta, Rafael, Florencio Lopez-de-Silanes, and Andrei Shleifer, 1999, "Corporate Ownership Around the World," *Journal of Finance* 54, pp. 471–517.

_____, 2002, "Investor Protection and Corporate Valuation," *Journal of Finance* 57, pp. 1147–1170.

La Porta, Rafael, Florencio Lopez-de-Silanes, Andrei Shleifer, and Robert W. Vishny, 1997, "Legal Determinants of External Finance," *Journal of Finance* 52, pp. 1131–1150.

_____, 1998, "Law and Finance," *Journal of Political Economy* 106, pp. 1113–1155.

_____, 2000a, "Agency Problems and Dividend Problems Around the World," *Journal of Finance* 55, pp. 1–33.

_____, 2000b, "Investor Protection and Corporate Governance," *Journal of Financial Economics* 53, pp. 3–27.

Lane, Philip R., and Gian Maria Milesi-Ferretti, 2006, "The External Wealth of Nations Mark II: Revised and Extended Estimates of Foreign Assets and Liabilities, 1970–2004,"

IIIS Discussion Paper No. 126, International Monetary Fund.

Leeson, Nicholas, with Edward Whitley, 1996, *Rogue Trader: How I Brought Down Barings Bank and Shook the Financial World*. London: Little, Brown & Co.

Lipsey, Robert E., 2001, "Foreign Direct Investment and the Operations of Multinational Firms: Concepts, History, and Data," National Bureau of Economic Research working paper no. 8665.

———————, 2002, "Home and Host Country Effects of FDI," National Bureau of Economic Research working paper no. 9293.

Obstfeld, Maurice, 1998, "The Global Capital Market: Benefactor or Menace?" *The Journal of Economic Perspectives*, pp. 9–30.

Quinn, Dennis, and Maria Toyoda, 2004, "Does Capital Account Liberalization Lead to Growth?" working paper.

Rodrik, Dani, 1998, "Why Do More Open Economies Have Bigger Governments?" *Journal of Political Economy* p. 106.

Rodrik, Dani, and Francisco Rodriguez, 1999, "Trade Policy and Economic Growth: A Sceptic's Guide to the Cross-National Evidence," CEPR Discussion Paper 2143.

Rogoff, Kenneth, July 24, 2004, "The Sisters at 60," *The Economist,* pp. 63–65.

Sachs, Jeffrey D., and Andrew M. Warner, 1995, "Economic Convergence and Economic Policies," National Bureau of Economic Research Working Paper W5039.

Stiglitz, Joseph E., 2002, *Globalization and Its Discontents*. New York: W.W. Norton and Company.

Wacziarg, Romain, 2001, "Measuring the Dynamic Gains from Trade," *World Bank Economic Review 15,* pp. 393–429.

Wacziarg, Romain, and Karen Horn Welsh, 2003, "Trade Liberalization and Growth: New Evidence" National Bureau of Economic Research working paper no. 10152.

Chapter

2

The Foreign Exchange Market

*C*hapter 1 describes the growth of international trade and the globalization of capital markets that has occurred over the past 30 years. Because different countries use different kinds of money, or currencies, the international buying and selling of goods or assets requires the conversion of one type of currency for another. So whether you are a Dutch exporter selling Gouda cheese to a U.S. supermarket for dollars, or a U.S. mutual fund investing in Mexican stocks, you will need to find a way to exchange foreign currency into your own currency and vice versa. These exchanges of monies occur in the **foreign exchange market**.

This chapter introduces the institutional structure that allows corporations, banks, international investors, and tourists to convert one money into another money. We discuss the size of the foreign exchange market, where it is located, and who the important market participants are. We then examine in detail how prices are quoted in the foreign exchange market, and in doing so, we encounter the important concept of **arbitrage**. Arbitrage profits are earned when someone can buy something at a low price and sell it for a higher price without bearing any risk.

Most of the transactions in the foreign exchange markets occur between traders at large financial institutions. In this chapter, we study how these people trade with one another, and we consider the clearing mechanisms by which funds are transferred across countries and the risks these fund transfers entail. We also examine how foreign exchange traders try to profit by buying foreign money at a low price and selling it at a high price.

Finally, the chapter introduces the terms used to discuss movements in exchange rates. Unfortunately, international finance sometimes seems like a language course, but mastering this language is important because it allows you to understand and discuss the current and historical experiences of various countries. Developing the ability to use this language correctly also makes it easier to discuss the risks involved in doing business in an increasingly global marketplace.

2.1 THE ORGANIZATION OF THE FOREIGN EXCHANGE MARKET

The foreign exchange (sometimes abbreviated "forex") market typically conjures up images of a hectic trading room, full of computers and information networks, with traders talking excitedly on telephones. This image is a reality on the trading floors of the world's major banks and other financial institutions that make up the **interbank market**. It may help to think of the interbank market as the wholesale part of the forex market where banks manage inventories of currencies. There is also a less hectic retail side of the forex market,

Exhibit 2.1   The Structure of the Foreign Exchange Market

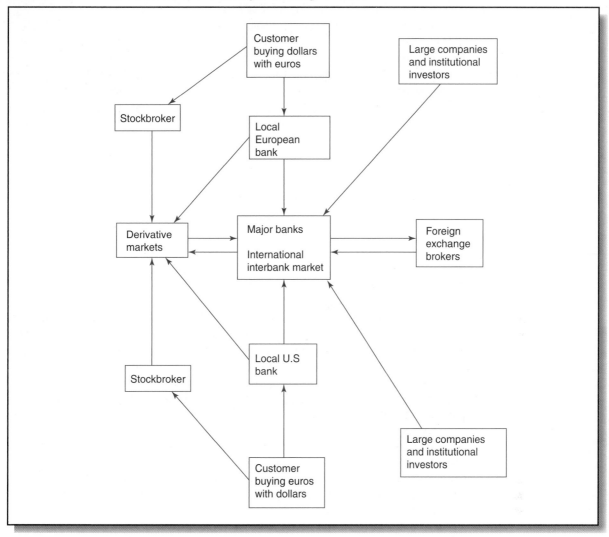

Note: Adapted from Federal Reserve Bank of St. Louis, March 1984, *Review* p. 9.

where the customers of the foreign exchange dealers buy and sell foreign currencies. These customers are the multinational corporations that market goods and services throughout the world and the institutional investors and money managers that invest capital throughout the world.

Exhibit 2.1 displays the various components of the foreign exchange market. In the middle of the diagram sits the interbank market, which accounts for about 80% of all transactions. The interbank foreign exchange market is a very large, diverse, over-the-counter market, not a physical trading place where buyers and sellers gather to agree on a price to exchange currencies. Traders, who are employees of financial institutions in the major financial cities around the world, deal with each other primarily over the phone or via computer, with written confirmations of transactions occurring only later.

The major financial centers where currencies are traded include New York, Chicago, and Los Angeles in the United States; Wellington, New Zealand; Sydney, Australia; Tokyo and Osaka in Japan; Hong Kong, China; Singapore; Frankfurt, Germany; Zurich, Switzerland; Copenhagen, Denmark; Paris, France; and London, England. Of these, London, New York, and Tokyo are the most important. Because of the geographical spread of these "money centers," the foreign exchange market operates 24 hours per day in the sense that there is always someone somewhere who stands ready to buy and sell currencies.

Because most transactions in the interbank market are large trades with values of $1 million or more, most retail investors and small businesses cannot access the foreign exchange market directly. As a result, many in need of foreign exchange deal with small regional banks or branches of money center banks that quote less advantageous rates than would be prevalent in the interbank market. Some enterprising firms have set up services to bundle many small orders together to bring a sizable order to the foreign exchange market and obtain competitive interbank pricing. Retail investors also participate in the foreign exchange markets through their stockbrokers, who can place orders in derivative markets on futures and options exchanges. As Exhibit 2.1 shows, large multinational corporations, such as IBM, and very large money-management firms, such as the mutual fund company Fidelity, can directly access the foreign exchange interbank market. Some multinational companies even have their own foreign exchange trading desks. We will discuss the role of foreign exchange brokers (on the right in Exhibit 2.1) later in the chapter.

Size of the Market

The foreign exchange market is often said to be the largest market in the world, measured by dollar volume of trade. This volume has increased rapidly since the 1970s. In 1973, the estimated daily volume of currency trading was roughly $10 to $20 billion. By the late 1980s, daily volume had grown to around $500 billion. By September 1993, the estimated daily volume in all currencies had grown to over $1 trillion, and the Bank for International Settlements (2005) estimated that daily trading volume in April 2004 was $1.9 trillion. This dollar volume of trade dwarfs the corresponding dollar volume of transactions on stock markets such as the New York Stock Exchange (NYSE), where average daily dollar volume is roughly $75 billion. Of course, the $1.9 trillion includes all markets and all currencies around the world, not just trade conducted in New York. Exhibit 2.2 gives an idea of the relative trading activity in the major financial centers around the world and how it grew between 1992 and 2004.

The United Kingdom, with London as the major financial center, is the dominant market, accounting for 31% of all trading in 2004, followed by the United States, with the bulk

Exhibit 2.2 Foreign Exchange Trading Activity Around the World

	April 1992		April 1998		April 2004	
Country	Amount (billions $)	Percentage Share	Amount (billions $)	Percentage Share	Amount (billions $)	Percentage Share
United Kingdom	291	27.0%	637	32.5%	753	31.3%
United States	167	15.5%	351	17.9%	461	19.2%
Japan	120	11.1%	136	6.9%	199	8.3%
Singapore	74	6.9%	139	7.1%	125	5.2%
Germany	55	5.1%	94	4.8%	118	4.9%
Switzerland	66	6.1%	82	4.2%	79	3.3%
Hong Kong	60	5.6%	79	4.0%	102	4.2%
Others	244	22.7%	440	22.6%	569	23.6%
Total	**1,077**	**100.0%**	**1,958**	**100.0%**	**2,406**	**100%**

Notes: Amounts are average daily turnover in billions of U.S. dollars. The numbers are not adjusted for cross-border interdealer double-counting, which explains why the total turnover in 2004 is about $500 billion higher than $1.9 trillion. The data are from Bank for International Settlements, March 2005, "Central Bank Survey of Foreign Exchange and Derivatives Market Activity, 2004," Table B-6.

Source: Copyright © 2005 Bank for International Settlements. All rights reserved. Reprinted by permission.

of the trades occurring in New York. The dominance of the two major markets has increased since 1992.

Types of Contracts Traded

Many different types of trades can be made in the foreign exchange market. In this chapter, we examine the **spot market**, where "spot" implies the market for immediate exchanges of monies. Another part of the interbank foreign exchange market involves trade in swaps and forward contracts, transactions that involve exchanges of currencies in the future. We discuss these types of trades in Chapter 3. A third part of the market involves derivative securities such as foreign currency futures and options. These contracts are discussed in Chapter 20.

When currencies in the interbank spot market are traded, certain business conventions are followed. For example, when the trade involves the U.S. dollar, business convention dictates that spot contracts are settled in 2 business days—that is, the payment of one currency and receipt of the other currency occurs in 2 business days. One business day is necessary because of the back-office paperwork involved in any financial transaction. The second day is needed because of the time zone differences around the world.

Several exceptions to the 2-business-day rule are noteworthy. First, for exchanges between the U.S. dollar and the Canadian dollar or the Mexican peso, the rule is 1 business day. Second, if the transaction involves the dollar and the first of the 2 days is a holiday in the United States but not in the other settlement center, the first day is counted as a business day for settlement purposes. Third, Fridays are not part of the business week in most Middle Eastern countries, although Saturdays and Sundays are. Hence, non–Middle Eastern currencies settle on Fridays, and Middle Eastern currencies settle on Saturdays.

Foreign Exchange Dealers

The main participants in the foreign exchange market are the commercial banks, investment banks, and brokerage firms in the major financial cities around the world. Traders at these banks and firms function as **foreign exchange dealers**, simultaneously "making a market" in several currencies. These **market makers** stand ready to buy and sell the currencies in which they specialize. By standing ready to transact with retail customers or other dealers, they provide **liquidity** to the market—that is, they make it easier and less costly to match buyers and sellers. When there are large numbers of buyers and sellers, markets are very liquid, and transaction costs are low. The foreign exchange markets for the major currencies of the world, such as the markets for the U.S. dollar, the euro, the Japanese yen, and the British pound, are among the most liquid markets in the world.

Forex dealers try to buy a foreign currency at a low rate and sell the foreign currency at a higher rate, thus making a profit. Hence, their provision of liquidity does not go unrewarded. We will examine the size of these profits in Section 2.3.

Foreign Exchange Brokers

Foreign exchange brokers do not attempt to buy low and sell high. Instead, brokers fulfill the role of a financial intermediary. They match buyers and sellers but do not put their own money at risk. They then receive a brokerage fee on their transactions.

Forex brokers typically have many lines of communication open to various foreign exchange dealers, and they provide information to dealers on the best available prices. Foreign exchange dealers often use these brokers to unwind very large positions in a particular currency in order to preserve their anonymity. For example, suppose that Citibank finds itself stuck with a very large amount of Australian dollars toward the end of the day. Citibank would like to sell Australian dollars for U.S. dollars before the end of the trading day. Without anonymity in trading, competing dealers would try to profit from the knowledge that Citibank has a short-term excess supply of Australian dollars. If Citibank were to call JPMorgan Chase, for example, the prices quoted to Citibank would likely be unfavorable. By contrast, a broker may be able to negotiate trades with several foreign exchange dealers, thereby "unwinding" the large position in Australian dollars in small portions, while preserving Citibank's anonymity.

Computerized Trading Systems

One of the most important advances in technology in the foreign exchange market has been the development of computerized trading systems. In 1992, Reuters, a large financial information provider, launched the first anonymous electronic brokering system for trading spot foreign exchange. The system, now called Dealing 3000, offers live exchange rates on a computer window for more than 30 currencies. To complete a deal, a user must press two keys. The Dealing 3000 system checks for mutual credit availability between the initiator of the deal and the counterparty of the deal, and if credit for both parties is available, the deal is executed immediately. There are currently thousands of key trading stations in all major countries that use the Dealing 3000 system.

A major competitor of Reuters is Electronic Brokering Service (EBS), which began trading in 1993. EBS is a partnership of major money center banks and the Minex Corporation of Japan. Trading is conducted over a proprietary computer network that links workstations at hundreds of banks all over the world. Currency prices are displayed on the computer screen, and deals are completed by keystroke or by automatic deal matching within the system. The parties to the transaction are revealed only after the trade is completed, so each counterparty must have its creditworthiness prescreened.

The Internet revolution has not bypassed the foreign exchange market. A number of relatively small firms now offer online foreign exchange dealing operations, often offering direct access to retail investors, hedge fund managers, and corporations. The major foreign exchange dealers have developed, or are in the process of developing, web-based systems of their own. It remains to be seen whether these developments will fundamentally change the old phone-dominated trading environment.

Other Participants in the Forex Market

The central banks of different governments around the world periodically participate in the foreign exchange market as they try to influence the foreign-exchange value of their currencies. (We will discuss how this works in Chapter 5.) Other participants include multinational corporations, which need to exchange currencies to conduct their international trade, institutional investors buying and selling foreign securities, hedge funds speculating on currency movements, and smaller domestic banks that service firms or individuals wanting to exchange currencies. If the trades are large enough, the highly liquid interbank market can be tapped. The more removed from the interbank market participants are (see Exhibit 2.1), the more steps the participants must take to exchange their currencies, and the higher the transaction costs.

The Competitive Marketplace

Retail customers pay only slightly more than participants in the interbank market if the foreign exchange market is competitive. In what economists refer to as a *perfectly competitive market*, many firms compete with one another, and the cost of entering the market is low. Competition is most intense when the product being sold is the same across the firms. We already know that the foreign exchange market satisfies this condition: A dollar is a dollar and a euro is a euro wherever and by whomever they are bought or sold. In such markets, prices are driven down, and firms are unable to earn abnormally high profits. On the other hand, when the number of firms in a market is small and entering the market is costly, firms possess

Exhibit 2.3 The Top 20 Dealers in the Foreign Exchange Market

Rank 2005	Company	Market Share	Rank 2004
1	Deutsche Bank	16.72	2
2	UBS	12.47	1
3	Citigroup	7.50	3
4	HSBC	6.37	5
5	Barclays Capital	5.85	7
6	Merrill Lynch	5.69	10
7	JPMorgan Chase	5.29	4
8	Goldman Sachs	4.39	6
9	ABN Amro	4.19	11
10	Morgan Stanley	3.92	13
11	Royal Bank of Scotland (RBS)	3.62	9
12	Lehman Brothers	2.46	14
13	Dresdner Kleinwort Wasserstein (DrKW)	2.37	12
14	Credit Suisse First Boston (CSFB)	2.36	8
15	Royal Bank of Canada	1.77	17
16	Bank of America	1.60	15
17	State Street	1.35	16
18	Calyon	1.15	—
19	BNP Paribas	1.09	18
20	Société Générale	0.80	20

Note: Based on the Foreign Exchange Polls by Euromoney in 2005.

market power, which leads to less competitive pricing. Exhibit 2.3 lists the major players in the foreign exchange market and their market shares.

The foreign exchange market used to be fiercely competitive, with new firms muscling their way into the top 20 foreign exchange dealers every year. The top 4 dealers would account for less than 30% of the trading and the top 20 for less than 75% of the trading. Nevertheless, Citigroup, helped by its global presence, would consistently be the top foreign exchange dealer. In recent years, the situation has changed dramatically. Exhibit 2.3 shows that there has been tremendous consolidation in foreign exchange trading, with the top 4 dealers now accounting for over 40% of trading volume and the top 20 for over 90%. Moreover, two European banks, Deutsche Bank and UBS, have made significant investments in foreign exchange trading and have overtaken Citigroup as the major foreign exchange dealers. They account for almost 30% of the trading volume.

Exhibit 2.3 also shows that quite a few investment banks, such as Merrill Lynch and Goldman Sachs, are now top-20 forex dealers. This change may reflect a change in the dominant clientele of foreign exchange dealers. Before the 1980s, international trade was the main source of non-bank demand and supply. Since then, the explosion in international capital flows has made professional money managers increasingly important participants in the forex market. These clients demand different kinds of services, including advice and trading to manage risk, and investment banks generally have more of this expertise than commercial banks.

Despite the somewhat increased market shares of the major traders, no single dealer dominates the market, and the foreign exchange market remains very competitive. We examine how this competition affects pricing later in this chapter, when we discuss bid–ask spreads.

2.2 CURRENCY QUOTES AND PRICES

You now know about the participants in the forex market and its organization but have yet to learn about the currencies that are traded and how their prices are quoted. Because more than 150 countries in the world have their own currencies, it makes sense that currency trading is governed by an intricate set of conventions and practices.

Exchange Rates

An **exchange rate** is the relative price of two monies, such as the Japanese yen price of the U.S. dollar, the U.S. dollar price of the euro, or the euro price of the Mexican peso. Rather than write out the full name of these currencies, contractual parties use abbreviations. In banking and commercial transactions, it is important that all parties understand which currencies are being used. Hence, there is a need for standardization of the abbreviations. The International Organization for Standardization (called ISO from the Greek word for equal) sets these standards. Exhibit 2.4 provides a list of some of the ISO currency abbreviations used to represent the different currencies. In most cases, the abbreviation is the ISO two-digit country code plus a letter from the name of the currency.

For example, the notation for the U.S. dollar is USD, the British pound is GBP, the Japanese yen is JPY, and the euro is EUR. In examples throughout the book, we use these codes to illustrate the units involved in different transactions. At other times, though, common symbols for the major currencies are used. For example, the symbol for the U.S. dollar is $, the symbol for the pound is £, the symbol for the euro is €, and the symbol for the Japanese yen is ¥.

If it takes 100 yen to purchase 1 dollar, we can write

$$JPY100 = USD1$$

The exchange rate can be written as ¥100/$1, or simply as ¥100/$, where the 1 dollar in the denominator is implicit. Similarly, if it takes 1.75 U.S. dollars to purchase 1 British pound, then

$$USD1.75 = GBP1$$

and the exchange rate can be written as $1.75/£.

Exchange Rate Quotes

Because exchange rates are relative prices, they can be expressed in two ways. Exchange rates can be quoted in direct terms as the domestic currency price of the foreign currency or in indirect terms as the foreign currency price of the domestic currency.

Because direct prices are, perhaps, the most natural way to discuss exchange rates, let's consider **direct quotes** first. For example, in Germany, people discuss the euro prices of various goods and assets. If you were in Germany, you might inquire, "How many euros does it take to purchase that car?" or "What does that car cost?" In each case, you want to know the number of euros that must be given up to purchase a specific car. An economist would say the answer to these questions is the value of the car in terms of the euro.

Now, suppose you were in Germany, and you wanted to travel to Britain. If you thought you might need 1,000 British pounds on your trip, it would also be natural for you to inquire, "How many euros does it take to purchase 1,000 British pounds?" or "What do 1,000 British pounds cost?" In each case, you want to know the number of euros that must be given up to purchase this specific number of British pounds. Once again, economists would say that the answer is the value of 1,000 British pounds in terms of the euro.

If the euro price of the pound is €1.40/£, the cost of 1,000 pounds in euros is

$$£1,000 \times (€1.40/£) = €1,400$$

Notice that with direct exchange rates, converting from a foreign currency amount (in this case, the British pound) into a domestic currency value (in this case, the euro) simply involves multiplying the amount of foreign currency by the exchange rate expressed in units of domestic currency per foreign currency.

For the U.S. dollar, it is common for many exchange rates to be quoted in **indirect quotes**, such as ¥100/$ for the Japanese yen or CHF1.8/$ for the Swiss franc. These exchange rates represent the amount of foreign currency that is equivalent to 1 dollar, which is also the amount of foreign currency required to purchase 1 dollar. Most people commonly use indirect

Exhibit 2.4 Currencies and Currency Symbols

Country	Currency	ISO Currency Code
Argentina	New Peso	ARS
Australia	Dollar	AUD
Austria	Euro (€)	EUR
Bahrain	Dinar	BHD
Belgium	Euro (€)	EUR
Brazil	Real	BRL
Canada	Dollar	CAD
Chile	Peso	CLP
China	Renminbi	CNY
Colombia	Peso	COP
Czech Republic	Koruna	CZK
Denmark	Krone	DKK
Ecuador	U.S. Dollar	USD
European Union	Euro (€)	EUR
Finland	Euro (€)	EUR
France	Euro (€)	EUR
Germany	Euro (€)	EUR
Greece	Euro (€)	EUR
Hong Kong	Dollar	HKD
Hungary	Forint	HUF
India	Rupee	INR
Indonesia	Rupiah	IDR
Ireland	Euro (€)	EUR
Israel	Shekel	ILS
Italy	Euro (€)	EUR
Japan	Yen (¥)	JPY
Jordan	Dinar	JOD
Korea, Rep. of	Won	KRW
Kuwait	Dinar	KWD
Lebanon	Pound	LBP
Malaysia	Ringgit	MYR
Malta	Euro(€)	EUR
Mexico	Neuvo Peso	MXN
Netherlands	Euro (€)	EUR
New Zealand	Dollar	NZD
Norway	Krone	NOK
Pakistan	Rupee	PKR
Peru	New Sol	PEN
Philippines	Peso	PHP
Poland	New Zloty	PLN
Portugal	Euro(€)	EUR
Russia	Ruble	RUB
Saudi Arabia	Riyal	SAR
Singapore	Dollar	SGD
Slovak Rep.	Koruna	SKK
South Africa	Rand	ZAR
Spain	Euro (€)	EUR
Sweden	Krona	SEK
Switzerland	Franc	CHF
Taiwan	Dollar	TWD
Thailand	Baht	THB
Turkey	Lira	TRL
United Arab Emirates	Dirham	AED
United Kingdom	Pound (£)	GBP
United States	Dollar ($)	USD
Uruguay	New Peso	UYU
Venezuela	Bolivar	VEB

terms to express the exchange rates between Asian and Latin American currencies and the U.S. dollar. Adopting a common way of quoting prices clearly facilitates communication between traders in the United States and those in other countries.

Because exchange rates are the relative prices of monies, an exchange rate expressed in direct terms is the reciprocal (inverse) of the exchange rate expressed in indirect terms. For example, suppose it takes 100 yen to purchase 1 dollar—that is, the exchange rate in indirect terms from the U.S. perspective is ¥100/$. Then, the exchange rate in direct terms from the U.S. perspective, which is the dollar price of the Japanese yen, is the reciprocal of the exchange rate quoted in indirect terms:

$$1/(¥100/\$) = \$1/¥100 = \$0.01/¥$$

The reciprocal nature of direct and indirect terms often confuses students. Earlier in the chapter, we converted money between euros and British pounds when traveling between Germany and Britain. Now, suppose you are in the United States, and you want to travel to Japan. If you were advised that you needed 500,000 yen for your trip, it would be natural for you to inquire, "How many dollars does it take to purchase 500,000 yen?" Now, though, because the exchange rate is typically quoted as ¥100/$, the dollar cost of the ¥500,000 is

$$¥500,000/(¥100/\$) = \$5,000$$

Notice that with the exchange rate quoted as an indirect price, converting from a foreign currency amount (the yen, in this case) into a domestic currency value (the dollar, in this case) involves dividing the amount of foreign currency (the yen) by the exchange rate expressed in units of foreign currency per domestic currency (¥/$). Because such currency conversions lie at the heart of all international financial transactions, it clearly pays to be careful to remember how the exchange rate is being quoted before converting from one currency into another.

The indirect method of quoting exchange rates is also commonly referred to as a **European quote** (the amount of foreign currency needed to buy dollars) because most former European currencies, such as the Deutsche mark and the French franc, were quoted this way relative to the dollar. The phrase **American quote** refers to the dollar price of a foreign currency—that is, the number of dollars it takes to purchase one unit of the foreign currency. Exchange rates of the British pound versus the dollar and the euro versus the dollar are commonly expressed directly in dollars per pound (for example, as $1.65/£) and in dollars per euro (for example, $1.15/€).

The following table summarizes the different ways of quoting exchange rates:

DIRECT AND INDIRECT, EUROPEAN AND AMERICAN QUOTES		
	In the U.S.	In Britain
$/£	Direct	Indirect
$/£	American	American
£/$	Indirect	Direct
£/$	European	European
	In Thailand	In the European Union
Thai baht/€	Direct	Indirect

When you are in the United States, quoting the pound exchange rate as $/£ means you are using domestic currency per foreign currency; it is a direct quote. Similarly, when you are in Thailand, quoting the euro exchange rate as Thai baht/€ is an example of a direct quote. When you are in Europe, quoting the Thai baht as Thai baht/€ is an example of an indirect quote because you use foreign currency per domestic currency. The terminology *American* and *European* only refers to exchange rates relative to the dollar.

Exhibit 2.5 Currency Quotes in the *Wall Street Journal*

Exchange Rates — *February 16, 2006*

The foreign exchange mid-range rates below apply to trading among banks in amounts of $1 million and more, as quoted at 4 p.m. Eastern time by Reuters and other sources. Retail transactions provide fewer units of foreign currency per dollar.

Country	U. S. $ EQUIVALENT		CURRENCY PER U.S. $	
	Thu	Wed	Thu	Wed
Argentina (Peso)-y	.3261	.3256	3.0665	3.0713
Australia (Dollar)	.7389	.7383	1.3534	1.3545
Bahrain (Dinar)	2.6537	2.6528	.3768	.3770
Brazil (Real)	.4726	.4681	2.1160	2.1363
Canada (Dollar)	.8638	.8633	1.1577	1.1583
1-month forward	.8644	.8640	1.1569	1.1574
3-months forward	.8659	.8654	1.1549	1.1555
6-months forward	.8680	.8674	1.1521	1.1529
Chile (Peso)	.001908	.001884	524.11	530.79
China (Renminbi)	.1242	.1241	8.0487	8.0557
Colombia (Peso)	.0004437	.0004437	2253.78	2253.78
Czech. Rep. (Koruna)				
Commercial rate	.04194	.04187	23.844	23.883
Denmark (Krone)	.1593	.1592	6.2775	6.2814
Ecuador (US Dollar)	1.0000	1.0000	1.0000	1.0000
Egypt (Pound)-y	.1742	.1745	5.7412	5.7300
Hong Kong (Dollar)	.1289	.1288	7.7608	7.7614
Hungary (Forint)	.004730	.004735	211.42	211.19
India (Rupee)	.02260	.02264	44.246	44.170
Indonesia (Rupiah)	.0001085	.0001084	9217	9225
Israel (Shekel)	.2133	.2119	4.6887	4.7192
Japan (Yen)	.008498	.008485	117.67	117.86
1-month forward	.008529	.008514	117.25	117.45
3-months forward	.008598	.008583	116.33	116.51
6-months forward	.008704	.008690	114.89	115.07
Jordan (Dinar)	1.4114	1.4115	.7085	.7085
Kuwait (Dinar)	3.4240	3.4231	.2921	.2921
Lebanon (Pound)	.0006649	.0006649	1503.99	1503.99
Malaysia (Ringgit)-b	.2688	.2687	3.7202	3.7216
Malta (Lira)	2.7706	2.7688	.3609	.3612

Country	U.S. $ EQUIVALENT		CURRENCY PER U.S. $	
	Thu	Wed	Thu	Wed
Mexico (Peso)				
Floating rate	.0954	.0949	10.4844	10.5385
New Zealand (Dollar)	.6695	.6738	1.4937	1.4841
Norway (Krone)	.1473	.1463	6.7889	6.8353
Pakistan (Rupee)	.01670	.01669	59.880	59.916
Peru (new Sol)	.3046	.3042	3.2830	3.2873
Philippines (Peso)	.01935	.01941	51.680	51.520
Poland (Zloty)	.3159	.3153	3.1656	3.1716
Russia (Ruble)-a	.03543	.03542	28.225	28.233
Saudi Arabia (Riyal)	.2667	.2666	3.7495	3.7509
Singapore (Dollar)	.6115	.6139	1.6353	1.6289
Slovak Rep. (Koruna)	.03182	.03175	31.427	31.496
South Africa (Rand)	.1651	.1648	6.0569	6.0680
South Korea (Won)	.0010261	.0010276	974.56	972.95
Sweden (Krona)	.1268	.1274	7.8864	7.8493
Switzerland (Franc)	.7629	.7629	1.3108	1.3108
1-month forward	.7651	.7650	1.3070	1.3072
3-months forward	.7699	.7698	1.2989	1.2990
6-months forward	.7771	.7771	1.2868	1.2868
Taiwan (Dollar)	.03086	.03091	32.404	32.352
Thailand (Baht)	.02540	.02542	39.370	39.339
Turkey (New Lira)-d	.7527	.7493	1.3285	1.3345
U.K. (Pound)	1.7395	1.7406	.5749	.5745
1-month forward	1.7396	1.7407	.5748	.5745
3-months forward	1.7407	1.7417	.5745	.5742
6-monhs forward	1.7434	1.7443	.5736	.5733
United Arab (Dirham)	.2722	.2723	3.6738	3.6724
Uruguay (Peso)				
Financial	.04140	.04140	24.155	24.155
Venezuela (Bolivar)	.000466	.000466	2145.92	2145.92
SDR	1.4311	1.4337	.6988	.6975
Euro	1.1893	1.1887	.8408	.8413

Special Drawing Rights (SDR) are based on exchange rates for the U.S., British, and Japanese currencies, Source: International Monetary fund.
a-Russian Central Bank rate. b-Government rate. d-Rebased as of Jan. 1, 2005. y-Floating rate.

Source: Copyright © 2006 Reuters.com

Major financial newspapers such as the *Wall Street Journal* and the *Financial Times* provide daily lists of foreign exchange rates. Exhibit 2.5 presents a typical listing from the *Wall Street Journal*. These exchange rates are supplied to the *Wall Street Journal* from the interbank market by Reuters and other sources.

Notice that the four columns contain information on exchange rates for two different days, Wednesday and Thursday, February 15 and 16, 2006. One set of quotes is in direct terms from the U.S. perspective (American quotes) and is reported as "U.S. $ equiv." These columns indicate the number of U.S. dollars equivalent to one unit of the other currency, which is also the U.S. dollar price of one unit of the other currency. The second set of quotes is in indirect terms from the U.S. perspective (European quotes). These columns are labeled "Currency per U.S. $," which is the foreign currency price of 1 U.S. dollar.

Notice that many of the exchange rates in the columns listed "Currency per U.S. $" are greater than one in value (although there are a number of exceptions, including the British pound and the SDR[1]). Most people find this way of discussing exchange rates superior to discussing small fractions. It is much easier to state the yen rate as "117.67 yen per dollar"

---

[1]SDR stands for *Special Drawing Right*, a unit of account created by the International Monetary Fund. The SDR is a composite of several major currencies. The dollar value of the SDR is found by multiplying the specific amounts of the different currencies that compose the SDR by the respective dollar exchange rates and summing the dollar values. The IMF and the SDR are discussed in Chapter 5.

(¥117.67/$) than it is to state its reciprocal, which is "Eight thousand, four hundred, ninety-eight millionths of a dollar per yen" ($0.008498/¥). No doubt this is why indirect terms have become the common way of discussing many dollar exchange rates.

Most of the quotations in Exhibit 2.5 represent spot exchange rates. Notice also that the currencies of Britain, Canada, Japan, and Switzerland have quotes for 1-month, 3-month, and 6-month forward contracts. These financial instruments are discussed in Chapter 3.

Vehicle Currencies and Currency Cross-Rates

Why do we focus so much on the U.S. dollar exchange rates versus other currencies of the world? Is it simply the prominence of the U.S. economy, or is there an economic reason? The answer involves the concept of a vehicle currency. A **vehicle currency** is a currency that is actively used in many international financial transactions around the world. The transaction costs of making markets in many currencies has led to the use of only a few currencies as the major vehicles for international transactions.

For example, if there are N different currencies issued by various countries throughout the world, there are $N(N - 1)/2$ possible exchange rates. With more than 150 different currencies, there are more than 11,175 possible exchange rates. Because the demands to trade between many of these different currency pairs are often low or nonexistent, there is no direct market made. Rather, traders make a direct market in one or two important currencies, referred to as *vehicle currencies*. Currently, the U.S. dollar serves as the world's primary vehicle currency, but in the nineteenth century, the world's vehicle currency was the British pound.

Exchange rates between two currencies that do not involve the dollar are often called **cross-rates**. Exhibit 2.6 provides examples of cross-rates taken from the *Wall Street Journal* for February 16, 2006.

The rows represent "direct quotes" from the perspective of the country whose currency begins the row. For example, 117.67 is the Japanese yen price of 1 dollar. The columns thus represent the indirect quotes from the perspective of the country whose currency is at the top of the column. For example, the Swiss franc column tells you how many foreign currency units it takes to buy 1 Swiss franc.

Although there appears to be a trend toward more cross-rate transactions, an estimated 89% of all transactions have the dollar as one side. Some analysts think the euro, which replaced 11 different currencies in Europe in 1999, may someday replace the dollar as a vehicle currency. In fact, a Bank for International Settlements (2005) survey of foreign exchange activity revealed that about 37% of all trades that occurred during 2004 involved the euro.

Triangular Arbitrage

Triangular arbitrage is a process that keeps cross-rates (such as euros per British pound) in line with exchange rates quoted relative to the U.S. dollar. A trader can conduct a triangular arbitrage in many ways. For example, a trader might start by directly buying a currency such

Exhibit 2.6 Cross-rates Quotes in the *Wall Street Journal*

Key Currency Cross Rates				Late New York Trading Thursday, February 16, 2006			
	Dollar	Euro	Pound	SFranc	Peso	Yen	CdnDlr
Canada	1.1577	1.3768	2.0138	0.8832	0.11042	.00984	...
Japan	117.67	139.95	204.70	89.774	11.224	...	101.647
Mexico	10.4844	12.4691	18.238	7.9985	...	.08910	9.0564
Switzerland	1.3108	1.5589	2.2801	...	.12502	.01114	1.1323
U.K.	.57490	.6837	...	.4386	.05483	.00489	.49658
Euro	.84080	...	1.4626	.64147	.08020	.00715	.72631
U.S.	...	1.1893	1.7395	.76290	.09538	.00850	.86380

Source: Copyright © 2006 Reuters.com

as the pound with euros and then simultaneously selling the pounds for dollars and selling the dollars for euros. In other words, instead of exchanging just two currencies, the trader exchanges three (hence the term "triangular" arbitrage). If the number of euros the trader has at the end of these three transactions is greater than the number of euros at the beginning, there is a profit. An alternative approach would be to buy pounds indirectly with euros by first buying dollars and then buying pounds and selling the pounds for euros. Once again, the trader would want to have more euros at the end than at the beginning.

If either of these sets of transactions can be done profitably, the trader can generate pure arbitrage profits—that is, earn risk-free profits. Obviously, in perfectly competitive financial markets, it is impossible to earn arbitrage profits for very long. If the euro price of the pound were not equal to the euro price of the U.S. dollar multiplied by the U.S. dollar price of the pound, arbitrage activity would immediately restore equality between the quoted cross-rate and the cross-rate implied by two dollar quotes:

$$(\text{Euros/Pound}) = (\text{Euros/Dollar}) \times (\text{Dollars/Pound})$$

In other words, the direct quote for the cross-rate should equal the implied cross-rate, using the dollar as an intermediary currency.

To see how a triangular arbitrage works, suppose that the euro price of the pound quoted in the market is €1.4381/£. Also, suppose that this quoted cross-rate is lower than the indirect rate, using the dollar as the intermediary currency. That is,

$$(\text{Euros/Pound}) < (\text{Euros/Dollar}) \times (\text{Dollars/Pound})$$

This means there is some room to make a profit. In this situation, buying the pound first with euros (or selling euros for pounds), and then selling the pound for dollars, and finally selling that number of dollars for euros would make a profit because we would be buying the pound at a low euro price and selling the pound at a high euro price.

To check this logic, let's go through the steps in a triangular arbitrage.

Example 2.1 A Triangular Arbitrage

Suppose David Sylvian, a trader at the foreign exchange desk of Goldman Sachs in London, observes the following exchange rates of the euro relative to the pound and the dollar and the dollar relative to the pound:

EUR1.4381/GBP or GBP0.6954/EUR
EUR0.8408/USD or USD1.1893/EUR
USD1.7395/GBP or GBP0.5749/USD

Determine the arbitrage profits when the trader starts with EUR10,000,000 and buys GBP. Exhibit 2.7 presents the situation in a triangle diagram.

The exchange rates beneath the arrows in Exhibit 2.7 indicate the relevant prices, denominated in the currency at the next node (the buyer's node), of selling one unit of the currency at the starting node (the seller's node). You can use these prices to follow along on the transactions, recognizing that in some cases, we want to buy a currency, and in others, we want to sell.

Step 1. The revenue in pounds of selling EUR10,000,000 at the direct cross-rate would be

EUR10,000,000 × (GBP0.6954/EUR) = GBP6,954,000

Step 2. Because the exchange rate of dollars per pound is (USD1.7395/GBP), we would be able to sell GBP6,954,000 for dollars to get

GBP6,954,000 × (USD1.7395/GBP) = USD12,096,483

Exhibit 2.7 Triangular Arbitrage Diagram

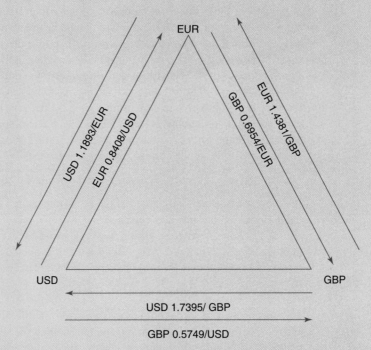

Note: The exchange rates beneath the arrows indicate the revenue to the seller from selling the currency at one node to purchase the currency at another node. For example, at the EUR node, selling the euro yields 0.6954 GBP going in the clockwise direction, and it yields 1.1893 USD going in the counterclockwise direction.

Step 3.   Then, because the exchange rate of euros per dollar is EUR0.8408/USD, we would sell the USD12,096,483 for euros to get

$$\text{USD12,096,483} \times (\text{EUR0.8408/USD}) = \text{EUR10,170,722}$$

If we had truly been able to make these transactions simultaneously, we would have made

$$\text{EUR10,170,722} - \text{EUR10,000,000} = \text{EUR170,722}$$

for an instantaneous rate of return of

$$1.71\% = (\text{EUR170,722/EUR10,000,000}) \times 100$$

Example 2.1 demonstrates how triangular arbitrage provides an instantaneous opportunity for profit *if* these are the actual market quotes. The data for the dollar exchange rates we used are, in fact, from Exhibit 2.5—quotes from the *Wall Street Journal* on February 16, 2006. We can use them to calculate the cross-rate of EUR/GBP using the dollar as an intermediary currency:

$$(\text{EUR0.8408/USD}) \times (\text{USD1.7395/GBP}) = \text{EUR1.4626/GBP}$$

This is 1.70% larger than the rate quoted in Example 2.1 of EUR1.4381/GBP. Traders in the foreign exchange market will quickly capitalize on such a situation, figuring out in what direction to move around the triangle in order to make a profit. David Sylvian made money by selling euros for pounds rather than by going in the counterclockwise direction; he first sold euros for dollars and then obtained pounds with dollars. He knew this was the way to go because he compared the direct revenue in pounds (GBP0.6954/EUR) with the implied one we computed:

$$1/[\text{EUR}1.4626/\text{GBP}] = \text{GBP}0.6837/\text{EUR})$$

Exhibit 2.8 summarizes David's arbitrage activities, and it also shows how he would have lost money if he had chosen to go in the wrong direction.

Exhibit 2.8   Good and Bad Triangular Arbitrages

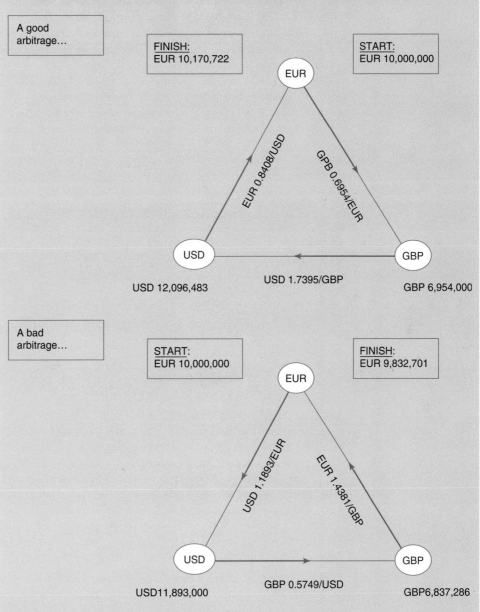

Note: The arrows indicate selling of the currency at the starting node for the currency at the ending node. The exchange rates express the amount of ending node currency obtained from selling one starting node currency.

Three things are important to note about triangular arbitrage. First, to be an effective arbitrage, the transactions must all be conducted simultaneously. Because it is not physically possible to do all three transactions simultaneously, there is some risk involved in any attempted triangular arbitrage because prices might change between transactions. Second, as traders place orders to conduct the arbitrage (see the top panel of Exhibit 2.8), market forces are created that bring the quoted cross-rate back into alignment with the indirect cross-rate—the rate we calculated. In our example, we have

$$\text{GBP0.6954/EUR} > \text{GBP0.5749/USD} \times \text{USD1.1893/EUR}$$

As traders buy pounds with euros to conduct the arbitrage, the supply of euros (that is, the demand for pounds) increases in this market, which tends to drive down the GBP/EUR rate. Selling pounds for dollars tends to drive up the GBP/USD rate because it increases the supply of pounds (demand for dollars) in this market, and selling dollars for euros tends to drive up the USD/EUR rate because it increases the supply of dollars (that is, the demand for euros) in this market. Eventually, the two sides of the equation will once again equal one another. At that point, arbitrage profits will no longer be possible.

The third point is that the arbitrage need not start by using the euro to purchase pounds. The triangular arbitrage would be profitable starting from any of the currencies, as long as we trade in the same direction and go completely around the triangle.

Let's illustrate this last point and review triangular arbitrage one more time.

Example 2.2 Another Triangular Arbitrage

Suppose David Sylvian starts with GBP10,000,000. How can he make a profit?

Step 1. David already knows he has to move in the clockwise direction to make a profit. Consequently, he will buy USD with his pounds, obtaining

$$\text{GBP10,000,000} \times (\text{USD1.7395/GBP}) = \text{USD17,395,000}$$

Step 2. He can now sell USD17,395,000 for euros at EUR0.8408/USD, yielding

$$\text{USD17,395,000} \times (\text{EUR0.8408/USD}) = \text{EUR14,625,716}$$

Step 3. David finally sells the EUR14,625,716 for pounds at GBP0.6954/EUR, yielding

$$\text{EUR14,625,716} \times (\text{GBP0.6954/EUR}) = \text{GBP10,70,722}$$

Note that David again ends up with a 1.71% instantaneous profit.

Because we used actual dollar quotes, we can check whether the direct cross-rate satisfies the triangular arbitrage condition. Going back to Exhibit 2.6, which reports actual direct cross-rates, we see that the reported cross-rate is EUR1.4626/GBP. So, for this real-world example, the quoted direct cross-rate and the one computed using the dollar as an intermediary currency are the same. We see that triangular arbitrage indeed works.

Example 2.3 Ringgits and Bahts

Suppose you would like to know the Thai baht (THB) price of the Malaysian ringgit (MYR). For these emerging market currencies, it is unlikely that cross-rate quotes will be available except possibly at Thai or Malaysian banks. However, quotes relative to the dollar are easy to find. For example, the February 16, 2006, Reuters quotes were as follows:

$$MYR3.7202/\$$$

$$THB39.370/\$$$

By using triangular arbitrage, we would expect the THB/MYR exchange rate to be

$$(THB39.370/\$)/(MYR3.7202/\$) = THB10.5828/MYR$$

Of course, in our examples, we ignored transaction costs. In the forex market, the major source of transaction costs is the bid–ask spread, which we discuss in detail in the next section. Nevertheless, as you will see, the bid–ask spreads in the spot foreign exchange market are quite small and are often ignored in the discussions in this book. We also assume that triangular arbitrage works perfectly from now on.

2.3 INSIDE THE INTERBANK MARKET I: BID–ASK SPREADS AND BANK PROFITS

A foreign exchange trader is typically responsible for buying and selling a particular currency or a small group of currencies and holds an inventory of those currencies. One reason for the activity in the interbank market is that forex traders at one bank use forex traders at other banks to adjust their portfolios of positions in various currencies in response to transactions that arise from their customers in the corporate market. They also trade with other banks to try to make a profit, and their desired positions in various currencies change in response to the news events of the day.

For example, suppose corporate customers want to buy yen from a trader at Deutsche Bank. After completing the corporate trade, the trader may enter the interbank market to buy yen from Mizuho Financial to replenish his inventory of yen. Alternatively, if the corporate customers are selling yen to the trader, he may sell some of the yen to other banks. If a particularly large order comes in, the trader's inventory will be imbalanced, and the trader is likely to use the interbank market to "pass along" the order. The repeated passing of inventory imbalances among dealers has been dubbed "hot potato trading" and may be one reason for the large volumes we see in the interbank market (see Lyons, 1997).

Ultimately, traders in the interbank market simultaneously buy and sell various foreign currencies with the goal of generating profits. To do so, they quote two-way prices. The **bid rate** is the rate at which they want to buy a currency (to remember this, think *b* for buy), and the **ask rate** is the rate at which they sell currency (think *s* for sell). The difference between these two rates is known as the **bid–ask spread**.

Bid–Ask Spreads

Let's illustrate the concept of bid–ask spreads with a numeric example. A yen–dollar trader would quote a bid price of yen per dollar at which she is willing to buy dollars in exchange for yen of, say, ¥104.30/$. The trader would then quote a higher ask price (also called the **offer price**) at which she is willing to sell dollars for yen, say, at an exchange rate of ¥104.40/$. In this latter transaction, the trader can be said to be offering dollars, the currency in the denominator, to the market, and she is willing to accept yen in return. We can summarize the reciprocal nature of bid–ask spreads with a line diagram, as represented in Exhibit 2.9.

Exhibit 2.9   The Reciprocal Nature of Bid and Ask Exchange Rates

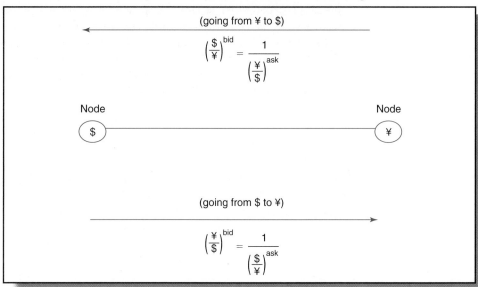

Note: The exchange rates beneath the arrows indicate the revenue to the seller of selling the currency at his node to obtain the currency at the other node. We take the perspective of a corporation or an individual at the starting node and a bank trader at the ending node.

Each node in the diagram represents a currency at a point in time. In Exhibit 2.9, we have only the dollar and the yen at the current time period. The arrows indicate the direction of sale. The exchange rates under the arrows are direct revenues to the seller (in terms of the currency at the next node) from selling one unit of the currency at the starting node. We take the perspective of the seller being a corporation or a client (with foreign currency) and the buyer being a bank trader. In selling yen for dollars, the seller will receive the bid price of $(\$/¥)^{\text{bid}}$, which is the reciprocal of the bank's ask yen price per dollar. That is

$$(\$/¥)^{\text{bid}} = 1/(¥/\$)^{\text{ask}}$$

The person selling yen to the bank for dollars gets the lower bid price because the bank trader buying yen with dollars wants to make a profit when reselling the yen she obtains. Similarly, in going from dollars to yen, the seller of dollars to the bank receives the bank's bid price of $(¥/\$)^{\text{bid}}$, which Exhibit 2.9 demonstrates is the reciprocal of the bank's ask price of dollars for yen. That is,

$$(¥/\$)^{\text{bid}} = 1/(\$/¥)^{\text{ask}}$$

If you are confused about whether to use the bid or ask exchange rate in a particular transaction, just remember that you will *always* transact with the bank to your disadvantage. If you are purchasing dollars with yen, you will have to pay the high price of ¥/$, which is the bank's ask price for dollars. Similarly, if you are selling dollars to the bank to obtain yen, you will get the low price of ¥/$, which is the bank's bid price for dollars.

Example 2.4   Yen–Dollar and Dollar–Yen Bid and Ask Rates

Suppose a trader quotes the yen–dollar exchange rate as ¥110.25–110.33/$. This means that the bid rate is ¥110.25/$ because the trader is willing to buy 1 dollar in return for 110.25 yen. He is also willing to sell a dollar in return for 110.33 yen because the ask rate is ¥110.33/$. What are the $/¥ bid and ask rates? The ask rate is the rate at which the dealer is willing to sell yen for dollars. We know that rate has to be higher than the rate at which the dealer is willing to buy yen for dollars. Consequently, if we take the inverse of the yen/dollar bid rate, we will obtain the dollar/yen ask rate. The dollar/yen ask is therefore $1/[¥110.25/\$] = \$0.009070/¥$. Following similar reasoning, the $/¥ bid rate is $[1/¥110.33/\$] = \$0.009064/¥$.

The Magnitude of Bid–Ask Spreads

Given the competitive nature of the foreign exchange market, it is not surprising that in normal times, bid–ask spreads are very low. Consequently, a trader who tries to make a lot of money quickly by setting a large bid–ask spread would soon find out that no one wanted to trade at those prices. But how big are actual bid–ask spreads?

For the major currencies and large transaction sizes, bid–ask spreads are now within 5 "pips." **Pip** is trader jargon for the fourth decimal point in a currency quote. For example, Exhibit 2.5 shows that the USD/EUR quote on February 16, 2006, is $1.1893/€. Assuming a spread of 4 pips and taking the $1.1893/€ rate as the midpoint, the ask rate is $1.1895/€, and the bid rate is $1.1891/€. Therefore, one pip reflects 1/100 of a U.S. cent in this case. However, to get an idea of transaction costs involved in trading currencies, it's better to express the bid–ask spread in percentage points. The percentage bid–ask is computed as:

$$\text{Percentage spread} = 100 \times (\text{ask} - \text{bid})/\text{ask}$$

Historical data for the 1980s and the 1990s reveal bid–ask spreads in the 0.05% to 0.07% range for the major currencies, but they can be substantially lower in the high-volume environment of the market today. For the USD/EUR quotes mentioned previously, the spread is

$$100 \times \frac{1.1895 - 1.1891}{1.1895} = 0.03\%$$

The difference between the ask price and the bid price actually represents two transaction costs. In the first transaction, you buy from a bank at its ask price; then you turn around and sell to another bank at its bid price. To understand how small these transaction costs are, consider the following example.

Example 2.5   Paying the Bid–Ask Spread

Suppose the treasurer of a U.S. company purchases pounds with dollars in anticipation that the manufacturing manager will want to purchase some British goods, but the treasurer is told immediately after the purchase of the pounds that the deal for the goods is off. The treasurer then sells the pounds back to the bank for dollars. Because the treasurer bought pounds at the bank's ask price of $/£ and immediately sold the pounds back to the bank at the bank's bid price of $/£, the treasurer has made two transactions and has lost the bid–ask spread on every pound bought and sold. (Of course, this presupposes that the quoted exchange rates did not change.)

Assume that the percentage bid–ask spread the treasurer faced for the pound–dollar exchange rate is 0.06%. If the ask rate is $1.50/£, then the bid rate is $1.4991/£ because

$$100 \times [(\$1.50/£) - (\$1.4991/£)]/(\$1.50/£) = 0.06$$

Thus, if the treasurer bought, say, £1,000,000 at $1.5000/£, the cost would have been

$$£1,000,000 \times (\$1.5000/£) = \$1,500,000$$

Selling £1,000,000 back to the bank at the bank's bid price for pounds of $1.4991/£ would provide

$$£1,000,000 \times (\$1.4991/£) = \$1,499,100$$

Hence, the treasurer would lose $900 on the two transactions, which is 0.06% of $1.5 million.

Although the spread in the interbank market is very small, spreads for exchanging physical currencies in the tourist market are often 3% or more. Banks and currency exchanges quote larger bid–ask spreads in this market because they must hold physical inventories of different monies, and these inventories are not interest bearing. They must also transact with brokers who move physical amounts of currencies between different countries in response to excess supplies and demands. It is interesting to note that using credit cards when traveling as a tourist actually saves on transaction costs because the credit card companies give their customers an exchange rate that is quite close to the interbank rate on the day of the transaction. Unfortunately, some card companies have now started to charge fees for international transactions.

Bid–Ask Spreads All Day Around the World

Bid–ask spreads fluctuate during the day. Hence, there are times when the foreign exchange market is more competitive and times when it is less advantageous to trade. Several studies have confirmed that, generally speaking, the presence of additional dealers and increased trading activity lowers spreads (see Hartmann, 1998; and Huang and Masulis, 1999). This behavior is evident from detailed studies by Goodhart and Demos (1990) and Bollerslev and Domowitz (1993), based on a database of continuously recorded bid and ask quotations for exchange rates obtained from Reuters's network screens for the period April 9, 1989, to June 30, 1989. During this time period, there were 305,604 quotes on Reuters's screens from 125 participating banks. Consider the time-of-day pattern for the bid–ask spreads of the exchange rate of the former currency of Germany, the Deutsche Mark (DEM) versus the dollar, starting at midnight, Greenwich Mean Time. When it is midnight in Greenwich, England, it is morning in the Pacific and Asian markets. The first market activity is in Sydney and Wellington, and it is quickly followed by trading in Tokyo, Hong Kong, and Singapore. An abrupt decline in trading and widening of bid–ask spreads occurs at hour four, which is lunchtime in those markets. Market intensity picks up again in the afternoon of the Far Eastern trading session, and it continues as Hong Kong and Singapore close and Frankfurt and London open. Trading intensity increases when New York opens and overlaps with European activity, and trading declines after New York closes until the Far Eastern markets open again.

With the exception of late Friday, which is already Saturday in the Tokyo and Sydney markets, there is no discernable difference in the pattern of trading across weekdays. Over the weekend, there is very little activity until late Sunday, when the usual pattern described begins again.

Trading is geographically widely dispersed, with no center having more than 13.5% of quotes. The top five markets (with percentage of quotes in parenthesis) are Hong Kong (13.5%), London (12.7%), Frankfurt (11.8%), Singapore (11.0%), and New York (9.1%).[2]

The patterns in bid–ask spreads are typically slightly U-shaped in European markets, particularly in the smaller centers. The bid–ask spread is higher at the beginning and end of the European trading day than it is in the middle. In New York, the spread is highest at the

---

[2]Tim Bollerslev and Ian Domowitz (1993) note that this attribution of activity may be misleading in the sense that the entire market for DEM/$ quotes is not being captured; only the Reuters share is captured. Yet many of the patterns described here were confirmed in a study by Takatoshi Ito and Yuko Hashimoto (2006) using yen-dollar data from EBS instead of Reuters.

beginning of the trading day; it declines during the middle of the day; and it increases slightly at the close. The bid–ask spread in Tokyo and Singapore is essentially flat except for a spike at lunchtime, when the market effectively shuts down. That is, traders post high spreads that nobody would want to trade at before going out for lunch. Trading in New York continues during lunchtime, with no discernible increase in spreads, confirming the unhealthy lunch habits of U.S. traders who simply continue to trade while eating at their desks.

POINT–COUNTERPOINT

Are Speculative Trading Profits in the Foreign Exchange Market Excessive?

The top foreign exchange dealers, such as UBS, Deutsche Bank, and Citigroup, reportedly earn over $1 billion per year from foreign exchange trading. Our two sidekick brothers engage in a heated discussion of this fact. Ante Handel views these profits as a typical example of speculative excess. "Compare the dollar volume of interbank foreign exchange trading to the dollar volume of international trade flows," he fumes. "The difference is enormous. All that trading only makes the banks rich, and it causes exchange rates to be more volatile than they should be, which hurts our exporters. The government ought to tax speculative trading and make sure our banks simply support our exporters, who need these foreign currencies," he concludes.

Freedy Handel, on the other hand, claims that foreign exchange dealers are primarily market makers who trade with one another to adjust their portfolios in response to fundamental buy and sell transactions from the corporate world. "These banks' profits are simply the normal reward for providing liquidity in a market, and liquidity is of vital importance to the well-being of our economy," he politely argues.

As often happens, their cousin, Suttle Trooth, comes in and reconciles their differences by analyzing the available facts. "First," Suttle says, "Freedy, you are wrong in presuming that banks do not speculate. There is plenty of evidence that they do." (In this book, we will encounter several examples of speculative trading strategies that major banks follow in order to profit from exchange rate movements. As indicated in Section 2.1, large banks may attempt to exploit information from their order flow to predict exchange rate movements and develop a position before their competitors do. Many banks apparently attempt to profit from short-term, within-the-day, trading strategies.)

"Second," Suttle continues, "Ante, you are wrong to conclude that the profits are necessarily due to speculative excess. If most of the enormous trading volume in the foreign exchange market is trading between banks, you should realize that as a whole, the interbank market cannot profit from interbank trades. Interbank trading is a 'zero sum' game: Some other bank must lose every dollar one bank gains. If Ante's view is right for, say, Citigroup, some other banks must have together lost close to $1 billion in foreign exchange trading. While this is possible, other banks, like Citigroup, also find it profitable to have forex trading rooms."

"Third," Suttle goes on, "Freedy might be right to think that market making alone may indeed lead to substantial profits for foreign exchange dealers because of the huge trading volumes. Let's make a quick back-of-the-envelope computation." Suttle produces the following numbers. Suppose that 20% of all trading is between banks and their customers. In 2004, Citibank's share of the total market is 7.50%. Hence, if total volume in the foreign exchange market is $1.9 trillion, the volume of transactions per day handled by Citibank is

$$0.0750 \times \$1.9 \text{ trillion} = \$142.5 \text{ billion}$$

However, 80% of these transactions involve other foreign exchange dealers, and we assume that overall, Citibank does not earn money on these deals. However, it does earn the bid–ask spread from dealing with corporate customers and other customers, which represents 20% of their market or $0.20 \times \$142.5$ billion $= \$28.50$ billion.

If a typical bid–ask spread is 0.03%, the profit potential from pure market making is

$$\$28.5 \text{ billion/day} \times \frac{1}{2} \times 0.03/100 \times 250 \text{ trading days} = \$1.069 \text{ billion/year}$$

The $\frac{1}{2}$ arises because the volume applies to both sell and buy transactions, and Citigroup needs a round-trip transaction to earn the full spread.

For a number of reasons, this estimate probably understates Citigroup's earnings from providing liquidity services in the foreign exchange market. First, we used the interbank spread in the spot market for the major currencies, and we know spreads with retail customers tend to be higher than in the interbank market. Second, spreads are much higher for less liquid minor currency markets, such as emerging currencies, in which Citigroup tends to have a larger market share. Finally, spreads are larger on the part of the foreign exchange trading volume that involves forward contracts and other derivative contracts. Given our computations, it seems very likely that the bulk of Citigroup's profits arise from its market-making function and not from its taking of speculative positions.

A study by Federal Reserve economist John Ammer and IMF economist Allan Brunner (1997) confirms Suttle's rough computations. In the study, Ammer and Brunner examined the sources of foreign exchange profits for seven of the largest foreign exchange dealers among U.S. commercial banks between the years 1984 and 1993, using survey data collected by federal agencies. They found that speculative position taking was, on average, not a major source of earnings from foreign exchange trading for the banks in their sample. Instead, the banks' trading profits derived from conventional market making. As always, there are some caveats to their study. It is possible, for example, that the banks in the sample were systematically earning profits on intraday positions that Ammer and Brunner could not observe. Nevertheless, a later study of one foreign exchange dealer confirmed that most profits come from market making activities versus speculation (see Lyons, 1998).

While Suttle's arguments have reconciled our two brothers on their main points of disagreement, Suttle has to concede that he is not sure whether the taking of speculative positions by banks could drive up exchange rate volatility, as Ante claimed. He promises to revisit this issue in later chapters.

2.4 INSIDE THE INTERBANK MARKET II: COMMUNICATIONS AND FUND TRANSFERS

The enormous volume of trade in the foreign exchange market requires an extensive communication network between traders and a sophisticated settlement system to transfer payments in different currencies between the buyers and sellers in different countries.

Communication Systems

Until the introduction of computers in the 1970s, the participants in the foreign exchange market communicated with their clients and each other on the telephone and via telex. Today, traders watch information displayed on computer screens, provided by major commercial information distributors such as Reuters and Bloomberg. The firms distributing financial information have long provided information about market prices of different currencies that is *not* contractually binding. Traders then contact each other to obtain actual prices and negotiate deals. For example, suppose Citibank wants to obtain a large number of euros. Citibank has three avenues to conduct a trade. First, it may contact traders at other major banks, such as ABN-AMRO. Second, it may contact a foreign exchange broker to obtain quotes and broker a deal. Third, Citibank may be part of an electronic brokerage system (see the discussion in "Computerized Trading Systems," earlier in this chapter).

When the traders agree on the telephone, banks communicate and transfer funds electronically through computer networks. The most important interbank communications network is the **Society of Worldwide Interbank Financial Telecommunications (SWIFT)**, which began operations in Europe in 1973 and is jointly owned by more than 2,000 member banks. The SWIFT network links more than 7,500 financial institutions in more than 200 countries. Banks use SWIFT to send and receive messages pertaining to foreign exchange transactions, payment confirmations, documentation of international trade, transactions in securities, and other financial matters. In particular, SWIFT is used to confirm foreign exchange deals agreed upon on the phone. In 2005, SWIFT's global network processed more than 2 trillion messages.

After the verbal deal is electronically confirmed over SWIFT, the deal also has to be settled. Citibank will transfer dollars to ABN-AMRO in the United States, and Citibank will receive euros from ABN-AMRO in Europe. The transfer of dollars will be done through the **Clearing House Interbank Payments System (CHIPS)**, and the transfer of euros will be done through the **Trans-European Automated Real-time Gross Settlement Express Transfer (TARGET)**.

CHIPS is a private-sector system, owned and operated by The Clearing House Interbank Payments Company L.L.C. (CHIPCo), whose membership consists of many of the world's largest commercial banks. CHIPS is an electronic payment system that transfers funds and settles transactions in U.S. dollars. It is the central clearing system in the United States for international transactions, handling the bulk of all dollar payments moving between countries around the world. On a typical day in New York, well over $1.3 trillion in business payments pass through CHIPS computers. This amount corresponds to more than 285,000 international transactions, such as foreign trade payments, foreign exchange transfers, securities settlements, and money market transactions, as well as a growing number of domestic payments. CHIPS participants receive same-day settlement of funds through a special Fedwire account at the Federal Reserve Bank of New York.

Fedwire is a real-time gross settlement (RTGS) system operated by the Federal Reserve System of the United States. Fedwire links the computers of more than 7,000 U.S. financial institutions that have deposits with the Federal Reserve System. Transactions on Fedwire instantly move dollar balances between financial institutions. A transfer occurs when the originating office transmits a message to a Federal Reserve Bank, indicating who the paying and receiving banks are. The Federal Reserve Bank then debits the account of the paying bank and credits the account of the receiving bank.

Transactions on CHIPS are facilitated with a universal identifier (UID), a unique identification number for a bank or a corporation that tells the CHIPS system what private account and bank information to use for sending or receiving payments. Because Citibank owes dollars to ABN-AMRO, it uses ABN-AMRO's UID to ensure that it is paying to the right account.

Cross-border transactions in euros are facilitated through TARGET, which is the euro counterpart of Fedwire. Each of the European countries using the euro has its own central bank and a domestic RTGS system. TARGET links these systems to each other and to the European Central Bank in an international RTGS system. Hence, ABN-AMRO would indicate to TARGET that it was paying euros to a particular European Citibank office, and TARGET would debit ABM-AMRO's account and credit that of Citibank.

Exhibit 2.10 summarizes the communication systems used in the foreign exchange market, using two banks, Citibank and ABN-AMRO, as an example.

Cross-Currency Settlement (or Herstatt) Risk

Of course, the settlement of a foreign exchange trade requires the payment of one currency and the receipt of another. However, the settlement procedures described previously do not guarantee that the final transfer of one currency occurs if and only if the final transfer of the other currency occurs as well. Because foreign currency transactions often involve the payment systems of two countries in different time zones, simultaneous exchange of

Exhibit 2.10   Communication Systems in the Forex Market

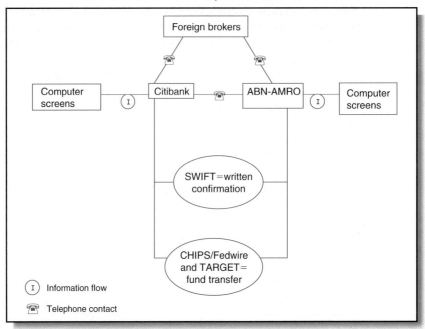

currencies is difficult. The risk that only one leg of the transaction may occur is very real. It is known as **cross-currency settlement risk**, or **Herstatt risk**.

The term *Herstatt risk* derives from the first modern occurrence of settlement risk. On June 26, 1974, Bankhaus Herstatt, a small bank in Cologne, Germany, went bankrupt at a very inopportune time for some of its foreign exchange trading partners. Herstatt had purchased Deutsche marks with dollars, and it was expected to wire dollars to various trading partners in the United States that day in return for the Deutsche marks. But that same day, the German regulatory authorities withdrew Herstatt's banking license and ordered it into liquidation after several of its U.S. counterparties in the foreign exchange market had irrevocably paid Deutsche marks to Herstatt. However, Herstatt had not yet delivered the U.S. dollars it owed its trading partners because the U.S. trading day had only just begun. After Herstatt's closure, its New York correspondent bank suspended outgoing U.S. dollar payments from Herstatt's account.

Herstatt risk is thus the risk that a bank will fail to deliver on one side of a foreign exchange deal even though the counterparty to the trade has delivered its promised payment. With the growing volumes of foreign exchange trading, the major central banks have understandably been worried about the ramifications of another Herstatt crisis. In particular, there is fear among government authorities that a large settlement failure could create an international liquidity crisis and jeopardize the health of the worldwide financial system. A liquidity crisis arises when participants in the financial marketplace fear that their counterparties may be insolvent—that is, will not be able to repay their debts. This happens when the debts of these counterparties exceed their assets. As a result, they do not pay their own debts.

Indeed, after the 1974 Herstatt event, several U.S. banks suddenly faced a short-term liquidity crisis because the millions of dollars they expected to receive failed to materialize. Daily gross funds transfers in the United States fell by half. Fortunately, the crisis was short-lived. The banks gradually regained confidence in each other, and normal operations soon resumed, indicating that the banks were basically solvent despite their losses from Herstatt's failure to deliver.

With the explosion in trading volume that is occurring today, systemic risk is much larger. Central banks worry that foreign exchange trading is so large that even highly capitalized major banks could be wiped out by a Herstatt-style event. Despite these concerns, little regulatory action has been undertaken to address the problem, although the Bank for International Settlements (BIS) has prepared several reports on the issue and has formulated a number of proposals designed to minimize Herstatt risk (see Committee on Payment and Settlement Systems, 1996).

Recently, foreign exchange dealers themselves, encouraged by the BIS, have developed a number of practices to limit settlement risk. First, banks now have strict limits on the amount of transactions they are willing to settle with a single counterparty on a given day. This generally helps curtail Herstatt risk.

Second, banks have started to engage in a variety of netting arrangements, in which they agree to wire the net traded amounts only at the end of a trading day. That is, a series of gross currency payments going both ways are converted into a single netted payment. When Citibank owes JPMorgan Chase $50 million from one foreign exchange transaction, and JPMorgan Chase owes Citibank $30 million from another transaction, it sounds reasonable to have only one wiring of funds from Citibank to JPMorgan Chase for the net amount of $20 million rather than to have JPMorgan Chase wire $30 million to Citibank and Citibank wire $50 million to JPMorgan Chase. Bilateral netting reduces the amount of settlement risk by lowering the number and size of payments that would otherwise be needed to settle the underlying transactions on a trade-by-trade basis. SWIFT has recently started to offer netting services for its users.

In the 1990s, several financial institutions set up organizations that offered multilateral (that is, involving multiple parties) netting services. The multilateral systems take all of a given bank's foreign exchange payments with other members of the system and then net them down to a single payment. This results in a further reduction in the number of payments actually required at the end of the day.

To illustrate these various netting arrangements, suppose that, in addition to Citibank and JPMorgan Chase, Bank of America participates in a multinetting system. Suppose Bank of America owes Citibank $30 million and is owed $20 million by JPMorgan Chase. Exhibit 2.11 illustrates this numeric example to demonstrate how gross flows, in which every payment is made, differ from the payments made under both bilateral and multilateral netting.

When there is no netting at all, the gross flows equal the sum of all transactions $(30 + 20 + 50 + 30 = 130)$. Under bilateral netting, Citibank and JPMorgan Chase recognize that one payment between them (20 million from Citibank to JPMorgan Chase) settles their net position, reducing the gross flows to 70 million. With all three banks in the netting organization, JPMorgan Chase does not have to pay anything because it owes Bank of America 20, but it is owed 20 by Citibank. The netting organization simply settles the overall net debt and credit positions, significantly reducing the amount of payment flows between banks.[3]

Third, settlement risk is eliminated if the exchange of the two monies happens simultaneously. The dream of a global clearing bank that would ensure the simultaneous settlement of all currency transactions between members of its system became a reality with the establishment of CLS Bank in 2002. CLS Bank (where CLS stands for *Continuous Linked Settlement*) is owned by 71 of the world's largest financial groups. CLS Bank collects details of all the currency trades between its member banks, uses multilateral netting to figure net payments for each bank, and finalizes pay-ins and pay-outs to the system over a 5-hour window. This window represents the overlapping hours of the participating settlements systems. While CLS Bank is a private institution, its creation and operation require unprecedented cooperation between central banks, as the accounts that the financial institutions hold at central banks are used for all the transactions.

2.5 DESCRIBING CHANGES IN EXCHANGE RATES

Section 2.3 explains how exchange rates are quoted at one point in time. Now, we turn to the topic of how to describe changes in exchange rates that occur over time. The first thing to remember about describing changes in exchange rates is that they are relative prices.

---

[3]These issues are also discussed in Chapter 20.

Exhibit 2.11 Netting Arrangements

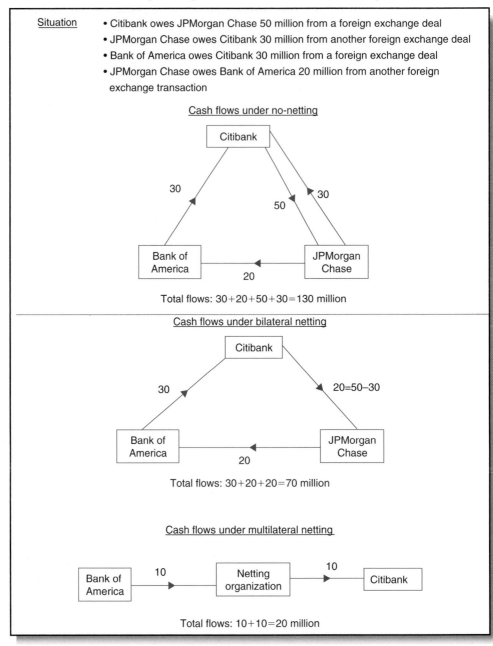

Situation
- Citibank owes JPMorgan Chase 50 million from a foreign exchange deal
- JPMorgan Chase owes Citibank 30 million from another foreign exchange deal
- Bank of America owes Citibank 30 million from a foreign exchange deal
- JPMorgan Chase owes Bank of America 20 million from another foreign exchange transaction

Cash flows under no-netting

Citibank

30

50

30

Bank of America

20

JPMorgan Chase

Total flows: 30+20+50+30=130 million

Cash flows under bilateral netting

Citibank

30

20=50−30

Bank of America

20

JPMorgan Chase

Total flows: 30+20+20=70 million

Cash flows under multilateral netting

Bank of America

10

Netting organization

10

Citibank

Total flows: 10+10=20 million

Consequently, there are always two ways to describe the same situation. After the change in the exchange rate, it will always be true that it takes relatively less of one currency to purchase the other currency and relatively more of the latter currency to purchase the former.

Consider an example. Suppose the exchange rate between the dollar and the yen changes from ¥120/$ to ¥100/$. Because it now takes fewer yen to purchase the dollar, the yen is said to have *strengthened*, or appreciated, in value relative to the dollar. The dollar consequently is said to have *weakened*, or depreciated, in value relative to the yen. After this depreciation of the dollar, it will take more dollars to purchase a given number of yen. Formerly, at ¥120/$, it took $8,333.33 to purchase ¥1,000,000. Now, at ¥100/$, it takes $10,000.00 to purchase

¥1,000,000. The terms **appreciation** and **depreciation** are typically used to describe changes in exchange rates when exchange rates are allowed to be flexible—that is, to fluctuate freely in response to changes in demand and supply.

Sometimes the government authorities of a country "fix," or "peg," the exchange rate of their money relative to a foreign money. (We discuss how they do this in Chapter 5.) Discrete changes in the values of exchange rates under such a fixed exchange-rate system are called **devaluations** and **revaluations** of the currencies. If the monetary authorities increase the domestic currency price of foreign exchange, they are *devaluing* their money. Such actions increase the domestic currency prices of foreign monies and are often the result of a failure in government policy. One famous historical devaluation occurred in November 1967, when Britain devalued the pound relative to the dollar by changing the price from $2.80/£ to $2.40/£, or by over 14% ((2.40 − 2.80)/2.80 = −14.29%).

If the dollar prices of foreign imports into Britain remain constant after such a devaluation, the pound prices of foreign goods will rise with the devaluation. This is because, after the devaluation, it takes more pounds to purchase a given number of dollars. Similarly, if the pound prices of British export goods remain constant after the devaluation, the dollar price of British goods will fall after the devaluation.

The simple logic that a devaluation increases the prices of foreign goods relative to domestic goods for domestic residents and decreases the relative prices of domestic goods to foreign buyers makes devaluations a tempting way for government authorities to try to "cure" unemployment problems in a country at the expense of the country's consumers. By devaluing their currency, which changes the relative prices of goods, the government induces more foreign demand for the domestic goods produced in its country. Unfortunately, the policy does not always work because the prices of goods are not fixed. They can adjust rapidly in response to devaluations. In addition, if a devaluation does work, it can lead to a cycle of competitive devaluations as countries across the world try to gain a competitive advantage in international trade.

If the authorities of a country decrease the domestic currency price of foreign exchange, they are said to be *revaluing* the country's money. For example, in October 1969, Germany lowered the DM price of the dollar from DM4/$ to DM3.66/$, a change of 8.5% = 100 × (4 − 3.66) / 4.0. This action decreased the DM cost of imports to Germany and increased the dollar cost of goods exported from Germany. If a revaluation changes the relative prices across countries, it benefits domestic

Example 2.6 Baseball Caps in Turkey

Suppose a Turkish importer buys American baseball caps for $10 per cap. The current exchange rate is 685,000 Turkish lira (TRL) per dollar, and the baseball caps are put up for sale in Ankara, with a 50% markup over the export price. Hence, the price of the baseball caps for Turkish consumers is

$$\$10 \times TRL685,000/\$ \times 1.50 = TRL10,275,000$$

The Turkish lira was pegged to a "basket" (combination) of the dollar and the euro until February 23, 2001. A political crisis earlier that week led to a financial crisis: Interest rates soared, and the Turkish stock market plummeted. On February 23, the Turkish government let the lira "float," or fluctuate, rather than keep it pegged to the dollar–euro basket. In just 1 day, the value of the dollar increased to TRL962,499/$, which represents a 40.51% increase in the value of the dollar relative to the lira. If the baseball cap export price and the markup remain unchanged, the Turkish lira price becomes

$$\$10 \times TRL962,499\$ \times 1.50 = TRL14,437,402$$

This increase in price should certainly decrease the demand for baseball caps in Turkey.

consumers but hurts domestic workers and producers. This is because the goods and services produced in the country have to compete with imports that have become cheaper after the revaluation.

Rates of Appreciation and Depreciation

Now that you know how to describe the movements in exchange rates, you can quantify those changes. The rate of appreciation or depreciation of one currency relative to another can be calculated as the percentage rate of change of the exchange rate:

$$100 \times \frac{(\text{New exchange rate} - \text{Old exchange rate})}{\text{Old exchange rate}}$$

It is important to note that technically, the description of an appreciation or a depreciation refers to the currency that is in the denominator of the exchange rate. For example, for dollar–pound exchange rates, the percentage change in the exchange rate describes an appreciation or a depreciation of the pound:

$$\text{Percentage appreciation or depreciation of the pound} = 100 \times \frac{(\text{new \$/£}) - (\text{old \$/£})}{(\text{old \$/£})}$$

For example, if the exchange rate changes from \$2.00/£ to \$2.50/£, the pound is said to have appreciated relative to the dollar by 25%:

$$25\% = 100 \times \frac{(\$2.50/£) - (\$2.00/£)}{(\$2.00/£)}$$

Now, let's examine the rate of depreciation of the dollar relative to the pound in the same situation. Unfortunately, it will turn out to be a slightly different percentage change. Because the old exchange rate of pounds per dollar is £1/\$2.00 = £0.50/\$, and the new exchange rate is £1/\$2.50 = £0.40/\$, the dollar is said to have depreciated relative to the pound by 20%, because

$$100 \times \frac{(£0.40/\$) - (£0.50/\$)}{(£0.50/\$)} = -20\%$$

The fact that these rates of appreciation and depreciation are not the same causes some confusion. The explanation for the difference begins with the observation that the exchange rate quoted in American terms is the reciprocal (inverse) of the exchange rate quoted in European terms. Let $S(t,\$/£)$ be the dollar–pound exchange rate at time t. Then, the rate of appreciation of the pound relative to the dollar is $\frac{S(t + 1,\$/£) - S(t,\$/£)}{S(t,\$/£)}$. If we want to find the rate of appreciation of the dollar relative to the pound, we must consider European terms. Let us denote these exchange rates with a different symbol, $E(t, £/\$)$. Then, the rate of appreciation of the dollar relative to the pound is $\frac{E(t + 1,£/\$) - E(t,£/\$)}{E(t,£/\$)}$. But, by definition, the European and American quotes are each other's reciprocal, $S(t,\$/£) = 1/[E(t,£/\$)]$. Hence, the rate of appreciation of the dollar relative to the pound can be re-written as $\frac{[1/S(t + 1,\$/£)] - [1/S(t,\$/£)]}{[1/S(t,\$/£)]}$. If we multiply the numerator and the denominator ofthe rate of appreciation of the dollar by $S(t,\$/£)$, we find

$$\frac{S(t,\$/£)}{S(t + 1,\$/£)} - 1 = \frac{S(t,\$/£) - S(t + 1,\$/£)}{S(t + 1,\$/£)}$$

Hence, the numerator in the rate of appreciation of the dollar is the negative of the numerator in the rate of appreciation of the pound, but the denominators are different. One uses the exchange rate at time t and the other uses the exchange rate at time $t + 1$.

While the distinction in terminology (that appreciation or depreciation refers to the currency in the denominator of the exchange rate) may seem like little more than an annoying and potentially confusing curiosity, the different descriptions are sometimes used for political purposes, which makes the distinction important to understand.[4] In Greece, before the advent of the euro, for example, different newspapers tended to describe the change in the exchange rate in the way that was most favorable to the political party that the newspaper supported. For example, suppose the Greek drachma value of the dollar rose from GRD200/$ to GRD220/$. Newspapers that wanted to heighten concern about the event would report "Dollar Strengthens Relative to Drachma by 10%," while newspapers that wanted to reduce concern would announce "Drachma Weakens Relative to Dollar by 9%." You should be able to explain why these statements actually describe the same event.

Continuously Compounded Rates of Appreciation (Advanced)

It turns out that using continuously compounded rates of change reconciles the two descriptions of the same event and makes them equal but opposite in sign. Let's look at what happens to the description as we change the time interval over which the event happened. For example, if the appreciation of the pound, from $2.00/£ to $2.50/£, took place over the course of a year, we would say that the annual rate of appreciation of the pound was 25%. That is, to go from the old rate at the end of a year to the new rate at the end of the current year requires multiplication by 1.25:

$$(\$2.00/£) \times (1.25) = (\$2.50/£)$$

If portfolio decisions are made monthly, we might also be interested in describing the rate of appreciation on a compound monthly basis while still expressing the percentage change at an annual rate. In this case, we ask what value of a in $[1 + (a/12)]$ when raised to the 12th power satisfies the following equation:

$$(\$2.00/£)[1 + (a/12)]^{12} = (\$2.50/£)$$

To solve for a, we first divide both sides by $2.00/£ and then take the $(1/12)$ power on each side:

$$[1 + (a/12)] = [(\$2.50/£)/(\$2.00/£)]^{1/12}$$

Try this with your calculator. Then subtract 1 and multiply by 12. The answer is $a = 0.2256$, or an annualized compound monthly rate of appreciation of the pound of 22.56%. The annualized compound monthly rate of depreciation of the dollar, d, can analogously be calculated as

$$(£0.50/\$)[1 - (d/12)]^{12} = (£0.40/\$)$$

and we find through similar steps that $d = 0.2208$, or 22.08%. Notice that the difference in the two descriptions of the same event is now smaller.

If we drive the compounding interval smaller and smaller, we will eventually ask what continuous rate of appreciation of the pound relative to the dollar over the course of a year caused the pound to strengthen from $2.00/£ to $2.50/£. Continuous compounding uses the symbol e, which represents the base of natural logarithms, and the value of e rounded to three decimal places is 2.718.[5]

Now, the annualized continuously compounded rate of appreciation of the pound is the value of a that satisfies

$$(\$2.00/£)e^a = \$2.50/£$$

---

[4]Thanks to Ekaterini Kryiazidou for this example.
[5]The appendix to this chapter discusses logarithms and continuous compounding.

To solve for the value of a, we take the natural logarithm of both sides of the equation and find

$$a = \ln(\$2.50/\pounds) - \ln(\$2.00/\pounds) = 0.2231$$

or 22.31%. Similarly, the annualized continuously compounded rate of depreciation of the dollar is the value of d that satisfies

$$(\pounds0.50/\$)e^{-d} = \pounds0.40/\$$$

To solve for the value of d, we take the natural logarithm of both sides of the equation and find

$$d = -[\ln(\pounds0.40/\$) - \ln(\pounds0.50/\$)] = 0.2231$$

or 22.31%. With continuous compounding, the rates of appreciation of the pound and depreciation of the dollar are the same.

2.6 SUMMARY

This chapter introduces the institutions and contracts that form the basis of the world's international financial system. The main points in the chapter are as follows:

1. The foreign exchange market is a large, over-the-counter market composed of banks and brokerage firms and their customers in the financial centers of countries around the world. Volume of trade in the market is estimated to be over $1.5 trillion on active days.

2. The foreign exchange market is very competitive, with no single bank dominating the worldwide trading of currencies.

3. Exchange rates—that is, the prices of currencies—are relative prices. They can be quoted in direct terms as the domestic currency price of the foreign currency (sometimes called *American terms* in the United States) or in indirect terms as the foreign currency price of the domestic currency (sometimes called *European terms* in the United States).

4. Exchange rates between two currencies that do not involve the dollar are called *cross-rates*. Triangular arbitrage keeps cross-rates in line with exchange rates quoted relative to the U.S. dollar.

5. Traders quote two-way prices in a bid–ask spread. They attempt to buy one currency at their low bid price and to sell that currency at their higher ask, or offer, price. Competition keeps bid–ask spreads in the market quite small.

6. In the interbank market, traders agree on currency transactions by phone or through electronic trading systems. Confirmation and settlement of a trade occurs later through SWIFT and CHIPS.

7. Settlement risk, the risk that one leg of the currency transaction may not occur, is also called Herstatt risk.

8. Changes in flexible exchange rates are described as currency appreciations and depreciations. When it takes fewer yen to purchase the dollar, the yen is said to have *strengthened*, or *appreciated*, in value relative to the dollar. The dollar consequently has *weakened*, or *depreciated*, in value relative to the yen. It will take more dollars to purchase a given number of yen. Discrete changes in the values of exchange rates under a fixed exchange-rate system are called *devaluations* and *revaluations* of the currencies.

QUESTIONS

1. What is an exchange rate?
2. What is the structure of the foreign exchange market? Is it like the New York Stock Exchange?
3. What is a spot exchange-rate contract? When does delivery occur on a spot contract?
4. What was the Japanese yen spot price of the U.S. dollar on February 16, 2006?
5. What was the U.S. dollar spot price of the Swiss franc on February 16, 2006?
6. How large are the bid–ask spreads in the interbank spot market? What is their purpose?
7. What was the euro price of the British pound on February 16, 2006? Why?
8. If the direct euro price of the British pound is higher than the indirect euro price of the British pound using the dollar as a vehicle currency, how could you make a profit by trading these currencies?

9. What is an appreciation of the dollar relative to the pound? What happens to the dollar price of the pound in this situation?

10. What is a depreciation of the Thai baht relative to the Malaysian ringgit? What happens to the baht price of the ringgit in this situation?

PROBLEMS

1. Mississippi Mud Pies, Inc., needs to buy 1,000,000 Swiss francs (CHF) to pay its Swiss chocolate supplier. Its banker quotes bid–ask rates of CHF1.3990–1.4000/USD. What will be the dollar cost of the CHF1,000,000?

2. If the Japanese yen–U.S. dollar exchange rate is ¥104.30/$, and it takes 25.15 Thai bahts to purchase 1 dollar, what is the yen price of the baht?

3. As a foreign exchange trader, you see the following quotes for Canadian dollars (CAD), U.S. dollars (USD), and Mexican pesos (MXN):

   CAD1.419/USD
   MXN6.4390/CAD
   MXN8.7535/USD

   Is there an arbitrage opportunity, and if so, how would you exploit it?

4. The Mexican peso has weakened considerably relative to the dollar, and you are trying to decide whether this is a good time to invest in Mexico. Suppose the current exchange rate of the Mexican peso relative to the U.S. dollar is MXN9.5/USD. Your investment advisor at Goldman Sachs argues that the peso will lose 15% of its value relative to the dollar over the next year. What is Goldman Sachs's forecast of the exchange rate in 1 year?

5. Deutsche Bank quotes bid–ask rates of €0.9850 – 0.9855/$ and ¥104.30 − 104.40/$. What would be Deutsche Bank's direct asking price for yen (€/¥)?

6. Western Mining of Australia has called Mitsubishi Tokyo Financial to get its opinion about the Japanese yen–Australian dollar exchange rate. The current rate is ¥67.72/A$, and Mitsubishi thinks the Australian dollar will weaken by 5% over the next year. What is Mitsubishi's forecast of the future exchange rate?

BIBLIOGRAPHY

Ammer, John, and Allan D. Brunner, 1997, "Are Banks Market Timers or Market Makers? Explaining Foreign Exchange Trading Profits," *Journal of International Financial Markets, Institutions and Money* 7, pp. 43–60.

Bank for International Settlements, May 2005, "Central Bank Survey of Foreign Exchange and Derivatives Market Activity, 2004," Bank for International Settlements.

Bollerslev, Tim, and Ian Domowitz, September 1993, "Trading Patterns and the Behavior of Prices in the Interbank Deutsche Mark/Dollar Foreign Exchange Market," *Journal of Finance* pp. 1421–1443.

Braas, Alberic, and Charles N. Bralver, 1990, "An Analysis of Trading Profits: How Most Trading Rooms Really Make Money," *Journal of Applied Corporate Finance* 2, pp. 85–90.

Chakrabarti, Rajesh, 2000, "Just Another Day in the Interbank Foreign Exchange Market," *Journal of Financial Economics* 56, pp. 29–64.

Committee on Payment and Settlement Systems of the Central Banks of the Group of Ten Countries, March 1996, "Settlement Risk in Foreign Exchange Transactions," http://riskinstitute.ch/140530.htm.

Goodhart, Charles, and Antonis Demos, Winter 1990, "Reuters Screen Images of the Foreign Exchange Markets: The Deutsche Mark/Dollar Spot Rate," *The Journal of International Securities Markets* pp. 333–348.

Hartmann, Philip, 1998, "Do Reuters Spreads Reflect Currencies' Differences in Global Trading Activity?" *Journal of International Money and Finance* 17, pp. 757–784.

Huang, Roger D., and Ronald W. Masulis, 1999, "FX spreads and dealer competition across the 24-hour trading day," *Review of Financial Studies* 12, pp. 61–93.

Ito, Takatoshi, and Yuko Hashimoto, 2006, "Intra-Day Seasonality in Activities of the Foreign Exchange Markets: Evidence from the Electronic Brokering System," NBER Working Paper W12413.

Lyons, Richard K., 1998, "Profits and Position Control: A Week of FX Dealing," *Journal of International Money and Finance* 17, pp. 97–115.

Lyons, Richard K., May 1997, "A Simultaneous Trade Model of the Foreign Exchange Hot Potato," *Journal of International Economics* pp. 275–298.

Appendix

Logarithms

Logarithms are useful because they simplify growth calculations. The logarithm of a number is taken with respect to a particular base number, such as base 10 or base 2. The logarithm of a number X under base B is the number Y to which the base number B must be raised to make it equal to X. That is, because

$$B^Y = X$$

Base B logarithm of X is Y.

For example, if the base number is 10, and $X = 1,000$, then $Y = 3$, because $10^3 = 1,000$. Thus, in base 10, we say the logarithm of 1,000 is 3, and we can write $\log_{10}(1,000) = 3$. Similarly, if the base number is 2, and $X = 256$, then $Y = 8$, because $2^8 = 256$. Therefore, in base 2, we say the logarithm of 256 is 8, and we can write $\log_2(256) = 8$.

In finance, we often encounter the *natural logarithm*. Natural logarithms arise because of continuous compounding and discussions of growth at continuous rates.

Banks usually quote interest rates at annual rates such as 10%, and they specify a compounding period, which might be annual, semiannual, monthly, daily, or even continuously. We know that the more often the bank credits interest to our account, the more money we will have at the end of a year because we will earn interest on previously credited interest. For example, if the quoted interest rate is 10%, at the end of 1 year, we will have the following amounts, depending on the compounding interval:

Compounding Interval	Amount in 1 Year
Annual	$(1 + 0.1) = 1.1$
Semiannual	$(1 + (0.1/2))^2 = 1.1025$
Quarterly	$(1 + (0.1/4))^4 = 1.1038$
Monthly	$(1 + (0.1/12))^{12} = 1.1047$
Daily	$(1 + (0.1/365))^{365} = 1.10516$

The return from continuously compounding at an interest rate, i, is obtained by taking the limit as the number of compounding intervals goes to infinity:

$$\lim_{n \to \infty}(1 + (i/n))^n = e^i$$

where e turns out to be the number that is the base for natural logarithms, which is approximately equal to 2.71828. In our example with a 10% annual interest rate, the amount of money in 1 year if interest is continuously compounded is $e^{0.1} = 1.1052$.

The natural logarithm of 1.1052 is 0.1 because raising 2.71828 to the 0.1 power is 1.1052. Sometimes people write $\exp(i)$ rather than e^i to mean evaluate the exponential function, $\exp(i)$, at the value of i, which means simply to raise the number e to the i-th power.

Because raising the number e to a power tells you how much your principal grows when it is compounded continuously at a certain interest rate, the exponential function can be used to describe other growth rates, such as rates of appreciation or depreciation of currencies and rates of inflation. For example, if the dollar price of the pound were to grow at a continuous rate of 5% during 2006, then the exchange rate at the end of the year would be

$$S(\$/\pounds)_{2006} = S(\$/\pounds)_{2005}\, e^{0.05}$$

There are several useful properties of natural logarithms, which are represented by ln and their base number, e, that we will exploit:

1. $\ln(e(A)) = A$
2. $e(\ln(A)) = A$
3. If $A = BC$, then $\ln(A) = \ln(B) + \ln(C)$
4. If $A = B/C$, then $\ln(A) = \ln(B) - \ln(C)$
5. If $A = B^C$, then $\ln(A) = C\ln(B)$

We can combine these properties to establish that differences in natural logarithms are growth rates or percentage differences at continuous rates.

For instance, you can use the rules to demonstrate that

$$\ln[S(\$/\pounds)_{2006}] - \ln[S(\$/\pounds)_{2005}] = 0.05$$

Chapter 3

Forward Markets and Transaction Exchange Risk

*K*ashima, a Japanese oil refinery, imports crude oil, refines it, and sells the refined oil in the Japanese market. Kashima's revenues are in yen, but its costs are in dollars because contracts in the world crude oil market are dollar denominated. Consequently, an adverse movement in the yen–dollar exchange rate, in this case a weakening of the yen, significantly increases Kashima's yen costs for its oil. Kashima's dollar-denominated contracts for the delivery of oil in the future give Kashima an exposure to losses from movements in exchange rates. In general, when the delivery of and payment for goods takes some time, future fluctuations in exchange rates give rise to potential losses, and possible gains, for the parties involved. The possibility of taking a loss in such a transaction is called **transaction exchange risk**.

In Chapter 2, we examined the organization of the spot foreign exchange market, in which the exchange of currencies typically happens in 2 business days. This chapter examines the **forward foreign exchange market** (or the *forward market*, for short). It is the market for exchanges of currencies in the future.[1] One of the major reasons for the existence of forward markets is to manage foreign exchange risk in general and transaction exchange risk in particular.

The forward markets for foreign exchange allow corporations, such as Kashima, to protect themselves against transaction exchange risks by **hedging**.[2] To hedge against such risks, the corporation enters into an additional contract that provides profits when the underlying transaction produces losses. To evaluate the costs and benefits of hedging for a future transaction involving foreign currencies, the hedging party must have some way to quantify the degree of uncertainty it faces about future spot exchange rates. It accomplishes this by figuring out the likelihood of observing various ranges for future exchange rates.

We begin the chapter by defining *transaction exchange risk* and continue by formalizing how to think about the uncertain future exchange rate movements that cause it. Next, we introduce forward contracts and discuss how transaction exchange risk can be hedged using these contracts. We then provide more details about the conventions and trading practices of the forward exchange market. Finally, we introduce the concept of a forward premium, which describes how forward rates are related to spot rates, a relationship that we will come back to many times throughout the book.

---

[1]This chapter studies the interbank forward markets. The other type of market for the exchange of currencies in the future is the organized futures foreign exchange market, which is discussed in Chapter 20.
[2]In Chapter 17 we explore more generally why firms might want to hedge currency risk.

Corporations, institutional investors, and individuals incur transaction exchange risk if they enter into a transaction in which they are required to pay or to receive a specific amount of foreign currency at a particular date in the future. Because the future spot exchange rate cannot be known with certainty, and the exchange rate can move in an unfavorable direction, such a transaction could lead to a loss. Our next task is to determine the precise nature of the risks associated with these transactions.

Suppose Motorola, a U.S. firm, is importing some electronic equipment from Hitachi, a Japanese company. Motorola orders the equipment and promises to pay a certain amount of yen in, say, 90 days. Suppose that Motorola does nothing between the time that it enters into the transaction and the time that the payment of yen is scheduled to occur. Motorola consequently will be required to purchase the amount of yen that it owes Hitachi with dollars in the future spot market. If the dollar weakens unexpectedly relative to the yen, Motorola will end up paying more dollars than it expected to pay.

Analogously, suppose Sun, a U.S. firm, exports workstations to Europe and agrees to receive euro payments in the future, when it delivers the workstations. If Sun does nothing between the time that it enters into the contracts and the dates of delivery and payment, Sun will convert the euros into dollars in the future spot market. If the euro depreciates unexpectedly, Sun will receive fewer dollars for the transaction than it had anticipated receiving.

Whenever you engage in an international financial transaction that involves an exchange of currencies in the future, you will almost always be unsure about what the spot exchange rate will be in the future when you conduct this transaction. This is true even under regimes of fixed exchange rates because political and economic events can always trigger devaluation or revaluation of the domestic currency relative to foreign currencies. Under the flexible exchange rate system that has characterized the foreign exchange markets for the major currencies for more than 30 years, exchange rates fluctuate a good deal from day to day. As a financial manager, you must be able to gauge where the exchange rate might head and how likely such fluctuations may be. This range of possible future values for the exchange rate and the likelihood of their occurring will give you an idea of the foreign exchange risk your firm faces and whether it's a good idea to hedge.

Often, people in corporations discuss the possibility or magnitude of a potential foreign exchange loss by valuing the foreign currency that is scheduled to be paid or received in the future at today's spot exchange rate. However, this is not the proper way to think about transaction exchange risk *unless there is no expected change to the exchange rate*. The potential loss or the possible gain from uncertain future exchange rates is appropriately measured relative to the expected future spot rate.

To see why, let's look at an example regarding transaction exchange rate risk at a fictitious company, Fancy Foods. We will return to this example in the next section, after we have discussed how to formally describe uncertainty in future spot rates.

Example 3.1   Transaction Exchange Risk at Fancy Foods

Suppose Fancy Foods, a U.S. firm, is importing meat pies from the British firm Porky Pies. Assume that Fancy Foods is obligated to pay £1,000,000 in 90 days, in return for meat pies that will be delivered at that time by Porky Pies. Suppose that Fancy Foods has no pounds currently and is going to wait until 90 days in the future to purchase pounds. How many dollars does Fancy Foods expect to have to pay? If Fancy Foods waits until 90 days from now to transact, it will have to purchase the £1,000,000 at whatever the spot exchange rate is at that time. Its dollar cost will consequently be

$$\text{Realized dollar cost in 90 days} = S(t + 90,\$/£) \times (£1,000,000)$$

Suppose the current exchange rate is $1.50/£ and that Fancy Foods expects the pound to appreciate relative to the dollar by 2% over the next 90 days. Then the expected value of the future spot rate in 90 days is $1.53/£ = ($1.50/£) × (1 + 0.02). Hence, Fancy Foods expects to pay

$$(\$1.53/£) \times (£1,000,000) = \$1,530,000$$

This is the amount that will be paid *if* Fancy Foods's expectations are realized and the pound actually appreciates by 2%. But in currency markets, as in most other financial markets, what is expected usually does not happen. If the pound appreciates relative to the dollar by more than 2%, the future exchange rate will be higher than $1.53/£, and Fancy Foods will have to pay more dollars to offset its pound liability. On the other hand, if the dollar strengthens relative to the pound or does not weaken from the current spot rate of $1.50/£ to the expected spot of $1.53/£, Fancy Foods will experience a gain because the number of dollars required to eliminate the pound obligation will be reduced relative to what it expected.

If, instead, another U.S. company, Nancy Foods, agrees to receive some number of British pounds 90 days in the future in return for delivering frozen quiches to the British firm Quirky Pies, our calculations of gains and losses will be exactly the opposite: A depreciation of the pound relative to the dollar will cause Nancy Foods to receive fewer dollars than it expected to receive. Conversely, if the pound appreciates (that is, if the dollar weakens) by more than is expected, Nancy Foods will experience a gain because it has a pound asset.

3.2 DESCRIBING UNCERTAIN FUTURE EXCHANGE RATES

To quantify the potential losses or gains due to a transaction exchange risk, we must think more about describing the uncertainty surrounding *future* spot exchange rates. Although we do not know exactly what value exchange rates will have in the future, we can quantify the possible changes that may occur and thus quantify how much risk we are bearing in international financial transactions. In doing so, we will, unfortunately, have to use a host of statistical concepts that you may or may not be familiar with. The appendix "A Statistics Refresher," at the end of this chapter, should bring you up to speed.

Assessing Exchange Rate Uncertainty Using Historical Data

We can use historical data to get an idea not only of what has happened in the past but what might happen in the future. Exhibit 3.1 presents a histogram of monthly percentage changes in the exchange rate of the U.S. dollar relative to the British pound, with rates in conventional American terms as $/£. The exhibit also superimposes on the graph a normal distribution curve, with the same **mean** and **standard deviation** as the data. We will explore this in more detail shortly.

Exhibit 3.1   Dollar–Pound Monthly Exchange Rate, 1975–2005

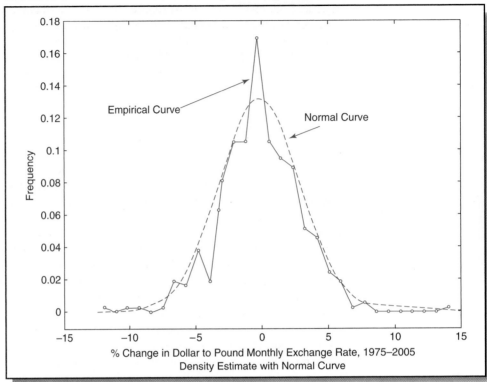

Notes: We compute percentage changes of exchange rates for the dollar–pound as $s(t) = \dfrac{S(t) - S(t-1)}{S(t-1)}$, where
$S(t)$ is the exchange rate at time t (the end of a month). The graph creates a histogram of the $s(t)$ data. We consider
small bins (ranges) of possible percentage changes (for example, between –0.167% and 0.167%) and compute the
number of observations within a bin. The dots on the graph represent the midpoints of the bins and their frequency
(number of observations divided by the total number of observations). The curve connecting the dots is the histogram. The smooth curve corresponds to a normal distribution with the same mean and standard deviation as the
sample data. (The formula for this curve is $\dfrac{1}{\sqrt{2\pi\sigma^2}} e^{-\frac{1}{2}\left(\frac{s-\mu}{\sigma}\right)^2}$ where μ is the mean and σ is the standard deviation;
e is the number 2.71828 (see the appendix to Chapter 2); and π is the number 3.14159.)

The data in Exhibit 3.1 cover the period January 1975 to December 2005, or 372 observations. With the spot exchange rate at time t denoted $S(t)$, the percentage change in the
exchange rate between time period $t - 1$ and time period t is calculated as

$$s(t) = [S(t) - S(t-1)]/S(t-1) \tag{3.1}$$

and we report $100 \times s(t)$. Remember that Chapter 2 notes that these percentage rates of
change in exchange rates are called *appreciations* of the pound (if positive) and *depreciations*
of the pound (if negative).

The horizontal axis in Exhibit 3.1 describes the percentage changes historically observed for
the $/£ rate, which range from about -12% to $+14.5\%$. To create the histogram, we create ranges
("bins") of equal width. These ranges are represented by the space between the dots along the
curve. The dot is graphed for the midpoint of the bin. The vertical axis represents the frequency or
probability of occurrence for each bin. The average (mean) monthly percentage change was
-0.04% for the dollar–pound. Because the mean "centers" the distribution, and because the

distribution is bell shaped, observations near the mean are likely to occur. The standard deviation is a measure of the dispersion of possibilities *around* the mean. For the percentage changes in the exchange rates, the standard deviation was 3.04%. Exchange rate changes within 1 standard deviation of the mean (between $-0.04\% - 3.04\% = -3.08\%$ and $-0.04\% + 3.04\% = 3.00\%$) are more likely to occur than changes further away from the mean. For the curve in Exhibit 3.1, it appears that exchange rate changes 2 standard deviations away from the mean (either smaller than $-0.04\% - (2 \times 3.04\%) = -6.12\%$ or larger than 6.04%) seem not very likely to occur because the probability estimates on the vertical axis become very small.

We use probability distributions to describe uncertain future exchange rates more formally. You have no doubt encountered probability distributions used to describe the uncertainty in other financial applications, such as describing the short-term returns on investments in equity or long-term bonds. Analogously, we can summarize our ignorance about what will happen to the exchange rate in the future with a probability distribution.

The second curve in Exhibit 3.1 represents a normal distribution. Exhibit 3.1 reveals that the assumption of a normal distribution, characterized by a bell-shaped curve, is very reasonable for the pound, as it is for all major currencies for monthly rates of change. However, we will encounter situations in which this assumption is not appropriate. For example, many emerging market currencies exhibit probability distributions that are distinctively non-normal. An example is Exhibit 3.2, which shows the distribution for monthly percentage changes of the Mexican peso relative to the U.S. dollar (MXN/USD) and the normal distribution with the same mean and standard deviation.

The historical distribution in Exhibit 3.2 is obviously not symmetric. Using historical data, we calculate a mean of 0.98% and a standard deviation of 5.24%. But the most prominent feature of the historical distribution is the long right-hand tail. Statisticians say the distribution is skewed to the right. This indicates that large depreciations or devaluations of the peso relative to the dollar have occurred, and the absence of a large left-hand tail indicates that

Exhibit 3.2 Peso–Dollar Monthly Exchange Rate, 1994–2005

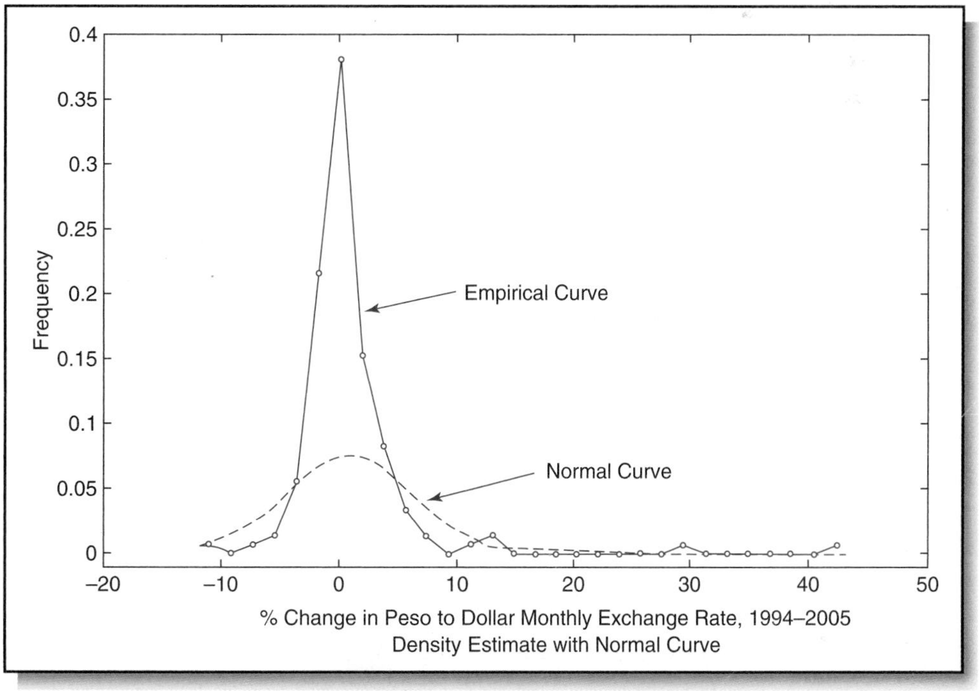

Notes: We perform the same exercise as in Exhibit 3.1 but for peso–dollar exchange rates.

there have been no analogously large appreciations or revaluations of the peso. Also, many more of the observations are centered around the mean (relative to the normal distribution) because the Mexican peso has been pegged to one particular value for various time intervals. We will come back to this issue in Chapter 5, when we talk about alternative exchange rate arrangements. For now, you should remember that a normal probability distribution is a reasonable description of monthly percentage changes for the major floating currencies, but it is not a good description of emerging market currencies.

The Probability Distribution of Future Exchange Rates

Exhibits 3.1 and 3.2 are based on historical data. Financial managers are also interested in the probability distribution of *future* spot exchange rates. Given that we observe an exchange rate of $S(t)$ today, we can find the probability distribution of future exchange rates in, say, 90 days from the probability distribution of the percentage change in the exchange rate. From Equation (3.1) we see that the possible future spot exchange rates are

$$S(t+90) = S(t) \times [1 + s(t+90)] \tag{3.2}$$

where $s(t+90)$ denotes the percentage change in the exchange rate over the next 90 days, $s(t+90) = [S(t+90) - S(t)]/S(t)$.

Exhibit 3.3 provides an example of a probability distribution for the spot exchange rate between the U.S. dollar and the British pound at time $t + 90$, which is 90 days in the future relative to today. As drawn, Exhibit 3.3 represents the typical bell-shaped curve of a normal distribution.

Conditional Means and Volatilities

Because the probability distribution of the future exchange rate depends on all the information available at time t, we say that it is a **conditional probability distribution** (see the appendix to this chapter). Consequently, the mean, which is the expected value of this distribution, is

Exhibit 3.3 Probability Distribution of $S(t+90)$

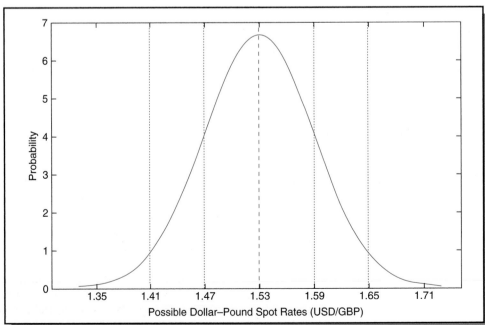

also referred to as the **conditional mean**, or the **conditional expectation**, of the future exchange rate. Because the conditional expectation of the future exchange rate plays an important role in what is to follow, we can use the following symbolic notation to represent it:

Conditional expectation at time t of the future spot exchange
rate at time $t + 90 = E_t[S(t+90)]$

One nice feature of the normal distribution is that the probability of any range of possible future exchange rates is completely summarized by its mean and the standard deviation, which is also often referred to as **volatility**. The conditional mean ties down the location of the probability distribution; the conditional standard deviation describes how spread out the distribution is. Notice that if the mean and the standard deviation of $s(t+90)$ are denoted μ and σ, then from Equation (3.2), we see that the conditional mean and conditional standard deviation of $S(t+90)$ are $[S(t)(1+\mu)]$ and $[S(t)\sigma]$, respectively.

Let's look at how Exhibit 3.3 is constructed. Suppose, as in Example 3.1, that the current exchange rate is \$1.50/£, and that people expect the pound to appreciate relative to the dollar by 2% over the next 90 days. The conditional expectation of the future spot rate in 90 days is then \$1.53/£ = (\$1.50/£) × (1 + 0.02). Suppose that the standard deviation of the rate of appreciation over the next 90 days is 4%. Because 4% of \$1.50/£ is \$0.06/£, the standard deviation of the conditional distribution of the expected future spot exchange rate is \$0.06/£. To summarize,

	Formula	Example
Conditional expectation of the future exchange rate (mean)	$S(t) \times (1+\mu)$	\$1.50/£ × (1 + 0.02) = \$1.53/£
Conditional volatility of the future expected exchange rate (standard deviation)	$S(t) \times \sigma$	\$1.50/£ × 0.04 = \$0.06/£

Armed with the conditional mean and conditional standard deviation of the future exchange rate, we can determine the probability that the future exchange rate will fall within any given range of exchange rates. For example, for the normal distribution, slightly more than two-thirds, or 68.26%, of the probability distribution is within plus or minus 1 standard deviation of the mean. In our example, this range is from

$$\$1.47/£ = \$1.53/£ - \$0.06/£$$

to

$$\$1.59/£ = \$1.53/£ + \$0.06/£$$

Consequently, the area under the curve between the two vertical lines emanating from \$1.47/£ and \$1.59/£ represents 68.26% of the total area. Also, for the normal distribution, 95.45% of the probability distribution is within plus or minus 2 standard deviations of the mean. Thus, the range of future exchange rates that encompasses all but 4.55% of the future possible values of dollar–pound exchange rates is \$1.41/£ to \$1.65/£.

Assessing the Likelihood of Particular Future Exchange Rate Ranges

Given our assessment of the probability distribution of future exchange rates, we can also determine the probability that the exchange rate in the future will be greater or less than a particular future spot rate. For example, suppose we want to know how likely it is that the pound will strengthen over the next 90 days to at least an exchange rate of $1.60/£. Because $1.60/£ is $0.07/£ greater than the conditional mean of $1.53/£ and the standard deviation is $0.06/£, we want to know how likely it is that we will be 0.07/0.06 = 1.167 standard deviations above the mean. For the normal distribution, this probability is 12.16%—that is, the probability of the exchange rate rising to $1.60/£ or higher from $1.50/£ is 12.16%.

Now that you can describe the possible changes in exchange rates that you may experience, you are in a better position to define and understand the concept of transaction exchange risk, so let's revisit the Fancy Foods example.

Example 3.2 Transaction Exchange Risk at Fancy Foods Revisited

Fancy Foods must pay Porky Pies £1,000,000 in 90 days, and the current exchange rate is $1.50/£. The conditional distribution of future $/£ rates is based on the information that the firm has when it is making its decision. Let's assume that the firm bases its decision on the probability distribution in Exhibit 3.3. Our calculations of the range of possible future exchange rates calculated earlier tell us that with 95.45% probability, the exchange rate will fall between $1.41/£ and $1.65/£. Hence, there is a 95.45% chance that Fancy Foods will pay between $1,410,000 = $1.41/£ × £1,000,000 and $1,650,000 = $1.65/£ × £1,000,000 to offset its pound liability. Remember that Fancy Foods expects to pay $1,530,000. If the dollar weakens to $1.65/£, we can think of Fancy Foods as losing

$$\$1,650,000 - \$1,530,000 = \$120,000,$$

compared to what it expected to pay. In contrast, if the dollar strengthens to $1.41/£, we can think of Fancy Foods as gaining

$$\$1,530,000 - \$1,410,000 = \$120,000,$$

compared to what it expected to pay. Of course, Fancy Foods is exposed to potentially larger losses and possibly bigger gains because something more extreme than this range of exchange rates could happen, but the probability of such extreme events is less than 4.55 if our probability distribution accurately reflects rational beliefs about the future.

3.3 HEDGING TRANSACTION EXCHANGE RISK

Fancy Foods can totally eliminate the risk of loss due to a change in the exchange rate if it uses a **forward contract**. Let's see why.

Forward Contracts and Hedging

A forward contract between a bank and a customer calls for delivery, at a fixed future date, of a specified amount of one currency against payment in another currency. The exchange rate specified in the contract, called the **forward rate**, is fixed at the time the parties enter into the contract. If you owe someone foreign currency at some date in the future, you can "buy the foreign currency forward" by contracting to have a bank deliver a specific amount of foreign currency to you on the date that you need it. At that time, you must pay the bank an amount of domestic currency equal to the forward rate (domestic currency/foreign currency) multiplied by the amount of foreign currency. Because the total amount you would owe the bank is determined today, it does not depend in any way on the actual value of the future exchange rate. Thus, using a forward contract eliminates transaction exchange risk.

Similarly, if you are scheduled to receive some foreign currency on a specific date in the future, you can "sell it forward" and entirely eliminate the foreign exchange risk. You contract to have the bank buy from you the amount of foreign currency you will receive in the future on that date in the future. Your forward contract establishes today the amount of domestic currency that you will receive in the future, which is equal to the forward exchange rate (domestic currency/foreign currency) multiplied by the amount of foreign currency you will be selling. The amount of domestic currency that you receive in the future consequently does not depend in any way on the future spot exchange rate.

Notice that in both cases, you have completely hedged your transaction exchange risk. Basically, you eliminate your risk by acquiring a foreign currency asset or liability that exactly offsets the foreign currency liability or asset that is given to you.

Hedging Currency Risk of Fancy Foods

Consider again Example 3.1, in which Fancy Foods owes Porky Pies £1,000,000 in 90 days. Let the forward rate at which Fancy Foods can contract to buy and sell pounds be $1.53/£. Fancy Foods can wait to transact in 90 days, but it risks losing money if the pound strengthens against the dollar. Contracting to buy £1,000,000 at $1.53/£ from a bank in the forward market gives Fancy Foods a foreign currency asset that is equivalent to its foreign currency liability. Fancy Foods's £1,000,000 liability from its business transaction is offset by a £1,000,000 asset, which is the bank's promise to pay Fancy Foods on the forward contract. Fancy Foods is left with an offsetting dollar liability of $1,530,000 = ($1.53/£) × (£1,000,000). We can summarize this position using the asset and liability accounts on Fancy Foods's balance sheet:

FANCY FOODS PARTIAL BALANCE SHEET	
Assets	**Liabilities**
£1,000,000 due from the bank in 90 days	£1,000,000 payable to Porky Pies in 90 days
	$1,530,000 payable to the bank in 90 days

Hedging at Nancy Foods

Now let's consider Nancy Foods, which is scheduled to receive £1,000,000 from Quirky Pies in 90 days. The sale of the pies gives Nancy Foods a foreign currency asset. Entering into a forward contract to sell £1,000,000 to the bank provides Nancy Foods with an equivalent foreign currency liability and a domestic currency asset. This hedges its foreign exchange risk. In this example, Nancy Foods's asset and liability positions would look like this:

NANCY FOODS PARTIAL BALANCE SHEET	
Assets	**Liabilities**
£1,000,000 receivable from Quirky Pies in 90 days	£1,000,000 payable to the bank in 90 days
$1,530,000 receivable from the bank in 90 days	

These asset and liability accounts demonstrate that using forward contracts can turn the underlying British pound asset or liability that arises in the course of a U.S. firm's normal business transactions into a dollar asset or liability that has no foreign exchange risk associated with it.

Exposure of Hedged Versus Unhedged Strategies

Exhibit 3.4 summarizes the exposures to transaction exchange risk of various strategies for buying or selling foreign currency. On the horizontal axis of Exhibit 3.4 (Panel A) are the future spot rates that can be realized in terms of the domestic currency (for example, dollars) per unit of foreign currency (for example, pounds). As you move to the right, the price of the foreign currency (pounds) in terms of the domestic currency (dollars) rises. In other words, the pound is appreciating in value. On the vertical axis are the domestic currency costs per unit of foreign currency (if you must buy the foreign currency in the future) or the domestic currency revenue per unit of foreign currency (if you must sell the foreign currency in the future). Hence, we can represent the domestic currency revenue or cost of hedging or not hedging as a function of the actual value of the future spot exchange rate using simple lines.

Exhibit 3.4 Gains and Losses Associated with Hedged Versus Unhedged
Contracts

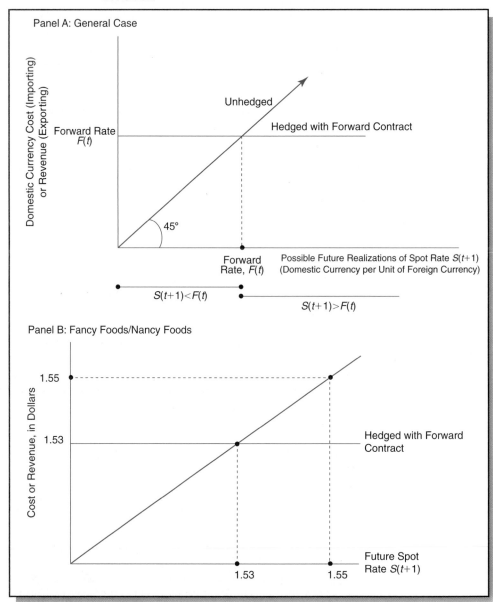

The 45-degree line represents the unhedged strategy. If you must buy foreign currency in the future and you are unhedged, your cost will fluctuate one-for-one with the domestic currency price of foreign currency that is realized in the future. As the domestic currency weakens, your cost rises, and as the domestic currency strengthens, your cost declines. Your risk is unlimited in the sense that your cost keeps rising one-for-one with the future exchange rate. Conversely, your costs decline directly with any strengthening of the domestic currency relative to the foreign currency. Theoretically, your costs could fall to zero, although it's highly unlikely that the domestic currency would strengthen to that extent.

The horizontal line in Exhibit 3.4 represents the strategy of hedging with a forward contract. If an international transaction requires you to buy foreign currency in the future, and you completely hedge by buying a forward contract today, your cost will be the same (equal to the forward rate) no matter what spot exchange rate is realized in the future. You bear no risk because the price you will pay is completely unaffected, even if the domestic currency weakens relative to the foreign currency. But the price you pay also cannot decline if the domestic currency strengthens relative to the foreign currency.

In Panel B, we consider the cases of Fancy Foods and Nancy Foods. Suppose that after 90 days, when the contracts must be settled, the spot rate is $1.55/£. If the companies entered a forward contract at $1.53/£, this is entirely immaterial. Fancy Foods will avoid paying $1.55/£ as it has locked in $1.53/£, and Nancy Foods will receive only $1.53/£, even though it could have done better in the spot market by selling its pounds at $1.55/£.

The Costs and Benefits of a Forward Hedge

In light of the discussion of hedging transaction exchange risk, what is the appropriate way to think about the cost of a forward hedge? First, it is important to ascertain when the cost is computed. Are we looking *ex post* (after the fact) and examining whether we paid more or less with our forward contract than we would have paid had we waited to transact at the realized future spot rate? Or are we thinking of cost in an *ex ante* (before the fact) sense, in which case we have to examine the expected cost? In the latter case, you should remember that if you do not hedge, you will bear the foreign exchange risk, and the actual exchange rate at which you will transact in the future is very likely not going to be the expected future spot rate.

If you are buying foreign currency with domestic currency because your underlying transaction gives you a foreign currency liability, you will be glad to have hedged *ex post* if the future spot rate (domestic currency/foreign currency) is above the forward rate. You will have regrets *ex post* if the future spot rate is below the forward rate. These costs and benefits are summarized in Exhibit 3.5.

When you are trying to determine whether to hedge, how the forward rate relates to the expected future spot exchange rate dictates whether there is an expected cost or an expected benefit to hedging. If you are buying foreign currency because your underlying transaction gives you a foreign currency liability, you will think that there is an expected cost to hedging if the expected future spot rate of domestic currency per unit of foreign currency is below the forward rate (domestic currency/foreign currency). Hedging would require you to transact at a domestic

Exhibit 3.5 Costs and Benefits of Hedging

	$F(t,k) < S(t + k)$	$F(t,k) > S(t + k)$
Foreign currency asset	Cost of hedging	Benefit of hedging
Foreign currency liability	Benefit of hedging	Cost of hedging

Notes: The spot rate and the forward rate are in domestic currency per unit of foreign currency. $F(t,k)$ is the forward rate at time t for delivery at time $t + k$. The costs or benefits are calculated *ex post*, after the realization of $S(t+k)$. If we replace $S((t+k)$ by $E_t[S(t+k)]$, they become expected costs or benefits.

currency price higher than you expect to have to pay if you do not hedge. Conversely, you will think there is an expected benefit to hedging if the expected future spot rate (domestic currency/foreign currency) is above the forward rate. In this case, hedging allows you to purchase foreign currency with domestic currency more cheaply than you would have expected to have to pay. Of course, complete hedging removes all potential benefits as well as all possible losses.

Notice that when we compare the forward rate to the expected future spot rate, the expected cost or benefit of hedging generated by this discussion is not a current-period cash flow. How can we determine the cost to us today of hedging or not hedging? The correct answer is that we must discount the future payments; that is, we must figure out the appropriate present values. We know that the payment associated with the forward contract will take place for certain in the future period, and in Chapter 6, we will discuss present-value techniques that allow us to determine the present value of the payment today. Determining the value today for a future cash flow from an uncertain distribution is quite another story. We must determine the discount rate that is appropriate for discounting the expected value of an uncertain future cash flow, a process we discuss in Chapter 13. As you will see, the problem of determining the *ex ante* cost of a hedge is complicated because we are comparing an uncertain payoff in one situation with a certain payoff in another situation.

Examples of Using Forward Contracts to Hedge Transaction Risk

Let's look at some examples to see the nature of different exposures, the extent of the possible losses, and how the exposures might be fully hedged with forward contracts.

Example 3.3 Hedging Import Payments

Assume that you are the financial manager of Zachy's, a wine store in Scarsdale, New York, that imports wine from France. You have just contracted to import some Chateau Margaux wine, and your invoice is for €4 million. You have agreed to pay this number of euros when you have received the wine and determined that it is in good condition. Payment of the euros and delivery of the wine are scheduled for 90 days in the future. The following data are available:

$$\text{Today's spot rate} = \$1.10/€$$

$$\text{Today's 90-day forward rate} = \$1.08/€$$

What is the source of your transaction exchange risk, and how much could you lose? First, as the U.S. importer, you have a euro-denominated liability because you have agreed to pay euros in the future. You are exposed to losses if the euro strengthens relative to the dollar unexpectedly to, say, $1.12/€. In this case, the dollar cost of the euros would be higher. If you do nothing to hedge your risk, your loss is theoretically unlimited in the sense that the dollar cost of the euros could go to infinity because the dollar amount that you will pay is $S(t+90,\$/€) \times €4$ million. Although this extreme loss is very unlikely, there is always some downside risk due to possible weakening, or depreciation, of the dollar relative to the euro.

You can eliminate the transaction exchange risk completely by buying €4 million in the forward market. The dollars that will be paid in 90 days are

$$(€4,000,000) \times (\$1.08/€) = \$4,320,000$$

Notice that the cash inflow of euros that you generate from the forward contract (€4,000,000) exactly matches the cash outflow of euros that you have from your underlying transaction. In other words, you have neutralized the euro liability that arises from your business by acquiring an equivalent euro asset, which is the promise by the bank to deliver euros to you. Hence, as long as you trust the bank that is your counterparty, you are not exposed to the risk of loss from fluctuations in exchange rates.

Of course, if you buy euros forward and the dollar strengthens substantially over the next 90 days (for example, to $1.05/€), you will still have to buy your euros from the bank at the forward price of $1.08/€ because that is the price you agreed to in the contract with the bank. In this sense, the forward contract eliminates your risk of loss, but it does so by keeping you from participating in possible gains in the future.

Example 3.4 Hedging Export Receipts

Now, place yourself in the position of Shetland Sweaters, a British manufacturer. Consider your transaction exchange risk if you agree to ship sweaters to Japan and are willing to accept ¥500,000,000 in payment from the Japanese sweater importer Nobu Inc. Delivery of the goods and receipt of the yen are scheduled for 30 days from now, and the following data are available:

$$\text{Today's spot rate} = ¥176/£$$

$$\text{Today's 30-day forward rate} = ¥180/£$$

What are the nature and extent of your transaction exchange risk? Because you have agreed to accept yen in payment for your sweaters, you have a yen-denominated asset. You are exposed to losses if you wait to sell the yen in the future spot market and the yen depreciates, or weakens, unexpectedly relative to the pound. In this case, the yen you receive in payment for your sweaters will purchase fewer pounds than you expect. If you do nothing between the time you enter into the contract and the time you receive your yen, you risk everything in the sense that, theoretically, the pound value of your yen receivable could go to zero. Although that is very unlikely, there certainly is a downside risk due to a possible weakening of the yen relative to the pound. Of course, there is also a possible gain if the yen strengthens relative to the pound.

How can you fully hedge, or eliminate, this transaction risk from your business? You can eliminate the risk of loss by selling ¥500,000,000 in the forward market for pounds. The pounds that will be received in 30 days are

$$¥500,000,000/(¥180/£) = £2,777,778$$

Notice again that your contractual yen cash outflow (¥500,000,000) to pay the bank for the forward purchase of pounds in 30 days exactly matches the cash inflow of yen that you will have from your underlying transaction. You have neutralized the foreign exchange exposure of your business by acquiring a foreign currency liability that is exactly equivalent to your foreign currency asset. Your promise to deliver yen to the bank is your yen liability. Hence, as long as you are willing to trust that the bank will be able to deliver pounds to you in the future and that Nobu Inc. will pay yen for the goods, you are not exposed to risk of loss due to an unanticipated change in the exchange rate.

Of course, if the yen strengthens relative to the pound over the next 30 days, you will still have to sell your yen at the forward price specified by your agreement with the bank because the forward contract is not contingent on the future exchange rate. The rate is carved in stone, so to speak, by your contract with the bank. In this sense, the forward contract eliminates your risk of loss, but it does so by not allowing you to participate in possible gains in the future.

POINT-COUNTERPOINT

"Refining" a Hedging Strategy

With the *Financial Times* in hand, Ante Handel bursts into his brother's room, shouting, "I told you non-financial companies should stay out of the forex markets! Another Japanese company has been pounded in the forward market. Kashima Oil has just announced a loss of ¥61.9 billion. At least it is only half the loss that other Japanese oil refinery, Showa Shell, had to swallow last year. I wonder what the stock market will think of this baby. Showa's equity value dropped in half when the news of their foreign exchange loss broke!"

Ante's brother, Freedy, responded surprisingly fast. "Come off it. Kashima is an oil refinery. They were just trying to hedge their currency risk. Oil is priced in dollars, and they were buying dollars in the forward market, and the exchange rate moved against them. It's just bad luck. It could have gone the other way."

Fortunately, their cousin, Suttle Trooth, had overheard everything through the thin walls of their dorm rooms, and he was intrigued. "This is not so simple," he thought. "Should an oil company be hedging in the foreign exchange market? What really happened? Did they simply get a bad shock?" Rather than disturb the raucous discourse of the two brothers, Suttle put on his headphones, cranked up his iPod, and started searching the Internet. The facts soon became clear.

Suttle quickly learned that the Japanese oil refineries, Showa Shell and Kashima, are exposed to foreign exchange risk. All contracts in the oil business are settled in dollars, implying that these companies have dollar costs because they import crude oil, and they have yen revenues because they sell their refined oil in Japan. Showa Shell and Kashima face the risk that their costs will escalate if the dollar appreciates unexpectedly. To hedge that risk, both companies routinely buy dollars in the forward market for several months and sometimes years ahead. It happened to be the case that the forward yen price of the dollar was usually lower than the prevailing spot rate when most of these contracts were struck. So the forward contracts reduced the cost of the dollars relative to the prevailing spot rate and protected the companies against the risk of a dollar appreciation. However, the relevant comparison rate to judge the *ex post* benefit of the hedge is the future exchange rate at which crude oil would have been bought had the oil refineries not hedged. Often, the dollar did not appreciate relative to the yen. On the contrary, the yen often appreciated substantially more than was predicted by the forward rate—that is, the actual yen price of the dollar in the future turned out to be lower than the forward rate the companies had agreed to. After the fact, it was clear that the companies would have been better off not to hedge. They would have had lower yen costs by buying the dollars they needed in the spot market with the stronger yen.

Unfortunately, as Suttle read on, he learned that these companies did not just hedge. People in the companies' finance departments who were authorized to make forward contracts expected the dollar to appreciate. They thought they could profit from this outlook, and they agreed to forward contracts for much more than the actual currency exposure the companies had from their underlying oil businesses. In other words people at both companies were **speculating** in an effort to make a profit! When the yen continued to appreciate and the speculators' losses mounted, they did not disclose these losses to their superiors. They instead hid the losses from the companies' accounting statements and simply entered into additional forward contracts with their banks, hoping that the yen would eventually fall in value. Showa's total losses finally amounted to ¥125 billion and Kashima's to ¥152.5 billion.

Hedging Versus Speculating. Suttle Trooth decided to analyze this case step by step. The first thing to do is to separate the hedging part from the speculation part. Pure speculation in the currency markets does not seem to be a great idea for any corporate finance department. In addition, not disclosing mounting losses to your shareholders is illegal in most countries. So on that part, Ante is right, Suttle mused. Kashima should not have dabbled in foreign exchange markets the way it did. Not surprisingly, Japan's regulatory authorities cracked down on the practice of nondisclosure, and new disclosure rules regarding unrealized losses or profits from forward contracts in the foreign exchange markets were instituted in the wake of the oil companies' debacles.

To Hedge or Not to Hedge? Now, Suttle wondered whether hedging made sense in this case. Why was Freedy so convinced this was absolutely a normal thing to do? Certainly, if Kashima has a number of contracts to buy oil in the future with dollars, and we view this as a source of transaction exposure, it makes sense to hedge, right? After all, Kashima has a dollar liability, and by buying dollars forward, it obtains a dollar asset in exchange for a yen liability. This allows it to lock in the future transaction price in yen, getting rid of the effect of uncertain future exchange rates. Of course, *ex post* there may be a cost to hedging because the yen may keep appreciating, but at least they do not lose sleep over exchange rate movements, and they can better budget future operations.

But Suttle Trooth had a nagging feeling this might not be the full story. You see, Kashima's and Showa Shell's whole businesses are structured around buying oil with dollars, refining the oil, and selling it for yen in the local Japanese market. Not only do they do this now, but they plan to be doing the same thing for the conceivable future. In other words, their exchange rate exposures do not just arise from a single transaction. Exchange rate movements can really affect the bottom line of the companies. Consequently, if they hedge, they should at least have a long-term hedging plan in place. Also, it may be that forward contracts are not the right hedging vehicles. Suttle had heard that these contracts are only liquid when the maturity is shorter than 1 year and that the transaction costs for longer-term contracts are higher. In lieu of forward contracts, are there other contracts out there for longer-term hedging?

If the companies think long term, don't they also need to worry about inflation and oil price movements? Maybe an increase in the oil price or an increase in the yen–dollar rate is not so bad for the oil refining companies if the general price level in Japan goes up, too, and they can pass the increase in their costs through to their customers in the form of higher yen prices for the refined oil they sell.

Suttle Trooth started to have some doubts about the benefits of hedging, even for firms such as Kashima and Showa Shell. He concluded that he better keep reading the international financial management text he had just picked up from his bookshelf.

We will discuss the fundamental issue of why a firm should or should not hedge in Chapter 17. By that time, we will have developed all the tools necessary to answer all of Suttle's questions.

3.4 THE FORWARD FOREIGN EXCHANGE MARKET

Now that you understand why forward contracts arose to manage foreign exchange risk, let's examine the organization of the forward market in more detail.

Market Organization

The organization of trading for future purchase or delivery of foreign currency in the forward foreign exchange market is similar to the interbank spot market discussed in Chapter 2. Whereas some traders focus on spot contracts, other traders focus on forward contracts.

As mentioned previously, forward contracts greatly facilitate corporate risk management, and bank traders happily quote forward exchange rates for their corporate and institutional customers. In the interbank market, however, such simple forward contracts, called **outright forward contracts**, are a relatively unimportant component of the foreign exchange market. In fact, a Bank for International Settlements (2005) survey found that only slightly more than 11% of all transactions in the foreign exchange market are outright forward contracts. The survey also found that forward contracts are much more often part of a package deal, called a **swap**. In fact, more than 50% of forex market transactions are swaps, and swap traders trade nothing but swaps. A swap transaction involves the simultaneous purchase and sale of a certain amount of foreign currency for two different dates in the future. Given the importance of swaps, we discuss the swap market after we describe some of the details regarding the trading of forward contracts.

Forward Contract Maturities and Value Dates

As explained previously, forward exchange rates are contractual prices, quoted today, at which trade will be conducted in the future. The parties agree to the price today, but no monies change hands until the maturity of the contract, which is called the **forward value date**, or **forward settlement date**.

The most active maturities in the forward market tend to be the even maturities of 30, 60, 90, and 180 days. Because the forward foreign exchange market is an over-the-counter market, however, it is possible for the corporate and institutional customers of banks and traders at other banks to arrange odd-date forward contracts with maturities of, say, 46 or 67 days.

The exchange of currencies in a forward contract takes place on the forward value date. Determination of the value date for a forward contract begins by finding today's spot value date. As we saw in Chapter 2, this is 2 business days in the future for trades between U.S. dollars and European currencies or the Japanese yen. Exchange of monies in a 30-day forward contract occurs on the calendar day in the next month that corresponds to today's spot value

Exhibit 3.6 Rules for Determining Forward Value Dates

A. *Spot value date is not the last day of the month.* We consider the example in the text in which today's date is July 30, and we consider a 30-day forward contract.
   1. Find today's spot value date. **Example: July 30**
   2. For an *X*-month forward contract, go to the calendar day *X* months in the future that corresponds to today's spot value date. **Example: August 30**
   3. Check if this is a legitimate business day in both countries. If it is, this is the forward value date. If not, proceed to step 4.
   4. If step 3 produces a non-business day because of a weekend or a bank holiday in either country, settlement of the forward contract occurs on the next available business day, unless this day would move settlement into the *X* + 1st month in the future. If so, go to step 5. **Example: August 31 if August 30 is a weekend day**
   5. To avoid settlement in *X* + 1st month in the future, the forward value day becomes the *previous* legitimate business day before the calendar day *X* months in the future corresponding to today's spot value date. **Example: August 29 if both August 30 and 31 are weekend days**
B. *Spot value date is the last day of the month.* If the spot value day is the last business day of the current month, the forward value day is the last legitimate business day of the month that is *X* months in the future. This is known as the *end–end rule*. **Example: Suppose today is July 29 and the spot value date is July 31. The value date for a 30-day contract is the last business day in August!**

date, assuming that it is a legitimate business day. So, if today is July 28 and the spot value date is July 30, the forward value date for a 30-day contract is August 30. If the forward value date is a weekend or a bank holiday in either country, settlement of the forward contract occurs on the next business day. If the next business day moves the settlement of the forward contract into a new month, the forward value day becomes the *previous* business day. For example, in our previous example, it is possible that August 30 and 31 are weekend days. In that case, the value date would be August 29. This rule is followed except when the spot value day is the last business day of the current month, in which case the forward value day is the last business day of the next month (this is referred to as the *end–end rule*).

The rules for determining the forward value date are summarized in Exhibit 3.6. Let's consider an example.

Example 3.5 Finding the Forward Value Date

Suppose we purchase euros with dollars in the spot market on Friday, November 9, 2007. The dollars will come from our Citibank account in New York, and the euros will be paid into our Deutsche Bank account in Germany. The spot value day for such a trade is Tuesday, November 13, 2007, a legitimate business day in both countries. If we also initiated a 30-day forward contract to buy euros with dollars on Friday, November 9, 2007, when would the exchange of currencies take place? We can find the forward value date by following the logic just described. Because the spot value date is November 13, 2007, the forward value date is Thursday, December 13, 2007, a legitimate business day in both countries. Notice that the exchange of currencies on the 30-day forward contract is actually 34 days in the future in this example.

Of course, you don't have to actually own the currency that you contract to deliver when entering into a forward contract. It may be that you expect to receive the currency in the future in the normal course of your business, or you may plan to acquire the currency in the spot market sometime between when the forward contract is made and when the exchange of monies takes place on the forward value date. Suppose you have contracted to deliver euros as part of a forward contract (as in the previous example), but you do not own any euros. When is the last day that you could purchase euros in the spot market? We know that you must have euros on Thursday, December 13, 2007. Thus, you could buy the euros in the spot market 2 business days before this day, or on Tuesday, December 11, 2007, which is 32 days in the future relative to the date the forward contract was initiated.

Forward Market Bid–Ask Spreads

We noted in Chapter 2 that bid–ask spreads are quite narrow in the spot market. In the forward market, however, they tend to widen as the maturity of the forward contract increases. Ninety-day forward contracts, for example, exhibit bid–ask spreads about 15% larger than spot contracts. Yet forward bid–ask spreads remain small and are typically less than 0.10% for the major currencies. For very long-dated contracts, especially extending beyond 1 year, bid–ask spreads are wider still.[3]

Liquidity in the Forward Market

The bid–ask spreads are larger in the forward market than in the spot market because the forward market is less liquid than the spot market. Remember that the liquidity of a market refers to how easy or costly it is for buyers and sellers to be matched. Liquid markets are markets in

---

[3]The high transaction costs in the long-term forward market contributed to the development of an entirely new market, the long-term currency swap market, which is discussed in Chapter 21.

which traders have the ability to buy and sell something without incurring large transaction costs and without significantly influencing the market price. The liquidity of the market depends on the number of people who are actively trading in the market and on the sizes of the positions they are willing to take. In very liquid markets, it is easy to find a buyer if you want to be a seller and vice versa. It is also easy to conduct large transactions without having to provide concessions to the party taking the opposite side of the transaction. Illiquid markets are sometimes referred to as *thin* markets.

The reasons forward markets are less liquid than spot markets are subtle and are best explained in the context of an example.

Example 3.6 The Source of Low Liquidity in the Forward Market

Suppose Canada Beer, a Canadian company, exports beer to the United States and receives regular payments in U.S. dollars. Suppose Canada Beer enters into a 30-day forward contract with Bank of America to sell USD1,000,000 in exchange for Canadian dollars. That is, Canada Beer is selling its dollar revenues forward for Canadian dollars. Assume that the forward rate is $0.90/CAD. We are interested in seeing what risk this transaction creates for Bank of America. Consider Panel A in Exhibit 3.7.

The forward contract implies that Bank of America is now short Canadian dollars in the forward market—that is, it owes Canadian dollars for future delivery. Conversely, in the forward contract, Canada Beer is long Canadian dollars and short U.S. dollars, but Canada Beer expects to receive U.S. dollar revenues from its beer sales, which hedges this position.

What are the risks involved for Bank of America? The most obvious risk is currency risk. In 30 days, Bank of America must deliver CAD1,111,111 = $1,000,000/($0.90/CAD) to Canada Beer in exchange for $1,000,000. In the mean time, the Canadian dollar may increase in value relative to the U.S. dollar, yet Bank of America will receive only the $1,000,000 specified in the forward contract. For example, suppose the spot exchange rate in 30 days moves up to $1.00/CAD. Then the cost of CAD1,111,111 would be $1,111,111, not the $1,000,000 Bank of America is receiving!

It is tempting to think that this position carries more transactions exchange risk than a spot position with delivery 2 days from now because adverse exchange rate movements are more likely over the longer time span. Although it is true that the size of possible adverse exchange rate movements increases over the longer time span, the forward position does not pose a larger currency risk than the spot position as long as the forward market is liquid enough to allow a fast reversal of the forward position. That is, if Bank of America thinks that it may take a loss on the forward contract because of an adverse movement in the Canadian dollar exchange rate, the bank will want to close its position by buying Canadian dollars forward for the remaining life of the contract. Let's reconsider Exhibit 3.7. In Case 1 (Panel B), Bank of America waits 1 day and sees the spot rate increase. It suddenly feels that the risk of a short position in Canadian dollars is not worth taking and will go long Canadian dollars in the interbank market with a 29-day contract. We assume that the forward rate for this contract is $0.92/CAD, making the dollar equivalent of CAD1,111,111 equal to CAD1,111,111 × $0.92/CAD = $1,022,222. In 29 days, Bank of America's counterparty bank will deliver the CAD1,111,111 to Bank of America, and Bank of America in turn will deliver them to Canada Beer. The forward price with the bank's counterparty is set only 1 day after the Canada Beer contract was signed. So the adverse currency movement

Exhibit 3.7 Risks in Forward Contracts

Panel A: Original Positions

BANK OF AMERICA

Assets	Liabilities
$1,000,000 due from Canada Beer in 30 days	CAD1,111,111 payable to Canada Beer in 30 days

CANADA BEER

Assets	Liabilities
$1,000,000 Export revenues in 30 days CAD1,111,111 due from Bank of America in 30 days	$1,000,000 payable to Bank of America

Panel B: Bank of America Risk Management—Case 1

BANK OF AMERICA

Assets	Liabilities
$1,000,000 due from Canada Beer in 29 days	CAD1,111,111 payable to Canada Beer in 29 days
CAD1,111,111 due from interbank counterparty in 29 days	$1,022,222 payable to interbank counterparty in 29 days

Panel C: Bank of America Risk Management—Case 2

BANK OF AMERICA

Assets	Liabilities
$1,000,000 due from Canada Beer in 30 days	CAD1,111,111 payable to Canada Beer in 30 days
CAD1,111,111 payable to interbank counterparty in 30 days	$1,000,000 payable to interbank counterparty in 30 days

---

Notes: Since the forward rate is $0.90/CAD, the amount of Canadian dollars involved in the forward contract is $\dfrac{\$1,000,000}{\$0.90/CAD} = CAD\ 1,111,111$. We assume that the next day's forward rate for a 29-day contract is $0.92/CAD.

pertains only to 1 day. Nevertheless, because the Canadian dollar strengthened in that 1 day, Bank of America has already lost $1,022,222 − $1,000,000 = $22,222 on the deal. In fact, more often than not, banks will immediately hedge their positions with corporate customers, as illustrated in Panel C of Exhibit 3.7. As soon as the trader records the trade with Canada Beer, he may start looking for a counterparty in the interbank market to conclude a 30-day forward contract to buy Canadian dollars.

As long as forward contracts are traded actively enough for this transaction to occur at fair prices, the bank does not have to worry much about the currency risk in the forward contract. But there is another risk that Bank of America faces: Bank of America expects that Canada Beer will deliver U.S. dollars to it in exchange for Canadian dollars. But Canada Beer may not honor the forward contract if it goes bankrupt between now and 30 days from now. This is an example of default risk. Recall from Chapter 2 that counterparty default occurs when the party on the other side of a contract fails to deliver what it promised. If Canada Beer does not deliver the U.S. dollars, Bank of America does not need to deliver the Canadian dollars to Canada Beer, but Bank of America was counting on having U.S. dollars in its portfolio, not additional Canadian dollars. In fact, if it indeed hedged the original transaction as in Exhibit 3.7, it will receive Canadian dollars from its bank counterparty and must wire U.S. dollars to that bank. Hence, if Bank of America does not want to build up an inventory of Canadian dollars, it will have to sell Canadian dollars for U.S. dollars in the spot market if Canada Beer defaults. This spot transaction will occur about 28 days from now, so that it settles 2 business days later, at the same date the forward contract with the bank counterparty does. In other words, currency risk reappears because the future Canadian versus U.S. dollar exchange rate may be disadvantageous for Bank of America.

There are two main reasons why forward markets are less liquid than spot markets. First, banks are exposed to counterparty default risk for a much longer time interval in a forward contract than in a spot contract. In fact, banks are so worried about counterparty default risk in forward contracts that they impose limits on the total magnitude of the contracts (the "positions") traders can enter into with their counterparty banks in the interbank market. The limits vary with the creditworthiness and reputation of the other trading bank. In retail transactions, the dealer bank also often requires the non-bank counterparty either to maintain a minimum deposit balance with the dealer bank, to accept a reduction in its normal credit line, or to provide some other form of collateral. Second, because increased counterparty default risk reduces liquidity, banks now find it more difficult to manage open positions in forward contracts. Because it may take longer to find a counterparty with whom to trade at reasonable prices, forward contracts are more susceptible to foreign exchange risk. This reduces liquidity even more.

Given these concerns, the lack of liquidity in the interbank forward market and the resulting increase in bid–ask spreads are not so surprising. In addition, some contracts are less heavily traded than others and are therefore less liquid. As a result, the bid–ask spread for these contracts is greater. Odd-maturity forward contracts—that is, contracts that don't have standard value dates 30, 60, or 90 days in the future—are an example.

Net Settlement

Most outright forward contracts are settled by payment and delivery of the amounts in the contract. It is possible, however, to settle a contract by paying or receiving a net settlement amount that depends on the value of the contract. For example, suppose you think you will owe a Mexican company MXN20,000,000 in 30 days, and you would like to pay with dollars. You could enter into a forward contract to purchase MXN20,000,000 with dollars at a forward rate of, say, MXN10/USD. On the settlement day of the forward contract, you could expect to receive MXN20,000,000 from the bank and expect to pay $2 million for it:

$$MXN20,000,000/(MXN10/USD) = USD2,000,000$$

Suppose that 1 business day before the forward value date, the spot exchange rate is MXN12/USD. Suppose you also learn that you no longer need to purchase MXN20,000,000 because the underlying transaction has been cancelled. Must you still follow through with the forward contract, paying the USD2 million and receiving the MXN20,000,000 that you will now have to sell for dollars? It turns out that the bank will let you make a net payment. Notice that the MXN20,000,000 is now worth only

$$\frac{MXN20,000,000}{MXN12/USD} = USD1,666,667$$

Hence, if you pay the bank

$$USD2,000,000 - USD1,666,667 = USD333,333$$

this is equivalent to carrying out the original transaction and then entering into a new spot transaction in which you immediately sell the MXN20,000,000 back to the original seller of pesos at the current spot rate. Net settlement is often used in the forex futures market, which we discuss in Chapter 20.

The Foreign Exchange Swap Market

Most of the trading of forward contracts happens in the swap market. We now discuss in more detail what swap contracts are, how swap rates are quoted, and why swaps are so popular.

There are four basic types of swaps:

1. The purchase of foreign currency spot against the sale of foreign currency forward.
2. The sale of foreign currency spot against the purchase of foreign currency forward.
3. The purchase of foreign currency short-term forward against the sale of foreign currency long-term forward.
4. The sale of foreign currency short-term forward against the purchase of foreign currency long-term forward.

The most common example of a swap is the combination of a spot and a forward contract (types 1 and 2).

The main reason swaps are so popular is that simultaneous spot and forward transactions in opposite directions occur quite naturally. In Chapter 6, we discuss interest rate arbitrage, and we show that arbitrage transactions in the money markets across two countries involve spot and forward transactions in opposite directions. Similarly, in Part IV we discuss investments in international bond and equity markets. Many portfolio managers want to invest in the bond and equity markets of foreign countries without being exposed to changes in the values of those countries' currencies. To buy a foreign equity, these people must first buy the foreign currency in the spot market. To hedge the currency risk, they sell that currency forward. Hence, it is again natural to combine the spot and forward transaction in one trade.

Banks also actively use swaps to manage the maturity structure of their currency exposure. If they think they have too much exposure at one particular maturity, they can conveniently switch their position to another maturity, using a single swap transaction without changing their overall exposure to that currency. For example, when a bank has a short Swiss franc position of CHF1,000,000 (that is, when it sold CHF1,000,000 forward for dollars) with a maturity of 180 days and would like to shorten the maturity of these contracts to 90 days, it can simply enter into a swap to buy CHF1,000,000 at a 180-day value date and sell CHF1,000,000 at a 90-day value date. Because of the existence of the swap market, these transactions can be carried out with one phone call to a swap trader.

How Swap Prices Are Quoted

Before we examine the details of the cash flows associated with a swap, let's look at how prices are quoted. We will focus on swaps involving a spot transaction and a forward transaction. The following is an example of a swap quote:

Spot	30-day
¥/$ 104.30–40	80/85

A quote mentions the spot rates (first column) and the swap points (second column). The spot rates quoted by a bank in this example are ¥104.30/$ bid and ¥104.40/$ ask. Remember that the bank's bid price is the rate at which the bank buys dollars from someone in exchange for yen. In contrast, the bank's ask or offer price is the rate at which the bank sells dollars to someone and receives yen from them. The **swap points** are a set of basis points that must be either added to or subtracted from the current spot bid and ask prices to yield the actual 30-day bid and ask forward prices.

A Rule for Using Swap Points

A confusing aspect of moving from swap quotes to outright forward quotes is knowing whether to add the swap points to or to subtract the points from the bid and ask prices. Here's the rule: If the first number in the swap quote is smaller than the second, you add the points to the spot bid and ask prices to get the outright forward quotes; if the first number in the swap points is larger than the second, you subtract the points.

Let's examine the logic behind this rule, using the sample prices. With the swap points quoted as 80/85, the points should be added, so the outright forward quotes for 30 days would be

$$\text{¥104.30/\$ spot bid} + \text{¥0.80/\$} = \text{¥105.10/\$ forward bid for dollars}$$

and

$$\text{¥104.40/\$ spot ask} + \text{¥0.85/\$} = \text{¥105.25/\$ forward ask for dollars}$$

Notice that adding the swap points in this case makes the bid–ask spread in the forward market larger than the bid–ask spread in the spot market, which it should be.

When the first swap point quote is larger than the second, the points must be subtracted. Traders could quote negative numbers to indicate subtraction, but they follow a different convention. Rather than quote negative numbers when they want to indicate that the forward exchange rates are less than the spot prices, traders are assumed to understand that a swap quote of, say, 70/65 indicates that the swap points must be subtracted from the spot bid and ask rates. In this second example, the outright forward quotes for 30 days would be

$$\text{¥104.30/\$ spot bid} - \text{¥0.70/\$} = \text{¥103.60/\$ forward bid for dollars}$$

and

$$\text{¥104.40/\$ spot ask} - \text{¥0.65/\$} = \text{¥103.75/\$ forward ask for dollars}$$

Notice that in both of these examples, the bid–ask spread in the forward market is 15 points, which is larger than the 10-point spread in the spot market. If we had, in error, added the points in the second example, the forward market bid–ask spread would have fallen to 5 points, which is less than the 10-point spot bid–ask spread. This would tell us that we made an error because we know that the forward market is less liquid than the spot market. Hence, if you are having trouble remembering the rule and are trying to determine whether to add the swap points or to subtract them, you can always check to make sure that the forward bid–ask spread is larger than the spot bid–ask spread.

Cash Flows in a Swap

Let's consider an example of a swap to see what the cash flows look like.

Example 3.7 Swapping into Dollars and Out of Yen

Suppose Nomura, a Japanese investment bank, wants to have a dollar asset exposure of $10,000,000 for a duration of 30 days, while being short an equivalent amount of yen. To do so, Nomura will buy dollars in the spot market in exchange for yen, but Nomura will contract to sell dollars for yen 30 days from now using a forward transaction. Both transactions can be combined in a swap. Nomura swaps into $10,000,000 and out of an equivalent amount of yen for 30 days. Suppose Goldman Sachs is Nomura's counterparty. Let's examine the cash flows, assuming that the prices are the same as the ones we just discussed. That is, the spot rates are ¥104.30/$ bid and ¥104.40/$ ask, and the swap points are 80/85. The swap diagram in Exhibit 3.8 summarizes the cash flows.

Exhibit 3.8 Cash Flows in a Spot-Forward Swap

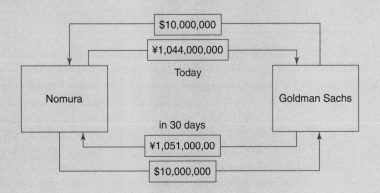

Because Nomura is buying $10,000,000 from Goldman Sachs in today's spot market, Nomura's cost will be the Goldman Sachs spot ask rate of ¥104.40/$. Hence, Nomura must pay ¥1,044,000,000 to Goldman Sachs for $10,000,000 because

$$\$10,000,000 \times (¥104.40/\$) = ¥1,044,000,000$$

When Nomura returns the $10,000,000 to Goldman Sachs in 30 days, how many yen will Goldman Sachs return to Nomura? Notice that in 30 days, Goldman Sachs will be buying dollars from Nomura, and Goldman Sachs will do so at its forward bid price of ¥105.10/$ = ¥104.30/$ + ¥0.80/$. Hence, Nomura will receive

$$\$10,000,000 \times (¥105.10/\$) = ¥1,051,000,000$$

In this example, Nomura gains access to $10,000,000 for 30 days and gives up ¥1,044,000,000 for 30 days, whereas Goldman Sachs gives up $10,000,000 for 30 days in exchange for the use of ¥1,044,000,000. When Nomura returns the $10,000,000 to Goldman Sachs, Goldman Sachs gives Nomura more yen than Nomura originally gave Goldman Sachs. The difference is precisely

$$¥1,051,000,000 - ¥1,044,000,000 = ¥7,000,000$$

Why is Goldman Sachs willing to pay Nomura ¥7,000,000 more than the amount Nomura paid Goldman Sachs in the spot market for the use of the $10,000,000? The answer is related to the interest rates on the two currencies.

Fundamentally, in a swap, each party is giving up the use of one currency and gaining the use of a different currency for the period of time of the swap. The two parties could charge each other the going market rates of interest on the respective currencies for this privilege. Instead of doing this, however, swaps are priced so that the party that is borrowing the high-interest-rate currency pays the party that is borrowing the low-interest-rate currency the difference in basis points. We will see in Chapter 6 precisely how the swap rates are related to the interest differential between the two currencies. Here we merely note that the yen must be the high-interest-rate currency relative to the dollar in this example because Goldman Sachs had the use of yen while Nomura had the use of dollars, and Goldman Sachs paid Nomura more yen in the future than the amount of yen Nomura paid Goldman Sachs for use of the dollars.

3.5 FORWARD PREMIUMS AND DISCOUNTS

Now that you understand how forward contracts are traded, it is time to introduce some important terminology regarding the relationship between forward and spot exchange rates.

If the forward price of the euro in terms of dollars (that is, USD/EUR) is higher than the spot price of USD/EUR, the euro is said to be at a **forward premium** in terms of the dollar. Conversely, if the forward price of the euro in terms of dollars (USD/EUR) is less than the spot price of USD/EUR, the euro is said to be at a **forward discount** in terms of the dollar. Remember, as with the terms *appreciation* and *depreciation*, the terms *forward premium* and *forward discount* refer to the currency that is in the denominator of the exchange rate.

Because the forward premium and forward discount are related to the interest rates on the two currencies, these premiums and discounts are often expressed as annualized *percentage*s. That is, the difference between the forward rate and the spot rate is divided by the spot rate and then multiplied by the reciprocal of the fraction of the year over which the forward contract is made. The result is then multiplied by 100 to convert it to a percentage:

$$\% \text{ per annum forward premium or discount of an } N \text{ day forward rate}$$

$$= \left(\frac{\text{forward} - \text{spot}}{\text{spot}} \right) \times \left(\frac{360}{N \text{ days}} \right) \times 100 \qquad (3.3)$$

Here, N is the number of days in the forward contract. A 360-day year is used for most currencies, corresponding to the conventions for quoting interest rates. Exceptions to this convention include the British pound, the Irish punt, and the Kuwaiti dinar, which are quoted on a 365-day year. Multiplying by 100 converts to percentage per annum and makes forward premiums and discounts comparable to interest rates quoted on a per annum basis.

We explore the formal linkage between the forward premium or discount and the interest differential between the two currencies in Chapter 6. Intuitively, however, you should realize that there must be a strong link among the spot rate (the relative price of two monies for immediate trade), the forward rate (the relative price of two monies for trade at a future date), and the two interest rates, which are the time values of the two monies between today and the future date.

Exhibit 3.9 Historical Means of Forward Premiums or Discounts

	$/£	$/€	¥/$
30-day forward (mean)	−1.432%	0.713%	−3.782%
30-day forward (2005 mean)	−1.302%	1.260%	−3.478%
90-day forward (mean)	−1.385%	0.728%	−3.750%
90-day forward (2005 mean)	−1.110%	1.375%	−3.562%

Notes: We report the sample means of the time series of forward premiums for three currencies during the sample period 1975–2005 and for 2005. We use daily data. A negative sign indicates that the currency in the denominator is at a discount. The forward premiums and discounts are annualized.

Sizes of Forward Premiums or Discounts

Exhibit 3.9 presents some information on historical forward premiums and discounts for several of the major currencies versus the dollar. We use the Deutsche mark to fill in data for the euro prior to 1999.

Both for 30-day and 90-day yen–dollar contracts, the average forward premium is negative. In other words, on average, the dollar traded at a discount in the forward market versus the yen. The yen-denominated forward prices of the dollar were about 3.8% lower than the spot prices. For the euro and the pound, the exchange rates are expressed in $/€ and $/£. For the dollar–euro rates, the 30-day forward premium of 0.713% indicates that the euro was at a small premium versus the dollar, and the negative values for the dollar–pound rates indicate that the pound traded at a forward discount relative to the dollar. The discount was 1.432% for 30-day forward contracts and 1.385% for 90-day contracts. These numbers only represent averages (the means) because the forward discount changes over time. For example, Exhibit 3.9 shows that in 2005, the dollar forward discount on the pound and the yen discount on the dollar were close to the historical average, while the dollar premium on the euro was over 0.60% more than the historical average.

Forward Premiums and Swap Points

Because forward contracts are typically traded as part of a swap, the swap points tell us whether the denominator currency is at a premium or a discount. Consider the example given using the JPY/USD exchange rate. If the dollar is at a forward premium, it is more expensive to purchase dollars in the future, so the forward rate should be larger than the spot rate. This happens if the swap points are added to the spot rates to yield larger forward rates. Hence, when the first number in the swap points is less than the second number, as in our earlier example of 80/85, the swap points should be added, and the currency in the denominator is at a premium. If there is a discount on the dollar, the first number in the swap price will be greater than the second number, as in the second example of 70/65, and the swap points should be subtracted.

In the swap in Example 3.7, the dollar is at a premium relative to the yen because the forward rate is larger than the spot rate (the swap points were added to the spot rate). In this example, Nomura bought USD10,000,000 at the spot ask and sold them at the forward bid. Because of the forward premium on the dollar, the example involves an additional positive yen cash flow at maturity to Nomura because the company bought dollars in the spot market, and the dollar is the low-interest-rate currency. That is, Nomura gets more yen back than it paid the bank to begin with. Thus, Nomura is said to be "earning the points," or "dealing in its favor." Conversely, if the dollar were at a discount, a swap of the first type in which dollars were purchased at the spot ask and sold at the forward bid would require the return of the yen principal plus a negative yen cash flow at maturity. In this case, one is consequently said to be "paying the points," or "dealing against oneself." Let's look at the cash flows for this swap.

Example 3.8 Swapping Out of Dollars and into Yen

Example 3.7 generated a positive yen cash flow by swapping into dollars and out of yen when the dollar was at a premium. If the dollar is at a discount, swapping out of dollars today and into yen generates a positive yen cash flow. A good rule to remember is that swapping into the currency that is at a premium generates a positive cash flow. Suppose that IBM wants to swap out of $10,000,000 and into yen for 30 days. Nomura quotes the spot rates ¥104.30/$ bid and ¥104.40/$ ask and swap points of 70/65. In this example, IBM is selling $10,000,000 to Nomura in the spot market. Consequently, the amount of yen IBM receives is now determined by Nomura's spot bid rate of ¥104.30/$. In the first leg of the swap, IBM would receive

$$\$10,000,000 \times (¥104.30/\$) = ¥1,043,000,000$$

When IBM gets its $10,000,000 back in 30 days, how many yen will it have to pay the bank? Because in the future Nomura is selling dollars to IBM for yen, Nomura will charge its forward ask price of ¥103.75/$ (¥104.40/$ − ¥0.65/$). Hence, IBM will pay Nomura

$$\$10,000,000 \times (¥103.75/\$) = ¥1,037,500,000$$

In this example, IBM gives up $10,000,000 for 30 days, and it receives ¥1,043,000,000 for 30 days. Nomura receives $10,000,000 for 30 days and in exchange gives up the use of ¥1,043,000,000. At the swap contract's maturity, IBM has to give Nomura only ¥1,037,500,000 rather than the original ¥1,043,000,000, which means that IBM gets to keep

$$¥1,043,000,000 − ¥1,037,500,000 = ¥5,500,000$$

Once again, we would like to know why Nomura is willing to accept ¥5,500,000 less in return when it buys $10,000,000 from IBM for 30 days. As we hinted at before, the answer must be related to the interest rates on the two currencies. In this case, the dollar interest rate must be higher than the yen interest rate.

3.6 CHANGES IN EXCHANGE RATE VOLATILITY (ADVANCED)

Now that you understand conditional distributions of future exchange rates, we want to discuss what economists know about how these distributions change over time. Exhibit 3.1 uses monthly percentage changes in exchange rates to describe the probability distribution of the $/£ rate. The standard deviation of this distribution can be used to characterize the volatility of the conditional distribution. Understanding volatility is critical in judging transaction exchange risk. Because asset markets in general, and the foreign exchange market in particular, appear to go through periods of tranquility and periods of turbulence, a single historical calculation of volatility is probably a bad estimate of the prospective volatility, looking forward from any particular point in time. Exhibit 3.1 uses information from several different decades. Perhaps the exchange rate volatility is higher now than it was in the 1990s for some currencies but not for others. Or perhaps the current year is more volatile than the previous year. In this case, using a probability distribution based on a historical standard deviation will underestimate the true uncertainty about future exchange rates.

Volatility Clustering

Many financial researchers have spent considerable computer time examining exchange rate data, and they have come to the conclusion that exchange rate volatility is not constant over time. In fact, as is true for the returns on many assets, percentage changes in exchange rates show a pattern known as **volatility clustering**. When volatility is high, it tends to remain high for a while; periods of low volatility are likewise persistent. To illustrate this pattern, we use daily data on the dollar/pound exchange rate to compute monthly standard deviations. That is, for each month in our sample, we use the available daily observations to compute the sample standard deviation for each month. Exhibit 3.10 plots these monthly standard deviations.

The graph clearly reveals quiet periods (for example, 1977–1979 or 1999) and turbulent periods (for example, 1985 and 1991–1993) during which volatility exceeded 20% at times.

A number of models have been developed to fit the observed pattern of volatility clustering in these data. The most successful model to date is the GARCH model developed by Tim Bollerslev (1986).[4] Remember that the squared value of the volatility is the variance. Let v denote the variance. The relevant variance for assessing our uncertainty about future exchange rate changes is the conditional variance, $v(t) = var_t[s(t+1)]$ (see the appendix to this chapter). Let us denote the deviation of the actual percentage change in the exchange

Exhibit 3.10 Monthly Standard Deviations of Daily Rates of Appreciation

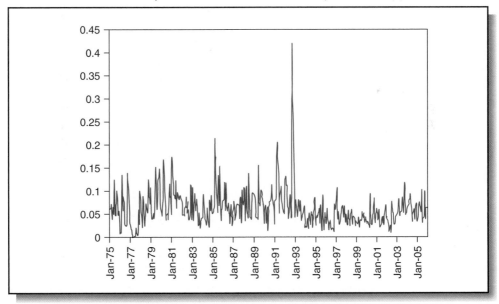

Notes: We use daily percentage changes in the $/£ exchange rate to compute the standard deviation, or volatility, for each month. The graph plots these volatilities, annualized to be comparable to the way volatilities are discussed in financial markets. The data span January 1, 1975, through the end of 2005.

---

[4]GARCH is an acronym that stands for Generalized Auto-Regressive Conditional Heteroskedasticity. A conditionally heteroskedastic time series does not have a constant variance. The future of an auto-regressive process depends on its own past. You will be happy to know that other models of conditional heteroskedasticity, such as SPARCH, QGARCH, and FIGARCH models, are gaining in popularity, but we will not discuss them here. A precursor to the GARCH model was Robert Engle's ARCH model, for which Engle won the Nobel Prize in Economics in 2003.

rate from its conditional expectation by $e(t) = s(t) - E_{t-1}[s(t)]$. We can interpret $e(t)$ as an economic shock that represents "news" because that part of the exchange rate change was not expected to occur. For example, suppose you expected the exchange rate change over the past month to be 5%, but it was actually 7%. The additional 2% change is "news" to you; it is an unexpected change in the exchange rate. The GARCH model for the conditional variance is

$$v(t) = a + b\,v(t-1) + c\,e(t)^2$$

The constants a, b, and c are parameters that can be estimated from the data; b reflects the sensitivity of the current conditional variance to the past conditional variance; c reflects its sensitivity to current news; and a is the minimum variance we would predict even if the past volatility and news terms are zero. Depending on the frequency of the data, b is between 0.85 and 0.95 (see Baillie and Bollerslev, 1989), and c is much lower (for example, between 0.05 and 0.15).

This model accommodates persistence in volatility. If the conditional variance is high today, it is likely to be high tomorrow. This persistence in $v(t)$ can generate the patterns of volatility clustering we see in the data. If we are in a quiet period today, but the exchange rate suddenly and unexpectedly moves in either direction, volatility immediately shifts to a higher level for a while through the e^2-term. This shift will tend to persist because of the feedback the model allows through the $b\,v(t-1)$ term. That is, because $v(t)$ is now higher, $v(t+1)$ will be higher as well because b is positive. Let's illustrate this positive feedback effect with an example.

Example 3.9 Positive Feedback in Volatility

Suppose last month's dollar–euro exchange rate stood at $1.00/€ , and the market expected no change for the next month. However, after a number of opaque statements by the policymakers in Europe, the euro has weakened to $0.90/€ . Note that this depreciation of the euro, $\left(s(t) = \dfrac{0.90 - 1.0}{1.0} = -0.10\right)$, is unexpected, and hence it constitutes news (an $e(t)$-shock). What does the GARCH model predict next month's currency volatility to be, assuming that $a = 0.00072$, $b = 0.90$, and $c = 0.05$ and the previous market volatility of the $/€ rate of depreciation was 8.0%? The GARCH model predicts $v(t)$, according to

$$v(t) = a + b\,v(t-1) + c\,e(t)^2$$
$$= 0.00072 + 0.90\,(0.08)^2 + 0.05(-0.10)^2 = 0.00698$$

Hence, volatility today, which is the square root of v_t, is 8.35% ($\sqrt{0.00698}$). The large unexpected depreciation drives up volatility by 0.35%. Whatever the "shock" next month, today's volatility increase will tend to persist. If the GARCH model is correct, next month's volatility will be $v(t+1) = 0.00072 + 0.90(0.0835)^2 + 0.05(e(t+1))^2$. Today, we do not know what next month's shock will be, but we assign a high weight ($b = 0.90$) to this period's higher volatility in computing next period's volatility. This is why we say the coefficient b implies positive feedback, or persistence, for the volatility process.

Other Volatility Models

Not everyone is convinced that GARCH is the right volatility model (see Andersen and Bollerslev, 1998a), but alternative models have not garnered as much attention. One alternative approach is to use "implied volatility," where the future conditional variance is backed out from option prices and an option-pricing model called the Black-Scholes model. (We discuss this model in Chapter 20 when we discuss options.) Others have investigated models accommodating discrete shifts in volatility, which market participants try to predict using so-called jump models (Jorion, 1988) or regime-switching models (Bekaert and Hodrick, 1993; Engel and Hamilton, 1993).

Although some of these statistical models capture the volatility patterns well, they do not tell us why volatility moves the way it does. This is a topic of very active research. Possibilities include the clustering of macroeconomic news events (see Andersen and Bollerslev, 1998b), the reaction of risk-averse agents to small changes in uncertainty regarding macroeconomic fundamentals (Bekaert, 1996; Hodrick, 1989), and the trading process itself (Laux and Ng, 1993).

3.7 SUMMARY

The purpose of this chapter is to introduce forward foreign exchange markets and to examine their use in hedging transaction exchange risk. The following are the main points in the chapter:

1. A transaction exchange risk arises when an individual or a firm enters into a transaction in which it is required to receive or pay a specific amount of foreign currency at some date in the future. If the firm does nothing to hedge the risk, there is a possibility that the firm will incur a loss if the exchange rate moves in an unfavorable direction.

2. One can fully hedge a transaction exchange risk by either buying or selling foreign currency in the forward foreign exchange market. If you are importing (exporting) goods and will contractually owe (receive) foreign currency, you have a foreign currency–denominated liability (asset) and must acquire an equivalent foreign currency–denominated asset (liability) to be hedged. Buying (selling) foreign currency from (to) the bank in the forward market provides the hedge.

3. Outright forward exchange rates are contractual prices at which trade will be conducted in the future. The parties agree to the price today, but no currencies change hands until the maturity, or value, date in the future.

4. Bid–ask spreads in the forward market are larger than in the spot market because the forward market is less liquid.

5. A swap involves the simultaneous purchase and sale of a certain amount of foreign currency for two different value dates. Traders quote swap rates as the number of basis points that must be either added to the spot bid and ask rates or subtracted from the spot rates. When the points must be added, they are quoted with the smaller number first, and when they must be subtracted, they are quoted with the smaller number second. This ensures that the bid–ask spread in the forward market is always larger than the spread in the spot market.

6. If the forward price of a currency is higher than the spot price, that currency is said to be trading at a forward premium. If the forward price of a currency is lower than the spot price, that currency is said to be trading at a forward discount.

QUESTIONS

1. What is a forward exchange rate? When does delivery occur on a 90-day forward contract?

2. Using the data in Chapter 2, what was the dollar price of a forward contract to buy euros in 90 days on Thursday, February 16, 2006?

3. If the yen is selling at a premium relative to the euro in the forward market, is the forward price of EUR/JPY larger or smaller than the spot price of EUR/JPY?

4. What do we mean by the expected future spot rate?

5. How much of the probability distribution of future spot rates is between plus or minus 2 standard deviations?
6. If you are a U.S. firm and owe someone ¥10,000,000 in 180 days, what is your transaction exchange risk?
7. What is a spot–forward swap?
8. What is a forward–forward swap?

PROBLEMS

1. If the spot exchange rate of the yen relative to the dollar is ¥105.75, and the 90-day forward rate is ¥103.25/$, is the dollar at a forward premium or discount? Express the premium or discount as a percentage per annum for a 360-day year.
2. Suppose today is Tuesday, January 13, 2009. If you enter into a 30-day forward contract to purchase euros, when will you pay your dollars and receive your euros? (Hints: February 13, 2009, is a Friday, and the following Monday is a holiday.)
3. As a foreign exchange trader for JPMorgan Chase, you have just called a trader at UBS to get quotes for the British pound for the spot, 30-day, 60-day, and 90-day forward rates. Your UBS counterpart stated, "We trade sterling at $1.7745-50, 47/44, 88/81, 125/115." What cash flows would you make and receive if you do a forward foreign exchange swap in which you swap into £5,000,000 at the 30-day rate and out of £5,000,000 at the 90-day rate? What must be the relationship between dollar interest rates and pound sterling interest rates?
4. Consider the following spot and forward rates for the yen–euro exchange rates:

Spot	30 days	60 days	90 days	180 days	360 days
146.30	145.75	145.15	144.75	143.37	137.85

Is the euro at a forward premium or discount? What are the magnitudes of the forward premiums or discounts when quoted in percentage per annum for a 360-day year?

5. As a currency trader, you see the following quotes on your computer screen:

Exch. Rate	Spot	1-month	2-month	3-month	6-month
USD/EUR	1.0435/45	20/25	52/62	75/90	97/115
JPY/USD	98.75/85	12/10	20/16	25/19	45/35
USD/GBP	1.6623/33	30/35	62/75	95/110	120/130

a. What are the outright forward bid and ask quotes for the USD/EUR at the 3-month maturity?
b. Suppose you want to swap out of $10,000,000 and into yen for 2 months. What are the cash flows associated with the swap?
c. If one of your corporate customers calls you and wants to buy pounds with dollars in 6 months, what price would you quote?
6. Intel is scheduled to receive a payment of ¥100,000,000 in 90 days from Sony in connection with a shipment of computer chips that Sony is purchasing from Intel. Suppose that the current exchange rate is ¥103/$, that analysts are forecasting that the dollar will weaken by 1% over the next 90 days, and that the standard deviation of 90-day forecasts of the percentage rate of depreciation of the dollar relative to the yen is 4%.

a. Provide a qualitative description of Intel's transaction exchange risk.
b. If Intel chooses not to hedge its transaction exchange risk, what is Intel's expected dollar revenue?
c. If Intel does not hedge, what is the range of possible dollar revenues that incorporates 95.45% of the possibilities?

BIBLIOGRAPHY

Andersen, Torben G., and Tim Bollerslev, 1998a, "Answering the Skeptics: Yes, Standard Volatility Models Do Provide Accurate Forecasts," *International Economic Review* 39, pp. 885–905.

Andersen, Torben G., and Tim Bollerslev, 1998b, "Deutsche Mark–Dollar Volatility: Intraday Activity Patterns, Macroeconomic Announcements, and Longer Run Dependencies," *Journal of Finance* 53, pp. 219–265.

Baillie, Richard, and Tim Bollerslev, 1989, "The Message in Daily Exchange Rates: A Conditional Variance Tale," *Journal of Business and Economic Statistics* 7, pp. 297–305.

Bank for International Settlements, May 2005, "Central Bank Survey of Foreign Exchange and Derivatives Market Activity, 2004," Bank for International Settlements.

Bekaert, Geert, 1995, "The Time-Variation of Expected Returns and Volatility in Foreign Exchange Markets," *Journal of Business and Economic Statistics* pp. 397–408.

Bekaert, Geert, 1996, "The Time-Variation of Risk and Return in Foreign Exchange Markets: A General Equilibrium Perspective," *Review of Financial Studies* 9, pp. 427–470.

Bekaert, Geert, and Robert J. Hodrick, 1993, "On Biases in the Measurement of Foreign Exchange Premiums," *Journal of International Finance and Money* 12, pp. 115–138.

Bollerslev, Tim, 1986, "Generalized Autoregressive Conditional Heteroskedasticity," *Journal of Econometrics* 31, pp. 307–327.

Cornell, Bradford, and Marc R. Reinganum, 1981, "Forward and Futures Prices," *Journal of Finance* 36, pp. 1035–1045.

Cox, John C., Jonathan E. Ingersoll, and Stephen A. Ross, 1981, "The Relation Between Forward Prices and Futures Prices," *Journal of Financial Economics* 9, pp. 321–346.

Dawkins, William, October 5, 1994, "Tokyo to Lift Veil on Currency Risks: Unrealized Losses Will Have to be Revealed," *Financial Times*, p. 32.

Engel, Charles, and James Hamilton, 1993, "Long Swings in the Dollar: Are They in the Data and Do Markets Know It?" *American Economic Review* 80, pp. 689–713.

Hodrick, Robert J., 1989, "Risk, Uncertainty, and Exchange Rates," *Journal of Monetary Economics* 23, pp. 433–459.

Hardy, Quentin, April 11, 1994, "Foreign Exchange Trading Pounds Japan's Kashima," *Wall Street Journal*, p. A7.

Jorion, Philippe, 1988, "On Jump Processes in the Foreign Exchange and Stock Markets," *Review of Financial Studies* 1, pp. 427–445.

Laux, Paul A., and Lilian K. Ng, 1993, "The Sources of GARCH: Empirical Evidence from an Intraday Returns Model Incorporating Systematic and Unique Risks," *Journal of International Money and Finance* 12, pp. 543–560.

Poon, Ser-Huang, and Clive W.J. Granger, 2003, "Forecasting Volatility in Financial Markets: A Review," *Journal of Economics Literature* 41, pp. 478–539.

Appendix

A Statistics Refresher

Statistics is a very valuable tool in business, and you will encounter the concepts discussed here on many occasions throughout the book. Let's start with an exchange rate example. Exhibit 3A.1 provides historical data on the euro–dollar exchange rates from January 2004 to December 2005. We record the end-of-month exchange rate and therefore have a total of 24 observations. The last column records the percentage change in the exchange rate from one month to the next. We denote the exchange rate itself by $S(t)$, where t indicates the date, and we denote the percentage rate of change of the exchange rate, by

$$s(t) = 100 \left[S(t) - S(t-1) \right] / S(t-1)$$

One goal of statistics is to use past data to describe what the future will be like. Eventually, we would like to attach "likelihoods of occurrence" to different possible realizations of the future exchange rate. We will start by looking at simple properties of the past data. In statistics, we would say we have T (in this case 24) observations on a time series $\{s(t), t = 1, \ldots, T\}$ or $\{S(t), t = 1, \ldots, T\}$. The average, or **sample mean**, of a time series is the sum of all these observations divided by T. Focusing on $s(t)$, we denote this sample mean by $\hat{\mu}$, and in symbols it is given by

$\hat{\mu} = (1/T) \sum_{t=1}^{T} s(t)$. The sample mean for our example is 0.30%. To the extent that the future is like the past, the sample mean may tell us something about the central tendency of future rates of depreciation. But we know it will not tell us enough because we see months in which the dollar appreciated by 4.5% and months in which the dollar depreciated by more than 4%, and these observations are quite different from the mean of 0.30%. One way to summarize how spread out our past observations were and how spread out they may be in the future is to compute the standard deviation of our $s(t)$ time series. The standard deviation is a measure of the dispersion of possibilities around the sample mean. The sample standard deviation is the square root of the **sample variance**. In symbols, the sample variance is computed as

$$\hat{\sigma}^2 = \frac{1}{T-1} \sum_{t=1}^{T} [s(t) - \hat{\mu}]^2.$$

An extreme observation relative to the sample mean in either direction (such as 4.5% in this example) makes the sample variance bigger. The sample variance squares the deviations from the mean so that an extreme positive observation, such as 4.5%, does not get partially cancelled out by an extreme negative observation, such as −5%.

Exhibit 3A.1   Euro/$ Data

Date	Level	% Change
1/30/2004	0.805	1.534
2/27/2004	0.805	−0.016
3/31/2004	0.814	1.107
4/30/2004	0.834	2.514
5/31/2004	0.819	−1.834
6/30/2004	0.822	0.370
7/30/2004	0.831	1.055
8/31/2004	0.823	−0.934
9/30/2004	0.805	−2.150
10/29/2004	0.786	−2.362
11/30/2004	0.752	−4.288
12/31/2004	0.736	−2.222
1/31/2005	0.767	4.273
2/28/2005	0.753	−1.794
3/31/2005	0.769	2.132
4/29/2005	0.775	0.673
5/31/2005	0.810	4.552
6/30/2005	0.826	1.990
7/29/2005	0.823	−0.329
8/31/2005	0.813	−1.235
9/30/2005	0.829	2.007
10/31/2005	0.835	0.659
11/30/2005	0.848	1.594
12/30/2005	0.848	−0.051
Mean:	**0.805**	**0.302**
Std:	**0.031**	**2.152**

Note: Data from Datastream.

Common sense suggests that such extreme observations are less likely to occur than observations near the mean, and statistical analysis bears this out. To find out how much less likely these observations might be, we can construct a **histogram** of the data. A histogram groups our observations into intervals of equal magnitude and records the number of observations in each interval. We do this in Exhibit 3A.2.

The intervals are represented on the horizontal axis—we show the midpoint of each interval—and the number of observations in each interval on the vertical axis. In this example, the width of an interval is 1.7680%. Often we denote the number of observations as a fraction of the total, and it is then called the *frequency of occurrence*. For example, given our limited sample, there is a 4.17% frequency that euro–dollar changes belong in the lowest bin—that is, are lower than $-1.6361\% - 1.7680\%/2 = -2.5201\%$ (that is,

1 observation out of 24). A histogram expressed in frequencies is also called a **frequency distribution**.

It turns out that many natural and economic data show frequency distributions that can be approximated by smooth curves and simple mathematical expressions. Such a smooth curve is called a **probability distribution**, and the mathematical formula that describes it is often called a **density function**. Probability distributions summarize information about the likelihood of different events (for example, future exchange rates) occurring. It is easiest to think about probability distributions when there are a finite, distinct number of possible events. In this case, the probability distribution describes the events and their associated probabilities and the distribution is said to be *discrete*.

There are several important things to remember about probabilities. First, if there is more than one thing that can happen in the future, the probability of each future event must be a fraction between 0 and 1. Second, if we know all the possible future events, the sum of the probabilities of all the events must be 1 because one of the events will actually happen.

Now that you understand the concept of a probability distribution, we can also more formally define the mean, or **expected value**, and the **variance**, associated with a distribution. The expected value is easily defined in the case of discrete probability distributions. The expected value of the future events is the sum of the values in each state of the world, say x_k in state k, multiplied, or "weighted," by the probability of that particular state, say p_k. That is, the expected value of event x is

$$E(x) = (p_1 x_1 + p_2 x_2 + \ldots + p_N x_N)$$

Notice that if there are N possible events that are equally likely, the probability of any one event is $(1/N)$. In this case, the expected value is the average of the possible outcomes. The sample mean implicitly assigns an equal weight to each observation. When the probabilities of the events differ, the expected value is the *probability-weighted average* of the possible events.

The variance, $V(x)$, is the expected value of the squared deviations from the means:

$$\begin{aligned} V(x) &= E[(x - E[x])^2]. \\ &= p_1(x_1 - E[x])^2 + p_2(x_2 - E[x])^2 \\ &\quad + \ldots + p_N(x_N - E[x])^2 \end{aligned}$$

The sample variance we defined is an estimate of this variance, treating each observed exchange rate change as having equal probability of occurrence. The square root of the variance is called the *standard deviation*, or *volatility*, when it concerns financial data.

Exhibit 3A.2 Euro–Dollar Monthly Percentage Changes

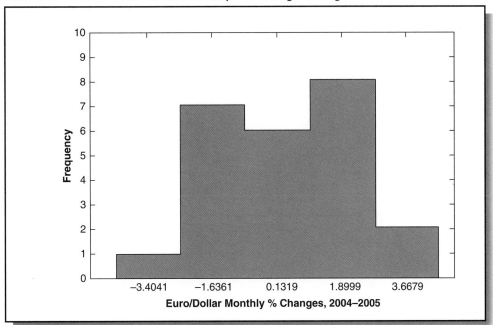

Euro/Dollar Monthly % Changes, 2004–2005

Example 3A.1   Calculating with a Discrete Distribution

Suppose there are only three possible exchange rate changes, which are equally likely to occur: -5, 0, and 8 (in percentages). The probability distribution refers to the events $[-5, 0, 8]$ and the associated probabilities $[1/3, 1/3, 1/3]$.

The mean is $(1/3)(-5) + (1/3)(0) + (1/3)(8) = 1$.

The variance is $(1/3)(-5-1)^2 + (1/3)(-1)^2 + (1/3)(8-1)^2 = 86/3$.

The standard deviation therefore equals $\sqrt{86/3} = 5.35\%$.

If the possible exchange rate percentage changes were $[-3, 0, 3]$ instead, you should demonstrate to yourself that the mean would be 0, and the standard deviation would be smaller (2.45%).

Although discrete distributions are useful in many circumstances, describing uncertainty of future rates of depreciation for flexible exchange rates should allow for all possible values over a very wide range. This is best done using a continuous probability distribution and a density function that expresses probabilities of occurrence for any range of depreciation between $-\infty$ and $+\infty$.

In Exhibit 3A.3, for example, we draw a smooth bell-shaped curve that seems to roughly approximate a histogram rather well. In fact, the approximation would become more accurate if we had many more data points on exchange rate changes and let the intervals in which we measure the frequencies become smaller and smaller. The probability distribution described by the curve in Exhibit 3A.3 is called the **normal distribution**, and it describes many phenomena well. (For example, the heights of people in the general population are normally distributed.)

The normal distribution has a number of important characteristics. First, it is symmetric around its mean—that is, the same amount of the probability distribution of possibilities is below as above the mean. If the mean is 0.30, statisticians would say that the probability of

Exhibit 3A.3 Euro–Dollar Monthly Percentage Change Normal Density, 2004–2005

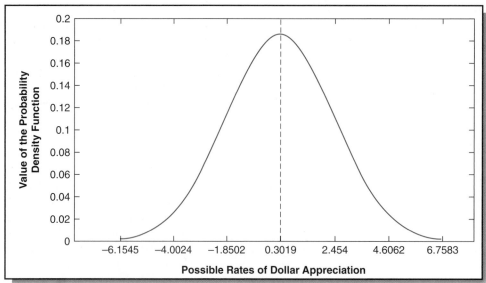

observing $s(t)$ larger than 0.30 is 50%. Because the normal distribution is symmetrical, the mean and median of the distribution of the future exchange rate coincide. The **median** is the exchange rate that has 50% of the possible exchange rates above it and 50% of the possible exchange rates below it. Not all distributions are symmetrical. For example, suppose that, as in Example 3A.1, there are only three possible exchange rate changes (-5.00%, 0%, and 8.00%), which are equally likely to occur. The mean exchange rate change is 1%, but the median exchange rate change is 0%, which is lower than the mean. The distribution is said to be *positively skewed* in this case.[5]

Second, the normal probability distribution is completely summarized by its mean and its standard deviation. When a statistician is given the mean and standard deviation of the normal distribution, she has all the information necessary to assess the probability of any range of possible exchange rate changes. These probabilities can be assessed using computers or tables that are reported in any statistics textbook. For example, suppose the possible euro–dollar exchange rate changes are well described by a normal distribution with a mean of 0.30% and a standard deviation of 2.15%. How likely is it that we will observe an exchange rate change larger than 8% or an exchange rate change smaller than -5%? We

can look up the answer in any statistics book. Most books describe the probabilities for standard normal distributions—this is, normal distributions with a mean of 0 and a standard deviation of 1. To use the tables in statistics books, we must "standardize" our numbers by figuring out how many standard deviations from the mean the number we are interested in is. For example, an exchange rate change of 8% is $\dfrac{8\% - 0.30\%}{2.15\%} = 3.58$ standard deviations from the mean. According to the table, there is only a 0.02% chance that an exchange rate change will occur that is larger than that. Likewise, an exchange rate change smaller than -5%, which is 2.46 standard deviations away from the mean, has a 0.69% probability of occurrence.

Throughout this book, we are interested in describing our uncertainty about future exchange rates. To do so, we look at the distribution of exchange rate changes, conditional on the information we have today (which includes the current exchange rate). Because the probability distribution of the future exchange rate depends on all the information available at time t, we say that it is a *conditional probability distribution*. Consequently, the expected value of this distribution is also referred to as the *conditional expectation* of the future exchange rate (conditional mean). Likewise, we can define a

---

[5]The mean is the first moment or the center of the distribution, and the variance is the second moment around the mean, and it measures the dispersion of the distribution. Skewness is the third moment around the mean, and it measures asymmetry. For the normal distribution, skewness is 0. Another moment of interest in financial data is the fourth moment around the mean, called kurtosis. Kurtosis measures how "fat" the tails of the distribution are, that is, it measures the likelihood of extreme outcomes.

conditional standard deviation, or **conditional volatility**, as the square root of the conditional variance. With $E_t[S(t+1)]$, the conditional mean of exchange rate changes, the conditional variance $v(t)$ is

$$v(t) = E_t\{s(t+1) - E_t[s(t+1)]\}^2$$

The conditional means and volatilities of future exchange rate changes and their distribution allow us to make inferences about future exchange rates. Because $s(t+1) = [S(t+1) - S(t)]/S(t)$, we can solve for the future exchange rate as a function of future exchange rate changes and the current exchange rate (which is part of our information set). That is,

$$S(t+1) = S(t)[1 + s(t+1)]$$

Hence the conditional mean of the future exchange rate will simply be

$$E_t[S(t+1)] = S(t)[1 + E_t[s(t+1)]]$$

Note that we do not take an expectation of the current exchange rate because it is a part of our information set today.

Likewise, the conditional volatility of the future exchange rate will be $S(t)\sqrt{v(t)}$.[6]

If the distribution of exchange rate changes never varied over time, there would be no need to distinguish between the conditional and the unconditional distributions we talked about earlier. However, throughout this book, you will see how both the mean and volatility can, and do, vary through time. Section 3.6 summarizes recent research on how the volatility of exchange rate changes seems to move through quiet and turbulent periods.

You may wonder why we did not look at the distribution of actual exchange rates instead of percentage changes in exchange rates. This is because it is more reasonable to assume that percentage changes in exchange rates are drawn from some well-defined probability distribution, such as the normal distribution, than to assume that the levels of exchange rates are from a common distribution. The logic that leads us to use percentage changes in exchange rates in describing future distributions of exchange rates is the same as the logic that dictates using rates of return on stocks rather than the levels of stock prices to describe future distributions of stock prices. Both the stock price and the exchange rate are asset prices, and the percentage changes in asset prices provide part of the rate of return to holding the asset. For most of our applications, we are interested in how much the exchange rate is likely to change from today's level.

---

[6]If we take a random variable, say x, with a certain distribution and multiply it by a constant, say b, the variance of bx is $V(bx) = b^2V(x)$. From the perspective of today's information set, $S(t)$ is a constant because it is known, and the conditional variance is $S(t)^2v(t)$.

Chapter 4

The Balance of Payments

*T*he first three chapters of this book provide insights into the nature of foreign exchange markets and foreign exchange risks. To understand these concepts more deeply, you need to understand the economic forces that cause exchange rates to fluctuate. Exchange rates respond to demand and supply to trade currencies. These demands and supplies arise from international trade flows and international capital flows.

Plenty of useful information about these international flows is provided by the balance of payments, which records the payments between residents of one country and the rest of the world over a given time period. As such, it helps shed a great deal of light on the supply and demand for various currencies, the possible evolution of their exchange rates, and the global financial marketplace in general.

Balance of payments statistics are discussed daily by politicians, the news media, and currency analysts at corporations, commercial banks, investment banks, and mutual funds. Currency traders eagerly await the release of new balance of payments statistics because they know exchange rates will move with the new information. We will see how the balances on various subaccounts are linked to domestic and international saving and investment decisions and ultimately how they may determine a country's financial and economic health. For example, multinational firms should recognize that persistent current account deficits in developing countries can signal that currency devaluations are likely to occur there, with potentially dire economic ramifications. In developed countries, persistent current account deficits can lead legislators to unleash protectionist policies, such as tariffs and embargoes on imported goods and services. Every company in the world doing business with China keenly follows the effect that the U.S. trade deficit with China is having on the two countries' trade policies.

4.1 THE BALANCE OF PAYMENTS: CONCEPTS AND TERMINOLOGY

A country's **balance of payments (BOP)** records the value of the transactions between its residents, businesses, and government with the rest of the world for a specific period of time, such as a month, a quarter, or a year. Hence, the balance of payments summarizes the international flows of goods and services and changes in the ownership of assets across countries.

Major Accounts of the Balance of Payments

There are two major BOP accounts: the current account and the capital account. In recent years, most countries have renamed the capital account as the "financial account" in order to comply with the desires of the International Monetary Fund (IMF). Because the terminology *capital account* has a long tradition and continues to be used in the financial press, we continue to use it here.

The **current account** records the following:

1. Goods and services transactions (**imports**, which are purchases of goods and services from foreign residents; and **exports**, which are sales of goods and services to foreign residents).
2. Transactions associated with the income flows from the ownership of foreign assets (dividends and interest paid to domestic residents who own foreign assets as well as dividends and interest paid to foreign residents who own domestic assets).
3. Unilateral **transfers** of money between countries (foreign aid, gifts, and grants given by the residents or governments of one country to those of another).

The **capital account** records the purchases and sales of foreign assets by domestic residents as well as the purchases and sales of domestic assets by foreign residents. The definition of an asset is all inclusive: It is any form in which wealth can be held. It encompasses both financial assets (bank deposits and loans, corporate and government bonds, and equities) and real assets (factories, real estate, antiques, and so forth). Hence, the capital account records all changes in the domestic ownership of the assets of other nations as well as changes in the foreign ownership of the assets of the domestic country.

One type of capital account transaction merits special attention: transactions involving the purchase or sale of official international reserve assets by a nation's central bank. International reserves are the assets of the central bank that are not denominated in the domestic currency. Gold and assets denominated in foreign currency are the typical international reserves. Exhibit 4.1 surveys the various types of transactions and accounts of the BOP and splits the capital account into two parts: a regular account and an **official settlements account**, or **official reserves account**. The regular capital account records all transactions

Exhibit 4.1 Summary of the Accounts of the Balance of Payments

Debits (recorded with a −)	Credits (recorded with a +)
I. CURRENT ACCOUNT	
(A) TRADE BALANCE	
(Transactions in goods, services, and transfers)	
Imports to the United States	Exports from the United States
(B) INVESTMENT INCOME ACCOUNT	
Payment by the United States of dividends and interest to foreigners	Receipt by the United States of dividends and interest from foreigners
II. CAPITAL ACCOUNT	
Capital Outflows	Capital Inflows
Increase in U.S. ownership of foreign assets	Increase in foreign ownership of U.S. assets
Decrease of foreign ownership of U.S. assets	Decrease in U.S. ownership of foreign assets
III. OFFICIAL RESERVES ACCOUNT	
Increase in official reserves of the U.S. central bank	Decrease of official reserves of the U.S. central bank
Decrease in dollar reserves of foreign central banks	Increase in dollar reserves of foreign central banks

Notes: This exhibit summarizes the various accounts of the balance of payments and indicates the types of transactions that are booked there. We use the U.S. perspective, but the structure applies to any country.

other than those involving international reserves. We discuss the official settlements account in detail in Section 4.2. Throughout this chapter, Exhibit 4.1 provides a useful guide.

A Double-Entry Accounting System

The balance of payments uses a double-entry system. Each transaction gives rise to two entries: One entry is a credit, and the other entry is a debit of equal value. The rules for determining credits and debits on the balance of payments are analogous like those in financial accounting. Any transaction resulting in a payment to foreigners is entered in the BOP accounts as a debit. Any transaction resulting in a receipt of funds from foreigners is entered as a credit. In presentations of the balance of payments that merely list the values of the items, it is traditional that credit items are listed with a positive + sign and debit items are listed with a negative – sign.

An Intuitive Rule for Determining Credits and Debits

Determining which items are credits and which are debits is very intuitive when you suppose that all transactions between the residents of a country and the rest of the world must be conducted with foreign money, which flows through the foreign exchange market. Thus, a credit transaction on a country's balance of payments corresponds to an inflow, or source, of foreign currency, whereas a debit transaction constitutes an outflow, or use, of foreign currency:

In summary:

1. **Credit transactions** give rise to *conceptual inflows or sources of foreign exchange*. The purchases of goods and assets by foreign residents from domestic residents are credits because they are a source of foreign exchange. That is, they increase the supply of foreign money in the foreign exchange market.
2. **Debit transactions** give rise to *conceptual outflows or uses of foreign exchange*. The purchases of goods and assets by domestic residents from foreign residents are debits because they cause an outflow of foreign exchange. Debit transactions increase the demand for the foreign money in the foreign exchange market.

Let's apply these rules in some example situations to make sure that you understand them and the double-entry system.

Current Account Transactions

Every current account transaction can be considered to have a corresponding flow of foreign money associated with it, and this flow of foreign money is recorded as a capital account transaction. To illustrate the double-entry system, let's begin with two simple examples that illustrate the recording on the BOP of export and import transactions.

Example 4.1 Commercial Exports of Goods

Suppose the U.S. computer maker Dell sells $20 million of computers to Komatsu, a Japanese manufacturer of construction and mining equipment. Komatsu pays Dell by transferring dollars from its dollar-denominated bank account at Citibank in New York to Dell's bank account. What are the credit and debit items on the U.S. balance of payments?

First, a U.S. firm is selling goods to a foreign firm. This transaction is an export of goods from the United States and is a credit on the U.S. balance of payments because it gives rise to a conceptual inflow of foreign money—in this case yen—to the United

States. Second, in this example, Komatsu already owned dollars and thus did not need to enter the foreign exchange market, but the payment of dollars by Komatsu does reduce the foreign ownership of U.S. assets. This action is a debit transaction because if it were done as a separate transaction, Komatsu would have taken the dollars it owned and converted them back into yen, which would have increased the demand for yen in the foreign exchange market. In summary, we record the following transactions on the U.S. BOP:

U.S. BOP	Credit	Debit
Computer purchase by Komatsu from Dell (Current account; U.S. goods export)	$20 million	
Citibank foreign deposit decrease (Capital account; capital outflow from the U.S.)		$20 million

If these transactions were listed without the credit and debit titles, the export of goods would receive a $(+)$, and the capital outflow item would receive a $(-)$. Example 4.2 examines the impact the import of a foreign service has on France's balance of payments.

Example 4.2 Commercial Imports of Services

Suppose LVMH, a French luxury goods company, buys €1.5 million of consulting services from the British subsidiary of the Boston Consulting Group (BCG). LVMH pays by writing a check on its euro-denominated bank account at its Paris bank, Société Générale, and BCG deposits the check in its euro-denominated bank account at a different Paris bank, BNP Paribas. What are the credit and debit items on the French balance of payments?

First, a French firm, LVMH, is buying services from a foreign firm, BCG. This is a French import of services. This gives rise to an outflow of funds from France, so it is a debit on the current account of the French balance of payments. BCG could have demanded British pounds, which would have forced LVMH to enter the foreign exchange market to purchase pounds thus increasing the demand for pounds. Second, the receipt of the euro funds by the British firm increases foreign (British) ownership of French assets. This is a credit transaction on the capital account of the French balance of payments because if it were done as a separate transaction, the British firm would have had to buy euros directly with pounds, which would have supplied foreign currency to the French foreign exchange market. Hence, the underlying transaction by BCG of depositing the euro-denominated check in a Paris bank is one that conceptually supplies foreign money to France and is thus a credit on the French balance of payments.

In summary, the transactions on the French BOP are as follows:

French BOP	Credit	Debit
LVMH purchase of consulting services from BCG (Current account; French import of services)		€1.5 million
BNP Paribas foreign deposit increase (Capital account; capital inflow to France)	€1.5 million	

If these transactions were listed without the credit and debit titles, the import of services would receive a $(-)$, and the capital inflow item would receive a $(+)$.

Interest and Dividend Receipts and Payments

The current account also records receipts and payments of dividend and interest income across countries. Dividends from foreign stocks and interest income on foreign bonds give rise to inflows of foreign money and are therefore credit items on the balance of payments. These investment income flows are also recorded on the current account of the balance of payments because they are considered returns to the owners of capital for the services of productive capital. The service flows from capital assets are comparable to the service flows from labor, such as the consulting services LVMH purchased from BCG in Example 4.2.[1]

It is important to distinguish between these income flows that are returns to previously made investments from the values of the outstanding assets. The outstanding asset or stock position is analogous to an item on the balance sheet of a firm. Changes in the ownership of assets are booked on the capital account.

Example 4.3 is a concrete example of how investment income is recorded on the Belgian balance of payments.

Example 4.3 The Receipt of Income from Foreign Assets

Consider a Belgian resident who in previous years made substantial investments in British government bonds. Each year, the Belgian receives £500,000 of coupon payments from her British bonds. Suppose that these payments are paid to her London bank, where she keeps a pound-denominated bank account. What are the credit and debit items on the Belgian balance of payments?

When the Belgian resident receives coupon payments from the British government, these receipts are credits to Belgium's current account in the investment income account (see Exhibit 4.1). They provide an inflow of foreign currency to Belgium. The fact that the Belgian resident receives the pounds and deposits them at a London bank implies that there is an increase in Belgian ownership of foreign assets. This is a debit on the capital account of the Belgian balance of payments because if the Belgian resident had set out to increase the value of her pound bank account in London directly, she would have had to use euros to purchase pounds in the foreign exchange market. Hence, the increase in Belgian ownership of foreign assets would have increased the demand for foreign exchange, and it is consequently a debit item on the Belgian balance of payments. In summary, if the euro–pound exchange rate is €1.5/£, so that £500,000 represents €750,000, the transactions on the Belgian BOP would be as follows:

Belgian BOP	Credit	Debit
Coupon receipts from British Treasury (Current account; interest income)	€750,000	
London Bank, foreign deposit increase (Capital account; capital outflow from Belgium)		€750,000

Transfer Payments Between Countries

The last items recorded on the current account of the balance of payments are transfers between countries. Transfers are indicated as unilateral transfers in the U.S. BOP and unrequited transfers in the IMF's *Balance of Payments Manual*. Both terms indicate that the items are given by the individual, without an explicit receipt of an item of equivalent value in return. Typical examples

---

[1]In fact, the economics of the transaction in Example 4.2 can describe the payment for consulting services as a payment for the use of an individual's human capital, which is the stock of education and knowledge that allows the person to provide valuable advice.

are a U.S. resident sending a gift to her relatives in the "old country" or foreign aid from one country to another. Clearly, gifts to foreign countries or to a family abroad lead to an increase in the demand for foreign exchange and, by our rule, must be debit items on the U.S. BOP.

You may be thinking that because the gift is a debit, there must be a way of describing this transaction that makes it seem more like an import of goods or services to United States, which is also a debit item on the U.S. BOP. There is a way—you just need to understand the motivation behind the transaction. Presumably, the U.S. resident hoped that the gift would improve relations with her foreign relatives. That is, she sought to import goodwill to the United States. Hence, the gift is an import of goodwill and is therefore a debit (on the current account).

To clarify how transfers are recorded on the BOP, let's look at an example that considers the Japanese balance of payments.

Example 4.4 Gifts to Foreign Residents

Consider the effect on the Japanese BOP of a gift of $2 million by a Japanese firm to a U.S. university to create an endowed chair. Suppose, also, that the Japanese firm finances the gift by selling U.S. Treasury bonds in which it had previously invested. What should we record as credit and debit items on Japan's balance of payments?

The action by the Japanese firm clearly uses $2 million of foreign exchange from the Japanese government's perspective. Hence, by our rule, the gift must be a debit item on the Japanese balance of payments because it leads to an outflow of foreign exchange. Notice that the gift by the Japanese firm improves relations with the U.S. university and is a Japanese import of goodwill from the United States.

Now, consider the offsetting credit transaction on the Japanese balance of payments. The Japanese firm sold U.S. Treasury bonds, which reduces the Japanese ownership of foreign assets. This transaction is a credit on the capital account of the Japanese balance of payments because it supplies dollars to the Japanese foreign exchange market.

In summary, if the yen–dollar exchange rate is ¥100/$, in which case the $2 million equals ¥200 million, the transactions would be as follows:

Japanese BOP	Credit	Debit
Gift by Japanese firm to U.S. university (Current account; Japanese import of goodwill)		¥200 million
Sale of U.S. Treasury bonds (Capital account; capital inflow to Japan)	¥200 million	

We turn now to transactions in assets that are recorded on the capital account.

Capital Account Transactions

Some capital account transactions arise naturally, as demonstrated in the case of payment flows associated with current account transactions. However, some transactions involve situations in which both entries are recorded exclusively on the capital account. For example, suppose a Mexican resident buys a U.S. Treasury bond. You can think of this as Mexico "importing" a foreign asset (a bond). Thus, the transaction should have the same sign as an import of a regular good. This transaction is therefore a debit on the Mexican capital account because it represents an outflow, or use, of foreign exchange. In other words, this transaction gives rise to an increase in the demand for foreign currency— dollars in this case—because the Mexican resident needs dollars to purchase the U.S. Treasury bond. Notice that in presentations of the balance of payments in which credits are given a $+$ sign and debits are given a $(-)$, the acquisition of foreign assets by a Mexican resident would be a debit and would receive a − sign, even though Mexican ownership of foreign assets is increasing!

Capital Outflows

There is an alternative way of describing the acquisition of foreign assets. When the residents of Mexico purchase foreign assets rather than invest in domestic assets, there is said to be a **capital outflow** from Mexico. In this case, the "capital" refers to the money that could have financed an investment in Mexico. Because this money is no longer available to finance local investment projects, local governments often try to discourage this outflow of capital, which is often called **capital flight** when it occurs rapidly in response to a deteriorating investment climate in the home country.

Capital Inflows

If a U.S. resident purchases Mexican Cetes (Treasury bills), Mexico is said to have a **capital inflow**. This transaction is recorded as a credit on the Mexican balance of payments because it supplies foreign money to Mexico's foreign exchange market. Generally, capital inflows to Mexico occur when foreigners buy Mexican assets or when Mexicans reduce the amount of wealth they hold abroad (for example, a Mexican sells U.S. stocks).

Summarizing Capital Account Transactions

All the transactions discussed so far are easily matched with the capital account categories mentioned in Exhibit 4.1, when viewed from the Mexican perspective. The U.S. purchase of Cetes corresponds to an "increase in foreign ownership of assets in Mexico," and the Mexican selling of U.S. stocks corresponds to a "decrease in Mexican ownership of foreign assets." Both are capital inflows to Mexico. Similarly, capital outflows from Mexico (debits on the Mexican BOP) happen when Mexicans increase their assets abroad, as they do when buying U.S. Treasury bonds, or when foreigners decrease their ownership of assets in Mexico.

We have now discussed how the buying and selling of assets is recorded on the Mexican BOP, but what about the payment flows associated with these transactions? When a Mexican resident buys a U.S. Treasury bond, he must pay in dollars. This reduction of his dollar holdings is a Mexican capital inflow ("decrease in Mexican ownership of foreign assets") and provides the credit transaction that balances the debit transaction of the original foreign bond purchase. Similarly, when a U.S. investor buys Cetes (a capital inflow into Mexico), he must pay in Mexican pesos. If we conceptually assume that he had a peso-denominated account with a Mexican bank, the reduction in his peso bank account is a capital outflow, which is the debit on the Mexican BOP that balances the credit generated when the American purchases a Cetes.

Official Reserves Account Transactions

Changes in the **official international reserves** of a country's central bank are also recorded on the country's balance of payments—in this case, in the country's official reserves account. The rules for determining credits and debits are identical to the rules that govern the private sector's capital account. If the central bank acquires international reserves, a debit is entered on the official settlements account, just as it is recorded on the private capital account if private residents acquire foreign assets. Once again, this debit receives a (−) in a presentation of the BOP that just lists items even though the reserves of the central bank are increasing. If, on the other hand, the central bank draws down its international reserves, there is a credit on the official settlements account, just as there is on the private capital account if private residents sell their foreign assets. In this case, the transaction would be recorded with a (+) even though the central bank's reserves are declining.

Implications for Fixed Exchange Rates

In some developing countries, the central bank fixes the exchange rate at a particular value relative to the dollar, for example, and the country's residents are required to deal directly with the central bank to conduct international transactions. If a resident of the country wants to purchase U.S. equities, the person must first purchase dollars from the central bank with local currency at the fixed exchange rate determined by the central bank. The official settlements account records a credit that offsets the debit associated with the use of the dollars (the increase in foreign assets represented by the equity purchase). Conversely, when residents of this country acquire dollars in international transactions, they must also sell the dollars to the central bank for local currency at the fixed exchange rate. In this way, the central bank's stock of dollars increases, and the transaction is recorded as a debit on the official settlements account, offsetting the private sector's credit transaction that originally gave rise to the dollars.

4.2 SURPLUSES AND DEFICITS IN THE BALANCE OF PAYMENTS ACCOUNTS

Because the balance of payments system uses a double-entry accounting system, the value of credits on a country's balance of payments must equal the value of its debits. The overall balance of payments therefore must always sum to zero. Nevertheless, the total value of credits generated by a particular set of economic transactions, such as the sales of goods and services *to* foreigners (exports), need not be equal to the value of debits generated by the purchase of goods and services *from* foreigners (imports). If credit transactions on a particular account are greater than debit transactions on that account, the account is said to be in **surplus**. If debit transactions on a particular account are greater than credit transactions on that account, the account is said to be in **deficit**.

An Important Balance of Payments Identity

Because the two major accounts of the balance of payments are the current account and the capital account, we see immediately that a current account deficit must have a capital account surplus as its counterpart. In other words, if we list credit items with a + sign and debit items with a – sign, we can add the accounts, and they must sum to zero:

$$\text{Current account} + \text{Capital account} = 0$$

If we highlight the transactions that change a country's stock of international reserves at its central bank as a separate part of the balance of payments, as in Exhibit 4.1, we have

$$\text{Current account} + \text{Regular capital account} + \text{Official settlements account} = 0 \qquad \textbf{(4.1)}$$

To better understand the economic meaning of the various surpluses and deficits, we next study the U.S. BOP statistics in more detail. We then look at the special role of the official settlements account balance. Finally, we investigate recent BOP statistics around the world. Detailed statistics of the U.S. BOP are provided in Exhibit 4.2 and 4.3. Exhibit 4.4 presents the data from these exhibits for 2005 in the format of Exhibit 4.1. In the following text, we discuss the various subaccounts, one by one.

The U.S. Current Account

Let's look at the current account of the United States and its various subcategories, which are shown in Exhibit 4.2.

Exhibit 4.2 The U.S. Current Account, 1970–2005 (Millions of Dollars; Credits, +; Debits, −)

Year	Goods Exports	Goods Imports	Balance on Goods	Services Balance on Services	Balance on Goods and Services	Income Receipts and Payments Receipts	Income Receipts and Payments Payments	Balance on Income	Unilateral Current Transfers, Net	Balance on Current Account
1970	42,469	−39,866	2,603	−349	2,254	11,748	−5,515	6,233	−6,156	2,331
1975	107,088	−98,185	8,903	3,503	12,404	25,351	−12,564	12,787	−7,075	18,116
1980	224,250	−249,750	−25,500	6,093	−19,407	72,606	−42,532	30,073	−8,349	2,317
1985	215,915	−338,088	−122,173	295	−121,880	98,542	−72,819	25,723	−21,998	−118,155
1990	389,307	−498,337	−109,030	30,172	−78,857	171,742	−143,192	28,550	−26,654	−76,961
1995	575,845	−749,574	−173,729	77,782	−95,947	211,502	−190,955	20,547	−34,057	−109,457
2000	771,994	−1,224,417	−452,423	73,742	−378,681	352,997	−331,215	21,782	−53,442	−410,341
2005	894,631	−1,677,371	−782,740	66,011	−716,729	474,647	−463,353	11,293	−86,072	−791,508

Note: Data are from the U.S. Department of Commerce, Bureau of Economic Analysis, Survey of Current Business, April 2006.

Goods

The first category in Exhibit 4.2 is "exports and imports of goods." This account covers trade in commodities such as oil or wheat and in physical goods such as cars, airplanes, DVD players, and computers. The goods can be raw materials, semi-finished goods, or finished goods. In 2005, the U.S. exported $895 billion of goods and imported $1,677 billion of goods. Because debits (imports) exceeded credits (exports) by $783 billion, we say the United States had a $783 billion **merchandise trade balance deficit** in 2005.

Services

We only show the net amount, or balance, on the services account, which was a $66 billion surplus in 2005. Typically, economists classify services as economic transactions that must be produced and utilized at the same time. Services thus include the export and import of education, financial services, insurance, consulting, telecommunications, medical services, royalties on films, and the fees and royalties repatriated to U.S. corporations. Fees and royalties repatriated to U.S. corporations are earned when the corporations license technology to their foreign subsidiaries or to other foreign companies.

In the U.S. current account, services also include military transactions even when they involve purchases of goods. Because personnel at U.S. military bases in foreign countries are considered to be U.S. residents, their purchases of local goods and services, including supplies for the bases themselves, are imported goods. The primary U.S. military exports are sales of aircraft.

Another important subcategory of services is travel and transportation. When foreigners spend more while traveling in the United States for food, lodging, recreational activities, and gifts than U.S. residents spend while traveling in foreign countries, this account is in surplus. Because it is impossible to know how much each foreign tourist spends, the U.S. Department of Commerce estimates expenditures on this account by multiplying an average expenditure obtained from surveys by the known number of travelers (obtained from immigration and naturalization statistics).

Balance on Goods and Services

The sum of the net positions on the goods account and the services account gives the balance on the goods and services account, which was −$717 billion in 2005. Notice that the value of this account has become more negative over time, and we therefore say that the deficit on this account has grown over time.

Investment Income

The next columns in Exhibit 4.2 report income receipts and payments, which are the dividend and interest income received by U.S. residents (credits) because of their ownership of assets in foreign countries as well as the dividend and interest income paid to foreigners (debits) who own U.S. assets. In 2005, the United States received $475 billion of investment income from foreigners and made $463 billion of payments to foreigners, for a net figure of $11.3 billion, which represents a surplus on this account.

Unilateral Current Transfers, Net

The second-to-last column in Exhibit 4.2 is "Unilateral Current Transfers, Net." The figure for 2005 is –$86 billion. This indicates that the U.S. government and other U.S. residents gave more money to foreign countries and residents as gifts and grants than the United States received from abroad. The deficit on this account represents a net import of goodwill into the United States.

Balance on Current Account

When the investment income account and the unilateral transfers account are added to the balance on goods and services, the result is the *current account surplus or deficit*, which is recorded in Exhibit 4.2 as the balance on the current account. Exhibit 4.2 indicates that the 2005 U.S. current account balance was –$791.5 billion. Consequently, we say there was a current account deficit of $791.5 billion.

The U.S. Capital and Financial Accounts

Exhibit 4.3 presents the details of the U.S. capital and financial accounts. As noted earlier, the current account and the capital account must sum to zero. Hence, if there is a current account deficit, it must be financed by a capital account surplus.

A surplus in the capital account can occur in several ways. First, there could be a decrease in U.S. private and official assets abroad. A country might sell its foreign assets to finance a current account deficit, just as an individual might consume more than his current income by selling his or her assets. Such sales of foreign assets are credits on the capital account.

Exhibit 4.3 The U.S. Capital and Financial Account, 1970–2005 (Millions of Dollars; Credits, +; Debits, −)

| Year | U.S.-owned assets abroad, net [increase/financial outflow (−)] | | | | Foreign-owned assets in the U.S., net [increase/financial inflow (+)] | | | | Statistical discrepancy |
	Total	U.S. official reserve assets	Other U.S. Government assets	U.S. private assets	Total	Foreign official assets	Other foreign assets	Capital account transfers	Total (sum of all items with the sign reversed)
1970	–8,470	3,348	–1,589	–10,229	6,359	6,908	–550	—	–219
1975	–39,703	–849	–3,474	–35,380	17,170	7,027	10,143	—	4,417
1980	–85,815	–7,003	–5,162	–73,651	62,612	15,497	47,115	—	20,886
1985	–44,752	–3,858	–2,821	–38,074	146,115	–1,119	147,233	315	16,478
1990	–81,234	–2,158	2,317	–81,393	141,571	33,910	107,661	–6,579	23,204
1995	–352,376	–9,742	–941	–341,650	465,684	109,880	355,804	372	–4,223
2000	–606,489	–290	–341	–605,258	1,015,986	37,640	978,346	837	7
2005	–426,801	14,096	5,539	–446,436	1,212,250	199,495	1,012,755	–4,351	10,410

Note: Data are from the Department of Commerce, Bureau of Economic Analysis, Survey of Current Business, April 2006.

A second way that a current account deficit can be financed is through a net increase in foreign private and official assets in the United States. Just as an individual might consume more than her income by taking out a loan or selling someone their assets, a country might borrow from abroad or sell assets to foreigners. For the United States, these activities correspond to an increase in foreign claims on the United States. Any combination of these capital account transactions that results in a capital account surplus of the appropriate magnitude will also finance the current account deficit. From Exhibit 4.4 we see that the particular combination of capital account transactions that financed the current account deficit in 2005 was an increase in foreign ownership of U.S. assets that was much larger than the increase in U.S. ownership of foreign assets.

U.S.-Owned Assets Abroad, Net

The total of credits and debits recorded for changes in "U.S.-Owned Assets Abroad, Net" was –$427 billion for 2005. This indicates that during 2005, although some U.S. residents sold foreign assets and others bought foreign assets, on net, U.S. residents increased their

Exhibit 4.4 U.S. Balance of Payments Accounts for 2005 (Billions of Dollars)

	Credits	Debits
Current Account		
[A] Trade Account		
Exports/Imports of Goods	894.5	–1,677.5
Exports/Imports of Services	66	
Net Unilateral Transfers		–86
Trade Balance		**–803**
[B] Investment Income Account		
Receipts on U.S. Assets Abroad	475	
Payments on Foreign Assets in the U.S.		–463.5
Investment Account Balance		**11.5**
Current Account Balance [A] + [B]		**–791.5**
Regular Capital Account		
U.S. Assets Abroad (net) of which:		–441
Other U.S. Government Assets	+5.5	
U.S. Private Assets		–446.5
Foreign Private Assets in the U.S.	+1,013	
Capital Account Transfers, Net		–4
Balance on Regular Capital Account	**+568**	
Official Settlements Account		
U.S. Official reserve Assets	+14	
Foreign Official Assets	+199.5	
Balance on Official Settlements Account	**+213.5**	
Balance on Capital Account	**+781.5**	
Statistical Discrepancy		
(Sum of all the items with sign reversed)	+10	

Note: Data are from the Department of Commerce, Bureau of Economic Analysis, Survey of Current Business, April 2006.

outstanding stock of claims on foreigners by $427 billion. This represents a capital outflow from the United States.

Foreign Assets in the U.S., Net

The category "foreign assets in the U.S., net" shows that foreign residents increased their claims on the United States by $1,212 billion in 2005, which constitutes a capital inflow to the United States.

Capital Account Transfers

In 1997, the U.S. Department of Commerce began separating capital transfers—primarily transactions involving the forgiveness of debt and the value of goods and assets accompanying migrants as they cross borders—from other unilateral transfers involving current income. The latter transactions continue to be recorded on the current account. The transactions involving debt forgiveness and the value of assets accompanying migrants are now recorded on the capital account. In 2005, that amount was –$4 billion. The terminology can get a bit confusing here. The U.S. balance of payment statistics uses the word *capital account* very narrowly to indicate the category "capital account transfers," whereas the financial account records all transactions that belong in what we called the "capital account." We will therefore refer to the transactions booked under the capital account in the United States as "capital account transfers."

Balance on the Capital Account

By adding together the debits that result from the increase in U.S.-owned foreign assets (–$427 billion), the credits from the increase in foreign ownership of U.S. assets ($1,212 billion), and the debits from the capital account transfers (–$4 billion), the balance on the capital account in 2005 was a surplus of $781 billion ($1,212 billion – $427 billion – $4 billion). Remember, for balance of payments purposes, the concept of *capital* refers to liquid purchasing power. Capital must flow into a country if it has a current account deficit, and capital flows out of a country if it has a current account surplus.

The Statistical Discrepancy

Exhibits 4.2 and 4.3 show that in 2005, the value of the U.S. current account was –$791.5 billion, and the value of the U.S. capital account was $781 billion. Hence, the sum of the two accounts is –$10.5 billion. However, we explained that because of the double-entry system, the sum of the current account and the capital account should be zero. Why then was it –$10.5 billion in 2005? The fact is that the government misses some transactions, and it estimates other transactions.

To make the balance of payments add to zero, government statisticians must add a balancing item (or fudge factor) equal to the sum of all the measured items with the sign reversed. The technical term for the balancing item in the U.S. accounts is the **statistical discrepancy**. Formerly, this balancing account was called "errors and omissions," and such a term is often encountered in other presentations of the balance of payments. The statistical discrepancy is reported in column 10 of Exhibit 4.3 as $10.4 billion.

Because the statistical discrepancy is the sum of all the measured items with the sign reversed, the United States was missing over $10 billion of credits in 2005. These credits are probably capital account transactions such as unmeasured U.S. sales of foreign assets and unmeasured purchases of U.S. assets by foreign residents.

Does the World Have a Current Account Deficit?

Because one country's borrowing is another country's lending, theoretically, the sum of all the individual current account balances of countries across the world should also sum to zero. Unfortunately, as the data in Exhibit 4.5 reveal, there is a problem with this logic.

Exhibit 4.5 World Current Account Balance
(Billions of U.S. Dollars)

1980	−38.5
1981	−68.3
1982	−100.2
1983	−62.1
1984	−73.4
1985	−80.8
1986	−76.7
1987	−62.3
1988	−78.9
1989	−96.2
1990	−126.0
1991	−118.2
1992	−104.2
1993	−57.4
1994	−50.6
1995	−39.4
1996	−49.8
1997	−4.6
1998	−81.3
1999	−126.8
2000	−163.8
2001	−163.4
2002	−132.2
2003	−97.7
2004	−64.8
2005	−87.1*

Notes: Data for 1980 to 1994 are from Madura, p. 319; data for 1993 to 2002 are from International Monetary Fund, *World Economic Outlook*, September 2004. The * indicates an estimated number.

Beginning in the early 1980s, economists noted that the world as a whole has often run a current account deficit, which is impossible unless we're trading with Mars. The large, consistently negative sign for the global balance suggests that the discrepancy cannot simply be due to measurement errors because if it were, the balance would be positive about as often as it is negative. Why, then, is total world current account almost always negative?

An IMF study John Motala (1997) offers several reasons. Many individuals try to escape taxes on the income from their investments. Hence, they may fail to report the interest income they earn on their foreign securities, which would constitute a credit for their home country's current account balance. Unrecorded earnings in the international shipping business may also account for a large part of the missing surplus. In fact, much of the world's merchant shipping fleet is registered in countries that do not report maritime freight earnings to the IMF. Once again, these would be credits on the service account of the balance of payments. Finally, countries that receive foreign aid may fail to fully account for official aid disbursements.

More recently, the *Economist* offered several additional reasons. First, freer trade has made it more difficult for governments to measure sales accurately. Second, sales over the Internet can escape detection.

The Official Settlements, or Reserves, Account

In our discussion of the U.S. capital account so far, we have not made any distinction between the transactions of private individuals and those of the government. The U.S. Department of Commerce breaks the total net change in U.S. assets abroad into transactions in three categories: transactions in "U.S. official reserve assets" (column 3 of Exhibit 4.3), transactions in "other U.S. governmental assets" (column 4 of Exhibit 4.3), and transactions in "U.S. private assets" (column 5 of Exhibit 4.3).

The U.S. official reserves account measures changes in the official stock of international reserve assets, consisting of gold, foreign currencies, special drawing rights, and the U.S. reserve position with the IMF. In 2005, there was a surplus on this account of $14 billion. The surplus indicates that official reserves were decreased by that amount. Transactions in other U.S. governmental assets are primarily the changes in the outstanding quantities of official loans to foreigners and of capital subscriptions to international financial institutions. In 2005, there was a surplus on this account of $5.5 billion. Here, the surplus indicates that U.S. official loans to foreigners were reduced by this amount, which amounts to a capital inflow. Column 5 of Exhibit 4.3 indicates a deficit of $446 billion in transactions in U.S. private assets. The deficit in this account indicates the net amount by which private U.S. residents increased their ownership of foreign assets, which amounts to a capital outflow.

Similarly, the U.S. Department of Commerce decomposes the total net change in Foreign-owned U.S. assets into transactions in "Foreign official assets" and "other foreign assets." In 2005, foreign official assets in the United States increased by $199.5 billion, whereas foreign private individuals increased their ownership of U.S. assets by $1,013 billion. The former category is important for the United States because other countries use dollar-denominated assets as international reserves. Hence, the increase in foreign official assets indicates that the dollar reserves of foreign central banks increased substantially.

Although the Department of Commerce separately records transactions in U.S. international reserves and foreign official assets within the capital account, it does not separate this account into an official settlements account as we did in Exhibit 4.1. So, we do it ourselves in Exhibit 4.4. Exhibit 4.4 shows that in 2005, the balance on the official settlements account was a $213.5 billion surplus: The U.S. central bank decreased its official reserves by $14 billion (a credit), and the central banks across the world increased their dollar assets by $199.5 billion (a credit). This buildup in dollar reserves by central banks around the world has been going on for a while and is primarily concentrated in Southeast Asia, particularly China.

BOP Deficits and Surpluses and the Official Settlements Account

One often hears that the central bank gained international reserves because the balance of payments was in "surplus." This statement refers to the fact that if the sum of the private and government transactions on the other accounts (the current and regular capital account) is positive, the central bank must have increased its holdings of foreign money. Hence, there is a deficit on the official settlements account when the other accounts are in surplus.

Conversely, if private residents and government agencies other than the central bank have more debits than credits in their accounts, the central bank must be in surplus. It will be supplying foreign assets out of its stock of international reserves. Because the central bank is losing international reserves (that is, it is reducing its ownership of foreign assets), the official settlements account is credited, but there is said to be a deficit on the balance of payments. This indicates that private residents and other government agencies of the country are purchasing more goods, services, and assets from abroad than foreigners are purchasing domestic goods, services, and assets.

The official settlements account plays a critical role if a central bank wants to maintain a "fixed" exchange rate, a situation we discuss in detail in Chapter 5. To fix the exchange rate, the central bank must be prepared to buy and sell its domestic currency with its stock of international reserves. However, if the central bank depletes its stock of international reserves, which is what occurred in Mexico in 1994, the central bank will not be able to maintain the fixed exchange rate, and the country will be forced to devalue its currency. Hence, looking closely at a country's balance of payments and the variation over time in the country's stock of international reserves can help exporters, importers, and investors get an idea about how probable a devaluation of the currency will be in the future. We explore these issues in more detail in Chapter 5.

Balance of Payment Statistics Around the World

Although we have focused the discussion so far in this chapter on the United States, the principles are applicable to the balance of payments statistics of all countries. Exhibit 4.6 presents data for the current account balances of the G7 countries, which are the United States, the United Kingdom, Germany, Japan, Italy, France, and Canada.

Each of these balances is expressed as a percentage of the country's **gross domestic product** (**GDP**), the value of all final goods and services produced within a country. (See the appendix to this chapter for a review of GDP and a country's national income and product accounts.) Notice that in any given year, some of the G7 countries have a current account deficit, whereas other countries have a current account surplus. This situation is to be expected because a country with a current account deficit must borrow from or sell assets to another country to finance the deficit.

Several features of these data are noteworthy. First, during the 45 years accounted for in Exhibit 4.6, the largest current account deficit as a percentage of GDP is the 5.7% value for the United States in 2004. The largest surplus is Japan's 4.8% in 1989. Second, deficits and surpluses are quite persistent. Third, there is a persistently large current account surplus in Japan and a large current account deficit in the United States. Japan and the United States are also important trading partners, and it is indeed the case that a substantial part of these two countries' current account balances is linked to their bilateral **trade balance**. This situation first occurred in the early 1980s, and its persistence remains somewhat puzzling to many economists.

The balance of payments is also a critical set of statistics for developing countries. In Exhibit 4.7 we show current account balances between 1990 and 2004 for some Southeast Asian countries.

In 1997, several of these countries faced severe currency and banking crises. You might wonder whether large current account deficits in these countries helped trigger the crises. Note that Singapore, Hong Kong, and China all had only small current account deficits or even surpluses prior to the crises and that these countries did not experience large depreciations of their currencies. After the crises, the crisis countries experienced large current account reversals, moving from large deficits to large surpluses. The surpluses in emerging Asia, Japan, and the oil-producing countries (benefiting from increases in oil prices) therefore form the counterpart to the sizable U.S. current account deficit. The fact that these surpluses and the deficit in the United States are so large has led economists and reporters alike to refer to them as "global imbalances." To evaluate whether this moniker is accurate, you must understand how current accounts and the balance of payments evolve over time.

Exhibit 4.6 Current Account Balances for the G7 Countries as a Percentage of GDP

Year	United States	United Kingdom	Japan	Italy	Germany	France	Canada
1960	0.6	–1.0	0.5	0.6	1.6	2.2	–3.2
1961	0.8	0.0	–1.7	0.8	1.0	1.6	–2.3
1962	0.7	0.4	0.1	0.4	–0.1	1.6	–2.0
1963	0.8	0.3	–1.0	–0.9	0.2	0.8	–1.2
1964	1.2	–1.3	–0.5	0.8	0.2	0.4	–0.6
1965	0.9	–0.4	1.1	2.5	–1.3	1.5	–1.9
1966	0.5	0.1	1.3	2.2	0.3	0.8	–1.9
1967	0.4	–0.9	0.0	1.5	2.2	0.7	–0.9
1968	0.2	–0.8	0.8	2.3	2.3	0.1	–0.4
1969	0.2	0.6	1.3	1.8	1.4	–0.3	–1.4
1970	0.4	1.3	1.0	0.8	0.6	0.8	0.9
1971	0.1	1.8	2.5	1.4	0.4	0.9	0.1
1972	–0.3	0.1	2.3	1.5	0.6	1.0	–0.6
1973	0.7	–2.0	0.0	–1.7	1.5	0.6	–0.1
1974	0.5	–4.5	–1.0	–4.4	2.7	–1.3	–1.4
1975	1.4	–2.0	–0.1	–0.3	1.2	0.9	–3.5
1976	0.5	–1.6	0.7	–1.3	0.8	–0.9	–2.6
1977	–0.5	0.0	1.5	1.0	0.8	–0.1	–2.4
1978	–0.5	0.5	1.7	2.1	1.4	1.4	–2.3
1979	0.1	0.2	–0.9	1.6	–0.5	0.9	–2.3
1980	0.4	1.5	–1.0	–2.4	–1.7	–0.6	–0.9
1981	0.2	2.5	0.5	–2.4	–0.6	–0.8	–2.7
1982	–0.2	1.5	0.7	–1.8	0.8	–2.1	0.4
1983	–1.1	0.8	1.8	0.2	0.9	–0.8	0.2
1984	–2.4	–0.3	2.8	–0.8	1.4	0.0	0.2
1985	–2.9	0.3	3.6	–1.0	2.4	0.1	–1.0
1986	–3.4	–1.1	4.3	0.4	4.3	0.5	–2.6
1987	–3.5	–2.2	3.6	–0.3	4.1	–0.2	–2.2
1988	–2.4	–4.9	2.8	–0.8	4.3	–0.3	–2.7
1989	–1.8	–5.6	2.0	–1.5	4.8	–0.5	–3.6
1990	–1.3	–3.4	1.5	–1.5	3.5	–0.8	–3.5
1991	0.1	–1.5	2.0	–2.1	–1.0	–0.5	–3.8
1992	–0.8	–1.7	3.0	–2.4	–0.9	0.3	–3.7
1993	–1.3	–1.7	3.1	0.8	–0.7	0.7	–3.9
1994	–1.7	–0.2	2.8	1.3	–1.0	0.5	–2.4
1995	–1.5	–0.5	2.2	2.3	–0.8	0.7	–0.7
1996	–1.6	–0.1	1.4	3.2	–0.3	1.3	0.6
1997	–1.7	–0.2	2.3	2.9	–0.4	2.6	–1.3
1998	–2.5	–0.5	3.0	1.9	–0.7	2.6	–1.3
1999	–3.3	–2.7	2.6	0.7	–1.2	2.9	0.3
2000	–4.3	–2.6	2.5	–0.5	–1.6	1.4	2.8
2001	–3.9	–2.2	2.1	–0.1	0.2	1.6	2.3
2002	–4.6	–1.6	2.8	–0.8	2.2	1.0	1.9
2003	–4.8	–1.5	3.2	–1.3	2.1	0.4	1.5
2004	–5.7	–2.0	3.7	–0.9	3.8	–0.4	2.3

Note: Data are from the Organization for Economic Co-operation and Development, 2006.

Exhibit 4.7 Current Account Balances for Developing Asian Economies as a Percentage of GDP

	Korea	Indonesia	Malaysia	Philippines	Singapore	Thailand	China
1990	−0.8	−2.6	−2.0	−6.1	8.5	−8.5	3.1
1991	−2.7	−3.3	−8.5	−2.3	11.4	−7.7	3.3
1992	−1.2	−2.0	−3.7	−1.9	12.1	−5.7	1.3
1993	0.2	−1.3	−4.5	−5.5	7.3	−5.1	−2.0
1994	−1.0	−1.6	−6.1	−4.6	16.3	−5.6	1.4
1995	−1.7	−3.2	−9.7	−2.7	17.3	−8.1	0.2
1996	−4.1	−3.4	−4.4	−4.8	15.2	−8.1	0.9
1997	−1.6	−1.6	−5.9	−5.2	17.9	−2.1	3.8
1998	11.7	3.8	13.2	2.3	25.4	12.8	3.3
1999	5.5	3.7	15.9	9.5	25.0	10.2	1.6
2000	2.4	4.8	9.4	8.4	11.6	7.6	1.9
2001	1.7	4.2	8.3	1.9	13.8	5.4	1.5
2002	1.0	3.9	8.4	5.8	13.4	5.5	2.8
2003	2.0	3.4	12.9	1.8	24.1	5.6	3.2
2004	4.1	1.2	12.6	2.7	30.5	4.5	4.2

Notes: For Korea, data are from the Organization for Economic Co-operation (2006). For the other countries, data are from the IMF's *World Economic Outlook,* September 2004. For China, the numbers are from the OECD until 1996 and are from the *World Economic Outlook* thereafter. For Singapore, the numbers from 2000 onward are computed using Singapore's official statistics.

4.3 THE DYNAMICS OF THE BOP

Now that you understand the meaning of the surpluses and deficits on various subaccounts of a country's BOP, it is time to reflect on the economic importance of these surpluses and deficits. For example, the experience of Southeast Asia in the late 1990s shows how large current account deficits led to an accumulation of foreign debt that eventually became unsustainable and led to currency crises in Thailand, Malaysia, Indonesia, and South Korea. We leave the discussion of these currency crises to Chapter 10; here we discuss how current account deficits today affect the balance of payments in the future and ultimately the country's debt position relative to the rest of the world.

The Trade Account and the Investment Income Account

In Exhibits 4.1 and 4.4, we intentionally lumped in the current account all the items other than those associated with flows of investment income into what can be called the **trade account** of the balance of payments. The flows of payments that service assets and liabilities were put into the **international investment income account**. The current account is the sum of the trade account and the investment income account:

$$\text{Current account} = \text{Trade account} + \text{International investment income account} \qquad \textbf{(4.2)}$$

Note that the "trade account" in this case is not the same thing as the goods or merchandise trade balance, which the Department of Commerce calculates. The trade account includes transactions in the economic services such as education, banking, tourism, shipping, insurance and transfers that the merchandise trade balance does not. This breakdown of the balance of payments is desirable because it will help us discuss the dynamics of the balance of payments and the accumulation of international assets or debt.

Investment income flows come from previously made foreign direct investments and previously made portfolio investments. Recall from Chapter 1 that a *foreign direct investment (FDI)* implies that an investor has a long-term interest in a business enterprise in a foreign country and some ability to affect how the company is managed, whereas a *portfolio investment* is typically thought to be more short term in nature and does not involve control over a foreign company. Income from previous FDI is the return a parent firm earns on its foreign affiliates, including the dividends repatriated (returned) from those affiliates plus the interest paid by affiliates to the parents on loans made by the parents. Dividends and interest earned on equity and debt securities are examples of portfolio investment income.

There is considerable estimation involved in determining the flows of income related to portfolio investments. In the United States, the Department of Commerce uses information from the monthly and quarterly Treasury International Capital reporting system to estimate the outstanding stocks of various asset classes. It then uses market interest rates and bond yields to estimate the income flows to these asset classes.

Countries as Net Creditors or Net Debtors

A country's balance of payments records the flows of goods and assets over a period of time, just like the income statement of a firm. A country's **net international investment position**, or **net foreign assets**, with the rest of the world is similar to a firm's balance sheet. It is the difference between the value of a country's ownership of foreign assets and the value of the foreign ownership of the country's assets at a given point in time. If the net international investment position is positive, the country is often referred to as a *net creditor*, and if the net international investment position is negative, the country is often called a *net debtor*, even though the investments in question are not restricted to debt securities.

The statement that a country such as Brazil is a net debtor means that ownership of foreign assets by Brazilian residents is less than foreign ownership of Brazilian assets. This typically implies that the country has a deficit on its investment income account, which in this case may also be called its debt service account.

Suppose that a country is a net debtor and that it cannot take on additional foreign debt because foreign lenders do not want to increase their claims on the country. As a consequence, the country's capital account cannot be positive. From Equation (4.1) we see that the country's current account cannot be negative, because it must be equal and opposite in sign to the capital account. From Equation (4.2) we see that the country's trade account must be in surplus if there is a deficit on the investment income account. Because the country must pay more interest and dividends to foreigners than it receives from them in asset income, the country must sell more goods and services abroad than it buys from abroad. We will see shortly that this means the country must consume less than its income.

Now, consider a country such as Japan that is a net creditor to the rest of the world. It has a positive international investment income account. From Equation (4.2) we see that Japan could have a trade balance deficit while still having a balanced current account. This means that Japan could import more goods and services from abroad than it exports out of the country without incurring foreign debt or selling assets to foreigners because it has a surplus on its investment income account.

Data on International Investment Positions

Exhibit 4.8 shows the international investment positions of the United States, other industrialized countries, and developing countries. They are expressed as a percentage of GDP.

Exhibit 4.8 International Investment Positions

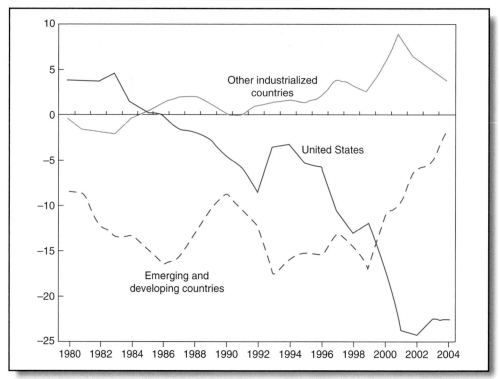

Note: The chart plots aggregate net asset positions for the two country groups and the United States, divided by each group's/country's GDP. The group "other industrialized countries" includes all industrialized countries except the United States. The graph is taken from Philip Lane and Gian Maria Milesi-Ferretti (2005).

Industrialized countries besides the United States have positive international investment positions. One big contributor to this state of affairs is Japan, which has a large positive international investment position arising from its persistent current account surpluses. Developing countries typically run current account deficits, leading to negative international investment positions, but since 1998, there has been a reversal, and persistent current account surpluses have increased the average investment position, bringing it close to zero. China stands out among these countries, as it has consistently run current account surpluses and has a fairly large positive international investment position. China's net international investment position amounted to about $380 billion at the end of 2005.

At the end of 2006, the U.S. Department of Commerce Bureau of Economic Analysis estimates that the net international investment position of the United States was –$2,539 billion. This figure is negative because foreign-owned assets in the United States ($16,294) were substantially larger than U.S.-owned assets abroad ($13,755). In fact, as Exhibit 4.8 shows, the estimated U.S. net international investment position turned negative in the mid-1980s.

Of course, because current account deficits must be balanced by capital account surpluses, the deterioration in the U.S. international investment position parallels the deterioration of its current account that we discussed earlier. Yet, a change in the international investment position cannot only be due to actual international transactions (selling and buying of assets across borders) but must also be due to valuation adjustments attributable to changes in the market prices of assets and changes in exchange rates. For example, even though the United States ran a current account deficit of almost $800 billion in 2005, the U.S. Department of Commerce reports that its investment position worsened by only $330 billion.

The strengthening of the dollar during 2005 also lowered the value of U.S.-owned assets abroad, leading to a further deterioration of the U.S. net international investment position. Nevertheless, the local currency capital gains that the United States earned on its investments in foreign bonds and equities substantially exceeded the capital gains that foreigners had on their U.S. assets, which reduced the deterioration in the U.S. net international investment position that would have been implied by its current account deficit. The continuing globalization of the world economy has made the outstanding stocks of foreign assets and liabilities much larger than they used to be, causing such valuation effects to be relatively more important than they once were. See Pierre-Olivier Gourinchas and Hélène Rey, 2005, and Philip Lane and Gian Maria Milesi-Ferretti, 2005, for recent analyses stressing the importance of these valuation effects.

Many economists worry about the large negative international investment position of the United States because they worry about its implications for the U.S. current account. In theory, the magnitude of a country's international investment position should determine the balance on the investment income account. For example, suppose that interest on all assets is 5%. Then, a –$2,539 billion net international investment position implies a deficit on the international investment income account of 0.05 × $2,539 billion = $126.95 billion.

From Exhibit 4.4, though, we see that the United States had a surplus on its investment account in 2005. In fact, until very recently, the United States managed to combine a negative net international investment position with a surplus on its investment account. Some economists called it the best deal in international finance: Americans borrowed trillions of dollars from abroad to buy big SUVs and build fancy homes, but as their international debts mounted, the nation's payments on its net foreign debt barely budged.

Some economists went as far as to suggest that the United States might not really have a negative international investment position. The United States must have some income-producing assets abroad, such as managerial and technological know-how transferred to foreign subsidiaries, that the official statistics have missed. In a 2005 article, economists Ricardo Hausmann and Frederico Sturzenegger call this invisible wealth "dark matter," after the mass in the universe that can be identified only by its gravitational pull.

The truth is more mundane. The U.S. net income balance has remained positive until recently because of a composition effect and a return effect. The composition effect arises because the U.S. portfolio of assets abroad contains a relatively large share of higher-risk, higher-yielding FDI, while a relatively large share of foreign liabilities is made up of lower-risk, lower-yielding portfolio debt. The return effect arises because there has been a large and persistent yield differential between U.S. direct investment abroad and FDI in the United States. One recurring explanation for why the return on U.S. FDI would be relatively high is that FDI in the United States is relatively young compared with U.S. direct investment abroad, and it appears that the income generated by new investments increases over time. A study by the Bank for International Settlements (2006) also suggests that foreign MNCs have tax incentives to minimize income reported in the United States, lowering the measured yield on their investments.

It is rather obvious that as the U.S. net international investment position continues to deteriorate, the net income balance cannot remain in surplus. As a matter of fact, in 2006, the U.S. investment income account turned negative. This has fueled intense debate over the sustainability of the situation.

First, the net international investment position has grown considerably as a percentage of the total wealth of the country. The U.S. Bureau of Economic Analysis estimates total U.S. "tangible" (that is, excluding intangibles such as human capital) wealth at the end of 2006 to be $44,432 billion. Hence, the ratio of the outstanding net foreign liability position, $2,539 billion, to the tangible wealth of the United States is 5.7%. In 1998, this figure was 5.9%. Thus, although the net international investment position has deteriorated substantially, wealth in the U.S. has grown also. When viewed as a percentage of the GDP, the current account deficit in 1998 was less than 3% of GDP, but at the end of 2006, it stood at 6.1% of GDP.

Second, observers are worried about the changing composition of foreigners' claims on the United States. Since 2000, foreigners have primarily bought U.S. bonds, especially Treasury bonds, with central banks in Asia particularly keen on building up official reserves denominated in dollars. So the United States borrows money relatively cheaply and then invests in risky assets. What might happen if foreign central banks suddenly diversify out of U.S. bonds? To better understand the macroeconomic background to these figures, it is necessary to understand the relationship between income, saving, and investment, to which we now turn.

4.4 SAVINGS, INVESTMENT, INCOME, AND THE BOP

In this section we explore how current account surpluses and deficits are linked to the saving and spending patterns of a country, including its government. Understanding these links allows us to see how the policies of different governments around the world affect the international economic environment and the determination of exchange rates, a topic we take up in Chapter 10. The discussion that follows uses the information in a country's **national income and product accounts** (**NIPA**). The appendix to this chapter reviews the most important concepts.

Linking the Current Account to National Income

From NIPA, we know that gross national income (GNI) equals gross domestic product (GDP) plus net foreign income (NFI):

$$\text{Gross national income} = \text{Gross domestic product} + \text{Net foreign income}$$
$$\text{GNI} = \text{GDP} + \text{NFI} \tag{4.3}$$

If we subtract the country's total expenditures—that is, its consumption purchases (C), investment purchases (I), and government purchases (G)—from both sides of Equation (4.3), and we use the definition of GDP as the sum of C, I, G, and NX (net exports), we obtain:

$$\text{Gross national income} - \text{National expenditures} = \text{Net exports} + \text{Net foreign income}$$
$$\text{GNI} - (\text{C} + \text{I} + \text{G}) = \text{GDP} + \text{NFI} - (\text{C} + \text{I} + \text{G}) = \text{NX} + \text{NFI} \tag{4.4}$$

The right-hand side of Equation (4.4) is of course the current account of the balance of payments (CA) because net exports correspond to the overall trade balance, and net foreign income represents the investment account.[2]

Thus, we now have an important national income accounting identity:

$$\text{Gross national income} - \text{National expenditures} = \text{Current account}$$
$$\text{GNI} - (\text{C} + \text{I} + \text{G}) = \text{CA} \tag{4.5}$$

From Equation (4.5) we see that if a country has a current account surplus, it must have national income that exceeds national expenditures. If a country has a current account deficit with the rest of the world, the country's expenditures exceed its income.

Because the overall balance of payments must always balance, if a country has a current account surplus, it must have a capital account deficit. Remember that the capital account records transactions that generate changes in ownership of net foreign assets. Let's denote the stock of net foreign assets by NFA and changes in NFA by ΔNFA. The symbol Δ indicates the change in a stock variable from the end of the previous period to the end of the current period. A capital account deficit means that the debit items on the capital account (increases in the domestic ownership of foreign assets) must outweigh credit items on the capital account

---

[2]In fact, this is true only if we ignore transfers. In our definition of the trade balance, we have included transfers that are not part of net exports but of net foreign income.

(increases in the foreign ownership of domestic assets). Hence, a current account surplus is associated with an increase in net foreign assets. Therefore, we can write

$$\text{Current account} = \text{Change in net foreign assets}$$
$$CA = \Delta NFA \qquad (4.6)$$

If there is a current account surplus, the economy is adding net foreign assets. Substituting from Equation (4.5) into Equation (4.6),

$$\text{National income} - \text{National expenditures} = \text{Change in net foreign assets}$$
$$GNI - (C + I + G) = \Delta NFA \qquad (4.7)$$

This identity makes perfectly good intuitive sense. Just as an individual whose income is greater than her expenditures must be acquiring assets, similarly, if a country has total income that is greater than the country's total expenditures, the country must be acquiring assets. Of course, the only assets that the country can acquire are those of foreign countries. Hence, the country's net foreign assets must increase when its expenditures are less than its income. Viewed this way, the concept of net foreign assets is simply the net debtor or net creditor position of the country.

National Savings, Investment, and the Current Account

Another way to understand the current account is to see that it is the difference between national savings and national investment. If an individual consumes more (less) than her income, her savings are negative (positive). In the case of a country, both the private (C) and public (G) sectors consume. So, by definition, national savings are equal to national income minus the consumption of the private and public sectors:

$$\text{National savings} = \text{Gross national income} - \text{Consumption of the private and public sectors}$$

In symbols, this becomes:

$$S = GNI - C - G \qquad (4.8)$$

After substituting the definition of GNI from Equation (4.3), we find

$$S = GDP + NFI - C - G$$

Substituting the components of GDP gives

$$S = C + I + G + NX + NFI - C - G$$

Upon canceling out the consumption terms and rearranging terms, we find

$$S - I = NX + NFI = CA \qquad (4.9)$$

$$\text{National saving} - \text{National investment} = \text{Current account}$$

If a country's purchases of investment goods are more than its savings, the country must run a current account deficit; that is, the country's investment spending must be financed from abroad with a capital account surplus.

Current Accounts and Government Deficits

It is often argued that current account deficits are caused by government budget deficits. We now show that there is indeed an identity that links current accounts and government budget deficits, although the identity does not at all suggest causality from government budget deficits to current account deficits.

Consider total national savings; it consists of private savings and government savings. Private savings are what is left over after households spend out of their disposable income. Total disposal income for the residents of the country is gross national income, plus the transfer payments received from the various levels of government (TR), plus interest on government debt (iD), but minus taxes (T) paid to the government. Hence, we have

$$\text{National income} + \text{Transfers} + \text{Interest on government debt} - \text{Taxes} = \text{Consumption} + \text{Private saving}$$

Using symbols, we have

$$GNI + TR + iD - T = C + S^P \qquad \textbf{(4.10)}$$

where S^P is private savings. But we know that GNI is linked to the current account:

$$GNI = C + I + G + NX + NFI = C + I + G + CA \qquad \textbf{(4.11)}$$

By rearranging terms and canceling the two consumption terms, we find

$$(\text{Private saving} - \text{Investment}) + (\text{Taxes} - \text{Transfers} - \text{Interest on government debt} - \text{Government purchases}) = \text{Current account}$$

or

$$(S^P - I) + (T - TR - iD - G) = CA \qquad \textbf{(4.12)}$$

The first term in parentheses on the left-hand side of Equation (4.12) is **net private saving**, which is the difference between **private saving** and the private sector's expenditures on investment goods. The second term is **national government saving**, which is the **surplus on the government budget**. If there is a deficit on the government budget because total government expenditures (including spending on goods and services, transfer payments, and interest on government debt) exceed taxes, government saving is negative. There are a number of ways to interpret Equation (4.12).

If the current account is negative, private savings are inadequate to finance both private investment purchases and the government budget deficit. Therefore, foreign funds (borrowing from the rest of the world in the form of an accumulation of foreign debt) are required. Equation (4.12) also indicates that the government and private industry are competitors in capital markets for the pool of private savings: If the government borrows more of that capital, there is less capital available for private investment.

Because Equation (4.12) is an identity, a government budget deficit must be matched by some combination of higher private saving, lower investment, or a current account deficit. So it is quite conceivable that a large government deficit will be associated with a large current account deficit. This was the case in the United States, for example, during the 1980–1985 period, when the federal budget deficit coincided with a large current account deficit. But must it be the case?

What Causes Current Account Deficits and Surpluses?

Why did France run a current account deficit during most of the 1980s but a current account surplus in the 1990s, whereas the opposite happened in Germany (refer to Exhibit 4.6)? The discussion in this section reveals that it must be related to savings and investment decisions by the citizens and governments of these countries.

Let's start with governments. If a government chooses not to finance its current purchases of goods and services, its transfer payments, and the interest payments on outstanding government debt from its current tax receipts, the government must either issue more government debt to be held by the public or print money. On the other hand, if current tax receipts exceed current government outlays, government debt can be retired or money can be removed from the economy.

To induce investors to hold its debt, a government must pay a competitive interest rate on its outstanding stock of government bonds. In the future, though, these interest payments must be financed through some form of taxation, including possibly money creation. For every dollar of taxes not raised this period, the government must raise 1 dollar plus interest in the future. This long-run budget constraint is called an **intertemporal budget constraint**.

Hence, we are left with a puzzle. Why does a country's government not balance its current total expenditures with its current tax receipts? The answer is that the economic costs of distortions due to taxes are minimized if the government sets permanent tax rates that balance the government budget only over the long run and not every period. Roughly, this appears to be what governments try to do.

Suppose, for example, there were a recession. During a recession, people's incomes fall, so the government's tax revenues fall as well. Hence, if the government were to attempt to balance the budget during the recession, it would have to cut spending and increase tax rates. However, governments are often reluctant to cut spending because spending stimulates the economy. Raising taxes during a recession is also likely to put a serious damper on the economy and would be politically unpalatable. Therefore, instead of adjusting their spending and tax rates, governments tend to run deficits during recessions and surpluses during economic booms.

Ricardian Equivalence

Another serious problem in understanding how government budget deficits affect the economic behavior of the overall economy is the important idea of **Ricardian equivalence** between government debt and taxes.[3] The issue is the extent to which taxpayers look into the future and see their future tax liabilities increasing when the government runs a deficit (that is, the government dissaves). If private saving increases one for one with any government budget deficit, budget deficits have no real effect. In particular, from Equation (4.12) we see that the current account of the balance of payments would not be affected by government saving and dissaving if taxpayers are Ricardian. Alternatively, it may be that taxpayers feel wealthier when governments run budget deficits because some future generation is going to have to pay the increased taxes. In this case, government budget deficits reduce national savings and cause current account deficits.

Individuals' Intemporal Budget Constraints

Individuals are also subject to intertemporal budget constraints when it comes to their consumption and savings decisions. The decision of how much to work, how much to consume, and how to invest any accumulated wealth is heavily influenced by the prices and opportunities that individuals have in current markets and by their expectations of what those prices and opportunities are likely to be in the future. For example, high interest rates might induce people to save more rather than to consume. And good investment opportunities in other countries might lead to a capital outflow.

Investment Spending

The last of the components that determine the current account is private investment in businesses and residential housing. Businesses continually evaluate investment projects. They contemplate adding new product lines and changing their scales of operation to generate additional future income. When firms consider investment projects, they are subject to an intertemporal

---

[3]The effect is named after the economist David Ricardo (1772–1823), who first analyzed arguments for the equivalence of government debt and taxes in his *Principles of Political Economy and Taxation* (1817). Although the effect bears his name, Ricardo did not believe that the result would hold in actual economies. In particular, he argued that high public debt could create an incentive for both labor and capital to migrate abroad to avoid future taxes necessary to service the public debt. See Ricardo (1951), pp. 247–249.

budget constraint as well. An investment project is worth doing only if it is a positive net present value project. We will explain this concept in more detail in Chapter 15; for now, assume that it means that the project's expected return in future periods must provide adequate compensation to those who have supplied the capital to the firm. Put differently, businesses invest in new projects by purchasing new plants and equipment when managers believe the returns on projects will be high relative to the cost of capital required to launch them. Analogously, new residential housing is constructed only when expected rents in the future provide the developer with an expected return that exceeds the cost of the project. The cost of funding a project rises with higher interest rates so that higher interest rates typically decrease investments.

Investment expenditures are also highly pro-cyclical because during expansions in the business cycle, businesses perceive the expected returns on investments to be large relative to the cost of capital. When a country is growing rapidly, much current investment is required to provide the goods and services that people will demand in the future. If a country's growth prospects slow down, or if there is fear of possible tax increases on the income earned from capital, investment will decline. When the desired investments by the businesses of a particular country exceed the desired savings of its citizens and government, the country must borrow from abroad and run a current account deficit.

As you can see, it is very difficult to disentangle the exact determinants of the current account because it depends on so many individual decisions. Taxes, interest rates, the relative expected investment returns in different countries, and business cycles all play a role.

POINT-COUNTERPOINT

Is the U.S. Current Account Deficit Excessive?

It is a sunny Sunday afternoon in New York, and Ante and Freedy Handel are enjoying some Central Park greenery at the Boathouse Café while digesting a refreshing beer. Ante is perusing some statistics on the bilateral U.S.–Japan and U.S.–China current account deficits for his international finance class, when he suddenly blurts out, "This is a crazy, untenable situation. If we do not do something about this U.S. current account deficit, the dollar will tank. Did you know that these large cumulative deficits have made the United States a huge debtor relative to the rest of the world?"

Because Freedy was enjoying the sunshine too much to put up a fight, Ante was able to continue: "The Japanese protect their businesses and dump their products here at cheap prices to keep their workers employed. The Chinese simply exploit their workers, making them work long hours for next to nothing. That is the main cause of it all: unfair competition. I tell you what we should do. We should slap tariffs on these Japanese and Chinese products. We have got to force them to open up their markets more to American products or pay the price. We should refuse to trade with China as long as it doesn't enact decent social laws for its workers."

Now, Freedy had finally had too much. He countered, "Ante, you can't be serious. Free trade has been the cornerstone of world economic growth for the past few decades, and you propose to turn back the clock? The U.S. current account deficit does not matter at all. Remember, it is just national savings minus national investment. Americans do not save very much, and they love to consume foreign goods and gadgets. They are enjoying the current account deficit enormously. Look at the beer you are drinking. It isn't Budweiser, my friend, but a much better-tasting Belgian Stella. Besides, the flip side of the current account deficit is the capital account surplus; that just means that foreigners are buying U.S. stocks and bonds more than Americans are investing overseas. Do you know why? Foreigners buy U.S. assets because they are considered to be very attractive investments with high expected returns."

"Wow, I never heard you spout so much," blurted Ante. "It must be that foreign beer! I cling to my story. If we do not clean this mess up, we will be sorry one day because it already costs $5 for this Stella, and soon it will be $10."

Freedy was about to answer, when a familiar voice shouted, "Hey, guys, what are you up to?" As Suttle Trooth walked up to their table, Freedy said. "Hey, look Ante, he's drinking foreign beer, too, although it's only a Heineken. I see that deficit going up even more!"

After hearing the topic of discussion, Suttle said, "Well guys, this time you picked an important and complex issue. Let me tell you what I think. Ante, you cite the lack of openness of foreign markets as a cause of U.S. large trade balance deficit. Such an argument misses the point that the Chinese savings rate is much larger than the U.S. savings rate, and the Japanese savings rate used to be much higher. It is not clear how more openness in Chinese and Japanese markets would change the excess of gross savings over gross investment in those countries or America."

Freedy is definitely right that current account deficits reflect an imbalance between savings and investment. For instance, Chinese government policies may indeed have a rather profound effect on the saving rate of its citizens, which is now close to 50%. For example, a better social safety net would reduce the need to save as much for a rainy day.

A good first perspective to see if a current account deficit is good or bad is to check the source of the deficit. Is there too much investment perhaps, or too little savings? In the latter case, maybe it's good to differentiate private savings from government savings or the budget deficit. The bottom line is that if we are to understand the current account, we must understand the determinants of private saving, private investment, and government budget surpluses and deficits.

Perhaps U.S. consumers currently find interest rates and the expected returns on assets too low to induce them to reduce consumption and increase their savings. It might also be that the United States represents a very attractive investment opportunity for foreign and U.S. investors alike. Hence, it is conceivable that the U.S. current account reflects a large pool of profitable investment opportunities that cannot be financed by domestic savings alone, given the consumption preferences of U.S. citizens.

To sum up, when a country runs a current account deficit, it borrows from foreigners. If the foreign funds are profitably invested, there is no reason for concern. These investments will increase domestic growth and generate returns that can be used to pay off the foreign debt.

This is not always the case, though. Many economists argue that the large current account deficits in Southeast Asia in the mid-1990s were unsustainable because they represented investment projects that offered low or negative returns. Also, many of the projects were in the real estate sector, which doesn't generate the foreign currency needed to repay foreign debt. In the early 1990s in Mexico, large government deficits were coupled with a boom in private consumption, which also led to unsustainable current account deficits.

Of course, it is true that Americans do not save very much, and the Chinese do. Japan's savings rate has halved over the past 20 years, and its government now runs big government deficits. Yet Japan still runs a large current account surplus. Perhaps the situation will reverse itself automatically as soon as Japanese investment demand picks up. Come to think of it, this example shows that government deficits and surpluses do not automatically create current account deficits and surpluses. Nevertheless, the fact that the United States now runs large government deficits cannot exactly help close the U.S. current account deficit.

Many of the concerns that apply to less-developed countries also do not apply to the United States. Those countries have foreign-currency-denominated debt. That means they have to earn foreign currency to pay back the debt, and if they cannot, a genuine crisis results. For the United States, foreigners often accept dollars in payment and hold dollar-denominated assets, so the United States can simply pay back in its own currency. Of course, Ante is right that the cumulative deficits could become so large that foreigners suddenly perceive the debt to be unsustainable and refuse to further finance U.S. current account deficits. If that happens, Ante is probably right that the dollar would likely depreciate to induce higher expected returns on U.S. assets and to make U.S. goods more attractive to foreigners so that the current account deficit can be reversed. One reason for concern therefore is that a good portion of the recent deficits have been financed by the Japanese and Chinese central banks buying Treasury bonds. They may no longer be willing to hold such large positions in U.S. bonds.

Suttle said, "There is inherently nothing good or bad about a current account deficit. Personally, I think emerging markets should run current account deficits because they have better growth opportunities than the developed world. It makes sense for them to import foreign capital to help them grow. Clearly, as the many recent crises have amply demonstrated, though, this growth strategy is not without problems."

"Thanks, Suttle," said Ante. "Now, I feel much more comfortable drinking foreign beer. Let's have another one."

Assessing the Openness of International Capital Markets

In a closed economy, national saving and national investment are forced to move together. When two variables move perfectly together, statisticians say their correlation is one. However, access to international capital markets allows the correlation between national savings and national investment to be less than one. An increase in savings can finance a foreign project rather than a domestic one, and domestic investment can be conducted by raising funds from the savings of other countries rather than from domestic savings.

In an important, but controversial, article in 1980, Martin Feldstein and Charles Horioka demonstrated that there was a very strong correlation between the average national savings rate and the average national investment rate in 16 countries. This suggests that countries with relatively high average savings rates also have relatively high investment rates. Feldstein and Horioka concluded that international capital markets were not very open and international capital mobility was quite low during their sample period. More recent studies largely confirm the significant positive correlation between the national savings rates and national investment rates of developed countries. Are the Feldstein and Horioka findings that international capital markets are not very open accurate? Or can the data be interpreted another way? There are several important caveats to the Feldstein and Horioka interpretation that have been noted in the literature. One line of argument asserts that the high correlation between savings and investment could be produced by common forces that move both variables even though the international capital market is open and competitive. For example, Maurice Obstfeld (1986) argues that high rates of population growth tend to lead to high investment because capital is needed to equip young workers. But young workers also must save for their retirements. However, if the population is growing, its demographic makeup will be such that the savings of the young will outweigh the "dissaving," or spending, of older, retired generations. Hence, both saving and investment will be higher in quickly growing countries than in slowly growing countries.

Other authors (see Marianne Baxter and Mario Crucini, 1993; and Enrique Mendoza, 1991) argue that economic shocks affecting productivity can increase both saving and investment over the business cycle. The argument goes like this: An increase in productivity causes output and income to increase. Some of the increase in income is consumed, but some of it is saved because the shock is not expected to be permanent. But because productivity is temporarily high and is expected to be high for awhile, it is also a good time to invest. Hence, investment and saving both increase.

Finally, Jeffrey Frankel (1991) has argued that high correlations between national investment rates and national saving rates should not really be surprising because the world economy during the 1960s, 1970s, and even much of the 1980s and 1990s was not characterized by perfect capital mobility. That is, capital markets were not completely open around the world. For example, there were significant barriers to international investment in many European countries and Japan that persisted well into the 1980s. (See also Chapter 1.) Hence, it would stand to reason that in countries in which the saving rates are high, investment rates would be high as well because there is nowhere else for the capital to go. Frankel argues that to assess how integrated the world's capital markets are, we must look at the various rates of return offered around the world and not merely the flows of saving and investment stressed by Feldstein and Horioka. We examine the evidence about international capital market equilibrium in Chapter 13.

4.5 SUMMARY

This chapter introduced the concepts associated with a country's balance of payments and its net international investment position and examined how these concepts are related to national income and product accounts. Knowledge of this information is useful in discussions of the determination of exchange rates. The main points in the chapter are the following:

1. A country's balance of payments records the economic transactions between its residents and government and those of the rest of the world.
2. There are two major accounts on the balance of payments: the current account and the capital account.
3. The current account records transactions in goods and services, transactions that are associated with the income flows from asset stocks, and unilateral transfers.
4. The capital account, which is also called the financial account in some presentations of the BOP, records the purchases and sales of assets, that is changes in the domestic ownership of the assets of other nations and in the foreign ownership of assets of the domestic country.
5. The balance of payments uses a double-entry accounting system. Each transaction gives rise to two entries—a credit and a debit of equal value.
6. The purchases of goods and assets by foreign residents from domestic residents are recorded as credits. Credit transactions result in an inflow, or source, of foreign currency.
7. The purchases of goods and assets by domestic residents from foreign residents are debits. Debit transactions result in an outflow, or use, of foreign currency.
8. Sales of domestic goods and services to foreign residents are domestic exports. Sales of domestic assets to foreigners are capital inflows to the home country. Both types of transaction are credits on the domestic balance of payments.
9. Purchases of foreign goods and services by domestic residents are domestic imports. Purchases of foreign assets by domestic residents are capital outflows from the home country. Both types of transaction are debits on the domestic balance of payments.

10. If the sum of the credits on a particular account is greater than the sum of the debits on that account, the account is said to be in surplus. If the sum of the debits on a particular account is greater than credits on that account, the account is said to be in deficit.
11. The current account is sometimes decomposed into the sum of the trade account and the international investment income account. The trade account is a broader concept than the merchandise trade balance because the former includes trade in economic services such as education, banking, tourism, shipping, insurance, and transfers, whereas the latter does not.
12. International reserves are the assets of a country's central bank that are not denominated in the domestic currency. Gold and assets denominated in foreign currency are the typical international reserves.
13. The official settlements account of the capital account measures changes in the international reserves that a country's central bank holds. If a central bank wants to maintain a fixed exchange rate, it must use its international reserves to fix the price of the domestic currency in terms of a foreign currency. International reserves will rise and fall with the surpluses and deficits on the current account and the private capital account.
14. Because many balance of payments entries are estimated, the sum of the current account and the capital account does not always equal zero as it should in a double-entry system. If the sum of the current and capital accounts is not zero, statisticians add a balancing item equal to the sum of all the measured items with the sign reversed. This term is called the statistical discrepancy or errors and omissions.
15. The balance of payments records flows of goods and assets over a period of time, just like the income statement of a firm. By analogy, just as a firm has a balance sheet, at a point in time, a country owns a certain stock of foreign assets, and foreigners own a certain stock of domestic assets. The difference between the values of these two stocks is called net foreign assets. Consequently, at any given point in time, a country has an international investment

position; it is either a net creditor or a net debtor with the rest of the world.

16. The value of all the final goods and services produced within a country is called the country's gross domestic product (GDP).

17. The value of what is produced in a country must be purchased either by domestic residents or foreign residents. Hence, the country's total consumption purchases, C, plus its total government purchases, G, plus its total investment purchases, I, plus the value of its net exports, NX, must equal its GDP: GDP = C + I + G + NX

18. The value of all the final goods and services must be paid to factors of production. In an open economy, net factor income from abroad (NFI) from either labor that works in foreign countries or capital that is invested in foreign countries provides a flow of resources that separates gross national income (GNI) from GDP (GNI = GDP + NFI).

19. By subtracting a country's total expenditures on consumption, investment, and government purchases from its gross national income, we are left with net exports plus net factor income from abroad, which is equal to the current account (CA) of the balance of payments: GNI − (C + I + G) = CA.

20. If a country has a current account surplus, it must have national income that exceeds national expenditures. If a country has a current account deficit, the country's expenditures exceed its income.

21. The owners of a country's factors of production receive its national income plus transfer payments from the government and interest on government debt, but they must pay taxes to the government. After-tax disposable income must be either spent on consumption or saved in some form of asset: GNI + TR + iD − T = C + S.

22. Net private saving, which is the private saving in excess of expenditures on investment goods plus national government saving, which is taxes minus total government spending or the surplus on the government budget, equals the current account of the balance of payments.

23. Because national savings and national investment decisions affect a country's current account, interest rates and other rates of return around the world influence, and in turn are influenced by, the current account.

24. Martin Feldstein and Charles Horioka demonstrated that there is a very strong cross-sectional correlation between the national savings rate and the national investment rate of countries. They argued that this is evidence of strong international capital market imperfections, but there is a large debate regarding this interpretation.

QUESTIONS

1. What are the major accounts of the balance of payments, and what transactions are recorded on each account?

2. Why is it important for an international manager to understand the balance of payments?

3. What are the rules that determine the residency requirements on the balance of payments?

4. Which items on the balance of payments are recorded as credits, and which items are recorded as debits? Why?

5. How are gifts and grants handled in the balance of payments?

6. What does it mean for a country to experience a capital inflow? Is this associated with a surplus or a deficit on the country's capital account?

7. If you add up all the current accounts of all countries in the world, the sum should be zero. Yet this is not so. Why?

8. What is the investment income account of the balance of payments?

9. What is the official settlements account of the balance of payments? How are official settlements deficits and surpluses associated with movements in the international reserves of the balance of payments?

10. What is the meaning of an account labeled "statistical discrepancy" or "errors and omissions"? If this account is a credit, what does that imply about the measurement of other items in the balance of payments?

11. Why must the national income of a closed economy equal the national expenditures of that economy? What separates the two concepts in an open economy?

12. Explain why private national saving plus government saving equals the current account of the balance of payments.

13. It has been argued that the high correlation between national saving and national investment that Feldstein and Horioka first measured in 1980 is not evidence of imperfect capital mobility. What arguments can you offer for why they might have misinterpreted the data, and what do recent investigations of this issue imply about the degree of capital mobility throughout the world?

PROBLEMS

1. Suppose that the following transactions take place on the U.S. balance of payments during a given year. Analyze the effects on the merchandise trade balance, the international investment income account, the current account, the capital account, and the official settlements account.

   a. Boeing, a U.S. aerospace company, sells $3 billion of its 747 airplanes to the People's Republic of China, which pays with proceeds from a loan from a consortium of international banks.

   b. Nikko, a Japanese investment bank, purchases $70 million of 30-year U.S. Treasury bonds for one of its Japanese clients. Nikko draws down its account with the First National Bank of Chicago to pay for the bonds.

   c. General Motors, a U.S. automobile company, sends a dividend check for $25,255 to a Canadian investor in Toronto. The Canadian investor deposits the check in a U.S. dollar-denominated bank account at the Bank of Montreal.

   d. The U.S. Treasury authorizes the New York Federal Reserve Bank to intervene in the foreign exchange market. The New York Fed purchases $5 billion with Japanese yen and euros that it holds as international reserves.

   e. The president of the United States sends troops into a Latin American country to establish a democratic government. The total operation costs U.S. taxpayers $8.5 billion. To show their support for the operation, the governments of Mexico and Brazil each donate $1 billion to the United States, which they raise by selling U.S. Treasury bonds that they were holding as international reserves.

   f. Honda of America, the U.S. subsidiary of the Japanese automobile manufacturer, obtains $275 million from its parent company in Japan in the form of a loan to enable it to construct a new state-of-the-art manufacturing facility in Ohio.

2. Consider the situation of La Nación, a hypothetical Latin American country. In 2006, La Nación was a net debtor to the rest of the world. Assume that all of La Nación's foreign debt was dollar denominated, and at the end of 2006, its net private foreign debt was $75 billion and the official foreign debt of La Nación's treasury was $55 billion. Suppose that the interest rate on these debts was 2.5% per annum (p.a.) over the London Interbank Offering Rate (LIBOR), and no principal payments were due in 2007. International reserves of the Banco de Nación, La Nación's central bank, were equal to $18 billion at

the end of 2006 and earn interest at LIBOR. There were no other net foreign assets in the country. Because La Nación is growing very rapidly, there is great demand for investment goods in La Nación. Suppose that residents of La Nación would like to import $37 billion of goods during 2007. Economists indicate that the value of La Nación's exports is forecast to be $29 billion of goods during 2007. Suppose that the Banco de Nación is prepared to see its international reserves fall to $5 billion during 2007. The LIBOR rate for 2007 is 4% p.a.

   a. What is the minimum net capital inflow during 2007 that La Nación must have if it wants to see the desired imports and exports occur and wants to avoid having its international reserves fall below the desired level?

   b. If this capital inflow occurs, what will La Nación's total net foreign debt be at the end of 2007?

3. True or false: A trade balance deficit can never have a capital account deficit as its counterpart under truly flexible exchange rates (that is, the government does not intervene to fix the price of foreign exchange). Explain your answer.

4. True or false: If a country is a net debtor to the rest of the world, its international investment service account is in deficit. Explain your answer.

5. Choose a country and analyze its balance of payments for the past 10 years. Good sources of data include official bulletins of the statistical authority of a country or its central banks; *International Financial Statistics*, which is a publication of the IMF (www.imf.org), and the *Main Economic Indicators*, which is a publication of the Organization for Economic Co-operation and Development (www.oecd. org).

   a. Examine how trade in goods and services has evolved over time. Is the country becoming more or less competitive in world markets?

   b. Consider the relationship between the country's net foreign asset position and its international investment income account.

   c. If the country has run a current account deficit, what capital inflows have financed the deficit? If the country has run a current account surplus, how have the capital outflows been invested?

6. Pick a country and search the internet for newspaper or magazine articles that contain information related to the balance of payments of the country and corresponding movements in the foreign exchange value of the country's currency. Does an unexpectedly large

current account deficit cause the country's currency to strengthen or weaken on the foreign exchange market?

7. What are the effects on the British balance of payments of the following set of transactions? U.K. Videos imports £24 million of movies from the U.S. firm Twenty-First Century Wolf (TFCW). The payment is denominated in pounds, is drawn on a British bank, and is deposited in the London branch of a U.S. bank by TFCW because TFCW anticipates purchasing a film studio in the United Kingdom in the near future.

8. What are the effects on the French balance of payments of the following set of transactions? Les Fleurs de France, the French subsidiary of a British company, The Flowers of Britain, has just received €4.4 million of additional investment from its British parent. Part of the investment is a €0.9 million computer system that was shipped from Britain directly. The €3.5 million remainder was financed by the parent by issuing euro denominated Eurobonds to investors outside of France. Les Fleurs de France is holding these euros in its Paris bank account.

9. In December 1994, a major earthquake rocked Kobe, Japan, destroying the housing stock of more than 300,000 people and ruining bridges, highways, and railroad tracks. What impact, if any, do you think this event had on the Japanese current account deficit? Why?

10. After running high current account surpluses in the second half of the 1980s, Germany ran sizable deficits in the early 1990s. The most important reason for the current account deficit was the surge in demand from eastern Germany after reunification, causing imports to rise sharply. At the same time, Germany went from being a net creditor country to being a net debtor. Explain why this is a logical implication of the current account deficits. Interest rates in Germany were historically high during this period. Why might that have been the case? Could East Germany have been developed without running a current account deficit? How?

BIBLIOGRAPHY

Abel, Andrew B., and Ben S. Bernanke, 2004, *Macroeconomics*, 5th ed., Reading, MA: Addison-Wesley.

Barro, Robert J., 1993, *Macroeconomics*, 4th ed., New York: Wiley.

Baxter, Marianne, and Mario J. Crucini, 1993, "Explaining Saving–Investment Correlations," *American Economic Review* 83, pp. 416–436.

Bank for International Settlements (BIS), 2006, *76th Annual Report*, Basle, Switzerland: BIS.

Coakley, Jerry, Farida Hasan, and Ron Smith, 1999, "Saving, Investment, and Capital Mobility in LDCs," *Review of International Economics* 7, pp. 632–640.

Eisner, Robert, and Paul Pieper, 1984, "A New View of the Federal Debt and Budget Deficits," *American Economic Review* 74, pp. 11–29.

Feldstein, Martin, and Philippe Bacchetta, 1991, "National Savings and International Investment," in B. Douglas Bernheim and John B. Shoven, eds., *National Saving and Economic Performance*, Chicago: University of Chicago Press, pp. 201–220.

Feldstein, Martin, and Charles Horioka, 1980, "Domestic Savings and International Capital Flows," *Economic Journal* 90, pp. 314–329.

Frankel, Jeffrey A., 1991, "Quantifying International Capital Mobility in the 1980's," in B. Douglas Bernheim and John B. Shoven, eds., *National Saving and Economic Performance*, Chicago: University of Chicago Press, pp. 227–260.

Froot, Kenneth A., ed., 1993, *Foreign Direct Investment*, Chicago: The University of Chicago Press for the National Bureau of Economic Research.

Gourinchas, Pierre-Olivier, and Hélène Rey, 2005, "International Financial Adjustment," National Bureau of Economic Research working paper 11155.

Hausmann, Ricardo, and Frederico Sturzenegger, 2005, "U.S. and Global Imbalances: Can Dark Matter Prevent a Big Bang?" Harvard University working paper.

International Monetary Fund (IMF), 1993, *Balance of Payments Manual*, Washington, DC: IMF.

International Monetary Fund, 1989–2004, *World Economic Outlook*, Washington, DC: IMF.

Lane, Philip R., and Gian Maria Milesi-Ferretti, August 2005, "A Global Perspective on External Positions," IMF working paper.

Mendoza, Enrique G., 1991, "Real Business Cycles in a Small Open Economy," *American Economic Review* 81, pp. 797–818.

Motala, John, 1997, "Statistical Discrepancies in the World Current Account," *Finance and Development,* pp. 24–25.

Nguyen, Elena L., 2006, "The International Investment Position of the United States at Yearend 2005," *Survey of Current Business,* pp. 9–19.

Obstfeld, Maurice, 1986, "Capital Mobility in the World Economy: Theory and Measurement," *Carnegie-Rochester Conference Series on Public Policy* 24, pp. 55–104.

Obstfeld, Maurice, and Kenneth Rogoff, 1994, "The Intertemporal Approach to the Current Account," National Bureau of Economic Research working paper no. 4893.

Obstfeld, Maurice, and Alan M. Taylor, 2004, *Global Capital Markets: Integration, Crisis, and Growth,* Japanese–U.S. Center Sanwa Monographs on International Financial Markets. Cambridge, UK: Cambridge University Press.

Organization for Economic Co-operation and Development, 2006, *OECD Factbook 2006*, Brussels, Belgium: OECD.

Organization for Economic Co-operation and Development, National Accounts, Brussels, Belgium: OECD.

Ott, Mack, 1989, "Is America Being Sold Out?" *Review*, Federal Reserve Bank of St. Louis, pp. 47–64.

Ricardo, David, 1817, *On the Principles of Political Economy and Taxation*, London: John Murray.

Ricardo, David, 1951, *On the Principles of Political Economy and Taxation*, Piero Sraffa, ed., Cambridge, UK: Cambridge University Press.

Taylor, Alan M., 1994, "Domestic Saving and International Capital Flows Reconsidered," National Bureau of Economic Research working paper no. 4892.

United Nations (UN), National Accounts Statistics, New York: The UN.

U.S. Department of Commerce, *Survey of Current Business*, various issues dealing with direct foreign investment and the international investment position of the United States, which is typically reported in the August issue.

U.S. Department of Commerce, 1990, *The U.S. Balance of Payments: Concepts, Data Sources, and Estimating Procedures.* Washington, DC: U.S. Government Printing Office.

Appendix

A Primer on National Income and

The **natio**
resources o
the country
for their fu
accumulati
sure their n
States, nat
income a
reported by
income ac
the *Nation*
Cooperati
National A

There
production
a quarter
accrue to
and capita
idents of
services.
of final go
of all the
within a c
domestic
capital go
depreciat
country p

uctures that have worn out during a given period. cting a measure of this depreciation from a coun- DP gives us a country's net domestic product. In ollows, however, we will ignore depreciation and on GDP.

s Domestic Production
Expenditures

ases of goods and services fall under four general ries of expenditures: personal consumption expen- s, gross private domestic investment, government ases, and net exports of goods and services.

sumption Expenditures (C)

ersonal consumption expenditures of domestic res- s are the purchases of final goods (such as cars and ng) and services (such as education or the imputed value of owner-occupied housing). In most devel- countries, roughly two-thirds of GDP is purchased mestic consumers.

ss Private Domestic Investment (I)

s private domestic investment includes investment orporations (that is, purchases of new machines buildings), residential investment (including the construction of both single family homes, and multifamily buildings such as apartments), and the change in business inventories. Business inventories are stocks of finished goods, goods in process, and raw materials for the production process. The change in business inventories measures the investment firms have made in the current period to improve the firms' profitability in future periods. For example, if firms add finished goods to their stocks of inventories, this is positive investment, and if firms draw down their stocks of finished goods, this is negative investment. In developed countries, gross private domestic investment (I) ranges between 15% and 30% of GDP.

Government Purchases (G)

The different levels of government of a country—federal, state or provincial, and local—purchase a substantial amount of the final goods and services that are produced in a country. In the United States, government purchases of goods and services equal approximately 20% of GDP, but in a small European country, such as Sweden, they equal approximately 25%.

Overall outlays of the federal government, which are the total expenditures in the government budget, are much larger than a government's purchases of goods and services. This is because federal government outlays include transfer payments and interest on the federal debt. Examples of transfer payments in the United States include Social Security, Medicare benefits, and welfare. Although these programs provide income to the recipients of the transfers, the programs do not provide additional income to the economy. The government merely taxes some individuals in the economy and transfers the money to other individuals in the economy.

Net Exports (NX)

If the economy were completely closed to international trade, the value of what is produced as final goods and services would equal the value of the purchases of goods and services for consumption, investment, and government. What is produced as a final good would either be sold to someone in the economy or placed into business inventories. But in an open economy, the foreign sector can buy some of an economy's final goods and services. In the United States, the fraction of exports to GDP sold to foreigners is lower than in many other major countries, but it has been growing rapidly and now exceeds 10% of GDP. In a smaller, more open economy, such as that of Sweden, the fraction of exports to GDP is almost 40%.

Because the consumers, businesses, and various governmental organizations of a country need not limit their expenditures to goods and services that are produced in that country, part of a country's total purchases of goods and services for consumption, investment, and government will be imports of foreign goods and services. Net exports are exports minus imports, and they roughly correspond to the trade balance concept introduced in Section 4.1.

Gross Domestic Product and Expenditures

Our discussion of the relationship between the value of what is produced in a country and the purchases of various goods and services by individuals in the country can be summarized in our first fundamental national income identity:

Gross domestic product = Consumption + Investment + Government + Net exports

or, using symbols:

$$GDP = C + I + G + NX \qquad (4A.1)$$

Basically, this equation states that the value of what is produced in a country, GDP, equals the total purchases of final goods and services of individuals, firms, and the government of the country plus the purchases by foreigners of domestic exports, but minus the value of what is imported into the country because these are goods and services that are not produced in the country. There are of course serious measurement issues in quantifying GDP.

In 2006, the Greek statistical office reminded us of this fact by suddenly declaring GDP to be 25% higher. The change was designed to better capture a fast-growing service sector, including parts of the illegal economy, such as prostitution and money laundering. Although this led the Financial Times to write "Oldest profession helps boost Greek national output by 25%," the potential consequences were quite important: The higher GDP meant that the ratio of Greece's budget deficit to its GDP would also be lower. Thus, Greece would not be subject to certain European Union (EU) limits on the size of this ratio. However, the higher Greek GDP also meant that Greece would lose some financial aid from the EU.

From Gross Domestic Product to Gross National Income

In a closed economy, the value of GDP must equal the income of the factors of production in the economy. Thus, the value of what is produced domestically (GDP) would equal the gross national income (GNI) of the country. In an open economy that trades and invests with other countries in the world, GNI need not equal GDP.

There are three reasons why GNI does not equal GDP in an open economy. First, the capital and labor used to produce the goods in the domestic country need not be owned by domestic residents. Hence, the income that accrues to the factors of production used in producing goods in the country would go to foreign residents and not domestic residents.

For example, Germany has historically imported many temporary workers from eastern Europe. These foreign workers take substantial amounts of their wage income back to their home countries. Similarly, in most countries, some fraction of the capital stock that is used to produce output in the country is owned by foreign residents. In the United States, Japanese car manufacturers have made substantial investments in production facilities. As a result, many of the Toyotas and Hondas sold in the United States are actually "made in America" with American labor, but the income attributable to the capital stock goes to the owners of the equity of these firms, who are primarily Japanese.

The second related reason why GDP does not equal GNI in an open economy is that capital and labor owned by the country can be located and used to produce goods in different countries. Hence, the income of the residents of the country is augmented relative to the value of the goods produced in the country by the income from these factors of production located abroad. For example, Japan has a large capital investment in foreign countries that adds to its income. Pakistan also generates important income from workers who supply labor in other countries. In recent years, Ireland's GDP has been much higher than its GNI because the country has attracted a great deal of foreign investment, drawn to Ireland by its low corporate tax rates. Consequently, much of Ireland's GDP is accounted for by non-Irish factors of production.

The third reason why GNI does not equal GDP is that the country may receive unilateral transfers (gifts and grants) from abroad or may give unilateral transfers to other countries. Gifts from abroad increase a country's income.

In summary, in an open economy, net factor income from abroad plus net unilateral transfers from abroad, which we combine and define as **net foreign income (NFI)**, provide a flow of resources that separates the income of the country from the value of final goods and services produced in a country. Thus, we have our second open-economy national income accounting identity:

Gross national income = Gross domestic product + Net foreign income

$$GNI = GDP + NFI \qquad (A.2)$$

Notice that both net factor income and net unilateral transfers from abroad can be either positive or negative. Hence, net foreign income can be either positive or negative.

For many countries, such as the United States and Japan, the primary source of net factor income from abroad is the asset income generated by the country's net international investment position.

5

Exchange Rate Systems

*C*urrencies such as the euro, the yen, and the dollar trade freely in the world's foreign exchange markets, and their values fluctuate from minute to minute. Monetary authorities in Hong Kong, on the other hand, have kept the Hong Kong dollar at HKD7.80 = USD1 since 1983. Between these extremes of freely floating exchange rates and fully fixed exchange rates are a wide variety of exchange rate systems. Understanding how these systems differ is critically important because the differences affect the currency risks that international businesses face.

This chapter examines the many different currency arrangements in place around the world and considers their pros and cons. An important part of this discussion involves understanding the key role that central banks and their international reserves play in the exchange rate system of any country.

This chapter also describes how European countries created the European Monetary Union and came to adopt the euro as a common currency. This discussion is topical for three reasons. First, other countries continue to adopt the euro as their currency; second, other groups of countries in other parts of the world may someday follow a similar scheme; and third, some European politicians would do away with the euro and return to domestic currencies. Understanding the constraints that adopting the euro has placed on different countries helps us consider the desirability of such a system.

5.1 ALTERNATIVE EXCHANGE RATE ARRANGEMENTS AND CURRENCY RISK

In this section, we first survey the spectrum of existing exchange rate arrangements. Then we summarize how different systems impose different currency risks on international businesses. Finally, we reflect on past and future trends in exchange rate arrangements.

Exchange Rate Systems Around the World

Exhibit 5.1 surveys the current arrangements in place across the world, using information from the International Monetary Fund (IMF).

Although the IMF distinguishes more categories, the exchange rate systems in the world can be split up into roughly three categories: floating currencies, fixed or pegged currencies, and currencies in target zones or crawling pegs.

Floating Currencies
At one extreme are the exchange rate systems in which countries allow the value of their currency to be determined freely in the foreign exchange markets around the world without any

Exhibit 5.1 Exchange Rate Systems Around the World

Fixed Rate System		
No Separate Legal Tender	**Currency Boards**	**Conventional Pegs Against a Single Currency**

No Separate Legal Tender	Currency Boards	Conventional Pegs Against a Single Currency	
Dollarized	Bosnia and Herzegovina	Aruba	Maldives
Ecuador	Brunei Darussalam	Azerbaijan	Mauritania
El Salvador	Bulgaria	The Bahamas	Namibia
Kiribati	Djibouti	Bahrain	Nepal
Marshall Islands	Estonia	Barbados	Netherlands, Antilles
Micronesia	Hong Kong SAR	Belarus	Oman
Palau	Lithuania	Belize	Pakistan
Panama		Bhutan	Qatar
San Marino		Cape Verde	Saudi Arabia
Timor-Leste		Comoros	Seychelles
ECCU		Egypt	Solomon Islands
Antigua and Barbuda		Eritrea	Suriname
Dominica		Guyana	Swaziland
Grenada		Honduras	Syrian Arab Republic
St.Kitts and Nevis		Iraq	Trinidad and Tobago
St. Lucia		Jordan	Turkmenistan
Vincent & the Grenadines		Kuwait	Ukraine
CFA Franc Zone		Latvia	United Arab Emirates
Benin		Lebanon	Venezuela
Burkina Faso		Lesotho	Vietnam
Cote D'Ivoire		Macedonia, FYR	Zimbabwe
Guinea Bissau		**Against a Composite**	
Mali		Fiji	
Niger		Libyan Arab Jamahiriya	
Senegal		Morocco	
Togo		Samoa	
Cameroon		Vanuatu	
Central African Republic		China	
Chad			
Republic of Congo			
Equatorial Guinea			
Gabon			
Euro Area			
Austria			
Belgium			
Cyprus			
Finland			
France			
Germany			
Greece			
Ireland			
Italy			
Luxembourg			
Malta			
The Netherlands			
Portugal			
Spain			
Slovenia			

Target Zones		Managed Floats		Independently Floating
Conventional	**Crawling Pegs**			
Denmark	Bolivia	Afghanistan	Madagascar	Albania
Hungary	Botswana	Algeria	Malawi	Armenia
Slovak Republic	Costa Rica	Angola	Malaysia	Australia
Tonga	Iran	Argentina	Mauritius	Brazil
Cyprus	Nicaragua	Bangladesh	Moldova	Canada
		Burundi	Mongolia	Chile
		Cambodia	Mozambique	Rep. of Congo
		Colombia	Myanmar	Iceland
		Croatia	Nigeria	Israel
		Czech Republic	Papua New Guinea	Japan
		Dominican Rep.	Paraguay	Korea
		Ethiopia	Peru	Mexico
		The Gambia	Romania	New Zealand
		Georgia	Russian Fed.	Norway
		Ghana	Rwanda	Philippines
		Guatemala	Sao Tome & Principe	Poland
		Guinea	Serbia & Montenegro	Sierra Leone
		Haiti	Singapore	Somalia
		India	Sri Lanka	South Africa
		Indonesia	Sudan	Sweden
		Jamaica	Tajikistan	Switzerland
		Kazakhstan	Thailand	Tanzania
		Kenya	Tunisia	Turkey
		Kyrgyz Republic	Uruguay	Uganda
		Lao	Uzbekistan	United Kingdom
		Liberia	Rep. of Yemen	United States

Note: The information is based on the IMF's 2006 Annual Report (Appendix-Table II-9) with updates by the authors.

government restrictions. These currencies are said to be **floating currencies**, and major currencies such as the dollar, yen, euro, and pound fall into this category, as do the currencies of other developed countries, such as the Australian dollar and the Swedish krona. Currencies of developing countries, such as the South African rand and the Turkish lire, also fall into this category.

Fixed, or Pegged, Currencies

At the other extreme from floating systems are the exchange rate systems of countries with **fixed currencies**, or **pegged currencies**. In these systems, the governments attempt to make sure the values of their currencies trade at particular "pegged" values in the foreign exchange market, relative to another currency or a "basket" of currencies. A **basket of currencies** is a composite currency consisting of various units of other currencies. The two most well-known examples of currency baskets are the **special drawing right (SDR)**, which is a unit of account created by the IMF (see Section 5.5), and the historical **European currency unit**

(ECU), which was formerly a unit of account in the European Monetary System (see Section 5.6). The SDR is sometimes used to denominate contracts, as Example 5.1 demonstrates.

Example 5.1   The Thai Baht Value of the SDR

As an exporter of rice from Thailand, ThaiRice contracted to receive the Thai baht (THB) value of SDR 1 million on April 24, 2007, for its rice exports. How many baht were ThaiRice to be paid?

Whenever a contract is denominated in a basket of currencies such as the SDR, the value of the SDR in terms of a particular currency, such as the Thai baht, is found by multiplying the exchange rates of the baht versus the individual currencies by the given amounts of each currency in the basket. The SDR consists of the following amounts of four major currencies: €0.3519, ¥27.2, £0.1050, and \$0.5821. The exchange rates for these currencies on April 24, 2007, were THB43.6679/EUR, THB0.2710/JPY, THB64.3741/GBP, and THB32.1600/USD.

Thus, on April 24, 2007, the Thai baht value of the SDR was

$$(\text{THB43.6679/EUR} \times €0.3519) + (\text{THB0.2710/JPY} \times ¥27.2)$$
$$+ (\text{THB64.3741/GBP} \times £0.1050) + (\text{THB32.1600/USD} \times \$0.5821)$$
$$= \text{THB48.2176/SDR}$$

Because ThaiRice was receiving the Thai baht value of SDR 1 million, ThaiRice received

$$\text{THB48.2176/SDR} \times \text{SDR 1 million} = \text{THB 48,217,600 million}$$

On July 22, 2005, China changed its exchange rate system from a peg of the yuan relative to the dollar to a peg of the yuan relative to a basket of currencies including the major ones (dollar, euro, and yen) and a number of Asian currencies. Following the lead of Singapore, China has not disclosed the amounts of the currencies in the basket. Other examples of pegged currencies include the Namibian dollar, which is pegged to the South African rand, and the Latvian lat, which is pegged to the euro.

Special Pegged Arrangements

Apart from conventional pegs, the IMF distinguishes a number of special categories. The first category in Exhibit 5.1 is exchange arrangements with no separate legal tender. These systems include arrangements such as the CFA franc zone and the euro, where a regional central bank controls the exchange rate system for several countries. The CFA franc zone, for example, is a group of 14 African countries with two currencies, the West African CFA franc (with currency symbol XOF), which is used in eight countries, and the Central African CFA franc (with currency symbol XAF), which is used in six countries. The values of the CFA francs are pegged to the euro at 655.957 CFA francs = EUR1. The area is called the *franc zone* because prior to pegging to the euro in 1999, the countries pegged their currencies to the French franc. CFA is an acronym that originally stood for *Colonies Françaises d'Afrique* ("French colonies of Africa") and now stands either for *Coopération Financière en Afrique Centrale* ("Financial

Cooperation in Central Africa") in the West African countries and *Communauté Financière d'Afrique* ("Financial Community of Africa") in the central African countries.

A fixed, or pegged, exchange rate fully hinges on the commitment of a country's central bank to defend the currency's value. Some countries have created **currency boards** to accomplish this. A currency board limits the ability of the central bank to create money (see Section 5.4). The most well-known currency board is run by Hong Kong. After suffering severe **inflation** in the 1980s, in 1991, Argentina adopted a currency board, which pegged the Argentine peso at 1 ARS = 1 USD. The system was abandoned in January 2002 as the Argentine economy fell into crisis, and the peso lost 75% of its value over the course of a few months.

Target Zones and Crawling Pegs

Besides the categories already discussed, the IMF distinguishes some other categories, including *target zone systems* and *crawling pegs systems*. In such systems, the currency has limited flexibility. The exchange rate is either kept within a fixed band (the target zone), or exchange rate changes are kept lower than preset limits that are adjusted regularly, typically with inflation (crawling pegs). For example, in 2007 the currency of Cyprus, the Cypriot pound, moved in a 15% band around the value of the euro. The ability of Cyprus to remain in this band was a condition for eventually joining the euro system, and the Cypriot pound was replaced by the euro in January 2008.

Currency Risks in Alternative Exchange Rate Systems

It seems as though an exporter or importer would face more uncertainty conducting business in a country with a flexible exchange rate than in a country with a target zone, or even better, a pegged exchange rate system; unfortunately, things are not that simple.

Quantifying Currency Risks

We know from the discussions in Chapters 2 and 3 that the transaction exchange risk faced by an importer or exporter depends on the conditional distribution of the future exchange rate. We recognized that the conditional distribution of exchange rate changes summarizes the relative likelihoods of various exchange rate changes. It is easier to assess the conditional distribution of exchange rate changes in some regimes than in others.

A critical characteristic of the conditional distribution is its dispersion, typically measured by the standard deviation (also called volatility). Exporters and importers can use this volatility to help quantify a possible range of future exchange rates, and hence quantify their currency risks. Exhibit 5.2 provides a general guide to the currency risks related to various exchange rate regimes.

A second important characteristic of the conditional distribution of future exchange rate changes is its skewness. Skewness tells us whether the likelihood of large changes in the exchange rate in a particular direction are more likely than in the other direction.

Currency Risks in Floating Exchange Rate Systems

A completely pure floating rate system does not really exist. In reality, the central banks *intervene* periodically in the foreign exchange market. That is, they buy and sell their own currencies to attempt to affect their values. Whether such a **dirty float currency system** is more or less volatile than a true floating system depends on whether you believe central bank intervention decreases or increases exchange rate volatility. In any case, one advantage of the floating exchange rate system is that history provides us with data which indicate how volatile currencies have been in the past and we can infer from those data how volatile they may be in the future.

In Chapter 2, we computed an estimate of this volatility using historical data for the major currencies, and we found it to be around 11%. Although this volatility varies through

Exhibit 5.2 Currency Risk in Alternative Exchange-rate Systems

	Central Bank Objective	Exchange-rate Volatility		Inflation Variability	Countries Adhering to System
		Historical	Latent		
Pure Floating	Domestic	—	—	—	0
Dirty Float	Domestic and Exchange rate	Large	None	Large	79
Target Zone or Crawling Bands/Pegs	Domestic and Exchange rate	Small	Large	Small	10
Pegged Exchange Rates	Exchange rate	None	Large	Small	48
Currency Board	Exchange rate	None	Small	Small	7
Dollarized	Domestic	None	Small	Small	9
Monetary Union	Domestic	None	Very small	?	15

Notes: The first column indicates whether the central bank must focus its policy on exchange rates or domestic objectives, such as high employment. We classified "managed floating systems" under dirty float, but some of these currencies may more appropriately fit into the pegged or target zone categories. We did not classify the currencies in the ECCU and EFA zones. The two exchange rate volatility columns classify the various currency systems according to the expected magnitude of volatility. The next column does the same with respect to inflation variability. The last column records the number of countries in each currency system, using the information provided in Exhibit 5.1.

time, because most major currencies have been freely floating since 1973, the historical data are useful in pinning down a realistic volatility number. However, if you randomly pick two countries in the world that have substantial trade with one another, chances are their currencies are not floating relative to one another.

The risks of a large movement of the exchange rate in one direction or another in a floating exchange rate system are reasonably symmetrical unless a currency has strengthened or weakened systematically for several years, as the dollar did in the early 1980s. Then, the risk of a large reversal in direction typically begins to manifest itself—often while the currency continues to defy this prediction.

Currency Risk in Target Zones

Target zones try to limit exchange rate variability and achieve inflation convergence within the participating countries. As long as the exchange rate remains within the preset band, day-to-day currency fluctuations are bound to be smaller than what is observed for floating currencies. However, when the monetary authorities devalue or revalue a currency (by resetting the bands), suddenly a very large currency movement occurs. The effect of this behavior for currency risk is best illustrated with an example.

Consider the exchange rate between the French franc and the German Deutsche mark (FRF/DEM) between 1979 and 1999. The annualized historical volatility of the rate of change of the FRF/DEM exchange rate was 3.01%. This is much lower than the 11% observed for the major floating currencies such as the $/£ and $/¥. This seems to suggest that the European Monetary System—the target zone system under which the franc and Deutsche mark traded at the time—successfully reduced the volatility of the exchange rate between the two currencies to below what it would have been in a floating currency system. However, the comparison is somewhat strained.

The United States and the United Kingdom and the United States and Japan do not have similarly close geographical proximity and trading relationships as France and Germany do. A more comparable country duo, which has not established a formal currency system between them, is Canada and the United States. The volatility of changes in the CAD/USD exchange rate is only 4.53%, which is closer to the volatility of the FRF/DEM series than to the volatility of the major currencies.

Exhibit 5.3 Contrasting the FRF/DEM and CAD/USD Exchange Rates

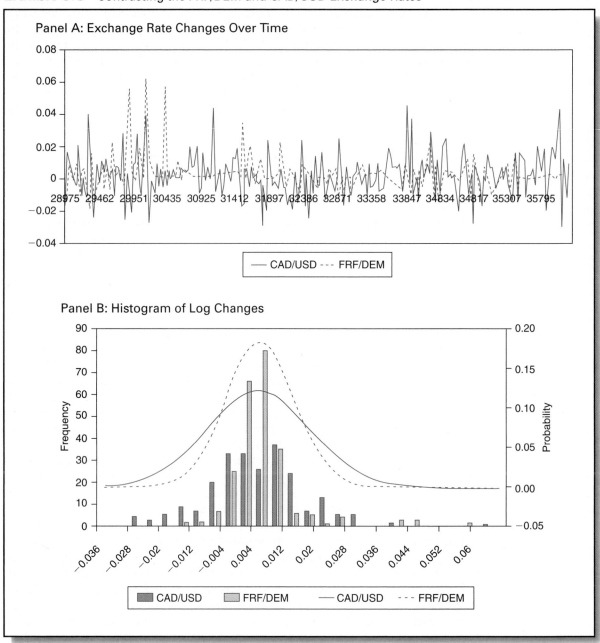

Notes: In Panel A, we graph monthly exchange rate changes over time (using data from April 1979 to December 1998), whereas in Panel B, we show histograms for logarithmic differences. These logarithmic differences are relatively close to the simple percentage differences computed as $[S(t+1)/S(t)]-1$, with $S(t)$ the spot rate. For each histogram, we also graph the normal distribution with the same mean and standard deviation as the data.

When we graph the CAD/USD and the FRF/DEM exchange rate changes (see Exhibit 5.3), we see that the volatility came in bursts for the FRF/DEM exchange rate. When there was a speculative crisis and the weak currency was eventually devalued, volatility suddenly and sharply increased.[1] For example, the exchange rate would abruptly move to

---

[1]See Geert Bekaert and Stephen Gray (1998) for a detailed study of the currency volatility around speculative crises in the FRF/DEM market.

the edge of the band. Indeed, the FRF witnessed devaluations of as much as 5.75%. Such large, 1-day movements do not tend to occur with floating exchange rates, where a weak currency may lose ground more gradually. As a result, more extreme observations occurred for FRF/DEM exchange rate changes than for CAD/USD exchange rate changes. If more extreme observations are observed than what we would see in a normal distribution, the distribution is said to exhibit "fat tails," or leptokurtosis (see Chapter 3). We can see this fat tail, or leptokur-tic, behavior clearly in the histograms in Panel B of Exhibit 5.3. From the perspective of a multinational business, dealing with such exchange rate behavior is much more difficult than dealing with the smoother changes over time characterizing flexible exchange rates changes. If the possibilities of devaluations or revaluations are not symmetrical, the conditional distribu-tion will also be skewed. This risk also arises in pegged exchange rate systems, as you will see.

Currency Risk in Pegged Exchange Rate Systems

The difficulties in assessing currency risk are amplified in pegged exchange rate systems. If the peg holds for a long time, historical volatility appears to be zero, but this may not accu-rately reflect underlying tensions that may ultimately result in a devaluation of the currency. Hence, the true currency risk does not show up in day-to-day fluctuations of the exchange rate. We therefore say this situation exhibits "latent volatility."

The key reason we discovered that the behavior of the FRF/DEM exchange rate was not all that different from the behavior of the CAD/USD exchange rate is that we used a long enough historical period, so that a number of devaluations of the FRF were part of the sample. In pegged exchange rate systems, such history is sometimes completely lacking. For example, before the Thai baht succumbed to speculative pressure in 1997, it had only been devalued twice in the course of 30 years and not at all in the 10 years prior to the crisis. From these few observations, it was impossible to determine the true latent volatility of the baht in 1997. What can be done is to look at other countries with similar systems and policies. Economists have built sophisticated models to forecast devaluations and quantify currency risk, which we will discuss in Chapter 10. The great challenge of these models often is to be forward looking without the benefit of a long span of historical data.

Fortunately, it is usually clear in a pegged exchange rate system whether the pegged currency will be devalued or revalued. This one-sided view helps importers and exporters to assess who is facing the greater risk. However, it is still difficult to know the probabilities associated with devaluations or revaluations and the potential magnitudes of these changes.

Currency Risk in Currency Boards and Monetary Unions

Currency boards attempt to further limit the risk of devaluation by severely reducing the scope of a country's monetary policy in exchange rate matters. The problem is that currency boards frequently collapse. For example, the currency boards of all the former British colonies ceased to exist after the colonies became independent, although their demise was not always accompanied by a currency crisis. As noted previously, in 2002, the currency board in Argentina that began in 1991 came under persistent pressure, leading the government to aban-don it. Meanwhile, the country plunged into a deep economic crisis.

The only truly credible fixed exchange rate regime may well be a common currency in a monetary union, such as the euro. (We study the European experience with currency arrange-ments in the final section of this chapter and offer a brief introduction to monetary unions there.) Nevertheless, even a monetary union can be broken apart, so while the probability of devaluation under such a system is quite low, it is not zero.

The lessons from this analysis are clear: For currencies that are not freely floating, the historical volatility of their exchange rates may not be an accurate measure of currency risk. Even though such exchange rate systems might provide short-term exchange rate stability, they do not guarantee the absence of currency risk. Currencies in pegged exchange rate sys-tems can still be devalued, and even currency boards can be, and have been, abandoned.

Exhibit 5.4 Exchange Rate Arrangements

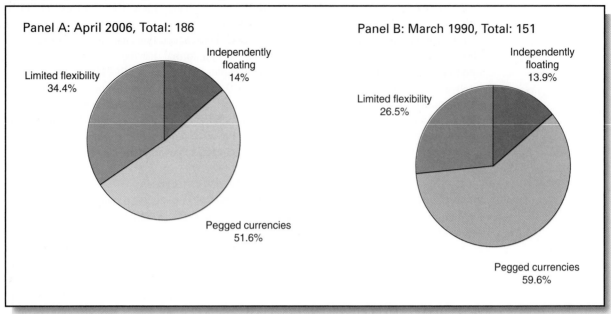

Panel A: April 2006, Total: 186

Limited flexibility
34.4%

Independently
floating
14%

Pegged currencies
51.6%

Panel B: March 1990, Total: 151

Independently
floating
13.9%

Limited flexibility
26.5%

Pegged currencies
59.6%

Note: Data are from various Annual Reports from the IMF.

Trends in Currency Systems

Exhibit 5.4 puts the currencies into the three categories mentioned earlier, comparing the current situation (Panel A) with the situation of 1990 (Panel B). Needless to say, there have been many changes in recent years.

First of all, there are now more currencies than there used to be. One main reason for this is the splitting of the Soviet Union into separate states, each with its own currency. Second, pegged currency systems still dominate, but they are less dominant than they used to be. The world has seen a modest increase in limited-flexibility systems and in floating exchange rate systems.

Exchange rate systems are in constant flux, and international businesses must be watchful for potential dramatic events. If there is one prediction we can venture to make from studying the recent history of currency systems, it is that there is a trend toward the extremes. Countries seem to opt for a very credible fixed exchange rate system, such as a currency board or monetary union, or a free-float system. The popularity of pegged and target zone systems seems to be declining. When doing business with countries operating such systems, the potential for regime shifts seems large.

5.2 CENTRAL BANKS

To understand how the major currency systems operate, you must first have a basic understanding of the functioning of central banks.

The Central Bank's Balance Sheet[2]

Exhibit 5.5 shows a simplified central bank balance sheet.

---
[2]See Frederic Mishkin (1992) for more details about central banks and monetary policy.

Exhibit 5.5 Central Bank Balance Sheet

Assets	Liabilities
Official international reserves	Deposits of private financial institutions (Bank reserves)
Domestic credit	Currency in circulation
• Government bonds	Other
• Loans to domestic financial institutions	
Other	

Bank Reserves and Currency in Circulation

The first item on the liabilities side of the balance sheet in Exhibit 5.5 consists of the reserves that financial institutions have on deposit at the central bank. Many countries require their banks to hold a certain percentage of the deposits the banks accept from the public as reserves at the central bank. These reserves are called **required reserves**, and they are often non-interest bearing. Even if the central bank did not force banks to hold reserves, banks would still hold a certain amount of reserves to facilitate transfers across banks and because they always face withdrawals, many of which have to be met immediately. Currency that is physically held by banks, called *vault cash* because it is stored in bank vaults overnight, is also part of reserves.

The other liability of the central bank is currency in circulation, which includes the coins and bills used by the public. Because the central bank operates the only authorized printing press in the country, it can actually print money to pay its bills or to acquire assets.

The sum of the two central bank liabilities is called the **monetary base** of the country, or simply *base money*. If the central bank buys an asset (for example, a government bond) from a financial institution, it credits the financial institution's reserve account at the central bank for the purchase price of the bond. Because this financial institution can now use this credit to its account to lend money to individuals and businesses, the central bank has, essentially, created money. Although definitions of *money* in a modern economy vary, we define it here as the sum of bills in circulation and demand deposits at commercial banks (a measure called M1).

One dollar of additional base money will eventually lead to much more than 1 dollar of actual money. Further money creation happens as financial institutions lend out part of the additional reserve dollar. This money in turn will be deposited at some financial institution, swelling its total deposit base, which increases the reserves of that bank. The bank will not leave that money idle but will lend it out and keep a fraction as reserves. Consequently, the process of money creation continues. Monetary economists call the fact that 1 dollar of additional base money leads to multiple dollars of new money the money multiplier effect. The money multiplier effect is smaller when financial institutions fail to lend out new deposits or when people hold cash rather than demand deposits.

Domestic Credit

The asset side of the central bank's balance sheet in Exhibit 5.5 records its investment portfolio. One important category here is domestic government bonds. In the United States and many other countries, these assets are used to influence the money supply through **open market operations**, which are the purchases or sales of government bonds by the central bank. In the United States, the Federal Reserve (the Fed) is the central bank, and if the Fed buys a U.S. Treasury bond, it pays by crediting the account of the bank selling the bond. By doing so, it injects dollars into the financial system. The converse is also true; the central bank can reduce the money supply by selling government bonds to the public. Open market operations are the main channel through which the Federal Reserve in the United States affects the money supply.

The interest rate at which the Fed's supply of reserves matches the financial institutions' demand is called the federal funds rate. It is also the rate at which banks lend reserves to each other overnight. Using open market operations, the Fed can control the federal funds rate, which in turn affects the interest rates at which banks lend to households and firms.

Another category of assets on a central bank's balance sheet that is often extremely important for developing countries is "credit to the domestic financial sector," which corresponds to "loans to domestic financial institutions" in Exhibit 5.5. The central bank in most countries is also a lender of last resort—that is, it can and should extend credit to the banking sector to prevent bank runs in times of panic and financial crisis. Inflationary problems often arise, though, when financial institutions become dependent on the central bank for funds.

Official Reserves

The item "official international reserves" on the balance sheet in Exhibit 5.5 is at the core of the role central banks play in the foreign exchange market. **Official reserves** consist of three major components: foreign exchange reserves, gold reserves, and IMF-related reserve assets. (We discuss the last two items in Section 5.4.) Around the world, **foreign exchange reserves** constitute the largest component of official reserves, accounting for 88.42% of total reserves in March 2006. Gold accounted for 10.42% and IMF-related reserve assets for 1.16% of total reserves. The relative importance of gold has gradually decreased over time.

What is the composition of international reserves around the world? Recall from Chapter 4 that international reserves are the foreign currency–denominated assets (bonds, deposits, and credit lines) that the central bank holds. In terms of currency denomination, the dollar is the dominant foreign reserve asset held by most central banks around the world. Exhibit 5.6, constructed from information in various issues of the IMF's Annual Report, indicates that the dollar's dominance has waned in recent times, falling from close to 80% in 1975 to about 65% today.

Other important reserve assets are the euro, the pound sterling, and the yen. A much-discussed issue is whether the arrival of the euro will cause the relative importance of the dollar to decrease (see Gabriele Galati and Philip Wooldridge, 2006; and Elias Papaioannou, Richard Portes, and Gregorios Siourounis, 2006). Comparing the 1999 and 2005 numbers, it does appear to be the case that the share of the euro has increased relative to that of the dollar, but at times during the 1980s and 1990s, the total share of international reserves of the currencies replaced by the euro (the Deutsche mark, French franc, and ECU) was higher than that of the euro today.

This stock of foreign currency–denominated assets is depleted or increased when a central bank intervenes in the foreign exchange market. If the central bank buys its currency in the foreign exchange market, its international reserves are depleted, and if the central bank sells its currency in the foreign exchange market, its international reserves are increased.

In terms of asset mix, central banks usually limit the risk level of their portfolios and typically do not invest in equities. Most official reserves are in the form of Treasury bills and bonds of other countries, ranging from very short-term to medium-term paper, although in recent years, some central banks have become a bit more adventurous in their portfolio choices.

Whereas 10 years ago, the largest stock of official reserves was found in developed countries, in March 2006, developing countries held more than 60% of the global stock of reserve assets. After currency crises in Mexico in 1994, Southeast Asia in 1997, and Russia in 1998, many developing countries built up substantial reserves, partially as an insurance policy against future crises. Traditionally, the level of reserves is compared to the amount of imports a country must fund. However, in an increasingly financially globalized world, reserves can

Exhibit 5.6 Foreign Exchange Reserves

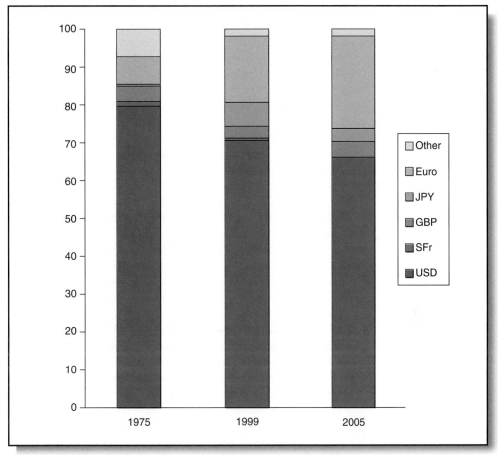

Notes: The data are from Table I-2 in the IMF Annual Reports, various issues. For 1975, the numbers for the euro reflect the sum of reserve positions in the Deutsche mark and the French franc.

also protect against sudden stops in capital flows from abroad (see Olivier Jeanne and Romain Ranciere, 2006). China, in particular, has built up substantial reserves, which at the end of March 2006 stood at $875 billion and later came to exceed $1 trillion, as the following feature on China's central bank shows.

The Trillion-Dollar Portfolio of the Chinese Central Bank

In early 2007, the People's Bank of China (PBOC), the central bank of the People's Republic of China, held a whopping $1 trillion-plus stash of foreign exchange reserves, predominantly denominated in dollars. In Chapter 4, we discussed how many economists worry that China (as well as other countries) may diversify its reserves into other currencies, with potentially dire consequences for the value of the dollar. Of course, if the yuan were to rise sharply against the dollar, the PBOC would incur huge losses on its dollar portfolio. Less well known is that the PBOC in fact makes hefty profits. According to one estimate (see "China's Reserves, A Money Machine," 2007), the PBOC made a profit of $29 billion in 2006. The main reason is that the interest it pays on its liabilities (mostly reserves of domestic financial banks) is much lower than the interest it receives on its foreign exchange reserves (mostly invested in U.S. Treasury bills and bonds). The yuan-denominated domestic bonds issued or sold to sterilize increases in foreign exchange reserves also carried a much lower interest rate than the American interest rate received on the international reserves. Consequently, its huge stack of dollar assets has proved rather profitable to the PBOC, so far.

Money Creation and Inflation

The central bank's right to create money is a valuable tool. Central banks finance their physical operations and pay their staff from the interest income on their assets, which are obtained by printing money. Any residual income is given to the country's treasury. The value of the real resources that the central bank obtains through the creation of base money is called **seigniorage**. By setting the amount of nominal money circulating in the economy at each point in time, the bank establishes the growth rate of the nation's money supply over time. Monetary authorities hope to use their policies to promote growth, lower unemployment, or pursue other goals. However, the demand for money ultimately depends on the number of real transactions in the economy and how much money is needed to facilitate these transactions.

For example, if the authorities double the money supply in the hope of stimulating the economy, they may only succeed in doubling the overall level of prices in the economy. The increase in the money supply is unlikely to make people consume more or work harder. But with more money supporting the same number of real transactions, prices will inevitably rise. Whereas economists have formulated theories in which changes in the supply of money do have real effects on the economy in the short run, it is generally believed that the long-run impact of additional money growth on real activity is negligible. This long-run property of the growth in the money supply is called *money neutrality*.

Central banks often forget that printing money cannot solve real problems. For example, governments occasionally use open market operations to monetize fiscal deficits. Suppose a government runs a large budget deficit because its expenditures exceed its revenues. The deficit must be financed by the sale of government bonds to the public. If the bonds are bought by the central bank, the central bank's holdings of government bonds increase, and the money supply expands. The deficit is monetized. A government that "runs the printing presses" to finance its deficits undermines its central bank's ability to control the money supply and creates inflation.

This problem was acute in many Latin American economies in the 1970s and 1980s. Countries such as Argentina and Bolivia eventually faced hyperinflation (triple-digit annual inflation or worse) because they printed too much money. Similarly, if central banks frivolously extend credit to the banking sector, the money supply will likely expand beyond the amount that individuals and firms need to conduct transactions, and inflation will be the inevitable result.

The Impossible Trinity

Standard open-economy macroeconomic theory holds that there is an intrinsic incompatibility between perfect capital mobility (that is, no capital controls), fixed exchange rates, and domestic monetary autonomy (that is, using monetary policy to achieve domestic policy goals such as low inflation and/or unemployment). Only two of these three policies are possible. If a country wants to fix its exchange rate and has perfect capital mobility, capital flows will determine the country's money supply, making it impossible to run an independent monetary policy.

Some economists argue that capital controls can be a way around the impossible trinity, but in practice, such policies do not always work. Even when a currency is flexible, problems can arise. For example, in December 2006, Thailand imposed capital controls on foreign capital inflows (essentially slapping a tax on foreign portfolio investment into Thailand) after facing a strong appreciation of the Thai baht that hurt Thai exporters. The Thai authorities did not want to lower local interest rates to lessen the attractiveness of foreign investment in Thailand. Why? Because that would boost local demand and further overheat the economy. As you will see in the next section, any effort by the central bank to intervene to lower the value of the baht would have a similar effect. After the equity market declined by 15% in 1 day in response to the imposition of capital controls, the controls were hastily removed from equity investments and relaxed for debt investments.

Foreign Exchange Interventions

Central banks sometimes intervene in foreign exchange markets to affect exchange rates. By supplying more of their currency, they weaken it; and by demanding their currency, they strengthen it. Exhibit 5.7 shows the effects of two different types of interventions on a central bank balance sheet.

With either intervention, the central bank ends up buying foreign currency. (In practice, central banks do not just buy foreign currency; they eventually buy foreign currency assets that earn interest, such as foreign bonds.) There are two types of interventions, depending on whether the interventions are "sterilized." We discuss the non-sterilized intervention first and then explain sterilization.

Non-Sterilized Interventions

Consider the situation in Exhibit 5.7. Imagine that the Fed wants to depreciate the value of the dollar relative to the yen, to make U.S. products more attractive to potential Japanese buyers.

Suppose the exchange rate is ¥100/$. The Fed buys ¥5,000 million in the foreign exchange market, using the services of a major U.S. commercial bank. How does the Fed pay for the yen? It simply credits the account of the commercial bank at the Federal Reserve by $50 million = (¥5,000 million)/(¥100/$). The commercial bank in turn wires ¥5,000 million to the Federal Reserve. This transaction decreases the assets of the commercial bank by ¥5,000 million, but it increases the assets of the central bank by $50 million.[3] The ultimate effect of this **non-sterilized intervention** is to increase the foreign assets on the left-hand side of the balance sheet of the central bank and to increase the U.S. money supply. Essentially, the

Exhibit 5.7 Sterilized and Non-Sterilized Foreign Exchange Intervention

Panel A: A Non-Sterilized Intervention

Central Bank Balance Sheet				Financial Intermediary Balance Sheet			
Assets		**Liabilities**		**Assets**		**Liabilities**	
International reserves	+50	Deposits of financial institutions	+50	Reserves at Federal Reserve	+50		
Domestic credit	0			Foreign currency interbank deposits	−50		
				Government bonds	0		

Panel B: A Sterilized Intervention

Central Bank Balance Sheet				Financial Intermediary Balance Sheet			
Assets		**Liabilities**		**Assets**		**Liabilities**	
International reserves	+50	Deposits of financial institutions	+50	Reserves at Federal Reserve	+50 −50		
				Foreign currency interbank deposits	−50		
Domestic credit	**−50**		**−50**	Government bonds	**+50**		
	0		0		0		

Note: The Fed buys USD 50 million worth of yen on the foreign exchange market in Panel A. In Panel B, the bold transaction shows how the Fed sterilizes the original transaction by selling government bonds to financial intermediaries.

---

[3]The commercial bank will, in turn, use its yen account at some major Japanese financial institution to pay the Federal Reserve.

Fed has paid the financial intermediary by creating additional base money equal to $50 million. By increasing the demand for yen and increasing the supply of dollars to the foreign exchange market, the Fed hopes to lower the JPY/USD exchange rate.

Sterilized Interventions

An unwelcome side effect of a non-sterilized foreign exchange intervention is the effect on the money supply. A higher money supply eventually leads to higher inflation, and the foreign exchange objective of the central bank's policy may conflict with its domestic goal of price stability. A potential solution is to "sterilize" the foreign exchange intervention—that is, to remove the new money from circulation to remove the inflation threat. **Sterilized interventions** involve conducting an offsetting open market transaction to restore the monetary base to its original size.

A sterilized intervention is shown in Panel B of Exhibit 5.7. Here the government uses an open market transaction to offset the effect of the foreign exchange intervention on the domestic money supply. That is, at the same time as the central bank buys ¥5,000 million for $50 million, it sells $50 million worth of domestic government bonds in the secondary market for government bonds. Because a financial institution will pay for these bonds using its reserve account at the central bank, money is taken out of circulation at the same time that money is injected into circulation through the foreign exchange intervention. These two transactions cancel each other out, as Exhibit 5.7 shows. The net effect is that the central bank has replaced domestic bonds with foreign assets, but there is no effect on the money supply. The private sector now holds more domestic bonds and fewer foreign currency bonds.

How Do Central Banks Peg a Currency?

While most central banks—even those with free-floating currencies—often intervene in the foreign exchange market, some central banks go further and attempt to fix the value of their currencies relative to a benchmark currency. How does a central bank peg a currency? To establish and maintain a fixed value when a currency is freely traded, the central bank has to be willing to "make a market" in its currency. The central bank has to be willing and able to supply its currency when there is excess demand for it (buying the foreign currency), and if there is excess private supply of the currency, the central bank must demand any excess supply that arises (selling its foreign currency reserves). As the central bank buys or sells the foreign currency, its international reserves increase or decrease.

Pegging the Exchange Rate

Suppose, hypothetically, that the Bank of England, the central bank of the United Kingdom, wants to peg the value of the pound relative to the dollar at a level of $\overline{S} = \$1.25/£$. We represent the aggregate demand and supply for the pound in Exhibit 5.8.

The horizontal axis represents quantities of pounds demanded or supplied in the foreign exchange market over some time interval, such as a quarter or a year. The vertical axis represents the price of the pound in terms of the dollar—in other words the dollar/pound exchange rate, S.

Why is the demand (supply) schedule downward (upward) sloping? Let us assume that the United Kingdom and the United States are the only countries in the world and assume for simplicity that the demands to trade currencies arise only from importers and exporters. The quantity of pounds demanded by U.S. importers will go down as the dollar price of the pound (the exchange rate) increases. If the U.K. product prices remain fixed, a higher dollar/pound exchange rate raises the dollar prices of U.K. goods to U.S. importers. Consequently, the demand schedule for pounds, Demand$_£$, is downward sloping. Similarly, the supply of pounds to the foreign exchange market—for example, by U.K. importers needing dollars to import goods or services from the U.S.—will tend to increase the higher the exchange rate (the more dollars a pound buys) because the price of U.S. goods is going down from the U.K. perspective. The supply schedule, Supply$_£$, is therefore upward sloping. The equilibrium exchange

Exhibit 5.8   Fixing the $/£ Exchange Rate

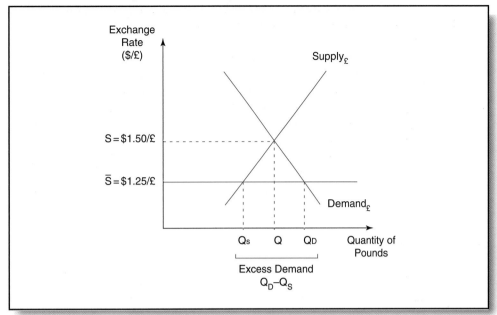

rate, the exchange rate that equates the private sector's demand and supply schedules, is denoted by S and equals $1.50/£. If the exchange rate were freely floating without government intervention, this would be the market exchange rate.

The level at which the government wants to fix the value of the pound, $\overline{S}$, is represented by a horizontal line. In this case, the value is below the equilibrium exchange rate. At $\overline{S}$, there is an excess demand for pounds, and the pound is undervalued relative to its equilibrium value. Hence, if the Bank of England wants to keep the exchange rate at that level, it will have to supply these excess pounds (represented by $Q_D - Q_S$) to the foreign exchange market and obtain foreign currency (dollars) in return. In other words, this situation leads to the Bank of England building up additional foreign reserves.

Exhibit 5.8 also summarizes the essence of the economic content of the balance of payments (BOP) statistics we discussed in Chapter 4. The demand for pounds over a certain time interval is every item that gives rise to a credit on the BOP, a source of foreign currency. The supply of pounds over that same time interval is every item that gives rise to a debit item, a use of foreign currency. In a purely floating exchange rate system, the exchange rate is always at its equilibrium value, S; the private sector's balance of payments is always balanced; and there is no need for central bank intervention. However, if the Bank of England wants to peg the currency at $\overline{S}$ its foreign exchange reserves will increase when there is excess private-sector demand for pounds, and there will be an official settlements deficit because the Bank of England is building up foreign assets.

5.3 FLEXIBLE EXCHANGE RATE SYSTEMS

Although the central banks of the major developed countries mostly let competitive market forces determine the values of their exchange rates, they nonetheless have a variety of tools at their disposal to influence the path of exchange rates. For example, they can use domestic monetary policy (by varying the money supply or interest rates under their control); they can attempt to restrict capital movements; or they can tax or subsidize international trade to influence the demand for foreign currency. We will come back to these alternative tools later on in this chapter. Here we focus on direct foreign exchange intervention—that is, the sale or purchase of foreign assets against domestic assets by the central bank.

The Effects of Central Bank Interventions

Despite their prevalence, foreign exchange interventions are a controversial policy option for central banks. In one view, intervention policy is not only ineffective in influencing the level of the exchange rate but also dangerous because it can increase foreign exchange volatility. Others argue that intervention operations can influence the level of the exchange rate and can "calm disorderly markets," thereby decreasing volatility. Yet others, including Nobel Prize–winning economist Milton Friedman (1953), argue that interventions are ineffective and a waste of taxpayers' money.

To better understand this debate, let's look at how interventions can affect exchange rates. We can distinguish two main channels through which foreign exchange interventions can affect exchange rates: a direct channel and an indirect channel. The direct channel stresses the importance of the volume and the intensity of the intervention operations themselves, whereas the indirect channel stresses the importance of the market response to the intervention and how expectations of private investors and their investment portfolios may be altered as a result. We summarize these channels in Exhibit 5.9, which takes us through the potential effects of the Fed buying euros. In the discussion here, we move from left to right in the diagram.

Exhibit 5.9   The Effects of Foreign Exchange Interventions

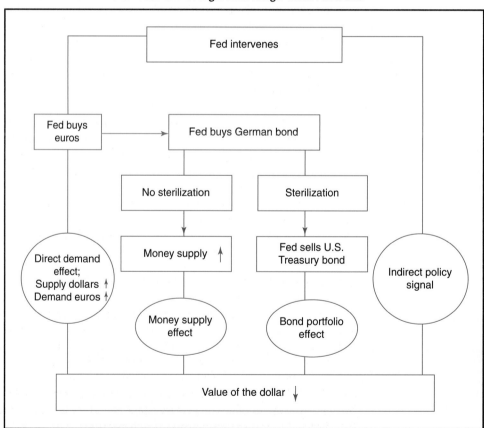

Note: The Federal Reserve buys euros to attempt to reduce the value of the dollar relative to the euro. Because it wants to hold interest-bearing instruments, it uses the euro to buy a 5-year Bund, a German government bond with a maturity of 5 years.

Direct Effects of Interventions

The direct channel is easiest to understand. The central bank's action directly affects the supply and demand of foreign currency. In our example (see Exhibit 5.9), the supply of dollars to the foreign exchange market increases, and the demand for euros increases. Most economists believe that the direct effects of interventions must be negligible. Why? Because the magnitude of interventions is typically like a drop in the ocean of overall foreign exchange trading. The daily trading volume in the foreign exchange markets across all currencies mostly exceeds $2 trillion per day, whereas interventions rarely exceed $1 billion at a time. Of course, when the intervention is not sterilized, buying euros has the same effect as an expansion of the U.S. money supply (see Section 5.2). However, the U.S. money supply also dwarfs the size of a typical intervention so that this money supply effect is likely to be small as well. Moreover, both the Fed and the European Central Bank routinely *sterilize* their interventions, implying that the money supply is typically not affected by direct interventions.

Although sterilized interventions have no effect on the domestic money supply, they do change the composition of the assets held by private investors. For example, a purchase of foreign currency (the euro, in our example) in return for dollars would increase the U.S. money supply and must be offset with a sale of government bonds, which reduces the U.S. money supply, if the intervention is sterilized. The net effect is that domestic bonds replace foreign currency bonds in the private-sector portfolio, which we term the *bond portfolio effect*. In Exhibit 5.9, Bunds, German government bonds, disappear out of the private sector's bond portfolio and are replaced with U.S. Treasury bonds. The central bank forces this change in portfolio composition upon private investors, who may require changes in the prices and expected returns on the bonds before they are willing to buy them. Whether these changes in portfolio composition generate any direct effect on the exchange rate is questionable, given the size of bond portfolios worldwide relative to the typical size of an intervention. The U.S. bond market alone, for example, has a market capitalization of close to $8 trillion.

Recent research suggests that interventions may still be effective in generating short-term effects on the exchange rate because much of the huge trading volume in the foreign exchange market represents "hot-potato trading." This term refers to the repeated passing of inventory imbalances between dealers in response to customer orders they receive (see Richard Lyons, 1997). For example, if a bank buys euros from a large multinational company that is selling euros, the bank's currency inventories will now be out of balance. The bank will try to rebalance its foreign exchange portfolio by selling the euros to another dealer. That bank will now be out of balance, and it will try to sell euros to another bank, and so on. If the central bank is intervening to reduce the value of the euro by selling euros to several dealers, it may be difficult for the commercial banks to achieve rebalancing without lowering the value of the euro. In this sense, "smallish" interventions may still have an exchange rate effect by squeezing foreign exchange inventories at dealer banks.

Indirect Effects of Interventions

Even though an intervention may fail to move the exchange rate directly, it can still alter people's expectations and affect their investments, thus helping to push the exchange rate in the direction the central bank desires. For example, the intervention may be a signal to the public of the central bank's monetary policy intentions, or it may signal the central bank's inside information about future market fundamentals, such as future GDP growth.

Alternatively, the central bank may signal to investors that a currency's exchange rate is deviating too far from its long-run equilibrium value. However, the market might not take a mere announcement of a policy change seriously because "talk is cheap," as the saying goes. By contrast, an actual intervention makes the signal more credible because the central bank is putting its own resources on the line when it intervenes. When a central bank incorrectly assesses the equilibrium value of the exchange rate, the intervention will result in the loss of money. For example, if the bank buys foreign currency when it feels the foreign currency is undervalued and bound to appreciate, but subsequently the appreciation does not occur, the bank will not profit from the purchase. The marketplace, recognizing these costs, is likely to take the central bank's policy statement more seriously if it is backed up by intervention. This reasoning, though, makes the secretive interventions of central banks, which occur regularly, quite mysterious.

Empirical Evidence on the Effectiveness of Interventions

After the advent of floating exchange rates in 1973, which we will discuss in more detail in Section 5.4, countries attempted to adopt currency stabilization policies at the national level, with the expectation that exchange rate stability would emerge as a byproduct. By the fall of 1985, it was apparent that such stability was not forthcoming, and exchange rates were much more variable than policymakers had envisioned. Several years of undisciplined and uncoordinated national policies had created huge current account imbalances and a sizable misalignment of the dollar, which had appreciated strongly since the end of 1979. As a result, since 1985, interventions by the major central banks have occurred regularly.

Two celebrated cases of internationally coordinated interventions were the Plaza Accord of September 1985, which tried to lower the value of the dollar after its sustained rise during the first half of the 1980s; and the Louvre Accord, which tried to stabilize the dollar's value in 1987. In 1994 and 1995, the central banks of Germany, Japan, and the United States coordinated a massive intervention that increased the value of the dollar on the foreign exchange markets. Indeed, economists Kathryn Dominguez and Jeffrey Frankel (1993) argue that coordinated intervention by a number of central banks is more effective than a unilateral intervention by a single central bank. Such a move demonstrates that central banks agree that there is a problem with the exchange rate and are willing to do something about it.

Nonetheless, the effectiveness of central bank intervention in bringing exchange rates back to the long-run equilibrium values appears weak. One problem in judging the success of an intervention is the inability to control for market fundamentals. For example, common sense suggests that interventions that fly in the face of powerful economic fundamentals are unlikely to work. Although the Plaza Accord was deemed successful because the dollar did indeed decline in its wake, the decline in the value of the dollar had already started, and the Plaza Accord may have just endorsed a market movement already under way.

Dominguez and Frankel (1993) draw an engaging analogy between the foreign exchange market and a cattle drive. In the analogy, the market is the herd of steers, and the central banks are the herd dogs. In any cattle drive, the steers clearly outnumber the herd dogs in both size and number, yet the dogs can still influence the steers' path by barking and nipping at their heels. The steers at the edge of the pack influence the rest of the herd to stay on the right path. In much the same way, central banks, while clearly outnumbered in terms of market participants and the sheer volume of market trading activity, may be able to exert a greater influence on exchange rates than their size and number would suggest because they can affect market expectations.

It is somewhat easier to test whether a central bank intervention has served to stabilize exchange rates than to influence the level of exchange rates. However, the empirical evidence so far suggests that central bank interventions have increased or not changed volatility rather than decreased it (see Michel Beine, Jerome Lahaye, Sebastien Laurent, Christopher Neely, and Franz Palm, 2006; Catherine Bonser-Neal and Glenn Tanner, 1996; and Kathryn Dominguez, 1998).[4] One problem with assessing the efficacy of intervention to reduce volatility is the possibility that central banks intervene during periods that are relatively more volatile.

---

[4]This is true despite central bankers themselves believing that their interventions do not increase volatility. See the survey in Christopher Neely (2006).

A final perspective is to try to assess directly whether central bank interventions indeed waste taxpayers' money by examining the profitability of interventions. In Mongolia, the answer is clear. In 1990 and 1991, inexperienced foreign exchange dealers in Mongolia's central bank lost some $90 million, a sum equivalent to virtually all their poor country's foreign currency reserves. In contrast, a study on the United States by Michael Leahy (1995) found that interventions by the Federal Reserve between 1973 and 1992 was profitable! Given the inconclusiveness of much of the research in this area, the debate on the usefulness of interventions in otherwise freely floating currencies will probably continue for a long time to come.

5.4 FIXED EXCHANGE RATE SYSTEMS

Until 1971, an essentially fixed exchange rate system based on gold dominated the international monetary system. From then onward, fixed exchange rate systems have been primarily prevalent in developing countries.

The International Monetary System Before 1971: A Brief History

The Gold Standard

At the start of the eighteenth century, Great Britain made its paper currency notes exchangeable for gold, thereby establishing the first official **gold standard**. By the end of the nineteenth century, all major industrial countries had adopted the gold standard. Because coins and bills could be converted into gold at fixed rates at central banks, the gold standard essentially resulted in a system of fixed exchange rates among the major countries. Central banks also used gold to pay for balance of payments deficits. That is, gold was sent from the deficit country (which faced an excess demand for the foreign currency) to the surplus country. This transfer helped restore equilibrium on the balance of payments because the loss of international reserves by deficit countries also meant that their money supply decreased, putting downward pressure on prices. Lower prices increased demand for the country's products from foreign residents, which automatically improved the BOP.

Hyperinflation and the Interwar Period

During World War I, the gold standard was suspended as governments printed massive amounts of paper money to finance their war efforts. The result was substantial inflation, with Germany as the most dramatic example. Germany faced hyperinflation between 1919 and 1923, with prices rising by a factor of 481.5 billion in those 4 years alone! People literally had to take wheelbarrows full of money to the store to make their purchases.

The interwar period was an era of international economic disintegration punctuated by the Great Depression starting in 1929. Some countries allowed their currencies to float in the foreign exchange markets. Others maintained some form of gold standard; for example, the United States and Great Britain restored gold convertibility at prewar parities after the war. That is, the number of dollars or pounds needed to obtain an ounce of gold was kept at the same value as before the war. However, gold standard countries regularly devalued their currencies relative to gold and hence relative to other currencies. These devaluations were intentionally aimed at making locally produced goods more competitive—that is, cheaper for foreign buyers. At the same time, protectionist measures were taken, aimed at keeping out foreign products. International cooperation and coordination of economic policies declined precipitously, and international tensions grew.

The Bretton Woods System

In 1944, the International Monetary Fund (IMF) was created by an international agreement called the **Bretton Woods agreement** because it was signed at Bretton Woods, New Hampshire. The participating countries agreed to an exchange rate regime that linked their exchange rates to the dollar. The dollar itself had a fixed gold parity ($35 per ounce).

The Bretton Woods agreement grew out of a desire to avoid the monetary chaos of the interwar period. Fixed exchange rates were meant to provide stability and discipline, but the Great Depression had convinced the IMF's architects that fixed exchange rates should not come at the price of long-term domestic unemployment. Therefore, the IMF agreement incorporated some flexibility into the application of the fixed exchange rate system. When a country ran into a temporary balance of payments problem (a current account deficit) that threatened the currency peg, it could draw on the lending facilities of the IMF to help it defend the currency.

Each IMF member contributed both gold and its own national currency to the fund. A member was entitled to use its own currency to temporarily purchase gold or foreign currencies from the fund equal in value to its gold contribution. Further gold or foreign currencies (up to a limit) could be borrowed from the fund, but only under increasingly stringent IMF supervision of the borrower's macroeconomic policies. This *IMF conditionality* (see also Chapter 1) is still applied to countries when they borrow from the IMF. In addition, the Bretton Woods agreement pegged the world's currencies to the dollar, but they could fluctuate in a 1% band around the chosen parity value. (We will discuss recent examples of target zones in the next section.) Countries were also allowed to change their parities when their balances of payments were considered to be in "fundamental disequilibrium." Unfortunately, it was difficult to know what this latter term meant, and policymakers in different countries debated who should do the adjustments and who was at fault for protracted balance of payments deficits.

Individual Incentives Versus Aggregate Incentives

Because the United States was required to trade gold for dollars with foreign central banks, it maintained a large pool of gold reserves. During the 1950s, the world demand for international reserves grew more rapidly than world gold supplies, and foreign countries happily accumulated interest-earning dollar international reserves without converting them into gold at the Federal Reserve. As these dollar claims became larger and larger relative to the size of the U.S. gold reserves, though, the public's confidence in the dollar–gold parity understandably fell. The market began to predict a devaluation of the dollar in terms of gold, which increased the incentive of individuals to hold gold, not dollars.

If individual foreign countries exercised their right to convert their dollar claims into gold at the Federal Reserve, the United States would eventually not be able to honor all these requests and would be forced to abolish convertibility at $35 an ounce. Yet, if the aggregate of all countries did not ask to convert their dollar assets into gold, the system could continue indefinitely, with dollar assets forming the foundation of international reserves. Some countries, such as France, found this politically unacceptable.

Special Drawing Rights

In 1968, the IMF created special drawing rights (SDRs) as an alternative reserve asset with the same gold value as the dollar, in an attempt to provide an internationally acceptable asset other than the dollar. However, the United States kept running BOP deficits, and the pressure on the U.S. gold reserves continued to mount, prompting President Nixon to abolish the convertibility of the dollar into gold in August 1971.

An international agreement reached in December 1971 at the Smithsonian Institution in Washington, DC, devalued the dollar by about 8% relative to most other currencies, but

Exhibit 5.10   Pegging an Exchange Rate in a Developing Country

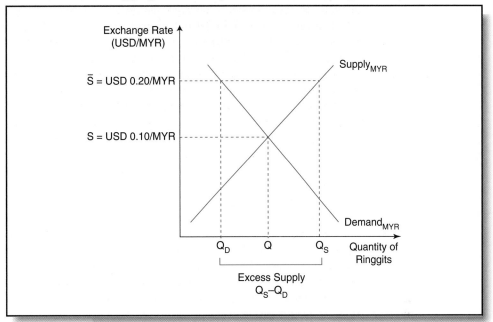

speculation against the dollar continued. By March 19, 1973, the Bretton Woods system collapsed, and the currencies of Japan and most European currencies began to float freely relative to the dollar.

The value of the SDR remained expressed in gold until 1976, after which time it became a basket currency, consisting of fixed amounts of five major currencies: the dollar, the Deutsche mark, the French franc, the yen, and the pound. (With the creation of the euro, the SDR is now based on four currencies.) Since then, gold has lost its official role in the international monetary system, although most central banks continue to keep part of their official reserves in the form of gold.

Although gold reached a high price of almost $700 per ounce in 1980, it was less than $300 from 1998 until early 2002. Sales of gold reserves by central banks were partly to blame for the fall in price. Since then, the price of gold has increased considerably, exceeding $691 per ounce in April 2007. Those who bought gold at $35 per ounce and held it for 39 years have earned a rate of return of 7.95% per annum, although there was clearly much volatility.

Pegged Exchange Rate Systems in Developing Countries

As we saw in Exhibit 5.1, many developing countries have pegged exchange rate systems. Essentially, the government tries to fix the exchange rate without allowing any room for movement. It is often the case that the authorities in these countries set the exchange rate at a level that is clearly higher than the level that would exist in a free market—that is, they overvalue the local currency. This situation is opposite that in Exhibit 5.8, in which the equilibrium exchange rate is below the pegged value. Exhibit 5.10 repeats Exhibit 5.8 for the Malaysian ringgit, with S being 0.10 dollars per ringgit (10 ringgits to the dollar) and $\bar{S}$ equal to 0.20 dollars per ringgit (5 ringgits to the dollar).

At 0.20 dollars per ringgit, there is an excess supply of Malaysian ringgits ($Q_S - Q_D$): Everybody wants to turn in ringgits to the central bank, receive dollars, and invest them abroad. The fixed exchange rate undervalues the foreign currency and overvalues the domestic currency, thereby subsidizing buyers of foreign currency (such as importers and those investing abroad) and taxing sellers of foreign exchange (such as exporters and foreign buyers of domestic assets). (The *Point–Counterpoint* feature in this chapter further analyzes the ramifications of such an overvalued exchange rate.)

Needless to say, this situation is not tenable indefinitely. Because of the implicit tax on sellers of foreign exchange, exporters would fail to repatriate their foreign currency earnings, and because of the subsidies to buyers of foreign exchange, domestic residents would invest in foreign assets (a phenomenon known as capital flight; see Chapter 4). At the exchange rate the central bank wants to maintain (0.2 dollars per ringgit), the supply of ringgits to the central bank is larger than the demand for ringgits; or, equivalently, the demand for foreign currency from the central bank is larger than the supply of foreign currency to the central bank. The country runs a BOP deficit, and the central bank must artificially restore equilibrium by using its own international reserves to satisfy the excess demand. If this situation persists, the central bank's foreign reserves will dwindle fast.

The only way to sustain such a system is to impose exchange controls. The central bank of the developing country must ration the use of foreign exchange, manage who gets access to it, and restrict capital flows; in short, it must strictly control financial transactions involving foreign currencies. More often than not, the currencies of developing countries are inconvertible, which makes the use of exchange controls easier.[5] The inconvertible currencies of developing countries are primarily traded by the central bank of the country or by a number of financial institutions with strict controls on their use of foreign currency.

Illegal Currency Markets

The private market response to the incorrectly valued exchange rate is often the development of an illegal or parallel exchange rate market. In these illegal markets, foreign currencies command a higher domestic-currency price than the one offered by the central bank. The differences between official and illegal market rates can often be staggering. The situation in Zimbabwe in January 2008 is particularly striking. The official exchange rate is 30,000 Zimbabwe dollars per 1 U.S. dollar. Nevertheless, in the illegal market 1 U.S. dollar trades for 2.5 million Zimbabwe dollars. Tourists often take advantage of the illegal market rate simply by selling dollars to dealers stationed in front of their hotel, but such activity sometimes results in severe penalties.

While maintaining capital controls may be feasible when currencies are inconvertible, it is much harder for countries with freely traded currencies because the government can exert less direct control over the use of its currency. Nevertheless, capital controls were the norm in many European countries during the 1970s and 1980s (see Section 5.6).

POINT-COUNTERPOINT

The Burden of the Baguette

Freedy, Ante, and Suttle are in Paris, where they are visiting their cousin Jean Patie, who grew up in France, received his MBA at Columbia Business School in May 1993, and then decided to go back to France. Jean suggested that they meet at Chez Jerry, a cozy bar on the Place du Tertre, and over a delightful glass of Sancerre, Ante asks Jean what life was like when Jean took his first job.

"Well," Jean begins, "I spent half of my time in Africa, as I was working for Painargent, a French company that exported sourdough baguettes to African countries. Their main markets

---

[5]A convertible currency is one that may be freely used in international transactions by citizens of any country. After World War II, Europe only restored currency convertibility (and then mostly only for current account transactions) in 1958.

were the 14 French-speaking African countries in the Communauté Financière d'Afrique."[6] "Hey," Freedy interjects, "we just learned about those countries in the international finance class that Ante and I are taking. Those countries all peg the CFA franc to the euro, right?" Jean responds, "Very good, Freedy. So, if you guys are such international finance hot shots, are you up for a little quiz?" Ante and Freedy respond enthusiastically, with shouts of "Bring it on," as Suttle just smiles.

Jean begins, "Well, when I left school, the CFA countries had been pegging their exchange rate versus the French franc, without devaluation, for an impressive 45 years. My new employers spoke volumes about how wonderful the stability of the fixed exchange rate was for business. Painargent even accepted CFA francs from the African importers because they were fully convertible into French francs at the fixed exchange rate. Because of the stability of the CFA franc's value, exchange rate issues really had not played any part in Painargent's business."

Jean continued, "When I was hired, economic growth in the CFA region had recently lagged behind economic growth in other countries. Many in the region blamed an overvalued CFA franc, and some politicians were calling for a devaluation of the CFA franc relative to the French franc. These politicians noted that non-CFA neighbors Nigeria and Ghana had recently devalued their own currencies, which seemed to improve the competitiveness of their exports and provided additional jobs in their export industries. Nevertheless, some of my bosses at Painargent expressed anger at those CFA *canailles* and said that devaluation would crush Painargent's profit margin." Ante and Freedy, remembering their international finance class, nod approvingly. Jean asks Ante, "What would devaluation mean for Painargent?"

Ante quickly responds, "A CFA devaluation would mean that every CFA franc Painargent earns would turn into fewer French francs, resulting in lower French franc revenues." Freedy, quick to show that he had been paying attention in class, adds, "A CFA devaluation would definitely have cut into Painargent's profits because its costs were probably primarily wages paid to French bakers, and wages would not be affected by the devaluation. Thus, profits would fall."

Jean then asks, "So, did the CFA countries devalue or not?" Ante agitatedly exhorts, "Surely they did not devalue! The system worked well for over 45 years, it brought stability to the region, and besides, devaluation would have been a disaster for too many people. Think of all the French companies, like Painargent, with assets, real and financial, in the CFA countries. It would have been devastating for them to have to endure devaluation!" Freedy is less sure. "If their currency was really overvalued, this would have put pressure on their foreign reserves because foreign goods would have appeared cheaper than domestic goods. People in the CFA countries would also have swapped out of the overvalued currency and bought foreign exchange if they thought devaluation might occur. The central bank would have to supply that foreign exchange to keep the exchange rate fixed, but their reserves would have been limited. Devaluation was probably inevitable," he concludes.

While Ante and Freedy continue their heated discussion about the likelihood of devaluation, Jean notices that his other cousin, Suttle, has decided to join in. "Come on over, Suttle, and make these guys shut up. I do not want to talk economics all afternoon!"

After a short briefing, Suttle interjects, "Let me make a simple suggestion. Let's list who gains and who loses by the devaluation. Once we figure this out, it should be easy to infer what was likely to happen." Ante gushes, "Good idea! Here is why they would never devalue: French businesses such as Painargent would never tolerate the loss of stability and monetary discipline that the fixed CFA franc brought. Moreover, these firms would be willing to use a lot of political capital to prevent devaluation because such an event would mean an instant loss of wealth for these companies." Suttle nods. "You're right, cousin, but I think the decision

---

[6]The countries are Benin, Burkina Faso, Cameroon, Central Africa Republic, Comoros Islands, Congo, Cote d'Ivoire, Equatorial Guinea, Gabon, Mali, Niger, Senegal, Chad, and Togo.

to devalue was not entirely up to the French businesses. I think it is also important to think about the rich Africans, including the ones wielding political power and the civil servants. Devaluation would reduce their purchasing power abroad as the CFA franc would buy fewer French francs, and hence, fewer bottles of Moët et Chandon and fewer vacations in Saint-Tropez. It would also make French schools more expensive for their kids." Ante, now ecstatic, shouts, "And import prices would rise, which fuels inflation. It would also be harder for the CFA governments and firms to repay any debt denominated in foreign currency because it would cost more in local currency."

"Hold it," cries a surprisingly agitated Freedy. "A government simply cannot keep the exchange rate at what is clearly not its equilibrium value without severe exchange controls that would eventually cripple the country. If the CFA countries had lost their competitiveness relative to the countries with which they trade, a devaluation would make imports more expensive, but exports to the rest of the world would be cheaper, leading to a competitive edge for local businesses." Suttle notes, "Yes, that is true, too." Jean adds, "At the time there were also lots of rumors of rich Africans spotted arriving in Marseilles with suitcases stuffed full of CFA francs that they immediately converted to French francs while the rate was good." Freedy interjects, "Right, we learned that such capital flight removes critical capital, which could be used to finance development. Moreover, it is likely that the IMF and the World Bank probably were insisting on devaluation before they would lend more money to those countries."

"Hmmm, this is a hard one," Suttle admits. "I am not convinced that devaluation helps in the long run. After all, import prices will likely rise, and that in turn may put upward pressure on other prices and wages. If that is true, the competitive advantage for local firms gets squandered pretty quickly. In the short run, however, appropriate government policies can make sure the higher import prices do not filter through immediately into higher wage demands. I'm not sure I know how this one turned out," he muses.

Finally, Jean decides it is time to explain what happened. "Well, the devaluation happened shortly after I started working. In January 1994, the exchange rate was changed from 50 CFA francs per French franc to 100 CFA francs per French franc, a 100% increase in the value of the French franc relative to the CFA franc. The results of the devaluation were decidedly mixed. After years of dismal growth, the Ivory Coast, for example, started growing again, but in Cameroon, problems persisted, and inflation was rife.[7] The profitability of Painargent was definitely affected for a few years, but we persisted as best we could. We raised our baguette prices as much as we could, and we had to fire some of our bakers. We also started selling more in Nigeria."

Why Not Simply Float?

Why do countries go through the trouble of trying to keep the exchange rate fixed at a particular value instead of letting market forces determine the correct value of their currency? As the *Point–Counterpoint* feature discusses, the political elite may prefer a strong exchange rate for their own private benefit, potentially to the detriment of the country's citizens. However, the economics profession has most definitely not reached a consensus about the choice of the exchange rate regimes. The most-often-quoted advantages ascribed to fixed exchange rates can be summarized with two words: discipline and stability.

Discipline refers to the "straitjacket" that a fixed-rate regime imposes on fiscal and monetary policies. If a country with a fixed exchange rate runs higher inflation than its trading

---

[7]See "After a Devaluation, Two African Countries Fare Very Differently" (1995), and Loffi Amegbeto and Alex Winter-Nelson (1996).

partners, it loses competitiveness (see Chapters 8 and 9). The fear of this occurring should discourage over-expansionary fiscal or monetary policies, which in turn, should keep inflation down. According to fixed-rate proponents, the currency volatility that characterizes floating exchange rates can hardly be beneficial for international trade. Fluctuating currencies make importers more uncertain about the prices they will have to pay for goods in the future and exporters more uncertain about the prices they will receive. Of course, this argument can be easily countered by noting that this risk can be rather cheaply hedged (for example, using forward contracts) and by noting that the stability offered by pegged exchange rate systems appears more illusory than real. In fact, the 1990s witnessed a number of important currency crises where speculators successfully attacked pegged currencies.

These currency crises are not isolated phenomena. Michael Klein and Nancy Marion (1997) examine the duration of exchange rate pegs in seventeen Central and South American countries from 1957 to 1995. The average duration of a fixed-rate regime is 32.2 months, and the median is only 10 months. More than half of the pegs were over by the end of their first year! Most fixed-rate periods end with a devaluation of the currency and a continuation of the pegged system, but often a new exchange rate regime is adopted. The risk that the currency will devalue plagues any system in which exchange rates are not allowed to trade at market values.

If pegged systems have such low duration and devaluations occur frequently, can they really be expected to yield the benefits of inflation credibility and exchange rate stability the authorities expect? Many believe that such systems are doomed to failure. In recent times, a number of governments have resorted to an alternative monetary system, the currency board, which enhances the credibility of the peg. In their quest for exchange rate stability, the European Union countries went one step further and established a monetary union, where one central bank issues one currency for all the participating countries. Other countries have adopted the currency of a larger country, a phenomenon known as *dollarization*. We discuss currency boards and dollarization next but defer the discussion of monetary unions to Section 5.6, where we survey Europe's experimentation with different currency arrangements.

Currency Boards

A currency board is a type of fixed exchange rate system, a monetary institution that issues base money (notes and coins, and required reserves of financial institutions) that is fully backed by a foreign reserve currency and fully convertible into the reserve currency at a fixed rate and on demand. Hence, the domestic currency monetary base is 100% backed by assets payable in the reserve currency. In practical terms, this requirement bars the currency board from extending credit to either the government or the banking sector. Exhibit 5.11 shows the balance sheet of a currency board.

In the past, currency boards have existed in more than 70 countries. The first currency board was established in the British Indian Ocean colony of Mauritius in 1848, and currency boards were subsequently adopted in many British colonies and a few other countries. However, when those countries became independent after World War II, most of them decided to replace their currency boards with central banks. More recently, currency boards have been adopted by Hong Kong (1983), Argentina (1991–2001), Estonia (1992), Lithuania (1994), Bulgaria (1997), and Bosnia (1997).

Exhibit 5.11 The Balance Sheet of a Currency Board

Assets	Liabilities
International reserves	Currency in circulation
	Required reserves of financial institutions

In recent policy debates, currency boards are often mentioned as a miracle cure for cutting inflation without high costs to the economy. The main success story is Hong Kong (see Yum Kwan and Francis Liu, 1996). The Hong Kong Monetary Authority has kept the Hong Kong dollar at HKD7.8/USD since 1983, and it successfully weathered the Southeast Asian currency crisis of 1997. Argentina's experience offers a cautionary tale. Argentina's Convertibility Law of April 1991 instituted a currency board. In the 1980s, inflation in Argentina averaged 750.4% per year; in the 1990s, inflation averaged 2.4% per year. The reason some believe a currency board imparts more monetary credibility than a conventional exchange rate peg is that a currency board has no discretionary powers. Its operations are completely passive and automatic. It cannot lend to the government and hence cannot monetize fiscal deficits. This also means that a currency board cannot rescue banks when they get into trouble. In other words, a currency board cannot function as a lender of last resort.

It has to be said that the practical implementations of currency boards are not always this strict. For example, the reserve requirements for Argentinean banks were quite high; hence, the central bank could inject liquidity into the banking system by lowering reserve requirements, and it did so following the Mexican crisis in 1994.

Whether a currency board is more credible than a standard pegged exchange rate system is hard to determine from the limited historical experiences we have. Speculators attacked the Argentine peso, in the wake of the Mexican currency crisis, and they attacked the Hong Kong dollar in the wake of the Southeast Asian currency crisis, but the currency boards survived. During this time, as always in speculative crises, interest rates did increase, and the economies suffered. Whether other systems would have generated smaller economic costs is difficult to guess.

Argentina's good luck did not last. While Argentina enjoyed the success of a seemingly well-functioning currency board, its government was able to borrow at competitive rates, and the country's public debt grew substantially. In addition, a crisis in Brazil in 1999 led to a large devaluation of the Brazilian real, making Argentine exports less competitive. Also, the dollar was strong relative to the euro, which undermined the competitiveness of Argentine exports to Europe. The Argentine economy began to sputter, with economic growth becoming negative, making the public debt burden suddenly seem much less sustainable. In mid-2001, the government started to tinker with the currency board (introducing a special exchange rate for international trade transactions, for example) in the hope of improving Argentina's international competitiveness. But the policy changes only managed to further undermine the confidence of investors in the sustainability of the currency board.

Argentina had trouble meeting interest payments on its international bonds, and in November 2001, the country effectively defaulted on its international debt. This led to a bank run by Argentine citizens, who dumped their pesos in favor of dollars. The government responded by restricting bank deposit withdrawals. Soon the country was engulfed in a deep economic crisis, with looting and rioting accompanying close to 20% unemployment rates.

In January 2002, the new interim president of Argentina, Eduardo Duhalde, abandoned the currency board and devalued the peso to 1.4 pesos per dollar for most transactions, while allowing all other transactions to be made at market rates. Other ill-devised temporary measures to deal with the crisis (converting debts denominated in dollars to debts denominated into pesos, for example) only further deepened the economic crisis. The year 2002 was disastrous for Argentina: Output collapsed, and inflation increased to double-digit levels. The idea that a currency board entailed no currency risk was buried with it. The peso was eventually allowed to float, and it depreciated by over 100%.[8]

---

[8]See Rudiger Dornbusch (2001) for more detail about the pros and cons of currency boards. See www.imf.org/external/np/pdr/lessons/100803. htm for an in-depth analysis of the Argentinean crisis and the role the IMF played.

Dollarization

Interestingly, Argentina's Minister of Finance, Domingo Cavallo, who was the architect of the Convertibility Plan, ascribed Argentina's initial success in controlling inflation and maintaining the exchange rate peg not as much to the currency board as to the dual-currency feature of the system. During the hyperinflation of the 1970s, Argentina's money was superseded by the U.S. dollar. The phenomenon of foreign currencies (often the dollar) driving out local currencies as a means of payment (at least for big transactions) and a savings vehicle is known as **dollarization**.[9] "Unofficial" dollarization occurs when residents of a country extensively use foreign currency alongside or instead of the domestic currency. Although many countries in Latin America are partially dollarized, the foreign currency need not be the dollar, as, for example, the euro is often the currency of choice in the countries of the Balkan peninsula in southeastern Europe.

That unofficial dollarization indeed occurs around the world can be gauged by estimating the sheer use of dollars by nonresidents. Researchers at the Federal Reserve System estimate that foreigners hold 55% to 70% of U.S. dollar notes.

"Official" dollarization occurs when foreign currency has exclusive or predominant status as full legal tender. In Andorra, a small country in the Pyreneés, between France and Spain, both the French franc and the Spanish peseta were legal tender prior to 1999. Andorra now uses the euro. Similarly, the 1991 Convertibility Law in Argentina officially condoned the use of the dollar, allowing Argentines to open checking and savings accounts in the currency of their choice and to conduct most transactions in the currency of their choice.

Most officially dollarized countries, however, are tiny, using the currency of the "mother" country from colonial times or from a large neighboring country. Kiribati, a Polynesian island, for example, uses the Australian dollar, but it issues its own coins. The largest and most well-known dollarized country is Panama, where dollarization has existed since 1904. In the past few years Ecuador (in 2000) and El Salvador (in 2001) have officially adopted the U.S. dollar as their currency. In contrast to a currency board, a dollarized system can no longer collect seigniorage. This may discourage larger countries such as Mexico and Argentina from adopting such a system.

5.5 LIMITED-FLEXIBILITY SYSTEMS: TARGET ZONES AND CRAWLING PEGS

In between fixed and floating exchange rate systems are systems where exchange rate fluctuations are kept within a certain range.

Target Zones

The Bretton Woods system in effect between 1944 and 1971 (see Section 5.4) is an example of a **target zone system**. Whereas the dollar was fixed relative to gold (at $35 per ounce), all other currencies had particular dollar par values (that is, each had an exchange rate versus the dollar), but the actual exchange rates were allowed to move within a range of 1% on either side of these par values. The most famous target zone system in recent times is the European Monetary System (EMS), and, given its historical importance, we discuss it in greater detail later. More recently, a number of other countries, including Croatia, Hungary, and Vietnam, have adopted such systems.

To see how a target zone operates, consider Exhibit 5.12, which once again looks at the French franc–Deutsche mark (FRF/DEM) exchange rate between early 1987 and August 1993.

---

[9]A detailed study of the dollarization phenomenon is provided in Kurt Schuler (2000). Sebastian Edwards (2001) provides a rather skeptical view of the economic benefits of dollarization.

Exhibit 5.12 An Example of a Target Zone

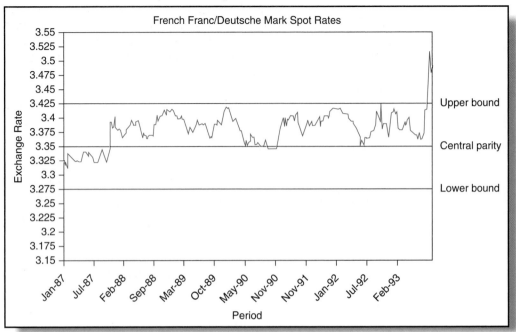

Although the exchange rate shows substantial variability, it fluctuates within a band until the very end of that period. The EMS specified a central rate, or central parity of FRF3.3539/DEM, but the exchange rate was allowed to fluctuate in a 2.25% band around this value.

Example 5.2 Determining the Intervention Exchange Rates

Let's use the preceding FRF/DEM example to determine the intervention exchange rates. With the central parity set at FRF3.3539/DEM, the monetary authorities need to determine the exchange rates for the upper and lower intervention limits such that the band is 2.25% band around the central parity. The computation also must guarantee that the width of the band is the same, no matter how the exchange rates were expressed (in FRF/DEM or DEM/FRF).

Let S be the central parity in FRF/DEM, let the upper intervention limit be $(1 + y)S$, and let the lower intervention limit be $S/(1+y)$. Clearly, expressing exchange rates in DEM/FRF by taking reciprocals results in the same intervention points. Then, because the width of the band is 4.5% of the central parity, we can solve the following equation for y:

$$(1 + y)S - S/(1+y) = 0.045S$$

The solution is $y = 0.022753$. Thus, the upper value of the band is $1.022753 \times$ (FRF3.3539/DEM) = FRF3.4302/DEM, and the lower value of the band is (FRF3.3539/DEM)/1.022753 = FRF3.2793/DEM.

During this period, French francs and Deutsche marks were freely traded in the foreign exchange market. What keeps the actual exchange rate in the prespecified band around some rate specified by the monetary authorities? As long as private market participants deem the central rate reasonable and recognize a credible commitment by the monetary authorities to defend the rate, market participants will not expect the currency value to go outside the bands, and no currency crisis will occur. A previously announced strategy of monetary policy is *credible* if it remains an optimal strategy for the central bank over time. A strategy will continue to be optimal if it is more costly for policymakers to abandon their commitment to the strategy rather than to honor it. Unless a strategy is credible, the private sector's expectations and consequent behavior will not support the strategy's goal, and it will not be achieved.

Hence, a crucial element for the stability of a target zone system is the perception on the part of investors and speculators that the authorities are committed to defend their exchange rate. This holds all the more for a pegged exchange rate system, which can be thought of as a target zone with a very thin band. From our description of how a central bank functions, we know that such an exchange rate target necessarily means that the authorities will not be able to use monetary policy to reach other goals, such as pushing the economy toward full employment. When the commitment of the authorities becomes less certain—for example, because of unfavorable domestic economic conditions—a currency can come under pressure and move toward the edge of the band. In Exhibit 5.12, the franc is the weak currency when the exchange rate approaches the higher edge of the band.

Speculative Attacks

Policymakers invariably blame downward pressure on the foreign exchange value of their currency on nasty speculators. We will discuss speculation explicitly in Chapter 7, so here we just give a verbal description. During a speculative attack, speculators hope to profit from a devaluation of the currency or a resetting of the bands of a target zone by massively borrowing the weak currency and investing the proceeds in assets (typically short-term money market instruments) denominated in the strong currency. If the amount of the devaluation exceeds any differential between the interest they pay and the interest they receive, speculators win.

Defending the Target Zone

To defend their currency, the monetary authorities in the countries with weaker currencies have three basic mechanisms available. First, they can simply intervene in the currency markets. When a central bank intervenes to support its currency, it buys its own currency with official reserves. An intervention by the central bank of the weak currency country, if not sterilized, reduces the money supply. The reduced liquidity in the money market tends to put upward pressure on interest rates. This raises the costs of speculators (which include financial institutions), who try to borrow the money to invest abroad.

The second defense mechanism of the central bank is to raise the interest rates they control (typically, the rate at which banks can borrow at the central bank), both to make currency speculations more costly and to signal commitment to the central rate.[10] The behavior of central banks and private market participants results in higher short-term interest rates, which drive up the cost of speculation. The magnitude of the interest rate hike needed to stave off a speculative attack depends on the probability that the currency will devalue and hence on the credibility of the authorities. We cover this issue in more detail in Chapter 7.

Although a policy of high interest rates discourages speculation, it also increases the short-term funding costs for businesses borrowing money, which is a drag on the economy. Not surprisingly, many countries resort to a third line of defense: limiting foreign exchange

---

[10]Earlier we argued that monetary authorities can set the rate of money growth, unless they focus on another policy goal, in which case money growth becomes endogenous (see Section 5.2).

transactions through capital controls. **Capital controls** are the set of regulations pertaining to flows of capital into and out of the country. At the simplest level, the authorities may tax or simply prohibit the purchase of most foreign securities by the country's residents. At one time, Italy and Spain, countries that had participated in the EMS, forced purchasers of foreign currency or foreign assets to make a non-interest-bearing deposit at their central banks equal to 50% of the value of the foreign investment. Such rules considerably increase the cost of speculation but at a loss of freedom for the citizens of the country.

Lead–Lag Operations

Most countries with capital controls also impose restrictions on trade financing. Whereas currency speculation may conjure up images of wicked financiers plotting the fall of a currency behind a computer screen, often a more serious problem currencies face arises from the financing practices of exporters and importers. In international business, it is customary for exporters to allow their customers to pay some time after the goods have been shipped or even after they have arrived. When devaluation is expected, exporters from the country tend to extend the maturity of these "trade credits" (because they hope to exchange currency they receive for a greater amount of local currency than they could have before the devaluation). This is called a **lag operation** because it postpones the inflow of foreign currency. Conversely, domestic importers prepay for goods that they plan to purchase from abroad in order to beat the increase in costs the devaluation will impose on them. This effectively grants a credit to foreign exporters and is therefore called a **lead operation**. Lead and lag operations often put pressure on the foreign reserves of the central bank because the volume of foreign trade is large relative to the reserves of the central bank for small open economies.

Exhibit 5.12 suggests that, whatever the defense mechanisms, they successfully defended the FRF/DEM exchange rate between January 1987 and the end of July 1993. Nevertheless, the EMS witnessed occasional speculative crises, and the bands were often reset. At the end of the sample, we see an example of a speculative crisis, with the exchange rate exploding out of the band. We discuss the EMS experience in more detail in Section 5.6.

Crawling Pegs

In many developing countries, where inflation is especially a problem, the bands have been allowed to move ("crawl") over time. Such mini-devaluations or resets of the bands take place quite frequently, sometimes even daily, and are mostly preannounced.

To understand the logic behind this system, you must understand the effects of inflation on a quasi-fixed exchange rate system. (These issues are addressed in more detail in Chapters 8 and 9.) We will consider the example of Mexico and the United States. Suppose the Mexican central bank wants to fix the Mexican peso's value relative to the dollar, as it has tried to do many times in the past. If the exchange rate remains fixed, and Mexico experiences higher inflation than the United States, it will lose competitiveness because the prices of Mexican goods will increase relative to the prices of U.S. goods. The resulting reduction in Mexican exports to the United States is likely to hurt Mexico's economy severely because the United States is its largest trading partner.

Knowing the perverse effects of the loss of competitiveness that high inflation entails, governments and private agents (firms, wage earners) alike should be motivated to follow non-inflationary policies. Hence, the fixed exchange rate can potentially buy inflation credibility, and Mexico can "import" low inflation from the United States by pegging its currency to the U.S. dollar. Again, credibility is key, and in developing countries, maintaining the same level of inflation as in developed countries is a tall order. Also, the consequences of the loss of competitiveness are particularly dire. Anticipating a gradual loss of competitiveness, a **crawling peg** system adjusts the fixed rate or band over time, where the adjustment is often a function of the inflation differential between the developing country and the country to which its currency is pegged.

Exhibit 5.13   An Example of a Crawling Peg

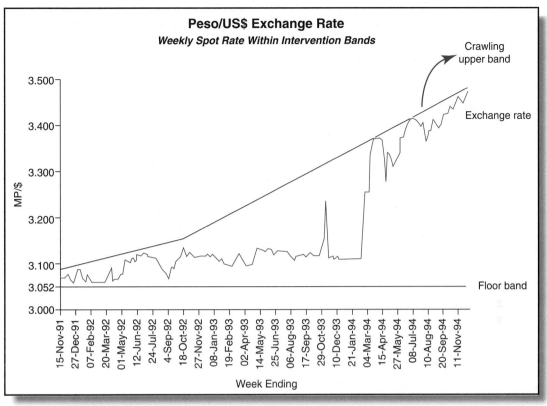

Exhibit 5.13 offers a real-word illustration. From November 1, 1991, to December 21, 1994, the Mexican peso traded within a formal intervention band set by the Bank of Mexico relative to the dollar. The floor of the band remained fixed at MXP3.052/USD, while the upper band rose (allowing for peso depreciation) at a predetermined rate: increasing at MXP0.0002/USD per day from November 11, 1991, to October 20, 1992, and MXP0.0004/USD per day from October 21, 1992, to December 21, 1994. The history of the crawling peg in Mexico ended with the famous currency crisis in December 1994 and early 1995.

It turns out that the changes in the band did not fully correct for the inflation difference between the United States and Mexico, and Mexican firms gradually lost competitiveness. With a large current account deficit and insufficient capital inflows, Bank of Mexico intervention in the foreign exchange market was necessary. By December 1994, international reserves had dwindled until they were almost depleted. An attempt to devalue the peso by 15% in December only caused a run on the currency, and Mexico was forced to float the peso. Currently, the Mexican peso floats freely.

Countries that have had more success implementing crawling pegs include Chile (1984–1999), Colombia (1994–1999), and Poland (1991–2001).

A number of economists, including John Williamson (1987) and Ronald McKinnon (1988), have proposed target zones of the crawling variety for the major currencies (yen, dollar, euro), citing the high costs of currency misalignment when the exchange rate is left to market forces. There is a historical precedent for this desire. The Louvre Accord of 1987 involved an unpublished agreement between the finance ministers and central banks of the G5 countries (United States, United Kingdom, Germany, Japan, and France) and Canada to set up target zones for the major currencies and to defend them by intervening in the foreign exchange market. However, the accord crumbled in October 1987 when the U.S. stock market crashed, leading to a sharp decrease in U.S. interest rates and in the value of the dollar.

5.6 HOW TO SEE AN EMU FLY: THE ROAD TO MONETARY INTEGRATION IN EUROPE

One of the most important financial developments in recent years is the emergence of the European Monetary Union (EMU), with the euro as a common currency, first for 11 countries and now for 15 countries. All of the 27 countries that are members of the EU are eligible to join the monetary union if they comply with certain monetary requirements. Although the United Kingdom and Denmark participated in the Maastricht Treaty (see later on in this section) and the European Monetary System (EMS), they negotiated exemptions from the requirement that they adopt the euro as their currency. Any country that has joined the EU since the 1993 implementation of the Maastricht Treaty has had to pledge to adopt the euro in due course.

The importance of these developments and the fact that other regions of the world may set up similar currency systems prompts us to describe the developments in some detail. In particular, regional associations of countries promoting free trade and other forms of economic and political cooperation in Latin America (Mercosur), Asia (the ASEAN countries), and Africa (the East African Community [EAC] countries) are prime candidates for a similar currency arrangement some time in the foreseeable future.[11] Because the euro did not arrive overnight, this section presents a historical case study that chronicles the history of currency systems in Europe, starting with the EMS and leading to the introduction of the euro.

The European Monetary System (EMS)

The desire for currency stability in Europe dates back many decades. It was actively pursued in the context of the European Community (EC). One obvious reason that these countries desired monetary stability is that most western European countries are not only quite open to foreign trade but their main trading partners are also their neighboring countries, making potential costs of exchange rate variability particularly acute within Europe. Another reason the EC countries wanted to limit exchange rate fluctuations was to facilitate the operation of a common market for agricultural products. Finally, the desire for an exchange rate arrangement in Europe should also be viewed as an integral part of the wider drive toward economic, monetary, and political union between European countries in the EC.

From 1944 to 1973, stability was supplied by the Bretton Woods system of fixed exchange rates. While old plans to establish a monetary union got bogged down during the breakup of the Bretton Woods system, the EC countries kept their currencies in a target zone system and eventually established the **European Monetary System (EMS)** in 1979. All EC countries joined, though Britain, characteristically, did not fully participate until 1990. The EMS had three components: the Exchange Rate Mechanism (ERM), a set of intervention rules and intervention financing mechanisms, and a set of rules for realignments. We discuss each in turn.

---

[11]The Mercosur countries are Brazil, Bolivia, Chile, Argentina, Paraguay, and Uruguay. The ASEAN countries are Brunei Darussalam, Cambodia, Indonesia, Laos, Malaysia, Myanmar, the Philippines, Singapore, Thailand, and Vietnam. The EAC countries are Kenya, Uganda, Tanzania, Burundi, and Rwanda.

The ERM

The ERM was a grid of bilateral fixed exchange rates, called "central parities," from which exchange rates could deviate by 2.25% on each side, with the exception of the Italian lira, which was allowed a margin of 6%. The ERM gradually included more countries.

Intervention Rules

Interventions were compulsory whenever either bilateral margin was reached. Both central banks were required to intervene. The central bank of the strong currency was required to grant the central bank of the weak currency an unlimited credit line to assist in the defense of its currency. Of course, a central bank could intervene to support its currency before the outer limits were reached. Francesco Giavazzi and Alberto Giovannini (1989) report that such intra-marginal interventions were even more frequent than the required marginal interventions.

Realignment Rules

When the bilateral central parity could not be sustained at reasonable cost, the finance ministers of the EMS countries gathered secretively to establish new central parities, devaluing the weaker currencies and revaluing the stronger currencies.

On ECUs, Euros, and Franken

Many non-Europeans mistakenly believed the ECU to be the cornerstone of the system. The ECU was a currency basket, consisting of specified amounts of each member currency. The amounts of currencies included in the basket were last changed in 1989, after which the Maastricht Treaty prevented any further changes. Because of this, the currencies of Austria and Finland, which joined the EC later, were never part of the ECU basket.

We show the composition of the ECU basket in Exhibit 5.14. For example, in an ECU, there were 1.332 French francs and 0.6242 Deutsche marks. These amounts were revised every 5 years to reflect the economic importance of each country. If we take the central rates

Exhibit 5.14 Composition of the ECU Basket

Currency	Amounts of Currencies Included in the ECU Basket [a]	ECU Central Rates [b]	Relative Weight of Each Currency in the ECU Basket (in %)	
			9-21-89	10-22-98
Deutsche mark	0.6242	1.97738	30.09	31.57
French franc	1.332	6.63186	19	20.08
British pound	0.08784	0.653644	13	13.44
Italian lira	151.8	1957.61	10.16	7.75
Dutch guilder	0.2198	2.22799	9.4	9.87
Belgian and Luxembourg franc	3.431	40.7844	7.89	8.41
Spanish peseta	6.885	168.22	5.31	4.09
Danish krone	0.1976	7.54257	2.45	2.62
Irish punt	0.008552	0.796244	1.1	1.07
Portuguese escudo	1.393	202.692	0.8	0.69
Greek drachma	1.44	357	0.8	0.41

[a] As of September 21, 1989.
[b] As of October 23, 1998.
Note: Data are from the Bank for International Settlements.

of one currency relative to all other countries, we can determine what weight the currency has in the basket.

Example 5.3   The Weight of the DEM in the ECU

To determine the weight of the DEM in the ECU basket of currencies, we start by adding up the DEM value of all the currencies in the basket, using the exchange rates from the bilateral grid of central rates specified in the ERM in Exhibit 5.14:

$$DEM0.6242 + [FRF1.332 \times (DEM0.2982/FRF)] + [GBP0.08784$$
$$\times DEM3.0252/GBP] + \ldots + [GRD1.44\ GRD \times (DEM0.0055/GRD)]$$
$$= DEM1.97738/ECU$$

Because an ECU contains DEM0.6242 directly, the proportionate weight of the DEM in the ECU in this case is $(0.6242 / 1.97738) = 31.57\%$.

Exhibit 5.14 also reports the ECU central rates, the values of the currencies expressed in ECU. This shows a primary role of the ECU in the ERM, to be the unit of account, or numeraire. By expressing all central rates in terms of the ECU, the whole complex bilateral grid of central rates is no longer needed. For example, if we know the exchange rates of FRF/ECU and DEM/ECU, we can easily compute the FRF/DEM central rate, as

$$(FRF6.63186/ECU) / (DEM1.97738/ECU) = FRF3.35386/DEM$$

However, the actual market exchange rates often differed from the central rates because exchange rates only needed to stay within a 2.25% band around the central rates. This also meant that the market weights in the ECU basket could differ from the official weights. In fact, with the basket amounts fixed, stronger currencies slowly gained weight in the basket.

Apart from its role as a numeraire, the ECU was also an important reserve asset and a settlement instrument for transactions among the EC's central banks. It was also the unit of account for all intervention mechanisms.

In addition, companies started to use the ECU for invoicing and in their financial statements, and denominating contracts in ECUs became important in financial markets. There were ECU-denominated deposits and short-term loans, bonds were issued in ECU, and derivative contracts traded on exchanges allowed traders to bet on the direction of ECU interest rates. As a consequence, banks started to quote ECU-denominated exchange rates without strict reference to its synthetic value—that is, the value of the ECU in terms of the market value of the constituent currencies. Soon, this "private" ECU no longer necessarily had a value of 1 to 1 with the market-determined value of the basket of currencies.

The Treaty of Maastricht in 1991, which mapped out the road to monetary integration, named the ECU as the single European currency, and when the single currency came into existence, on January 1, 1999, its external value was set equal to the theoretical value of one ECU. However, the new currency is not called the ECU, but the euro. This is somewhat surprising because the name "euro" confusingly adds to a list of existing but quite different "Euro-financial assets" such as Eurobonds and Eurocurrencies (see Chapter 11).

The Politics of Naming the Euro

The seemingly insignificant issue of the single currency's name is a nice illustration of the amazing development in Europe that brings together very different cultures in one monetary arrangement. Despite the familiarity of Europeans with the ECU and its use in scores of financial contracts, the Germans, who were very attached to their beloved Deutsche mark, felt that the name "ECU" sounded too French. The name of an old French coin also was the écu. Rumor has it that to ensure that the name "euro" would replace the name "ECU," the Germans pushed for an alternative name, the "Franken." Appalled, the French agreed to a compromise.

Was the EMS Successful?

The main goal of the EMS was to reduce exchange rate volatility and consequently to narrow inflation and interest differentials between countries. Was it successful?

Day-to-Day Variability Was Down

Overall, the EMS record was mixed. First, although the day-to-day variability of European exchange rates decreased beginning in 1979, large currency movements still occurred because of realignments and the currency crises of 1992 to 1993. The realignments were frequent at first, but they became less and less frequent over the years. Interestingly, the Deutsche mark never devalued during the history of the EMS. With the exception of the Dutch guilder, the currencies of other countries in the EMS fell by more than 20% relative to the Deutsche mark through seven realignments in the early 1980s.

Inflation and Interest Differentials Narrowed

Although inflation and interest rate differentials did narrow during the EMS period, the EMS might not have been the main cause of the narrowing. For instance, inflation cooled down in most countries around the world during the 1980s. After the currency realignments mentioned earlier, two traditionally weak currencies, the Belgian franc and the Danish krone, actually became "hard" currencies.

A country's monetary and fiscal authorities practice a hard currency policy when they try to prevent their currency from depreciating by maintaining staunch anti-inflationary monetary and fiscal policies. The benefit of such a policy in the context of the EMS was lower interest rates, which meant important interest rate savings for a high public debt country such as Belgium. Unfortunately, the Maastricht Treaty started a period of currency turmoil that peaked in September 1992, when the pound and the lira were forced to leave the system. This currency turmoil led to a widening of the bands to 15% on each side of the central rates in August 1993.

Asymmetric Adjustments

The original plans for the EMS envisioned a symmetric system with the ECU as the center of the EMS and the adjustment burden in times of crises shared across countries. An anatomy of the realignment episodes and the turbulent events in the 1990s strongly indicates an asymmetric system with an anchor role for the Deutsche mark. That is, the Bundesbank, the German central bank, maintained the purchasing power of the Deutsche mark, and the other countries adopted monetary and financial market policies that were consistent with maintaining a stable exchange rate vis-à-vis the Deutsche mark. In tense and speculative times, countries with weak currencies intervened in the currency markets and increased their interest rates.

Some claim the system proved beneficial to inflation-prone countries, such as Italy and France, by improving the credibility of authorities in pursuing non-inflationary policies. The EMS made it costly for an economy to experience inflation because it led to an erosion of the competitiveness of the country's currency between realignments. It could also lead to a permanent erosion of the currency if the realignment didn't compensate fully for the inflation that had occurred, which was often the case. Others admit that the Bundesbank played a central and at times disciplinary role in the EMS, but they believe that in times of crises, the Bundesbank stubbornly stuck to its policies, even if that put the entire adjustment burden on the other countries. For example, the Bundesbank only intervened when it was required to do so according to the EMS rules.

The Maastricht Treaty and the Euro

In 1991, the European heads of state met in Maastricht in the Netherlands to map out the road to economic and monetary union, including a single EC currency, to be reached by 1999. When a number of countries establish a **monetary union**, they fix their exchange rates relative to one another, possibly by introducing a single currency, and they establish a single central bank to conduct a single monetary and exchange rate policy across the region. Historical examples of monetary unions include the Latin Monetary Union (France, Belgium, Switzerland, Bulgaria, and Greece) from 1865 until 1873, Belgium and Luxembourg from 1921 until 1999, and Ireland and the United Kingdom briefly before Ireland joined the EMS in 1979. The Maastricht Treaty in 1991 embarked on what is the most important monetary union ever.

The Maastricht Treaty specified a number of criteria that member countries had to satisfy in order to be able to join the monetary union. These "convergence criteria" were to be measured 1 year before the start of the EMU and were as follows:

1. Inflation within 1.5% of that of the three best-performing states.
2. Interest rate on long-term government bonds within 2% of the long-term interest rates of the three best-performing countries in terms of inflation.
3. A budget deficit of less than 3% of gross domestic product.
4. Government debt less than 60% of gross domestic product.
5. No devaluation within the exchange rate mechanism within the past 2 years.

The convergence criteria garnered a lot of controversy, and the fiscal criteria almost became a stumbling block for the EMU. At one point, only one country readily qualified for EMU entry—tiny Luxembourg—and even Germany barely made it.

The road to EMU was completed in three stages. In Phase I, all remaining restrictions on the movement of capital and payments between member states and between member states and third countries were removed. This phase was completed by January 1, 1994.

In Phase II, a new European Monetary Institute (EMI) was created, with headquarters in Frankfurt, Germany, to administer the EMS and prepare the ground for the European Central Bank to be established in Phase III by strengthening the coordination of monetary policies of the member states. Phase II also introduced EC supervision of fiscal policy of the member states and forbade monetary financing of budget deficits. Central banks of the member countries were also made politically independent.

In Phase III, the European Central Bank (ECB) replaced the EMI. The European System of Central Banks (ESCB), composed of the ECB and the national central banks, conducts monetary and exchange rate policy for the whole of the single-currency area. Its primary objective, as specified in the Maastricht Treaty, is to maintain price stability. This phase started on January 1, 1999, at which time the conversion rates into the euro were fixed. The United Kingdom and Denmark opted out. Greece joined in January 2001, after it satisfied the convergence criteria, and Slovenia joined in January 2007. Cyprus and Malta joined in January 2008.

Whereas the different national currencies immediately ceased to exist, the notes and coins remained legal tender until early 2002. From then onward, new euro notes and coins replaced the national notes and coins.

ERM II

When a country joins the EU, it negotiates a time at which it joins the ERM II, which is a requirement that the country establish a central parity for its currency versus the euro and pledge to remain within a plus or minus 15% band. While the Danish krone is allowed to fluctuate within 15%, the Danish Central Bank is currently conducting monetary policy to hold the currency within a tighter 2.25% band.

If a country successfully keeps its currency within the ERM II band for 2 years and satisfies the other Maastricht criteria, it is eligible to adopt the euro as its currency and become a member of the **eurozone**. The EMU may eventually include most countries in Europe and may inspire other regions to form monetary unions, but are they really a good idea?

Pros and Cons of a Monetary Union (Advanced)

Since the signing of the Maastricht Treaty, economists have heatedly debated whether monetary union in Europe makes economic sense. The debate typically centers on the question of whether Europe is, or is not, an optimum currency area.

Optimum Currency Areas

In 1961, Robert Mundell, a Nobel prize–winning economist, published a theory of **optimum currency areas**. Mundell defines an optimum currency area as one that balances the microeconomic benefits of perfect exchange rate certainty against the costs of macroeconomic adjustment problems.

Sharing a currency across a border enhances price transparency (that is, makes prices easier to understand and compare across countries), lowers transactions costs, removes exchange rate uncertainty for investors and firms, and enhances competition. These gains are already being realized throughout Europe—for example, car prices have decreased and converged across Europe. The European Commission has estimated these microeconomic gains to amount to 0.5% of GDP of the entire EU—a substantial sum.

The potential cost of a single currency is the loss of independent monetary policies for the participating countries. Losing this monetary independence is especially grave if a region is likely to suffer from *asymmetric economic shocks*. Asymmetric shocks can include a sudden fall in demand for a country's main export product or a sudden increase in the price of one of the main inputs for a country's manufacturing sector, where the shocks affect that country differently from the other countries in the single-currency area. In a monetary union, the affected country no longer has the ability to respond to economic shocks by relaxing its monetary policy. The country also cannot devalue its currency. The inability to react with monetary policy is thought to deepen recessions and exacerbate unemployment.

The optimum currency area theory concludes that for a currency area to have the best chance of success, asymmetric shocks should be rare. This is likely to be the case when the economies involved face similar business cycles and have similar industrial structures. Failing that, other mechanisms must absorb the shocks. This requires mobility of labor and capital.

An analogy to the United States is useful. For example, if California experiences lower demand from Asia, which increases unemployment in California, while Texas booms due to high oil prices, workers moving from California to Texas can restore unemployment rates back to normal. Such labor mobility will be enhanced if wages are flexible. Wages would be increasing in Texas and decreasing in California. Moreover, federal fiscal transfers to California may help it get out of the economic doldrums.

Is Europe an Optimum Currency Area?

Many prominent U.S. economists conclude that Europe is not particularly well suited to be a monetary union: The shocks hitting European countries are quite asymmetric; labor mobility is very limited due to cultural, linguistic, and legal barriers between countries; and the EC budget is too small to transfer huge resources into recessionary areas. An adjustment to a bad shock requires a relative price change, which can be more quickly accomplished by an exchange rate change.

Proponents of the EMU argue that the skeptics have too much confidence in the real effects of monetary or exchange rate policy. They argue that devaluing a currency may only cause local inflation, and the competitive advantage gained may be very temporary. Furthermore, the proponents question the effectiveness of labor mobility as a shock absorber, even in the United States. The theory talks about temporary business cycle shocks that would require a temporary movement into regions where work is abundant and productivity high, and vice versa. But even in the United States, such a temporary migration of workers across states is unlikely to occur on a large scale because moving is so costly.

Undeterred, some economists have argued that the United States would have been better off with different currencies across its regions or even states. Taking the argument to Europe, some have even argued that it would be better to have two currencies in Italy: a "north-lira" for the wealthy northern part, and a "south-lira" for the poorer south. Skeptical European economists question how a different exchange rate could possibly solve the structural economic problems Southern Italy faces (see, for example, Martin Feldstein, 1992; Paul Krugman, 1992; and Hugh Rockoff, 2000).

Finally, it is quite conceivable that when countries are within a monetary union, the nature of economic shocks starts to change, and they become less asymmetric (see Jeffrey Frankel and Andrew Rose, 1998). While it will take considerably more time for the full effects of the euro to unravel, a recent survey by Francisco Paolo Mongelli and Juan Luis Vega (2006) suggests that initial concerns regarding the effects of EMU on member countries have been dispelled. For example, trade and financial integration have been enhanced, and business cycle synchronization remains high.[12] Conveniently, the architects of the single-currency arrangements have made no provision, legal or practical, for any participant's withdrawal or expulsion.

5.7 SUMMARY

This chapter has analyzed the large variety of currency arrangements around the world. The main points in the chapter are:

1. There are three main currency systems: floating exchange rates, target zones, and pegged or fixed exchange rate systems. Different systems entail different currency risks.
2. Currency risk can be summarized by a forward-looking conditional distribution of exchange rate changes and the distribution's volatility (dispersion) and skewness. This distribution will be a function of the exchange rate system and will be more difficult to estimate when currencies are not freely floating.
3. In most societies, the government, mostly through a central bank, has control over the money supply. When too much money is issued relative to the demand for money, inflation results.
4. The central bank's balance sheet contains currency in circulation and reserves held by financial institutions

as its main liabilities. Together these are called base money. The assets of the central banks are foreign currency–dominated securities (official reserves), domestic government bonds, and loans to the domestic financial sector.
5. When a currency is freely floating, no official reserves are needed, but in reality, pure freely floating exchange rate systems do not exist. Instead, governments either intervene to influence a currency's value (dirty float) or formally try to peg the exchange rate (fixed exchange rate system) or limit its variability within certain bands around a central value (target zone or crawling peg when the bands are automatically reset over time).
6. In dirty float systems, interventions to affect the value of the currency are often sterilized; that is, the central bank performs an open market operation that counteracts the effect of the original intervention on the money supply. There is no consensus on whether central banks can really affect the level

---

[12]Gikas Hardouvelis, Dimitrios Malliaropoulos, and Richard Priestley (2007) argue that the adoption of the euro and the process of economic and monetary integration preceding it have led to lower costs of equity capital.

and volatility of exchange rates through their interventions.

7. To peg a currency, the government must make a market in foreign currencies buying any private excess supply of foreign currency and delivering additional foreign currency if there is excess demand for it.

8. After World War II, the world at large experimented with a fixed exchange rate system, the Bretton Woods system, based on gold and the dollar. This system lasted until 1971.

9. Currently, many developing countries peg their exchange rates, often at unrealistically high values. Devaluations and currency crises resulting in changes in the exchange rate regime occur regularly.

To increase credibility, a number of governments have introduced currency boards, where base money is backed 100% by foreign currency–denominated assets.

10. Target zones have gained popularity in recent years. The most important example in recent history is the European Monetary System, which operated between 1979 and 1999. Exchange rates were maintained between bands of 2.25% around central rates.

11. The European Union experimented with various exchange rate systems in an attempt to limit exchange rate variability. Since 1999, 15 countries in Europe are now joined in a monetary union with a single currency, the euro, and a single monetary policy.

QUESTIONS

1. How can you quantify currency risk in a floating exchange rate system?
2. Why might it be hard to quantify currency risk in a target zone system or a pegged exchange rate system?
3. What is likely to be the most credible exchange rate system?
4. How can a central bank create money?
5. What are official international reserves of the central bank?
6. What is likely to happen if a central bank suddenly prints a large amount of new money?
7. What is the effect of a foreign exchange intervention on the money supply? How can a central bank offset this effect and still hope to influence the exchange rate?
8. How can a central bank peg the value of its currency relative to another currency?
9. Describe two channels through which foreign exchange interventions may affect the value of the exchange rate?
10. What was the Bretton Woods currency system?

11. How do developing countries typically manage to keep currencies pegged at values that are too high? Who benefits from such an overvalued currency? Who is hurt by an overvalued currency?
12. What are the potential benefits of a pegged currency system?
13. Describe two different currency systems that have been introduced in countries such as Hong Kong and Ecuador to improve the credibility of pegged exchange rate systems.
14. What is the difference between a target zone and a crawling peg?
15. How can central banks defend their currency—for example, if the currency is within a target zone or pegged at a particular value?
16. What was the EMS?
17. What is a basket currency?
18. What did the Maastricht Treaty try to accomplish?
19. What is an optimum currency area?
20. Do you believe its monetary union will be beneficial for Europe?

PROBLEMS

1. Toward the end of 1999, the central bank (Reserve Bank) in Zimbabwe stabilized the Zimbabwe dollar, the Zim for short, at Z$38/USD and privately instructed the banks to maintain that rate. In response, at the end of 1999, an illegal market developed wherein the Zim traded at Z$44/USD. Are you surprised at rumors that claim corporations in Zimbabwe were "hoarding" USD200 million? Explain.

2. In Chapter 3, we described how exchange rate risk could be hedged using forward contracts. In pegged

or limited-flexibility exchange rate systems, countries imposing capital controls sometimes force their importers and exporters to hedge. First, assuming that forward contracts are to be used, and an exporter has future foreign currency receivables, what will the government force him to do? Second, how does this help the government in defending their exchange rate peg?

3. In years past, Belgium, a participant of the former EMS, and South Africa operated a two-tier, or dual,

exchange rate market. The two-tier market was abolished in March 1990 in Belgium and in March 1995 in South Africa. Import and export transactions were handled on the official market, and capital transactions were handled on the financial market, where the "financial" exchange rate was freely floating. Discuss why such a system may prevent speculators from profiting when betting on a devaluation.

BIBLIOGRAPHY

"After a Devaluation, Two African Countries Fare Very Differently," May 10, 1995, *Wall Street Journal*.

Amegbeto, Koffi, and Alex Winter-Nelson, 1996, "Currency Devaluation and Resource Mobilization. A Computable General Equilibrium Analysis of Adjustment in Cameroon," University of Illinois working paper.

Beine, Michel, Jerome Lahaye, Sebastien Laurent, Christopher J. Neely, and Franz C. Palm, August 2006, "Central Bank Intervention and Exchange Rate Volatility, Its Continuous and Jump Components," working paper.

Bekaert, G., and S. Gray, 1998, "Target Zones and Exchange Rates: An Empirical Investigation," *Journal of International Economics* 45, pp. 1–45.

Bonser-Neal, Catherine, and Glenn Tanner, 1996, "Central Bank Intervention and the Volatility of Foreign Exchange Rates: Evidence from the Options Markets," *Journal of International Money and Finance* 15, pp. 853–878.

Canto, Victor, and Arthur Laffer, November–December 1991, "Everything You Always Wanted to Know About the European Monetary System, the ECU and ERM, but Didn't Know Who to Ask," *Financial Analysts Journal*, pp. 22–24.

"China's Reserves: A Money Machine," January 27, 2007, *The Economist*, p. 76.

De Grauwe, Paul, 1988, "Is the European Monetary System a DM Zone?" unpublished working paper.

De Grauwe, Paul, 1992, "The Economics of Monetary Integration," Oxford: Oxford University Press.

Dominguez, Kathryn M., 1998, "Central Bank Intervention and Exchange Rate Volatility," *Journal of International Money and Finance* 17, pp. 161–190.

Dominguez, Kathryn, and Jeffrey Frankel, 1993, "Does Foreign Exchange Intervention Matter? The Portfolio Effect," *American Economic Review* 83, pp. 1356–1369.

Dornbusch, Rudiger, June 2001, "Fewer Monies, Better Monies," National Bureau of Economic Research working paper.

Edwards, Sebastian, May 2001, "Dollarization and Economic Performance: An Empirical Investigation," National Bureau of Economic Research working paper.

Eichengreen, Barry, 1992, *Golden Fetters*, Oxford: Oxford University Press.

Feldstein, Martin, 1992, "The Case Against EMU," *The Economist*, pp. 23–26.

Folkerts-Landau, David, and Donald J. Mathieson, 1989, "The European System in the Context of the Integration of European Financial Markets," International Monetary Fund occasional paper no. 66.

Frankel, Jeffrey A., and Andrew K. Rose, 1998, "The Endogeneity of the Optimum Currency Area Criteria," *Economic Journal* 108, pp. 1009–1025.

Fratianni, Michele, Jürgen Von Hagen, and Christopher Waller, 1992, "The Maastricht Way to EMU," *Essays in International Finance* 187.

Friedman, Milton, 1953, "The Case for Flexible Exchange Rates," *Essays in Positive Economics*, Chicago: University of Chicago Press, pp. 157–203.

Galati, Gabriele, and Philip Wooldridge, 2006, "The Euro as a Reserve Currency: A Challenge to the Pre-eminence of the Dollar," Bank of International Settlements working paper no. 218.

Giavazzi, Francesco, and Alberto Giovannini, 1989, *Limiting Exchange Rate Flexibility: The European Monetary System*, Cambridge, MA: MIT Press.

Giavazzi, Francesco, and Marco Pagano, 1988, "The Advantage of Tying One's Hand: EMS Discipline and Central Bank Credibility," *European Economic Review* 32, pp. 1055–1075.

Gros, Daniel, and Niels Thygesen, 1988, "The EMS: Achievements, Current Issues and Directions for the Future," CEPS Papers, No. 35, Brussels: Centre for European Policy Studies.

Hardouvelis, Gikas A., Dimitrios Malliaropulos, and Richard Priestley, 2007, "The Impact of EMU on the Equity Cost of Capital," forthcoming, *Journal of International Money and Finance*.

Jeanne, Olivier, and Romain Ranciere, 2006, "The Optimal Level of International Reserves for Emerging Market Countries: Formulas and Applications," International Monetary Fund working paper.

Klein, Michael W., and Nancy P. Marion, 1997, "Explaining the Duration of Exchange Rate Pegs," *Journal of Development Economics* 54, p. 387.

Krugman, Paul, 1992, "Second Thoughts on EMU," *Japan and the World Economy* 4, pp. 187–200.

Kwan, Yum K., and Francis T. Liu, 1996, "Hong Kong's Currency Board and Changing Monetary Regimes," National Bureau of Economic Research working paper no. 5723.

Leahy, Michael P., 1995, "The Profitability of U.S. Intervention in the Foreign Exchange Markets," *Journal of International Money and Finance* 14, pp. 823–844.

Lyons, Richard K., May 1997, "A Simultaneous Trade Model of the Foreign Exchange Hot Potato," *Journal of International Economics* 42, pp. 275–298.

"Maastricht at a Glance," October 17, 1992, *The Economist,* pp. 60–61.

McKinnon, Ronald, Winter 1988, "Monetary and Exchange Rate Policies for International Financial Stability: A Proposal," *Journal of Economic Perspectives* 2, p. N.1.

Mishkin, Frederic S., 1992, *The Economics of Money, Banking, and Financial Markets*, 3rd ed., New York: HarperCollins Publishers.

Mongelli, Francesco Paolo, and Juan Luis Vega, March 2006, "What Effects Is EMU Having on the Euro Area and Its Member Countries? An Overview," European Central Bank working paper 599.

Mundell, Robert, 1961, "A Theory of Optimum Currency Areas," *The American Economic Review*, LI, No. 4, pp. 509–517.

Neely, Christopher J., 2006, "Authorities' Beliefs About Foreign Exchange Intervention: Getting Back Under the Hood," working paper.

Papaioannou, Elias, Richard Portes, and Gregorios Siourounis, 2006, "Optimal Currency Shares in International Reserves: The Impact of the Euro and the Prospects for the Dollar," European Central Bank working paper.

Prasad, Eswar, Thomas Rumbaugh, and Qing Wang, 2005, "Putting the Cart Before the Horse? Capital Account Liberalization and Exchange Rate Flexibility in China," International Monetary Fund policy discussion paper.

Rockoff, Hugh, 2000, "How Long Did It Take the United States to Become an Optimal Currency Area," working paper.

Rosenberg, Michael, 1992, "Central Bank Intervention and the Determination of Exchange Rates," Merrill Lynch.

Roubini, Nouriel, "The Case Against Currency Boards," http://www.geocities.com/Eureka/Concourse/8751/jurus/vs-cbs.htm.

Sargent, Thomas, 1999, "A Primer on Monetary and Fiscal Policy," *Journal of Banking and Finance* 23, pp. 1463–1482.

Sargent, Thomas, and Neil Wallace, 1981, "Some Unpleasant Monetarist Arithmetic," *Federal Reserve Bank of Minneapolis Economic Review*.

Schuler, Kurt, 2000, "Basics of Dollarization," Joint Economic Committee Staff Report, U.S. Congress, www.globalpolicy.org/nations/sovereign/dollar/2000/01basics.htm.

Svensson, Lars E. O., 1992, "The Foreign Exchange Risk Premium in a Target Zone with Devaluation Risk," *Journal of International Economics* 33, pp. 21–40.

Von Hagen, Jurgen, and Manfred J. M. Neumann, 1994, "Real Exchange Rates within and between Currency Areas: How Far Away is EMU?" *Review of Economics and Statistics*, pp. 236–244.

Williamson, John, May 1987, "Exchange Rate Management: The Role of Target Zones," *American Economic Review* 77, p. N.2.

Chapter 6

Interest Rate Parity

*K*im Deal, a portfolio manager for UBS, a European bank, is considering two alternative investments of €10 million. Either she will invest in euro deposits for 1 year, or she will invest in yen deposits for 1 year. In the latter case, she knows that she must worry about transaction foreign exchange risk, and she has decided to fully hedge her investment. The relative return of these two investments is driven by four variables: the euro interest rate, the spot yen/euro rate, the forward yen/euro rate, and the yen interest rate.

Interest rate parity describes a no-arbitrage relationship between spot and forward exchange rates and the two nominal interest rates associated with these currencies. The relationship is called **covered interest rate parity**. This chapter shows that interest rate parity implies that forward premiums and discounts in the foreign exchange market offset interest differentials to eliminate possible arbitrage that would arise from borrowing the low-interest-rate currency, lending the high-interest-rate currency, and covering the foreign exchange risk. Interest rate parity is a critical equilibrium relationship in international finance.

The availability of borrowing and lending opportunities in different currencies allows firms to hedge transaction foreign exchange risk with money market hedges. We will also demonstrate that when interest rate parity is satisfied, money market hedges are equivalent to the forward market hedges of transaction exchange risk that were presented in Chapter 3. Moreover, we can use interest rate parity to derive long-term forward exchange rates. Knowledge of long-term forward rates is useful in developing multiyear forecasts of future exchange rates, which are an important tool in the valuation of foreign projects.

6.1 THE THEORY OF COVERED INTEREST RATE PARITY

In international money markets, the interest rate differential between two currencies approximately equals the percentage spread between the currencies' forward and spot rates. If this is not the case, traders have an opportunity to earn arbitrage profits. In this section, we first derive intuition for this interest rate parity relationship using a number of examples, and then we derive it formally. We end the section by illustrating how an arbitrage would result when the parity relationship is violated. For students rusty on concepts related to interest rates, the box on *The Time Value of Money* in this chapter provides a brief review.

Example 6.1 Kim Deal's Investment Opportunities

Let's consider the situation of Kim Deal, the European-based portfolio manager we met in the introduction. Kim is trying to decide how to invest €10 million, and she must choose between 1-year euro deposits and 1-year yen investments. In the latter case, she knows she must worry about transaction foreign exchange risk, but she also understands that she can use the appropriate forward contract to eliminate it.

Suppose Kim has the following data:

EUR interest rate:	3.5200% per annum (p.a.)
JPY interest rate:	0.5938% p.a.
Spot exchange rate:	¥146.0300/€
1-year forward exchange rate:	¥141.9021/€

Which of these bank investments should Kim choose to get the highest euro return?

To do the analysis, let's first calculate the euro return from investing in the euro-denominated asset. If Kim invests €10,000,000 at 3.52%, after 1 year she will have

$$€10,000,000 \times 1.0352 = €10,352,000$$

Next, let's calculate the euro return if Kim invests her €10,000,000 in the yen-denominated asset. This analysis requires three steps:

Step 1. Convert the euro principal into yen in the spot foreign exchange market. The €10,000,000 will buy

$$€10,000,000 \times (¥146.03/€) = ¥1,460,300,000$$

at the current spot exchange rate. This is Kim's yen principal.

Step 2. Calculate yen-denominated interest plus principal. Kim can invest her yen principal at 0.5938% for 1 year. Hence, Kim knows that in 1 year she will have a return of yen principal plus interest equal to

$$¥1,460,300,000 \times 1.005938 = ¥1,468,971,261$$

Step 3. Hedge the transaction exchange risk with a 1-year forward contract.

Kim knows that if she does nothing today to eliminate the transaction foreign exchange risk, she will sell the ¥1,468,971,261 at the future spot rate in 1 year to get back to euros, and she will bear the foreign exchange risk that the yen will weaken relative to the euro. Kim also realizes that this unhedged investment does not have the same risk characteristics as the euro-denominated bank investment. The unhedged investment is subject to foreign exchange risk; the euro investment returns a sure amount of euros. As we saw in Chapter 3, the transaction foreign exchange risk can be eliminated by selling yen forward for euros. In this case, Kim would contract to sell ¥1,468,971,261 for euros at the 1-year forward rate of ¥141.9021/€. In 1 year she would receive

$$¥1,468,971,261/(¥141.9021/€) = €10,352,005$$

So, even though she has the opportunity to invest euros at 3.52% versus investing yen at 0.5938%, Kim is slightly better off making the yen-denominated investment and covering the foreign exchange risk. But the difference between the two euro returns is an additional €5 of interest on €10,000,000 after 1 year for the yen investment, and this is 5 thousandths of a basis point. We conclude that the two returns are essentially the same.

The Intuition Behind Interest Rate Parity

Two Ways to Buy a Currency Forward

Suppose BMW wants to purchase dollars with euros in 90 days to fulfill a commercial obligation. This can be done in two ways. One way is for BMW to enter into a forward foreign exchange contract to buy dollars with euros at the 90-day forward rate. The second way for BMW to buy dollars with euros in 90 days requires three transactions: Because BMW does not want to pay euros today, BMW can (1) borrow euros for 90 days, (2) use the borrowed euros to buy dollars in the spot foreign exchange market, and (3) invest those dollars for 90 days. At the end of 90 days, BMW will owe interest plus principal on the euros that it borrows, and BMW will receive interest plus principal on the dollars that it invests. Notice that BMW acquires dollars in 90 days and the only cash flow that requires a euro payment by the company also takes place in 90 days. The fact that two methods exist for purchasing dollars with euros in 90 days means that the two methods must cost the same amount of euros. Otherwise, there would be an arbitrage opportunity.

Note that the first method to buy euros forward involves the forward exchange rate between the euro and the dollar. The second transaction involves the spot exchange rate and the interest rates in both euro and dollar money markets.

Why There Must Be Interest Rate Parity

Forward exchange rates allow investors to contract to buy and sell currencies in the future. Because the future value of one unit of currency depends on the interest rate for that currency, the forward exchange rate must be linked to the current spot exchange rate and to the nominal interest rates in the two currencies. Interest rate parity relates the spot and forward exchange rates and the nominal interest rates denominated in the two currencies. Instead of memorizing a formula that will require you to remember which way spot and forward rates are quoted, think of interest rate parity as the equality of the returns on comparable money market assets when the forward foreign exchange market is used to eliminate foreign exchange risk. With interest rate parity satisfied in Example 6.1, the two euro-denominated returns were equal.

Interest rate parity will hold if markets are efficient and there are no government controls to prevent arbitrage. In the absence of these conditions, traders could make an extraordinary profit via **covered interest rate arbitrage**. Once again, the term *covered* means the investment is not exposed to transaction foreign exchange risk. The return Kim Deal obtained by investing in yen, for example, and "covering" the yen exchange rate risk is sometimes called the *covered yield*. The next example demonstrates how to exploit the covered yield if interest rate parity is not satisfied.

Example 6.2   Kevin Anthony's Arbitrage Opportunity

Suppose Kevin Anthony has $10,000,000 to invest, and suppose that Kevin has the following data:

USD interest rate:	8.0% p.a.
GBP interest rate:	12.0% p.a.
Spot exchange rate:	$1.60/£
1-year forward exchange rate:	$1.53/£

Doing the calculations analogous to Example 6.1 indicates that if Kevin invests his $10,000,000 in the dollar asset at 8%, he will have

$$\$10,000,000 \times 1.08 = \$10,800,000$$

If Kevin converts his $10,000,000 into pounds, he'll get

$$\$10,000,000/(\$1.60/£) = £6,250,000$$

at the current spot exchange rate, which he can invest at 12% to get

$$£6,250,000 \times 1.12 = £7,000,000$$

of pound principal plus interest. Selling this amount forward gives a dollar return of

$$£7,000,000 \times (\$1.53£) = \$10,710,000$$

So, even though Kevin has the opportunity to invest in pounds at 12% versus investing dollars at 8%, he is better off making the dollar-denominated investment. But would Kevin stop there?

Let's allow Kevin to borrow or lend at the dollar interest rate of 8% and the pound interest rate of 12%. Now, instead of simply choosing to invest in dollars instead of pounds, Kevin can borrow pounds and invest in dollars. Will it make sense for him to do this?

For each £1,000,000 that Kevin borrows, in 1 year he will owe

$$£1,000,000 \times 1.12 = £1,120,000$$

Let's see how many pounds he will have after 1 year if he converts the pound principal to dollars in the spot market, invests the dollars at 8%, and covers the foreign exchange risk by selling the dollar interest plus principal in the forward market. Once again, this takes three steps:

Step 1. Convert from pounds to dollars at the spot rate of $1.60/£:

$$£1,000,000 \times (\$1.60/£) = \$1,600,000$$

Step 2. Calculate dollar interest plus principal at 8%:

$$\$1,600,000 \times 1.08 = \$1,728,000$$

Step 3. Cover the foreign exchange risk by engaging in a forward contract to sell the dollar interest plus principal at $1.53/£:

$$\$1,728,000/(\$1.53/£) = £1,129,411.76$$

The covered interest arbitrage produces a riskless profit of

$$£1,129,411.76 - £1,120,000.00 = £9,411.76$$

for every £1,000,000 that is borrowed.

If interest rates and spot and forward exchange rates were actually as they are in Example 6.2, many banks and investors would borrow pounds, convert to dollars, invest the dollars, and sell the dollar interest plus principal in the forward market for pounds. This arbitrage activity would quickly eliminate the profit opportunity. The additional demand to borrow pounds would drive up the pound interest rate. The sale of pounds for dollars would lower the dollar–pound spot exchange rate. The lending of dollars would lower the dollar interest rate, and the forward purchase of pounds with dollars would raise the dollar–pound forward exchange rate. Each of these movements would reduce the arbitrage profits that are present at the current prices.

The Time Value of Money

Interest rates provide market prices for buying and selling a given currency between different points in time. If you sell someone a dollar for 1 year (that is, you lend them $1), they must pay you $1 plus the 1-year dollar interest rate after 1 year. Similarly, if you buy pounds from someone today, promising payment in pounds in 1 year (that is, you borrow pounds), the price paid in 1 year for £1 today is £1 plus the 1-year pound interest rate. Thus, interest rates provide prices for moving currencies between different time periods. Interest rates are therefore said to be the *time values* of monies.

The two fundamental concepts associated with the time value of money are **present value** and **future value**. The following are examples of each.

Example 6.3 Lisa Dowling's Lottery Choices

Suppose Lisa Dowling has just won the London daily lottery and has been offered a choice of prizes. The lottery is willing to pay her either £100,000 today or £110,000 in 1 year. Suppose that London banks are paying 11% interest on deposits for the next year. Which offer should she accept and why?

First, we know that if Lisa deposits £100,000 in the bank today, she will receive an amount of pounds in 1 year, denoted FV (for future value), equal to

$$FV = £100,000 + 0.11 \times £100,000 = £100,000 \times 1.11 = £111,000$$

$$FV = \text{Return of Principal} + \text{Interest on Principal}$$

We say that £111,000 is the future value in 1 year of £100,000 today when the interest rate is 11% p.a. Because this is more than the lottery has promised her in 1 year, she should take the money today.

Future value (FV) is also sometimes called *compound value*. In our example, Lisa receives only one interest payment because there is a 1-year horizon and because the interest rate is quoted as a simple interest rate per annum. If the interest rate were quoted with a compounding frequency more than once per year, or if the horizon were longer than 1 year, Lisa would receive several interest payments and would earn interest on the earlier interest. Interest that is earned on interest is called **compound interest**.

An alternative way to analyze Lisa's choice is to ask how much money she must set aside today if she wants to have £110,000 in 1 year. This approach calculates the present value (PV) of the future cash flow promised by the lottery. We want to know the amount of pounds, denoted PV, that is equal to £110,000 in 1 year after Lisa earns interest on the PV pounds at 11% p.a. Algebraically, we have

$$PV \times 1.11 = £110,000$$

Solving for PV gives the present value of the future pounds:

$$PV = £110,000 / 1.11 = £99,099.10$$

$$PV = \frac{\text{Future Value}}{1 + \text{Interest Rate}}$$

Lisa's decision is still the same. She should take the £100,000 today. If she wants to have £110,000 in 1 year, she can deposit £99,099.10 in the bank, and she can spend the residual £900.90 today. When interest rates appear in the denominator of a present value relation, as in the formula here, they are often called **discount rates**. Both present value analysis and future value analysis lead Lisa to the same solution. This is true in all problems involving the time value of cash flows, whether they are denominated in pounds, dollars, or yen. Because the interest rates denominated in different currencies are not the same, we must use an interest rate quoted on a particular currency to understand the time value of that currency.

Deriving Interest Rate Parity

A General Expression for Interest Rate Parity

Now let's consider the derivation of interest rate parity in algebraic terms. Our goal is to derive an expression that summarizes the relationship between the interest rates denominated in two different currencies and the spot and forward exchange rates between those currencies when there are no arbitrage opportunities in the money markets. The notation is as follows:

i = the domestic currency interest rate appropriate for one period
$i*$ = the foreign currency interest rate appropriate for one period
S = the spot exchange rate (Domestic currency/Foreign currency)
F = the one-period forward exchange rate (domestic currency/foreign currency)

Consider an investor who has one unit of domestic currency and is considering only two alternative investments at time t. Alternative 1 is to invest one unit of domestic currency in order to earn domestic currency interest along with the return of principal. Alternative 2 is to convert the unit of domestic currency into foreign currency, invest the foreign currency to earn foreign currency interest, and then eliminate the foreign exchange risk by contracting to sell the foreign currency principal plus the interest earned on it in the forward market in exchange for domestic currency to be received in the future. Each of the investments returns domestic currency in one period:

Alternative 1: Invest one unit of domestic currency. Get $[1 + i]$ units of domestic currency (the return of the principal plus interest) after the investment period.

Alternative 2: Covert the one unit of domestic currency into foreign currency to get $[1/S]$ units of foreign currency in today's spot market. This amount is the foreign currency principal. Invest the $[1/S]$ units of foreign currency to get $[1/S] \times [1 + i^*]$ units of foreign currency (the return of the principal plus interest) after the investment period.

Because the amount of foreign currency principal plus interest that will be returned in the future is known today, a contract can be made to sell the foreign currency in the forward market for domestic currency to produce $[1/S] \times [1 + i] \times F$ units of domestic currency after the investment period.

Because Alternatives 1 and 2 are both made with one unit of domestic currency, and because both provide a certain return of domestic currency at the end of the investment period, the domestic currency returns must be equal. Hence, the equality of the two returns is

$$[1 + i] = [1/S] \times [1 + i^*] \times F \qquad \text{(6.1)}$$

This is one way to represent interest rate parity.

Interest Rate Parity and Forward Premiums and Discounts

Although Equation (6.1) provides a relationship between the two interest rates and the spot and forward exchange rates that satisfies interest rate parity, people usually talk about interest rate parity in an alternative equivalent way. By using a little algebra, we can derive a relationship between the interest differential between the two currencies and the forward premium or discount. First, divide both sides of Equation (6.1) by $[1 + i^*]$:

$$\frac{1 + i}{1 + i^*} = \frac{F}{S}$$

(6.2)

Then subtract 1 from both sides of Equation (6.2) and apply a different common denominator on each side:

$$\frac{1 + i}{1 + i^*} - \frac{1 + i^*}{1 + i^*} = \frac{F}{S} - \frac{S}{S}$$

After simplifying, the result is an expression of interest rate parity that is valid when the exchange rates are expressed in direct terms as domestic currency per unit of foreign currency:

$$\frac{i - i^*}{1 + i^*} = \frac{F - S}{S}$$

(6.3)

Notice that the right-hand side of Equation (6.3) is the forward premium on the foreign currency and that the numerator of the left-hand side is the interest differential between the domestic and foreign currencies. It is often said casually that interest rate parity requires equality between the interest rate differential and the forward premium or discount in the foreign exchange market. For simple interest rates, the expression of interest rate parity in Equation (6.3) demonstrates that this statement is an approximation because it ignores the term $[1 + i^*]$ in the denominator on the left-hand side. But the approximation is reasonably good because this term is close to 1, especially if the maturity is short.

From our expression for interest rate parity, Equation (6.3), we learn that if the domestic currency interest rate is greater than the foreign currency interest rate, the foreign currency must be at a premium in the forward market. That is, the forward exchange rate (Domestic currency/Foreign currency) must be greater than the spot exchange rate. Analogously, if the domestic interest rate is less than the foreign interest rate, the foreign currency must sell at a discount in the forward market. Let's examine the intuition behind these results.

Notice from our original expression for the equality of the two investment opportunities in Equation (6.1) that when the foreign currency is at a premium (that is, the forward rate is above the spot rate), an individual buying foreign currency in the spot market and contracting to sell it forward locks in a domestic currency capital gain. This capital gain contributes an additional return on the foreign investment. But when domestic interest rates are higher than foreign interest rates, a capital gain on the foreign currency is required to equate the two returns. Conversely, when the foreign currency interest rate is above the domestic currency interest rate, a domestic investor must suffer a capital loss when buying foreign currency in the spot market and selling it forward. Otherwise, foreign investments would be very attractive. The capital loss arises because the forward rate, expressed in (Domestic currency/Foreign currency), is less than the spot rate. In this scenario, the domestic investor locks in a capital loss when buying foreign currency spot and contracting to sell it forward.

Let's revisit Kim Deal's situation and calculate the forward premium on the yen. This requires that we work with the reciprocals of the exchange rates quoted as yen per euro. The forward premium on the yen is therefore

$$\frac{F - S}{S} = \frac{\dfrac{1}{¥141.9021/€} - \dfrac{1}{¥146.03/€}}{\dfrac{1}{¥146.03/€}} = 2.91\%$$

By investing now in the yen and selling the yen proceeds forward after 1 year, Kim will earn this premium. Of course, this premium compensates her for the lower interest rate that yen investments offer. Notice that the interest rate differential (Euro − Yen) is 3.52% − 0.5938% = 2.93%, which is approximately equal to the forward premium.

Interest Rate Parity with Continuously Compounded Interest Rates (Advanced)

In Chapter 2, we introduced continuously compounded interest rates and natural logarithms. When interest rates are continuously compounded, interest rate parity has a particularly elegant representation. Now, let i and i^* represent domestic currency and foreign currency interest rates quoted on a continuously compounded basis. Investing one unit of domestic currency provides $\exp[i]$ units of domestic currency after one period. If we instead convert the one unit of domestic currency into foreign currency, invest the foreign currency, and cover the foreign exchange risk, we will have a domestic currency return of $[1/S] \exp[i^*] F$. Now, equating the two domestic currency returns, we get

$$\exp[i] = [1/S] \times \exp[i^*] \times F. \tag{6.4}$$

Taking natural logarithms of both sides of Equation (6.4) and rearranging terms, we have

$$i - i^* = \ln[F] - \ln[S]. \tag{6.5}$$

The left-hand side of Equation (6.5) is the interest differential between the continuously compounded interest rates, and the right-hand side is the forward premium, or discount, expressed in continuously compounded terms. Hence, interest rate parity is exactly characterized by the equality of the continuously compounded interest differential and the continuously compounded forward premium or discount.

Covered Interest Arbitrage

In Example 6.2, the data violated the interest rate parity condition, and Kevin Anthony preferred the direct dollar investment because he achieved a higher dollar return than was available in the covered pound investment. In symbolic terms, we had

$$[1 + i(\$)] > [1/S] \times [1 + i(£)] \times F \tag{6.6}$$

where the dollar interest rate is $i(\$)$, the pound interest rate is $i(£)$, and the units of the exchange rates are dollars per pound. In numbers, we had:

$$1 + 0.08 > \frac{1}{\$1.60/£} \times [1 + 0.12] \times \$1.53/£ = 1.071$$

Example 6.2 drew out the implication of Equation (6.6). Investors facing these interest rates and exchange rates would be able to profit by borrowing pounds, converting the pounds into dollars in the spot market, investing the dollars, and contracting in the forward market to cover the foreign exchange risk by selling the dollar amount of principal plus interest. To see this, multiply both sides of the inequality in Equation (6.6) by S and by $[1/F]$ to get

$$S \times [1 + i(\$)] \times [1/F] > [1 + i(£)]. \tag{6.7}$$

The right-hand side of the inequality in Equation (6.7) is the cost per pound to an investor who borrows pounds. For Kevin Anthony, this was £1.12. The left-hand side is the pound return per pound invested from converting the borrowed pound into dollars, investing the dollars, and contracting to sell dollar interest plus principal forward for pounds. For Kevin, the transaction would yield £1.1294. The inequality indicates that there is an arbitrage possibility at these interest rates and exchange rates, amounting to 0.94 pounds per £100 borrowed in Kevin's case.

Because the lending return is greater than the borrowing cost, a covered interest arbitrage opportunity would be available. Everyone would want to borrow an infinite amount of pounds, convert those pounds to dollars, invest the dollars, and sell the dollars forward for pounds. Clearly, such interest rates and exchange rates would not be in equilibrium.

A Box Diagram

The idea of covered interest arbitrage can be represented in a box diagram that is similar to the diagrammatic representation of triangular arbitrage in Exhibit 2.7. Exhibit 6.1 presents a box diagram that represents covered interest arbitrage.

In Exhibit 6.1, each node represents either dollars or pounds today or dollars or pounds in a future period. As in Exhibit 2.7, the arrows indicate the direction of movement from

Exhibit 6.1 Diagram of Covered Interest Arbitrage

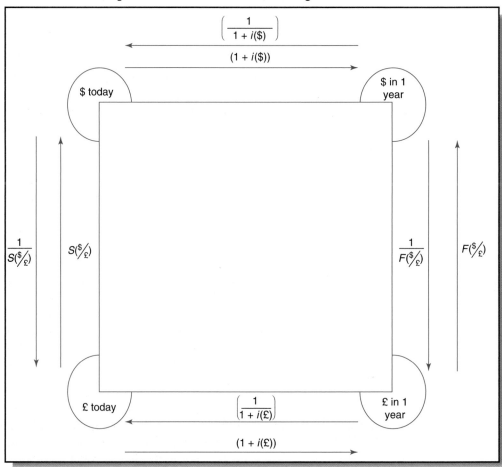

Note: The exchange rates and interest rates associated with each arrow indicate the funds obtained in the currency at the arrow's point from selling one unit of the currency at the arrow's tail. For example, at the $ today node, selling 1 dollar for $ in 1 year gives $(1 + i(\$))$ dollars in 1 year.

one node to another, and they are labeled with the associated revenue or price in terms of the currency at the final node as a result of delivering one unit of currency at the initial node. The interest rates provide the prices for moving monies between today and the future. The exchange rates provide the revenues of moving from one currency to another currency either today for the spot rate or in the future period for the forward rate.

For example, if you are at the node representing pounds today, and you want to invest 1 pound for the future period, the pound revenue tomorrow is $[1 + i(£)]$. Similarly, if you place yourself in the future period at the dollar node, and you pay 1 dollar, you must have received $\dfrac{1}{1 + i(\$)}$ dollars in the current period. Obtaining dollars today with payment of dollars in the future is equivalent to borrowing dollars today. You will owe interest plus principal on your loan at maturity. Hence, in order for the repayment to work out to be $1, you borrow only $\dfrac{1}{1 + i(\$)}$ today. If you are at the node representing dollars today, the number of pounds a dollar yields is $\dfrac{1}{S(\$/£)}$, and if you are at the future pound node, the dollars available from 1 pound are $F(\$/£)$.

In the covered interest arbitrage described for Kevin Anthony in Example 6.2, we moved clockwise around the box, starting from the future pound node. We first bought current pounds (that is, we borrowed a fraction of a pound by promising to repay 1 pound in the future) and used the borrowed pounds to buy dollars today, yielding the dollar principal of $\dfrac{S(\$/£)}{1 + i(£)}$. We then sold our current dollars for dollars in the future (by investing the dollars today), and we sold future dollars for future pounds by using a forward contract. This set of transactions made a profit.

If we start at the future pound node and move completely around the box in a clockwise direction, selling one unit of currency at each node, we will sell 1 future pound. The total revenue of selling this 1 future pound is found by multiplying the four prices of selling one unit together:

$$(\text{Current } £ \ / \ \text{Future } £) \times (\text{Current } \$ \ / \ \text{Current } £) \times (\text{Future } \$ \ / \ \text{Current } \$)$$

$$\times \ (\text{Future } £ \ / \ \text{Future } \$) = \left[\frac{1}{1 + i(£)} \right] \times [S(\$/£)] \times [1 + i(\$)] \times \left[\frac{1}{F(\$/£)} \right] \quad \textbf{(6.8)}$$

The expression on the right-hand side of Equation (6.8) gives us more than one. (To see this, divide both sides of the inequality in Equation (6.7) by the value on the right-hand side.) We made a profit when we did the arbitrage because we were able to sell 1 pound in the future for more than 1 pound in the future. You should convince yourself that, with these prices, you could start at any node and move around the box in the clockwise direction to make a profit because the price of one unit starting at any node will always be more than one with this particular violation of interest rate parity.

Let's look again at the Kevin Anthony situation (Example 6.2). Exhibit 6.2 shows Kevin Anthony starting with $10,000,000 today. He can invest those dollars at 8% to yield $10,800,000 in 1 year. Selling these dollars forward for pounds will yield £7,058,823.5 in the future. Because Kevin can assure himself of that many pounds, he can presently borrow the present value of £7,058,823.5, which is £6,302,521. But that amount of pounds is currently worth $10,084,034. That is $84,034 more than Kevin invested, so he locks in a tidy profit. Note that for this arbitrage to work, Kevin must engage in all these transactions simultaneously before prices move. Traders in the external currency market—a market we discuss in the next section—become adept at such transactions.

Exhibit 6.2 Kevin Anthony's Arbitrage

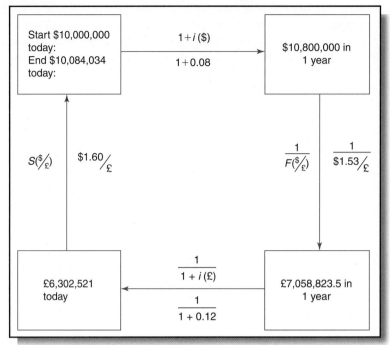

Note: Kevin starts with $10,000,000 today in the upper-left column and moves clockwise, contracting around the box to end up with $10,084,034 today.

6.2 COVERED INTEREST RATE PARITY IN PRACTICE

As we saw in Chapter 2, there are transaction costs in the foreign exchange market. Clearly, these must be taken into account when we evaluate the possibility of arbitrage opportunities. One type of transaction cost arises because it is not possible for individuals to borrow and lend at the same interest rate. The lending rate that banks charge their customers is above the rate that the banks are willing to pay on deposits. To appreciate the magnitude of these transaction costs and how they prohibit profitable covered interest arbitrage, we first discuss the *external currency market*, the interbank market most closely related to the foreign exchange market.

The External Currency Market

The **external currency market** is a bank market for deposits and loans that are denominated in currencies that are not the currency of the country in which the bank is operating. Its settlement procedures are identical to those of the foreign exchange market and its interest rates flicker on the same computer screens.

The first of these deposits and loans were called eurodollars because they were dollar-denominated deposits at European banks. Although the external currency market was once limited to eurodollars, the idea quickly spread. Now, there are external currency markets for many currencies in financial centers around the world. A few of the examples include pound-denominated deposits and loans made by banks in Frankfurt, euro deposits and loans made by banks in Hong Kong or Tokyo, and yen deposits and loans made by banks in Paris or New York. Many market participants still use the terminology *euro-currency* for this market, but given its international nature and especially the emergence of the euro as a currency in continental Europe, *external currency market* now seems more appropriate.

One reason that the external currency market continues to prosper and grow is that the banks accepting the deposits and making the loans are subject to the regulations of the government of the country in which the bank is operating, not the government of the country that issues the money in which the deposits and loans are denominated. These regulations include how much banks must keep on reserve with their nation's central bank (see Chapter 5). Because reserve requirements are often lower for foreign currency deposits than for domestic currency deposits, banks can lend out a larger part of these deposits. Thus, the foreign currency deposits are potentially more profitable.

The demand by domestic banks to meet the foreign competition from the external currency market has also resulted in some government authorities allowing external currency deposits that are internal to the country issuing the currency. In short, the domestic bank gets to act like a foreign bank in the domestic country. For example, U.S. financial regulations allow U.S.-chartered depository institutions to establish international banking facilities (IBFs) that accept dollar deposits from and make dollar loans to non-citizens of the United States. The IBF is not a separate physical or legal entity, but its asset and liability accounts are segregated from the rest of the bank's. The IBF's accounts are subject to different regulations and reserve requirements.

Transaction Costs in the External Currency Market

In practice, the reduced regulatory burden and the strong competition in the external currency market have resulted in very small spreads between the interest rates at which banks are willing to pay for deposits and the interest rates that banks charge for loans. This has lowered transaction costs. Exhibit 6.3 provides information from the *Financial Times* of June 27, 2006, which reports external currency interest rates in the form of a bid–ask spread. The quotations indicate that in normal times, the spreads are quite narrow. For example, at the 3-month maturity, banks are willing to make Canadian dollar (CAD) loans at $4\frac{3}{8}$, or 4.375%, and accept CAD deposits at $4\frac{5}{16}$, or 4.3125%. These interest rates are quoted in percentage points per annum. To determine the appropriate interest rate for a 3-month basis, we must "de-annualize" the quoted interest rates by dividing by 100 (to convert from a percentage quotation to a decimal value) and then multiply by the fraction of a year over which the investment is made.

Most annualized external currency interest rates are based on a 360-day year, except for the pound sterling, which is quoted on a 365-day year. The interest received is the annualized interest rate multiplied by the ratio of actual days of deposit to the postulated number of days in a year. Thus, if the 3-month CAD deposit actually corresponds to 90 days, the de-annualized deposit interest rate is

$$4.3125 \times (1/100) \times (90/360) = 0.010781$$

Exhibit 6.3 Interest Rates in the External Currency Market

Jun 26	Short term	7 days notice	One month	Three months	Six months	One Year
Euro	$2^{27}/_{32}-2^{13}/_{16}$	$2^{7}/_{8}-2^{27}/_{32}$	$2^{15}/_{16}-2^{27}/_{32}$	$3^{1}/_{32}-2^{31}/_{32}$	$3^{7}/_{32}-2^{1}/_{8}$	$3^{15}/_{32}-2^{7}/_{16}$
Danish Krone	$2^{7}/_{8}-2^{11}/_{16}$	$3^{1}/_{16}-2^{7}/_{8}$	$3^{1}/_{32}-2^{15}/_{16}$	$3^{3}/_{32}-2$	$3^{3}/_{32}-3^{3}/_{16}$	$3^{3}/_{32}-3^{15}/_{32}$
Sterling	$4^{9}/_{16}-4^{17}/_{32}$	$4^{5}/_{8}-4^{17}/_{32}$	$4^{21}/_{32}-4^{19}/_{32}$	$4^{11}/_{16}-4^{21}/_{32}$	$4^{13}/_{16}-4^{3}/_{4}$	$5^{3}/_{32}-4^{31}/_{32}$
Swiss Franc	$1^{1}/_{4}-1^{3}/_{32}$	$1^{7}/_{16}-1^{3}/_{8}$	$1^{7}/_{16}-1^{3}/_{8}$	$1^{1}/_{2}-1^{7}/_{16}$	$1^{21}/_{32}-1^{19}/_{32}$	$1^{15}/_{16}-1^{7}/_{8}$
Canadian Dollar	$4^{1}/_{4}-4^{3}/_{16}$	$4^{9}/_{32}-4^{3}/_{16}$	$4^{11}/_{32}-4^{1}/_{4}$	$4^{3}/_{8}-4^{5}/_{16}$	$4^{1}/_{2}-4^{13}/_{32}$	$4^{11}/_{16}-4^{5}/_{8}$
US Dollar	$5^{3}/_{32}-4^{31}/_{16}$	$5^{5}/_{16}-5^{9}/_{32}$	$5^{11}/_{32}-5^{9}/_{32}$	$5^{11}/_{32}-5^{9}/_{32}$	$5^{5}/_{8}-5^{9}/_{16}$	$5^{25}/_{32}-5^{11}/_{16}$
Japanese Yen	$^{1}/_{16}-^{1}/_{32}$	$^{1}/_{8}-^{1}/_{16}$	$^{3}/_{16}-^{1}/_{8}$	$^{3}/_{8}-^{5}/_{16}$	$^{7}/_{16}-^{11}/_{32}$	$^{5}/_{8}-^{9}/_{16}$
Singapore $	$3^{3}/_{8}-3^{1}/_{8}$	$3^{7}/_{16}-3^{3}/_{16}$	$3^{1}/_{2}-3^{1}/_{4}$	$3^{1}/_{2}-3^{1}/_{4}$	$3^{25}/_{32}-3^{11}/_{16}$	$3^{25}/_{32}-3^{11}/_{16}$

Source: Reuters. Short term rates are call for the US Dollar and Yen, others: two days' notice.

Source: From the June 27, 2006, *Financial Times*. Copyright © 2006 Financial Times.

For the 3-month CAD borrowing rate, the de-annualized interest rate is

$$4.375 \times (1/100) \times (90/360) = 0.010938$$

Hence, for each CAD1,000,000 that you deposit, you would receive

$$CAD1,000,000 \times 1.010781 = CAD1,010,781$$

in principal and interest after 90 days, and for each CAD1,000,000 you borrow, you would owe

$$CAD1,000,000 \times 1.010938 = CAD1,010,938$$

in 90 days. You would lose CAD157, or 0.0157%, of your principal in the two transactions, which is a bid–ask spread comparable to the ones in the foreign exchange market. Notice that this bid–ask spread is simply one-fourth of the quoted annualized spread of 0.0625%.

These deposit and lending quotations are available in the interbank market on the same telecommunications networks as the spot and forward quotations discussed in Chapters 2 and 3. The minimum amount traded in the external currency markets is typically $1 million. The maximum amount varies because lending banks limit the amount they will loan to borrowing banks, depending on their default risk.

How the External Currency Market Affects Other Capital Markets

External currency quotations in the interbank market actually form the basis for the interest rates at which investors and corporations can borrow and lend. An investor or a corporation that wants to participate in this market will typically be charged a small commission on deposits. For example, from Exhibit 6.3, if a bank quotes that it will accept 3-month CAD deposits at 4.3125% in the interbank market, the deposit interest rate that is available to a corporate customer may be $\frac{1}{16}$% less, or 4.25%.

The loan rate that banks and other financial intermediaries charge to investors and corporations is typically quoted as a fixed spread or margin over the external currency market interbank rate. Governments and corporations borrow at spreads that depend on their creditworthiness. For example, if the spread is 1.0% over the interbank ask rate (the rate at which the bank lends money), and the 3-month interbank borrowing rate for Canadian dollars in Exhibit 6.3 is 4.375%, the corporation would borrow at 5.375% = 4.375% + 1.0%.

Interbank interest rates in various cities around the world are often the basis for interest rates in contractual loan agreements. The most important of these rates is the **London Interbank Offer Rate (LIBOR)**.[1] Borrowing agreements involving corporations and sovereign nations often specify that the interest rate on a loan is a fixed spread over LIBOR. The determination of the spread depends on the possibility that the borrower will default on the loan. We will examine these issues in detail in Chapter 14. The LIBOR rate also plays a large role in the swap market, which we will discuss in Chapter 21.

Covered Interest Arbitrage with Transaction Costs (Advanced)

In the presence of transaction costs in the spot and forward foreign exchange markets and the external currency markets, the absence of profitable covered interest arbitrage opportunities can be characterized by two inequalities. Arbitrage must be impossible by borrowing in the domestic money market and lending in the foreign money market and by borrowing in the

---

[1]The British Banker's Association (BBA) officially defines U.S. dollar LIBOR as the arithmetic mean of 16 multinational banks' interbank offered rates. These rates are sampled by the BBA in London at approximately 11 A.M. London time. Similarly, there is a euro LIBOR, which is also obtained from the mean of the 16 banks' euro interest rates, and there is a Japanese yen LIBOR, which is the mean of 8 banks' yen interest rates. Because of the prominence of London as a financial center, London interest rates are often used as reference rates in loan agreements, but other reference rates exist. These other interbank offer rates include CIBOR (Copenhagen), FIBOR (Frankfurt), HELIBOR (Helsinki), HIBOR (Hong Kong), MIBOR (Madrid), PIBOR (Paris), and SIBOR (Singapore), among others. With the advent of the euro as a new currency in 1999, EURIBOR (Euro Interbank Offered Rate) became the new money market reference rate for the euro. The rate is the average of rates quoted by a number of banks with the largest volume of business in the eurozone money markets.

foreign money market and lending in the domestic money market. In each case, the transaction foreign exchange risk must be eliminated with the appropriate forward market transaction.

Consider an attempted arbitrage out of domestic money and into foreign money. This would involve borrowing domestic money at the ask interest rate, converting the domestic currency into foreign currency at the ask rate of domestic currency per foreign currency in the spot foreign exchange market, lending the foreign currency at the bid interest rate, and selling the foreign currency principal plus interest in the forward foreign exchange market at the bid rate of domestic currency per foreign currency. For no profitable arbitrage to exist, this set of transactions must be done at a loss or at least at no gain. Similarly, one would attempt arbitrage by borrowing foreign currency at the ask interest rate, converting into the domestic currency at the spot bid rate of domestic currency per foreign currency, lending the domestic currency at the bid interest rate, and selling the domestic currency principal plus interest at the forward ask rate of domestic currency per foreign currency. If there are no profit opportunities in the market, this attempted arbitrage must also be done at a loss or at least at no gain.

We can express these two inequalities symbolically by defining the dollar bid and ask interest rates, $i(\$)^{bid}$ and $i(\$)^{ask}$, the pound bid and ask interest rates, $i(\pounds)^{bid}$ and $i(\pounds)^{ask}$, and the bid and ask spot and forward exchange rates of dollars per pound, S^{bid}, S^{ask}, F^{bid}, and F^{ask}. The appropriate modifications to the box diagram in Exhibit 6.1 are made in Exhibit 6.4. Thus, if

Exhibit 6.4 Covered Interest Rate Parity with Bid–Ask Rates

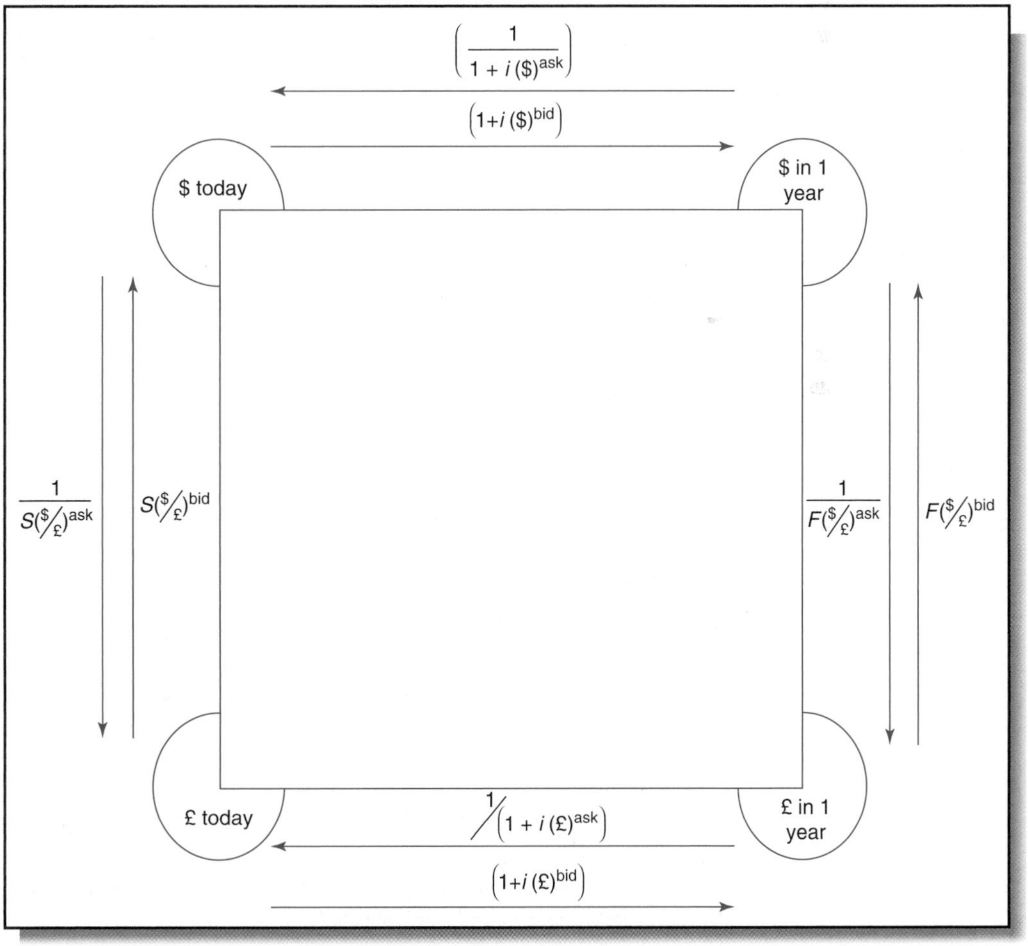

Note: The exchange rates and interest rates associated with each arrow indicate the funds obtained in the currency at the arrow's point from selling one unit of the currency at the arrow's tail. For example, at the $ today node, selling 1 dollar for $ in 1 year gives $(1 + i(\$)^{bid})$ dollars in 1 year.

we go clockwise around the box in Exhibit 6.4, starting at £ in 1 year, we borrow pounds, convert from pounds to dollars in the spot market, lend the dollars, and sell the dollars forward for pounds. The failure of this attempt to do covered interest arbitrage out of pounds into dollars can be summarized by the fact that the revenue of selling 1 pound in the future is less than 1:

$$\frac{1}{[1 + i(\pounds)^{\text{ask}}]} \times [S^{\text{bid}}] \times [1 + i(\$)^{\text{bid}}] \times \frac{1}{F^{\text{ask}}} < 1 \qquad (6.9)$$

Alternatively, rearranging the terms in the inequality in Equation (6.9), we see that the pound borrowing cost is greater than the benefit of converting the pounds to dollars, lending the dollars, and selling the dollars forward for pounds:

$$[1 + i(\pounds)^{\text{ask}}] > S^{\text{bid}} \times [1 + i(\$)^{\text{bid}}] / F^{\text{ask}} \qquad (6.10)$$

The failure of an attempt to do covered interest arbitrage out of the dollar into the pound is summarized by going counterclockwise around the box in Exhibit 6.4. We start at the future dollar node and find out that the future revenue of selling 1 future dollar is less than 1:

$$\frac{1}{[1 + i(\$)^{\text{ask}}]} \times \frac{1}{S^{\text{ask}}} \times [1 + i(\pounds)^{\text{bid}}] \times F^{\text{bid}} < 1 \qquad (6.11)$$

Alternatively, rearranging the terms in the inequality in Equation (6.11), we see that the dollar borrowing cost is greater than the benefit of converting the dollar to pounds, lending the pounds, and selling the pounds forward for dollars:

$$[1 + i(\$)^{\text{ask}}] > [1/S^{\text{ask}}] \times [1 + i(\pounds)^{\text{bid}}] \times F^{\text{bid}} \qquad (6.12)$$

Example 6.4 An Attempt at Arbitrage Using Dollars and Yen

We can use the data from Exhibit 6.3 together with the spot and forward exchange rates that also appear in the *Financial Times* to examine how much would have been lost in attempting to arbitrage between, say, the U.S. dollar and the yen at the 3-month maturity. The relevant data are as follows:

	Bid	Ask
Spot exchange rates (¥/$):	116.325	116.365
Forward exchange rates (¥/$):	114.800	114.870
Dollar interest rates:	5.4375	5.46875
Yen interest rates:	0.3125	0.3750

To make the magnitudes interesting, let's first borrow $10,000,000. If we convert this to yen, we do so at the bank's bid price for dollars:

$$\$10,000,000 \times \yen 116.325/\$ = \yen 1,163,250,000$$

This is our yen principal. We can invest this amount for 3 months at 0.3125% p.a. The appropriate yen interest rate is therefore

$$0.3125 \times (1/100) \times (90/360) = .000781$$

Hence, in 90 days we will have

$$¥1,163,250,000 \times 1.000781 = ¥1,164,158,789$$

Now, we must determine the forward rate at which we can contract to sell yen for dollars. Remember, the bank will charge us a high price to buy dollars. Therefore, the right rate is the yen forward ask price of 114.87¥/$. Hence, we could have contracted to sell our yen principal plus interest for dollars to get

$$(¥1,164,158,789) / (¥114.87/\$) = \$10,134,576$$

Our dollar borrowing rate is 5.46875% p.a., or an interest factor of

$$5.46875 \times (1/100) \times (90/360) = 0.0136719$$

Thus, if we borrow $10,000,000 for 3 months, we will owe

$$\$10,000,000 \times 1.0136719 = \$10,136,719$$

Notice that if we were to do these transactions, we would lose

$$\$10,136,719 - \$10,134,576 = \$2,143.00$$

Notice also that the loss is 0.021% = 2,143/10,000,000 × 100 of the principal that we borrow. This is the equivalent of four transaction costs of 0.0054% each.

Given that we lose money by attempting arbitrage by borrowing dollars, let's try to make money by doing a covered interest arbitrage that begins by borrowing yen. For example, we could borrow ¥10,000,000 for 3 months at 0.375% p.a. (the bank's lending rate), in which case we will owe

$$¥10,000,000 \times [1 + (0.375/100) \times (90/360)] = ¥10,009,375$$

in 3 months. We can convert our 10,000,000¥ to dollars at 116.365¥/$ in the spot market (the bank's ask rate) to get

$$¥10,000,000 / (¥116.365/\$) = \$85,936$$

as our dollar principal. If we invest this for 3 months at 5.4375% p.a. (the bank's deposit rate), we will receive

$$\$85,936 \times [1 + (5.4375/100) \times (90/360)] = \$87,104$$

in 3 months. We can contract to sell these dollars for yen in the forward market at 114.80¥/$ (the bank's forward bid rate) to lock in a yen return of

$$\$87,104 \times (¥114.80/\$) = ¥9,999,539$$

Notice that this amount (¥9,999,539) is ¥9,836 less than what we will owe (¥10,009,375). Hence, no profitable arbitrage opportunities exist in this case.

An Empirical Test

In the previous section, we derived two inequalities that the various bid and ask interest rates, forward rates, and spot rates must satisfy in order to prevent arbitrage. Let's rearrange the inequalities in Equations (6.9) and (6.11) to put them in terms of interest differentials and forward premiums, as in Equation (6.3). The inequality in Equation (6.9), rewritten for the dollar relative to a general foreign currency (FC), becomes

$$\frac{i(\$)^{\text{bid}} - i(FC)^{\text{ask}}}{1 + i(FC)^{\text{ask}}} < \frac{F^{\text{ask}} - S^{\text{bid}}}{S^{\text{bid}}} \tag{6.13}$$

This inequality indicates that it is impossible to borrow the foreign currency and do a covered interest arbitrage into dollars. Inequality (6.11) becomes

$$\frac{i(\$)^{ask} - i(FC)^{bid}}{1 + i(FC)^{bid}} > \frac{F^{bid} - S^{ask}}{S^{ask}} \qquad (6.14)$$

This inequality indicates that it is impossible to borrow dollars and do a profitable covered interest arbitrage into the foreign currency.

Exhibit 6.5 graphically represents the two covered interest parity inequalities with transaction costs, Equations (6.13) and (6.14), using $/£ data.

The horizontal axes represent the forward premiums (or discounts, if negative) on the foreign currencies in terms of the dollar, constructed with the appropriate bid and ask exchange rates. The vertical axes represent the corresponding adjusted interest rate differentials of the dollar interest rate minus the foreign currency rate, constructed with the appropriate bid and ask interest rates. Pairs of observations on forward premiums and adjusted interest differentials are plotted in the graph. In the absence of both transaction costs and covered interest rate arbitrage opportunities, interest rate differentials and forward premiums equal each other on the 45-degree line, as the equality in Equation (6.3) indicates. Let's consider a concrete example. The data points in both panels of Exhibit 6.5 representing July 6, 2006, were computed from the following exchange rate and interest rate data:

$S^{bid} = \$1.8378/£$ $S^{ask} = \$1.8380/£$
$F^{bid} = \$1.841863/£$ $F^{ask} = \$1.842113/£$
$i(\$)^{bid} = \$5.45\%$ $i(\$)^{ask} = 5.53\%$
$i(£)^{bid} = \$4.64\%$ $i(£)^{ask} = 4.69\%$

The inequality in Equation (6.13) indicates that the observations on interest differentials and forward premiums constructed with the appropriate bid–ask rates would plot below the 45-degree line if it is impossible to do a covered interest arbitrage out of the foreign currency and into dollars. This is what we find in Panel A. Evaluating the left-hand side of Equation (6.13) for the data of July 6, 2006, we find:

$$\frac{\left[5.45\% - 4.69\%\right]}{1 + \dfrac{4.69\%}{4}} = 0.7512\%$$

Note that interest rates are per annum (hence, we divide 4.69% by 4) in the denominator, but we leave the interest rate differential in annualized terms. For the right-hand side, we find (annualized)

$$400 \times \frac{1.842113 - 1.8378}{1.8378} = 0.9387\%$$

Hence, this observation is indeed below the 45-degree line in Panel A. Now, consider an attempted arbitrage in the other direction, out of dollars and into the foreign currency. The inequality in Equation (6.14) indicates that the observations on interest differentials and forward premiums constructed with the appropriate bid–ask rates would plot above the 45-degree line if it is impossible to do a covered interest arbitrage out of dollars and into the foreign currency. This is what we observe in Panel B. Let's go to the data example again. For the left-hand side of Equation (6.14), we find:

$$\frac{5.53\% - 4.64\%}{\left[1 + \dfrac{4.64\%}{4}\right]} = 0.8798\%$$

Evaluating the right-hand side of Equation (6.14) yields

$$400 \times \frac{1.841863 - 1.8380}{1.8380} = 0.8407\%$$

Consequently, this interest rate differential is indeed above the forward premium.

Exhibit 6.5 $/£ Covered Interest Arbitrage into £

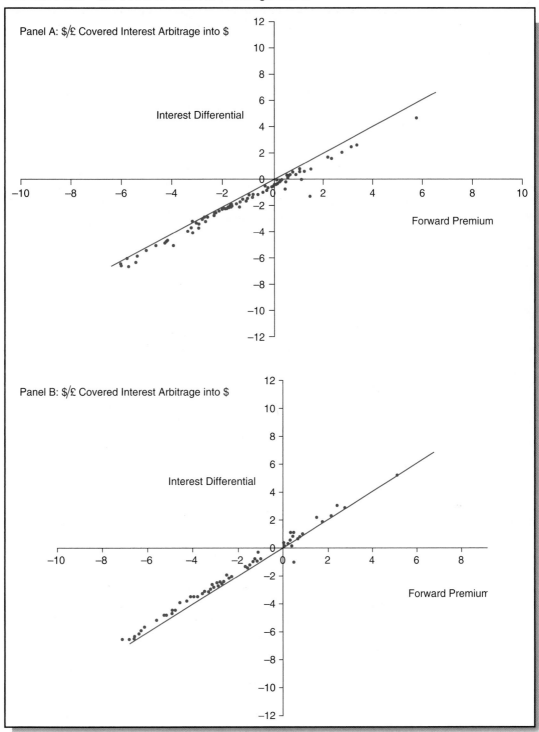

Notes: The data are spot rates and 3-month external currency market interest rates and forward rates from Global Insight from 1981 to October 2006. The vertical axis displays the interest rate differential computed as $\dfrac{i(\$)^{\text{bid}} - i(\pounds)^{\text{ask}}}{1 + i(\pounds)^{\text{ask}}}$ in Panel A and as $\dfrac{i(\$)^{\text{ask}} - i(\pounds)^{\text{bid}}}{1 + i(\pounds)^{\text{bid}}}$ in Panel B. The horizontal axis displays the forward premium computed as $\dfrac{F^{\text{ask}} - S^{\text{bid}}}{S^{\text{bid}}}$ in Panel A and as $\dfrac{F^{\text{bid}} - S^{\text{ask}}}{S^{\text{ask}}}$ in Panel B. All exchange rates are expressed in $/£.

Other Empirical Results

We noted previously that the transaction costs involved in covered interest arbitrage are generally small in the major currency foreign exchange and money markets. This means that the observations are close to the 45-degree line. Although our data indicate a few violations of interest rate parity, how likely are you to observe violations of interest rate parity in the real world, and what would cause such violations to occur?

Because the settlement procedures in the external currency markets are identical to the settlement procedures in the forward markets, and because transaction costs are small, banks operating in this market should arbitrage away all deviations from covered interest rate parity. In fact, it is often the case that banks use interest rate parity to quote forward rates in outright forward transactions.

Empirical studies that are careful to collect data correctly confirm that interest rate parity holds in the external currency markets. That is, high interest rates on a currency are offset by forward discounts, and low interest rates are offset by forward premiums. Profitable arbitrage opportunities arise only in very turbulent market periods, and even then, the profitability tends to be small; it grows even smaller as the maturity of the contract becomes shorter (see Mark Taylor 1987, 1989).

6.3 PROBLEMS RELATED TO TESTING INTEREST RATE PARITY

Suppose you are working in a large international bank and observe foreign exchange prices and interest rates that appear to provide an arbitrage opportunity. Are there any factors that might make you stop and think before plunging headlong into a large arbitrage? In other words, might the arbitrage opportunity really not be present? There are three reasons apparent arbitrage opportunities might not result in riskless profitable trades: default risk, exchange controls, and political risk. We discuss each of these factors next.

Default Risks

In all our derivations so far, we have ignored the possibility that one of the counterparties may fail to honor its contract. When this possibility is reflected in interest rates, we may find an apparent deviation from interest rate parity that does not represent a riskless arbitrage opportunity. Default risk or credit risk is the possibility that a borrower will not be able to repay the lender the entire amount promised in a loan contract. Let's explore the implications of default risk in more detail.

Because there is always some risk that a bank will fail, depositors must assess the possibility that they will not be repaid. To make a rational investment, the depositors must determine what possible events in the future could trigger a default, and they must ascertain what probabilities are associated with these events. The expected return to the investors or lenders is calculated by summing the returns in each state of the world with each return multiplied, or "weighted," by the probability of that particular state.

For example, let p denote the probability that the borrowing bank will default. The resulting probability that the borrowing bank will not default is therefore $(1 - p)$. Suppose also, for simplicity, that if the borrowing bank defaults, the bank making the deposit will receive nothing. When the borrowing bank does not default, the depositing bank will receive $(1 + i)$, where i is the promised interest rate on the deposit of one unit of currency. Then the expected return to the depositing bank is

$$[(1 - p) \times (1 + i)] + (p \times 0) = (1 - p) \times (1 + i)$$

If depositors require a particular expected return in order to make a deposit, riskier banks (ones with larger values for p) must offer higher deposit rates to increase the expected return on their deposits in order to compete effectively for funds. Therefore, observing different interest rates on bank deposits denominated in the same currency in the interbank market need not be evidence of market inefficiency. If we see a deviation from interest rate parity, we cannot be certain that we are observing a true profit opportunity without knowing more about the particular banks making the quotations.

There may also be some risk of default on the forward contracts (again, because some banks are risky), and this could also lead to deviations from interest rate parity that do not represent arbitrage opportunities. Banks must continually assess the risk of their counterparties; a bank's risk managers put limits on the amount of trading that can be done with any particular counterparty.[2]

Exchange Controls

Another problem with empirical analysis of interest rate parity is caused by **exchange controls**. The governments of countries periodically interfere with the buying and selling of foreign exchange. They may, like the United Kingdom in the mid-1970s, prohibit domestic residents from buying more than a certain small amount of foreign currency to make investments overseas. Other countries, like Switzerland, have at various times taxed the inflow of foreign investment into their country. During the 1970s, the Swiss had a 10% tax on the principal of any investment by a foreign national in Switzerland. Whenever you examine historical data on interest rates and exchange rates, you should be aware that not taking into account exchange controls or differential taxes can cause the appearance of a covered interest arbitrage opportunity that really doesn't exist.

One way to understand the effects of exchange controls and differential taxes on foreign versus domestic investors is to examine internal interest rates within a country versus external interest rates outside of the country. These differentials have narrowed greatly in recent years. Exhibit 6.6 presents historical data on external and internal French franc (FRF) interest rates.

Exhibit 6.6 External and Internal FRF Interest Rates and Difference

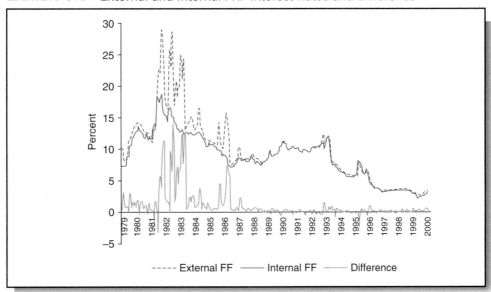

Note: The data are monthly observations on 3-month interest rates taken from Datastream.

---

[2]Banks rely on information from firms that rate the creditworthiness of financial institutions and corporations. See Chapter 14 for additional discussion of these issues.

The graphs present the 3-month interest rates on external bank deposits and Treasury bills.[3] Although the differences are not large in normal times, the large FRF differentials in the early 1980s suggest that borrowing at the domestic franc interest rate and lending at the external franc interest rate should have generated hefty profits. Because interest rate parity holds with respect to the external interest rates but not with respect to the domestic rates, foreigners would have attempted to profit by borrowing francs in the French domestic market, exchanging them for other currencies, and investing the proceeds while covering the exchange rate risk using a forward contract. However, this arbitrage possibility was precluded by the exchange controls in place in France at the time. As we discussed in Chapter 5, capital controls were gradually abandoned in western Europe after 1985, and the differential between domestic and offshore interest rates decreased. Although the external currency market is often viewed as being outside the regulatory control of the authorities issuing the currency, the settlement of transfers between external accounts usually involves the central bank of the country. Exchange controls can therefore be used to shut down the trade of a currency in the external currency market. This happened in Malaysia in 1998. Because of perceived speculation against the ringgit, the Malaysian government announced exchange control measures that replaced a liberal regulatory structure of the external currency market with a highly restrictive one in which the settlement of payments between external Malaysian ringgit accounts required prior approval of the Governor of Bank Negara, the Malaysian central bank. Without assurance that approval would be given, the external currency market for ringgits and all other trades related to it were shut down. Trading stopped, and all outstanding contracts were settled or closed out.

Political Risk

Even without exchange controls, foreign investors may rationally believe that a government will impose some form of exchange controls or taxes on foreign investments in the future. Or, perhaps the government will declare a "bank holiday," closing the nation's banks for a period of time.[4] All such events would affect an investor's return. The possibility of any of these events occurring is called **political risk**, which we will discuss in more detail in Chapter 14.

An example of a realization of political risk occurred in 1982 in Mexico. When the Mexican government encountered difficulty making its scheduled interest and principal payments on its foreign debt, it froze $12 billion of USD accounts at Mexican banks. It then converted those dollar deposits into peso deposits at an unfavorable peso/dollar exchange rate. The net result was an immediate loss of 50% of the dollar principal on these investments. When this event was coupled with previous devaluations of the peso relative to the dollar, the dollar value of the deposits was only about 20% of the original dollar principal (see Darrell Delamaide, 1985).

Because the market knew that such an event was possible, Mexican banks had to offer higher interest rates on their U.S. dollar accounts than were available on federally insured U.S. bank deposits. For many years before the actual event, Mexican interest rates on dollar deposits were often 200 to 300 basis points higher than rates on U.S. bank deposits. Some

---

[3]In the United States, the difference between the 3-month Treasury bill and interest rate and the corresponding LIBOR is known as the TED spread. The name originated at the Chicago Mercantile Exchange, which traded futures on both T-Bills and eurodollars. The price of a Treasury bill typically exceeds the price of a eurodollar deposit reflecting the lower interest rate that the government security offers because of its lower default risk. The TED spread became particularly large in 2007 during the subprime mortgage crisis.

[4]*Bank holidays* are situations in which governments close banks for periods of time to allow information to be obtained about the solvency of various banks—that is, whether the value of their assets exceeds the value of their liabilities.

investors argued that these Mexican bank deposits were great investments, and they were, for those who got out before the policy change.

The Thrilla in Manila

Another famous example of political risk affecting domestic versus external interest rates is the "Thrilla in Manila" case.[5] In June 1983, Wells Fargo Asia Ltd., a subsidiary of the U.S. bank Wells Fargo, deposited $2 million in the form of 6-month deposits at Citibank's Manila branch in the Philippines. The interest rate on these 6-month deposits was higher than what Citibank was offering in the United States. On October 15, 1983, the Philippine government imposed exchange controls that prevented foreign currency payments to foreign banks without prior approval. When Wells Fargo's deposits came due in December 1983, Citibank did not deliver the deposits to Wells Fargo, citing the exchange controls. Later on, with the Philippine government's approval, the Manila branch of Citibank repaid part of the deposits using the Citibank's worldwide assets. However, Wells Fargo felt that Citibank New York should have repaid the full value of the funds and sued Citibank. After a drawn-out legal battle, the court finally sided with Wells Fargo.

From a purely financial perspective, the court's decision was surprising because the higher deposit rate in Manila reflected the political risk that the Philippine government might impose some form of exchange controls. If Wells Fargo wanted to minimize political risk, it could have either deposited the money in New York or taken out an insurance contract that would have reimbursed the bank in the event that a political risk was realized in Manila. However, taking either of those routes would have earned Wells Fargo a lower return than the interest rate offered by Citibank Manila.

Legally, however, the case was much more complex, revolving around issues such as where creditors can collect debts from entities that are branches or subsidiaries of international financial institutions. These issues likely contributed to the surprising outcome of the case.

POINT—COUNTERPOINT

Mexican Cetes or U.S. T-bills?

Ante and Freedy are working on a case for their international finance class. Their professor has asked them to examine some data from June 20, 1995, to look for arbitrage opportunities between Mexico and the United States. Ante storms into Freedy's room with *Wall Street Journal* quotes in his hand and shouts, "Here is the definite proof. Markets are totally inefficient. Look at these prices. People must have made a killing investing in Cetes. These Mexican treasury bills were offering 44.85% p.a. on a 3-month deposit. And look, the Mexican peso–U.S. dollar forward rate was really attractive, so they could have covered the currency risk cheaply and locked in immediate profits of 1.2% per dollar invested." Freedy peruses the data and urges Ante to stay calm so he can explain why this apparent arbitrage opportunity may have been pretty illusory.

Ante says, "Look, the USD T-bill rate was 5.60% p.a., so you could borrow a dollar at 1.4% for 3 months. Because the spot rate was MXP6.25/USD, each dollar borrowed yielded 6.25 Mexican pesos. By investing these pesos at the Cetes rate of 44.85%, they would have grown to

$$\text{MXP6.25} \times (1 + 44.85/400) = \text{MXP6.95078}$$

---

[5]The original "Thrilla in Manila" was a grueling heavyweight boxing match in which Muhammad Ali defeated Joe Frazier on September 30, 1977.

With the forward at a rate of MXP6.775/$, one could sell them for dollars to lock in the profit.[6] In other words, for each dollar that someone borrowed, they got

$$MXP6.95078/(MXP6.775/USD) = USD1.0259$$

back, and they only need \$1.014 to pay back the 1-dollar loan. So their profit was a whopping \$1.0259 − \$1.014 = \$0.0119 per dollar invested. Now that was a money machine, buddy!"

Freedy is totally puzzled. "But that is impossible. Financial markets would not tolerate a money machine. Traders would quickly take advantage of the situation and, via arbitrage, eliminate any opportunity for profit. Maybe these Mexican peso investments were much less liquid than other contracts, or maybe these are just typos in the newspaper. I bet you this opportunity was gone the next day."

At this point Suttle leisurely walks in, sighing, "Are you guys at it again? What are you fighting about now?" After hearing both Ante's and Freedy's accounts of the great Mexican investment opportunity, Suttle smiles and says there is nothing mysterious about those rates. "It was not a money machine, and it wasn't explained by transaction costs. The higher Cetes rates simply reflected country risk or default risk on the part of the Mexican government. The U.S. government may be expected to always repay its dollar debts, but this is not necessarily true for the governments of developing countries," he says. "As you may remember, Mexico had come close to totally running out of official international reserves at the end of 1994, and it was building up its international reserves during 1995, after having been bailed out by an international aid package early in 1995. In this context, the interest rate differential can be split up into two parts. One part is the Mexican interest rate that would result if the Mexican government had the same credit risk as the U.S. government. This rate can be inferred from spot and forward exchange rates (if conducted with creditworthy counterparties) and the U.S. T-bill rate. The remainder is an additional return offered by the Mexican government to compensate for the political risk that investors perceive to be present," he continues.

Seeing Ante's and Freedy's puzzled faces, Suttle decides to use the actual numbers. "So, if we look at the numbers, the Cetes investment, hedged for foreign currency risk, represents a 10.37% annualized return (2.5945% times 4), which is 4.77% higher than the U.S. Treasury bill rate of return. Because the investment is totally hedged against foreign currency risk, this extra reward must be due to default risk, and it is typically called the **country risk premium**. I remember that for 1993 and 1994, country risk premiums on 3-month Mexican Cetes averaged 2.25%," he finally offers (see Ian Domowitz, Jack Glen, and Ananth Madhavan, 1998). Ante and Freedy know that Suttle has taught them a very valuable lesson!

Epilogue:

The Mexican government did not default on the Cetes investments discussed here. Consequently, Ante was right, *ex post*, that investors would have found them to be a good investment relative to USD T-bills. Nevertheless, government defaults do happen. For example, both Russia and Ecuador defaulted in the late 1990s on obligations to foreign investors that had similar risk characteristics to Mexican Cetes investments in 1995, and Argentina also defaulted on its international debt in 2002. It is therefore difficult to know exactly whether Ante or Freedy is right in an *ex ante* sense.

---

[6]The forward exchange rate used here is actually calculated from the price of the peso futures contract trading on the Chicago Mercantile Exchange. (See Chapter 20 for a full account of futures contracts and exchanges.) For our purposes, it is important to realize that the forward rate and the futures rate are virtually identical for identical maturities and that the counterparty in the futures contract (the Chicago Mercantile Exchange) is very likely to honor its contract with you.

If you have an open position (either an account receivable or an account payable) denominated in foreign currency, you are exposed to transaction foreign exchange risk. When interest rate parity holds, there are two equivalent ways to hedge your transaction exchange risk:

1. Having an appropriate forward contract to buy or sell the foreign currency
2. Borrowing or lending the foreign currency coupled with making a transaction in the spot market

We examined the first technique in Chapter 3. Now let's look at the second, which is also known as a **synthetic forward**. There are several reasons for using such hedges. First, in some currency markets (for instance, those in certain developing countries), forward contracts may not be available. Nevertheless, a forward contract can be manufactured using a **money market hedge**. Second, individual companies are not able to borrow and lend at the interest rates available in the interbank market, which means the two strategies may not be equivalent, depending on the forward quote that the company receives. Third, when time horizons are long, forward contracts can be expensive as the bid–ask spread widens substantially. It may therefore be advantageous to consider borrowing and lending to hedge one's currency risk. We discuss this long-term issue explicitly in Section 6.5. For now, we focus on short-term money markets hedges to get the logic correct.

The general principal is that if the underlying transaction gives you a liability (an account payable) denominated in foreign currency, you need an equivalent asset in the money market to provide a hedge. If, on the other hand, the underlying transaction gives you an asset (an account receivable) denominated in foreign currency, you need an equivalent liability in the money market to provide a hedge.

Hedging a Foreign Currency Liability

Example 6.5   Zachy's Money Market Hedge

Assume, as in Chapter 3, that you are managing Zachy's Wine and Spirits, and you have just contracted to import some Chateau Margaux wine from France. As before, the wine is valued at €4 million, and you have agreed to pay this amount when you have received the wine and determined that it is in good condition. Payment of the money and delivery of the wine are scheduled for 90 days in the future. You are looking at the following data:

Spot exchange rate:	$1.10/€
90-day forward exchange rate:	$1.08/€
90-day dollar interest rate:	6.00% p.a.
90-day euro interest rate:	13.519% p.a.

Remember that because the underlying transaction gives you a euro-denominated account payable, you are exposed to losses if you do not hedge and the euro appreciates, or strengthens, relative to the dollar. In this case, the dollar cost of the euros would be higher in the future, which would increase the cost of your wine.

In Chapter 3 we eliminated this risk by buying euros forward. Numerically, the dollar cost, which is paid in 90 days, is

$$€4,000,000 \times (\$1.08/€) = \$4,320,000$$

Let's look at the alternative money market hedging strategy. Because you have a euro liability, you must acquire an equivalent euro asset. You can do this by buying the present value of your euro liability at the spot exchange rate and investing these euros in a money market asset. You then use the principal plus interest on this euro asset to offset your underlying euro liability at maturity. Consequently, it is the present value of the euros that you owe in the future that you should buy today.

The present value of €4,000,000 at 13.519% p.a. is

$$€4,000,000/[1 + (13.519/100)(90/360)] = €3,869,229.71$$

This amount of euros must be purchased in the spot foreign exchange market. Hence, at the spot exchange rate of $1.10/€, the dollar cost today is

$$€3,869,229.71 \times \$1.10/€ = \$4,256,152.68$$

Notice that with the money market hedge, the payment is made today unless you borrow dollars. To compare the money market hedge to the forward market hedge, we must take the present value of the $4,320,000 at 6% p.a.:

$$\$4,320,000 / [1 + (6/100)(90/360)] = \$4,256,157.64$$

At these interest rates and exchange rates, the two strategies are basically equivalent. The dollar present value of the cost of the forward contract is only $4.96 more expensive ($4,256,157.64 − $4,256,152.68).

Hedging a Foreign Currency Receivable

Example 6.6 A Shetland Sweater Exporter's Money Market Hedge

In Example 6.5, you had a foreign currency liability that arose because you were importing wine. Now, consider the example in Chapter 3 of the British manufacturer Shetland Sweaters. As in that example, you have agreed to ship sweaters to Japan, and you will receive ¥500,000,000 in payment. Shipment of the goods and receipt of the yen are scheduled for 30 days from now, and the following data are now available:

Spot exchange rate:	¥179.5/£
30-day forward exchange rate:	¥180/£
30-day sterling interest rate:	2.70% p.a.
30-day yen interest rate:	6.01% p.a.

As a British exporter of sweaters, you have a yen-denominated account receivable, which is your yen asset. If you do nothing to hedge the transaction foreign exchange risk, you are exposed to losses if the yen depreciates, or weakens, relative to the pound. In this case, the yen receivable will purchase fewer pounds when you receive the yen payment.

In Chapter 3 we eliminated the transaction foreign exchange risk by selling the yen forward for pounds. The amount of pounds that will be received in 30 days from the forward contract is

$$(¥500,000,000) / (¥180/£) = £2,777,778$$

Now, consider the alternative money market hedge. You must acquire a yen liability that is equivalent in value to your yen asset. You do this by borrowing the present value of your yen asset and using the yen that you receive from selling your sweaters to pay off the principal and interest on your yen loan. To be hedged, you must convert the yen principal that is borrowed into pounds at the spot exchange rate.

The present value of ¥500,000,000 at 6.05% p.a. is

$$¥500,000,000 / (1 + (6.01/100)(30/360)) = ¥497,508,313$$

By borrowing ¥497,508,313 for 1 month at 6.01% p.a., you will owe ¥500,000,000 in 30 days, which is the amount you will receive for selling your sweaters. Your pound revenue is found by selling the ¥497,508,313 for pounds in the spot market at ¥179.5/£, which is

$$¥497,508,313 / (¥179.5/£) = £2,771,634$$

We can compare this revenue to the revenue available from the forward hedge in 30 days by taking the future value of the £2,771,634. We can invest pounds at 2.70% p.a. Hence, the future value of the pounds received today is

$$£2,771,634 \times (1 + (2.7/100)(30/365)) = £2,777,785$$

Hence, at these interest rates and exchange rates, the money market hedging strategy is basically equivalent to the forward hedging strategy.

6.5 THE TERM STRUCTURE OF FORWARD PREMIUMS AND DISCOUNTS

Does interest rate parity hold at long horizons? This is an important question because many international investment projects involve currency exposures that extend over many years. If an exposure is longer term, the short-term money market contracts we discussed earlier might be inadequate. However, before we investigate interest rate parity over longer time frames, we need to explain the term structure of interest rates. Whereas the interest rates for short-term maturities are readily available in the marketplace, we will see that interest rates for longer maturities must be derived from the prices of coupon bonds. Long-term interest rates are useful in terms of computing the present value of cash flows of long-term projects.

After we look at the term structures of interest rates for two currencies, we can combine them with interest rate parity to examine the term structure of the forward premiums or discounts between two currencies. That is, we investigate how international interest rate differentials change with different maturities. These computations can be useful for MNCs seeking financing in international bond markets. Recent empirical evidence suggests that covered interest rate parity does not hold perfectly at longer horizons. In Chapter 12, we discuss how MNCs can exploit these deviations from parity to lower their financing costs.

The Term Structure of Interest Rates

Spot Interest Rates

It is generally true that the time values of different monies for a particular maturity are not equal. The 1-year interest rate on U.S. dollars might be 5%, whereas the 1-year interest rate on Japanese yen might be 1.5%. Similarly, the time value of one currency, say the U.S. dollar, at one maturity

Exhibit 6.7   Term Structures for Four Currencies

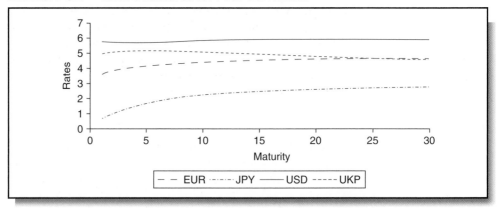

Notes: The term structure data are taken from swap rates (see Chapter 21) for different currencies on July 6, 2006, reported in *The Financial Times*. These rates are comparable to yields to maturity for domestic bonds. On the vertical axis, the yields are expressed in annualized terms. The horizontal axis displays the maturity expressed in years.

is usually not equal to the time value of the U.S. dollar at a different maturity. The 1-year U.S. dollar interest rate might be 5%, whereas the 30-year U.S. dollar interest rate might be 7.5%.

When there are no intervening cash flows between the time a deposit is made and the maturity of the deposit, the interest rates are said to be **spot interest rates**. Interest rate parity only applies to spot interest rates. The **term structure of interest rates** for a particular currency is a description of the different spot interest rates for various maturities into the future. For shorter maturities, these spot interest rates are directly observable because they are widely quoted by banks. However, for longer maturities, we usually have to derive the spot interest rates from the market prices of coupon-paying bonds. Typically, the interest rates are quoted on an annual basis—that is, they reflect the return earned per year.

Exhibit 6.7 presents term structures of interest rates for the U.S. dollar (USD), the euro (EUR), the British pound (GBP), and the Japanese yen (JPY) that prevailed on July 6, 2006. Note that the yen interest rates are the lowest at all maturities, and the interest rates for the yen's shorter maturities are lower than the interest rates for longer maturities. Consequently, we say that the term structure of interest rates for the yen is rising, or upward sloping. Note that the pound interest rates are higher at shorter maturities but slightly lower at very long maturities. Consequently, we say that the pound term structure is downward sloping. Term structures such as these are said to be *inverted* because they usually slope upward. The U.S. term structure appears flat: Long-term rates are only slightly above short-term rates.

To understand how to determine spot interest rates from bond prices, let's review some additional terminology associated with bond pricing.

A Review of Bond Pricing

Bonds are financial contracts that obligate the bond issuer to pay the bondholder a sequence of fixed contractual payments until the maturity of the bond. These payments represent the return of principal and interest on the principal. Most bonds with maturities of longer than 1 year have coupon payments that provide the bondholder with intervening interest payments between the purchase of the bond and the maturity date. For example, the coupon payments on U.S. government bonds and American corporate bonds are made every 6 months. A 7% bond with a final payment of $1,000 would pay $35 of coupon interest every 6 months because

$$(.07/2) \times \$1,000 = \$35$$

The simplest bonds, though, are **pure discount bonds**. Such bonds promise a single payment of, say, $1,000 or €1,000 at the maturity of the bond. The terminal payment is called the *face value* of the bond. The bonds are sold at a discount on the face value such that the difference between the face value of the bond and the market price of the bond when it is purchased provides an interest return to the buyer. Long-maturity pure discount bonds are often called *deep-discount bonds*, *zero-coupon bonds*, or simply *zeros* to emphasize that the only cash flow to the bondholder is the final face value on the bond. Consequently, we can now define the spot interest rate as the market interest rate that equates the price of a pure discount bond to the present value of the face value of the bond.

Example 6.7   Pure Discount Bonds and Spot Interest Rates

Suppose the market price of a 10-year pure discount bond with a face value of $1,000 is $463.19. What is the spot interest rate for the 10-year maturity expressed in percentage per annum?

We want to find the spot interest rate, say $i(10)$, such that when $463.19 is invested today, it can grow at the compound rate of $i(10)$ to be equal to $1,000 after 10 years:

$$\$463.19 \, [1 + i(10)]^{10} = \$1,000$$

The solution is

$$i(10) = (\$1,000/\$463.19)^{1/10} - 1 = 0.08$$

The spot interest rate for the 10-year maturity is 8% p.a., and at this rate, the future value of $463.19 in 10 years is $1,000, and the present value of $1,000 to be received 10 years from now is $463.19 today.

We can put the finding from Example 6.7 in more general terms. Let $B(n)$ equal the current market price of a pure discount bond with n periods to maturity, and let M be the face value of the bond that will be paid at maturity. Let the spot interest rate today for maturity n be $i(n)$. Then the market price of the bond is the present discounted value of the face value of the bond at the given spot interest rate:

$$B(n) = \frac{M}{[1 + i(n)]^n}$$

In some environments, the interest rate $i(n)$ is called a *discount rate*. Mostly, the face values and the prices of bonds are available as information in the market. Then, we can calculate the spot interest rate by solving the following equation for $i(n)$:

$$[1 + i(n)]^n = \frac{M}{B(n)}$$

To solve this equation, we must raise each side to the 1/n power and then subtract 1 from both sides:

$$i(n) = \left[\frac{M}{B(n)}\right]^{1/n} - 1$$

Yields to Maturity
Another piece of readily available information about a bond is its **yield to maturity**. This is the single common discount rate that equates the present value of a sequence of coupon payments and the final, face-value payment to the current price of the bond.

Let $B(n,C)$ denote the current market price of an n-period bond with a face value of M and a periodic coupon payment of C. The yield to maturity on this bond, denoted $y(n)$, is the single discount rate or interest rate that equates the present value of the n coupon payments plus the final principal payment and the current market price:

$$B(n, C) = \frac{C}{[1 + y(n)]} + \frac{C}{[1 + y(n)]^2} + \cdots + \frac{C}{[1 + y(n)]^n} + \frac{M}{[1 + y(n)]^n} \qquad \textbf{(6.15)}$$

Notice that the discount rate is the same for each of the coupons and the final principal, but 1 plus the discount rate is raised to various powers to reflect the number of periods the coupon payments are away from today (see Frank Fabozzi, 1996).

Yields to maturity are straightforward to calculate for a variety of maturities, and market participants often discuss the **yield curve**. Just as the term structure of interest rates refers to the relationship between maturity and spot interest rates for different maturities, the yield curve is the relationship between maturity and the yields on bonds of those maturities. When the term structure of interest rates slopes upward, the yield curve generally slopes upward as well.

Deriving Long-Term Spot Interest Rates

For pure discount bonds, the yield to maturity is the spot interest rate for that maturity because there are no cash flows between now and the maturity date. When there are intervening coupon payments and the spot interest rates for different maturities are not all equal, there must be a difference between the yield to maturity on the bond and the spot interest rate for the maturity of the bond.

Example 6.8 Spot Interest Rates Versus Yields to Maturity

Consider a 2-year bond with face value equal to $1,000, an annual coupon of $60, and a market price of $980. Suppose the 1-year spot interest rate, $i(1)$, is 5.5%. The current 2-year spot interest rate is found as the solution, $i(2)$, to the following equation:

$$\$980 = \frac{\$60}{1.055} + \frac{\$1060}{1 + i(2)^2}$$

By solving the equation, we find $i(2) = 7.1574\%$.

The yield to maturity is a complicated average of the spot interest rates for the various maturities of the coupon payments and the final repayment of principal. It would be the discount rate $y(2)$ that solves[7]

$$\$980 = \frac{\$60}{[1 + y(2)]} + \frac{\$1060}{[1 + y(2)]^2}$$

The value of $y(2)$ is 7.11%, which is intermediate between the two spot rates but much closer to $i(2)$ because most of the cash flows of the bond occur in the second year.

---

[7]In this simple example, we could analytically solve for $y(2)$, but when there are many periods involved, the yield to maturity must typically be found with computational numeric methods. One easy way is with Microsoft Excel. The yield to maturity is the internal rate of return (IRR) on the negative cash flow incurred when the bond is purchased followed by the positive cash flows from holding the bond to maturity.

The solution procedure applied here indicates that spot interest rates are the appropriate discount rates for the cash flows that take place at a particular maturity. The logic of this conclusion is clearer if you think of a long-term bond with coupon payments and a final principal payment as the sum of several pure discount bonds. Consider each maturity at which a cash flow occurs to be a separate bond. The value of each pure discount bond is found by taking the present value of the single payment with the appropriate spot interest rate for that maturity. The market value of the bond is then the sum of the present values of the different promised payments.

Generally, let $i(t,j)$ denote the spot interest rate at time t for maturity j periods into the future. Consider the present value at time t, $PV(t)$, of a sequence of known cash flows, denoted $C(t+j)$, for values of j between 1 and n periods into the future. By discounting each cash flow with its appropriate pure discount rate, we find the present value at time t as

$$PV(t) = \frac{C(t+1)}{[1 + i(t, 1)]} + \frac{C(t+2)}{[1 + i(t, 2)]^2} + \cdots + \frac{C(t+n)}{[1 + i(t, n)]^n}$$

Because calculating present values in different currencies is a fundamental part of international finance, understanding the different term structures of spot interest rates for different currencies is quite important.

Long-Term Forward Rates and Premiums

Let's develop the relationship between long-term forward exchange rates and spot exchange rates with an example. Let $i(2,¥)$ and $i(2,\$)$ denote the spot interest rates today for the 2-year maturity for Japanese yen and U.S. dollar investments, respectively. Let S be the spot exchange rate of yen per dollar today, and let $F(2)$ denote the outright forward rate today for delivery in 2 years. If there are no opportunities for arbitrage, the outright forward rate of yen per dollar for the 2-year maturity must be

$$F(2) = S \times \frac{[1 + i(2, ¥)]^2}{[1 + i(2, \$)]^2} \tag{6.16}$$

To see why this must be true, consider that a Japanese investor must be indifferent between investing in yen for 2 years and getting $[1 + i(2, ¥)]^2$ for each yen or converting the yen into dollars and getting $1/S$ dollars for each yen, investing these dollars for 2 years to have $(1/S)[1 + i(2, \$)]^2$ dollars after 2 years, and contracting to sell these dollars forward at $F(2)$ to get a yen return of $F(2)(1/S)[1 + i(2, \$)]^2$. Equating these returns and solving for $F(2)$ gives Equation (6.16). Example 6.9 is a numeric example that illustrates these issues.

Example 6.9 The 2-Year Forward Rate

Let the spot exchange rate be $S = ¥110/\$$, and let the spot interest rates for the 2-year maturity be $i(2,\$) = 5\%$ p.a. and $i(2,¥) = 4\%$ p.a. Suppose you invest ¥10,000,000 in a 2-year yen pure discount bond. At the end of 2 years, your investment will grow to

$$¥10,000,000 \times (1.04)^2 = ¥10,816,000$$

At the current spot exchange rate, the dollar cost of ¥10,000,000 is

$$¥10,000,000 / (¥110/\$) = \$90,909.09$$

If you invest $90,909.09 in a 2-year dollar pure discount bond, at the end of 2 years you will have

$$\$90,909.09 \times (1.05)^2 = \$100,227.27$$

This analysis indicates that you can either invest $90,909.09 today to buy ¥10,000,000 and invest it for 2 years to have ¥10,816,000, or you can invest the $90,909.09 in the dollar bond for 2 years to get $100,227.27. You will prefer the yen investment if you can contract today in the forward market to convert from yen back to dollars at $F(2)$ and have more dollars than $100,227.27. You will be indifferent if the forward sale of ¥10,816,000 for dollars provides you with the same dollar return as investing directly in dollars. That is, only if the forward rate satisfies

$$¥10,816,000 / F(2) = \$100,227.27$$

will you be indifferent between the two investments. If we solve this equation for the forward rate, we find

$$F(2) = ¥10,816,000 / \$100,227.27 = ¥107.9147/\$$$

or, rounding to the nearest one-hundredth of a yen, $F(2) = ¥107.91/\$$. If the forward exchange rate quoted today for transactions in 2 years is greater than ¥107.91/$, a dollar investor would receive more dollars by investing in the dollar bond than by investing in the yen bond. Investors of yen would also receive more yen by investing in the dollar bond than by investing in the yen bond. They would, of course, have to sell the dollars forward for yen. This is the same type of arbitrage argument that was used earlier when short-term interest rate parity was developed. Analogously, if the forward exchange rate quoted today for transactions in 2 years is less than ¥107.91/$, a dollar investor would receive more dollars by investing in the yen bond and contracting to sell yen forward for dollars than by investing directly in the dollar bond. Investors of yen would also receive more yen by investing in the yen bond than by investing in the dollar bond and contracting to sell dollars forward.

What would happen if the forward rate did not satisfy Equation (6.16), implying that there was a difference in returns available in the market? For example, suppose that the dollar and yen interest rates and the spot and forward exchange rates favored investing in the dollar bond over the yen bond. Investors would move funds out of Japanese yen bonds and into U.S. dollar bonds. Changes in the demand for bonds denominated in different currencies would be accompanied by changes in demand for the currencies as investors sold one currency and bought another. This activity would set up a series of changes in the bond prices, interest rates, and the spot and forward exchange rates that would bring the market back to equilibrium.

If investors sold yen bonds, the prices of the yen bonds would fall, and their yields would rise. As money flowed out of Japan, the dollar would strengthen relative to the yen, causing the spot exchange rate of yen per dollar to rise as increased dollars were demanded with the yen to make investments in the dollar bond. As additional dollars flowed into the dollar bond market, the prices of dollar bonds would rise, causing their yields to fall. Finally, the forward rate of yen per dollar would fall as investors sold dollars forward to acquire yen in the future.

All four effects make investing in the yen asset more attractive and investing in the dollar asset relatively less attractive.

Notice that we have demonstrated how long-term investment considerations would move the outright forward exchange rate quoted today for delivery n periods from now to be equal to the spot rate today adjusted for the relative returns on pure discount bonds between now and n periods from now in the two currencies (in yen per dollar):

$$F(n) = S \times \frac{[1 + i(n, ¥)]^n}{[1 + i(n, \$)]^n}$$

Theoretically, this is the way that long-term forward contracts should be priced.

Of course, throughout this discussion, we have ignored bid–ask spreads on the transactions in the bond market as investors buy and sell bonds and on the transactions in the spot and forward foreign exchange markets. These transaction costs become larger as the maturities lengthen. They are also the source of the development of currency swaps, which are discussed in more detail in Chapter 21.

6.6 SUMMARY

This chapter investigates the relationship between nominal interest rates for two currencies and the corresponding spot and forward exchange rates. When the money markets are free from arbitrage, this relationship between these four variables is called *interest rate parity*. The main points in the chapter are the following:

1. The nominal interest rate is the time value of money. The future value (FV) of an amount of money is obtained by multiplying by 1 plus the interest rate: $[FV = \text{cash flow} \times (1 + i)]$. The present value ($PV$) today of an amount of money in the future is obtained by dividing by 1 plus the interest rate: $PV = \dfrac{\text{Future cash flow}}{1 + i}$.

2. Covered interest arbitrage is done in four steps: borrowing one currency, converting to a second currency, investing the second currency, and selling the interest plus principal on the second currency in the forward market for the first currency.

3. When domestic and foreign interest rates and spot and forward exchange rates are in equilibrium such that no covered interest arbitrage is possible, the interest rates and exchange rates are said to satisfy interest rate parity.

4. With exchange rates expressed directly as domestic currency per unit of foreign currency, interest rate parity is satisfied when the forward premium or discount on the foreign currency equals the interest differential between the domestic and foreign interest rates divided by one plus the foreign interest rate.

5. The external currency market is an interbank market for deposits and loans that are denominated in currencies that are not the currency of the country in which the bank is operating.

6. Bid–ask spreads in the external currency market (with the bank bidding for deposits and offering an interest rate on loans) are quite small in normal periods.

7. In the presence of transaction costs, interest rate parity is characterized by two inequalities, indicating that covered interest arbitrage leads to losses in both directions. That is, neither lending nor borrowing in a particular currency at the start of the attempted arbitrage leads to profits.

8. The empirical evidence indicates that interest rate parity is the norm, especially during tranquil periods and for short maturities. During turbulent periods, there appear to be occasional arbitrage opportunities that persist for several days and offer potential profits.

9. These profit opportunities may instead merely reflect the differential credit risks of the institutions quoting prices in the market. Credit risk or default risk is the chance that a counterparty will default on its side of a commitment.

10. Exchange controls involve taxes a government imposes on foreign investments, or regulatory restrictions on the use of foreign exchange. These controls and restrictions can lead to perceived interest rate parity violations that cannot actually be exploited.

11. Political risk arises when investors rationally believe a government may impose some form of exchange controls or taxes during the life of the investment or even seize the assets of investors. Political risk can cause deviations from interest rate parity that do not actually represent profit opportunities.

12. Transaction exchange risk can be hedged with money market hedges. A money market hedge establishes a foreign currency–denominated asset or liability that offsets the underlying transaction exposure. If interest rate parity is satisfied, a money market hedge is identical to a forward market hedge.

13. The only cash flow to the bondholder of a pure discount bond is the final face value of the bond. Spot interest rates are the discount rates that equate the prices of pure discount bonds to the present values of the face values of the bonds. Spot interest rates are the appropriate discount rates for cash flows with no uncertainty that take place at a particular maturity.

14. The term structure of interest rates for a particular currency represents the different spot interest rates for various future maturities.

15. A bond's yield to maturity is the single common discount rate that equates the present value of the sequence of all coupon payments and principal payments to the current price of the bond.

16. Using the spot exchange rate and the domestic and foreign spot interest rates for a particular maturity, we can derive the forward rate for that maturity.

QUESTIONS

1. Explain the concepts of present value and future value.

2. If the dollar interest rate is positive, explain why the value of $1,000,000 received every year for 10 years is not $10,000,000 today.

3. Describe how you would calculate a 5-year forward exchange rate of yen per dollar if you knew the current spot exchange rate and the prices of 5-year pure discount bonds denominated in yen and dollars. Explain why this has to be the market price.

4. If interest rate parity is satisfied, there are no opportunities for covered interest arbitrage. What does this imply about the relationship between spot and forward exchange rates when the foreign currency money market investment offers a higher return than the domestic money market investment.

5. It is often said that interest rate parity is satisfied when the differential between the interest rates denominated in two currencies equals the forward premium or discount between the two currencies. Explain why this is an imprecise statement when the interest rates are not continuously compounded.

6. What do economists mean by the external currency market?

7. What determines the bid–ask spread in the external currency market? Why is it usually so small?

8. Explain why the absence of covered interest arbitrage possibilities can be characterized by two inequalities in the presence of bid–ask spreads in the foreign exchange and external currency markets.

9. If volatility in foreign exchange markets increases, what do you think happens to the bid–ask spread? Why?

10. Describe the sequence of transactions required to do a covered interest arbitrage out of Japanese yen and into U.S. dollars.

11. Suppose you saw a set of quoted prices from a U.S. bank and a French bank such that you could borrow dollars, sell the dollars in the spot foreign exchange market for euros, deposit the euros for 90 days, and make a forward contract to sell euros for dollars and make a guaranteed profit. Would this be an arbitrage opportunity? Why or why not?

12. The interest rates on U.S. dollar–denominated bank accounts in Mexican banks are often several percentage points per annum higher than the interest rates on bank accounts in the United States. Can you explain this phenomenon?

13. What is a money market hedge? How is it constructed?

14. Suppose you are the French representative of a company selling soap in Canada. Describe your foreign exchange risk and how you might hedge it with a money market hedge.

15. What is a pure discount bond?

16. What is the term structure of interest rates? How are spot interest rates determined from coupon bond prices?

17. How does a coupon bond's yield to maturity differ from the spot interest rate that applies to cash flows occurring at the maturity of the bond? When are the two the same?

1. In the entry forms for its contests, Publisher's Clearing House states, "You may have already won $10,000,000." If the Prize Patrol visits your house to inform you that you have won, it offers you $333,333.33 each and every year for 30 years. If the interest rate is 8% p.a., what is the actual present value of the $10,000,000 prize?

2. Suppose the 5-year interest rate on a dollar-denominated pure discount bond is 4.5% p.a., whereas in France, the euro interest rate is 7.5% p.a. on a similar pure discount bond denominated in euros. If the current spot rate is $1.08/€, what is the value of the forward exchange rate that prevents covered interest arbitrage?

3. Carla Heinz is a portfolio manager for Deutsche Bank. She is considering two alternative investments of EUR10,000,000. Either she will invest in euro deposits or she will invest in Swiss francs (CHF) for 180 days. In the latter case, she knows that she must worry about transaction foreign exchange risk, so she has decided to fully hedge her investment. Suppose she has the following data:

180-day Swiss franc deposits: 8.0% p.a.
180-day euro deposits: 10.0% p.a.
Spot exchange rate: EUR1.1960/CHF
180-day forward exchange rate: EUR1.2024/CHF

Which of these deposits provides the higher euro return in 180 days? If these were actually market prices, what would you expect to happen?

4. If the 30-day yen interest rate is 3% p.a., and the 30-day euro interest rate is 5% p.a., is there a forward premium or discount on the euro in terms of the yen? What is the magnitude of the forward premium or discount?

5. Suppose the Swiss franc–dollar exchange rate is CHF1.4706/$ in the spot market, and the 180-day forward rate is CHF1.4295/$. If the 180-day dollar interest rate is 7% p.a., what is the annualized 180-day interest rate on Swiss francs that would prevent arbitrage?

6. As a trader for Bear Sterns you see the following prices from two different banks:
1-year euro deposits/loans: 6.0% –6.125% p.a.
1-year Malaysian ringgit
deposits/loans: 10.5% – 10.625% p.a.
Spot exchange rates:
       MYR 4.6602 / EUR – MYR 4.6622 / EUR
1-year forward exchange rates:
       MYR 4.9500 / EUR – MYR 4.9650 / EUR
The interest rates are quoted on a 360-day year. Is there an opportunity for covered interest arbitrage?

7. Assume that you are an importer of grain into Japan from the United States. You have agreed to make a payment in dollars, and you are scheduled to pay $377,287 in 90 days after you receive your grain. You face the following exchange rates and interest rates:

Spot interest rate: ¥106.35/$,
90-day forward interest rate: ¥106.02/$,
90-day dollar interest rate: 3.25% p.a.,
90-day yen interest rate: 1.9375% p.a.

a. Describe the nature and extent of your transaction foreign exchange risk.
b. Explain two ways to hedge the risk.
c. Which of the alternatives in part b is superior?

8. You are a sales manager for Motorola and export cellular phones from the United States to other countries. You have just signed a deal to ship phones to a British distributor. The deal is denominated in pounds, and you will receive £700,000 when the phones arrive in London in 180 days. Assume that you can borrow and lend at 7% p.a. in U.S. dollars and at 10% p.a. in British pounds. Both interest rate quotes are for a 360-day year. The spot exchange rate is $1.4945/£, and the 180-day forward exchange rate is $1.4802/£.

a. Describe the nature and extent of your transaction foreign exchange risk.
b. Describe two ways of eliminating the transaction foreign exchange risk.
c. Which of the alternatives in part b is superior?
d. Assume that the dollar interest rate and the exchange rates are correct. Determine what sterling interest rate would make your firm indifferent between the two alternative hedges.

9. Suppose that there is a 0.5% probability that the government of Argentina will nationalize its banking system and freeze all foreign deposits indefinitely during the next year. If the dollar deposit interest rate in the United States is 5%, what dollar interest would Argentine banks have to offer in order to attract deposits from foreign investors?

10. Suppose the market price of a 20-year pure discount bond with a face value of $1,000 is $214.55. What is the spot interest rate for the 20-year maturity expressed in percentage per annum?

11. Consider a 2-year euro-denominated bond that has a current market price of €970, a face value of €1,000, and an annual coupon of 5%. Suppose the 1-year euro-denominated spot interest rate is 5.5%. What is the 2-year euro-denominated spot interest rate?

BIBLIOGRAPHY

Aliber, Robert, 1973, "The Interest-Rate Parity Theorem: A Reinterpretation," *Journal of Political Economy* 81, pp. 1451–1459.

Clinton, Kevin, 1988, "Transaction Costs and Covered Interest Arbitrage: Theory and Evidence," *Journal of Political Economy* pp. 358–370.

Delamaide, Darrell, 1985, *Debt Shock: The Full Story of the World Credit Crisis*, New York: Anchor Books.

Domowitz, Ian, Jack Glen, and Ananth Madhavan, 1998, "Country and Currency Risk Premia in an Emerging Market," *Journal of Financial and Quantitative Analysis* 33, pp. 189–216.

Fabozzi, Frank J., 1996, *Bond Markets, Analysis and Strategies*, 3rd ed., Upper Saddle River, NJ: Prentice Hall, Inc.

Levich, Richard M., 1998, *International Financial Markets*, Boston: Irwin McGraw-Hill.

McBrady, Matthew R., 2005, "How Integrated are Global Bond Markets? Estimating the Limits of Covered Interest Arbitrage," working paper.

Sarver, Eugene, 1990, *The Eurocurrency Handbook*, 2nd ed., New York: New York Institute of Finance.

Stigum, Marcia, 1981, *Money Market Calculations: Yields, Breakevens and Arbitrage*, Homewood IL: Dow-Jones Irwin Publishing.

Solnik, Bruno, 2000, *International Investments*, 4th ed., Reading, MA: Addison-Wesley.

Taylor, Mark P., 1987, "Covered Interest Arbitrage: A High-Frequency, High-Quality Data Study," *Economica* 54, pp. 429–438.

Taylor, Mark P., 1989, "Covered Interest Arbitrage and Market Turbulence," *The Economic Journal* 99, pp. 376–391.

7

Speculation and Risk in the Foreign Exchange Market

*T*his chapter examines what happens if an investor chooses to speculate—that is, if an investor chooses not to hedge (or "cover") the foreign exchange risk on a foreign money market investment. The investor's return is uncertain and may be high if the foreign currency appreciates or low if the foreign currency depreciates. In this chapter, we discuss theories and techniques to help investors quantify the expected return and risk associated with such speculative foreign exchange investments. We address whether risk premiums on **uncovered investments in the foreign money market** induce people to bear these risks. Fully understanding this discussion requires an evaluation of the statistical methods that are used in this literature. It might help to reread the Appendix to Chapter 3 and to read Appendix 7.2 in this chapter. These methods can be used to understand the empirical evidence about the returns on investments in all asset markets.

7.1 SPECULATING IN THE FOREIGN EXCHANGE MARKET

Uncovered Foreign Money Market Investments

In Chapter 6 we examined covered investments in foreign money markets and found that if interest rate parity is satisfied, the domestic currency rate of return from investing in a foreign money market is the domestic currency interest rate. What happens if an investor does not cover his or her foreign exchange risk? Let's look at an example.

Example 7.1 Kevin Anthony's Uncovered Pound Investment

Recall the situation in Example 6.2 in which a portfolio manager, Kevin Anthony, was considering several ways to invest $10,000,000 for 1 year. The data are as follows:

> USD interest rate: 8.0% per annum (p.a.)
> GBP interest rate: 12.0% p.a.
> Spot exchange rate: $1.60/£

Remember that if Kevin invests in the USD-denominated asset at 8%, he will have

$$\$10,000,000 \times 1.08 = \$10,800,000$$

at the end of 1 year.

Suppose Kevin invests his $10,000,000 in the pound money market, but he decides not to hedge the foreign exchange risk. As before, we can calculate his dollar return in three steps.

Step 1. Convert dollars to pounds in the spot market. The $10,000,000 will buy

$$\frac{\$10,000,000}{\$1.60/\pounds} = \pounds6,250,000$$

at the current spot exchange rate. This is Kevin's pound principal.

Step 2. Calculate pound-denominated interest plus principal. Kevin can invest his pound principal at 12% for 1 year. Hence, Kevin knows that in 1 year he will have a return of pound principal plus interest equal to

$$\pounds6,250,000 \times 1.12 = \pounds7,000,000$$

Step 3. Sell the pound principal plus interest at the spot exchange rate in 1 year:

$$\text{Dollar proceeds in one year} = \pounds7,000,000 \times S(t+1,\$/\pounds)$$

If Kevin chooses not to hedge the foreign exchange risk, the dollars that he receives from his investment in the pound money market will be determined by the value of the future exchange rate.

It is customary to express the return to an investment per dollar invested. Let's denote the current spot rate by $S(t)$ and the future spot rate by $S(t + 1)$, remembering that the currency values are expressed in $/£. Following the three steps in Example 7.1, the dollar return on a pound money market investment, $r(t + 1)$, is as follows:

$$r(t+1) = \frac{1}{S(t)} \times [1+i(\pounds)] \times S(t+1) \tag{7.1}$$

where $i(\pounds)$ denotes the pound interest rate.

In Example 7.1, we obtain:

$$r(t+1) = \frac{1}{\$1.60/\pounds} \times 1.12 \times S(t+1) = 0.7 \times S(t+1).$$

Notice that $0.7 = \dfrac{\pounds7,000,000}{\$10,000,000}$ is the ratio of the amount of future pounds Kevin will have to the amount of dollars he invests today. The return on Kevin's investment is risky because the value of the future exchange rate is not known today. Kevin might also be interested in the excess return to this investment, denoted $\text{exr}(t + 1)$—that is, the return over and above what he could earn risk free domestically. The excess return (exr) is

$$\text{exr}(t+1) = \frac{S(t+1)}{S(t)} \times [1+ i(\pounds)] - [1+i(\$)] \tag{7.2}$$

$$= S(t+1) \times 0.7 - 1.08$$

where $i(\$)$ is the dollar interest rate.

Speculating with Forward Contracts

The Break-Even Spot Rate

Let's reconsider Equation (7.2). If Kevin has not hedged, he will hope that the pound appreciates as much as possible—that is, that $S(t + 1)$, the future \$/£ exchange rate, is as high as possible to give him a positive excess return. The future exchange rate for which Kevin breaks even between the pound and the domestic money market investment is the exchange rate for which Equation (7.2) is equal to zero. Let's call that rate S^{BE}:

$$S^{BE} = \frac{1.08}{0.7} = \$1.5429/£$$

$$= S(t) \times \frac{[1 + i(\$)]}{[1 + i(£)]} \tag{7.3}$$

From Chapter 6, we recognize that the formula in Equation (7.3) is nothing but the formula for the forward rate! Consequently, if the future exchange rate appreciates to above the level predicted by the forward rate, Kevin will make a positive excess return, but if the future exchange rate is less than the forward rate, Kevin will have a negative excess return. It is therefore not surprising that Kevin can speculate on the direction of the pound exchange rate using forward contracts rather than money market investments.

Comparing Forward Market and Foreign Money Market Investments

Forward contracts are pure bets—that is, no money changes hands when a forward contract is made. To make this forward contracting situation more concrete, let Mr. Buy represent the person who contracts to buy pounds with dollars in the forward foreign exchange market from Ms. Sell, who represents the person contracting in the forward market to sell pounds for dollars. Mr. Buy will pay $F(t)$ dollars in 1 year for every pound he buys forward, and he can sell each pound in the future spot market for dollars at a price of $S(t + 1)$. Ms. Sell, on the other hand, will buy her pounds in the future spot market at a dollar price of $S(t + 1)$, and she will sell each pound to Mr. Buy for $F(t)$. Therefore, on a per-pound basis, the dollar profits and losses are as follows:

$$\text{Mr. Buy's dollar profit or loss} = S(t+1) - F(t)$$

and

$$\text{Ms. Sell's dollar profit or loss} = F(t) - S(t+1)$$

These dollar profits and losses are graphed in Exhibit 7.1 as a function of the value of $S(t+1)$. Notice that the dollar profit of the person who buys foreign currency forward is the dollar loss of the person who sells foreign currency forward, and vice versa.

How does this **forward market investment** compare with Kevin Anthony's pound foreign money market investment? First, because no money changes hands up front in a forward contract, it makes sense to compare the **forward market return** to the excess return from the foreign money market investment derived in Equation (7.2). The excess return can be viewed as the return on a strategy in which Kevin borrows dollars in the domestic money market and invests them in the pound money market. Second, the forward market return is expressed per unit of foreign currency (the pound), whereas the money market return was expressed in domestic currency units (dollars). However, it is straightforward to convert the per-pound return into a per-dollar return by dividing by the current exchange rate. Third, because the forward contract sells £1 in the future, but Kevin's strategy invests money today, we must make a future value adjustment. We must scale up the forward market return by $[1 + i(£)]$ to compare it to a money market investment because 1 pound today is worth $[1 + i(£)]$ in the future.

Exhibit 7.1 Profits and Losses from Forward Market Speculation

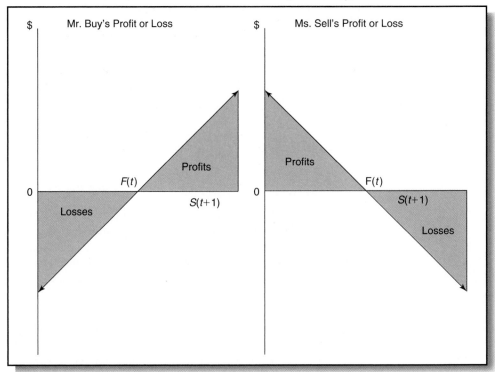

Because Kevin invests in the pound money market investment, the relevant comparison is with Mr. Buy's contract to buy pounds in the forward market. We first express Mr. Buy's profits on a per-dollar basis by dividing $S(t)$:

$$\text{Forward Market return (per dollar)} = \text{fmr}(t+1) = \frac{S(t+1) - F(t)}{S(t)} \qquad (7.4)$$

where we define the forward market return (per dollar) in Equation (7.4) as $\text{fmr}(t+1)$. From covered interest rate parity, we know

$$F(t) = S(t) \times \frac{[1+i(\$)]}{[1+i(£)]} \qquad (7.5)$$

Hence, solving Equation (7.5) for (F/S) and substituting into Equation (7.4), the forward market return (per dollar invested) is equivalent to:

$$\text{fmr}(t+1) = \frac{S(t+1)}{S(t)} - \frac{[1+i(\$)]}{[1+i(£)]}$$

Finally, when we multiply by $[1+i(£)]$ to make the number of invested units the same, we obtain

$$\text{fmr}(t+1) \times [1+i(£)] = \frac{S(t+1)}{S(t)}[1+i(£)] - [1+i(\$)]$$

This expression is exactly the excess return, $\text{exr}(t+1)$, from investing 1 dollar in the pound foreign money market financed by borrowing 1 dollar in the domestic money market, as derived in Equation (7.2). We have a relationship between the return in the forward market and the excess return in the foreign money market:

$$\text{fmr}(t+1) \times [1 + i(\pounds)] = \text{exr}(t+1)$$

Example 7.2 Forward Market Returns Versus Foreign Money Market Returns

Let's focus on Kevin Anthony's investment situation (see Example 7.1) and consider how the actual return from speculating in the foreign exchange market depends on the future value of the exchange rate. Here we set the forward rate equal to the break-even rate $1.5429/£ we computed in Example 7.1:

Future Value of the Exchange Rate	Forward Market Return (in Future Dollars)	Excess Foreign Money Market Return (in %)
$S(t+1)$	$S(t+1) - F(t)$ $= [S(t+1) - 1.5429]$	$\dfrac{S(t+1)}{S(t)}[1+i(\pounds)] - [1+i(\$)]$ $= [0.7\, S(t+1) - 1.08]$
1.65	0.1071	7.5
1.5429	0.0	0.0
1.50	−0.0429	−3.0

Note that the critical level of the future exchange rate that separates loss from profit is the forward rate. Moreover, the returns in the two columns are proportional $\left(\dfrac{0.075}{0.1071} = \dfrac{-0.03}{-0.0429} = 0.70\right)$ because they provide exposure to the same source of risk (dollar/pound exchange rate movements), but they are expressed in different units. When thinking about risky investments, we would like to know the expected return and risk of the investment. We start by examining the expected return.

Currency Speculation and Profits and Losses

The expected return to currency speculation clearly depends on expectations regarding the value of the future exchange rate. By and large, expected future spot rates of market participants are unobservable. Occasionally, however, we see some data on them.

Some Observable Expectations

Consider the information in Exhibit 7.2. In May 1995, the *Wall Street Journal* published the exchange rate forecasts of seven prominent commercial and investment banks that are active players in the foreign exchange market. These data are reproduced in Panel A of Exhibit 7.2. Because these banks have extensive experience dealing in the foreign exchange market, and because they systematically take long or short positions in various currencies in an attempt to make a profit, they ought to be able to forecast exchange rates if anyone can.

To put the forecasts in Exhibit 7.2 in perspective, you should also know that in May 1995, spot exchange rates were DEM1.4440/$ and ¥87.18/$, 3-month forward rates were DEM1.4377/$ and ¥86.11/$, and 6-month forward rates were DEM1.4321/$ and ¥85.08/$. Notice that the dollar was at a forward discount in both the Deutsche mark and yen foreign exchange markets because the forward rates are below the spot rates. Panel B of Exhibit 7.2 reports the expected percentage appreciation or depreciation of the dollar that are implicit in the various forecasts shown in Panel A.

Exhibit 7.2 Exchange Rates Forecasts from May 23, 1995: An Analysis

| Current Spot Rates | DEM 1.440/$ | | ¥87.18/$ | |
| Panel A: | DEM/$ Forecast | | Yen/$ Forecast | |
	3 Months	6 Months	3 Months	6 Months
Forward Rates	1.4377	1.4321	86.11	85.08
S. G. Warburg	1.40	1.53	88	103
Union Bank of Switz.	1.52	1.55	92	96
Goldman Sachs	1.39	1.47	85	95
Citibank	1.40	1.25	82	75
Paine Webber Intl.	1.45	1.40	92	90
Merrill Lynch	1.45	1.50	88	92
Swiss Bank Corp.	1.46	1.40	93	90

| | Percentage Dollar Appreciation Forecast | | | |
Panel B:	3 Months	6 Months	3 Months	6 Months
Forward Rate	−0.44	−0.82	−1.23	−2.41
S. G. Warburg	−3.05	5.96	0.94	18.15
Union Bank of Switz.	5.26	7.34	5.53	10.12
Goldman Sachs	−3.74	1.80	−2.50	8.97
Citibank	−3.05	−13.43	−5.94	−13.97
Paine Webber Intl.	0.42	−3.05	5.53	3.23
Merrill Lynch	0.42	3.88	0.94	5.53
Swiss Bank Corp.	1.11	−3.05	6.68	3.23
Ex post Spot Rates	1.4817	1.4131	96.52	100.65
Actual $ Appreciation	2.61	−2.14	10.71	15.45

| | Percentage Forecast Error | | | |
Panel C:	3 Months	6 Months	3 Months	6 Months
Forward Rate	3.05	−1.32	11.94	17.86
S. G. Warburg	5.66	−8.10	9.77	−2.70
Union Bank of Switz.	−2.65	−9.48	5.18	5.33
Goldman Sachs	6.35	−3.94	13.21	6.48
Citibank	5.66	11.30	16.66	29.42
Paine Webber Intl.	2.20	0.91	5.18	12.22
Merrill Lynch	2.20	−6.02	9.77	9.92
Swiss Bank Corp.	1.50	0.91	4.04	12.22

Note: From the *Wall Street Journal*, May 24, 1995, p. C1, and authors' calculations. The percentages in Panel B use forecasts in Panel A and the current spot rates reported on top of the table (e.g., for the forward rate,

$$-0.44 = \frac{1.4377 - 1.444}{1.444} \times 100).$$ The forecast errors of Panel C are most easily computed by subtracting the

forecasted dollar appreciation in Panel B from the actual dollar appreciation reported just above Panel C.

It is apparent that the forecasters disagreed not only with the forward rate that they all observed in the market, but they also disagreed with each other. For example, at the 3-month horizon, Goldman Sachs forecast that the dollar would depreciate relative to the DEM by 3.74% (from 1.4440 to 1.39), whereas UBS forecast that the dollar would appreciate by over 5%. At the 6-month horizon for the yen–dollar rate, the differences were even more pronounced. Citibank forecast that the dollar would depreciate by almost 14% (from ¥87.18/$ to ¥75/$), whereas S. G. Warburg forecast that the dollar would appreciate by over 18% (from ¥87.18/$ to ¥103/$).

Remember that to prevent arbitrage opportunities in the market, all these banks must quote forward rates that are essentially the same. Otherwise, someone could buy a currency forward from the bank quoting the low price and sell that currency forward to the bank quoting the high price and thereby lock in an arbitrage profit. Therefore, the large differences in opinion about future spot rates that we see in Exhibit 7.2 suggest that these banks would have been willing to trade in the forward market with each other and that both parties to the trade would have expected that they were going to profit.

Consider the following example of such a trade that could have taken place in the 6-month yen–dollar market.

Example 7.3 Exchange Rate Forecasts and Forward Market Speculation

In Panel A of Exhibit 7.2, Citibank forecasts that it will be able to buy dollars with yen in 6 months at ¥75/$, and Citibank can contract to sell dollars for yen in the forward market at ¥85.08/$. If a Citibank trader sells $10,000,000 forward, the expected yen profit is the difference between the price at which the trader sells dollars forward and the price at which the trader expects to be able to buy dollars in the future spot market times the size of the dollar trade:

Expected profit (in yen) $= (¥85.08/\$ - ¥75/\$) \times \$10,000,000 = ¥100,800,000$

To find the percentage return per yen invested, we must divide by the dollars sold forward and by the spot exchange rate:

$$\frac{¥100,800,000}{\$10,000,000} \times \frac{1}{¥87.18/\$} = 11.56\%$$

In contrast, S. G. Warburg forecasts that the dollar will strengthen to ¥103/$, the price at which it expects to be able to sell dollars for yen. Hence, an S. G. Warburg trader would be willing to take the other side of Citibank's $10,000,000 trade and would contract to buy dollars at the forward rate of ¥85.08/$. This trader's expected yen profit is the price at which the trader expects to be able to sell dollars in the future minus the forward price at which the trader contracts to buy dollars in today's forward market times the size of the dollar trade:

$$(¥103/\$ - ¥85.08/\$) \times \$10,000,000 = ¥179,200,000$$

When we divide by $10,000,000 and the spot rate, we find that this represents a 20.56% expected return.

Of course, both of these forecasts cannot be right. In 6 months, one of the traders will make a profit, and one will suffer a loss. We now know that the actual exchange rate 6 months later, in November 1995, turned out to be ¥100.65/$, as the dollar strengthened by 15.45% over the intervening 6-month period. If Citibank and S. G. Warburg had engaged in the forward transaction, Citibank would have lost:

$$(¥100.65/\$ - ¥85.08/\$) \times \$10,000,000 = ¥155,700,000$$

because in this example Citibank sold $10,000,000 forward at ¥85.08/$, and it would have had to buy dollars in the spot market at ¥100.65/$. Citibank's loss would have been S. G. Warburg's gain. In contrast, S. G. Warburg contracted to buy $10,000,000 at the forward price, and it would then have been able to sell those dollars at the higher spot price.

Panel C of Exhibit 7.2 provides the actual percentage **forecast errors**, which are calculated as the difference between the future spot rate and the forecast divided by the spot rate at the time the forecast was made. So, for example, at the 6-month horizon, Citibank's forecast error is $\dfrac{¥100.65/\$ - ¥75/\$}{¥87.18/\$} = 29.42\%$. It is striking that the forecast errors are quite large, especially for the yen. Clearly, even though Citibank's expected return, given its own forecast, was 11.56%, if it traded at these prices, it would have realized a return of $\dfrac{¥85.08/\$ - ¥100.65/\$}{¥87.18/\$} = -17.86\%$.

Quantifying Expected Losses and Profits

The previous sections have established that it is the uncertainty of future exchange rates that makes currency speculation risky. To quantify our uncertainty about future returns, we can use the concept of a conditional probability distribution from Chapter 3. Recall that we view today as being time t, and remember that the probability distribution of the spot exchange rate for some time in the future, as in Exhibit 3.1, describes the probabilities associated with all the possible exchange rates that may occur at that time. Because the probability distribution of future exchange rates is based on, or is said to be *conditioned on*, all the information that is available today, it is a *conditional probability distribution*.[1] The collection of all information that is used to predict the future value of an economic variable is typically called an **information set**. Also, recall that we refer to the expected value (the mean) of this probability distribution as the *conditional expectation of the future exchange rate*. As before, if we are looking at a 1-year time frame, we denote the conditional expectation at time t of the future spot exchange rate of dollars per pound at time $t+1$ as $E_t[S(t+1, \$/£)]$.

In Chapter 3, we argued that the distribution of exchange rate changes is relatively well described by a normal (that is, a bell-shaped) distribution, at least for exchange rates between the currencies of developed countries. Hence, in addition to the mean of the conditional distribution of the future spot exchange rate, we must also specify its standard deviation. Then we are ready to quantify the probability of losses and gains. Let's illustrate by revisiting Kevin Anthony's example.

Example 7.4 Kevin Anthony's Probability of Loss

Suppose Kevin expects the pound to depreciate relative to the dollar by 3.57% over the next year. Then, the conditional expectation of his future spot rate in 1 year is

$$\$1.60/£ \times (1 - 0.0357) = \$1.5429/£$$

which makes the conditional expectation of his uncertain dollar return equal to

$$£7,000,000 \times \$1.5429/£ = \$10,800,300$$

This return is the same as the return from his dollar investment because $\$1.5429/£$ is the break-even future exchange rate (S^{BE}) that equalizes the returns on dollar and pound investments.

Suppose Kevin thinks that the rate of appreciation of the pound relative to the dollar is normally distributed. From the symmetry of the normal distribution, he knows that there is a 50% probability that he will do better than the dollar investment and there is a 50% probability that he will do worse.

---

[1]At this point, one can think of the conditional probability distribution as reflecting the subjective beliefs of an individual investor—an importer or an exporter—about the uncertain future exchane rate. While in this chapter we mostly discuss the conditional mean of the probability distribution, Chapter 20 introduces foreign currency options whose prices depend on the entire shape of the probability distribution. Consequently, foreign currency option prices can be used to understand what the market thinks about the probabilities of various future exchange rates.

Kevin might also be interested in knowing the probability that he will lose some of his dollar principal. At what future value of the spot exchange rate $S(t + 1, \$/£)$ will Kevin just get his \$10,000,000 principal back? This value—let's call it $\hat{S}$—satisfies

$$(£7,000,000) \times \hat{S} = \$10,000,000$$

from which we find

$$\hat{S} = \frac{\$10,000,000}{£7,000,000} = \$1.4286/£$$

Kevin can calculate the probability that the future exchange rate will be lower than \$1.4286/£. To perform such a calculation, he needs to determine the standard deviation of the payoff on his investment. Suppose he thinks that the standard deviation of the rate of appreciation of the pound relative to the dollar over the next year is 10%. Because 10% of \$1.60/£ is \$0.16/£, the standard deviation of the conditional distribution of the future spot exchange rate is \$0.16/£ (see Chapter 3). He can calculate the probability of losing money by creating a **standard normal random variable**. A standard normal random variable has a mean of 0 and a standard deviation of 1, which we denote with *N(0,1)*, and we can calculate it by subtracting the mean of the future spot rate and dividing by the standard deviation. Thus,

$$\frac{S(t+1,\$/£) - \$1.5429/£}{\$0.16/£}$$

has a mean of 0 and a standard deviation of 1. We graph such a standard normal distribution in Exhibit 7.3. Then, the value of the standard normal variable associated with zero rate of return is

$$\frac{\$1.4286/£ - \$1.5429/£}{\$0.16/£} = -0.7144$$

Exhibit 7.3   Standard Normal Distribution

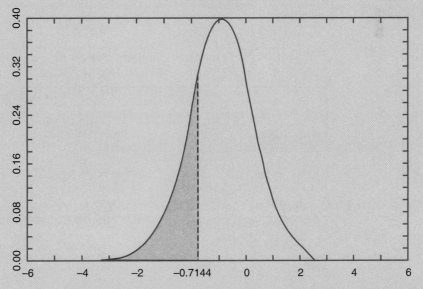

Notes: The horizontal axis represents possible values for a standard normally distributed variable (say, x). The vertical axis represents the value of the normal distribution function (say, y) for each x. In fact $y = \frac{1}{\sqrt{2\pi}} e^{-\frac{1}{2}x^2}$, where e is 2.71828. The area below –0.7144 represents 23.75% of the total area, which sums to 1.

From the probability distribution of a standard normal, we find that there is a 23.75% probability that a $N(0,1)$ variable will be less than –0.7144, or equivalently that $S(t + 1,\$/£)$ will be less than $1.4286/£. In the graph in Exhibit 7.3, the area below the curve to the left of –0.7144 is 23.75% (the total area sums to 1). Hence, 23.75% is the chance that Kevin will actually lose some of his dollar principal over the course of the next year.

Lessons from History: The Variability of Currency Changes and Forward Market Returns

If the variability of dollar/pound exchange rate changes were larger than the 10% Kevin originally anticipated, the conditional distribution for the future exchange rate would be more dispersed, and the probability that he would lose some of his principal would be larger than 23.75%. Is 10% a realistic number for the exchange rate variability?

Exhibit 7.4 shows the standard deviations of percentage changes in exchange rates and forward market returns for three exchange rates versus the U.S. dollar calculated with 30 years of actual data. It also presents the same information for the three corresponding non-dollar cross-rates. The three currencies are the Deutsche mark (the euro did not exist for most of the sample period), the British pound, and the Japanese yen.

Note that the annualized volatilities of percentage changes in the exchange rate are indeed around 10% (somewhere between 8.69% and 11.73%). In other words, Kevin Anthony guessed about right, and the computation in Example 7.4 is realistic.

The second column of Exhibit 7.4 gives an idea about how variable forward market returns are. The returns in this column are measured per domestic currency unit (either per dollar, yen, or pound). For the currency pairs denominated in dollars, the forward market return is

$$\frac{S(t+1) - S(t)}{S(t)} - \frac{F(t) - S(t)}{S(t)} = s(t+1) - fp(t) = \frac{S(t+1) - F(t)}{S(t)}$$

with all exchange rates measured in dollars per foreign currency [see Equation (7.4)]. Here $F(t)$ denotes the 1-month forward rate, $s(t + 1)$ is the percentage exchange rate change, and $fp(t)$ is

Exhibit 7.4 Standard Deviations of Monthly Percentage Changes in Exchange Rates and Forward Market Returns:

	Standard Deviation	
Exchange Rate	**Exchange Rate Change**	**Forward Market Return**
DEM/$	11.06	11.16
£/$	10.61	10.73
¥/$	11.73	11.90
DEM/¥	10.98	11.06
DEM/£	8.69	8.78
¥/£	11.69	11.80

Note: The table uses data from February 1976 to September 2006. The euro replaces the Deutsche mark (DEM) from January 1999 onward. The percentage change in the exchange rate is $s(t+1) = \dfrac{S(t+1) - S(t)}{S(t)} \times 100$, and

the forward market return is $100 \times [s(t+1) - fp(t)]$ with $fp(t) = \dfrac{F(t) - S(t)}{S(t)}$. To annualize the monthly standard deviations, we multiply them by the square root of 12, as is typical in financial markets. The data were obtained from Reuters and Global Insight.

the forward premium. The variability of the forward market returns is of the same order of magnitude as the variability of the exchange rate changes themselves, which are shown in column 1. Clearly, speculating in the foreign exchange market is not without risk of loss.

7.2 UNCOVERED INTEREST RATE PARITY AND THE UNBIASEDNESS HYPOTHESIS

Covered interest rate parity maintains that a domestic money market investment and a foreign money market investment have the same domestic currency return as long as the foreign exchange risk in the foreign money market investment is "covered" using a forward contract. Two related theories predict what may happen when exchange rate risk is, by contrast, not hedged. **Uncovered interest rate parity** maintains that the "uncovered" foreign money market investment, which has an uncertain return because of the uncertainty about the future value of the exchange rate, has the same *expected* return as the domestic money market investment. The **unbiasedness hypothesis** states that there is no systematic difference between the forward rate and the expected future spot rate and that, consequently, the expected forward market return is zero.

In this section, we develop both of these hypotheses in more detail. We start the section with a discussion of market efficiency in the foreign exchange market because any purported violation of uncovered interest rate parity or the unbiasedness hypothesis is often associated with an inefficient foreign exchange market.

Exchange Rate Forecasts and Market Efficiency

Forecast Errors

In the previous section, we showed that percentage changes in exchange rates and forward market returns (the differences between the percentage changes in exchange rates and the forward premiums) are very variable. This large variability suggests that the forecast errors in predicting exchange rates, using either the current exchange rate or the forward rate as the forecast, are very variable.

A forecast error is the difference between the actual future spot exchange rate and its forecast. One way to measure the magnitude of forecast errors is to examine their standard deviation. We cannot just measure the average forecast error because very large errors in either direction would tend to cancel each other out, potentially resulting in a small average error. Because the standard deviation squares the errors, large errors result in a large standard deviation. In other words, Exhibit 7.4 suggests that forecast errors, when using the current spot or forward rate, are large. Forecasts from commercial firms that sell exchange rate forecasts also have large standard deviations, and no one forecasting firm seems to be very successful over time.[2]

Is it reasonable to expect exchange rate forecasts to have these characteristics? We think the answer is yes because exchange rates are the relative prices of currencies, and currencies are assets. Thus, exchange rates are asset prices, and we should expect exchange rates to behave very much like other asset prices, such as stock prices, which are also very difficult to predict. If exchange rates were easy to predict, lots of easy money would be made betting that one currency would strengthen relative to another.

Market Efficiency and Forecasting

The fact that no one consistently and accurately predicts future exchange rates is neither necessary nor sufficient for the foreign exchange market to be considered efficient. Intuitively, a market is efficient when the expected profits from following a trading strategy

---

[2]The inability of advisory services to forecast exchange rates was first documented by Richard Levich (1980). In Chapter 10 we will return to how well or poorly forecasting services do.

merely compensate the investor for risks that are undertaken in exploiting the trading strategy. An inefficient market is one in which profits from trading are not associated with bearing risks and are therefore considered extraordinary.

Of course, we do hear stories that speculators periodically make a fortune in the foreign exchange market. For example, the hedge funds operated by George Soros reportedly made $2 billion in 1992, when Soros bet correctly that the British pound would weaken relative to the Deutsche mark. (Soros subsequently became known as "the man who broke the Bank of England.") What is less widely well known is that some years later, Soros lost over $1 billion because he incorrectly bet that the euro would strengthen relative to the dollar. This and other difficulties eventually led Soros to change his strategy and make more conservative, safer investments.

Uncovered interest rate parity and the unbiasedness hypothesis take a narrow view of market efficiency, however. After all, because currency speculation involves risk taking, isn't it conceivable that there is a positive expected return to be made from speculating in the foreign exchange market—despite what the uncovered interest rate parity and unbiasedness hypotheses say? As long as the expected return is commensurate with the risk taken, earning a return would therefore not be inconsistent with a wider notion of market efficiency. We explore this theory later in the chapter. In the meantime, let's explore uncovered interest rate parity and the unbiasedness hypotheses in more detail.

Uncovered Interest Rate Parity

Recall from Equation (7.1) that the uncovered dollar return to investing 1 dollar in the pound money market is

$$r(t+1) = \frac{1}{S(t)} \times [1 + i(\pounds)] \times S(t+1)$$

Because the current spot rate, $S(t)$, and the interest rate, $i(t, \pounds)$, are in the time t information set, the expected return on the uncovered investment is

$$E_t[r(t+1)] = \frac{1}{S(t)} \times [1 + i(\pounds)] \times E_t[S(t+1)] \qquad (7.6)$$

Uncovered interest rate parity is the hypothesis that the expected return on the uncovered foreign investment equals $[1 + i(t,\$)]$, the known return from investing 1 dollar in the dollar money market. If uncovered interest rate parity is true, there is no compensation to the uncovered investor for the uncertainty associated with the future spot rate, and expected returns on investments in different money markets are equalized. Equivalently, the speculative return on borrowing 1 dollar and investing it in the pound money market, $exr(t+1)$ [see Equation (7.2)], is expected to be zero, given current information.

Let's go back to the portfolio manager Kevin Anthony. The interest rate on the pound is 12%, but the interest rate on the dollar is only 8%. Uncovered interest rate parity suggests that it would be naïve to think that pounds therefore constitute a great investment for Kevin. In fact, the high yield on pounds implies that the market anticipates the pound to depreciate by just enough that the expected dollar return to currency speculation in the pound market is also 8%. In particular,

$$\frac{1}{\$1.60/\pounds} \times [1 + 0.12] \times E_t[S(t+1)] = 1 + 0.08$$

or

$$E_t[S(t+1)] = \frac{1.08}{1.12} \times 1.60 = \$1.5429/\pounds$$

That is, the pound is expected to depreciate by 3.57%:

$$\left(\frac{\$1.5429/\pounds - \$1.60/\pounds}{\$1.60/\pounds}\right) = -0.0357$$

The Unbiasedness Hypothesis

When the forward rate equals the expected future spot rate, the forward rate is said to be an **unbiased predictor** of the future spot rate. This equality is summarized by the unbiasedness hypothesis:

$$F(t, \$/\pounds) = E_t[S(t+1, \$/\pounds)] \qquad (7.7)$$

Covered interest rate parity and uncovered interest rate parity imply the unbiasedness hypothesis, which can be seen as follows (with S and F always referring to $/£ exchange rates):

$$E_t\left[\frac{S(t+1)}{S(t)}\right][1 + i(\pounds)] = [1 + i(\$)] = \frac{F(t)}{S(t)}[1 + i(\pounds)] \qquad (7.8)$$

$$\underbrace{\phantom{E_t\left[\frac{S(t+1)}{S(t)}\right][1 + i(\pounds)]}}_{\substack{\text{Uncovered Interest} \\ \text{Rate Parity}}} \qquad \underbrace{\phantom{[1 + i(\$)] = \frac{F(t)}{S(t)}[1 + i(\pounds)]}}_{\substack{\text{Covered Interest} \\ \text{Rate Parity}}}$$

By eliminating $S(t)$ and $[1+i(\pounds)]$ from both sides of the exterior equations, we recover the unbiasedness hypothesis.

Unbiased Predictors

Whenever you must predict something that is uncertain, such as the future spot rate, there will inevitably be a forecast error. You will make a mistake because you cannot know the new information that will occur during the forecasting interval, in this case, 1 year. An unbiased predictor implies that the expected forecast error is zero. In our setting, we forecast the future spot rate using the forward rate so that the forecast error is the difference between the two: $S(t+1) - F(t)$.

The unbiasedness hypothesis states nothing about the magnitude of the forecast errors, which can be large or small and which can vary over time. Instead, it has two important implications. First, given your current information, you should expect the forecast error to be zero. Second, on average, the forecast errors of an unbiased predictor may sometimes be negative and sometimes positive, but they are not systematically positive or negative, and they will average to zero.[3] If a forecast is biased, however, and you know what the bias is, you can improve your forecast by taking into account the bias. Currency speculators seek to exploit such biases.

The Unbiasedness Hypothesis and Forward Market Returns

The unbiasedness hypothesis in Equation (7.7) is often identified with market efficiency. In efficient capital markets, investors cannot expect to earn profits over and above what the market supplies as compensation for bearing risk. To link the unbiasedness hypothesis more explicitly with market efficiency, we revisit the example of Mr. Buy and Ms. Sell. Mr. Buy bought pounds in the 30-day forward market, and Ms. Sell sold pounds forward. Their profits or losses after 30 days, per pound bought and sold, were as follows:

$$\text{Mr. Buy's profit or loss} = S(t+30, \$/\pounds) - F(t, \$/\pounds)$$
$$= -[F(t, \$/\pounds) - S(t+30, \$/\pounds)] = -[\text{Ms. Sell's profit or loss}]$$

---

[3] The second implication follows from the first because of a famous statistical theorem called the law of iterated expectations.

The next step in the argument relating market efficiency and the unbiasedness hypothesis is to link these realized profits and losses to expectations of profits and losses.

The definition of *market efficiency* incorporates the hypothesis that people process information rationally and have common information on relevant variables that may help predict exchange rates; that is, they have a common information set. Together, these assumptions ensure that people have common expectations of the future. If the forward exchange rate were a biased predictor of the future spot rate, and people had the same expectation of the future spot rate, one side of the forward contract, either Mr. Buy or Ms. Sell, would expect a profit on the contract, and the other party to the forward contract would expect a loss. Hence, the argument goes, because no one would willingly enter into a forward contract if they expected to lose money, forward rates must be unbiased predictors of future spot rates if the market is efficient. That is, they must both expect zero profits:

$$E_t[S(t+30,\$/£)] - F(t,\$/£) = 0 = E_t[F(t,\$/£) - S(t+30,\$/£)] \qquad \textbf{(7.9)}$$

The Siegel Paradox (Advanced)

Suppose we consider Blake Bevins, Kevin Anthony's British counterpart, who is investing in the dollar money market. Let $\bar{S}(£/\$)$ and $\bar{F}(£/\$)$ denote the pound/dollar spot and forward exchange rates, so at each point of time $\bar{S}(£/\$) = \dfrac{1}{S(\$/£)}$. Now, apply Equation (7.7) from the British perspective:

$$\bar{F}(t) = E_t[\bar{S}(t+1)]$$

But, of course, $\bar{F}(£/\$) = \dfrac{1}{F(\$/£)}$, so that

$$E_t[\bar{S}(t+1,£/\$)] = \frac{1}{F(t,\$/£)} = \frac{1}{E_t[S(t+1,\$/£)]}$$

So, for the unbiasedness hypothesis to hold from both the British and American perspectives, it must be the case that

$$E_t[\bar{S}(t+1,£/\$)] = E_t\left[\frac{1}{S(t+1,\$/£)}\right] = \frac{1}{E_t[S(t+1,\$/£)]}$$

However, we know the latter equality is false because of a statistical property known as Jensen's inequality.[4]

Rather than get mired in statistical jargon, let's work out a simple numeric example. Suppose Kevin Anthony and Blake Bevins agree on the following possible scenarios for the future exchange rate:

	$S(t+1,\$/£)$	$\bar{S}(t+1,£/\$) = \dfrac{1}{S(t+1,\$/£)}$	Probability
Scenario 1	1.50	0.6667	0.714
Scenario 2	1.65	0.6061	0.286

---

[4]In fact, because $f(x) = \dfrac{1}{x}$ is a convex function, Jensen's inequality implies $E_t\left[\dfrac{1}{S(t+1)}\right] > \dfrac{1}{E_t[S(t+1)]}$

From Kevin's perspective, the expected future \$/£ exchange rate is

$$E_t[S(t+1,\$/£)] = 0.714 \times \$1.50/£ + 0.286 \times \$1.65/£ = \$1.5429/£$$

This is the forward rate derived earlier. According to Blake, the expected exchange rate in £/\$ terms is

$$E_t[S(t+1,£/\$)] = 0.714 \times £0.6667/\$ + 0.286 \times £0.6061/\$ = £0.6493/\$$$

Is this consistent with the \$1.5429/£ rate? The answer is no because

$$0.6493 \neq \frac{1}{1.5429} = 0.6481$$

We see that when the unbiasedness hypothesis is considered from the two different currency perspectives, it leads to an inconsistency. We cannot have two different forward rates in the market! This little conundrum is known as the Siegel paradox because Jeremy Siegel (1972) was the first to point out this inconsistency.

Whereas some have argued that the Siegel paradox invalidates the unbiasedness hypothesis as a reasonable theory, note that the difference between 0.6481 and 0.6493 is small: In percentage terms, it represents less than a 0.2% difference. Hence, we will ignore the Siegel paradox for the remainder of this book. Moreover, it is possible to formulate versions of the unbiasedness hypothesis either using logarithmic exchange rates or using real values that resolve the Siegel paradox (see Charles Engel, 1996).

7.3 RISK PREMIUMS IN THE FOREIGN EXCHANGE MARKET

Can forward rates be biased predictors of future spot rates? Put differently, can there be an expected forward market return, as we discussed earlier in the chapter? And if so, can the foreign exchange market still be considered an efficient market?

You might be surprised by the fact that there are many people like Mr. Buy and Ms. Sell who are quite willing to enter contracts, expecting a loss. Suppose you want to buy fire insurance for 1 year on your \$250,000 home. The insurance company charges you today and promises to pay you in the future if you suffer a certain type of loss—in this case, loss due to fire. Suppose everyone agrees that the probability of fire destroying your home is 0.01%. What insurance premium would you be willing to pay? If you are risk neutral, you would just be willing to pay the expected loss:

$$\$250,000 \times \frac{1}{10} \times 0.01 = \$250$$

However, if you confronted many people with this question, they would be willing to pay more than \$250 because they are risk averse. To avoid this devastating loss, they would gladly pay more than \$250. If they do, they willingly enter a contract with an expected loss because the expected value of the insurance (given the probability of a fire) is only \$250.

Similarly, going back to our example, either Mr. Buy or Ms. Sell may be paying the other person a **risk premium** in order to avoid further harm from large exchange rate movements. For example, Ms. Sell may be selling pounds forward because she is the treasurer of a large MNC that is expecting pound revenues 30 days from now. Remember that the forward rate is \$1.5429/£. Even if Ms. Sell expects the future spot rate to be higher than \$1.5429/£, she might still choose to hedge because there is a lot of uncertainty about the future value of the pound.

It is tempting to conclude that the potential for a risk premium on currency speculation must be linked to the variability of exchange rate changes. After all, the conditional distribution of the future exchange rate will be wider the more variable such changes are. However, this intuition is incorrect, as we now discuss.

What Determines Risk Premiums?

The risk premium on an asset is the expected return on the asset in excess of the return on a risk-free asset. Different assets can have different risks, and assets that are riskier must offer higher expected returns in order to induce investors to hold them. You may think that the riskiness of an investment in an asset is determined by the standard deviation or variance of the uncertainty associated with the payoff on the asset. However, this is not the case. The reason is that investors care about the expected return and risk of their whole portfolio of assets, not necessarily about the risk of an individual asset viewed in isolation.

Modern portfolio theory postulates that risk-averse investors like high expected returns on their portfolios, but they dislike a high variance in their portfolios. (That is, they don't like the value of their portfolios to go up and down very much.[5]) The question then becomes how an individual asset's return contributes to the variance of the kinds of portfolios investors are likely to hold. It turns out that part of the variance of an asset's return does not contribute to the portfolio's variance. This leads to an important decomposition of the uncertainty of the return on any asset.

Systematic and Unsystematic Risk

The uncertainty of a return can always be decomposed into a part that is *systematic* and a part that is *unsystematic*, which is also called *idiosyncratic*. That is,

Individual asset return uncertainty = Systematic risk + Idiosyncratic uncertainty

Systematic risk is the risk associated with an asset's return arising from the covariance of the return with the return on a large, well-diversified portfolio. The **covariance** of two random variables describes how the two variables move together, or *covary*, with each other. Often, we describe how things covary with each other in terms of correlation coefficients that are bounded between -1 and $+1$. If the returns on two assets are perfectly correlated (that is, they perfectly move in the same direction), their correlation coefficient is 1. By contrast, if the assets are not at all correlated (neither moves at all in relation to the other), their correlation coefficient is 0. If the coefficient is -1, the two asset returns always move in opposite directions. The correlation coefficient is the covariance of the two variables divided by the product of their standard deviations.

The large, well-diversified portfolio that investors should hold according to finance theory is called the **market portfolio**.[6] The market portfolio is a "representative" portfolio that reflects the financial assets in the market as a whole. It is the value-weighted collection of all available assets.

How does this decomposition relate to risk premiums? If the return on the asset contains only idiosyncratic uncertainty, there will be no increase in the expected return on the asset due to the uncertainty of the return. It will not command a risk premium! The asset will be priced to yield an expected return equal to the return on risk-free assets. An asset has only idiosyncratic uncertainty if its return does not covary with the returns on other assets.

These statements follow from a fundamental insight of portfolio theory: Idiosyncratic uncertainty can be diversified away. Even though investors do not like the uncertainty of their total portfolio and demand risk premiums on assets that contribute to the variance of the portfolio, assets whose returns contain only idiosyncratic uncertainty do not contribute to the variance of the portfolio and, consequently, do not command any risk premium. Because idiosyncratic uncertainty is diversifiable in large portfolios, it is also called *diversifiable uncertainty*, or *diversifiable risk*. Because systematic risk measures how much an asset's return co-moves with the market, it cannot be diversified away, and the risk involved commands a risk

---

[5]We have previously discussed the variance of a random variable and indicated that it is a measure of the dispersion of the probability distribution. This is a concept that is easy to demonstrate graphically because it is associated with the width of a bell-shaped curve. (See, for example, Exhibit 7.3.)

[6]Appendix 7.1 provides a review of portfolio theory and related statistical concepts, such as covariance, correlations, and betas, to allow you to examine the arguments implying that covariances among returns are the main sources of portfolio variance.

premium. For example, the variance of an individual stock return is partly driven by macroeconomic events such as the business cycle and interest rates that affect every stock. Such risks are systematic. The variance of the stock return is also partially driven by **idiosyncratic risks** that affect only that particular stock, such as the quality of the firm's management.

The CAPM

The theories we have been discussing are the foundation of the **capital asset pricing model (CAPM)**. William F. Sharpe was awarded the Nobel Prize in Economics in 1990 for its development. The CAPM holds that it is the covariance of an asset's return with the return on the market portfolio that determines the asset's systematic risk and hence its risk premium. The model also provides an easy-to-implement procedure to put an actual number on the premium, which we describe in detail in Chapter 13.

According to the CAPM, the systematic risk of an individual asset is fully described by its **beta** with respect to the market portfolio. The formula for the beta is simple:

$$\text{Beta on asset } i = \frac{\text{Covariance (Asset return } i, \text{ Market portfolio return)}}{\text{Variance (Market portfolio return)}}$$

Higher betas indicate higher systematic risk, and the CAPM postulates that

$$\text{Risk premium on asset } i = (\text{Beta on asset } i) \times (\text{Risk premium on market portfolio})$$

What is the intuition for the prediction about expected returns of the CAPM? Think of the return on the risk-free asset as the compensation provided to an investor for the time value of money that is required or demanded by the investor because the investor sacrifices the use of the money for a certain period. The investor requires compensation in excess of the risk-free rate (that is, a risk premium) if the beta of the asset is positive, as are the betas of most equity investments. Assets with positive betas contribute to the variance of the market portfolio, and the larger the beta, the more risky the asset and the higher its expected return must be. Notice that if an asset has a negative beta because the return on the asset is negatively correlated with the return on the market portfolio, the expected return on the asset is less than the risk-free rate. Investing in an asset that covaries negatively with the return on the market portfolio provides an investor with some portfolio insurance. When the rest of the investor's portfolio is doing poorly, the asset with the negative covariance generally pays high returns, and when the rest of the investor's portfolio pays high returns, the asset with the negative covariance generally pays relatively low returns. Investing in this asset thus dampens the volatility of the return on the total portfolio. Risk-averse investors are willing to "pay" for this reduction in the volatility of their overall portfolio by accepting an expected return that is less than the risk-free interest rate.

Applying the CAPM to Forward Market Returns

Because a forward contract is an asset, there is potential for a risk premium. How will this potentially bias the forward rate as a predictor of the future spot rate? Taking a position in a forward contract involves no investment of funds at the point in time when the contract is set, and there is no necessity for compensation to an investor for the time value of money. But the dollar profits and losses on the forward contract can still covary systematically with the dollar return on the market portfolio. Hence, if the profitability of Mr. Buy's purchase of foreign currency at the forward exchange rate covaries positively with the dollar return on the market portfolio, Mr. Buy will view the forward contract as risky and will demand an expected profit. As noted previously, though, Ms. Sell's profits and losses on the forward contract are the opposite of Mr. Buy's profits and losses. Hence, if Mr. Buy's dollar profit is positively correlated with the dollar return on the market portfolio, the covariance of the dollar profit on Ms. Sell's side of the forward contract is negatively correlated with the dollar return on the market portfolio. In this case, when Ms. Sell enters into the contract, she obtains an asset that reduces the variability of her overall portfolio. She consequently willingly holds this contract at an expected loss. Again, this is like portfolio insurance. From Ms. Sell's perspective, she pays up front by entering into a contract in which she expects to lose money. But she is compensated with profit on the forward contract when the rest of her portfolio does poorly. Consequently, there can be a risk premium that causes the forward rate to be a biased predictor of the future spot rate. According to the CAPM, such a risk premium should depend on the beta of the (excess) return to currency speculation.

Formal Derivation of CAPM Risk Premiums (Advanced)

The CAPM in Symbols

Let the dollar return for a 1-year holding period for an arbitrary asset j be $R_j(t+1)$, and let the risk-free return be $[1 + i(t,\$)]$. The CAPM predicts that the risk premium on an asset is equal to the beta of the asset multiplied by the amount by which the expected return on the market portfolio, $R_M(t+1)$, exceeds the return on the risk-free asset:

$$E_t\{R_j(t+1) - [1 + i(t,\$)]\} = \beta_j E_t\{R_M(t+1) - [1 + i(t,\$)]\} \qquad (7.10)$$

The beta of the jth asset is the covariance of the return on asset j with the return on the market portfolio, σ_{jM}, divided by the variance of the return on the market portfolio, σ_{MM}:

$$\beta_j = \frac{\sigma_{jM}}{\sigma_{MM.}}$$

Here, the variance (covariance) is a conditional variance (covariance) because it is based on the information at time t.

The CAPM and Forward Market Returns

Let's derive the implications of the CAPM for the risk premium on an unhedged investment of dollars in the British pound money market. The excess return on such an investment was defined in Equation (7.2), and we review it here for convenience:

$$\text{exr}(t+1) = \frac{S(t+1,\$/\pounds)[1+i(t,\pounds)]}{S(t,\$/\pounds)} - [1 + i(t,\$)] = R_\pounds(t+1) - [1 + i(t,\$)]$$

From Equation (7.9), the CAPM gives the expected excess return on this uncertain dollar investment:

$$E_t[\text{exr}(t+1)] = \beta_u E_t\{R_M(t+1) - [1 + i(t,\$)]\} \qquad (7.11)$$

The beta on the uncovered pound investment is

$$\beta_u = \frac{\text{COV}_t[R_\pounds(t+1), R_M(t+1)]}{\text{VAR}_t[R_M(t+1)]} \qquad (7.12)$$

where COV_t and VAR_t are shorthand for conditional covariance and variance, respectively, and the interest rates do not enter the expression because they are in the time t information set.

In Section 7.1, we derived the relationship between this excess money market return $[\text{exr}(t+1)]$ and the forward market return $[\text{fmr}(t+1)]$. In particular,

$$\text{fmr}(t+1) = \frac{\text{exr}(t+1)}{1 + i(t,\pounds)} \qquad (7.13)$$

The forward market return therefore also satisfies a CAPM relationship:

$$E_t[\text{fmr}(t+1)] = \beta_F E_t\{R_M(t+1) - [1 + i(t,\$)]\} \qquad (7.14)$$

Here, β_F is the beta on the forward contract to buy foreign currency in the forward market and sell it subsequently in the future spot market. Now, we can use the relationship between the forward market return and the excess return from investing in the pound money market in (7.13) and Equation (7.11) to derive

$$E_t[\text{fmr}(t+1)] = \beta_u \frac{E_t\{R_M(t+1) - [1 + i(t,\$)]\}}{1 + i(t,£)} \tag{7.15}$$

Hence, $\beta_F = \dfrac{\beta_u}{1 + i(t,£)}$. In other words, the expected returns on forward market contracts and money market investments are proportional because they have the same fundamental risk exposure but invest a different number of units.

Equations (7.14) and (7.15) indicate that forward rates will be biased predictors of future spot rates if there is systematic risk associated with the profits on a forward contract. In the case of the dollar/pound example, if the dollar weakens relative to the pound when the dollar payoff on the market portfolio is high, the risk premium would be positive, and the forward rate would be below the expected future spot rate. You would expect to profit by buying pounds forward, and you would expect to suffer a loss by selling pounds forward. If, on the other hand, the dollar strengthens relative to the pound when the dollar return on the market portfolio is high, the beta on the forward contract would be negative. Thus, the forward rate would be above the expected future spot rate, and there would be an expected loss from buying pounds forward and an expected gain from selling pounds forward.

7.4 UNCOVERED INTEREST RATE PARITY AND THE UNBIASEDNESS HYPOTHESIS IN PRACTICE

We have devoted considerable space to the development of uncovered interest rate parity and the unbiasedness hypothesis for good reason. Taking a stand on whether the theories actually hold is important when international financial managers are making their decisions. This section reviews situations in which this issue arises.

International Portfolio Management

When a U.S.-based portfolio manager buys Japanese equities, he hopes the Japanese equity market will perform well, but he is also exposed to foreign exchange risk in the yen–dollar market. As we will discuss in detail in Chapter 13, the return on a foreign bond and/or equity can be decomposed into two components: the (local) return on the foreign asset and the currency return. Global money managers may decide to speculate on a currency, or they may decide to hedge the currency risk. This decision will be greatly affected by whether they believe in the validity of uncovered interest rate parity and the unbiasedness hypothesis.

Exchange Rate Forecasting

Forecasting exchange rates is difficult, but it remains an activity that attracts many resources and much brainpower in the real world. If the unbiasedness hypothesis holds, the best forecast of the future exchange rate can be read from a table in your daily *Financial Times* or the *Wall Street Journal* because the answer lies in the forward rate. Chapter 10 examines the success of different forecasting models relative to the forward rate.

Exchange Rate Determination

Chapter 10 discusses some popular exchange rate determination theories. It turns out that many of the well-known theories linking exchange rate values to fundamentals such as trade balances, money supplies, and so forth, assume that uncovered interest rate parity holds. But if it does not hold, the validity of these theories is immediately in doubt. On the other hand, the empirical evidence that we present in Section 7.5 has motivated some macroeconomists to supplement macro-models with time-varying foreign exchange risk premiums.

The Cost of Hedging

Multinational corporations often hedge their transaction foreign exchange risk using forward contracts. Clearly they may be willing to pay a premium to insure against this risk. The following *Point–Counterpoint* makes a link between the unbiasedness hypothesis and a practical hedging situation. In a nutshell, when unbiasedness holds, multinationals effectively do not pay premiums to hedge their foreign exchange risk related to transactions. Of course, as we argued in Section 7.3, the existence of a premium is not necessarily inconsistent with market efficiency and may be fair compensation for risk insurance. Note also that a MNC may benefit from such premiums. For example, if the long position in a particular currency commands a premium, a MNC that hedges a short position will earn the risk premium.

POINT–COUNTERPOINT

The Cost of Hedging[7]

Not surprisingly, Ante's and Freedy's Uncle Fred is holding forth during dinner at the annual Handel family gathering at his estate in Chappaqua, New York. Uncle Fred is in the export–import business, is very well traveled, and loves recounting his on-the-road war stories. After a hilarious account of how a Dutch business associate recommended checking out the Walletjes (the red light district) in Amsterdam as the high point of Dutch architecture, he suddenly turns to Ante and Freedy: "Hey, how's that international finance class going? I hope well, because I've got a question for you from my business. Suppose I owe 10 million Swedish kronor, payable in 1 month. The company has the cash to buy kronor now, or it could wait until later. I figure we should put the money wherever in the world it would earn the highest interest rate, but my treasurer, one of those MBA hotshots, tells me that high interest rates are irrelevant because if the krona interest rate is higher than the dollar interest rate, the krona is expected to fall in value relative to the dollar. When I ask her what I should do, she says that it doesn't matter. 'Flip a coin,' she says. Is this why I'm paying her such a high salary? Anyway, young fellows, what do you think?"

As usual, Ante is quickest to respond: "You're absolutely right, Uncle Fred, you should fire that MBA. I am convinced that your business will do better if you put your cash balances in the currency that has the highest interest rate. That way, you will earn higher returns, which will lower the effective dollar cost of your foreign payables."

Freedy shakes his head. "Have you been sleeping in class, Ante? Remember the theory of uncovered interest rate parity? The MBA is right. On average, dollar returns will be equalized in different countries. If Uncle Fred puts his money in kronor when the interest rate is high, the krona will likely depreciate, wiping out the interest rate gain. Maybe he could make it easier on himself and just buy the kronor in the forward market."

"Hmm, this is a useful argument. Let's have our Amaretto in the living room. Maybe that will bring your thoughts together," sighs Uncle Fred. As they walk toward the comfortable, Italian-designed sofas, Suttle Trooth joins them from the kitchen.

---

[7]This *Point–Counterpoint* is motivated by the discussion in Kenneth Froot and Richard Thaler (1990).

"Hey guys, I overheard your conversation, and are you ever confused," says Suttle. "Let me explain to Uncle Fred what is going on. I brought some paper and a pencil because I want to write down a few things."

"Consider what Uncle Fred is saying," continues Suttle. "Suppose he keeps his money in dollars. Then, Uncle Fred incurs currency risk because he will have to convert the dollars into kronor 1 month from now at the exchange rate of $S(t+1,\$/\text{SEK})$. The dollar cost in 1 month of the krona payable will be

$$\text{SEK10 million} \times S(t+1,\$/\text{SEK})$$

If he converts his dollars now, he will not face any currency risk because he will know exactly how many kronor to convert so that they grow to SEK10 million in 1 month. That amount will be the present value of the SEK10 million, or

$$\text{SEK10 million} \times \frac{1}{1 + i(\text{SEK})}$$

The current cost in dollars of this amount of kronor is

$$\text{SEK10 million} \times \frac{1}{1 + i(\text{SEK})} \times S(t,\$/\text{SEK})$$

Because the first cost is dollars in 1 month and the second cost is dollars today, to compare the alternative strategies, we have to take both costs to the same point in time. Let's take the future value in dollars of the second strategy:

$$\text{SEK10 million} \times \frac{1}{1 + i(\text{SEK})} \times S(t,\$/\text{SEK}) \times [1 + i(\$)]$$

is what we obtain."

At this point, Freedy interjects, "Hey, those terms involving interest rates and the spot rate are equal to the forward rate, right?"

"Very good, Freedy, you've got it," replies Suttle. "The strategy of converting into kronor now is equivalent to a strategy of buying kronor in the forward market. Therefore, we can compare the performance of Uncle Fred's possible strategies by comparing the future exchange rate with the forward rate. Suppose dollar interest rates are higher than krona interest rates, in which case the krona trades at a forward premium. Then, Uncle Fred's proposal would have him not hedge, and he would keep his money in dollars. That strategy works great *if* the future USD/SEK exchange rate turns out to be lower than the forward rate. If it does, Uncle Fred's *ex post* costs will be relatively low."

"Very interesting, but all these equations do not appear to answer my question, now do they?" grumbled Uncle Fred.

"Hold on. I am not done yet," says Suttle. "Let's think about what you'd lose by hedging. We can call this the *cost of hedging*, if you wish. *Ex post*, the cost of having hedged can be either positive or negative because it will equal

$$F(t,\$/\text{SEK}) - S(t+1,\$/\text{SEK})$$

If the forward rate is higher than the future spot rate, you would indeed have been better off not to hedge and to have just taken the currency risk. Of course, you cannot necessarily know when this will occur, and there will certainly be instances in which the future spot rate ends up higher than the forward rate (when the SEK appreciates more than the forward rate indicates), in which case your *ex post* cost of hedging will be negative because you have higher costs by having not hedged. Now, what the MBA is trying to tell you is that the expected value of the cost of hedging is zero in an efficient market with no risk premium:

$$E[F(t,\$/\text{SEK}) - S(t+1,\$/\text{SEK})] = 0$$

This relationship is also known as the unbiasedness hypothesis. Equivalently, whether interest rates are higher or lower abroad does not matter because currency changes, on average, correct for this. If the unbiasedness hypothesis is correct, it won't matter whether you hedge or do not hedge your exposure. Also, Uncle Fred, your strategy won't make money on average because sometimes you will hedge and sometimes you will not, but the expected difference between the two is zero. So the expectation of the difference in the cost of the two strategies can be viewed as the expected cost of hedging, and it is zero—if unbiasedness holds."

Ante excitedly interjects, "But who says the market is efficient? These equations are derived by some ivory tower academics. Why should we expect them to characterize actual markets where real people have to trade?"

"Well, there is something to that point, I must admit," answers Suttle. "Some econometric tests have rejected the unbiasedness hypothesis, and the estimates actually indicate that Uncle Fred's high-yield strategy may work. But that need not mean the market is inefficient. If Uncle Fred does not hedge, he is exposed to currency risk. In other asset markets, such as equities, investors are compensated for taking on risk by receiving a higher expected return than the risk-free rate. We call this higher expected return a *risk premium*. There are probably risk premiums in the currency markets, too. If indeed there is a risk premium, there is an expected cost or an expected return to hedging. Suppose that a relatively high interest rate is providing compensation for both expected currency depreciation but also for risk. Uncle Fred's unhedged strategy is then associated with currency exposure when such exposure is very risky. To make this more concrete, suppose the dollar interest rate is higher than the krona interest rate. Uncle Fred won't hedge because he thinks $E[F(t) - S(t+1)] > 0$. There is a positive cost to hedging. But is that wise? Uncle Fred is not in the foreign exchange investment business, exchange rates are quite volatile, and not hedging may really hurt the bottom line, if the currency moves against him. When you hedge, you buy security! Don't you agree, Uncle?" asks Suttle, turning to see Uncle Fred comfortably snoring on the Italian sofa.

7.5 EMPIRICAL EVIDENCE ON THE UNBIASEDNESS HYPOTHESIS

Because we have data on exchange rates and forward rates, it should be possible to determine whether forward rates have indeed historically been unbiased predictors of future spot rates. In this section, we derive statistical tests of the unbiasedness hypothesis and apply them to actual exchange rate data. The discussion uses simple statistics reviewed in Chapter 3 and **regression analysis**. (Appendix 7.2 provides a primer on regression tests.)

The Quest for a Test

Although some early studies of the unbiasedness hypothesis were conducted directly using the variables in Equation (7.7), econometricians pointed out that these tests were statistically inappropriate.[8] A proper test transforms Equation (7.7) by dividing by $S(t,\$/\pounds)$ on both sides and by subtracting 1—with 1 written as $S(t,\$/\pounds)/S(t,\$/\pounds)$—from both sides of the equation. This is possible because the spot exchange rate at time t, $(S(t,\$/\pounds))$, is in the

---

[8]Because spot rates and forward rates move together over time in a very persistent fashion, econometricians showed that a test in levels of the variables would always fail to reject the unbiasedness hypothesis, even when the hypothesis was false. See Charles Engel (1996).

investors' information set. We obtain a new hypothesis—that the forward premium equals the expected rate of appreciation:

$$\frac{F(t,\$/£) - S(t,\$/£)}{S(t,\$/£)} = \frac{E_t[S(t+30,\$/£) - S(t,\$/£)]}{S(t,\$/£)} \tag{7.16}$$

In Equation (7.16), we use a 30-day (1-month) forward contract, as in the empirical test reported in the next section.

Using the notation for forward premiums and rates of appreciation in Equation (7.16), we get

$$fp(t,\$/£) = E_t[s(t+30,\$/£)] \tag{7.17}$$

The left-hand side of Equation (7.17) is the 30-day forward premium or discount on the pound. The right-hand side of Equation (7.17) is the expected rate of appreciation or depreciation of the pound relative to the dollar. It describes the percentage rate at which investors think the spot price will change over the course of the next 30 days. Equation (7.17) states that the unbiasedness hypothesis requires the forward premium or discount on the pound to be equal to the market participants' expectations about the rate of appreciation or depreciation of the pound relative to the dollar over the course of the next 30 days. If the hypothesis holds, the expected return to currency speculation will be exactly zero.

Incorporating Rational Expectations into the Test

Testing the unbiasedness hypothesis is not easy for several reasons (see Geert Bekaert, Mian Wei, and Yuhang Xing, 2007; Menzie Chinn, 2006; Charles Engel, 1996; and Robert Hodrick, 1987). The most difficult problem is that it contains a variable that cannot be observed by a statistician: the conditional expectation of the rate of appreciation of the pound relative to the dollar. This conditional expectation is formed by market participants on the basis of their information set. Hence, in order to test the unbiasedness hypothesis, a statistician must specify how investors and speculators form their expectations. Typically, when statisticians are confronted with an unobservable variable, they make an auxiliary assumption in order to develop a test of the underlying hypothesis.

As in most other areas of financial economics, the most popular auxiliary assumption is that investors have **rational expectations**. If investors have rational expectations, they do not make systematic mistakes, and their forecasts are not systematically biased. When investors have rational expectations, we can decompose the realized (observed) rate of appreciation into its conditional expectation plus an error term that does not depend upon time t information:

$$s(t+30,\$/£) = E_t[s(t+30,\$/£)] + \epsilon(t+30) \tag{7.18}$$

Realized appreciation = Expected appreciation + Forecast error

The error term can be viewed as news that moved the exchange rate, but the news, by definition, was unanticipated by rational market participants at time t.

Rational expectations imply that both the conditional mean, $E_t[\epsilon(t+30)]$, and unconditional mean, $E[\epsilon(t+30)]$, of the error term, $\epsilon(t+30)$, in Equation (7.18), are zero. Because it reflects unanticipated news, $\epsilon(t+30)$ should not be correlated with anything in the information set. Substituting the unbiasedness hypothesis of Equation (7.17) into Equation (7.18), we obtain

$$s(t+30,\$/£) = fp(t,\$/£) + \epsilon(t+30) \tag{7.19}$$

In Equation (7.19), one observable variable, the realized rate of appreciation, equals another observable variable, the forward premium, plus an unobservable error term whose unconditional mean is zero. It turns out that this equation can be used for two tests of the unbiasedness hypothesis, which we discuss next.

A Test Using the Sample Means

Data on Rates of Appreciation and Forward Premiums

Because the average or mean forecast error in Equation (7.19) should be zero, we can easily test the weakest implication of the unbiasedness hypothesis: The unconditional mean of the realized rate of appreciation should equal the unconditional mean of the forward premium.[9] The equality of these means or averages constitutes the **null hypothesis** (the hypothesis that is assumed to be true and is tested using data and a test statistic). Intuitively, to test the hypothesis, we compare the two sample means and check whether the difference between them is small or large in a statistical sense. The equality of the mean rate of appreciation and the mean forward premium is examined in Exhibit 7.5 which reports the results for three foreign currencies versus the dollar and for the three corresponding cross-rates, as in Exhibit 7.4.

Once again, the three currencies are the Deutsche mark, the British pound, and the Japanese yen, and the data are expressed in annualized percentage terms. Consequently, the value of −2.39 for the mean rate of change of the yen relative to the dollar indicates that during the sample period the yen strengthened relative to the dollar at an average annual rate of 2.39%.

The sample means of the realized rates of appreciation range from −2.65% for the yen value of the pound to 1.98% for the DEM value of the yen. We can conclude that the mean of a time series is significantly different from zero at the 95% confidence level if the sample mean is more than 1.96 standard errors from zero. Said differently, we are then 95% sure that the true mean is not zero. The standard error of the sample mean depends on the volatility of the time series and the number of observations.[10] In all cases the volatilities of the rates of appreciation are large. The large volatility of the realized rate of appreciation inflates the standard errors associated with the mean rate of appreciation making it difficult to precisely estimate the mean. Thus, not a single mean rate of depreciation is sufficiently large relative to its standard error that we can be more than 90% confident that it is significantly different from zero.

The sample means of the forward premiums range from −5.60% for the yen value of the pound to 2.24% for the pound value of the dollar. Because the volatilities of the forward premiums are much smaller than those of the rates of appreciation, all the sample means of the forward premiums are large relative to their respective standard errors. Hence, we can be quite confident that all the unconditional means of the forward premiums are not zero. For example, the pound appears robustly at a forward discount relative to all other currencies.

The Test

The third column of Exhibit 7.5 tests the hypotheses that the means of the 1-month forward premiums are equal to the means of the 1-month rates of appreciation on a currency-by-currency basis. The third column is labeled "Difference" to indicate that it represents the (*ex post*) rate of appreciation minus the (*ex ante*) forward premium. If the null hypothesis is true, the mean of the difference should be zero. In no case is there sufficient evidence to reject the null hypothesis with 90% confidence. The largest confidence level is only 0.81 for the DEM

---

[9]The sample mean of time series $\{x_t\}$ using T observations is $\frac{1}{T}\sum_{t=1}^{T}x_t$.

[10]The usual standard error of the sample mean for a time series is $\sigma/\sqrt{T}$, where $\sigma^2 = \sum_{t=1}^{T}(x_t - \hat{\mu})^2/T$ denotes the sample variance of the series, and $\hat{\mu}$ denotes the sample mean of the series. For this to be the correct standard error, the time series must be serially uncorrelated, that is, the observation at time t must not be correlated with the observation at time $t + 1$. The standard errors reported here are slightly different because they are calculated using the methods of Lars Hansen (1982) and accommodate both serial correlation and conditional heteroskedasticity (see Chapter 3).

Exhibit 7.5 Means of Monthly Rates of Appreciation, Forward Premiums, and the Differences Between the Two

	Mean		
Exchange Rate	Rate of Appreciation (S.E.) Conf.	Forward Premium (S.E.) Conf.	Difference (S.E.) Conf.
DEM/$	−1.09 (2.07) 0.40	−1.57 (0.27) 1.00	0.48 (2.12) 0.18
£/$	0.82 (1.99) 0.32	2.24 (0.24) 1.00	−1.42 (2.05) 0.51
¥/$	−2.39 (2.20) 0.72	−3.37 (0.25) 1.00	0.98 (2.29) 0.33
DEM/¥	1.98 (2.07) 0.66	1.81 (0.20) 1.00	0.17 (2.11) 0.06
DEM/£	−1.58 (1.67) 0.66	−3.80 (0.26) 1.00	2.22 (1.70) 0.81
¥/£	−2.65 (2.22) 0.77	−5.60 (0.17) 1.00	2.95 (2.27) 0.81

Notes: The table uses data from February 1976 to September 2006. The euro replaces the Deutsche mark (DEM) from 1999 onward. The monthly data are expressed as annualized percentage rates. S.E. stands for standard error and Conf. for confidence level. The standard error (reported in parentheses) measures the uncertainty we have about the accuracy of our estimate of the sample average. If we had an infinite amount of data, the standard error would be zero. As a technical note, the standard errors allow for conditional heteroskedasticity and two lagged autocorrelations in the errors. The confidence level of the test that the mean is zero is below the standard error. A confidence level of 0.9 indicates that we can be 90% sure that the null hypothesis of a zero mean is false.

and yen values of the pound. Of course, here again, the volatilities of the realized rates of appreciation make it difficult to precisely estimate the differences of the means.

Because of triangular arbitrage, only three of the six statistical tests we conducted provide independent information. If we test the difference between the mean rate of appreciation of the dollar relative to the yen and relative to the Deutsche mark, we have implicitly done the test statistic for the yen relative to the Deutsche mark. We can conduct a joint test that the means of the three forward premiums of the foreign currencies relative to the dollar are each equal to their respective mean rates of appreciation of the dollar. This joint test is a chi-square statistic with 3 degrees of freedom (see Appendix 7.2). Its value is 1.28, which corresponds to a confidence level of 0.27. We are only 27% confident that the null hypothesis is rejected by the data. Hence, there is essentially no evidence to suggest that the unconditional means of the forward premiums differ from the unconditional means of the rates of appreciation. Because the difference between $s(t + 1)$ and $fp(t)$ is the forward market return, this also means that, on average, forward market returns are zero.

Implications: High-Interest-Rate Currencies Depreciate

The zero unconditional means of the differences between the rates of appreciation and the forward premiums are also consistent with an important fact of international finance: Countries with high nominal interest rates have currencies that tend to depreciate in value over time relative to the currencies of countries with low nominal interest rates. From our discussion of interest rate parity in Chapter 6, you know that the forward premium on a foreign currency is equal to the interest differential between the domestic currency and the foreign currency. Hence, failure to reject the unbiasedness hypothesis with the test of unconditional means supports the proposed fact quite strongly. For example, the average forward discount on the Deutsche mark in terms of the yen is approximately 2%, which implies that DEM (now euro) interest rates were on average 2% higher than JPY interest rates. Exhibit 7.5 demonstrates that these higher DEM interest rates were providing compensation for the average depreciation of the Deutsche mark relative to the yen, which was approximately 2% as well. In other words,

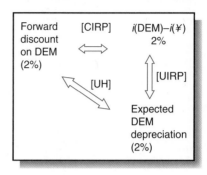

In assessing the validity of the unbiasedness hypothesis, it is important to remember that this first test is a very weak implication because it considers only the overall average performance of the theory. We can also derive tests that examine the implications of the theory at different points in time. Such an approach is important because it corresponds to what someone would do in an active international portfolio management situation.

Regression Tests of the Unbiasedness of Forward Rates

The Test

A straightforward way to use additional information to test the unbiasedness hypothesis is to use regression analysis. Suppose we write Equation (7.19) in the form of a regression, as in the following equation:

$$s(t+30) = a + b\,fp(t) + \epsilon(t+30) \qquad \text{(7.20)}$$

Here, a is the intercept, and b is the slope coefficient of the regression. The unbiasedness hypothesis implies that $a = 0$ and $b = 1$ because with these substitutions, Equation (7.20) reduces to Equation (7.19).

The Test Results

The regression tests of the unbiasedness hypothesis are presented in Exhibit 7.6, which presents the estimated parameters and their standard errors for regressions using the same six exchange rates as in Exhibit 7.5—that is, the value of the dollar in terms of the Deutsche mark, the British pound, and the Japanese yen and the three corresponding cross-rates.

The standard errors are presented in parentheses below the estimated coefficients. The confidence levels of the tests that $a = 0$ and that $b = 1$ are presented below the standard errors. Values of the confidence level that are above 0.90 indicate that we can reject the null hypothesis with 90% confidence.

Notice that all six of the estimated values of b are significantly different from unity. Perhaps more surprisingly, notice that all the estimated slope coefficients are negative. The estimated values of b range from -3.17 for the yen value of the pound to -0.55 for the Deutsche mark value of the pound. Consequently, the regressions suggest the existence of a **forward rate bias**; the forward rate does not equal the expected future spot rate.

The fact that negative values of b are found in the cross-rate regressions strongly supports the position that the explanation of this phenomenon for the dollar exchange rates should not be sought in a story about common movements of the dollar relative to other currencies, nor

Exhibit 7.6 Regression Tests of the Unbiasedness Hypothesis

$$s(t+30) = a + b\,fp(t) + \epsilon(t+30)$$

Currency	Const. (S.E.) Conf. ($a = 0$)	Forward Premium (S.E.) Conf. ($b = 1$)	R^2
	Coefficients on Regressors		
DEM/$	−2.59 (2.48) 0.70	−0.96 (0.83) 0.98	0.006
£/$	4.17 (2.20) 0.94	−1.50 (0.84) 1.00	0.013
¥/$	−10.99 (2.79) 1.00	−2.55 (0.67) 1.00	0.033
DEM/¥	4.60 (2.30) 0.95	−1.45 (0.89) 0.99	0.007
DEM/£	−3.69 (2.56) 0.85	−0.55 (0.64) 0.98	0.003
¥/£	−20.40 (5.18) 1.00	−3.17 (0.88) 1.00	0.026

Notes: The table reports data from February 1976 to September 2006. The euro replaces the Deutsche mark (DEM) from 1999 onwards. Data on rates of appreciation and the forward premiums are annualized. The parameter estimates are obtained using ordinary least-squares regression for each equation. The standard error (S.E.) is in parentheses below the estimate. The confidence level of the test is below the standard error. The tests are that the constant is zero and that the slope coefficient is one. The last column reports the R^2: how much of the variation in $s(t+30)$ is explained by the variation in $fp(t)$. The standard errors correct for heteroskedasticity and allow for serial correlation (2 lags) in the error terms.

should it be due strictly to U.S. policy. Apparently, the explanation must encompass the behavior of all major foreign exchange markets.[11]

Notice also that the explanatory power of the regressions, which is measured by the R^2 values, is quite low. The largest R^2 is 3.3%. The appropriate way to interpret this finding is that there is some ability of the forward premium to predict the rate of appreciation, but the unanticipated component in the rate of appreciation is large relative to its predictable component.

A Popular Interpretation

People familiar with the results of the regressions just presented often argue that the negative slope coefficients imply that a forward discount on the dollar in terms of a foreign currency signals that the foreign currency is going to weaken relative to the dollar, in contrast to the prediction of the unbiasedness hypothesis, which implies that the foreign currency is going to strengthen relative to the dollar. Because a forward discount on the dollar implies that the foreign interest rate is lower than the U.S. interest rate, these people argue that investors should do the **"carry trade"**—that is, borrow in the foreign currency to earn both the higher yield and the expected capital appreciation of the dollar implied by the regression. Unfortunately, this interpretation of the regression is wrong because it ignores the value of the constant term.

---

[11]The results for these cross-rate regressions confirm the findings of Geert Bekaert (1995), but they contrast with those of Peter Bossaerts and Pierre Hillion (1991), who examine exchange rates denominated in French francs for a shorter sample period of June 1, 1973, to June 13, 1988. The results for emerging markets are also more supportive of the null hypothesis (see Ravi Bansal and Magnus Dahlquist, 2000).

Exhibit 7.7 Interpreting the Unbiasedness Regression

	$fp(t)$	a	b	$E_t[s(t+1)]$
Uncovered interest rate parity/unbiasedness hypothesis	−3.37%	0	1	−3.37%
Naive interpretation	−3.37%	0	−2.55	8.60%
Actual interpretation	−3.37%	−10.99	−2.55	−2.39%

Notes: The three different lines compare expected exchange rate appreciation using information in the forward premium and three different assumptions. The first line assumes uncovered interest rate parity holds. The second line uses the regression reported in Exhibit 7.6 for ¥/$ but sets the constant equal to 0. The third line uses the actual regression results.

Exhibit 7.7 shows the importance of the constant in the regression, using the yen/dollar equation as an example. We consider a forward discount on the dollar of 3.37%, the sample average (see Exhibit 7.5), implying that Japanese yen interest rates were on average 3.37% less than U.S. dollar interest rates. We use the regression with the estimated coefficients to determine an estimate of expected dollar depreciation or appreciation:

$$E_t[s(t+1)] = \hat{a} + \hat{b}\ fp(t)$$

On the first line of Exhibit 7.7, we repeat the prediction of the theory: If the dollar is at a 3.37% discount, it should be expected to depreciate by 3.37%. If we were to use the regression and ignore the constant as in the computation on the second line, the prediction is an 8.59% appreciation of the dollar, so that the dollar indeed gives a higher yield and is expected to appreciate substantially. However, the correct interpretation is on the third line of Exhibit 7.7: The dollar is still expected to weaken, but only by 2.40%. This is the average depreciation of the dollar (39%; see Exhibit 7.5), and most importantly, it is lower than the depreciation the forward discount suggests. However, the regression still implies that a speculator should buy dollars forward if he believes the prediction of the regression will be borne out. That is,

$$E_t[fmr(t+1)] = E_t[s(t+1) - fp(t)]$$
$$(\text{Expected forward market return}) = -2.39\% - (-3.37\%)$$
$$= 0.98\%$$

The expected forward market return from buying dollars forward is positive!

Notice that the regression evidence qualifies the use of the unbiasedness hypothesis. Treasurers in MNCs and global portfolio managers must realize that there is a potential cost to hedging foreign currency risk because the forward rate is not necessarily the best forecast of the future exchange rate.

7.6 ALTERNATIVE INTERPRETATIONS OF THE TEST RESULTS

In this section we examine three possible explanations of the results from the preceding section: the presence of a foreign exchange risk premium discussed in Section 7.3, the presence of irrational investors, and peso problems.

Risk Premiums

In the discussion of risk premiums earlier in this chapter, we noted that there are good theoretical reasons that the unbiasedness hypothesis may not hold. Nevertheless, the estimated slope coefficients are quite far from the values they would have if the unbiasedness hypothesis were true. Can we learn anything from the regression evidence about the nature and magnitude of potential risk premiums? It turns out that if we maintain the assumption of rational expectations so that the regression residual is uncorrelated with anything in the information set, we can say quite a bit about the relative variabilities of risk premiums, expected rates of appreciation, and forward premiums.

Decomposing the Forward Premium

Let's consider the alternative hypothesis in which the unbiasedness hypothesis is false. We can now decompose the forward premium on a foreign currency into an expected rate of appreciation of the currency plus a risk premium:

$$fp(t) = E_t[s(t+1)] + rp(t) \qquad \textbf{(7.21)}$$

$$\text{Forward premium} = \text{Expected rate of appreciation} + \text{Risk premium}$$

In Equation (7.21), the risk premium is $E_t[F(t) - S(t+1)]/S(t)$, the expected profit in terms of the numerator currency of selling $[1/S(t)]$ units of foreign currency in the forward market. In that sense, the risk premium is a return in units of numerator currency.

To understand this point, consider one of the numeric examples mentioned in Section 7.1. Suppose a yen investor is selling the dollar forward. Recall that the 6-month forward rate was ¥85.08/$, and the expected spot rate according to Citibank was ¥75/$. Then, Citibank's expected yen profit per dollar sold forward was

$$¥10.08/\$ = (¥85.08/\$ - ¥75/\$)$$

However, the yen investor is interested in calculating her return per yen invested. Because the current spot rate was ¥87.18/$, the expected return per yen invested was

$$11.56\% = (¥10.08/\$)/(¥87.18/\$)$$

Now, let's use these numbers to understand what the decomposition of the forward premium tells us if we believe that forward premiums can only reflect either expected currency depreciation or a risk premium. The forward discount on the dollar was 2.41%, and Citibank predicts a depreciation of the dollar of 13.97%. So, according to Citibank, the 2.41% forward discount on the dollar reflects a 13.97% expected depreciation of the dollar and an 11.56% risk premium on selling dollars in the forward market. Note that

$$-2.41\% = -13.97\% + 11.56\%$$

According to this view, if selling the dollar forward did not command such a large risk premium, the interest differential, $i(¥) - i(\$)$, would have to be much more negative to reflect the expected depreciation of the dollar relative to the yen. Note that both the expected depreciation (13.97%) and the risk premium (11.56%) are much larger in magnitude than the forward discount (-2.41%). This seems to be at odds with the intuition of many economists, who think that most of the forward premium variation is a reflection of expected currency depreciation. What we would like to do now is to summarize the information present in the regression evidence regarding the relative magnitude of forward premiums, risk premiums, and expected currency depreciation.

The Variability of the Forward Premium and Its Components[12]

The variabilities of forward premiums on the major currencies are about 3% (on an annualized basis). It turns out that the regression evidence presented in Exhibit 7.6 implies that both the variability of expected exchange rate changes and risk premiums are often (much) larger than the variability of forward premiums. Let's see why.

If we take the regression to be truth, what is the variance of expected exchange rate changes? Let's go through the computations step by step:

$$VAR[E_t[s(t+1)]] = VAR[a + b\,fp(t)]$$
$$= b^2 VAR[fp(t)]$$

Hence, if $b^2 > 1$, which is the case for £/$, ¥/$, DEM/¥ and ¥/£ rates, expected exchange rate changes are more variable than forward premiums. To find the variance of the risk premium, note that the risk premium is exactly the negative of the expected forward market return: $rp(t) = -E_t[\text{fmr}(t)]$, defined earlier.

So, if we compute the variability of the expected forward market return, we have also found the variability of the risk premium because $VAR(z_t) = VAR(-z_t)$.

Now, we know

$$E_t[\text{fmr}(t+1)] = E_t[s(t+1)] - fp(t)$$
$$= a + (b - 1)\,fp(t)$$

Hence,

$$VAR(E_t[\text{fmr}(t+1)]) = (b - 1)^2 VAR[fp(t)]$$

Consequently, as long as b is negative, which is the case for all currencies, the implied variability of the risk premium is not only larger than the variance of the forward premium, it is also larger than the implied variability of the expected exchange rate changes.

If risk premiums are more variable than expected currency appreciation, a particular movement in the interest rate may more likely be driven by a change in the risk premium than by a change in the expected rate of appreciation of the currency. Whereas this regression evidence seems to be consistent with our assessment of the numeric analysis of Citibank's forecasts, it is counterintuitive to most economists. Formal models of risk, such as the CAPM, have a hard time generating this kind of behavior (see, for example, Geert Bekaert, 1996; Giorgi De Santis and Bruno Gerard, 1999; and Alberto Giovannini and Philippe Jorion, 1989). Not surprisingly, some economists have therefore argued that the evidence coming from the regressions should be interpreted differently. We now discuss two such alternative explanations.

Do Survey Data Reveal Irrational Expectations?

Jeffrey Frankel and Kenneth Froot (1990) were among the first to argue that the assumption of rational expectations might be too strong. By using survey data in which people are asked directly about their expected rates of appreciation, Frankel and Froot sought to measure expected rates of appreciation and risk premiums directly. More recent work by Menzie Chinn and Jeffrey Frankel (2002) largely confirms their findings.

Frankel and Froot analyze data taken from a survey by the *Economist*, and their sample period is June 1981 to August 1988 with observations on 3-, 6-, and 12-month forecasts. They consider regressions that are pooled across several currencies like the following:

$$s(t+k)^e = a + b\,fp(t,k) + \varepsilon(t) \tag{7.22}$$

---

[12]Eugene Fama's 1984 study was the first to recognize that the estimated slope coefficients in tests of the unbiasedness hypothesis can be interpreted to provide information about the variability of risk premiums and the variability of expected rates of appreciation.

in which $s(t + k)^e$ is the survey measurement at time t of the expected rate of appreciation over the next k months, and $fp(t,k)$ is the corresponding forward premium at time t for the k-month horizon. The estimated values of the b values, with standard errors in parentheses, are 1.123 (0.143) for the 3-month forecast, 1.113 (0.096) for the 6-month forecast, and 1.005 (0.099) for the 12-month forecast. Clearly, the estimated b values are insignificantly different from 1. Frankel and Froot interpret this finding to mean that all the variation in the forward premium is due to variation in the expected rate of appreciation. This is in sharp contrast to the conclusions drawn from the unbiasedness hypothesis regressions. These results suggest that the survey data provide biased forecasts of future rates of appreciation.

Notice that if the forward premium contains no risk premium and is consequently the market's expected rate of appreciation, and if the survey data accurately measure the market's expected rate of appreciation, not only would the slope coefficient in Equation (7.22) be 1, but the R^2 from the regression would be 1 as well. This is not the case. The R^2 values are 0.36 for the 3-month, 0.58 for the 6-month, and 0.53 for the 12-month forecasts. Frankel and Froot cite measurement errors in the survey data for the failure of the R^2 to be 1.

Problems with Interpreting Survey Data

One of the potential problems with asking individual people about their expectations is that economists want to understand how their actions collectively affect the market as a whole. While understanding the responses to direct questions may be interesting in and of itself, no one expects a great basketball player, such as Steve Nash, to be able to explain why he can shoot basketballs as well as he can. The physiology and physics of the problem are overwhelmingly complex, and Steve's answer would not necessarily have much scientific content. Similarly, we may not learn very much by asking people questions about their expectations if their investment actions are not consistent with their answers.

A second problem is that survey participants may not have the proper incentive to tell the truth. For example, if you think that your response to a survey will reveal information that others can use to profit at your expense, you will be less likely to respond sincerely.

A third problem with survey data is that they can be very disparate. Faced with a disparity of forecasts, a statistician must choose something that represents the "market's forecast." Typically, the median forecast is chosen. Ideally, however, we are interested in the marginal investor's expectation. Why is the median of the survey's responses an indication of the opinion of the marginal investor? In fact, several researchers, including Graham Elliott and Takatoshi Ito (1999) and Ronald MacDonald and Ian Marsh (1996), using data sets covering different currencies and different sample periods, show that forecasters are quite heterogeneous.

These very different forecasts also result in different forecasting performance. The forecasts of some forecasters would result in profitable trades, but the forecasts of others would have no economic value. We discuss the profitability of trading strategies in more detail in Chapter 10.

Peso Problems

Statistical Problems with Unbiasedness Hypothesis Regressions

Exhibit 7.8 presents information on the evolution of the slope coefficients from Equation (7.20) over time. The first estimate in the graph uses 5 years of monthly data. The next estimate results from rolling the data forward by 1 month and reestimating the regression, again with 5 years of data.

In the regression analysis of the unbiasedness hypothesis, the estimates of the slope coefficient, b, are very far from 1, but Exhibit 7.8 indicates that there is dramatic instability in these coefficients across 5-year intervals. During the major appreciation of the dollar relative to the other major currencies in the early 1980s, the estimated slope coefficient decreased from -5 to -10. Clearly, this was probably because of the unexpectedly strong appreciation of the dollar and not a response to an increase in the variability of risk premiums. A potential

Exhibit 7.8 Rolling Monthly 5-Year Regression: Monthly Spot Rate % Change Versus Monthly Forward Premium, February 1976–September 2000

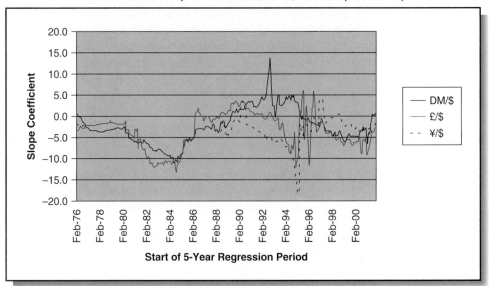

explanation of the evidence is that there is a problem with the assumptions underlying the statistical analysis of the data. We now consider one such explanation.

Peso Problems

A phenomenon called the **peso problem** arises when rational investors anticipate events that do not occur during the sample or at least do not occur with the frequency the investors expect. This invalidates statistical inferences conducted under the rational expectations assumption based on data drawn from the period. The peso problem got its name from the experience of Mexico during 1955–1976. During this period, the Mexican authorities were attempting to peg the peso–dollar exchange rate at MXP12/USD, and they did so successfully between 1955 and 1975. Suppose we assume that the market sets the forward rate in such a way that it is an unbiased predictor of the future spot rate—that is, we assume that the unbiasedness hypothesis holds. Now, let's see if a statistician would conclude that the forward rate is an unbiased or a biased predictor using the Mexican data.

Let S_{peg} be the peso–dollar exchange rate at which the Mexican authorities are currently pegging. Let S_{dev} be the rate that the Mexican authorities will choose if they devalue the peso, so $S_{dev} > S_{peg}$. Suppose that the Mexican authorities successfully peg the peso to the dollar between time T_0 and time T_2, when they eventually devalue the peso. Suppose also that the market knew during the time period between T_0 and T_2 that the Mexican authorities might devalue the peso at any time. It is assumed that everyone knew the value of S_{dev}. Let $prob_t$ be the probability that the market assigns to the event that the peso will be devalued during the next month. Then, the 1-month forward rate is an unbiased predictor of the future spot rate when it is the probability-weighted average of the two possible events:

$$F(t) = E_t[S(t+1)] = (1 - prob_t)S_{peg} + prob_t\,S_{dev} \qquad (7.23)$$

The forward rate is the probability of no devaluation multiplied by the current exchange rate plus the probability of a devaluation multiplied by the new exchange rate. To be concrete, let's assume a value for $S_{dev} = $ MXP18/\$; which represents a 50% appreciation of the dollar relative to the peso. As Equation (7.23) makes clear, as the market's assessment of the strength of the government's commitment to the peg changes over time, prob_t will change, and so will the forward rate. As long as the devaluation does not materialize, the dollar will trade at a forward premium relative to the peso (in pesos per dollar, $F > S_{peg}$), and peso money market investments will carry higher interest rates than dollar investments.

If the statistician takes data from an interval of time during which no devaluation occurs, say, between T_0 and T_1, where $T_1 < T_2$, and compares forward rates with realized future spot rates, the person will conclude that the forward rate is a biased predictor of the future spot rate. During the statistician's sample, the realized future spot rate is always below the forward rate. Hence, the statistician rejects the null hypothesis that the forward rate is an unbiased predictor of the future spot rate. The statistician has rejected the null hypothesis, but the null hypothesis is true.

How did the statistician go wrong? In other words, what led to the peso problem in this case? When we do statistical analysis on a financial time series using the rational expectations assumption, we assume that a reasonably long sample of returns is representative of the true distribution of returns that investors thought they faced when they made their investments. For the forward market example, we would assume that the *ex post* spot rates reflect all the possible events that investors thought might happen when they entered into their forward contracts. If there are important events that investors thought might happen but that did not happen, or if relatively rare events happened too frequently, the historical sample means, variances, and correlations in the data may tell us very little about the means, variances, and correlations of returns that investors thought they faced. The historical means, variances, and correlations may also be relatively uninformative about the moments that investors will face in the future. It is in this sense that the past performance of foreign investments, whether they are hedged or unhedged, may be poor indicators of the returns that investors can expect in the future.

In the case of the Mexican peso, even though the forward rate seemed to be a biased predictor of the future spot rate over 20 years, the devaluation eventually occurred in 1976, thereby validating the prediction embedded in the forward rate.

Argentina in 2000

Any episode in which investors expect a devaluation or change in regime gives rise to potential peso problems. A more recent example is Argentina at the beginning of the twenty-first century. As we discussed in Chapter 5, Argentina's monetary stabilization plan in the early 1990s included introducing a currency board that tied the Argentine peso (ARS) to the U.S. dollar at an exchange rate of ARS1/USD1. If the currency board were fully credible and there were no chance of a devaluation, ARS interest rates would equal USD interest rates, and there would be no forward discount on the peso [see Equation (7.23)]. Let's look at some actual data from 2000.

On June 21, 2000, the 3-month USD interest rate quoted in Argentina was 6.71%, and the 3-month ARP interest rate quoted by Argentinean banks was 7.33%. What explains the difference? It must have been that investors in the Argentine money market attached some probability to the currency board being abandoned and the peso being devalued relative to the dollar.

Suppose investors think a 5% devaluation to ARS1.05/USD is possible. What is the probability of this happening if uncovered interest rate parity holds? First, we must calculate the expected future exchange rate, which is the probability weighted average of the current rate and the possible future rate where prob is the probability of a devaluation:

$$E_t[S(t+1, \text{ARS/USD})] = [(1 - \text{prob}) \times \text{ARS1.0/USD}]$$
$$+ (\text{prob} \times \text{ARS1.05/USD}) \qquad \textbf{(7.24)}$$

Uncovered interest rate parity states that the return to investing in the Argentine peso is the same as the expected return from investing in the USD, which potentially involves an expected dollar appreciation. That is, 1 plus the peso interest rate, $i(\text{ARS})$, equals the expected return from converting pesos into dollars at $S(t, \text{ARS/USD})$, investing in dollars at the interest rate $i(\text{USD})$, and converting back from dollars to pesos at $S(t + 1, \text{ARS/USD})$:

$$[1 + i(\text{ARS})] = \frac{1}{S(t,\text{ARS/USD})} \times [1 + i(\text{USD})] \times E_t[S(t+1, \text{ARS/USD})]$$

Solving for the expected future exchange rate gives

$$E_t[S(t+1, \text{ARS/USD})] = S(t,\text{ARS/USD}) \times \frac{1 + i(\text{ARS})}{1 + i(\text{USD})}$$

Because $S(t, \text{ARP/USD})$ is 1 in this example, the ratio of the interest rates (plus 1) immediately gives the expected exchange rate:

$$E_t[S(t+1, \text{ARS/USD})] = \frac{1 + \dfrac{0.0733}{4}}{1 + \dfrac{0.0671}{4}} = 1.001524 \tag{7.25}$$

Note that we put the annualized interest rates on a 3-month basis using the conventions of the external currency market (see Chapter 6). By plugging this estimate of the expected exchange rate into Equation (7.24) and solving for the probability of a devaluation, prob, we find

$$\text{prob} = \frac{1.001524 - 1}{1.05 - 1} = 0.0305 = 3.05\%$$

We can do a similar computation for a 10% devaluation, which yields an even smaller probability, namely, 1.52%.

Thus, if uncovered interest rate parity and the unbiasedness hypothesis are good descriptions of reality, the slightly positive 3-month interest differential implies that the chances of a 5% or 10% devaluation were small in June 2000.

However, devaluation probabilities did not stay small. A number of macroeconomic developments and adverse stocks eroded the confidence in Argentina's currency board toward the end of 2000. Interest rate differentials with the United States soared, reaching a high of 20% during 2001. The large interest rate differentials reflected people's belief that the currency board might not last, and it did not. In April 2001, the currency board was replaced by a peg relative to a basket of the dollar and the euro, and different exchange rates for exports and imports were introduced. By December 2001, a financial crisis erupted, forcing the government to freeze bank deposits. In January 2002, the peso became a floating currency. By the end of 2002, the exchange rate was 3.3 pesos to the dollar.

Swedish Interest Rates of 500%

During currency crises, short-term interest rates often become exorbitantly high while long-term interest rates rise only a little, which means there is a large inversion of the term structure of interest rates. This peculiar pattern occurred in Sweden at the height of a currency crisis in Europe in 1992. The Riksbank, Sweden's central bank, raised its marginal lending rate on overnight borrowing to a staggering 500% p.a.—its highest level ever. The marginal lending rate is the rate that applies to the "last resort" financing offered by the Riksbank to Swedish financial institutions when other sources of overnight liquidity have dried up. The marginal lending rate typically provides a ceiling for the overnight market interest rate. Although only a small fraction of the Riksbank's borrowers had to pay the high rate, it still caused the *average* bank borrowing rate to rise to 38%. Yields on 3-month treasury bills rose to 35% from 25% the previous day, and yields on 6-month bills rose to 30% from 22%. Yields on 5-year government bonds actually fell slightly, from 12.58% to 12.30%.

Does an interest rate of 500% p.a. make any sense at all? Was this simply an attempt by the Swedish government to foil speculation against the krona? After all, a high borrowing rate would make speculation prohibitively expensive. In fact, imposing high interest rates is a tactic that central banks have used successfully since Premier Raymond Poincaré first used it in France in 1924 to prevent speculation against the franc. (This event came to be called "Poincaré's Bear Squeeze.") It turns out that we can fully understand these interest rate hikes if we use our theory of uncovered interest rate parity and the idea behind the peso problem.

Although the Swedish krona was pegged against the ECU, let us assume for simplicity that it was pegged against the DEM (which had by far the largest weight in the ECU basket). We will try to convince you that a large fraction of the higher short-term and long-term krona interest rates can be accounted for by what is often called a **devaluation premium**—that is, an interest rate that reflects the expected depreciation of a currency. Furthermore, devaluation premiums can also explain the inverted yield curve.

Let's revisit our simple model for exchange rate expectations. For the Swedish krona, there are two possible events:

1. A devaluation with probability of occurrence equal to prob
2. No devaluation with probability of occurrence equal to $(1 - \text{prob})$.

When the Swedish central bank successfully holds the peg, the exchange rate remains equal to the current spot rate. Let Z% denote the magnitude in percentage terms of a devaluation of the krona versus the DEM if the pegged exchange rate does not hold. Then, interest rate differentials tell us something about the probability of devaluation, prob, and the percentage magnitude of the devaluation, Z%. Consider the expected returns in Swedish krona on two investments for a period of n days, with interest rates measured at annual rates and with exchange rates measured in Swedish krona per Deutsche mark as follows:

$$\text{Krona investment: } 1 + i(\text{SKR})\frac{n}{360}$$

$$\text{DEM investment: } \frac{\left[1 + i(\text{DEM})\frac{n}{360}\right] \times E_t[S(t+n,\text{SEK/DEM})]}{S(t,\text{SEK/DEM})}$$

According to uncovered interest rate parity, these two investments yield the same expected return. Because there are two possible events for the krona—a devaluation or no devaluation—the expected spot rate is simply

$$E_t[S(t+n,\text{SKR/DEM})] =$$
$$(1 - \text{prob}) \times S(t,\text{SEK/DEM}) + \text{prob} \times S(t,\text{SEK/DEM}) \times (1 + Z\%)$$

Therefore, by equating the two rates of return, substituting for the expected spot rate, and solving for the intensity of the devaluation (which is the probability of the devaluation multiplied by the size of the devaluation), we find

$$\text{prob} \times Z\% = \frac{1 + i(\text{SEK})\frac{n}{360}}{1 + i(\text{DEM})\frac{n}{360}} - 1$$

or by placing the right-hand side over a common denominator, we find

$$\text{prob} \times Z\% = \frac{\left[i(\text{SEK})\frac{n}{360}\right] - \left[i(\text{DEM})\frac{n}{360}\right]}{1 + i(\text{DEM})\frac{n}{360}}$$

Consequently, if krona interest rates are higher than Deutsche mark interest rates, there is a chance of a devaluation of some magnitude. The higher the interest differential, the higher the market assesses the chance and/or the magnitude of a devaluation.

Now, suppose at the height of a currency crisis, prob (the likelihood of a devaluation) is very close to 1, say, 0.8. Speculators are quite confident the currency will be devalued, but they are not absolutely sure it will be. Consequently, the interest rate differentials can be used to infer the expected percentage magnitude of the currency devaluation:

	i(SEK)	I(DEM)	Prob × Z%	Z%, if prob = 0.8
1 month	35%	4%	2.57%	3.22%
3 months	20%	4.5%	3.83%	4.79%

These numbers do not look unreasonable at all.

Why do devaluation expectations of a few percentage points lead to such high interest rates, and why is the effect so much larger for short maturities than for long ones? The inverted yield curve and the large magnitude of the short interest rates are simply a consequence of annualizing interest rates. To make this concrete, suppose that international speculators expect a 5% devaluation within a week. Whatever Swedish money market investments they hold, they face an imminent capital loss of 5%. Speculators will consequently demand higher interest rates to protect themselves against this possibility. If the interest rate applies to a 1-year maturity, this interest rate increase will be approximately 5%. But when the investment is very short term (such as 1 week), an extra 5% p.a. only means a small increase in the actual return. This won't compensate investors for the capital losses they will suffer as a result of a devaluation. Let the probability of a devaluation be 0.8, and let the DEM interest rate be 3% at the weekly horizon and 5% at the annual horizon. Whatever the investment, prob × Z = 0.8 × 5% ≡ 4%. According to the formula, we have:

$$\text{Devaluation premium} = 1 \text{ week investment} = 1 \text{ year investment}$$

$$4\% = \frac{i(\text{SEK},1 \text{ week})\dfrac{7}{360} - 3\%\dfrac{7}{360}}{1 + 3\%\dfrac{7}{360}} = \frac{i(\text{SEK},1 \text{ year}) - 5\%}{1 + 5\%}$$

Clearly, i(SEK, 1 week) will have to increase by much more than i(SEK, 1 year) to compensate for the expected devaluation of 4%. In particular, we can solve for i(SEK, 1 week) = 208.83% p.a., and i(SEK, 1 year) = 9.20% p.a. Clearly, the yield curve would be very inverted in this case.

7.7 SUMMARY

This chapter analyzes speculative currency investments. Its main points are as follows:

1. To speculate in currency markets, you can either invest in the money market of the currency you are bullish on (financing the investment with borrowed domestic currency, for example) or buy that currency in the forward market. Only when the realized future spot exchange rate is actually above the forward rate (domestic currency per foreign currency) will a speculative currency strategy make money.

2. Exchange rates are asset prices, the relative prices of two currencies, and they are therefore difficult to forecast.

3. The expected return and volatility of a speculative currency investment depend on the mean and the standard deviation, respectively, of the conditional distribution of the future spot exchange rate.

4. Uncovered interest rate parity states that the expected return on an unhedged investment of domestic currency in the foreign money market will equal the domestic interest rate.

5. The unbiasedness hypothesis states that the forward rate equals the expected future spot rate—that is, what the market expects the spot rate to be on the day your forward contract comes due, $F(t) = E_t[S(t + 1)]$. The average forecast error of an unbiased predictor is zero when the average is computed over a large enough sample of forecasts.

6. Both uncovered interest rate parity and the unbiasedness hypothesis are consistent with a narrow view of market efficiency—that is, that there is no expected return to currency speculation. A broader view of market efficiency maintains that the expected profits from a trading strategy should merely compensate the investor for the risk she has taken.

7. The capital asset pricing model (CAPM) provides a theoretical reason why forward rates would be biased predictors of future spot rates and yet the market would still be considered to be efficient. The bias would be attributable to a risk premium, arising from the correlation between forward market returns and the market portfolio return.

8. Whether uncovered interest rate parity or the unbiasedness hypothesis holds has important implications for portfolio management, exchange rate forecasting, and theories of exchange rate determination.

9. If there is a difference between the expected future spot exchange rate and the forward rate for that maturity, hedging transaction foreign exchange risk produces a different revenue or cost than that expected to occur without hedging.

10. If investors have rational expectations, they do not make systematic mistakes when forecasting exchange rates. The actual future rate of appreciation then equals its conditional expectation plus an error term that has a conditional mean of 0; that is, only news makes future exchange rates different from their expected values.

11. The weakest implication of the unbiasedness hypothesis is that the unconditional mean of the forward premium should equal the unconditional mean of the realized rate of appreciation. The data appear consistent with the fact that high-interest-rate or forward-discount currencies tend to depreciate relative to low-interest-rate or forward-premium currencies.

12. Regression tests of the unbiasedness hypothesis indicate that it is strongly inconsistent with the data: Slope coefficients in regressions of the *ex post* rate of appreciation on the forward premium are negative rather than equal to 1. One explanation is that the variances of foreign exchange risk premiums are larger than the variances of the expected rates of appreciation.

13. A phenomenon called the peso problem arises when rational investors anticipate events that do not occur during the sample, or at least not do not occur with the frequency they expect. In such a situation, a statistical analysis of returns can be badly biased.

14. In fixed-rate regimes, interest rate differentials provide information about the intensity of a devaluation— that is, the probability of the devaluation multiplied by the magnitude of the devaluation.

QUESTIONS

1. What are two ways to speculate in the currency markets without investing any money up front?

2. What do financial economists mean when they discuss the conditional expectation of the future spot exchange rate?

3. What is the main determinant of the variability of forward market returns?

4. Describe how you construct the uncertain yen-denominated return from investing 1 yen in the Swiss franc money market.

5. What is a hedged foreign currency investment? What happens if you hedge your return in Question 4?

6. What does it mean for the forward exchange rate for a particular horizon, such as 90 days, to be an unbiased predictor of the future spot exchange rate?

7. Why is it true that the hypothesis that the forward exchange rate is an unbiased predictor of the future spot exchange rate is equivalent to the hypothesis that the forward premium (or discount) on a foreign currency is an unbiased predictor of the rate of its appreciation (or depreciation)?

8. It is often claimed that the forward exchange rate is set by arbitrage to satisfy (covered) interest rate parity. Explain how interest rate parity can be satisfied

and how the forward exchange rate can be set by speculators in reference to the expected future spot exchange rate.

9. It is sometimes asserted that investors who hedge their foreign currency bond or stock returns remove the foreign exchange risk associated with the investment, reduce the volatility of their domestic currency returns, and thus get a "free lunch" because the mean return in domestic currency remains the same as the mean return in the foreign currency. Is this true or false? Why?

10. It is often argued that forward exchange rates should be unbiased predictors of future spot exchange rates if the foreign exchange market is efficient. Is this true or false? Why?

11. What is the prediction of the CAPM for the relationship between the forward exchange rate and the expected future spot exchange rate?

12. If the CAPM explains deviations of the forward exchange rate from the expected future spot exchange rate, explain why one party involved in a forward contract would be willing to enter into a contract with an expected loss.

13. Why is it only the covariance of an asset's return with the return on the world market portfolio that determines whether there is a risk premium associated with the asset's expected return?

14. What is the rational expectations hypothesis, and how is it applied to tests of hypotheses about expected returns in financial markets?

15. Suppose that the forward premium on the foreign currency at each moment in time equals the conditional expectation of the future rate of appreci-

ation of the foreign currency relative to the domestic currency at that moment in time. If we form the average realized rate of appreciation from a large sample of data and compare it to the average forward premium, what should be true?

16. Explain how you would use a regression to test the unbiasedness hypothesis.

17. Suppose you run a regression of the realized rate of appreciation of a foreign currency on a constant and the forward premium on the foreign currency. What interpretation can you give to the estimated slope coefficient? If the slope coefficient is negative, is it true that the forward premium is predicting the wrong sign for the rate of appreciation?

18. Let the forward premium be equal to the expected rate of appreciation of a foreign currency relative to the domestic currency plus a forward market risk premium. What does a negative slope coefficient imply about the variability of risk premiums relative to variability of expected rates of appreciation?

19. In order to examine issues such as the unbiasedness hypothesis, some financial economists have used survey data in which people are asked directly about their expectations of future rates of appreciation. Are there potential problems with this approach?

20. What is a peso problem? Explain the term within the context of its original derivation. Now, explain how peso problems can generally plague the study of financial market returns.

21. How can you use interest rate differentials to understand the probability of a devaluation and the potential magnitude of the devaluation?

PROBLEMS

1. Over the next 30 days, economists forecast that the pound may weaken relative to the dollar by as much as 7%, or it may strengthen by as much as 6%. The possible values for the rate of change of the dollar–pound spot exchange rate are −7%, −5%, −3%, −1%, 0%, 2%, 4%, and 6%. Suppose that each of these values is equally likely. What are the mean and standard deviation of the future spot exchange rate if the current rate is $1.5845/£?

2. Consider the following hypothetical facts about Mexico: The peso recently lost over 40% of its value relative to the dollar. Over the course of the next 90 days, the Mexican government risks losing control of the economy. If it does, the Mexican peso will lose

33% of its value relative to the U.S. dollar, and the Mexican stock market will fall by 39%. There is a 35% chance that the authorities will lose control of the economy. Alternatively, the U.S. Congress may vote to help Mexico by offering collateral for Mexican government loans. In that case, the Mexican peso will gain 27% in value relative to the U.S. dollar, and the Mexican stock market will rise by 29%. As a U.S. investor with no current assets or liabilities in Mexico, you have decided to speculate. Calculate your expected dollar return from investing dollars in the Mexican stock market for the next 90 days.

3. Suppose that you observe a 90-day forward rate of $1.19/€. The current spot rate is $1.20/€, and you

expect that the spot rate that will be realized 90 days in the future is $1.21/€. If you wanted to speculate in the forward market by either buying or selling $10,000,000, what contract would you make? What would be your expected profit on the contract? If the standard deviation of the rate of appreciation of the dollar relative to the euro is 3% over this period, what range of possible profits and losses covers 95% of the possibilities that you may experience?

4. Consider the following facts about Switzerland: The current spot exchange rate is CHF1.7/USD. Over the next 90 days, there is a 30% probability that the Swiss franc will strengthen relative to the dollar by 5%, and there is a 70% chance that the Swiss franc will weaken by 3%. What is the expected future spot exchange rate of dollars per Swiss franc? If the current forward rate is CHF1.71/USD, calculate your expected dollar profit from contracting either to buy or to sell CHF10,000,000 for USD in the 90-day forward market. If only one of these two events can occur, how much will you actually win or lose in 90 days?

5. Suppose the continuously compounded rate of appreciation of the dollar relative to the yen over the next 90 days has a mean of −1% and a standard deviation of 3%. Use a spreadsheet program to graph the distribution of the future yen–dollar exchange rate. If the current spot exchange rate is ¥99/$, and the 90-day forward rate is ¥98.30/$, what is the expected profit or loss in yen on a forward contract that sells $5,000,000 forward?

6. Suppose that the spot exchange rate is $1.55/£, that the beta on a forward contract to buy pounds with dollars is −1.5, and that the expected dollar rate of return on the market portfolio in excess of the dollar risk-free interest rate is 7%. What is the expected profit or loss on a forward purchase of £1,000,000? Explain how this can be an equilibrium.

7. Consider the implication of a regression of the rate of depreciation of the dollar relative to the yen on a constant and the forward discount on the dollar. Suppose the estimated slope coefficient is −2, and the standard deviation of the forward discount, measured on an annualized basis, is 2.5%. What is a lower bound for the variability of the risk premium in the yen–dollar forward market?

8. Suppose the British pound (GBP) is pegged to the euro (EUR). You think there is a 5% probability that the GBP will be devalued by 10% over the course of the next month. What interest differential would prevent you from speculating by borrowing GBP and lending EUR?

BIBLIOGRAPHY

Baillie, Richard, and Tim Bollerslev, 2000, "The Forward Premium Anomaly Is Not as Bad as You Think," *Journal of International Money and Finance* 19, pp. 471–488.

Bansal, Ravi, and Magnus Dahlquist, 2000, "The Forward Premium Puzzle: Different Tales from Developed and Emerging Economies," *Journal of International Economics* 51, pp. 115–144.

Bekaert, Geert, 1995, "The Time-Variation of Expected Returns and Volatility in Foreign-Exchange Markets," *Journal of Business and Economic Statistics* 13, pp. 397–408.

Bekaert, Geert, 1996, "The Time Variation of Risk and Return in Foreign Exchange Markets: A General Equilibrium," *Review of Financial Studies* 9, pp. 427–470.

Bekaert, Geert, and Robert J. Hodrick, 1993, "On Biases in the Measurement of Foreign Exchange Risk Premiums," *Journal of International Money and Finance* 12, pp. 115–138.

Bekaert, Geert, and Robert J. Hodrick, 2001, "Expectations Hypotheses Tests," *Journal of Finance* 56, pp. 1357–1394.

Bekaert, Geert, Min Wei, and Yuhang Xing, 2007, "Uncovered Interest Rate Parity and the Term Structure," *Journal of International Money and Finance*," 26(6), 1038–1069.

Black, Fischer, 1989, "Universal Hedging: Optimizing Currency Risk and Reward in International Equity Portfolios," *Financial Analysts Journal* 45, pp. 16–22.

Black, Fischer, 1990, "Equilibrium Exchange Rate Hedging," *Journal of Finance* 45, pp. 899–907.

Bossaerts, Peter, and Pierre Hillion, 1991, "Market Microstructure Effects of Government Intervention in the Foreign Exchange Market," *Review of Financial Studies* 4, pp. 513–541.

Chinn, Menzie, 2006, "The (Partial) Rehabilitation of Interest Rate Parity in the Floating Rate Era: Longer Horizons, Alternative Expectations, and Emerging Markets," *Journal of International Money and Finance* 25, pp. 7–21.

Chinn, Menzie, and Jeffrey A. Frankel, 2002, "Survey Data on Exchange Rate Expectations: More Currencies, More Horizons, More Tests," in Bill Allen and David Dickinson, eds., *Monetary Policy, Capital Flows and Financial Market Developments in the Era of Financial Globalisation: Essays in Honour of Max Fry*. London: Routledge.

De Santis, Giorgio, and Bruno Gérard, 1998, "How Big Is the Premium for Currency Risk?" *Journal of Financial Economics* 49, pp. 375–412.

Elliott, Graham, and Takatoshi Ito, 1999, "Heterogeneous Expectations and Tests of Efficiency in the Yen/Dollar Forward Exchange Rate Market," *Journal of Monetary Economics* 43, pp. 435–456.

Engel, Charles, 1996, "The Forward Discount Anomaly and the Risk Premium: A Survey of Recent Evidence," *Journal of Empirical Finance* 3, pp. 123–191.

Fama, Eugene, 1984, "Forward and Spot Exchange Rates," *Journal of Monetary Economics*, pp. 319–338.

Frankel, Jeffrey, and Kenneth Froot, 1990, "Exchange Rate Forecasting Techniques, Survey Data, and Implications for the Foreign Exchange Market," in D. Das, ed., *Current Issues in International Trade and International Finance*. Oxford, UK: Oxford University Press.

Froot, Kenneth A., and Richard H. Thaler, 1990, "Foreign Exchange," *Journal of Economic Perspectives* 4, pp. 179–192.

Giovannini, Alberto, and Philippe Jorion, 1989, "The Time-Variation of Risk and Return in the Foreign-Exchange Stock Markets," *Journal of Finance* 44, pp. 307–325.

Green, Philip, 1992, "Is Currency Trading Profitable? Exploiting Deviations from Uncovered Interest Rate Parity," *Financial Analysts Journal* pp. 82–86.

Hansen, Lars Peter, 1982, "Large Sample Properties of Generalized Method of Moments Estimators," *Econometrica* 50, pp. 1029–1054.

Hodrick, Robert J., 1987, *The Empirical Evidence on the Efficiency of Forward and Futures Foreign Exchange Markets*, in Jacques Lesourne and Hugo Sonnenschein, eds., *Fundamentals of Pure and Applied Economics*, Chur, Switzerland: Harwood Academic Publishers.

Keane, Michael P., and David E. Runkle, 1990, "Testing the Rationality of Price Forecasts: New Evidence from Panel Data," *American Economic Review* 80, pp. 714–735.

Levich, Richard M., 1980, "Analyzing the Accuracy of Foreign Exchange Advisory Services: Theory and Evidence," in Richard M. Levich and Clas Wihlborg, eds., *Exchange Risk and Exposure*, Lexington, MA: D. C. Heath.

MacDonald, Ronald, and Ian W. Marsh, 1996, "Currency Forecasters Are Heterogeneous: Confirmation and Consequences," *Journal of International Money and Finance* 15, pp. 665–685.

Sharpe, William F., 1964, "Capital Asset Prices: A Theory of Market Equilibrium Under Conditions of Risk," *Journal of Finance* 19, pp. 425–442.

Siegel, Jeremy J., 1972, "Risk, Information, and Forward Exchange," *Quarterly Journal of Economics* 86, pp. 303–309.

Appendix 7.1

The Portfolio Diversification Argument and the CAPM

If an investor places all her wealth in only one asset, the expected return on that asset and the variance of the return on that asset dictate the mean and variance of the investor's portfolio. The purpose of this appendix is to review how the mean and variance of a portfolio are determined when there is more than one asset in the portfolio. To do this easily, we must develop some notation. Let R_i be the return on asset i and denote the mean return on asset i as $E(R_i)$, where we recognize that the mean of the return is its expected value. Let σ_{ij} denote the covariance between asset i and asset j. The covariance is a measure of the degree to which two returns move together, and it is found by taking the expectation

of the product of the deviations of the returns from their respective means:

$$\sigma_{ij} = E\left[[R_i - E(R_i)][R_j - E(R_j)] \right]$$

Because the covariance involves the product of two random variables and the order of multiplication is not important, $\sigma_{ij} = \sigma_{ji}$. Also, from the definition of variance, which is the expected value of the squared deviation around the mean, we have

$$\sigma_{ii} = E\left[[R_i - E(R_i)]^2 \right]$$

The square root of the variance is the standard deviation. Often, people find it more intuitive and convenient to think in terms of correlations between returns on assets rather than covariances because the correlation is a number between −1 and 1. The correlation coefficient, ρ_{ij}, is defined to be the covariance divided by the product of the standard deviations of the two assets:

$$\rho_{ij} = \frac{\sigma_{ij}}{\sqrt{\sigma_{ii}}\sqrt{\sigma_{jj}}} \qquad (7A.1)$$

Now that we have the notation, we can examine the mean and variance of the return on a portfolio of several assets. Let w_i denote the share of the investor's wealth that is invested in asset i. Let's also begin with just two assets in the portfolio. Suppose the investor puts a share of her wealth equal to w_1 in asset 1 and the remainder of her wealth in asset 2, such that $w_2 = 1 - w_1$.

The actual return on the portfolio, R_p, will be the weighted average of the returns on the two assets, where the weights are the shares of invested wealth:

$$R_p = w_1 R_1 + w_2 R_2 \qquad (7A.2)$$

Hence, to find the mean return on the portfolio, we take the expectation of the realized return in Equation (7A.2), and we find

$$E(R_p) = w_1 E(R_1) + w_2 E(R_2)$$

Just as the actual return is a weighted average of the actual individual returns, the expected return on the portfolio is the same weighted average of the expected returns on the assets in the portfolio.

The variance of the return on the portfolio $V(R_p)$ is the expectation of the squared deviation of the return from its mean as in the following:

$$V(R_p) = E\left[[R_p - E(R_p)]^2 \right] =$$
$$E\left[[(w_1 R_1 + w_2 R_2) - (w_1 E(R_1) + w_2 E(R_2))]^2 \right]$$
$$\qquad (7A.3)$$

By multiplying out and rearranging the terms in Equation (7A.3), we find that

$$V(R_p) = w_1^2 E\left[[R_1 - E(R_1)]^2 \right]$$
$$+ w_2^2 E\left[[R_2 - E(R_2)]^2 \right]$$
$$+ 2w_1 w_2 E\left[[R_1 - E(R_1)][R_2 - E(R_2)] \right]$$
$$= w_1^2 \sigma_{11} + w_2^2 \sigma_{22} + 2w_1 w_2 \sigma_{12}$$

Let's do a calculation with some real numbers to see how the mean and variance of a portfolio are related to the means and variances of the individual assets. Suppose that the expected return on asset 1 is 15%, and its standard deviation is 22%, whereas the expected return on asset 2 is 16%, and its standard deviation is 24%. Suppose also that the correlation between the returns on the two assets is 0.4, and remember from Equation (7A.1) that the covariance is the correlation multiplied by the product of the two standard deviations. Hence, the covariance between the return on asset 1 and the return on asset 2 is

$$\sigma_{12} = (0.4)(0.22)(0.24) = 0.02112$$

Now we can calculate the mean and variance of any portfolio composed of assets 1 and 2. Suppose we put 35% of our wealth in asset 1 and 65% in asset 2. The mean return on our portfolio is then

$$E(R_p) = (0.35)(0.15) + (0.65)(0.16) = 0.1565$$

and the variance of the return on our portfolio is

$$V(R_p) = (0.35)^2(0.22)^2 + (0.65)^2(0.24)^2$$
$$+ 2(0.35)(0.65)(0.02112)$$
$$= 0.039875$$

The standard deviation of our portfolio is therefore

$$\sqrt{0.039875} = 0.1997$$

or 19.97%.

The ratio of the mean to the standard deviation of an asset or a portfolio is a measure of the trade-off an investor faces between return and risk. The ratio of the mean of asset 1 to the standard deviation of asset 1 is $0.68 = 15\%/22\%$, and the ratio of the mean of asset 2 to the standard deviation of asset 2 is $0.67 = 16\%/24\%$. The ratio of the mean of our portfolio to the standard deviation of our portfolio is $0.78 = 15.65\%/19.97\%$. By diversifying across the two assets, we have improved our risk–return trade-off. Also, note that the standard deviation of the portfolio is lower than the standard deviations of both individual assets. Diversification makes some risk disappear.

Because there are many more than two assets in the world, we next want to examine what happens if we put a small amount of our wealth in each of N assets. To simplify the analysis even more, let's put an equal share, $w_i = (1/N)$, in the N different assets. Determining the mean return of our portfolio is easy because it is just the weighted, linear combination of the expected returns on the N assets, as in Equation (7A.2):

$$E(R_p) = \sum_{i=1}^{N} w_i E(R_i) = \sum_{i=1}^{N} \frac{E(R_i)}{N}$$

Consequently, the portfolio's mean return is the average of the mean returns on the N assets.

The variance of the return on an N-asset portfolio is as follows:

$$V(R_p) = E[R_p - E(R_p)]^2$$

$$= E\left[\sum_{i=1}^{N} w_i[R_i - E(R_i)] \sum_{i=1}^{N} w_i[R_i - E(R_i)] \right]$$
(7A.4)

If you multiply out the terms involving the summations on the right-hand side of Equation (7A.4), you will find that you must take the sum of the expectations of N^2 terms. There will be N variances that arise from the multiplication of the return on an asset with itself, and there will be $N(N - 1)$ other terms that are covariances. So, there will be $N(N - 1)/2$ distinct covariance terms because $\sigma_{ij} = \sigma_{ji}$. In Equation (7A.4), the weights are multiplied by each other, but because the weights on the equal-weighted portfolio are the same, each of the N^2 terms in Equation (7A.4) is multiplied by $1/N^2$. Therefore,

$$V(R_p) = \frac{1}{N^2} \sum_{i=1}^{N} \sigma_{ij} + \frac{2}{N^2} \sum_{i=1}^{N-1} \sum_{j=i+1}^{N} \sigma_{ij}$$
(7A.5)

The double summation term, $\sum_{i=1}^{N-1} \sum_{j=i+1}^{N} \sigma_{ij}$, is multiplied

by 2 because the summation involves only the distinct $N(N - 1)/2$ covariances. Let's define the average variance as

$$\Lambda_i = \frac{1}{N} \sum_{i=1}^{N} \sigma_{ii}$$

and the average covariance as

$$\Lambda_{ij} = \frac{1}{N(N - 1)/2} \sum_{i=1}^{N-1} \sum_{j=i+1}^{N} \sigma_{ij}$$

Equation (7A.5) implies that the portfolio variance can be written as

$$V(R_p) = \frac{1}{N} \Lambda_i + \left(1 - \frac{1}{N} \right) \Lambda_{ij}$$
(7A.6)

Notice that as N gets large in Equation (7A.6), the importance of the average variance of the returns on the N investments in the determination of the variance of the return on the portfolio goes to zero. Thus, as N gets large, the variance of the return on a highly diversified portfolio is driven to be equal to the average covariance of the assets in the portfolio. If asset returns were uncorrelated, the average covariance would be zero, and a highly diversified portfolio would produce an essentially riskless return, even though each of the individual asset returns were drawn from a random distribution with finite variance. Notice also that assets with negative covariances are very important because they reduce the average covariance of the portfolio.

From Equation (7A.6) it is clear that the individual variance of an asset will not affect the overall variance of the portfolio, and the individual variance consequently should not affect the expected return that a risk-averse investor demands to hold that particular asset. This intuition leads directly to the CAPM as a relationship describing how expected returns are determined. Essentially, the CAPM builds on the intuition that an investor will add an asset to his or her portfolio until it cannot further improve the risk–return trade-off of the portfolio. We elaborate on this intuition in Chapter 13.

Although the large portfolio in our analysis was arbitrary, the fundamental insight of the CAPM was that with a few additional assumptions, it would have to be the case that, in equilibrium (that is, when all investors are happily holding the existing assets in the marketplace at their current prices, without feeling the need to trade them), the well-diversified portfolio that every investor would hold would be the market portfolio. All investors would hold some fraction of their wealth in the market portfolio, with more risk-averse investors holding smaller fractions and more risk-tolerant investors holding larger fractions and possibly borrowing to invest in the market.

Appendix 7.2

A Regression Refresher

In Section 7.5, we tested the unbiasedness hypothesis with a model in this form:

$$\frac{S(t+1) - S(t)}{S(t)} = a + b\frac{F(t) - S(t)}{S(t)} + \epsilon(t+1)$$

This is an example of a linear regression model, where a dependent (or explained) variable $y(t+1) = \frac{S(t+1) - S(t)}{S(t)}$ is regressed on a independent variable,

or explanatory variable $x(t) = \frac{F(t) - S(t)}{S(t)}$. Hence, the

regression can be written as

$$y(t+1) = a + b\,x(t) + \epsilon(t+1)$$

The regression describes the amount of the movement or variation in $y(t+1)$ that can be explained linearly by movement or variation in $x(t)$. We want to find values of the parameters a and b that make $a + b\,x(t)$, a linear function of $x(t)$, as close to $y(t+1)$ as possible. The fit is unlikely to be perfect, so there will be an error (or disturbance) term, which we call $\epsilon(t+1) = y(t+1) - a - b\,x(t)$.

Econometricians have developed several methods to find "estimates," or values for the parameter, a and b, given data on $y(t+1)$ and $x(t)$. For any given sample of data, these estimates are just numbers and are typically represented by putting a caret symbol over the parameter symbol; for example, $\hat{a}$ and $\hat{b}$ would be estimates of a and b. With such estimates, we can compute the actual errors the model makes in predicting $y(t+1)$:

$$\hat{\epsilon}(t+1) = y(t+1) - \hat{a} - \hat{b}\,x(t)$$

These actual errors are called *residuals*.

The formula by which the data are transformed into an actual estimate is called an **estimator**, and the most popular estimator for the linear regression model is the **OLS estimator**. OLS stands for *ordinary least squares* because the estimator minimizes the sum of the squared residuals. That is, the estimates of a and b are such that the sum of the squared residuals, $\sum_{t=1}^{T}\hat{\epsilon}(t+1)^2$, is as low as possible, and we are assuming that we have $T+1$ total observations, of which only T will be used in the regression.

To illustrate this concretely, let's use some actual data on exchange rates and forward premiums and run a regression. Exhibit 7A.1 shows monthly data on dollar/euro exchange rates and forward premiums between March 31, 2001, and April 30, 2003, for a total of 26 data points ($T+1$ is 26 here).

Note that monthly exchange rate changes are often quite large and mostly positive during this sample. They represent our $y(t+1)$ observations. The forward premiums represent our $x(t)$ observations. We have to be careful with the timing to match up, say, the April 2001 exhange rate change with the forward premium for the end of March 2001. The forward premiums are quite small because they are in monthly percentages. The predominantly negative values suggest that for most of the sample period, the euro was trading at a discount, which means that euro interest rates were higher than dollar interest rates.

Exhibit 7A.2 presents a scatter plot of the data, with the exchange rate changes on the vertical axis and the forward premiums on the horizontal axis. The OLS estimator attempts to fit a linear line through this scatter plot such that the sum of the squared deviations between the actual data and the regression line are minimized. The corresponding fitted values that lie on the regression line are also on the graph.

Concretely, the OLS estimator resulting from this procedure for the slope of the line is as follows:

$$\hat{b} = \frac{\frac{1}{T}\sum_{t=1}^{T}[y(t+1) - \bar{y}\,][x(t) - \bar{x}\,]}{\frac{1}{T}\sum_{t=1}^{T}[x(t) - \bar{x}\,]^2}$$

where $\quad \bar{y} = (1/T)\sum_{t=1}^{T}y(t+1)$
and $\quad\quad \bar{x} = (1/T)\sum_{t=1}^{T}x(t)$

are the sample means, and $\hat{a} = \bar{y} - \hat{b}\,\bar{x}$ is the constant. Note that the numerator of $\hat{b}$ represents an estimate of the covariance between $y(t+1)$ and $x(t)$, whereas the denominator represents an estimate of the variance of $x(t)$. Hence, the slope coefficient b is the covariance of the dependent variable and the independent variable divided by the variance of the independent variable:

$$b = \frac{\text{cov}[y(t+1), x(t)]}{\text{var}[x(t)]}$$

Exhibit 7A.1 Data on Exchange Rates (USD/EUR) and Forward Premiums (USD/EUR)

Date	Exchange Rate	Exchange Rate Change (in %)	Forward Premium (in %)
3/31/2001	0.8792	−5.08	0.0232
4/30/2001	0.89	1.2135	−0.0024
5/31/2001	0.8575	−3.7900	−0.0489
6/30/2001	0.8495	−0.9417	−0.0581
7/31/2001	0.8747	2.8809	−0.0647
8/31/2001	0.9167	4.5816	−0.0755
9/30/2001	0.9098	−0.7584	−0.0921
10/31/2001	0.9049	−0.5414	−0.1088
11/30/2001	0.8885	−1.8458	−0.1138
12/31/2001	0.886	−0.2821	−0.1279
1/31/2002	0.8617	−2.8200	−0.1337
2/28/2002	0.8659	0.4850	−0.1296
3/31/2002	0.8702	0.4941	−0.1263
4/30/2002	0.904	3.7389	−0.1288
5/31/2002	0.9376	3.5836	−0.1321
6/30/2002	0.9921	5.4933	−0.1329
7/31/2002	0.9835	−0.8744	−0.1321
8/31/2002	0.9826	−0.0915	−0.1321
9/30/2002	0.9812	−0.1426	−0.1288
10/31/2002	0.9844	0.3250	−0.1296
11/30/2002	0.9946	1.0255	−0.1545
12/31/2002	1.0483	5.1225	−0.1354
1/31/2003	1.0815	3.0698	−0.1313
2/28/2003	1.0759	−0.5204	−0.1255
3/31/2003	1.08	0.3796	−0.1130
4/30/2003	1.1086	2.5798	

Notes: The forward premiums are computed using 1-month interest rates for the dollar and the euro. All data are from the website of the European Central Bank, http://www.ecb.int/stats/mb/eastats.html.

When we carry out the actual regression with the data given in Exhibit 7A.2, we find:

$$\hat{a} = -0.042 \quad \hat{b} = -7.26$$
$$(1.011) \qquad (8.90)$$
$$[0.033] \qquad [0.646]$$
$$R^2 = 2.69\%$$

An OLS regression also yields a standard error for the estimates, which gives an idea of how confident we are in the estimates. We report standard errors in parentheses below the parameter estimates as shown in the previous equation; that is, the standard error of $\hat{a}$ is 1.011, for example.

Even if $y(t + 1)$ and $x(t)$ are totally independent, they may appear to be related just by chance. Use of the standard error together with the coefficient estimate allows computation of a confidence level for b to be different from a particular value. For example, the unbiasedness hypothesis in the context of the regression model represents the statistical null hypothesis $\hat{b} = 1$. We would like to know whether $\hat{b}$ is close to or far away from 1 in a statistical sense.

If we want to test whether b is 1, we compute the square of $\hat{b} - 1$ divided by the standard error of $\hat{b}$. Let us introduce the test statistic z:

$$z = \left[\frac{\hat{b} - 1}{se(\hat{b})} \right]^2$$

If $\hat{b}$ is truly close to 1, the value of z should be small, and if the true value of b is not equal to 1, the z statistic should be large. However, the true b may be far from 1, but the estimate may be very noisy—that is, the standard error may be big. In this case, our test statistic z will be small as well.

In our sample regression, the standard error for $\hat{b}$ is 8.90; hence, $z = 0.861$. Standard errors are inversely

Exhibit 7A.2 Exchange Rate Changes on Dollar/Euro

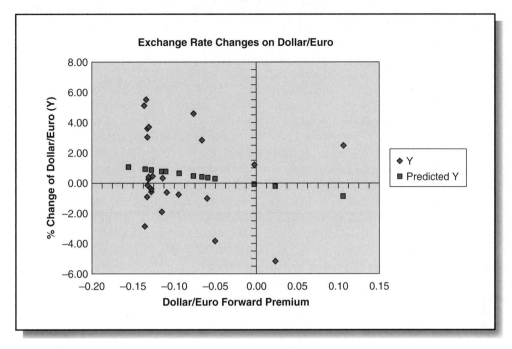

related to the size of the sample, and our sample here is very short. Even though $\hat{b}$ is far from 1, the large standard error keeps z relatively low. But at what value of z do we reject the null hypothesis?

If the sample is large, econometricians have actually figured out that the statistic z should follow a particular statistical distribution if the null hypothesis is correct. This distribution is a chi-square distribution with degrees of freedom equal to the number of restrictions tested. Exhibit 7A.2 graphs a $\chi^2(1)$ distribution: a chi-square distribution with 1 degree of freedom. Even if the null hypothesis is true, sometimes, by chance, large

Exhibit 7A.3 Chi-Square Distribution

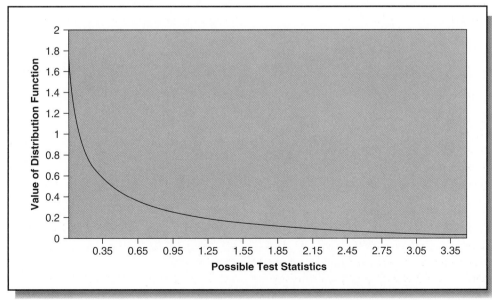

values of z might occur, but they are not very likely. The higher z is, the less likely it is that z comes from a $\chi^2(1)$distribution. For example, if z is 10, it is extremely unlikely to have come from a $\chi^2(1)$distribution. In fact, there are only 5% of the observations of a chi-square statistic with 1 degree of freedom that should be above the value 3.841. Hence, if our test statistic yields a value higher than 3.841, we would be more than 95% confident that the null hypothesis is rejected because there is more than a 95% chance that a $\chi^2(1)$ variable is lower than the z statistic. Statisticians often focus on "5% level" tests. The value 3.841 is called the critical value of the $\chi^2(1)$ distribution for a 5% test, and when z exceeds the critical value, we say that the null hypothesis is rejected at the 5% level. In the chapter itself, we primarily focus on these confidence levels. In this example, the confidence level is 0.646. We report these confidence levels in square brackets above. Consequently, we are not very confident at all that the hypothesis is rejected, given the limited data we have.

The null hypothesis must not necessarily be about just one coefficient. We can also test multiple restrictions together (for instance, $\hat{a} = 0$ and $\hat{b} = 1$), and the resulting statistic will follow a chi-square distribution with degrees of freedom equal to the number of restrictions tested.

Finally, the regression output typically also provides the R^2 statistic. This statistic measures how much of the variation of the dependent variable is explained by the regression model. Concretely, it is computed as the variance of $\hat{a} + \hat{b} \; x(t)$ divided by the variance of $y(t+1)$. The R^2 is very low in our example because the regression is predictive: We use a variable at time t to predict changes in an asset price at time $t+1$. Most of the variation in the exchange rate will be driven by news which is by definition unpredictable. In Exhibit 7A.3, the poor R^2 is obvious as the data points are often quite far away from the regression line.

Chapter 8

Purchasing Power Parity and Real Exchange Rates

*T*his chapter begins our exploration of the relationship between exchange rates and the prices of goods in different countries. We start this discussion with a theory known as **purchasing power parity (PPP)**, which is a simple model of the determination of exchange rates.[1] PPP is often used as a benchmark model when people describe what value they think an exchange rate should have or where they think an exchange rate will be in a few years or in the "long run."

Why should you study the theory of purchasing power parity? First, PPP provides a baseline forecast of future exchange rates that is usually considered whenever it is necessary to forecast future cash flows in different currencies, especially when inflation rates differ across these countries. Consequently, PPP plays a fundamental role in corporate decision making, such as the international location of manufacturing plants, and other international capital budgeting issues. Second, understanding the theory of purchasing power parity is important because deviations from PPP significantly affect the profitability of firms. For example, pricing products internationally, analyzing long-term international contracts, hedging the cash flows of an ongoing international operation, and evaluating the performance of foreign subsidiaries all require an analysis in terms of deviations from PPP. Third, PPP is particularly useful in assessing cost-of-living differences across countries. If you are going to work in a different country, and your salary is denominated in a foreign currency, you would like to know what standard of living you will experience.

As we will see when we look at the data, PPP does not hold very well in the short run. The deviations from the theory are sometimes so large that some economists dismiss the theory, at least as far as the determination of exchange rates is concerned. Nevertheless, for the world's major currencies, we will also see that PPP has some validity in the long run. It even works reasonably well over shorter horizons, whenever inflation dominates the economic environment.

Because purchasing power parity involves comparing the **purchasing power** of a money within a country to the purchasing power of that money when spent in a different country, we need to examine how to measure these purchasing powers. When economists convert from monetary magnitudes into units of purchasing power, they say they are converting from nominal units into real units. This chapter also introduces the real exchange rate. You will see that deviations from PPP can also be described as fluctuations in real exchange rates.

To understand these ideas, we first need to discuss price levels and price indexes.

---

[1] Rudiger Dornbusch (1988) provides the history of economic thought on the ideas associated with purchasing power parity. He notes that the earliest references to the subject are from sixteenth-century Spain and seventeenth-century England. Gustav Cassel (1916) is generally credited with coining the name for the theory. Kenneth Rogoff (1996) provides a survey of the voluminous economic literature on the subject.

8.1 PRICE LEVELS AND PRICE INDEXES

The General Idea of Purchasing Power

Economists usually measure the purchasing power of a country's currency in two steps:

1. First, economists calculate the monetary value, or **nominal price**, of a typical bundle of consumption goods in a country. We call this the price of the country's consumption bundle, and it represents the country's **price level**. Specifically, the price level is the weighted average of the nominal prices of the goods and services consumed in the economy. The weights of the goods and services usually represent the percentage shares of the goods and services in the consumption bundle. That is, if shoes constitute 1% of the typical consumer's budget, the price of shoes receives a weight of 0.01 in constructing the weighted average of all prices. When the price level of an economy is rising, **inflation** is occurring. Conversely, when the price level is falling, **deflation** is occurring.

2. Second, economists figure out what the purchasing power of the country's money is—that is, what a unit of currency will actually buy, given the price level in the country. To do this, they take the reciprocal, or inverse, of the price level. Taking the reciprocal of the price level gives the purchasing power of the currency. The purchasing power measures the amount of goods that can be purchased per unit of currency.

Calculating the Price Level

Rather than associate the price level with a country, for notational purposes, we associate the price level with the currency of a country. Hence, for the United States, we can write the price level as

$$P(t,\$) = \sum_{i=1}^{N} w_i P(t,i,\$)$$

where $P(t,i,\$)$ represents the dollar price of good i at time t, w_i represents the weight or consumption share of good i, and $P(t,\$)$ is the dollar price level, the weighted average of the dollar prices of the N different goods and services.

For example, the price level in the United States or Japan indicates how many dollars or yen it takes to purchase the consumption bundle of goods and services in either country. It might take something like \$15,000 to purchase the consumption bundle in the United Sates and ¥1,600,000 to purchase a similar bundle in Japan. This is why the price level is also known as the cost of living.

Calculating a Price Index

Unfortunately, governments usually do not provide information on consumer price levels. Instead of reporting data on price levels, governments usually provide information on price indexes. A **price index** is the ratio of a price level at one point in time to the price level in a designated base year. Typically, the ratio of the two price levels is multiplied by 100. That is, the dollar price index in year $t + k$ with year t as a base year is

$$PI(t + k,\$) = \left(\frac{P(t + k,\$)}{P(t,\$)}\right) \times 100 = \left(\frac{\sum_{i=1}^{N} w_i P(t + k,i,\$)}{\sum_{i=1}^{N} w_i P(t,i,\$)}\right) \times 100$$

Because price indexes are ratios of price levels at different points in time, they directly reflect the amount of inflation (that is, the percentage change in the average of all nominal

Exhibit 8.1 Price Indexes for the G7 Countries, 1960–2005

Year	United States	Canada	France	Germany	Italy	Japan	United Kingdom
1960	27.6	24.6	17.2	39.4	9.8	21.2	13.2
1965	29.4	26.8	20.5	45.1	12.4	28.4	15.6
1970	36.1	32.3	25.2	50.9	14.0	36.9	19.6
1975	49.9	45.8	38.5	67.8	24.0	63.3	36.1
1980	76.5	69.7	63.3	82.6	51.0	87.2	70.7
1985	100.0	100.0	100.0	100.0	100.0	100.0	100.0
1990	121.4	124.1	116.3	107.7	131.2	107.0	133.4
1991	126.5	131.3	120.0	110.7	139.8	110.5	141.3
1992	130.3	133.4	122.9	115.1	147.3	112.4	146.5
1993	134.2	135.6	125.5	120.0	154.4	113.8	149.1
1994	137.5	135.6	127.8	123.8	159.7	113.3	153.0
1995	141.7	139.2	129.9	126.2	168.6	113.5	158.4
1996	145.5	141.2	132.9	127.9	175.5	113.5	161.8
1997	148.7	143.5	134.2	129.9	177.7	116.0	165.9
1998	151.2	145.3	135.4	131.6	181.7	116.6	172.9
1999	154.4	147.2	135.9	132.1	184.4	116.1	175.1
2000	159.0	150.0	138.0	133.9	188.3	115.2	179.9
2001	164.2	155.0	140.8	137.3	194.0	114.3	183.4
2002	165.9	157.0	142.9	138.6	198.1	113.5	185.3
2003	169.4	161.1	145.7	139.9	203.5	113.0	190.6
2004	175.0	165.0	149.2	142.3	208.3	113.0	196.4
2005	179.4	167.8	151.8	144.9	212.0	112.4	202.1

prices) between the base year (in the denominator of the ratio) and the current year (in the numerator of the ratio). If the price index today is 115, we know that prices are 15% higher than they were in the base year, and economists say the cost of living has increased by 15% because it takes 15% more money to purchase the consumption bundle.

Exhibit 8.1 provides some information on consumer price indexes for the G7 countries—the United States, Canada, France, Germany, Italy, Japan, and the United Kingdom—from 1960 to 2005. We can use these data to understand the historical inflationary experiences in these countries.

Example 8.1 Calculating an Annual Rate of Inflation

Notice that if the base year in a price index for year t, $PI(t)$, is the same as the base index for the next year, $PI(t+1)$, the ratio of the two price indexes measures 1 plus the rate of inflation between the 2 years because the two base-year price levels will cancel each other out:

$$\frac{PI(t+1)}{PI(t)} = \frac{P(t+1)}{P(t)} = [1 + \pi(t+1)]$$

where $\pi(t+1) \equiv \dfrac{P(t+1) - P(t)}{P(t)}$.

Now let's use the data in Exhibit 8.1 to determine the rate of inflation in Italy between 1990 and 1991. The values of the Italian price indexes for 1990 and 1991 were 131.1 and 139.8, respectively. We find the percentage rate of inflation by subtracting 1 from the ratio of the price indexes and multiplying by 100:

$$\left(\frac{139.8}{131.2} - 1\right) \times 100 = 6.55\%$$

You will see later in the chapter that the high annual inflation rates in Italy during the 1970s and 1980s were associated with a significant weakening of the Italian lira relative to the currencies of lower inflation countries like Germany and the United States.

Example 8.2 Calculating the Cumulative Rate of Inflation

How do we determine the total amount of inflation between 1985 and 2005 for the United States, and how can we calculate the average annual rate of inflation during that same period? First, because 1985 is the base year, we know that 1985 = 100. Because the U.S. price index in 2005 was 179.4, we know that the average dollar prices of goods and services in 2005 were 79.4% higher than were the prices in 1985. Over the 20 years, prices increased at a compound annual rate of inflation of slightly less than 3% because

$$\left(\frac{179.4}{100}\right)^{1/20} = 1.0297$$

8.2 THE PURCHASING POWER OF A CURRENCY

Internal Purchasing Power

Now that we know how to measure a country's price level and inflation's impact on it, we can measure and discuss the purchasing power of a dollar, first internally in the United States and then externally, outside the United States. The units of the **internal purchasing power** of a dollar are the amount of goods and services that can be purchased with a dollar in the United States. That is, the amount of goods that corresponds to the purchasing power of 1 dollar is measured by taking the reciprocal of the U.S. price level. Because the units of the U.S. price level are dollars per U.S. consumption bundle, the units of purchasing power (the reciprocal of the price level) are U.S. consumption bundles per dollar. The internal purchasing power of a dollar at time t is $1/P(t,\$)$.

Example 8.3 Calculating the Purchasing Power of $1,000,000

Suppose the price level in the United States is $15,000 for the average consumption bundle. What is the purchasing power of $1,000,000?

The purchasing power of 1 dollar is (1/$15,000), so the purchasing power of $1,000,000 is

$$\frac{1}{\$15,000} \times \$1,000,000 = 66.67 \text{ consumption bundles}$$

In other words, $1,000,000 is enough to purchase 66.67 consumption bundles.

External Purchasing Power

The units of the **external purchasing power** of a dollar are the amount of goods and services outside the United States that can be purchased with a dollar, say, in the United Kingdom. Calculating the external purchasing power of a dollar in Britain therefore involves two steps. First, it is necessary to purchase some amount of pounds with the dollar. Second, it is necessary to examine the purchasing power of those pounds in Britain.

One dollar buys $1/S(t,\$/£)$ pounds if $S(t,\$/£)$ represents the spot exchange rate of dollars per pound. The purchasing power of the pound may be measured by taking the reciprocal of the price level in Britain, $1/P(t,£)$, which represents the number of consumption bundles that can be bought per pound in Britain. Therefore, the external purchasing power of the dollar in Britain is

$$\frac{1}{S(t,\$/£)} \times \frac{1}{P(t,£)}$$

We check the units on the external purchasing power calculation:

$$\frac{\text{Pounds}}{\text{Dollar}} \times \frac{\text{UK consumption bundles}}{\text{Pound}} = \frac{\text{UK consumption bundles}}{\text{Dollar}}$$

as is required by the concept of the external purchasing power of a dollar in Britain.

Now that we can calculate the purchasing power of the dollar in two countries, we can examine what happens when we equate the two.

8.3 ABSOLUTE PURCHASING POWER PARITY

The Theory of Absolute Purchasing Power Parity

One version of PPP, called **absolute purchasing power parity**, states that the exchange rate will adjust to equalize the internal and external purchasing powers of a currency. The internal purchasing power is calculated by taking the reciprocal of the price level, and the external purchasing power is calculated by first exchanging the domestic money into the foreign money in the foreign exchange market and then calculating the purchasing power of that amount of foreign money in the foreign country. Hence, the prediction of absolute PPP for the dollar–pound exchange rate is found by equating the internal purchasing power of a dollar to the external purchasing power of a dollar:

$$\frac{1}{P(t,\$)} = \frac{1}{S^{\text{PPP}}(t,\$/£)} \times \frac{1}{P(t,£)} \qquad (8.1)$$

where $S^{\text{PPP}}(t,\$/£)$ signifies the dollar–pound exchange rate that satisfies the PPP relation. By solving Equation (8.1) for $S^{\text{PPP}}(t,\$/£)$, we find

$$S^{\text{PPP}}(t,\$/£) = \frac{P(t,\$)}{P(t,£)} \qquad \text{(8.2)}$$

You should think of absolute PPP as a theory that makes a prediction about what the exchange rate should be given the price levels in two countries. Equation (8.2) predicts that the dollar–pound exchange rate should be equal to the ratio of the price level in the United States to the price level in the United Kingdom. The key here is that differences in prices across countries should be reflected in the relative price of the currencies—that is, in the exchange rate. Later, we will look at how well or poorly the theory works by comparing actual exchange rates to the predictions of PPP. First, let's explore the foundations of the theory of absolute PPP.

Goods Market Arbitrage

Suppose the internal purchasing power of the dollar is less than its external purchasing power in a foreign country. What could you do to make a profit? If the dollar buys more goods abroad than it does at home, it ought to be possible to take some amount of dollars, buy goods abroad, ship the goods to the United States, and sell them for more dollars than your original dollar expenditure.

To demonstrate this arbitrage, consider the following example.

Example 8.4   A Goods Market Arbitrage

Suppose that the U.S. price level is $15,000/consumption bundle and that the U.K. price level is £10,000/consumption bundle. Let the exchange rate be $1.4/£. Rather than compute the purchasing power of 1 dollar, consider the internal and external purchasing powers of $1 million. The internal purchasing power of $1 million in the United States is

$$\$1,000,000 \times \frac{1}{\$15,000/\text{consumption bundle}} = 66.67 \text{ consumption bundles}$$

The external purchasing power of $1 million in the United Kingdom is found in two steps. First, convert the $1 million into pounds to get

$$\$1,000,000 \times \frac{1}{\$1.4/£} = £714,286$$

Then, find the purchasing power of £714,286 in the United Kingdom:

$$£714,286 \times \frac{1}{£10,000/\text{consumption bundle}} = 71.43 \text{ consumption bundles}$$

Because the external purchasing power of the dollar in the United Kingdom is higher than the internal purchasing power of the dollar in the United States, we can profit by buying goods in the United Kingdom and shipping them to the United States for resale. If we buy goods in the United Kingdom, we can purchase 71.43 consumption bundles with our $1 million. If we sell the 71.43 consumption bundles in the United States at $15,000/consumption bundle, we will receive

$$\$1,071,450 = (71.43 \text{ consumption bundles}) \times (\$15,000/\text{consumption bundle}).$$

Thus, by buying goods at low prices and selling goods at high prices we have generated a 7.145% rate of return on our $1 million investment.

Example 8.4 demonstrates another way of looking at PPP. If absolute PPP holds, the costs of the consumption bundles in different countries are equal when expressed in a common currency. When absolute PPP does not hold, there is a potential opportunity for goods market arbitrage.

Such goods market arbitrage would, of course, be subject to somewhat larger transaction costs than the financial arbitrages we discussed in previous chapters. For example, there would be transaction costs associated with physical shipment of goods between countries. Also, if you attempted to do this type of goods market arbitrage, you would obviously have to buy a particular commodity versus a consumption bundle.

8.4 THE LAW OF ONE PRICE

The Perfect Market Ideal

If markets are competitive, we should not be able to make a profit reselling goods between countries. In fact, if there were no transaction costs, arbitrage would drive the price of any good quoted in a common currency to be the same around the world. The **law of one price** says that the price of a commodity, when denominated in a particular currency, is the same wherever in the world the good is being sold. (PPP is an extension of the law of one price. Only instead of looking at a single good and its various prices around the world, when we are looking at PPP, we are looking at the prices of a bundle of goods.)

For example, in the absence of arbitrage possibilities, the dollar price of a barrel of oil should equal the dollar price of the British pound multiplied by the pound price of a barrel of oil:

$$\frac{\$}{\text{Barrel of oil}} = \frac{\$}{£} \times \frac{£}{\text{Barrel of oil}}$$

If there were a difference between the dollar price of a barrel of oil in New York and the exchange rate of dollars per pound multiplied by the pound price of a barrel of oil in London, someone could buy oil at the low dollar price and sell oil at the high dollar price just as in Example 8.4. But, as you learned, even in the highly competitive forex markets of Chapter 3, actual markets have transaction costs.

Why Violations of the Law of One Price Occur

No good or service will literally always satisfy the law of one price. However, obvious violations of the law of one price do not necessarily represent unexploited profit opportunities. Why might the prices of goods and services deviate from the law of one price?

Tariffs and Quotas

One obvious reason for violations of the law of one price is because countries impose different tariffs on imports, taxes and/or subsidies on exports, quotas on imports and exports, and other non-tariff barriers to trade. Governments often tax international shipments of goods at their borders to generate revenue, and, more likely, to protect their industries.

For example, until the year 2003, Malaysian tariffs on imported car parts and fully assembled cars ranged from 42% to 300%. These tariffs protected the Malaysian national car companies, Proton and Produa, from foreign competition and allowed the automakers to establish as much as an 80% market share in their home market.

If we measure prices of goods in different currencies with these taxes incorporated into the prices, there will be deviations from the law of one price. For example, if there is a 100% tariff on imported cars, we should expect the domestic price of imported cars to be twice the world price, and the world price should be the exchange rate multiplied by the foreign currency price of the cars.

There are many dramatic examples of the failure of the law of one price, but two particularly striking ones involve food and the protection of domestic agricultural interests. In Japan, importing rice is severely restricted. In April 1999, the Japanese government converted from a quota system, which limited the physical amount of rice that could enter the country, to a tariff such that kilogram of imported rice cost ¥351.17. The tariff was determined by averaging wholesale prices of rice in Japan under the quota system with the average world price of rice. The world price of rice fluctuates with supply and demand, but it is often less than ¥250 per kilogram. Given the high tariff on rice imports, it is not surprising that less than 8% of Japan's domestic rice consumption is met by imports.[2] Similarly, although sugar seems quite inexpensive in the United States, the dollar price of sugar in the United States is actually substantially above the world price. In January 2007, raw, unrefined sugar sold in world markets for $0.12 per pound. However, because the U.S. Department of Agriculture limits the amount of sugar that can be imported into the United States, the domestic price remains above $0.20 per pound. U.S. consumers pay much more for sugar than the rest of the world, and, as a result, more sugar is produced in the United States than would be without the quota.

Transaction Costs That Prevent Trade

In theory, all goods and services can potentially be traded across countries, but when transaction costs in international markets are prohibitively large, goods become non-traded. The quintessential example of a non-traded good is a haircut. If the dollar price of the euro multiplied by the euro price of Italian haircuts is lower than the dollar price of haircuts in the United States, you might consider getting your hair cut by an Italian barber. But the transaction costs of doing so are simply prohibitive. The true economic cost of the Italian haircut must include the costs of the trip to Italy. Given that this cost is high, when you are at home, you get your hair cut locally, and when you are in a foreign country and need a haircut, you pay the foreign currency price of haircuts. This foreign currency price multiplied by the domestic currency price of foreign currency might be very different from the domestic currency price of your usual haircut.

Notice that a haircut is a service that is performed by an individual; it is not a commodity that can be shipped from place to place. Of course, if the law of one price for services is violated in one direction by a large enough magnitude for a sufficiently long time, suppliers of these services will migrate from one country to another. If giving haircuts provides a higher real income in the United States than it does in Italy, for example, barbers will move from Italy to the United States. But migration is a slow way to equalize wages across countries.

Thus, if wages are not equalized by international trade, we should expect some violations of the law of one price for traded retail goods because the sale of a retail good in a particular country always involves a certain amount of service. The goods must be shipped to retail outlets, and the retailer must hire someone to sell the goods. Because these services cannot be exported or imported, there can be differences in the prices of retail goods that arise purely from the fact that the purchase of the goods involves the purchase of some non-traded services.

Speculation

Another reason for deviations from the law of one price in the goods market is that it is often difficult to find a buyer for a particular good at a point in time. In addition, because it takes time to ship goods between countries, a speculative element is introduced into the goods market arbitrage transaction. You may think or expect that you will be able to sell the goods for a profit in a particular country after buying them in a different country, but only if you are able to contract with a buyer at a specified price when you initially purchase the goods will you be sure to earn an arbitrage profit. If no contractual relationship is possible, there is a potential risk that either the market price for the commodity in the country of sale or the exchange rate between the two currencies may change. In such a circumstance, you are speculating that you will make a profit, and the transaction is risky. It is no longer an arbitrage.

---

[2]The Japanese government argues that it must be self-sufficient in the country's food staple.

Noncompetitive Markets

Deviations from the law of one price also arise when goods are sold in noncompetitive markets. Under pure competition, individual buyers and sellers of goods do not influence the prices of the goods. In the absence of pure competition, though, firms may be able to effectively segment markets in different countries. This allows firms to charge different prices in different countries, a practice that is called **pricing to market**. (Chapter 9 explores some formal models of pricing to market.) Segmenting markets is especially easy if the goods are marketed through dealerships established in foreign countries. For example, when the dollar was very strong in the mid-1980s, the dollar prices of European luxury cars in the United States were much higher than the dollar values of the foreign currencies multiplied by the foreign currency prices of the cars in the countries of production. In other words, you could travel abroad, convert your dollars to a foreign currency, and purchase a foreign car much more cheaply than you could purchase the same car in the United States.

Why can't you arbitrage this situation? The problem is that automobile manufacturers in foreign countries typically only sell one car to an individual foreign buyer. The buyer then has to take receipt of the car in the foreign country. Many individuals did take advantage of this opportunity to purchase cars cheaply and simultaneously enjoyed vacations in the foreign countries.

However, given such an apparent arbitrage opportunity, ideally you would like to make some real money by purchasing more than just one car: You would like to call the BMW factory in Germany, buy enough cars to establish a dealership in the United States, ship the cars to the United States, and sell the cars for less than their current dollar prices at established BMW dealers. Unfortunately, BMW's managers will not be willing to sell you more than one car. The managers are probably happy with their current dealer network and with the profitability of their exports. If they wanted to sell more cars to Americans, they could open more dealerships or ship more cars to their existing U.S. dealers and charge lower dollar prices (versus selling cars to you in Germany so you could profit from the price difference).

Sticky Prices

The last reason that there may be observed deviations from the law of one price arises from the fact that the nominal, or money, prices of many goods are set by firms for various lengths of time. Unlike exchange rates and the prices of financial assets such as stocks and bonds, which change continuously, the nominal prices of many goods and services are not changed very often. Economists say the prices of such goods and services are "sticky."

One reason for **sticky prices** was noted by Arthur Okun (1981), who distinguished between auction goods and customer goods. Auction goods are traded on organized exchanges and are homogeneous commodities, such as wheat, soybeans, gold, and oil. Customer goods are heterogeneous products that are highly differentiated and require marketing through established customer relations. Examples of customer goods include items from refrigerators to automobiles.

Auction goods should be expected to satisfy the law of one price much more consistently than customer goods. One reason has to do with the menu costs related to customer goods. **Menu costs** refer to the costs that a firm incurs in changing its prices. The classic example is a restaurant that must print up a new menu whenever the manager wants to change prices. If inflation is low, the restaurant may leave its prices unchanged for several months or even years, replacing the menus only as they become too dirty to use. But if inflation is high, the restaurant will find it optimal to print new prices weekly or even daily. If inflation is extreme enough, the restaurant could even adjust prices hourly on a chalkboard. The frequent adjustment of prices due to inflation is costly to consumers, who have no idea from one time to the next how much a particular item will cost.

Menu costs are ubiquitous. They arise whenever the marketing of a good requires the producer or retailer of the good to provide price information to potential customers in advance of the sale of the good. Whenever a good is sufficiently complex that buyers would like to be able to do comparison shopping, retailers find it in their interests to set prices in advance and to leave their prices fixed for some period of time. Hence, changes in the exchange rate create deviations from the law of one price with regard to customer goods because firms do not continuously adjust the prices of their goods.

How Wide Is the Border?

Because of tariffs, noncompetitive markets, sticky prices, and the other sources of deviations we just discussed, the prices of comparable goods differ across cities within a country as well as across countries. Charles Engel and John Rogers (1996) examine the failure of the law of one price using U.S. and Canadian data for 23 North American cities and 14 disaggregated commodities, such as men's and boy's apparel, footwear, medical care, and other goods. Their statistical analysis indicates that a substantial amount of the variation in the relative prices of similar goods across cities is attributable to the distance between the cities. But crossing a border between countries adds as much variability to the relative prices of similar goods as does adding 2,500 miles to the distance between two cities within the same country. Clearly, borders between countries, and in particular, the change in currencies that occurs with crossing the border, matter a great deal.[3]

In the same way the deviations we just discussed affect the law of one price, they likewise affect PPP. In the following *Point–Counterpoint*, our friends Ante, Freedy, and Suttle discuss the theory of PPP and opportunities (or the lack thereof) related to the law of one price.

POINT–COUNTERPOINT
Making Money on Deviations from the Law of One Price

Ante, Freedy, and Suttle are savoring one of the first sunny days during their trip through Belgium. To their surprise, they regularly spot young, hip Belgians driving convertible Ford Escorts, which is not a particularly sensible car for such a rainy, foggy country. It looks like a real craze among the trendsetters. Ante, jolting his elbow in Freedy's ribs, points to the road and exclaims, "Wow, look, there's another convertible Ford Escort. This is really amazing. Hey, I think I have a business plan. Escorts are dirt cheap in the United States. Let's buy them there, have them made into convertibles, and sell them here to these crazed Belgians. I'm sure we can make a killing."

Freedy, still catching his breath after Ante's push, feebly responds, "Do you ever pay attention in class? Remember PPP. We would not make a profit. I bet if we convert the dollar prices and our conversion costs into euro prices using the dollar/euro exchange rate, we would probably come out at what the local dealers charge here in Belgium. Goods market arbitrage ensures that there are no abnormal profits."

Ante retorts, "PPP is a useless theory. Goods markets aren't at all like asset markets. Goods markets are totally inefficient, so exchange rates really bear no relationship to goods prices because you can't arbitrage in the goods market."

Freedy shouts back, "Oh yeah? Well, I think PPP is pretty elegant economics, and people wouldn't have talked about it for nearly 100 years if it didn't work quite well."

Ante responds, "Elegant schmelegant! What's the point of learning something that just doesn't work?!"

Suttle, somewhat mesmerized by two young women in a Ford Escort, responds slowly to the escalating argument. "Look guys, you are both right and both wrong," states Suttle. "Freedy, you're right: The PPP theory is good basic economics. But it isn't the whole story. There is some validity to Ante's point, too: Arbitrage in the goods market is a lot more costly

---

[3]In a related study, Engel and Rogers (2001) use data on U.S. consumer prices to determine why there is variability in prices of similar goods across U.S. cities. They find that variability is actually larger for traded goods than for non-traded goods and attribute this finding to greater price stickiness for non-traded goods. Distance between cities accounts for a significant amount of the variations in prices between pairs of cities, but nominal price stickiness is more important.

than arbitrage in asset markets. As for the Ford Escorts, I am not sure that Ante's proposal is a good business plan, but it might be. Ford Escorts do not have a 'bottom of the line, cheap car' image here in Europe as they do in the United States. They are considered trendy luxury cars here. I checked yesterday, and Ford is charging premium prices for these convertibles compared to the dollar price divided by the exchange rate of dollars per euro. Clearly, Ford is exploiting a difference in tastes across countries that they may even have created with Ford's advertising. But segmentation of the markets can only work to a point."

"What Ante is proposing is exactly how goods arbitrage makes PPP work in the long run," continues Suttle. "If Ford sets its Belgian price too high, someone will set up a business to exploit the price differential, which moves us closer to the law of one price because that person will have to undercut Ford's price to attract customers. Of course, as Ante admitted, setting up such a business is costly, and Ford will do everything to stop it. Ford is also limited by the competitive response of other automakers who will quickly rush similar convertibles to the market if there is too much profit."

Ante smiles and says, "See, maybe we should do it anyway! But one thing I do remember from our international finance class is that changes in exchange rates cause big changes in relative prices across countries. I guess a big move in the exchange rate while we are setting up our business could get us into serious trouble. I'm not sure I want the foreign exchange risk."

Suttle nods, "Yes, you're right about that. Changes in exchange rates can create big changes in relative prices, and people respond to such changes by shifting their consumption patterns. Managers try to find different suppliers, and they may even relocate production facilities to cheaper countries. All this takes some time. Maybe if we look at the data, we'll get an idea for how well or poorly the PPP theory works in the short run and the long run."

8.5 Describing Deviations from PPP

Overvaluations and Undervaluations of Currencies

Before we look at actual exchange rates and PPP predictions, we first need to discuss some additional terminology. A currency is said to be **overvalued** if its external purchasing power is greater than its internal purchasing power. An **undervalued** currency's external purchasing power is less than its internal purchasing power. Because purchasing power parity makes one prediction for the actual exchange rate between two currencies, if currency A is overvalued relative to currency B, currency B must be undervalued relative to currency A.

An easy way to remember which currency is overvalued and which currency is undervalued is to add the phrase "on foreign exchange markets" to the statement. For example, the dollar is "overvalued on foreign exchange markets" if the dollar's external purchasing power is greater than its internal purchasing power.[4]

Example 8.5 Overvaluation of the Dollar Implies Undervaluation of the Pound

In this example, we'll check our ability to manipulate internal and external purchasing powers by verifying that if the dollar is overvalued relative to the pound, as in Example 8.4, the pound must be undervalued relative to the dollar.

---

[4]The terms *overvalued* and *undervalued* are also employed in discussions of the relationship of a particular exchange rate to other theories of exchange rate determination. An overvalued currency must weaken on the foreign exchange markets to return to the prediction of the theory, and an undervalued currency must strengthen.

Recall that the dollar price level is \$15,000/consumption bundle, the pound price level is £10,000/consumption bundle, and the exchange rate is \$1.4/£. The statement that the dollar is overvalued relative to the pound implies that the external purchasing power of the dollar is greater than its internal purchasing power. As in Example 8.4, we calculate the external purchasing power of \$1 million in the United Kingdom as

$$\$1,000,000 \times \frac{1}{\$1.4/£} \times \frac{1}{£10,000/\text{consumption bundle}}$$
$$= 71.43 \text{ consumption bundles}$$

This is larger than the internal purchasing power of \$1 million in the United States, which is

$$\$1,000,000 \times \frac{1}{\$15,000/\text{consumption bundle}} = 66.67 \text{ consumption bundles}$$

Thus, the dollar is overvalued on the foreign exchange market. Now let's look at the pound. Is the pound over- or undervalued on the foreign exchange market? The internal purchasing power of £1,000,000 is

$$£1,000,000 \times \frac{1}{£10,000/\text{consumption bundle}} = 100 \text{ consumption bundles}$$

but the external purchasing power of the pound in the United States is

$$£1,000,000 \times \frac{\$1.4}{£} \times \frac{1}{\$15,000/\text{consumption bundle}}$$
$$= 93.33 \text{ consumption bundles}$$

Because the internal purchasing power of the pound is greater than its external purchasing power, the pound is undervalued on the foreign exchange market. Hence, the statement that the dollar is overvalued relative to the pound is equivalent to the statement that the pound is undervalued relative to the dollar.

Predictions Based on Overvaluations and Undervaluations

The logic of overvaluations and undervaluations of currencies leads to predictions of currency depreciation or appreciation. If a currency is overvalued on foreign exchange markets, it must weaken, or suffer depreciation on the foreign exchange markets if the exchange rate is to return to the prediction of PPP. This weakening, or depreciation, of the currency lowers its external purchasing power and returns the external purchasing power of the currency to its internal purchasing power. Conversely, a currency that is undervalued on foreign exchange markets must strengthen, or experience an appreciation, on foreign exchange markets if its external purchasing power is to increase to equal its internal purchasing power. Of course, currency appreciations and depreciations are not the only way that an exchange rate can return to the PPP relationship. There can be differences in the rates of inflation, which will affect PPP calculations as well.

Example 8.6 Using PPP Deviations to Predict Currency Appreciations

If the yen is undervalued relative to the euro, what prediction would you make regarding the movement of the exchange rate (in ¥/€) if you think a correction back to PPP is imminent? If the yen is undervalued (on foreign exchange markets) relative to the euro, the external purchasing power of the yen in Europe is less than the yen's internal purchasing power in Japan. This can be corrected by an appreciation, or strengthening, of the yen relative to the euro, which causes the exchange rate measured in ¥/€ to fall.

8.6 THE MACPPP STANDARD

The Big Mac as a Price Index

Shortly, we will examine data on absolute PPP using conventional consumer price indexes (CPIs). One criticism of using CPI data is that the consumption bundles of the different countries are not the same. Fortunately, *The Economist* calculates implied PPP exchange rates for a large number of countries, using a bundle of goods that is the same around the world—namely, a McDonald's Big Mac sandwich.

There are several advantages to using the Big Mac as an index of prices. First, McDonald's strives to make the sandwich the same way in all its outlets. Just as with the consumer price level, there are particular weights that McDonald's places on each item in the Big Mac, and these weights are the same across countries. Specifically, the commodity bundle is "two all-beef patties, special sauce, lettuce, cheese, pickles, and onions on a sesame seed bun." Second, McDonald's uses local suppliers for the goods entering the index, which reduces the role of international transportation costs.

Each spring since 1986, *The Economist* has had its correspondents sample the prices of Big Macs in local currencies in a large number of countries. Implied PPP exchange rates for various currencies relative to the dollar are calculated by taking the ratio of the local currency price of the Big Mac to its average dollar price in four U.S. cities.

Although the Big Mac PPP standard, called **MacPPP**, may seem somewhat foolish or silly in light of the fact that one cannot transport fresh Big Macs across countries, the deviations of actual exchange rates from the implied PPP values are actually about the same size as those that arise using more conventional consumer price indexes. Also, the degree of overvaluation or undervaluation of particular currencies has been used by *The Economist* to make a few interesting predictions that have had some accuracy, as you will see.

Comparing Prices Across Countries

Exhibit 8.2 gives MacPPP values for 2006 from *The Economist*.

Local Currency and Dollar Prices

The first column in Exhibit 8.2 shows the prices of Big Macs in the local currencies of the countries in which they are sold. For example, the average price of a Big Mac in the United States was $3.15, whereas it cost ¥250 in Japan. The second column gives the dollar price of a Big Mac in the different countries calculated as the local currency price of a Big Mac divided by the exchange rate of local currency per dollar. This is the price that an American traveling in that country might calculate. Because the yen–dollar exchange rate was ¥114.31/$, the dollar cost of a Big Mac in Japan was

$$\frac{(¥250/\text{Big Mac})}{(¥114.31/\$)} = \$2.19/\text{Big Mac}$$

The most expensive Big Mac for a person paying in U.S. dollars was in Switzerland, where it cost $4.93. The cheapest Big Mac for a dollar purchaser was in China, where it cost only $1.30.

Exhibit 8.2 MacPPP in 2006

| | | Big Mac Prices | | Exchange Rates | | % Under (−)/Over (+) |
		Local Currency	Dollars	PPP	Actual	Valuation against the Dollar
United States[*]	dollar	3.15	3.15	1.00	1.00	
Argentina	peso	4.75	1.55	1.51	3.06	−51
Australia	dollar	3.25	2.44	1.03	1.33	−22
Brazil	real	6.2	2.74	1.97	2.26	−13
Britain†	pound	1.88	3.32	1.68	1.76	5
Canada	dollar	3.52	3.01	1.12	1.17	−5
Chile	peso	1560	2.98	495.24	522.75	−5
China	yuan	10.5	1.30	3.33	8.06	−59
Czech Republic	koruna	62	2.60	19.68	23.84	−17
Denmark	krone	27.75	4.49	8.81	6.18	43
Egypt	pound	9.25	1.61	2.94	5.74	−49
Euro area‡	euro	2.91	3.51	1.08	1.21	12
Hong Kong	dollar	12	1.55	3.81	7.75	−51
Hungary	forint	560	2.71	177.78	206.96	−14
Indonesia	rupiah	14600	1.54	4634.92	9460.00	−51
Japan	yen	250	2.19	79.37	114.31	−31
Malaysia	ringgit	5.5	1.47	1.75	3.75	−53
Mexico	peso	28	2.66	8.89	10.54	−16
New Zealand	dollar	4.45	3.08	1.41	1.45	−2
Peru	sol	9.5	2.76	3.02	3.45	−12
Philippines	peso	82	1.56	26.03	52.58	−50
Poland	zloty	6.5	2.09	2.06	3.12	−34
Russia	ruble	46	1.60	14.60	28.67	−49
Singapore	dollar	3.6	2.20	1.14	1.64	−30
South Africa	rand	13.95	2.29	4.43	6.08	−27
South Korea	won	2500	2.56	793.65	977.45	−19
Sweden	krona	33	4.28	10.48	7.71	36
Switzerland	franc	6.3	4.93	2.00	1.28	56
Taiwan	dollar	75	2.35	23.81	31.95	−25
Thailand	baht	60	1.51	19.05	39.76	−52
Turkey	lire	4.1	3.07	1.30	1.34	−3
United States[*]	dollar	3.15	3.15	1.00	1.00	
Venezuela	bolivar	5900	2.26	1873.02	2615.92	−28

[*]Average of New York, Chicago, San Francisco, and Atlanta

†Exchange rate: dollars per pound.

‡Weighted average of member countries. Exchange rate: dollars per euro

Note: Data are from *The Economist*, April 2006.

The Implied PPP Exchange Rates

The third column of Exhibit 8.2 gives implied PPP exchange rates of the currency versus the dollar. This is the ratio of the local currency price of the Big Mac to the dollar price of the Big Mac in the United States, except for Britain and the euro area, in which case the implied PPP is expressed in dollars per pound and dollars per euro, respectively. The fourth column provides the actual exchange rate measured in local currency per dollar, except for the British pound and the euro, which are again expressed as dollars per pound and dollars per euro. If McDonald's priced Big Macs to always satisfy the law of one price, implied PPP exchange rates in the third column would equal the exchange rates in the fourth column. The fact that implied PPP exchange rates differ from the actual exchange rates indicates that the local currencies are either overvalued or undervalued relative to the dollar, and the fifth column presents the overvaluation or undervaluation of the local currency in percentage points.

Overvaluations and Undervaluations

The overvaluation or undervaluation of the local currency indicates the percentage appreciation or depreciation of the dollar that would be required to return the actual exchange rate to the implied PPP value. For example, the fifth column indicates that the yen is 31% undervalued because with the actual exchange rate at ¥114.31/$, a 31% depreciation of the dollar versus the yen would be required to decrease the exchange rate to the implied PPP value of ¥79.37/$. Similarly, the Swiss franc is 56% overvalued because with an actual exchange rate at CHF1.28/USD, a 56% appreciation of the U.S. dollar relative to the Swiss franc would be required to increase the exchange rate to the implied PPP value of CHF2.00/USD.

Some Predictions of Currency Appreciations

At this point, if you are getting the feeling that PPP does not work well, you are right! There are relatively large deviations of actual exchange rates from the theory. Before you decide that the theory is totally bunk, consider some predictions that *The Economist* made using its MacPPP standard.

Predicting British Heartburn

In April 1991, *The Economist* noted that the implied PPP of the Deutsche mark relative to the British pound was DEM2.58/£. However, the central parity value of the two currencies in the European Exchange Rate Mechanism (ERM) was set by the governmental authorities at DEM2.95/£ when Britain entered the ERM in October 1990. Given this difference of more than 14% between the implied PPP and the central parity exchange rate, *The Economist* noted that the pound was overvalued, and the DEM was undervalued. *The Economist* also suggested that the British Treasury would eventually get "severe heartburn" if it tried to defend the actual exchange rate rather than devalue the pound within the ERM.

The logic of the argument is as follows: As we discussed in Chapter 5, the ERM required countries to buy their currencies with foreign currencies if the currency weakened by a certain amount relative to the central parity. The maximum deviation of the pound from its central parity with the DEM was DEM2.78/£ (6% below the central parity), which is substantially above the MacPPP value. Thus, if the pound began to weaken in the ERM to correct its overvaluation, the British Treasury would be forced to buy pounds with Deutsche marks. Given the limited amount of DEM that the Bank of England had in its international reserves, the market could force a devaluation of the pound by borrowing pounds and lending DEM. Investors would expect to profit from the devaluation because the pounds they would borrow would be easy to repay with the appreciated Deutsche marks they would own. The only way this would not occur would be if pound-denominated interest rates were increased sufficiently by the Bank of England to make it unattractive to borrow pounds and attractive for investors to hold pound-denominated assets.

Indeed, in September 1992, British authorities were essentially forced to withdraw from the ERM. On September 15, 1992, the exchange rate was DEM2.7912/£. On September 16, it fell to DEM2.7500/£, and the authorities chose to abandon the ERM rather than increase pound interest rates and sell additional international reserves. After they abandoned the ERM and allowed the exchange rate to float, the pound weakened further on September 17 to DEM2.64/£, and by September 28, it stood at DEM2.51/£. Before abandoning the ERM, it is estimated that the Bank of England lost over $12 billion of international reserves trying to defend the pound. Because these are resources that could have been used to pay for British government spending, not only did the British Treasury get a bad a case of heartburn, so did British taxpayers.

Predicting Initial Weakness of the Euro

The Economist used MacPPP to predict that the euro would weaken relative to the dollar in its first year of trading after the creation of the euro in January 1999, in contrast to the prediction of many economists, who thought that the European Central Bank would want to see the euro strengthen. *The Economist*'s prediction was correct, and the euro depreciated by 13% during 1999, which caused *The Economist* to note, "Burgernomics is far from perfect, but our mouths are where our money is" (*The Economist*, April 29, 2000).

The Econometric Evidence

More formal statistical studies by economists also support the usefulness of MacPPP (see Robert Cumby, 1996; Lilian Ong, 1997; and Michael Pakko and Patricia Pollard, 1996). Cumby (1996) finds that deviations from MacPPP are temporary. After allowing for a constant deviation, he estimates that one-half of the deviation from parity disappears in 1 year. Cumby's evidence also indicates that both the exchange rate and the prices of the burgers are adjusting to eliminate the deviation. The prediction is that a 10% undervalued currency tends to appreciate over the next year by 3.5%.

8.7 EXCHANGE RATES AND ABSOLUTE PPPs USING CPI DATA

Interpreting the Charts

One disadvantage of the MacPPP analysis is its comparatively short time span because *The Economist* only started calculating MacPPP in 1986. Exhibits 8.3 through 8.9 present data for actual exchange rates and the predictions of absolute PPP calculated from consumer price indexes for several of the world's major currencies, including some historical information about European currencies before the advent of the euro. The values of these currencies are continued after 1999 using their euro values and the $/€ exchange rate. In Exhibits 8.3 through 8.9, the solid line represents the actual exchange rate, and the dashed line is the implied exchange rate from the prediction of PPP.

Exhibit 8.3   Actual USD/GBP and PPP Exchange Rates

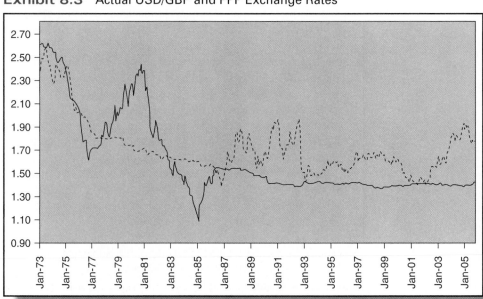

Overvaluations and Undervaluations

In examining the deviations from PPP in Exhibits 8.3 through 8.9, it is important to remember how the exchange rate is quoted. For example, the dollar–pound exchange rate is quoted directly as the amount of dollars it takes to purchase 1 pound, whereas the other exchange rates relative to the U.S. dollar are quoted indirectly as the amount of that currency that it takes to purchase 1 dollar. The PPP prediction for the dollar–pound exchange rate is therefore $P(t,\$)/P(t,£)$, whereas the PPP predictions for the other currencies relative to the dollar are the ratios of the foreign price levels to the U.S. price level. Hence, the dollar is undervalued when the actual exchange rate $S(t,\$/£)$ is above the PPP prediction, $P(t,\$)/P(t,£)$, because the dollar must strengthen relative to the pound if the undervaluation (on foreign exchange markets) is to be corrected. For the other currencies versus the dollar—say, the yen/dollar rate—the dollar is overvalued when the actual exchange rate, $S(t,¥/\$)$, is above the PPP prediction, $P(t,¥)/P(t,\$)$, because the dollar must weaken relative to the yen if the overvaluation of the dollar (on foreign exchange markets) is to be corrected by a movement in the exchange rate.

Fixing When PPP Held

The data in Exhibits 8.3 through 8.9 begin in January 1973, which is 2 months before the final collapse of the Bretton Woods fixed exchange rate system; and the data end in October 2005. Because the prices of goods are obtained as consumer price indexes rather than price levels, it is necessary to take a stand on when the actual exchange rate satisfied the PPP relationship in order for the units of the ratio of the prices to correspond to the units of the exchange rate. The data are plotted such that absolute PPP is assumed to have held in June 1973, 3 months after the collapse of the Bretton Woods fixed exchange rate system. The choice of this date is motivated by the following argument.

Economists often assert that one of the reasons for the collapse of the Bretton Woods system was that the dollar had become overvalued on foreign exchange markets. This situation arose when the governmental authorities of the countries in the Bretton Woods system prevented their dollar exchange rates from changing, but inflation in the United States was higher than inflation in other countries, particularly Germany. With constant exchange rates, a higher U.S. inflation rate eroded the internal purchasing power of the dollar more than the foreign inflation rates eroded the external purchasing powers of the dollar. Economists argued at the time that the dollar was approximately 10% overvalued. It turns out that is about how much the dollar depreciated in the 3 months between the beginning of generalized floating rates in March 1973 and June 1973, when absolute PPP is presumed to have held in the figures.

Dollar–Pound Data

How well or poorly does the theory of absolute PPP work? Clearly, there are large and persistent deviations of actual exchange rates from the predictions of PPP. For example, the data for the $/£ rate in Exhibit 8.3 indicate that the pound was 29.9% overvalued in October 1980, but by February 1985, it was 45.3% undervalued.[5]

Because the ratio of the price levels in the two countries changed only slightly over this period, almost all of the change is due to the movement of the exchange rate from $2.40/£ to $1.10/£. Once the dollar peaked in strength in 1985, though, it began to depreciate, and by August 1990, the pound was again more than 25% overvalued relative to the dollar. At the end of the sample in October 2005, the pound was 20% overvalued.

---

[5]The percentage overvaluation or undervaluation is computed as the percentage change in the exchange rate that is required if the actual exchange rate is to return to the PPP value. Consistent with the discussion in Chapter 2, these are the amounts by which the denominator currency in the exchange rate is overvalued or undervalued. For example, if the actual exchange rate is $1.50/£, and the PPP exchange rate is $1.80/£, the pound is 20% undervalued because the percentage appreciation of the pound required to go from the actual exchange rate to the PPP exchange rate is $[(\$1.80/£)/(\$1.50/£) - 1] \times 100 = 20\%$.

Exhibit 8.4 Actual DEM/USD and PPP Exchange Rates

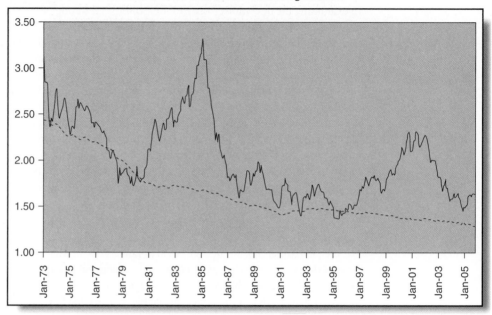

Deutsche Mark–Dollar Data

The extreme overvaluation of the dollar relative to the PPP prediction that peaks in 1985 is repeated for the exchange rates of the other European currencies relative to the dollar. For the DEM/$ rate, in Exhibit 8.4, which is continued with data from the euro, we see that in February 1985, the dollar was overvalued by 45.8% because this is the amount the dollar would have had to weaken if the actual exchange rate were to adjust to its PPP value. This is precisely what happened over the course of the next 2 years.

For the DEM/$ rate, the implied PPP value in January 1973 was DEM2.43/$, and in October 2005, it was DEM1.30/$. This is a cumulative weakening of the dollar relative to the DEM of 46.5%, or 1.9% per year.[6] This decline in the PPP exchange rate indicates that U.S. inflation was on average 1.9% per year higher than German inflation during this 33-year period. Although the actual exchange rate declined to its PPP value in 1996, the dollar strengthened substantially relative to the DEM after the creation of the euro in January 1999. In October 2000, the dollar was 41.2% overvalued relative to the prediction of PPP, and it began to weaken. By the end of the sample in October 2005, the dollar was still 20.7% overvalued.

Yen–Dollar Data

The data for the yen–dollar exchange rates in Exhibit 8.5 differ somewhat from the previous ones. First, notice that the PPP line is upward sloping from 1973 to 1977, and then it is downward sloping thereafter.

Because the PPP line corresponds to $P(t,¥)/P(t,\$)$, the positive slope indicates that Japanese inflation was higher than U.S. inflation during the first part of the sample, whereas the negative slope of the ratio of the price levels indicates that Japanese inflation was lower than U.S. inflation during the second part of the sample.

The data on the ¥/$ rate indicate that the dollar was undervalued in October 1978 by 65%, with the implied PPP rate at ¥300/$ and the actual rate at ¥182/$. By 1982, the PPP value had fallen to ¥250/$, and the exchange rate had risen to that value as well. Once the dollar peaked in strength in 1985, though, it began to depreciate relative to the yen. At the end of the sample

---

[6]To find the annualized rate of depreciation of the dollar, we solve for d in the following equation: $(\text{DEM2.43}/\$)$ $(1-d)^{33} = \text{DEM1.30}/\$$ or $d = \{[(\text{DEM1.30}/\$)/\text{DEM2.43}/\$]^{1/33} - 1\}$.

Exhibit 8.5   Actual JPY/USD and PPP Exchange Rates

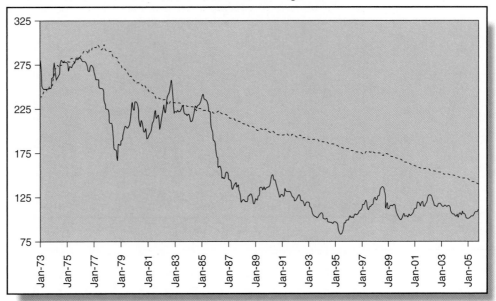

in October 2005, at a PPP value of ¥146.6/$, the dollar was undervalued relative to the yen by 26.7% because the actual exchange rate was ¥115.7/$. In other words, those converting dollars into yen for expenditures in Japan found that their purchasing power was quite a bit lower than they were used to in the United States.

Canadian Dollar–U.S. Dollar Data

Exhibit 8.6 presents data for countries that share a common border, and here PPP works slightly better. The data for the Canadian dollar versus the U.S. dollar indicate that the maximal deviation from PPP was a 34.6% overvaluation of the U.S. dollar relative to the Canadian dollar in March 2002.

Exhibit 8.6   Actual CAD/USD and PPP Exchange Rates

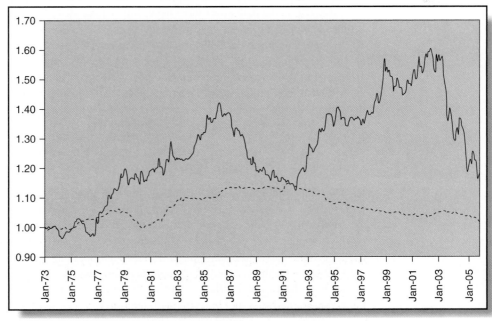

Exhibit 8.7   Actual FRF/DEM and Implied PPP Exchange Rates

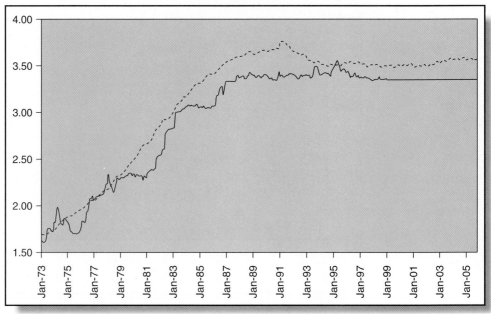

The overall flatness of the PPP line indicates that although U.S. and Canadian inflation rates were not identical period by period, they averaged essentially the same value over the sample period. Thus, the nominal weakening of the Canadian dollar during the 1990s led directly to a deviation from PPP, but by November 2007, the Canadian dollar had strengthened to CAD0.9853/USD returning the two currencies to parity.

French Franc–Deutsche Mark Data

The data for the French franc versus the Deutsche mark in Exhibit 8.7 indicate that the maximal deviation was a 14.4% undervaluation of the DEM in February 1976.

After 1982, the deviations were never larger than 10%. During the 33-year sample, the actual FRF/DEM exchange rate increased from FRF1.6/DEM to FRF3.35/DEM. This is a 109% strengthening of the DEM relative to the franc. This percentage is also essentially the amount by which the ratio of the price levels increased. Cumulatively, French inflation was 109% higher than German inflation. Notice also, from the change in the slope of the PPP line in 1990, that the French rate of inflation became slower than the German rate of inflation at that time. This phenomenon reflects the problems with inflation that afflicted the German economy because of the reunification of East and West Germany.

Italian Lira–Deutsche Mark Data

For the Italian lira relative to the Deutsche mark in Exhibit 8.8, we see very small deviations prior to 1980. Thereafter, the DEM became progressively more undervalued relative to the lira.

By April 1991, the undervaluation of the DEM was 37.6%, and it remained above 36% until September 1992, when Italy withdrew from the ERM. Subsequent movements of the exchange rate were within 26% of the PPP prediction. Although the gentle upward slope of the PPP line after the creation of the euro indicates that the Italian inflation rate was slightly higher than the German inflation rate, at the end of the period, the DEM was still 25.6% undervalued relative to its PPP value with the lira.

Exhibit 8.8 Actual ITL/DEM and PPP Exchange Rates

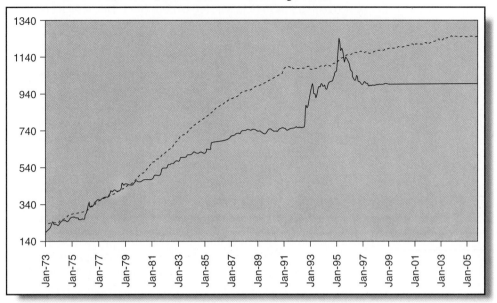

Mexican Peso–Dollar Data

All the exchange rates that have been discussed so far are for major developed countries. The last exchange rate we'll look at is the Mexican peso relative to the dollar, in Exhibit 8.9, where the exchange rates are in new pesos per dollar extrapolated into the past.

The first thing to notice about Exhibit 8.9 is the periods of long stability when Mexico pegged the peso to the dollar, as discussed in Chapter 5. The collapses of the fixed rates are also quite apparent. The second important point about this exhibit is that the vertical scale is now a logarithmic one, in which the same vertical increment measures the same multiplicative increase or percentage rate of change. We need to use this graphical technique in order to see

Exhibit 8.9 Actual MXP/USD and PPP Exchange Rates

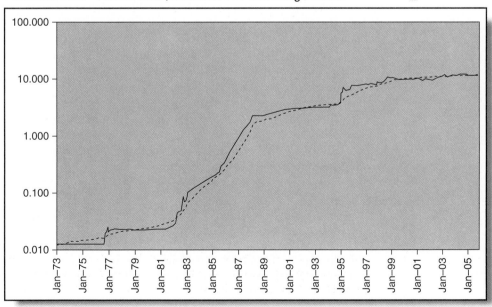

the early years of the period because the exchange rate (measured in current units) went from MPX0.0125/$ in 1973 to MPX10.67/$ in 2000. This is an increase of 853% over the 27 years, or 28.4% per year. The fact that the dollar was overvalued by only 8% relative to the peso after this enormous movement in the exchange rate is a testimony to the long-run validity of PPP. The overvaluation of the peso prior to the 1976 and 1982 devaluations is also clearly present in the data. The data indicate that the peso was overvalued by 28% in 1976 and by 26% in 1982 prior to the devaluations, whereupon it was subsequently undervalued by 17% in 1976 and 22% in 1982 after the devaluations. In 1994, the data indicate that the peso was only 5% overvalued when the market forced the devaluation. The maximum deviation of the exchange rate from the PPP calculation occurred in 1986, when the dollar was 44% stronger relative to the peso than indicated by the PPP value of the exchange rate.

8.8 EXPLAINING THE FAILURE OF ABSOLUTE PPP

Exhibit 8.3 shows that there are large, persistent deviations of actual exchange rates from the predictions of absolute PPP. Because PPP is ultimately based on the law of one price, we know that anything that causes deviations from it can also cause deviations from PPP. As we saw, the factors causing deviations from the law of one price are quite numerous. These factors include things like tariffs, quotas, and transaction costs. But there are other factors that cause deviations from absolute PPP as well.

Changes in Relative Prices

Changes in the relative prices of goods can cause deviations from PPP if price indices do not have the same weights across countries. To see this, suppose all goods are traded and assume that the prices of all goods satisfy the law of one price. But assume that tastes differ across countries so that expenditure shares on goods differ and let the price levels reflect the differences in consumption bundles. Typically, the residents of a country consume a larger share of the goods and services produced in that country than of imported goods and services. Consequently, the price indexes of each country will have a larger weight on goods produced at home and a smaller weight on imported goods. Changes in the relative prices will then lead to deviations from PPP.

A Burgers-and-Sushi World

Consider a simple example of the problem of changes in relative prices. Suppose there are only two countries, the United States and Japan, and to keep things really simple, assume that people consume only two goods, hamburgers and sushi. Let the United States produce only hamburgers, with a dollar price of $10, and let Japan produce only sushi, with a yen price of ¥5,000. Assume the exchange rate is ¥100/$. The U.S. price level will put a weight of 60% on the dollar price of hamburgers because U.S. consumers prefer hamburgers to sushi and a weight of 40% on the dollar price of sushi (the yen price of sushi divided by the yen–dollar exchange rate). Thus, the U.S. price level will be

$$P(t,\$) = 0.60 \times \$10 + 0.40 \times \frac{¥5,000}{¥100/\$} = \$26$$

Now, suppose the Japanese price level places a weight of 35% on the yen price of hamburgers (the dollar price of hamburgers multiplied by the yen–dollar exchange rate) because Japanese prefer sushi and a weight of 65% on the yen price of the sushi. Thus, the Japanese price level will be

$$P(t,¥) = 0.35 \times (¥100/\$) \times \$10 + 0.65 \times ¥5,000 = ¥3,600$$

The ratio of the price level in Japan to the price level in the United States is

$$\frac{P(t,¥)}{P(t,\$)} = \frac{¥3,600}{\$26} = ¥138.5/\$$$

Thus, even though the law of one price is satisfied in each country, the dollar appears to be 38.5% undervalued on the foreign exchange market. The problem is the difference in consumption shares. You should convince yourself that if the consumption shares were the same in both countries and if the law of one price held, then PPP would be satisfied.

It is now straightforward to understand how a change in relative prices can cause a change in the deviation between the exchange rate and measured PPP even though all goods are traded and all prices satisfy the law of one price. Suppose that there is a shift in demand away from U.S. hamburgers and toward Japanese sushi. With no changes in the supplies of the two goods, the relative price of sushi must rise both in the United States and in Japan. The increase in the relative price can be accomplished by an appreciation of the yen relative to the dollar, with no change in the dollar price of hamburgers and no change in the yen price of sushi. Suppose the yen appreciates to ¥90/$. With unchanged dollar prices of hamburgers and yen prices of sushi, the appreciation of the yen decreases the yen price of hamburgers in Japan and increases the dollar price of sushi, thereby making sushi relatively more expensive in both Japan and the United States. The U.S. price level will now be

$$P(t,\$) = 0.60 \times \$10 + 0.40 \times \frac{¥5,000}{¥90/\$} = \$28.22$$

and the Japanese price level will now be

$$P(t,¥) = 0.35 \times (¥90/\$) \times \$10 + 0.65 \times ¥5,000 = ¥3,565$$

The ratio of the price level in Japan to the price level in the United States is

$$\frac{P(t,¥)}{P(t,\$)} = \frac{¥3,565}{\$28.22} = ¥126.33/\$$$

Thus, even though the law of one price continues to be satisfied in each country, the dollar now appears to be 40.4% undervalued on the foreign exchange market because $(126.33 - 90)/90 = 0.404$. The shift in demand toward Japanese goods and away from U.S. goods causes the apparent undervaluation of the dollar to increase, but there is no opportunity for a goods market arbitrage.

Non-Traded Goods

Similar problems with absolute PPP arise when there are changes in the relative prices of traded and non-traded goods. Earlier in the chapter, we noted that when transaction costs are prohibitive, goods become non-traded. Because these goods are also included in the consumption bundles of individuals in the different countries, the prices of non-traded goods affect the price levels of the countries. Changes in the relative prices of traded and non-traded goods in two countries will cause deviations from absolute PPP that do not represent arbitrage opportunities.

Housing

Housing and other types of real estate are particularly important non-traded goods. If the price of housing in a country rises, with the price of other goods held constant, the relative price of housing rises, and the internal purchasing power of the country's money falls. Nevertheless, there need be no effect on the exchange rate. Consequently, after an increase in the relative price of housing in a country, the currency of that country will appear more overvalued (or less undervalued) on foreign exchange markets than before the increase in housing prices.

Technological Change

Why would the relative prices of non-traded goods rise compared to traded goods? Differential rates of technological change, which are also called productivity improvements, provide one answer. As the personal computer industry has aptly demonstrated over the past 25 years, improvements in technology in a competitive market force the prices of PCs to fall rapidly over time. The same is true of goods in other markets. If technology increases faster in traded goods industries than in non-traded goods industries, which is reasonable to expect if non-traded goods are services, we would expect that the relative price of non-traded goods would rise over time.[7] This effect can impart a systematic bias in PPP calculations.

PPP Deviations and the Balance of Payments

Our last explanation for deviations from absolute PPP is that they arise as equilibrium changes in the relative prices of goods across countries in a process that involves the balance of payments. The balance of payments of a country represents the aggregate amounts of goods and services that are bought and sold between the residents of a country and the rest of the world. We studied the accounting aspects of the balance of payments in Chapter 4. In Chapter 10, we will formally discuss the relationship between deviations from PPP and the balance of payments. Here, we merely note that when a currency is overvalued relative to a PPP calculation, the external purchasing power of that currency increases, which shifts the nation's expenditures from domestic to foreign goods. This weakens the competitive position of domestic firms relative to foreign firms.

8.9 COMPARING INCOMES ACROSS COUNTRIES

Before we leave the subject of absolute PPP, we want to examine one particularly important use of PPP data: comparing nominal incomes across countries. Let's consider an extended example to make things easier.

Comparing Incomes in New York and Tokyo

The Salary Offers

Suppose you are considering working in New York for Citigroup and have been offered $100,000 per year. Goldman Sachs has also offered you a job working in Japan for the next 2 years at ¥15,000,000 per year. Suppose you are indifferent between living in New York and living in Tokyo. Either sounds okay to you. The question then becomes, which job makes you better off financially—working in New York or Tokyo?

A Naïve Calculation

You might be tempted to make the decision by simply comparing the dollar value of the yen salary offer to your current dollar salary by converting the yen salary into dollars at the current exchange rate. If the current exchange rate is ¥100/$, the ¥15,000,000 is worth $150,000. If you used this approach, you would accept the job offer to work in Japan.

Incorporating Purchasing Power

By now, you should realize that this is a naïve calculation because if you must live and work in Japan, you will not consume goods by purchasing them with $150,000. You will spend your yen salary to purchase goods and services that are priced in yen, just as you are currently spending your dollar salary to buy goods and services that are priced in dollars. To do a proper comparison, you

---

[7]Bela Belassa (1964) and Paul Samuelson (1964) were the first to demonstrate that differential rates of technological change could produce systematic deviations from PPP. David Hsieh (1982) provides some empirical support for this idea, as do Matthew Canzoneri, Robert Cumby, and Behzad Diba (1999).

must determine the command over goods and services that you will have based on the purchasing powers of the nominal salaries in each country. If you knew the price level in the United States, $P(t,\$)$, you could divide your \$100,000 salary by the price level to determine its command over goods and services. Similarly, if you knew the price level in Japan, $P(t,¥)$, you could divide your ¥15,000,000 salary by the Japanese price level to determine its command over goods and services in Japan. From a financial viewpoint, you would be indifferent between working in New York and working in Japan if the purchasing powers of your two salaries were the same—that is, if

$$\frac{(\$100,000 \text{ salary})}{P(t,\$)} = \frac{(¥15,000,000 \text{ salary})}{P(t,¥)}$$

Working with the PPP Rate

What if the prices levels are not available, but the PPP exchange rate is available? Multiplying on both sides of the previous equation by the price level in Japan gives

$$(\$100,000 \text{ salary}) \times \frac{P(t,¥)}{P(t,\$)} = ¥15,000,000 \text{ salary}$$

This equation states that you would be indifferent between the two jobs if your dollar salary multiplied by the PPP exchange rate, $[P(t,¥) / P(t,\$)]$, equals your yen salary offer. Suppose the PPP exchange rate is ¥160/\$. To achieve the same purchasing power in Japan as you currently have in the United States, you need a salary of

$$(¥160/\$) \times \$100,000 = ¥16,000,000$$

But the problem is that you were only offered a salary of ¥15,000,000.

Alternatively, if you divide your yen salary offer by the PPP exchange rate of yen per dollar, you get a dollar equivalent of your yen salary. Then, when you determine your command over goods and services by mentally dividing the dollar equivalent salary by the dollar price level, the resulting units are consumption bundles in Japan. The implied dollar salary is

$$\frac{¥15,000,000}{¥160/\$} = \$93,750$$

This calculation states that the purchasing power you would have in Japan from a ¥15,000,000 salary is equivalent to the purchasing power that you would have in the United States from a \$93,750 salary. As you can see, if the PPP exchange rate were ¥160/\$, you should turn down the offer to work in Japan or demand a higher yen salary.

Given the occasional large percentage differences between actual exchange rates and implied PPP exchange rates that we saw in Exhibits 8.3 through 8.9, converting a foreign currency–denominated salary into dollars using an actual exchange rate versus a PPP exchange rate will sometimes produce quite substantively different results. The numerical example in this section demonstrates that if the dollar is undervalued relative to the foreign currency, the dollar-equivalent salary of a foreign currency offer is lower when you use the PPP exchange rate rather than the actual exchange rate.

Conversely, whenever the dollar is overvalued relative to a foreign currency, converting a foreign currency salary into dollars with the actual exchange rate will result in a smaller dollar salary than if the PPP exchange rate were used. However, although your salary in dollars will seem low, the dollar prices of goods and services purchased in the country will also seem quite low relative to comparable items in the United States. In such cases, dividing by the implied PPP exchange rate again provides a better estimate of the standard of living that you will face in the country, were you to be stationed there and paid in the foreign currency. This is particularly important if you are considering job offers in emerging market countries, whose currencies often appear to be undervalued relative to the dollar.

Comparing GDPs Using PPP Exchange Rates

Exhibit 8.10 presents a comparison of gross domestic product (GDP) per capita for the OECD countries in 2006, measured in U.S. dollars, using a three-year average of current exchange rates in the first column and PPP exchange rates in the second column. The last row indicates that the United States produced final goods and services in 2006 that were worth $44,970 per person. When the currency of a country is stronger in foreign exchange markets than its PPP exchange rate, as in the case of the Japanese yen, the dollar value of the country's GDP per capita when measured by current exchange rates is larger than when measured by PPP exchange rates. Notice that the dollar value of Japan's GDP falls from $38,410 per capita in the first column to $33,150 in the second column. The fact that the euro strengthened considerably relative to the dollar between 2004 and 2006 and was overvalued relative to PPP leads the European countries to have higher incomes measured in dollars than in PPP. Conversely,

Exhibit 8.10 GDP per Capita for OECD Countries in 2006 Using Exchange Rates and PPP Values

OECD Country	In U.S. Dollars, Based on Market Exchange Rates	In U.S. Dollars, Based on PPP Exchange Rates
Australia	35,990	34,060
Austria	39,590	35,130
Belgium	38,600	35,090
Canada	36,170	34,610
Czech Republic	12,680	21,470
Denmark	51,700	36,460
Finland	40,650	35,150
France	36,550	33,740
Germany	36,620	31,830
Greece	21,690	24,560
Hungary	10,950	18,290
Iceland	50,580	36,560
Ireland	45,580	35,900
Italy	32,020	30,550
Japan	38,410	33,150
Korea	17,690	23,800
Luxembourg	76,040	59,560
Mexico	7,870	11,410
Netherlands	42,670	37,580
New Zealand	27,250	27,220
Norway	66,530	43,820
Poland	8,190	14,830
Portugal	18,100	21,580
Spain	27,570	28,030
Sweden	43,580	35,070
Switzerland	57,230	40,930
Turkey	5,400	9,060
United Kingdom	40,180	35,580
United States	44,970	44,970

Source: Organization for Economic Cooperation and Development

when a currency is weaker in foreign exchange markets than its PPP exchange rate, as in the cases of Mexico, Korea, and Turkey, the dollar value of the country's GDP per capita when measured by current exchange rates is smaller than when measured by PPP exchange rates.

The discussion in this section about comparing incomes across countries strongly suggests that the PPP exchange rates are the appropriate ones to use when comparing standards of living across countries.

8.10 Relative Purchasing Power Parity

Section 8.8 discusses reasons why absolute PPP generally will not hold. In addition, Exhibits 8.3 through 8.9 demonstrate that currencies are often substantially undervalued and overvalued relative to the predictions of absolute PPP. Another form of PPP, called **relative purchasing power parity**, takes market imperfections into account, and it acknowledges that because of these imperfections, a consumption bundle will not necessarily have the same value from country to country. However, according to the theory of relative PPP, exchange rates adjust in response to differences in inflation rates across countries to leave the differences in purchasing power unchanged. If the percentage change in the exchange rate just offsets the differential rates of inflation, economists say that relative PPP is satisfied. To help you better understand these concepts, let's use a numerical example.

Example 8.7 The Warranted Change in the Exchange Rate

Suppose, as in Example 8.4, that the price level in the United States is initially ($15,000 / U.S. consumption bundle), the price level in the United Kingdom is initially (£10,000 / U.K. consumption bundle), and the exchange rate is $1.40/£. We determined that absolute PPP is violated. The pound is undervalued on foreign exchange markets because the implied PPP exchange rate of

$$\frac{\$15,000}{£10,000} = \$1.50/£$$

is not equal to the actual exchange rate. The pound would have to strengthen relative to the dollar by 7.14% to correct its undervaluation because

$$\frac{\$1.50/£}{\$1.40/£} = 1.0714$$

Now, suppose that during the following year, the rate of U.S. inflation is 3%, and the rate of U.K. inflation is 10%. From the definition of *inflation* we know that the new price level in the United States is 3% higher:

$$\$15,000 \times 1.03 = \$15,450$$

and the new price level in the United Kingdom is 10% higher:

$$£10,000 \times 1.10 = £11,000$$

Hence, the new implied PPP exchange rate is

$$\frac{\$15,450}{£11,000} = \$1.4045/£$$

If the pound remains 7.14% undervalued on the foreign exchange market, as it was before, the pound must weaken relative to the dollar for relative PPP to be satisfied. The new exchange rate should equal

$$S(t+1,\$/\pounds) = \frac{\$1.4045/\pounds}{1.0714} = \$1.3109/\pounds$$

The pound depreciates relative to the dollar by 6.36% because the actual exchange rate moves to $1.3109/£ from $1.40/£, and

$$\frac{\$1.3109/\pounds}{\$1.40/\pounds} = 0.9364 = 1 - 0.0636$$

Notice also that 0.9364 is the ratio of 1 plus the rate of inflation in the United Kingdom divided by 1 plus the rate of inflation in the United States because

$$\frac{1.03}{1.10} = 0.9364$$

Intuitively, the pound is losing purchasing power over goods and services due to U.K. inflation of 10% per year, and the dollar is losing purchasing power over goods and services due to U.S. inflation of 3% per year. A 6.36% depreciation of the pound relative to the dollar is therefore required to make the loss of the dollar's external purchasing power equal to the loss of its internal purchasing power.

A General Expression for Relative PPP

The example in the preceding section demonstrates that relative PPP requires that 1 plus the rate of appreciation of the pound relative to the dollar should equal 1 plus the rate of inflation in the United Kingdom divided by 1 plus the rate of inflation in the United States.

The Logic of Relative PPP

Relative PPP is derived from the following economic reasoning: Inflation lowers the purchasing power of money. If the amount of inflation in the foreign country differs from the inflation rate in the domestic country, a change in the nominal exchange rate to compensate for the differential rates of inflation is warranted so that the loss of internal purchasing power due to domestic inflation equals the loss of external purchasing power due to foreign inflation and the change in the exchange rate. If the exchange rate satisfies this warranted value, relative purchasing power is satisfied.[8]

A Symbolic Representation of Relative PPP

In general symbolic terms, if $s(t+1, \text{DC}/\text{FC})$ denotes the percentage rate of change of the domestic currency (denoted DC) per unit of foreign currency (denoted FC) from time t to $t+1$, and if $\pi(t+1, \text{DC})$ and $\pi(t+1, \text{FC})$ represent the corresponding rates of domestic and foreign inflation, respectively, then relative PPP requires that

$$1 + s\left(t+1, \frac{\text{DC}}{\text{FC}}\right) = \frac{1 + \pi(t+1, \text{DC})}{1 + \pi(t+1, \text{FC})} \tag{8.3}$$

---

[8]It was this formulation of the theory that the Swedish economist Gustav Cassel (1918) called *purchasing power parity*. Cassel was writing about the reestablishment of exchange rates after World War I because foreign exchange markets had closed during the War. Prior to the war, the countries of the world were on the gold standard, and their exchange rates were fixed. Cassel (p. 413) wrote:

> The general inflation which has taken place during the war has lowered this purchasing power in all countries, though in a different degree, and the rate of exchange should accordingly be expected to deviate from their old parities in proportion to the inflation of each country. At every moment the real parity is represented by this quotient between the purchasing power of the money in one country and the other. I propose to call this parity *"purchasing power parity."*

If we subtract 1 from each side of Equation (8.3) and place terms over a common denominator, we get

$$s\left(t+1, \frac{DC}{FC}\right) = \frac{\pi(t+1, DC) - \pi(t+1, FC)}{1 + \pi(t+1, FC)} \qquad (8.4)$$

Equation (8.4) states that the rate of appreciation of the foreign currency relative to the domestic currency is equal to the difference between the domestic rate of inflation and the foreign rate of inflation divided by one plus the foreign rate of inflation.

Because $[1 + \pi(t+1, FC)]$ is often close to one if the foreign inflation rate is low, some presentations of relative PPP ignore this term in the denominator of Equation (8.4) and state that relative PPP requires equality between the rate of appreciation of the foreign currency relative to domestic currency and the difference between the domestic and foreign inflation rates. Equation (8.4) indicates that this statement is an approximation, albeit a pretty good one if the foreign inflation rate is small.

Of course, because the graphs in Exhibit 8.3 indicate that deviations from absolute PPP change over time, relative PPP also does not hold in the data. The rate of change of the exchange rate does not equal the inflation differential between two currencies.

Relative PPP with Continuously Compounded Rates of Change (Advanced)

The discussion of relative PPP suggests ignoring the denominator of Equation (8.4) as a reasonable approximation. We encountered a similar approximation in the discussion of interest rate parity in Chapter 6. There, we noted that if we measure the forward premium on the foreign currency and the domestic and foreign interest rates in continuously compounded terms, it is an exact statement to state that interest rate parity requires equality between the forward premium on the foreign currency and the interest differential between the domestic and foreign interest rates. Analogously, if we measure the rate of appreciation of the foreign currency relative to the domestic currency and the domestic and foreign inflation rates as continuously compounded rates of change, relative PPP requires equality between the rate of appreciation of the foreign currency and the difference between the domestic and foreign rates of inflation. We demonstrate this equality by using the dollar–pound exchange rate and the respective rates of inflation.

If there are obstacles to international trade that prevent absolute PPP from holding, we can introduce a factor k such that the internal purchasing power of the money equals k times the external purchasing power of the money:

$$\frac{1}{P(t,\$)} = k \times \frac{1}{S(t,\$/£)} \times \frac{1}{P(t,£)} \qquad (8.5)$$

where $S(t,\$/£)$ now denotes the actual exchange rate and not the implied PPP value. By rearranging Equation (8.5) we have

$$\frac{S(t,\$/£) \times P(t,£)}{P(t,\$)} = k \qquad (8.6)$$

If the amount of overvaluation or undervaluation of the dollar relative to the pound is the same at time $t + 1$, we have

$$\frac{S(t+1,\$/£) \times P(t+1,£)}{P(t+1,\$)} = k \qquad (8.7)$$

Hence, the ratio of Equation (8.6) to Equation (8.7) is

$$\frac{S(t+1, \$/£)}{S(t,\$/£)} \times \frac{P(t+1, £)/P(t,£)}{P(t+1, \$)/P(t,\$)} = 1 \qquad (8.8)$$

Now, if $s(t+1,\$/\pounds)$ denotes the continuously compounded rate of change of the dollar–pound exchange rate over the time interval from t to $t+1$, then $[S(t+1,\$/\pounds)/S(t,\$/\pounds)] = \exp[s(t+1,\$/\pounds)]$. Similarly, let $\pi(t+1,\pounds)$ and $\pi(t+1,\$)$ now denote the continuously compounded rates of inflation over the time interval from t to $t + 1$ in the pound and dollar prices of goods, respectively. Then, $P(t+1,\pounds)/P(t,\pounds) = \exp[\pi(t+1,\pounds)]$, and $P(t+1,\$)/P(t,\$) = \exp[\pi(t+1,\$)]$. Substituting these exponential expressions into Equation (8.8) gives

$$\frac{\exp[s(t+1,\$/\pounds)] \times \exp[\pi(t+1,\pounds)]}{\exp[\pi(t+1,\$)]} = 1 \tag{8.9}$$

If we apply the rules for taking natural logarithms from the appendix to Chapter 2 to Equation (8.9), we find

$$s(t+1,\$/\pounds) + \pi(t+1,\pounds) - \pi(t+1,\$) = 0$$

or, rearranging terms, we find

$$s(t+1,\$/\pounds) = \pi(t+1,\$) - \pi(t+1,\pounds) \tag{8.10}$$

Equation (8.10) expresses relative PPP in its continuously compounded version. The rate of appreciation of the pound versus the dollar equals to the rate of dollar inflation minus the rate of pound inflation when all the rates of change are continuously compounded.

8.11 THE REAL EXCHANGE RATE

While discussions of purchasing power parity have been around since Swedish economist Gustav Cassel coined the term in 1918, the concept of the **real exchange rate** is much newer, as it entered the jargon of international finance in the late 1970s. Nonetheless, the real exchange rate is important because it affects domestic versus foreign prices and thereby influences the competitiveness of firms; this is explored in Chapter 9. Here, we introduce the concept of the real exchange rate.

The Definition of the Real Exchange Rate

The real exchange rate, say, of the dollar relative to the euro, will be denoted $RS(t,\$/\euro)$. It is defined to be the nominal exchange rate multiplied by the ratio of the price levels:

$$RS(t,\$/\euro) = \frac{S(t,\$/\euro) \times P(t,\euro)}{P(t,\$)} \tag{8.11}$$

Notice that the real exchange rate would be 1 if absolute PPP held because the nominal exchange rate, $S(t,\$/\euro)$, would equal the ratio of the two price levels, $P(t,\$)/P(t,\euro)$. Similarly, if absolute PPP is violated, the real exchange rate is not equal to 1. Also, the real exchange rate is constant if relative PPP holds, as we see in the next example.

Example 8.8 A Constant Real Exchange Rate

Suppose that the U.S. price level is initially $15,000/U.S. consumption bundle and the price level in Europe is initially €12,000/European consumption bundle. With the nominal exchange rate equal to $1.30/€, the real exchange rate equals

$$RS(t,\$/\euro) = \frac{\$1.30/\euro \times \euro12,000}{\$15,000} = 1.04$$

Suppose that over the next year there is 4% inflation in the United States, there is 8% inflation in Europe, and the nominal exchange rate changes so that relative PPP is satisfied. Then, as equation (8.3) indicates, the new nominal exchange rate is

$$S(t,\$/€) = \frac{\$1.30/€ \times 1.04}{1.08} = \$1.2519/€$$

The euro weakens by 3.7%. With 4% U.S. inflation, the new U.S. price level is $15,600 = $15,000 \times 1.04$, and with 8% European inflation, the new European price level is €12,960 = €12,000 \times 1.08$. The new real exchange rate is the same as it was before, because

$$RS(t+1,\$/€) = \frac{\$1.2519/€ \times €12,960}{\$15,600} = 1.04$$

Because the real exchange rate is not equal to 1 in Example 8.8, absolute PPP does not hold. But because relative PPP holds in Example 8.8, the deviations from absolute PPP are constant in percentage terms. This keeps the real exchange rate constant. If deviations from absolute PPP vary over time, relative PPP does not hold, and the real exchange rate fluctuates. Essentially, the real exchange rate describes deviations from absolute PPP, and changes in the real exchange rate represent deviations from relative PPP.

Real Appreciations and Real Depreciations

Of course, when the concept of the real exchange rate took hold, people naturally began to refer to **real appreciations** and **real depreciations** of different currencies. The concepts of real appreciations and real depreciations are useful because they help us describe real exchange risk, which we will examine in Chapter 9.

In Chapter 2, we defined the percentage rate of change in the nominal exchange rate of the dollar relative to the pound by $s(t+1,\$/£) = [S(t+1,\$/£) - S(t,\$/£)]/S(t,\$/£)$. If the percentage change in $S(t,\$/£)$ was positive, we called it a nominal appreciation of the pound. We also defined an appreciation by $a(t+1,\$/£) = s(t+1,\$/£)$, when $s(t+1,\$/£) > 0$. Similarly, we defined a nominal depreciation of the pound by $d(t+1,\$/£) = -s(t+1,\$/£)$, if $s(t+1),\$/£) < 0$. For example, if the percentage change in the dollar–pound exchange rate was -5%, we said that the pound had depreciated by 5%.

The Percentage Change in the Real Exchange Rate
We can define the percentage rate of change in the real exchange rate by

$$rs(t+1,\$/£) = \frac{RS(t+1,\$/£) - RS(t,\$/£)}{RS(t,\$/£)} \tag{8.12}$$

If the right-hand side of Equation (8.12) is positive, we have a real appreciation of the pound:

$$ra(t+1,\$/£) = rs(t+1,\$/£), \text{ if } rs(t+1,\$/£) > 0$$

and if the real exchange rate falls, we have a real depreciation of the pound:

$$rd(t+1,\$/£) = -rs(t+1,\$/£), \text{ if } rs(t+1,\$/£) < 0$$

Because the ratio of the new real exchange rate to the old real exchange rate equals 1 plus the rate of change of the real exchange rate, we have

$$[1 + rs(t+1,\$/£)] = \frac{RS(t+1,\$/£)}{RS(t,\$/£)} \tag{8.13}$$

To understand what leads to real appreciations and depreciations, we must substitute the definition of the real exchange rate from Equation (8.11) into Equation (8.13):

$$[1 + rs(t+1,\$/£)] = \frac{[S(t+1,\$/£) \times P(t+1,£)/P(t+1,\$)]}{[S(t,\$/£) \times P(t,£)/P(t,\$)]} \tag{8.14}$$

Now we group the exchange rate terms, the pound price-level terms, and the dollar price-level terms together to get the following:

$$[1 + rs(t+1,\$/£)] = \frac{[S(t+1,\$/£)/S(t,\$/£] \times [P(t+1,£)/P(t,£)]}{[P(t+1,\$)/P(t,\$)]}$$

After substituting the definitions of the ratios of variables at time $t + 1$ to those at time t, we find

$$[1 + rs(t+1,\$/£)] = \frac{[1 + s(t+1,\$/£)] \times [1 + \pi(t+1,£)]}{[1 + \pi(t+1,\$)]} \tag{8.15}$$

The left-hand side of Equation (8.15) is 1 plus the percentage rate of change of the real dollar–pound exchange rate. The right-hand side equals 1 plus the percentage rate of change of the nominal dollar–pound exchange rate multiplied by 1 plus the U.K. rate of inflation, $\pi(t+1,£)$, divided by 1 plus the U.S. rate of inflation, $\pi(t+1,\$)$.

What Leads to Real Appreciations or Depreciations

Because the real exchange rate is composed of three variables that can all move simultaneously, many combinations of changes lead to a real appreciation of the pound. The three basic movements are as follows:

1. An increase in the nominal exchange rate ($/£), holding the dollar prices and pound prices of goods constant.
2. An increase in the pound prices of goods, holding the exchange rate and the dollar prices of goods constant.
3. A decrease in the dollar prices of U.S. goods, holding the exchange rate and the pound prices of goods constant.

Because relative PPP implies that there is a constant real exchange rate, we know that $rs(t+1,\$/£) = 0$ in this case. We can therefore use this information to solve Equation (8.15) to find that the required percentage change in the nominal exchange rate that just keeps the real exchange rate constant is

$$[1 + s(t+1,\$/£)] = \frac{[1 + \pi(t+1,\$)]}{[1 + \pi(t+1,£)]} \tag{8.16}$$

Equation (8.16) provides the warranted percentage rate of change of the dollar–pound exchange rate that leaves the real exchange rate unchanged. If the nominal appreciation is larger than the amount that is warranted by the right-hand side of Equation (8.16), there is a real appreciation of the pound. Conversely, if the actual rate of appreciation of the pound relative to the dollar falls short of the warranted amount on the right-hand side of Equation (8.16), there is a real depreciation of the pound.

Example 8.9 A Variable Real Exchange Rate

When the real exchange rate was constant in Example 8.8, the annual U.S. rate of inflation was 4%, the annual European rate of inflation was 8%, and the dollar–euro exchange rate offset the inflation differential, with the euro depreciating by 3.7%. Suppose that the euro actually depreciates in nominal terms by 2% relative to the dollar during the year of these inflations. Is this nominal depreciation of the euro associated with a real depreciation of the euro or a real appreciation?

From Equation (8.16) we know that the warranted rate of depreciation of the euro relative to the dollar is 3.7% because

$$\frac{[1 + \pi(t+1,\$)]}{[1 + \pi(t+1,€)]} = \frac{1.04}{1.08} = 0.963 = 1 - 0.037$$

Because the nominal rate of depreciation of the euro relative to the dollar is only 2%, there has been a real appreciation of the euro. The new real exchange rate is now greater than it was before. With the new nominal exchange rate of

$$(\$1.30/€) \times (1 - 0.02) = \$1.2740/€$$

the new real exchange rate is

$$RS(t+1,\$/€) = \frac{\$1.2740/€ \times €12,960}{\$15,600} = 1.0584$$

The old real exchange rate was 1.04. There is a real appreciation of the euro, and there is a real depreciation of the dollar, even though the dollar appreciated relative to the euro in nominal terms. The nominal dollar value of the euro just did not fall enough when compared to the respective rates of inflation of the two currencies. Because the euro only weakened by 2% instead of the 3.7% that was warranted by the inflation differential, the euro actually strengthened in real terms.

Notice from Equation (8.15) that real appreciations and real depreciations can occur even if the nominal exchange rate does not change. If the exchange rate is fixed between two currencies, but the prices of goods measured in these currencies rise at different rates because of differences in rates of inflation, the high-inflation country will experience a real appreciation of its currency, and the low-inflation country will experience a real depreciation.

Trade-Weighted Real Exchange Rates

To this point, we have considered only bilateral real exchange rates. Many governments calculate a **trade-weighted real exchange rate**. The numerator of a trade-weighted real exchange rate contains the sum of the nominal exchange rates for different currencies multiplied by the price levels of different countries weighted by the proportion of trade conducted with that country. A trade-weighted real exchange rate makes good economic sense because a given currency rarely strengthens or weakens relative to all foreign currencies by the same amount, and real exchange rates are critical determinants of international trade. For example, if we are interested in describing the extent to which a depreciation of the domestic currency would affect a country's trade balance, we must know how much trade the country is doing with other nations and how much the depreciation is increasing the relative prices of the goods of those countries.

How Real Exchange Rates Changes Can Affect Pegged Currencies: The Case of Argentina

In Chapter 5, we noted that when Carlos Menem took office as the president of Argentina in July 1989, inflation was running at a staggering 200% per month. By August 1992, the inflation rate was 1.5% per month, and in 1999, it was 1.6% per annum. What happened to the real exchange rate after the currency board was adopted? Although the peso was pegged to the dollar on January 1, 1992, for the next 3 years, the rate of inflation in Argentina continued at a faster pace than the rate of inflation in the United States. Hence, the peso appreciated in real terms.

Exhibit 8.11 provides an illustration of the data.

Exhibit 8.11 Actual ARS/USD and PPP Exchange Rates

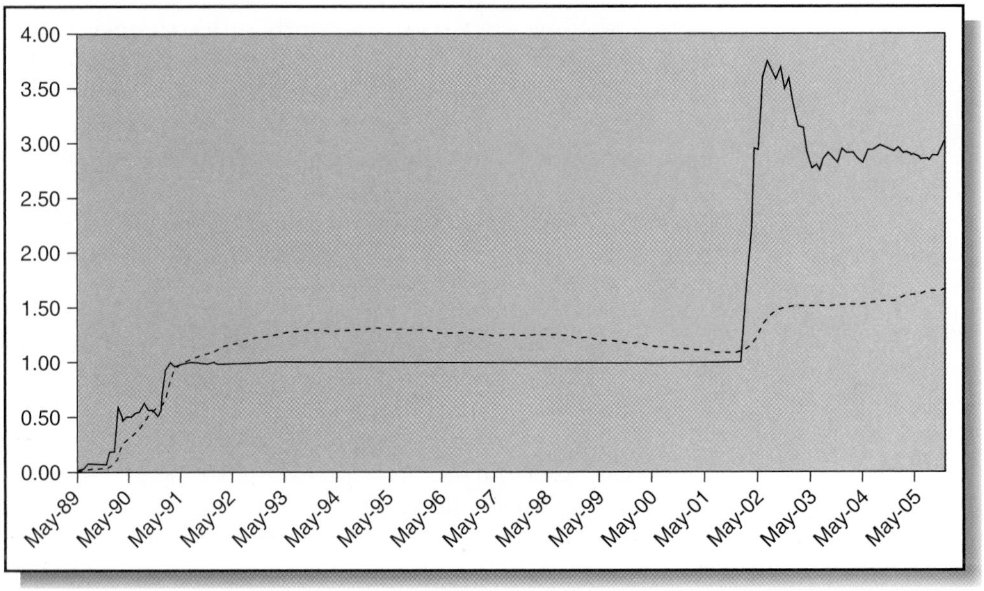

The nominal exchange rate was pegged at 1, but the ratio of Argentine peso prices of goods to U.S. dollar prices of goods peaked in 1995. Because the ratio of the price levels was 1.2 at that time, there was a 20% cumulative real appreciation of the peso. However, after 1995, the declining price ratio indicates that Argentine inflation was actually less than U.S. inflation, implying that the Argentine peso was depreciating in real terms. The currency board provided an important nominal anchor for the economy and engendered stability. Unfortunately, a real appreciation is bad for the exports of a country, as we will discuss in Chapter 9.

8.12 SUMMARY

This chapter explores the theory known as purchasing power parity and a related concept, the real exchange rate. The main points in the chapter are as follows:

1. Absolute PPP states that the nominal exchange rate adjusts to equate the internal purchasing power of a nation's currency to the external purchasing power of that currency.

2. The internal purchasing power of a currency is the amount of goods and services that a unit of the currency can buy in the country that issues that money. The consumer price level of a country measures the amount of money that is necessary to purchase a typical bundle of consumption goods in that country. The internal purchasing power of a currency is consequently the reciprocal of the price level.

3. The external purchasing power of a currency is the amount of goods and services that a unit of the money can buy in a foreign country after converting from the domestic money into the foreign money.
4. Inflation (increases in a nation's price level) lowers the purchasing power of a country's currency. In contrast, deflation (decreases in a nation's price level) increases the purchasing power of a country's currency.
5. The law of one price means that the price of a commodity denominated in a particular currency is the same wherever in the world the good is being sold. If markets are competitive and there are no transaction costs or information costs, goods market arbitrage drives the price of the good quoted in a common currency to be the same around the world.
6. Violations of the law of one price are caused by transaction costs; barriers to trade such as tariffs, quotas, and government regulations; and noncompetitive markets. When transaction costs or barriers to trade in international markets are prohibitive, goods become non-traded. For these goods, the law of one price won't hold.
7. A currency is said to be overvalued on foreign exchange markets if its external purchasing power is greater than its internal purchasing power. A currency is undervalued on foreign exchange markets if its external purchasing power is less than its internal purchasing power. Overvalued currencies must weaken to return to the prediction of PPP, whereas undervalued currencies must strengthen to return to PPP.

8. Deviations from absolute PPP are large and persistent. For the major currencies, deviations from PPP of 35% or more are not uncommon, and such discrepancies between the market exchange rate and the PPP prediction often persist for 5 or more years. In the long run, however, the deviations tend to subside and reverse sign.
9. Equilibrium changes in relative prices, especially between the prices of traded and non-traded goods, explain some of the observed deviations from absolute PPP.
10. The theory of relative purchasing power acknowledges that a consumption bundle will not necessarily be the same from country to country. However, it holds that exchange rates will adjust in response to differential inflation rates occurring in countries.
11. The real exchange rate of a domestic currency relative to a foreign currency is defined to be the nominal exchange rate (in domestic currency per unit of foreign currency) multiplied by the ratio of the price levels in the two countries:

$$RS = \frac{S(\text{DC/FC}) \times P(\text{FC})}{P(\text{DC})}$$

12. If the percentage change in the nominal exchange rate (domestic currency per unit of foreign currency) exceeds the rate of change that is warranted by differential inflation rates between two countries (that is, the differential inflation rate that satisfies relative PPP), there is a real appreciation of the foreign currency and a real depreciation of the domestic currency.

QUESTIONS

1. What does the purchasing power of a money mean? How can it be measured?
2. Suppose the government releases information that causes people to expect that the purchasing power of a money in the future will be less than they previously had expected. What will happen to the exchange rate today? Why?
3. What is the difference between a price level and a price index?
4. What do economists mean by the law of one price? Why might the law of one price be violated?
5. What is the value of the exchange rate that satisfies absolute PPP?
6. If the actual exchange rate for the euro value of the British pound is less than the exchange rate

that would satisfy absolute PPP, which of the currencies is overvalued and which is undervalued? Why?
7. What market forces prevent absolute PPP from holding in real economies? Which of these represent unexploited profit opportunities?
8. Why is it better to use a PPP exchange rate to compare incomes across countries than an actual exchange rate?
9. What is relative PPP, and why does it represent a weaker relationship between exchange rates and prices than absolute PPP?
10. What is the real exchange rate, and how are fluctuations in the real exchange rate related to deviations from absolute PPP?

11. If the nominal exchange rate between the Mexican peso and the U.S. dollar is fixed, and there is higher inflation in Mexico than in the United States, which currency experiences a real appreciation and which experiences a real depreciation? Why? What is likely to happen to the balance of trade between the two countries?

PROBLEMS

1. If the consumer price index for the United States rises from 350 at the end of a year to 365 at the end of the next year, how much inflation was there in the United States during that year?

2. As a wheat futures trader, you observe the following futures prices for the purchase and sale of wheat in 3 months: $3.00 per bushel in Chicago and ¥320 per bushel in Tokyo. Delivery on the contracts is in Chicago and Tokyo, respectively. If the 3-month forward exchange rate is ¥102/$, what is the magnitude of the transaction cost necessary to make this situation not represent an unexploited profit opportunity?

3. Suppose that the price level in Canada is CAD16,600, the price level in France is EUR20,750, and the spot exchange rate is EUR1.57/CAD.
   a. What is the internal purchasing power of the Canadian dollar?
   b. What is the internal purchasing power of the euro in France?
   c. What is the implied exchange rate of EUR/CAD that satisfies absolute PPP?
   d. Is the Canadian dollar overvalued or undervalued relative to the euro?
   e. What amount of appreciation or depreciation of the Canadian dollar would be required to return the actual exchange rate to its PPP value?

4. Suppose that the rate of inflation in Japan is 2% in 2009. If the rate of inflation in Germany is 5% during 2009, by how much would the yen strengthen relative to the euro if relative PPP is satisfied during 2009?

5. One of your colleagues at Deutsche Bank thinks that the dollar is severely undervalued relative to the yen. He has calculated that the PPP exchange rate is ¥140/$, whereas the current exchange rate is ¥105/$. Because interest rates are 3% p.a. lower in Japan than in the United States, he thinks that this is a good time to speculate by borrowing yen and lending dollars. What do you think?

6. In August 1992, the lira–dollar exchange rate was ITL1103/$, which was ITL497 below its implied PPP value. By what percentage was the dollar undervalued? Subsequently, the dollar strengthened relative to the lira and was near its PPP value at the creation of the euro in January 1999. The PPP exchange rate increased from ITL589/$ in 1973 to ITL1680/$ in 1999. What annualized inflation differential between Italy and the United States accounts for this change over the 27-year period?

7. Suppose that you are trying to decide between two job offers. One consulting firm offers you $150,000 per year to work out of its New York office. A second consulting firm wants you to work out of its London office and offers you £100,000 per year. The current exchange rate is $1.65/£. Which offer should you take, and why? Assume that the PPP exchange rate is $1.40/£ and that you are indifferent between working in the two cities if the purchasing power of your salary is the same.

8. Suppose that in 2008, the Japanese rate of inflation is 2%, and the German rate of inflation is 5%. If the euro weakens relative to the yen by 10% during 2008, what would be the magnitude of the real depreciation of the euro relative to the yen?

BIBLIOGRAPHY

Belassa, Bela, 1964, "The Purchasing Power Parity Doctrine: A Reappraisal," *Journal of Political Economy* 72, pp. 584–596.

Canzoneri, Matthew B., Robert E. Cumby, and Behzad Diba, 1999, "Relative Labor Productivity and the Real Exchange Rate in the Long Run: Evidence for a Panel of OECD Countries," *Journal of International Economics* 47, pp. 245–266.

Cassel, Gustav, 1916, "The Present Situation of the Foreign Exchanges," *Economic Journal* 26, pp. 319–323.

Cassel, Gustav, 1918, "Abnormal Deviations in International Exchanges," *Economic Journal* 28, pp. 413–415.

Cumby, Robert E., 1996, "Forecasting Exchange Rates and Relative Prices with the Hamburger Standard: Is What You Want What You Get with McParity?" National Bureau of Economic Research working paper no. 5675.

Dornbusch, Rudiger, 1988, "Purchasing Power Parity," in R. Dornbusch, ed., *Exchange Rates and Prices*, Cambridge, MA: The MIT Press.

Engel, Charles, and John Rogers, December 1996, "How Wide Is the Border?" *American Economic Review* 86, pp. 1112–1125.

Engel, Charles, and John Rogers, 2001, "Violating the Law of One Price: Should We Make a Federal Case Out of It?" *Journal of Money, Credit and Banking* 33, pp. 1–15.

Glen, Jack D., 1992, "Real Exchange Rates in the Short, Medium, and Long Run," *Journal of International Economics* 33, pp. 147–166.

Hsieh, David A., 1982, "The Determination of the Real Exchange Rate: The Productivity Approach," *Journal of International Economics* 12, pp. 355–362.

Lothian, James R., and Mark P. Taylor, 1996, "Real Exchange Rate Behavior: The Recent Float from the Perspective of the Past Two Centuries," *Journal of Political Economy* 104, pp. 488–509.

Okun, Arthur, 1981, *Prices and Quantities*, Washington, DC: Brookings Institution.

Ong, Li Lian, 1997, "Burgernomics: The Economics of the Big Mac Standard," *Journal of International Money and Finance* 16, pp. 865–878.

Pakko, Michael R., and Patricia S. Pollard, 1996, "For Here or to Go? Purchasing Power Parity and the Big Mac," *Federal Reserve Bank of St. Louis Review* 78, pp. 3–21.

Rogoff, Kenneth, 1996, "The Purchasing Power Parity Puzzle," *Journal of Economic Literature* 34, pp. 647–668.

Samuelson, Paul, 1964, "Theoretical Notes on Trade Problems," *Review of Economics and Statistics* 46, pp. 145–154.

The Economist, "Big MacCurrencies," April 1991, April 2000, April 2006.

9

Measuring and Managing Real Exchange Risk

*I*n 1997, Garuda Indonesia, an Indonesian airline company, got hit by exchange rate "lightning." The currency crisis that swept Southeast Asia caused a severe devaluation of the Indonesian rupiah. Because Garuda had incurred dollar-based costs for its fuel and borrowed in dollars to finance its planes, the devaluation caused a severe cost shock. Following the devaluation, the income the company collected in rupiah from its flights became minuscule compared to what it owed its creditors, as stable dollar costs exploded when measured in rupiah. But the bad news didn't stop there. As a recession began to plague the Indonesian economy, Garuda saw its revenues drop precipitously as fewer tickets were purchased. The fall in demand for Indonesian air travel meant that Garuda would be unable to increase its fares to attempt to recover its profitability. Because the 1997 devaluation of the Indonesian rupiah was not immediately accompanied by offsetting changes in the prices of goods, the devaluation caused a deviation from purchasing power parity (PPP) and led to a real depreciation of the rupiah.

This chapter investigates how managers respond to fluctuations in real exchange rates and develops the concept of real exchange risk. We first demonstrate how the real exchange rate arises naturally in understanding the profitability of exporters and importers. Then we examine how to share real exchange risk in a long-term contract. Whenever firms from different countries that do not share a common currency enter into a long-term contract, real exchange risk must be allocated in some way. The next set of issues involves pricing-to-market. We examine why firms violate the law of one price when selling in the domestic and foreign markets, and we explore how firms' prices respond optimally to fluctuations in real exchange rates. You should come away with an understanding of why prices of imported goods don't fluctuate as much as the exchange rate. Another issue covered here is evaluating the performance of foreign subsidiaries. Fluctuations in real exchange rates make foreign subsidiaries more or less profitable. How can you design a compensation system for foreign subsidiaries that rewards good management and not just luck due to favorable movements in real exchange rates? The chapter ends with some general advice for how managers can respond to changes in real exchange rates.

9.1 HOW REAL EXCHANGE RATES AFFECT REAL PROFITABILITY

The easiest way to understand how changes in the real exchange rate affect a firm's profitability is to consider the real profitability of a firm. **Real profitability** refers to the purchasing power of a firm's nominal profits. It is obtained by dividing the firm's nominal profits by the price level. A firm's shareholders care only about the firm's real profits, not its nominal profits, because ultimately they care only about how much they can consume—not how much money they have.

The Real Profitability of an Exporting Firm

Consider the real profitability of Apples Galore, a U.S. exporter that sells apples in both the United States and Britain. Suppose that Apples Galore produces apples in the United States and incurs only dollar costs. Let's begin by calculating its nominal profit.

Calculating a Firm's Nominal Profit

The nominal profit that Apples Galore earns is the sum of its domestic sales and foreign sales minus its nominal costs:

$$\text{Firm's Nominal Profit} = \text{Dollar revenue from firm's U.S. sales}$$
$$+ \text{Dollar revenue from firm's UK sales} - \text{Firm's dollar costs}$$

Apples Galore's dollar revenue from its U.S. sales is its dollar price of apples, $P(A,\$)$, multiplied by the quantity of apples the firm sold, $Q(A,\text{U.S.})$:

$$\text{Dollar revenue from firm's U.S. sales} = P(A,\$) \times Q(A,\text{U.S.})$$

The dollar revenue from Apples Galore's UK sales is the nominal exchange rate of dollars per pound multiplied by the price per pound the apples were sold for, $P(A, £)$, multiplied by the quantity of apples the firm sold in the United Kingdom, $Q(A,\text{UK})$:

$$\text{Dollar revenue from UK sales} = S(\$/£) \times P(A,£) \times Q(A,\text{UK})$$

Apples Galore's dollar cost of production is the firm's average dollar cost per apple, $C(A,\$)$, multiplied by the total quantity of apples it sold in both the U.S. market and the British market:

$$\text{Dollar cost of production} = C(A,\$) \times [Q(A,\text{U.S.}) + Q(A,\text{UK})]$$

Relative Prices and Components of Real Profit

Now we can find Apples Galore's real profits by dividing its nominal profit by the price level in the United States, $P(\$)$. We'll consider U.S. revenue, U.S. costs, and UK revenue, in that order. The first term is

$$\text{Real revenue from U.S. sales} = \frac{P(A,\$) \times Q(A,\text{U.S.})}{P(\$)} = \frac{P(A,\$)}{P(\$)} \times Q(A,\text{U.S.})$$

On the right-hand side is the **relative price** of apples in the United States multiplied by the quantity of apples sold. The relative price affects the **demand curve** for apples and determines, along with other variables like people's income, how many apples will be sold. We can think of Apples Galore as setting its relative price to determine how much it will be able to sell. To keep the relative price of apples constant, the firm must ensure that the nominal price of the apples increases at the U.S. rate of inflation.

Next, consider Apples Galore's real costs. By dividing the firm's dollar cost of production by the price level in the United States, we get the real value of its nominal costs:

$$\text{Real costs} = \frac{C(A,\$)}{P(\$)} \times [Q(A,\text{U.S.}) + Q(A,\text{UK})]$$

The firm's total real costs amount to the average real cost per apple, $[C(A,\$)/P(\$)]$, multiplied by the amount of apples it produced and sold in both countries. If its nominal average cost per unit increases at the U.S. rate of inflation, its real average costs are constant, and the Apples Galore's total real costs are the same when the same amount is produced.

A Firm's Real Export Revenue

Now consider Apples Galore's real export revenue. The real value of the exporter's sales is found by dividing its nominal export revenue by the price level in the United States:

$$\text{real revenue from UK sales} = \frac{S(\$/£) \times (P(A,£) \times Q(A,\text{UK}))}{P(\$)}$$

If we multiply and divide the right-hand side of the firm's real revenue from its UK sales by the UK price level, $P(£)$, and we rearrange terms, we have

$$\text{real revenue from UK sales} = \frac{S(\$/£) \times P(£)}{P(\$)} \times \frac{P(A,£)}{P(£)} \times Q(A,\text{UK})$$

Apples Galore's real revenue from the UK involves three terms. The first is the real exchange rate, $[S(\$/£) \times P(£)/P(\$)]$; the second is the relative price of apples in the United Kingdom, $[P(A,£)/P(£)]$; and the third is the quantity of apples the firm sold in the United Kingdom, $Q(A,\text{UK})$. Each of these terms is a real concept.

In order to sell the same amount of apples in the United Kingdom, if everything else in the UK demand curve is the same as before, Apples Galore must keep its relative price constant. This would require the firm to increase its pound-denominated price of apples by the same percent as the UK rate of inflation. If the firm does this and the same amount is sold, and if the real exchange rate is constant, the same real revenue will occur. Clearly, an increase in the real exchange rate, which is a real appreciation of the pound, increases the real revenue the company earns from the United Kingdom and allows the firm to become more competitive in the United Kingdom because it can lower its relative price of apples.

How the managers of the firm choose to respond with their relative prices to changes in the real exchange rate is known as **exchange rate pass-through**. We will study more about pricing in the face of real exchange rate changes in Section 9.4. Now, though, let's consider the nature of risk that a firm faces from real exchange rate changes.

9.2 REAL EXCHANGE RISK AND THE PROFITABILITY OF DOMESTIC AND FOREIGN FIRMS

The phenomenon whereby the profitability of a firm can change because of fluctuations in the real exchange rate is called **real exchange risk** (or **operating exposure** or **economic exposure**). Although the example in the previous section focuses on an exporting firm, firms that sell products domestically but that have imported costs can also experience real exchange risk. Why is this so?

The value of a firm is represented by the present value of its expected future profitability. If there are changes in exchange rates that affect a firm's cash flows, either through changes in the demand for its products or through changes in the costs of its inputs, the firm faces a real exchange risk. Before we examine discounted profitability, let's examine how changes in real exchange rates cause changes in a firm's profitability.

In general, a real depreciation of the domestic currency hurts importing firms and helps exporting firms. A firm can even have an exposure to real exchange rates without having direct exposure to foreign currency cash flows because, for example, a real appreciation of the domestic currency hurts domestic import–competing firms who must then compete against less expensive imports. Because many firms have important imported parts and materials, real exchange rate changes can also affect the cost structure of a firm. Exactly how a firm is affected depends on the firm's type of business—that is, it depends on whether it is a net exporter of goods, a net importer of goods, or an import competitor. It also depends on the firm's competitive situation, by which we mean the degree of monopoly power that the firm commands for its products.

The Real Exchange Rate Risk of a Net Exporter

Let's look at a **net exporter** of goods. Suppose an exporting firm faces a nominal depreciation of the foreign currency. If the firm does nothing, the depreciation of the foreign currency will lower the nominal value of the revenue it earns from its exports receipts. The firm can avoid this fall in profitability by increasing the foreign currency price of its product, but its ability to do so will be limited by the competitive situation of the firm. Because the foreign demand for the firm's product depends on the product's relative price in the foreign country, we know that the firm will sell less of its product if it raises the price in the foreign country by more than the foreign rate of inflation. However, if the magnitude of the depreciation of the foreign currency *just equals* foreign inflation minus domestic inflation (that is, if relative PPP holds), then increasing the nominal foreign price of the product in the foreign market by the same amount as at the foreign rate of inflation will cause the domestic currency value of the firm's foreign revenue to increase at the domestic rate of inflation. Thus, the firm's real revenue from exporting would not be affected.

Example 9.1 A Greek Cell Phone Exporter

Olympia Communication Exporters (OCE) manufactures cellular phones in Greece and sells them in the United States. Today's dollar price of an OCE phone is $79.00, and the company is selling 2,000,000 phones per year. The current exchange rate is $1.25/€. Hence, OCE's euro revenue this year is

$$\frac{\$79.00}{\text{phone}} \times (2{,}000{,}000 \text{ phones}) \times \frac{1}{\$1.25/€} = €126{,}400{,}000$$

Economists are forecasting 5.5% inflation for the United States and 1% inflation for Europe. They also expect the dollar to weaken to

$$\frac{\$1.3057}{€} = \frac{\$1.25}{€} \times \frac{1.055}{1.01}$$

and the change just offsets the inflation differential and leaves the real exchange rate unchanged. If the demand curve is constant in the United States, what dollar price should OCE charge if it wants to earn the same real revenue and sell the same quantity of phones in the United States?

The answer is that the price of a phone should increase by 5.5%, to

$$(\$83.35/\text{phone}) = (\$79.00/\text{phone}) \times (1.055)$$

in which case the nominal revenue will increase to

$$\frac{\$83.35}{\text{phone}} \times 2{,}000{,}000 \text{ phones} \times \frac{1}{\$1.3057/€} = €127{,}670{,}981$$

Notice that €127,670,981 is 1% higher than €126,400,000. An increase of 1% in nominal revenue is required to keep the firm's real revenue constant.

A Competitive Dilemma

Any increase in the dollar–euro exchange rate above $1.3057/€, the value that kept the real exchange rate constant in Example 9.1, creates a dilemma for Olympia Communication Exporters. If the firm does not increase the price of its phones above $83.35 each, the euro value of the company's revenue will decrease. However, if the company increases the price of its phones above the U.S. rate of inflation, the firm will sell fewer phones. Either way, though, a real depreciation of the dollar hurts OCE's real profitability.

The choice that OCE should make in terms of raising its relative price depends on its competitive situation. We know that OCE will be less profitable after a real depreciation of the dollar, but we don't know by how much. A major factor determining the response of the firm is the elasticity of the product's demand curve. Elasticity measures the percentage change in the quantity of the product demanded when the percentage relative price of the product changes. The more *inelastic* a product's demand curve, the less the quantity of it sold falls when its price rises. In other words, the drop-off in sales will be relatively little. In contrast, the more *elastic* a product's demand curve, the more the quantity sold will fall when the product's price rises. In other words, the more elastic the demand curve, the more likely it is that consumers will switch products or not buy the product at all when the relative price increases. In addition, the more competitive the market is for a product, the more elastic is the product's demand curve.

Because cellular phones are manufactured by many different companies around the world, the market is quite competitive. Hence, it is unlikely that OCE would have much market power to raise its relative price without suffering a large fall in its sales. Thus, it is likely that OCE would not increase its price very much above what is warranted by U.S. inflation. However, if the OCE phone has some unique features that make the demand for its phone more inelastic (that is, less responsive to price changes), the company will not lose as much profitability because it can pass through more of the change in the exchange rate to the product's price.

The Real Exchange Risk of a Net Importer

The next example demonstrates how the real profits of a **net importer**—that is, a firm with more imported inputs than exports—are affected by a change in the real exchange rate.

Example 9.2 A Malaysian Airline Company

Trans-Malaysian Airlines (TMA) flies mostly domestic routes within Malaysia. It imports its fuel from a Singaporean oil company that charges $3.50/gallon. Last year, TMA imported 250,000,000 gallons of fuel, and the Malaysian ringgit–U.S. dollar exchange rate was MYR4/USD. Thus, TMA's annual nominal costs for fuel were

$$\frac{\$3.50}{\text{gallon}} \times 250{,}000{,}000 \text{ gallons} \times \frac{\text{MYR4}}{\text{USD}} = \text{MYR3.5 billion}$$

Last year, TMA's nominal revenues minus its other MYR-denominated costs were MYR4.0 billion. Then, last year's profit was

$$\text{MYR4.0 billion} - \text{MYR3.5 billion} = \text{MYR0.5 billion}$$

Suppose TMA is regulated and cannot increase its MYR ticket price by more than the Malaysian rate of inflation, which is 15% this year. If holding the relative price constant results in the same demand for its flights, then TMA will have the same number of passengers this year, and its revenue will increase by 15%. Suppose that its other MYR-denominated costs also increase by 15%. However, suppose the dollar price of fuel increases by the U.S. rate of inflation, which is 4%. By how much will real profits fall if there is a 10% real appreciation of the dollar relative to the ringgit?

One way to proceed is to calculate the new nominal MYR/USD exchange rate implied by the 10% real appreciation of the dollar. Because Malaysian inflation (15%) is higher than U.S. inflation (4%), we know that the dollar should appreciate in nominal terms even if there is no real dollar appreciation. One plus the warranted rate of nominal dollar appreciation due strictly to the inflation differential is (1.15 / 1.04). The new nominal exchange rate must be 10% higher than this to induce a 10% real appreciation of the USD, so the new nominal exchange rate will be

$$\frac{\text{MYR4}}{\text{USD}} \times \frac{1.15}{1.04} \times 1.10 = \frac{\text{MYR4.8654}}{\text{USD}}$$

The new price of fuel is \$3.50/gallon $\times$ 1.04 = \$3.64/gallon. Because the same number of gallons will be required as there is no change in the demand for flights, the new fuel costs will be

$$\frac{\$3.64}{\text{gallon}} \times 250{,}000{,}000 \text{ gallons} \times \frac{\text{MYR4.8654}}{\text{USD}} = \text{MYR4.428 billion}$$

TMA's revenues and its other costs, which are both MYR denominated, are now 15% higher, due to inflation in Malaysia. Because revenues net of other costs were MYR4.0 billion last year, this year they will be MYR4.0 billion $\times$ 1.15 = MYR4.6 billion. Hence, nominal profits will be

$$\text{MYR4.6 billion} - \text{MYR4.428 billion} = \text{MYR0.172 billion}$$

Recall that TMA's nominal revenues last year were MYR0.5 billion. As you can see, instead of nominal profits increasing by 15% as they would have without the real depreciation of the ringgit, nominal profits have actually fallen by 65.6% because $0.656 = [(0.5 - 0.172)/0.5]$. Notice also that real profits have fallen by 70.1% because $0.701 = [(0.5 - (0.172/1.15))/0.5]$.

A real appreciation of the dollar clearly has a severe effect on the real profitability of Trans-Malaysian Airlines because it increases TMA's costs, and the regulation prevents the company from passing any of its increased costs due to a change in the exchange rate on to its customers in the form of higher prices.

Of course, an increase in the relative price of tickets decreases the demand for air travel. If TMA could increase its relative price, it would have to decide how much of the real appreciation of the dollar it could pass through to its customers in the form of higher prices. The answer depends on the elasticity of TMA's demand curve. The less competitive the market, the more inelastic the demand curve (that is, the less responsive consumers are to increased fares) and the more TMA's increased costs could be passed on to customers in the form of higher ticket prices.

The Real Exchange Risk of an Import Competitor

The firms we have described so far all engage in operational transactions that require the exchange of foreign currency. Each firm therefore directly experiences a change in profitability with a change in the real exchange rate. It may seem surprising to you, however, that a firm can have an exposure to real exchange risk even though the company has no explicit cash flows denominated in foreign currency. Consider the following example of an **import competitor**.

Example 9.3 Miami Beach Restaurants

Restaurants in Miami Beach, Florida, accept only dollars from their customers. They buy all their food from suppliers who accept only dollars, and they pay their employees in dollars. Consequently, the restaurants have no explicit foreign currency cash flows and no foreign currency–denominated assets and liabilities. Nevertheless, the Miami Beach restaurants experience fluctuations in their profitability because the demand from their patrons depends on the value of the dollar on the foreign exchange markets.

For example, when the dollar is weak and European currencies are strong, more European tourists enjoy vacations in Miami Beach because U.S. vacations are relatively inexpensive from the European perspective. Likewise, when the dollar is weak on foreign currency markets, more U.S. residents demand vacations in Miami Beach because European trips are relatively more expensive for them. Hence, demand for the restaurants' services is high when the dollar is weak. In contrast, when the dollar is strong, Americans view European vacations as relative bargains, and Europeans view trips to the United States as relatively expensive. As a result, relatively fewer Europeans travel to Miami Beach for vacations and eat in Miami restaurants. As you can see, changes in the real exchange rate can alter the demand for products that are neither exported nor imported, such as restaurant meals.

Measuring Real Exchange Risk Exposure

Most nominal exchange rate changes are large relative to the associated changes in the price levels of countries. Hence, most changes in the nominal exchange rate are highly correlated with changes in the real exchange rate, especially in the short run. Most large changes in the nominal exchange rate are therefore associated with changes in relative prices, and most nominal exchange rate changes generate a fair amount of real operating exposure. Real exchange risk means that a firm's operating cash flows are affected by a change in the real exchange rate. Not only does this directly affect the firm's current profitability, it also affects its future profitability. Thus, our definition of real exchange rate exposure must include future periods as well as the current period.

The Present Value of a Firm's Profits

Let $CF(t+j)$ represent the expected value at time t of after-tax profits for period $t+j$, and let r represent the appropriate discount rate. Then, the present value of the firm's future after-tax profits at time t is

$$V(t) = \sum_{j=1}^{\infty} \frac{CF(t+j)}{(1+r)^j}$$

The real exchange risk of this firm is the change in $V(t)$ with an unexpected change in $RS(t)$.

We focus on the unanticipated change in the real exchange rate because the effects of any anticipated change would already be incorporated into the market value of the firm. By considering the present value of the firm's profits, we recognize that changes in the exchange rate are quite persistent and thus will have persistent effects into the future. A real strengthening of the domestic currency is bad for a net exporter in the current period. Moreover, because changes are so persistent, the next period's profits are also likely to be low because the domestic currency is expected to continue to be strong. The next example works through a case in which the change in the real exchange rate is expected to persist indefinitely.

Example 9.4 A French Cheese Exporter

Fromagerie du Provence exports sheep's milk cheese to the United States. Last year, Fromagerie du Provence sold 1.5 million kilos of cheese at $10 per kilo, for total revenue of $15 million. The company had dollar costs of $1 million associated with its U.S. distribution network, which left it with $14 million in net revenue earned from its U.S. exports. Because the current exchange rate was $0.85/€, Fromagerie du Provence's net export revenue in euros (that is, the euro value of the dollar revenue minus the company's dollar costs) was equal to

$$\$14,000,000/(\$0.85/€) = €16,470,588$$

The company's euro-denominated costs of production in France were €13.5 million, and it has no sales outside the United States. Hence, its euro-denominated profits were

$$€16,470,588 - €13,500,000 = €2,970,588$$

Suppose financial analysts forecast a constant real exchange rate and recognize that if the company maintains a constant relative price in the United States, it will sell the same amount of cheese every year. Suppose nominal costs in the United States and France are also expected to rise at the respective rates of inflation, in which case real costs are constant.

In this situation, the purchasing power of real net revenue in today's dollars will be $14 million every year in the future. With a constant real exchange rate, the real euro profits will be €2,970,588. If the real discount rate is 8%, the real value of the firm in terms of its future profits will be the following infinite sum:[1]

$$\frac{€2,970,588}{1.08} + \frac{€2,970,588}{1.08^2} + \cdots = \frac{€2,970,588}{.08} = €37,132,350$$

Suppose analysts also think that if the real dollar–euro exchange rate changes, the change will be permanent. In this situation, we can consider how a 1% appreciation of the euro would affect the value of the firm. First, the new nominal exchange rate would increase to $(0.85/€) \times 1.01 = \$0.8585/€$. We can consider this to be a real appreciation of the euro as well because prices are being held constant as the company does not respond to real appreciations. If Fromagerie du Provence does not adjust the price of its product, the appreciation of the euro would lower the company's net revenue by 1%, to

$$\$14,000,000/(\$0.8585/€) = €16,307,513$$

---

[1]This particular infinite sum is a perpetuity, which is straightforward to evaluate. The appendix to Chapter 15 describes how the perpetuity formula is derived.

and its euro profits would fall to

$$€16,307,513 - €13,500,000 = €2,807,513$$

which is a fall of 5.5%.

An unanticipated 1% real appreciation of the euro that was expected to be permanent would therefore lower all future net revenues to €2,807,513. Thus, the value of the firm would fall to (€2,807,513/0.08) = €35,093,913, or by 5.5%.

Notice that the real exposure of Fromagerie du Provence arises from its large net dollar revenues and the assumed permanence of the exchange rate change, which creates the large exposure. Extrapolating from our 1% change, we see that a 10% real depreciation of the dollar, which is not an extreme event, would cause the value of the firm to fall by 55%. Of course, this example treats the change in the real exchange rate as permanent. This assumption conflicts with the empirical evidence presented in Chapter 8, which shows that although changes in real exchange rates are highly persistent, they appear to reverse themselves slowly over time. Thus, the actual exposure would be less than what is calculated here.

Who Doesn't Have Real Exchange Risk?

Given the broadness of the definition of real foreign exchange risk, it is quite unlikely that a firm would not have any real operating exposure. What would be required for this to be the case? If a firm is not to be exposed to the effects of changes in real exchange rates, its future revenues and its future costs must be isolated from the effects of foreign currency fluctuations.

Conceptually, there is only one way that such a situation could occur in an environment in which real exchange rates fluctuate: The firm must be completely domestic. It must be something like the corner barbershop. But even in this case, large changes in real exchange rates will have an effect on the entire wage structure of the economy and hence on the wages a barber can command. Barbers are also mobile across countries, and people respond eventually to differential living standards by migrating between countries. Therefore, although the corner barbershop may not have much short-run exposure to real foreign exchange risk, it may have a relatively large exposure to prolonged real appreciations and depreciations of the domestic currency.

POINT–COUNTERPOINT

On Producing BMWs in the United States

It is December, and Ante, Freedy, and Suttle are driving through South Carolina on their way to Florida for a quick vacation when Ante spots the BMW plant in Spartanburg. Ante blurts out, "Why on earth would a high-quality German company like BMW want to sully their reputation by producing cars in South Carolina? They must have gotten some enormous tax breaks to induce them to locate there."

Freedy steadies the steering wheel and replies, "What do you mean? American workers are every bit as good as German workers. They're cheaper, too, at current exchange rates. From the German perspective, German workers cost over €30 per hour while Americans work for €24.50. Obviously, BMW saw a cost advantage. BMW is also very zealous about its quality. It wouldn't build a facility if it wasn't sure that it could produce high-quality cars."

Ante can hardly control himself as he shouts, "That cost advantage will quickly evaporate if the dollar strengthens versus the euro."

Suttle, who had been sleeping in the backseat, says, "Guys, must you always fight about international finance? There are elements of truth in what both of you are saying. It is true that BMW looks at the costs of workers when making a plant location decision. It also tries to get as many tax breaks from the local authorities as possible. After all, it has invested over $1.7 billion in the South Carolina plant during the past 10 years and is providing thousands of jobs directly, not to mention the jobs of parts suppliers. But Ante is certainly right that an appreciation of the dollar versus the euro would raise the perceived euro-denominated cost to BMW of producing products in the United States because the workers there are unlikely to take a pay cut just because the dollar strengthens. Nevertheless, you're both missing a major point."

Suttle continues, "One of the main reasons BMW built the Spartanburg plant is foreign exchange risk. If BMW builds a car in Germany and exports it to the United States, BMW has euro costs and dollar revenues. A weakening of the dollar creates a big loss of profit if BMW cannot increase the dollar price of the car to offset the depreciation of the dollar. The potential loss is huge because the entire dollar revenue of the car is exposed to shifts in the exchange rate. On the other hand, if BMW builds a car in the United States and sells it there, BMW incurs dollar costs and dollar revenues. A depreciation of the dollar still creates a loss of value when the profits are converted into euros, and there is still pressure to increase the dollar price of the car to offset dollar depreciation, but the real exchange rate exposure is only on BMW's profit, its dollar revenues minus its dollar costs."

Suttle finishes by saying, "Ante, you're also right that BMW took a big risk that the quality of the cars would be up to the standards of the cars produced in Germany. But that was a risk worth taking because of the enormity of the foreign exchange risk."

9.3 SHARING THE REAL EXCHANGE RISK: AN EXAMPLE

This section examines an extended case that is designed to help you understand how real exchange risk can be shared between firms that do not share a common currency.

Safe Air's Situation

John Cromwell is the 54-year-old CEO of Safe Air, Inc., a small, publicly traded U.S. corporation that sells compressed air tanks to fire departments. Safe Air has been in business for 35 years and has been publicly traded for over 20 years. During this period, it has successfully introduced more than a dozen innovations that have saved many lives. Firefighters need a source of air to breathe while fighting a fire. They typically wear an air tank equipped with a regulator (an air delivery system) and a face mask as a normal part of their equipment.

Cromwell is proud of his product and the historic profitability of his firm. Recently, though, Safe Air's board of directors has begun to question Cromwell's leadership because earnings have been declining. Cromwell thinks he is too young to retire, and being forced out by the board would be humiliating. If he could just figure out a way to cut current costs and keep them more under his control, he is confident the board would retain him for another 6 years. Consequently, he has recently been evaluating several offers that he solicited from potential suppliers.

Metallwerke A.G.'s Proposal

Metallwerke, A.G., a German firm that manufactures air tanks, has submitted one attractive contractual offer to Cromwell. Cromwell has stated on numerous occasions that Safe Air has no expertise in the manufacturing of air tanks. It consequently has always purchased its tanks from an external supplier. Safe Air's current supplier is a U.S. firm, and Safe Air is invoiced for the basic tank in dollars.

Cromwell is intrigued by the possibility of locking in dollar prices from a low-cost foreign supplier like Metallwerke. He has also evaluated the quality of Metallwerke's product and thinks the quality of the German firm's tank is as good as, if not superior to, that of Safe Air's current U.S. supplier. If the Metallwerke air tank works better than his current tank, he knows that fire departments will probably pay more for the improved performance.

Cromwell also knows that if Metallwerke's supply price is right, costs can be reduced, and Safe Air's profitability would be enhanced. No matter who the supplier is, though, Cromwell knows that Safe Air's resources will be required to produce, advertise, and distribute the modified air tank. Also, all of Safe Air's sales are likely to be to U.S. fire departments. The sales will consequently all be done at a retail dollar price.

The Indexing Formula

Because Cromwell had never done an international deal before, in the initial stages of the negotiations with Metallwerke, he demanded that they quote a dollar-denominated base price for the tank. Gerhard Spiegel, the CEO of Metallwerke, agreed in principle, and expressed his general willingness to accept payment in dollars. But Spiegel is eager to sign a 10-year contract that sets a base dollar price for the tank and provides an **indexing formula** that allows for annual changes in the base dollar price under certain contingencies. The contingencies are the following: (1) The base dollar price will be increased at the annual rate of inflation, as indicated by the U.S. producer price index; and (2) if the dollar depreciates relative to the euro, the percentage change in the base dollar price will equal the U.S. rate of inflation plus an additional percentage equal to one-half the rate of depreciation of the dollar relative to the euro.

In the past, Safe Air's cost of the basic air tank has mostly increased with the rate of inflation in the United States, and Safe Air has typically been able to pass this increased cost along to its fire department customers by increasing its retail price at the rate of inflation. But occasionally, Safe Air's cost increases from its suppliers have exceeded the U.S. rate of inflation. This has resulted in several unprofitable periods, each lasting more than 3 years.

The demand for air tanks from fire departments is not very cyclical because they need new air tanks as the old ones wear out. Nevertheless, Safe Air management has always recognized that the fire department buyers are quite sensitive to price. Cromwell knows this limits the ability of his firm to pass along cost increases. He also does not think that the board of directors at Safe Air will tolerate another unprofitable period without a change in senior management.

The Consultant's Task

You are a consultant, trying to help Cromwell decide what to do. As he talked to you on the telephone yesterday about Metallwerke's offer, you could sense the concern in Cromwell's voice. He stated that the initial base price quoted by Spiegel is quite attractive. Nevertheless, he is wary of signing a contract that is proposed completely by his German counterpart. He thinks there must be a way to redesign it to be more favorable to Safe Air, and he wants you to find it.

As you prepare for a meeting with Cromwell, you know that the profitability of both firms must be considered in any long-term contract. You also know that somebody must bear the risk that the dollar will weaken relative to the euro, which must be what Spiegel is worried about. But something about the current contract seems fishy. If a weak dollar is so bad for Metallwerke, shouldn't a strong dollar be good? Why isn't this mentioned in any way?

As a consultant to Safe Air, your task is to evaluate the desirability of this contract, to redesign it to be more favorable to Safe Air, and to figure out some way of explaining the issues to Cromwell and possibly to the company's board of directors.

Basic Data and Analysis

Based on the data that Cromwell's assistant e-mailed to you, you have set out some basic prices and notations (the zeros indicate current-period values) related to the deal proposed by Metallwerke:

Safe Air's contractual base purchase price = $B(0,\$) = \$400$ per tank
Safe Air's other variable production costs = $C(0,\$) = \$313$ per tank
Safe Air's retail sales price = $T(0,\$) = \$820$ per tank
Safe Air's profit margin = $M(0,\$) = 15\%$
U.S. price level = $P(0,\$) = \$50$ per U.S. general good
Exchange rate = $S(0,€/\$) = €2/\$$
German price level = $P(0,€) = €100$ per German general good
Metallwerke's profit margin $M(0,€) = 15\%$
Metallwerke's production cost = $C(0,€) = €696$ per tank

Profitability Under a Simple Contract with Constant Prices

Let's first look at the profitability of the firms if they were to sign a long-term contract that simply fixes the dollar price of the tank at $400, no matter what the exchange rate. This is a contract that Cromwell would understand and like. Recall that he wanted to lock in a dollar price for the tank.

Assuming that the sales price of the tank is kept constant at $400, Exhibit 9.1 shows the risks the two companies would face under three alternative scenarios corresponding to the following three exchange rates: €2/$, €1.8/$ (which represents a 10% depreciation of the dollar), and €2.2/$ (which represents a 10% appreciation of the dollar).

Because Exhibit 9.1 assumes that the nominal exchange rate is changing with nominal prices fixed, the real exchange rate is also changing by 10%. Exhibit 9.1 indicates that in this case, each firm will earn a 15% profit margin when the exchange rate is €2/$. The ratio of Safe Air's retail sales price to its total production costs per tank in this case will be

$$\frac{\$820}{(\$400 + \$313)} = 1.15$$

The ratio of Metallwerke's euro sales price per tank to its production costs per tank will be

$$\frac{(€2/\$) \times \$400}{€696} = 1.15$$

We know that the profit margin of each firm will be constant if their sales prices increase at the same rates as their costs of production. But because the $400 Metallwerke charges Safe Air isn't being changed in Exhibit 9.1, the German company's profit margin

Exhibit 9.1 Profitability When the Price per Tank Is Contractually Fixed

	Safe Air (dollars)			Metallwerke (euros)		
	€1.8/$	€2.0/$	€2.2/$	€1.8/$	€2.0/$	€2.2/$
Sales						
Exported		0	0	720	800	880
Local	820	820	820			
Costs of goods sold						
Imported	(400)	(400)	(400)			
Local	(313)	(313)	(313)	(696)	(696)	(696)
Operating profit	107	107	107	24	104	184
Profit margin	15%	15%	15%	3.4%	15%	26.4%

Exhibit 9.2 Profitability Under Metallwerke's Proposed Contract

	Safe Air (dollars)			Metallwerke (euros)		
	€1.8/$	€2.0/$	€2.2/$	€1.8/$	€2.0/$	€2.2/$
Sales						
Exported		0	0	756	800	880
Local	820	820	820			
Costs of goods sold						
Imported	(420)	(400)	(400)			
Local	(313)	(313)	(313)	(696)	(696)	(696)
Operating profit	87	107	107	60	104	184
Profit margin	11.9%	15%	15%	8.6%	15%	26.4%

falls to 3.4% when the dollar weakens by 10%. On the other hand, Metallwerke's profit margin rises to a whopping 26.4% when the dollar strengthens by 10%. In other words, with a constant dollar price, if the dollar weakens, Safe Air won't suffer, but Metallwerke will see its profits decline drastically. By contrast, if the dollar strengthens, Safe Air won't be any more profitable, but Metallwerke will be very profitable. What should the two companies agree to do?

Exhibit 9.2 provides an analysis of the profitability of the two firms under Metallwerke's proposed contract. As in Exhibit 9.1, exchange rates are allowed to change, but nominal prices other than the tank price are held constant. If you compare Exhibit 9.2 to Exhibit 9.1, you'll notice that the price Safe Air has to pay per tank rises by 5%, to $420, when the dollar weakens by 10%. This causes Safe Air's profit margin to fall to 11.9%, but it causes Metallwerke's profit margin to rise to 8.6% (from 3.4% in Exhibit 9.1). Notice that the increased profitability of Metallwerke when the dollar strengthens is not shared with Safe Air, however.

Sharing the Exchange Rate Risk with Constant Prices

Let's examine a contract that shares the foreign exchange risk. Exhibit 9.3 demonstrates what happens if the firms agree to share the exchange rate risk equally. As before, if the dollar depreciates, the base price of the tank will increase by one-half the percentage rate of the dollar depreciation. If the dollar appreciates, though, the base price of the tank will decrease by one-half the percentage rate of dollar appreciation.

In this case, the price Safe Air pays per tank when the dollar strengthens by 10% is $380, and Safe Air's profit margin increases to 18.3%. Metallwerke still has an increase in profitability, but only to a margin of 20.1%.

Exhibit 9.3 Profitability Under a Contract That Shares Real Exchange Risk

	Safe Air (dollars)			Metallwerke (euros)		
	€1.8/$	€2.0/$	€2.2/$	€1.8/$	€2.0/$	€2.2/$
Sales						
Exported		0	0	756	800	836
Local	820	820	820			
Costs of goods sold						
Imported	(420)	(400)	(380)			
Local	(313)	(313)	(313)	(696)	(696)	(696)
Operating profit	87	107	127	60	104	140
Profit margin	11.9%	15%	18.3%	8.6%	15%	20.1%

Analyzing Contracts When Inflation and Real Exchange Rates Are Changing

We noted that Exhibits 9.1 through 9.3 hold the prices of labor and the retail price of the tank constant. In such a situation, the change in the nominal exchange rate *is* a change in the real exchange rate. When other prices are moving, however, it is important to distinguish contractually between movements in nominal and real exchange rates. It will turn out that if the base price increases at the U.S. rate of inflation, only movements in the real exchange rate are a source of risk.

Profits with a Constant Real Exchange Rate

To see how profits are affected by the terms of the contract when *all* prices are allowed to move, we next examine the real costs, real revenues, and the real profits of the two firms under various future scenarios. We begin the scenarios using a constant real exchange rate as a benchmark. Starting there makes sense—not because real exchange rates are constant but because if the contract doesn't work well in this simple environment, you know it won't work well in the real world, in which large, unpredictable, and highly persistent fluctuations in real exchange rates occur.

In doing the analysis, it will be useful to have some notation for the percentage rates of change of several key variables. The percentage rate of change of any variable Z from period 0 to period 1 is $\% Z = [Z(1) - Z(0)]/Z(0)$. Let's define the following variables:

U.S. rate of inflation $= \pi(\$) = \%P(\$)$
German rate of inflation $= \pi(€) = \%P(€)$
Rate of appreciation of the dollar versus the euro $= a(€/\$) = \%S(€/\$)$,
    if $\%S(€/\$) > 0$
Rate of depreciation of the dollar versus the euro $= d(€/\$) = -\%S(€/\$)$,
    if $\%S(€/\$) < 0$
Rate of change of Safe Air's contractual base price per tank $= \%B(\$)$
Rate of change of the Safe Air's retail sales price per tank $= \%T(\$)$
Rate of change of the Safe Air's production cost per tank $= \%C(\$)$
Rate of change Metallwerke's production cost per tank $= \%C(€)$

Notice that because the contract calls for base-price adjustments if the dollar depreciates, the symbol for the rate of depreciation of the dollar, d, is defined to be positive.

Safe Air's Real Cost per Tank

The period 0 real imported cost per tank for Safe Air is the base dollar price of the tank divided by the U.S. price level. An additional R before a symbol denotes a real variable that is obtained by dividing the nominal variable by the appropriate price level for that currency. Thus, Safe Air's real imported costs equal the following U.S. general goods per tank:

$$RB(0,\$) = \frac{B(0,\$)}{P(0,\$)} = \frac{\$400 \text{ per tank}}{\$50 \text{ per U.S. general goods}} = 8 \text{ U.S. general goods per tank}$$

In period 1, the base dollar price per tank that Safe Air pays will increase by $\%B(\$)$ percent, and the U.S. price level will increase $\pi(\$)$ percent because of inflation. Hence, the period 1 real imported cost for Safe Air will be

$$RB(1,\$) = \frac{B(1,\$)}{P(1,\$)} = \frac{B(0,\$) \times (1 + \%B(\$))}{P(0,\$) \times (1 + \pi(\$))} = RB(0,\$) \times \frac{(1 + \%B(\$))}{(1 + \pi(\$))}$$

Only if the percentage rate of change of the base price equals the U.S. rate of inflation will Safe Air's real imported cost per unit not change. Increases in the base price that are larger (smaller) than the U.S. rate of inflation increase (decrease) real imported part costs.

Safe Air's other variable production costs per unit in period 0 in real terms are similarly found to be the following:

$$RC(0,\$) = \frac{C(0,\$)}{P(0,\$)} = \frac{\$413 \text{ per tank}}{\$50 \text{ per U.S. general goods}} = 8.26 \text{ U.S. general goods per tank}$$

In the next period, real production costs will be

$$RC(1,\$) = \frac{C(1,\$)}{P(1,\$)} = \frac{C(0,\$) \times (1 + \%C(\$))}{P(0,\$) \times (1 + \pi(\$))} = RC(0,\$) \times \frac{(1 + \%C(\$))}{(1 + \pi(\$))}$$

If Safe Air's nominal production costs increase at the same rate as the U.S. rate of inflation, its real production costs will be constant. However, if Safe Air's nominal production costs increase faster than the U.S. rate of inflation, its real production costs will increase.

Safe Air's Real Revenue per Tank

The real revenue per tank sold by Safe Air is determined by dividing the tank's retail dollar sales price by the U.S. price level:

$$RT(0,\$) = \frac{T(0,\$)}{P(0,\$)} = \frac{\$820 \text{ per tank}}{\$50 \text{ per U.S. general goods}} = 16.4 \text{ U.S. general goods per tank}$$

These are the real resources available to the firm from selling an air tank. In period 1, Safe Air will be able to change its retail price by $\%T(\$)$, and the U.S. price level will increase $\Pi(\$)$ percent because of inflation. Hence, the period 1 real revenue per unit for Safe Air will be

$$RT(1,\$) = \frac{T(1,\$)}{P(1,\$)} = \frac{T(0,\$) \times (1 + \%T(\$))}{P(0,\$) \times (1 + \pi(\$))} = RT(0,\$) \times \frac{(1 + \%T(\$))}{(1 + \pi(\$))}$$

Only if Safe Air is able to increase its retail dollar sales price at the U.S. rate of inflation, as measured by the rate of change of the U.S. price level, will its real revenue per unit remain constant because both the numerator of RI and the denominator of RI will rise at the same rate.

Metallwerke's Real Revenue per Tank

The real revenue per tank for Metallwerke is the exchange rate, €/\$, multiplied by the dollar price per tank the company charges Safe Air, divided by the German price level:

$$RR(0, \text{€}) = \frac{S(0,\text{€}/\$) \times B(0,\$)}{P(0,\text{€})} = \frac{(\text{€}2/\$) \times (\$400 \text{ per tank})}{\text{€}100 \text{ per German general goods}}$$
$$= 8 \text{ German general goods per tank}$$

Notice that 8 German general goods per tank is the same amount of goods and services that Safe Air sacrifices when it pays dollars. This is true because the current exchange rate of €2/\$ equals the ratio of the price levels, (€100 per German general good) / (\$50 per U.S. general good). Hence, absolute PPP is satisfied.

In period 1, Metallwerke's new real revenue will be

$$RR(1,\text{€}) = \frac{S(1,\text{€}/\$) \times B(1,\$)}{P(1,\text{€})}$$
$$= \frac{S(0,\text{€}/\$) \times [1 + \%S(\text{€}/\$)] \times B(0,\$) \times [1 + \%B(\$)]}{P(0,\text{€}) \times [1 + \pi(\text{€})]}$$
$$= RR(0,\text{€}) \times \frac{(1 + \%S(\text{€}/\$)) \times (1 + \%B(\$))}{(1 + \pi(\text{€}))}$$

What percentage rate of change of the base price is required to keep Metallwerke's real revenue constant? Only if the percentage change in the base price satisfies

$$[1 + \%B(\$)] = \frac{[1 + \pi(\text{€})]}{[1 + \%S(\text{€}/\$)]}$$

will Metallwerke's real revenue be constant. Notice that this analysis indicates that Metallwerke would like to increase the base price of the tank to offset both the German rate of inflation and any depreciation of the dollar relative to the euro. But this is not how the proposed contract is written. We will return to this issue later, after examining how the real costs of the German firm change over time.

Metallwerke's Real Cost per Tank

Metallwerke's real cost per tank is the nominal euro cost of production divided by the German price level:

$$RC(0,\text{€}) = \frac{C(0,\text{€})}{P(0,\text{€})} = \frac{\text{€}696 \text{ per tank}}{\text{€}100 \text{ per German general goods}}$$
$$= 6.96 \text{ German general goods per tank}$$

The real production cost for the German firm per tank is constant as long as its euro cost of production rises at the German rate of inflation:

$$RC(1, \text{€}) = \frac{C(1,\text{€})}{P(1,\text{€})} = \frac{C(0,\text{€}) \times [1 + \%C(\text{€})]}{P(0,\text{€}) \times [1 + \pi(\text{€})]} = RC(0, \text{€}) \times \frac{[1 + \%C(\text{€})]}{[1 + \pi(\text{€})]}$$

Evaluating Metallwerke's Proposal

Suppose that relative purchasing power parity holds and that the U.S. rate of inflation happens to be greater than the German rate of inflation. For example, let the U.S. rate of inflation be 10%, and let the German rate of inflation be 5%. Then, we know that the dollar will depreciate relative to the euro, and the percentage change in the exchange rate will be

$$[1 - d(\text{€}/\$)] = \frac{[1 + \pi(\text{€})]}{[1 + \pi(\$)]} = \frac{(1 + 0.05)}{(1 + 0.1)}$$

Solving for d, we find

$$d(\text{€}/\$) = 0.0455$$

Under the terms of the contract Metallwerke is proposing, the percentage change in the base price of the air tank will equal the rate of inflation in the United States, 10%, plus an additional adjustment equal to one-half of the 4.55% rate of depreciation of the dollar relative to the euro, or

$$[1 + \%B(\$)] = [1 + \pi(\$) + d(\text{€}/\$)/2] = (1 + 0.1 + 0.0228)$$

Solving for $\%B(\$)$, we find

$$\%B(\$) = 0.1228$$

or a 12.28% increase in the base price of the tank.

From our analysis of Safe Air's real costs, we know that if the base price increases at this rate, the company's real cost per unit will increase:

$$RB(1,\$) = RB(0,\$) \times \frac{(1 + \%B(\$))}{(1 + \pi(\$))} = RB(0,\$) \times \frac{1.1228}{1.10} = RB(0,\$) \times 1.0207$$

With this change in the base dollar price, Safe Air's real cost of acquiring an air tank from Metallwerke will increase by 2.07%.

Let's see what Metallwerke's real per-tank revenue will be under the terms of its proposed contract. From our earlier analysis, we know that

$$RR(1,\text{€}) = RR(0,\text{€}) \times \frac{(1 + \%S(\text{€}/\$)) \times (1 + \%B(\$))}{(1 + \pi(\text{€}))}$$

$$= RR(0,\text{€}) \times \frac{(1 - 0.0455) \times (1 + 0.1228)}{(1 + 0.05)}$$

$$= RR(1,\text{€}) = RR(0,\text{€}) \times 1.0207$$

Hence, Metallwerke's real revenue will rise by the same 2.07% that Safe Air's real cost will increase.

What would happen if the rate of increase in the base price were just equal to the rate of inflation in the U.S.? In this case, with $\%B(\$) = \pi(\$)$, we can see that

$$RR(1,\text{€}) = RR(0,\text{€}) \times \frac{(1 + \%S(\text{€}/\$)) \times (1 + \Pi(\$))}{(1 + \pi(\text{€}))} = RR(0,\text{€})$$

because, under our assumption that relative PPP holds, the change in the exchange rate will be just what is required to offset the differential rates of inflation.

In this case, if Safe Air's other production costs and the retail price of the tank are increasing at the U.S. rate of inflation, Safe Air will be in the same real situation as it was before. Similarly, if Metallwerke's production costs increase with German inflation, it is straightforward to show that Metallwerke will be in the same real situation as before. Hence, we find that if the real exchange rate is constant, the base tank price could be increased just at the U.S. rate of inflation leaving Safe Air's real cost of a tank constant and the change in the nominal exchange rate would offset any differential rate of inflation between the United States and Germany, leaving Metallwerke's real revenue constant.

In summary, if the base price of the air tank increases with the U.S. rate of inflation, a nominal depreciation of the dollar lowers Metallwerke's real revenue only if it is greater in magnitude than what is warranted by the inflation differential between the United States and Germany. This potential loss of real revenue is the risk that Metallwerke should want to hedge against when it enters into a long-term contract. It is an exposure to real exchange risk.

Designing a Contract That Shares the Real Exchange Risk

Making sure that the Metallwerke/Safe Air contract is not biased if the real exchange rate is constant should not be the end of the story. Both companies are exposed to real foreign exchange risk if relative PPP is violated and real exchange rates fluctuate. As discussed in Chapters 8, such violations of PPP are the rule rather than the exception. Hence there is a real foreign exchange risk related to this long-term contract. Both companies would presumably prefer some protection against major swings in the real exchange rate. Both would prefer a contract that maintains a constant real price of the air tank over the 10-year horizon, thereby providing constant real costs to Safe Air and constant real revenues to Metallwerke.

Unfortunately, this is impossible to accomplish for both companies without contracting to give the risk to a third party. If Safe Air cares about the real value of the dollars it pays, and if Metallwerke cares about the real value of the euros it receives after converting from dollars, and if there are fluctuations in the real exchange rate, someone must bear the risk of fluctuations in the real exchange rate.

A Contract That Shares the Risk

As discussed earlier in the chapter, it is possible to share real exchange risk almost equally between two parties. Recall that the percentage change in the real exchange rate—the real rate of appreciation of the dollar relative to the euro—can be measured in the following way:

$$[1 + \%RS(\text{€}/\$)] = \frac{[1 + \%S(\text{€}/\$)] \times [1 + \pi(\$)]}{[1 + \pi(\text{€})]}$$

Here $\%\Delta RS$ represents the real rate of appreciation or depreciation of the dollar relative to the euro, which can be either positive or negative. Then, let the base dollar price of the product increase one for one with the U.S. rate of inflation and make an additional adjustment to the base price for changes in the real exchange rate. Make the base price higher by one-half of any real depreciation of the dollar relative to the euro, but make the base price lower by one-half of any real appreciation of the dollar relative to the euro:

$$(1 + \%B(\$)) = [1 + \pi(\$)] \times [1 - (\%RS(\text{€}/\$)/2)]$$

Now, Safe Air's real cost is

$$RB(1,\$) = RB(0,\$) \times \frac{[1 + \%B(\$)]}{[1 + \pi(\$)]} = RB(0,\$) \times [1 - (\%RS(\text{€}/\$)/2)]$$

It is constant if the real exchange rate is constant, $\%RS(\text{€}/\$) = 0$. It increases by one-half of the rate of real depreciation when the dollar weakens in real terms relative to the euro—that is, when $\%RS(\text{€}/\$) < 0$. By contrast, Safe Air's real cost decreases when the dollar strengthens in real terms relative to the euro—that is, when $\%RS(\text{€}/\$) > 0$.

Now consider Metallwerke's real revenue under the revised contract. We know that

$$RR(1,\text{€}) = RR(0,\text{€}) \times \frac{(1 + \%S(\text{€}/\$)) \times (1 + \%B(\$))}{(1 + \pi(\text{€}))}$$

which we can rewrite substituting the new terms of the contract as

$$RR(1,\text{€}) = RR(0,\text{€}) \times \frac{(1 + \%S(\text{€}/\$)) \times (1 + \pi(\$)) \times [1 - \%RS(\text{€}/\$)/2]}{(1 + \pi(\text{€}))}$$

Because $[1 + \%RS(\text{€}/\$)] = [1 + \%S(\text{€}/\$)] \times [1 + \pi(\$)]/[1 + \pi(\text{€})]$, we have

$$RR(1,\text{€}) = RR(0,\text{€}) \times [1 + \%RS(\text{€}/\$)] \times [1 - \%RS(\text{€}/\$)/2)]$$

Because

$$[1 + \%RS(\text{€}/\$)] \times [1 - \%RS(\text{€}/\$)/2)]$$

$$= 1 + \%RS(\text{€}/\$) - \%RS(\text{€}/\$)/2 - [\%RS(\text{€}/\$)]^2/2$$

$$= 1 + \%RS(\text{€}/\$)/2 - [\%RS(\text{€}/\$)]^2/2$$

the percentage change in Metallwerke's real revenue is approximately $\%RS(\text{€}/\$) / 2$, ignoring the second-order term, which is two orders of magnitude smaller than the other terms. Consequently, Metallwerke's real revenue goes up by one-half of any real appreciation of the dollar when $\%RS > 0$, and it goes down by one-half of any real depreciation of the dollar when $\%RS < 0$.

Understanding the Contract

The reason that the redesigned contract shares the real exchange risk is that if the dollar depreciates relative to the euro by more than is warranted by the differential rates of inflation, Metallwerke's real revenue falls. The redesigned contract forces the nominal base price to increase in this situation, which causes Safe Air to bear part of the loss. But if the euro weakens relative to the dollar by more than the inflation differential, Metallwerke's real revenue rises. The redesigned contract makes Metallwerke share this gain with Safe Air by lowering the rate at which the dollar base price is increasing.

Would the Redesigned Contract Be Adopted?

Whether the redesigned contract would actually be adopted by the firms as a way of sharing real exchange risk depends on several factors. First, as the real exchange rate changes, how are Safe Air's other production costs and Metallwerke's costs changing?

Other Factors Affecting Costs

Suppose that when the dollar is weak in real terms relative to the euro, Safe Air faces additional cost pressures from its workers because their nominal wages buy fewer foreign goods. In contrast, Metallwerke's real costs may be relatively low when the euro is strong in real terms. German workers will have higher purchasing power given their nominal euro wage rates. The opposite situations would be true when the dollar is strong in real terms relative to the euro. In this case, the real profits of both firms would be smoother if Safe Air were to agree to a smaller increase in the base price per tank when the dollar is weak. In return, however, Safe Air would have to accept less of a decrease in the base price per tank when the dollar is strong. Such an agreement might nonetheless be acceptable to Safe Air because the pressure on its domestic costs will be less when the dollar is strong. (Safe Air's workers won't be demanding higher wages, for example.) The additional income Metallwerke earns when the dollar is strong comes at the right time for the German tank maker because it will face additional pressure on its domestic costs due to the weakening of the euro. (Metallwerke's employees will demand higher wages, for example.)

Competitiveness and Pricing Ability

Does Safe Air have any ability to adjust its retail price at a rate different from the U.S. rate of inflation? Is the retail demand for air tanks completely independent of the forces causing the change in the real exchange rate? If Safe Air truly cannot adjust its retail price except at the U.S. rate of inflation and if its demand is completely driven by replacement, then these factors are unimportant.

The situation is different if Safe Air has foreign competitors in the United States who price more aggressively when the dollar is strong and who fade away when the dollar is weak. In this case, Safe Air would like its retail sales price increase to be less than the U.S. rate of inflation when the dollar is strong. This might be accomplished by having Safe Air receive more than one-half of the benefit of a strong dollar. In return, Safe Air could accept more of an increase in the base dollar price it pays for tanks when the dollar is weak. In contrast, if a strong dollar is somehow linked to an increased demand for Safe Air's product, it may not be necessary for the company to pay a lower price for its tanks when the dollar is strong because demand is strong anyway.

Relative Bargaining Strength

The last issue that determines how the contract will be written is the relative bargaining strength of the two firms. As the contract was initially written, Metallwerke received all the benefit of a strong dollar, and when the dollar was weak, Safe Air still had to share part of the cost. This may be the best that Cromwell can do, given his precarious position with the board of directors. If Spiegel knows that his initial base price is attractive, he may be able to force

Cromwell to accept a current benefit in exchange for possible problems in the future. In contrast, if Metallwerke really needs Safe Air's business, Spiegel might be more willing to accept a fixed-price contract and bear the risk while hoping that the dollar will strengthen.

9.4 PRICING-TO-MARKET STRATEGIES

The next aspect of managing real exchange risk that we discuss is the issue of **pricing-to-market**. The discussion in Chapter 8 on the sources of deviations from the law of one price for particular goods notes that whenever the market for a good is not fully competitive, producers have an incentive to charge different prices in different countries.

Some Examples of Pricing-to-Market Strategies

Luxury Cars in the 1980s
As noted earlier, during the mid-1980s, the dollar was very strong in real terms relative to European currencies. As a result, U.S. consumers could travel to Europe, exchange their dollars, and buy European luxury cars for 30% to 40% less than the same cars cost in the United States. Apparently, the European manufacturers found it in their interest to fatten their profit margins on the cars they sold in the United States rather than lower their dollar prices to gain additional U.S. market share.

Japanese Consumer Electronics
The mirror image of the 1980s luxury cars situation occurred in the United States during 1987–1988, when the dollar became very weak in real terms relative to the yen. However, Japanese manufacturers of consumer electronics did not find it in their interest to increase the dollar prices of their products sold in the United States because they believed it would cost them substantial market share. Instead, they kept their dollar prices low and allowed their profit margins to deteriorate. Consequently, the yen prices of consumer electronics in the United States fell substantively below the yen prices of the same goods in Japan. In response, enterprising Japanese consumers traveled to the United States, purchased electronic goods, and shipped them back to Japan.

French Handbags
Another pricing-to-market example is from an article from the July 14, 2001, *The Economist*, which notes that handbags manufactured by the French luxury goods producer Louis Vuitton cost 40% more in Japan than in Europe at that time. Enterprising Hong Kong Chinese merchants were trying to arbitrage this differential by sending employees to purchase handbags in Europe and reselling them in Japan, much to the chagrin of the French handbag maker. The problem in Europe was how to tell an arbitrageur from a legitimate tourist. Do you draw the line at the purchase of 5 bags or 10?

The Concept of Pricing-to-Market
These examples illustrate a phenomenon that economists call pricing-to-market, which means that producers charge different prices for the same good sold in different markets. In each of these examples, producers were charging different prices in different countries and only allowed a fraction of any change in the real exchange rate to affect the prices of their products sold abroad. The goal of this section is to understand why this occurs. We do this by examining how a monopolist responds to fluctuations in real exchange rates.[2]

---

[2]The issues in this section are explored more formally in Richard Marston (1990), which provides a static, one-period profit maximization, and in Kenneth Kasa (1992), which provides a dynamic formulation of the problem.

Pricing-to-Market by a Monopolist

A Monopolistic Exporter

Consider the problem of a domestic **monopolist**, a sole producer who sells a non-storable good to both the domestic market and the foreign market. The monopolist faces a different demand curve in each market, and as the price of the product increases in each market, the monopolist will sell fewer units there. We can think of the monopolist as either choosing the domestic and foreign prices of the goods it will supply to each market and letting the quantities it sells in each market be determined by the respective demand curves, or alternatively, we can think of the monopolist as choosing the quantities to supply to each market with the demand curves then determining the prices.

Example 9.5 A Monopolist Seller in Two Markets

Demand Curves

Suppose a monopolist faces the same linear demand curve in the domestic and foreign markets. The domestic demand curve is

$$Q = 1,000 - P$$

where Q is the quantity sold in the domestic market, and P is the domestic relative price. At a price of zero, the monopolist could sell 1,000 units. As the monopolist increases the price, the number of units sold decreases until none are sold at a price of 1,000. The demand curve in the foreign market is similarly

$$Q^* = 1,000 - P^*$$

where Q^* represents the quantity sold in the foreign market at the foreign relative price of P^*.

Domestic and Foreign Revenues

From the domestic demand curve, we find that $P = 1,000 - Q$, and revenue from domestic sales is

$$P \times Q = (1,000 \times Q) - Q^2$$

From our earlier analysis, we know that when the monopolist sells output in the foreign market, the domestic real value of revenue from foreign sales is the real exchange rate, RS, multiplied by the foreign relative price, multiplied by foreign sales, or by substituting $P^* = 1,000 - Q^*$, we find

$$RS \times P^* \times Q^* = (RS \times 1,000 \times Q^*) - RS \times Q^{*2}$$

Cost of Production

Suppose that the **marginal cost** of production is constant, and let this per-unit cost of production be 500. Then the total cost of production is the per-unit cost multiplied by the total quantity produced for sale in each of the two markets:

$$500 \times (Q + Q^*)$$

Profit-Maximizing Quantities

A profit-maximizing monopolist produces an amount of a good such that the **marginal revenue** earned from each market is equal to the common marginal cost.[3] The marginal revenue from domestic sales is $1,000 - 2Q$, and the marginal revenue from the foreign market is $RS \times 1,000 - RS \times 2Q^*$. Thus, the monopolist should sell a quantity in the domestic market that satisfies

$$1,000 - 2Q = 500$$

or, by solving for Q, we find

$$Q = (1,000 - 500)/2 = 250$$

The optimal quantity in the foreign market satisfies

$$RS \times 1,000 - RS \times 2Q^* = 500$$

[solv]ing for Q^*, we find

$$Q^* = [1,000 - (500/RS)]/2$$

[Equilibriu]m with RS = 1

[...r]eal exchange rate is initially equal to 1. In this case, the monopolist [...] each market by charging the relative price of 750 in each country. The [...wo]uld be

[(750 × 2]50) + (750 × 250) − [500 × (250 + 250)] = 125,000

[... summ]arizes this equilibrium in the domestic and foreign markets.

[...] Monopolistic Exporter

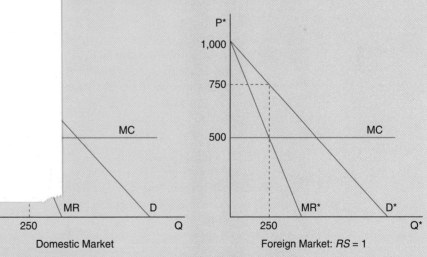

Domestic Market

Foreign Market: $RS = 1$

The Equilibrium with a Real Appreciation

Now, suppose there is a 20% real appreciation of the foreign currency such that the new real exchange rate is 1.2. The real appreciation benefits the exporting monopolist because total real revenue in the foreign country is now

$$1.2 \times (1,000 - Q^*) \times Q^*$$

---

[3]Marginal revenue is the derivative of total revenue with respect to the quantity sold.

How will the monopolist respond to this new environment? By equating the foreign marginal revenue to the unchanged domestic marginal cost of 500 and solving for Q^*, we find

$$Q^* = [1,000 - (500 / 1.2)]/2 = 291.7$$

Exhibit 9.5 summarizes the new foreign equilibrium.

Exhibit 9.5 A Monopolistic Exporter When $RS = 1.2$

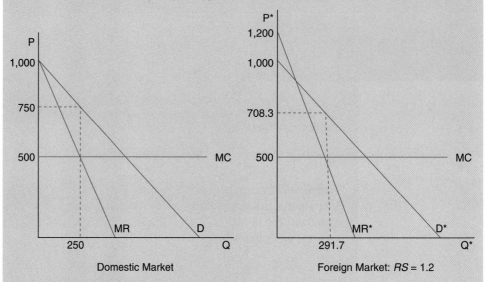

Domestic Market   Foreign Market: $RS = 1.2$

In order to sell the 291.7 units in the foreign market, the monopolist must lower the foreign price per unit to

$$P^* = 1,000 - 291.7 = 708.3$$

Because the marginal cost of production is constant, the domestic price per unit remains at 750, and the domestic sales remain at 250.

Notice that although the foreign currency appreciates by 20%, the monopolist only decreases the relative price in the foreign market by 5.6% because the ratio of the new foreign price to the old foreign price is

$$708.3/750 = 0.944$$

The 5.6% pass-through reduction in the relative foreign price resulting from the 20% appreciation of the foreign currency is quite small. Put differently, the domestic currency price that is equivalent to the new foreign price multiplied by the real exchange rate has increased drastically from 750 to

$$1.2 \times 708.3 = 850$$

Because the actual domestic price stays constant at 750, the law of one price is now violated.

Violations of the Law of One Price

The solution shown in Exhibit 9.5 demonstrates the point that whenever demand curves differ across countries, a monopolist finds it in his interest to violate the law of one price. Because the demand curves depend only on the relative price of the product in the consumer's country and not on the relative prices in other countries, these deviations from the law of one price do not trigger arbitrage in the goods markets. Implicit in the formulation of the demand curves are some costs that prevent this arbitrage.

The real appreciation of the foreign currency makes the monopolist more profitable. Even if the monopolist lowered the foreign relative price by the full amount of the foreign currency appreciation to $625 = 750/1.2$, in which case the law of one price would not be violated, the monopolist's profits would still increase because foreign sales would increase to $375 = 1,000 - 625$. At these prices and quantities, total profit would increase to

$$(750 \times 250) + (1.2 \times 625 \times 375) - [500 \times (250 + 375)] = 156,250$$

or by 25%, because the ratio of new profit to old profit is $156,250/125,000 = 1.25$. But the monopolist can do even better by violating the law of one price. At the new optimal prices and quantities, total profit increases to

$$(750 \times 250) + (1.2 \times 708.3 \times 291.7) - [500 \times (250 + 291.7)] = 164,583.3$$

or by 31.7%, because the ratio of new profit to old profit is $164,583.3/125,000 = 1.317$. By acting optimally, the exporting monopolist exploits the real appreciation of the foreign currency to become even more profitable.

A Monopolistic Net Importer

Now, consider how a monopolist who is a net importer responds to changes in the real exchange rate.

Example 9.6 A Monopolist with Imported Costs

The Demand Curve
Consider a monopolist who faces a domestic demand curve given by

$$Q = 1,000 - P$$

where Q is the quantity demand at the domestic relative price, P.

Domestic and Foreign Costs
The cost of production involves domestic costs per unit of C and a foreign cost per unit produced of C^*. Total cost is the sum of domestic costs, $C \times Q$, and the domestic value of foreign costs. To find the domestic value of foreign costs, we must multiply total foreign costs, $C^* \times Q$, by the real exchange rate, RS. Hence, total real domestic costs are

$$(C \times Q) + (RS \times C^* \times Q)$$

Because $P = 1,000 - Q$, total revenue is

$$P \times Q = 1,000 \times Q - Q^2$$

and marginal revenue is $1,000 - 2Q$. Marginal cost is $C + (RS \times C^*)$.

The Equilibrium

Suppose that initially $C = 250$, $C^* = 200$, and $RS = 1$. Then, the profit-maximizing decision of the monopolist is to set marginal revenue equal to marginal unit cost:

$$1,000 - 2Q = 250 + (1 \times 200) = 450$$

or, solving for Q, we find

$$Q = (1,000 - 450)/2 = 275$$

The monopolist would produce 275 units and sell them in the domestic market at the relative price of 725. The initial equilibrium is given in Exhibit 9.6.

Exhibit 9.6   A Monopolist with Imported Costs

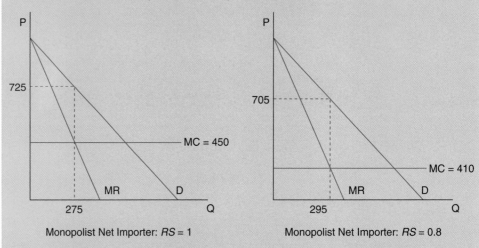

Monopolist Net Importer: $RS = 1$ Monopolist Net Importer: $RS = 0.8$

A Real Depreciation

Now, suppose there is a 20% real depreciation of the foreign currency such that the new real exchange rate is 0.8. This causes the domestic value of the monopolist's foreign costs to fall by 20%, to $0.8 \times 200 = 160$. The decrease in marginal cost to $250 + 160 = 410$ (versus 450) causes the monopolist to increase his production. The optimal quantity now sets marginal revenue, which is again $1,000 - 2Q$, equal to the new marginal cost:

$$1,000 - 2Q = 250 + (0.8 \times 200) = 410$$

or

$$Q = (1,000 - 410)/2 = 295$$

In order to sell 295 units, the monopolist decreases the domestic relative price to 705.

Pass-Through Pricing

How much of the cost saving shown in the preceding section is passed through to consumers? The monopolist's marginal cost has fallen by 8.9% because the ratio of new marginal cost to the old is $(410/450) = 0.911$. But the percentage reduction in the domestic price is only 2.8% because the ratio of the new price to the old price is $(705/725) = 0.972$. Thus, once again, the pass-through is less than one for one. In this case, the monopolist increases his profits because the real depreciation of the foreign currency lowers the cost of his imports. With a real exchange rate of 1, profits were

$$(725 \times 275) - [(250 \times 275) + (1 \times 200 \times 275)] = 75{,}625$$

With a real exchange rate of 0.8, profits are

$$(705 \times 295) - [(250 \times 295) + (0.8 \times 200 \times 295)] = 87{,}025$$

Notice that profits have risen by 15.1% because the ratio of new profits to old profits is $(87{,}025/75{,}625) = 1.151$. If the monopolist had passed through the full cost saving of 8.9% from the exchange rate to the domestic price, the new price would have been $0.911 \times 725 = 660.5$, and the new quantity sold would have been $1{,}000 - 660.5 = 339.5$. Hence, profits would have been

$$(660.5 \times 339.5) - [(250 \times 339.5) + (0.8 \times 200 \times 339.5)] = 85{,}045$$

As you can see, the monopolist's profits would, again, increase (from 75,262 to 85,045) with the complete pass-through of the reduction in foreign costs to the domestic price. However, the monopolist can do better by passing less of the savings on to consumers. Instead, he charges domestic consumers a relatively higher price per unit than with complete pass-through and produces fewer units, thereby earning 87,025 instead of just 85,045.

Empirical Evidence on Pricing-to-Market

The examples just examined demonstrate what could happen in monopolistic environments. Although there are few monopolists in actual markets, economists do generally find strong evidence that the exports of various countries are priced to market suggesting that firms do have some market power.

For example, an early study by Richard Marston (1990) examined the determination of the domestic currency price in the foreign market relative to the domestic currency price in the domestic market for a number of goods for the period from 1980 to 1987, using data from the Bank of Japan. The pricing-to-market elasticities measure the effects of a change in the real exchange rate on the different relative prices. The elasticities are generally significantly different from 1 for all goods categories examined by Marston, except for cameras and small trucks. For small passenger cars, large trucks, agricultural tractors, motorcycles, color TVs, and copying machines, the estimated pricing-to-market elasticities are roughly 0.5. This indicates that a real appreciation of the yen of 10% lowers the export prices of these products relative to their domestic prices by 5%.

Michael Knetter (1993) found strong evidence that annual price adjustments for the exports of Germany, Japan, the United Kingdom, and the United States, when expressed in the importer's currency, do not fully reflect changes in exchange rates between the exporter's currency and the currency of the destination market. Knetter found that different amounts of an exchange rate change are allowed to pass through to local currencies for the exports of different countries. For Germany, the estimates indicate that only 11% of an exchange rate change passes through to local currency prices; for Japan, the estimated pass-through is 21%; for the United Kingdom, the estimate is 33%; and for the United States, the estimate is 55%. One surprising finding of Knetter's study is that pricing-to-market is found to be an important phenomenon in German exports of relatively homogeneous chemical product categories, including aluminum dioxide, synthetic dyes, special dyes, titanium oxide pigments, aluminum hydroxide, vitamin A, and vitamin C. Another surprising finding is that exports of large German automobiles show no evidence of pricing-to-market. On the other hand, there is strong evidence of pricing-to-market in the automobile exports of Japan and the United Kingdom.

A more recent study by researchers at the Board of Governors of the Federal Reserve found that pass-through to U.S. import prices in the 1980s was typically about 50%. In the 1990s and 2000s, the figure has fallen to closer to 20%.[4] While understanding why it has fallen is a difficult problem, the economists attribute the change to a reduced share of commodity-intensive industrial supplies in U.S. imports and the increased presence of Chinese exporters to the U.S. market. Because China was pegging the yuan to the dollar during this period, any depreciation of the dollar versus third currencies that would have potentially led to an increase in dollar prices of third-country exports to the United States was held in check by competition from China.

9.5 EVALUATING THE PERFORMANCE OF A FOREIGN SUBSIDIARY

The fact that fluctuations in real exchange rates affect the profitability of doing international business severely complicates the process of evaluating the performance of managers of foreign subsidiaries.[5] We know that a real depreciation of the local currency hurts the performance of a net importing company because it increases the company's costs. Conversely, a real depreciation of the local currency improves the operating performance of a net exporting company because it increases the company's revenues.

Because fluctuations in real exchange rates are large and difficult to forecast, the operating performance of foreign subsidiaries will be quite variable. How can we design a system to determine good management from bad management in such an environment?

Three Types of Subsidiaries

Consider the initial situations of three different Japanese subsidiaries operating in Thailand, where the local currency is the baht. The three firms are ThaiComp, which is a net importer; WeRToys, which is a net exporter; and RiceNoodle, which neither imports nor exports.

The Net Importer

ThaiComp imports personal computer (PC) parts, assembles the PCs in Thailand, and sells most of its PCs in Thailand. ThaiComp exports some computers to Malaysia, Indonesia, and China. Because the computer maker is a net importer, its costs increase more than its revenues when there is a real depreciation of the baht. The Japanese owners of ThaiComp then experience an additional loss in real terms when they convert baht profit into yen.

The Net Exporter

WeRToys is a toy production and exporting company. Although it also sells some toys in the local Thai market, and it, too, has some imported inputs, WeRToys's export sales produce a large fraction of its revenues. Consequently, its operating performance improves with a real depreciation of the baht, but its Japanese owners experience less of this increase in real profitability when the yen strengthens.

The Neutral Firm

RiceNoodle is a restaurant chain that serves the Thai market. It has no export revenues, no direct foreign costs, and no foreign competition. Consequently, RiceNoodle's real profit, which is its baht profit divided by the Thai price level, should not be affected by changes in the real exchange rate. However, a real depreciation of the baht relative to the yen does adversely affect the real value of RiceNoodle's profits for the company's Japanese owners.

---

[4]See Mario Marazzi, Nathan Sheets, Robert Vigfusson, Jon Faust, Joseph Gagnon, Jaime Marquez, Robert Martin, Trevor Reeve, and John Rogers (2005).

[5]The approach in this chapter is based on the analysis in Donald Lessard and David Sharp (1984).

Exhibit 9.7 Operating Profit with a One-to-One Real Exchange Rate Between the Baht and the Yen

	RiceNoodle		ThaiComp		WeRToys	
	Real Baht	**% of Sales**	**Real Baht**	**% of Sales**	**Real Baht**	**% of Sales**
Sales						
Exported	0	0	696	30	1,607	70
Local	2,303	100	1,607	70	696	30
Costs of goods sold						
Imported	0	0	(900)	(39)	(825)	(36)
Local	(1,725)	(75)	(825)	(36)	(900)	(39)
Local fixed costs	(350)	(15)	(350)	(15)	(350)	(15)
Operating profit in real baht	228	10	228	10	228	10
Operating profit in real yen	228	10	228	10	228	10

Initial Operating Profitability

Exhibit 9.7 shows the operating profits earned by the three firms when the real exchange rate (baht/yen) equals 1.

For each subsidiary, the real revenues, real costs, and real operating profits are presented, along with the percentage of total revenue that each category represents. Real units are found by deflating nominal variables denominated in baht by the Thai price level. Exhibit 9.7 indicates that each firm has real revenue of 2,303. Notice that RiceNoodle gets 100% of this revenue from sales in Thailand. ThaiComp gets 70% of its real revenue in the local Thai market and 30% from exports out of Thailand. In contrast, WeRToys gets 30% of its real revenue from the Thai market and 70% from exports. Each firm initially has real costs of goods sold equal to 1,725. Of this, ThaiComp's local costs are only 825, whereas its imported costs are 900. These figures are reversed for WeRToys, whose local costs are 900 and whose imported costs are 825. All three firms have real local fixed costs of 350. By subtracting costs of goods sold and fixed costs from total revenue, we find that each firm has an initial real operating profit of 228, which is 10% of real revenue.

The last line of Exhibit 9.7 evaluates the real operating profit of the three subsidiaries in real yen by dividing by the real exchange rate. Although this conversion has no effect when the real exchange rate is 1, a real depreciation of the baht will involve an increase in the real exchange rate of baht per yen and a consequent lowering of real profitability when the baht are converted into yen. So, even though RiceNoodle is not exposed directly to foreign exchange risk, the Japanese owners of RiceNoodle will still suffer a decline in yen revenue when there is a real depreciation of the baht (as we will see in Exhibit 9.8).

Actual Versus Forecasted Operating Results

If we want to evaluate the performance of a foreign subsidiary's managers, we first need to look at the subsidiary's expected operating results. This represents the managers' best forecasts of what will happen in the upcoming year and how the subsidiaries will respond to changing economic circumstances. For simplicity, assume that Exhibit 9.7 also represents what is expected to happen during the coming year—that managers expect the same real earnings in the year to come, and they do not expect the real exchange rate to change. (Of course, in actual practice, managers generally expect these variables to change.)

Exhibit 9.8 presents the actual operating results for the three firms in the following year. Suppose that during the year, there is a 10% real appreciation of foreign currencies relative to the Thai baht. Thus, the real exchange rate is now 1.1. Let's examine how each firm is doing.

Exhibit 9.8 Actual Operating Profit After a 10% Real Appreciation of the Yen

	RiceNoodle		ThaiComp		WeRToys	
	Real Baht	**% of Sales**	**Real Baht**	**% of Sales**	**Real Baht**	**% of Sales**
Sales						
Exported	0	0	830	35	1,900	75
Local	2,188	100	1,526	65	648	25
Costs of goods sold						
Imported	0	0	(980)	(42)	(945)	(37)
Local	(1,656)	(76)	(810)	(34)	(969)	(38)
Local fixed costs	(333)	(15)	(349)	(15)	(355)	(14)
Operating profit in real baht	199	9	217	9	279	11
% change in real baht profit	(12.7)		(4.8)		22.4	
Operating profit in real yen	181	9	197	9	254	11
% change in real yen profit	(20.6)		(13.5)		11.4	

RiceNoodle's Results

RiceNoodle's real sales are down somewhat relative to what was expected, but its costs are also lower. Real operating profit is 199, down 12.7% from 228. Because the change in the real exchange rate is not supposed to affect RiceNoodle, the local Thai managers must accept responsibility for the shortfall in baht profit relative to what was forecast. Presumably, this would affect the current compensation these managers receive, and continued substandard performance of this kind would probably result in a change in local management. Notice also that real operating profit in yen is even lower because of the real depreciation of the baht. Real operating profit in yen is now 181, down 20.6% from 228. Now, let's consider the other two firms.

Results at ThaiComp and WeRToys

Exhibit 9.8 indicates that the 10% real appreciation of the yen has hurt the profitability of ThaiComp. Real baht operating profit has fallen by 4.8%, to 217 from 228. The increase in imported costs has caused operating profit to fall to 9% of sales from 10%. In contrast, the real baht operating profit of WeRToys has risen by 22.4%, from 228 to 279, and its operating profit is now 11% of total revenue.

The last two lines of Exhibit 9.8 show how converting the baht operating profits of the foreign subsidiaries into real yen by dividing by the real exchange rate lowers the profitability of these firms as well. ThaiComp's real operating profit in yen has fallen by 13.5%, and the good performance of WeRToys, when evaluated in Thai baht, is reduced to an 11.4% increase when converted to real yen.

A naïve interpretation of these annual performances (either in real baht or real yen) would award a substantial bonus to the managers of WeRToys, who produced a profit that impressively exceeded what was forecast. Of course, it would be recognized that the operating environment for WeRToys was favorable, in light of the unanticipated 10% real depreciation of the baht. Still, it would be argued that some of the increase in operating performance was due to superior management. The managers of WeRToys would try to take as much credit for this good performance as possible, arguing that a 22.4% increase in real baht profitability cannot be due strictly to chance.

Evaluating the performance of ThaiComp would be a problem. The managers of ThaiComp would claim that the firm's poor performance was due strictly to the real depreciation of the

Exhibit 9.9 Operating Profit After a 10% Real Appreciation of the Yen: No Response by Managers

	RiceNoodle		ThaiComp		WeRToys	
	Real Baht	% of Sales	Real Baht	% of Sales	Real Baht	% of Sales
Sales						
Exported	0	0	766	32	1,768	70
Local	2,303	100	1,607	68	696	30
Costs of goods sold						
Imported	0	0	(990)	(42)	(908)	(37)
Local	(1,725)	(75)	(825)	(35)	(900)	(37)
Local fixed costs	(350)	(15)	(350)	(15)	(350)	(14)
Operating profit in real baht	228	10	208	8	306	12
% change in real baht profit	0		(8.8)		34.2	
Operating profit in real yen	207	10	189	8	278	12
% change in real yen profit	(9.2)		(17.1)		21.9	

baht. A debate might ensue regarding whether a 4.8% fall in profitability should be expected for this type of firm operating in this adverse environment.

Comparing the Optimal Response with No Response by Managers

The previous section highlights the problem of evaluating the performance of the foreign subsidiaries only with *ex post* information. Because we know ThaiComp will do relatively poorly and WeRToys will do relatively well when the baht suffers a real depreciation, merely observing the direction of the change in operating profit gives no indication of how well the firms' managers are performing. What we need to know is how poorly ThaiComp would be expected to do and how well WeRToys would be expected to do, contingent on a 10% real depreciation of the baht.

Comparisons with No Operating Responses

One starting point would be to evaluate the operating performance of the firms if there were no operating responses by their managers. This perspective is presented in Exhibit 9.9.

With no operating responses, the firms would charge the same relative prices in their local and export markets. They would presumably sell the same quantities, and they would have the same costs of production as in their respective expected budgets in Exhibit 9.7. Differences in sales, costs of goods sold, and profitability would arise merely because each of the figures associated with international transactions—export sales and imported costs—would be multiplied by the new real exchange rate of 1.1.

Now look at Exhibits 9.7 and 9.9. Comparing the two exhibits shows that a 10% real depreciation of the baht, with no operating response by managers, would cause ThaiComp's operating profit in real baht to fall from 228 to 208. The fall of 20 arises, because imported costs rise from 900 to 990, 20 more than the increase in exports from 696 to 766. WeRToys's real baht operating profit would rise from 228 to 306. The increase of 78 arises because at the original one-to-one exchange rate, export revenue (1,607) exceeds imported costs (825) by 782, and the exchange rate has increased by 10%.

It's critical for the Thai managers of the three firms to understand how their imports and exports are affected by real exchange rates changes. In other words, they need to think

Exhibit 9.10 Operating Profit After a 10% Real Appreciation of the Yen: Managers Respond Optimally

	RiceNoodle		ThaiComp		WeRToys	
	Real Baht	**% of Sales**	**Real Baht**	**% of Sales**	**Real Baht**	**% of Sales**
Sales						
Exported	0	0	815	35	1,848	74
Local	2,303	100	1,522	65	644	26
Costs of goods sold						
Imported	0	0	(969)	(41)	(920)	(37)
Local	(1,725)	(75)	(807)	(35)	(913)	(37)
Local fixed costs	(350)	(15)	(350)	(15)	(350)	(14)
Operating profit in real baht	228	10	211	9	309	12
% change in real baht profit	0		(7.5)		35.5	
Operating profit in real yen	207	10	192	9	281	12
% change in real yen profit	(9.2)		(15.8)		23.2	

through what their reactions will be. By responding appropriately to these changes, the firms should be able to achieve higher profits than those shown in Exhibit 9.9.[6]

Comparisons with Optimal Responses

Earlier in this chapter, we indicated that the firms' responses to a real depreciation of the baht would involve an appropriate pricing-to-market strategy. That is, in response to a real depreciation of the baht, the firms should try to shift some sales from the Thai market to the export market. This could be accomplished by increasing the relative price charged in the Thai market and decreasing the relative price charged in the export market. The increase in the import costs of production also dictates reducing the overall quantity of production for ThaiComp because its costs have increased more than the benefit of additional international sales. WeRToys, on the other hand, should expand production.

Exhibit 9.10 provides this contingent forecasting information associated with the managers' anticipated responses to a 10% real depreciation of the baht.

Notice that revenues from export sales are higher for ThaiComp and WeRToys than in Exhibit 9.9 and that their revenues from local sales are lower than in Exhibit 9.9. Also, ThaiComp's local costs of production and imported costs of production are lower in Exhibit 9.10 than in Exhibit 9.9. These lower costs reflect the decreased output of the firm. Overall, with an optimal response by ThaiComp to the real depreciation of the baht, the operating profit in real baht is 211, which is 1% higher than the corresponding value in Exhibit 9.9. WeRToys, the net exporter, can also do better. Exhibit 9.10 indicates that WeRToys can produce an operating profit in real baht of 309, which is slightly better than the corresponding value of 306 in Exhibit 9.9.

Who Deserves a Bonus?

The question of which of the three Thai companies deserves a bonus is now easily assessed. Exhibit 9.11 compares the actual operating results (shown in Exhibit 9.8) after a 10% real appreciation of the yen to the anticipated operating responses (shown in Exhibit 9.10) that are

---

[6]Richard Marston's (2001) research indicates that the first-order effect of a real depreciation with an optimal operating response is still given by the effect of the real exchange rate on the net exposure of the firm because the firm has already optimized quantities it is selling in each market. Hence, changes in the quantities produced and sold in the different markets will not produce large improvements in operating profit.

Exhibit 9.11 Actual versus Optimal Operating Profit After a 10% Real Appreciation of the Yen

	RiceNoodle		ThaiComp		WeRToys	
	Real Baht		Real Baht		Real Baht	
	Optimal	Actual	Optimal	Actual	Optimal	Actual
Sales						
Exported	0	0	815	830	1,848	1,900
Local	2,303	2,188	1,522	1,526	644	648
Costs of goods sold						
Imported	0	0	(969)	(980)	(920)	(945)
Local	(1,725)	(1,656)	(807)	(810)	(913)	(969)
Local fixed costs	(350)	(333)	(350)	(349)	(350)	(355)
Operating profit in real baht	228	199	211	217	309	279
% change in real baht profit	0	(12.7)	(7.5)	(4.8)	35.5	22.4
Operating profit in real yen	207	181	192	197	281	254
% change in real yen profit	(9.2)	(20.6)	(15.8)	(13.5)	23.2	11.4

contingent upon the same 10% real appreciation of the yen. Notice that only ThaiComp's actual results are better than the optimal result. Managers can do better than they anticipate, because they have additional information and can respond to it.

RiceNoodle's local sales were less than anticipated, but so were its costs. Unfortunately, its operating profit falls short of what was expected, conditional on operating in the new environment.

WeRToys actually sold more goods than was anticipated, both in Thailand and as exports from Thailand. Unfortunately, all of its costs, imported, local, and fixed, were higher than they should have been. Its overall profit of 279 falls substantially short of the 309 that should have been produced.

ThaiComp, on the other hand, was operating in an adverse environment. Its actual local revenues were higher, as were its exports. Its imported costs and its local fixed costs were also higher than expected. Overall, though, ThaiComp's real operating profit of 217 exceeds the 211 that was forecast for this situation. After converting to real yen, its operating profit of 197 exceeds the contingent value of 192. Clearly, the management of ThaiComp deserves a bonus for their superior performance.

Assessing the Long-Run Viability of a Subsidiary

The contingent forecasting approach can be used to assess the long-run viability of a subsidiary as it is currently being managed. Suppose that, at the real exchange rate of 1, the Thai baht is currently 10% undervalued relative to the Japanese yen. We know that in the long run, such an undervaluation is likely to be corrected. This will provide a favorable shock to the profitability of ThaiComp, the net importer, as the baht strengthens in real terms; but it will hurt the long-run profitability of WeRToys, the net exporter.

Exhibit 9.12 provides the anticipated operating responses for the three firms, contingent on a 10% real depreciation of the yen to a new real exchange rate of 0.9 (baht/yen). The figures incorporate the optimal operating responses of each firm.

RiceNoodle has no exposure to real exchange rates, so its real operating profit in Thailand is anticipated to remain at 228 baht. However, when the profits are converted into real yen, the appreciation of the baht raises the value to 253 yen.

Compared to the base case in Exhibit 9.7 with a real exchange rate of 1, the real appreciation of the baht increases ThaiComp's real operating profit in Thailand from 228 to 251.

Exhibit 9.12 Operating Profit After a 10% Real Depreciation of the Yen: Managers Respond Optimally

	RiceNoodle		ThaiComp		WeRToys	
	Real Baht	% of Sales	Real Baht	% of Sales	Real Baht	% of Sales
Sales						
Exported	0	0	574	25	1,361	65
Local	2,303	100	1,687	75	745	35
Costs of goods sold						
Imported	0	0	(822)	(36)	(725)	(34)
Local	(1,725)	(75)	(838)	(37)	(878)	(42)
Local fixed costs	(350)	(15)	(350)	(15)	(350)	(17)
Operating profit in real baht	228	10	251	11	153	7
% change in operating profit	0		10.1		(32.9)	
Operating profit in real yen	253	10	279	11	170	7
% change in real yen profit	11		22.4		(25.4)	

When this is converted to real yen, the real profits increase to 279, which is 22.4% higher than the base case.

In contrast, a real appreciation of the baht hurts WeRToys. Even with optimal operating responses, the firm's real operating profit in Thailand would be expected to fall from 228 in the base case to 153. The conversion to real yen increases this to 170 yen, but this still represents a 25.4% fall in real operating profit. Because the operating margin is now only 7%, WeRToys looks like a marginal business unless an alternative operating strategy can be found to increase its profitability.

9.6 STRATEGIES FOR MANAGING REAL EXCHANGE RISK

Given that real exchange rates fluctuate, how should the management team of a large multinational firm respond to various real exchange risks? The most important point is that managers must recognize that the influences of real exchange rates are pervasive. They directly affect foreign pricing and domestic costs of foreign imports, but they also affect the nature of competition between firms in different countries.

Obviously, financial managers must understand these risks, but hedging against adverse real exchange risks is complicated. Consequently, we devote Chapter 17 to a more formal analysis of that issue. Here we merely note that financial hedging can help by assuring the firm of cash flow when changes in exchange rates would otherwise make the firm unprofitable.

It is also important for marketing and operations managers to understand the nature of real exchange risks that the firm faces. The managers of the firm must be aware that fluctuations in real exchange rates will create problem situations and profit opportunities that call for appropriate managerial responses.

Transitory Versus Permanent Changes in Real Exchange Rates

One key element that influences a firm's optimal response to a given change in the real exchange rate is the length of time that the change in the real exchange rate is expected to persist. How long a real depreciation is expected to last can affect both the amount of the exposure and managers' possible responses to that exposure. The time frame of the change in the exchange rate affects the firm's response because it is costly to change the operations of the firm. The next sections explore how managers can respond to real exchange rates in a dynamic way.

Production Management

How can a firm's production processes be designed to reflect real foreign exchange risk? Certainly, the production schedule, the sourcing of inputs, and even the location of production facilities ought to be sensitive to prospective fluctuations in real exchange rates.

Production Scheduling

Production scheduling must be sensitive to the real exchange rate because its fluctuations affect the demand for the firm's products. Many firms build up inventory to meet their transitory fluctuations in demand because it is usually less costly to run a smooth production process than a fluctuating one. Inventories accumulate during periods of slack demand, and inventories fall during periods of high demand, but production remains steady. In Example 9.5, we saw how a real appreciation of the foreign currency motivates a monopolist to increase its exports to foreign markets. In that example, per-unit costs were constant. However, if per-unit costs increase with the amount of production because of overtime pay and increased maintenance costs related to machines when output increases, the monopolist can earn more revenue in the foreign market simply by selling more of the product out of inventory than by increasing production. The major factor that determines by how much the firm will increase the sale of its goods in inventory versus increasing production depends on the persistence of the change in the real exchange rate. The more persistent the change, the longer the firm expects to have high demand, and the more the firm will want to increase its production rather than sell out of inventory. If the change in the exchange rate were perceived as permanent, the firm would want to permanently adjust its prices and production.

Input Sourcing

The sources of materials and intermediate parts in the production process should be sensitive to the real exchange rate. When the domestic currency is strong, domestic companies should use foreign inputs because they will be relatively inexpensive. But these foreign sources should be lined up in advance to take full advantage of the fluctuations in exchange rates.

One mitigating influence that prevents manufacturers from changing between domestic and foreign suppliers is the value the firm puts on its long-term relationships with its suppliers. Having a stable and reliable source of parts or materials is a valuable asset. If the firm shifts to a foreign supplier today, there is no guarantee that its current domestic supplier will still be interested in servicing the firm's business in the future. Thus, managers must assess how long the domestic currency is expected to remain strong. If the firm switches too quickly to a foreign supplier in response to a transitory real appreciation of the domestic currency, it may ultimately end up with no domestic suppliers or with unreliable suppliers when the domestic currency depreciates and foreign supplies are no longer competitively priced.

Using foreign suppliers can also either mitigate or exacerbate a firm's exposure to real exchange risk. For example, if a firm is exporting a lot to a country that has a foreign supplier, using the supplier would mitigate the real exchange risk. But if using the foreign supplier adds a new source of real exchange risk, the domestic firm's managers must think about this dimension as well as the respective domestic and foreign costs.

Plant Location Decisions

If a multinational firm has production operations in several countries, it is natural for the managers to shift production among the plants to minimize costs. As real exchange rates fluctuate,

Exhibit 9.13 A Production Manager's Responses to Real Exchange Rates

Production Issue	Response to a Transitory Rate Change	Response to a Persistent Rate Change
Production scheduling	Let inventory fluctuate	Change production amount
Input sourcing	Use domestic suppliers	Switch to foreign suppliers
Plant location	Use domestic plants	Set up a foreign plant

the firm can increase production in countries whose currencies have depreciated in real terms, and it can decrease production in countries whose currencies have strengthened in real terms. However, because opening a plant abroad represents a long-term investment, management should be reasonably sure that the current cost advantage that the country enjoys is not likely to be undone by a real appreciation of the foreign currency. It may be that the currency has experienced a temporary real depreciation that is likely to be reversed within a few years.

In the 1990s, Japanese and European car manufacturers such as Toyota and BMW invested in U.S. production facilities to hedge against the adverse effects of a real depreciation of the dollar. With their production facilities located in the market of their sales, only their sales profits were exposed to the risk of dollar depreciation. In contrast, when these firms merely export products to the United States, their revenues are entirely exposed to possible losses if the dollar depreciates.

A firm's ability to shift production around the world is also limited by the cost structure of its plants. If a firm operates a plant that is too small, it loses the economies of scale it could have obtained by operating a larger plant, and this increases its costs per unit. Thus, instead of limiting its real exchange risk by operating smaller plants in different countries, a firm might choose to achieve economies of scale by operating a single large plant.

A good example of this situation occurred after Jaguar was privatized in 1984. At the time, Jaguar had only one plant, which was located in the United Kingdom. Because over 50% of its sales were made in the United States, when the dollar weakened in the late 1980s, Jaguar's revenues plummeted. One way to limit the exposure of Jaguar's U.S. dollar revenue stream would have been to build a production facility in the United States. But the economies of scale Jaguar needed to remain profitable didn't allow for this.

In 1989, Jaguar became the takeover target of General Motors and Ford. These companies realized that Jaguar was more valuable as part of a larger company than as an independent entity. Ford subsequently purchased Jaguar and began sourcing additional parts from the United States. Unfortunately, even after massive capital investments, Jaguar never achieved the profitability that Ford predicted.

These issues are summarized in Exhibit 9.13.

Marketing Management

How can marketing strategy and pricing policy be designed to offset real foreign exchange risk? Pricing policies, promotional strategies, market entry decisions, and even product development should be designed with exchange rate changes in mind.

Pricing Policies

We have already discussed some specific examples of pricing-to-market. In general, however, when a currency depreciates, exporters to that country face a trade-off: They can maintain either their profits or their market shares, but not both. If the firm increases its foreign currency price to maintain its profit, it will lose sales to foreign rivals. If the firm maintains a given foreign currency price, it will maintain its market share but lose profit. Research indicates that the optimal thing for firms to do lies somewhere between the two extremes. Faced with a real depreciation of the foreign currency, an exporter typically increases its relative price in the foreign country but not by the full percentage of the depreciation. The firm loses market share and earns a smaller profit on all sales.

A couple of factors affect this strategy, however. One is the elasticity of demand for the exporter's product. If demand is highly elastic, the firm's loss of market share will be large when the product's price is increased. In this case, the exporter needs to lean toward not increasing its prices. By contrast, if demand is highly inelastic, the exporter can afford to increase its prices by a greater amount. Another factor has to do with the nature of the firm's cost structure. For example, if there are important economies of scale in production, the firm's costs will increase significantly if it reduces production. Hence, the firm will hold down foreign price increases in response to a foreign currency depreciation to keep the demand for its products high. In contrast, if the firm's costs are less affected when the company loses market share, the firm may be able to reduce the quantities it produces and increase its prices.

The Frequency of Price Adjustments

A marketing consideration that should be addressed is how frequently prices are adjusted. Demand for a product often depends on the stability of its price. Consumers want to be able to compare items in different stores, and this takes time. Potential customers want to know nominal prices in advance, and this requires advertising. Customers hate surprise price increases. Given that consumers like price stability, foreign exporters are faced with the decision of how frequently to adjust prices in response to exchange rate changes. Firms consequently develop boundaries for exchange rate fluctuations that will not trigger a change in the firm's foreign currency prices. Then, only sufficiently large changes in exchange rates cause the firm to change its product price.

Market Entry Decisions

Firms often introduce new products in foreign markets when the foreign currencies are strong in real terms. Doing so allows a firm to set a comparatively low foreign currency price for a product so that it can better compete and become an established player in the market. For example, the large real appreciation of the dollar from 1980 to 1985 gave Honda and Toyota a golden opportunity to penetrate the U.S. market with low dollar prices that translated into high yen revenues. The Japanese companies were able to establish a reputation in the United States for providing high-quality, low-priced cars. This reputation persisted in the United States, even after a substantial real appreciation of the yen.

Brand Loyalty

Brand loyalty describes a situation in which consumers continue to purchase a brand they have purchased in the past even though it costs more now.[7] Developing brand loyalty clearly helps in situations of real exchange risk because consumers will not switch to competitors' products that enjoy a temporary pricing benefit from a favorable fluctuation in the exchange rate. Thus, it is important for a domestic company to develop loyal customers—especially when it's facing competition from abroad. But the firm must also recognize that in entering a foreign market, it will have to win over the customers who are loyal to brands in their home countries. That said, entering a foreign market when the foreign currency is strong in real terms makes a lot of sense because the firm can use advertising campaigns and low foreign prices to get consumers to try its product without sacrificing too much profit. Establishing a

---

[7]Is brand loyalty a rational phenomenon? Whenever consumers cannot easily find out information about how a new product will perform without experiencing the product, it is costly for consumers to switch brands. In such a situation, brand loyalty is a rational economic phenomenon. Economists use the term *experience goods* for this situation, and in such markets, future demand depends on current market share. (See Kenneth Froot and Paul Klemperer [1989], for a formal analysis of these effects.)

Exhibit 9.14 A Checklist for Managers of Real Exchange Risk

Production inputs—Source inputs from suppliers in countries suffering real depreciations of their currencies.

Production location—Shift production to plants located in countries suffering real depreciations of their currencies or countries with low-cost production.

Pricing-to-market—Allow a real appreciation of the foreign currency to increase the profitability of foreign sales but lower foreign prices to expand market share.

Market entry—Begin selling in foreign markets after a real appreciation of the foreign currency.

Brand loyalty—Create loyal customers who will not "buy foreign" when the domestic currency strengthens in real terms.

Price consistently—Recognize that exchange rates will be more volatile than prices of goods. Be prepared for short-run swings in profitability due to exchange rates.

Hedging—Use derivative securities such as forward contracts or options to hedge foreign exchange risk to assure cash flow when changes in exchange rates would make the firm unprofitable.

Currency of denomination of debt—Denominate long-term debt in foreign currencies in which the firm has substantial assets or sales to reduce exposure to foreign exchange risk.

large foreign market share when the foreign currency is strong in real terms means that a large number of foreign customers will have tried the firm's product. These foreign customers will not all be lost when the foreign currency depreciates in real terms and the firm is forced to raise foreign currency prices.

The discussion in this section is summarized in Exhibit 9.14.

9.7 Summary

This chapter introduces the idea of real exchange risk. The main points in the chapter are as follows:

1. Real exchange risk, which is also called real operating exposure and real economic exposure, is the variability in the present value of a firm's profits that is caused by unpredictable fluctuations in real exchange rates.

2. A real depreciation of the domestic currency makes domestic exporters and import competitors more profitable because it shifts demand to the domestic market.

3. The pass-through to product prices from changes in real exchange rates is not one-to-one if goods markets are not perfectly competitive because producers optimally adjust their profits in response to fluctuations in the real exchange rate.

4. Real exchange risk is present in any long-term contract between parties from two countries that do not share a common currency. Making product prices in the contract contingent upon the real exchange rate helps firms share the real operating risk.

5. Evaluating the performance of a foreign subsidiary is complicated by fluctuations in real exchange rates. Establishing contingent forecasts based on optimal responses by managers can help determine how they have performed under a variety of exchange rate scenarios.

6. Managers can utilize pricing, promotional, and product development strategies to help reduce real exchange risks. The extent to which they are able to utilize these strategies depends on a firm's economies of scale and the elasticity of its demand curve.

7. Fluctuations in real exchange rates affect the cost of operating in different countries. A firm's input sources and plant location decisions need to take this into account.

Questions

1. As the vice president of finance for a U.S. firm, what do you say to your production manager when he states, "We shouldn't let foreign exchange risk interfere with our profitability. Let's simply invoice all our foreign customers in dollars and be done with it."

2. Lands' End is a U.S. mail-order company that sells clothing primarily from catalogs. Initially, all its catalog prices were quoted in U.S. dollars, but recently, the company has expanded and begun printing catalogs with prices denominated in British

pounds. Given that the company wants to stand behind its prices for several months, what should the company do if the dollar–pound exchange rate changes?

3. What do economists mean by *pricing-to-market*?

4. Why does a monopolist not charge the same price for the same good in two different countries?

5. What determines how much a foreign producer allows the dollar price of a product sold in the United States to be affected by a change in the real exchange rate?

6. Why is the pass-through from changes in exchange rates to changes in the prices of products not one-for-one?

7. Given that real exchange rates fluctuate, when would be the best time to enter the market of a foreign country as an exporter to that market?

8. You have been asked to evaluate possible sites for an Asian production facility that will manufacture your firm's products and sell them to the Asian market. What real exchange rate considerations should you entertain in your evaluation?

PROBLEMS

1. Suppose that you have one domestic production facility that supplies both the domestic and foreign markets. Assume that the demand for your product in the domestic market is $Q = 2,000 - 3P$ and in the foreign market, demand is given by $Q^* = 2,000 - 2P^*$. Assume that your domestic marginal cost of production is 600. If the initial real exchange rate is 1, what are your optimal prices and quantities sold in the two markets? By how much will you change the relative prices of your product if the foreign currency appreciates in real terms by 10%? What will you do to production?

2. How would you respond in Problem 1 if the marginal cost of production were increasing? Why?

3. Suppose you are a monopolist who faces a domestic demand curve given by $Q = 1,000 - 2P$. Your domestic cost of production involves domestic costs per unit of 300 and a foreign cost per unit produced of 150. If the real exchange rate is 1.1, what would be the price you would charge and the quantity you would sell? How do these variables change when the real exchange rate increases by 10%?

BIBLIOGRAPHY

Bodnar, Gordon M., Bernard Dumas, and Richard C. Marston, 2002, "Pass-Through and Exposure," *Journal of Finance* 57, pp. 199–231.

Bodnar, Gordon M., and Richard C. Marston, 2001, "A Simple Model of Foreign Exchange Exposure," in Takashi Negishi, Rama Ramachandran, and Kazuo Mino, eds., *Economic Theory, Dynamics and Markets: Essays in Honor of Ryuzo Sato*, New York: Kluwer Academic Press.

Campa, José Manuel, and Linda S. Goldberg, 2005, "Exchange Rate Pass-Through into Import Prices," *Review of Economics and Statistics* 87, pp. 679–690.

Campa, José Manuel, and Linda S. Goldberg, 2006, "Distribution Margins, Imported Inputs, and the Sensitivity of the CPI to Exchange Rates," Federal Reserve Bank of New York staff report no. 247.

Dornbusch, Rudiger, 1987, "Exchange Rates and Prices," *American Economic Review* 77, pp. 93–106.

Feenstra, Robert C., 1989, "Symmetric Pass-Through of Tariffs and Exchange Rates Under Imperfect Competition: An Empirical Test," *Journal of International Economics* 27, pp. 25–45.

Fisher, Eric, 1989, "A Model of Exchange Rate Pass-Through," *Journal of International Economics* 26, pp. 119–137.

Froot, Kenneth A., and Paul D. Klemperer, 1989, "Exchange Rate Pass-Through When Market Share Matters," *American Economic Review* 79, pp. 637–653.

Kasa, Kenneth, 1992, "Adjustment Costs and Pricing-to-Market: Theory and Evidence," *Journal of International Economics* 32, pp. 1–30.

Knetter, Michael, 1989, "Price Discrimination by U.S. and German Exporters," *American Economic Review* 79, pp. 198–210.

Knetter, Michael, 1993, "International Comparisons in Pricing-to-Market" *American Economic Review* 83, pp. 473–486.

Krugman, Paul, 1987, "Pricing-to-Market When the Exchange Rate Changes," in Sven W. Arndt and J. David Richardson, eds., *Real-Financial Linkages Among Open Economies*, Cambridge, MA: MIT Press.

Lessard, Donald R., and David Sharp, 1984, "Measuring the Performance of Operations Subject to Fluctuating Exchange Rates," *Midland Corporate Finance Journal* 2, pp. 18–30.

Mann, Catherine, 1986, "Prices, Profit Margins, and Exchange Rates," *Federal Reserve Bulletin* 72, pp. 366–379.

Marazzi, Mario, Nathan Sheets, Robert Vigfusson, Jon Faust, Joseph Gagnon, Jaime Marquez, Robert Martin, Trevor Reeve, and John Rogers, 2005, "Exchange Rate Pass-Through to U.S. Import Prices: Some New Evidence," Board of Governors of the Federal Reserve System international finance discussion paper no. 833.

Marston, Richard C., 1990, "Pricing-to-Market in Japanese Manufacturing," *Journal of International Economics* 29, pp. 217–236.

Marston, Richard, 2001, "The Effects of Industry Structure on Economic Exposure," *Journal of International Money and Finance* 20, pp. 149–164.

Shapiro, Alan C., 1984, "The Evaluation and Control of Foreign Affiliates," *Midland Corporate Finance Journal* 2, pp. 13–25.

Williamson, Rohan, 2001, "Exchange Rate Exposure and Competition: Evidence from the Automobile Industry," *Journal of Financial Economics* 59, 441–475.

The Economist, "A Different Kind of Package Holiday," July 14, 2001, U.S. edition.

Yang, Jiawen, 1997, "Exchange Rate Pass-Through in U.S. Manufacturing Industries," *Review of Economics and Statistics* 79, pp. 95–104.

Chapter 10

Exchange Rate Determination and Forecasting

*D*uring April 1995, the value of the dollar in terms of the Japanese yen hovered around ¥80/$. On December 20, 2001, it was ¥128.55/$. In other words, the dollar strengthened by over 60% in 5½ years. What drives such extraordinary changes in relative currency valuations, and can we predict their direction and magnitude? Economists have developed many different models to explain why exchange rates fluctuate, but no one has yet discovered the truth. In fact, even the ability to explain exchange rate movements after the fact is quite limited. Nevertheless, because exchange rates are so important, financial institutions devote substantial resources to producing forecasts for their clients, and forecasting firms successfully market currency forecasts.

In Chapter 3, we saw how currency forecasts help a firm to quantify its transactions exposure. Multinational firms also use currency forecasts to value foreign projects they are undertaking, to develop their international operational strategies, to establish prices for their products in foreign markets, and to manage their working capital. International portfolio managers use exchange rate forecasts to evaluate the desirability of investing in particular foreign equity and bond markets. These managers also use currency forecasts to help decide whether to hedge the currency risks related to the portfolios they manage.

Should managers purchase sophisticated currency forecasts? If markets are relatively efficient, it should be difficult to produce better short-term forecasts than forward exchange rates portend or better long-term forecasts than uncovered interest rate parity predicts. In particular, we will see that if covered and uncovered interest rate parity, the unbiasedness hypothesis, and purchasing power parity were to hold, managers would not be willing to pay for currency forecasts. However, there is considerable evidence that these parity conditions do not always hold, especially in the short run. Therefore, currency forecasts are potentially valuable so we review techniques that are used to forecast exchange rates. We discuss two categories: fundamental analysis and technical analysis, and we examine their empirical performance. Because of the dramatic currency crises in a number of developing countries with pegged systems in the 1990s, forecasts in these systems are of special interest.

10.1 PARITY CONDITIONS AND EXCHANGE RATE FORECASTS

The covered interest rate parity (CIRP) relationship, discussed in Chapter 6, links forward rates, spot rates, and interest rate differentials. Uncovered interest rate parity (UIRP), discussed in Chapter 7, which is sometimes referred to as the *international Fisher relationship* (named for the economist Irving Fisher), links expected exchange rate changes and interest rate differentials, whereas the unbiasedness hypothesis links forward rates and expected future exchange rates. Purchasing power parity (PPP), discussed in Chapter 8, provides a link between inflation rates and rates of change of exchange rates. To close the loop between expected future exchange rate changes, forward rates, interest rates, and rates of inflation, we need another well-known relationship: the *Fisher hypothesis*. After discussing the Fisher hypothesis, we demonstrate how all the parity conditions together lead to a world in which currency forecasting is not necessary. This hypothetical world constitutes an interesting benchmark for judging the potential value of currency forecasts.

The Fisher Hypothesis

Interest Rates and Inflation

The interest rates we have discussed thus far are nominal interest rates. That is, they promise a nominal or money rate of return. For example, if the interest rate on a 1-year dollar money market deposit is 8%, you anticipate receiving $1.08 in 1 year for every dollar you deposit today. Irving Fisher (1930), an eminent American economist, noted that nominal interest rates should reflect expectations of the rate of inflation. This is easy to understand.

Your happiness with the 8% return you earned on your money market deposit will depend on how prices in the economy evolve over the year. If prices increase by less than 8%, the purchasing power of your $1.08 then will be greater than the purchasing power of your $1.00 today. You will experience a positive real return. Conversely, if prices increase by more than 8%, your purchasing power will be lower. You will have a negative real return. Thus, if you expect prices to increase by more than 8% over the course of the year, you will be reluctant to accept an 8% deposit rate because the 8% return is insufficient to maintain the purchasing power of the money you are lending.

Whenever someone lends money and is scheduled to receive nominal or monetary interest as a return in the future, the lender faces a risk that the money denominated in the contract may lose purchasing power during the time of the loan because of inflation. In Chapter 8, we noted that if $P(t)$ is the price level of the United States at time t, then $\dfrac{\$1}{P(t)}$ is the purchasing power of 1 dollar, which is the amount of goods and services that 1 dollar can buy. We saw that inflation, which is the rate of increase of the price level, drives down the purchasing power of the money.

Real Rates of Return

As a lender, you care about the real return on your investment, which is the return that measures your increase in purchasing power between two periods of time. If you invest $1, you sacrifice $\dfrac{\$1}{P(t)}$ real goods now. But in 1 year, you get back $\dfrac{1+i}{P(t+1)}$ in real goods, where i is the nominal rate of interest. We calculate the real return by dividing the real amount you get back by the real amount that you invest. Thus, if r^{ep} is the *ex post* real rate of return, we have

$$1 + r^{ep} = \frac{\left(\dfrac{1+i}{P(t+1)}\right)}{\left(\dfrac{1}{P(t)}\right)} = \frac{(1+i)}{\left(\dfrac{P(t+1)}{P(t)}\right)} \tag{10.1}$$

Notice that the real rate of return depends on the realization of the rate of inflation because $P(t+1)/P(t) = 1 + \pi(t+1)$, where $\pi(t+1)$ is the rate of inflation between time t and $t+1$. For simplicity, we drop the time notation and simply write Equation (10.1) as

$$1 + r^{ep} = \frac{(1 + i)}{(1 + \pi)} \qquad (10.2)$$

If we subtract 1 from each side of Equation (10.2), we have

$$r^{ep} = \frac{(1 + i)}{(1 + \pi)} - \frac{(1 + \pi)}{(1 + \pi)} = \frac{i - \pi}{(1 + \pi)} \qquad (10.3)$$

which is often approximated as

$$r^{ep} = i - \pi \qquad (10.4)$$

The approximation involves ignoring the term $(1 + \pi)$ in the denominator of Equation (10.3), which is close to 1 if inflation is not too high. Equation (10.4) states that the *ex post* real interest rate equals the nominal interest rate minus the actual rate of inflation.[1] In other words, if the nominal interest rate is, say, 8%, and the actual rate of inflation is, say, 3%, your *ex post* real interest rate will be 5%.

The Ex Ante Real Interest Rate

Because the inflation rate is uncertain at the time an investment is made, the lender cannot know with certainty the real rate of return on the loan. By taking the expected value of both sides of Equation (10.4), conditional on the information set at the time of the loan, we derive the lender's expected real rate of return, which is also called the **expected real interest rate**, or the *ex ante real interest rate*, which we denote r^e:

$$r^e = E_t[r^{ep}] = i(t) - E_t[\pi(t+1)] \qquad (10.5)$$

If we rearrange the terms in Equation (10.5), we have

$$i(t) = r^e + E_t[\pi(t+1)] = r^e + \pi^e \qquad (10.6)$$

where we define π^e as expected inflation, $E_t[\pi(t+1)]$.

Equation (10.6) states that the nominal interest rate is the sum of the expected real interest rate and the **expected rate of inflation**. This decomposition of the nominal interest rate is often referred to as the **Fisher hypothesis**, or the *Fisher equation*.

If expected real interest rates are similar across countries, countries with high expected inflation rates will have high nominal interest rates, and countries with low expected inflation rates will have low nominal interest rates. The real interest rate is important because it influences investment decisions. Firms will want to borrow money and invest in projects only if the expected rate of return on the investment is greater than the real interest rate.

---

[1] An alternative interpretation of Equation (10.4) that involves no approximations uses the continuously compounded nominal interest rate and rate of inflation. The continuously compounded real rate of return, r^{ep}, is

$$\exp(r^{ep}) = \exp(i)\frac{P(t)}{P(t+1)}$$

Hence, by taking the natural logarithm of both sides of the equation and defining the continuously compounded rate of inflation, $\pi = \ln[P(t+1)] - \ln[P(t)]$, we have

$$r^{ep} = i - \{\ln[P(t+1)] - \ln[P(t)]\} = i - \pi$$

See the appendix to Chapter 2 for a review of continuous compounding.

Example 10.1 The Real Interest Rate in Mexico

Suppose the nominal interest rate in Mexico is 10%, and the expected rate of inflation in Mexico is 7%. What is the expected real rate of return in Mexico? From Equation (10.5) we have

$$r^e = 10\% - 7\% = 3\%$$

By investing in an asset that pays a nominal interest rate of 10% when the expected rate of inflation is 7%, the investor expects to earn a 3% real rate of return. In other words, the investor expects to have 3% more purchasing power over goods and services at the end of the year for every Mexican peso invested than she currently has from these pesos.

The Fisher hypothesis is a reasonable approximation for thinking about a long-run link between inflation and interest rates. Exhibit 10.1 graphs average long-term government bond yields in the 1990s for nine countries on the vertical axis versus the countries' average inflation rates during the same period on the horizontal axis.

As the Fisher hypothesis suggests, the relationship is clearly positive, and the slope of the regression line is insignificantly different from 1. That is, for each additional 1% of inflation, the nominal government bond yield is about 1% higher. Hence, for long-term averages, real interest rates appear to be equal across countries. The intercept on the vertical axis of 3.63%

Exhibit 10.1 Long-Term Government Bond Yields and Inflation Rates (for Nine Countries, 1990–2000)

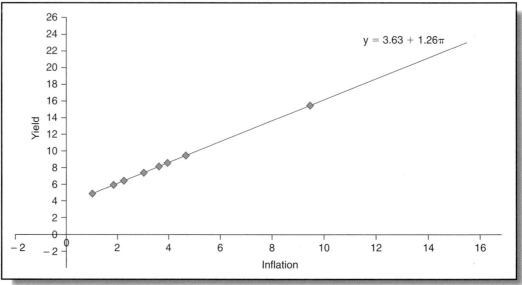

Note: The vertical axis measures average government bond yields for 1990–2000. The horizontal axis measures the average annual inflation rate over the same period. The line represents a regression of yield (y) on inflation (π). The diamonds represent observations for nine countries: the United States, Canada, Japan, France, Germany, Italy, the United Kingdom, South Africa, and Thailand. It appears as if only eight countries are represented on the graph because the observations for Canada and Germany are practically on top of one another. Data are from International Financial Statistics of the IMF.

is also a very reasonable estimate of the real interest rate. We will discuss short-term real interest rate differentials shortly.

The International Parity Conditions

The covered interest rate parity (CIRP), uncovered interest rate parity (UIRP), and purchasing power parity (PPP) relationships, together with the Fisher hypothesis, are sometimes referred to as the **international parity conditions**. To review these conditions, consider the numeric example in Exhibit 10.2, which examines exchange rates, interest rates, and expected inflation rates for the United Kingdom and Switzerland. Exchange rates are measured as Swiss francs per British pound, CHF/GBP.

Exhibit 10.2   An Example of International Parity Conditions: The United Kingdom and Switzerland

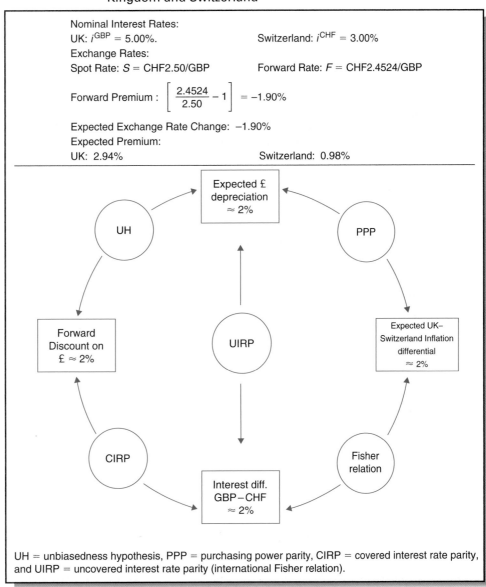

Nominal Interest Rates:
UK: i^{GBP} = 5.00%.   Switzerland: i^{CHF} = 3.00%
Exchange Rates:
Spot Rate: S = CHF2.50/GBP   Forward Rate: F = CHF2.4524/GBP

Forward Premium : $\left[\dfrac{2.4524}{2.50} - 1\right]$ = −1.90%

Expected Exchange Rate Change: −1.90%
Expected Premium:
UK: 2.94%   Switzerland: 0.98%

Expected £ depreciation ≈ 2%

UH

PPP

Forward Discount on £ ≈ 2%

UIRP

Expected UK–Switzerland Inflation differential ≈ 2%

CIRP

Fisher relation

Interest diff. GBP−CHF ≈ 2%

UH = unbiasedness hypothesis, PPP = purchasing power parity, CIRP = covered interest rate parity, and UIRP = uncovered interest rate parity (international Fisher relation).

Notes: Data on interest rates and exchange rates are from *The Financial Times*, May 8, 2001.

CIRP

At the bottom of the diagram in Exhibit 10.2, we find a 2% nominal interest differential between the countries. From covered interest parity, we can relate the interest differential to the forward premium:

$$\text{Forward premium} = \text{Annualization factor} \times \frac{\text{Forward rate} - \text{Spot rate}}{\text{Spot rate}}$$

For 1-year contracts, the annualization factor is 1, and the forward premium is −1.90%. Because the United Kingdom has the higher interest rate, its currency must be at a discount in the forward market; otherwise, an arbitrage opportunity exists.

UIRP or Unbiasedness

If the forward rate is an unbiased predictor of the future spot rate, the forward discount on the pound means that the market expects the pound to depreciate by the amount of the forward discount, which brings us to the top of the diagram. We could have also moved to the top directly by observing that the higher interest rate on the pound must mean that British investors in Swiss francs expect a capital gain on holding Swiss francs to increase their expected return up to the higher pound return.

PPP

Relative PPP requires that the expected change in the exchange rate reflects the differential in inflation rates, so if the British pound is expected to weaken versus the Swiss franc, British inflation is expected to be higher than Swiss inflation by about 2%. This brings us to the right-hand side of Exhibit 10.2, where the inflation differential is 1.96% (also about 2%). (The small difference in percentage calculations arises because we are using inflation rates calculated in simple percentage terms. The percentage changes are identical if the computations use continuously compounded rates.)

To see this, remember from Chapter 8 that relative PPP predicts

$$\frac{S(t+1)}{S(t)} - 1 = \frac{1 + \pi(\text{SW})}{1 + \pi(\text{UK})} - 1 = \frac{\pi(\text{SW}) - \pi(\text{UK})}{1 + \pi(\text{UK})}$$

Because of the presence of UK inflation in the denominator, the inflation differential is slightly larger than the percentage rate of change of the exchange rate. Now we know that inflation is the fundamental reason for the higher British nominal interest rates observed in the first place. The United Kingdom has higher expected inflation than Switzerland, which brings us back to the bottom of the exhibit through the Fisher relationship.

Real Interest Rates and the Parity Conditions

Real Interest Rate Parity

What are the real interest rates in the United Kingdom and Switzerland? According to Equation (10.5), the real interest rate is

$$r^e = \frac{1 + i}{1 + \pi^e} - 1$$

Plugging in the numbers for both the United Kingdom and Switzerland gives real interest rates of 2% in both cases. This is no coincidence. If the parity conditions all hold simultaneously, real interest rates are equal across countries. If uncovered interest rate parity and PPP hold, the nominal interest rate differential between the United Kingdom and Switzerland reflects only an expected inflation differential. Then, by rearranging terms, we find that the real return is the same in each country.

In a world where all the parity conditions hold, multinational business would be rather simple. International pricing would be easy because prices in foreign countries would move in line

Exhibit 10.3 Real Interest Rates at Different Maturities

	3 Months	1 Year	3 Years	5 Years
United States	1.67	2.33	3.28	4.08
United Kingdom	2.09	1.85	2.93	4.03
Germany	3.20	3.09	4.09	4.83

Notes: The exhibit lists average *ex post* real interest rates computed as the interest rate at time *t* for a particular horizon (say 1 year) minus realized inflation occurring between time *t* and time *t* plus the horizon; see Equation (10.1). The data are monthly zero coupon interest rates between 1972 and 1996, taken from Geert Bekaert, Robert Hodrick, and David Marshall (2001), and the inflation numbers are computed from the consumer price indexes for the various countries.

with domestic prices after currencies were converted. You would not have to worry about the currency denomination of debts because the real cost of funding would be the same everywhere in the world. Finally, if a company wanted to know what the future exchange rate was likely to be—for example, to help quantify its transaction exposure—the best predictor for the future exchange would be the forward rate because the unbiasedness hypothesis holds. International investors would not need to worry about predicting currency values either. A higher nominal interest rate in one country would simply reflect the fact that the country's currency was expected to depreciate.

Testing Real Interest Rate Parity

Unfortunately, the world is not as simple as we've just described. From the empirical evidence discussed in previous chapters, we know that the international parity conditions except CIRP are best viewed as long-run relationships. In the short run, there are significant deviations from these conditions. In the long run, we know that PPP holds better and that high interest rate currencies depreciate relative to low interest rate currencies. Hence, it would seem more likely that real interest rate parity holds in the long run, as in Exhibit 10.2. Nevertheless, studies have found that it holds neither in the short run nor the long run.

Exhibit 10.3 shows average *ex post* real interest rates for the United States, the United Kingdom, and Germany for different investment time frames.

Real interest rates tend to increase over time, which reflects the extra return investors demand for holding longer-term investments. Real interest rates are highest in Germany and lowest in the United States at the 3-month horizon, and they are lowest in the United Kingdom at all other horizons. However, in no case are the rates perfectly equal to one another, even at the 5-year horizon. It is possible that these differences are an artifact of our small sample of data. Perhaps Germany will eventually experience higher inflation or U.S. and UK rates of inflation will be surprisingly low to eliminate the spread between real interest rates.

Assessment

All things considered, it is unlikely that equality of real interest rates across countries is a good description of reality, especially in the short run. There are good reasons for this. First, PPP deviations are sizable and prolonged. Consequently, identical nominal returns imply very different real returns for investors in different countries. Second, as our discussion of forward market risk premiums showed, returns in different currencies can have different currency risk premiums. Third, real returns across countries can differ because of political risks or the threat of capital controls, which prevent investors from taking advantage of higher returns in other countries. This is particularly true in developing countries.[2]

---

[2]Indeed, research by Charles Himmelberg, Glenn Hubbard, and Inessa Love (2002) indicates that failure to protect the rights of investors can significantly increase the cost of capital in some countries. Consistent with this, Charles Lee and David Ng (2006) find significantly lower price–earnings ratios in countries with high incidences of corruption after controlling for a large variety of economic influences.

Of course, real interest rate differentials between countries reflect differential risks, but they also offer multinational businesses opportunities—for example, opportunities to reduce costs of funds or to invest excess cash more profitably. Knowing the source of an observed real interest rate differential is important to making the right decisions. When the parity conditions break down, forecasting becomes important. The next section reviews the types of forecasting techniques managers use.

10.2 CURRENCY FORECASTING TECHNIQUES

There are probably as many exchange rate forecasting techniques as there are exchange rate forecasters. Nevertheless, Exhibit 10.4 attempts to group them according to the data and techniques used.

The parity conditions suggest the forward rate as a predictor. If no forward market exists for a particular currency, nominal interest rates and UIRP can be used to extract a market-based forecast.

Other forecasting techniques do not rely directly on the predictions embodied in forward rates and interest rates and can be split into two main categories: *fundamental analysis* and *technical analysis*. We briefly describe these in turn and end this section with a discussion of how we should evaluate the quality of a forecast. Sections 10.3 and 10.4 then provide more detail about these two forecasting techniques.

Fundamental Exchange Rate Forecasting

One class of forecasting techniques uses fundamental factors to predict exchange rates. **Fundamental analysis** techniques are typically based on formal economic models of exchange rate determination, which link exchange rates to macroeconomic fundamentals such as money supplies, inflation rates, productivity growth rates, and the current account. The models involve parameters that govern the relationship between the exchange rate and the fundamentals. For example, if the current account deficit as a percentage of GDP increases by x%, the model predicts that the domestic currency will depreciate relative to the foreign currency by b multiplied by x%. The parameter b has to be determined, and this is typically accomplished by estimating the relationship from the data using econometric techniques such as regression analysis. Alternatively, some forecasters simply examine economic information and use educated analysis to derive an exchange rate forecast based on their judgment of

Exhibit 10.4 Categories of Exchange Rate Forecasting Techniques

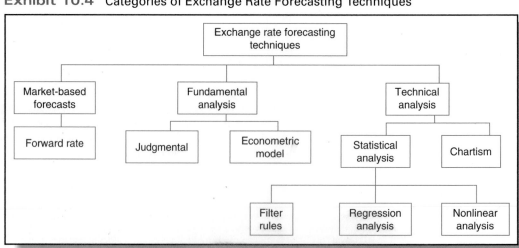

future macroeconomic relationships. Fundamental analysis is typically concerned with multi-year forecasts because the fundamental economic forces operate at that horizon.

Exchange Rate Forecasting with Technical Analysis

Technical analysis is not based on formal exchange rate determination models and is usually used for short-term forecasts. Technical analysts use only past exchange rate data, and perhaps some other financial data, such as the volume of currency trade, to predict future exchange rates. Consequently, all the information about the future exchange rate is believed to be present in past trading behavior and past exchange rate trends.

The original technical analysts were called *chartists*. Chartists restricted themselves to studying graphs of past exchange rates. Now, technical analysis refers to the use of any type of financial data to predict future exchange rates outside the confines of a fundamental model. Some technical analysts employ rather sophisticated econometric techniques to discover what they hope are predictable patterns in exchange rates. Therefore, we distinguish between chartists and *statistical technical analysts*.

Why Technical Analysis Might Work

Technical analysis is often derided in academic circles because it is not based on any economic theory and is thought to be inconsistent with efficient markets. Nevertheless, it is important to discuss technical analysis for four reasons.

First, forex dealers make extensive use of technical analysis. A 1992 study by economists Mark Taylor and Helen Allen found that forex traders in London primarily rely on technical analysis for short-term forecasting, whereas they rely more, but not exclusively, on fundamental forecasting for longer-run forecasts. Other surveys conducted among Hong Kong traders by Yu-Hon Lui and David Mole (1998) and German foreign exchange professionals in banks and fund management by Lukas Menkhoff (1998) found similar results.

Second, fundamental analysis has some inherent problems. Fundamental forecasters must pick the right exchange rate model. Then, the model's fundamental variables must be forecast. Moreover, the macroeconomic inputs to fundamental analysis are not all available at frequent intervals. Some variables are measured weekly, some monthly, and some only quarterly or even annually, and the measurements are often poor (recall the discussion of the missing current account surplus in Chapter 4) and are frequently subject to revision. The data used by technical analysts are of much higher quality and are available much more frequently, often on a daily or even intra-daily basis.

The third reason technical analysis may be of value in forecasting is that the forward rate may not be an unbiased predictor of the future spot rate, even in an efficient market. As indicated in Chapter 7, rational risk premiums can separate forward rates from expected future spot rates. Moreover, we see differences of opinion on the future direction of exchange rates, even among relatively specialized foreign exchange experts. Consequently, it is conceivable that technical analysis might uncover a predictable component in exchange rate changes not present in forward rates.

A fourth reason technical analysis may have value is that if a sufficiently large segment of the trading world is using technical analysis, demands and supplies to trade currencies will be buffeted by these traders even if they are irrational. A truly rational trader would therefore need to know technical analysis to understand why other irrational traders are doing what they are doing.

Evaluating Forecasts

What constitutes a good forecast? In general, it depends on how the forecast will be used. Ultimately, exchange rate forecasts are "good" when they lead to "good" decisions. Next, we distinguish three dimensions of the quality of a forecast.

Accuracy

One dimension of forecast quality is the accuracy of the forecast. Suppose that today is time t, and we are forecasting over a k-period horizon (say k months). Let $S(t+k)$ be the actual exchange rate at time $t+k$, and let $\hat{S}(t+k)$ be the forecast at time t. The closer $\hat{S}(t+k)$ is to $S(t+k)$, the more accurate the forecast, and the smaller the forecast error:

$$e(t+k) = S(t+k) - \hat{S}(t+k)$$

Of course, we cannot judge a forecaster by just one forecast because he or she may have just been lucky. Instead, we need a substantial record of forecasts and realizations:

$$\{\hat{S}(t+k), \ S(t+k)\}$$

where $t = 1, \ldots T$ for a total of T observations, to allow statistical analysis. Accuracy of the forecasting record cannot simply be judged by taking the average forecast error, however, because a forecaster producing huge errors with opposite signs could end up with a small average error.

Two Measures of Accuracy

The two summary measures most frequently used are the **mean absolute error (MAE)** and the **root mean squared error (RMSE)**:

$$\text{MAE} = \frac{1}{T}\sum_{t=1}^{T}|e(t+k)|$$

$$\text{RMSE} = \sqrt{\frac{1}{T}\sum_{t=1}^{T}e(t+k)^2}$$

The MAE is the average of the absolute values of the forecast errors. The RMSE is the square root of the average squared forecast errors. It has the same units as the standard deviation of exchange rate changes.

In comparing forecasts, a number of obvious benchmarks come to mind. For example, we could simply replace the forecast with the current exchange rate or with the current forward rate with maturity k. We hope that a forecaster's MAE or RMSE is smaller than such simple forecasts. If it weren't, why would we need to pay money for it?

Forecast accuracy is economically meaningful in a number of settings. For example, suppose Liberty Shipping, a U.S. firm, is evaluating a foreign investment project that will generate foreign currency profits. Liberty Shipping must forecast the future dollar cash flows generated by the project by converting future foreign currency profits into future dollars that will be discounted at an appropriate discount rate to determine whether the investment project will be profitable. Suppose that its calculations lead Liberty Shipping to accept the project and make the investment. Then, however, a currency crisis erupts in the country in which Liberty Shipping invested, and the currency depreciates significantly. If local competition prevents Liberty Shipping from passing through the currency loss in the form of higher local prices, the currency crisis will depress the company's dollar earnings, and the investment decision will have been a disaster. Here accuracy matters. A more accurate assessment of the future would have led Liberty Shipping to forgo the investment.

Even if the foreign currency appreciates after the investment is made and the investment decision looks good, forecasting inaccuracy still matters. A better exchange rate forecast might have caused the firm to invest more in the foreign country. Pricing decisions and long-term strategic planning are other examples in which the accuracy of exchange rate forecasts matters a great deal. Note that in many of these cases, firms may be more concerned with predicting the real exchange rate rather than the nominal exchange rate.

Being on the Right Side of the Forward Rate

There are situations in which accuracy may not be the most relevant quality measure. Simply being on the right side of the forward rate is enough. If the forecast relative to the forward rate suggests a long position in the forward market, and the future exchange rate is indeed above the forward, the forecast was on the right side of the forward rate. Conversely, if the forecast relative to the forward rate suggests a short position in the forward market, and the future exchange rate is below the forward rate, the forecast was not on the right side of the forward rate. We illustrate this with an example.

Example 10.2   Currency Forecasts at Fancy Foods

Chapter 3 introduced the situation of Fancy Foods, which owes Porky Pies £1,000,000 in 90 days. The current exchange rate is $1.50/£, and the forward rate is $1.53/£. To decide whether to hedge its currency exposure, suppose Fancy Foods can enlist the services of two forecasting companies, Forexia and Trompe Le Monde. Forexia predicts that the exchange rate will be $1.65/£, whereas Trompe Le Monde predicts that the exchange rate will be $1.51/£. After 90 days, the exchange rate turns out to be $1.55/£. Which forecast is more accurate? Which forecast is more economically useful to Fancy Foods?

To find out, let's examine how Fancy Foods uses forecasts in its hedging decision. Suppose Fancy Foods hedges when the forecast of the future spot rate is above the forward rate, and it does not hedge when the forecast is less than the forward rate because it thinks the dollar cost of the pounds will be lower than if it uses the forward rate. The following table summarizes the situation:

	Forexia	Trompe Le Monde
Forecast	$1.65/£	$1.51/£
Forecast relative to forward rate (forward rate: £1.53/$)	Higher	Lower
Decision	Hedge	Do not hedge
Forecast error	−$0.10/£	$0.04/£
Ex post cost relative to forward rate	Zero	Higher

So, although Trompe Le Monde's forecast turns out to be more accurate, it leads Fancy Foods not to hedge because it predicts an exchange rate lower than the forward rate. Because the pound actually appreciates to a level above the forward rate, not hedging proves costly. Not hedging would cost Fancy Foods £1,000,000 × $(1.55 − 1.53)/£ = $20,000. The prediction of Forexia, which is quite inaccurate, would lead Fancy Foods to hedge, which *ex post* leads to a lower pound cost than if the pounds had to be purchased at the future spot rate.

Example 10.2 shows that it is often more important to be on the correct side of the forward rate than to be accurate. It is also important to realize that the relevant benchmark is the forward rate, not the current spot rate, because the forward rate is the available rate for future transactions.

Percentage Correct

To evaluate a forecasting record, the percentage of times the forecaster was on the correct side of the forward rate seems to be a natural indicator. Because just flipping a coin could lead to a 50% correct record, this "percentage correct signals" statistic should be strictly larger than

50% for the forecaster's services to add value to your decision-making process. We can view this as a test of market timing ability.[3]

Profitability

Technical analysts assert that the percentage-correct-signals metric does not accurately measure how well they perform. They claim that they can give valuable advice and should not be required to be right more than 50% of the time. This is true because the overall size of the profits and losses a company earns as a result of the advice matters, too. A technical forecaster's performance may be characterized by a relatively small number of successful forecasts in which large profits are made and a relatively large number of incorrect predictions in which small losses are incurred. As long as you do not lose too much money when you are wrong and you make a lot of money when you are right, you can be wrong more than 50% of the time and still be valuable.

To evaluate forecasters on this basis, we can simply compute the profits or losses made based on a forecaster's advice and compare those returns to the returns on alternative investments that do not require forecasts. Again, it is important to determine that the profits are not simply due to chance. We illustrate this later in the chapter, in the context of an actual study. We are now ready to examine fundamental and technical forecasts in more detail.

10.3 FUNDAMENTAL EXCHANGE RATE FORECASTING

This section examines forecasting techniques that rely on models of exchange rate determination and fundamental economic factors. From the parity conditions, we know that exchange rates are likely to be influenced by interest differentials, relative price levels, and inflation rates. Interest rates and the current account are the most talked-about fundamental factors, judging from countless articles in the financial press.

The first subsection discusses the asset market approach to exchange rate determination, which relies heavily on the link between interest rate differentials and expected exchange rate changes, as reflected by uncovered interest rate parity. Next, we discuss how real interest rate differentials and real exchange rates are related. These models are entirely silent about the current account. We then discuss the intuitive links between current accounts, real exchange rates, and interest rates. This allows a discussion of the other fundamental factors that affect exchange rates. We end the section by reviewing how well formal fundamental models of exchange rates have fared in helping to predict future exchange rates.

The Asset Market Approach to Exchange Rate Determination

Chapter 9 notes that the equity value of a firm is the expected discounted value of all future cash flows accruing to the firm's shareholders. The model predicts that the market value of a firm's equity fluctuates daily as people revise either their expectations about the firm's future

---

[3]Roy Henrikkson and Robert Merton (1981) developed market-timing tests for stock market returns, where forecasters predict the stock market to go up or down. However, stock returns are expected to be positive, so always predicting the market to go up is likely to lead to a better-than-50%-correct forecasting record. Similarly, if it rains on 80% of the days, a weather forecaster has an 80% success rate by always forecasting rain. Analogously, if during the period that you record the forecasting performance, the forward rate is consistently below the spot rate, a forecaster who ends up with a 100% correct forecasting record may have superior forecasting knowledge or may have simply failed to change his forecast, and this laziness led to the perfect record. Because the market direction did not change, there is little information on timing the market in this sample. Henrikkson and Merton show how to correct for such a bias. Basically, you should add the proportion of correct forecasts conditional on the eventual spot rate being above the forward rate to the proportion of correct forecasts conditional on the eventual spot rate being below the forward rate. If the sum of these proportions is higher than 1, there is evidence of market timing ability. Indeed, our lazy forecaster, who just got lucky, would end up with a score of 1.0 and would not be dubbed a forecasting genius with such a test.

cash flows to shareholders or the required rate of return at which these cash flows are discounted. Although expected capital gains provide part of the required rate of return, even a 15% per annum expected capital gain translates into an expected rate of change of only $15\%/365 = 0.04\%$ per day. We know that the standard deviation of equity rates of return is usually great than 1% per day. Thus, the model predicts that most changes in equity values are due to new information. This is what we expect when asset markets are working well.

The Exchange Rate as an Asset Price

The asset market approach to exchange rate determination recognizes that the exchange rate is the relative price of two monies, and it notes that monies are assets, which makes the exchange rate an asset price. Hence, exchange rates should fluctuate quite randomly, and the value of an exchange rate of, say, dollars per euro should be determined by people's willingness to hold the outstanding supplies of dollar-denominated assets and euro-denominated assets. These demands, in turn, depend on the expectations of the future values of these assets.

We can capture this reasoning in a very simple equation:

$$\ln[S(t)] = \text{fund}(t) + aE_t[\ln[S(t+1)]] \tag{10.7}$$

In Equation (10.7), $\ln[S(t)]$ is the logarithm of the current exchange rate expressed as domestic currency per foreign currency, $\text{fund}(t)$ is the generic name we use to indicate the value of market fundamentals at time t, and the coefficient a is a discount factor that is less than 1 but may be very near 1.

Equation (10.7) states that the exchange rate depends on current fundamentals and on what people think the exchange rate will be in the next period. In the equity-pricing model, the fundamentals are the cash flows to shareholders, and an equation similar to (10.7) describes equity pricing.

If we iterate Equation (10.7) one step forward to solve for $\ln[S(t+1)]$ and plug the result back into that equation, we obtain the following:

$$\ln[S(t)] = \text{fund}(t) + aE_t[\text{fund}(t+1) + aE_{t+1}[\ln[S(t+2)]]] \tag{10.8}$$

Because expectations at time t of expectations at some future time reduce to expectations at time t, as in $E_t[E_{t+1}[\ln[S(t+2)]]] = E_t[\ln[S(t+2)]]$, if we keep iterating Equation (10.8) forward, we obtain the following:[4]

$$\ln[S(t)] = \text{fund}(t) + \sum_{j=1}^{\infty} a^j E_t[\text{fund}(t+j)] \tag{10.9}$$

Hence, the current exchange rate embeds all information about current and expected future fundamentals, and the exchange rate changes as the fundamentals change or as we get news about future fundamentals. Note that even a small change in current fundamentals may induce a large change in the exchange rate if it also changes the expected value of all future fundamentals. Thus the value of the exchange rate may move a lot in response to what seems to be a small piece of news.

Many exchange rate models fit this framework. We begin with a discussion of the monetary approach model.

The Monetary Approach

One of the best-known asset market models is the monetary exchange rate model. In this model, the menu of assets is fairly simple. There are distinct demands for non-interest-bearing domestic and foreign currencies. The demand for nominal money arises from the demand for **real money balances**. That is, people are only concerned with the real value of the nominal money they are holding.

---

[4]This property of expectations is known as the *law of iterated expectations*, and it follows from the fact that we necessarily have less information now (at time t) than we will have in the future (at time $t+1$).

The demand for real money balances (or *real balances*, for short) is assumed to depend positively on the aggregate real income of the country and negatively on the nominal interest rate. Real income positively affects the demand for money because the higher the real income, the greater the number of monetary transactions required to support the real transactions of this economy. A higher interest rate negatively affects the demand for money because there is a higher opportunity cost of holding real money balances. People will want to earn interest on their money rather than hold it. This requires that they invest it. If mon(t) is the logarithm of the domestic money supply, inc(t) is the logarithm of domestic real income, p(t) is the logarithm of the domestic price level, and i(t) is the domestic currency nominal interest rate, then equilibrium in the domestic money market can be described by setting the logarithm of the supply of real money equal to the demand for real balances:

$$\text{mon}(t) - p(t) = b_0 + b_1\text{inc}(t) - b_2 i(t) \qquad (10.10)$$

where the b coefficients are positive numbers. The foreign money market equilibrium can be defined analogously using an asterisk (*) to represent a foreign value:

$$\text{mon}^*(t) - p^*(t) = b_0 + b_1\text{inc}^*(t) - b_2 i^*(t) \qquad (10.11)$$

If we assume that the b parameters are the same in the two countries, and we take the difference between Equations (10.10) and (10.11) and solve for the difference in price levels, we find

$$p(t) - p^*(t) = [\text{mon}(t) - \text{mon}^*(t)] - b_1[\text{inc}(t) - \text{inc}^*(t)] + b_2[i(t) - i^*(t)] \qquad (10.12)$$

To turn Equation (10.12) into a theory of the exchange rate, we substitute in purchasing power parity, $\ln[S(t)] = p(t) - p^*(t)$, and uncovered interest rate parity, $i(t) - i^*(t) = E_t[\ln[S(t+1)] - \ln[S(t)]]$. After these substitutions, Equation (10.12) becomes

$$\ln[S(t)] = [\text{mon}(t) - \text{mon}^*(t)] - b_1[\text{inc}(t) - \text{inc}^*(t)] + b_2[E_t(\ln[S(t+1)] - \ln[S(t)])] \qquad (10.13)$$

If we solve Equation (10.13) for the logarithm of the current exchange rate, we get an equation exactly like Equation (10.7), where the fundamentals are given by

$$\text{fund}(t) = (\text{mon}(t) - \text{mon}^*(t)) - b_1(\text{inc}(t) - \text{inc}^*(t)) \qquad (10.14)$$

and the discount factor is $a = b_2/(1 + b_2)$.

Equations (10.9) and (10.14) indicate that the domestic currency weakens if the domestic money supply increases today or if news arrives that leads people to believe that the future domestic money supply will increase. In contrast, the domestic currency strengthens if the foreign money supply increases today or if news arrives that causes people to think that foreign money supplies will be higher in the future. These effects arise directly from the influence of money on prices with the demand for money held constant. The domestic currency also weakens if domestic real income falls, if foreign real income rises, or if news arrives that causes people to expect lower domestic real growth or faster foreign real growth.

Sticky Prices and Overshooting

The predictions of the monetary model are quite reasonable at long horizons, but as a short-run theory, the monetary model's reliance on PPP is questionable. Several extensions of the monetary model have been developed. The most important ones relax the assumption of PPP. If nominal prices of goods do not adjust immediately to an increase in the money supply or to other shocks (that is, information events) that hit the economy, economists say prices are "sticky." A number of famous models of exchange rate determination, such as the Rudiger Dornbusch model (1976), incorporate this feature. Models with sticky prices predict more volatility in nominal and real exchange rates than occurs in the monetary model because asset prices, including the exchange rate, do all of the adjusting to the shocks that hit the economy, whereas nominal prices in the goods markets only adjust slowly over time.

Responses to an Increase in the Money Supply

Consider how the economy responds to a permanent increase in the money supply. According to the monetary model, in the long run, an increase in the money supply causes a depreciation of the domestic currency by the same percentage that the money supply increases. What happens in the short run? The paths for the money supply, the price level, the domestic interest rate, and the exchange rate are presented in Exhibit 10.5, where t_0 is the time of the change.

Because asset prices are flexible, the asset markets will remain in equilibrium. Now, from Equation (10.10), we know that an increase in the nominal money supply with goods prices fixed increases the supply of real balances. For the money market to remain in equilibrium, the demand for real balances must increase, which requires either an increase in real income or a decrease in the nominal interest. If real income is also exogenous in the short run and cannot adjust, the nominal interest rate must decrease. Thus, the increase in the money supply causes the domestic interest rate to fall. Exhibit 10.5 indicates this fall and a subsequent rise over time as the economy adjusts to equilibrium.

The Link with UIRP

Now, let's think about how the exchange rate responds to the increase in the money supply. Because we just established that the domestic interest rate is lower than the foreign interest rate, we know from uncovered interest rate parity that the domestic currency must be expected to appreciate. The domestic interest rate is lower than the foreign rate, so people must think the domestic currency will strengthen. But if people are rational, they know that in the long run, the domestic currency will be weaker than it was before the increase in the money supply. The only path for the exchange rate that allows for a long-run depreciation of the domestic currency and an expected appreciation in the short run is for the domestic currency to immediately weaken by more than it will weaken in the long run. Thus, the exchange rate overshoots its new equilibrium. Notice that in Exhibit 10.5, the exchange rate jumps when the money supply is increased and subsequently falls over time toward its new higher or equilibrium value.

Exhibit 10.5   Responses of Variables to an Increase in the Money Supply

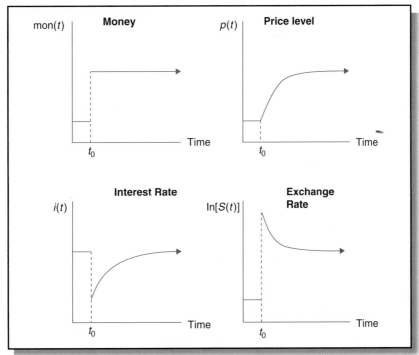

The Path of Prices

Because the increase in the money supply also causes prices to increase in the long run, expected inflation rises in the short run. Exhibit 10.5 shows that prices begin to rise and eventually converge to their new higher level over time. Because the nominal interest rate has fallen and expected inflation has risen, the real interest rate is lower. Because the nominal depreciation of the domestic currency occurs with no changes in prices, the nominal depreciation of the domestic currency coincides with a real depreciation. Subsequently, as the domestic currency appreciates and inflation increases domestic prices, there is a real appreciation of the domestic currency until the economy returns to equilibrium. Thus, the model predicts that low real interest rates are associated with expected real appreciations of those currencies.

We next turn to the issue of the strength of the relationship between real exchange rates and real interest rates across countries.

The Real Exchange Rate and the Real Interest Rate Differential

As exchange rates began to float in 1973, the real exchange rates between the dollar and other major currencies and the real interest rate differentials between the United States and other countries have tended to move together, as Exhibit 10.6 shows (see Hali Edison and Dianne Pauls, 1993).

Exhibit 10.6   Movements in the Real Dollar Exchange Rate Relative to the Real Interest Rate Differential

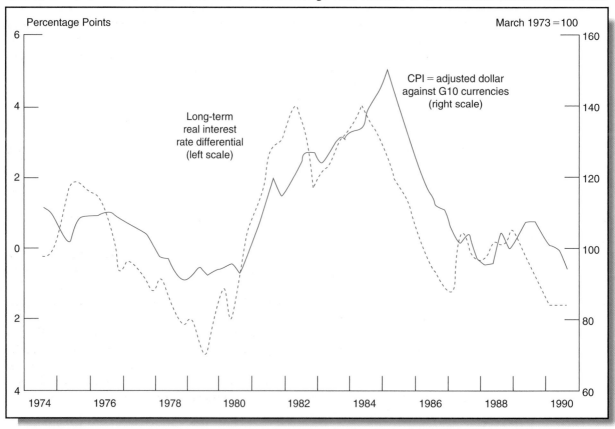

Note: The solid line is the trade-weighted real exchange rate of the dollar relative to the other currencies of the G10 countries, as calculated by the U.S. Federal Reserve Board. An increase in the real exchange rate represents a real appreciation of the dollar. The dotted line is the differential between the real interest rate on U.S. dollar long-term bonds and a weighted average of the real interest rates on the other G10 countries' long-term bonds. The plot is taken from Edison and Pauls (1993).

The solid line in Exhibit 10.6 represents the trade-weighted real exchange rate of the dollar relative to other G10 currencies, as calculated by the U.S. Federal Reserve Board. The real exchange rate is defined using the nominal exchange rate expressed as foreign currency per dollar. Hence, increases in the real exchange rate in Exhibit 10.6 represent real appreciations of the dollar relative to foreign currencies, and decreases in the real exchange rate represent real depreciations of the dollar. The dotted line in Exhibit 10.6 represents the differential between the real interest rate on U.S. dollar-denominated long-term bonds and a weighted average of the real interest rates on the other G10 countries' long-term bonds. The dotted line represents an estimate of the expected real rate of return on U.S. dollar-denominated investments minus an estimate of the expected real rate of return on foreign-currency-denominated investments from the foreign perspective.[5]

It is apparent from Exhibit 10.6 that when the dollar is relatively strong in real terms, the U.S. real interest rate seems relatively high compared to foreign real interest rates. Also, conversely, when the dollar is relatively weak, the real interest rate differential of the United States seems relatively low. Why should the level of the real exchange rate be related to the differential between the real interest rates on different currencies?

Converting UIRP to Real Terms

To see why the level of the real exchange rate should be related to the differential between the real interest rates on different currencies, we need to convert uncovered interest rate parity from a relationship between nominal interest rates and nominal rates of depreciation into a relationship between real interest rates and expected real rates of depreciation. We do this by adding the expected (logarithmic) inflation differential between the home and foreign countries, $E_t[\pi(t+1) - \pi^*(t+1)]$, to both sides of the uncovered interest rate parity expression, $i^*(t) - i(t) = E_t[s(t+1)]$, where $s(t+1) = \ln[S(t+1)] - \ln[S(t)]$ with exchange rates measured as foreign currency per unit of domestic currency:

$$i^*(t) - E_t[\pi^*(t+1)] - (i(t) - E_t[\pi(t+1)])$$
$$= E_t[s(t+1)] + \pi(t+1) - \pi^*(t+1)]$$

From the definitions of the real interest rate and of the rate of change of the real exchange rate, this equation reduces to the following:

$$r^{e*}(t) - r^e(t) = E_t[rs(t+1)] \tag{10.15}$$

where $r^e(t)$ denotes the domestic real interest rate, $r^{e*}(t)$ denotes the foreign real interest rate, and $rs(t)$ denotes the rate of exchange of the real exchange rate.

Equation (10.15) indicates that when the foreign real interest rate is greater than the domestic real interest rate, the domestic currency is expected to appreciate in real terms, as we saw earlier in the Dornbusch model. Conversely, if the domestic currency is expected to weaken in real terms, the right-hand side of Equation (10.15) is negative, and the domestic real interest rate must be above the foreign real interest rate.

Equation (10.15) establishes a link between the expected real interest rate differential and the expected rate of change of the real exchange rate. So, we have not yet generated the relationship between the level of the real exchange rate and the real interest rate differential that is expressed in Exhibit 10.6, but we are close to establishing a direct link. One way to establish this link is to think about where the real exchange rate is now compared to where it will be in the long run.

---

[5]Because real interest rates depend on expected rates of inflation, which are not observed, Edison and Pauls (1993) estimate the expected rates of inflation at time t by taking averages of the realized rates of inflation on either side of time t. These measures of expected inflation are then subtracted from the observed nominal interest rates on long-term bonds to measure the expected real rates of return.

Implications of an Autoregressive Process for the Real Exchange Rate

Suppose, as we argued in Chapter 8, that the real exchange rate moves around over time, but it is expected to return eventually to its unconditional mean. When the real exchange rate experiences transitory deviations from an unconditional mean, we can model the real exchange rate as an **autoregressive process**. In an autoregressive process, the current value of a variable is a function of past observed values of the variable, its unconditional mean, and a zero mean shock. The simplest autoregressive process is a first-order process, which we can represent in the following equation:

$$\ln[RS(t+1)] = \overline{RS} + \rho(\ln[RS(t)] - \overline{RS}) + \epsilon(t+1) \tag{10.16}$$

In Equation (10.16), $\overline{RS}$ represents the long-run equilibrium of the logarithm of the real exchange rate, which is its unconditional mean. The innovation in the real exchange rate is $\epsilon(t+1)$. This innovation represents the change in the real exchange rate that is due to new information between period t and period $t+1$, and it consequently has a mean of zero. The coefficient ρ, which is between 0 and 1, tells us how fast the real exchange rate converges to its unconditional mean. If ρ is close to 1, deviations of the real exchange rate from its long-run equilibrium can be quite persistent.[6]

By subtracting $\ln[RS(t)]$ from each side of Equation (10.16), we get

$$\ln[RS(t+1)] - \ln[RS(t)] = (\rho - 1)(\ln[RS(t)] - \overline{RS}) + \epsilon(t+1) \tag{10.17}$$

Taking the expected value of Equation (10.17) relates the expected rate of change of the real exchange rate to the deviation of the current real exchange rate from its long-run equilibrium value:

$$E_t[\ln[RS(t+1)] - \ln[RS(t)]] = (\rho - 1)(\ln[RS(t)] - \overline{RS}) \tag{10.18}$$

Substituting from Equation (10.18) into Equation (10.15) and multiplying both sides by –1 gives

$$r^e(t) - r^{e*}(t) = (1 - \rho)[\ln[RS(t)] - \overline{RS}] \tag{10.19}$$

Equation (10.19) indicates that when the real exchange rate is above its long-run equilibrium—that is, when $[\ln[RS(t)] - \overline{RS}] > 0$ and the domestic currency is strong—the real interest rate in the home country is greater than the real interest rate in the foreign country because ρ is less than 1. Hence, we have demonstrated that when the dollar is strong in real terms relative to foreign currencies, the real interest rate on dollar assets should be above the real interest rate on the foreign currency assets. Conversely, when real interest rates in the United States are relatively low, the dollar should be weak in real terms and expected to appreciate.

Empirical Evidence

Although the *Economist* and others in the popular press routinely write about the strength of the relationship between real interest rates and the level of the real exchange rate, academic researchers who have examined the relationship between the real value of the dollar and the

---

[6]The magnitude of ρ also depends on the interval over which the change in the real exchange rate is being measured. To understand why, recognize that the expected deviation of the real exchange rate from its long-run value is $E_t[\ln[RS(t+1)] - \overline{RS}] = \rho[\ln[RS(t)] - \overline{RS}]$, from which it follows that the expected deviation k periods into the future is $E_t[\ln[RS(t+k)] - \overline{RS}] = \rho^k[\ln[RS(t)] - \overline{RS}]$. Consequently, if it takes a certain amount of real calendar time for a deviation of the real exchange rate to be expected to adjust one-half of the way back to the mean, the value of ρ must depend on the time interval of measurement. For example, suppose it takes 6 years to eliminate one-half of the divergence of the real exchange rate from its long-run value. Then, if we have annual data, the appropriate value of ρ that satisfies $\rho^6 = 0.5$, or $\rho = (0.5)^{(1/6)} = 0.891$. If we have quarterly data, the appropriate value of ρ would be $\rho^{24} = 0.5$, $\rho = (0.5)^{(1/24)} = 0.972$ because there are 24 quarters in the 6-year interval, and with monthly data, the appropriate value of ρ is $\rho^{72} = 0.5$, or $\rho = (0.5)^{(1/72)} = 0.990$.

real interest rate differential have found the relationship to be weak.[7] What problems could account for this failure?

One explanation comes from the fact that real exchange rates are very persistent, which makes the ρ coefficient in Equation (10.19) very close to 1. If ρ is almost equal to 1, $1 - \rho$ is very close to 0. Therefore, even though the real exchange rate might be very far from its long-run equilibrium level, the short-term real interest rate differential would not be required to reflect much of this deviation because it will take a long time for the real exchange rate to return to its long-run value. "Noise" in the data, due perhaps to our inability to measure expected rates of inflation, could easily mask the true relationship.

A second, related, explanation for the problems that people have in finding a statistical relationship between the real interest rate differential and the real exchange rate is caused by the presence of the risk premium in the foreign exchange market, which we have ignored in our derivations. Time variation in risk premiums could also mask a significant relationship between the expected real interest rate differential and the level of the real exchange rate.

A third explanation is that there are statistical problems in investigating the relationship, such as the peso problem discussed in Chapter 7.

The Real Exchange Rate and the Current Account

Now that we have successfully linked real interest rate differentials and the level of the real exchange rate, albeit more in the long run than the short run, we are in a position to discuss how other important market fundamentals help to determine the real exchange rate simultaneously with the determination of the current account of the balance of payments. Recall from Chapter 4 that the balance of payments is an identity in which the sum of the current account and the capital account must be zero. Hence, the value of the current account surplus or deficit equals the value of the capital account deficit or surplus, respectively. The real exchange rate and other variables adjust to ensure that the balance of payments balances. Hence, economic shocks to the accounts of the balance of payments affect the real exchange rate.

These shocks may come from the "real" side of the balance of payments, the trade balance, which records exports and imports, and from the "financial" side to the balance of payments, the capital account, which records purchases and sales of assets. Models of the real exchange rate recognize that real exchange rates affect these two parts of the balance of payments differently.[8] We next discuss how exchange rates affect the two parts of the balance of payments, and we then examine how putting the two pieces together gives a fundamental solution for the real exchange rate and the current account of the balance of payments.

The Trade Balance and Real Exchange Rates

When currencies strengthen in real terms, foreign goods become less expensive than domestic goods. Hence, a real appreciation is typically associated with a deterioration of the trade balance—that is, a rise of imports relative to exports. Conversely, a real depreciation of a country's currency enhances a country's competitiveness in world markets and improves the trade balance. In this case, exports typically increase relative to imports.

---

[7]For example, John Campbell and Richard Clarida (1987), Richard Meese and Kenneth Rogoff (1988), and Hali Edison and Dianne Pauls (1993) perform various statistical tests that are designed to find the relation between real exchange rates and the real interest rate differential. Each pair of authors concludes that the relation is very weak. Marianne Baxter (1994) finds statistical support for a long-run relation but not a short-run relation between the level of the real exchange rates and real interest rate differentials. The more recent evidence remains mixed; see, for instance, Avik Chakrabarti (2006), who finds no link, and Robert Sollis and Mark Wohan (2006), who do find a link.
[8]An interesting formal model that simultaneously determines both the real exchange rate and the current account is the seminal analysis of Michael Mussa (1984).

Remember that the current account of the balance of payments is the trade balance plus the flows of income that are generated by a country's net international investment position—that is, by its net foreign assets. At a point in time, the domestic economy owns a stock of net foreign assets, which can be either positive or negative. If net foreign assets are positive, the domestic economy receives interest income, and if net foreign assets are negative, the domestic economy must pay interest. Because the current account of the balance of payments is the trade account plus the flow of interest earnings or payments on net foreign assets, the current account is related negatively to the country's real exchange rate through its effect on the trade balance.

The Capital Account and Real Exchange Rates

The real exchange rate also influences the capital account. Recall from Chapter 4 that the capital account records changes in the net foreign assets of a country. If a country has a capital account deficit, it is acquiring net foreign assets, and if the country has a capital account surplus, it is losing net foreign assets. Chapter 4 also notes that the excess of a country's gross national income over its gross national expenditure is related by an identity to the rate of change of net foreign assets. Thus, the economic forces that determine a country's desired excess of income over expenditures determine the country's acquisition or loss of net foreign assets. When a country's income exceeds its expenditures, or when savings exceeds investment, the country builds up net foreign assets. This requires that the country run a capital account deficit and a current account surplus.

One of the most important variables that affects the aggregate saving and investment of a country is the real interest rate. Because higher real interest rates increase saving and decrease real investment, higher real interest rates are associated with capital account deficits and current account surpluses. From the previous section, we know that higher real interest rates are also associated with temporarily higher real exchange rates so that the currency can be expected to depreciate in real terms over time. This is also important for the demands for assets because it ensures that the perceived rate of return on assets denominated in different currencies is the same. Thus, we have another relationship between the real exchange rate and the balance of payments, but this time, real appreciations are associated with current account surpluses.

Equilibrium

The equilibrium determination of the current account and the exchange rate is presented in Exhibit 10.7. The value of the current account surplus is on the horizontal axis, and the real exchange rate is on the vertical axis, where the units of the real exchange rate are such that an increase in the real exchange rate corresponds to a real appreciation of the domestic currency. The line labeled TT indicates the influence of the real exchange rate on the current account through the trade balance channel. It is negatively sloped because an increase in the real exchange rate (that is, an appreciation of the home currency) causes imports to rise relative to exports, which lowers the current account surplus. The line labeled AA indicates the influence of the real exchange rate on the current account from the savings and investment channel. It is positively sloped because an increase in the real exchange rate (an appreciation of the home currency) is associated with an expected real depreciation and thus with a higher real interest rate at home than abroad. The increase in the real interest rate decreases investment and increases saving, which creates a larger current account surplus.

The intersection of the TT and AA lines is the equilibrium current account (CA^E) and real exchange rate (RS^E). It is important to remember that the current account and the real exchange rate are jointly determined. Variables that shift demand between domestic and foreign goods will shift the TT line, whereas variables that affect savings and investment will shift the AA line. Hence, a particular current account balance may be consistent with various levels of the real exchange rate. We next consider which variables shift the relationships between the real exchange rate and the current account.

Exhibit 10.7 Equilibrium Determination of the Current Account and the Exchange Rate

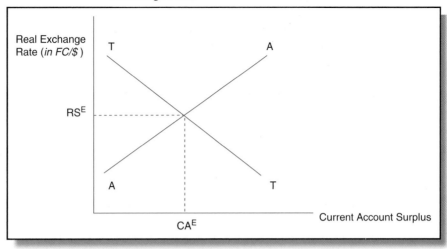

Variables That Affect the Real Exchange Rate–Current Account Equilibrium

Net Foreign Assets

As the domestic economy acquires net foreign assets, residents of the country feel comparatively wealthy and increase their expenditures relative to their incomes. As a result, domestic saving falls relative to investment as wealth is accumulated. Conversely, saving tends to rise relative to investment as a country's net foreign assets fall. People are less wealthy and cut back on their expenditures. Hence, we should expect a natural correction of current account deficits because they represent a loss of wealth to foreigners. These arguments imply that an increase in net foreign assets shifts the AA line up, and a decrease in net foreign assets shifts the AA line down. There is a natural dynamic interaction between the real exchange rate and the accumulation of net foreign assets.

Government Spending and Budget Deficits

An increase in government spending or a decrease in taxes that causes a budget deficit increases aggregate demand in the economy. This causes the real interest rate to rise, which reduces investment and encourages private saving. Hence, the AA line shifts up because the interaction of savings and investment that produces a given current account deficit now requires a stronger currency. The shift up in the AA line means that in equilibrium the domestic currency appreciates in real terms, and the current account deficit increases as the real interest rate increases.

These effects of government spending are consistent with the experience of the United States in the early 1980s. When President Reagan increased government spending and decreased taxes, real interest rates increased, the dollar experienced a massive real appreciation, and U.S. current account deficits grew to unprecedented levels.

Technological Change and Productivity Growth

Traders keenly await news announcements reporting growth numbers or other indicators of real economic activity, such as figures on housing starts, industrial production, unemployment, and retail sales. How do these information signals enter the model?

New information that signals increases in future GDP encourages firms to invest more today. Consumers also feel wealthier, so they want to consume more. Hence, the AA line must again rise to ration investment and consumption, and the increase in AA causes a real appreciation and a current account deficit. The counterpart of the current account deficit is an inflow of foreign capital, which finances some of the investment and allows consumption to be higher than it otherwise could be. An example of this effect is the sustained strength of the dollar during 1995 through 2000 and the corresponding large U.S. current account deficits. These effects were thought to be the result of the attractive growth potential associated with the U.S. economy during the information technology boom.

Portfolio Shifters

The AA line represents asset market equilibrium in all countries. If something shifts the asset demands of international investors from the foreign countries' assets to the domestic country's assets, the exchange rate and current account will be affected. Suppose there is news of reduced profitability abroad. Investors will want to shift out of foreign assets into domestic assets. The AA line must shift up because the domestic currency must appreciate, and the domestic country must experience a current account deficit. Changes in risk tolerances of investors would have similar consequences. Of course, the relationships here are very complex, but you can think of these forces as things that shift the AA line. Things that increase the demand for domestic assets shift AA up, and things that decrease the demand for domestic assets shift AA down.

Clearly, the determination of real exchange rates is very complex because it involves current market fundamentals and expectations about future fundamentals that were just discussed. We now analyze whether fundamental models can improve our forecasting ability.

Forecasting Performance of Fundamental Exchange Rate Models

Forecasting Models and Benchmarks

To analyze the forecasting power of fundamental models of exchange rate determination, we follow the analysis of economist Richard Meese (1990). Meese evaluates models that link the current spot rate to relative money supplies, interest differentials, relative industrial production, inflation differentials, and the difference in cumulated trade balances, which represents the level of net foreign assets. He estimates the parameters of these models and uses them to predict future exchange rate values. Because the predictions are "out of sample" experiments, he uses the actual values for the fundamentals in the future combined with the parameters to get a prediction of the exchange rate. This gives the fundamental models an advantage relative to the other models considered, which use only current information to predict future exchange rates because the fundamental information is not known when the forecast would have to be made. If a caret symbol denotes a forecast and k is the forecast horizon, the other models considered are:

Random walk: $\qquad \hat{S}(t+k)=S(t)$

Unbiasedness hypothesis: $\qquad \hat{S}(t+k)=F(t,k)$

Univariate autoregression: $\qquad \hat{S}(t+k) = \mu \cdot \dfrac{1-\rho^k}{1-\rho} + \rho^k \cdot S(t)$

Vector autoregression: $\qquad$ A generalization of the autoregression to include other lagged variables

Here $F(t,k)$ is the forward rate at time t for horizon $t + k$, and the forecast from the univariate autoregression solves $\hat{S}(t+k) = E_t[S(t + k)]$, where the autoregression specifies $S(t+1) = \mu + \rho S(t) + \epsilon(t+1)$. Because $E_t[\epsilon(t+j)] = 0$, for $j > 0$, we can recursively substitute into the autoregression to write it as $S(t+k) = \mu(1 + \rho + \cdots + \rho^k) + \rho^k S(t) +$ news, where the news is unpredictable with time t information.

Empirical Results

Meese computed the root mean squared error (RMSE) for the predictions at various horizons. Surprisingly, he found that the random walk model beat all the other models in 10 of the 12 cases considered. Particularly surprising was that the fundamental models did not even perform better at long horizons. This result, first uncovered by Meese and Kenneth Rogoff in 1983, has long puzzled international economists. Nevertheless, it has been confirmed by a large number of researchers over the years.

It is only in recent years that some research has started to appear that finds predictable components in exchange rates linked to fundamentals. A study by Nelson Mark (1995) reports evidence that deviations from the exchange rate's fundamental value (as measured by a model similar to the one used in Meese, 1990) has predictive power for exchange rate movements 12 and 16 quarters in the future. At short horizons, it remains difficult to beat the random walk model. The results suggest that exchange rates slowly adjust to changes in fundamentals, and there are many important fundamentals to model.

10.4 TECHNICAL ANALYSIS

Whereas fundamental forecasters use macroeconomic data to forecast future exchange rates, technical analysts focus entirely on financial data. Next we examine different technical forecasting methods in order of increasing sophistication: chartism, filter rules, regression analysis, and nonlinear analysis. We then survey the academic evidence on the success of technical trading rules and end the section with a discussion of the effectiveness of exchange rate forecasting services that use technical analysis.

"Pure" Technical Analysis: Chartism

Chartists graphically record the actual trading history of an exchange rate and then try to infer possible future trends based on that information alone. Exhibit 10.8 graphs a daily exchange rate series, which we use to introduce some chartist terminology.

A **support level** is any chart formation in which the price has trouble falling below a particular level. A **resistance level** is any chart formation in which the price of an instrument has trouble rising above a particular level. Support levels and resistance levels define a trading range, which might be short term, medium term, or long term. When a trading range is broken, a sudden rise or fall in prices is expected and is called a **breakout**.

Chartists argue that a number of different patterns in data clearly signal future trends. One well-known pattern is the "head and shoulders," which indicates a pending fall in the exchange rate once "the neckline is pierced." Clearly, chartists do not believe in efficient financial markets but in markets that are driven by irrational whims that induce prolonged trends of rising or falling prices that are predictable.

Potentially Spurious Patterns

Because chartists rely on graphs to detect trends rather than on statistics, the patterns they identify may be spurious. For example, Exhibit 10.8 does not represent data corresponding to an actual exchange rate. The data are an artificial series based on the random walk model that we generated using a random number generator. The random walk model implies that $E_t[S(t+1)] = S(t)$. Thus, the model states that the best predictor for the future exchange rate is today's exchange rate, and the best prediction for the change in the exchange rate is zero.

Trading on a Random Walk

If exchange rates truly follow random walks, potentially profitable trading strategies nonetheless do present themselves. For example, whenever the forward rate did not equal the current spot rate, the forward rate would not be equal to the expected future spot rate, and you would

Exhibit 10.8 Exchange Rate Patterns Described by Chartists

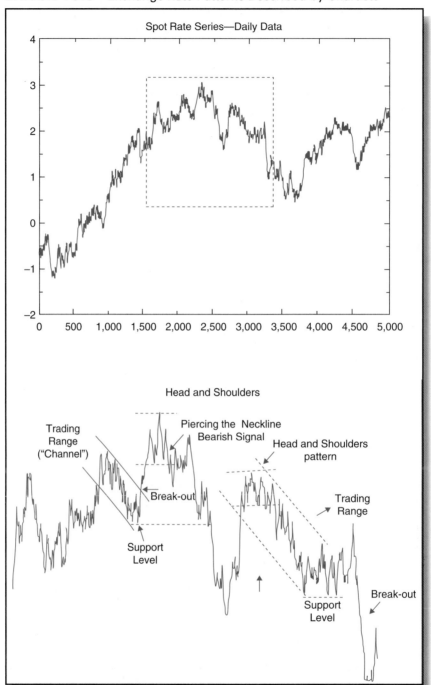

Note: The top graph shows a daily exchange rate series (about 250 days per year) over a time span of 20 years. The graph appears to display some clear trends. The bottom panel investigates these short-term trends more closely by lifting the part in the box at the top and blowing it up. The apparent trends are then interpreted using chartist jargon.

have an incentive to speculate in the forward market. For example, if the euro is at a discount relative to the dollar $(F(t) < S(t))$, and if the $/€ exchange rate follows a random walk, there is an expected profit to be made from buying euros forward. This is true because the future exchange rate at which you expect to sell euros for dollars in the future, which would be the current spot rate, is higher than the forward rate at which you can buy future euros with dollars today. Random walk behavior of exchange rates is consistent with the regression evidence from Chapter 7 that considered the unbiasedness hypothesis. There, we present evidence which suggests that investing in a currency trading at a forward discount is profitable.

Does Charting Work?

The recommendations of chartists are very subjective. As you see from the graph in Exhibit 10.8, it is possible for the eye to pick up what seem to be predictable patterns that are simply not there. Moreover, it is difficult to statistically analyze the predictions chartists make. For example, we must formalize what it means to see a head-and-shoulders pattern or another rule in a formula that can be applied to the data. One interesting study by Kevin Chang and Carol Osler (1999) compared the profitability of the head-and-shoulders pattern with other trend-predicting rules. Although Chang and Osler found that trading on the head-and-shoulders patterns is profitable, the profitability is dominated by other, simpler trading rules, which we discuss next.

Filter Rules

Filter rules are popular methods for detecting trends in exchange rates. In general, filter rules are trading strategies based on the past history of an asset price that provide signals to an investor as to when to buy a currency (that is, go long in that currency) and when to sell a currency (that is, go short in that currency). We investigate two often-used techniques, which we describe from the perspective of a dollar-based investor who is examining exchange rates in dollars per foreign currency.

x% Rules

An $x\%$ rule states that you should go long in the foreign currency (buy) after the foreign currency has appreciated relative to the dollar by $x\%$ above its most recent trough (or support level) and that you should go short (sell) whenever the currency falls $x\%$ below its most recent peak (or resistance level). Common $x\%$ rules are 1%, 2%, and so forth. The bottom panel of Exhibit 10.9 illustrates this rule for an upward trend of the currency.

Moving-average Crossover Rules

Moving-average crossover rules use moving averages of the exchange rate. An n-day moving average is just the sample average of the last n trading days, including the current rate. A (y, z) moving-average crossover rule uses averages over a short period (y days) and over a long period (z days). The strategy states that you should go long (short) in the foreign currency when the short-term moving average crosses the long-term moving average from below (above). Common rules use 1 and 5 days (1, 5), 1 and 20 days (1, 20), and 5 and 20 days (5, 20). Panel A of Exhibit 10.9 shows how the short-run moving average line, which in this case is the exchange rate itself because we are using a 1-day rule, more rapidly picks up the upward trend in the left-hand portion of the graph and cuts through the long-run moving average line from below, signaling a buy.

Filter Rule Profitability

How well do filter rules work? Filter rules have been widely studied. Studies by Richard Levich and Lee Thomas (1993) and Blake LeBaron (1999) report that following filter rules earns speculative profits that are statistically and economically significant. For example, the

Exhibit 10.9 How Filter Rules Work

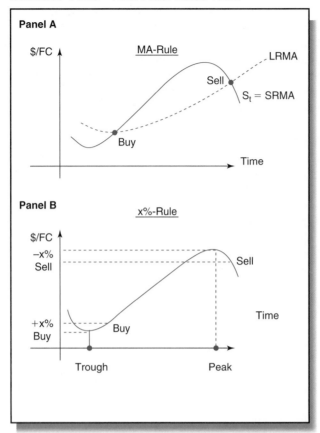

Note: In Panel A, the solid line represents the actual exchange rate, $S(t)$, which serves as the short-run moving average (SRMA). The dashed line is the long-run moving average (LRMA), averaging the current and past exchange rates. In Panel B, we graph only the exchange rate and illustrate the use of an x% filter rule.

Levich and Thomas study considered nine different filter rules for five currencies versus the dollar. The lowest average annual profit was 0.7%, and the highest was 11.1%. Generally, annual average profits were higher than 6%. How do the authors assess the statistical significance of these returns? We know that repeatedly flipping a fair coin sometimes results in a long sequence of heads, or many more heads than tails. Similarly, technical analysts boasting that their predictions have led to high returns might just have been lucky in applying their rules to a completely random series of exchange rate movements. Consequently, it is important to determine that the profits generated by the use of filter rules were not simply due to pure luck.

One way to determine the statistical significance of profits is to generate distributions of the profitability of the rules using artificial data in which the rules would not be profitable. Usually, economists assume that the unbiasedness hypothesis holds, and they generate artificial histories of spot rates and forward rates that satisfy the unbiasedness hypothesis. This can be accomplished using a technique called *bootstrapping*. In bootstrapping, the actual data are used to generate artificial exchange rate series, but the data are randomly scrambled so as to destroy any possible predictable patterns.[9] Hence, in the artificial data, there are no trends that can be consistently exploited.

---

[9]Many authors conduct their studies using logarithmic prices, rather than levels of prices. See Chapter 2 for a review of logarithms. Richard Levich and Lee Thomas apply bootstrapping to logarithmic differences of futures prices.

Every new artificial exchange rate series provides a path the exchange rate could have followed if it were really random and predictable only by the forward rate. Levich and Thomas generated 10,000 different artificial exchange rate data sets, applied the technical rules to the artificial data, and recorded the profits. This procedure generated an *empirical distribution* of profits for each filter rule and each exchange rate. Although the distributions are centered on zero, there were, nonetheless, cases in which the rules generated profits that were quite high—even as high as 5%—just by chance.

The profits of the original series are then compared to the profits from the randomly generated series. Under the null hypothesis of no filter rule profitability, the profits in the actual series should not have been significantly different from the profits generated in the artificial series. If the actual profits were higher than 95% of the simulated profits, the hypothesis that there is no exploitable trading information in the original data is rejected at the 5% marginal level of significance, or we say that we have 95% confidence that the profits were not due to chance.

Levich and Thomas find strong evidence against the hypothesis that there was no information in the original series that could have been exploited for profit using the filter rules. For the moving-average rules, in 12 out of 15 cases, the profits of the actual series ranked in the top 1% of all the simulated series. In other words, the profitability in the actual data was better than 99% of the profits that would have been found by chance if there were no trends to exploit.

Whereas the studies discussed here simply prespecify the trading rules, more recent studies have applied sophisticated computer techniques, such as genetic algorithms, to search for optimal trading rules. Without going into details, these techniques apply a Darwinian-like, natural-selection process to filter rules applied to past data that eventually breeds the "best" trading rules. (The *Point–Counterpoint* feature in this chapter discusses these kinds of "nonlinear" forecasting techniques in more detail.) Christopher Neely, Paul Weller, and Rob Dittmar (1997) found that adhering to such trading rules was, indeed, profitable. In a subsequent study conducted in 2001, Neely and Weller found that additional information about central bank interventions further improved profitability.

Assessment

There are some major limitations associated with the trading rule studies we just discussed. First of all, the studies focused on a relatively short time span because the period of floating exchange rates only began in 1973. The period was dominated by long swings in the value of the dollar: For example, the dollar appreciated measurably in the first half of the 1980s, and it then depreciated substantially in the second half of the 1980s.[10] During this period, trend-following systems may have had a comparatively easy time making profits. Note that the sample period of the Levich and Thomas study ends in 1990, the end of the "long swings" period. Indeed, newer work by Kuntara Pukthuanthong-Le, Richard Levich, and Lee Thomas, (2006) states that the era of easy profits from simple trend-following strategies is over, at least for the major currencies.

Second, most of the academic studies do not account for realistic transaction costs. Third, even if certain trading rules uncover significant profit opportunities, these profits might be normal compensation for bearing the risk of suffering currency fluctuations. Most of the empirical studies mentioned earlier did not attempt to account for risk, but even if they had, such corrections are typically imperfect. Fourth, studies such as these suffer from a problem called *data mining*. Researchers may have tried many filter rules that did not detect trends, but they failed to report them. The unsuccessful search for data rules should have been taken into account when the statistical significance of the rules was reported.

---

[10]Charles Engel and James Hamilton (1990) develop a statistical model that clearly identifies these long swings.

Regression Analysis

Trading Based on Regressions

The evidence against the unbiasedness hypothesis presented in Chapter 7 suggests that interest rate differentials may contain information about future exchange rates that can be profitably exploited. Alternatively, the profits may just arise from bearing currency risks. Both academic analysts and foreign exchange professionals have explored models that link future exchange rate changes to interest rate differentials and other easily available information (such as past exchange rates) to predict future exchange rates (see, for example, John Bilson, 1989; Craig Burnside, Martin Eichenbaum, Isaac Kleschelski, and Sergio Rebelo, 2006; Richard Clarida and Mark Taylor, 1997; Philip Green, 1992; and Miguel Villanueva, 2007). Most have used regression models.

Essentially, a regression can be used to link future returns on forward market positions $[s(t+1) - f_p(t) = \dfrac{S(t+1) - F(t)}{S(t)}]$ to current information, such as the forward premium $f_p(t) = [\dfrac{F(t) - S(t)}{S(t)}]$:

$$s(t+1) - f_p(t) = a + \gamma\, f_p(t) + e(t+1) \qquad (10.20)$$

Recall from Chapter 7 that the profit per dollar of buying the foreign currency forward is $\dfrac{S(t+1) - F(t)}{S(t)}$ because the numerator is the dollar profit per unit of foreign currency bought forward, and 1 dollar is equivalent to $1/S(t)$ units of foreign currency, and we use $s(t+1)$ to denote the percentage change in the exchange rate. In a trading strategy, the regression framework is used to find a value for the expected return on a forward position. If the expected return is positive (negative), the strategy goes long (short) the foreign currency.

To judge the usefulness of such a trading strategy, we compute the economic profits on returns it generates. Because different strategies may have different risks, it is customary to compare the Sharpe ratios of various investment strategies. The Sharpe ratio essentially represents the excess return per unit of volatility. Correcting for volatility is especially important for currency strategies, as they often employ "leverage." The following analysis reviews the important concepts of leverage and the Sharpe ratio.

The Return on Capital at Risk and Leverage

The profits we record each month are per dollar and are often called *return on capital at risk*. Remember, a forward contract does not necessitate an up-front investment because it is just a bilateral contract with a bank, but banks want to know that their counterparties can deliver on the contracts. Thus, the actual trading strategy is to invest in relatively riskless securities, such as Treasury bills, absorb potential losses, and then invest possible gains. If there is exactly 1 dollar invested in a Treasury bill for every dollar wagered in the forward market, the excess return on the trading strategy, the return over and above the return on the Treasury bill, will equal the return on capital at risk.

If forward contracts pertain to more dollars than there are in a riskless account, the trading strategy uses **leverage**. For example, if for every 1 dollar in the riskless account, 2 dollars are wagered in the forward market, the leverage ratio is 100%:

$$\text{Leverage} = \frac{\text{Capital at Risk} - \text{Capital owned}}{\text{Capital owned}} = \frac{\$2 - \$1}{\$1} = 100\%$$

Using leverage in a trading strategy scales up both its returns and its risk.

Example 10.3 Leverage and Returns

The forecasting company Trompe Le Monde uses a trading strategy in which, for each dollar placed in a money market deposit, a $3 short or long forward contract is taken out in the Swiss franc forward market. Here is an excerpt from Trompe Le Monde's trading record (all rates are USD/CHF):

Trade	Current Spot Rate	Forward Rate	Decision	Realized Future Spot Rate	Return on Capital at Risk	Actual Return
1	1.50	1.53	Short	1.52	0.67%	2.00%
2	1.52	1.55	Short	1.60	−3.29%	−9.87%
3	1.60	1.62	Short	1.54	5.00%	15.00%
4	1.54	1.53	Long	1.50	−1.95%	−5.84%
5	1.50	1.48	Long	1.48	0.00%	0.00%

The return on capital at risk is computed as $\dfrac{S(t+1) - F(t)}{S(t)}$ for a long position in the foreign currency in the forward market, and it is computed as $\dfrac{F(t) - S(t+1)}{S(t)}$ for a short position. This is the return for $1 invested in the forward market either by buying or selling forward. However, because Trompe Le Monde puts $1 in a money market deposit and $3 in the forward market position, the actual return is:

$$\text{Interest rate on money market} + 3 \times \text{Return on capital at risk}$$

(For simplicity, let's assume that the money market interest rate is zero.) In this case, the leverage ratio is 200%, so the levered returns are (1 + Leverage ratio) higher than the "returns on capital at risk."

Leverage implies that we should focus on the risk–return trade-off when investigating the profitability of regression-based trading strategies. The most popular measure is the **Sharpe ratio**, named after William F. Sharpe, a Nobel Prize–winning economist:

$$\text{Sharpe ratio} = \frac{\text{Average excess return}}{\text{Standard deviation of excess return}}$$

Example 10.4 The Sharpe Ratio of Trompe Le Monde's Trading Record

Let's return to Example 10.3 and compute the Sharpe ratio for Trompe Le Monde's five trades. Note that normally a larger sample (say, at least 20 observations) is used to compute statistics such as the Sharpe ratio. Because the money market interest rate is 0, the excess return equals the actual return. The average return is 0.26%, and the standard deviation is 8.49%. The Sharpe ratio is therefore 0.03. This means that the strategy earns 3 basis points more than the risk-free rate for every percentage of volatility risk it takes.

Regression-based Currency Strategies in Practice

The Sharpe ratio in Example 10.4 is very low. In other words, the average return is small compared to the variability of the return. Actual long-term investments in the stock market have Sharpe ratios that are about 10 times better; that is, the Sharpe ratio in the stock market tends to be about 0.30 versus the 0.03 found here.

Studies find that regression-based foreign exchange strategies produce Sharpe ratios similar to those available on actual stock return investments. Consequently, some hedge funds and investment banks (Deutsche Bank and Barclays Global Investors, for example) have used regression-based strategies to their advantage. These banks typically use multicurrency portfolios and optimization techniques to determine optimal positions and to control risk. (These optimization techniques are discussed in Chapter 13.) However, simpler approaches are also common. In September 2006, Deutsche Bank launched a currency fund that attempts to exploit the forward bias.

Deutsche Bank's strategy involves making a diversified investment in equally weighted long or short positions in 10 possible currencies versus the U.S. dollar. The 10 currencies are the euro and the currencies of Australia, Canada, Denmark, Great Britain, Japan, New Zealand, Norway, Sweden, and Switzerland. The strategy involves going long in the three currencies that trade at the steepest forward discounts versus the U.S. dollar (that is, currencies traded in countries where money market yields are higher than those in the United States) and going short in the three currencies that trade at the highest forward premiums versus the U.S. dollar (that is, currencies traded in countries where money market yields are lower than those in the United States). The long or short positions are determined at the beginning of each month and are closed at the end of each month. Apparently, the Sharpe ratio of such a strategy compares favorably to the Sharpe ratio of investing in an S&P 500 equity portfolio.

Although these results are interesting, it is important to realize that past performance need not repeat itself and that currency investing is risky. In particular, in Chapter 3, we indicated that the distribution of currency changes exhibits "fat tails"; that is, extreme outcomes (both positive and negative) are more likely than a normal distribution predicts. If a currency strategy's return exhibits fat tails, the Sharpe ratio might not adequately reflect the risk–return trade-off.

Evaluating Forecasting Services

One way to ascertain whether profits are being made in the foreign exchange market using technical analysis is to look at the forecasting records of actual forecasting services. Forex advisory services are a diverse lot. All of them generate exchange rate forecasts, but their clienteles, techniques, and forecast horizons differ. Some have expanded into giving advice on more complex hedging strategies; some manage their client's exposure for them; and some trade for their own account. However, most services use some form of technical analysis. Unfortunately, there exists scant empirical evidence on the forecasting ability of services such as these. In the late 1970s and early 1980s, *Euromoney* featured annual surveys on these advisory services, reporting and analyzing their performance. However, by the end of the 1980s, *Euromoney* had to discontinue the forex advisory survey because of lack of useful replies.

Robert Cumby and David Modest (1987) examined the advice of seven technical advisory services by conducting hypothetical trades based on their advice. The two major findings were that the advisors performed poorly on the "percentage correct signals" measure, meaning that their recommendations were more likely to be wrong than right. Second, following the advice would have earned profits in 34 of the 39 cases they examined, but the results were not as good for subsamples.

Some of the techniques used by forecasting services are very simple and easy to implement. As a potential user of advisory services, it is pertinent to ask whether these services are really worth their money. As a general rule, it is wise to be skeptical when past returns look too good. Remember that "news" is the main factor driving exchange rates, and news is by definition largely unpredictable! Moreover, investments with high expected returns are typically risky strategies. If free lunches exist, they are usually hard to find.

Chaos, Genetic Engineering, and Neural Networks

"Come on, Ante. It will not be that bad," Freedy implored. Ante could not shake off the dreadful prospect of seeing Covis Estello at their high school reunion. Although the brothers acknowledged that Covis was smart, they had often made fun of him in high school, frequently calling him Mr. Super-Geek. Now, Ante was holding an article from the newspaper describing Mr. Estello's prowess in developing systems to trade currencies. Estello's expertise was apparently in the area of chaos theory and neural network systems, and he had reputedly "trained" different models using "genetic algorithms."

"I have no clue what he's doing, but he seems to be able to predict currency values, and he is clearly way richer than we will ever be," Ante lamented.

Freedy sighed and cautioned, "Come on, you know predicting currency values is incredibly difficult. I actually think he may just be lucky. Foreign exchange markets are very efficient. It's very hard to make abnormal returns in these markets. I think Covis used some mathematical hocus-pocus to convince investors to give him money, took some risks with other peoples' money, and got lucky. If I'm right, we'll soon see an article titled "The Rise and Fall of Estello.""

"Well, that won't happen before our class reunion, and besides, to me his profits are exactly proof that markets are totally inefficient," retorted Ante. "Clearly, super-nerd Covis must have devised some complex system to find trends in exchange rates, and now he is making oodles of money while we are studying efficient markets!"

At that moment, Suttle Trooth agitatedly rushed into the room. "Hey guys, did you read the article about Covis? What a success story! Come on, Ante, aren't you happy with our old friend's success?" Suttle smirked as he saw Ante frowning.

Freedy immediately asked, "Please explain to us what all this math junk is about. I can't figure out how Covis can make money if markets are efficient, yet I've got a lot of faith in efficient markets."

Suttle relaxed and said, "Well, these are very complex issues. If markets are efficient, you're right that it would be quite difficult to make tons of money trading currencies. There certainly wouldn't be any easy trends to exploit. But even if we believe in efficient markets, the theories we studied in school make a number of doubtful or at least brave assumptions. First of all, speculating in currency markets exposes you to risk, and any profits may just be compensation for bearing currency risk. Remember, the risk premium can also move around and change signs. If that is the case, predictable patterns in exchange rates, picked up by Estello's system, may just reflect time-varying risk premiums—that is, he goes long in currencies that are especially risky. If this is the case, it would not be surprising that one of these days, he may suffer a serious loss.

"Second," continued Suttle, "economists often assume that all traders have the same information, act in their self-interest, and agree on the model generating exchange rates and the market fundamentals. We all know that this is not literally true. For example, some commercial banks use the superior information they have from the flow of forex orders they take from their multinational clients. This might help them get an idea of short-run patterns. In U.S. equity markets, such trading is called front-running, and it is illegal, but in the unregulated currency markets, anything goes. Other economic models only make sense if there are traders who are not trading on their private information. In addition, smart people can exploit 'noise traders' who systematically lose money. Noise traders could be acting irrationally; they could also be a central bank that is not profit maximizing and therefore could be exploited.

"Work in psychology and economics now shows all sorts of behavioral biases that may lead to non-rational trading behavior that more rational traders could exploit. Furthermore, we know that exchange rates are influenced by monetary policy, and many relevant elements of policy making are really not publicly known. It is possible that some experts learn more about these policies or they can predict policy changes better than others. Finally, even if you are right in the long run, the market might turn against you in the short run. A trader must have sufficient capital to ride out a string of losses, or he may go broke before the profits start rolling in."

"But how exactly does Covis make money?" Freedy interjected.

Suttle answered, "Well, I do not know much about the mathematical models he uses except for the fact that they are inherently nonlinear—that is, they involve quadratic and cubic functions and the like. A chaos system, which is one of the models mentioned in the article, is actually a deterministic system with no news or shocks at all. The future is thought to be a deterministic, nonlinear function of the past. If you can figure out the relationship, you can perfectly predict the future. Although chaos theory seems to have some useful applications in biology and physics (it's apparently great in explaining fluid dynamics), I haven't seen any really useful applications in economics and finance.

"News is what drives asset prices! Moreover, chaos systems are extremely sensitive to initial conditions and yield vastly different predictions, depending on small perturbations to initial conditions. How will Covis ever know he has found the right system? A small data error could lead him astray. However, I see more of a future in these neural network systems," continued Suttle. "A neural network is another kind of nonlinear model, where depending upon the outcome of some criterion (say above or below 0), a particular function gets switched on. From what I can tell, genetic algorithms are tools to help determine the best trading rules for a given set of historic data. They are really a computer research procedure that uses the Darwinian principle. Essentially, the computer randomly generates a number of potential trading rules. The best trading rules ('survival of the fittest') have the best chance of surviving to the next round (they 'reproduce'). These rules are mixed with some randomly generated new rules (there is 'mutation'). Eventually, the program identifies trading rules that are very profitable.

"What is problematic about all these models," said Suttle, "is that they are heavily parameterized. What I mean is that the mathematical model requires the specification of a lot of parameters. For a particular sample of data, it will always be the case that some nonlinear function describes the data very well. The key issue is whether it works in the real world with real trading and real money. And even if it does work well for a while, is it really skill, or is it simply luck? That may take years to figure out. Hence, I'm not so sure that Covis has any particular skill. The jury is still out. Moreover, if he is successful, and there is something in the data the market participants did not know, his trading will make markets more efficient, which will kill the profit opportunity. Undervalued currencies will be bought and overvalued currencies will be sold."

Freedy shouted, "See, I told you, in the end, markets are efficient! Unfortunately, Ante, Covis will still be the man at the school's reunion." Ante just sighed.

10.5 PREDICTING DEVALUATIONS

So far, we have discussed currency forecasting for floating exchange rates. Unfortunately, nearly 60% of currency systems in the world do not fit into this category. We now focus our discussion on the special forecasting problems that arise in pegged systems, but note that many of these ideas also apply to the target zones and currency boards discussed in Chapter 5.

In a pegged system, the forecasting issues are whether there will be a devaluation, and, if so, how large it will be. We first review the major theories on why pegged systems break down. Then we discuss various forecasting techniques, both in situations where good financial data are available and in cases where they are lacking. We also recount the currency devaluations that occurred in Europe in 1992, Mexico in 1994–1995, and Southeast Asia in 1997 and the havoc they wrought.

What Causes a Currency Crisis?

The spectacular currency crises just mentioned have revived interest in the causes of speculative attacks that typically accompany the failure of a pegged exchange rate. When a speculative attack is successful, the currency either experiences a large devaluation (which happened many times during the European Monetary System [EMS]), or the exchange rate is floated (as happened in Mexico in 1994). For multinational businesses, such occurrences are very important not only because the companies have direct currency exposures in the devaluing countries but also because currency crises are usually accompanied by economic upheaval. This can lower the value of the local assets that the companies own, affect their production, and adversely affect their local and worldwide sales. There are two main reasons pegged currencies succumb to speculative pressures.

Macroeconomic Conditions

The first explanation for why pegged currencies succumb to speculative pressures, building on the seminal work of Paul Krugman (1979) and Robert Flood and Peter Garber (1984), argues that if a government follows policies inconsistent with its currency peg, a speculative attack is unavoidable. Speculators will attack the system and attempt to profit by selling the local currency and buying the foreign currency. The country's central bank, in this case, will lose foreign reserves defending the peg until a critical level of low reserves is reached, at which point, the bank is forced to abandon the peg. Whereas initial models focused on expansionary monetary policies, expansionary fiscal policies can also lead to speculative attacks.

These models argue that devaluations are predictable. Growing budget deficits, fast money growth, and rising wages and prices should precede them. If prices rise faster in the local economy than foreign prices are rising while the nominal exchange rate remains unchanged, the local currency is appreciating in real terms. Hence, currency overvaluations should also be a signal of an imminent crisis. The combination of government budget deficits and real exchange rate overvaluations also usually leads to large current account deficits. Consequently, if the theory is correct, speculative pressures should be predictable from economic data.

Self-fulfilling Expectations

The second explanation for why pegged currencies succumb to speculative pressures recognizes that speculative attacks sometimes seem to come out of the blue. The crisis may be a self-fulfilling prophecy caused by the "animal spirits" of investors, as the famous economist John Maynard Keynes once phrased it.

Although the formal models outlining these ideas are too abstract to recount here, consider the following argument: Suppose a significant group of investors simply starts speculating against a currency, which causes a substantial capital outflow from the country under attack. Other investors, seeing the capital outflow, think the currency will collapse, so they, too, sell the currency, leading to yet more capital outflow. If the central bank becomes overwhelmed, and the country's currency is devalued, this validates the fears of investors, even though there was no fundamental economic reason for dropping the peg.[11]

More recent studies on the issue recognize that fundamental economic variables enter the picture. Basically, a deterioration of a fundamental such as the country's employment rate makes defending the nation's currency more costly and eventually leads to a crisis. However, the actual occurrence and timing of the crisis are still determined by the animal spirits of speculators.

---

[11]Technically, such self-fulfilling attacks are possible in models with multiple equilibriums. There is a stable equilibrium in which the government follows the right policies consistent with the peg, but there is also another equilibrium in which the speculators attack the currency and the government accommodates the lower exchange rate. See, for example, Maurice Obstfeld (1986) and Bernard Bensaid and Olivier Jeanne (2000).

Contagion

The phenomenon known as **contagion** is an increase in the probability that a speculative attack on a currency will occur merely as a result of other currency crises. For example, in September 1992, the British pound first devalued and then left the EMS altogether. The pound suffered a large depreciation in value relative to most European currencies. A few months later, speculators attacked the Irish punt, which was still in the EMS, and the Irish authorities were forced to devalue as well. Because Ireland did not appear to be experiencing any economic problems, many market observers ascribed the Irish devaluation to contagion from the United Kingdom.

If speculative attacks are merely self-fulfilling prophesies as in the models of Maurice Obstfeld (1986) and Bernard Bensaid and Olivier Jeanne (2000), contagion is easy to understand. If speculators successfully attack one currency, they may as well try another. Nevertheless, contagion may be a rational response and even predictable for a variety of reasons. For example, when the British pound devalues but the Irish punt does not devalue, the Irish punt experiences a real appreciation relative to the pound. Because a real appreciation adversely affects the competitive position of Irish exporters, it causes economic and political pressure to devalue.

Another situation in which contagion is rational but the first crisis is not the cause of the second crisis arises when two currencies are attacked sequentially because the second country is experiencing similar negative macroeconomic conditions or it is following similar inconsistent policies.

Empirical Evidence on the Predictability of Currency Crises

The theory on currency crises clearly suggests that certain macroeconomic signals predict devaluations or currency crises. What macroeconomic variables have proved useful predictors of devaluations? Although the many empirical studies do not always agree, a number of economic variables consistently show up as useful predictors. These include PPP-based measures of currency overvaluation, current account balances and monetary growth rates (see Barry Eichengreen, Andrew Rose, and Charles Wyplosz, 1995; Gerardo Esquivel and Felipe Larrain, 2000; Ilan Goldfajn and Rodrigo Valdes, 1998; and Michael Klein and Nancy Marion, 1997).

A number of economists and investment banks have built econometric models to predict currency crashes using similar economic variables. The model is estimated using data from various countries on past devaluations. The input of current values of the macroeconomic variables associated with a country then delivers the probability of a devaluation occurring. Some models in this class (for instance, Geert Bekaert and Stephen Gray, 1998) combine financial data, such as interest rate differentials, and other macroeconomic information, such as cumulative inflation differentials. If liquid financial markets exist, information about forward rates or interest rates, currency option prices, and so on may prove useful in terms of forecasting devaluations. After all, the market prices should rapidly reflect all new economic information.

The Rocky 1990s: Currency Crises Galore

In 1992, speculators attacked a number of currencies in Europe, severely undermining and casting doubt on the progress toward monetary union in Europe. An exasperated Michel Sapin, French finance minister, was quoted in the *New York Times* on September 24, 1992, "I will fight, we will fight, France and Germany will fight this speculation, which is based on no economic fundamentals. During the French Revolution such speculators were known as 'agioteurs' and they were beheaded."

But this was only the beginning of the very rocky decade. At the end of 1994, the Mexican peso collapsed, and in its wake, other emerging market currencies and stock markets wobbled. In 1997, several Southeast Asian countries were forced to abandon their pegs relative to the dollar. We now chronicle these watershed events.

The Treaty of Maastricht and German Reunification

In December 1991, representatives from the EC countries signed the Treaty of Maastricht, which still required approval by referendum in some countries. The treaty mapped out the road to a monetary union. Even before this historic event, the first signs of currency turmoil began, not in countries that were part of the EMS at the time but in Scandinavia. Finland, Sweden, and Norway had adopted pegs to the ECU, hoping to strengthen their application for EC membership and signaling their determination to keep inflation down. In November 1991, the collapse of the former Soviet Union obliterated a large portion of Finland's foreign trade, and the markka devalued by 12.3%. This caused a shake-up in the EMS, as weaker currencies dropped in value against the Deutsche mark. On June 2, 1992, voters in Denmark narrowly rejected the Treaty of Maastricht, which rattled the confidence of those proposing EMU. On June 18, 1992, Irish voters accepted the treaty in a referendum.

Against this background, developments in Germany began to cast a shadow on the credibility of the treaty. In 1990, East and West Germany were reunified, and Germany struggled to absorb the Eastern Länder into the German economy. Inflation surged from increased demand and from wage increases in the former East Germany that exceeded growth in productivity. Moreover, the German money supply increased dramatically from the conversion of Ostmarks, the money of East Germany, into Deutsche marks at a 1 for 1 exchange rate, even though the purchasing power of the Ostmark was significantly less than that of the Deutsche mark. Sizable budget deficits arose when the government chose to finance the costs of the transition without raising taxes.

The Ostmark conversion, the loose fiscal policy, and the emergence of inflation worried the Bundesbank, Germany's largely independent central bank that has been obsessed with maintaining price stability ever since the hyperinflation of the 1920s. The Bundesbank stepped hard on the brakes and implemented a tight monetary policy of low money growth and high interest rates. The high interest rates in Germany caused a capital inflow and drove up the value of the mark.

The other countries in the EMS were confronted with a dilemma: raise interest rates to stay in the EMS and appreciate versus the dollar and other major currencies along with the Deutsche mark while seeing their economies suffer in the short run or keep interest rates low to stimulate their economies and risk future devaluation and possible failure of the EMU. With Britain in deep recession and other economies heading there, participants in the financial markets began to sense a dwindling belief in the commitment to the EMU.

The September 1992 Currency Crisis

In September 1992, speculative pressure on the weak currencies in Scandinavia and the Italian lira, the British pound, the Spanish peseta, and the Portuguese escudo came to a boiling point as the speculators won most of the battles. On September 8, 1992, Finland dropped its peg to the ECU, and the markka floated, promptly depreciating by 16% with respect to the mark. On September 16, 1992, a day now known as Black Wednesday, the British pound was forced out of the ERM and plummeted in value as billions of pounds were sold on the foreign exchange markets. One day later, the Italian lira, which had previously devalued, was suspended from the EMS, and the Spanish peseta and Portuguese escudo were devalued.

On September 20, 1992, French voters narrowly voted yes to the Treaty of Maastricht, but speculative pressure against the French franc, the peseta, the escudo, the Swedish krona, and the Irish punt continued to mount. Portugal and Ireland made use of their remaining capital controls to help contain the crises, and Spain reintroduced capital controls that had been lifted only 8 months before. France raised short-term interest rates, and both the Bundesbank and the Banque de France intervened heavily. It is generally believed that the defense of the French franc was more successful than that of the pound because the Bundesbank officially came to the franc's defense.

Although by the end of 1992, all countries except Britain and Denmark had ratified the Treaty of Maastricht, currency speculation claimed more victims in the last 2 months of the year. Both the Swedish krona and Norwegian krone dropped their ECU pegs, and the peseta and escudo were devalued. Meanwhile, the Bundesbank announced that it would keep official interest rates unchanged.

The Events of 1993

On January 1, 1993, Ireland lifted capital controls and started to rely on interest rates as its main defense mechanism against speculative attacks. From then onward, the punt faced almost continuous pressure, and eventually, on January 30, it was devalued by 10% versus the other countries' currencies. The fate of the Irish punt seemed a vindication of the 1985 Padoa-Schioppa report which had suggested that higher capital mobility would endanger the EMS—in other words, that there might be a trade-off between economic union and monetary union.

Although the Bundesbank began to ease interest rates in 1993, the currency turmoil was not over, and the peseta and escudo devalued once more on May 13, 1993. On May 18, 1993, the Danes voted in favor of the Treaty of Maastricht at the second referendum (56.8% yes votes), but the vote failed to quash speculation that the move to EMU was off the rails. Nevertheless, positive economic figures in France led to a virtual convergence of French short- and long-term interest rates to German levels, prompting some French journalists to propose the French franc as the new anchor of the ERM: the "franchor!"

But it was not to be. The Bundesbank cut interest rates all too gradually, and a streak of disconcerting statistics on the macroeconomic health of a number of European countries (in particular France) intensified speculative pressures during June and early July. On July 29, 1993, the Bundesbank snubbed market speculation that it would cut interest rates to save the ERM. Weak ERM currencies, including the French franc, came under tremendous pressure, and on July 30, the French franc dipped through the ERM floor several times. Governments in the ERM countries were no longer prepared to continue to defend their currencies, and on August 2, 1993, the European leaders decided to widen the parity bands to 15% on either side of the central rate, except for the Dutch guilder, which remained in a 2.25% band around the Deutsche mark. With perfect timing, the British parliament ratified the Treaty of Maastricht on August 3, 1993.

Although most currencies initially depreciated against the Deutsche mark after the widening of the bands, the values of most currencies returned to within their old bands by the end of 1993. Perhaps surprisingly, thereafter, the movement toward the single currency proceeded without too many hiccups. There were a few realignments in 1995, but the Austrian shilling and Finnish markka joined the EMS, and the Italian lira reentered without causing any problems. By 1999, the euro was introduced without problems, although all the old currencies continued to circulate, and the introduction of physical euros at the beginning of 2002 was also quite successful.

1994–1995: THE MEXICAN CRISIS AND THE TEQUILA EFFECT

As we discussed in Chapter 5, Mexico operated a crawling band exchange rate system. However, on December 20, 1994, the ceiling of the band was raised by approximately 13% in an attempt to stop the heavy losses of foreign exchange reserves sustained since mid-November. But the losses continued, and on December 22, the government effectively floated the peso.

Unfortunately, this currency crisis was only beginning. Investors around the world and Mexican residents dumped Mexican bonds and equities, putting enormous pressure on the exchange rate. The peso halved in value, as did the equity market. Interest rates spiked up. What was worse, in the course of 1994, the Mexican government had, as a signal of its commitment to the exchange rate band, issued bonds called Tesobonos. Tesobonos are Mexican Treasury bills denominated in dollars but paid in pesos. In effect, Tesobonos protect investors from currency risk. At the end of 1994, the Tesobonos outstanding was more than three times the value of the remaining foreign currency reserves of the Bank of Mexico, and, despite very high Tesobonos interest rates, no new foreign money was ready to be invested in Mexico. Mexico faced a very acute liquidity crisis, which threatened to affect other emerging markets as well.

With the private sector no longer willing to provide funds to Mexico, there was a feeling at the IMF and in the Clinton administration of the U.S. government that a support package of short-term emergency loans was necessary to get Mexico through its financing problems. Whereas the U.S. Congress voted down support for Mexico, the IMF and the Clinton administration, drawing on funds from the U.S. Treasury's Exchange Stabilization Fund, put together a bailout package worth some $50 billion that saved Mexico.

The Mexican currency crisis was a watershed event for emerging markets. Since the early 1990s, many emerging markets had witnessed large portfolio inflows from the developed world. The currency crisis in Mexico and its adverse effects on equity markets seemed to cause foreign capital to dry up not only for Mexico but also for other emerging markets, from Latin American to Asia and eastern Europe. This spillover of the Mexican crisis to other countries came to be known as the Tequila Effect and caused many economists and policymakers to reevaluate the benefits of unbridled capital flows.

Nevertheless, Mexico managed to rebound rather quickly, and the loans provided in the bailout package were duly repaid. Unfortunately, the Mexican crisis was only a warning sign for worse to come.

1997: The Southeast Asian Crisis

Since 1980, the countries of Southeast Asia, the so-called Asian Tigers, had engineered an economic miracle, growing their real GDPs by over 7% per year. But there were some uncanny parallels between their macroeconomic fundamentals and those of Mexico just before the crisis. Mexico had been running large current account deficits in the years preceding the currency crisis. For some of the Asian Tigers, their high economic growth also went hand-in-hand with growing current account imbalances. The current account imbalances were worst for Thailand, followed by Malaysia, the Philippines, Korea, and Indonesia. The other Asian countries—Taiwan, Singapore, China, and Hong Kong—on the other hand, ran current account surpluses or very small deficits. These countries all had relatively fixed exchange rate systems in place. Whereas Hong Kong was the only country running a currency board with dollars, other countries were formally pegging their exchange rate to a basket of currencies. However, the effective weight of the U.S. dollar in the basket was so high that the countries were essentially pegged to the U.S. dollar.

We show the historic evolution of some of these currencies relative to the dollar in Exhibit 10.10, in which the values of the currencies are normalized to equal 100 in January 1997.

All five currencies were within 10% of 100 during 1995–1996. In fact, the Malaysian ringgit moved in a 10% range of MYR(2.5–2.7)/USD for most of the years between 1990 and 1997. The Thai baht was effectively fixed in a narrow range of THB(25.2–25.6)/USD from 1990 until 1997. In the Philippines, the peso was practically fixed at PHP26.2/USD from spring 1995 until the beginning of 1997. The other countries followed more flexible exchange rate regimes.

Exhibit 10.10 indicates that these currencies experienced sharp depreciations in the second half of 1997. Thailand was the first country to be hit by the crisis. Intervention could not stem the outflow of capital in the first half of 1997, and by early July, the authorities were

Exhibit 10.10 Asian Exchange Rates

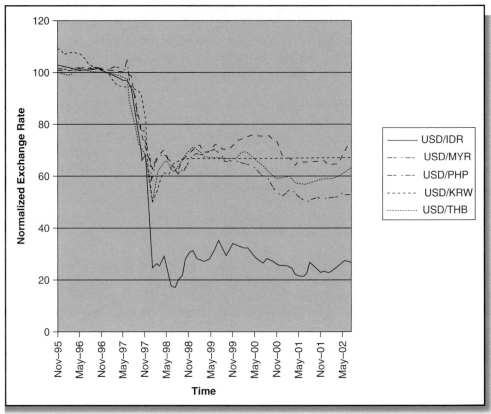

Note: The exchange rates are normalized to equal 100 in January 1997. The currencies are the U.S. dollar values of the Indonesian rupiah (IDR), the Malaysian ringgit (MYR), the Philippine peso (PHP), the Korean won (KRW), and the Thai baht (THB).

forced to let the baht float (or, rather, sink). Indonesia quickly became engulfed in the regional financial crisis, and its authorities allowed the rupiah to float freely in mid-August 1997. Sharp currency depreciations also occurred in Malaysia and the Philippines. Korea was the last to be hit by the crisis. Despite repeated exchange market intervention in the summer and autumn and a firming of interest rates, the Korean won's slide could not be arrested. By late November, the country seemed on the brink of defaulting on its short-term external liabilities.

All the countries facing currency crises were very heavily exposed to short-term foreign currency–denominated debt (typically dollars), but Korea was by far the most exposed. In June 1997, outstanding, short-term, foreign currency–denominated debt was more than 300% of Korea's official reserves. In Thailand and Indonesia, this ratio was also well over 100%. Of course, once the crisis hit and the currency depreciated, the value of the debt burden in local currency exploded.

The currency crises in Southeast Asia had wide repercussions, leading to corporate restructuring and bankruptcies. Rich businesspeople became poor overnight, fueling a thriving market for secondhand luxury goods. More importantly, economic growth was hampered, especially in Thailand and Korea, and unemployment rose. The Asian currency crises became real economic crises, causing the Asian miracle to come to a screeching halt.

10.6 SUMMARY

This chapter focuses on the determination of exchange rates and forecasting of exchange rates. The main points of the chapter are as follows:

1. Currency forecasts are useful in the international aspects of project evaluation, strategic planning, pricing, working capital management, and the analysis of portfolio investments.
2. The Fisher hypothesis states that the nominal interest rate equals the real interest rate plus the expected rate of inflation.
3. When all the international parity conditions hold, currency forecasting models have little value: The forward rate is the best predictor for the future spot rate, the current real exchange rate is the best predictor of the future real exchange rate, and costs of funding and returns to investment are equalized in real terms across countries (that is, real interest rates are equalized across countries).
4. Empirical evidence overwhelmingly rejects the notion of the equality of real interest rates across countries.
5. The two main forecasting techniques are fundamental analysis and technical analysis.
6. Fundamental analysis links exchange rates to fundamental macroeconomic variables such as GDP growth and the current account either through a formal model or through judgmental analysis.
7. Technical analysis uses financial data, such as past exchange rate data, to predict future exchange rates.
8. The root mean squared error (RMSE) can be used to judge the accuracy of forecasts. The percentage of correct signals relative to the forward rate can be used to judge the usefulness of hedging. The profits generated by using the forecasts can also be used to gauge their quality.
9. The asset market approach to exchange rate determination views the exchange rate as an asset price. Its value then depends on current fundamentals (such as relative money supplies and output levels of countries) and expected values of future economic fundamentals. Only a change in current fundamentals or news about future fundamentals changes the exchange rate.
10. Two of the most often-mentioned determinants of exchange rates are real interest rate differentials and current account balances. These variables are simultaneously determined.
11. The complexity of the relationships that determine the current account and the exchange rate may explain why fundamental exchange rate models perform rather poorly in forecasting future exchange rates.
12. Chartists record the actual trading history of an exchange rate and try to infer possible trends based on that information alone. It is unlikely that the naked eye can pick up trends in a randomly fluctuating series.
13. Filter rules, such as x% and moving-average rules, are trading rules designed to detect trend behavior in exchange rates. Although early empirical studies focusing on data from the 1980s found strong trends in exchange rates, more recent work has a more difficult time uncovering trend behavior.
14. More sophisticated technical analysis uses regression analysis or other econometric techniques to link exchange rates to financial data, such as forward premiums. Whether the trading strategies based on this analysis have led to profitable trading strategies and demonstrate market inefficiency has not been resolved.
15. When an exchange rate is pegged, multinational businesses must assess the probability and magnitude of a possible devaluation. Poor macroeconomic fundamentals, such as an overvalued currency, high money growth rates, and large current account deficits, are warning signs of an imminent devaluation. To make devaluation predictions, formal models employ macroeconomic information, financial information (such as interest rate differentials), or both.

QUESTIONS

1. What is the difference between the *ex ante* and the *ex post* real interest rate?
2. Suppose that the international parity conditions all hold and a country has a higher nominal interest rate than the United States. Characterize the country's inflation rate compared to the United States, the country's expected exchange rate change versus the dollar, the country's currency forward premium (or discount) versus the dollar, and the country's real interest rate compared to the U.S. real interest rate.
3. How do fundamental analysis and technical analysis differ?

4. Would technical analysis be useful if the international parity conditions held? Why or why not?
5. Describe three statistics you should obtain from a currency-forecasting service in order to judge the quality of its currency forecasts.
6. Does a large increase in the domestic money supply always lead to a depreciation of the currency?
7. Is a current account deficit always associated with a strong real exchange rate (that is, one in which the currency is overvalued compared to the PPP prediction)?
8. Describe how three macroeconomic fundamentals affect exchange rates.
9. Which simple statistical model yields some of the best exchange rate predictions available? What does this imply for the value of models of exchange rate determination to multinational businesses?
10. What is chartism?
11. What is an $x\%$ filter rule?
12. What is a moving-average crossover rule?
13. Have forecasting services been successful in forecasting exchange rates?
14. Are devaluations of pegged exchange rates totally unexpected?
15. Construct a list of a country's economic statistics you would assemble to help determine the probability of a devaluation of its currency within the coming year.

PROBLEMS

1. Suppose the 1-year nominal interest rate in Zooropa is 9%, and Zooropa's expected inflation rate is 4%. What is the real interest rate in Zooropa?
2. You were recently hired by the Doolittle Corporation corporate treasury to help oversee its expansion into Europe. Blake Francis, the CFO, wants to hire a foreign exchange forecasting company. Blake has asked you to evaluate three different companies, and he has obtained information on their past performances. Out of a total of 50 forecasts for the $/€ rate, the companies reported the number of times they correctly forecast appreciations and depreciations:

	Correct Down Forecasts	Correct Up Forecasts
Morrissey Forex Advisors	20	5
Pixie Exchange Land	20	4
FOREX Cures	12	12

There are a total of 35 dollar appreciations (down periods) and 15 dollar depreciations (up periods) in the sample. Blake wants to know two things:

a. Can anything be said about the companies' forecasting ability with the available data?
b. What additional information should Blake try to obtain in order to form a better judgment?

3. Mini-Case: Currency Turmoil in Zooropa

Fad Gadget has never worked so hard in his entire life. It is near midnight, and he is still poring over statistics and tables. Fad recently joined Smashing Pumpkins, a relatively young but fast-growing British firm. Smashing Pumpkins produces and distributes an intri-cate device that turns fresh pumpkins into pumpkin pie in about 30 minutes. Recently, the firm has started exporting to Zooropa. Some of the largest and tastiest pumpkins are grown in Zooropa, and Zooropa's population boasts the highest per capita pumpkin consumption in the world. A recent analysis of the pumpkin market in Zooropa has left the company's senior managers very impressed with the profit potential.

Although Zooropa consists of 10 politically independent countries, their currencies are linked through a system called the Currency Rate Linkage System (CRLS) that works exactly like the former Exchange Rate Mechanism (ERM) of the EMS before the currency turmoil started in September 1992. The anchor currency is the banshee of Enigma, the leading country in Zooropa.

Initial contacts with importers in Zooropean countries indicated that they typically insist on payment in their own local currency. About a week ago, Cab Voltaire, the CEO of Smashing Pumpkins, expressed concerns about this development and asked Fad to lead a research team to further examine the present state of the currency system of Zooropa. Cab viewed the outlook for the banshee relative to the pound quite favorably and did not predict any substantial depreciation of the banshee against any other major currency. However, the precarious economic situation of some of the countries in Zooropa and the growing importance of speculative pressures in Zooropa's currency markets last week suddenly made him suspicious about the possibility of realignments within the system. He even doubted the long-term viability of the system. Cab instructed Fad to examine the following issues:

• Which currencies in the system exhibit the highest realignment risk?

- If a currency realigns and gets devalued, what are the effects on our sales and profit margins in this particular country? Can we take the realignment possibility into account in our pricing?
- Suppose a currency is forced to leave the CRLS. What are the effects on exchange rates, interest rates, and the outlook for sales in that country? What is the likelihood of this occurring for the different countries?

Fad Gadget felt nervous. A meeting was scheduled with Cab the day after tomorrow. He wanted to write a thorough and insightful report. At the last management meeting, he had the uneasy feeling that some senior managers doubted his abilities. Some managers were naturally suspicious of a young Australian newcomer with his MBA. His earring and punk hairdo did not exactly help either. His team of analysts had already assembled a table with relevant macroeconomic and financial data (see Exhibit 10.11). "If only I could use this to rank the different countries according to realignment risk," he thought. Place yourself in Fad Gadget's shoes and see what your ranking is.

Exhibit 10.11 Zooropa in Numbers

Country	Currency's CRLS Position	Currency's over/ undervaluation, %	Reserves, Import Coverage	Budget Deficit as % of GDP	Inflation rate, %	GDP Growth, %
Sinead	−6	−10	9	−1.9	3.6	2.4
Carmen	−36	−12	3.1	−2.3	2.7	2.0
Marquee	16	11	8.2	−4.9	5.7	2.0
Fries	−3	11	11.7	−5.4	9.5	2.8
Ney	−22	−2	2.5	−2.1	2.2	2.1
Helpisink	31	−18	1.3	−5.5	2.1	1.6
Benfica	30	−16	1.5	−3.4	3.5	1.6
Che ora	−90	3	2.6	−4.6	3.6	−0.8
Vachement	27	2	0.5	−11.3	5.2	1.3

Notes: The CRLS position measures the general strength or weakness of a currency within the target zone. A value of −100 means that the currency is at its lower bound and is weak relative to all other currencies in the zone. A value of 100 means that the currency is at its upper bound and is strong relative to all other currencies in the zone. The currency's over/undervaluation is relative to the prediction of purchasing power parity (PPP). It is computed by taking the percentage deviation from the prediction of PPP of the currency versus the banshee, the central rate in the system. A positive number means the currency is overvalued relative to PPP. Import coverage calculates the ratio of foreign exchange reserves at the central bank to average monthly imports. This indicates how many months of imports could be purchased by the foreign exchange reserves held at the central bank. The inflation rate and GDP growth rate are in percentage per annum.

BIBLIOGRAPHY

Baxter, Marianne, 1994, "Real Exchange Rates and Real Interest Differentials: Have We Missed the Business Cycle Relationship?" *Journal of Monetary Economics* 33, pp. 5–37.

Bekaert, Geert, and Stephen Gray, 1998, "Target Zones and Exchange Rates: An Empirical Investigation," *Journal of International Economics* 45, pp. 1–35.

Bekaert, Geert, Robert J. Hodrick, and David Marshall, 2001, "Peso Problem Explanations for Term Structure Anomalies," *Journal of Monetary Economics* 48, pp. 241–270.

Bensaid, Bernard, and Olivier Jeanne, 2000, "Self-fulfilling Currency Crises and Central Bank Independence," *Scandinavian Journal of Economics* 102, pp. 605–620.

Bilson, John F.O., 1989, "Technical Currency Trading," manuscript.

Bilson, John F.O., David A. Hsieh, 1987, "The Profitability of Currency Speculation," *International Journal of Forecasting* 3, pp. 115–130.

Burnside, Craig, Martin Eichenbaum, Isaac Kleschelski, and Sergio Rebelo, 2006, "The Returns to Currency Speculation," National Bureau of Economic Research working paper 12489.

Campa, Jose M., and P.H. Kevin Chang, 1996, "Arbitrage-Based Tests of Target-Zone Credibility: Evidence from ERM Cross-rate Options," *American Economic Review* 86, pp. 726–740.

Campbell, John Y., and Richard H. Clarida, 1987, "The Term Structure of Euromarket Interest Rates: An Empirical

Investigation," *Journal of Monetary Economics* 19, pp. 25–44.

Chakrabarti, Avik, 2006, "Real Exchange Rates and Real Interest Rates Once Again: A Multivariate Panel Cointegration Analysis," *Applied Economics* 38, pp. 1217–1221.

Chang, P.H. Kevin, and Carol L. Osler, 1999, "Methodical Madness: Technical Analysis and the Irrationality of Exchange-Rate Forecasts," *Economic Journal* 109, pp. 636–661.

Clarida, Richard H., and Mark P. Taylor, 1997, "The Term Structure of Forward Premiums and the Forecastability of Spot Exchange Rates: Correcting the Errors," *Review of Economics and Statistics* 79, pp. 353–361.

Cumby, Robert E., and David M. Modest, 1987, "Testing for Market Timing Ability—A Framework for Forecast Evaluation," *Journal of Financial Economics* 19, pp. 169–189.

Diebold, Francis X., and James A. Nason, 1990, "Nonparametric Exchange-Rate Prediction," *Journal of International Economics* 28, pp. 315–332.

Dooley, Michael P., and Jeffrey R. Shafer, 1982, "Analysis of Short-Run Exchange Rate Behavior: March 1973 to November 1981," in D. Bigman and T. Taya, eds., *Exchange Rate and Trade Instability: Causes and Consequences*, Cambridge, MA: Ballinger.

Dornbusch, Rudiger, 1976, "Expectations and Exchange-Rate Dynamics," *Journal of Political Economy* 84, pp. 1161–1176.

Edison, Hali J., and B. Dianne Pauls, 1993, "A Re-assessment of the Relationship Between Real Exchange Rates and Real Interest Rates: 1970–1990," *Journal of Monetary Economics* 31, pp. 165–187.

Eichengreen, Barry, Andrew K. Rose, and Charles Wyplosz, 1995, "Exchange Market Mayhem: The Antecedents and Aftermaths of Speculative Attacks," *Economic Policy* 21, pp. 251–312.

Eichengreen, Barry, Andrew K. Rose, and Charles Wyplosz, 1996, "Contagious Currency Crises," National Bureau of Economic Research working paper.

Engel, Charles M., and James Hamilton, 1990, "Long Swings in the Dollar—Are They in the Data and Do Markets Know It?" *American Economic Review* 80, pp. 689–713.

Esquivel, Gerardo, and Felipe Larrain, 2000, "Determinants of Currency Crises," *Trimestre Economico* 67, pp. 191–237.

Fisher, Irving, 1930, *The Theory of Interest as Determined by Impatience to Spend Income and Opportunity to Invest It.* New York: MacMillan.

Flood, Robert, and Peter Garber, 1984, "Collapsing Exchange Rate Regimes, Some Linear Examples," *Journal of International Economics* 17, pp. 1–13.

Gencay, Ramazan, 1999, "Linear, Non-linear and Essential Foreign Exchange Rate Prediction with Simple Technical Trading Rules," *Journal of International Economics* 47, pp. 91–107.

Glick, Reuven, and Michael Hutchinson, 2005, "Capital Controls and Exchange Rate Instability in Developing Countries," *Journal of International Money and Finance* 24, pp. 387–412.

Goldfajn, Ilan, and Rodrigo O. Valdes, 1998, "Are Currency Crises Predictable?" *European Economic Review* 42, pp. 873–885.

Green, Philip, 1992, "Is Currency Trading Profitable? Exploiting Deviations from Uncovered Interest Parity," *Financial Analysts Journal* 48, pp. 82–86.

Henriksson, Roy D., and Robert Merton, 1981, "On Market Timing and Evaluation Performance, 2: Statistical Procedures for Evaluating Forecasting Skills," *Journal of Business* 54, pp. 513–533.

Himmelberg, Charles P., R. Glenn Hubbard, and Inessa Love, 2002, "Investor Protection, Ownership, and the Cost of Capital," Columbia Business School, unpublished manuscript.

Jorion, Philippe, 1996, "Does Real Interest Parity Hold at Longer Maturities?" *Journal of International Economics* 40, pp. 105–126.

Kaminsky, Graciela L., Saul Lizondo, and Carmen M. Reinhart, 1998, "Leading Indicators of Currency Crises," *IMF Staff Papers* 45, pp. 1–48.

Klein, Michael W., and Nancy P. Marion, 1997, "Explaining the Duration of Exchange-Rate Pegs," *Journal of Development Economics* pp. 387–404.

Krugman, Paul, 1979, "A Model of Balance of Payments Crises," *Journal of Money and Credit and Banking* 11, pp. 311–325.

LeBaron, Blake, 1999, "Technical trading rule profitability and foreign exchange intervention," *Journal of International Economics* 49, pp. 125–143.

Lee, Charles, and David Ng, 2006, "Corruption and International Valuation: Does Virtue Pay?" working paper.

Levich, Richard, "How to Compare Chance with Forecasting Expertise," *Euromoney* February 1981, 3.

Levich, Richard, and Lee Thomas, 1993, "The Significance of Technical Trading-Rule Profits in the Foreign-Exchange Market—A Bootstrap Approach," *Journal of International Money and Finance* 12, pp. 451–474.

Lui, Yu-Hon, and David Mole, 1998, "The Use of Fundamental and Technical Analyses by Foreign Exchange Dealers: Hong Kong Evidence," *Journal of International Money and Finance* 17, pp. 535–545.

Malkiel, Burton, 2000, *A Random Walk Down Wall Street*, 7th ed., New York: W.W. Norton.

Mark, Nelson, 1995, "Exchange Rates and Fundamentals: Evidence on Long-Horizon Predictability," *American Economic Review* 85, pp. 201–218.

Marston, Richard C., 1997, "Tests of Three Parity Conditions: Distinguishing Risk Premia Systematic Forecast Errors," *Journal of International Money and Finance* 16, pp. 285–303.

Meese, Richard, 1990, "Currency Fluctuations in the Post–Bretton Woods Era," *Journal of Economic Perspectives* 4, pp. 117–134.

Meese, Richard, and Kenneth Rogoff, 1983, "Empirical Exchange-Rate Models of the Seventies—Do They Fit Out of Sample?" *Journal of International Economics* 14, pp. 3–24.

Meese, Richard, and Kenneth Rogoff, 1988, "Was It Real? The Exchange Rate Interest Rate Differential Relation over the Modern Floating Rate Period," *Journal of Finance* 43, pp. 933–948.

Menkhoff, Lukas, 1998, "The Noise Trading Approach—Questionnaire Evidence from Foreign Exchange," *Journal of International Money and Finance* 17, pp. 547–564.

Mishkin, Frederic S., 1984, "Are Real Interest Rates Equal Across Countries—An Empirical Investigation of International Parity Conditions," *Journal of Finance* 39, pp. 1345–1357.

Mussa, Michael, 1984, "The Theory of Exchange Rate Determination," in J.F.O. Bilson and R.C. Marston, eds., *Exchange Rate Theory and Practice*, Chicago: University of Chicago Press.

Neely, Christopher, and Paul Weller, 2001, "Technical Analysis and Central Bank Intervention," *Journal of International Money and Finance* 20, pp. 949–970.

Neely, Christopher, Paul Weller, and Rob Dittmar, 1997, "Is technical analysis in the foreign exchange market profitable? A genetic programming approach," *Journal of Financial and Quantitative Analysis* 32, pp. 405–426.

Obstfeld, Maurice, 1986, "Rational and Self-fulfilling Balance of Payments Crises," *American Economic Review* 76, pp. 72–81.

Ozkan, F. Gulcin, and Alan Sutherland, 1998, "A Currency Crisis Model with an Optimizing Policymaker," *Journal of International Economics* 44, pp. 339–364.

The Economist, "The Perils of Prediction," August 1, 1988, pp. 61–62.

Pukthuanthong-Le, Kuntara, Richard M. Levich, and Lee R. Thomas III, 2006, "Do Foreign Exchange Markets Still Trend?" working paper.

Rose, Andrew K., and Lars E.O. Svensson, 1994, "European Exchange Rate Credibility Before the Fall," *European Economic Review* pp. 1185–1216.

Rosenberg, Michael, 1996, *Currency Forecasting*, Chicago, IL: Irwin.

Sapin, Michel, 1992, "Quote of the Day," *The New York Times,* September 24, p. A6.

Sollis, Robert, and Mark E. Wohar, 2006, "The Real Exchange Rate–Real Interest Rate Relation: Evidence from Tests for Symmetric and Asymmetric Threshold Cointegration," *International Journal of Finance and Economics* 2, pp. 139–153.

Stockman, Alan C., 1987, "The Equilibrium Approach to Exchange Rates," *Federal Reserve Bank of Richmond Economic Review* pp. 12–30.

Svensson, Lars E.O., 1993, "Assessing Target Zone Credibility: Mean Reversion and Devaluation Expectations in the ERM, 1979–1992," *European Economic Review* 37, pp. 763–802.

Taylor, Mark P., and Helen Allen, 1992, "The Use of Technical Analysis in the Foreign Exchange Market," *Journal of International Money and Finance* 11, pp. 304–314.

Villanueva, O. Miguel, 2007, "Forecasting Currency Excess Returns: Can the Forward Bias Be Exploited?" *Journal of Financial and Quantitative Analysis*, forthcoming.

Chapter 11

International Debt Financing

*I*n 2000, France Telecom raised €5.4 billion in the international bond market with the help of four financial institutions: Morgan Stanley Dean Witter, an American investment bank; Deutsche Bank, a German universal bank; BNP Paribas, a large French bank; and Barclays, a British bank. Most of the bonds were issued in the Eurobond market. That is, they were not targeted to a specific country. Others were issued in the UK domestic bond market. This **global bond** deal was lauded as one of the corporate bond deals of the year in the February 2001 issue of *Euromoney*, a magazine specializing in international finance. The deal vividly illustrates how large companies use the international debt markets to pull in as many investors as possible to meet their financing needs. If France Telecom had tried to raise €5.4 billion in France alone, it would have faced a much higher cost of funding, and it might not have been able to raise nearly as much capital. The goal of this chapter is to explain the various funding sources for debt that are available to MNCs in an increasingly globalized world and to examine why MNCs choose the different financing options they choose.

11.1 THE GLOBAL SOURCES OF FUNDS FOR INTERNATIONAL FIRMS

The sources of funds for a MNC (and its subsidiaries) can be split into two major categories: cash that is internally generated by the MNC and cash that is externally provided from the debt markets or the equity markets. Exhibit 11.1 surveys the various sources of funds for a MNC, starting on top with internal sources of funds reinvested in the company.

The potential sources of external capital are extremely wide ranging. Both bonds and stocks (debt and equity financing) can be issued by a firm and sold to investors, typically through the financial intermediation of an investment bank. These externally issued securities are often tradable in secondary markets.

In contrast, loans are obtained from specialized financial intermediaries, typically commercial banks, and the lender monitors the financial behavior of the firm to make sure she will get repaid. For all three types of external sources of funds (bank loans, debt securities, and equity), MNCs and their affiliates can tap either domestic or international markets. *Euromarket* refers to the external, or offshore, market for borrowing and lending that we first encountered in Chapter 6.

A foreign affiliate of a MNC can obtain funds from within the MNC or from the same external sources as mentioned in Exhibit 11.1. The affiliate's external borrowing ability may be enhanced when the parent company guarantees the loan. In addition to using debt and

Exhibit 11.1   Sources of Long-Term Capital
for a Multinational Corporation

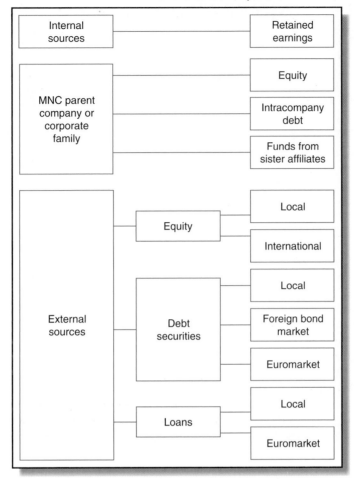

equity, MNCs often transfer funds across their affiliates by leading and lagging the payments of intracompany accounts.[1]

The Financing Mix Around the World

The financial appetites of countries differ, and their firms use a different mix of funds to finance their activities. This is, of course, reflected in the way local affiliates of MNCs finance themselves. By and large, internally generated cash is the main source of funding for a MNC. To get a rough idea of the main differences across countries, Exhibit 11.2 shows the evolution of the relative size of the equity, bond, and loan markets for the United States, Euroland, and Japan during the 1990s.

It is clear that public markets (equity and bonds) dominate the financial mix in the United States.[2] In fact, since 1995, loans have become relatively less important in the United States. In Japan, the bond market is the largest source of funds, but loans still account for over 30% of assets.

The Japanese corporate finance model of the 1970s and 1980s, in which companies relied heavily on bank funds and banks in turn invested heavily in equities, led to a banking and

---

[1]The use of leading and lagging payments to transfer funds between affiliates of a MNC is explicitly discussed in Chapter 19.
[2]The dominance is even more outspoken for pure corporate financing because the bond data also include government bonds, but the corporate bond market is largest in the United States.

Exhibit 11.2
Financing Mixes
Around the World

	2000			1995			1990		
	Equity	Bond	Loan	Equity	Bond	Loan	Equity	Bond	Loan
United States	45.0	45.9	9.1	36.3	49.5	14.2	27.1	53.8	19.1
Euroland	23.4	26.8	49.8						
Germany				2.1	11.0	86.9	1.8	10.0	88.2
France				17.1	35.3	47.6	15.1	27.6	57.3
Italy				10.5	55.4	34.1	9.3	47.7	43.0
Japan	24.8	43.6	31.6	27.6	37.3	35.2	33.4	29.8	36.8

Note: The data from BIS (see http://www.bis.org/statistics/secstats.htm), and represent a global comparison of the size of bank loans versus public securities markets in percentage of total financial assets, 1990 to 2000.

economic crisis in the 1990s, which continued into the 2000s. As the Japanese economy suffered falling product prices (deflation), the Japanese stock and real estate markets crashed, which eroded the capital base of many banks. Simultaneously, many bank loans became nonperforming, further eroding the health of the banking system.

With banks unable or unwilling to supply new loans, Japanese MNCs entered international markets. It is fair to say that the high-quality Japanese MNCs, such as Sony, Toyota, and Canon, were much less affected by this crisis than were purely domestic firms. In fact, it is conceivable that the increased access to direct debt finance of the well-performing companies, such as many export-oriented companies, worsened the balance sheet of the banks, leaving them lending to companies with a lower ability to repay their debts.

In Europe, loans dominate as a financing source. However, in the early 1990s, it was obvious that the loan market was becoming relatively less important in Germany, France, and Italy. Whatever the country, debt financing in the form of either bonds or bank loans dominates the external financing that corporations seek. We now take a closer look at the different types of debt instruments that exist in global capital markets.

11.2 THE CHARACTERISTICS OF DEBT INSTRUMENTS

The main characteristics differentiating debt instruments are the currency in which they are denominated, their maturity, the nature of their interest payments, their tradability, and their international character. This large variety of debt instruments arose as MNCs sought various ways to minimize their cost of debt and avoid financial distress. The cost of a debt is simply the after-tax interest and repayment of principal that must be paid to service the debt.

Financial distress occurs when debt repayment is stopped or has become difficult. Although financial distress need not always lead to bankruptcy, it may make it more difficult and more costly for a firm to get financing, and it can adversely affect a firm's share price and the demand for its products.

Currency of Denomination

When a purely domestic company issues debt denominated in a foreign currency, it faces the risk that the foreign currency will appreciate relative to the domestic currency, which would increase the cost of repaying the debt. However, for a MNC, it is quite natural to borrow in different currencies because the firm's revenues are also likely denominated in foreign currencies.

Exhibit 11.3 Centralized and Decentrailized Debt Denomination

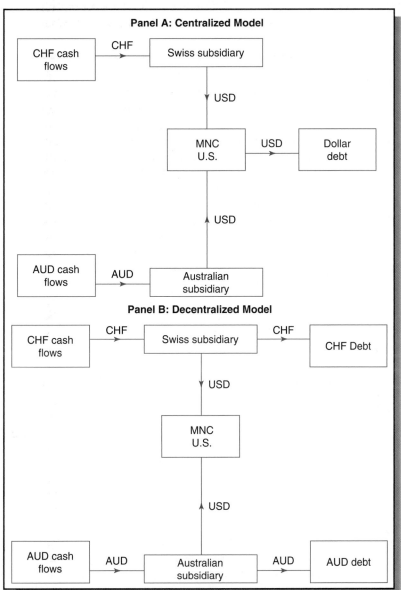

Note: The arrows indicate the direction of payment flows, either revenues or interest payments going from one entity to the other.

Centralized Versus Decentralized Debt Denomination

A U.S.-based MNC may, for example, prefer incurring dollar-denominated debt and therefore "centralize" its debt financing. We illustrate this **centralized debt denomination** model in Exhibit 11.3, using the example of a U.S. MNC with Swiss and Australian subsidiaries. Note that the debts for both the parent company and its foreign subsidiaries are denominated in dollars.

Alternatively, the parent company may maintain a **decentralized debt denomination** model, borrowing in the countries and currencies where the subsidiaries operate or to which it exports. In the decentralized model, also illustrated in Exhibit 11.3, the debt service payments (interest payments and principal repayment) are denominated in the currency in which the subsidiary's revenues are received. This is an example of balancing foreign assets against foreign liabilities and is often called a **balance-sheet hedge**.

From the perspective of a MNC, its subsidiary in a foreign country is an asset that generates foreign currency revenues. To hedge the risk of the foreign currency depreciating, which decreases the asset's value, a corporation should have an equivalent liability also denominated in that foreign currency. In this way, foreign currency debt forms a natural hedge for the cash flows from the subsidiary's operations.

Consider the example shown in Exhibit 11.3. Suppose the Australian dollar appreciates relative to the U.S. dollar. In the decentralized model, the Australian dollar debt becomes more costly to service in terms of the U.S. dollar. However, as long as the appreciation does not coincide with a major recession that reduces the demand for Australian products, the Australian dollar revenues are higher than before in terms of U.S. dollars. And because the AUD revenues will be used to pay off the AUD debt, the firm is not adversely affected. Now, suppose the Australian dollar weakens. This puts a strain on the subsidiary's profits when expressed in U.S. dollars. But again, it does not make the AUD debt more of a burden for the parent company. Hence, the decentralized model naturally hedges foreign exchange risk.

In contrast, with the centralized model, if the AUD depreciates, the subsidiary's revenues go down when expressed in U.S. dollars. This reduces the profits the parent firm earns when expressed in U.S. dollars. And because the U.S. debt is expressed in dollars, that debt becomes more difficult to pay. Of course, as we have learned, it is possible for a MNC following the centralized model to hedge against such a situation by using forward contracts.

Is Issuing Debt in Low–Interest Rate Countries a Good Idea?

At first glance, the answer to this question would seem to be yes. To finance its operations, the MNC from Exhibit 11.3 might want to borrow money in yen (versus Australian or U.S. dollars) because Japanese interest rates are extremely low. Still, there is no free lunch here. The final cost of the loan will involve the change in the exchange rate and the interest rate. If uncovered interest rate parity (UIRP) holds, the expected cost of the loan should equal the cost of a domestic currency loan. Of course, a loan denominated in a currency in which the MNC does not generate cash flows brings with it exchange rate uncertainty. Yet, MNCs often do rightfully borrow in unusual currencies for a variety of reasons, including the following:

- As we discussed before, UIRP may not hold, and high–interest rate currencies may not depreciate as much as suggested by the interest rate differential. Consequently, a low–interest rate borrowing strategy might be a good idea. If the low–interest rate currency does not appreciate as predicted by the interest rate differential, the MNC will have lowered its cost of debt.
- MNCs do not necessarily face the offshore interest rates that lie at the core of our discussion of the parity conditions. Investors often require rates above the risk-free rate, depending on the ability of the MNC to repay the debt. Because these **credit spreads** can differ in different markets, it may be beneficial for the corporation to issue debt in other currencies.
- Regulatory peculiarities, including tax differences, may make issuing debt in particular currencies unusually inexpensive.

Debt Portfolios

If you are the manager of a MNC, you could decide to issue debt in several currencies in order to diversify your company's currency exposure. Nonetheless, when MNCs source debt in other currencies, they typically hedge the currency risk. This can be done using forward contracts or currency swaps.

Maturity

Companies tend to structure their borrowing so that large principal repayments are not clustered together. That helps limit their refinancing risk: They do not have to come up with a large amount of cash at a point in time when cash flows are potentially low and market conditions for issuing more debt are unfavorable. Instead, firms spread out the due dates on loans and debt instruments. Some firms engage in maturity matching. They attempt to finance current assets (such as accounts receivable and inventories) with short-term debt and to finance fixed assets (investments) with long-term debt.

When companies issue long-term debt, the maturity is typically governed by standards in the particular debt market in which they issue the debt or by investor demand. For example, Eurobonds mostly mature in less than 10 years, and typically in exactly 5 years. However, in early 2003, several large European corporations, including Olivetti and France Telecom, issued 30-year bonds. By contrast, U.S. corporate bonds can have quite long maturities, typically 20 to 30 years. In fact, when the maturity is less than 10 years, the bonds are called *notes*. In 1993, the Walt Disney Company issued $300 million worth of bonds with a maturity of exactly 100 years. The Disney 100-year bonds were immediately dubbed "Sleeping Beauties" after the fairy tale princess and heroine in the popular Disney animated film by the same name (because she slept for 100 years under a magic spell). Later in that same year, Coca-Cola and ABN AMRO, a Dutch financial institution, issued similar bonds. Of course, the record for the longest maturity goes to perpetual bonds, or consols, which never pay back the face value of the bond and have been issued by companies as diverse as the Canadian Pacific Corporation, a Canadian railway company, and AEGON, a Dutch insurance company.

The Nature of Interest Rate Payments: Fixed-Rate Versus Floating-Rate Debt

Borrowers pay the interest on debt instruments at regular intervals (for example, annually or semiannually), and the amount may be fixed (**fixed-rate debt**), or it may vary, or float, over time (**floating-rate debt**), based on changes in the prevailing reference interest rate, typically a short-term borrowing rate in the interbank market such as LIBOR (see Chapter 6).

When to Use Floating Rate Debt
The choice between fixed- and floating-rate debt depends on a variety of factors. When short-term interest rates are below long-term interest rates, you might be tempted to conclude that MNCs should choose floating-rate debt to reduce their immediate funding costs. However, higher long-term rates likely reflect investors' expectations that short-term rates will rise, so it is not at all clear that *ex post* the company will save on financing costs. Let's illustrate this with a numeric example.

Example 11.1 Cost of Debt Comparisons Across Maturities

Dig-It-Up is a multinational mining company based in Canada that has mines in Australia as well. Dig-It-Up wants to borrow CAD2,000,000 for 2 years. Dig-It-Up's treasury department claims to be able to borrow at the following annual interest rates:

	1 year	2 years
CAD	3%	5%

These rates are for zero-coupon bonds, which we initially discussed in Chapter 6. The borrower does not have to make regular interest payments on the bonds, but it must pay back the principal plus all the compound interest at maturity. For example, if Dig-It-Up borrowed CAD2,000,000, the principal and interest it would have to repay in 2 years would be:

$$CAD2,000,000 \times [1 + 0.05]^2 = CAD2,205,000 \qquad \text{(11.1)}$$

If the company does not want to incur either interest rate or currency risk, it should lock in a loan for 2 years at the 5% rate. However, the 3% 1-year rate looks more attractive initially. Wouldn't borrowing the money for 1 year at a 3% interest rate and then renewing the loan for another 1 year lower the cost of debt for Dig-It-Up? The problem, of course, is that we do not know what the interest rate will be 1 year in the future.

What would be the cost of the short-term debt renewed after 1 year for Dig-It-Up? After 1 year, Dig-It-Up would have to repay the loan plus 3% interest. It would do so by borrowing that amount with another 1-year loan, at the prevailing interest rate, whatever it is. After 2 years, Dig-It-Up would then have to repay the principal plus interest. That is, with the unknown future interest rate denoted as i_{fut}, the total repayment would be

$$CAD2,000,000 \times [1 + 0.03] \times [1 + i_{fut}] \qquad \text{(11.2)}$$

When we compare Equation (11.1) with Equation (11.2), we see that the second option involves interest rate risk. The option could turn out to be cheaper, but it might not. We can compute a breakeven rate by equating the two equations and solving for the i_{fut} that makes the *ex post* cost of the two loans the same. If we do so, we find that i_{fut} satisfies

$$[1 + 0.03] \times [1 + i_{fut}] = 1.05^2$$

By solving for i_{fut}, we find

$$i_{fut} = 1.05^2/1.03 - 1 = 7.04\%$$

The interpretation is simple. As long as the 1-year interest rate 1 year from now remains below 7.04%, the company would be better off having borrowed in the short-term market rather than in the long-term market. This might look like an extreme change in the prevailing interest rate, but such a change can, indeed, happen. If the firm borrows in the short term, it risks having to refinance at a rate higher than 7.04% in 1 year.

The Expectations Hypothesis

The **expectations hypothesis**, or *expectations theory*, of the term structure is the best-known theory governing the relationship between long rates and expected future short rates. In fact, the expectations theory maintains that the breakeven rate is exactly the rate that the market expects for future short-term borrowing. If this were not the case, many companies would borrow short term, and short-term rates would increase because of the heavy demand for funds borrowed.

The theory also implies that long-term interest rates are a weighted average of the current short-term rate and expected future short-term rates. In the example, the long-term rate, 5%, is in between the current short rate of 3% and the higher expected future short rate of 7.04%. In this case, Dig-It-Up should be indifferent between borrowing short term or long term. Why? Because the savings the company realizes at the start of the borrowing period will be lost when short-term rates rise later on, as expected. The empirical evidence regarding the expectations hypothesis is mixed, however. In some countries, such as the United Kingdom, the theory describes the data well, while in other countries, such as the United States, there appears to be some evidence against the theory.

That said, it is possible that borrowing at a floating rate—which is what Dig-It-Up would essentially be doing if it took out two short-term loans—would give the company a natural hedge, if its cash flows were positively correlated with interest rates—that is, if interest rates and cash flows tended to be procyclical. In other words, the company is likely to experience high interest rate expenses on its floating debt when its revenues are high and low interest rate expenses when its revenues are poor.[3] Large companies and MNCs can constantly modify the fixed-rate versus floating-rate composition of their debt by making use of the swap markets. In fact, as we will see in Chapter 21, they frequently do.

Intermediated and Direct Debt

When debt is intermediated, a financial institution such as a commercial bank or an investment bank first attracts funds from investors and then lends money to the borrower, for example the MNC. One of the major trends in recent years has been for large MNCs to issue bonds directly to investors. The process whereby corporate borrowing takes the form of a tradable security issued in the public market, rather than a non-tradable loan provided by financial intermediaries is called **financial disintermediation**. Note that even though financial institutions do not provide the funds directly to corporations issuing bonds, they typically still play an intermediary role in selling the securities to the investing public.

There are many reasons for financial disintermediation. One is simply the deregulation taking place in countries, such as that in the United States in 1981 and Japan in 1986. This deregulation removed restrictions that had allowed banks to attract low-cost funds from depositors. Moreover, banks had to give in to regulatory demands for a stronger capital base (for example, through the Basel Accord requirements, discussed later in the chapter), which pushed up their cost of funds. Finally, the information revolution also means that information regarding any company can be found much more easily than in the past, which is a necessary ingredient for a successful direct debt market.

Private Placements

Privately placed bonds lie somewhere between loans and bonds. **Private placement bonds** are not sold to the market at large but are placed privately with sophisticated, well-endowed investors, such as pension funds, life insurance companies, or university endowments. Consequently, they are less tradable than standard bonds. In the United States, private placements are regulated by the Securities Act of 1933 and must conform to a number of conditions:

- They must be sold to a limited number of large and sophisticated investors.
- Investors must have access to substantial financial information regarding the company.
- Investors must purchase the securities for their own investment portfolios and not for resale, and they must be capable of sustaining losses.

These conditions ensure that the investors are sufficiently informed and qualified to judge the merits of the investment.

The International Character of Debt

In Chapter 6, we encountered the concept of an external capital market. An *external debt market* is a market where debt is placed outside the borders of the country issuing the currency. In contrast, an *internal debt market* is a market where debt is denominated in the currency of the host country and placed within that country.

In the long-term debt markets, it is customary to make a distinction between domestic and international bonds. **Domestic bonds** are issued and traded within the internal market of a single country and are denominated in the currency of that country. **International bonds** are traded outside the country of the issuer.

---

[3]In fact, nominal interest rates in the United States tend to be countercyclical, but real interest rates are procyclical (see Andrew Ang, Geert Bekaert, and Min Wei, 2007).

There are two types of international bonds. **Foreign bonds** are issued in a domestic market by a foreign borrower, denominated in the domestic currency, marketed to domestic residents, and regulated by the domestic authorities. For example, in 2003, the Tennessee Valley Authority, a U.S. power company, issued a foreign bond (denominated in British pounds) in the UK corporate bond market. Over the years, various foreign bonds have earned nicknames. For example, there are Yankee bonds in the United States, bulldog bonds in the United Kingdom, Samurai bonds in Japan, Matadors in Spain, and Rembrandts in the Netherlands.

The other type of international bond is a **Eurobond**, which is denominated in one or more currencies but is traded in external markets outside the borders of the countries issuing the currencies. For example, in 2003, Medco Energi Internasional, Indonesia's largest oil and gas company, issued a Eurobond, denominated in dollars, that was sold to investors in the United States, Asia, and Europe.

We can split up bond issues in a particular country with the following diagram:

	Issued by Residents	Issued by Nonresidents
Domestic currency	A. Domestic bond	B. Foreign bond
Foreign currency	C. Eurobond	D. Eurobond

The sum of segments B and D is sometimes called the *external*, or *cross-border*, bond market. The international bond market comprises segments B, C, and D. The next section provides much more detail on the international bond market.

11.3 A Tour of the World's Bond Markets

Size and Structure of the World Bond Market

Exhibit 11.4 reports the amounts outstanding in the world's various bond markets for the years 2000 and 2006. In most countries, government bonds constitute the most important segment of the bond market. The largest government market in 2000 was in the United States with over USD8 trillion outstanding. In 2006, the government bond markets of Euroland and Japan were more similar in size to the United States, but the U.S. data for 2006 exclude agency debt, which is now included in the corporate category. Together, these countries account for more than 85% of the global bond market. Government bonds are defined broadly and include federal, state, and local government issues. In emerging markets, government issues made up 72% of total local currency debt in 2000, with this share decreasing to 56% by 2006. Overall, countries with large government sectors tend to have large government bond markets.

Corporations can issue bonds in the domestic or international bond markets. However, the domestic bond market is still the larger of the two. With USD7.8 trillion outstanding in 2000 and over USD20 trillion in 2006, the U.S. corporate bond market is the largest in the world, but other markets have seen rapid development in this segment recently, as financial disintermediation has continued. The international bond market represents about 25% of the global bond market, but this share has been rapidly growing over time, as Exhibit 11.5 shows.

Because of its growing importance, we devote a separate subsection to the international bond market. We first discuss some important features of domestic bond markets, which will prove useful when we discuss international bonds.

Domestic Bond Markets

Domestic bonds are regulated by the domestic governments of the countries in which they are issued. These agencies include the Securities and Exchange Commission (SEC) in the United

Exhibit 11.4 The Size and Structure of the World Bond Market (in billions of U.S. dollars)

Panel A: End of 2000

Country	Total Outstanding	% World Bond Mkt	Government U.S. $ bn	% of Gov	Corporate U.S. $ bn	% of Corp	Foreign U.S. $ bn	% of For	Eurobond US $ bn	% of Total
United States	15,417.5	49.1	8,025.9	46.0	4,515.9	57.4	495.4	60.8	2,380.3	45.3
Euroland	6,223.8	19.8	3,125.0	17.9	1,027.7	16.9	0.0	0.0	1,771.1	33.7
Japan	5,549.3	17.7	3,995.6	22.9	973.0	12.4	72.6	8.9	508.1	9.7
United Kingdom	1,065.3	3.4	416.7	2.4	70.6	0.9	122.3	15.0	455.7	8.7
Canada	540.6	1.7	385.0	2.2	103.4	1.3	0.4	0.0	51.8	1.0
Switzerland	277.5	0.9	45.6	0.3	89.1	1.1	113.4	13.9	29.4	0.8
Australia	182.1	0.6	69.7	0.4	80.5	1.0	6.6	0.8	30.3	0.6
Total Developed	29,804.1	95.0	16,314.6	93.5	7,422.5	94.4	815.1	100.0	5,251.9	100.0
Emerging Markets	1,598.7	5.0	1,161.7	6.5	437.0*	5.6	NA	NA	NA	NA
Total	31,402.8	100.0	17,476.3	100.0	7,859.5	100.0	815.1	100.0	5,251.9	100.0

Panel B: End of 2006

Country	Total Outstanding	% World Bond Mkt	Government U.S. $ bn	% of Gov	Corporate U.S. $ bn	% of Corp	International U.S. $ bn	% of For
United States	26,735.8	38.9	6,230.3	26.0	16,085.2	61.2	4,420.3	24.0
Euroland	18,780.0	27.3	5,758.4	24.0	4,927.7	18.8	8,093.9	43.9
Japan	8,676.0	12.6	6,747.8	28.1	1,653.4	6.3	274.8	1.5
United Kingdom	10,813.6	15.7	835.1	3.5	402.5	1.5	2,060.1	11.2
Canada	1,335.9	1.9	613.8	25.5	370.2	1.4	351.9	1.9
Switzerland	555.7	0.8	111.3	4.6	112.0	4.3	332.4	1.8
Australia	847.6	1.2	95.9	0.0	362.9	1.4	398.8	2.2
Total Developed	62,000.6	90.0	20,655.4	86.0	24,700.0	94.0	16,645.2	90.2
Emerging Markets	5,988.4	8.7	3,353.1	14.0	1,576.9	6.0	1,058.4	5.7
Total	68,734.3	100.0	24,008.5	100.0	26,276.9	100.0	184,448.9	100.0

Note: For Panel A, Merrill Lynch (2001). In the United States, agency debt is included in the government category. Panel B is compiled from data in the *BIS Quarterly Review*, June 2007, Tables 12–16. (Copyright © 2007 Source Media, Inc.) Corporate issuance comprises domestic bonds issued by corporations and financial institutions. International issues by international agencies and offshore countries are not part of the developed or emerging market category totals. The BIS makes no distinction between foreign bonds and Eurobonds. Agency debt is not included in the government category for the United States.

*Asia only.

States, the Financial Services Authority (FSA) in the United Kingdom, and the Ministry of Finance (MOF) and the Financial Services Agency (FSA) in Japan.

In the United States, a company issuing debt securities to the public in amounts greater than $1.5 million is required to prepare and file a registration statement with the SEC that includes a financial history of the company, the state of its existing business, and how the funds raised through the public offering are to be used. After the registration statement is filed with the SEC, there is a waiting period of 20 days during which the SEC reviews the accuracy and completeness of the registration statement. The issue is priced and sold after the waiting

Exhibit 11.5 The Internationalization of the World Bond Market

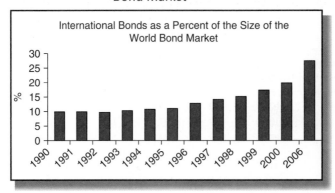

Note: Data are from Merrill Lynch (2001) and author computations based on *BIS Quarterly Review*, June 2007.

period. Exceptions to this rule include short-term securities maturing within 9 months and private placements.

New public issues in Japan must be approved by the MOF. The registration process forces the issuers to maintain records of the owners of corporate and government bonds, thereby facilitating the calculation and payment of accrued interest. The registration also facilitates tax collection on the semiannual interest that the bonds pay.

Unlike the United States and Japan, governments and corporations in most western European countries issue bearer bonds. Bearer bonds are not registered, meaning the name and country of residence of the owner are not on the certificate. To receive interest, the bearer cuts an interest coupon from the bond and redeems the value of the coupon at the banking institution listed on the bond as a paying agent. The principal advantage of bearer bonds is that they retain the anonymity of the bondholder, which makes them perfect for tax evasion. Because it is inconvenient to present bond coupons for payment of interest, bearer bonds are usually issued with annual coupons.

Domestic bond market prices and yield quotation conventions and withholding taxes differ from country to country. In many countries, corporate bonds are traded over the counter by commercial and investment banks as well as listed on the local stock exchange.

The International Bond Market

The Foreign Bond Market

Foreign bonds (bonds issued by nonresidents in a country's domestic capital market) are subject to domestic regulations rather than the trading conventions of the borrower's country. For example, in the United States, foreign bonds must go through the SEC's registration process, just like domestic bonds do. This is a costly process and requires disclosure of financial information.

To make the U.S. bond market more competitive with the less-regulated Eurobond market, the SEC allows shelf registration and instituted Rule 144A. With **shelf registration**, which the SEC began to allow in 1982, an issuer can preregister a securities issue and then shelve the securities for later sale, when financing is actually needed. This has allowed foreign companies to issue bonds quickly in the United States when they need financing. However, it has not eliminated the information disclosure that many foreign borrowers find expensive and/or objectionable. As a result, **Rule 144A** was enacted in 1990. Rule 144A allows qualified institutional investors in the United States to invest in private placement issues that do not have to meet the strict information disclosure requirements of publicly traded issues.

The Eurobond Market[4]

Eurobonds (which are issued simultaneously in the capital markets of several nations) need not comply with the regulatory restrictions that apply to domestic issues. For example, in June 2002, General Electric Capital Corporation (GE Capital) issued a Eurobond with the following characteristics:

Amount: €2billion
Maturity: 5 years
Price: €995.18 per €1,000 face value
Annual coupon: 5.125%
Syndicate led by Dresdner and Morgan Stanley
Fees: 0.275%
Fixed re-offer price

As is typical, these were bearer bonds, and they were sold by an international group of banks (a *syndicate*; syndicates are described later in this chapter) led by Dresdner and Morgan Stanley. Most of the buyers of the bonds were residents of the United Kingdom, Germany, and the Netherlands. The fixed re-offer price is the price at which the bonds can be traded until they have been placed with end investors.

Major MNCs; national or regional governments and government agencies, such as the U.S. Federal National Mortgage Association ("Fannie Mae"); and supranational organizations, such as the World Bank, the Asian Development Bank, and organizations associated with the European Union, all issue Eurobonds. In fact, the most important borrowers in the international bond market (which combines Eurobonds and foreign bonds) are financial institutions. As Exhibit 11.6 shows, issues by financial institutions accounted for well over 50% of

Exhibit 11.6 Borrowers in the International Bond Market (amounts outstanding, March 2007, in billions of U.S. dollars)

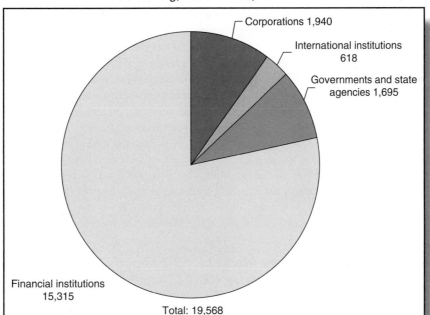

Corporations 1,940
International institutions 618
Governments and state agencies 1,695
Financial institutions 15,315
Total: 19,568

Note: Compiled from *BIS Quarterly Review*, March 2007, Tables 12A through 12D.

---

[4]Some of the data and facts in this section are based on Anouk Claes, Mark DeCeuster, and Ruud Polfliet (2002), which offers a comprehensive study of the Eurobond market between 1980 and 2000.

the $19.5 trillion outstanding in March 2007, and this has always been the case. Corporate borrowers have about $2 trillion outstanding, governments about $1.7 trillion, and international institutions about $0.6 trillion. The share of corporate borrowing has steadily increased.

A withholding tax on interest payments in the U.S. domestic and foreign bond markets fueled the growth of the Eurobond market in the 1960s. Because taxes can be avoided on bearer bonds, investors are willing to accept lower yields on them. Many U.S. firms have taken advantage of this opportunity to lower their funding cost. The financial infrastructure in London (where most of the trading in Eurobonds takes place) and the liquidity of the London market have also helped the Eurobond market flourish.

Although these withholding taxes and other burdensome regulations have since been abolished, the Eurobond market continues to thrive because, unlike any other capital market, it remains largely untaxed, unregulated, and convenient. Despite attempts to improve the competitive position of the U.S. bond market relative to the Eurobond market via shelf registration, Rule 144A, and so forth, the SEC disclosure requirements and registration procedure remain time-consuming and burdensome for some U.S. and non-U.S. issuers.

The Primary Market for Eurobonds

When a bond issue is large, the borrower often benefits by issuing the bonds in a variety of locations. A borrower wanting to issue a Eurobond contacts an investment banker to serve as lead manager (or *bookrunner* in the UK) of a group of investment and commercial banks that will bring the bonds to market. This group is called a **syndicate**. From 1980 to 2000, more than 90% of Eurobond issues were coordinated by a single bookrunner. The lead manager usually invites co-managers to form a managing group to help negotiate terms with the borrower, ascertain market conditions, and manage the issuance.

The banks in the managing group, along with the other banks in the underwriting syndicate, serve as underwriters for the issue. That is, they commit their own capital to buy the issue from the borrower at a discount, which is called the underwriting spread. Most of the underwriters, along with other banks, are also part of the group that sells the bonds to the investing public. The various members of the underwriting syndicate receive a portion of the spread, depending on the number and the type of functions they perform. The lead manager obviously receives the full spread, but a bank serving only as a member of the selling group receives a smaller portion.

Since 1989, most Eurobond syndicates have used the fixed-price re-offer method to issue bonds. In this system, syndicate members agree to sell bonds only at a predetermined price until the lead manager feels the deal is largely placed, or until the market moves significantly. Then "the deal breaks syndicate," and bonds are free to trade at whatever level the market sets, depending on supply and demand. However, the lead manager is expected to carry on buying the bonds at the re-offer price. One problem with this system appears to be that some syndicate members do not attempt to distribute the bonds to institutional or retail investors but sell their allotments back to the lead manager anonymously, in the meantime pocketing the underwriting fees. It takes about 5 to 6 weeks from the date the borrower decides to issue Eurobonds until the net proceeds from the sale are received.

The Secondary Market for Eurobonds

Eurobonds initially purchased in the primary market from a member of the selling group may be resold prior to their maturity dates to other investors in the secondary market. The secondary market for Eurobonds is an over-the-counter market, comprising market makers and brokers connected by an array of telecommunications equipment, with principal trading in London. However, important trading is also done in other major European money centers, such as Zurich, Luxembourg, Frankfurt, and Amsterdam. Many commercial banks, investment banks, and securities trading firms hold large portfolios of Eurobonds. These institutions act as market makers in the Eurobond market: They quote two-way (buy and sell) prices on the bonds and stand ready to trade at these prices. Most of the secondary-market Eurobond transactions are cleared through Euroclear, which is a bank in Brussels that is owned by the many financial institutions using its services and that specializes in multiple cross-border settlement services.

Global Bonds

A 10-year $1.5 billion offering by the World Bank in 1989 was the first global bond issued simultaneously in a domestic market and in the Eurobond market. This is particularly important in the United States because U.S. investors can generally only buy Eurobonds after a 40-day waiting period due to the fact that they are not registered. Borrowers issuing global bonds must be large and creditworthy, and they must borrow in actively traded currencies. Darius Miller and John Puthenpurackal (2005) analyzed a large number of global bond issues and found that such bonds lower borrowing costs by approximately 20 basis points relative to nonglobal bonds.

Dragon Bonds

A **Dragon bond** is a Eurobond targeted at the Asian market (outside Japan) with Asian syndication. Lehman Brothers launched Dragon bonds in the early 1990s, with the first Dragon bond issued in November 1991 by the Asian Development Bank. Whereas Dragon bonds are launched during Asian market hours and listed in Hong Kong and Singapore, they are cleared in Europe through major clearance organizations such as Euroclear and Clearstream (see "Where Be Dragons?" 1994). Secondary market trading is also still concentrated in Europe, primarily in London.

The Blurring of the Distinctions in the International Bond Market

The acceleration of globalization, including tax harmonization, financial deregulation, and the widespread relaxation of capital controls, has blurred traditional distinctions between domestic and international bonds, especially in Euroland. Panel A of Exhibit 11.4 uses the official definitions of the BIS, long a leading source for international debt statistics. It divides the Eurobond market according to the currency of issue. However, the increased globalization of the world's bond markets has caused what were once distinctive market features to be more common across markets. Prime examples of this evolution are the global bonds discussed previously. In addition, global consolidation of the financial service industry and opportunities for foreign intermediaries to participate fully in domestic issuance make national distinctions somewhat nebulous. Finally, some statistical offices do not provide sufficient information to distinguish between foreign and traditional Eurobonds. As a result, the more recent BIS data used in Panel B no longer make this distinction.

The Types of Debt Instruments in the International Bond Market and Their Prevalence

Three main types of bonds are issued in the international bond market. We discuss them in the order of their relative importance and end the section by discussing the currency denomination of international bonds.

Straight Fixed-Rate Issues

Straight fixed-rate bond issues have a set maturity date at which the issuer promises to repay the principal or face value of the bond. During the life of the bond, fixed coupon payments, which are a percentage of the face value, are paid as interest to the bondholders. These bonds are sometimes called *bullet bonds*.

A very special category of straight fixed-rate bonds is zero-coupon bonds. Zero-coupon bonds are sold at a discount from face value and do not pay any coupon interest over their life (see also Chapter 6). At maturity, the investor receives the full face value. Zero-coupon bonds have been denominated primarily in U.S. dollars and Swiss francs. Zero-coupon bonds are

Exhibit 11.7 Types of International Bonds Issued in the Marketplace (in billions of U.S. dollars)

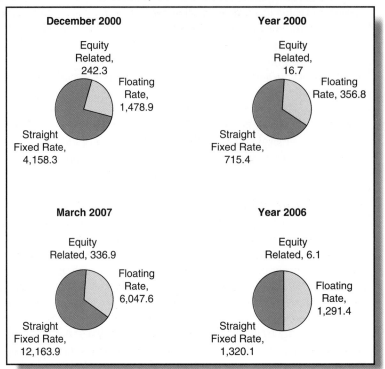

Notes: Data are from *BIS Quarterly Review*, March 2007, Table 13B. The pies on the left represent amounts outstanding, and the pies on the right refer to new issues during that particular year. The pies appear to have only two parts, because the equity related fractions are too small to illustrate.

attractive to investors who want to avoid the reinvestment risk of coupon receipts at possibly lower interest rates. Under U.S. tax law, interest on a zero-coupon bond is taxable as it accrues, even though there is no actual cash flow to the investor.

Exhibit 11.7 shows that the vast majority of international bonds outstanding in both 2000 and 2007 were straight fixed-rate bonds, with a share of about 70%.

Floating-Rate Notes

In contrast to straight fixed-rate bonds, floating-rate notes (FRNs) constitute about 25% of the total amount of international bonds outstanding. FRNs are typically medium-term bonds, with maturities between 1 and 10 years and with coupon payments indexed to a reference interest rate. Common reference rates are 3-month and 6-month LIBOR, and coupons are paid quarterly or semiannually, consistent with the maturity underlying the reference rate. As an example, let's consider an FRN issued by GE Capital in June 2002, simultaneously with the fixed-rate bond we discussed before. These are its characteristics:

Amount: €1 billion
Maturity: 2 years
Reference rate: 3-month Euribor[5]
Spread: 15 basis points, or 0.15%
Price: €999.42 per €1,000 face value
Fees: 0.125%
Fixed re-offer price

---

[5]*Euribor* is the benchmark Eurocurrency interest rate for the euro.

Most companies pay a spread above the relevant LIBOR rate, which reflects the company's credit risk (see Section 11.5). In this case, the spread was first set at 15 basis points, but at the time of the actual issue date, the effective spread was increased roughly to 18 basis points by reducing the price of the bond to €999.42 instead of €1,000. That is, the percentage less than face value that the investor pays is $\frac{1,000 - 999.42}{1,000} = \frac{0.58}{1,000}$, which is approximately 6 basis points (or 3 basis points per year), which effectively increases the yield on the bond to the investor.

At the beginning of every 3-month period, the next quarterly coupon payment is *reset* to be $\frac{1}{4} \times$ (Euribor + 0.15%) of face value, where Euribor is the annual percentage rate. As an example, in June 2002, the 3-month Euribor stood at 3.441%. Consequently, the coupon interest rate on a €1,000 face value for the FRN was

$$\tfrac{1}{4} \times (0.03441 + .0015) \times €1,000 = €8.98$$

Equity-Related Bonds

As Exhibit 11.7 shows, equity-related bonds are a small but growing component of the international bond market. This category of bonds consists of two closely related securities: convertible bonds and bonds with warrants. A **convertible bond** is a straight bond that is convertible into equity prior to maturity. The number of shares into which each bond is convertible is fixed when the bond is issued. Alternatively, the bond can have an attached **warrant**, which grants the bondholder the right to purchase a certain amount of common stock of the company at a specified price. Investors accept a lower coupon rate on convertible bonds than on the comparable straight fixed-coupon bonds because of the added option value of the conversion feature. Bonds with warrants are quite similar to convertible bonds, both giving the investor an equity option, but the warrant is detachable and can trade separately from the bond.

The difference between the market value of the convertible bond and that of the straight bond involves the value of the equity option. Convertible securities and warrants make sense whenever it is difficult to assess the risk of debt, such as when the firm is involved in projects with very uncertain cash flows and whenever investors are worried that managers may not act in their interests. The convertible bond gives investors a piece of the action when the projects turn out to be successful. For rapidly growing firms with heavy capital expenditures, the lower interest rates paid on these bonds can be particularly helpful, but the low coupon rate is of course obtained by giving away a valuable equity option.

In international markets, these bonds were very popular in the 1980s among Japanese companies. Many of the embedded equity options subsequently proved to be worthless when the Japanese bull market crashed toward the end of the 1980s. In 2002, convertible bonds made a comeback in the Euroyen bond market, and several leading companies—including Fujitsu, Japan's largest computer maker; Mitsubishi, the country's leading trading house; Orix, Japan's largest leasing company; and Nikon, the camera and chip equipment maker—all issued equity-linked debt in the month of May alone.

Currency of Denomination

Historically, the dollar has been the dominant currency of issuance in international bond markets. As Exhibit 11.8 indicates, issuance in euros dominated issuance in U.S. dollars.

Before the advent of the euro, the most important currency of issue in Europe was the Deutsche mark. In addition, the European currency unit—the basket currency that was the forerunner of the euro—was also popular in the Eurobond market. The only other currencies that are widely issued are the pound, yen, and Swiss franc (in that order). Viewed over a 20-year period, yen-dominated bonds come second after dollar-denominated bonds, but yen issues sharply decreased during the late 1990s.

A very special type of international bond is a **dual-currency bond**, which became popular in the mid-1980s. A dual-currency bond is a straight fixed-rate bond issued in one currency,

Exhibit 11.8 Currency of Issuance in the International Bond Market (March 2007, outstanding amounts, in billions of U.S. dollars)

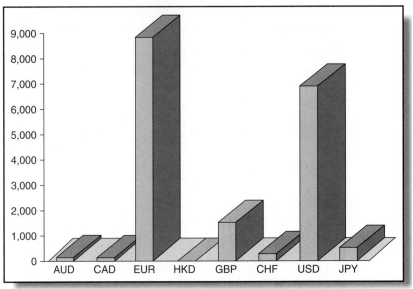

Note: Compiled based on *BIS Quarterly Review*, March 2007, Table 13B.

say yen, which pays coupon interest in that same currency, but the promised repayment of principal at maturity is denominated in another currency, say U.S. dollars. The interest rates on these bonds are often higher than those on comparable straight fixed-rate bonds. The amount of the dollar principal repayment at maturity is set when the bond is issued. Frequently, however, the amount allows for some appreciation in the exchange rate of the stronger currency.

The dual-currency bond can be viewed as a combination of a straight yen bond and a long-term forward contract to sell the dollar principal back for yen. The market value of a dual-currency bond in yen should therefore equal the sum of the present value of the yen coupon stream discounted at the yen market rate of interest plus the dollar principal repayment, converted to yen at the forward exchange rate, and discounted at the yen market rate of interest. Whether the bond is *ex post* a good investment depends on the movement of the dollar relative to the yen over the life of the bond.

Japanese firms have historically been large issuers of dual-currency bonds, with coupon payments in yen and the principal repayment in U.S. dollars. Use of yen/dollar dual-currency bonds can be an attractive way for Japanese MNCs to establish or expand U.S. subsidiaries. The yen proceeds can be converted to dollars to finance the capital investment in the United States, and during the early years, the coupon payments can be made by the parent firm in yen. At maturity, the dollar principal repayment can be made from dollar profits earned by the subsidiary.

Example 11.2   Reverse Dual-Currency Bonds

On March 16, 1997, the Inter-American Development Bank, a development bank focused on the social and economic development of Latin America and the Caribbean, issued a "reverse" dual-currency Japanese yen/Australian dollar bond. Here are the characteristics of the bond:

Aggregate face value: JPY15 billion
Face value per bond: JPY500,000

Interest: 3% (to be paid in Australian dollars)
Maturity: March 17, 2007 (10-year bond)
Exchange rate used for interest rate payments: JPY94.15/AUD

This bond is not registered but is a bearer bond, as is typical in the Eurobond market. Because the face value is in one currency and the interest rate payments are in another, the bond is clearly a dual-currency bond. However, the bond is different from typical dual-currency bonds in two ways. First, both the initial amount and the final redemption value are in the same currency. The spot exchange rate when the bond was issued was JPY94.15/AUD, so the equivalent Australian dollar amount is AUD159.32 million. Second, historically, most dual-currency bonds paid interest in the "strong" currency (the currency with the lower interest rate that was trading at a premium), whereas this bond pays interest in the weaker currency.

To analyze this bond and compare it with either a debt instrument issued entirely in yen or entirely in Australian dollars, the cash flows have to be converted to one currency. The correct way to do this is to use forward exchange rates. For example, to compute the actual yen interest rate on this bond, the five Australian dollar payments have to be converted into yen, using the 1-, 2-, 3-, 4-, and 5-year JPY/AUD forward exchange rates. Let's illustrate this for the interest payment occurring in 1998 for one bond. At the time of the issue, the 1-year JPY/AUD forward exchange rate was JPY98/AUD. So, we obtain

$$\text{Australian interest} = 0.03 \times (\text{JPY500,000})/(\text{JPY94.15/AUD}) = \text{AUD 159.32}$$

$$\text{Equivalent yen interest} = \text{AUD 159.32} \times (\text{JPY98/AUD}) = \text{JPY 15,613}$$

In Section 11.5 we show how, when all the cash flows are expressed in one currency, the cost of debt can be expressed in percentage per annum and then compared to alternative financing instruments of similar maturity and in the same currency.

11.4 INTERNATIONAL BANKING

The growth and increasing integration of the world economy since the end of World War II has been paralleled by an expansion of global banking activities as commercial banks have followed their customers into foreign markets. We use two criteria to differentiate international from domestic banking activities: the location and the counterparty. If either the borrower or the depositor is a nonresident, the transaction is viewed as international. However, a transaction is also typically categorized as international if it occurs in a non-domestic currency. To demonstrate the importance of international banking in numbers, Exhibit 11.9 reports the international claims (lending) for the majority of the world's banks, split out by borrowing country.

These claims are on a worldwide consolidated basis, covering all "international" contractual lending by the head office and its branches and subsidiaries. More specifically, it includes

- Cross-border claims in all currencies (that is, the borrower is a foreign entity relative to the bank's country)
- Local claims (the borrower is domestic) in non-local currencies
- Local currency positions of reporting banks' foreign affiliates with local residents

The five main countries of international banking activity are the United States, the United Kingdom, Germany, Japan, and France. This reflects the roles of New York, London, Frankfurt,

Exhibit 11.9 Consolidated Foreign Claims of Reporting Banks (by borrowing country), Ending in December 2006

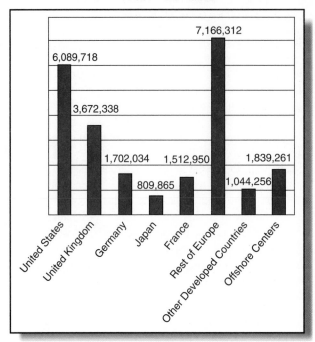

Note: This exhibit was constructed using data from Table 9A, "Consolidated Foreign Claims of Reporting Banks on Individual Countries," *BIS Quarterly Review*, March 2007, pages A54–A61.

Paris, and Tokyo as major international financial centers, and it also correlates with the sizes of these countries' economies. Lots of activity also happens in offshore banking centers, with the Cayman Islands accounting for almost 30%. We will come back to the distinction between international financial centers and offshore centers shortly.

In this section, we first offer a brief survey of banks as important multinationals. We then summarize some important international banking regulation, known as the BIS standards. Finally, we survey the different organizational forms through which international banks assist their multinational clients, clarifying the differences between, for example, branches, subsidiaries, and offshore banking centers.

Banks as MNCs

Commercial banks usually develop a complete line of financial services to facilitate the overseas trade of their customers. In addition to commercial credit, these ancillary financial services include market making and trading in spot and forward currencies (see Chapters 2 and 3), international trade financing (see Chapter 18), and risk management services (see Chapter 17).

Unlike domestic banks, international banks participate in the Eurocurrency market and are frequently members of international loan syndicates, lending out large sums of money to MNCs or governments. An international bank might also engage in the underwriting of Eurobonds and foreign bonds, which are investment-banking activities. Banks that perform both traditional commercial banking and investment banking functions are called **merchant banks**. Banks that provide a wide array of services, including securities activities, are known as **universal banks**, or **full-service banks**.

The formation of the European Union and intensifying global competition have led to mergers and acquisitions in the banking industry. The merger and acquisition activity was particularly hectic at the end of the 1990s. For example, following the formation of the EU, banks were allowed to operate within Europe using a single banking license instead of needing licenses in each and every country in which they did business. It was generally expected that this relaxation in the rules would result in a consolidation of the banking industry in Europe, as large banks gobbled up small banks. However, that really did not happen. By and large, banks didn't consolidate from country to country but, instead, consolidated *within* countries. It is certainly possible that these domestic mergers were an effort by domestic banks to stave off being taken over by "foreigners" (foreign banks).

The exception was in central Europe, where almost all the major banks in the region are now in foreign hands. When the Iron Curtain came down in 1989, central Europe was stuck with an inefficient and rudimentary financial system after years of communism. Central European governments soon realized that an influx of foreign capital and banking know-how and technology were badly needed. They consequently encouraged the foreign acquisition of their domestic banks.

Exhibit 11.10 lists the 25 largest banks in the world, based on market capitalization. Nine of the top 25 are Anglo-Saxon banks. Many of the 25 largest banks are the result of past mergers. For example, the Japanese bank ranked number 8, Mitsubishi UFJ Financial Group,

Exhibit 11.10 The Largest Banks, Ranked by Market Capitalization

Ranking, Feb-07	Bank	Country	Assets (in billions of U.S. dollars)	Market Capitalization (in billions of U.S. dollars)
1.	Citigroup	United States	1,884.32	247.42
2.	Bank of America	United States	1,459.74	226.61
3.	HSBC Holdings	United Kingdom	1,860.76	202.29
4.	ICBC	China	800.04	176.03
5.	JPMorgan Chase	United States	1,351.52	170.97
6.	Bank of China	China	585.55	143.80
7.	CCB-China Construction Bank	China	568.21	126.55
8.	Mitsubishi UFJ Financial	Japan	1,585.77	124.55
9.	Royal Bank of Scotland	United Kingdom	1,705.35	124.13
10.	Wells Fargo	United States	482.00	117.19
11.	UBS	Switzerland	1,776.89	116.84
12.	Banco Santander	Spain	945.86	115.75
13.	Wachovia	United States	707.12	105.42
14.	BNP Paribas	France	1,898.19	97.03
15.	UniCredito Italiano	Italy	922.79	96.24
16.	Barclays	United Kingdom	1,949.17	94.79
17.	Intesa Sanpaolo	Italy	321.64	92.74
18.	BBVA—Banco Bilbao Vizcaya	Spain	536.05	82.55
19.	Mizuho Financial	Japan	1,269.60	81.31
20.	HBOS	United Kingdom	1,156.61	79.83
21.	Société Générale Group	France	1,259.32	77.62
22.	Sumitomo Mitsui Financial	Japan	901.71	73.38
23.	Sberbank	Russia	87.43	67.92
24.	Deutsche Bank	Germany	1,485.58	65.15
25.	ABN Amro	The Netherlands	1,302.19	64.92

Note: Data from Forbes.com *The Global 2000*, http://www.forbes.com/lists/2007/18/biz_07forbes2000_The-Global-2000-Rank.html. Reprinted by permission of Forbes Magazine © 2007 Forbes LLC.

combined the Mitsubishi Tokyo Financial Group and the UFJ group. As another example, the bank ranked number 20, Mizuho Financial Group, combined the previous institutions Sumitomo Mitsui Banking, Dai-Ichi Kangyo Bank, Fuji Bank, Industrial Bank of Japan, and Mitsubishi Trust and Banking. Whereas some markets are already highly concentrated (such as Belgium, Canada, and Sweden), other markets (such as the United States) have more dispersed banking markets. In these latter markets, further consolidation can be expected to occur. A relatively new phenomenon is the ascent of Chinese banks, with ICBC (Industrial and Commercial Bank of China) taking the fourth spot and two other Chinese banks in the top 10. This is partially the result of the spectacular performance of the Chinese stock market in 2006.

Consolidation of international banking took an interesting twist in 2007, with Barclays, the 17th-largest bank, bidding €63.9 billion for ABN AMRO, the 26th-largest bank. This bid was topped by a consortium led by Royal Bank of Scotland (the 9th-largest bank), which bid €70.5 billion. Under the RBS bid, Fortis NV of Belgium would take ABN AMRO's Dutch operations, Banco Santander Central Hispano SA would take ABN AMRO's Brazilian and Italian operations, and RBS would get the rest, including ABN AMRO's investment banking arm. Either deal would be the largest in the financial industry.

Types of International Banking Offices

Exhibit 11.11 provides an overview of the organizational forms that banks may use for their international banking activities. As the exhibit shows, U.S. banks may not conduct international business on U.S. soil. The remainder of this section details the differences between the various entries in Exhibit 11.11.

Correspondent Banks

Recall from Chapter 2 that when commercial banks do not have their own banking operation in a major financial center, they establish a correspondent relationship with a local bank to conduct trade financing, foreign exchange services, and other activities on their behalves. Correspondent relationships allow a bank to service its multinational corporate clients without having to locate their banking personnel in many countries. However, the **correspondent bank** may not be able to give the same level of services as it would if it had its own facilities.

Representative Offices

A **representative office** is a small service facility that is staffed by parent bank personnel and designed to assist the clients of the parent bank in their dealings with the bank's correspondents or with information about local business practices and credit evaluation of the MNC's foreign customers. Although it does not provide direct banking functions to the MNCs, it represents a higher level of service than pure correspondent banking.

Exhibit 11.11 Organizational Structure of International Banking

	International Bank							
Characteristic	Domestic Bank	Correspondent Bank	Representative Office	Foreign Branch	Subsidiary/ Affiliate Bank	Offshore Bank	International Banking Facility	Edge Act Bank
Location	Domestic	Foreign	Foreign	Foreign	Foreign	Foreign	Domestic	Domestic
Loans/deposits to foreigners	No	—	No	Yes	Yes	Yes	Yes	Yes
Separate legal entity	No	—	No	No	Yes	No	No	Yes

Note: This exhibit was inspired by Exhibit 6.2 in Cheol Eun and Bruce Resnick (1997), p. 145.

Foreign Branches

A **foreign branch of a bank** is legally a part of the parent bank, but it operates like a local bank. A foreign branch allows the parent bank to offer its domestic, foreign, and international customers direct, seamless service in multiple countries. However, setting up a foreign branch is much more expensive than partnering with a correspondent bank. Foreign branch banks are also subject to both the banking regulations of their home countries *and* the countries in which they operate. However, foreign branches of U.S. banks are not subject to U.S. reserve requirements and are not required to have federal deposit insurance, which guarantees depositors up to $100,000 if the bank fails. Banks fund the Federal Deposit Insurance Corporation (FDIC) by paying insurance premiums expressed as a percentage of their deposits. Hence, both reserve requirements and deposit insurance drive up the cost of funds for banks and would prevent branches of U.S. banks from operating on the same level playing field as the local banks. Conversely, when a foreign bank locates a branch in the United States, the branch is treated like a domestic bank, and it is subject to all the same U.S. regulations.

Subsidiary and Affiliate Banks

Like a branch, a **subsidiary bank** is also wholly or partly owned by a parent bank, but it is incorporated in the foreign country in which it is located. An **affiliate bank** is only partly owned but not controlled by a foreign parent bank. Affiliate and subsidiary banks are subject to the banking laws of the countries in which they are incorporated. Prior to the repeal of the Glass Steagall Act in 1999, that meant, for example, that a U.S. parent bank was prohibited from engaging in investment banking activities, but its subsidiaries located abroad were not. Nevertheless, U.S. parent banks generally preferred to expand their operations overseas via branch banks.

Offshore Banking Centers[6]

An **offshore banking center** is a center that satisfies most of a number of conditions. First, the bulk of financial activity on both sides of the bank's balance sheet—that is, both borrowing and lending—is offshore, that is with nonresidents as counterparties. Second, the transactions are typically initiated outside the financial center. Third, the majority of the financial institutions involved are controlled by nonresidents doing business primarily with nonresidents. Finally, the centers typically offer low or zero taxation, moderate or light financial regulation, banking secrecy, and anonymity on transactions.

Offshore banking centers can be found in Aruba, the Bahamas, Bahrain, Barbados, Bermuda, the Cayman Islands, Hong Kong, Lebanon, Liberia, the Netherlands Antilles, Panama, Singapore, Vanuatu, and the West Indies, among other countries. Offshore banks engage in foreign currency loans, the floating of Eurobonds, over-the-counter trading in derivatives, and deposit taking from individual customers seeking to lower their tax liabilities. In some countries, international banks establish "shell branches," which have only a very limited physical presence in these nations—sometimes only post office boxes!

Clearly, a lack of financial regulation can lead to tax evasion and financial crime. Consequently, various international organizations, such as the BIS, the OECD, and the European Union, have joined forces in an effort to supervise the activities taking place in these centers. A major impetus to these efforts was the collapse of BCCI (Bank of Credit and Commerce International) in 1991. For years, BCCI (dubbed by some as the "Bank of Crooks and Criminals International") laundered drug money, faked loans, and hid losses without regulators noticing.

In the wake of the terrorist attacks of September 2001, the United States substantially expanded its antiterrorism legislation, including the power to seize money from foreign banks doing business in the United States, without notifying the foreign government. So far, the new tool has primarily been used in fraud and money-laundering cases (see Eric Lichtblau, 2003).

---

[6]This section is based primarily on "Offshore Financial Centers," 2000.

Edge Act Banks

Edge Act banks are federally chartered subsidiaries of U.S. banks that are physically located in the United States but are allowed to engage in a full range of international banking activities. Such activities include accepting deposits from foreign customers, trade financing, and transferring international funds. Edge Act banks are not prohibited from owning equity in U.S. corporations, as are domestic commercial banks. Consequently, U.S. parent banks own foreign subsidiaries and affiliate banks through an Edge Act setup.

International Banking Facilities

An **international banking facility (IBF)** is a separate set of asset and liability accounts that is segregated on the parent bank's books, so it is not a unique physical or legal entity. Any U.S.-chartered depositary institution (including a U.S. branch, a subsidiary of a foreign bank, or a U.S. office of an Edge Act bank) can operate an IBF. An IBF operates as a foreign bank in the United States and is consequently not subject to domestic reserve requirements or FDIC insurance regulation. However, IBFs may only accept deposits from non-U.S. citizens and make loans to foreigners. The bulk of an IBF's activities relate to interbank business.

The U.S. Federal Reserve established IBFs in an effort to allow U.S. banks to recapture business lost to offshore banks. Other countries created similar institutions. Examples include the Japanese Offshore Market (JOM) and the Bangkok International Banking Facilities in Thailand. These initiatives, along with the relaxation of financial regulations worldwide to allow offshore banking activities to be conducted by domestic banks, have slowed the growth of genuine offshore banking activities.

Small Belgian Bank Carves Out a Niche[7]

At first glance, central Europe looks like a very attractive market for international banks. Not only are these countries developing rapidly, but they will likely register significantly higher economic growth rates than the western European markets. The relative size of the banking sector is also likely to grow significantly. Moreover, these countries will develop closer and closer trade ties with western European countries, which will intensify when these countries are admitted to the European Union. In other words, European multinationals may do more and more business in central Europe and will require a local banking presence.

Expansion into eastern Europe could take the form of any of the alternatives discussed previously, from representative offices to subsidiaries or affiliates. However, the dominant method to gain a presence in the central European banking community has been through acquisitions of local banks. Somewhat surprisingly, the large international banks have not been the main acquirers, but, as Exhibit 11.12 shows, a number of medium-sized players with regional focus have led the way.

The only major international bank with a significant presence in central Europe is omnipresent Citibank. The top bank in the area, however, is KBC, a small Belgian bank. This bank has basically viewed central Europe as a second home market, in which it has systematically sought to build up market share through acquisitions. Whereas the prices paid for these local banks are indeed lower than for banks of comparable level in western Europe, many of the central European banks had a large number of bad loans on their books. In some instances, governments took over the bad loans when KBC acquired the banks. KBC now owns banks such as CSOB, the largest bank in the Czech Republic, Kredytbank, the fifth-largest bank in Poland; and it has a large minority participation (34%) in NLB, the largest bank in Slovenia. In all these markets, KBC is trying to push its "bank assurance" business model, where banking and insurance products are bundled and cross-sold through banking and insurance institutions.

---

[7]See "Central Europe: Second Home Market for KBC" (2002) and Ingo Walter and Roy Smith (2000).

Exhibit 11.12 Most Important Banks in Central Europe in 2000

		Market Share in Central Europe (in %)	Total Assets in Central Europe (in millions of EUR)	Central Europe as % of Total Assets
1	KBC (Belgium)	11.7	20,448	11
2	Hypovereinsbank (Germany)	9.9	17,360	2
3	UniCredito (Italy)	7.7	13,526	7
4	Société Générale (France)	7.7	13,526	3
5	Citibank (U.S.)	7.6	13,313	1
6	Erste Bank (Austria)	7.4	12,248	19
7	BCVIntesa (Italy)	5.4	9,479	3
8	ING (Netherlands)	4.4	7,668	2
9	RZB (Austria)	4.0	6,923	19
10	Commerzbank (Germany)	3.8	6,710	1

Note: Based on *The Banker* (2001) and authors' computations from the KBC Economic and Financial Bulletin (May 2002). Copyright © 2001 Financial Times.

It remains to be seen whether "bigger" is really "better." Bigger is better when there are economies of scale or scope. Economies of scale arise when the large fixed costs associated with production are borne by a larger, higher-revenue organization. Economies of scope arise when there are competitive benefits to be gained by selling a broader rather than narrower range of products. The best-known example of a financial group that has resolutely chosen to try to achieve economies of scope is Citigroup. Citigroup is involved in normal commercial banking activities, investment banking, asset management (for institutional and retail investors, including mutual funds), and insurance.

International Banking Regulation

The increasing globalization of the world's financial markets and the growth of international banking activities created the need for an international supervisory framework for two main reasons. First, banks hold capital (equity capital and other reserves) to protect depositors against losses. Recall that a bank's assets consist of the securities it buys and the loans it provides. The liabilities of the bank are the deposits it accepts from its customers, the borrowing the bank does in securities markets, and the bank's equity capital. The important role banks play in allocating capital in most countries makes their business losses resulting from companies not repaying their loans a regulatory concern; and most countries require banks to have a minimum capital-to-asset ratio as a safety cushion against losses.

As discussed earlier, the failure of one bank can set off a bank run—as worried depositors withdraw funds at many banks. Even in a well-developed country such as the United States, the state of Rhode Island experienced a bank panic in January 1991, and in the U.K. Northern Rock, a bank specializing in mortgage lending, experienced a run in 2007. Central banks are concerned that without international regulations to ensure that an adequate level of capital is maintained in the international banking system, bank failures could lead to a global financial crisis or at least could spill over into other countries.

Second, the variety of different national regulations potentially gives an unfair advantage to banks from countries with laxer regulatory standards, and this could decrease the soundness and safety of the international banking system overall. International regulations can create a more level playing field. A case in point occurred during the 1980s. During this time, central bankers from the G10 countries became worried that increased international competition in the banking industry due to globalization and deregulation had eroded the capital base of international banks. Japanese banks, for example, had aggressively built up their international loan portfolios by making low-cost loans. These banks gained market share, but subsequently many of them went bankrupt. This background set the stage for the 1988 Basel Accord.

International Capital Adequacy: The 1988 Basel Accord

The **Basel Accord** of 1988 requires internationally active banks in the G10 countries to hold capital equal to at least 8% of a basket of assets measured in different ways, according to their riskiness. The accord was put together by the Basel Committee on Banking Supervision, a committee of banking supervisory authorities that was established in 1975 by the central banks of the G10 countries. It consists of senior banking supervisors and representatives of the central banks of Belgium, Canada, France, Germany, Italy, Japan, Luxembourg, the Netherlands, Sweden, Switzerland, the United Kingdom, and the United States. It usually meets at the BIS in Basel, Switzerland.

The 1988 Basel Accord was primarily concerned with default or credit risk. To measure the riskiness of a bank's asset portfolio, the assets are classified into four buckets, according to debtor category. The first category requires no capital charge and consists of items such as Treasury bills and bonds, which have zero credit risk. Claims on other banks receive only a 20% weighting, meaning that only 20% of the claim is counted against the 8% capital requirement. Some claims receive a 50% weighting, but virtually all claims on the non-bank private sector receive a 100% weight and hence the full capital charge.

One difficulty in establishing the riskiness of a bank's activities is that many bank activities are not recorded on the balance sheet. These so-called off–balance sheet activities involve trading financial instruments and generating income from fees and loan sales. Good examples include foreign exchange trading activities and interest rate and currency swaps. The Basel Accord attempted to establish ways to measure the riskiness of these activities, using complex conversion factors. Over time, it was also recognized that the regulatory framework should not only apply to credit risk but to market risk as well. Market risk is the risk of losses in trading positions when prices move adversely. In 1996, the Basel Accord was amended, and trading positions in bonds, equities, foreign exchange, and commodities were removed from the credit risk category and given explicit capital charges. During the 1990s, well over 100 countries adopted the measures set forth in the Basel Accord, making it the world standard on banking regulation.

A New Capital-Adequacy Framework

Although it was successful, the Basel Accord was also subject to criticism. First, the simple bucket approach with a flat 8% charge for loans made to the private sector gave banks an incentive to move high-quality assets off their balance sheets. The enormous growth in **asset securitization**—the packaging of assets or obligations (mortgages or car loans, for example) into securities for sale to third parties—played a large role in this development. Banks found that they could sell a portfolio of higher-quality loans for an amount slightly greater than the value of the original loans, making the banks profits and reducing their capital charges. Of course, the practice also reduced the average quality of bank loan portfolios. Second, financial institutions gradually developed more sophisticated and realistic models to measure risk than the simple approach adopted in the Basel Accord. Finally, the 1988 accord did not sufficiently recognize the use of techniques to mitigate credit risk, such as collateral, guarantees, or hedges.

In response to these criticisms, the Basel Committee started work on a new accord, Basel II, in 1999, hoping to implement it in each country by the end of 2006, but although it has been created, as of late 2007, it had not been implemented. The new accord has three pillars. The first pillar still requires the bank capital ratio (the ratio of bank capital to risk-weighted assets) to be 8%. However, now three types of risk are explicitly and separately recognized: credit risk, market risk, and operational risk. This last risk category is new. Operational risk is the risk of direct or indirect loss resulting from inadequate or failed internal processes, people, and systems or from external events, such as computer failure, poor documentation, or fraud. The committee expects operational risk to account for about 20% of the overall capital requirements.

Changes to the old accord had already allowed banking institutions to choose between the Basel Committee guidelines to measure market risk or to use internally developed models. In 1994, JPMorgan made its internally developed model (RiskMetrics) publicly available and introduced the *VaR* terminology. VaR stands for **value at risk**. It measures the dollar loss that a given portfolio position can experience with 5% probability over a given length of time. If the weekly VaR is $100,000, it means that the position (or set of positions) could lose $100,000 in about 1 out of 20 weeks. Using the logic developed in Chapter 3, the VaR depends on the conditional volatility of the underlying asset returns. Importantly, internal models of risk take into account the risk reduction allowed by holding a diversified portfolio of imperfectly correlated assets.

For credit risk measurement, the new accord gives banks two options: They can use either a standardized approach for credit risk measurement or an "internal-rating-based approach." The standardized approach maintains the old framework, but now the differentiated risk weightings are based on a rating provided by an external credit assessment institution. Moreover, these weightings take into account the use of collateral, guarantees, and hedging techniques. Under the internal-ratings-based approach, banks are allowed to use their internal estimates of creditworthiness to assess the credit risk of their portfolios, subject to strict methodological and disclosure standards.

The second pillar of the accord involves a supervisory review process. That is, bank supervisors must ensure that each bank has sound internal processes in place to assess capital adequacy commensurate with its risks. The final pillar stresses market discipline through disclosure. The new accord describes disclosure requirements related to the internal risk assessment methods a bank uses to compute its capital adequacy. This information is essential to ensure that market participants (including the multinational clients of the banks) better understand the bank's risk profile and solvency.

A large debate has ensued about whether the new system will lead to more or less capital in the banking system (see, for example, "Basel Accord," 2001, and "Deep Impact," 2003). Some observers feel that the internal-ratings-based approach will lead to less capital because most quantitative models overestimate the power of diversification to reduce risk. It is often the case that, when there is crisis or market meltdown, many assets go down in value together and that many banks hold similar positions. This increases the riskiness of bank portfolios.

Also, there is some doubt as to whether the regulators in various countries will be up to the task of supervising sophisticated internal risk assessment models developed by their banks. Recent estimates suggest that the overall minimum regulatory capital will remain about the same, with lower charges for credit risk offset by the new charge for operational risk. Nevertheless, American supervisors have said that Basel II will be mandatory for only 10 internationally active American banks, whereas the European Union is committed to writing Basel II into EU law.

11.5 INTERNATIONAL BANK LOANS

In addition to tapping the bond markets, MNCs can also obtain loans from their banks. We next discuss several of the options and end with a discussion of how the differences between alternative financing options have become blurred.

Eurocredits

In Chapter 6, we discussed the interbank market known as the Eurocurrency market—the market where banks borrow from and lend to each other for short periods of time outside the jurisdiction of their countries. Banks operating in the Eurocurrency market are known as **Eurobanks**. Eurobanks not only make short-term loans but also extend them to other financial institutions and to corporations, sovereign governments, and international organizations at medium to longer maturities. These long-term debts are known as **Eurocredits**.

There are two characteristics that differentiate Eurocredits from similar debt instruments offered by domestic banks. First, the loans tend to be extended by a consortium or syndicate of banks that share the risk of the loan. Second, Eurocredits are typically issued at floating interest rates. That is, the rate charged is typically LIBOR plus a spread that reflects the credit risk of the borrower.

Example 11.3 The Role of Floating-Rate Debt

Suppose ABN AMRO, a Dutch international bank, pays 1.85% on eurodollar deposits with 6-month maturities. If ABN AMRO lends dollars for 6 months at 1.95%, it earns the spread (that is, 10 basis points). Also, assume that ABN AMRO has extended a 5-year Eurocredit denominated in dollars to the Swedish company Ericsson. Ericsson borrows for 5 years because it may need capital long term, and it may be concerned about an increase in credit spreads or that it could be denied credit when it tries to roll over short-term debt. Assume that the 5-year U.S. Treasury bond yield is 5%. If the interest rate on the loan is fixed, ABN AMRO will charge 5% plus a spread to account for Ericsson's credit risk. If the rate is floating, ABN AMRO will charge LIBOR (that is, 1.95%) plus a credit spread, but the rate will be reset every 6 months.

Suppose that the credit spread both for a 5-year floating-rate loan and for a fixed-rate loan to Ericsson is 1%. At first glance, it would appear that ABN AMRO might be better off to offer Ericsson a fixed-rate loan. The bank would then not only earn the credit spread but also earn the difference between the short- and long-term interest rates (5% versus 1.85%).[8]

Many banks often practice this maturity transformation that is taking in short-term deposits and providing long-term loans, which is sometimes called "riding the yield curve." However, this strategy is not without risk. It works only if average long-term rates are higher than short-term rates. Whereas this tends to be true in most countries, on average, it is not always true. In fact, we already discussed how the expectations hypothesis theory states that when short-term rates are lower than long-term rates, the market anticipates an increase in short-term rates. Hence, by extending a fixed-rate loan, ABN AMRO incurs the risk that short-term interest rates will rise and that in the future, it must pay its depositors a much higher interest rate than the current 1.85%, and even higher than the 5% + 1% = 6% they obtain from Ericsson.

By extending a floating-rate loan, ABN AMRO simply cashes in the credit spread on the Ericsson loan as long as the firm continues to pay interest on the loan. Hence, floating-rate loans protect banks against interest rate risk.

Types of Eurocredits

There are two main types of Eurocredits: term credits and revolving credits. A *term loan* is a loan with a fixed maturity for a fixed amount. In contrast, a *credit line* allows the borrower to withdraw as a loan any amount of money up to a fixed limit. In a term loan, the borrower has a fixed draw-down period (the "grace period") over which it may take up the loan. A term credit does not involve any other regular expenses except for the interest rate expense. With revolving credit, the borrower has the right to borrow up to a "committed" amount at the prevailing interest rate, plus a preset credit spread during an agreed-upon period specified in the

---

[8]Note that the interest rate for Treasury bills at the short end would be lower than 1.85% because banks have credit risk, and the U.S. government does not.

loan. However, the bank charges a commitment fee for the unused portion of the committed amount.

For instance, a borrower may have the right to issue 6-month promissory notes (I-owe-you documents) worth up to CHF50 million at an interest rate of 6-month LIBOR plus 1.00% per annum. This is similar to a standard credit line, except that it cannot be revoked during the lifetime of the loan. The commitment of the credit line is potentially very valuable when a company's credit standing deteriorates. Because a MNC can always borrow elsewhere if the market-required spread drops, the fixed spread can be viewed as an option contract.

Syndicates

A syndicate consists of a group of banks that take different roles in the debt-arranging process:

- The lead manager negotiates with the borrower for tentative terms and conditions. When there seems to be a preliminary agreement on details, the lead manager prepares a placement memorandum. The placement memorandum describes the borrower, including the borrower's financial condition, and gives details about the proposed loan. The lead manager then invites other banks to participate in the loan.
- Because the funding is not yet arranged at the time of the negotiations, the lead manager often contacts a smaller number of managing banks to underwrite the loan—that is, to guarantee to make up for the shortage of funds if there is a shortage.
- The banks that provide the actual funding are called *participating banks*.
- The *paying agent* is the bank that receives the service payments from the borrower and distributes them to the participating banks.

Any given bank can play multiple roles. For instance, the lead bank is almost invariably also the largest underwriter (hence the name *lead manager*) and often provides funding as well. The main objective of syndication is to spread the risks of default. Because of the paying agent system, if the borrower defaults, the default is considered against all banks of the syndicate. This structure ensures that the borrower does not pay off the larger banks while ignoring the smaller debt holders. As in domestic banking, the borrower often signs promissory notes, one for each payment. The advantage of receiving promissory notes is that they are negotiable. That is, if the lending bank needs funds, it can pass on the promissory note to another financial institution as security for a new loan, or it can sell the promissory note.

If demand by other banks to take part in the loan is good, then the amount of the loan may be increased if the borrower wishes. On the other hand, if there is insufficient demand, the managing banks (with the lead manager) may have to make up the difference. If the managing banks have previously guaranteed to the borrower the full amount of the proposed loan, the credit is said to be "fully underwritten." On the other hand, if the credit is on a "best efforts" basis, the managing banks have only promised to try their best. If there is not sufficient demand in the latter case, the size of the loan may be scaled down, or the terms may be changed.

Fees and Borrowing Costs

There are several types of costs to a Eurocredit borrower in addition to the obligation to repay the loan principal. These costs can be divided into two categories: periodic costs and the up-front cost.

The up-front cost is typically a one-time fee of 1.0% to 2.5% of the total amount of the credit, which is paid to the lead manager and managing banks for organizing and managing the loan. This amount is deducted from the principal; that is, a 1% fee means that the borrower receives only 99% of the face value of the loan. In practice, the managing banks pass along a portion of this fee to the participating banks.

Periodic costs include the interest paid on the amount of the credit actually in use. If the interest agreement calls for 6-month LIBOR plus a 1.5% margin, the borrower makes periodic interest payments on the amount of the credit drawn (that is, the amount of the loan the borrower has actually received) equal to the new 6-month LIBOR established at the beginning of the current 6-month period, plus 1.5%. In addition, there will be a commitment fee (probably in the range of 0.25% to 0.75%) to be paid periodically on the unused portion of the credit in the case of a revolving credit. Finally, there is usually a small fee paid to the paying agent bank to cover administrative expenses. In summary:

$$\begin{aligned}\text{Periodic costs} =\ &(\text{Amount of total credit drawn}) \times (\text{Reference rate} + \text{Margin})\\ &+ (\text{Amount of total credit not drawn}) \times (\text{Commitment fee})\\ &+ \text{Agent fee}\end{aligned}$$

The reference rate is usually LIBOR, in the case of a floating-rate loan, or the long-term rate paid by a government of excellent credit standing, in the case of a fixed rate loan. The margin, or spread above the reference rate, depends on the quality of the borrower, the political risk of his or her country, the maturity, and the up-front cost.

In recent years, many large banks have specialized in managing loans as middlemen. That is, they lead manage syndicated loans to receive up-front fees for their management services; afterward, they sell off much of their share in the loan to other smaller banks or thrift institutions. This practice has stemmed not only from the comparative advantage of some banks in providing management services but also from new regulatory guidelines, in particular the Basel Committee standards previously discussed.

In principle, the fees are compensation for the services of the intermediaries, while the spread is a compensation for default risk. However, one can trade a higher up-front fee for a lower spread and vice versa. For instance, borrowers often accept a high up-front fee in return for a lower spread because the spread is sometimes seen as a quality rating. Importantly, both fees and credit spread must be taken into account to determine the effective cost of a loan, as we demonstrate in Section 11.6.

History and Size of Eurocredits

Exhibit 11.13 shows the international syndicated credit facilities signed for selected years starting in 1980. At the beginning of the 1980s, the market for international syndicated loans was already well established. What was perhaps remarkable is the importance of borrowers from developing countries as opposed to developed markets. Equally striking is how the market almost completely dried up around 1985. We will come back to these facts in Chapter 14 because they are intimately related to the Debt Crisis, a phenomenon that dominated the economies of many developing countries in the 1980s. The market then picked up again and grew rather dramatically starting in 1990 and continuing over the past decade, with borrowers increasingly coming from the developed markets and increasingly from the corporate sector. For example, in the mid-1990s, the new loans primarily refinanced outstanding loans or

Exhibit 11.13 International Syndicated Credits (in billions of U.S. dollars)

	1980	1985	1995	2000	2006
Total	82.8	19.0	370.2	1,464.9	2,121.2
Developed countries	39.9	9.5	329.4	1,331.7	1,822.3
Developing countries	41.9	9.3	40.8	94.5	237.6

Notes: Data are from *BIS Quarterly Review*, various issues. The two numbers do not necessarily add to the total because of two omitted categories, offshore centers and international institutions.

financed acquisitions, infrastructure projects, or the restructuring of national industries such as telecommunications. In 2000, a syndicated loan of $30 billion, the largest ever, supported the hostile takeover of Mannesmann A.G. by Vodafone. In 2006, the total market size exceeded $2 trillion.

The Secondary Market

Another major development since the early 1980s has been the increasing tendency for banks to trade Eurocredits in the secondary market. Although there are few statistics on the total size of the secondary market, the main impetus for this market was the debt problem of developing countries in the 1980s. In addition, the Basel agreements on capital adequacy also presented many banks with the choice of increasing capital or removing assets from their balance sheets. Many banks appear to have chosen to adopt the latter option to some degree and to use the secondary market in Eurocredit debt to offload some loans from their balance sheets.

The Euronote Market

The Euronote market is a clear example of the blurring of the distinctions between loan and security markets. The main distinction in this market is between short-term Euronotes (Euro-commercial paper and other short-term paper) and medium-term notes, although the option to issue short-term paper included in several medium-term note programs is creating some overlap between the two market segments in terms of actual drawings.

Euronotes

International banks responded to the competition from the Eurobond market by creating facilities for sales of short-term, negotiable promissory notes, called **Euronotes**. In a basic Euronote facility, a syndicate of banks commits to distribute for a specified period, typically 5 to 7 years, the borrower's notes (the "Euronotes"), with maturities ranging between 1 month, 3 months, 6 months, and 12 months. In case the notes cannot be placed in the market, the syndicate banks in many Euronote facilities stand ready to buy them at previously guaranteed rates. Such facilities have names, such as note issuance facility (NIF), standby note issuance facilities (SNIFs), or revolving underwriting facility (RUF). They give borrowers long-term continuous access to short-term money underwritten by banks at a fixed spread. Euronotes are more flexible than floating-rate notes and usually cheaper than syndicated loans. Banks eager to beef up their earnings without fattening their loan portfolios (which would then require them to add expensive equity capital) made Euronote facilities an important segment of the Euromarket. More recently, the notes have appeared in non-underwritten form, called Euro-commercial paper (Euro-CP).

Euro Medium-Term Notes

Since the mid-1980s, a growing number of firms have been bypassing financial intermediaries and issuing **Euro-medium-term notes (Euro-MTNs)** directly to the market. Euro-MTNs bridge the maturity gap between Euro-CP and the longer-term international bond, with maturities as short as 9 months to as long as 10 years. Let's look at some of the basic characteristics of a Euro-MTN. First, the Euro-MTN is a facility with notes offered continuously or periodically rather than all at once, like a bond issue. Therefore, Euro-MTNs give issuers the flexibility to take advantage of changes in the shape and level of the yield curve and of the specific needs of investors with respect to amount, maturity, currency, and interest rate form (fixed or floating).

Second, unlike conventional underwritten debt securities, medium-term notes can be issued in relatively small denominations. This makes the medium-term debt market more flexible than the Eurobond and Eurocredit markets. Third, the costs of setting up a Euro-MTN program are much smaller than the total cost of a Eurobond issue, although its basic characteristics (coupon structure rates, maturity) are similar. Fourth, medium-term notes are not underwritten; securities firms place the paper as agents instead. Fifth, unlike public bond issues, the amounts and timing of medium-term notes sales are not disclosed. Such a lack of visibility allows companies to raise funds quickly and discreetly, without the risk of a complex public offering.

For example, it is conceivable that a MNC may optimally need, at a particular moment, USD10 million of 6-month money, USD21.0 million of 16-month money, and USD15.5 million of 24-month money. The bond market—with its high issuance costs—could not economically supply such small or precise amounts of debt, but a Euro-MTN program offers the flexibility to accomplish this precise financing need.

The Major Debt Arrangers

The success of Euronotes and Euro-MTNs has blurred the line between bond and loan markets. As a result, today, the loan and securities divisions of most major financial institutions are no longer separate and distinct. When a MNC must raise money, bankers may offer the MNC loans, or they may offer to issue a Eurobond or initiate a Euronote facility. In arranging security issues, banks earn fee income. Whereas loans allow banks to earn the spread between the interest rate they charge and the interest they pay depositors in addition to fee income, they also incur a capital charge in the BIS capital adequacy framework, which banks may want to avoid. In fact, there appears to be a trend toward relationship lending, where banks provide loans only when the borrower conducts securities or advisory business with the bank.

Exhibit 11.14 shows the top 15 global debt arrangers. "Debt" in the table combines Eurocredits, international bonds, and medium-term notes. The top 15 banks account for close

Exhibit 11.14 Top Arrangers of International Debt

Bookrunners	January 1, 2007–June 30, 2007					January 1, 2006–June 30, 2006				
	Proceeds ($M)	Rank	Mkt. Share	No. of Issues	Discl. Fees ($M)	Proceeds ($M)	Rank	Mkt. Share	No. of Issues	Discl. Fees ($M)
Citigroup	362,802.6	1	8.4	952	657.5	312,125.8	1	8.4	971	845.4
JPMorgan Chase	320,781.4	2	7.5	807	773.6	244,374.7	2	6.6	811	450.7
Deutsche Bank	282,527.7	3	6.6	801	283	242,135.3	3	6.5	772	282.1
Merrill Lynch	261,535.8	4	6.1	653	874.3	203,753.9	7	5.5	580	516.1
Morgan Stanley	246,475.0	5	5.7	691	615.3	228,670.7	4	6.1	680	684.8
Barclays Capital	228,812.5	6	5.3	551	66.7	159,811.1	10	4.3	553	80.6
Lehman Brothers	223,932.1	7	5.2	541	477.4	218,238.1	5	5.9	578	397.1
Credit Suisse	195,000.0	8	4.5	572	449.1	190,739.1	8	5.1	590	394.8
Goldman Sachs	192,196.4	9	4.5	491	593.9	206,229.8	6	5.5	498	787
UBS	177,306.2	10	4.1	646	554.5	157,342.8	11	4.2	628	435.1
Bank of America	175,534.0	11	4.1	453	259.7	145,478.6	12	3.9	478	225.9
Royal Bank of Scotland	168,434.8	12	3.9	426	30.3	171,796.4	9	4.6	404	32
HSBC	115,384.4	13	2.7	386	70	113,752.3	13	3.1	424	139.4
Wachovia	103,607.5	14	2.4	236	227.7	62,267.1	17	1.7	188	179.3
ABN AMRO	102,257.8	15	2.4	294	43.4	86,885.9	15	2.3	290	70.7
Industry Total	**4,304,656.0**		**100.0**	**10,453.0**	**7,817.9**	**3,722,388.8**		**100.0**	**10,361.0**	**7,875.1**

Note: Data from *Investment Dealers' Digest*, Global Debt and Equity League Table A1, Second Quarter, July 2007. Full credit for an issue is given to bookrunners (equal if joint). Copyright © 2007 Source Media, Inc.

to 60% of the market in arranging global debt. Not surprisingly, there is regional specialization; for example, Deutsche Bank is the number one when western European borrowers are considered; but JPMorgan Chase and Citigroup have been in the top 5 for quite some time.

11.6 COMPARING THE COSTS OF DEBT

In this section, we first review how the costs of debt of various instruments can be compared. We then reflect on the fundamental sources of the costs of debt. This brings us to the topic of a firm's credit risk and how banks measure it. Finally, we reflect on how firms can minimize their costs of debt in international financial markets and illustrate this process with some examples.

When you compare the cost of alternative debt instruments, it is important to compare "oranges with oranges." In Chapter 6, we reviewed the term structure of interest rates. Interest rates for short maturities may be lower or higher than interest rates for longer maturities. Similarly, Chapter 6 revealed interest rates on different currencies to be very different. According to the expectations theory of interest rates and foreign exchange, these differences reflect expected movements in asset prices, which should eventually equalize the cost of debt for a given maturity. We already illustrated how low–interest rate currency debt does not mean cheap debt and used a numeric example to show how debt costs of different maturities cannot be compared (see Example 11.1).

As you can see, it is important to compare debt instruments of nearly similar amounts that have the same maturity and cash flow patterns, are expressed in the same currency, and share the same interest rate structure. Take, for example, Eurobonds versus U.S. bonds: Because fixed-rate Eurobonds normally pay their coupons once a year, whereas U.S. bonds pay semiannually, to compare the cost of debt between the two, the interest rates have to be expressed on the same basis. A semiannual yield can be annualized by using the formula

$$\text{Annual yield} = (1 + \text{Semiannual yield})^2 - 1$$

Typically, the semiannual yield will be expressed in per annum terms; that is, to obtain the semiannual yield, one takes the annualized yield and divides by 2. For example, suppose that a Eurobond carries an annual interest rate cost of 7.00%, and a U.S. corporate bond carries an interest rate of 6.95%. Both have a maturity of 5 years; but in the U.S. corporate bond market, coupons are paid semiannually, whereas in the Eurobond market, coupons are paid annually. To compare the two bonds, we must therefore annualize the U.S. corporate bond rate:

$$\text{Semiannual yield} = \frac{6.95\%}{2} = 3.457\%$$

$$\text{Annual yield} = (1 + 0.03475)^2 - 1 = 7.07\%$$

So, this U.S. corporate bond actually has a slightly higher interest rate cost.

The All-in-Cost Principle

To compare alternative debt securities, the **all-in-cost (AIC) principle** is typically used. The AIC is the discount rate or internal rate of return that equates the present value of all the future interest rate and principal payments to the net proceeds (face value minus fees) received by the issuer.

To illustrate the AIC principle, we revisit the Eurobond issued by GE Capital described in Section 11.3. The bond has a face value of €2 billion; the maturity is 5 years; the price is €995.18 per €1,000 face value; the coupon is 5.125%, and the fees are 0.275%. To compute the AIC, we must trace the actual cash flows to and from GE Capital, which look as follows:

Year	Cash Flows	Cash Flows in Present Value Terms
0	1,984.86	1,984.86
1	(102.50)	(97.34)
2	(102.50)	(82.44)
3	(102.50)	(87.79)
4	(102.50)	(83.37)
5	(2,102.50)	(1,624.03)
		0.00

GE Capital's Cash Flow (in millions of euros)

The net proceeds of the loan are less than €2,000 million for two reasons: GE Capital must pay 0.275% on €2,000 million (which is €5.5 million!) in fees to pay for the syndication, and the bond sold for 99.518% of face value. Hence the net amount is

$$€2,000 \text{ million} \times [0.99518 - 0.00275] = €1,984.86 \text{ million}$$

The annual coupon payment is simply €2,000 million × 0.05125 = €102.50 million; the last payment (year 5) reflects the repayment of the principal plus the last coupon payment.

The AIC is the internal rate of return of all the cash flows; in other words, it is the interest rate that makes the initial proceeds equal to the present value of all the future payments GE Capital must make. In mathematical terms, the internal rate of return, y, solves

$$1,984.86 = \frac{102.50}{(1 + y)} + \frac{102.50}{(1 + y)^2} + \frac{102.50}{(1 + y)^3} + \frac{102.50}{(1 + y)^4} + \frac{2,102.50}{(1 + y)^5}$$

Software programs such as Excel have built-in commands (IRR) that compute internal rates of return for a given set of cash flows. It turns out that the equation is satisfied for $y = 5.30\%$. In the right-hand column of the cash flow table, we filled out the present values for each cash flow. Because the cash flows (coupon payments) are the same in nominal terms between years 1 and 4, their present value decreases over time. When we add all the present values of all the cash outflows, discounted at the rate of 5.30%, we obtain 1,984.97. The difference between this amount and 1,984.86 is due to rounding error. Because $y = 5.30\%$ makes the present value of the cash outflows equal to the net proceeds of the loan, the loan for GE Capital is said to have an AIC of 5.30%. If GE Capital wants to borrow in dollars, at fixed interest rates, for 5 years, it should try to borrow at the lowest possible AIC.

Components of the All-in Cost

The AIC has three components: The "default free" interest rate, the credit spread, and transaction costs. The default free interest rate is the rate available on risk-free government securities of the same maturity. For the GE Capital example, the relevant government rate would be a government bond issued by a Euroland government with 5 years to maturity. The euro–denominated benchmark bonds typically referred to in the Eurobond market are Bunds, German government bonds. The 5-year interest rate at the time GE Capital issued the bond was 4.67%. Hence, GE Capital paid 5.30% − 4.67% = 0.63%, or 63 basis points above the government rate.

This differential has two sources. The first is simply transaction costs. The fees that GE Capital paid to arrange the bond reduced its net proceeds and increased the effective interest rate payable on the loan. To see how much these transaction costs contribute, we must compute the rate the company would pay if the fees were zero. That is, we repeat the computation using the table, but we replace the initial proceeds by 1,990.36 = 2,000 × 0.99518. The internal rate of return now becomes 5.24%. Hence, transaction costs add only

5.30% − 5.24% = 6 basis points to the AIC of the loan. Nevertheless, this is a significant cost for GE Capital because it amounts to €5.5 million.

The final component of the cost is the credit spread, the difference between the borrowing cost of the government and the borrowing cost of GE Capital, in this case 5.24% − 4.67% = 0.57%, or 57 basis points. The credit spread reflects the market's assessment of the ability of the company to repay its debt and is typically closely associated with a company's **credit rating**.

To sum up, the cost of a loan can be split up into three components:

$$\text{Total cost} = \text{Risk-free rate} + \text{Credit spread} + \text{Transaction cost}$$

$$5.30\% = 4.67\% + 0.57\% + 0.06\%$$

Credit Ratings

Companies compete in providing information on the creditworthiness of corporate and government borrowers. Moody's Investors Service and Standard & Poor's (S&P) are the best-known credit-rating organizations that provide credit ratings on U.S. domestic bonds and most international bonds, too. They classify bond issues into categories based on the creditworthiness of the borrower. The ratings are based on an analysis of current information regarding the likelihood of default and the specifics of the debt obligation. The ability of a firm to service its debt depends on the firm's financial structure, its profitability, the stability of its cash flows, and its long-term growth prospects. The ratings only reflect creditworthiness—not exchange rate uncertainty.

In addition to Moody's and S&P, the European Rating Agency (Eurorating) and the Japan Credit Rating Agency (JCR) are major rating agencies. Until a few years ago, the capital markets in Europe and Japan were less "credit risk" sensitive than the U.S. capital market, making it possible to tap the capital market without an official rating. The corporate bond and Eurobond markets have now matured to the point that this has become very difficult.

Ratings Schemes

The ratings schemes used by Moody's and S&P are summarized in Exhibit 11.15. Moody's rates bonds into nine major categories, from Aaa, Aa, A, Baa, and Ba down to C; S&P uses AAA, AA, A, and BBB down to C. Ratings of Aaa to Baa for Moody's and AAA to BBB for S&P are known as investment-grade ratings. For these issues, interest payments and principal appear safe at the time of the rating. Many prominent institutional investors such as pension funds are only allowed to purchase investment-grade bonds. As a result, MNCs have a huge incentive to achieve investment-grade ratings. For bonds rated lower than investment grade, investors should assign some substantial probability to future payment problems, and hence these issues are called "speculative." Within each of the nine categories, Moody's has three numeric modifiers, 1, 2, and 3, to place an issue, respectively, at the upper, middle, or lower end of the category, whereas S&P uses + and − modifiers.

Government borrowers are called **sovereign borrowers**. Sovereign borrowing is a sizable portion of the international bond market. In rating a sovereign borrower, S&P analyzes its degree of political and economic risk. (Chapter 14 discusses these topics in detail.) The rating assigned to a sovereign government is particularly important because it affects the ratings applied to corporations within that country.

Minimizing the Cost of Debt Internationally

Why Source Debt Internationally?

This chapter illustrates the rich diversity of global debt markets. Nevertheless, we have also cautioned that this world of opportunities does not necessarily mean that an MNC can easily lower its cost of capital by sourcing debt internationally.

If an MNC wants to minimize its fixed-interest cost of debt for a given maturity and currency of denomination, the AIC measured in the headquarters' currency is the correct number

Exhibit 11.15 Credit Ratings for Bond Issuers

Credit quality	Standard & Poor's	Moody's
Investment grade		
	AAA	Aaa
Highest quality	AA+	Aa1
	AA	Aa2
High quality	AA−	Aa3
	A+	A1
Highest middle quality	A	A2
	A−	A3
	BBB+	Baa1
Middle quality	BBB	Baa2
	BBB−	Baa3
Speculative		
	BB+	Ba1
Predominantly speculative	BB	Ba2
	BB−	Ba3
	B+	B1
Low quality	B	B2
	BB−	B3
Very low quality	CCC	Caa
Highly speculative	CC	Ca
Lowest quality	C	C
In default		
	D	

Note: Data are from "Corporate Bonds on the Way to Maturity" (2002). Courtesy of KBC Group.

to minimize. We already discussed that when UIRP does not hold, sourcing debt in low–interest rate countries may be less costly, but it also entails risk. In fact, an unexpected appreciation of the currency beyond the built-in appreciation implied by the forward rate will increase the MNC's cost of debt relative to borrowing at home.

Many companies issue debt in foreign currencies but hedge the currency risk. In fact, Matthew McBrady and Michael Schill (2005) studied the currency composition of international bonds in detail and found concrete evidence that firms try to source debt in the currencies that produce the lowest AICs after hedging. In the previous section, we learned that the AIC has three components. Hence, there are three channels through which foreign borrowing can lower the AIC:

1. Transaction costs are lower.
2. The credit spread is lower.
3. The "hedged" foreign interest rate is lower than the local risk-free rate.

Whereas the first channel is pretty easy to understand, it will be helpful to go back to the Dig-It-Up example to illustrate the second and third channels.

Example 11.4 International Credit Spreads and the AIC

Suppose we supplement the data for 1-year borrowing for Dig-It-Up, the Canadian MNC from Example 11.1, as follows:

	LIBOR (r)	Dig-It-Up's Rates (i)
CAD	2.50	3.00
AUD	4.75	5.00

The column labeled Dig-It-Up's Rates refers to the actual 1-year borrowing rates that Dig-It-Up faces in both markets compared to the LIBOR rates that are for AAA credits. Hence, Dig-It-Up faces a 50 basis-point credit spread in CAD, but only a 25 basis-point spread in AUD. In what currency should Dig-It-Up borrow if the borrowing transaction costs are similar? Because Dig-It-Up is Canadian based, if it borrows in AUD, it must hedge the currency risk by buying AUD forward. Assume that the spot rate is AUD1.10/CAD. If covered interest rate parity holds, the forward rate (see Chapter 6) will be

$$F = S \times \frac{[1 + r(\text{AUD})]}{[1 + r(\text{CAD})]} = \frac{\text{AUD1.10}}{\text{CAD}} \times \frac{1.0475}{1.025} = \frac{\text{AUD1.1241}}{\text{CAD}}$$

The relevant interest rates for the covered interest rate parity (CIRP) relation are the LIBOR rates, $r(\text{AUD})$ and $r(\text{CAD})$.

Because interest rate parity is satisfied, we know that a AAA company borrowing at 4.75% in Australia dollars would face an effective Canadian dollar interest rate of 2.50% when hedging the AUD currency risk by buying the necessary AUD funds in the forward market to pay off the loan. Of course, if CIRP were not to hold, this is another way to capitalize on different borrowing costs across countries. For the developed countries, we argued that CIRP holds up very well, but for many emerging markets, this may not be the case.

However, Dig-It-Up does not have a AAA credit rating, and so it faces the higher borrowing costs displayed in the table. The "hedged" CAD borrowing cost for Dig-It-Up when borrowed in AUD can be calculated by examining the hedged costs of repayment. Dig-It-Up would borrow AUD1.10 to get CAD1. It would owe interest at 5%, and it can hedge the AUD interest and principal payment by buying AUD at the forward rate of AUD1.1241/CAD. Its hedged borrowing cost will therefore be

$$\text{AUD1.10} \times [1 + 0.05] \times \frac{1}{\text{AUD1.1241/CAD}} - 1 = 2.75\%$$

Note that 2.75% is lower than 3.00% by 25 basis points, the cost of borrowing directly in CAD. The reason is that Dig-It-Up faces a credit spread in Australia that is 25 basis points lower than in Canada!

Example 11.4 suggests that in efficient, integrated markets, credit spreads ought to be equalized across countries; otherwise, companies should all borrow in the countries where credit spreads are lowest and then hedge the exchange rate risk. This reasoning is correct for the example, but the statement is generally only true for "multiplicative" credit spreads rather than the "absolute" credit spreads that are commonly used. The absolute credit spread simply reflects the difference between the company's interest rate and the risk-free rate, whereas the multiplicative spread is somewhat smaller, reflecting the (gross) rate at which the risk-free rate must be scaled up to obtain the company's interest rate. Our example lists absolute credit spreads (designated acsp):

$$\text{acsp}(\text{CAD}) = i(\text{CAD}) - r(\text{CAD}) = 0.50\%$$

$$\text{acsp}(\text{AUD}) = i(\text{AUD}) - r(\text{AUD}) = 0.25\%$$

However, the credit spreads across currencies are really only comparable when expressed in multiplicative form. The multiplicative credit spread (mcsp) in this case is defined as

$$1 + i(\text{CAD}) = [1 + \text{mcsp}(\text{CAD})] \times [1 + r(\text{CAD})]$$

$$1 + i(\text{AUD}) = [1 + \text{mcsp}(\text{AUD})] \times [1 + r(\text{AUD})]$$

Only if mcsp(CAD) = mcsp(AUD) will the cost of borrowing in CAD and in AUD while hedging the currency risk be equivalent. To see this, note that the cost of borrowing in AUD, while hedging the currency risk, is

$$[1 + i(\text{AUD})] \times \frac{S(\text{AUD/CAD})}{F(\text{AUD/CAD})}$$

with S and F representing the spot and forward rates. Using CIRP, we obtain

$$[1 + i(\text{AUD})] \times \frac{[1 + r(\text{CAD})]}{[1 + r(\text{AUD})]} = [1 + \text{mcsp}(\text{AUD})] \times [1 + r(\text{CAD})]$$

This value equals $[1 + i(\text{CAD})]$ only if mcsp(AUD) = mscp(CAD). For our example, note that

$$\text{mcsp}(\text{CAD}) = \frac{1.03}{1.025} - 1 = 0.49\%$$

$$\text{mcsp}(\text{AUD}) = \frac{1.05}{1.0475} - 1 = 0.24\%$$

In other words, absolute, or multiplicative credit spreads, are almost indistinguishable when interest rates are low. However, at higher interest rate levels, discrepancies between relative and absolute credit spreads increase.

Example 11.5 Credit Spreads at High Interest Rate Levels

Suppose the 1-year interest rate on Mexican pesos (for a AAA credit) is 50% and that a multinational corporation faces a 1-year MXN borrowing cost of 60%. Hence, the absolute credit spread is

$$\text{acsp}(\text{MXN}) = 60\% - 50\% = 10\%$$

and the multiplicative credit spread is

$$\text{mcsp}(\text{MXN}) = 6.67\% = \left[\frac{1 + 0.60}{1 + 0.50} - 1 \right] \times 100$$

If the interest rate for a company with a AAA credit rating in the United States is 5%, the risky company's borrowing cost in the United States will be identical to its borrowing cost in Mexico as long as its multiplicative credit spread in the United States is also 6.67%.

Suppose the interest rate in the United States is 5% for AAA-rated companies. Then, the USD interest rate equivalent to 60% in Mexico is $1.05 \times 1.0667 = 12\%$. Hence, the absolute credit spread in U.S. dollars that is equivalent to an absolute credit spread of 10% in Mexican pesos is only $12\% - 5\% = 7\%$!

Credit Spreads Across Countries

There are many reasons companies face different (multiplicative) credit spreads in different markets. One reason is that credit perceptions differ across markets. For example, in the not-so-recent past, European and Japanese retail investors were less concerned about credit risks, especially when the brand-name products produced by a MNC were familiar in the market-place. Ford Motor Credit, for example, successfully raised €1.5 billion in the international bond markets in 2003 even though some U.S. credit analysts were worried about a deterioration of Ford's creditworthiness. European retail and institutional investors were obviously less concerned. As a result, Ford was able to lower the yield offered on the bonds relative to what it would have been in the U.S. corporate bond market.

Similarly, many European and Japanese-based companies have faced lower credit risk ratings in international markets than in their domestic markets. Hence, borrowing costs differ in international markets for these companies as well.

In contrast, in the early 1990s in Japan, the so-called industrial banks, such as Industrial Bank of Japan, Nippon Credit Bank, and Bank of Tokyo, played a large role in Japan's financial system. Their task was to help finance the growth of industry in Japan by providing loans to industrial companies. They usually issued 5-year bonds to finance themselves, but they also explored international capital markets to source debt. Interestingly, Japanese investors did not differentiate between the different banks, with the debentures trading at very narrow spreads relative to Japanese government bonds of similar maturity.

For their international borrowing, many of the industrial banks got credit ratings from Moody's and S&P, and the credit ratings of the banks differed substantially. In fact, some of the banks were rated AAA, whereas others were rated only AA−. Hence, the borrowing costs of the various industrial banks were very different in international markets.

If credit spreads are larger in one country than in others, investors would like to borrow in countries with low interest rates and invest (lend) in countries with high interest rates while hedging their currency risk. This is exactly the kind of arbitrage that keeps CIRP holding in well-developed markets. However, the arbitrage is not so easy in this case for several reasons. First, transactions costs can be significant when the securities are traded in the secondary market. Second, the arbitrage is risky because the company involved may go bankrupt. If that happens, the arbitrageur could presumably cancel the two transactions with the company (borrowing and lending for the same amounts). However, he or she will still be left with an open forward contract that must be paid. This leaves the arbitrageur exposed to currency risk. Nevertheless, arbitrage clearly takes place in international markets, and, as it does, the credit rate differentials between local and international markets narrow.

Oftentimes, differences in credit spreads reflect regulatory arbitrage or tax loopholes. Exxon successfully exploited such a loophole in 1984. The company was able to issue dollar-denominated zero-coupon bonds in the Eurobond market at a rate lower than the U.S. Treasury interest rate. Exxon simply borrowed money in the Eurobond market and invested it in U.S. Treasury bonds, pocketing a gain of $19 million in the process. The source of this peculiar situation was a combination of the name recognition Exxon had with Eurobond investors, the fact that Exxon did not have many outstanding Eurobond issues (so the bonds were relatively scarce), and a regulatory loophole in Japan that drove up the demand for the bonds by Japanese investors. Why were Japanese investors so interested in Exxon's zero-coupon bonds? Because when the bonds were redeemed at maturity, the capital gain on the money received was nontax-able in Japan. In contrast, regular interest payments associated with coupon bonds were taxable.

Another classic example is the acquisition of Nabisco by R.J. Reynolds (RJR) in 1985. For part of the financing, RJR issued a number of Eurobonds in various currencies, including dual-currency bonds, all hedged back to dollars. By exploiting regulatory differences across markets, RJR was able to decrease its borrowing costs substantially.

Finally, there are cyclical variations in credit spreads that are not necessarily perfectly correlated across countries. Credit spreads tend to be countercyclical, widening in economic downturns and falling in economic booms. MNCs can react to such cycles in an effort to exploit them, but in some cases, the firms will be faced with higher borrowing costs they need to try to avert. For example, in 2000, on top of a rise in the general level of interest rates, credit spreads widened, making it increasingly difficult for lower-rated issuers to borrow in the long-term bond market. As a result, many of these companies relied more heavily on bank financing and floating-rate debt. In general, opportunities to lower the cost of debt through credit spread arbitrage are decreasing over time because of the ongoing globalization process.

POINT–COUNTERPOINT

Financing Chocolate Globalization

When Suttle bursts into Freedy's room one sunny afternoon, he finds Ante and Freedy glued to the computer screen, surrounded by heaps of paper. "Hey guys, fancy a quick afternoon coffee?" Freedy and Ante both sigh, and Freedy says, "I am afraid we've got to really continue working because we must finish this case for tomorrow's class on corporate finance. And, unfortunately, we are not making much progress right now."

"Well, maybe I can help. What is it about?" Suttle asks. Ante throws a small package of papers Suttle's way. "Here, read for yourself," says Ante. "The more I learn about finance, the less I understand what the heck is going on." Suttle is soon engaged in reading the case while Ante and Freedy wrestle with their spreadsheets.

The case is about the financing of an acquisition of a private U.S. chocolate company, Worshey's, by a Swiss, multinational food product company, Cote D'Argent, with its own line of chocolate products. The financial team of Cote D'Argent is looking at three possibilities: a straight Eurobond in euros, a straight Eurobond denominated in yen, and a yen/euro dual-currency bond. All bonds have a maturity of 5 years, with annual coupons. The case asks which type of bond the company should pick and why. It also asks why there might be differences in financing costs across the three different instruments. Suttle finds it so fascinating that he starts to really investigate the numbers of the case. The details on the three bonds are as follows:

Face value	Euro Eurobond €100 million	Yen Eurobond ¥14 billion	Yen/Euro Dual-Currency Eurobond ¥14 billion
Price as a % of face value	100%	101%	98%
Fees	1.25%	0.90%	0.90%
Coupon (annual)	4.10%	1.00%	2.00%
Final redemption	Par	Par	€104.90 million

The two yen-related bonds would be arranged through a syndicate run by Kozuma, a Japanese investment bank. Kozuma is negotiating aggressively with Cote D'Argent to consider the yen instruments. Kozuma is also suggesting that Cote D'Argent should immediately hedge out the currency risk by using forward contracts and is offering the following exchange rates (in yen/euros):

Spot exchange rate: 140.00
1-year forward rate: 136.78
2-year forward rate: 133.03
3-year forward rate: 128.87
4-year forward rate: 124.50
5-year forward rate: 120.12

The Eurobond issue in euros would be run by a syndicate headed by Kneutsche Bank, a German universal bank.

After digesting the numbers, Suttle asks, "What are your conclusions so far?" Ante excitedly points toward the spreadsheets onscreen: "Either the case is not realistic, or we have made a huge mistake: The dual-currency bond is too good to be true! I first thought that taking on yen debt would be great: The interest rate is so low! However, Freedy convinced me that Cote D'Argent might not want to take on currency risk, and the low interest rates simply reflect the fact that the yen trades at a huge forward premium relative to the euro. You can see from the forward exchange rates that there is a large implicit yen appreciation, from ¥140/€ to almost ¥120/€. So, we decided to compute the cost of debt for hedged cash flows using the forward exchange rates to convert yen into euros."

"Wow, I am impressed," Suttle says. "Did you also take the fees into account?"

"Oh yeah!" answers Freedy "We computed the all-in cost as you should. Here are our spreadsheets."

Suttle takes a peek at the spreadsheets, which present Cote D'Argent's cash flows:

I. Euro Eurobond

Year	Euro Cash Flows
0	$100 - 1.25 = 98.75$
1	(4.10)
2	(4.10)
3	(4.10)
4	(4.10)
5	(104.10)
All-in cost	4.38%

II. Yen Eurobond

Year	Yen Cash Flows (¥ millions)	Exchange Rate (¥/€)	Euro Cash Flows (€ millions)
0	$14{,}000 \times (1.01 - 0.0090) = 14{,}014$	140.00	100.10
1	(140)	136.78	(1.024)
2	(140)	133.03	(1.052)
3	(140)	128.87	(1.086)
4	(140)	124.50	(1.124)
5	(14,140)	120.12	(117.72)
All-in cost			4.11%

Interest in yen is 1%. The last column is the second column divided by the third column.

III. Yen/Euro Dual-Currency Eurobond

Year	Yen Cash Flows (¥ millions)	Exchange Rate (¥/€)	Euro Cash Flows (€ millions)
0	$14{,}000 \times (0.98 - 0.0090) = 13{,}594$	140.00	97.10
1	(280)	136.78	(2.048)
2	(280)	133.03	(2.104)
3	(280)	128.87	(2.172)
4	(280)	124.50	(2.248)
5	(280)	120.12	(2.331) + (104.90)
All-in cost			3.73%

Interest in yen is 2%. The last column is the second column divided by the third column, except for the final principal payment, which is already in euros.

Suttle inquires, "So, the AIC is the internal rate of return that equates the present value of the future cash outlays with today's euro revenues, net of fees, right?"

"Yeah, of course," shouts Ante. "Maybe you can tell me why the dual-currency bond is so cheap. Clearly, Kozuma either made a mistake, or they are plain stupid to have given Cote D'Argent a deal like that. If Japanese investors really invest in this bond, they must be pretty irrational."

Freedy interjects, "Well, I think that is the wrong perspective. Perhaps the Japanese investors simply want some exposure to long-term euro risk, plus they are getting a nice coupon. They might be betting that the €104.90 million that they are getting back in 5 years will be still worth ¥14,000 million, in which case they get a great deal, relative to the 1% bond. But the forward value of the €104.90 million is only €104.90 million × ¥120.12/€ = ¥12,601 million, so they are definitely taking a risk."

After Suttle takes another look at the spreadsheets, he summarizes the situation: "I think your computations are right, and yes, both yen alternatives are cheaper than the euro alternative, with the dual-currency bond clearly offering the lowest cost of debt to Cote D'Argent. The company should use that bond to finance the acquisition.

"Why can there be such substantial differences? I think there are grains of truth in what both of you are saying," continues Suttle. "It is possible that Japanese investors, which are probably the target market for the dual-currency bonds, are indeed blinded by the high yen coupon rate because interest rates in Japan are very close to zero. They are likely aware of the currency risk, though. If you use the 5-year forward rate to convert the face value of the bond into euros, the euro payment at the end would have to be ¥14,000 million /(¥120.12/€) = €116.55 million, not €104.90 million, in order for Japanese investors to be guaranteed that they get their principal back. Japanese investors are really betting on the euro being stronger than implied by forward rates.

"I believe there is some empirical evidence for the fact that high-yield currencies do not depreciate by as much as implied by forward exchange rates, but it is not clear that investors would like to speculate on this with a bond," says Suttle. "Besides, smart investors could try to set up an arbitrage with the dual-currency bond. The yield is too low, so you'd like to sell the bond and 'buy' the underlying cash flows in, say, Treasury markets and exchange rate markets. However, such arbitrage is not risk free because Cote D'Argent may default on the bond. Moreover, transaction costs in long-date forward contracts are high. Also, there might not be a very liquid secondary market for these bonds. Hence, I am not so worried about the 27 basis-points difference between the yen Eurobond and the euro Eurobond. It might be due to a difference in credit perceptions in Europe and Japan and may be hard to arbitrage. Cote D'Argent's chocolate is really popular in Japan, so some investors might very well like to buy the company's bonds. It is also striking that the fees Kozuma demands are lower than the fees for the euro Eurobond. It may be that this is part of a relationship-banking ploy. Kozuma might be keen to work with Cote D'Argent in an effort to do other, more profitable business with the company later on. However, the fact that the dual-currency bond is another 40 basis points cheaper is surprising. It is possible that for some Japanese investors, the dual-currency bond is advantageous from a tax or competitive viewpoint. For example, the dual-currency bond may be viewed as entirely domestic, even though, in truth, it is not."

"All right, Suttle. I think we've got it solved. Let's go for coffee," Ante declares.

"And let's have a nice bar of Cote D'Argent chocolate with it," Freedy yells. "What I really wonder about is why such a fine chocolate company would want to acquire such a horrible Worshey's product."

"You Euro-snob," shouts Ante. "I love my Worshey's!"

11.7 SUMMARY

This chapter analyzes debt financing in a global world. Its main points are the following:

1. Debt is only one source of funds for MNCs. MNCs can also issue equity or finance projects using their internally generated funds.

2. Debt instruments differ in currency of denomination, maturity, nature of interest rate payments, tradability, and international character.

3. Under a decentralized debt-denomination model, MNCs issue debt in different currencies to hedge the cash flows they earn in these currencies from their foreign subsidiaries. If the debt is centralized—that is, issued in the currency of the MNC's headquarters—the profits from the MNC's foreign subsidiaries are subject to additional currency risk.

4. Issuing debt in low–interest rate currencies does not reduce a company's debt costs if international markets are efficient.

5. MNCs can issue short-term or floating-rate debt, or they can issue long-term fixed-rate debt. As with the currency of denomination, there is no free lunch here: If short-term rates are lower than long-term rates, this may be an indication of impending interest rate increases.

6. MNCs can borrow from a financial institution, in which case the debt is called *intermediated debt*. Alternatively, they can issue securities to investors in the capital markets. The trend toward direct issues is called *financial disintermediation*.

7. International bonds are traded outside the country of the issuer. If they are issued in a particular domestic bond market, they are called *foreign bonds*. If they are issued simultaneously in various markets, outside the specific jurisdiction of any country, they are called *Eurobonds*.

8. The foreign bond and Eurobond markets make up about 25% of the global bond market.

9. Because foreign bonds are subject to local regulations, in some countries, such as the United States, they require a lengthy registration process.

10. Eurobonds are placed among investors with the help of a syndicate of financial institutions. Typically these bonds are bearer bonds (not registered).

11. The acceleration of globalization, including tax harmonization, financial deregulation, and the relaxation of capital controls, has blurred traditional distinctions between domestic and international bonds. Global bonds, for example, are issued simultaneously in a domestic market and in the Eurobond market.

12. Bonds can have a fixed interest rate (straight issues), no interest at all (zero-coupon bonds), or a floating interest rate that varies with LIBOR rates. Convertible bonds allow the holder to convert the bonds into shares, or stock. Dual-currency bonds are issued in one currency and pay interest in that currency, but the final principal payment is in another currency.

13. Banks are MNCs and are subject to international banking regulation in the form of capital adequacy standards set by the Basel Committee.

14. To engage in international banking activities, banks may use correspondent banks, representative offices, foreign branches, affiliate banks, or subsidiary banks. These different organizational forms determine the degree of service and control exercised by the parent bank.

15. Offshore banking centers conduct international banking activities in a "lightly" regulated setting. International banking activities can also be organized in the United States via an Edge Act bank or international banking facility.

16. Eurocredits are long-term bank loans extended by a syndicate of banks in countries other than the country in whose currency the loans are denominated. Most Eurocredits are of the floating-rate variety, with the interest rates set at a spread above LIBOR.

17. Euronotes and Euro-medium-term notes give borrowers access to short- or long-term loans via the intermediation of financial institutions. These securities blur the distinctions between debt and loan markets.

18. To compare the cost of debt across markets, debt instruments must have approximately the same maturity, be expressed in the same currency, and be of the same rate structure (fixed or floating), and their interest rates must be expressed on the same basis (that is, annualized appropriately).

19. The all-in cost is the discount rate, or internal rate of return, that equates the present value of all future interest rate and principal payments to the net proceeds received by the issuer. The AIC can be split up into three components: the risk-free rate, the credit spread, and transaction costs.

20. S&P and Moody's rate the credit risk of debt instruments based on the creditworthiness of the borrower.

21. MNCs should minimize the AIC of their debts expressed in the local currency of the country in which they are headquartered. Opportunities to reduce these costs appear to be related to differences in credit spreads across countries.

22. As markets become more internationally integrated, opportunities to lower the cost of capital in global markets may diminish.

QUESTIONS

1. What are the three main sources of financing for any firm?
2. What is the difference between a centralized and decentralized debt denomination for a MNC?
3. Will a MNC issuing debt in low–interest rate currencies necessarily lower its cost of funds? Why?
4. Should a MNC borrow primarily short term when short-term interest rates are lower than long-term interest rates? Or should it keep the maturity the same but use a floating-rate loan rather than a fixed-rate loan? Explain.
5. What is financial disintermediation?
6. What are the two main segments of the international bond market, and what types of regulations apply to them?
7. What is the difference between a foreign bond and a Eurobond?
8. Why might U.S. investors continue to purchase Eurobonds, despite the fact that the U.S. corporate bond market is well developed?
9. What is a global bond, and what role does the global bond market play in the blurring of the distinctions in the international bond market?
10. What are the differences between a straight bond, a floating-rate note, and a convertible bond?
11. What is a dual-currency bond?

12. What kind of activities do international banks engage in?
13. Why is there a need for international banking regulation?
14. What are the differences between credit risk, market risk, and operational risk?
15. Which activity would require the largest capital charge under the 1988 Basel Accord: a loan to another bank or a loan to a large MNC? Would this necessarily be true under the Basel II?
16. What is VaR?
17. What is the difference between a foreign branch and a subsidiary bank?
18. What is an offshore center?
19. What is the difference between an Edge Act bank and an international banking facility?
20. What is the difference between a Eurocredit, a Euronote, and a Euro-medium-term note?
21. Why are Eurocredits not extended by one bank but by a large syndicate of banks?
22. What is the all-in cost of a 5-year loan? What are its main components?
23. What is a credit rating? What is a credit spread?
24. Should corporations issue bonds in countries where they face the lowest credit spreads? Be very specific about the concept of credit spread you use.

PROBLEMS

1. In 1985, R.J. Reynolds (RJR for short) acquired Nabisco Brands and financed the deal with a variety of financial instruments, including three dual-currency Eurobonds. The first dual-currency bond, lead-managed by Nikko, raised JPY25 billion (equivalent to USD105.5 million at the time of issue). Coupons were paid in yen, but the required final principal payment was not JPY25 billion but USD115.956 million. The coupon was 7.75%, even though a comparable fixed-rate Euroyen bond at that time carried only a 6.375% coupon. The actual 5-year forward rate at the time was around JPY200/USD.

   a. Given the "fat" coupon, is this bond necessarily a great deal for the investors?
   b. At maturity, in August 1990, the exchange rate was actually JPY144/USD. Was the bond a good deal for investors?

2. GBA Company wishes to raise $5,000,000 with debt financing. The funds will be repaid with interest in 1 year. The treasurer of GBA Company is considering three sources:

   i. Borrow USD from Citibank at 1.50%
   ii. Borrow EUR from Deutsche Bank at 3.00%
   iii. Borrow GBP from Barclays at 4.00%

If the company borrows in euros or British pounds, it will not cover the foreign exchange risk; that is, it will change foreign currency for dollars at today's spot rate and buy foreign currency back 1 year later at the spot rate prevailing then. The GBA Company has no operations in Europe.

A representative of GBA contacts a local academic to provide projections of the spot rates 1 year in the future. The academic comes up with the following table:

Currency	Spot Rate	Projected Rate 1 Year in the Future
USD/GBP	1.50	1.55
USD/EUR	0.95	0.85

a. What is the expected interest rate cost for the loans in EUR and GBP?

b. What are the projected USD/GBP rate and USD/EUR rate for which the expected interest costs would be the same for the three loans?

c. Should the country borrow in the currency with the lowest interest rate cost? Why or why not? Would your answer change if GBA did generate cash flows in the UK and continental Europe?

3. FE Company wishes to raise $1,000,000 with debt financing. The treasurer of FE Company considers two possible instruments:

   i. A 2-year floating-rate note at 1% above the 1-year dollar LIBOR rate on which interest is paid once a year

   ii. A 2-year bond with an interest rate of 5%

   Currently, the dollar LIBOR is 1.50%.

   a. Is it obvious which security the Treasurer should pick?

   b. Suppose the Treasurer believes that the 1-year LIBOR rate 1 year from now will rise to 4.50%. Which security has the lowest expected AIC if borrowing fees are similar for the two instruments?

4. K3 Company wants to borrow $100 million for 5 years. Investment bankers propose to either do a syndicated Eurocredit or issue a Eurobond. The Eurocredit would be denominated in dollars, but the Eurobond would be denominated in different currencies for different markets (these issues are called tranches):

   Terms: Syndicated Eurocredit
   Amount: USD100 million
   Upfront fees: USD1.25%
   Interest rate: Interest payable every 6 months; LIBOR plus 1.00%
   Terms: Eurobond
   Tranche 1: USD 50 million, Interest rate: 3.50%
   Tranche 2: ¥5,952 million (equivalent of USD50 million), Interest rate 1.5%

   a. What are the net proceeds in USD for K3 for the Eurocredit loan?

   b. Assuming that the 6-month LIBOR in USD is currently at 2.00%, what is the effective annual interest cost for K3 for the first 6 months of the loan?

   c. Compute an effective annualized interest rate cost (all-in cost) for the USD tranche of the Eurobond.

   d. What information would you need to obtain the dollar all-in cost of the yen tranche?

   e. What elements would you take into account to choose between the two possibilities?

5. Suppose Intel wishes to raise USD1 billion and is deciding between a domestic dollar bond issue and a Eurobond issue. The U.S. bond can be issued at a 5-year maturity with a coupon of 4.50%, paid semiannually. The underwriting, registration, and other fees total 1.00% of the issue size. The Eurobond carries a lower annual coupon of 4.25%, but the total costs of issuing the bond runs to 1.25% of the issue size. Which loan has the lowest all-in cost?

BIBLIOGRAPHY

Ang, Andrew, Geert Bekaert, and Min Wei, 2008, "The Term Structure of Real Rates and Expected Inflation," *Journal of Finance*, forthcoming.

"Basel Accord," March 2001, *Euromoney,* pp. 49–53.

Bekaert, Geert, Robert Hodrick, and David Marshall, 2001, "Peso Problem Explanations for Term Structure Anomalies," *Journal of Monetary Economics* 48, pp. 241–270.

"Central Europe: Second Home Market for KBC," May 2002, *KBC Economic and Financial Bulletin*.

Claes, Anouk, Mark J.K. DeCeuster, and Ruud Polfliet, 2002, "Anatomy of the Eurobond Market, 1980–2000," *European Financial Management* 8, pp. 373–386.

"Corporate Bonds on the Way to Maturity," March 2002, *Kreditbank Economic Financial Bulletin,* p. 5.

"Deep Impact," May 10, 2003, *The Economist*, p. 78.

Eun, Cheol, and Bruce Resnick, 1997, *International Financial Management*, Boston: Irwin-McGraw-Hill.

Gadanecz, Blaise, 2004, "The Syndicated Loan Market: Structure, Development and Implications," *BIS Quarterly Review*, pp. 75–89.

"The Great League Table Debate," June 2001, *Euromoney*, pp. 116–130.

Jeanneau, Serge, 2002, "Recent Initiatives by Basel-Based Committees and the Financial Stability Forum," *BIS Quarterly Review*, pp. 57–100.

Lichtblau, Eric, 2003, "U.S. Cautiously Begins to Seize Millions in Foreign Banks," *New York Times*, May 30, p. A16.

McBrady, Matthew R., 2002, "How Integrated Are Global Bond Markets?" working paper.

McBrady, Matthew R., and Michael J. Schill, 2005, "The Currency Denomination Decision: Do Firms Seek Bargains in International Bond Markets?" working paper.

Merrill Lynch, April 2001, *Size and Structure of the World Bond Market: 2001*.

Miller, Darius P., and John J. Puthenpurackal, 2005, "Security Fungibility and the Cost of Capital: Evidence from Global Bonds," *Journal of Financial and Quantitative Analysis* 40, pp. 849–872.

Morris, Jennifer, 2001, "France Telecom Spreads Bets," *Euromoney*, February.

"The New Basel Accord: An Exploratory Note," January 2001, Bank for International Settlements discussion paper.

"Offshore Financial Centers," June 2002, International Monetary Fund background paper.

"Walt Disney Company's Sleeping Beauty Bonds—Duration Analysis," 1994, Harvard Business School case, 9-294-038.

Walter, Ingo, and Roy Smith, 2000, *High Finance in the Euro Zone*, London: Pearson Education, Ltd.

"Where Be Dragons?" August 1994, *Euromoney*, pp. 78–79.

"Who Needs Syndicates?" 1995, *Euromoney*, pp. 30–36.

Chapter 12

International Equity Financing

*W*hen a company lists its shares on a stock market, it seeks to access capital from a wide pool of investors. Apart from this **primary market** at the time of an initial public offering, the daily trading of a corporation's shares among investors (the **secondary market**) provides an objective, forward-looking valuation of the company's activities. One important aspect of this activity is that it determines the cost of additional equity capital: the more investors are willing to pay for a company's shares, the cheaper will be additional capital when the company issues additional shares. Consequently, everything that affects stock market prices is important for a capital-hungry MNC. (However, we leave a formal discussion of the international cost of capital to Chapter 13.) Another benefit of listing on a public stock exchange is that the presence of a stock market price can be used to align the interests of managers with the interests of shareholders in management compensation schemes.

This chapter examines how and why MNCs list their shares on international equity markets. Most MNCs list their shares on the stock exchanges of the countries in which they are headquartered. However, many MNCs also list their shares on stock exchanges located in other countries. For example, in 2001, the total value of shares traded in the stock of Nokia on the New York Stock Exchange (NYSE) reached $30 billion. Such a large volume for a single company is not unusual for the NYSE. IBM's total NYSE trading volume during 2001 was well over $100 billion, for instance. Nevertheless, Nokia, which is one of the world's premier mobile phone companies, is headquartered in Finland, in contrast to IBM, which is a U.S. company. Even though U.S. investors can directly buy Nokia stock on the Finnish stock exchange in what is called *cross-border trading*, Nokia must find this international ("cross-exchange") stock listing valuable. Why? After first giving you a tour of the world's stock exchanges and how they work, we explore the advantages and disadvantages of cross-listing.

12.1 A TOUR OF INTERNATIONAL STOCK MARKETS

The Size of Stock Markets

As Exhibit 12.1 indicates, the U.S. stock market capitalization was almost 40% of the world's stock market capitalization at the end of 2005. The second-largest market is that of Japan, which is followed by the exchanges of the United Kingdom, France, and Canada.

Exhibit 12.1 Market Capitalizations and Turnovers of Stock Exchanges

	Market Capitalization (in millions of U.S. dollars)						Turnover		
	1991 (% of world total)		2000 (% of world total)		2005 (% of world total)		1991	2000	2005
Australia	148,511	1.31%	372,794	1.16%	804,015	1.81%	0.32	0.61	0.84
Austria	7,689	0.07%	29,935	0.09%	126,309	0.28%	0.92	0.31	0.37
Belgium	71,319	0.63%	182,481	0.57%	269,834	0.61%	0.09	0.21	0.38
Bermuda		0.00%	2,146	0.01%	2,125	0.00%		0.06	0.03
Canada	266,874	2.35%	841,385	2.61%	1,482,185	3.33%	0.29	0.75	0.61
Cayman Islands		0.00%	250	0.00%	2,217	0.00%		0.00	
Cyprus	1,290	0.01%	11,516	0.04%	5,853	0.01%	0.05	0.80	0.26
Denmark	44,841	0.40%	107,666	0.33%	162,732	0.37%	0.21	0.85	0.65
Finland	14,271	0.13%	293,635	0.91%	198,652	0.45%	0.11	0.70	1.26
France	348,083	3.07%	1,446,634	4.48%	1,667,652	3.75%	0.33	0.75	0.76
Germany	393,454	3.47%	1,270,243	3.94%	1,221,106	2.75%	0.96	0.84	1.57
Hong Kong	121,986	1.08%	623,398	1.93%	1,054,999	2.37%	0.32	0.61	0.44
Iceland		0.00%	4,439	0.01%	27,799	0.06%		0.54	0.68
Ireland		0.00%	81,882	0.25%	114,086	0.26%		0.18	0.59
Italy	158,865	1.40%	768,364	2.38%	798,073	1.80%	0.16	1.01	1.62
Japan	3,130,863	27.60%	3,157,222	9.79%	7,542,716	16.97%	0.32	0.85	0.62
Kuwait		0.00%	20,772	0.06%	294,058	0.66%		0.20	0.18
Luxembourg	11,308	0.10%	34,016	0.11%	51,248	0.12%	0.01	0.04	0.01
The Netherlands	136,158	1.20%	640,456	1.99%	542,679	1.22%	0.29	1.06	1.06
New Zealand	14,336	0.13%	18,613	0.06%	40,592	0.09%	0.20	0.58	0.51
Norway	22,043	0.19%	65,034	0.20%	190,952	0.43%	0.53	0.92	1.23
Portugal	9,613	0.08%	60,681	0.19%	70,743	0.16%	0.29	0.90	0.50
Singapore	47,367	0.42%	152,827	0.47%	257,341	0.58%	0.38	0.60	0.45
Spain	147,928	1.30%	504,219	1.56%	959,910	2.16%	0.27	1.96	1.63
Sweden	100,913	0.89%	328,339	1.02%	366,053	0.82%	0.21	1.18	1.11
Switzerland	173,881	1.53%	792,316	2.46%	935,448	2.10%	0.40	0.77	1.04
U.A.E.		0.00%	23,262	0.07%	132,413	0.30%		0.01	0.22
UK	987,952	8.71%	2,567,992	7.99%	3,058,182	6.88%	0.32	0.71	1.86
U.S.	4,087,660	36.03%	15,104,037	46.82%	17,000,864	38.24%	0.53	2.11	1.46
World Total	**11,345,733**		**32,260,433**		**44,459,895**				

Notes: The data are taken from the World Federation of Exchanges, Datastream, and the S&P/IFC database. Turnover is value traded during the year divided by total market capitalization.

The relative market capitalizations of the different exchanges around the world are in constant flux, however. For example, at one point in the 1980s, Japan's stock market was the world's largest. The dominance of Japan's stock market was also somewhat artificial because cross-holding grossly inflated the numbers.

Cross-holding refers to the practice of one firm owning shares in another firm. If both of these firms are listed on an exchange, and one calculates total market capitalization by merely multiplying the total number of shares outstanding by the market price per share, the market capitalization will be overstated because part of the value of the shares is essentially double-counted. Let's illustrate this with a hypothetical example.

Example 12.1 Cross-holding of Shares

Assume that Companies A and B are each worth $100. Hence the total market capitalization of the two companies is $200. Suppose both companies are fully equity financed, so we can represent their balance sheets as follows:

Company A		Company B	
Assets	Liabilities	Assets	Liabilities
$100	$100	$100	$100

Here liabilities represent owner's equity, and assets represent plant and equipment. If there is no intercorporate share ownership, $200 represents the true value of the assets of both companies and, consequently, the true value of their shares. Now, suppose Company A issues $50 in new shares and buys $50 of the outstanding shares of Company B in the secondary stock market. Whereas the balance sheet of Company B remains unchanged, the balance sheet of Company A becomes

Company A		
	Assets	Liabilities
Physical Assets	$100	$150
Investment in Co. B	$50	

The market capitalization of Company A therefore increases by 50%, to $150, and total market capitalization of shares that have been issued by corporations increases by 25%, to $250. Of course, the true value of the assets remains $200 because no new assets were created by this transaction. To get the correct market capitalization, one must value only the shares that are held by the public, in which case we find a valuation of $50 for Company B and $150 for Company A, for a total of $200.

Cross-holding is especially common in Japan and in many European countries, such as Germany and Belgium, where banks are permitted to hold substantial and sometimes controlling interests in non-banking firms. The institutions that construct the major international stock market indices, such as Morgan Stanley Capital International (MSCI), now routinely correct for such cross-holdings.

Stock Markets and the Economy

Exhibit 12.1 shows that the total capitalization of the world's stock markets has almost quadrupled in value over 15 years. This is due to a combination of relatively good stock returns during this period and a high level of new stock listings, many associated with the dot-com boom.

Notice that large, free-market economies tend to have large stock markets. Dividing a country's stock market capitalization by its GDP provides an alternative perspective. As Exhibit 12.2 shows, the U.S. capital market is very large compared to the U.S. economy. This is due in part to the fact that proportionately more U.S. firms prefer to go public than do European firms, which are more often privately owned. Many European companies rely much more heavily on bank financing than in the United States. It is common for European banks to own shares of their client companies, whereas that is prohibited in the United States. Moreover, it is still the case that more enterprises in Europe are partially government owned (railroads, for example) and hence are not listed on exchanges. All this is changing, however, and the two models are converging.

Many government companies have been privatized throughout Europe. The late 1990s Internet craze also may have jump-started an equity culture in Europe, with young, rapidly

Exhibit 12.2 Market Capitalization as a Percentage of GDP

Developed Markets		Emerging Markets	
Australia	113.59	Argentina	62.71
Austria	41.09	Brazil	59.63
Belgium	72.51	Chile	118.43
Canada	131.22	China	17.19
Denmark	63.60	Colombia	34.75
Finland	102.47	Czech Republic	28.51
France	78.78	Egypt	85.66
Germany	43.59	Hungary	29.84
Greece	64.25	India	133.58
Hong Kong	593.62	Indonesia	28.95
Ireland	57.05	Iran	22.30
Italy	46.17	Israel	99.30
Japan	161.54	Korea	105.64
Luxembourg	160.83	Malaysia	138.24
The Netherlands	86.96	Malta	77.02
New Zealand	37.41	Mexico	31.12
Norway	64.54	Morocco	52.32
Portugal	38.52	Pakistan	41.19
Singapore	220.37	Peru	35.17
Spain	85.25	Philippines	40.77
Sweden	102.53	Poland	31.06
Switzerland	254.92	Russia	79.13
UK	138.96	Slovenia	24.54
U.S.	136.15	South Africa	229.33
		Sri Lanka	28.52
		Taiwan	130.21
		Thailand	70.15
		Turkey	44.55
		Venezuela	5.02

Notes: The data are for the end of 2005. Stock market capitalizations are from the World Federation of Exchanges. GDP numbers are from the International Financial Statistics, except for Taiwan, where a GDP number was obtained from the statistical office.

growing companies eager to tap equity capital. In addition, the Glass-Steagall Act passed in 1933 in the United States to separate commercial from investment banking has been dismantled, allowing U.S. financial institutions to become more like their European counterparts in terms of combining banking, insurance, and investment banking activities.

Nevertheless, the capitalizations of some exchanges in Europe represent more than 100% of the GDP in the nations in which they are located. The exchanges in Finland, Luxembourg, Sweden, Switzerland, and the United Kingdom are examples. In Asia, the countries with the largest stock markets in terms of GDP are Hong Kong, Singapore, and Japan.

The Organization and Operation of Stock Markets

Legal Organization

Legally, stock markets can be organized as private or public organizations, called *bourses*. A **private bourse** is owned and operated by a corporation founded for the purpose of trading securities. In many countries, several private exchanges compete with one another. This is the situation in the United States, Japan, and Canada. In the United Kingdom, one dominant exchange has emerged. This model also characterizes the stock markets in Australia and the Far East. In Germany, Austria, Scandinavia, and the Netherlands, banks are the major, and sometimes only, securities traders. These exchanges have thus become known as **banker's bourses**.

In **public bourses**, the government appoints brokers, typically ensuring them a monopoly over all stock market transactions. Belgium, France, Spain, Italy, Greece, and some Latin American countries are among the nations with public bourses. However, waves of deregulation in the 1980s and 1990s resulted in the dismantling of this structure in most countries. Today, most bourses are either private bourses or banker's bourses. In all countries, however, both private and public bourses are typically subject to a substantial amount of government regulation. Note that privately owned exchanges may or may not represent companies that are publicly traded on the stock market. We defer discussing the recent trend toward stock exchanges listing on the stock market to a later section of this chapter.

Trading Practices
The trading practices of a market are more important than how the market is organized because trading practices more directly affect price discovery and liquidity. Price discovery is the process by which information is revealed. A good trading process leads to "fair," or "correct," prices that cannot be manipulated to the advantage of individual traders. However, stock market manipulation still exists, as the box in this chapter illustrates. In a liquid market, trading happens quickly, and large quantities of securities can be traded without the price being affected. Transaction costs are also low in liquid markets. International stock markets present an opportunity to learn about the importance of trading arrangements in ensuring price discovery and liquidity. There are two major trading arrangements utilized by international stock markets: **price-driven trading systems** and **order-driven trading systems**.

Price-driven Trading Systems
The foreign exchange market is a good example of an over-the-counter, price-driven system in which market makers stand ready to buy at their bid prices and sell at their ask prices. Similar price-driven stock market systems exist for stocks. The NASDAQ (National Association of Securities Dealers Automated Quotations) in the United States and London's SEAQ (Stock Exchange Automated Quotation) are examples.

The NASDAQ system is a complex communications network that centralizes a geographically dispersed market. Bid and ask stock prices for more than 6,500 actively traded stocks are continuously quoted by more than 500 competing NASDAQ market makers who deal in any stocks they choose. From computer terminals connected to NASDAQ's mainframe computer, brokers are able to see the current bid and ask prices for all NASDAQ stocks, quoted on the screen, by competing market makers (dealers). An investor's broker can execute a trade online through NASDAQ's computer or call a NASDAQ dealer with a bid or an ask price at which she wants to transact. At SEAQ, any member of the exchange is free to register as a market maker for any shares. In practice, only a few brokers act as market makers, and most market makers tend to specialize in particular groups of shares. Market makers are obliged to display prices for a minimum trade size (number of shares) on SEAQ screens available to all members of the stock exchange. A market maker's name, her quotes, and the maximum size of the transactions for which these quotes are valid are displayed on the screens. When a member of the exchange contacts a market maker by phone to conduct a transaction, the transaction price may be better than the price quoted on the screen but never worse (within the maximum transaction size) because the market maker has already committed to the price. For less liquid stocks, the quotes are only indicative and are not firm. Executed transactions must be reported on SEAQ screens within a couple of minutes. London is a major market for international stock trading for two primary reasons. First, its market makers have a high level of expertise and are able to provide a high degree of liquidity at low trading costs. Second, trades on the SEAQ are not taxed under British law. Not surprisingly, a significant portion of French, German, Swiss, Dutch, and Italian shares are bought and sold on SEAQ.

Stock Market Manipulation in China[1]

On April 1, 2003, a Beijing court handed down long-awaited sentences in one of the largest stock-manipulation cases in history. Several men were convicted of manipulating the stock of China Venture Capital Group and were sentenced to jail terms ranging from 2 to 4 years and fines of up to ¥500,000.[2] Yet the alleged masterminds of the scheme, Lu Liang and Zhu Huanliang, have not yet been captured and incarcerated.

At the beginning of 1998, China Venture Capital was a company listed on the Shenzhen Stock Exchange (one of the three stock exchanges in China), with a stock price around ¥10. In early 1998, Zhu, a major stock market player, contacted Lu, an established business journalist, to help him unwind his money-losing investment in China Venture Capital. At that time, Zhu controlled about 40% of China Venture Capital's outstanding shares.

As part of the deal, from December 1998 to May 1999, Lu began to build up his inventory of stock, buying first primarily from Zhu and eventually arranging to purchase 34.61% of the restricted shares owned by the government and assuming complete control of the board of directors. Now, Lu was ready to start the manipulation of the China Venture Capital stock in earnest. First, Lu was able to mislead the investing public with various company press releases, thereby significantly increasing the stock price. Second, Lu actively used large-size "wash trades" to increase the stock price and to produce the impression of high trading volume.[3] Apparently, Lu gave specific instructions to his head trader to execute buy trades to attract attention and to execute sell trades while avoiding attention. As a result of this manipulation, the stock price reached over ¥84 per share. Lu then took over other companies and formed new business ventures using the stock of China Venture Capital to finance his acquisitions.

Eventually, the scheme collapsed when traders and investors began to learn the truth. Interestingly, Lu facilitated the collapse by doing an interview with a reputable finance and economics magazine, which ultimately cast light on the deception. China Venture Capital's stock price rapidly sank back to ¥10. While Lu was under house arrest, he managed to escape, and his whereabouts are unknown to this day.

Although this box is about China, it is important to note that price manipulation may occur in many less developed markets. For example, Asia Khwaja and Atif Mian (2003) demonstrate that brokers in Pakistan earn significantly higher returns on their trades than on trades intermediated for outside investors. They use detailed transactions to show that the returns are due to a "pump and dump" price manipulation scheme.

Order-driven Trading Systems

In an **order-driven trading system**, orders are batched together and then auctioned off at an equilibrium market price. Such an auction may happen once per day, a few times per day, or more continuously. A good example of an order-driven system is the Tokyo Stock Exchange (TSE), which is the largest exchange in Japan. The TSE lacks market makers. Instead, trading

---

[1]This box is based on Guojun Wu and J. He (2003).

[2]The currency symbol ¥ stands for yuan and coincides with the symbol for Japanese yen. The Chinese currency is more formally referred to as the renminbi, and the ISO currency code is CNY.

[3]A *wash trade* is a strategy of simultaneously buying and selling the same stock. Of course, when the manipulator sells, he hopes the stock price does not drop by more than the amount it went up when shares were bought.

happens electronically and automatically, and orders are matched according to the following precedence rules, which are standard on order-driven markets:

- *Price priority:* The highest bid (buy) and the lowest ask (sell) have priority over all other orders.
- *Time priority:* Orders at the same price are treated on a first-come, first-served basis.
- *Order priority:* Market orders (orders to buy or sell at the market price) have priority over limit orders (orders to buy or sell at a maximum or minimum price).

The NYSE is an interesting combination of a price-driven system and an order-driven system. Each stock is assigned to a single specialist, who is physically located at one of the exchange's trading posts on the trading floor. The specialist acts as an auctioneer, setting a market-opening price based on an auction. The specialist also maintains a book of limit orders (called a **limit order book**). These are orders collected from floor brokers and from an electronic system called Super Dot. If the specialist does not intervene in the market to trade on her own behalf, the transaction price is determined in a simple auction process involving the limit order book and the trading crowd (floor brokers and specialists at the trading post). However, the specialist is also a market maker and can trade for her own account.

Automation and Electronic Trading

Over the past two decades, stock trading has become increasingly computerized and automated. In order-driven systems, it is straightforward to automate the trading rules adopted by the exchange to arrive at transaction prices. By recording all orders and making them public instantly, automation could appear to contribute greatly to the transparency of the market. However, this transparency has costs because of the presence of two types of traders: liquidity traders and informed traders. Liquidity traders trade for exogenous reasons, not because they have private information regarding the value of a stock. Examples of liquidity traders include retail investors who need money for a down payment on a house, pension funds or mutual funds that must invest their participants' inflows and reinvest dividends received, and index funds that track particular stock market indexes and consequently must trade the whole portfolio of stocks in the indexes. Informed traders trade on the basis of private information regarding the value of the stock.

An automated system with an open order book allows informed traders to wait behind their screens for the incoming orders of uninformed traders to obtain better pricing. Informed traders are themselves reluctant to reveal their information and consequently do not enter large orders (usually called a block) into an automatic trading system. In many countries, blocks of stock are therefore traded "upstairs," meaning in the offices away from the floor and via telephone through negotiation rather than through an automated system.

The first European stock exchange to adopt an electronic trading system was the Paris Bourse, with its CAC (*Cotation Assistée et Continue*) system, which was later replaced by the NSC (*Nouveau Système de Cotation*), or Super-Cac. The market is fully automated, and there is no longer any floor trading. The Paris Bourse does allow block trades to be negotiated outside the NSC. Germany has multiple exchanges, but the largest one by far is the Frankfurt Stock Exchange, operated by the Deutsche Börse. Here, floor trading (used especially for block trading and for less active stocks) and an electronic, automatic trading system (XETRA, or Exchange Electronic Trading) coexist. In Tokyo, the system of floor trading described earlier now coexists with a new automatic execution system. In 1997, the London Stock Exchange also introduced an order-driven electronic trading system known as SETS (Stock Exchange Electronic Service). While SETS is used for major British stocks with large transaction volume, the SEAQ system remains in force for all stocks.

The United States, in fact, has been a bit behind on the automation front. The specialist system with human interaction and expert judgment still accounts for the bulk of NYSE trading, but as of January 24, 2007, all NYSE stocks can also be traded via its electronic Hybrid Market. Customers can now send orders for immediate electronic execution. The SEC also approved a system whereby the U.S. exchanges and the NASDAQ must electronically disseminate transaction data within 90 seconds of a trade execution. In addition, since 1993, all exchange members must report all transactions conducted outside business hours or in foreign markets.

Even though the NYSE isn't fully automated, private electronic communication networks (ECNs) have rapidly developed in the United States. An ECN lists the prices of securities trading on other exchanges and either lets its subscribers trade directly with one another or uses some form of an order-crossing network. As a result, investors get slightly better buy and sell prices. Examples of ECNs are INSTINET, a member of the Reuters family of companies, and POSIT, from the Investment Technology Group (ITG).

The Globalization of Exchanges

As mentioned at the outset of the chapter, Nokia and other companies list their shares on several exchanges around the world. This is called **cross-listing**, and it is an important phenomenon that has led to the globalization of exchanges during the past two decades. Exchanges have also managed to achieve a measure of globalization simply by extending their trading hours to make their markets more accessible to foreign traders located in other time zones. In addition, some exchanges have merged or created alliances with foreign exchanges to automatically cross-list their stocks. For example, because electronic trading systems all over Europe drastically reduced the cost of trading on all national stock markets relative to SEAQ, SEAQ subsequently sought to form alliances with other, more-automated exchanges.

In 2000, the stock exchanges of Amsterdam, Brussels, and Paris merged to form Euronext. Euronext then absorbed the Lisbon exchange and LIFFE, the London derivatives market. Euronext became a company listed in Paris. Its goal was to provide a pool of liquidity through a common order book, one set of clearing hours, a single settlement procedure, and one screen-based electronic system for any company listed with one of the exchanges that are part of Euronext. The main competition of Euronext on the European continent is Eurex, which combines the German and Swiss exchanges.

In March 2007, consolidation took a big leap forward with the merger of the NYSE and Euronext to form a new company called NYSE Euronext, Inc. The consolidation is primarily a response to an increasingly competitive environment where exchanges face competition from other exchanges and alternative trading systems. Such competition has also driven another major trend that will make mergers even easier going forward: **demutualization**. *Demutualization* refers to the process of converting exchanges from nonprofit, member-owned organizations to for-profit investor-owned, and typically publicly traded companies. Examples include the Australian Stock Exchange (1998), the Toronto Stock Exchange (2000), Euronext (2000), NASDAQ (2000), and the NYSE (2005).

Turnover and Transaction Costs

The last columns in Exhibit 12.1 list turnover in 1991, 2000, and 2005. **Turnover** is the total volume of trade done on an exchange (measured in dollars) during the year divided by the exchange's total market capitalization (also in dollars) at the end of the year. For example, if every share traded exactly once during the year on an exchange, turnover would be 1, or 100%. Turnover is often considered to be an indicator of liquidity, although it can also simply reflect the arrival of news that instigates trades. The United States has the highest turnover of all the countries, followed by Spain, Italy, Germany, and the United Kingdom, which all have turnover rates of over 100%. In contrast, small markets, such as Austria and Belgium, and newer markets, such as Bermuda and Kuwait, have much smaller turnover.

Turnover is inversely related to the costs of trading stocks because high trading costs cause investors to trade less. **Trading costs** can be split up into three components. First, the investor making a trade may have to pay brokerage commissions and other fees, but these are typically relatively small, especially for large orders. Second, securities have bid and ask prices, so the investor must buy from the trader at the trader's high sell price and must sell to the trader at the trader's low bid price. Third, when the market is not very liquid, and an investor's trade is a relatively large one, it can adversely affect the price the investor gets (that is, cause it to rise when the investor buys or to fall when the investor sells). This latter effect is called **market impact**.

Market impact costs are difficult to estimate. Exhibit 12.3 shows the estimated total trading costs for developed markets using two different sources. The first estimates of costs, broken down by market capitalization, are from Salomon Smith Barney for 2000. The total cost combines half the bid–ask spread and an estimate of the market impact cost. The markets with the smallest transactions costs are the United States, France, the Netherlands, Spain, Finland, and Switzerland. The trading costs for large stocks in these countries are lower than 20 basis points. So, for a trade involving $100,000 of stock, transactions costs are less than $200. The trading costs for small-cap stocks are significantly larger in most countries, primarily because they have much wider bid–ask spreads.

The last column in Exhibit 12.3 reports average trading costs over the course of a 2-year period. The estimated costs include brokerage commissions, bid–ask spreads, and market impact costs. Seven countries have trading costs of less than 40 basis points: Belgium, France,

Exhibit 12.3 Trading Costs in Developed Markets

	Large-Cap Stocks			Small-Cap Stocks			Alternative Marketwide Estimate
	Bid/Ask	Market Impact	Total	Bid/Ask	Market Impact	Total	
Australia	19	18	37	52	12	64	54.7
Austria	28	27	55	37	14	51	43.8
Belgium	27	19	46	59	18	77	35.0
Canada	23	21	44	63	17	80	52.4
Denmark	54	42	96	82	14	96	40.7
Finland	9	10	19	68	17	85	43.4
France	10	7	17	33	10	43	29.5
Germany	35	8	43	43	33	76	37.7
Greece	25	58	83	56	39	95	65.5
Hong Kong	45	27	72	63	28	91	59.8
Ireland	48	139	187	120	48	168	130.7
Italy	15	11	26	26	11	37	34.8
Japan	20	17	37	21	19	40	41.3
The Netherlands	9	5	14	20	6	26	42.2
New Zealand	53	42	95	60	33	93	47.2
Norway	32	32	64	59	32	91	44.6
Portugal	12	20	32	26	7	33	62.7
Singapore	44	34	78	63	35	98	77.5
Spain	8	7	15	21	9	30	41.9
Sweden	18	14	32	48	11	59	35.8
Switzerland	7	5	12	27	7	34	38.5
UK	27	9	36	79	9	88	54.5
U.S.	11	8	19	27	10	37	38.1
Average	**25**	**25**	**50**	**50**	**19**	**69**	**50.1**

Notes: Columns (2) through (7) are taken from E. Sorensen and L. Price (2000) and are based on a transaction costs survey carried out by Salomon Smith Barney in 2000. The last column is from a study by Ian Domowitz, Jack Glen, and Ananth Madhavan (2000). The cost reported includes the three components of transactions costs: direct fees, bid–ask spreads, and an estimate of price impact. The data are based on average costs collected for September 1996 through December 1998 by Elkins/McSherry (See Elkins/McSherry.com).

Italy, Germany, the United States, Sweden, and Switzerland; only one country (France) has trading costs lower than 30 basis points. Whereas the relative rankings of the countries' trading costs in the two studies do not match exactly, they are qualitatively consistent with one another. It may surprise you that the United States does not have the lowest trading costs, but the totals are averages across all markets, encompassing both the very low-cost NYSE and the, back then, somewhat more expensive NASDAQ market (see Hendrik Bessembinder, 1998).

Research has shown that trading costs are "priced." That is, stocks with otherwise similar characteristics and promised cash flows trade at different prices when their trading costs and liquidity are different. Investors demand a higher expected return on stocks with higher trading costs or lower liquidity, and hence the prices of these stocks are lower. The cross-country differences in trading costs therefore provide an incentive to international firms to list their stocks on exchanges with lower transaction costs. Cross-listing may reduce their expected return, increase their stock prices, and thus lower their costs of capital.

Emerging Stock Markets

In the early 1990s, emerging countries began embarking on a trade and financial liberalization process. They relaxed restrictions on the foreign ownership of assets and improved the regulation of their capital markets. The results were dramatic. Not only did capital flows to emerging markets increase dramatically, but their composition changed substantially, as equity and fixed income investments increasingly replaced commercial bank debt. For example, in 1985, Mexico's equity market capitalization was 0.71% of GDP, and it was only accessible by foreigners through the Mexico Fund traded on the NYSE. In 2001, Mexico's equity market capitalization rose to over 20% of GDP, and U.S. investors directly held about 25% of the market. (See Geert Bekaert and Campbell Harvey, 2003, for more details about the liberalization process in emerging markets.)

Stock Market Size

The stock markets of developing countries are often referred to as **emerging markets**, and the young stock markets of the least developed countries are called **frontier markets**. Exhibit 12.4 shows the sizes of various emerging and frontier markets.

In 1991, the largest emerging and frontier markets, each representing between 0.85% and 1.50% of world market capitalization, were Mexico, Korea, South Africa, and Taiwan. At that time, because of a political boycott, foreigners were not able to invest in South Africa (making its shares not "investable"), and its stock was not part of any established index. South Africa is one of the largest emerging markets today, representing 1.24% of world market capitalization in 2005. India has thousands of companies listed on its 24 exchanges, but Korea and Russia are larger in terms of market capitalization. Taiwan remains one of the larger emerging markets, representing 1.07% of world market capitalization.

Overall, emerging markets did not perform as well as the U.S. stock market in the 1990s, which is reflected in the overall lower percentage of market capitalizations by 2000. A big exception is China, which now has three different stock exchanges—in Shanghai, Shenzhen, and Hong Kong. The Hong Kong market has been in existence so long and Hong Kong is sufficiently high income that it is actually considered a developed market.

Emerging markets are extremely volatile. Consequently, the relative returns earned on these exchanges can vary greatly. For example, the wave of currency crises in Southeast Asia in the 1990s halted the spectacular growth of markets there. Similarly, the stock markets in Argentina and Brazil fell by 48.72 % and 30.66%, respectively, amid the economic crisis in 2002.[4] But prior to that crisis, the two exchanges had risen rapidly in size. In both 2003 and 2005, many emerging markets dramatically increased in value, explaining why for many emerging markets, the percentage market capitalization relative to world market capitalization has increased since 2000.

---

[4]These numbers were computed from the MSCI indices.

Exhibit 12.4 Market Characteristics in Emerging Markets

Market Capitalization in Millions of U.S. Dollars

	1991 (% of world total)		2000 (% of world total)		2005 (% of world total)	
Argentina	18,509	0.16%	166,068	0.51%	95,960	0.22%
Bahrain		0.00%	6,624	0.02%	17,365	0.04%
Bangladesh	269	0.00%	1,186	0.00%	3,300	0.01%
Botswana	261	0.00%	978	0.00%	2,257	0.01%
Brazil	42,759	0.38%	226,152	0.70%	474,647	1.07%
Bulgaria		0.00%	617	0.00%	5,086	0.01%
Chile	27,984	0.25%	60,401	0.19%	136,493	0.31%
China	2,028	0.02%	580,991	1.80%	295,754	0.67%
Colombia	4,036	0.04%	9,560	0.03%	42,498	0.10%
Costa Rica		0.00%	2,029	0.01%	1,511	0.00%
Cote d'Ivoire	541	0.00%	1,185	0.00%	1,854	0.00%
Croatia		0.00%	2,742	0.01%	12,918	0.03%
Czech Repub.		0.00%	11,002	0.03%	34,886	0.08%
Egypt	2,651	0.02%	28,741	0.09%	79,509	0.18%
Estonia		0.00%	1,846	0.01%	389	0.00%
Ghana	76	0.00%	502	0.00%	10,094	0.02%
Greece	13,118	0.10%	110,839	0.34%	145,121	0.33%
Hungary	505	0.00%	12,204	0.04%	32,576	0.07%
India	47,730	0.42%	148,064	0.46%	1,069,046	2.40%
Indonesia	6,823	0.05%	28,834	0.08%	81,428	0.18%
Iran	34,282	0.30%	34,041	0.11%	36,440	0.08%
Israel	6,176	0.05%	64,081	0.20%	122,578	0.28%
Jamaica	1,034	0.01%	3,582	0.01%	6,643	0.01%
Jordan	2,512	0.02%	4,943	0.02%	37,644	0.08%
Kazakhstan		0.00%	1,342	0.00%	10,529	0.02%
Kenya	453	0.00%	1,283	0.00%	6,384	0.01%
Korea	96,373	0.85%	171,587	0.53%	718,011	1.61%
Latvia		0.00%	563	0.00%	775	0.00%
Lebanon		0.00%	1,583	0.00%	4,810	0.01%
Lithuania		0.00%	1,588	0.00%	5,099	0.01%
Malaysia	58,627	0.52%	116,935	0.36%	180,518	0.41%
Malta		0.00%	2,009	0.01%	4,097	0.01%
Mauritius	312	0.00%	1,331	0.00%	2,330	0.01%
Mexico	98,178	0.87%	125,204	0.39%	239,128	0.05%
Morocco	1,528	0.01%	10,899	0.03%	27,220	0.06%
Namibia		0.00%	311	0.00%	121,338	0.27%
Nigeria	1,882	0.02%	4,237	0.01%	22,244	0.05%
Oman		0.00%	3,463	0.01%	15,269	0.03%
Pakistan		0.00%	6,581	0.02%	45,317	0.10%
Panama		0.00%	2,794	0.01%	5,963	0.01%
Papua N.G.		0.00%		0.00%	6,138	0.01%
Peru	1,118	0.01%	10,562	0.03%	24,140	0.05%
Philippines	11,386	0.10%	51,554	0.16%	39,818	0.09%
Poland	144	0.00%	31,279	0.10%	93,602	0.21%
Romania		0.00%	1,069	0.00%	15,858	0.04%
Russia	244	0.00%	38,922	0.12%	604,210	1.36%

(continued)

Exhibit 12.4 (continued)

Market Capitalization in Millions of U.S. Dollars

	1991 (% of world total)		2000 (% of world total)		2005 (% of world total)	
Saudi Arabia	48,213	0.42%	67,171	0.21%	650,107	1.46%
Serbia		0.00%		0.00%	5,365	0.01%
Slovakia		0.00%	742	0.00%	2,458	0.01%
Slovenia		0.00%	2,547	0.01%	7,899	0.02%
South Africa	168,497	1.49%	204,952	0.64%	549,310	1.24%
Sri Lanka	1,936	0.02%	1,074	0.00%	5,720	0.01%
Swaziland	27	0.00%	73	0.00%	196	0.00%
Taiwan	124,864	1.10%	247,602	0.77%	476,018	1.07%
Thailand	35,815	0.32%	29,489	0.09%	123,885	0.28%
Trin. & Tobago	671	0.01%	4,330	0.01%	9,982	0.02%
Turkey	15,703	0.14%	69,659	0.22%	161,538	0.36%
Ukraine		0.00%	1,881	0.01%	6,820	0.02%
Venezuela	11,214	0.10%	8,128	0.03%	5,475	0.01%
Zambia		0.00%	236	0.00%	2,517	0.01%
Zimbabwe	1,394	0.01%	2,432	0.01%	1,094	0.00%
World Total	**11,345,733**		**32,260,433**		**44,459,895**	

	Turnover			Market Concentration	
	1991	2000	2005	2000	2005
Argentina	0.26	0.04	0.08	67.6	80.6
Bahrain		0.04	0.04	82.4	
Bangladesh	0.01	0.65	0.06		
Botswana	0.03	0.05			
Brazil	0.31	0.45	0.35	34.6	52.4
Bulgaria		0.09	0.15		
Chile	0.07	0.10	0.14	67.6	45.6
China	0.40	1.24	0.79	9.5	32.6
Colombia	0.05	0.04	0.16	68.0	62.8
Costa Rica		0.00	0.13		
Cote d'Ivoire	0.01	0.03			
Croatia		0.07	0.06		
Czech Repub		0.60	1.17	97.6	
Egypt	0.05	0.39	0.33	48.0	47.3
Estonia		0.18			
Ghana	0.00	0.02	0.01		
Greece	0.19	0.86	0.45	24.6	57.6
Hungary	0.23	1.01	0.74	88.9	95.5
India	0.48	3.44	0.44	48.9	36.5
Indonesia	0.43	0.53	0.51	44.3	53.2
Iran	0.15	0.15	0.22		37.0
Israel	1.36	0.37	0.40	58.3	47.6
Jamaica	0.09	0.02			
Jordan	0.17	0.08	0.63	58.3	
Kazakhstan		0.07	0.10		
Kenya	0.02	0.04	0.08		
Korea	0.89	6.22	1.69	18.4	40.2

Exhibit 12.4 (continued)

	Turnover			Market Concentration	
	1991	**2000**	**2005**	**2000**	**2005**
Latvia		0.40			
Lebanon		0.07	0.19		
Lithuania		0.13			
Malaysia	0.18	0.50	0.29	19.9	36.8
Malta		0.09	0.04		99.0
Mauritius	0.02	0.06	0.07		86.3
Mexico	0.32	0.36	0.24	66.5	63.5
Morocco	0.03	0.10	0.29	74.5	
Namibia		0.07	0.00		
Nigeria	0.00	0.06	0.09	53.8	
Oman		0.16	0.24	54.6	
Pakistan		5.01	3.10	91.9	
Panama		0.06	0.05		
Papua N.G.			0.00		
Peru	0.12	0.14	0.11	67.9	62.2
Philippines	0.13	0.16	0.18	42.7	60.8
Poland	0.19	0.47	0.33	25.1	65.1
Romania		0.22	0.16		
Russia		0.52	0.24	93.9	
Saudi Arabia	0.05	0.26	1.70	67.3	
Serbia			0.10		
Slovakia		1.21	0.03	43.0	
Slovenia		0.18	0.17		63.8
South Africa	0.05	0.38	0.37	30.9	44.1
Sri Lanka	0.05	0.13	0.19	68.5	51.1
Swaziland	0.00	0.00	0.00		
Taiwan	2.93	3.97	1.23	29.5	34.9
Thailand	0.84	0.79	0.77	37.7	47.1
Trin. & Tobago	0.12	0.03			
Turkey	0.55	2.57	1.24	43.3	50.8
Ukraine		0.15			
Venezuela	0.29	0.08	0.05	67.0	
Zambia		0.03	0.01		
Zimbabwe	0.06	0.11		47.6	

Notes: Computations are based on data from the World Federation of Exchanges, Datastream, and the S&P/IFC database.

If we go back to Exhibit 12.2, we can see the size of the stock markets relative to the size of the economies. Generally, the ratios of stock market capitalization to GDP are smaller in emerging markets than in developed markets. In fact, market capitalization to GDP is often viewed as an indicator of stock market development. From this perspective, the best-developed emerging and frontier stock markets are South Africa, Malaysia, India, Taiwan, Chile, and Korea, with ratios of over 100%. Chile is the only Latin American country on this list. Its stock market development has been bolstered by a social security system that forces workers to save for retirement through several investment funds.

Transaction Costs and Liquidity in Emerging Markets

Transaction costs and liquidity differ greatly across emerging markets. For example, Exhibit 12.4 shows that Taiwan and Israel have unusually large turnover. In 1991, only four markets had turnover exceeding 0.50, and they were primarily located in Asia (Israel, Korea, Taiwan, and Thailand). India was the country with the fifth-largest turnover (0.48). Today, however, some of the new markets also exhibit large turnover, especially in Eastern Europe. More than 10 countries now have turnover larger than 0.50. The five countries with the highest turnover for 2005 were Pakistan, Saudi Arabia, Korea, Turkey, and Taiwan.

Exhibit 12.4 also reports the market capitalization represented by the 10 most actively traded stocks. This is a measure of market concentration. Most developed markets have low market concentration. For example, in the United States, the 10 most active stocks represent less than 10% of total market capitalization. Exhibit 12.4 shows that the 10 most active stocks in most emerging markets represent around 50% of market capitalization. The figure exceeds 90% in Malta and Hungary. Generally, the Latin American markets appear more concentrated than the Southeast Asian markets.

Exhibit 12.5 shows estimates of total trading costs for a number of emerging markets. It is immediately apparent that transaction costs in emerging markets are significantly higher than in developing markets. The average trading cost across the emerging markets is 97 basis points, whereas it is only 50 basis points, on average, for developed countries. Even within emerging markets, transaction costs are negatively correlated with the size and development of the market. A surprising exception is Korea, one of the premier emerging markets, which features very high trading costs, primarily because of high market impact costs. Emerging markets with relatively low transaction costs, below 70 basis points, are Brazil, Greece, Mexico, and Turkey.

Exhibit 12.5 Trading Costs in Emerging Markets

Country	Total Trading Costs, 1996–1998
Argentina	76.9
Brazil	58.0
Chile	84.3
Colombia	97.5
Czech Republic	143.7
Greece	65.5
Hungary	143.4
India	71.6
Indonesia	100.9
Korea	197.5
Malaysia	88.7
Mexico	61.7
Peru	95.8
Philippines	112.7
South Africa	81.6
Taiwan	74.6
Thailand	89.1
Turkey	64.6
Venezuela	134.1
Average	**97.0**

Notes: The data are taken from Ian Domowitz, Jack Glen, and Ananth Madhavan (2000) and represent average one-way equity trading costs for September 1996 to December 1998. The original data were provided by Elkins/McSherry Co. The trading costs are expressed in basis points.

Research by Geert Bekaert, Campbell Harvey, and Christian Lundblad (2007) suggests that financial liberalization in emerging markets has significantly lowered transaction costs and that higher transaction costs are associated with higher costs of capital. This provides a powerful incentive for firms in emerging markets to cross-list stocks in more liquid, developed markets.

Casablanca: From a Sleepy Place to a Thriving Modern Market?[5]

Casablanca typically conjures up the image of the classic movie, starring Humphrey Bogart as Rick Blaine, an American who runs Rick's Café Americain in Casablanca, Morocco. In the early days of World War II, Morocco was a French protectorate and was thus under German control. There was active trading in "letters of transit" that allowed the bearer to travel around German-controlled Europe and to neutral Lisbon, Portugal, and then to the United States. Gambling was tolerated, although it was officially banned; and special discounts were extended to Rick's friends. In short, Rick's Café could serve as a good metaphor for an emerging market: Just as Rick could "fix" the roulette wheel to help his friends, so it may be that trading practices in emerging markets are not as fair as in the developed world.

The Casablanca Stock Exchange (CSE) is a typical emerging financial market that went through momentous change between 1990 and 2000. In the 1980s, the Moroccan stock exchange was a backwater in many ways. It was a state institution, with very few listed stocks and almost no participation of individual investors in the stock market. Institutional investors would often trade blocks on the upstairs market, but this upstairs market—in which trades were based on mutual agreements—was neither transparent nor standardized. The exchange was extremely illiquid, and most stocks did not trade for weeks. Foreign investors were not prohibited from buying Moroccan stock, but foreigners stayed away because of the archaic structure, the low trading volume, and the possibilities of market manipulation.

In 1989, Morocco announced an ambitious privatization and economic liberalization program, which also included financial market reforms that would greatly alter the operation of the stock exchange starting in 1993. The stock exchange was privatized and reformed. The reforms created a dealer/market-maker structure in which more disclosure was required from both listed companies and market makers.

The new reforms began to attract foreign investors, and in 1996, the CSE was included in the International Finance Corporation (IFC) emerging markets database. The number of individual investors increased considerably, reaching 300,000 in 1996. Exhibit 12.6 shows that these reforms had a profound effect on the stock market. Trading volume and liquidity exploded. Finally, on December 17, 1996, the CSE adopted the screen-driven trading system of the Paris Bourse. It is generally believed that such structural changes should greatly affect the quality of the market and lower its cost of trading. There is no doubt, as Exhibit 12.6 amply illustrates, that the reforms immediately increased turnover and liquidity, but did trading costs fall? Unfortunately, researchers do not have data on bid–ask spreads, let alone estimates of market impact. However, two researchers, Eric Ghysels and Mouna Cherkaoui (2003), nonetheless attempted to infer what the trading costs were, using the trading data of several stocks before and after the reforms. Surprisingly, Ghysels and Cherkaoui found that, at least until 1996, trading costs on the CSE actually increased after the reforms.

There are multiple interpretations of these results. Let's round up the usual suspects. First, although liquidity improved, until 1996, the CSE remained a relatively illiquid market compared to other markets, and trading was thin. Second, foreign investors (especially new arrivals) are sometimes among the least informed of market participants. *Casablanca* presents a case in point: When Captain Renault asks Rick what an ex-pat like him is doing in

---

[5]The analysis in this box builds heavily on the article by Eric Ghysels and Mouna Cherkaoui (2003).

Exhibit 12.6 Casablanca Stock Exchange: Basic Indicators

Year	Number of Trading Sessions	Average Daily Trading Volume	Total Market Capitalization	Ratio of Market Capitalization to GDP	Market Index
1989	248	123	5.0	2.6	122.65
1990	244	510	7.8	3.5	158.68
1991	243	428	12.4	5.0	187.55
1992	248	626	17.0	6.6	207.88
1993	248	4,611	25.7	10.0	259.78
1994	251	7,235	39.0	13.1	342.39
1995	251	20,730	50.4	17.5	342.39
1996	247	19,510	75.6	23.0	447.13

Notes: From Ghysels and Cherkaoui (2003). The entries to the table provide annual summary statistics of basic indicators. The average daily volume is in millions of Moroccan dirhams (MAD), the local currency. The total market capitalization is expressed in billions of MAD, and the market index value is taken on the last day of the year.

Casablanca, he answers that he came for his health, saying, "I came to Casablanca for the waters." Renault exclaims, "The waters? What waters? We're in the desert!" Rick laconically replies, "I was misinformed." Likewise, perhaps CSE dealers possessed a tremendous amount of market power relative to foreign traders and were able to pass along higher costs to them. A third possibility is that the Ghysels and Cherkaoui model misestimated true trading costs.

If the results are accurate, however, there are a few important lessons from this detailed example. First, jumps in turnover and trading are not necessarily associated with lower trading costs, although they typically are. Second, although reforms might encourage foreign investors to participate in a market, by themselves, they do not seem to bring down trading costs. What might have an effect on trading costs, however, is automated trading. Only after screen-driven trading was introduced to the CSE in late 1996 did transaction costs fall. Research by Ian Domowitz, Jack Glen, and Ananth Madhavan (2000) shows more generally that automated systems are associated with lower costs.

12.2 INTERNATIONAL CROSS-LISTING AND DEPOSITARY RECEIPTS

An increasing number of MNCs are finding ways to broaden their investor bases and raise capital by cross-listing their shares on foreign exchanges. For example, Royal Dutch Shell is headquartered in Amsterdam and is listed on the Amsterdam, London, and New York exchanges. Novartis, a pharmaceutical company headquartered in Basel, Switzerland, is traded on the Swiss Exchange in Zurich and in New York.

The number of cross-listed firms grew quickly in the 1990s. Exhibit 12.7 shows the percentage of total turnover due to trading of foreign companies in various countries. In London, 42% of trading pertains to foreign companies. Other markets with large foreign presence include the Swiss exchange, the Johannesburg Stock Exchange in South Africa, and the Argentinean stock exchange.

In the 1990s, cross-listing grew the fastest in the United States, especially at the NYSE. However, the 2002 Sarbanes-Oxley Act, aimed at improving corporate governance and accounting standards (see Chapter 1), proved quite costly, and the NYSE has seen fewer and

Exhibit 12.7 Percentage of Turnover by Foreign, Cross-Listed Companies

Exchange	Turnover Percentage	Exchange	Turnover Percentage
Americas		Oslo Børs	13.40
Mexican Exchange	16.33	Spanish Exchanges (BME)	0.83
Nasdaq	5.93	Swiss Exchange[b]	93.11
NYSE	8.77	Tehran SE	0.00
TSX Group Toronto	0.37	Tel Aviv SE	0.00
Buenos Aires SE	37.65	Vienna	2.42
Colombia SE	0.00	Warsaw SE	1.20
Lima SE	11.25		
Santiago SE	0.10	**Asia—Pacific**	
Sao Paulo SE	0.07	Australian SE	4.13
		Colombo SE	0.00
Europe—Africa—Middle East		Hong Kong Exchanges	0.14
Athens Exchange	3.45	Bombay SE	0.00
Budapest SE	0.00	National Stock Exchange India	0.00
Deutsche Börse	9.77	Jakarta SE	0.00
Euronext	0.50	Korea Exchange[c]	0.00
Irish SE	3.87	Bursa Malaysia	1.43
Istanbul SE	0.00	New Zealand Exchange	8.57
Borsa Italiana	5.07	Osaka SE	0.03
JSE South Africa	24.91	Philippine SE	0.16
Ljubljana SE	0.00	Shanghai SE	0.00
London SE	41.95	Shenzhen SE	0.00
Luxembourg SE	1.26	Taiwan SE Corp.	0.09
Malta SE	0.00	Thailand SE	0.00
Mauritius SE	15.03	Tokyo SE	0.03
OMX[a]	5.13		

Notes: The data are for the first 7 months of 2006 and were provided by the World Federation of Exchanges (http://www.world-exchanges.org). Due to different reporting rules and calculation methods, turnover figures across changes are not entirely comparable.

[a]OMX includes the Copenhagen, Helsinki, Stockholm, Tallinn, Riga, and Vilnius Stock Exchanges.

[b]Swiss Exchange turnover also includes shares traded on Virt-x.

[c]Korea Exchange includes Kosdaq market data.

fewer foreign firms cross-list, while some existing firms have de-listed. For example, in 2007, SGL, a German graphite and carbon fiber materials maker, de-listed from the NYSE in order to cut the costs associated with complying with Sarbanes-Oxley regulations.

How Do Firms Cross-list?

Companies seeking a listing overseas must satisfy two requirements. First, they must comply with the standards set for cross-listing by the exchanges. For example, the Tokyo Stock Exchange listing criteria and associated fees are steeper for non-Japanese companies than for domestic companies. Second, a company that wants to cross-list must adhere to the securities regulations of the country in which it wants to list its shares. This may require registering with the country's securities commission and reconciling the company's financial accounts with the market standards of that nation.

Cross-listed stocks can be traded directly on a national stock market, but most often they are traded in the form of a depositary receipt. A **depositary receipt (DR)** represents a number of original shares held in custody by a financial institution in the country of the exchange. The best-known depositary receipts are American depositary receipts (ADRs) and global depositary receipts (GDRs), which we discuss next.

American Depositary Receipts

An **American Depositary Receipt (ADR)** represents a specific number of shares in the home market that are held in custody by a U.S. depositary bank. The depositary bank converts all dividends and other payments into U.S. dollars and charges a small custodial fee for its services. The Bank of New York dominates the ADR custodial market, with a market share of well over 50%, but JPMorgan Chase, Citibank, and Deutsche Bank are also important players. Whereas most non-U.S. companies use ADRs, a minority of companies, mostly Canadian ones, use ordinary listings, which means they are traded entirely like U.S. companies and face very similar SEC registration and adherence to the reporting requirements of U.S. generally accepted accounting principles (GAAP).

Types of ADRs

The listing of foreign shares in the United States is subject to a detailed set of rules. Exhibit 12.8 gives an overview of the various types of ADRs and the rules that apply to them. Generally speaking, requirements involve registering with the SEC and furnishing an annual report with a reconciliation of financial accounts with GAAP.

A major distinction among the types of ADRs is whether the listing is associated with raising capital in the United States. No new capital is being raised when firms list a Level I or Level II ADR. That is, no new shares are being issued by the company. Only existing shares are being traded. **Level I ADRs** trade over the counter (OTC) in New York in what is called **pink sheet trading** and are not listed on a major U.S. stock exchange. The OTC market is composed of a network of broker/dealers who complete transactions via telephone or computer rather than in a centralized marketplace. (Pink sheets are weekly publications covering OTC securities and their market makers.) Level I ADRs face few requirements. They must register with the SEC but are not required to comply with GAAP. Basically, the firms file their home country accounting statements with adequate English translations. **Level II ADRs** trade on the NYSE, the NASDAQ, or the AMEX, and hence must satisfy the exchange's listing requirements. Firms issuing Level II ADRs must register with the SEC and must also file a form to comply with GAAP ("Form 20-F"). Typically, a firm first uses a Level I ADR. Then, it moves to a Level II.

Exhibit 12.8 Types of ADRs

	Description	Trading Location	GAAP Requirement	Percent of Current ADRs/Total Number
Level I	Unlisted	OTC pink sheets	No GAAP reconciliation required	54%/1,084
Level II	Listed on major U.S. exchange	NYSE, AMEX, or NASDAQ	Only partial reconciliation for financials	
Level III	Offered and listed on major U.S. exchange	NYSE, AMEX, or NASDAQ	Full SEC compliance, including full U.S. GAAP reconciliation for financials	28%/576
Rule 144A (RADR)	Private U.S. placement to qualified institutional buyers (QIBs)	U.S. private placement market using PORTAL	No U.S. GAAP reconciliation required	18%/369

Note: Data are from Darius Miller (2000). The numbers in the last column apply to the end of the 1990s.

Level III ADRs trade on one of the major exchanges, and they are also issued to raise capital in the United States. This implies that the SEC disclosure and GAAP requirements are even more stringent. Finally, **Rule 144 ADRs (RADRs)** are capital-raising ADRs whereby the securities are privately placed with qualified institutional investors, such as pension funds and insurance companies. As a result, the SEC and GAAP requirements are minimal. The drawback is that RADRs are very illiquid, much like the private placements discussed in Chapter 11. RADRs can only trade through the PORTAL system, which is a screen-based automated trading system established by the National Association of Securities Dealers.

Another important distinction is between sponsored and unsponsored ADRs. Sponsored ADRs are created by the bank at the request of the foreign company that wants to cross-list. The sponsoring bank often offers ADR holders an assortment of services, including investment information and portions of the annual report, translated into English. The depositary fees are paid by the foreign company. Unsponsored ADRs are put in place by a U.S. financial institution, without the direct involvement of the foreign company. Consequently, the foreign company may not provide investment information on a regular basis or in a timely manner. ADR investors pay the depositary fees on unsponsored ADRs. Today, the bulk of depositary receipt programs are sponsored.

The Road to a Successful ADR Listing

The following 19 steps to a successful ADR listing in the United States are excerpted from "Solving the ADR Puzzle" (Bank of New York et al., 2002):

1. Appoint an independent accountant/auditor with expertise in international offerings and U.S. capital markets.
2. Appoint an external legal counsel specializing in U.S. securities law to advise on SEC filings, prospectus (if any), and other related matters.
3. If the listing involves a U.S. public offering, appoint an underwriter(s)/investment bank(s) with appropriate transaction experience, sector or industry knowledge, and U.S. distribution capabilities. Investment banks will often make a "pitch" for the underwriter role in what is known as a "beauty contest." An important consideration is the likelihood of good after-market support.
4. Appoint a depositary bank with a significant amount of ADR listing experience, appropriate infrastructure, a knowledgeable staff, and technical capabilities.
5. Select a financial printer, which will manage the confidential document creation, revision, SEC filings, printing, and distribution. If necessary, foreign-language translations can also be arranged by the financial printer.
6. Appoint an investor-relations firm that specializes in U.S. listings of non-U.S. companies. Seek an international communications firm with experience in advising and assisting non-U.S. companies. Choose a firm with free access to senior counselors in both the United States and your country.
7. Apply for an exchange listing with the exchange on which you wish to list your stock. The procedure will differ, depending on the exchange. For example, the application to the NYSE will also involve selecting a specialist firm.
8. If the listing involves a U.S. public offering, prepare Form F-1, a SEC registration statement required for any non-U.S. company making its first offering of securities in the United States. The document describes in detail the securities and the transaction being undertaken. It will have been in preparation for several months, and it will be submitted for review and comments by the SEC's corporate finance division together with the prospectus for the offering, if any.

9. Send deposit agreement and Form F-6, submitted by the depositary bank, to the company for review. The documentation describes in detail all the activities undertaken by the depositary bank as agent on behalf of the company and has by now become standard documentation.

10. Have the investor relations firm prepare for the listing day event with detailed recommendations, including a publicity strategy, which should include a tactical plan for special events and media tour aimed at key audiences in the United States and the domestic market.

11. If the listing involves a U.S. public offering, prepare a Red Herring (preliminary prospectus). The company and underwriters print preliminary copies of the prospectus, which will be used to sell the shares to potential investors. Final prices are not contained in this document.

12. File Form F-1 (offerings only). With full and final response to SEC comments, company and counsel make final revisions to the registration statement, which the financial printer will then file with the SEC.

13. Request a CUSIP number from Standard & Poor's. This is a security identification code that provides financial intermediaries with a uniform number that identifies a company through all phases of securities processing and recording. Underwriters request a unique security identification number for the new ADR from the requisite authority.

14. Finalize an exchange listing agreement. All parties agree to the documentation, and the issuer promises to abide by the regulations of the chosen stock exchange.

15. Agree with the depositary bank on the final details of the documentation, which is then filed with Form F-6 with the SEC for review and comments. The review usually takes about 4 weeks.

16. If the listing involves a U.S. public offering, the price of the issue must be determined. Underwriters make final decisions regarding the price of the issue, taking into consideration market conditions and investor demand.

17. If the listing involves a U.S. public offering, schedule the closing, which involves the company, its underwriters (if any), the depositary, and legal counsel for all parties. The underwriters transfer the proceeds for the share sale to the company (or other selling party), and the company transfers ordinary shares to the sub-custody account of the depositary.

18. Conduct listing day events. This may involve significant promotional activities and media coverage.

19. Trading of ADRs commences!

Global Depositary Receipts

Many of the ADRs discussed so far are also part of a **global depositary receipts (GDR)** program. GDRs are like ADRs, but they can trade across many markets and settle in the currency of each market. One important GDR program was Telmex, the Mexican telephone company, which in 1991 became the first-ever international offering of equity shares in a public utility by a developing country. As a more recent example, Deutsche Bank launched an unsponsored GDR program in 2002 for the shares of Bashneft, the seventh-largest crude oil producer in Russia.

Global depositary receipts are not always associated with existing companies seeking to increase their shareholder base and raise additional capital. They can also be associated with companies wanting to tap the equity market for the first time. Some companies issue stock locally but also target foreign investors, especially foreign institutional investors. When a firm issues shares in multiple foreign markets, sometimes simultaneously with distribution in the domestic market, the issue is part of the **Euro-equity market**. Like the Eurocurrency and Eurobond markets discussed in Chapter 11, the Euro-equity market involves international issues originated and sold anywhere in the world, even though **external equity market** would be a more appropriate name (see Chapter 6).

Recent research suggests that the primary equity markets have become more and more globalized, with over 15% of all IPOs of non-U.S. companies including a U.S. listing. The wave of privatizations of government enterprises that occurred in Europe in the 1980s and in emerging markets in the 1990s is an important factor behind this development. The accompanying equity issues—such as those of British Telecom in December 1984; YPF, Argentina's state-owned oil company, in 1993; and, more recently, many companies in Eastern Europe, such as Hungary's OTP Bank in 1995—are so large that it was desirable to involve foreign investors directly. Interestingly, it appears that involving U.S. investment banks in the IPO process as underwriters has benefits in that it leads to better (that is, higher) prices for the new shares.

Size and Growth of the Depositary Receipt Market[6]

While in the 1990s, ADRs dominated the cross-listing market, this has recently changed. Of a total of 1,984 sponsored depositary receipt programs outstanding at the end of 2006, 34% are still Level I ADRs, and 24% are U.S.-listed ADRs, but over 42% are now part of GDR programs.

There has been phenomenal growth in depositary receipt (DR) programs. According to data from the Bank of New York ("Depositary Receipts, 2006 Year-End Market Review," 2007), there have been between 85 and 189 new DR programs per year every year since 1992. Part of this growth was accounted for by firms from emerging markets attempting to raise capital in the largest capital market in the world, following large-scale liberalization programs in these countries. As of June 2006, the Bank of New York data indicate that India now accounts for more of the total outstanding DR programs than any other country. Along with India, the United Kingdom and Australia round out the top three countries. Russia, Taiwan, Hong Kong, and Brazil each account for 5% to 6% of the total number of DR programs.

Russian companies primarily list on the London Stock Exchange (LSE). In fact, non-U.S. stock exchanges, in particular Luxembourg and London, have become the most important listing markets, overtaking the United States. However, in terms of trading activity, the NYSE remains the largest market for DR trading by a substantial margin, representing nearly two-thirds of worldwide DR trading value in 2006.

Among the most actively traded DRs in the United States during 2006 were Nokia, the Finnish cell phone company; BP, the British oil company; Teva Pharmaceuticals, an Israeli pharmaceutical company; Baidu.com, a Chinese Internet company; and Petrobras, a Brazilian oil company.

POINT–COUNTERPOINT

The Pricing of Royal Dutch and Shell

Ante is poring over the financial pages of the newspaper, searching for the prices of the ADRs for Royal Dutch and Shell, when Freedy yells, "You're not still trying to find arbitrage opportunities, are you? You know international financial markets are efficient."

Ante replies, "You may think markets are efficient, but you haven't read this article by Ken Froot and Emile Dabora (1999) in the *Journal of Financial Economics*. They've really uncovered a whopper of an issue. I'm going to get rich!"

Ante then lays out the facts for Freedy: "A corporate charter has linked Royal Dutch Petroleum (RDP), a Dutch company, and Shell Transport and Trading (STT), a UK company,

---

[6]Most of the data discussed here are based on Bank of New York (2007).

since 1907. All the operating units of the two companies use the same brand name, Shell, and after cash distributions to shareholders are decided, 60% of the cash goes to RDP shareholders, and 40% goes to STT shareholders. This arrangement looks more like one company with two classes of equity. RDP is listed on nine exchanges in Europe, and its ADR trades on the NYSE in the United States. STT is listed in London, and its ADR also trades on the NYSE."

After Freedy hears the details, he asks, "So, what is the big deal? I suppose you've found some price discrepancies between the RDP price in Amsterdam and its ADR price in New York. Or is STT's London price not equal to its ADR price in New York? Which is it? You know, you've got to get the prices into a common currency, and the ADR may be for more than one share."

Ante replies, "Well, you're right about those issues. The price of one share of RDP in Amsterdam should be the price of one ADR share in New York multiplied by the €/$ exchange rate. Also, the STT ADR represents six STT shares in London, so $/ADR should equal $(\$/\pounds) \times (\pounds/\text{share}) \times 6$. When Froot and Dabora did those calculations, the prices were usually within 2% or 3% of each other. Plus, it was hard to get the timing of the quotes on the stocks, the ADRs, and the exchange rates all at the same time. So, I know I can't make money on those tiny differences. The real issue is the difference between the prices of Shell and Royal Dutch."

Freedy takes the bait. "What do you mean? If there are X shares of RDP outstanding and Y shares of STT, and if RDP shareholders get 60% of the cash flows, and STT shareholders get 40% of the cash flows, the price of one share of RDP should equal $(Y/X) \times (60/40) \times$ (Price of one STT share). Tell me that Froot and Dabora did this and found a big difference."

Ante grins, "That is exactly right. There are 536,074,088 shares of RDP outstanding, and there are 3,314,503,242 shares of STT outstanding. So, one RDP share should have the same value as $(3{,}314{,}503{,}242/536{,}074{,}088) \times (60/40) = 9.2744$ STT shares. Or, since 6 STT shares = 1 STT ADR, one RDP ADR = 1.5457 STT ADR. When Froot and Dabora examined those prices, the prices were often as much as 15% different. I can drive a truck through that spread!"

As usual, Suttle is listening in and feels it is time to enter the conversation. "So, Ante, what is your big plan?" he asks.

Ante replies, "Well, if STT is selling at a 15% discount to RDP, I'll just buy STT and short RDP and pocket the difference: It is an arbitrage!"

"Ah," says Suttle. "You make it sound so easy. But what if the discount gets bigger?"

"What do you mean?" Ante asks. "I still make money, don't I?"

"Actually, Ante, if the discount gets bigger, you would lose money," says Suttle. "Remember, at some point, you have to cover your short position. If the price of RDP went up by more than the price of STT, this would widen the discount, and you would lose. You'd also lose if RDP fell in value by less than STT fell. Once there is a discount, the arbitrage is risky."

Ante replied, "Well, I'm going to have to think about that."

Epilogue

In 2005, Royal Dutch and Shell unified into Royal Dutch Shell, plc, with headquarters in The Hague. The new company now has two classes of shares, A and B shares. They trade on both the London Stock Exchange and Euronext Amsterdam and in the form of ADRs in New York. The two classes of shares have identical rights except in relation to the source of dividend income, where, for tax purposes, A shares have a Dutch source and B shares have a UK source.

DRs are very convenient for investors because they provide the opportunity for international diversification at low cost. DRs overcome obstacles such as foreign custody arrangements and are conveniently denominated and pay dividends in the local currency. Essentially, DRs trade, settle, and clear in the same manner as domestic securities, and there is no difference between the way an investor buys and sells a DR versus any other domestic stock.

But what are the advantages for the cross-listing company? Cross-listing is beneficial because it enhances shareholder value primarily by reducing the cost of capital (which in turn increases the stock price) and by allowing the MNC to exploit growth opportunities with additional foreign capital. Most of the empirical research has focused on foreign companies listing in the United States. Although the estimates differ somewhat across studies, the introduction of an ADR for a typical company translates into a lower cost of capital by between 1% and 3% (see, for example, Stephen Foerster and Andrew Karolyi, 1999, 2000, and Darius Miller, 2000). There are a host of potential reasons cross-listing may reduce the cost of capital, including improved liquidity, a wider shareholder base, different pricing because the cross-listing integrates the stock in global capital markets, and improved corporate governance enforced by the country in which the MNC cross-lists.

Cross-listing is not free, though. It costs money paid in exchange fees and road shows, and, more importantly, it may impose a level of scrutiny on the company's managers that they dislike. Exhibit 12.9 gives an overview of the pros and cons of cross-listing from the perspective of the cross-listing firm. The next two sections explain these benefits and costs in more detail and summarize the vast literature on the effects of cross-listing.

The benefits of cross-listing may not be limited just to the firms that cross-list. Michael Urias (1995) and Nuno Fernandes (2005) show that firms in the home country that do not cross-list but that are correlated with stocks that do (for example, because they are in the same industry) may also experience positive price effects. In this case, the benefits of ADR-issues may "spill over" into the local market.

Why Firms Choose to Cross-list

Liquidity

It is now widely recognized that liquidity is priced in stocks. More liquid stocks have lower expected returns and hence higher prices than less liquid stocks (see, for instance, Yakov Amihud and Haim Mendelson, 1986).[7] Thus, cross-listing on a larger, more liquid market that lowers transaction costs for investors and improves liquidity induces lower expected returns and, hence, increases the stock price.

While there is a debate about the relative importance of this liquidity effect, research has shown that typically, after listing abroad, stocks experience an increase in total trading volume and a significant decrease in home market bid–ask spreads, due in large part to competition from the new market. If trading in the foreign market also leads to more efficient price discovery and fewer opportunities to exploit insider trading, there is an additional benefit to cross-listing. Indirectly, the fact that the price effects of U.S. companies listing in Toronto, Tokyo, or European exchanges are small shows that liquidity is an important benefit of cross-listing.

---

[7]This is less obvious than it seems, especially in a market with many securities, such as the U.S. market. If a security is less liquid but still desirable in investors' portfolios, investors who know that they may have to sell the security in a relatively short period will attempt to get the same risk exposure using a closely related but more liquid security. Investors with longer investment horizons should then buy up the lower-priced low-liquidity assets. These clientele effects may serve to make the "liquidity premium" smaller than it otherwise would be.

Exhibit 12.9   The Costs and Benefits of Cross-listing

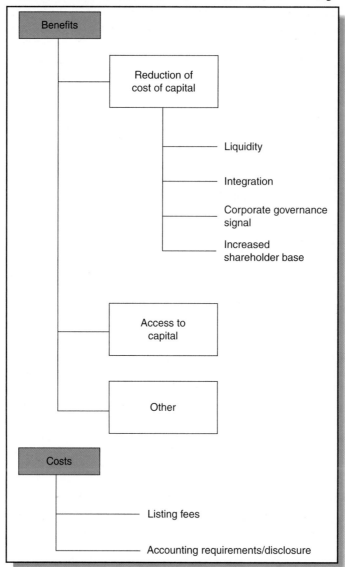

Nevertheless, some policymakers are quite concerned about possible adverse effects of multi-market trading. If cross-listing causes trading to migrate to the new market, firms that do not cross-list may become even less liquid as the home market traders and other people working on the local exchange are made worse off.

Wider Shareholder Base

The listing of an ADR is usually thought to widen a corporation's shareholder base, and this in itself may generate a price effect. Robert Merton (1987) developed a theory in which investors consider only a subset of the available securities when constructing their portfolios. They may be unaware of the other securities because of information problems, for example, or because the costs of trading these stocks might be prohibitive. In this case, stocks with a wide shareholder base are less risky, have lower expected returns than stocks with narrow shareholder bases, and receive higher prices.

If cross-listing through a depositary receipt literally expands the shareholder base, we should see an increase in stock price and lower expected returns going forward. This argument is particularly important because institutional investors in various countries are often restricted either legally or through their charters with respect to their foreign investments. However, cross-listed securities are often viewed as domestic investments, and, hence, may be the only way that some institutional investors may diversify internationally.

Market Integration

Markets are integrated when securities of similar risk have the same expected returns, whatever the market in which they trade (see Chapter 13 for more details). A firm located in a country that is not fully integrated in the world capital markets typically faces a higher cost of capital because the firm's equity risk has to be borne mostly by investors in its own country. If the firm finds a way to make it less costly for foreign investors to hold its shares, these investors share some of the firm's risk and therefore the cost of capital falls.

Investment barriers segment domestic capital markets from global capital markets. Investment barriers are usually grouped into "direct" and "indirect" barriers (see Geert Bekaert, 1995; and George Nishiotis, 2004). Direct barriers comprise regulatory frictions from foreign exchange controls, foreign ownership restrictions, and taxes and trading costs. For example, during much of the 1990s, the Korean authorities restricted foreign ownership in Korean companies to 10% of total market capitalization. Indirect barriers arise when countries fail to subject their companies to stringent disclosure requirements and investor protection is poor. These factors might play a large role in the investment decisions of international investors.

A U.S. or foreign listing makes its shares more accessible to foreign investors and can be viewed as a liberalization of investment. In some cases, the government literally relaxes restrictions for cross-listing stocks in order to facilitate cross-border arbitrage between the stock prices in the local and foreign markets. For example, even though Chile imposed capital flow and dividend repatriation restrictions on foreign investors in the mid-1990s (that is, foreigners could not repatriate capital or dividends for at least 1 year after the initial investment), these restrictions were lifted for the many Chilean companies cross-listing in the United States during that time. Consequently, cross-listing should lead to higher prices upon announcement of the listing and lower expected returns afterward. Consistent with this hypothesis, firms from emerging markets typically experience larger cross-listing price effects than firms from developed markets because emerging markets are more likely to be segmented from world capital markets.

Corporate Governance Signal

Indirect barriers can be reduced through better corporate governance (see Chapter 1). In corporate finance theory, it is now generally accepted that many firms are plagued by agency problems where controlling shareholders or managers try to appropriate funds from the firms. These private benefits of control may lead a firm to make suboptimal decisions (for its shareholders) with respect to investment, recruiting, and so on. In countries with poor investor protection and poor accounting standards, which includes not only emerging markets but also many European countries, these private benefits of control may be substantial and can depress stock prices.

When a firm cross-lists in a market with better investment protection, accounting standards, and disclosure requirements, firms commit themselves to an increased level of monitoring of both management and controlling shareholders. If they list in the United States, they also subject themselves to the litigious U.S. legal system. The reduction in deadweight costs resulting from agency problems increases the present value of future cash flows. The signal of improved management quality that the listing brings lowers the corporate governance discount, allowing the firm to face a lower cost of capital going forward.

This kind of reasoning, known as the "bonding hypothesis," played a major role in the NYSE listing of Kookmin Bank, the largest Korean bank, in November 2001. Kim Jung-tae, president and CEO, explains: "After Korea's financial crisis in 1997, many foreign investors were suspicious of Korean banks' books, and we wanted to clarify the situation by going abroad, especially on the NYSE. I think we have been fully tested in terms of accounting transparency and asset quality under more conservative U.S. GAAP. Our primary purpose is to be as open as possible."

Research by Craig Doidge, Andrew Karolyi, and René Stulz (2004) and William Reese and Michael Weisbach (2002) argues that a substantial part of the higher valuation enjoyed by cross-listing emerging market firms is due to the corporate governance channel. Recent research by Mark Lang, Karl Lins, and Darius Miller (2002) also suggests that more stringent disclosure requirements have an important side benefit: They improve analysts' earnings forecasts and therefore lead to more accurate prices.

Capital Needs and Growth Opportunities

Companies in emerging markets and small countries often outgrow their home markets and use cross-listing to raise capital to continue to grow. In addition, the worldwide privatization boom mentioned earlier created very large companies in very capital-intensive sectors, such as telecommunication, energy, and transportation. The size of these companies, compared to their home markets, virtually required that they raise capital outside their home countries. For example, Korea Telecom Corporation started its privatization process with a domestic IPO in 1998, and it quickly issued an ADR in May 1999.

When companies face constraints in the external financing markets, they can invest more only if they can generate more internal cash flows. Such a constrained firm's real investments will then be sensitive to cash flow growth. Financing constraints are most likely to exist in less financially developed markets. Karl Lins, Deon Strickland, and Marc Zenner (2005) show that foreign firms listing in the United States become much less financially constrained and substantially increase funds raised in the debt and equity markets. Both access to foreign investment banks with the ability to certify the quality of a deal and greater competition among providers of underwriting services help to reduce the cost of raising external capital.

Other Benefits of Cross-listing

When SAP, a German-based software company, listed on the NYSE in 1999, it not only wanted to enhance shareholder value but also wanted to strengthen its commercial profile in the United States. A foreign firm that has a U.S. customer base can increase brand awareness through a cross-listing, given the road show and publicity it entails and the continued increased media attention a listed security garners.

Marco Pagano, Ailsa Roell, and Josef Zechner (2002) even claim that firms with cross-listings increase their foreign sales as a percentage of total sales by approximately 20%. Of course, it might be the case that cross-listing firms cross-listed because they planned to expand their international activities and desired access to international capital markets to facilitate the expansion of their operations.

Increasingly, ADRs play a role in cross-border acquisitions. For example, in September 2000, Stora Enso Corporation, a paper company based in Finland, acquired Consolidated Papers, Inc., a U.S. company, in a $5 billion deal. For half of the offer, Stora Enso offered its own shares in the form of ADRs. Another example involves AngloGold, a South African mining company that began with a Level I ADR in June 1998 and soon after listed on the NYSE, bringing a real lion to the bell podium of the NYSE. Whereas this event clearly scored much media coverage, the main intent of the listing, according to CEO Bobby Godsell, lay elsewhere: He claimed in interviews that the firm's ADR program played a critical role in the firm's acquisition program. In 2004, AngloGold merged with the Ashanti

Goldfields Corporation of Ghana to create AngloGold Ashanti, the world's second-largest gold producer.

Finally, ADRs may help in the human resources department because they make it easier to set up a stock or stock option remuneration plan for top talent working in the United States.

Why Firms Decide Against Cross-listing

As we have said, listing on a foreign exchange is not costless. There are direct one-time costs, such as registration and listing fees, and there are the perennial costs of additional reporting and disclosure requirements. These latter factors are the primary inhibitors that keep more companies from listing abroad. When Daimler-Benz cross-listed its stock on the NYSE, it was not happy to find out it had to disclose the pay packages of its management. German and Swiss firms also tend to "smooth" reported earnings using various hidden accounting reserves; they cannot do this under U.S. GAAP. Among other things, smooth earnings help to reduce taxes when tax rates are progressive, as demonstrated in Chapter 17.

In their 2004 study, Craig Doidge, Andrew Karolyi, and René Stulz argue that cross-listing, while good for a firm, may not be beneficial for the controlling shareholders who may have to give up some of their private control benefits through the disclosure that is required under U.S. GAAP. By listing in the United States, a foreign firm increases the rights of its shareholders, especially its minority shareholders. It also constrains a controlling shareholder's ability to extract private benefits from control. From this perspective, it is not surprising that not every large foreign firm cross-lists its stock in the United States.

Which firms will cross-list? It seems likely that cross-listing will be done by firms with good growth opportunities that need funds to invest but find it difficult to finance their growth with internal funds or through debt. In these firms, the private benefits of control are relatively modest, and the controlling shareholders benefit from trying to grow the firm. Consequently, the growth opportunities of cross-listed firms should be valued more highly because they can better take advantage of these opportunities and because a smaller part of the cash flows of these firms is expropriated by controlling shareholders.

That costs matter is clear from the recent U.S. experience. Three out of four new DR listings in 2006 were completed on non-U.S. exchanges. Many feel that this shift may reflect the costs of litigation and corporate governance regulations when listing in the United States in the wake of the Sarbanes-Oxley Act.

CASE STUDY

The world's first truly global share
BACKGROUND

Daimler-Benz AG, the famous manufacturer of Mercedes-Benz cars, was founded in 1895 in Stuttgart, Germany. By the 1980s, it had become one of Germany's largest industrial companies. In 1997, net sales were over $68 billion, and the company's market capitalization was $36 billion on December 31, 1997. The company had more than 550,000 shareholders, with its shares distributed across 14 stock exchanges around the world, including the NYSE, where its ADR was listed in 1993. In addition to cars, it produced motor parts, trucks, and power systems; it also had a financial services and consulting division.

In 1997, Chrysler Corporation was the smallest but most efficient of America's big three car producers. Based in Auburn Hills, Michigan, Chrysler operated in two principal industry segments: automotive operations of cars, trucks, and related parts and financial services. It had $61 billion in net sales in 1997, and its market capitalization was $23 billion on December 31, 1997. Its shares, held by 135,000 shareholders, were traded worldwide, including in Frankfurt, Berlin, and Munich in Germany.

In May 1998, Daimler-Benz AG decided to merge with Chrysler Corporation. The two companies announced that their merger would create a global, diversified manufacturer and distributor of automobiles, diesel engines, aircraft, helicopters, space and defense systems, and other products and services. On November 17, 1998, trading commenced for DaimlerChrysler AG shares on stock exchanges around the world. The new symbol for the share was DCX. The type of shares DaimlerChrysler issued was new, and these shares were called **global registered shares (GRSs)**. A GRS is an ordinary share of a company that trades and transfers freely across national borders. On U.S. exchanges, a GRS is quoted, traded, and settled in U.S. dollars. Unlike an ADR, a GRS is an actual share of the company, not a receipt representing the ordinary shares deposited in trust. Daimler-Benz and Chrysler managers agreed to design and implement a global share as the only equity vehicle to be issued to all DaimlerChrysler stockholders with their merger transaction. Richard Grasso, CEO of the NYSE, hailed the event as a landmark for the globalization of stock markets, saying, "The security will trade in the U.S. in dollars, on the Deutsche Börse in Deutsche marks, and in 16 other markets around the world in whatever currency these markets would choose. We created for the first time a concept where equity could follow the sun" (see Andrew Karolyi [2003]).

Exhibit 12.10 is a schematic of the GRS facility. The left side of the schematic outlines the structure required to execute the GRS program in North America, and the right side outlines the structure for Europe and Asia, including Frankfurt, seven other German regional exchanges, and six other major world exchanges. All share registration and transfer was handled, respectively, by the U.S.-based and German-based agents/registrars. Establishment of the Europe/Asia segment required the introduction of registered shares instead of more common bearer shares in Germany. The Depositary Trust Company (DTC) in the United States and Deutsche Börse Clearing (DBC) in Germany handled the settlement and book entry of shares. To establish the GRS, the SEC approved an electronic link between DTC and DBC so that cross-border transactions could be cleared and settled in either the United States or Germany, ensuring complete transparency.

GRSs Versus ADRs

It is difficult to describe the GRS facility and its benefits without recognizing the limitations of the ADR and vice versa. ADRs represent negotiable claims on home-market ordinary shares (in bearer or registered form) issued by a U.S. depositary bank and coordinated in the home market through a local, custodial bank affiliate. Settlement of cross-border trades takes place daily through ADR issuances or cancellations ("conversions") conducted by the depositary bank, and fees for such transactions amount to about 5 cents per share. The ADRs are, of course, quoted, traded, and settled in U.S. dollars, and dividends are paid in U.S. dollars through the bank. Finally, the depositary bank maintains ownership records and processes corporate actions.

The GRS has "fewer moving parts" and does not require the intervention of a depositary bank. The per-share fee for conversion is subsumed by a single $5 settlement cost to the DTC that is independent of the number of shares. Hence, GRS may be less expensive to trade. At the same time, there is no depositary bank to oversee the coordination of the transfer, clearing, and settlement procedures of the GRS or to process corporate actions. In addition, ADRs provide the flexibility of bundling (or unbundling) a number of home-market shares into a receipt and therefore ensure that the shares trade in a price range that closely mirrors that of the company's competitors. This may help create additional liquidity. Finally, share ownership is more direct with a GRS than with an ADR. Holding a GRS gives investors the same voting privileges, rights to receive dividends, and so forth, whereas the depositary intermediary may impose certain restrictions.

Exhibit 12.10 The DaimlerChrysler Global Registered Share

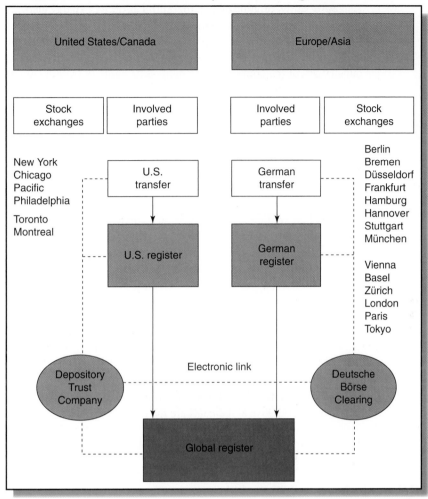

Note: Adapted from Karolyi (2003), p. 413. Reprinted from *Journal of Corporate Finance*, 9(4),
G. Andrew Karolyi, "DaimlerChrysler AG, The First Truly Global Share," p. 413, Copyright © 2003,
with permission from Elsevier.

WAS THE DAIMLERCHRYSLER GRS A SUCCESS?

Karolyi (2003) uncovered three main findings related to the DaimlerChrysler merger. First,
the program was associated with greater trading activity and enhanced liquidity. Trading
volumes were higher, and intraday bid–ask spreads were lower. Second, a significant number of orders eventually migrated back to the Frankfurt exchange during the first 6 months.
By 2006, the NYSE retained only 5% of total global trading volume of the stock. A possible explanation for the low NYSE volume is that DaimlerChrysler was dropped from the
S&P 500 index because it was no longer considered a U.S. stock. (The S&P 500 index is
composed of the 500 companies that S&P considers to be the largest, most liquid companies in a cross-section of industries in the United States.) Third, the return volatility of
DaimlerChrysler significantly increased after the issue of the GRS. Although the increase
in trading volume and decrease in the bid–ask spreads of the DaimlerChrysler stock were
both comparable to those experienced by other cross-listing firms, the extent of the migration

of order flow back to the Frankfurt exchange and the increase in volatility are unusual. Karolyi's study should temper the enthusiasm of experts who have touted the GRS as a cheaper and easier cross-border facility.

In 2007, this particular cross-border marriage ended in divorce, as DaimlerChrysler sold its Chrysler unit to a Cereberus Capital Management, a private equity firm, retaining only 19.9% of the company and changed its name to DaimlerAG. ■

12.4 STRATEGIC ALLIANCES[8]

Some projects are financed by multiple but separate companies. The best-known form of cooperation is probably the **joint venture**. A joint venture occurs when two or more independent firms form and jointly control a different entity, which is created to pursue a specific objective. The new entity tries to combine the strengths of each partner.

The joint venture is an example of a **strategic alliance**, which is an agreement between legally distinct entities to share the costs and benefits of what is hoped to be a beneficial activity. The activity typically involves large investments, but the level of collaboration is typically fairly low and focused on a well-defined set of activities, services, or products. Strategic alliances are most appropriate for companies wanting to exchange technical expertise or when there are legal, regulatory, or cultural constraints that might prevent, say, an acquisition of one company by another.

A good example of a strategic alliance involved Novartis, a Swiss pharmaceutical company, and Vertex, a U.S. biotechnology research company. In 2001, Novartis basically funded Vertex's research with total funds involving some $215 million over 6 years and further licensing fees of up to $600 million. In exchange, Novartis retained the worldwide distribution and development and marketing rights to eight potentially marketable drugs. This example is not an isolated case. Interfirm collaborative agreements are the norm in the biotech industry, but they also occur in a broad range of other industries. Exhibit 12.11 shows that there has been substantial growth in the number of joint ventures and strategic alliances taking place in recent years.

Exhibit 12.11   The Growth of Strategic Alliances

| | Domestic Deals | | | | Foreign Deals with U.S. Firms | | | | Totals | |
| | | | Cross-border | | | | Cross-border | | | |
Year	Joint Ventures	Strategic Alliances	Deals	Partners	Joint Ventures	Strategic Alliances	Deals	Partners	Domestic Deals	+ Deals with U.S. Firms
1985	50	152	25	177	48	314	1	343	202	564
1990	515	165	65	395	557	1,451	15	1,307	680	2,688
1995	917	2,426	478	1,165	1,328	510	118	1,688	3,343	5,181
1997	680	2,039	369	950	679	371	87	946	2,719	3,769
1999	454	2,577	299	848	565	984	49	1,428	3,031	4,580

Notes: This table presents a summary of strategic alliance and joint venture activity by year for agreements in which the alliance activity took place in the United States and for agreements involving U.S. firms that took place abroad. Joint ventures are collaborative agreements in which a third-party comprising members of the initiating firms is founded to oversee the agreement's activities. In a strategic alliance, only a contract is signed; no legally distinct control structure is established. "Year" refers to the year in which the agreement was announced. "Cross-border" refers to agreements that operate across different national borders; cross-border deals operate in more than one country, whereas cross-border alliance-partners refers to agreements struck between firms originating in different countries, regardless of whether the alliance itself is cross-border. The column headed "+ Deals with U.S. Firms" is the sum of domestic deals (joint ventures + strategic alliances) plus foreign deals involving U.S. firms. The table is adapted from Robinson (2006).

---

[8]Much of the material in this section is based on David Robinson (2006).

An interesting question is why certain activities are organized through strategic alliances rather than inside one firm. Why did Novartis choose to conduct this research through an arms-length contract with another firm instead of internally? David Robinson (2006) suggests an intriguing possibility. Robinson claims that strategic alliances are more often than not used to finance "underdog projects." Underdog projects have potentially very high payoffs but very low success probabilities; that is, they are very risky ventures. Even though underdog projects may have equal or higher expected value compared to other projects, managers in the relevant divisions may be unwilling to supply effort, fearing that the headquarters of the firm may take resources away from the underdog project. Through an alliance with a smaller, outside firm undertaking the underdog project, a centralized, large firm (the "parent") guarantees that the project gets some basic financing because the alliance is a legally enforceable contract between two legally distinct entities. In exchange, the parent gets a fraction of the revenues the project earns while giving the stand-alone firm undertaking the underdog project options to extra funds when the project's prospects improve.

12.5 SUMMARY

This chapter examines equity financing in a global market. The main points of the chapter are as follows:

1. A multinational corporation can obtain additional funds by issuing shares to its existing shareholders or to new shareholders. Most MNCs have shares listed on the stock market of the country in which they are headquartered, but many list their shares on several stock exchanges around the world, with the U.S. stock exchanges being most popular.

2. The largest stock markets are in the United States, the United Kingdom, and Japan. These markets are also large relative to the GDP of their respective countries, unlike European stock markets. In Europe, bank financing is a relatively more important source of funding for companies.

3. Most stock markets are private organizations or are owned by a set of financial institutions (banker's bourses), although many of the most prominent ones are now publicly traded corporations.

4. A trading system may be order driven or price driven. In a price-driven system, dealers who act as market markers for certain stocks stand ready to buy at a bid price and sell at an ask price. NASDAQ in the United States is such a system. In an order-driven system, share prices are determined in an auction that brings together the supply and demand of shares. The TSE in Tokyo is an example of an order-driven system. The NYSE has elements of both systems.

5. Stock markets around the world have become increasingly automated.

6. Stock markets have consolidated in response to competitive pressures to allow international investors more time to trade and to automatically cross-list shares.

7. Turnover is the total volume traded on an exchange during a year divided by the exchange's market capitalization. It is often viewed as a liquidity indicator. The United States has the largest turnover of all developed stock markets.

8. Turnover is negatively related to trading costs, which consist of brokerage commissions, bid–ask spreads, and market impact (the fact that the price may move against you when you trade a large order).

9. Emerging stock markets are the stock markets of developing countries, which developed rapidly during the 1990s, following a process of financial liberalization. Among the largest emerging markets today are India, South Africa, Taiwan, Korea, Russia, and Brazil.

10. Transaction costs in emerging markets are larger and turnover is generally lower than in developed markets.

11. When foreign companies list their shares in the United States, they typically use American depositary receipts (ADRs), which are held in custody by a depositary bank and represent a certain number of original shares issued in the home stock market.

12. ADR programs come in three varieties: Level I (not exchange traded), Level II (exchange traded), and Level III (exchange traded and capital raising). In addition, private placements occur through Rule 144.

13. Global depositary receipts (GDRs) are similar to ADRs. However, they can be traded on many exchanges in addition to U.S. exchanges.
14. Cross-listing a stock can lower a company's cost of capital through several channels, including improved liquidity and better corporate governance. It can heighten the awareness of the firm's brands, provide direct access to foreign capital, and make future capital access easier.
15. Global registered shares (GRSs) trade simultaneously in different markets around the world, in different currencies, with the shares being completely fungible across markets.
16. A strategic alliance is an agreement between legally distinct companies to share the costs and benefits of a particular investment.

QUESTIONS

1. What are the differences between public, private, and banker's bourses?
2. What is the difference between a price-driven trading system and an order-driven trading system? Which system lends itself most easily to automation?
3. Do we have a global stock market, as we have a global foreign exchange market?
4. What is turnover?
5. What are the three primary components of transaction costs in trading stocks?
6. Does high turnover always signal lower transaction costs?
7. What is the difference between an ADR and a GDR?
8. What motivates companies to cross-list their shares?
9. Has cross-listing been beneficial for most listed companies? If yes, why doesn't every company cross-list?
10. What is the difference between a GDR and a GRS?
11. What is a strategic alliance?
12. What is a joint venture?

PROBLEMS

1. The following table shows how average share prices jump (in percentage) after the announcement that the stocks will be cross-listed (see Darius Miller, 2000). The price response should be interpreted as corrected for risk and market movements that happened on the same day:

	All ADR Issues	Capital Raising	Non-Capital Raising
Emerging markets	1.5	0.9	2.8
Developed markets	0.9	0.7	0.9
Total	1.2	0.8	1.4

Although these numbers appear small, it is important to realize that announcements of equity issues, which are by definition capital raising, in a domestic context lead to an average negative return response of 2% to 3% (see, for instance, Ronald Masulis and Ashok Korwar, 1986). The main reason is that capital-raising equity issues are viewed as a signal by the managers that the firm may be overvalued in the stock market.

Given what you learned in this chapter, answer the following:
   a. Why is there a positive price response when a company's shares are cross-listed?
   b. Why might the response for emerging-market firms be larger than for developed-market firms?
   c. Without knowing that equity issues in a domestic context are associated with negative price responses, is the difference between capital-raising and non-capital-raising ADRs a surprise? Why or why not?
2. Suppose you are a U.S.-based investor, and you would like to diversify your stock portfolio internationally. What advantages do ADRs offer you? Would it be wise to restrict your international portfolio to only ADRs?

BIBLIOGRAPHY

Aggarwal, Reena, 2002, "Demutualization and Corporate Governance of Stock Exchanges," *Journal of Applied Corporate Finance* 15, pp. 105–113.

Alexander, Gordon, Cheol Eun, and Sundaram Janakiramanam, 1998, "International Listings and Stock Returns: Some Empirical Evidence," *Journal of Financial and Quantitative Analysis* 23, pp. 135–152.

Amihud, Yakov, and Haim Mendelson, 1986, "Asset Pricing and the Bid–Ask Spread," *Journal of Financial Economics* 17, pp. 223–249.

Baker, H. Kent, John R. Nofsinger, and Daniel G. Weaver, 2002, "International Cross-listing and Visibility," *Journal of Financial and Quantitative Analysis* 37, pp. 495–521.

Bank of New York, 2007, "The Depositary Receipt Markets: The Year in Review—2006."

Bank of New York, Gavin Anderson & Company, Van der Molen Specialists, PricewaterhouseCoopers, and Bowne, 2002, "Solving the ADR Puzzle: The Expert Guide to Building a Successful ADR Program," www.adrbny.com/files/2002_VDM_Guide_.pdf.

Bekaert, Geert, 1995, "Market Integration and Investment Barriers in Emerging Equity Markets," *World Bank Economic Review* 9, pp. 75–107.

Bekaert, Geert, and Campbell R. Harvey, 2003, "Emerging Markets Finance," *Journal of Empirical Finance* 10, pp. 3–55.

Bekaert, Geert, Campbell R. Harvey, and Christian Lundblad, 2007, "Liquidity and Expected Returns: Lessons from Emerging Markets," *Review of Financial Studies* 20(6), pp. 1783–1831.

Bessembinder, Hendrik, 1998, "Trade Execution Costs on NASDAQ and the NYSE: A Post-reform Comparison," working paper.

Chowdhry, Bhagwan, and Vikram Nanda, 1991, "Multimarket Trading and Market Liquidity," *Review of Financial Studies* 4, pp. 623–656.

Derrabi, Mohamed, Erik de Bodt, and Robert Cobbaut, 1999, "*Periode de Transaction, Volatilite et Correlation Serielle des Rendements Intrajournaliers: Unce Analyse du Marche Continu de Casablanca*," discussion paper, Centre d'Economie et Gestion Financiere, Université Catholique de Louvain.

Doidge, Craig, Karolyi G. Andrew, and René M. Stulz, 2004, "Why Are Foreign Firms Listed in the U.S. Worth More?" *Journal of Financial Economics*, pp. 205–238.

Domowitz, Ian, Jack Glen, and Ananth Madhavan, 1998, "International Cross-listing, Ownership Rights and Order Flow Migration: Evidence from Mexico," *Journal of Finance* 53, pp. 2001–2028.

Domowitz, Ian, Jack Glen, and Ananth Madhavan, 2000, "Liquidity, Volatility and Equity Trading Costs Across Countries and Over Time," working paper.

Errunza, Vihang, and Darius Miller, 2000, "Market Segmentation and the Cost of Capital in International Equity Markets," *Journal of Financial and Quantitative Analysis* 35, pp. 577–600.

Fernandes, Nuno, 2005, "Market Liberalization: Spillovers from ADRs and Implications for Local Markets," working paper.

Foerster, Stephen, and G. Andrew Karolyi, 1993, "International Listings of Stocks: The Case of Canadian and the U.S.," *Journal of International Business Studies* 24, 763–784.

Foerster, Stephen, and G. Andrew Karolyi, 1999, "The Effects of Market Segmentation and Investor Recognition on Asset Prices: Evidence from Foreign Stocks Listing in the U.S.," *Journal of Finance* 54, 981–1013.

Foerster, Stephen, and G. Andrew Karolyi, 2000, "The Long Run Performance of Global Equity Offerings," *Journal of Financial and Quantitative Analysis* 35, pp. 499–528.

French, Kenneth, and James Poterba, 1991, "Were Japanese Stock Prices Too High?" *Journal of Financial Economics* 29, pp. 337–363.

Froot, Kenneth, and Emile Dabora, 1999, "How Are Stock Prices Affected by the Location of Trade?" *Journal of Financial Economics* 53, pp. 189–216.

Ghysels, Eric, and Mouna Cherkaoui, 2003, "Emerging Market and Trading Costs: Lessons from Casablanca," *Journal of Empirical Finance* 10, pp. 169–198.

Howe, John S., and Kathryn Kelm, 1987, "The Stock-Price Impacts of Overseas Listings," *Financial Management* 16, pp. 51–56.

Jones, Charles, 2002, "A Century of Stock Market Liquidity and Trading Costs," working paper.

Karolyi, G. Andrew, 1998, "Why Do Companies List Their Shares Abroad? A Survey of the Evidence and Its Managerial Implications," *Salomon Brothers Monograph Series* 7.

Karolyi, G. Andrew, 2003 "DaimlerChrysler AG, the First Truly Global Share," *Journal of Corporate Finance* 9, pp. 409–430.

Khwaja, Asia I., and Atif Mian, 2003, "Trading in Phantom Markets: In-Depth Exploration of an Emerging Stock Market," working paper.

Lang, Mark H., Karl V. Lins, and Darius Miller, 2002, "ADRs, Analysts, and Accuracy: Does Cross Listing in the U.S. Improve a Firm's Information Environment and Increase Market Value?" *Journal of Accounting Research* pp. 317–346.

Lesmond, Desmond A., 2005, "Liquidity of Emerging Markets," *Journal of Financial Economics* 77, pp. 411–452.

Leuz, Christian, 2003, "Discussion of ADRs, Analysts, and Accuracy: Does Cross Listing in the U.S. Improve a Firm's Information Environment and Increase Market Value?" *Journal of Accounting Research* 41, pp. 347–362.

Lins, Karl V., Deon Strickland, and Marc Zenner, 2005, "Do Non-U.S. Firms Issue Equity on U.S. Stock Markets to Relax Capital Constraints?" *Journal of Financial and Quantitative Analysis* 40, pp. 109–133.

Ljungqvist, Alexander P., Tim Jenkinson, and William J. Wilhelm, 2004, "Global Integration in Primary Equity Markets: The Role of U.S. Banks and U.S. Investors," *Review of Financial Studies* 39, pp. 613–630.

Lowengrub, Paul, and Michael Melvin, 2002, "Before and After International Cross-listing: An Intraday Examination of Volume and Volatility," *Journal of International Financial Markets, Institutions and Money* 12, pp. 139–156.

Lynch, Anthony, and Richard R. Mendenhall, 1997, "New Evidence on Stock Price Effects Associated with Changes in the S&P 500 Index," *Journal of Business* 70, pp. 351–384.

Masulis, Ronald W., and Ashok N. Korwar, 1986, "Seasoned Equity Issues: An Empirical Investigation," *Journal of Financial Economics* 15, pp. 91–118.

McDonald, Jack, 1989, "The Mochiai Effect—Japanese Corporate Cross-Holdings," *Journal of Portfolio Management* 16, pp. 90–94.

Megginson, William L., and Jeffry M. Netter, 2001, "From State to Market: A Survey of Empirical Studies on Privatization," *Journal of Economic Literature* 39, pp. 321–389.

Merton, Robert C., 1987, "A Simple Model of Capital-Market Equilibrium with Incomplete Information," *Journal of Finance* 42, pp. 483–510.

Miller, Darius, 2000, "Return Behavior and Pricing of American Depositary Receipts," *Journal of International Financial Markets, Institutions and Money* 9, pp. 43–67.

Nishiotis, George P., 2004, "Do Indirect Investment Barriers Contribute to Capital Market Segmentation?" *Journal of Financial and Quantitative Analysis* 39, pp. 613–630.

Pagano, Marco, Ailsa Roell, and Josef Zechner, 2002, "The Geography of Equity Listings: Why Do European Companies List Abroad?" *Journal of Finance* pp. 2651–2684.

Reese, William A., and Michael S. Weisbach, 2002, "Protection of Minority Shareholder Interests, Cross-listings in the United States, and Subsequent Equity Offerings," *Journal of Financial Economics*, pp. 65–104.

Robinson, David T., 2006, "Strategic Alliances and the Boundaries of the Firm," working paper.

Shleifer, Andrei, 1986, "Do Demand Curves for Stocks Slope Down?" *Journal of Finance* 41, pp. 579–590.

Siegel, Jordan, 2005, "Can Foreign Firms Bond Themselves Effectively by Renting U.S. Secuirities Laws?" *Journal of Financial Economics* 75 (2), pp. 319–359.

Smith, Katherine, and George Sofianos, 1997, "The Impact of an NYSE Listing on Global Trading of Non-U.S. Stocks," New York Stock Exchange working paper.

Solnik, Bruno, 2000, *International Investments*, 4th ed., New York: Addison-Wesley.

Sorensen, E.H., and L.J. Price, March 13, 2000, *The Salomon Smith Barney Global Equity Impact Cost and Market Liquidity Monitor*. New York: Citigroup.

Urias, Michael, 1995, "Essays on the Effects of Cross-Border Investments in Emerging Markets," Ph.D. dissertation, Stanford University.

Werner, Ingrid, and Allan W. Kleidon, 1996, "UK and U.S. Trading of British Cross-listed Stocks: An Intraday Analysis of Market Integration," *Review of Financial Studies* 9, pp. 619–664.

Wu, Guojun, and J. He, 2003, "The Life of a Manipulated Stock," working paper.

Zenner, Marc and Todd Hazelkorn, 2001, "The Benefits of ADRs (and Other Cross-listings)," Salomon Smith Barney report.

Chapter 13

International Capital Market Equilibrium

A manager should allocate capital to an investment project when the present value of the net cash flows generated by the project exceeds the current investment outlay. Applying this net present value principle requires a discount rate. It is one of the hallmarks of modern finance that this discount rate—the cost of equity capital—is set by investors in the capital markets. When investors finance a firm by purchasing its equity shares, they are forgoing the opportunity to invest in the equities of many other firms. Investors therefore demand to be compensated for the opportunity cost of their investment with an appropriate expected rate of return. Consequently, the manager of a firm in a capital budgeting situation should set the discount rate for a project to be the expected return for the firm's investors as if they were investing directly in that project.

Chapter 11 showed that the international bond market sets the cost of a company's debt equal to the risk-free (government) interest rate on bonds plus a risk premium to compensate for the possibility that the company may default on the debt. The appropriate rate for discounting the equity cash flows of any project similarly depends on how risky the investors in the firm view the cash flows from that particular project to be. However, thinking about risk in increasingly more global equity markets is difficult because there are many more factors involved.

How, then, do investors determine the riskiness of an investment, and how do managers know the required rate of return on a risky investment? Unfortunately, there are no easy answers to these questions, and there are competing theories. This chapter develops the theories necessary to determine the cost of equity capital. It then demonstrates how these theories apply in an international context. Because investors set the cost of equity capital, we start with a detour through the fascinating world of international investing and the theory of optimal portfolio choice.

13.1 RISK AND RETURN OF INTERNATIONAL INVESTMENTS

The old saying "Don't put all your eggs in one basket" should entice investors to explore foreign stocks, perhaps in exotic places. As Chapter 12 indicates, global stock markets offer investors an incredible menu of choices, offering potentially higher rates of return and different types of risks. To understand the benefits and pitfalls of international investments, we

457

must fully understand what determines risk and return in international markets. This necessitates that we understand how currency fluctuations affect international investments.

The Two Risks of Investing Abroad

When a U.S. investor is bullish about the British stock market, she must realize that investing in the British equity market also implies an exposure to the British pound. Let us analytically derive the dollar return on British equity investment. First, we set up some notation. Let $S(t)$ be the \$/£ exchange rate, and let $s(t+1) = [S(t+1) - S(t)]/S(t)$ indicate the percentage appreciation of the pound relative to the dollar. We are interested in the dollar rate of return on British equity, which we denote by $r(t+1,\$)$. This return will have two components, the pound rate of return on British equity, denoted by $r(t+1, £)$, and the percentage change in the value of the pound, $s(t+1)$. This reasoning is identical to the derivation of the return on a foreign money market investment in Chapter 6. In this case, however, we replace the foreign interest rate with the foreign equity rate of return. We first convert from dollars to pounds to get $1/S(t)$ pounds, which we will invest. After investing these pounds, they each earn the pound return $1 + r(t+1, £)$ in the equity market. Subsequently, the total pound return is sold for dollars at $S(t+1)$. Thus, the dollar return on a British equity investment is

$$1 + r(t+1,\$) = [1/S(t)] \times [1 + r(t+1, £)] \times S(t+1)$$

Subtracting 1 from each side and using $\dfrac{S(t+1)}{S(t)} = 1 + s(t+1)$ gives

$$r(t+1,\$) = [1 + r(t+1, £)] \times [1 + s(t+1)] - 1$$

or

$$r(t+1,\$) = r(t+1, £) + s(t+1) + r(t+1, £) \times s(t+1)$$

We see that the dollar rate of return on a foreign investment depends on the local equity rate of return plus the currency return plus a cross-product term (the product of the two rates of return). The cross-product term is often small relative to the other two terms because it is percentages of percentages, and it is thus often ignored.

Example 13.1 Determining the Dollar Return of a British Equity Investment

Rob Dickinson of the Catherine Wheel Fund is bullish on British equity and wants to invest \$10 million in the British equity market. The spot exchange rate is \$1.6/£. At that exchange rate, Rob can convert \$10 million into \$10/(\$1.6/£) = £6.25 million. He then invests the £6.25 million in the British equity market. Suppose he plans to hold on to the investment for 1 year. During this time, he hopes to earn dividends plus a capital gain—the return an investor gets when he is able to sell a stock for more than what he paid for it. Let's consider three scenarios for the return in the British equity market: an increase in the market value of the stock by 10%, a decrease of 10%, and no change.

After earning the British equity return, Rob can then sell his pound return, which is (£6.25 million) $\times [1 + r(£)]$, for dollars. An appreciation of the pound will enhance his dollar return. In contrast, a depreciation of the pound will diminish his dollar return. Let's consider three possible scenarios for the change in the value of the pound as well: a 10% appreciation (to $1.6/£ × 1.10 = $1.76/£), a 10% depreciation (to $1.6/£ × 0.9 = $1.44/£), and no change. Consequently, there are a total of nine possible outcomes:

		DOLLAR–POUND EXCHANGE RATES		
		10% Depreciation of the Pound $1.44/£	No Change $1.60/£	10% Appreciation of the Pound $1.76/£
POUND	£5.625 million (−10%)	$8.1 million −19%	$9.0 million −10%	$9.9 million −1%
STOCK RETURNS	£6.25 million (0%)	$9.0 million −10%	$10.0 million 0.0%	$11.0 million 10%
	£6.875 million (+10%)	$9.9 million −1%	$11.0 million 10%	$12.1 million 21.0%

The numbers in each cell illustrate the formula for the exact dollar return—that is, the exact percentage change, including the cross-product term. If the news is good all around and the pound and the British equity market both appreciate by 10%, the approximation yields an estimated 20% return. The true number is 21% because the cross-product term is $0.10 \times 0.10 = 0.01$ in this case. Analogously, if the British equity market indeed increases by 10%, as Rob hopes, but at the same time the pound depreciates by 10%, then perhaps you would guess that the return would be zero, as the approximation suggests. The true answer is −1% because now the cross-product term is a negative 1%. For return horizons of 3 months or less, though, the cross-product term is likely to be small, and we often ignore it in computations.

The Volatility of International Investments

Exhibit 13.1 lists several characteristics of the equity markets of the G7 countries. The data are from Morgan Stanley Capital International (MSCI) and are for the sample period starting in January 1980 and ending in July 2006. We first focus on the three volatility columns. Remember that volatility, $\text{Vol}[r]$, is defined to be the standard deviation, which is the square root of the variance, $\text{Var}[r]$; it indicates how much returns vary around the mean or average return.

The Volatility of Currency and Equity Returns

For a U.S. investor, such as fund manager Rob Dickinson in Example 13.1, international investments appear to have two problems. First, focusing on the volatilities expressed in the foreign currencies, the volatilities of equity returns in foreign currencies exceed the volatility of U.S. equity returns. In fact, the U.S. market appears to be the least volatile market, with a volatility of only 15.0%. The second-least-volatile market is the UK, with a volatility of 16.3%. The other three European markets have volatilities exceeding 20%.

Second, currency changes are pretty variable themselves, with volatilities of around 11%, for the most part. The numbers in the sixth column of Exhibit 13.1 confirm this. The only exception is the substantially lower volatility of the Canadian dollar, which is driven by the close economic ties between the United States and Canada and episodes during which Canadian monetary policy focused on exchange rate stability.

Exhibit 13.1   Characteristics of Foreign Equity Returns, 1980–2006

	Means			Volatilities		
	Market Return	Currency Return	Dollar Return	Market Return	Currency Return	Dollar Return
U.S.	13.38	0.00	13.38	15.01	0.00	15.01
Canada	11.51	0.32	12.18	16.86	5.31	19.34
Japan	7.92	3.43	11.59	18.83	11.53	23.17
UK	14.54	−0.17	14.15	16.33	10.54	18.37
France	14.79	−0.25	14.09	20.17	10.93	21.23
Germany	12.28	1.15	13.09	21.04	11.04	22.22
Italy	17.62	−1.73	15.36	24.58	10.66	25.10

Notes: The original data are monthly total equity returns (including capital gains and dividends) taken from Morgan Stanley Capital International (MSCI) for the period January 1980 to July 2006. Means are in annualized percentage (monthly means multiplied by 12). Volatilities are converted to annualized percentages by multiplying the monthly volatilities by $\sqrt{12}$. There are three columns for both means and volatilities. The first column pertains to returns in the foreign currency (for example, the Japanese yen for Japan), the second column pertains to currency returns (the change in the value of the foreign currency relative to the dollar), and the third column contains characteristics of dollar returns.

Adding Up Volatility

We know that the volatility of the exchange rate will affect the volatility of the dollar return on a foreign equity. But the volatility of the dollar return on foreign equity is generally much less than the sum of the exchange rate and local equity return volatility. That is, whereas the approximate return to a foreign investment is the sum of a local equity and currency return component, $r(t+1,\$) = r(t+1, \text{FC}) + s(t+1)$, with FC denoting foreign currency, volatility is not additive. In particular, volatility is the square root of the variance, and the variance of the sum of two variables involves their covariance. Thus,

$$\text{Var}[r(t+1, \text{FC}) + s(t+1)] = \text{Var}[r(t+1, \text{FC})] + \text{Var}[s(t+1)]$$
$$+ 2\,\text{Cov}[r(t+1, \text{FC}), s(t+1)]$$

Recall that the covariance of two variables equals the **correlation** between the variables multiplied by the product of the two volatilities, and the correlation is a number between −1 and 1 that indicates how closely related are the variations in the two variables. Rewriting the variance as a function of the correlation, ρ, is informative:

$$\text{Var}[r(t+1,\text{FC}) + s(t+1)] = \text{Var}[r(t+1,\text{FC})] + \text{Var}[s(t+1)]$$
$$+ 2\rho\text{Vol}[r(t+1, \text{FC})]\text{Vol}[s(t+1)]$$

Suppose the correlation is 1. Then, because the variance is the square of the volatility and using $(A + B)^2 = A^2 + B^2 + 2AB$, we know that

$$\text{Var}[r(t+1,\text{FC}) + s(t+1)] = \text{Vol}[r(t+1,\$)]^2$$
$$= [\,\text{Vol}[r(t+1,\text{FC})] + \text{Vol}[s(t+1)]\,]^2$$

Hence, in this case, the volatility of the dollar return on foreign equity is indeed the sum of the foreign equity volatility and currency return volatility. Because of the perfect correlation, there is no natural diversification advantage to having exposure to two sources of risk. However, as long as $\rho < 1$, the total dollar volatility will be less than the sum of the two volatilities.

Exhibit 13.1 shows that the volatilities of dollar-denominated equity returns are often not much above the original volatility in the local currency. This indicates that the correlation between exchange rate changes and local equity market returns is low. It is sometimes argued

Exhibit 13.2 Correlations of Equity Returns in Foreign Currencies with $/FC Returns

Country	Correlation
Canada	0.35
Japan	0.08
UK	–0.13
France	–0.16
Germany	–0.17
Italy	–0.15

Notes: The original monthly data are taken from MSCI and cover the period January 1980 to July 2006.

that it should be negative, appealing to the competitiveness ideas of Chapter 9. When countries experience real depreciations (usually brought about by nominal exchange rate depreciations), firms in that country might also experience a boost to competitiveness and profitability, which might increase local stock market values. Under this scenario, the exchange rate and the stock market move in opposite directions. In most countries, the correlation between exchange rate changes and local stock market returns is indeed negative. See Exhibit 13.2.

In Japan and Canada, the correlation is positive. For these countries, the primary forces may be foreign capital flows that push up the values of the foreign currencies and the stock market simultaneously when investors enter the capital markets. Similarly, when foreign investors repatriate capital, stock prices fall, and the currencies weaken. Nevertheless, the main conclusion of Exhibit 13.2 is that currency returns and foreign currency–denominated equity returns show little correlation.

Expected Returns

Average Returns

We have already learned that in efficient markets, risky securities should earn returns higher than the risk-free rate. In Exhibit 13.1, we also report the average returns earned in the various markets for a period of over 20 years. We denote the average, or mean, return, which is a measure of the expected return, by $E[r]$. If these returns are representative of true expected returns, they do not indicate that volatility is rewarded in the international marketplace. Whereas the most volatile market (Italy) does have the highest average return both in lira (over 17%) and in dollars (over 15%), the two low-volatility markets (the United States and the United Kingdom) have relatively high average returns as well. Moreover, although Japan is a comparatively high-volatility country, it has low average stock market returns. Something else must drive average returns. We explore this issue later in this chapter.

Currency Components of Returns

Exhibit 13.1 splits up the average dollar return into the average equity return in the foreign currency and the average currency return. The currency returns range between −1.7% (Italy) and 3.4% (Japan). It should not be a surprise that countries such as Japan and Germany feature positive currency returns, and countries such as France, Italy, and the United Kingdom feature negative currency returns. In the long run, currency changes reflect nominal interest rate differentials (recall our discussion of uncovered interest rate parity in Chapter 7), and these interest rate differentials partially reflect inflation differentials. For example, Japan and Germany are both countries with historically low inflation and interest rates. In contrast, prior to the adoption of the euro, France, Italy, and the United Kingdom historically experienced relatively high inflation and high nominal interest rates.

Exhibit 13.3 Sharpe Ratios for the G7, 1980–2006

Country	Sharpe Ratio
U.S.	0.49
Canada	0.32
Japan	0.24
UK	0.44
France	0.38
Germany	0.32
Italy	0.37

Notes: Ratios are computed as the average return from Exhibit 13.1 minus 6% (our estimate for the risk-free rate) divided by the volatilities in Exhibit 13.1.

Sharpe Ratios

Investors naturally like high returns and dislike losses. The more variable the returns, the greater the probability of loss. Recall from Chapter 10 that the Sharpe ratio is one summary statistic of the risk–return trade-off inherent in a security or a portfolio of securities. The Sharpe ratio is measured as the average excess return relative to the volatility of the return:

$$\text{Sharpe ratio} = \frac{E[r] - r_f}{\text{Vol}[r]}$$

where r_f is the risk-free rate. It would be natural for investors to choose portfolios with high Sharpe ratios because investors want a high excess return (as measured by the numerator of the Sharpe ratio) and a low volatility (as measured by the denominator of the Sharpe ratio). The historical Sharpe ratios for the G7 countries are presented in Exhibit 13.3.

Note that the U.S. equity market produces the highest Sharpe ratio, with only the United Kingdom getting somewhat close. It is tempting to conclude that because the U.S. equity market offers the best possible Sharpe ratio, international diversification is a bust for U.S. investors. It is also tempting to conclude that Japan is the worst place to invest because it offers the lowest Sharpe ratio. The next section shows that these conclusions are naïve and erroneous.

13.2 THE BENEFITS OF INTERNATIONAL DIVERSIFICATION

Risk Reduction Through International Diversification

Exhibit 13.4 is taken from a classic study by Bruno Solnik (1974a). Solnik was one of the first researchers to demonstrate the considerable benefits of diversifying a portfolio internationally. The horizontal axis in Exhibit 13.4 depicts the number of stocks in a particular portfolio, and the vertical axis shows the typical variance of a portfolio, with the number of stocks on the horizontal axis. For the top line, Solnik considered a universe of only U.S. stocks. He computed the average variance of a typical individual U.S. stock and normalized that number to 100. He then considered equally weighted portfolios of two stocks (one-half each), found the typical variance of this portfolio to produce a second point on the graph, and so on.

Because of the imperfect correlation between stocks, the portfolio variances decline with the addition of stocks. The graph shows that the portfolio variance falls quickly as more

Exhibit 13.4 Solnik's Case for International Diversification

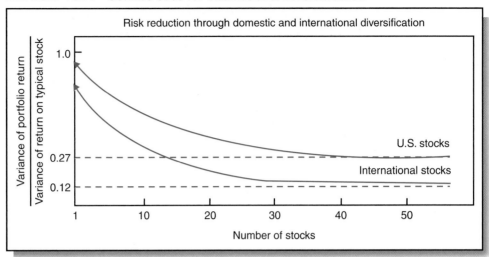

stocks are added, but after including around 20 to 30 stocks, it becomes difficult to reduce the variance further. The curve finally settles at a level of about 27% of the beginning variance. In other words, more than 70% of the variance of a typical stock can be eliminated through diversification. The part of the variance that can be diversified away is called **nonsystematic variance**.

The lower line in Exhibit 13.4 repeats the exercise, but now stocks can be added from the U.S. and the major European stock markets. Because there is even less correlation between U.S. and European stocks, the variance of the equally weighted portfolios goes down much more quickly as more stocks are added. The variance of the portfolio falls to barely 10% of the variance of a typical domestic stock.

Recall that the appendix to Chapter 7 formally demonstrates that in a large, equally weighted portfolio, the variance equals the average covariance among the stocks in the portfolio. Consequently, the variance of U.S. portfolios cannot be reduced further because there are systematic sources of variation that affect all stocks in the United States in the same way. The macroeconomic forces driving stock returns are factors that affect the cash flow prospects of firms and the discount rates used by investors to value these cash flows. We know that stock returns are sensitive to interest rates, which, in turn, depend on monetary policies and business cycles. Business cycles of course affect cash flow prospects, but they may also affect discount rates, as investors may become more risk averse in recessions and less risk averse during booms. These risks cannot be diversified away in a single domestic portfolio.

Notice, though, that when foreign stocks are added to the portfolio, these risks can, to some extent, be diversified away because U.S. monetary policies and business cycles are not perfectly correlated with those of the rest of the world. However, for the most part, stocks are positively correlated, so you cannot diversify away all of a portfolio's variance, no matter how many international stocks you add to the portfolio. Because the average covariance is positive, even a large portfolio of international stocks will have a positive variance. We call the variance that cannot be diversified away the **systematic variance** or **market variance**. The important insight here is that when an investor holds a diversified portfolio, a stock's contribution to the variance of the portfolio depends on its covariance relative to the other stocks in the portfolio.

Has Idiosyncratic Variance Increased?

The variance of a firm's return can be split up into an idiosyncratic component and a systematic component, with the latter variance being the source of risk. For a typical firm, the **idiosyncratic variance** constitutes about 75% of the total variance of the firm's return. This may sound like a lot, but Solnik's graph in Exhibit 13.4 shows that this idiosyncratic variance disappears relatively quickly when a portfolio is constructed with securities that are less than perfectly correlated. Researchers John Campbell, Martin Lettau, Burton Malkiel, and Yexiao Xu (2001) argue that the general level of idiosyncratic risk in the U.S. market substantially increased from the early 1960s to 1997, whereas the level of long-run systematic risk roughly remained constant. One potential explanation is the tendency of companies to focus on a few core activities rather than on diverse activities, as was popular in the 1960s. Another reason is that many companies are going public sooner—a phenomenon first noticed during the dot-com boom in the 1990s. The fact is, however, that smaller and younger firms often have a much more uncertain future than mature, established companies and therefore possess much higher levels of idiosyncratic risk. The technology sector is also one of the most volatile industries. It is also conceivable that young firms have higher levels of systematic risk and the authors did not allow for the possibility that the distribution of the exposures to **market risk** changed over time, which may have biased their results.

If Campbell et al. are right, their results are quite important for asset management because they imply that more stocks will be needed before full diversification is reached than the 20 to 30 stocks Solnik suggested. Recent work by Geert Bekaert, Robert Hodrick, and Xiaoyan Zhang (2006) casts some doubt on the robustness of these results and finds little evidence of a trend upward in idiosyncratic volatility, either in the United States or in any of the other G7 countries.

International Return Correlations

Exhibit 13.5 reports a full correlation matrix of the stock market returns of 23 developed countries. The sample period starts in 1980 for most countries. The correlations range from 0.14 for Japan and Greece to 0.75 for Germany and the Netherlands. It is striking that the stock returns of countries that are in close geographic proximity to one another and have significant exports and imports to one another seem to correlate more highly. This is true for Canada and the United States, and it is also true for European Union countries (in particular, Belgium, France, Germany, and the Netherlands). Hong Kong and Singapore are also highly correlated, at 0.72. This suggests that trade increases correlations, presumably because importing and exporting firms are affected by the economic factors in the other countries.

The lowest correlations all involve Greece. Greece has a correlation of less than 0.20 with Japan, Hong Kong, and Singapore. Even within Europe, Greece does not correlate very highly with most other markets. Interestingly, the highest correlation it has with any other country is with Portugal, another ex-emerging market. Portugal naturally correlates most closely with its neighbor and trading partner Spain.

What Drives Correlations of Returns?

Apart from trade patterns, what drives the different return co-movements we observe in Exhibit 13.5? To analyze this, it is best to first think of pure fundamental factors. Think of a country as a set of firms. Then figure that each firm is priced rationally, using a discounted cash flow analysis. In such a world, common variations in discount rates and common variations in expected cash flow growth rates will lead to correlations among the firms.

The first fundamental factor that may drive the correlations of stock returns in different countries is their industrial structures. Firms in the same industry are likely to be buffeted by the same shocks affecting cash flows and profitability. Moreover, it is likely that their systematic risks also move together, so both their discount rates and expected cash flow variations are closely related. Both Canada and Australia have many firms operating in the mining

Exhibit 13.5 Correlation Matrix for Developed Countries

	AT	BE	CA	DK	FI	FR	DE	GR	HK	IE	IT	JP	NL	NZ	NO	PT	SG	ES	SE	CH	UK	US
AU	0.23	0.34	0.62	0.32	0.43	0.40	0.37	0.23	0.46	0.46	0.28	0.34	0.46	0.68	0.52	0.30	0.51	0.43	0.46	0.41	0.55	0.48
AT		0.45	0.28	0.35	0.22	0.47	0.57	0.39	0.28	0.44	0.33	0.22	0.46	0.36	0.41	0.43	0.35	0.38	0.31	0.52	0.38	0.21
BE			0.39	0.52	0.28	0.70	0.66	0.38	0.29	0.56	0.45	0.37	0.68	0.25	0.56	0.47	0.34	0.49	0.43	0.64	0.57	0.47
CA				0.44	0.50	0.49	0.45	0.22	0.47	0.42	0.39	0.35	0.59	0.46	0.55	0.36	0.53	0.43	0.51	0.48	0.58	0.73
DK					0.38	0.52	0.56	0.28	0.28	0.55	0.43	0.35	0.57	0.28	0.52	0.49	0.36	0.47	0.46	0.54	0.48	0.44
FI						0.45	0.49	0.21	0.35	0.40	0.44	0.32	0.48	0.35	0.47	0.35	0.33	0.47	0.63	0.33	0.47	0.51
FR							0.73	0.39	0.32	0.53	0.53	0.41	0.70	0.30	0.58	0.51	0.39	0.58	0.55	0.64	0.61	0.54
DE								0.39	0.36	0.58	0.48	0.32	0.75	0.32	0.54	0.50	0.43	0.56	0.61	0.68	0.55	0.52
GR									0.18	0.35	0.36	0.14	0.35	0.23	0.31	0.49	0.16	0.42	0.33	0.31	0.27	0.22
HK										0.37	0.30	0.27	0.46	0.38	0.41	0.31	0.72	0.38	0.40	0.35	0.49	0.42
IE											0.41	0.45	0.65	0.38	0.54	0.50	0.43	0.61	0.55	0.52	0.69	0.55
IT												0.37	0.48	0.30	0.36	0.48	0.34	0.52	0.48	0.39	0.42	0.33
JP													0.41	0.35	0.32	0.30	0.39	0.43	0.39	0.41	0.42	0.31
NL														0.43	0.64	0.57	0.49	0.55	0.59	0.71	0.71	0.65
NZ															0.45	0.38	0.50	0.47	0.47	0.40	0.43	0.35
NO																0.45	0.45	0.46	0.55	0.55	0.59	0.52
PT																	0.26	0.64	0.54	0.52	0.46	0.35
SG																		0.45	0.48	0.40	0.50	0.55
ES																			0.57	0.50	0.54	0.46
SE																				0.53	0.54	0.54
CH																					0.61	0.53
UK																						0.61

Notes: The countries are Australia (AU), Austria (AT), Belgium (BE), Canada (CA), Denmark (DK), Finland (FI), France (FR), Germany (DE), Greece (GR), Hong Kong (HK), Ireland (IE), Italy (IT), Japan (JP), the Netherlands (NL), New Zealand (NZ), Norway (NO), Portugal (PT), Singapore (SG), Spain (ES), Sweden (SE), Switzerland (SWI), the United Kingdom (UK), and the United States (US). The data are monthly dollar returns from MSCI for the period January 1980 to July 2006, although for some countries the sample starts later.

industry, for example. This might explain why Australia is highly correlated with Canada but not with Germany.

A long debate has ensued about the importance of industry factors when it comes to return correlations across countries. Some researchers have found that industry factors are starting to dominate country factors (see Robin Brooks and Marco Del Negro, 2004, for example). It used to be the case that country factors clearly dominated when markets were less integrated and discount rates were not highly correlated across countries. Moreover, limited trade across countries and relatively independent monetary policies implied that business cycles showed little correlation across countries, resulting in low correlations among cash flows in different countries. Consequently, policies affecting the degree of integration and the independence of business cycles appear to be important determinants of cross-country correlations. For example, the adoption of a common currency has helped synchronize business cycles in Europe. In contrast, emerging markets typically act more independently of integrated countries. This may explain why Greek stock market returns have historically not been highly correlated with the returns of other countries, although that is likely to change with Greece's continued integration into the European Union.

Finally, irrational investor behavior may induce excess correlations across equity markets, especially during crisis periods. We already talked about this contagion phenomenon in Chapter 5 and simply repeat that increased volatility may lead to temporarily increased correlations.

Asymmetric Correlations?

Because the correlations overall are so far from unity, there are ample opportunities for investors to internationally diversify their portfolios. Some investors may be less impressed and argue that they really only care about diversification when their home market is going down. François

Longin and Bruno Solnik (2001) confirm what casual observations may have led you to suspect: International diversification benefits evaporate when you need them the most—that is, in bear markets. To demonstrate this rather annoying fact, Longin and Solnik computed "bear market correlations" (correlations using returns below the average for both of the stock markets) and "bull market correlations" (correlations using returns above the average) for various developed markets.

The results are striking: The bear market return correlations are much higher than the bull market correlations. This finding does not justify staying at home with your equity portfolio, however. Research by Andrew Ang and Geert Bekaert (2002) shows that these asymmetric correlations do not negate the benefits of international diversification. Even with correlated bear markets, investors are better off diversifying internationally because perfectly correlated bear markets have really never occurred, and because bear markets are relatively short-lived.

The Effect of International Diversification on Sharpe Ratios

Portfolio Risk and Return

Exhibit 13.3 shows the U.S. Sharpe ratio to be historically higher than the Sharpe ratios for the other G7 countries. Even so, international diversification makes perfect sense for U.S. investors. This is because it is not the Sharpe ratio of the foreign asset that the U.S. investor should care about but the Sharpe ratio of the portfolio that results from international diversification. Intuitively, because equity markets in other countries are not perfectly correlated with the U.S. market, part of their volatility disappears through portfolio diversification.

Let's consider formally how international diversification affects Sharpe ratios. Imagine putting a fraction w of your all-U.S. portfolio in international equity. Let's denote the U.S. return by r and the foreign return (in dollars) by r^*. The expected return of the new portfolio is $(1 - w)E[r] + wE[r^*]$. That is, the expected return of a portfolio of assets is the weighted average of the expected returns on the individual assets with the weights equal to the fraction of wealth invested in each asset. Expected returns aggregate linearly. As we already know, volatility does not aggregate linearly. The volatility of the new portfolio equals

$$\{(1 - w)^2 \mathrm{Var}[r] + w^2 \mathrm{Var}[r^*] + 2w(1 - w)\mathrm{Cov}[r, r^*]\}^{1/2}$$

Because the covariance is a function of the correlation, correlations really matter.

When Does International Diversification Improve the Sharpe Ratio?

Suppose you start with an all-U.S. portfolio. Recall that the U.S. Sharpe ratio is given by $E[r - r_f]/\mathrm{Vol}[r]$, and the Sharpe Ratio on the foreign equity is $E[r^* - r_f]/\mathrm{Vol}[r^*]$. We denote the correlation between the U.S. and foreign returns as ρ. From a zero investment in foreign equities, the Sharpe ratio goes up when you add a little bit of foreign equity exposure, if the following condition holds:

$$\frac{E[r^*] - r_f}{\mathrm{Vol}[r^*]} > \rho \frac{E[r] - r_f}{\mathrm{Vol}[r]} \tag{13.1}$$

The appendix to this chapter proves this statement formally, but the result is quite intuitive: When you add a little bit of the foreign asset to your portfolio, the portfolio's Sharpe ratio improves upon the Sharpe ratio of the U.S. portfolio, when the Sharpe ratio of the new asset is higher than the Sharpe ratio of the U.S. portfolio multiplied by the correlation between the U.S. return and the international return. In other words, the lower the correlation with the U.S. market, the lower the Sharpe ratio of the foreign market needs to be for it to become an investment that increases your Sharpe ratio. This is because markets that have low correlation with the U.S. market are the best diversifiers of a U.S. portfolio. Another way to see this is to bring ρ to the other side and notice that it is not the foreign asset's volatility that matters when computing the return:risk ratio but, rather, volatility adjusted for correlation (ρ Vol[$r*$]). The lower ρ is, the lower this adjusted risk number becomes and the easier it is to exceed the U.S. Sharpe ratio.

Investment Hurdle Rates

With the correlations from the preceding section in hand, we can compute hurdle rates on international investments for U.S.-based investors. The hurdle rate is the lowest possible expected return that must be earned in the foreign market for investors with purely domestic assets to improve their Sharpe ratio when they invest in that foreign market. Let's look at this in detail.

We have reasonably trustworthy data on correlations and volatility. We have already noted that it is difficult to estimate expected returns from the data with any accuracy, and we will return to this issue later on. Nonetheless, in light of these problems, we perform the following computation. Given a certain expected return on the U.S. market, what is the minimum expected return we must have on the foreign market in order to improve our Sharpe ratio by investing a little bit of our wealth in the foreign security? We call this expected return the *hurdle rate*.

Concretely, if we look at Equation (13.1), we fill in $E[r]$ with a reasonable number (for instance, 10%), and we use the data to estimate correlations and volatilities, leaving $E[r*]$ as an unknown variable. The minimum $E[r*]$ we need for the Sharpe ratio with foreign investment to be at least as large as the U.S. Sharpe ratio is the one that equates the two sides of the equation. That is,

$$\text{Hurdle rate} = \rho \frac{E[r]}{\text{Vol}[r]} \text{Vol}\,[r*] + r_f$$

The hurdle rate is higher when the U.S. market has a high Sharpe ratio, the foreign market is more volatile, or there is high correlation between foreign and U.S. stock returns.

Whereas Exhibit 13.1 reports the dollar volatilities of the various international equity market returns, and Exhibit 13.3 reports their Sharpe ratios, Exhibit 13.6 reports their correlations with the U.S. market. The market returns of Canada and the United Kingdom have the highest correlations with U.S. returns, whereas Japanese and Italian market returns have correlations barely above 30%. For France and Germany, the correlations are around 50% to 55%. The hurdle rates for the countries with low correlations will be low. Let's illustrate the computation of the hurdle rate for Japan, when the expected return for the United States is 10% ($E[r] = 10\%$). The number is

$$0.06 + 0.31 \times \frac{0.10 - 0.06}{0.1501} \times 0.2317 = 0.0791, \text{ or } 7.91\%$$

Exhibit 13.6   Correlations Between Foreign and U.S. Equity Market Returns, 1980–2006

Country	Correlation
Canada	0.73
Japan	0.31
UK	0.61
France	0.54
Germany	0.52
Italy	0.33

Notes: All returns have been converted to U.S. dollars. The original monthly data are taken from MSCI.

Exhibit 13.7 Hurdle Rates for Foreign Investments

Country	E[r] = 10%	E[r] = 12%
Canada	9.74%	11.62%
Japan	7.91%	8.88%
UK	8.97%	10.45%
France	9.08%	10.62%
Germany	9.08%	10.62%
Italy	8.22%	9.33%

Notes: The hurdle rate equals $r_f + \rho \dfrac{E[r] - r_f}{\mathrm{Vol}[r]} \mathrm{Vol}[r^*]$. The correlation number is taken from Exhibit 13.4; the volatility numbers (in dollars) are taken from Exhibit 13.1 (both for the United States and the foreign country); r_f is set at 6%; and $E[r]$ is the U.S. expected return specified on top of the two columns. Data are from MSCI, and the sample is 1980:01–2006:06.

The first number (0.06) is the risk-free rate, and the second number (0.31) is the correlation between the Japanese and U.S. equity returns, which multiplies the U.S. Sharpe ratio at $E[r] = 10\%$ and the volatility of the Japanese equity return (0.2317). Hence, a U.S. investor should put some money in Japanese equity even if he believes the expected return on Japanese equity is 2.19% (10% − 7.91%) lower than in the U.S. equity market.

Hurdle rates for these same countries appear in Exhibit 13.7. The correct conclusion is that international diversification can easily improve performance for U.S. investors because the hurdle rates for expected dollar returns on foreign investments are low. In fact, they are lower than the expected return on the U.S. equity market in every case. It is difficult to imagine that foreign equity markets have such dramatically lower expected returns relative to the U.S. market. Italy and Japan have the lowest correlation with the United States and therefore offer the easiest performance enhancement.

How to Diversify at Home

Retail investors do not necessarily need to call a foreign broker to invest in far-flung places. Many investment vehicles can be used to accomplish international diversification. First of all, would Coca-Cola not constitute an ideal international investment? After all, Coke sells its flagship product in more than 200 countries around the world. Hence its cash flows must be influenced by the local economies of all those countries. It was long thought that a portfolio of multinational companies would capture the benefits of international diversification. While the recent literature does indicate that the stock returns of multinational companies behave quite internationally (see, for example, Jeff Diermeier and Bruno Solnik, 2001), restricting yourself to domestically traded multinational companies remains a flawed diversification strategy (see, for instance, the analysis in Patrick Rowland and Linda Tesar, 2004). The best diversification opportunities may be exactly the companies for which local factors remain important drivers of their returns.

Chapter 12 notes that many companies cross-list in the United States using ADRs. Why not simply buy these companies? Again, the problem is one of representation: The ADR companies tend to be the larger, more internationally focused companies, and they may not give you full exposure to the stock markets of the foreign countries.

Another possibility is to invest in **closed-end funds**, or **investment trusts**, which trade on the local equity market. These funds represent a fixed portfolio that may invest in the world markets, sometimes restricted to a region (Latin America, for instance) or a particular country, in which case they are called **country funds**. The only way to buy into this portfolio is for the investor to buy the fund from another investor selling it. Therefore, closed-end funds can trade at prices that are different from the value of the portfolio, especially when they invest in emerging markets. Hence, it is conceivable that closed-end fund returns fail to offer the same diversification benefits as the underlying portfolio (see Section 13.6). This is not a problem with **open-end funds**, where the portfolio grows with new investments and contracts with redemptions and the fund is not traded on an exchange. These represent the bulk of the international funds available to retail investors.

Finally, a hybrid alternative that is rapidly gaining popularity is the **exchange-traded fund (ETF)**, which trades on an exchange but where prices are kept close to the value of the underlying portfolio through arbitrage activities by a few institutional investors. As the availability of these vehicles expands, an internationally diversified portfolio is only a phone call away for U.S. investors.

13.3 OPTIMAL PORTFOLIO ALLOCATIONS

We have now established that diversifying internationally is likely to reduce risk and improve your Sharpe ratio. But how much should you invest internationally? This is a portfolio choice problem—one of the most fundamental finance problems, and one that brings us very close to a formula for the cost of equity capital.

To solve for the **optimal portfolio**, we must first specify what the feasible portfolios are. Feasibility is not a difficult concept: All portfolios that use up all wealth are feasible. Let's consider the G7 example. An investor can invest in the risk-free asset or in seven different equity markets. These different securities constitute the investor's set of ingredients. Just as ingredients can be mixed into a dish, securities can be combined into a portfolio. We can represent the investor's feasible portfolios by a series of wealth fractions—the proportions of wealth devoted to each asset—and these proportions must add to 1. For example, putting 50% of your portfolio in the risk-free asset and 50% in the U.S. equity market is a feasible portfolio. The combination of all feasible portfolios constitutes the investor's menu. Of course, there are an infinite number of possible portfolios, so to figure out which portfolio is best for a particular investor seems like a daunting task.

Luckily, finance theory has come up with some rather simple answers. We start by defining investors' preferences regarding risk and return, and then we consider a simplified set of ingredients: one risky asset and one riskless security. After we extend the ingredients to multiple risky assets, we can solve the portfolio problem. For example, we will find that no smart investor should ever choose the 50–50 portfolio we proposed.

Preferences

In economics, preferences are typically represented by **utility functions**. Typically, a utility function mathematically links the consumption of units of real goods to a level of satisfaction. Here, we specify a utility function for the individual investor in terms of the statistical properties of the portfolio that the investor holds—that is, expected returns and portfolio variance. We assume that investors would like to generate the highest possible expected return with as little variance as possible, but each investor may have a different risk tolerance. A simple function that captures the trade-off the investors face is

$$U = E[r_p] - \frac{A}{2}\sigma_p^2$$

where the subscript p indicates the portfolio, $E[r_p]$ is the expected return on the portfolio, and σ_p is the volatility of the portfolio. The parameter A in this **mean-variance preference** function indicates the penalty the investor assigns to the variance of the portfolio. The higher A is, the more the investor dislikes variance or risk; in other words, A characterizes the risk aversion of investors.

Example 13.2 The Investor's Utility Calculation

Suppose the expected return on a portfolio is 9.87%, and its standard deviation is 7.835%. For an investor with $A = 4$, utility equals

$$9.87\% - \frac{1}{2} \times 4 \times (7.835\%)^2 = 9.87\% - 1.23\% = 8.64\%.$$

One interpretation of this number is that the investor in this portfolio achieves the same utility as he would by investing in a completely risk-free portfolio with a return of 8.64%.

The Case of One Risky Asset

The portfolio problem is considerably simplified, and much intuition is gained if we begin by restricting the set of ingredients to one single risky asset and the risk-free asset. Let's introduce some notation. Let the risk-free return be r_f, let the risky return be r, and let the weight on the risky asset be w.

If w of the portfolio is invested in the risky asset, the remainder of the portfolio, the $1 - w$, is invested in the risk-free asset. Hence, the return on a portfolio is

$$r_p = w \times r + (1 - w) \times r_f = r_f + w \times (r - r_f)$$

The variable $r - r_f$ is the excess return. Therefore, the portfolio's expected return is $E[r_p] = r_f + w \times E[r - r_f]$, and it increases linearly with the weight in the risky asset when the expected excess return is positive. To find the variance of the portfolio return, note that the risk-free rate is known with certainty. Therefore, we simply have $\sigma_p^2 = w^2\sigma^2$, where σ^2 is the variance of the risky return, r. Hence, the volatility of the portfolio is $\sigma_p = w\sigma$, and the risk of the portfolio is also linear in w. Now we use this volatility expression to substitute for w in the expected return expression, and find

$$E[r_p] = r_f + \frac{E[r] - r_f}{\sigma}\sigma_p \tag{13.2}$$

This expression describes the relationship between the expected return on the portfolio and its standard deviation. Consequently, Equation (13.2) fully describes the "menu," or the possible risk–return combinations, for this simple case. Also, note that the relationship is of the form $y = a + bx$, with $y = E[r_p]$ and $x = \sigma_p$, which is the equation for a straight line.

We call the line describing the risk–return trade-off in the single risky asset case the **capital allocation line (CAL)** because it describes the ways capital can be allocated in the single risky asset case. The CAL is graphed in Exhibit 13.8.

Exhibit 13.8 The Capital Allocation Line

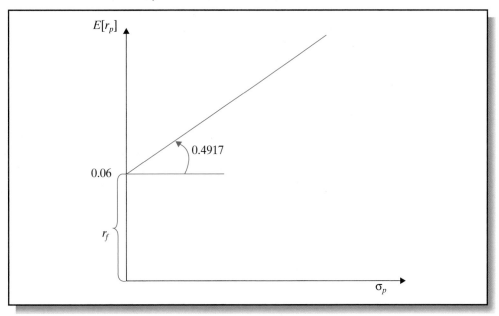

Notes: The vertical axis shows the expected return, and the horizontal axis is the standard deviation of the portfolio. The line is the capital allocation line of feasible risk–expected return patterns. It emanates at the risk-free rate (6% in this example) and slopes upward with the Sharpe ratio of the risky asset, $\dfrac{E(r) - r_f}{\sigma}$, as its slope.

Example 13.3 The Capital Allocation Line

Let's take the U.S. equity market as the risky asset, with expected return of 13.38%, and $\sigma^2 = (15.01\%)^2$ (see Exhibit 13.1) and let $r_f = 6\%$. Then, the CAL is given by

$$E[r_p] = 0.06 + SR \times \sigma_p \text{, with } SR = \frac{E[r] - r_f}{\sigma} = \frac{0.1338 - 0.06}{0.1501} = 0.4917, \text{ where}$$

we recognize SR as the Sharpe ratio, or the return premium per unit of risk.

The Optimal Portfolio

To find the optimal portfolio, we must combine the CAL menu with the investor's preferences. The mathematical problem to solve can be written as

$$\max_{w} U = \max_{w} \left[E[r_p] - \tfrac{1}{2}A\sigma_p^2 \right]$$

In words, we try to find the weight on the risky asset (w) that maximizes the utility function. We can substitute the expressions for $E[r_p]$ and σ_p^2 to obtain

$$\max_{w} \left[r_f + w[E[r] - r_f] - \tfrac{1}{2}Aw^2\sigma^2 \right]$$

To solve for the optimal w, denoted w^*, we must take the derivative of this function with respect to w and set it equal to zero, in which case we find

$$E[r] - r_f - Aw^*\sigma^2 = 0$$

Solving for the optimal portfolio gives a very intuitive solution:

$$w^* = \frac{E[r] - r_f}{A\sigma^2} \qquad (13.3)$$

The allocation to the risky asset is increasing in the expected return on the asset, decreasing in its variance, and decreasing in the risk aversion the agent displays.

Example 13.4 Calculations of Optimal Portfolios

Let's apply the formula for people who have different levels of risk aversion:

A	w^*	$E[r_p]$ (in %)	σ_p (in %)
1.0	3.28	30.21%	49.23%
2.0	1.64	18.10%	24.62%
3.0	1.09	14.04%	16.36%
4.0	0.82	12.05%	12.31%

To fill in the numbers of the table, we use the formula for w^*, and then the expected return is $E[r_p] = r_f + w^*E[r - r_f]$ and the volatility is $\sigma_p = |w^*|\sigma$.

Note that $w^* = 1$ implies that 100% of wealth is invested in the risky asset. As risk aversion increases, the weight on the risky asset decreases, which decreases the expected return and the standard deviation. Because we stay along the CAL, the risk–return trade-off (Sharpe ratio) remains the same because it is the slope of the line. Exhibit 13.9 demonstrates this graphically.

Exhibit 13.9 Optimal Portfolios

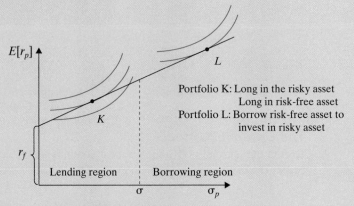

Portfolio K: Long in the risky asset
Long in risk-free asset
Portfolio L: Borrow risk-free asset to
invest in risky asset

Notes: Investors with different preferences toward risk and return invest in different portfolios, represented by different points on the capital allocation line.

For low A, we are at a point such as L. The investor is more than 100% invested in the risky asset ($w > 1$), and the investor finances this position by borrowing. For example, for $A = 1$, the investor borrows $2.28 for every dollar of his own wealth invested, and he invests the $3.28 in the stock market. For high A, the investor combines stock investing with an investment in the T-bill—that is, $w < 1$. For example, for $A = 4.0$, the investor places 82% of her wealth in the risky asset and 18% in the risk-free asset.

The Mean Standard Deviation Frontier

What if there are multiple risky assets? Consider Exhibit 13.10. The circles represent the expected returns and standard deviations of various available assets. It is now not at all obvious how to proceed. Even with just two risky assets, many different capital allocation lines are available. After all, we could consider all feasible risky portfolios as "the risky asset." What is the optimal risky portfolio? Economist Harry Markowitz (1952) won the Nobel Prize in 1990 for showing us how to proceed.

First, we must get rid of a large number of "inefficient" portfolios by creating the mean standard deviation frontier. The **mean standard deviation frontier** is the locus of the portfolios in expected return–standard deviation space that have the minimum variance for each expected return. It is therefore also often referred to as the **minimum-variance frontier**. For two assets, the frontier would represent all possible portfolio combinations but would have a shape similar to the one graphed in Exhibit 13.10. Imagine combining a low expected return–low variance asset (say asset *X*) with a high expected return–high variance asset (say asset *Y*). Starting from a portfolio 100% in the low expected return asset, adding some of asset *Y* to the portfolio will increase the expected return of the portfolio in a linear fashion. However, unless assets *X* and *Y* have perfectly correlated returns, the standard deviation will not change in a linear fashion. In fact, it may even decrease at first, but in any case, when it starts to increase, imperfect correlation makes the standard deviation of the portfolio increase at a rate lower than linear, giving rise to the curved-shape also seen in Exhibit 13.10.

Creating the frontier for multiple assets as in Exhibit 13.10 is the solution to a complex mathematical problem. We want to minimize the return variance for a portfolio of *N* securities, for each possible expected return:

$$\min_{\{w_1,\ldots,w_N\}} \left[\sum_{i=1}^{N} w_i^2 \sigma_i^2 + \sum_{i=1}^{N} \sum_{j \neq i}^{N} w_i w_j \text{cov}[r_i, r_j] \right] \Rightarrow \text{Minimum variance}$$

such that

$$\sum_{i=1}^{N} w_i = 1 \Rightarrow \text{Feasible portfolio} \qquad \sum_{i=1}^{N} w_i E[r_i] = \bar{r} \Rightarrow \text{Target return}$$

Exhibit 13.10 The Mean Standard Deviation Frontier

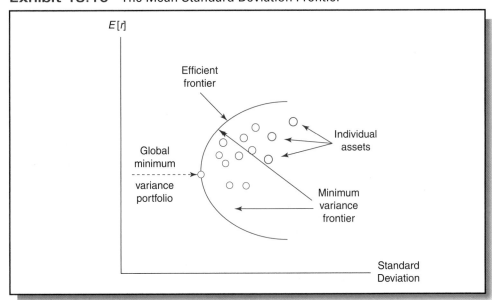

By varying $\bar{r}$, we trace out the frontier. Although analytical solutions are possible, using Excel Solver is a popular way of finding minimum-variance portfolios.

Two-Fund Separation

Interestingly, when this problem is solved for two target returns, we are done. This is called **two-fund separation**: The minimum-variance frontier is said to be spanned (or generated) by any two minimum-variance frontier portfolios. That is, if we find two portfolios—say, portfolio X with weights $[w_1^X, w_2^X, \ldots, w_N^X]$ and portfolio Y with weights $[w_1^Y, w_2^Y, \ldots, w_N^Y]$—that are on the frontier, we can generate the whole frontier by taking combinations of these two portfolios. If there are only two assets, then the mean standard deviation frontier can be found by simply mixing the two assets in all possible combinations with weights adding up to 1. Two-fund separation says that with multiple assets, all portfolios on the frontier can be viewed as a mix of any two frontier portfolios.

The Efficient Frontier

Once we have determined the mean standard deviation frontier, we can focus on a rather limited set of possible portfolios. Clearly, no one will want to invest in a portfolio on the inside of the frontier: You can either lower risk at the same expected return or increase the expected return at the same risk. Also, no one will invest in a portfolio on the portion of the frontier below the global minimum-variance portfolio, which is indicated on Exhibit 13.10. The **global minimum-variance portfolio** is the portfolio with the least variance among all possible portfolios. If you are below that portfolio, you can increase expected return without increasing volatility.

What remains is the upper portion of the frontier, starting at the global minimum-variance portfolio. This set of risky portfolios is called the **efficient frontier**. It yields a large number of "efficient" risky portfolios that could be combined with a risk-free asset to form a capital allocation line.

The Mean-Variance-Efficient Portfolio (the MVE)

Starting from the risk-free rate point on the vertical axis of 6%, we can consider any portfolio on the mean-standard deviation frontier as a potential risky asset and draw a line from the risk-free rate to the risky portfolio's point on the graph. This line constitutes a potential CAL (capital allocation line), and once we pick such a CAL, we know how to optimally combine the risky portfolio with the risk-free asset from our previous analysis. Remember that the slope of the CAL is the Sharpe ratio. Hence, different risky portfolios imply different CALs and thus different Sharpe ratios. People with utility functions that depend positively on the expected return and negatively on the variance of the portfolio would naturally prefer higher Sharpe ratios.

For example, consider Exhibit 13.11. It graphs the mean-standard deviation frontier for two assets—the U.S. and Japanese equity markets, using the expected return and volatility properties reported in Exhibit 13.1 and the correlation reported in Exhibit 13.6.

Clearly, there is a "best" CAL, and it is the CAL with the steepest slope, or highest Sharpe ratio. This is the line emanating from the risk-free return that rotates as far northwest as possible—that is, to the point where the line is tangent to the mean standard deviation frontier. This portfolio is called the **mean-variance efficient** or **MVE portfolio**, and it represents the risky portfolio maximizing the Sharpe ratio.

The theory is surprisingly powerful. It states that there is a superior risky portfolio that all investors will prefer: Of course, tastes or preferences still differ, and investors can combine

Exhibit 13.11 Finding the MVE Portfolio

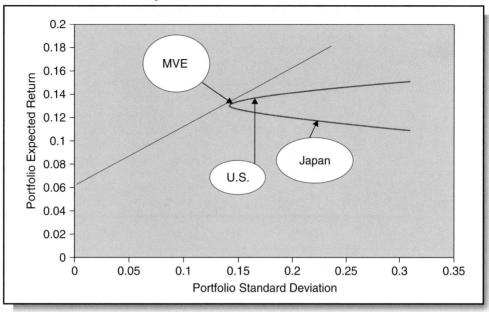

Notes: We form the mean-standard deviation frontier from two assets. The US portfolio has a mean return of 13.38% and a standard deviation of 15.01%. The Japanese portfolio has a mean return of 11.59% and a standard deviation of 23.17%. The correlation between the two returns is 0.31. The Mean Variance Efficient portfolio dominates either individual portfolio.

the MVE with the risk-free asset, depending on their preferences. Portfolios to the left of the triangle representing the MVE portfolio are for more risk-averse investors; portfolios to the right of the triangle will be chosen by less risk averse investors. Notice how the risky efficient frontier is completely below the CAL going through the MVE. By borrowing at the risk-free rate and investing more than 100% in the MVE portfolio, investors can achieve a much higher expected return for the same risk as they would if they only considered risky assets. The actual weight on the MVE portfolio versus the risk-free asset can be determined using the Equation (13.3).

13.4 THE CAPITAL ASSET PRICING MODEL

This section describes the most popular model underlying computations of the cost of capital: the capital asset pricing model (CAPM). We describe its origins, provide a formal derivation and interpretation, and discuss the difference between domestic and international CAPMs.

Assumptions and Origins

The **capital asset pricing model (CAPM)** is a model that underlies all modern financial theory. It was derived by William E. Sharpe (1964), John Lintner (1965), and Jan Mossin (1966), using principles of diversification, with simplified assumptions building on the original mean-variance optimization analytics developed by Markowitz. Markowitz and Sharpe won the 1990 Nobel Prize in economics for their efforts. The CAPM requires a long list of rather strong assumptions:

- There is a single-period investment horizon.
- Individual investors are price takers.
- Investments are limited to traded financial assets.
- There are no taxes and transaction costs.
- Information is costless and available to all investors.
- Investors are rational mean-variance optimizers.
- The expectations are homogeneous; that is, all investors agree on the expected returns, standard deviations, and covariances between security returns.

The CAPM then derives the optimal asset demands of all investors and derives restrictions on expected returns by imposing that markets have to clear (that is, supply must equal demand), or all assets must be willingly held.

Given these assumptions, it is perhaps not surprising that the CAPM yields strong predictions:

- All investors will hold the same portfolio for risky assets—the **market portfolio**.
- The market portfolio contains all securities, and the proportion of each security is its market value as a percentage of total market value.
- The risk premium on the market depends on the average risk aversion of all market participants.
- The risk premium on an individual security is a function of its covariance with the market portfolio.

While no one literally believes that the assumptions underlying the CAPM hold in the real world, the CAPM is one of the most useful models in finance. For example, it serves as a benchmark for evaluating portfolio managers, and it provided an impetus for the development of **index funds**. Index funds are open-end funds that passively track a stock index such as the S&P 500 without trying to outperform it. The CAPM also provides a starting point for estimates of expected returns for asset classes, even for active portfolio managers. Finally, the CAPM is the basis for cost-of-capital computations; it is this application of the CAPM that is most useful for this book. The next section provides a technical introduction to the main CAPM equation. The following sections help interpret it and illustrate its practical use in a global context, where exchange rate movements may complicate the model's application.

A Derivation of the CAPM (Advanced)

To derive the CAPM relation, we go back to the beginning of the chapter, where we looked at the diversification problem. Suppose we have a portfolio, p, and we consider adding a little bit of a new asset, say with a fraction, w. That is, the new portfolio has $(1 - w)$ in the old portfolio and w in the new asset. When we add a little bit of that new asset to the portfolio, when will the Sharpe ratio improve? The answer is that the Sharpe ratio will increase as long as the following condition holds:

$$SR_{NEW} \geq \rho \times SR_p$$

where ρ is the correlation between the portfolio, p, and the new asset, SR_{NEW}, is the Sharpe ratio of the new asset, and SR_p is the Sharpe ratio of the present portfolio. As we add more of the new asset, the correlation of the portfolio (now containing the new asset) with the new asset increases, and hence the condition becomes harder to satisfy. We should keep adding the asset until:

$$SR_{NEW} = \rho \times SR_p \tag{13.4}$$

At that point, further additions no longer increase the Sharpe ratio; that is, we will have reached the portfolio that maximizes the Sharpe ratio, the MVE portfolio. Rewriting Equation (13.4) using the definition of the Sharpe ratio is informative:

$$\frac{E(r_{\text{NEW}}) - r_f}{\sigma_{\text{NEW}}} = \rho \times \frac{E(r_p) - r_f}{\sigma_p} \quad \text{or}$$

$$\frac{E(r_{\text{NEW}}) - r_f}{\rho \times \sigma_{\text{NEW}}} = \frac{E(r_p) - r_f}{\sigma_p}$$

$(1 - \rho)\sigma_{\text{NEW}}$ of the total risk of the individual asset is diversified away in the portfolio because of imperfect correlation.

This relationship holds for any security, i, we consider adding to the MVE portfolio.

Because $\rho = \dfrac{\text{Cov}(r_i, r_p)}{\sigma_{\text{NEW}}\sigma_p}$, we find

$$\frac{E(r_i) - r_f}{\text{Cov}(r_i, r_p)} = \frac{E(r_p) - r_f}{\sigma_p^2} \tag{13.5}$$

This equation also implies that the expected excess returns per unit of covariance risk are the same for all assets and are equal to $\dfrac{E(r_p) - r_f}{\sigma_p^2}$. The relevant risk for a security is its covariance with the MVE portfolio. Rewriting Equation (13.5) gives

$$E(r_i) - r_f = \frac{\text{Cov}(r_i, r_p)}{\sigma_p^2} \times [E(r_p) - r_f] \tag{13.6}$$

Equation (13.6) establishes a relationship between the expected excess return on an individual asset and the expected return on the MVE portfolio.

We are almost finished. Let's review the major findings of the previous section on optimal asset allocation:

1. The efficient frontier is a set of "dominant" portfolios in risk–return space. Non-efficient portfolios would not be held by any mean-variance investor.
2. If there exists a risk-free asset, one portfolio of risky securities offers the best risk–return trade-off: the MVE portfolio.

Now, if everybody is a mean-variance investor facing the same frontier, what portfolio must the MVE be for there to be no excess demand or supply for any security? It must be the market portfolio—and that is what the CAPM says! The implication is

$$E(r_i) - r_f = \frac{\text{Cov}(r_i, r_m)}{\sigma_m^2} \times (E(r_m) - r_f)$$

where the subscript m represents the market portfolio. The relationship between the individual's security expected excess return and the market portfolio's expected return depends on the statistical construct $\dfrac{\text{Cov}(r_i, r_m)}{\sigma_m^2}$, which is called the *beta* (β) of security i.

Interpreting the CAPM

The CAPM is often used as a benchmark to determine the required rate of return on risky equity capital. The CAPM provides a formula for the required rate of return on an equity investment, which is its expected rate of return, $E(r_e)$.

The CAPM Equilibrium

Equity investors require compensation for the time value of money based on the risk-free rate, r_f. In addition, they require compensation for the systematic, or non-diversifiable, risk of the investment. Systematic risk is measured by the beta of the equity, β_e, multiplied by the risk premium on the market portfolio, $[E(r_m) - r_f]$. An equity's **beta** is the covariance of the rate of return on the equity with the rate of return on the market portfolio divided by the variance of the rate of return on the market portfolio:

$$\beta_e = \frac{\text{Cov}(r_e, r_m)}{\text{Var}(r_m)}$$

Hence, the CAPM states that

$$E(r_e) = r_f + \beta_e[E(r_m) - r_f] \tag{13.7}$$

The logic of the CAPM begins with the assumptions that investors prefer higher expected returns but that they are averse to risk. From the investor's perspective, risk is measured by the variance of the return on the overall portfolio. Given the expected future cash flows of the assets, changes in the market prices change the assets' expected returns and their variances and covariances. In equilibrium, the market prices of assets adjust such that the expected returns on the different assets and their variances and covariances allow the market portfolio to be willingly held by investors. This will happen when the expected excess returns per unit of covariance risk are equalized across assets and equal the expected excess return on the market divided by its variance (see Equation (13.5) in the section "A Derivation of the CAPM (Advanced)," earlier in this chapter). In equilibrium, all investors are thought to be holding the market portfolio because they are assumed to have the same expectations and the same investment opportunities.

The Risk Premium on the Market

The risk premium on the market portfolio is the amount by which the expected return on the market exceeds the risk-free rate. The CAPM actually predicts that this risk premium will depend on the average risk aversion in the market and the variance of the market portfolio return. To see this, consider Equation (13.3) but applied to the market portfolio. Because every investor chooses to combine the market portfolio with the risk-free asset according to her preferences, someone with average risk aversion, say $\bar{A}$, will hold exactly the market portfolio. Consequently, $w^* = 1 = \dfrac{1}{\bar{A}} \dfrac{E(r_m) - r_f}{\sigma_m^2}$, or

$$E(r_m) - r_f = \bar{A}\sigma_m^2 \tag{13.8}$$

Hence, the **market risk premium** balances the variance of the market portfolio to reflect the average risk aversion of the investors in the market.

Individual Expected Returns and the Role of Beta

Investors can reduce the contribution of the variance of a particular security to the total variance of their portfolios by diversifying their investments across a wide array of assets. In the CAPM equilibrium, such diversification leads to the proposition that if an equity return is not correlated with the return on the market portfolio, then the equity's expected return is equal to the risk-free rate because investors do not need to be compensated for bearing the uncertainty associated with the return on that particular asset. In Equation (13.7), if $\beta_e = 0$, then $E(r_e) = r_f$. The diversification argument shows that if an asset does not covary with the market portfolio, it becomes effectively riskless when it is held in a large, diversified portfolio that mirrors the market portfolio.

Equity returns that covary positively with the return on the market portfolio contribute to the variance of the return on the market portfolio. Consequently, these positive beta assets require an expected rate of return that is greater than the risk-free rate. On the other hand, an asset with a negative beta, whose return covaries negatively with the return on the market portfolio, actually reduces the overall variance of the portfolio. Investors are consequently willing to hold this asset even though its expected return is driven below the return on the risk-free interest rate in the competitive equilibrium. Most equities have positive betas, however, because the market environment tends to affect all stocks the same way.

Notice that the asset's beta is a measure of its relative risk because the beta is the covariance of the asset's return with the return on the market portfolio divided by the variance of the return on the market portfolio. If the beta is 1, the covariance of the asset's return with the return on the market portfolio equals the variance of the return on the market, and the asset's expected return is the same as the market's expected return. If the beta is larger than 1, the covariance is larger than the variance, and the asset is contributing a disproportionate share to the variance of the market portfolio. It must therefore be priced with an expected return that exceeds the expected return on the market portfolio.

Domestic Versus World CAPMs

In a **domestic CAPM**, the market portfolio is defined as the aggregate asset holdings of all investors in a particular country. Many real-world applications of the CAPM use domestic CAPMs. For example, the beta for a UK firm that is listed on the London Stock Exchange would be calculated relative to the value-weighted market return on the London Stock Exchange, and the beta for a Japanese firm that is listed on the Tokyo Stock Exchange would be calculated relative to the value-weighted market return on the Tokyo Stock Exchange.

What are the implications of this assumption? The domestic CAPM assumes that assets of a country are held only by investors who reside in that country. In such a case, there would be no international diversification of risk, and countries' capital markets would be completely internationally segmented. We discuss the concept of a segmented and integrated market more fully in Section 13.6. When the CAPM was first developed in the 1960s, international segmentation seemed reasonable because capital flows and portfolio investments were limited. Today, in an increasingly globalized world, it makes more sense to use an internationally diversified portfolio of securities as the market portfolio. This CAPM is called the **world CAPM**.

The Role of Exchange Rates

One major theoretical problem with using the world CAPM is that the development of the theory assumes that investors share the same expectations about the real returns on different assets. Given the observed deviations from purchasing power parity and fluctuations in real exchange rates discussed in Chapter 8, there is a substantial amount of evidence contrary to this premise. When real exchange rates fluctuate, investors in different countries have different perceptions about the real returns on different assets. Let's illustrate this with an example.

Let r_e be the real equity return on a U.S. security for a U.S.-based investor, and let r_f be the real risk-free rate in the United States. The world CAPM states

$$E(r_e) - r_f = \beta_e \left[E(r_m) - r_f \right] \tag{13.9}$$

where r_m is the real return on the world market portfolio. Because we are defining real returns for a U.S.-based investor, they are computed relative to the U.S. consumption basket, using the U.S. price level. For example, the real rate of return on equity, r_e, can be computed by subtracting 1 from 1 plus the nominal rate of return divided by 1 plus the U.S. rate of inflation: $\dfrac{1 + r_e(\$)}{1 + \pi(\$)} - 1$. Similarly, from Chapter 10, we know that r_f, the *ex ante* real interest rate, is the expected value of the *ex post* real interest rate:

$$r_f = r_f(\text{US}) = E\left[\frac{1 + i(\$)}{1 + \pi(\$)} - 1\right]$$

where $i(\$)$ is the nominal interest rate.

Now, what is the expected real return on the same U.S. security for a German investor? The German investor cares about real German returns, hence

$$\frac{1 + r_e(\text{€})}{1 + \pi(\text{€})} = \frac{[1 + r_e(\$)](1 + s)}{1 + \pi(\text{€})}$$

with s representing the percentage change in the euro–dollar exchange rate. But the expression for the dollar-based version of the CAPM contains the real return for the U.S. investor, $\dfrac{1 + r_e(\$)}{1 + \pi(\$)}$. This only equals the real return for the German investor when $\dfrac{1 + s}{1 + \pi(\text{€})} = \dfrac{1}{1 + \pi(\$)}$, or $1 + s = \dfrac{1 + \pi(\text{€})}{1 + \pi(\$)}$. In other words, the real returns for the U.S.-based and German-based investors are identical only when purchasing power parity (PPP) holds.

What about the risk-free rate? For the German-based investor, it should be defined relative to her consumption basket. Consequently, the *ex ante* German risk-free rate is $r_f(G) = E\left[\dfrac{1 + i(\text{€})}{1 + \pi(\text{€})}\right] - 1$. If we assume that PPP holds, we find that $r_f(G) = E\left[\dfrac{1 + i(\text{€})}{(1 + s)(1 + \pi(\$))} - 1\right]$. Of course, $E\left[\dfrac{1 + i(\text{€})}{1 + s}\right]$ is the dollar return on an investment in the euro money market. For the real interest rates to be equalized across countries, we need more than just PPP to hold. We also need the real expected returns on money market investments to be equal across countries—that is, we need a real version of uncovered interest rate parity to hold.[1] We conclude that translating the world CAPM to the other country's perspectives works only when all the international parity conditions hold.

So far we have focused on real returns as the theory demands. However, in practice, CAPMs are mostly applied using nominal returns. Let the nominal equity return be denoted by $r_e(\$)$, and let $i(\$)$ represent the money market interest rate in the United States. The world CAPM for the U.S.-based investor is then formulated as follows:

$$E[r_e(\$) - i(\$)] = \beta_e\,[E[r_m(\$) - i(\$)]] \qquad \textbf{(13.10)}$$

where the equity return is earned over a short interval such as 1 month, and the interest rate is the 1-month Treasury bill rate known at the beginning of the month. For such small intervals of time, the Equations (13.9) and (13.10) are indeed nearly equivalent. This is because, by definition, $r_e = \dfrac{1 + r_e(\$)}{1 + \pi(\$)} - 1 \approx r_e(\$) - \pi(\$)$. Moreover,

$$r_f = E\left[\frac{1 + i(\$)}{1 + \pi(\$)} - 1\right] \approx E[i(\$) - \pi(\$)].$$ It is easy to see that the inflation rates cancel out of the equation.

---

[1] In Chapter 10, we derived that real interest rates are equalized across countries when PPP, uncovered interest rate parity, and the Fisher hypothesis hold.

Of course, the beta computation in the two equations is different, involving real returns in Equation (13.9) and nominal excess returns in Equation (13.10). Because equity returns are much more variable than inflation and interest rates, these differences are immaterial from a practical perspective.

International CAPMs (Advanced)

The conditions for the world CAPM to apply to all countries are rather stringent. With deviations from the parity conditions, theory would suggest more complex models where inflation and exchange rate risks enter the expected return computation. Many models of international capital market equilibrium have been developed, but not one model has attained a dominant status.[2] Most models allow for currency risk premiums in one form or another.

An example of the most popular model in this class builds on the theories of Bruno Solnik (1974b) and Piet Sercu (1980) and forms the counterpart to the nominal returns model in Equation (13.10):

$$E[r_j(\$) - i(\$)] = \beta_j E[r_w(\$) - i(\$)] + \sum_{k=1}^{K} \gamma_{i,k} E[s_k(t+1) - fp_k(t)] \quad \textbf{(13.11)}$$

We assume that the dollar is the numeraire and that risk is measured for a U.S. investor.[3] The first term represents the standard world market risk; the other terms represent exchange rate risk, with s_k representing the rate of foreign currency appreciation and fp_k the forward premium on currency k. Exchange rates are thus measured as $ per currency, k. Investing in a foreign currency, k, may yield an expected excess return equal to $E[s_k(t+1) - fp_k(t)] = E\left[\dfrac{S_k(t+1) - F_k(t)}{S(t)} \right]$, with exchange rates as $/k$.

The γ's in Equation (13.11) measure the exposure of the firm's returns to exchange rate risk. For example, an exporter with many unhedged foreign currency receivables may exhibit positive γ's. That is, if these currencies appreciate substantially, the firm's return will be high as well. Of course, if uncovered interest rate parity holds, this model collapses to the world CAPM. To compute the cost of capital in such a setting, we must run a multivariate regression of excess returns for security j onto the world market return and various relevant currency returns. In practice, we use only a few major currencies or even a currency basket.

It is not clear whether the **international CAPM** is a better model than the world CAPM. Recent articles by Bernard Dumas and Bruno Solnik (1995) and Xiaoyan Zhang (2006) suggest that exchange rate risk is priced and that adding exchange rate factors to cost of capital computations is important. Other studies, such as that by John Griffin and René Stulz (2001), cast doubt on this conclusion. Because of the continuing academic controversy and the scant use of such models in practical capital budgeting situations, we do not further discuss these models.

13.5 THE CAPM IN PRACTICE

As we will explain in detail in Chapter 15, when a firm decides whether to allocate capital to a project, it must discount the project's cash flows at a discount rate equal to the expected return investors would require when investing in the project directly. The CAPM delivers such a discount rate. Thus, to be concrete about how to develop the cost of equity capital, we provide a recipe.

---

[2]See Michael Adler and Bernard Dumas (1983) for an early model and Andrew Karolyi and René Stulz (2002) for a more recent survey.
[3]One problem with the many variants of the international CAPM, including the one presented here, is that the exact outcome of the cost-of-capital computation may depend on the numeraire currency.

A Recipe for the Cost of Equity Capital

Recall the CAPM equation for security j:

$$E[r_j] - r_f = \beta_j [E(r_m) - r_f]$$

where $\beta_j = \dfrac{\text{Cov}(r_j, r_m)}{\text{Var}(r_m)}$. The recipe for finding the expected nominal return on security j is straightforward:

Step 1. Get data on the market portfolio return, the equity returns on security j, and the T-bill interest rate.

Step 2. Determine the market risk premium. The market risk premium is the expected excess return on a portfolio that approximates the market portfolio—in short, the market portfolio proxy.

Step 3. Obtain an estimate of β_j.

Step 4. Compute the expected return on security j as
T-bill rate (r_f) + Beta (β_j) × Market risk premium $[E(r_m - r_f)]$

This recipe reveals three problems in applying the CAPM to a practical capital budgeting situation: the choice of a benchmark (how to measure the market portfolio), the estimation of beta, and the determination of the risk premium on the market portfolio. We discuss each in turn.

The Benchmark Problem

The Market Portfolio

One problem that has plagued the CAPM since its early development is the issue of which portfolio to use as the market portfolio.[4] The theoretically correct value of the return on the market portfolio is the value-weighted return on all assets that are available for investors to purchase. If the return on the market portfolio is measured in dollars, it would consequently include the dollar-denominated returns on the equities of all the corporations of the different countries of the world, the dollar-denominated returns on the bonds of all the corporations and the governments of these countries, and the dollar-denominated returns on real estate and assets such as gold and land.

No one has ever attempted to use this version of the theory because its data requirements are too stringent. We simply do not have all the data. More importantly, though, financial markets are too imperfect to allow us to think that highly illiquid assets, such as real estate, would be bought and sold like stocks and bonds. Because data on the returns on corporate and government bonds in many countries are also difficult to obtain, in practice, people attempt to use the CAPM as if it were a theory that relates individual equity rates of return to a market portfolio composed of only equities.

World Market Proxies

When the CAPM is applied for a particular company's project, the proxy for the market portfolio should in theory represent the well-diversified portfolio that the firm's investors are holding. In practice, many U.S. companies use the U.S. stock market index as the market portfolio. With the increasing globalization of investors' portfolios (see Section 13.6), a world market index is becoming more and more appropriate. Although the availability of data on a world market index is imperfect, there are reasonable proxies available, such as the Morgan Stanley Capital International (MSCI) Index and the Financial Times Actuaries (FTA) Index.

---

[4]This issue is often called the "Roll critique" because Richard Roll was the first to write about the problems involved in testing the CAPM. Roll (1977) argued that statistical rejections of the theory could be incorrect if a statistician did not observe the true market portfolio.

Getting the Benchmark Wrong

We would like to know how large a mistake is made quantitatively if we use a country-specific CAPM (domestic CAPM) when the assets of the country are actually priced by investors with a world CAPM. If the assets of this country are actually priced internationally, the expected return on asset i, $E[r_i]$, satisfies the world CAPM:

$$E(r_i) = r_f + \beta_{im}[E(r_m) - r_f] \tag{13.12}$$

where r_m is the return on the world market portfolio and β_{im} is the beta of the return on asset i with the market return. We denote this "true" expected return or cost of equity capital by COE_i^{TR}. Now, suppose we postulate incorrectly that the expected return on asset i is determined by the covariance of the return on asset i with the return on the home market portfolio, r_h, as in the following version of a domestic CAPM:

$$E(r_i) = r_f + \beta_{ih}[E(r_h) - r_f] \tag{13.13}$$

Denote the cost of equity capital number resulting from this computation by COE_i^{FA}.

To compute the error in using Equation (13.13) rather than Equation (13.12), we first compute the correct expected return on the home market portfolio. The return on the home-country market portfolio is the value-weighted return on the individual assets in the country, and hence, it will also satisfy the world CAPM, as in Equation (13.12):

$$E(r_h) = r_f + \beta_{hm}[E(r_m) - r_f] \tag{13.14}$$

Will the application of a domestic CAPM lead to the correct expected returns for the individual stocks of this country? To find out, let's investigate the difference between the two costs of equity capital:

$$COE_i^{FA} - COE_i^{TR} = \beta_{ih}[E(r_h) - r_f] - \beta_{im}[E(r_m) - r_f]$$
$$= (\beta_{ih}\beta_{hm} - \beta_{im})[E(r_m) - r_f]$$

where we used Equations (13.13) and (13.14). Thus, we see that the expected return on asset i will be correct if $\beta_{im} = \beta_{ih}\beta_{hm}$. Example 13.5 provides some insight into when this expression is likely to be right and how badly things go if it is wrong.

Example 13.5 The Nestlé Cost of Equity Capital

René Stulz (1995) applies the analysis used here to derive two estimates of the expected return for the Swiss company Nestlé. Stulz estimates the beta of the Swiss franc return on Nestlé with respect to the Swiss franc return on the Swiss market portfolio (β_{ih}) to be 0.885. The beta of the Swiss franc return on Nestlé with respect to the Swiss franc return on the world market portfolio (β_{im}) using the world market index from the *Financial Times* is 0.585. The beta of the Swiss franc return on the Swiss market portfolio with respect to the Swiss franc return on the world market portfolio (β_{hm}) is 0.737. Hence, the pricing error in beta from using the domestic CAPM rather than the world CAPM is

$$\beta_{ih}\beta_{hm} - \beta_{im} = (0.885 \times 0.737) - 0.585 = 0.067$$

Stulz uses an expected excess return on the world market portfolio $(E(r_m) - r_f)$ of 6.22%, in which case the error for Nestlé from using a domestic CAPM instead of the global CAPM is $0.067 \times 6.22\% = 0.42\%$

Thus, using local pricing instead of global pricing implies an expected return for Nestlé that is 0.42% higher than it should be. If Nestlé is priced in the world market and not the local market, its required expected return should be the risk-free return on Swiss franc bonds plus a risk premium equal to the beta with the world market portfolio multiplied by the excess return on the world market portfolio, $0.585 \times 6.22\% = 3.64\%$. If Nestlé is priced in the local market, its required expected return would be the risk-free return on Swiss franc bonds plus a risk premium equal to $3.64\% + 0.42\% = 4.06\%$.

This example demonstrates that, at least for Nestlé, the error from using a domestic CAPM when the world CAPM is appropriate does not seem to be too big. Estimation error in the betas and the mean return on the world market portfolio could easily lead one to consider discount rates that are in this range when doing sensitivity analysis. In a similar exercise, Robert Harris et al. (2003) show that the world CAPM and the domestic CAPM led to similar cost-of-capital estimates for S&P 500 firms.

Beta Estimation

Recall that the beta for security j is given by $\beta_j = \dfrac{\text{Cov}[r_j, r_m]}{\text{Var}[r_m]}$. Astute readers will recognize that β_j can be viewed as the regression coefficient from regressing $r_j - r_f$ onto $r_m - r_f$ (see the appendix to Chapter 7). Suppose you have data on excess returns of security j, $r_j^e(t) = r_j(t) - i(t-1)$, and of the market, $r_m^e(t) = r_m(t) - i(t-1)$, where $i(t-1)$ is the risk-free rate from time $t-1$ to time t, the T-bill rate, and the returns are in nominal terms. How would you obtain β_j? You would run the regression:

$$r_j^e(t) = \alpha_i + \beta_j r_m^e(t) + \epsilon_j(t)$$

where $\epsilon_j(t)$ is the residual or error term in the regression. Exhibit 13.12 demonstrates graphically what we would find in a regression framework.

Exhibit 13.12 Estimating Beta

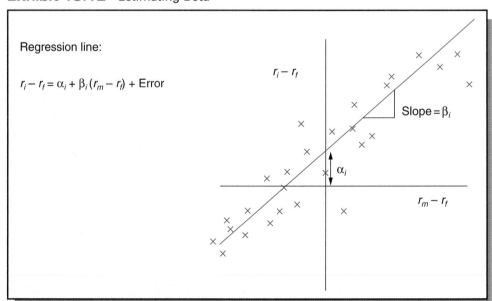

Note: CAPM implies $\alpha_i = 0$.

Many firms use the CAPM in their capital budgeting analyses. They can estimate the beta of a firm directly by choosing a portfolio to represent the market portfolio that is held by their investors and run the regression just described. They can also purchase beta estimates from companies that publish them, such as Value Line or Barra. Typically, the regression analysis uses only 60 months of data to accommodate the possibility that the risk profiles of companies change over time.

Estimating a beta using a regression is often imprecise because a firm's returns exhibit considerable idiosyncratic volatility. That is, much of the variation in a firm's return is driven by firm-specific events. This idiosyncratic volatility reduces the fit of the regression and increases the standard errors of the estimates. Therefore some beta providers (such as Merrill Lynch) shrink the estimates toward 1, which is the value we would expect without other information. Another approach is to use industry portfolios. If firms in the same industry have about the same systematic risk, their betas will be about the same as well. A portfolio of firms diversifies away a lot of idiosyncratic risk and is consequently much less variable than an individual firm's stock returns. Therefore, beta estimates from industry portfolios are more precise.

Example 13.6   Comparing Firm and Industry Betas

Yahoo's financial website (www.finance.yahoo.com) provides estimates of betas. Let's compare beta estimates obtained from there on November 10, 2003, with beta estimates we compute for industry portfolios. The Yahoo estimates use 5 years of individual stock returns on a monthly basis, whereas the industry estimates use a longer sample (40 years of data):

Firm	Yahoo Beta	Industry	Industry Beta
GM	1.185	Autos and Trucks	0.97
McDonald's	0.79	Restaurants	1.22
Wells Fargo	0.39	Banks	1.07
Microsoft	1.74	Software	1.07
Merck	0.30	Drugs	0.88

The individual stock betas vary between 0.30 (Merck) and 1.74 (Microsoft), whereas the industry estimates are much closer to 1.0.

There are good reasons for some companies to have betas that deviate from the industry average. For instance, they may have more or less financial leverage (debt value relative to equity value). If equity holders have to pay off bondholders before laying claim to the firm's assets, their claims are riskier. Nevertheless, betas of only 0.30 for Merck and 0.39 for Wells Fargo are almost surely due to unusual idiosyncratic movements of the firm's stock prices over the sample period and are unlikely to give rise to reliable cost-of-capital estimates.

The Risk Premium on the Market

Historical Estimates

Eugene Fama and Kenneth French (1997) argue that estimates of the cost of equity for industries are imprecise. In particular, a substantial part of the error comes from estimates of the risk premium on the market portfolio.

Exhibit 13.13   Equity Risk Premiums Around the World

Country	Mean	Standard Deviation
Australia	8.3	17.2
Belgium	4.4	23.1
Canada	5.5	16.8
Denmark	3.8	19.6
France	8.9	24.0
Germany	9.4	35.5
Ireland	5.5	20.4
Italy	10.3	32.5
Japan	9.3	28.0
The Netherlands	6.4	22.6
South Africa	7.9	22.2
Spain	4.9	21.5
Sweden	7.5	22.2
Switzerland	4.8	18.8
United Kingdom	5.9	20.1
United States	7.2	19.8
Average	6.9	22.8
World	5.7	16.5

Notes: Data are from Dimson, Marsh, and Staunton (2003). The Mean column reports the average return on equity in percentage per annum over and above a risk-free return for the period 1900 to 2002. The Standard Deviation column reports the annual standard deviation of these excess returns.

It is surprising how little consensus there is about the magnitude of the **equity risk premium**.[5] To estimate the risk premium, the first logical step is to look at history. Because stock returns are so volatile, it is important to take a long-run perspective.

Elroy Dimson, Paul Marsh, and Mike Staunton (2003) collected 100 years' worth of data for 16 countries. Exhibit 13.13 is based on their data and produces historical risk premiums for the 16 countries listed, which vary between 3.8% for Denmark and 10.3% for Italy.

The estimate for the United States is 7.2%, which is lower than the estimate that would be obtained with more recent data.

Caveats

The historical estimates we just looked at, even with such a long sample, are still prone to a large sampling error, and different subperiods give very different answers. For example, Jeremy Siegel (1992) examined U.S. data from 1800 to 1990, and found that from 1800 to 1888, the equity premium was slightly less than 2% per annum.[6] From 1889 to 1978, it was 7.04%, and from 1979 to 1990, it was 6.97%.

In fact, whereas the historical estimate of the risk premium is large, recent research has argued for smaller premiums going forward. For example, Fama and French (2002) argue that the high average realized equity returns are greater than what was expected over the past 50 years because the *ex post* returns include "large unexpected capital gains" caused by a decline in discount rates. James Claus and Jacob Thomas (2001) use analysts' forecasts to argue that the equity premium should be 3%, which is less than half the historical average.

It is certainly possible that there was a permanent decline in risk premiums. Investing in the stock market was traditionally difficult, costly, and limited to a select few, but now better

---

[5]A direct perspective on this issue can be gleaned from Ivo Welch's (2000) survey of the opinions of professional economists.

[6]Stephen Brown, William Goetzmann, and Stephen Ross (1995) argue that the equity markets of various countries have periodically closed or failed outright. Hence, they caution against interpreting the average return from a long uninterrupted stretch as in the Siegel data as an estimate of the expected *ex ante* return. If investors thought that the market might actually fail, but it did not, then the average return would be abnormally high.

technology, improved communication, an efficient mutual fund industry, and 401(k) legislation have increased stock market participation to close to 50% of the U.S. populace. Broadening the base of equity holders spreads risks and should decrease the risk premium. A decline in the risk premium produces a capital gain in stocks, but these high past returns signal future lower expected returns. Although there was a severe stock market correction in 2000 through 2002, the level of the stock market as measured by price–earnings ratios, for example, is still high relative to historical benchmarks. If the high stock market levels reflect permanently lower risk, we may have witnessed a permanent change in the price earnings ratio that reflects a lower equity premium going forward. Given this, we propose to use an equity premium between 4% and 8%.

The Need for Sensitivity Analysis

Clearly, there is variability in the estimate of the degree to which the market rate of return will exceed the risk-free rate. There is also variability in the estimates of any betas that can be calculated. In light of these imprecise estimates, doing sensitivity analysis when estimating the cost of equity capital is a good idea. The imprecision in the estimates of both the beta and the risk premium must be taken into account, which makes it difficult to give general guidance on a sensible range for **sensitivity analysis**. However, it is likely that the error in the risk premium dominates and requires the use of a fairly large range of values extending to $\pm 2\%$ around the estimates of the cost of capital.

13.6 INTEGRATED VERSUS SEGMENTED MARKETS

In this section, we first discuss investing in emerging markets and the critical role investment barriers play. We then discuss how integrated versus segmented markets affect a company's cost of capital. We end the section by describing the phenomenon of home bias.

Investing in Emerging Markets

Exhibit 13.14 reports characteristics of emerging market equity returns for the period 1988 to 2006. The average returns vary between 1.51% for China and a stellar 41.92% per annum for Russia. However, emerging market returns are very volatile, with most of annualized volatilities exceeding 30%. Russia's volatility is a whopping 62.76%. Nevertheless, the volatility of an index of emerging market returns measured in dollars is only 23%, which is about the same magnitude as that experienced by a developed country such as Japan.

The reduced volatility of the index reflects the low correlations across the markets and the substantial benefits of diversification. The last four columns report the correlations of emerging market returns with the stock returns of the United States, Japan, the United Kingdom, and Germany. The correlations are generally low and regularly below 25%. South Africa, one of the most developed of the emerging markets, exhibits a somewhat higher correlation (of over 40%) with all four developed markets. Such high correlations are rare for Japan, the United Kingdom, and Germany, but they occur for another eight emerging markets when their returns are correlated with U.S. returns. In the case of Japan, for instance, the only other correlation above 40% is with Korea, a close neighbor. Such low correlations should make it possible to construct low-risk portfolios.

It is therefore not surprising that early studies showed very significant diversification benefits for emerging market investments. However, these studies used market indexes compiled by the International Finance Corporation (IFC) that generally ignored the high transaction costs, low liquidity, and investment constraints associated with emerging market investments.

Exhibit 13.14 Average Returns and Volatilies in Emerging Markets

	Average Market Return	Volatility	Correlation with U.S. Returns	Correlation with Japanese Returns	Correlation with UK Returns	Correlation with German Returns
Argentina	34.34	58.25	0.23	0.02	0.11	0.11
Brazil	35.68	55.99	0.34	0.24	0.27	0.25
Chile	20.85	24.82	0.41	0.15	0.26	0.29
China	1.51	38.24	0.42	0.15	0.33	0.29
Colombia	19.65	33.31	0.17	0.10	0.21	0.22
Czech Republic	20.62	28.74	0.20	0.17	0.28	0.33
Egypt	25.18	33.02	0.20	0.17	0.17	0.18
Hungary	25.47	36.10	0.46	0.19	0.42	0.46
India	13.59	28.89	0.24	0.23	0.17	0.26
Indonesia	21.95	53.91	0.25	0.13	0.13	0.20
Israel	9.28	26.09	0.53	0.18	0.43	0.51
Jordan	8.89	17.84	0.09	0.08	0.08	0.03
Korea	15.02	39.86	0.35	0.45	0.30	0.22
Malaysia	11.32	31.22	0.33	0.23	0.31	0.32
Mexico	27.55	33.03	0.49	0.25	0.31	0.33
Morocco	14.59	18.80	0.05	0.10	0.19	0.18
Pakistan	16.22	39.32	0.10	0.04	0.12	0.12
Peru	20.01	31.09	0.23	0.31	0.23	0.25
Philippines	9.75	33.15	0.36	0.22	0.24	0.28
Poland	30.25	53.12	0.32	0.28	0.32	0.31
Russia	41.92	62.76	0.43	0.32	0.42	0.27
South Africa	16.53	27.28	0.43	0.45	0.45	0.44
Taiwan	13.61	39.16	0.28	0.21	0.16	0.29
Thailand	13.97	40.53	0.43	0.31	0.30	0.33
Turkey	29.02	61.96	0.26	0.12	0.22	0.31
Venezuela	19.08	49.05	0.24	0.16	0.17	0.17
EMF	16.10	23.02	0.59	0.40	0.46	0.47

Notes: For most emerging markets, the monthly data run from January 1988 to July 2006. All returns are in U.S. dollars. The last line reports characteristics for returns on the Emerging Market Index, a value-weighted average of all 26 country indexes.

Investment Barriers and Diversification

In the early 1990s, many emerging markets imposed severe investment restrictions on foreign investors. In Korea, most stocks were subject to strict foreign ownership restrictions (foreign ownership was limited to 10% of market capitalization for most stocks). Countries such as Chile prohibited foreign investors from immediately cashing in their capital gains and dividends. Given these conditions, it seems unlikely that the returns cited in the early diversification studies could actually have been captured by foreign investors.

Research by Geert Bekaert and Michael Urias (1996, 1999) examined the diversification benefits U.S. investors enjoyed through investing in a variety of different investment vehicles for emerging markets, such as closed-end funds, ADRs, and open-end funds. These assets are easily accessible to retail investors, and investment costs are comparable to the investment costs for U.S.-traded stocks. Historically, closed-end country funds have been an important means of access to restricted markets, while open-end funds and ADRs were relatively unimportant before 1993. Bekaert and Urias find that investors give up a substantial part of the diversification benefits by holding closed-end funds of the underlying portfolios to the point that the benefits from investing in U.S.-traded closed-end funds are not significant relative to an internationally diversified portfolio benchmark. Open-end funds, on the other hand, prove to offer substantial diversification benefits.

These results suggest that **investment barriers** may prevent the diversification benefits from emerging markets from being fully realized. It is therefore very unlikely that emerging markets satisfy the strong assumptions underlying the CAPM. In particular, emerging markets may not be completely integrated with world capital markets, making the world CAPM the wrong model to use. We now clarify the crucial distinction between integrated and segmented markets.

The Cost of Capital in Integrated and Segmented Markets

Markets are integrated when assets of identical risk command the same expected return, irrespective of their domicile. The governmental interferences with free capital markets in emerging markets can prevent market integration and effectively segment the capital markets of a country from the world capital market. If foreign investors are taxed or otherwise prohibited from holding the equities of a country, then that country's assets are not part of the world market portfolio, and that country is said to be segmented from international capital markets.

The implications of segmentation for determining the cost of capital are important. Suppose we want to figure out the expected return on the Colombian stock market. If the Colombian stock market is integrated with world capital markets, we can simply use the world CAPM and the world market return as the benchmark portfolio. However, such an exercise would yield a very low expected return for Colombia because the low correlation Colombia displays with the world market translates into a low beta. Whereas this may be the right computation to make in particular capital budgeting situations for foreigners, it clearly would yield a poor estimate of the true expected market return for local investors.

Campbell Harvey (1995) shows that the world CAPM provides a poor description of emerging market returns in general and that the domestic CAPM fares much better. Because the Colombian market is segmented, all securities will be priced according to their correlation with the Columbian market portfolio, but investors will not be able to diversify the risk of the Colombian market. Therefore, the expected return on the Colombian market will be a function of its own volatility. This follows from aggregating the CAPM to the market level, as in Equation (13.7):

$$E[r_j] = r_f + \beta_j E[r_{col} - r_f] \qquad (13.15)$$

for every j security in Colombia, where r_{col} is the return on the Colombian market. We know that the β_j is the covariance of security j with the market portfolio; hence, we can rewrite Equation (13.15) as

$$E[r_j] = r_f + \text{Cov}(r_j, r_{col}) \frac{E[r_{col} - r_f]}{\text{Var}(r_{col})}$$

The expected return on the market portfolio divided by its variance is typically called the price of risk. If investors hold only equities, Equation (13.8) shows that this price of risk equals the average risk aversion of the investors in Colombia. Let's denote this by A_{col}. Consequently, $E[r_j] = r_f + A_{col} \text{Cov}(r_j, r_{col})$, and aggregating over all securities in Colombia,

$$E[r_{col}] = r_f + A_{col} \text{Var}(r_{col})$$

Therefore, in **segmented markets**, expected and hence average returns should be related to the variance of returns rather than to the covariance with the world market return.

Example 13.7   The Expected Return in Colombia

From data on Colombian stock returns, we determine that its world market beta for the past 5 years is 0.4431. Given a risk-free rate of 6% and a world market premium of 5%, full integration dictates an expected return for the Colombian market of

$$6\% + 0.4431 \times 5\% = 8.22\%$$

While some foreign investors may find this cost-of-capital estimate low, most of the risk associated with investing in Colombia may indeed be political in nature and idiosyncratic to Colombia. Thus, it would not represent systematic risk.

However, if Colombia is truly segmented, the local expected return depends on the local market volatility, which stands at 33.31% in dollar terms (see Exhibit 13.14). Suppose the average risk aversion in Colombia is 2.0. Under a domestic CAPM for Colombia, the expected return on the Colombian market is

$$E[r_{\text{col}}] = 6\% + 2.0\,(0.3331)^2 = 28.19\%$$

Clearly, the cost-of-capital estimates from the domestic CAPM and the world CAPM are very different. The fact that the domestic CAPM expected return is so unrealistically high may suggest that the Colombian market is not fully segmented and that part of its variability is diversifiable.

Equity Market Liberalizations

Equity market liberalizations allow inward and outward foreign equity investment. The equity market liberalizations that took place in the late 1980s and early 1990s in many emerging markets form a nice laboratory to investigate the effects of potential integration into global capital markets.

If liberalization brings about integration with the global capital market, and if the world CAPM holds, what do we expect to happen? Suppose that the country is completely segmented from world capital markets before the liberalization. In this case, it is possible for the real interest rate in the country to be quite a bit higher than the world real interest rate. Also, the risk premiums associated with the equities in that country will be dictated by the variance of the return on that country's market portfolio. As we saw in Example 13.7, these risk premiums may be quite high.

Now, suppose the country unexpectedly opens its capital markets to the world economy. Two things will happen: First, the real interest rate in the country should fall dramatically because the country's residents are now free to borrow and lend internationally, and there is additional foreign supply of capital.[7] Second, the equities of the country will now be priced based on their covariances with the return on the world market portfolio, which are likely to be much smaller than the variance of the local market. Both of these effects will reduce the discount rate on the country's assets.

A big reduction in the discount rate, of course, causes the price of an asset to rise dramatically, which provides a big rate of return to the investors holding these assets. Simply put, foreign investors will bid up the prices of local stocks in an effort to diversify their portfolios, while all investors will shun inefficient sectors.[8] Thus, equity prices should rise substantially (as expected returns decrease) when a market moves from a segmented to an integrated state.

When a market is opened to international investors, though, the country's assets may become more sensitive to world events. In other words, their covariances with the rest of the world's assets may increase. Even with this effect, it is likely that these covariances will remain much smaller than the variance of the local market. The data bear out the theory. Studies by Han Kim and Vinjay Singal (2000), Peter Henry (2000), Geert Bekaert and Campbell Harvey (2000), and others show that equity market liberalizations were accompanied by positive returns to integration as foreign investors bid up local prices. Postliberalization returns, in contrast, were lower on average, as the theory predicts. While the exact estimates differ somewhat, liberalization causes the cost of capital to decline by at most 1%.

An interesting parallel occurs with respect to the price of a firm's shares following the issuance of an ADR. An ADR issued by a company headquartered in a country with investment restrictions can be viewed as a sort of liberalization of investment. For example, when Chile had

---

[7]It is conceivable that before the liberalization, the government may have kept interest rates artificially low—for instance, through interest rate ceilings—in which case the interest rate may rise upon liberalization.
[8]A more formal analysis can be found in Geert Bekaert and Campbell Harvey (2003), which builds on work by Vihang Errunza and Etienne Losq (1985).

repatriation restrictions in place, it had to lift the restrictions for those companies listing their shares overseas to allow cross-market arbitrage. When an ADR is announced, we therefore expect positive abnormal returns and lower expected returns after the liberalization. Several studies demonstrate that this effect is typically larger than 1%, and the studies find lower costs of capital after the ADR issuance. Of course, as we discussed in Chapter 12, there are many reasons, apart from liberalization, that ADR issues may result in a positive effect on the price of equity shares.

Many studies, as surveyed in Bekaert and Harvey (2003), have investigated the effects of liberalizations on other return characteristics. First, there is no significant impact on the volatility of market returns. Indeed, it is not obvious from finance theory that volatility should increase or decrease when markets are opened to foreign investment. On the one hand, markets may become informationally more efficient, leading to higher volatility as prices quickly react to relevant information, or hot speculative capital may induce excess volatility. On the other hand, in the preliberalized market, there may be large swings from fundamental values, leading to higher volatility. In the long run, the gradual development and diversification of the market should lead to lower volatility. Second, the correlation of the return and its beta with the world market increase after equity market liberalizations, and for some countries, the increase is dramatic. This is also consistent with these liberalizing emerging markets becoming more integrated with world capital markets.

Segmentation and Integration over Time

Although the empirical studies on the financial effects of equity market liberalizations confirm the intuition predicted by the simple CAPM, this does not mean that we are now living in a globally integrated capital market, especially in emerging markets. In fact, using official regulatory reforms to measure liberalization is fraught with difficulties because it is difficult to know what effectively segments a market from the global capital market. There are three different kinds of barriers. The first are legal barriers, such as foreign ownership restrictions and taxes on foreign investments. The second are indirect barriers arising from differences in available information, accounting standards, and investor protection. The third are emerging-market-specific risks (EMSRs) that discourage foreign investment. EMSRs include liquidity risk, political risk, economic policy risk, and perhaps currency risk.

In general, indirect barriers and EMSRs may make institutional investors in developed countries reluctant to invest in emerging markets and segment them from the world market. Geert Bekaert's (1995) evidence shows that indirect barriers, such as the lack of a high-quality regulatory and accounting framework, are particularly important. Nonetheless, measuring market integration purely by investigating the market's regulatory framework might not result in a true measure of integration. For example, regulatory restrictions might not have posed a barrier prior to liberalization because canny investors often find ways to circumvent them. Alternatively, there may be legal, indirect ways to access local equity markets, such as through country funds or ADRs. The Korea Fund, trading on the NYSE, is a good example; it was launched in 1986, well before the liberalization of the Korean equity market. Also, there are many kinds of investment barriers, and the liberalization process is typically a complex and gradual one. In short, determining whether a market is segmented, integrated, or something in between is far from easy.

A Model of Time-Varying Market Integration

We saw earlier how using a domestic CAPM would be inappropriate if a country's stock market were integrated into the world's equity market. In **integrated markets**, the covariance with the world market should determine the expected return on the domestic market. However, if the market is truly segmented, the variance of the return on the domestic market should affect the domestic expected return. Geert Bekaert and Campbell Harvey (1995) examine these issues of segmentation versus integration for a number of countries in an econometric framework that allows the degree of a country's integration with the world market to vary over time. Their model uses equity return data directly to determine the degree of market integration, therefore circumventing imperfections posed by regulatory reform dates. Their most important finding is that the degree of equity market integration seems to vary for all countries in the sample.

In many countries, with Thailand as a stark example, variation in the integration measure coincides with capital market reforms. In other countries, the regulatory framework and the de facto degree of integration do not coincide. For example, consider the market rate of return in some countries—such as Greece—whose markets are completely open to foreign investors. The market return was more sensitive to the variance of the return on the Greek market in some periods than to the covariance between the return on the Greek market and the return on the world market portfolio. Other stock markets in countries with strong legal restrictions seem to be priced internationally. Mexico, for example, has had rather strong legal restrictions on foreign investment, which would lead us to think that the variance of Mexico's stock market ought to be important when it comes to determining its expected return. But the analysis implies that Mexico is actually quite integrated with the world market. Consistent with this analysis, Exhibit 13.14 shows that Mexican equity returns have a 49% correlation with U.S. returns.

The Practical Implications of Segmentation and Time-Varying Integration

As a practical matter, when international managers choose a discount rate for the all-equity cash flows of a project, they must rely on a healthy dose of economic intuition and understand the meaning of historical statistics. Let's discuss two real-world examples.[9] The first involves a Mexican company and a Swiss company bidding for the Indonesian firm PT Semen Gresik in July 1998.

Indonesia liberalized in September 1990, and PT Semen Gresik had been publicly traded for some time prior to that. As part of your valuation, you must determine what the appropriate discount rate should have been. Will any of the historical return data be of use to you? The short answer is no. Unfortunately, the asset's historical average rate of return will be high to reflect the high risk premium typical for securities in segmented countries. Also, the historical average rate of return of Indonesian assets will include the one-time capital gain that occurred when the country opened up its international capital market.

What should you do? You should start asking yourself what your shareholders demand as a domestic currency return if they were to invest in this project directly. If your typical shareholder is thought to be well diversified internationally, then you can attempt to determine how the domestic currency return on this foreign asset will covary with the domestic currency return on the world market portfolio. This will lead you to a domestic currency discount rate. Because PT Semen Gresik is in the cement business, the bidders could obtain a first indication by using a portfolio of either Mexican or Swiss building firms to compute an appropriate discount rate. While these firms may correctly reflect the systematic risk of globally integrated cement firms, they are not likely fully representative of the cement business in Indonesia, even postliberalization. Therefore, the beta of PT Semen Gresik's returns with respect to the world market should likely enter the computations as well.

Now consider Westmore Coal Company, an actual U.S.-based firm that intended to invest $540 million in an electric power project located in Zhangze, China, in 1994. Not only were there no comparable publicly traded projects from which to compute betas, but China was a fully segmented country! As Exhibit 13.14 shows, local market volatility was very high, so the domestic discount rate would have been high, too. However, because Westmore Coal's shareholders were likely to be internationally diversified, the world CAPM should have been used. Because no data are available, the amount of risk premium that must be added to the risk-free rate becomes a business judgment that you should be able to defend. The equity risk

---

[9]Both examples are from Gordon Bodnar, Bernard Dumas, and Richard Marston (2003).

premium should be based on the type of business that the project represents. If the business is highly cyclical and its profits are likely to covary with the return on a world market portfolio, you add more than the average risk premium. If, on the other hand, the business is highly idiosyncratic, then not much of a risk premium may be warranted. In this case, it is likely that the power plant's cash flows in China show little correlation with the world market and that a lower risk premium is called for. This may be counterintuitive because a project in China may appear risky. However, the additional risks are likely of a political nature and should be assessed separately from the project's systematic risk. We discuss political risk in Chapter 14.

Home Bias and Its Implications

Unlike what the CAPM predicts, investors in different countries are generally not very well internationally diversified. In other words, most of their portfolios have a strong home bias. **Home bias** means that British investors, for example, hold a disproportionately large share of British assets compared to the world market portfolio. Exhibit 13.15 documents home bias using two different sources of data.

Exhibit 13.15   Home Biases in the United States and Other Nations

Panel A: Home Bias in the United States (1997)

	Percentage Shares Held in a Typical U.S. Portfolio	Bias
United States	89.9	
United Kingdom	1.82	0.79
Japan	1.14	0.88
France	0.71	0.75
Canada	0.59	0.75
The Germany	0.54	0.85
Italy	0.35	0.76
The Netherlands	0.89	0.55
Switzerland	0.52	0.79
Sweden	0.32	0.72
Spain	0.21	0.83
Australia	0.26	0.79
Hong Kong	0.23	0.87
Mexico	0.29	0.56
Brazil	0.26	0.76
India	0.05	0.91
China	0.02	0.98
Taiwan	0.04	0.97
Russia	0.07	0.87
South Africa	0.08	0.92

Panel B: Home Biases Around the World

	1991	2000
United States	4%	11%
Japan	12%	27%
The Netherlands	12%	62%
United Kingdom	23%	26%
Switzerland	11%	21%
Australia	14%	19%
Sweden	4%	25%

Notes: Panel A is based on Table 1 in Alan Ahearne, William Griever, and Francis Warnock (2004). The foreign equity shares are based on a 1997 comprehensive survey of U.S. residents' holdings of foreign securities. The Bias column is 1 minus foreign equity share divided by world market share. If U.S. investors would hold foreign securities in propositions equal to those in the world equity market benchmark, the bias would equal 0. Panel B is taken from a 2002 UBS Asset Management study. The numbers represent the proportion of foreign bonds and equities in the total equity and bond portfolios of residents in the foreign countries.

The data in Panel A are of the highest quality because they are based on a comprehensive survey of the equity holdings of U.S. residents, conducted by the U.S. Treasury in 1997. Panel B uses a private data source to give you some idea about the extent of home bias in other countries and the trend over time.

First, all around the world, people hold far less foreign securities than the world CAPM would dictate. Investors do not seem to take advantage of the considerable benefits to international diversification. Second, the bias is large. The second column in Panel A of Exhibit 13.15 measures home bias as 1 minus the ratio of the share of the foreign market in the U.S. portfolio to the share of the foreign market in the world market. The bias would be 0 if U.S. investors held the world market portfolio. The portfolio shares in each country would equal the shares of the countries in the world market portfolio. The bias measures the percentage by which the proportion held in the foreign country differs from its actual market capitalization share in the world market. The U.S. portfolio is most biased relative to emerging markets, such as China, South Africa, and Taiwan, and it is least biased relative to the Dutch and Mexican markets.

Third, from Panel B, we see that the best internationally diversified countries appear to be the Netherlands, followed by Japan. However, because the Netherlands constitutes only a very small fraction of the world market, the home asset bias is still considerable. Because the Dutch market represents approximately 2% of total world market capitalization, we can calculate the home bias using the data in Panel A. Foreign assets represent $1 - 2\% = 98\%$ of the world market portfolio for Dutch investors, and yet, Dutch residents devote only 62% of their portfolio to these securities, hence the bias is $1 - (62/98) = 36.7\%$. This bias is considerably smaller than the corresponding numbers for the UK and Japan, which are around 70%.

Finally, the data in Panel B suggest that the proportions of foreign securities in most country portfolios have dramatically increased over the past decade, more than doubling in most countries. Still, the phenomenon of home bias appears to be true for most countries in the world, and it is something that is not well understood by financial economists. Let's see if Ante and Freedy can shed any light on the puzzle.

POINT–COUNTERPOINT

What Breeds Foreign Investment?

"Hmm, they are delicious," Ante sighed, while he devoured his fourth Belgian Leonidas chocolate in a row. Ante and Freedy were sitting in the salon, digesting what their father had just told them about their trust fund. Dad wanted to increase the trust's allocation to foreign equities from 15% to 30% and wondered whether Ante and Freedy knew why U.S. investors were often reluctant to invest in foreign equities, despite their obvious diversification benefits. Ante and Freedy had agreed to study the issue, and to help their thinking, they had brewed nice, frothy cappuccinos using a fancy Italian machine their father had imported.

"You know," argued Freedy, "I could think of a number of rational reasons why U.S. investors might want to be home biased. Foreign equities have currency risk and hence more volatility than U.S. equities. The U.S. market is the most efficient market in the world, and transaction costs here are lower than they are elsewhere. Plus, it is very difficult to obtain reliable accounting information on foreign companies."

"No way," mumbled Ante, while enjoying his fifth Leonidas. "These foreign equities simply are underperforming the U.S. equity market. Besides, I do not feel comfortable having our money invested in unfamiliar companies."

At this point, Suttle, who had quietly sneaked into the room when he smelled the coffee, could no longer keep quiet. "Hey, guys! I happen to have just read some articles about the home bias phenomenon. Let me fill you in. First, currency risk is not what is stopping U.S. investors from investing abroad. Because currency changes show little correlation with local equity markets, they add little to the volatility that U.S. investors face when investing in foreign equity markets. Moreover, currency volatility can be hedged. Second, arguing that the U.S. market outperforms foreign markets is short-sighted and not even true historically, if you take a longer-term perspective. Third, transaction costs may play a role, but in order to generate the observed portfolio proportions of U.S. investors, U.S. investors would have to think that the average return on foreign stocks were 2% to 4% per annum less than the realized average returns on foreign assets. It may be that these figures represent U.S. investors' perceived transaction costs of foreign investing, but it is unlikely. Moreover, the huge volume of international capital flows is also inconsistent with the transaction costs story, as is the fact that foreign countries are home biased. Fourth, I do not like the information story: It is easy enough to obtain information on foreign companies or to set up or use local investment managers. However, it may be that the quality of the information and a poor regulatory framework in terms of investor protection and corporate governance keep out U.S. institutional investors. This may explain why foreign companies like to list ADRs and thus can be more easily included in institutional investors' portfolios."

Suttle continued, "Although these indirect barriers are clearly important, they cannot be the full story, given the cross-border flows and home biases in other countries. Clearly, direct barriers played a huge role, and many countries have only recently dismantled these barriers. In fact, there is a trend everywhere toward increased foreign holdings, so maybe investors are slowly adjusting toward rational asset allocation."

"Aha!" shouted Ante. "You do not really have a full, rational explanation for the phenomenon, do you, Suttle?"

"Well, you've got a point with that familiarity argument of yours," replied Suttle. "I just read a few articles that claim that U.S. investors even bias their domestic investments toward companies that are 'familiar' to them. One study showed that the ownership of the shares of regional telephone companies is dominated by people living in the area served by those companies. Another study showed that U.S. investment managers exhibit a strong preference for firms headquartered within a 500-mile radius of their offices."[10]

"Oh well, maybe people do not like foreign investments, but I will surely enjoy having another Italian coffee and Belgian chocolate," smirked Freedy.

Implications for Pricing

If investors are not fully internationally diversified, should we discard the world CAPM as the benchmark model? This is a difficult issue. However, it might not be necessary for every individual in the world to be fully internationally diversified for asset returns to be well described by a world CAPM. In fact, whereas it is true that emerging market returns do not look at all consistent with a world CAPM, the evidence against other stock markets is not strong. Campbell Harvey (1991) and Robert Hodrick, David Ng, and Paul Sengmueller (1999) show that a version of the CAPM in fact works well for most developed stock markets most of the time.

Time-varying Correlations

If markets are not perfectly integrated, the trend toward less home bias in Panel B of Exhibit 13.15 suggests that there is a move toward ever-increased integration, as investment barriers, both direct and indirect, are dismantled. François Longin and Bruno Solnik (1995) argue that increased integration may also increase the correlations across countries, making international diversification less viable. Exhibit 13.16 sheds some light on this issue. It reports

---

[10]These studies are by Gur Huberman (2001) and Joshua Coval and Tobias Moskowitz (1999), respectively.

Exhibit 13.16   Correlations Between Foreign and U.S. Equity Market Returns

	1970–1979	1980–1989	1990–1999	2000–2006	1970–2006
Canada	0.71	0.72	0.73	0.77	0.72
Japan	0.31	0.24	0.30	0.48	0.31
United Kingdom	0.45	0.56	0.58	0.80	0.53
France	0.40	0.44	0.55	0.78	0.50
Germany	0.29	0.36	0.51	0.78	0.46
Italy	0.17	0.24	0.32	0.60	0.29

Note: The data are from MSCI.

correlations for Japan, Canada, the United Kingdom, France, and Italy with the United States for every decade since 1970 and for the past 7 years. Until 1999, the correlations increase steadily for all countries except Japan. However, for all countries, the correlations are substantially higher during the past 7 years than they were before.

Whether the increases in correlations are due to increased market integration is now hotly debated in academic circles. The debate became very prominent when the countries in the European Union replaced their national currencies with the euro, hence removing a potential source of cross-country idiosyncratic fluctuations.

Why is it so difficult to determine whether the effect is permanent or temporary? The reason is that temporarily higher volatility in equity markets also tends to temporarily increase the correlations between markets, making it difficult to separate temporary from permanent correlation changes. The intuition for this fact is best understood if we consider two countries satisfying the world CAPM. As a consequence, part of the return variation in both countries is driven by the returns on the world market; and this joint exposure will likely induce positive correlation between the returns on the two stock markets. Intuitively, if the world market movements became extremely variable, they would dominate all return variation in the two stocks, and the correlation would converge to 1. This is relevant for the numbers produced in Exhibit 13.16, as the world market volatility at the end of the 1990s and early 2000s was indeed relatively high. A study by Geert Bekaert, Robert Hodrick, and Xiaoyan Zhang (2006) concludes that return correlations within Europe have permanently increased, but their tests do not reject the hypothesis that return correlations elsewhere have remained unchanged, once account is taken of temporary changes in volatility.

13.7 ALTERNATIVE COST-OF-CAPITAL MODELS

The Usefulness of the CAPM

Even though the CAPM is not without flaws, it is viewed as a reasonable model that can be used to estimate the required rates of return needed for capital budgeting. There are two basic ideas supporting this strategy.

First, as we discussed before, the average rate of return on equity investments has historically exceeded the average return on risk-free investments by a substantial margin. If we think that the past is a reasonable predictor of the future, then the cost of equity capital should incorporate some measure of this equity risk premium.

The second reason that people like to use the CAPM to develop costs of capital is that it incorporates an important lesson about diversification: There is no evidence that firms whose returns have had high historical standard deviations have had high average returns. In fact, recent research by Andrew Ang, Robert Hodrick, Yuhang Xing, and Xiaoyan Zhang (2006) shows just the opposite: Stocks with high idiosyncratic standard deviations have had low average returns.

When we consider the overall historical record, we conclude that the cost of equity capital should reflect a risk premium that compensates the firm's investors for the systematic risk present in the investment. Suppose, though, that the CAPM is wrong. In this case, it will either overstate or understate the market's required rate of return.

The Consequences of Using the Wrong Model

If a firm's managers use the CAPM and it overstates the market's required rate of return on a project, they will sometimes forgo profitable projects (that is, projects with positive net present value) that should have been undertaken. Eventually, the stock market will discipline these conservative managers by viewing them as underperformers. What about the reverse situation, in which the CAPM understates the risk premium on an asset, or project? In this case, the firm's managers will undertake some projects that are actually negative net present value, and thus, they will destroy shareholders' wealth. Likewise, eventually, the market will discipline these overly aggressive managers for their underperformance relative to what they promised shareholders.

Given that the CAPM may be incorrect and that recent empirical tests have not been kind to the CAPM, is there an alternative model to compute the cost of capital? We now discuss two models that have been proposed as alternatives to the CAPM.

The Arbitrage Pricing Theory

A serious competitor to the CAPM is the **arbitrage pricing theory (APT)**, which was originally developed by Stephen Ross.[11] The APT recognizes that the return on the market portfolio may not be the only potential source of systematic risks that affect the returns on equities. The APT postulates that other economy-wide factors can systematically affect the returns on a large number of securities. These factors might include news about inflation, interest rates, gross domestic product (GDP), or the unemployment rate. Changes in these factors will affect the future profitability of corporations, and they may affect how investors view the riskiness of future cash flows. This, in turn, will affect how investors discount future uncertain cash flows.

When there are economy-wide factors that affect the returns on a large number of firms, the influences of these factors on the return to a well-diversified portfolio are still present. The influences of the factors cannot be diversified away. Consequently, the risk premiums on particular securities are determined by the sensitivities of their returns to the economy-wide factors and by the compensations that investors require because of the presence of each of these different risks.

Theory (Advanced)

In the general k-factor model of the APT, a stock return can be written like this:

$$r(t) = E_{t-1}[r(t)] + \beta_1 F_1(t) + \beta_2 F_2(t) + \ldots + \beta_k F_k(t) + \epsilon(t) \qquad \textbf{(13.16)}$$

In Equation (13.16) the realized rate of return on the stock between time $t-1$ and time t is $r(t)$, and the expected rate of return based on time $t-1$ information is $E_{t-1}[r(t)]$. The innovation in

---

[11]For an introduction to the APT, see Chapter 11 of Stephen Ross, Randolph Westerfield, and Randolph Jaffee, 2001. The original research can be found in Stephen Ross, 1976.

the return, which is the part that cannot be predicted based on past information and which is therefore due to new information, is

Innovation or news in the stock return $= \beta_1 F_1(t) + \beta_2 F_2(t) + \ldots + \beta_k F_k(t) + \epsilon(t)$

The magnitude of the innovation in the return on this security depends on the news about the k different factors that potentially affect all securities, which are the $F_i(t)$'s for $i = 1, \ldots, k$; it also depends on the sensitivities of this equity return to each of these factors, the β_i's for $i = 1, \ldots, k$; and it depends on an innovation that is idiosyncratic to this particular stock, $\epsilon(t)$. In the most general model, the β's may also vary through time and hence may depend on time $t-1$ information.

Consider a cyclical technology stock such as Microsoft. When the economy unexpectedly does poorly, its prospects are hurt. Hence, if the first factor is GDP news, Microsoft's β with respect to GDP news is likely to be positive and large. This also means that Microsoft's return will tend to correlate with other stocks that also have a large exposure to GDP news. News about the health of Microsoft's CEO is specific, or "idiosyncratic," to Microsoft and is not a source of correlation with other stock returns.

Because the idiosyncratic uncertainty of a security can be diversified away just as in the CAPM, the idiosyncratic uncertainty does not contribute to the variance of the return on a large, well-diversified portfolio. In equilibrium, therefore, the idiosyncratic uncertainties associated with particular securities are not priced. That is, the presence of $\epsilon(t)$ in Equation (13.16) does not affect the expected rate of return on that equity.

The expected rate of return on an equity is affected, though, by the sensitivities of the security to the factors that may affect the returns on all assets. In equilibrium, all investors cannot avoid the systematic risks in the economy. Hence, there will be k different risk premiums associated with the k risk factors indexed by $i = 1, \ldots, k$ that reflect the aversion of investors to those sources of risk. To determine these risk premiums, researchers construct factor-mimicking portfolios—portfolios that correlate very highly (ideally perfectly) with the economic factors. Let $rp_i(t-1)$ denote the risk premium on factor i. Then, $rp_i(t-1)$ reflects the expected return, at time $t-1$, on the factor-mimicking portfolio for risk factor i, over and above the risk-free rate.

The derivation of the APT then requires that the expected equity return can be written as

$$E_{t-1}[r(t)] = r_{ft} + \beta_1[rp_1(t-1)] + \beta_2[(rp_2(t-1)] + \ldots + \beta_k[rp_k(t-1)]$$

The expected rate of return on a stock depends, first of all, on the risk-free rate, which provides compensation to an investor who holds the security for the time value of money, as in the CAPM. Because each of the k factors represents an economy-wide source of risk that cannot be diversified away, these risks require compensation in the form of risk premiums, which are the terms $rp_i(t-1)$ for $i = 1, \ldots, k$. Examination of Equation (13.16) indicates that the higher the sensitivities of the innovation in the return on the security to one of the systematic risk factors, as measured by the β_i's, the greater is the risk of that security. Because rational investors recognize that these risks are present, they require that the expected return on a risky security must compensate them for the risks they bear.

Researchers typically find that differences in expected returns on thousands of securities can be reasonably well explained by the presence of five factors (see Robert Korajczyk and Claude Viallet, 1992; and Nai-Fu Chen, Richard Roll, and Stephen Ross, 1986).

The Fama-French Factor Model

The Value and the Small Firm Effects

In a provocative 1992 paper, Eugene Fama and Kenneth French questioned the ability of the traditional CAPM to explain the cross-section of stock returns in U.S. data. They found that the market value of a firm's market equity (ME), which is its price per share multiplied by the number of shares outstanding (or the firm's market capitalization) and the ratio of the accounting book value of a firm to its market value (book equity to market equity [BE/ME]) contribute significantly to the explanation of average stock returns.[12]

During their sample, average returns on firms with small market capitalizations were higher than could be explained by their betas with the market portfolio. Perhaps small firms suffer from a greater lack of communication between the firm's managers and its investors. This asymmetric information could lead investors to require higher rates of return from small firms. Firms that have high ratios of the book value of their equity to the market value of their equity (so-called value firms) also have higher average returns than can be explained by the CAPM and have outperformed growth stocks (stocks with a low BE/ME). Interestingly, these firms often suffer from financial distress. If financial distress tends to systematically occur when investors are more risk averse or face bad times, it may cause investors to demand a risk premium for bearing this risk.

Fama and French's findings are still the subject of great debate in the economic literature, and not everyone believes the results will hold up to further scrutiny. First, many mutual fund companies offer value funds, which invest in high book-to-market stocks and small-cap funds, which are funds that invest in small-capitalization companies. Hence, individual investors can easily diversify their portfolios along size and value characteristics. Second, Andrew Ang and Joseph Chen (2007) found little evidence of a value effect in a larger sample than the one used by Fama and French (1992), and several other authors have suggested that the size effect disappeared in the 1980s.[13]

The Fama-French Three-Factor Model (Advanced)

Their empirical findings led Fama and French to develop a three-factor model to explain average equity returns (see Fama and French, 1995). The first factor-mimicking portfolio is the return on the value-weighted market portfolio in excess of the risk-free return, as in the CAPM. The second factor-mimicking portfolio is the difference in the return on a portfolio of small firms and the return on a portfolio of big firms (small minus big [SMB]), in which the ratio of BE/ME is held constant in each portfolio. The third factor-mimicking portfolio is the difference between the return on a portfolio of firms with high values of BE/ME and the return on a portfolio of firms with low values of BE/ME (high minus low [HML]), in which the size of firms is held constant in each portfolio. To find the sensitivities of a firm's equity return to the three factors, you merely run a regression, just as you do to find the beta in the CAPM. The difference is that now there are three explanatory variables instead of one. The average rates of return on the factor-mimicking portfolios can then be combined with the estimated sensitivities of the equity return to the returns on the factor-mimicking portfolios to provide an estimate of the required rate of return on the equity.

When Fama and French (1998) applied their model to international data,[14] they found that two factors—the return on the world market and a global version of the HML factor— sufficed to explain the cross-section of expected returns in 13 countries.

---

[12]Although firms with higher betas tend to have higher average returns, Eugene Fama and Kenneth French argue that the ability of beta to explain the cross-section of average stock returns is nil when the size of the firm's market equity and ratio of book equity to market equity are included as explanatory variables.

[13]To illustrate how divided the profession is on these issues, even the authors of this book disagree, with one of them arguing that there is a value effect to be explained and the other that it is most likely statistical baloney. We have booked a meeting with Suttle Trooth to help us out. We will let you know the outcome in the next edition.

[14]It must be said that the empirical evidence against the CAPM was marginal at best in most countries, with the exception of the United States. Nevertheless, the new proposed model clearly improved the fit with the data.

Example 13.8 The Cost of Equity Capital in the Fama-French Model

Suppose we want to estimate the cost of capital for a firm in Australia that has the same systematic risk as a portfolio of Australian stocks with high book-to-market levels. In Fama and French (1998), we find the following estimates:

	CAPM	TWO-FACTOR MODEL	
	Beta with Global Market	Beta with Global Market	Beta with HML Portfolio
Australian high book-to-market firms	0.84	0.90	0.59

If the current risk-free interest rate is 6%, and the world market equity risk premium is 5.7% (see Exhibit 13.13), from Equation (13.10), the required rate of return for the Australian firm from the CAPM is

$$r^{AUS} = 6\% + (0.84 \times 5.7\%) = 10.79\%$$

We estimate the premium on the value factor-mimicking portfolio to be 3%. Therefore, the required equity rate of return implied by the **Fama-French two-factor model** is

$$r^{AUS} = 6\% + (0.90 \times 5.7\%) + (0.59 \times 3.0\%) = 12.90\%$$

Notice that the two estimates of the required rate of return on the stock are very different. This is true because value firms in Australia have historically provided higher average rates of return than the CAPM would imply. Although the Fama-French model has become quite popular, it remains an empirical model, not grounded in formal theory. With remaining doubts about the validity of the model and no good story for why the value effect would persist, the Fama-French model has not yet been widely adopted in practice.

13.8 SUMMARY

This chapter develops the theories and background necessary to determine the cost of equity capital in global financial markets. Its main points are the following:

1. To determine the international cost of equity capital, we must first determine how investors view risk in a global investments context.

2. When investing abroad, an investor must assess both the returns of the international asset in its local currency and variations in the value of the foreign currency relative to the investor's home currency.

3. The volatility of an international equity investment is mostly determined by the volatility of the local equity market. Although exchange rate changes are quite variable, they are nearly uncorrelated with local stock returns.

4. International diversification results in portfolios with risk levels much lower than what can be achieved with domestic diversification alone. The main reason is that the stock market returns of different countries are not very highly correlated with one another, despite the fact that correlations among them tend to increase during bear markets.

5. Using available data on the volatilities of different markets and the correlation among them, investors can compute a "hurdle rate" of return for foreign investments. The hurdle rate is the expected return for which a small investment in the foreign equity market, starting from an all-U.S. portfolio, increases the Sharpe ratio for the portfolio.

6. Among the G7 countries, a U.S. investor can most easily improve her risk–return trade-off, as measured by the Sharpe ratio, by investing in Japan. Japan has a rather poor historical return record but

features the lowest correlation with U.S. returns among G7 countries.

7. It has become easier over time to invest internationally while remaining "at home," through investment vehicles such as closed-end funds, open-end funds, and ADRs.

8. A mean-variance investor likes high expected returns but assigns a penalty to portfolio variance. With a risk-free asset and just one risky asset available, she will invest more in the risky asset the lower her risk aversion, the higher the expected excess return on the asset, and the lower the variance on the asset.

9. The mean standard deviation frontier collects portfolios that minimize the portfolio variance for each possible expected return. The mean-variance-efficient (MVE) portfolio is the one portfolio on the frontier that maximizes the Sharpe ratio and is hence optimal. This portfolio defines the capital allocation line, which determines how the investor mixes the risk-free asset with the optimal risky portfolio, depending on her preferences.

10. The capital asset pricing model (CAPM) states that under some simplifying assumptions, the MVE portfolio ought to be the market portfolio, which contains all securities in proportion to their market capitalization.

11. The CAPM implies that the expected return of any security equals the risk-free rate plus the beta of the security multiplied by the market risk premium. The beta of the security is the covariance of its return with the return on the market portfolio divided by the variance of the market portfolio return.

12. In an international setting, the relevant benchmark for the market portfolio should be the world market portfolio, giving rise to the world CAPM. The world CAPM ignores exchange rate risk.

13. In an international setting, one should consider the complications arising from the fact that investors in different countries evaluate real returns using different consumption baskets and view money market investments in other countries as risky because of exchange rate risk. Although it is possible to adjust the CAPM for these considerations, the resulting international CAPMs are rarely used in practice.

14. To use the CAPM to obtain a cost of capital, we must determine the betas, the market risk premium, and a risk-free rate. The risk-free rate is mostly proxied by the Treasury bill rate. The beta is estimated from a regression of excess returns on the security in question onto excess returns on the market portfolio (proxied by the world market portfolio return, for example). Sometimes, industry portfolios are used to reduce the sampling error in estimating the betas. The risk premium on the market portfolio is the subject of much controversy. An estimate of 4% to 8% is reasonable. In any case, any cost-of-capital estimation and project evaluation should be accompanied by a sensitivity analysis.

15. Emerging equity markets display relatively low correlations with the stock markets of developed countries. Many of the emerging markets underwent a liberalization process in the 1990s that made their stock markets fully or partially accessible to foreign investors.

16. Equity markets are integrated when assets of identical risk command the same expected return, irrespective of their domicile. The many investment barriers in place in emerging markets have effectively segmented them from the global capital market. The liberalization process, however, has led to increased asset prices, higher correlations with the world market, and lower expected returns in emerging markets.

17. The benchmark used in the cost-of-capital computation should reflect the composition of the portfolio of the investors in the company, even when the project takes place in a potentially segmented emerging market. Historical data in these emerging markets may not be very useful for a cost-of-capital analysis if the market is truly segmented or if it underwent a liberalization process that caused a structural break in the return data.

18. Even in the developed world, investors have not fully internationally diversified. Instead, their portfolios are heavily invested in their home markets. This phenomenon is known as home bias.

19. There has been a gradual increase in the correlations between the G7 countries, potentially reflecting increased economic and financial integration.

20. Whereas the CAPM is the dominant model to determine the cost of capital, multifactor models building on the arbitrage pricing theory of Ross (1976) constitute an alternative approach. In such a model, the expected return on a stock depends on the risk-free rate, sensitivities to a number of systematic factors (such as GDP news), and the risk premiums related to these factors.

21. Fama and French (1992, 1995, 1998) proposed a factor model in which the factors measure the exposure of a stock to a portfolio going long in small stocks and short in large stocks and the stock's exposure to a portfolio long in high book-to-market stocks (value stocks) and short in low book-to-market stocks (growth stocks). There is some weak empirical evidence that small stocks and value stocks have outperformed large and growth stocks.

QUESTIONS

1. Is the volatility of the dollar return to an investment in the Japanese equity market the sum of the volatility of the Japanese equity market return in yen plus the volatility of dollar/yen exchange rate changes? Why or why not?
2. Why is the variance of a portfolio of internationally diversified stocks likely to be lower than the variance of a portfolio of U.S. stocks?
3. How can you increase the Sharpe ratio of a portfolio? What type of stocks would you have to add to it in order to do so?
4. Why is the hurdle rate in Section 13.2 lower for Japan than for Canada? Should U.S. investors still invest in Canada?
5. What is the mean standard deviation frontier, and what is the mean-variance-efficient (MVE) portfolio?
6. What is the prediction of the CAPM with respect to optimal portfolio choice?
7. What is the prediction of the CAPM with respect to the expected return on any security?
8. What is the beta of a security?
9. Why might it be useful to estimate the beta for a stock from returns on stocks within its industry rather than from the stock itself?
10. What does it mean for an equity market to be integrated or segmented from the world capital market?
11. What would you expect to happen to the risk-free rate and equity returns when a segmented country opens its capital markets to foreign investment?
12. What accounts for the home bias phenomenon?
13. Explain the basic principle of the APT.
14. Suppose AZT is a small value stock and that you use both the CAPM and the Fama-French model to compute its cost of capital. Under which model is the cost of capital for AZT likely to be higher?

PROBLEMS

1. The EAFE is the international index comprising markets in Europe, Australia, and the Far East. Consider the following annualized stock return data:

Average U.S. index return:	14%
Average EAFE index return:	13%
Volatility of the U.S. return:	15.5%
Volatility of the EAFE return:	16.5%
Correlation of U.S return and EAFE return:	0.45

   a. What would be the return and risk of a portfolio invested half in the EAFE and half in the U.S. market?

   b. Market watchers have noticed slowly increasing correlations between the United States and the EAFE index, which some ascribe to the increasing integration of markets. Given that the volatilities remain unchanged, is it possible that the volatility of a portfolio that is equally weighted between the two indexes has higher volatility than the U.S. market?

2. Let the expected pound return on a UK equity be 15%, and let its volatility be 20%. The volatility of the dollar/pound exchange rate is 10%.

   a. Graph the (approximate) volatility of the dollar return on the UK equity as a function of the correlation between the UK equity's return in pounds and changes in the dollar–pound exchange rate.

   b. Suppose the correlation between the UK equity return in pounds and the exchange rate change is 0. What expected exchange rate change would you need if the UK equity investment is to have a Sharpe ratio of 1.00? (Assume that the risk-free rate is 0 for a U.S. investor.) Does this seem like a reasonable expectation?

3. Suppose General Motors managers would like to invest in a new production line and must determine a cost of capital for the investment. The beta for GM is 1.185, the beta for the automobile industry is 0.97, the equity premium on the world market is assumed to be 6%, and the risk-free rate is 3%. Propose a range of cost-of-capital estimates to consider in the analysis.

4. Thom Yorke is a typical mean-variance investor. He likes high expected returns and hates high variability in his portfolio returns. He is currently invested 100% in a diversified U.S. equity portfolio. The expected return on the portfolio is 12.46%, and the portfolio's volatility (standard deviation) is 15.76%. Thom is considering adding some alternative investments to his portfolio. One investment he is considering is the STCMM fund, which invests in U.S. small-capitalization, high-technology firms. Yorke has determined that the expected return on the fund is 14.69%, that its volatility is 32.5%, and that its correlation with his current portfolio is 0.7274. He

is also intrigued by the LYMF fund, which invests in several emerging markets. The expected return on the fund is only 12%; it has 35% volatility and a correlation of 0.2 with his portfolio. The correlation of the LYMF fund with the STCMM fund is 0.15. Assume that the risk-free rate is 5%.

    a. If Yorke is interested in improving the Sharpe ratio of his portfolio, will he invest a positive amount in one of the funds? Which one? Carefully explain your reasoning.

    b. Suppose Yorke is moderately risk averse (meaning he hates variability quite a bit), but his friend, Nick Cave, is really quite risk tolerant and focuses primarily on expected returns. Both cannot short-sell securities, and both are thinking of splitting their entire portfolio between the U.S. portfolio that Yorke is currently holding, the STCMM fund, and the LYMF fund. They also do not invest in the risk-free asset and do not consider levering up risky portfolios. Compare the two investors' optimal holdings. Who will invest more in the LYMF fund, and who will invest more in the STCMM fund? Why?

5. International economists continue to be puzzled by the phenomenon that investors worldwide seem to be plagued by the home asset bias. Economists have pointed out that investors with **mean-variance preferences** (that is, they like higher expected returns and dislike higher volatility) ought to allocate much more of their wealth to foreign equities and bonds. Three explanations for the phenomenon are given below, all of them based on empirical facts. For each one of them, discuss whether the statements are true or false and in what sense they help rationalize or fail to rationalize the home bias puzzle. In answering the questions, assume that investors indeed have mean-variance preferences.

    a. Investors should not hold foreign equities because they are more volatile and have been yielding lower returns than U.S. stocks in recent years.

    b. Home bias arises because investors face an additional risk when investing internationally—namely, currency risk. Because currency risk makes returns more volatile but does not lead to a higher expected return, investing more in domestic assets is rational.

    c. Home bias arises because investors have a non-traded domestic asset that they care about as well—namely human capital. The returns to this asset can be thought of as labor income. It has been empirically determined that labor income correlates quite highly with U.S. stock returns.

6. Consider Softmike, a software company. Softmike's world market beta is 1.75. When a regression is run of Softmike's return on the world market return and the global HML factor, the betas are 1.50 and −1.2, respectively. Assume that the world equity premium is 6%, the HML premium is 3%, and the risk-free rate is 5%. Compute the cost of equity capital using both the CAPM and the Fama-French model. Is Softmike a value company or a growth company?

BIBLIOGRAPHY

Adler, Michael, and Bernard Dumas, 1983, "International Portfolio Choice and Corporation Finance—A Synthesis," *Journal of Finance* 38, pp. 925–984.

Ahearne, Alan G., William L. Griever, and Francis E. Warnock, 2004, "Information Costs and Home Bias: An Analysis of U.S. Holdings of Foreign Equities," *Journal of International Economics* 62, pp. 313–336.

Ang, Andrew, and Geert Bekaert, 2002, "International Asset Allocation with Regime Shifts," *Review of Financial Studies* 15, pp. 1137–1187.

Ang, Andrew, and Joseph Chen, 2007, "CAPM over the Long Run: 1926–2001," *Journal of Empirical Finance* 4, pp. 1–40.

Ang, Andrew, Robert Hodrick, Yuhang Xing, and Xiaoyan Zhang, 2006, "The Cross-Section of Volatility and Expected Returns," *Journal of Finance* 61, pp. 259–300.

Baele, Lieven, 2005, "Volatility Spillover Effects in European Equity Markets: Evidence from a Regime Switching Model," *Journal of Financial and Quantitative Analysis* 40, pp. 373–401.

Bekaert, Geert, 1995, "Market Integration and Investment Barriers in Emerging Equity Markets," *World Bank Economic Review* 9, pp. 75–107.

Bekaert, Geert, and Campbell R. Harvey, 1995, "Time-Varying World Market Integration," *Journal of Finance* 50, pp. 403–444.

Bekaert, Geert, and Campbell R. Harvey, 2000, "Foreign Speculators and Emerging Equity Markets," *Journal of Finance* 55, pp. 565–614.

Bekaert, Geert, and Campbell R. Harvey, 2003, "Emerging Markets Finance," *Journal of Empirical Finance* 10, pp. 3–55.

Bekaert, Geert, Campbell R. Harvey, and Angela Ng, 2005, "Market Integration and Contagion," *Journal of Business* 78, pp. 39–69.

Bekaert, Geert, Robert J. Hodrick, and Xiaoyan Zhang, 2006, "International Stock Return Comovements," Columbia Business School working paper.

Bekaert, Geert, and Michael Urias, 1996, "Diversification, Integration and Emerging Market Closed-End Funds," *Journal of Finance* 51, pp. 835–869.

Bekaert, Geert, and Michael Urias, 1999, "Is There a Free Lunch in Emerging Market Equities?" *Journal of Portfolio Management* 25, pp. 83–95.

Bodnar, Gordon M., Bernard Dumas, and Richard C. Marston, 2003, "Cross Border Valuation: The International Cost of Equity Capital," National Bureau of Economic Research working paper no. 6224.

Brealey, Richard A., and Stewart C. Meyers, 2003, *Principles of Corporate Finance*, 7th ed., Boston: McGraw-Hill/Irwin.

Brooks, Robin, and Marco Del Negro, 2004, "The Rise in Co-movement Across National Stock Markets: Market Integration or IT Bubble?" *Journal of Empirical Finance* 11, pp. 659–680.

Brown, Stephen J., William N. Goetzmann, and Stephen A. Ross, 1995, "Survival," *Journal of Finance* 50, pp. 853–873.

Campbell John Y., Martin Lettau, Burton G. Malkiel, and Yexiao Xu, 2001, "Have Individual Stocks Become More Volatile? An Empirical Exploration of Idiosyncratic Risk," *Journal of Finance* 56, pp. 1–43.

Carrieri, Francesca, Vihang Errunza, and Sergei Sarkissian, 2004, "Industry Risk and Market Integration," *Management Science* 50, pp. 207–221.

Chari, Anusha, and Peter B. Henry, 2004, "Risk Sharing and Asset Prices: Evidence from a Natural Experiment," *Journal of Finance* 59, pp. 1295–1324.

Chen, Nai-Fu., Richard Roll, and Stephen A. Ross, 1986, "Economic Forces and the Stock-Market," *Journal of Business* 59, pp. 383–403.

Claus, James, and Jacob Thomas, 2001, "Equity Premia as Low as Three Percent? Evidence from Analysts' Earnings Forecasts for Domestic and International Stock Markets," *Journal of Finance* 56, pp. 1629–1666.

Connor, Gregory, and Robert A. Korajczyk, 1986, "Performance Measurement with the Arbitrage Pricing Theory: A New Framework for Analysis," *Journal of Financial Economics* 15, pp. 373–394.

Cooper, Ian A., and Evi Kaplanis, 1994, "Home Bias in Equity Portfolios, Inflation Hedging, and International Capital Market Equilibrium," *Review of Financial Studies* 7, pp. 45–60.

Coval, Joshua D., and Tobias J. Moskowitz, 1999, "Home Bias at Home: Local Equity Preference in Domestic Portfolios," *Journal of Finance* 54, pp. 2045–2073.

De Santis, Giorgio, 1993, "Asset Pricing and Portfolio Diversification: Evidence from Emerging Financial Markets," World Bank Symposium on Portfolio Investment in Developing Countries, Washington, DC.

Diermeier, Jeff, and Bruno Solnik, 2001, "Global Pricing of Equity," *Financial Analysts Journal* 7, pp. 37–47.

Dimson, Elroy, Paul Marsh, and Mike Staunton, 2003, "Global Evidence on the Equity Risk Premium," *Journal of Applied Corporate Finance* 15.

Dumas Bernard, and Bruno Solnik, 1995, "The World Price of Foreign-Exchange Risk," *Journal of Finance* 50, pp. 445–479.

Errunza, Vihang, and Etienne Losq, 1985, "International Asset Pricing under Mild Segmentation: Theory and Test," *Journal of Finance* 40, pp. 105–124.

Errunza, Vihang, Kevin Hogan, and Mao-Wei Hung, 1999, "Can the Gains from International Diversification Be Achieved Without Trading Abroad?" *Journal of Finance* 6, pp. 2075–2107.

Fama, Eugene F., and Kenneth R. French, 1992, "The Cross-section of Stock Returns," *Journal of Finance* 47, pp. 427–465.

Fama, Eugene F., and Kenneth R. French, 1995, "Size and Book-to-Market Factors in Earnings and Returns," *Journal of Finance* 50, pp. 131–155.

Fama, Eugene F., and Kenneth R. French, 1997, "Industry Costs of Equity," *Journal of Financial Economics* 43, pp. 153–193.

Fama, Eugene F., and Kenneth R. French, 1998, "Value Versus Growth: The International Evidence," *Journal of Finance* 53, pp. 1975–1999.

Fama, Eugene F., and Kenneth R. French, 2001, "The Equity Premium," *Journal of Finance* 57 (2), pp. 637–659.

Ferreira, Miguel A., and Paulo M. Gama, 2005, "Have World, Country and Industry Risk Changed Our Time?" An Investigation of the Volatility of Developed Stock Markets," *Journal of Financial Quantitative Analysis 40*, pp. 195–222.

Forbes, Kristin J., and Roberto Rigobon, 2002, "No Contagion, only Interdependence: Measuring Stock Market Co-movements," *Journal of Finance* 57, pp. 2223–2261.

Griffin, John M., and René M. Stulz, 2001, "International Competition and Exchange Rate Shocks: A Cross-Country Industry Analysis of Stock Returns," *Review of Financial Studies* 14, pp. 215–241.

Harris, Robert S., Felicia Marston, Dev R. Mishra, and Thomas J. O'Brien, 2003, "*Ex ante* Cost of Equity Estimates of S&P 500 Firms: The Choice Between Global and Domestic CAPM," *Financial Management* 32, pp. 51–66.

Harvey, Campbell R., 1991, "The World Price of Covariance Risk," *Journal of Finance* 46, pp. 111–157.

Harvey, Campbell R., 1995, "Predictable Risk and Returns in Emerging Markets," *Review of Financial Studies* 8, pp. 773–816.

Henry, Peter B., 2000, "Stock Market Liberalization, Economic Reform, and Emerging Market Equity Prices," *Journal of Finance* 55, pp. 529–564.

Heston, Steve L., and K. Geert Rouwenhorst, 1994, "Does Industrial-Structure Explain the Benefits of International

Diversification," *Journal of Financial Economics* 36, pp. 3–27.

Hodrick, Robert J., David Ng, and Paul Sengmueller, 1999, "An International Dynamic Asset Pricing Model," *International Taxation and Public Finance* 6, pp. 547–620.

Huberman, Gur, 2001, "Familiarity Breeds Investment," *Review of Financial Studies* 14, pp. 659–680.

Jacquillat, Bertrand, and Bruno Solnik, 1978, "Multinationals Are Poor Tools for Diversification," *Journal of Portfolio Management* 4, pp. 8–12.

Karolyi, G. Andrew, and René M. Stulz, 2002, "Are Financial Assets Priced Locally or Globally?" National Bureau of Economic Research working paper no. 8994.

Kim, E. Han, and Vijay Singal, 2000, "Opening Up of Stock Markets: Lessons from Emerging Economies," *Journal of Business* 73, pp. 25–66.

Korajczyk, Robert A., and Claude J. Viallet, 1992, "Equity Risk Premia and the Pricing of Foreign Exchange Risk," *Journal of International Economics* 33, pp. 199–219.

Lewis, Karen K., 1994, "Puzzles in International Financial Markets," National Bureau of Economic Research working paper no. 4951.

Lewis, Karen K., 1999, "Trying to Explain Home Bias in Equities and Consumption," *Journal of Economic Literature* 37, pp. 571–608.

Lintner, John, 1965, "The Valuation of Risk Assets and the Selection of Risky Investments in Stock Portfolios and Capital Budgets," *Review of Economics and Statistics* 47, pp. 13–37.

Longin, François, and Bruno Solnik, 1995, "Is Correlation in International Equity Returns Constant? 1960–1990," *Journal of International Money and Finance* 14, pp. 3–26.

Longin, François, and Bruno Solnik, 2001, "Extreme Correlation of International Equity Markets," *Journal of Finance* 56, pp. 649–676.

Markowitz, Harry, 1952, "Portfolio Selection," *Journal of Finance* 7, pp. 77–91.

Merton, Robert C., 1973, "An Intertemporal Capital Asset Pricing Model," *Econometrica* 41, pp. 867–887.

Mossin, Jan, 1966, "Equilibrium in a Capital Asset Market," *Econometrica* 34, pp. 768–783.

Patro, Dilip K., and John K. Wald, 2005, "Firm Characteristics and the Impact of Emerging Market Liberalizations," *Journal of Banking and Finance* 29, pp. 1671–1695.

Roll, Richard, 1977, "A Critique of the Asset Pricing Theory's Tests," *Journal of Financial Economics* 4, pp. 129–176.

Ross, Stephen A., 1976, "The Arbitrage Theory of Capital Asset Pricing," *Journal of Economic Theory* 13, pp. 341–360.

Ross, Stephen A., and Michael M. Walsh, 1983, "A Simple Approach to Pricing Risky Assets with Uncertain Exchange Rates," *Research in International Business and Finance* 3, pp. 39–54.

Ross, Stephen A., Randolph W. Westerfield, and Jeffrey F. Jaffe, 2002, *Corporate Finance*, 6th ed., Boston: McGraw-Hill/Irwin.

Rowland, Patrick F., and Linda L. Tesar, 2004, "Multinationals and the Gains from International Diversification," *Review of Economic Dynamics* 7, pp. 789–826.

Sercu, Piet, 1980, "A Generalization of the International Asset Pricing Model," *Revue de l'Association Française de Finance* 1, pp. 91–135.

Sercu, Piet, and Raman Uppal, 1995, *International Financial Markets and the Firm*, Cincinnati: South-Western College Publishing.

Sharpe, William, 1964, "Capital Asset Prices: A Theory of Market Equilibrium Under Conditions of Risk," *Journal of Finance* 19, pp. 425–442.

Siegel, Jeremy J., 1992, "The Real Rate of Interest from 1800–1990: A Study of the U.S. and the U.K.," *Journal of Monetary Economics* 29, pp. 227–252.

Solnik, Bruno, 1974a, "Why Not Diversify Internationally Rather Than Domestically?" *Financial Analysts Journal*, pp. 48–53.

Solnik, Bruno, 1974b, "The International Pricing Risk: An Empirical Investigation of the World Capital Market Structure," *Journal of Finance* 29, pp. 365–378.

Solnik, Bruno, 1983, "International Arbitrage Pricing Theory," *Journal of Finance* 38, pp. 449–457.

Stulz, René M, 1995, "The Cost of Capital in Internationally Integrated Markets: The Case of Nestlé," *European Financial Management* 1, pp. 11–22.

Tesar, Linda L., and Ingrid M. Werner, 1992, "Home Bias and the Globalization of Securities Markets," National Bureau of Economic Research working paper no. 4218.

Tesar, Linda L., and Ingrid M. Werner, 1995, "Home Bias and High Turnover," *Journal of International Money and Finance* 14, pp. 467–492.

Warnock, Francis E., 2001, "Home Bias and High Turnover Reconsidered," Board of Governors of the Federal Reserve System working paper no. 702.

Warnock, Francis E., and C. Cleaver, 2002, "Financial Centers and the Geography of Capital Flows," Board of Governors of the Federal Reserve System working paper.

Welch, Ivo, 2000, "Views of Financial Economists on the Equity Premium and Other Issues," *Journal of Business* 73–74, pp. 501–537.

Zhang, Xiaoyan, 2006, "Specification Tests of International Asset Pricing Models," *Journal of International Money and Finance* 25, pp. 275–307.

Appendix

The Mathematics of International Diversification

Here, we formally prove two results that we used in this chapter.

RISK REDUCTION

Statement:

As long as the correlation coefficient between two assets is less than 1, the standard deviation of the portfolio will be less than the weighted average of the two individual standard deviations.

Proof: Let w and $1 - w$ denote the investment proportions in the two assets. Let σ_1 and σ_2 denote the two standard deviations of the two assets. We use two statistical properties:

1. The variance of a sum of two random variables equals the sum of the variances plus twice the covariance between the variables.
2. The correlation, ρ, between two variables is their covariance divided by the product of their standard deviations.

Hence, the variance of the portfolio with weights $\{w, 1 - w\}$ is:

$$w^2\sigma_1^2 + (1 - w)^2\sigma_2^2 + 2w(1 - w)\rho\sigma_1\sigma_2$$

We want to show $\{w^2\sigma_1^2 + (1 - w)^2\sigma_2^2 + 2w(1 - w)\rho\sigma_1\sigma_2\}^{.5} < w\sigma_1 + (1 - w)\sigma_2$. This is equivalent to

$$w^2\sigma_1^2 + (1 - w)^2\sigma_2^2 + 2w(1 - w)\rho\sigma_1\sigma_2$$
$$< w^2\sigma_1^2 + (1 - w)^2\sigma_2^2 + 2w(1 - w)\sigma_1\sigma_2$$

where the latter expression simply follows from squaring both sides.

Obviously, strict inequality follows from $\rho < 1$. In fact, given $\sigma_1 = \sigma_2 = \sigma$, we can show that the variance is minimized by setting $w = \frac{1}{2}$. The variance of the minimum-variance portfolio is then $\frac{1}{2}[1 + \rho]\sigma^2$. When ρ is smaller than 1, the variance of the portfolio is always smaller than the variance of either asset.

IMPROVING THE SHARPE RATIO

Statement:

If $\dfrac{E[r^*] - r_f}{\text{Vol}[r^*]} > \rho\dfrac{E[r] - r_f}{\text{Vol}[r]}$, the Sharpe ratio will improve when the asset with return r^* is added (marginally) to the portfolio with return r. Without loss of generality, we set the return on the risk-free asset equal to 0 in our proof.

Proof: The Sharpe ratio of the portfolio with w invested in the foreign asset is

$$SR = \frac{(1-w)E(r) + wE(r^*)}{\text{Var}(P)}$$

$$\text{Var}(P) = (1-w)^2\,\text{Var}(r) + w^2\,\text{Var}(r^*) + 2w\,(1-w)\text{Cov}(r, r^*)$$

We want to show that if the statement condition holds, then $\dfrac{\partial SR}{\partial w} > 0$ for small w (that is, when we set $w \equiv 0$). Taking the derivative and leaving out the (positive) denominator, we obtain:

$$\frac{\partial SR}{\partial w} > 0 \Leftrightarrow (E[r^*] - E[r])\text{Var}[P]^{\frac{1}{2}} - E[P]$$
$$\times \frac{1}{2}\text{Var}[P]^{-\frac{1}{2}} \times [-2\text{Var}[r] + 2\text{Cov}[r,r^*]] > 0$$

Evaluating this at $w = 0$ means that P equals the U.S. portfolio. Multiplying through with $\text{Var}[P]^{\frac{1}{2}}$ and simplifying, we obtain

$$E[r^*]\text{Var}[r] - E[r]\text{Cov}[r,r^*] > 0$$

or

$$\underset{\substack{\uparrow \\ \text{Foreign} \\ \text{Sharpe} \\ \text{ratio}}}{\frac{E[r^*]}{\text{Var}[r^*]^{\frac{1}{2}}}} > \underset{\substack{\uparrow \\ \text{Domestic} \\ \text{Sharpe} \\ \text{ratio}}}{\frac{E[r]}{\text{Var}[r]^{\frac{1}{2}}}} \times \underset{\substack{\uparrow \\ \text{Correlation,} \\ \text{CORR}(r,r^*)}}{\frac{\text{Cov}[r,r^*]}{\text{Var}[r]^{\frac{1}{2}}\text{Var}[r^*]^{\frac{1}{2}}}}$$

Chapter 14

Political and Country Risk

*O*n May 1, 2007, which is a traditional day for celebrating socialist causes, Venezuelan President Hugo Chavez announced that operating control of Venezuelan oil fields would transfer from international oil companies, such as ExxonMobil and ConocoPhillips of the United States, France's Total, Norway's Statoil, and Britain's BP, to Venezuela's government-owned oil company, Petroleos de Venezuela S. A. (PDVSA). This action was a realization of **political risk**, which is the risk that a government action will negatively affect a company's cash flows. In the most extreme form of political risk, governments seize property without compensating the owners in a total **expropriation** (or **nationalization**). For the international oil companies, the extent of the expropriation was uncertain as negotiations on how much they would be paid were still under way.

Country risk is a broad concept that encompasses both the potentially adverse effects of a country's political environment and its economic and financial environment. Understanding country risk and political risk is an important aspect of international capital budgeting and managing operations in other countries, especially developing countries.

This chapter discusses these risks and examines how they can be measured. It also explains which risks are diversifiable and which are not. Finally, it explores how multinationals, such as the international oil companies, can minimize and manage the risks.

14.1 POLITICAL RISK VERSUS COUNTRY RISK

This section explores the general differences between political risk and country risk. We begin with the broader concept of country risk.

Country Risk

As just explained, we use the term *political risk* to indicate the risk that a government action will negatively affect a company's cash flows. Country risk is broader because it includes the adverse political and economic risks of operating in a country. For example, a recession in a country that lowers its aggregate demand and reduces the revenues of exporters to that nation is a realization of country risk. Labor strikes by a country's dockworkers, truckers, and transit workers that disrupt production and distribution of products, thus lowering profits, also qualify as country risks. Clashes between rival ethnic or religious groups that prevent people in a country from shopping can also be considered country risks.

Besides affecting the profitability of firms, country risk also affects international investors who buy emerging-market securities (especially bonds) and the banks that lend to developing countries. In international bond markets, country risk refers to any factor related to a country that can cause a borrower to default on a loan. When country risk is taken in a narrow sense to be the risk associated with a government defaulting on its bond payments, it is called **sovereign risk**. More generally, country risk refers to the risk of private firms in these countries defaulting on their debts. Usually, the abilities of a private firm and its government to pay off international debt are highly correlated.

Financial and Economic Risk Factors

What factors do economists consider when thinking about country risk analysis? Let's first focus on sovereign risk and consider the benefits and costs of a country defaulting on its international debt. The benefit to a government of defaulting on debt to foreigners is that the country is wealthier today. It no longer has to make interest and principal payments to foreign creditors. The chief cost to a country that defaults is loss of reputation, which undermines its future access to international capital markets. Because this reputation cost is large, a country is likely to repay its debt as long as it generates enough cash flow to do so.

Of course, if an international debt is denominated in the currency of the borrowing country, the borrowing country can always repay the debt by printing more money. But this action will depreciate the local currency and is effectively equivalent to a partial default from the perspective of international investors. Consequently, most developing-country debt is denominated in developed-country currencies, such as the U.S. dollar. Hence, the capacity to repay foreign debt and, consequently, the probability of default ultimately depend on the country's ability to generate foreign exchange. Nevertheless, governments have still been known to refuse to pay their debts, even when they had foreign exchange available. It is this lack of willingness to pay that we call political risk.

To help investors discriminate between financially sound and financially troubled countries, a number of economic variables are used, including the following:

- The ratio of a country's external debt to its GDP
- The ratio of a country's debt service payments to its exports
- The ratio of a country's imports to its official international reserves
- A country's terms of trade (the ratio of its export to import prices)
- A country's current account deficit

These variables are directly related to the ability of the country to generate inflows of foreign exchange. Factors such as inflation and real economic growth are useful as well. Whereas a country's economic health may directly affect the cash flows of a multinational firm, it may also be informative about political risk in a narrow sense. The better a country's economic situation, the less likely it is to face political and social turmoil that will inevitably harm foreign (and domestic) companies.

Industry Factors and Country Risk

The industry in which a multinational corporation operates can affect its exposure to country risk. Often, policy changes are explicitly directed at certain industries (for instance, industries with valuable assets, such as oil companies). Calculating a company's industry-specific risk is not as straightforward as calculating more general country risks.

For example, if a multinational corporation dominates an industry with local competitors, it may be more subject to political risk than an MNC operating in an industry with primarily foreign companies as competitors. As another example, if a company is the source of considerable foreign exchange earnings for the host country or is the vehicle for important technology transfer, it might be less subject to government interference than one without such advantages.

Depending on its location within a country, the risks may be different. How much power do the country's regional governments have versus the national government? What is the attitude of local communities to the MNC's proposed projects? Are there any armed opposition groups in the area, and how do they view the presence of a foreign company? These are questions that managers must ask. Later on in the chapter, we mention a number of specialized organizations that can provide such an analysis.

Political Risk Factors

In this section, we provide a partial list of the most important factors an MNC should be aware of in assessing political risk.

Expropriation or Nationalization

The most extreme form of political risk is the possibility that the host country takes over an MNC's subsidiary, with or without compensation. This is the worst-case scenario for firms. Whereas outright expropriations have been rare in recent times, they used to be common: Regimes in Eastern Europe (after World War II) and in Cuba (in 1960) expropriated private businesses, both domestic and foreign. The ouster of the Shah of Iran by the Ayatollah Khomeini in 1979 also led to expropriations.

Contract Repudiation

In 1996, Mexico's Instituto Nacional de Ecologia (INE), an agency of the federal government, awarded Tecmed, a Spanish multinational corporation, a renewable license to operate a hazardous waste landfill in Mexico. In 1998, however, the INE suddenly refused to renew the license, and Tecmed faced the realization of political risk. Governments sometimes revoke, or repudiate, contracts without compensating companies for their existing investments in projects or services. This action can include the government defaulting on the payments associated with the contracts, canceling licenses (as Mexico did with Tecmed), or otherwise introducing laws and regulations that interfere with the contracts to which the government and the MNC agreed. Such acts are sometimes referred to as "creeping," or "indirect," expropriation because they deprive the company of the expected benefits of its investment.

In May 2006, Bolivia's new socialist president, Evo Morales, sent troops to the gas fields and put YPBF, a state company, in charge, repudiating existing contracts with multinationals such as Brazil's Petrobras, Spain's Repsol, and British Petroleum. Morales stopped short of a full nationalization, leaving a piece of the production in foreign hands.

Taxes and Regulation

Governments can dramatically change the "rules of the game" that were in place when an MNC first made its investment in the host country. This can take various explicit forms, such as unexpected increases in taxes, restrictions on hiring and firing local workers, and sudden stricter environmental standards. MNCs are also sometimes forced by governments to sell their equity stakes in local subsidiaries because of foreign ownership restrictions.

One set of regulations that MNCs find particularly problematic are regulations restricting the transfer of their profits earned abroad back to their home countries. Governments not only have the power to change the tax rates on these earnings, but they can completely block their transfer. This essentially forces the MNC to invest its funds locally, even if doing so is less profitable. Finally, governments often make decisions that can indirectly affect the cash flows of MNCs.

The situations in Peru and Chile provide examples of this type of political risk. Until 2004, international mining companies doing business in Peru and Chile enjoyed favorable tax treatment on the sale of their mineral concentrates, but in June 2004, Peru's congress approved a law to levy taxes on royalties (in this context, essentially taxes levied on minerals extracted in accordance with a mining license) of up to 3%. Chile's government proposed a similar law. These tax increases constitute a change in the rules of the game for the mining companies that will make them less profitable in the future.

Exchange Controls

Another political risk factor relates to exchange controls. Governments have been known to prevent the conversion of their local currencies to foreign currencies. In general, doing business in countries with inconvertible currencies puts an MNC at considerable risk.

An interesting case is the 2002 collapse of the Argentine currency board, which effectively ended the one-for-one convertibility of pesos into dollars. The Argentine government also curtailed bank deposit withdrawals and prohibited the unauthorized export of foreign currency from the country.

Corruption and Legal Inefficiency

Highly inefficient governments often increase the red tape companies have to deal with and hence increase their costs of doing business. Governments may also be corrupt and demand bribes. Transparency International (TI) produces an annual "Corruption Perceptions Index" for more than 150 countries, using expert assessments and opinion surveys. In 2005, Iceland was perceived as the least corrupt country; Chad and Bangladesh were perceived as the most corrupt.

TI also compiles information on which companies have the highest propensity to pay bribes and therefore undermine efforts of governments to improve governance. Multinationals from Russia, China, and India were the worst offenders in 2005, whereas Swiss and Swedish companies had the least tendency to pay bribes.

A country's legal system is an important factor in determining the overall quality of its institutions and how attractive it is for firms to do business there. Simeon Djankov, Rafael La Porta, Florencio Lopez-de-Silanes, and Andrei Shleifer (2003) used an interesting measure to gauge the quality and efficiency of the legal systems of 109 countries: They measured the time it takes to evict a tenant or clear a bounced check through the legal system. Exhibit 14.1 shows these measures for the G5 countries and for the best- and worst-performing countries on this score.

The United States and the United Kingdom seem to have the speediest legal systems among the G5 countries, but there are five countries (Uganda, Tunisia, Malawi, Swaziland, and Canada) where evicting a tenant happens even faster. In contrast, in Poland and Slovenia, it takes almost 3 years to either evict a tenant or collect on a bounced check. Such a tardy legal system poses a potential risk factor for MNCs.

Ethnic Violence, Political Unrest, and Terrorism

Significant MNC losses can occur due to internal civil strife or wars. An interesting historical case involves Consolidated Foods, Inc., which constructed a manufacturing plant in what the company perceived to be a "happy, sleepy country" in 1976. The country happened to be El Salvador, which within 2 years of the decision got embroiled in an internal war between the government and left-wing rebels. At one point, the rebels took about 120 employees of the company hostage. The plant was closed in 1979. More recently, in war-torn regions of Somalia and Iraq, companies have been forced to hire their own private armies in order to try to function normally. This, of course, is expensive.

Home-Country Restrictions

The politics of a company's home country can affect its cash flows from foreign operations. For example, after the Iranian Revolution in 1979, a U.S. embargo on Iran forced Coca-Cola to shut down its operations there. Coke later resumed operations in the country by the late 1980s, until President Clinton reimposed the embargo in 1995.

Exhibit 14.1   Legal System Quality

	Eviction of a Tenant (days)	Check Collection (days)
G5 Countries		
U.S.	49	54
UK	115	101
Germany	331	154
France	226	181
Japan	363	60
Countries with Slowest Evictions		
Poland	1,080	1,000
Slovenia	1,003	1,003
Lebanon	973	721
Morocco	745	192
Malta	730	545
Sri Lanka	730	440
Countries with Fastest Evictions		
Uganda	29	99
Tunisia	33	7
Malawi	35	108
Swaziland	40	40
Canada	43	421

Notes: The numbers represent the number of days it takes to evict a tenant or collect a bounced check through the court system. We report numbers for the G5 countries and the five countries with the longest and shortest durations. The source is Table 6 in Djankov, La Porta, Lopez-de-Silanes, and Shleifer (2003). Copyright © 2003 by the President and Fellows of the Massachusetts Institute of Technology. Reprinted by permission.

The Debt Crisis

The 1980s **Debt Crisis** was one of the defining historical episodes that made country risk analysis an important part of international banking and a critical component in international capital budgeting.

Origins of the Debt Crisis

From 1948 to the end of the 1960s, crude oil prices ranged between $2.50 and $3.00 per barrel. The Organization of Petroleum Exporting Countries (OPEC) was formed in 1960 to stabilize oil prices. In 1973, OPEC started curtailing production, which sent oil prices from $3.00 per barrel to over $12.00 per barrel by the end of 1974. Over the next few years, events in Iran and Iraq led to another round of increases in the price of crude oil, with prices eventually reaching $35 per barrel in 1981. Because these prices are all nominal, current-year prices, it helps to adjust them for inflation. In 1981, oil prices reached $60.00 per barrel measured in 2000 dollars.

Exhibit 14.2 summarizes how such a boon for oil-producing countries eventually led to a Debt Crisis for the developing countries. Rather than match the increases in income generated by the oil price jumps in 1973 and 1974 with increases in consumption and investment spending, the OPEC countries saved by making loans to international banks, often in the form of dollar deposits in the Eurocurrency markets at floating interest rates. The banks in turn loaned these "petrodollars," as they were called at the time, to developing countries, typically in the form of loans called eurocredits that were quoted at a spread above the floating interest rate they paid to the OPEC countries.

Banks viewed the lending as profitable and relatively riskless for three reasons. First, the loans were made at a spread over the banks' borrowing costs. Thus, the banks were not

Exhibit 14.2 The Origins of the Debt Crisis

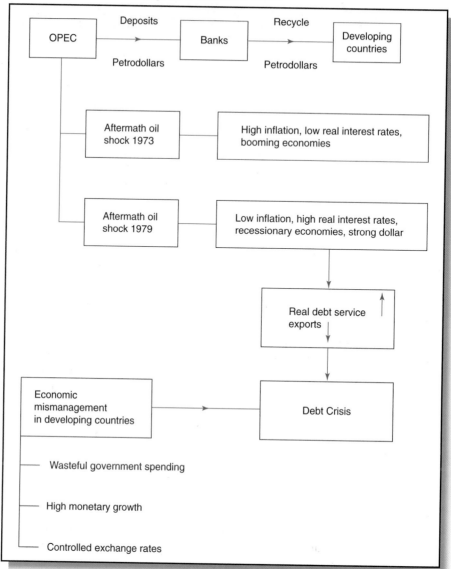

exposed to changes in interest rates, as they would have been if they had borrowed short term and had lent at long-term fixed rates. Second, the banks eliminated exchange rate exposure as the debts were denominated in dollars, which was the currency the OPEC countries had deposited. Third, the banks syndicated the loans, taking diversified exposures to a number of countries to avoid too much exposure to a single country. As a result, during the 1970s, the debt of non-OPEC developing countries owed to banks in industrialized countries, especially banks in the United States, increased significantly.

A mix of external shocks affecting industrialized countries and developing countries in the early 1980s and macroeconomic mismanagement in developing countries triggered the actual Debt Crisis. In contrast to the response to the first oil shock, the oil shock of the late 1970s was met with a staunchly anti-inflationary monetary policy in a number of countries, particularly in the United States under Paul Volcker, Chairman of the Board of Governors of the Federal Reserve System. The macroeconomic situation in the developed world was now totally different: Real interest rates were high, the global economy was in recession, and the dollar was strong. This situation contributed to low prices of commodities on the world markets and low demand for the exports of developing countries.

With the huge dollar appreciation and high dollar interest rates, the developing countries faced steep interest payments in dollars at the same time as their export revenues were falling. Suddenly, the default risk of the loan portfolios of international banks had greatly increased. The situation was exacerbated by the fact that developing countries had not used the money they borrowed very productively and had run unsustainable economic policies.

Ironically, however, the Debt Crisis actually started in Mexico, an oil-exporting country. On August 12, 1982, Mexico announced that it could no longer make its scheduled payments on its foreign debt. Mexico requested loans from foreign governments and the IMF, and it started negotiating with its commercial bank creditors. It was the start of a prolonged and deep crisis. By the end of the year, 24 other countries had requested restructuring on their commercial bank debts.

The debt of developing countries threatened to undermine the global financial system because many large banks, in particular the largest U.S. banks, had considerable exposures to Mexico and other debt-ridden developing countries—exposures that exceeded their capital. Moreover, developing countries lost access to much-needed international capital for a decade. As a result, they failed to register any substantive economic growth during the 1980s.

Managing the Debt Crisis

At the beginning of the Debt Crisis, advisory committees composed of the large banks, industrial-country governments, and the IMF arranged debt reschedulings and the extension of new credit. The hope was that economic recovery plus sensible economic policies in developing countries guided by the IMF would make the debt problem disappear. That is, the banks mistook the Debt Crisis for a "liquidity" problem. They were betting that the developing countries were only temporarily unable to repay their debts. Liquidity problems are much less worrisome than genuine insolvency. By 1984, the current account deficits run by developing countries had fallen, but at the cost of sharply reduced economic growth. The debt-rescheduling agreements proved a failure, and it was clear that the commercial banks wanted to decrease their exposure to high-debt developing countries.

The **Baker Plan**, instituted in 1985 and named for U.S. Treasury Secretary James Baker, constituted a second phase of the handling of the Debt Crisis. The Baker Plan relied heavily on countries agreeing to change their economic policies following guidelines set by the IMF in exchange for a modest amount of new loans extended to developing countries by private commercial banks and the World Bank. It assumed that with the right economic policies, these countries could "grow" themselves out of their excessive debts. Although some successful financing packages were agreed upon, the Baker Plan could not stop the banks from trying to reduce their exposure to developing countries.

According to a number of academic observers, the developing countries' reluctance to repay their debts was justified because they were suffering from "debt overhang"—the notion that a country saddled with a huge debt burden has little incentive to implement economic reforms or stimulate investment because the resulting increase in income will simply be appropriated by the country's creditors in the form of higher debt payments.[1] From this perspective, it is not surprising that some countries (Peru and Brazil, for example) stopped or severely restricted repaying their debts altogether. Moreover, the developing countries did not seem to implement the appropriate economic policies. By 1987, it became clear that the banks were not going to be repaid in full.

Debt- and Debt Service–Reducing Operations

Facing mounting debt stocks, many countries adopted debt-reducing policies. Stimulated by an active secondary market in developing-country debt, debt buybacks and debt–equity swaps proved popular. In a **debt buyback**, the country repays a loan at a discount.

---

[1]In Chapter 16, this debt overhang argument will resurface when we consider the investment incentives of private companies in severe financial distress.

In a **debt–equity swap**, an MNC that is willing to directly invest in a country buys the debt of the country from an original creditor at a market price that reflects a discount from face value. The MNC then presents the debt to the developing country's government and receives local currency (equal to the face value of the debt or at a discount less than the market discount). The MNC then uses the local currency to make the equity investment in the country.

Many MNCs have used debt–equity swaps to lower the cost of their investments (for example, in Mexico, Argentina, Brazil, and other countries). Debt–equity swaps were a central element of the efforts of Peru, Chile, and Argentina to privatize their government-operated industries. For example, in 1994, Peru partially raised money by offering debt–equity swaps in two government-owned and -operated mining companies, Tintaya and Cajamarquilla.

Some of the Debt Crisis debt-reduction arrangements were even accompanied by developmental aid for the troubled countries. For example, an international organization buying debt in the secondary market would exchange the debt for local currency at the country's central bank. The organization would then use the proceeds to finance development projects of an environmental, health, or educational nature. However, in addition to such "debt-for-do-good" swaps, there were also interesting "debt-for-do-bad" swap proposals. For example, in the mid-1980s, Colombian drug lords offered to buy back their country's debt in return for immunity from prosecution. The proposal was rejected.

Several economists argue that when a country uses its own resources to buy back its troubled debt at a discount, the country's creditors are the only ones that benefit. Here we use a simple numeric example to illustrate the main argument.

Example 14.1   Debt Buybacks in Brazar

Suppose that the country of Brazar has an outstanding debt of $100 billion. Creditors all agree that there is only a 25% probability that the debt will be repaid. They also estimate that if the country defaults, it will be possible to seize $20 billion of Brazar's international assets for distribution to creditors. Suppose the debt is payable next year, and to keep things simple, let the market interest rate be 0. What is the market value of the debt? We know that the value of the debt must be the expected value of the repayments:

$$V = 0.25 \times \$100 \text{ billion} + 0.75 \times \$20 \text{ billion} = \$40 \text{ billion}$$

Hence, $1 of debt sells for $0.40 in the market.

Suppose that the government of Brazar has some resources that it could use to buy back the debt. Given the steep 60% discount, Brazar may reason that a buyback is a good investment because it retires a dollar of debt for $0.40. Suppose Brazar has $8 billion. Can it buy back $20 billion of face-value debt at $0.40 on the dollar? The answer is no because creditors must be indifferent between selling the debt to Brazar in the buyback and holding the debt for the next year. They will figure out the new price of the debt after the buyback.

To determine how much the government must pay to buy back $20 billion of debt, we must first determine the new price of debt. Let's first assume that the amount that is recoverable in the bad state of the world remains $20 billion.[2] The new value of the debt is, therefore,

$$V_{\text{new}} = 0.25 \times \$80 \text{ billion} + 0.75 \times \$20 \text{ billion} = \$35 \text{ billion}$$

Hence, given that $80 billion of debt remains outstanding, the price per dollar of debt rises to $\frac{35}{80} = 0.4375$, or $0.4375 per dollar of debt. The creditors will want to sell only at this price. Who gains in this scenario? Let's consider the different parties:

---

[2]In reality, the country must use resources to repay the debt, which would likely reduce this amount. Research by Jeremy Bulow and Kenneth Rogoff (1988, 1991) shows that this effect is unlikely to overturn the main result of the example.

- The government pays $0.4375 \times 20 = \$8.75$ billion, not $8 billion and it reduces the market value of its debt from $40 billion to $35 billion, or by $5 billion.

- The creditors who sell their debt to the government realize a capital gain of 3.75 cents on the dollar. In sum, they gain $0.0375 \times \$20$ billion $= \$0.75$ billion.

- The creditors who hold out (do not sell) also receive a capital gain of 3.75 cents per dollar, for a total of $0.0375 \times \$80$ billion $= \$3$ billion.

The conclusion is pretty clear: The government overpaid by $3.75 billion ($8.75 − $5.00). Notice that the gain is nicely split up among the creditors who sell to the government and the holdout creditors.

A famous case that confirms this theory is the Bolivia debt buyback of 1988. The box below discusses this case in more detail.

The Bolivia Debt Buyback

In March 1988, Bolivia received $34 million from an anonymous group of countries to buy back part of its commercial bank debt. Whereas the market value of the debt before the buyback was around $50 million, the market value of debt after the buyback was $43.4 million, even though $34 million had been spent to reduce the debt. The reason was that the buyback increased the price of the debt on the secondary market from around 7 cents to the dollar to over 11 cents to the dollar. Although debt prices fluctuated daily, let's fix some prices to get a concrete idea of what happened.

Suppose the price just before the debt buyback is 7.25 cents on the dollar (the debt traded as low as 6 cents to the dollar at one point). The total outstanding face value of the debt was $670 million. Hence, the total market value of the debt was $0.0725 \times \$670$ million $= \$48.575$ million. The Bolivian government paid 11 cents on the dollar to buy back $308 million worth of debt. So, it paid $0.11 \times \$308$ million $= \$33.88$ million, about $34 million. However, the secondary market price of Bolivian debt then remained at or above 11 cents per dollar, so the value of the remaining debt was 0.11 ($670 million − $308 million) $= \$39.82$ million. Essentially, Bolivia paid $34 million to reduce the market value of its debt by a paltry $8.755 million. Clearly, commercial bank creditors reaped the bulk of the benefits.

The solution to this problem is to eliminate the debt entirely so that there are no holdout creditors benefiting from the debt buyback scheme. In March 1993, Bolivia eliminated $170 million of its commercial bank debt, leaving less than $10 million outstanding. The whole operation (primarily a debt buyback at 16 cents to the dollar) was financed by donations. Some banks, such as JPMorgan, chose to channel the money received into conservation and environmental projects run by the Nature Conservancy and the World Wildlife Fund. Although the whole operation clearly seemed a success, Bolivia still ended up with an outstanding debt of no less than $3.5 billion to various multilateral organizations, including the World Bank.

The Brady Plan

After years of muddling through the Debt Crisis, it became obvious that the real problem was a lack of solvency rather than a lack of liquidity on the part of developing countries. In 1989, the **Brady Plan**, developed by then U.S. Treasury Secretary Nicholas Brady, put pressure on banks to offer some form of debt relief to developing countries. The Brady Plan also called for an expansion in secondary market transactions aimed at debt reduction. In addition, the IMF and the World Bank were urged to provide funding for "debt or debt service reduction purposes." The first Brady package was arranged for Mexico in July 1989.

Negotiating a debt-reduction agreement is complex because numerous banks are involved, and "free-rider" problems exist. For example, small banks could refuse to put up new money, yet they still benefit from their share of interest rate payments that the new money makes possible. The Brady Plan approach offered banks a menu of different debt-reduction methods, including providing new loans. Each bank could choose the restructuring option that it found most suitable from a menu of possibilities established in a debt-reduction agreement between the debtor-country government and its creditor banks. The creditor banks, because of their large number, were represented by a bank advisory committee. In order to mitigate free-rider problems, no bank could opt out. Among the options available to the banks were the following:

- *Buybacks:* The debtor country was allowed to repurchase part of its debt at an agreed discount (a debt-reduction option).
- *Discount bond exchange:* The loans could be exchanged for bonds at an agreed discount, with the bonds yielding a market rate of interest.
- *Par bond exchange:* The loans could be exchanged at their face value for bonds yielding a lower interest rate than the one on the original loans.
- *Conversion bonds combined with new money:* Loans could be exchanged for bonds at par that yield a market rate, but banks had to provide new money in a fixed proportion of the amount converted (an option for banks unable or unwilling to participate in debt reduction or debt service reduction).

U.S. and Japanese banks primarily opted for discounts or par bonds.

The Brady Plan ended up securitizing the debt into easily tradable bonds, called **Brady bonds.** Quite a few Brady bonds have "official enhancements" attached to them, such as collateral provisions. (Collateral is an asset pledged as security for the repayment of a loan.) Hence, in exchange for a loan, a country could pledge collateral in the form of U.S. Treasury zero-coupon bonds, for example. The Brady Plan agreements also included financing arrangements to pay for the collateral and other up-front debt-reduction costs. Sources included the IMF, the World Bank, the Inter-American Development Bank, and the Japanese government, which would typically provide funds only if the country adhered to an IMF-supported structural adjustment program. Such a program typically involved economic policy recommendations such as currency devaluation, the lifting of export and import restrictions, the balancing of government budgets, and removal of price controls and state subsidies.

For many countries, the Brady bond market soon replaced the market for secondary bank loans and provided the impetus to an emerging-market bond market that is still in place today. Not only do sovereign borrowers now tap international bond markets, investors from industrialized countries have also started to invest in the local bond and money markets of many formerly heavily indebted developing countries. As a consequence, sovereign credit ratings have become more important. We discuss these debt markets in Section 14.3.

14.2 INCORPORATING POLITICAL RISK IN CAPITAL BUDGETING

When MNCs undertake international investments, they must forecast their future cash flows and discount them at an appropriate risk-adjusted discount rate. There is much confusion and disagreement about how political risks should enter these computations. Some researchers suggest using a discount rate adjustment to account for political risk; others feel that political risk should affect only cash flow projections.

Adjusting Expected Cash Flows for Political Risk

Consider a multinational corporation with a shareholder base that is globally diversified. In this case, the discount rate should reflect only international, systematic risks. Chapter 13 showed that systematic risks are typically related to how an MNC's return in a particular country covaries with the world market return. If the risk of loss from political risk does not covary with the world market return, no adjustment to the discount rate is necessary. Positive covariation between the cash flows from the project and the world market return increases the required global discount rate. Consequently, unless political risk, which adversely affects the MNC's investment returns, is systematically high when the world market return is low, political risk should not enter the calculation of the discount rate. Instead, the company's cash flows should be adjusted for the presence of political risk.

To fully understand this argument, consider a simple scenario. Suppose a company takes out an insurance policy against political risk and that the policy covers all contingencies and has no deductible. In this case, a company would simply compute its expected cash flows as if there were no political risk and then subtract the insurance premium it must pay each year from the cash flows of the project. The cash flows would then be discounted at the usual discount rate. It is, indeed, possible to purchase **political risk insurance**, and in some countries, such insurance is even subsidized by the government. (However, it is seldom the case that an investment can be fully insured. We discuss insurance and other ways companies can mitigate political risks in Section 14.4.)

If a company chooses not to purchase political risk insurance, when it forecasts its future cash flows, it must incorporate into the calculation how its cash flows might be affected by various political risks, such as expropriation, unexpected taxation, and so forth. In the following example, we show how this can be done.

Example 14.2 Oconoc's Project in Zuenvela

Suppose Oconoc, an American oil company, wants to do a joint project with Atauz Petrol, an oil company in the oil-producing country of Zuenvela. Oconoc's contribution to the project is $75 million, and Oconoc predicts that the project will yield it $50 million per year for 2 years. However, Zuenvela has a very unstable political system and in the past has witnessed widespread strikes. The president of Zuenvela, Ugo Vezcha, has expressed some dismay with the management of Atauz Petrol, and he has hinted that he might renationalize the company, which would have drastic consequences for Oconoc's cash flows. Given this information, the managers of Oconoc think that the probability that the government will expropriate the project is 12% each year. Furthermore, if the government interferes, the cash flows will be zero from then onward.

Exhibit 14.3 presents this analysis in a simple diagram. If there were no political risk, the value of the project would be easy to calculate. Let C be the expected cash flow, let r be the discount rate, and let V be the present value of the project. Then, we know that

$$V = \frac{C}{1 + r} + \frac{C}{(1 + r)^2}$$

With a 10% discount rate, we obtain

$$V = \frac{50}{1.1} + \frac{50}{1.1^2} = 86.78$$

Because the value of the project, $86.78 million, is greater than the cost of the project, $75 million, the net present value is $11.78 million; the project should therefore be undertaken.

Exhibit 14.3 Adjusting the MNC's Cash Flows for Political Risk

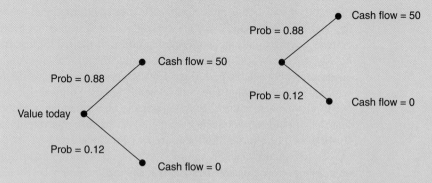

Notes: Expected cash flows are $50 million in period 1 and period 2. There is a 12% chance each period that the host government will expropriate the project. In this case, the cash flow to the MNC is 0.

However, the political risk adjustments change the computation considerably. Let's follow Exhibit 14.3 to make the adjustments. For the first year, there are two scenarios. There is a 0.88 chance that the cash flow of $50 million will be realized and a 0.12 chance that the project will return 0. For the second year, there are three scenarios: (1) expropriation in the first year implies no second-year cash flows; (2) no expropriation in the first year but expropriation in the second year, so no cash flows; and (3) no expropriation at all. The probability of the first scenario occurring is 0.12, the probability of the second scenario occurring is $0.88 \times 0.12 = 0.1056$, and the probability of the third scenario occurring is $0.88 \times 0.88 = 0.7744$. Note that to obtain the probabilities for the second year, we must multiply the probability of no expropriation in the first year by the probabilities of the second-year events. These three scenarios exhaust all possible outcomes, and hence, the probabilities must add to 1.

Bringing it all together, we obtain:

$$V = \frac{(0.88 \times 50) + (0.12 \times 0)}{1.1} + \frac{(0.88^2 \times 50) + (0.12 \times 0.88) \times 0 + (0.12 \times 0)}{1.1^2}$$

$$= 40 + 32 = 72$$

Hence, the value of the project is now less than its cost, and the project should not be undertaken because the net present value (NPV) is −$3.00 million.

An alternative way to compute the project's NPV is to calculate the probability weighted average of the scenario-specific NPVs. Let's first set up the different scenarios:

Scenarios	Probability	Value	NPV
No expropriation	0.7744	86.78	11.78
Expropriation in first year	0.12	0	−75
Expropriation in second year	0.1056	45.45*	−29.55
	1.00		

* This is $\frac{50}{1.1}$.

Only when there is no expropriation does the project capture the full NPV of $11.78 million computed before. When the project is expropriated in the second period, the company still receives cash flows in the first period, with a current worth of

$45.45 million. In sum, the NPV of the project is the probability weighted average of the three outcomes:

$$NPV = (11.78 \times 0.7744) - (75 \times 0.12) - (29.55 \times 0.1056)$$

$$= -3.00$$

If Oconoc's managers find it difficult to figure out the probability of expropriation, they can still do an informative analysis: They can find the expropriation probability that would cause the project to have an NPV of 0. That is, Oconoc management can solve for p such that

$$-75 + \frac{(1 - p)50}{1.1} + \frac{(1 - p)^2 50}{1.1^2} = 0$$

Such an equation can be solved analytically when a few periods are involved, as is the case here, but it soon becomes difficult to calculate for a large number of periods. However, because p is in the interval [0, 1], trial and error can yield a solution relatively quickly; in Microsoft Excel, the Goal Seek function can solve the equation. The solution here is $p = 9.48\%$. So, if management believes the expropriation probability is lower than 9.5%, it should take on the project.

Example 14.3 The Infinite Cash Flow Case

Most investments in the oil business generate cash flows over much longer periods of time than just 2 years. Let's investigate the extreme case that an oil investment generates an expected $50 million per year forever. The value of the project, not taking into account political risk, is

$$\frac{50}{1 + r} + \frac{50}{(1 + r)^2} + \frac{50}{(1 + r)^3} + \ldots = \frac{50}{r}$$

With a discount rate of 10%, the value of the project is $500 million.

How much will political risk reduce the value of the project? Let's assume that the probability of an adverse political event, again denoted by p, is constant over time. Note that the expected value of the project now decreases with time because it is less and less certain that the government won't seize the revenues earned from the project:

$$V = \frac{50(1 - p)}{1 + r} + \frac{50(1 - p)^2}{(1 + r)^2} + \frac{50(1 - p)^3}{(1 + r)^3} + \ldots$$

where p is the probability of expropriation ($p = 0.12$), and r is the discount rate ($r = 10\%$). To compute this infinite sum, we can use a trick we have used before. If $S = 1 + \lambda + \lambda^2 + \lambda^3 + \ldots$ and $\lambda < 1$, it is true that $S = \dfrac{1}{1 - \lambda}$. In our case, we have

$$V = \frac{50(1 - p)}{1 + r}[1 + \lambda + \lambda^2 + \ldots]$$

with $\lambda = \dfrac{1 - p}{1 + r}$. Hence, we obtain

$$V = \frac{50\,(1 - p)}{1 + r} \times \frac{1}{1 - \dfrac{1 - p}{1 + r}} = \frac{50\,(1 - p)}{r + p} = \frac{50\,(1 - 0.12)}{0.10 + 0.12} = 200$$

With 12% possibility of expropriation each period, the value of the project is reduced dramatically to $200 million.

General Formulas

In general, capital budgeting analysis must be adjusted for political risk as follows:

Step 1. Compute the discount rate, r, and future expected cash flows for period t, $C(t)$, as usual, without expropriation risk.

Step 2. Compute a series of expropriation probabilities, $p(t)$, for each future period.

Step 3. Let $\prod\limits_{n=0}^{t-1}(1 - p(t - n))$ be shorthand notation for $(1 - p(t))\,(1 - p(t - 1))\ldots$ $(1 - p(1))$, which is the probability that at time t, there has not yet been any expropriation.

For an investment of I, compute the NPV as

$$NPV = -I + \sum_{t=1}^{T} \frac{C(t)\,\prod\limits_{n=0}^{t-1}(1 - p(t - n))}{(1 + r)^t} \tag{14.1}$$

The formula assumes *total* expropriation. However, in many cases, the MNC might actually receive at least some compensation or experience only a reduction in its cash flow. If this is the case, additional terms are necessary to reflect these additional cash flows with their corresponding probabilities.

In the previous example, we had

- Infinite cash flows
- The same cash flows every period (C)
- The same probability of expropriation in each period

The formula then becomes

$$V = C \times \frac{1 - p}{r + p}$$

This represents a rather extreme estimate of the effect of political risk. It assumes that the MNC will receive no compensation and that the political risk will be present forever. However, in the case of an imminent crisis, it is likely that the political risk outlook will improve after a few years, so p will decrease over time if the crisis is resolved favorably.

Adjusting the Discount Rate Instead of Cash Flows

Many textbooks propose initially ignoring political risk and projecting an MNC's cash flows under the rosy scenario that no expropriation takes place. The books then suggest applying a discount rate scaled up to account for political risk. As the following example and formulas show, such a method can indeed yield exactly the same solution, as long as the new discount rate is

$$r^* = \frac{r + p}{1 - p} \tag{14.2}$$

Note that this formula is valid only in the special case we discussed—that is, the case in which cash flows occur forever and a constant probability of expropriation is assumed—and that a dramatically higher discount rate must be used. In our example, the discount rate adjusted for political risk is 25.0%. That is more than double the original 10% rate. However, as we just explained, it may well be the case that a country's political risk is unusually high for a short period of time but that the MNC's managers expect the situation to normalize after a few years if nothing happens during the crisis. The next example shows how to deal with a situation in which political risk subsides over time.

Example 14.4   Decreasing Political Risk

Say that Oconoc judges political risk to be negligible after 1 year. Either the company will be expropriated in the first year, or the populace of Zuenvela will have elected a more business-friendly president. In this case, the value of the project is

$$V = \frac{50 \times 0.88}{1 + r} + \frac{50 \times 0.88}{(1 + r)^2} + \frac{50 \times 0.88}{(1 + r)^3} + \cdots$$

The first cash flow calculation accounts for the probability of an adverse political event, but cash flows from the second period onward assume that there is no further political risk. However, there is only 0.88 probability that there are any positive cash flows from the second period onward. Hence, the value of the project is

$$V = \frac{44}{0.10}$$
$$= \$440 \text{ million}$$

Under this scenario for political risk, adjusting the discount rate from 10% to 11.36% would yield the "correct" discount rate. The new rate of 11.36% is the solution for r^* of $440 = \frac{50}{r^*}$.

More realistically, some probability of an expropriation after a first, tumultuous year would remain. Suppose the probability of expropriation decreases from 12% to 1% after the first year. We now obtain

$$V = \frac{50 \times 0.88}{1.1} + \frac{0.88 \times 0.99 \times 50}{1.1^2} + \frac{0.88 \times 0.99^2 \times 50}{1.1^3} + \cdots$$

$$= \frac{44}{1.1} + \frac{43.56}{1.1^2} \left[1 + \frac{0.99}{1.1} + \left(\frac{0.99}{1.1} \right)^2 + \cdots \right]$$

Applying our infinite sum formula with $\lambda = \frac{0.99}{1.1} = 0.9$, we obtain

$$V = \frac{44}{1.1} + \frac{43.56}{1.1^2} \times \frac{1}{1 - 0.9}$$

$$= \$400 \text{ million}$$

The remaining political risk reduces the value of the project further from $440 million to $400 million. Hence, the discount rate that would yield the correct project value would satisfy $400 = \frac{50}{r^*}$, implying $r^* = 12.50\%$. It is unlikely that one can guess the correct political risk–adjusted discount rate in this case.

Discount Rates for Emerging Markets and Political Risk

In Chapter 13, we argued that the discount rate for emerging market investments should be computed using the world CAPM, if the investing company has globally diversified investors. Because many emerging markets show low correlations with the world market, the standard procedure may lead to relatively low discount rates for emerging market investments, which strikes many practitioners and economists as counterintuitive. In fact, a practice has developed to adjust the standard CAPM-based discount rates with a number of fudge factors to make them more palatable (that is, higher). We discuss this in more detail in the *Point–Counterpoint* feature in this chapter. Of course, many of the perceived risks of investing in emerging markets are political in nature, and we argue here that from the perspective of global investors, idiosyncratic political risks should be perfectly diversifiable and, consequently, should not affect discount rates.

In reality, however, emerging markets are not yet fully integrated with global capital markets, and therefore it is possible that the CAPM does not capture all systematic risk factors. Perhaps political risk is one of these factors. Nevertheless, if the cost of capital is computed from the perspective of an MNC with globally diversified shareholders, political risk should really affect the discount rate only if it affects global discount rates and represents a global systematic risk. While recent crises in emerging financial markets, such as the 1998 Russia crisis, may have spilled over into other emerging markets and even have adversely affected the stock market performance in developed markets, hard evidence for such global contagion remains elusive. Therefore, it remains best to view political risk as country-specific risk that can be diversified away by global investors. For that reason, we recommend not adjusting the discount rate for pure political risk and using business risk only to increase the magnitude of the discount rate above the risk free rate. This will imply that emerging market investments may require surprisingly low discount rates. Political risk does reduce the value of the project, because it reduces the cash flows that the MNC expects to receive in the future.

14.3 COUNTRY AND POLITICAL RISK ANALYSIS

This section begins by discussing how one might acquire information on the factors that lead to various **country risk ratings**. It then discusses some of the organizations that provide political risk analysis. Finally, the section discusses sovereign credit ratings and information about default probabilities that is incorporated in market prices of government bonds.

Country Risk Ratings

The capital budgeting analysis in the previous section requires information about political risk probabilities and alternative expropriation scenarios. Many different organizations analyze the risk factors associated with doing business in countries around the world and come up with risk ratings for most countries. Some of these risk-rating organizations focus on financial and economic risks and others on political risk. As explained earlier in the chapter, political risks must be treated and managed differently than economic and financial risks.

How important political risk is relative to business risk depends on the particular activity of an MNC in a country. Imagine an MNC that establishes a foreign manufacturing plant to capitalize on cheap production costs and exports the goods produced to other countries. This MNC will be relatively less subject to local economic risk than it might otherwise be because the bulk of its customers lie outside the country. In other words, only the firm's costs—not its revenues—will be affected by economic risk. That said, the MNC might be quite vulnerable to political risks. In contrast, a firm that actually creates a local customer base in a foreign country might need to focus relatively more on economic risks because by creating local jobs and satisfying local customers, it may be less exposed to political risks. As you can see, ratings that do not distinguish between political and economic hazards are less useful for MNCs.

Political Risk Analysis

The primary objective of political and country risk analysis is to forecast losses stemming from these risks. Most risk-rating services forecast by linking certain measurable attributes to future political risk events.

Exhibit 14.4 shows two examples. Analysts have noted that ethnic conflicts in a country tend to adversely affect foreign investors, including MNCs. They have also noted that a good predictor of future ethnic conflict is the presence of ethnic fractionalization. For example, it is hard to imagine ethnic strife in a homogeneous country such as Sweden, but it is very likely to occur in Nigeria, where there are more than 250 different ethnic groups, several different religions, and at least five different languages spoken. Consequently, ethnic fractionalization is used as a risk attribute. Similarly, left-wing governments may be associated with actions that harm foreign investors, such as stricter labor regulations or outright nationalization. Countries with unstable governments and frequent, forced elections have a higher probability of electing left-wing officials within a particular period than countries with stable governments. This is true even if a right-wing government may be in power currently. Consequently, the frequency of government changes is used as a risk attribute. Generally, political risk services examine indicators of political risk, such as the following:

*   Political stability (for example, the number of different governments in power over time)
*   Ethnic and religious unrest; the strength and organization of radical groups
*   The level of violence and armed insurrections; the number of demonstrations
*   Property rights enforcement
*   The extent of xenophobia (fear of foreigners); the presence of extreme nationalism

The different political variables are then weighted and added to provide one country score. Of course, such weightings should be adjusted for a particular MNC's situation, which is not always possible. It is also clear that the relative importance of certain risk events has changed over time. For example, the Overseas Private Investment Company (OPIC), which is the U.S. government's political risk insurance company, has seen a distinct change in the

Exhibit 14.4 Risk Attributes and Political Risk Analysis

Societal attribute:	Ethnic fractionalization	Frequency of government changes
Political choice/action:	Ethnic conflict	Left-wing government
Effective outcome:	Civil strife damages	Labor regulations and nationalization
Loss to the MNC:	Damage to facilities	Increased costs Loss of total investment

Notes: Political risk analysis uses measurable "risk attributes" (at top) to predict risk events for MNCs (bottom).

nature of the claims it has paid over time. In the 1960s, there were a significant number of expropriations; in the 1970s and 1980s, there were many cases regarding inconvertible currencies; during the 1990s, the majority of claims were paid for damages due to civil strife.

There are, however, risk-quantifying approaches besides the attribute approach. Political Risk Services Group (PRS Group), a New York–based firm, forecasts the three most likely governments (regimes) to be in power in a country over 18 months to 5 years in the future, and it predicts how these governments will behave. Whereas PRS Group focuses on future risks, some ratings services focus on current conditions only. Of course, it is often the case that countries with precarious current political conditions also face high future political risks. It is important to realize that country and political risk analyses ultimately produce probabilistic forecasts. A high-risk country need not experience a political risk event. Let's examine some actual rating services in more detail.

Institutional Investor

Institutional Investor publishes a biannual country credit rating based on information provided by leading international banks. The banks grade each country (except their home countries) on a scale of 0 to 100, with 100 representing those with the least chance of default. The individual responses are weighted using a formula that gives more importance to responses from banks with greater worldwide exposure and more sophisticated country-analysis systems. The factors to which bankers pay the most attention in producing the country rating are its debt service, its political and economic outlook, its financial reserves, and its current account and trade account balances with other countries.

Economist Intelligence Unit

The composite risk indicator of the Economist Intelligence Unit (EIU), a sister company to the magazine *The Economist*, encompasses four types of risk: political risk (22% of the composite), economic policy risk (28%), economic structure risk (27%), and liquidity risk (23%). The political risk component is of the attribute type and includes two subcategories: political stability (war, social unrest, orderly political transfer, politically motivated violence, and international disputes), and political effectiveness (change in government orientation, institutional effectiveness, bureaucracy, transparency/fairness, corruption, and crime). The three other categories involve a mix of subjective elements, using opinions of country experts and objective economic statistics.

For example, the EIU's economic policy category focuses on a country's monetary policy, fiscal policy, exchange rate policy, and trade and regulatory policies. The economic structure category is defined in terms of the country's global environment, debt growth, financial structure, and current account balance. Finally, the liquidity risk category examines the imbalance between a country's assets and liabilities versus the rest of the world, using various economic statistics (such as the country's short-term debt as a percentage of its exports, for example). It also rewards countries that have steady and cheap access to the capital markets. The final score is between 0 (no risk) and 100 (highest risk) and is compiled for 100 countries on a quarterly basis. The EIU also provides detailed country reports on a quarterly basis.

Other Ratings Systems

The magazine *Euromoney* provides an overall country risk score based on nine individual variables that carry different weights. The two most important indicators, each with 25% weighting, are political risk and economic performance. The political risk assessment is based on scores given by country experts and banking officers, and it attempts to measure the risk of a country's nonpayment for goods and services, loans, trade-related finance and dividends, and the nonrepatriation of capital. The economic performance variable is based both on current GDP per capita figures and projections of future growth. The other indicators include indicators about the amount and status of the country's debt and its access to local and international finance.

S.J. Rundt & Associates relies on a global network of associates to provide scores on a total of 44 variables, grouped into three large categories: sociopolitical risk, domestic economic risk, and external-accounts risk. The average of the three composite scores provides the overall country risk score. A nice feature of S.J. Rundt's country reports is that they also provide the scores for all the underlying variables, so that they can be used in a company-specific analysis. As we argued before, the risks faced by, say, a mining operation in Papua-New Guinea are quite different from the risks faced by a distributor in Argentina.

Bank of America publishes a country risk monitor with a ranking for 80 countries, for both the current year and 5 years into the future. The analysis focuses primarily on the financial and banking industries. Analogously, the IHS Energy Group's Political Risk Ratings focus primarily on the risks for the petroleum industry. Control Risks Group (CRG) provides macro-level risk assessments in three major areas for 18 countries: political risk, security risk (focusing on terrorism, crime, and so on), and travel risk (similar to security risk but also including the possibility of strikes). CRG also specializes in customized political risk consulting, which necessarily also involves industry-specific risks. CRG relies on a team of analysts, editors, and local part-time analysts.

Hague, Mathieson, Mark, Kumar, and Hole (2004) examined which domestic economic variables most influenced a country's credit rating, using ratings by Institutional Investor, *Euromoney,* and the EIU. Their analysis revealed that a country's credit ratings were most affected by the ratio of its non-gold foreign exchange reserves to imports, the ratio of its current account balance to its GDP, and its growth rate and rate of inflation. Of these factors, inflation had the most impact. When it comes to their credit ratings, high-inflation countries seemed to be heavily penalized relative to countries with low or moderate inflation.

The PRS Group's ICRG Rating System

PRS produces the *International Country Risk Guide (ICRG)* monthly, along with the *Political Risk Yearbook*, and country fact sheets and data sets. We now focus on the ICRG ratings because they can be split up into economic, financial, and political risk components and their various subcomponents. The ICRG ratings, available since 1980, are developed from 22 underlying variables. The political risk measure is based on 12 different subcomponents, and the financial and economic risk measures are based on 5 subcomponents each. Exhibit 14.5 presents the different components and the points assigned to them in the ICRG system.

Financial and Economic Risk Factors
The financial and economic risk assessments are based solely on objective economic data. ICRG collects statistics on the variables listed in Exhibit 14.5 and then uses a fixed scale to translate particular statistics into risk points. For example, countries with foreign debt ratios smaller than 5% of GDP obtain a perfect 10 score on that indicator, while countries with a debt ratio of over 200% receive a score of 0.

The financial risk measure clearly aims to assess a country's ability to pay its foreign debts. The first indicator measures the size of a country's outstanding foreign debt as a percentage of the country's GDP. The second indicator is the country's foreign debt service as a percentage of its exports. The third indicator is the country's current account balance as a percentage of its exports. The fourth indicator is the country's official reserves divided by its average monthly merchandise imports; this is a measure of outflows of the country's foreign exchange relative to its sources of foreign exchange. The final component is a measure of exchange rate volatility. ICRG considers both large depreciations and appreciations of a currency to be "risky," but the former are considered the more risky of the two. The economic risk rating views highly developed countries (those with high levels of GDP per capita)—with high economic growth, low inflation, sound fiscal balances, and positive current balances—as having low economic risk.

Exhibit 14.5 The ICRG Risk Components

POLITICAL RISK COMPONENTS	
Component	**Points (max.)**
Government stability	12
Socioeconomic conditions	12
Investment profile	12
Internal conflict	12
External conflict	12
Corruption	6
Military in politics	6
Religious tensions	6
Law and order	6
Ethnic tensions	6
Democratic accountability	6
Bureaucracy quality	4
Maximum total points	**100**

FINANCIAL RISK COMPONENTS	
Component	**Points (max.)**
Foreign debt as a percentage of GDP	10
Foreign debt service as a percentage of XGS*	10
Current account as a percentage of XGS*	15
Net liquidity as months of import cover	5
Exchange rate stability	10
Maximum total points	**50**

ECONOMIC RISK COMPONENTS	
Component	**Points (max.)**
GDP per head of population	5
Real annual GDP growth	10
Annual inflation rate	10
Budget balance as a percentage of GDP	10
Current account balance as a percentage of GDP	15
Maximum total points	**50**

*XGS = exports of goods and services.

Note: From *International Country Risk Guide*, published by the PRS Group, Inc. Copyright © 2007. The PRS Group, Inc.

The Political Risk Components

Unlike the financial and economic risk indicators, the political risk rating depends on subjective information, with ICRG editors assigning points on the basis of a series of preset questions for each risk component. The various subcomponents are shown in Exhibit 14.5. Geert Bekaert, Cambell Harvey, and Christian Lundblad (2005) organize the 12 components into 4 categories, based on their content but also on an analysis of how correlated different components are across countries and time. Bekaert, Harvey, and Lundblad group the "law and order," "bureaucratic quality," and "corruption" variables into a "quality of institutions" measure. The "law and order" variable separately measures the quality of the legal system ("law") and the observance of the law ("order"). "Bureaucratic quality" measures the institutional quality and the strength of the bureaucracy, which can help provide a cushioning effect in case governments change. "Corruption" can add directly to the cost of doing business in a particular country, for instance, because bribes must be paid. However, the corruption variable also captures the actual or potential corruption in the form of excessive patronage, nepotism, job reservations, "favors-for-favors," secret party funding, and suspiciously close ties between politics and business. ICRG uses the length a government has been in power as an early indicator of potential corruption.

A second grouping Bekaert, Harvey, and Lundblad (2005) consider is "conflict" or "political unrest." The variables belonging in this category are "internal conflicts" (an assessment of internal political violence in the country), "external conflict" (an assessment of external disputes, ranging from full-scale warfare to economic disputes, such as trade embargoes), "religious tensions" (an assessment of the activities of religious groups and their potential to evoke civil dissent or war), and "ethnic tensions" (an assessment of disagreements and tensions between various ethnic groups that may lead to political unrest or civil war).

The sum of the subcomponents "military in politics" and "democratic accountability" is a good measure of the democratic tendencies of a country, which are correlated with political risk. A military takeover or threat of a takeover might represent a high risk if it is an indication that the government is unable to function effectively. This signals that the environment is unstable for foreign businesses.

The democratic accountability category measures how responsive the government is to its citizens. "Government stability" depends on a country's type of governance, the cohesion of its governing party or parties, the closeness of the next election, the government's command of the legislature, and the popular approval of the government's policies. Finally, Bekaert, Harvey, and Lundblad group the ICRG subcomponents "government stability," "socioeconomic conditions," and "investment profile" into one category. The "socioeconomic conditions" subcomponent attempts to measure the general public's satisfaction, or dissatisfaction, with the government's economic policies. Socioeconomic conditions cover a broad spectrum of factors, ranging from infant mortality and medical provision to housing and interest rates. Within this range, different factors have different weights in different societies.

Of particular interest for MNCs is the "investment profile" category. It has four subcomponents, including the risk of expropriation or contract viability, taxation, repatriation, and labor costs. For particular projects, these categories can be sufficient when it comes to assessing an MNC's pure political risk.

Overall Ratings

The points on the 12 categories within the "political risk" measure add up to 100, which constitutes the score for the political risk index. Analogously, the financial and economic risk indexes each carry 50 points. ICRG creates an overall index by adding up the three subindexes and by dividing by 2 so that the top score is 100. When all the subcomponents have been scored, ICRG then assigns the following degrees of risk to the composite score:

Very high risk	00.00% to 49.9%
High risk	50.00% to 59.9%
Moderate risk	60.00% to 69.9%
Low risk	70.00% to 79.9%
Very low risk	80.00% to 100%

The composite score is only an assessment of the country's current country risk situation. In addition, ICRG provides 1-year and 5-year risk forecasts. These forecasts include a worst-case forecast, a most-probable forecast, and a best-case forecast. The ICRG calls the difference between the worst and best case forecasts "risk stability" because it is an indication of the volatility of risk.

Example 14.5 A Cross-Country Example of ICRG's Political Risk Ratings

Exhibit 14.6 lists the political risk ratings and their subcomponents for a number of countries in Southeast Asia. For comparison, we also present the G5 countries, the country ranked the highest (Luxembourg), and the country ranked the lowest (Zimbabwe). Among the Southeast Asian countries, Singapore and Brunei have low overall country risk, whereas Myanmar and Indonesia have relatively high overall country risk.

Suppose a large U.S. MNC is considering setting up a textile production facility in Southeast Asia and is exploring options in Indonesia, Malaysia, Myanmar, and Vietnam. Among these four countries, Malaysia has the best overall political risk situation, but Vietnam is not much worse. Indonesia and Myanmar have the most risk overall. Note that these similar overall ratings hide very different performances on the subgroup measures discussed earlier. If democratic tendencies are important, both Myanmar and Vietnam score very poorly relative to Indonesia. However, Indonesia's political institutions are of very poor quality, pulling down its overall score.

Suppose the CEO is particularly concerned that profits will be able to be repatriated in the future and is concerned about the possibility that corruption will erode profits. We can specifically tailor the ICRG system to this situation by giving more weight to the "investment profile" and "corruption" categories.

The last column in Exhibit 14.6 uses the subcategories to create an alternative political risk index in which only the investment profile and corruption categories are considered. In this last column, we simply added the investment profile and corruption scores for each country and re-weighted the index to be between 0 and 100. Because the "investment profile" category receives double the points of corruption, the new index puts two-thirds of its weight on "investment profile" and one-third on "corruption," and it assigns a 0 weight to all other categories. Using this system, Malaysia remains the least risky country in which to invest, but Indonesia presents a larger risk than Vietnam, reversing the ordering obtained from the overall political risk index.

Exhibit 14.6 Country and Political Risk Ratings for Selected Countries

Country	Overall Country Risk	Political Risk	Quality of Institutions	Conflict	Democratic Tendencies	Socioeconomic Conditions	Investment Conditions/Corruption
U.S.	76.0	81.0	81.3	76.4	87.5	81.9	86.1
UK	83.8	86.0	90.6	79.2	100.0	86.1	91.7
France	79.0	78.0	65.6	75.0	83.3	84.7	83.3
Germany	81.8	83.0	84.4	84.7	91.7	77.8	91.7
Japan	86.5	85.5	78.1	88.9	91.7	83.3	83.3
Luxembourg	91.0	94.5	93.8	95.8	91.7	94.4	94.4
Zimbabwe	34.3	38.0	15.6	58.3	33.3	29.2	8.3
Brunei	88.3	82.0	71.9	88.9	41.7	93.1	77.8
Indonesia	61.3	51.5	31.3	59.7	54.2	51.4	38.9
Malaysia	75.8	71.5	53.1	81.9	58.3	73.6	61.1
Singapore	88.3	86.5	84.4	91.7	66.7	89.9	91.2
Vietnam	69.8	65.5	46.9	89.9	25.0	63.9	47.2
Myanmar	59.8	47.5	31.3	70.8	4.2	45.8	25.0
Philippines	70.0	68.0	43.8	78.4	75.0	67.7	67.7
Thailand	75.5	71.5	37.5	84.7	66.7	75.0	55.6

Notes: The ratings are taken from ICRG's website (www.prsgroup.com/ICRG.apx). The overall and political risk ratings are for September 2003, whereas the ratings for the four subgroups are for August 2003. These ratings were computed as the sum of the points for the several subcategories and multiplying the result by 100 total points, so that 100 would mean a perfect score (no risk). The last column results from adding the scores on the individual components "investment conditions" and "corruption" and re-normalizing to the [0,100] interval.

Country Credit Spreads

In Chapter 11, we defined the credit spread on a corporate bond as the difference between the yield (or all-in cost) on the bond and the yield on a comparable Treasury bond that is not subject to default risk. When a sovereign borrower issues bonds in its own currency, there is usually no default risk because the government can simply print money to pay back the debt holders. When sovereign borrowers issue bonds in a different currency, though, a default is possible because the government must earn foreign exchange to pay off the bondholders.

Government defaults have occurred regularly in international bond markets throughout the past 200 years. Russia defaulted on its debts in 1998, and Argentina defaulted in 2001. Because of the chance of default, the yields offered on international bonds are higher than the yields on the government bonds of the developed country issuing the currency. The difference between the two is called the **country credit spread**. For example, if the yield on a 5-year U.S. Treasury bond is 6%, and the yield on a 5-year dollar bond issued by the Brazilian government is 11%, the Brazilian country credit spread is 5%. These spreads, which vary over time as the bonds trade in secondary markets, are, of course, an indication of country risk.

Sovereign Credit Ratings

Today, major international rating agencies, such as Moody's, Standard & Poor's, and Fitch are rating more and more sovereign bond issues as the markets for them continue to grow. Exhibit 14.7 reports the October 2006 ratings on long-term foreign currency debt, provided by Fitch. Fitch uses a system similar to Standard & Poor's, with AAA being the best rating and D (default) the worst. An "investment-grade" rating extends from AAA to BBB.

Note that all developed countries, such as Canada and France, are rated investment grade, but not all are rated AAA. For example, political problems in Italy and economic problems in Japan have led to the slightly lower AA rating for those two countries. Whereas the debt of many developing countries is rated as "junk debt"—for example, Brazil (BB), Peru (BB+), Ukraine (BB−), and Vietnam (BB−)—countries such as Chile, Korea, Malaysia, and Mexico now receive investment-grade ratings.

An increasing number of firms in developing countries are also being rated as they seek to diversify their funding sources and access a wider investor base. These firms are not only using the Eurobond market but also other international bond markets, such as the Samurai bond market and the Yankee bond market. It is mostly the case that the credit ratings of private companies fall at or below the credit ratings of the governments of the countries in which the firms are domiciled. This "sovereign ceiling" makes sense in the case of foreign currency debt because the sovereign has first claim on available foreign exchange and controls the ability of residents to obtain funds to repay creditors.[3]

Why Is Sovereign Credit Risk Different?

Sovereign defaults are different from a company going bankrupt because it is very difficult to take a country to court, and there are no formal bankruptcy proceedings in place for sovereigns. Nonetheless, sovereigns still must worry about the consequences of defaulting because of the following issues:

- The assets of the country located in the jurisdiction of a creditor may be seized. For example, in early 1986, the Peruvian government brought home some $700 million worth of gold and silver it had been holding abroad. This was around the time it was restricting payments on its debt to a certain percentage of the country's export revenues.
- The country will not be able to borrow as readily in the future, which can have grave economic consequences.
- The country could find its ability to engage in international trade severely curtailed.

---

[3]Erik Durbin and David Ng (2005) note several recent exceptions to the sovereign ceiling.

Exhibit 14.7 Sovereign Credit Ratings by Fitch

Argentina	D	Italy	AA–
Armenia	BB–	Japan	AA
Aruba	BBB	Kazakhstan	BBB
Australia	AA+	Korea	A
Austria	AAA	Kuwait	AA–
Azerbaijan	BB	Latvia	A–
Bahrain	A–	Lebanon	B–
Belgium	AA+	Lesotho	BB–
Bermuda	AA+	Lithuania	A–
Bolivia	B–	Luxembourg	AAA
Brazil	BB	Malawi	CCC
Bulgaria	BBB–	Malaysia	A–
Cameroon	B	Mali	B–
Canada	AAA	Malta	A
Cape Verde	B+	Mexico	BBB
Chile	A	Moldova	B–
China	A	Mozambique	B
Colombia	BB	The Netherlands	AAA
Costa Rica	BB	New Zealand	AA+
Croatia	BBB–	Norway	AAA
Cyprus	A+	Panama	BB+
Czech Republic	A	Papua New Guinea	B
Denmark	AAA	Peru	BB+
Dominican Republic	B	Philippines	BB
Ecuador	B–	Poland	BBB+
Egypt	BB+	Portugal	AA
El Salvador	BB+	Romania	BB
Estonia	A	Russia	BBB+
Finland	AAA	San Marino	AA
France	AAA	Singapore	AAA
Gambia	CCC	Slovakia	A
Germany	AAA	Slovenia	AA
Ghana	B+	South Africa	BBB+
Greece	A	Spain	AAA
Hong Kong	AA–	Suriname	B
Hungary	BBB+	Sweden	AAA
Iceland	AA–	Switzerland	AAA
India	BBB–	Taiwan	A+
Indonesia	BB–	Thailand	BBB+
Iran	B+	Tunisia	BBB
Ireland	AAA	Turkey	BB–
Israel	A–	Ukraine	BB–
		UK	AAA
		U.S.	AAA
		Uruguay	B+
		Venezuela	BB–
		Vietnam	BB–

Notes: This table is extracted from Fitch's website (www.fitchratings.com) and represents the agency's
October 2006 ratings for long-term foreign currency debt of the various sovereign borrowers. The best rating is
AAA; the worst is D, similar to the Standard & Poor's rating system.

As we have explained, there are benefits to defaulting because the debt must no longer be
serviced. Servicing the debt can be painful if the country's income is low. One country that
has reneged on foreign obligations numerous times is Argentina. In 1930, an economic crisis
led to a military coup that ended 70 years of parliamentary government and led to a forced

debt restructuring. Argentina defaulted again after Mexico declared a debt moratorium in 1982. Finally, on Christmas Eve 2001, Argentina defaulted on $150 billion in foreign debt. The country then restructured its debt. The Argentine government offered a deal in which 76% of the defaulted bonds were exchanged for new bonds worth between 25% and 35% of the original value and with longer maturities. Payments on some of these bonds are indexed to the future economic growth of Argentina.

Taking Governments to Court

Bilateral investment treaties (BITs) have helped investors avoid legal problems associated with sovereign debt. A few decades ago, when foreign investors and multinationals were hurt by the actions of a foreign government, they had to rely on the foreign government's laws or persuade their own governments to intervene on their behalf. To encourage international capital investment, countries have recently begun entering into treaties with each other, promising mutual respect for and protection of investments in each other's territory. A BIT allows an individual investor to make his or her claims directly against a nation at a private international arbitration tribunal consisting of three independent arbitrators. The administering organization for many of these disputes is the **International Center for the Settlement of Investment Disputes (ICSID)**, an arm of the World Bank.

The standards of protection offered by BITs are quite broad. Indeed, the ICSID has made a number of precedent-setting arbitration awards. BIT arbitration now reaches far beyond cases in which expropriation or nationalization has occurred. It also encompasses any government action that deprives an investor of all or part of the economic value of an investment. This includes intangible assets such as contractual rights.

We started the chapter with the example of INE, an agency of the federal government of Mexico, refusing to renew Tecmed's license to operate a hazardous waste landfill. Tecmed argued that this act constituted an expropriation of its investment that was contrary to the provisions of the 1996 Spanish–Mexican BIT, and the company brought the case before the ICSID. The tribunal agreed and ordered Mexico to pay Tecmed damages in excess of $5 million plus compound interest.

Although there have been a number of cases in which investors such as Tecmed have won, there have also been cases in which investors have lost. In some instances, the issues involved are not simple but cut across a broad set of societal and cultural lines.

For example, in January 1997, the U.S.-based waste disposal company Metalclad Corporation filed a complaint with the ICSID, alleging that the Mexican state of San Luis Potosi had violated a number of NAFTA provisions when it prevented the company from opening a multimillion-dollar hazardous waste treatment and disposal site it had built near Guadalcazar. The site had previously been contaminated in 1990 when a Mexican company illegally dumped 55,000 drums—about 20,000 tons—of hazardous waste in a valley a few kilometers away from Guadalcazar. The drums were filled with industrial waste from Mexico City and other urban areas, and they were not covered or properly stored.

Metalclad had negotiated with the Mexican federal government to clean up the site in return for using it as a waste treatment and disposal site. The Mexican federal government saw Metalclad as a company that would clean up a horrible mess, but the local government and the people of Guadalcazar were not so sure.[4] The Governor of San Luis Potosi denied Metalclad the permit to operate when he rezoned the area of the site part of an ecological zone in response to an environmental impact assessment which revealed that the plant site lay atop an ecologically sensitive underground alluvial stream.

The Metalclad case raises complex social, legal, and economic issues. Perhaps the local population should have been consulted about the plans for establishing a toxic waste treatment

---

[4]See Heather Scoffield (1999).

facility in the area, but they never were. Legally, the case was brought against the Mexican federal government in defiance of a ruling by a local state, a factor that frightens environmentalists. "The decision is proof that NAFTA and the environment are at odds, and that municipalities will have a tough time turning away garbage if foreign corporations are involved," said Michelle Swenarchuk of the Canadian Environmental Law Association.[5] Although Metalclad sought $90 million in damages, the company received only $16.7 million. Grant Kesler, the CEO of Metalclad, stated, "This is a token amount of money that doesn't really reflect the value of the project." The company estimated that it had spent more than $20 million in planning, permitting, and construction. "The biggest losers of all," Mr. Kesler added, "are the people of Mexico who continue to have to live in a country that produces 10 million tons of hazardous waste a year and has only one facility in the whole country to handle it."[6]

Historical Background: Brady Bonds

The Brady bond market has become the largest and most liquid component of the emerging debt market. In February 1990, Mexico became the first country to issue Brady bonds, converting $48.1 billion of its eligible foreign debt to commercial banks into two types of the bonds. The principal on both types of bonds was fully collateralized in the form of U.S. Treasury zero-coupon bonds held at the New York Federal Reserve Bank. Mexico also guaranteed investors that 18 months' worth of interest payments would be paid on the bonds by depositing that amount as collateral with the New York Fed. Most other Brady deals were quite similar to Mexico's. Brady deals were concluded for Argentina, Brazil, Bulgaria, Costa Rica, the Dominican Republic, Jordan, Nigeria, the Philippines, Poland, Uruguay, and Venezuela.

Both investment banks and commercial banks initially participated as investors in the Brady bond market, and the investor base has widened to include mutual funds, money managers, insurance companies, and pension funds. The vast majority of outstanding Brady bonds are U.S. dollar denominated, and they tend to have very long maturities (20 to 30 years). The bonds are evenly divided between fixed and floating-rate instruments.

Brady bonds lend themselves to the same valuation techniques applied to more conventional fixed-income securities (see Chapters 6 and 11). The basic notion is that the price of a given bond represents the present value of its stream of future payments. However, as we hinted earlier in the chapter, Brady bonds have a number of special features:

- *Principal collateral:* All par and discount bonds are collateralized by U.S. Treasury zero-coupon securities having similar maturities.
- *Interest collateral:* For some bonds, the government issuing the Brady bonds deposits money with the New York Federal Reserve Bank in amounts covering 12 to 18 months' of interest payments on a "rolling" basis.
- *Sovereign portion:* The remaining cash flows are subject to sovereign risk.

The collateral enhancements imply that the difference between the yield-to-maturity on the Brady bond and a U.S. Treasury bond of comparable maturity (sometimes called the "blended" yield) cannot really be viewed as a country spread. Therefore, bond traders compute the "stripped yield," based on the yield-to-maturity of the unenhanced interest stream after removing the present value of the U.S. Treasury zero-coupon bond that collateralizes the principal and the present value of the guaranteed interest stream. This stripped yield is truly based on the credit quality, or sovereign risk, of the issuing nation.

Bonds sometimes also include detachable warrants or recovery rights predicated on a country's economic performance. Mexico's Value Recovery Rights (VRRs), for example, are based on numerous variables, including oil prices, GDP, and oil production levels. In June

---

[5]See Heather Scoffield (2000).
[6]See Anthony DePalma (2000).

2003, Mexico retired the last of $35 billion in Brady bonds, drawing an end to its disastrous debt default of the early 1980s.

Analyzing a Brady Bond

Consider a Brady bond issued by Peru with 10 years remaining until maturity. The bond was issued with an annual coupon of 7%. Also, assume that the par value of the bond and the following year's coupon payments are collateralized by U.S. Treasury bonds. Exhibit 14.8 contains all the information necessary to value the bond. If the Peruvian government does not default, the investor in this bond receives $7 (per $100 par) each year and receives $107 of interest and principal 10 years from now.

If this were a bond issued by the U.S. government, we would know how to value it from our discussion in Chapter 6. We would use the USD spot interest rates applicable to each year and then calculate the present value of the promised cash flows. Exhibit 14.8 also presents the U.S. spot rates. Note that interest rates for longer maturities are higher than those for shorter maturities. The value of such a hypothetical U.S. Treasury bond would then be

$$\text{Value} = \frac{7}{1 + 0.035} + \frac{7}{(1 + 0.0410)^2} + \ldots + \frac{107}{(1 + 0.065)^{10}} = 105.3724$$

Instead, the price of the Peruvian Brady bond is only $92. To analyze this bond, let's start by computing the yield-to-maturity, ignoring the collateral. Recall that the yield-to-maturity is the one yield that makes the present value of the cash flows equal to the price:

$$92 = \frac{7}{1 + ytm} + \frac{7}{(1 + ytm)^2} + \ldots + \frac{107}{(1 + ytm)^{10}}$$

Solving this equation gives $ytm = 8.20\%$. We can also compute the yield-to-maturity on a comparable bond issued by the U.S. Treasury. We computed that such a bond would cost 105.3724. Hence, the yield-to-maturity solves

$$105.3724 = \frac{7}{1 + ytm} + \frac{7}{(1 + ytm)^2} + \ldots + \frac{107}{(1 + ytm)^{10}}$$

The solution is $ytm = 6.26\%$.

From these computations, you might conclude that the country spread is $8.20\% - 6.26\% = 1.94\%$. However, this is incorrect because the 8.20% is a "blended," not a stripped, yield. The 8.20% yield does not take into account the fact that parts of the cash flows in the bond are collateralized and hence are risk free.

Exhibit 14.8   Analyzing a Brady Bond

Year	Dollar Cash Flows	Dollar Spot Rates	Present Value of the Cash Flows
1	7	3.50	6.76
2	7	4.10	6.46
3	7	4.65	6.11
4	7	5.05	5.75
5	7	5.55	5.34
6	7	5.85	4.97
7	7	6.05	4.64
8	7	6.25	4.31
9	7	6.35	4.02
10	107	6.50	57.00

Notes: The bond is trading at a price of $92 (per $100 par value) and carries a coupon of 7%. The second column lists the cash flows accruing to the bondholder when Peru does not default on its obligation. The third column lists the dollar spot interest rates. The fourth column computes the present value of the future cash flows, using these spot interest rates.

Let's look at the value of the collateral. The collateral consists of the first coupon payment and the par value of the bond. To find the current value, we simply use the USD spot interest rates:

$$\text{Value of collateral} = \frac{7}{1.035} + \frac{100}{1.065^{10}} = 60.0359$$

The value of the bond must be greater than this value. The price of $92 per $100 of par value can be thought of as consisting of $60.0359 for the cash flows collateralized by U.S. Treasury bonds and $31.9641 = $92 − $60.0359 for the other cash flows. These other cash flows are 9 coupons of $7 each, which are promised to be paid by the Peruvian government. The stripped yield therefore solves

$$31.9641 = \frac{7}{(1 + ytm)^2} + \frac{7}{(1 + ytm)^3} + \ldots + \frac{7}{(1 + ytm)^{10}}$$

Note that the first non-collateralized cash flow occurs in the second year. The solution for ytm in this equation is 12.88%. Hence, a better estimate of the country spread is 12.88% − 6.26% = 6.62%.[7]

Country Spreads and Political Risk Probabilities

Country spreads are often used in capital budgeting to account for political risk. Before summarizing some of the proposed uses of country spreads, let's first analyze under what circumstances country spreads may be useful.

First, recall that the country spread is an indication of the default risk of a bond. However, although a government might default on its bonds as a result of a political event, this does not necessarily mean that it will also expropriate the assets of the MNCs that lie within its borders.

Second, even if political risk and sovereign default risk are highly correlated, the nature of Brady bonds is such that the probabilities of default are not easily recovered from the yield spreads. It is best to use an example to illustrate the point. Consider the Peruvian bond we analyzed earlier. What is the probability that the Peruvian government will default each year? We can estimate this probability by making some additional assumptions. We first assume that when the Peruvian government reneges on the debt, it will pay foreign debt holders nothing. This is clearly unrealistic. In most cases of sovereign default, a restructuring happens (the Brady deals are but one example). In this case, foreign debt holders still recover some of their investment, as they did in 2005 when President Kirchner of Argentina negotiated extensively with foreign investors and the IMF to determine what, if anything, should be paid to foreigners holding defaulted Argentine debt. For the sake of this example, though, we set this recovery value to 0. (The next sub-section considers the case of nonzero recovery values.) We also assume here, for simplicity, that the probability of default is constant over time.

The cash flow diagram for the Peruvian bond is simple. The first period, it pays $7 for sure because that payment is collateralized. Therefore, it should not enter our computations at all. However, there is still a probability that the Peruvian government will default (for instance, on other bonds) in that year. We denote this probability by p. The second year, there is a probability of $(1 - p)^2$ that the bond will not be in default, and there is a probability of

---

[7]This calculation is not entirely correct because the timing of the cash flows in the 6.26% computation is more tilted toward the 10-year horizon (because there is a par value payment then) than in the computation for the Peruvian non-collateralized flows. To correct for that, we would have to compute the yield-to-maturity on a U.S. bond with a cash flow pattern similar to that of the non-collateralized portion of the Peruvian bond. To do so, we must first price the cash flows of $7 from year 2 to year 10 with the U.S. spot interest rates, and then we would compute the yield-to-maturity. It so happens that this yield is only 5.82%, so the country spread is even higher than the stripped yield indicates.

$(1 - p)p$ that there will be a default. This is the same reasoning used in Exhibit 14.3. For the third year, the probability of no default is $(1 - p)^3$, and the probability of default is $(1 - p)^2 p$. Following this same argument until the 10th year, it must be the case that

$$31.9641 = (1 - p)^2 \frac{7}{1.041^2} + (1 - p)^3 \frac{7}{1.0465^3} + \ldots + (1 - p)^{10} \frac{7}{1.065^{10}}$$

Here, we equate the value investors assign to the bond with the present value of the expected cash flows, discounted at U.S. risk-free rates. We can do this because the possibility of default is taken into account in the probabilities, and we assume that default is an idiosyncratic risk. As before, this equation can be solved for p, the probability of default. We find $p = 6.34\%$. If we believe sovereign risk as reflected in this default probability is perfectly correlated with the political risk embedded in a cash flow analysis for capital budgeting, this is the probability we should use.

Default Probabilities with Positive Recovery Values

In the previous section, we computed the probability of default by using the formula

$$\text{Stripped price} = \sum_{j=1}^{10} \frac{CF(j)(1 - p)^i}{[1 + i(j)]^j} \tag{14.3}$$

where

Stripped price = dollar price of the bond after subtracting the value of the collateral
$CF(j)$ = promised dollar cash flow at time j
$i(j)$ = U.S. dollar spot or zero-coupon interest rate for period j, conditional upon default at that time.
p = default probability

The assumptions are that the default probability is constant over time and the recovery value upon default is 0. In most cases of sovereign defaults, foreign investors have recovered some of their money after the governments renegotiated the terms of the debt jointly with investors and representatives of the World Bank and the IMF.[8] How much is recoverable depends on economic conditions. The recovery value therefore likely changes over time. When there is the possibility of recovery under default, the formula in Equation (14.3) becomes more complex:

$$\text{Stripped price} = \sum_{j=1}^{10} \frac{CF(j)(1 - p)^j + R(j)p(1 - p)^{j-1}}{[1 + i(j)]^j} \tag{14.4}$$

where $R(j)$ = expected recovery value for the bond in period j, conditional upon default at that time.

Let's apply this formula to the Peruvian bond example. The stripped bond promises nine payments of $7 per $100 par over 9 years. We computed the stripped price to be 31.9641. When there was no recovery, the default probability was 6.34%. Because recovery values increase the expected cash flows, the default probability will now be higher. In other words, assuming zero recovery underestimates the probability of the risk event occurring.

Let's work through an example. We assume that the Peruvian bond has the following expected recovery values:

Period 1: 8
Period 2: 8
Period 3: 4
Period 4: 4
Period 5 and thereafter: 0

---

[8] One problem has been that smallish minorities of creditors often block restructuring deals to which large majorities agree. Recently, some sovereign issuers have included "collective-action clauses" in their bonds that prevent this from happening.

Recall that the first coupon payment is collateralized. However, the Peruvian government can still announce that it will no longer service its debt and that it will default in period 1. We must now find a p that solves the following equation:

$$31.9641 = \frac{8 \times p}{1 + 0.035} + \frac{7 \times (1 - p)^2 + 8 \times p(1 - p)}{1.041^2}$$

$$+ \frac{7 \times (1 - p)^3 + 4 \times p(1 - p)^2}{1.0465^3} + \frac{7 \times (1 - p)^4 + 4 \times p(1 - p)^3}{1.0505^4}$$

$$+ \frac{7 \times (1 - p)^5 + 0 \times p(1 - p)^4}{1.0555^5} + \dots + \frac{7 \times (1 - p)^{10}}{1.065^{10}}$$

Solving this equation yields $p = 7.20\%$. This compares to an estimated p of only 6.34%, when recovery values were assumed to be 0.

CASE STUDY

The Mexican Peso Crisis and Country Risk

Determining the default probabilities related to Brady bonds is not always easy because their cash flows extend over such long periods of time. Let's revisit the country risk related to Tesobonos, securities issued by the Mexican government in the 1990s. Let's also discuss the correlation between currency risk and country risk in the context of the Mexican peso crisis in 1995.

In the early 1990s Mexico, which was recovering from the Debt Crisis, regained access to international capital flows and started to run a current account deficit. Domestic savings began to decline. This is very much like the situation in the United States then and today. In fact, it was jokingly suggested that Mexico was not only economically integrating with the United States but had also adopted the bad spending habits of U.S. citizens, as Mexican citizens were incurring substantial credit card debts. The Mexican current account deficit worsened over time, reaching 8% of Mexico's GDP by 1994. At the time, Mexico had a crawling peg exchange rate system (see Chapter 5), but the nominal exchange rate did not fully adjust with Mexican inflation. As a result, Mexico's real exchange rate appreciated, which further eroded Mexico's competitive trade position and encouraged Mexican consumers to buy international goods.

There were two other important developments in Mexico. First, Mexico had a weak banking system. Mexican banks had been privatized in the early 1990s, and they subsequently went on a lending boom. Nonperforming loans as a share of total loans increased from less than 5% in 1990 to around 10% in 1994. To keep its banks afloat, Mexico's central bank could not let interest rates rise too much. To do so would have threatened the economy and led to even more nonperforming loans. (At higher interest rates, borrowers with bad credit are the ones who still want to borrow money.)

Given Mexico's precarious economic situation, the demand for pesos was low. In order to prevent the peso from falling in value, Mexico's central bank used sterilized intervention. That is, because the bank was forced to use its foreign reserves to buy pesos, it simultaneously bought domestic bonds, increasing their prices and keeping their yields low. Understandably, foreign investors were not thrilled with the Mexican government's high-risk, low-yielding peso-denominated securities (called "Cetes"). This led to a second major development: From 1993 onward, the Mexican government started to rely more and more on the newly created Tesobonos to finance its public debt.

Tesobonos are treasury bills issued by the Mexican government, just as Cetes are, but they are effectively U.S. dollar denominated. That is, while both the purchase amount and the principal payment are denominated and made in pesos, the principal payment is fully indexed to the change in the exchange rate between the dollar and the peso.

Let's consider an example using a 3-month Tesobonos. Suppose the yield on the Tesobonos is 5%. If the Mexican peso exchange didn't change in value, the investor would receive

$$1 + \frac{0.05}{4} = \text{MXN}1.0125$$

after 3 months. Suppose though that the Mexican peso devalues by 5% over the 3-month period. Then, the amount paid to the investor will be

$$\left(1 + \frac{0.05}{4}\right) \times 1.05 = \text{MXN}1.063125$$

Note that this represents a 25.25% (6.3125×4) return on an annualized basis. While Tesobonos provided investors with protection against peso devaluation, they also guaranteed that a devaluation of the peso would be extremely costly to Mexico. In that sense, by shifting heavily toward short-term financing indexed to the dollar, the Mexican government signaled that it would not let the peso devalue. On December 30, 1994, $48.9 billion of Tesobonos were outstanding, and about one-third of them were held by foreigners.

The year 1994 was an election year for Mexico, and it proved disastrous for the country, both economically and politically. Economically, the current account worsened, the central bank steadily lost reserves, and foreign investors invested only in Tesobonos. Politically, 1994 was turbulent as well. Early in the year, the Chiapas Indians rebelled, and the presidential candidate most likely to win the election, Luis Donaldo Colosio, was murdered. This turmoil increased the political risk in Mexico, making it less attractive for international investors.

The situation became untenable on December 20, 1994. With international reserves in short supply, the Mexican government tried to devalue the peso by 13.67%, from MXN3.4662/$ to MXN3.94/$. However, the devaluation proved insufficient, and the Mexican government was forced to let the Mexican peso float. By the end of December 1994, the peso sank to above MXN5.20/$ and by March 1995, it was trading above MXN6/$. Interest rates on both Cetes and Tesobonos shot up. The central bank's official international reserves were insufficient to cover the amount of Tesobonos coming due in the following months. It became clear that Mexico faced an acute liquidity crisis. As we discussed in Chapter 10, the Mexican government was bailed out by a U.S. Treasury and IMF support package at the end of January 1995. The last Tesobonos were issued on February 17, 1995.

The Tesobonos and Cetes securities offer a unique opportunity to study the interaction of country risk and currency risk. The standard Mexican Treasury bills (Cetes) must reward investors for both currency risk and country risk; Tesobonos, however, need only reward investors for country risk because they are indexed to the U.S. dollar.

To put these ideas into symbols, let the U.S. interest rate be denoted by i_{US}, the Cetes rate by i_{CET}, and the Tesobonos rate by i_{TB}. The interest rates are all deannualized. Furthermore, we denote the country premium or country spread by copr and the currency or devaluation premium by cupr. We then define

$$1 + i_{CET} = (1 + i_{US}) \times (1 + \text{copr}) \times (1 + \text{cupr}) \qquad \textbf{(14.5)}$$
$$1 + i_{TB} = (1 + i_{US}) \times (1 + \text{copr})$$

Note that we define country and currency premiums multiplicatively rather than additively (see Chapter 11). The country risk premium is, of course, directly related to default probabilities. Let p be the probability that the Mexican government will not repay the Tesobonos investors, in which case we assume that recovery of interest and principal is 0. Then, it must be the case that

$$1 + i_{US} = (1 + i_{TB}) \times (1 - p) + 0 \times p \qquad \textbf{(14.6)}$$

Exhibit 14.9 Country and Currency Premiums around the Mexican Currency Crisis

| EXCHANGE RATE | | 3 MONTH INTEREST RATES | | | SPREADS | | |
| | | U.S. | Mexico | | Country Risk | Currency Risk | Default |
Month	Peso/$ Spot	T-bill	Cetes	Tesobonos	Premium	Premium	Probability
Dec-93	3.1070	3.054	10.370	5.090	2.021	5.569	0.5026
Jan-94	3.1065	2.992	10.890	4.670	1.666	6.148	0.4147
Feb-94	3.1900	3.435	9.340	5.050	1.601	4.237	0.3987
Mar-94	3.3586	3.538	10.120	6.790	3.223	3.274	0.7994
Apr-94	3.2700	3.940	16.450	7.750	3.773	8.535	0.9344
May-94	3.3200	4.260	16.770	7.190	2.899	9.411	0.7196
Jun-94	3.3900	4.240	17.000	7.000	2.731	9.828	0.6781
Jul-94	3.4000	4.354	17.190	7.250	2.865	9.763	0.7111
Aug-94	3.3785	4.655	13.820	7.240	2.555	6.463	0.6348
Sep-94	3.3955	4.768	13.100	6.790	1.998	6.205	0.4971
Oct-94	3.4335	5.121	14.350	6.730	1.589	7.494	0.3956
Nov-94	3.4475	5.423	14.760	7.500	2.049	7.126	0.5097
Dec-94	5.0750	5.682	31.990	10.490	4.741	20.95	1.171
Jan-95	5.7350	5.902	38.000	24.980	18.80	12.25	4.489
Feb-95	5.8750	5.870	57.000	16.990	10.96	38.38	2.667

Notes: The original source is Bloomberg, but the first five columns were taken from Kenneth Froot (1995). The last three columns represent the authors' own computations. The risk premiums are annualized, but the default probability applies to a 3-month horizon.

That is, the expected return on a U.S. T-bill investment or a Tesobonos investment is the same, taking default into account. After combining Equations (14.5) and (14.6), we obtain

$$1 + \text{copr} = \frac{1}{1 - p}$$

$$\text{or: copr} = \frac{p}{1 - p}$$

Equivalently, $p = \dfrac{\text{copr}}{1 + \text{copr}}$. The country risk premium embedded in Tesobonos provides immediate information on political risk probabilities.

Ian Domowitz, Jack Glen, and Ananth Madhavan (1998) studied 3-month and 6-month currency and country premiums in Mexico in 1993 and 1994. They found currency premiums, which averaged 7% to 8%, to be much bigger than country premiums, which averaged around 2.5%. They also found currency and country premiums to be only weakly positively correlated. Nevertheless, the correlation between the currency premiums and the country risk premium becomes extreme when it matters—that is, when the country is on the brink of a currency and/or debt crisis. This is vividly illustrated in Exhibit 14.9, which shows currency and country spreads before and during Mexico's 1994–1995 currency crisis.[9]

---

[9]Note that the country and currency premiums in the exhibit are annualized. That is, we multiplied them by 4 because we used 3-month Cetes and Tesobonos. When additive country and currency premiums are reported, one typically uses the annualized interest rates reported in the exhibit, so that the country risk spreads are already annualized. This annualization is not harmless. Three-month securities harbor information about currency and country risk within the 3-month period, not beyond. Consequently, the default probabilities reported in the last column use the actual 3-month country spreads (that is, the numbers in column 8 divided by 4). If we were to use annualized probabilities, the numbers would be higher. If the term structure of interest rates is relatively flat, these annualized probabilities will give a good indication of default risk over a 1-year period. However, in times of crisis, we often observe a downward-sloping term structure of interest rates, and the use of short-term rates may overestimate annual default probabilities.

In the beginning of 1995, Mexico suffered from extreme country and currency risk, with the currency premium exceeding 35% and the country premium exceeding 10%. This suggests that taking into account political risk should also affect the translation of foreign currency cash flows into dollar cash flows. This correlation between the two risks is mostly ignored in capital budgeting. Ignoring it, however, typically leads to conservative estimates of expected cash flows. Let us illustrate this with a numeric example.

Example 14.6 Stars and Bars Subsidiary Sale

Suppose it is the end of 1999, and Stars and Bars, a U.S. company, is planning to sell its Argentine subsidiary in 2 years. Given its projections for the local economy and the subsidiary's projected revenues and costs, the expected sales price is 50 million pesos. While the peso is trading at $1 per peso because of the Argentine currency board, Stars and Bars assigns a 20% chance to a collapse of the currency board regime, which will lead to a 25% devaluation of the peso. Hence, the expected dollar sales price is

$$(\text{ARS50 million} \times \frac{\$1.00}{\text{ARS}} \times 0.80) + (\text{ARS50 million} \times \frac{\$0.75}{\text{ARS}} \times 0.20)$$

$$= \$47.5 \text{ million}$$

Alternatively, note that the expected dollar–peso rate is $0.95/ARS = $(1.00 \times 0.80) +$ (0.75×0.20). Political risk analysts are also arguing that there is a 10% chance of total expropriation, in which case Stars and Bars would lose the full value of its subsidiary.

Following the recipe of this book, the expected cash flows are adjusted to reflect the expropriation probability:

$$(\$47.5 \text{ million} \times 0.90) + (0 \times 0.10) = \$42.75 \text{ million}$$

However, it is quite unlikely that expropriation will happen while the currency board is still in place. It is more likely that when Argentina gets into economic difficulties, it may first lift the currency board and devalue the currency. Then, if things get worse, it may also expropriate foreign investments. Hence, a more realistic scenario analysis is as follows:

	Probability	Dollar Sales Price
No devaluation, no expropriation	80%	$50 million
25% devaluation, no expropriation	10%	$37.5 million
25% devaluation and expropriation	10%	0

The expected sales price incorporating separate probabilities for devaluation and expropriation is as follows:

$$(\$50 \text{ million} \times 0.80) + (\$37.5 \text{ million} \times 0.10) + (0.0 \times 0.10) = \$43.75 \text{ million}$$

The analysis that ignored the correlation between political and currency risk underestimated expected cash flows by $1 million.

Epilogue
If Stars and Bars sold before the end of 2001, it would have received the full $50 million. However, at the end of January 2002, the currency board had collapsed, and the peso's value was reduced to $0.7143 per peso!

POINT–COUNTERPOINT

Cable Television in Argentina

"You are so naïve!" shouted Ante at Freedy. "That discount rate you've come up with is much too low. This is an emerging market, for crying out loud, so there has got to be an adjustment for political risk in your discount rate!"

Ante and Freedy already regretted having chosen to be in the same group to solve their international finance cases. Their case discussion on the Continental–Fintelco deal was due tomorrow, and they could simply not agree on the discount rate to be used for the cash flow analysis.

The case concerned Continental Cablevision, the third-largest U.S. cable operator, which was seeking to acquire a 50% stake in Fintelco, the number 3 cable company in Argentina, in early 1994. At the time, Argentina's president was Carlos Menem, who had overseen a profound transformation of Argentina's economy from a state-dominated closed economy suffering from hyperinflation to an open, deregulated economy in which the peso was pegged to the dollar through a currency board, and many state-owned companies had been privatized. Many risk factors remained. The stock market had been extremely volatile; inflation had been higher in Argentina than in the United States, leading to a loss of competitiveness, and presidential elections were scheduled for 1995. As part of the deregulation program, a treaty was in the works that would allow U.S. investors to own up to 100% of Argentine cable systems and 25% of broadcast television stations.

Ante and Freedy had worked hard on the case and had come up with a set of expected dollar cash flows. The only thing left to do was to discount them at an appropriate rate. Because they were supposed to value Fintelco assuming an all-equity deal, Freedy had suggested simply using the standard CAPM formula (see Chapter 13):

$$E[r_{\text{fin}}] = r_f + \beta_{\text{fin}} E[r_m - r_f]$$

where r_f is the risk-free rate, $E[r_m - r_f]$ is the risk premium on the world market, and β_{fin} is Fintelio's beta with the world market.

Freedy had suggested using a beta estimated from data on publicly traded U.S. cable companies. The number was 1.08. While Ante agreed with the use of a world market risk premium and a beta appropriate for cable companies, he had read a few articles on cost of capital computations for emerging markets and felt that two adjustments were necessary.

First, he wanted to increase the risk-free rate with the Brady bond country spread. The articles he read suggested that this was an appropriate adjustment for the political risk present in emerging markets. This would increase the discount rate by 3.5% in 1994. Second, he did not feel it would be appropriate to compare the cash flow risk of U.S. companies with the cash flow risk of Argentine companies. However, he had not been able to find data on publicly traded cable companies in Argentina. The beta of the Argentine market as a whole seemed to be quite unstable and had moved from being negative in the 1980s to close to 1.00 the past 5 years. Nevertheless, he felt they had to somehow adjust for the huge volatility of the Argentine market, which had been running over 60% on an annualized basis in the years before the time of the deal. One of the articles he read had suggested scaling up the beta for local companies with the ratio of the volatility of the local market to the volatility of the U.S. or world market.[10]

Freedy shouted at Ante, "If anything, my discount rate is too high! If we could compute betas of the local Argentine cable companies, they would be really low. I think that it provides a unique chance for the U.S. shareholders of Continental to diversify their cash flow risks."

Cousin Suttle Trooth leisurely walked into the room of the quarreling brothers, his smirk betraying a tired déjà vu feeling. "Did I hear someone mention political risk adjustments?

---

[10]Articles by Stephen Godfrey and Ramon Espinosa (1996) and Aswath Damadaran (2003) suggest both to increase the risk free rate by the country spread and to increase the risk premium by some function of the volatility ratio.

I know all about that! I once did a summer internship for OPIC, a U.S. political risk insurer," said Suttle.

Ante and Freedy simultaneously gasped: "You can insure your investments for political risk?"

"Sure you can," replied Suttle. "And it is done quite often, too."

Freedy, reasoning quickly, burst out: "Aha! So I am right. You do not need a discount rate adjustment!"

"Hold on, Cousin, it is not that simple!" said Suttle. "First of all, you should, of course, subtract any insurance premium from the expected cash flows. If your case says there was no insurance, you must still take political risk into account. In fact, full insurance is hard to get anyway. And there have been many cases in which political risk events wiped out whole investments. It is really an extremely bad negative cash flow scenario that many cash flow projections forget to take into account. So making no adjustment at all is probably worse than making an adjustment through the discount rate."

Ante was getting really agitated. "So, these professor guys talking about Brady bond spreads and risk premium adjustments do not know what they are talking about? Come on!" he said.

"Well, no, I did not say that," Suttle argued back. "It is very difficult to figure out what political risk events may occur, what their probabilities are, and whether there will be some compensation when they do occur. Therefore, some quite knowledgeable people have suggested that it is easier to scale up the discount rate with something that captures political risk in some sense like the country spread. However, it is quite hard to do even that right. Moreover, Freedy is absolutely right that the betas of local Argentine companies with the world market are likely low, and if the shareholders of the U.S. company are well diversified, the true discount rate should be low because the investment carries low systematic risk for them."

"Is there anything you do not know, cousin?" Ante sighed, as he turned on the TV—cable, of course.

Epilogue:

Continental Cable and Fintelco signed a joint venture agreement to go in effect in October 1994. However, Continental had trouble financing the deal because of the Mexican peso crisis. Eventually, the $80 million deal was financed using bank loans, part of them insured against political risk by OPIC.

Computing Political Risk Probabilities

In this book, we strongly recommend adjusting for political risk by changing the cash flow projections to reflect the probabilities of political risk. This, of course, requires computing the probabilities of political risk, which is easier said than done. In any case, cash flow scenarios for investments in high political risk countries should incorporate dramatic scenarios where part or all of the investment is lost due to a political risk event. To estimate political risk probabilities, we recommend using as much information as possible. There are essentially three sources of information that can be used, two of which we have already discussed extensively:

*   Country credit spreads
*   Political risk analysis and political risk ratings
*   Political risk insurance premiums

Even when a company does not intend to use political risk insurance or finds it unavailable for its project, the rates quoted for the insurance can be a useful indication. It can tell a firm's capital budgeting group about how much should be subtracted from expected cash flows to account for political risk. It is also possible that political risk insurance products provided by government organizations are priced below private market rates, in which case they should be purchased when available. We will discuss political risk insurance in Section 14.4, but now we discuss how to use country spreads and political risk ratings.

Using Country Spreads to Compute Political Risk Probabilities

Brady bonds and other dollar-denominated or major currency–denominated assets provide a market-determined assessment of a country's default risk that promptly reacts to new information. Although we do not recommend scaling up the costs of capital using a country spread, we do recommend analyzing these securities to uncover default probabilities, as we illustrated above. It is also important that stripped spreads be used. Because of the presence of collateralized cash flows, standard country spreads underestimate true default probabilities. In addition, when available, securities of different maturities should be examined to potentially detect horizon effects in a country's default probability.

We have already indicated some disadvantages of country spreads. In particular, the country risk premium reflects the ability and willingness of a country to repay debt; it therefore reflects both political and economic risks. In addition, Brady bond spreads may be influenced by the risk appetites of international investors, which have nothing to do with the likelihood of a political risk event in the bond-issuing country. Finally, countries that face increased political risks, such as African countries, are least likely to have any outstanding market debt because their ability to borrow from the rest of the world is limited.

Using Political Risk Ratings

Some of the political risk rating systems assign numeric scores to narrowly defined subcategories of political risk. They are therefore likely to be more informative than country spreads about the exact political risks a multinational corporation faces.

The subcategory risk ratings have two major disadvantages hampering their use. First, they are not determined by market forces, and little is known about how well the ratings truly predict political risk events. In addition, credit rating companies are often accused of lagging behind events and not being able to predict actual defaults. Second, although the ratings are numeric, they are not expressed in units (such as percentage discount rates) that are useful for capital budgeting purposes. The scores must somehow be converted into such units. Unfortunately, there simply does not seem to be an accepted method for accomplishing this.

14.4 Managing Political Risk

Political risk management means more than computing the probability of political risk events occurring. Even after a project is accepted and implemented, political risk must continue to be monitored. MNCs should plan ahead in terms of what they can do to minimize the chances that political risk events will materialize. They should also plan ahead in terms of what actions they will take if political risk events do materialize. In other words, they need to have a pre-developed exit strategy. We discuss these strategies and others in the following sections.

Structuring an Investment

When political risk is a factor, an MNC should structure its investment so as to minimize the chance that political risk events will adversely affect its cash flows. Here is a short list of actions that could be taken:

- *Focus on the short term:* The MNC can try to recover its invested cash flow quickly so as not to lose it. This can be done by repatriation or by selling off local assets to local investors or the government in stages rather than reinvesting funds for the long haul.
- *Rely on unique supplies or technology:* The MNC can make a government takeover difficult without its cooperation, for example, by relying on unique supplies coming in

from its headquarters, or unique technology that is difficult to operate without the collaboration of the MNC.

- *Use local resources:*   When the MNC hires local labor or borrows funds locally, it reduces the government's incentive to close down the plant.

- *Bargain with the government:*   Prior to making a major investment in a particular country, the MNC can improve its position by negotiating an agreement with the host country regarding the future convertibility of the funds the MNC earns and how they will be taxed, transferred, and so forth. This also allows the MNC to develop relationships with various government officials, which can come in handy if a political risk event occurs and a settlement must be negotiated. Nevertheless, bargaining with the current government can also backfire when the government turns over.

- *Hire protection:*   In the case of kidnapping possibilities or violence—for example, because of local warfare—MNCs can hire bodyguards or, at the extreme, employ private military companies for protection. With conflicts raging all around the globe, private military companies have become an important global business in their own right. Many private military companies are no longer small companies built by a few veteran soldiers but are sophisticated companies that offer a wide range of services. The oldest and most respected private military companies in the industry, MPRI, DynCorp, and Vinnel, have been purchased by industrial giants moving into the growing private military company market. MPRI was purchased by L3, DynCorp was purchased by CSC, and Vinnell was purchased by Northrop Grumman. Other well-known groups include Blackwater Security Consulting, CRG, and Janusian Security Risk Management Ltd, with portfolios of services including crisis management, kidnap and extortion management, fraud and insurance investigation, countersurveillance, and the defense of personnel and assets.

Insurance

Perhaps the clearest indication that political risk is a cash flow risk is that it is an insurable risk. If MNCs can fully insure themselves against all possible risk events and are fully compensated for their losses, subtracting the insurance premium from the expected cash flows suffices to account for political risk. The reality is much different, however. Full insurance is impossible to purchase. Because cash flows are uncertain, it is typically difficult to insure an amount more than the current investment. Nevertheless, political risk insurance is available from an increasingly wide variety of sources.

There are three potential sources of political risk insurance: international organizations aimed at promoting foreign direct investment (FDI) in developing countries, government agencies, and the private market. Among international organizations providing insurance, the World Bank's Multilateral Investment Guarantee Agency (MIGA), the Inter-American Development Bank (IDB), and the Asian Development Bank (ADB) are the best known. Most OECD countries have national agencies that provide domestic companies with political risk insurance. Examples include the Overseas Private Investment Corporation (OPIC; United States), Nippon Export and Investment Insurance (formerly EID/MITI; Japan), the Export Development Corporation (EDC; Canada), the Export Credits Guarantee Department (ECGD; United Kingdom), COFACE (France), and the Export Finance and Insurance Corporation (EFIC; Australia). The private market has grown significantly and now includes firms such as Lloyd's, American International Group (AIG), Sovereign Risk Insurance Ltd., and Zurich Emerging Markets Solutions.

Coverage is typically for three types of political risk events:

- Currency inconvertibility and non-transferability coverage protects companies against losses in case a company is unable to convert its foreign earnings to its home currency or otherwise transfer the earnings out of the host country. Currency inconvertibility and non-transferability coverage does not protect an investor against the devaluation of a country's currency.

- Expropriation coverage protects MNCs and lenders against confiscation, expropriation, nationalization, and other acts by the host government that adversely affect the MNC's cash flows. In addition to outright acts of nationalization and confiscation, "creeping expropriation" (a series of acts that cumulatively have an expropriatory effect), discriminatory legislation, the deprivation of assets or collateral, the repudiation of a concession, and the failure of a sovereign entity to honor an arbitration award issued against it can also be included in expropriation coverage.
- War and political violence coverage compensates a company when war or civil disturbances cause damage to the MNC's assets or cash flows. Political violence coverage does not cover losses due to labor strife or student unrest without a political objective. Political violence coverage has come back into the spotlight since the September 11, 2001, terrorist attacks on the United States.

Seldom is it true that 100% of losses are covered. Private insurers almost always impose limits on the amount of coverage they will provide. We now discuss two of the most important publicly provided political insurance programs: the OPIC in the United States and the MIGA run by the World Bank.

Political Risk Insurance for U.S. Companies

As mentioned earlier in the chapter, the U.S. government provides political risk insurance through the **Overseas Private Investment Corporation (OPIC)**. OPIC was established in 1971 as a self-sustaining government development agency. Its mission is to mobilize U.S. private capital and technological knowledge to aid the economic and social development of less developed countries with a particular focus on countries in transition from non-market to market economies. OPIC carries out this mission by providing financing through direct loans and loan guarantees and by leveraging private capital, using OPIC-supported funds. However, here we focus on its third task—the provision of political risk insurance.

By charging market-based fees for its products, OPIC operates at no net cost to taxpayers. While it has issued thousands of contracts and paid over $1 billion in claims, it has earned a profit in each year of its operation. OPIC has built up substantial reserves of over $4 billion. All its guaranty and insurance obligations are backed by its own reserves and by the full faith and credit of the U.S. government. OPIC insurance can cover up to $250 million per project for up to 20 years, and it can insure up to 90% of an eligible investment. For FDI, OPIC typically issues insurance commitments equal to 270% of the initial investment, with 90% representing the original investment and 180% to cover future earnings.

OPIC offers the three standard types of coverage: insurance against the risk of expropriation, political violence, and currency inconvertibility. OPIC has paid out claims under all three types of losses during its long history. With terrorist acts becoming more prevalent, OPIC has also started to offer stand-alone terrorism insurance. Terrorism coverage protects against violent acts with the primary intent of achieving a political objective, undertaken by individuals or groups that do not constitute national or international armed forces. OPIC has also started to support more and more small businesses in recent years, sometimes at reduced rates. OPIC's political risk insurance and financing have helped U.S. businesses of all sizes invest in more than 150 emerging markets and developing nations worldwide. In its history, OPIC has supported $164 billion worth of investments that have helped developing countries generate more than 732,000 host-country jobs and $13 billion in host-government revenues.[11]

Political Risk Insurance in Emerging and Transitioning Economies

Multilateral Investment Guarantee Agency (MIGA), part of the World Bank group, was established in 1988 to promote development by facilitating investment in emerging and transitioning economies. MIGA is able to provide political risk insurance for projects that cannot

---

[11]See United States Department of State (2006).

be easily covered elsewhere. In addition to the three types of risks covered by most other insurers (the risk of expropriation, political violence, and currency inconvertibility), MIGA also offers breach-of-contract insurance, a relatively new product that protects investors from losses arising from the host government's breach or repudiation of a contract with the investor. The investor must be able to invoke a dispute resolution mechanism (for example, an international arbitration) and obtain an award for damages. MIGA will pay compensation if the dispute resolution mechanism fails due to host government actions.

MIGA has a special interest in promoting investment in war-torn areas. For example, after the Serb–Croat conflict in the Balkans, it provided insurance for a number of investments in Bosnia-Herzegovina. This included an investment in 2000 by Coca-Cola in a bottling plant (Hadzici) near Sarajevo. MIGA also provided insurance for International Dialysis Center, a Dutch company, for its 2003 equity investment in a kidney dialysis center in Banja Luka. This project represents the first private investment in the health sector in all of the Balkans, but it still requires collaboration with the local government.

As of 2006, MIGA had issued more than 850 contracts worth more than $16 billion. Its largest exposures are in Brazil (7.5%), Bulgaria (6.9%), and Serbia and Montenegro (6.9%). MIGA insured Enron against expropriation risk for a power project in Java, Indonesia, in 1998. After the Indonesian government suspended the project, MIGA paid Enron $15 million for the losses it had sustained. The Indonesian government subsequently agreed to repay MIGA over a 3-year period.

Public Versus Private Insurance

Private insurers are playing an increasingly important role in the political risk insurance market. Nonetheless, public-sector insurers remain seemingly indispensable players, especially when it comes to long-term investment insurance in high-risk countries. Taxpayers may wonder why their tax dollars support an agency that provides a service that can be easily provided by private financial service companies. The basic idea is that political risk insurance facilitates FDI in less-developed countries and that FDI benefits both the developing countries and the countries that invest in them to the extent that governments should promote it.[12] Assuming that this is true, why then does OPIC have an advantage over say AIG? There are two related reasons.

First, the existence of a government-backed or international agency–backed political risk insurance program can act as a deterrent to rogue countries. When an OPIC or MIGA policy is in place, the host government may be less likely to interfere with the investment for fear of retribution from the United States or the World Bank. In other words, OPIC and other public insurers provide an umbrella of protection that helps to correct a market failure in the ability of host countries to make long-term commitments to honor contracts. Without such a policy in place, host countries will find it harder to resist domestic pressures to confiscate large amounts of foreign capital invested within their borders. In that sense, the presence of public PRI allows foreign investment projects to launch where they otherwise would never have been launched.

Second, when there is a claim, most public insurers try to recover the money from the respective governments of the countries in which the political risk event occurred. The claim then becomes the public debt of these developing countries to the U.S. government (in the case of OPIC) or another developed country. These governments have much more clout than private parties to recover their claims. For example, they can seize assets of the host countries on their territory, put pressure on the governments in trade matters, discourage further foreign direct investments, and so forth. It is striking that OPIC has operated for more than three decades on a self-sustaining basis and managed to accumulate more than $4 billion in reserves in the process. It is difficult to fathom that private-sector insurance providers would

---

[12]In economic jargon, FDI is a public good that generates positive externalities, benefits beyond those that accrue to the private parties involved (see Theodore Moran, 2003).

be able to replicate the deterrent function of the public-sector insurance providers or that their recovery rates for damages would compare favorably.

We now return to Oconoc's oil project in politically unstable Zuenvela to illustrate how political risk insurance affects capital budgeting.

Example 14.7 Political Risk Insurance at Oconoc

Barring political risk, the Oconoc project is very valuable, requiring a $75 million investment but generating a present value of $86.78 million. However, when political risk is taken into account, the NPV of the project becomes negative. Oconoc now considers obtaining political risk insurance from OPIC. OPIC has special rates for oil- and gas-sector companies. The ranges of the rates quoted on its website (www.opic.gov) for oil and gas development and exploration on August 15, 2004, were as follows:

Coverage	Rate Range
Inconvertibility	$0.20–$0.40
Expropriation	$1.35–$1.60
Political violence	$0.65–$0.85
Interference with operations	$0.35–$0.55

These rates are annual base rates per $100 of coverage. The actual rate depends on the particular situation in the country. Because the situation in Zuenvela is precarious, we assume that its rates are at the top of the range. Consequently, full coverage on all four types of coverage would cost $3.40 per $100 of coverage. Even though Oconoc may be particularly worried about expropriation, it might prefer to obtain full insurance because an unstable political situation can lead to riots and civil unrest, which can also jeopardize operations.

Let us assume that Oconoc takes out full coverage (that is, all four policies) and negotiates with OPIC to insure for $50 million. This is only two-thirds of the investment, rather than the more typical 90%, but it helps reduce the cost of the insurance. Given this situation, the annual insurance premium is $0.034 \times \$50$ million = $1.70 million.

Exhibit 14.10 describes the new cash flow pattern, which can be compared to that of Exhibit 14.3. In period 1, when there is an expropriation, Oconoc gets paid $50 million by OPIC, so its expected cash flows for that period are identical whether the political risk event is realized or not. Of course, this event then prevents Oconoc from continuing its operations and earning another $50 million in period 2. Moreover, Oconoc must pay the insurance premium of $1.70 million, which reduces its cash flow to $48.30 million. This is true whether or not expropriation occurs. There is still only a 0.88 probability that the cash flow in the second period is cashed in. Consequently, the present value computation becomes, using the discount rate of 10%, as before

$$V = \frac{48.30}{1.1} + 0.88 \times \frac{48.30}{1.1^2}$$

$$= 79.036$$

The present value of the project now becomes $79.036 million. Hence, the project now has a NPV of $4.036 million, so Oconoc should proceed with the project.

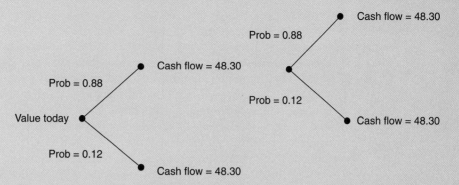

Exhibit 14.10 Political Risk Insurance and Capital Budgeting

Prob = 0.88   Cash flow = 48.30

Prob = 0.88   Cash flow = 48.30

Value today

Prob = 0.12

Prob = 0.12   Cash flow = 48.30

Prob = 0.12   Cash flow = 48.30

Notes: Expected cash flows are $50 million in period 1 and period 2. There is a 12% chance that the host government will appropriate the project. However, the company takes out political risk insurance, insuring $50 million at a $1.70 million premium per year. That is 48.30 = 50 − 1.70.

Does the fact that Oconoc turns a negative NPV project into a positive NPV project mean that the insurance company loses for sure? That is, for the insurance company, the expected value of the insurance claim must be negative. If this is true for all of the company's policies in different countries, and if the probabilities that we used accurately reflect the true probability of a risk event, then it seems as if OPIC should have to rely heavily on tax money. But as we learned, this is not the case. OPIC is actually profitable. The reason is that OPIC, in the case of expropriation, will simply turn the money it paid to Oconoc into a U.S. government claim on the Zuenvela government and use political pressure to recover its money. As history shows, OPIC's record in recovering money from offending host countries has been phenomenal.

Project Finance

At the end of the thirteenth century, a leading merchant bank in Florence, Italy, financed the development of silver mines in Devon, England, which were owned by the English Crown. In exchange for paying all the operating costs, the bank received a 1-year lease for the total output of the mines. However, if the extracted ore did not suffice to recover the bank's costs, it could seek no recourse from the Crown. This is an early example of **project finance**.

Project finance has two main characteristics. First, it is specific to a particular project, typically an industrial one. Second, the providers of the funds receive a return on their investment primarily from the cash flows generated by the project. That is, they have recourse only to the project's cash flows.

The project finance market has grown considerably in recent years. It is particularly prevalent in terms of power, telecom, infrastructure, and oil and gas projects. Project finance deals are typically long-term deals, with maturities mostly extending beyond 10 years and often beyond 20 years.

Famous examples of project finance transactions include the $16 billion Channel Tunnel (the "Chunnel") connecting France and the United Kingdom and the $4.4 billion Berlin–Brandenburg International airport. Although deals in developed countries still dominate, a growing number are taking place in developing countries. However, issuing bonds to finance projects in developing countries is sometimes problematic because of the "sovereign ceiling" that applies to credit ratings for such bonds (see section 14.3). If the country is not investment grade, it is difficult for the project finance bond to obtain an investment-grade rating, and without that, most institutional investors will not invest in these bonds.

Example 14.8 Petrozuata

Petrozuata is a joint venture between Maraven, a subsidiary of Venezuela's government-owned oil company, Petroleos de Venezuela S. A. (PDVSA), and Conoco, a U.S. oil company. Petrozuata was established in 1997 to develop the Orinoco oil belt in central Venezuela, the largest-known heavy and extra-heavy oil accumulation in the world. The project initially involved a $2.4 billion investment. It was part of PDVSA's long-term plan to expand domestic oil and gas production in Venezuela, which could not be accomplished without foreign funding.

Directing investments to Venezuela at that time was not obvious for a foreign oil company. In 1976, oil companies in Venezuela were the victims of a great deal of political turmoil. The Venezuelan government nationalized the domestic oil industry, integrating the Venezuelan assets of the multinationals Royal Dutch Shell, Exxon, Mobil, Conoco, and Gulf, among others, with those of PDVSA. According to some estimates, the government compensation package for the foreign oil companies amounted to only about 25% of the market value of their assets. In the early 1990s, the Venezuelan economy continued to depend heavily on its oil revenues, and it had witnessed two (failed) military coups.

Because the project was so large, planning its financing was an arduous and long process. Eventually, PDVSA decided to fund 60% of the project with debt and 40% with equity financing. Petrozuata's planning team also decided that project financing should be used on a stand-alone non-recourse basis. Moreover, the deal contained a special feature called a "cash waterfall."

The cash waterfall worked like this: Petrozuata's customers would deposit their dollar-denominated funds from the purchase of refined oil and by-products into an offshore account maintained by Bankers Trust, a U.S.-based bank. Bankers Trust would then disburse the cash according to a payment hierarchy, ensuring that the project debt would be serviced before money would be transferred to Venezuela to pay off the project's equity holders. It was hoped that this structure would help mitigate political risk and result in lower funding costs. By keeping dollar cash flows out of Venezuela, foreign exchange controls imposed by the Venezuelan government could not undermine the repayment of the debt.

The team considered bank loans, public bonds, and Rule 144A Bonds (private placement bonds, which we discussed in Chapter 11) as possible debt options to finance the deal. Of the three alternatives, the 144A bonds would raise money most quickly because they could be underwritten within a 6-month period and did not require an initial disclosure to the SEC. The main problem with this route, however, was that Rule 144A bonds can only be bought by institutional investors, and many institutional investors can buy only investment-grade debt.

At the time, PDVSA was a very well-run company. However, it had the same credit rating as Venezuela: a B rating from Standard & Poor's and Ba2 from Moody's. Even though the revenue cash flows from the project were protected by the cash waterfall structure, the Venezuelan government could still expropriate Petrozuata's oil fields. Consequently, some political risk remained. Eventually, the deal closed in June 1997. Petrozuata issued $1 billion worth of bonds with three different maturities in the Rule 144A market. S&P rated Petrozuata BBB–, Moody's rated it Baa1, and Duff and Phelps rated it BBB+ (investment grade). The project therefore was able to exceed the sovereign rating of the country, partly due to the special project finance structure.

The financing of the deal was considered a success, and the project itself also seems to have proceeded smoothly. However, the Venezuelan political front remains a rough ride. Former coup leader Hugo Chavez, now the president of the country, has made it more difficult for multinationals to invest there. Chavez initially meddled with the internal affairs of PDVSA, firing half of its workers, including nearly all the well-respected senior managers in 2003. In practice, this turned the control of PDVSA over to the presidency.

Then, on May 1, 2007, President Chavez announced that Venezuela was taking over control of all oil-production projects in the Orinoco belt. He stated in a speech, "Today is the end of that era when our natural riches ended up in the hands of anyone but the Venezuelan people."[13] The international oil companies were allowed to remain as minority partners, but as of June 2007, negotiations over the compensation that Venezuela would pay the oil companies for their loss of value had stagnated. Chavez declared, "Well if they do not want [to accept the terms], I told the minister to tell them they can go, that they should leave, that we, in truth, do not need them."[14] How these actions will affect the returns to the international investors who are holding Petrozuata's bonds remains to be seen.

The MidAmerican Energy Holdings Case

In the mid-1990s, two Indonesian subsidiaries of MidAmerican Energy Holdings Company entered into contractual arrangements with the wholly state-owned Indonesian electricity company PLN, the wholly state-owned natural resources company Pertamina, and the government of Indonesia. Under the contract terms, the subsidiaries were supposed to develop and operate a separate geothermal field, owned by Pertamina, for 42 years. The contracts also involved an energy sales contract, providing that PLN would purchase electricity generated from the field, and they established "unused capacity" fees even when no electricity was purchased. The development was to happen in stages. General Suharto had been governing Indonesia for over 30 years, and Indonesia did not rank highly on political risk ratings. MidAmerican took out political risk insurance policies with both OPIC and Lloyd's.

In September 1997, the Indonesian government issued a presidential decree essentially stopping the further development of the power projects, even though one of them was near completion. In 1998, PLN failed to make the first payment due under its contractual obligation. Moreover, the Indonesian government made it publicly clear that it viewed the power projects as unnecessary. As discussions with the Indonesian government proved fruitless, MidAmerican started arbitration proceedings, according to the stipulations in the contracts. In October 1999, the arbitration tribunal established that the Indonesian government had breached its contract with the MidAmerican subsidiaries and violated international laws it had signed and was therefore liable for damages to the two subsidiaries in the aggregate amount of $577 million. The government's defense was to assert that the contract was established as the result of corruption. Interestingly, the Indonesian government accused all international companies involved in power projects of "KKN" (corruption, cronyism, and nepotism), while trying to cancel the deals.

In the meantime, MidAmerican filed insurance claims, and by November 1999, OPIC and Lloyd's had paid a total of $290 million, with OPIC's share being $217.5 million. As a matter of normal practice, paid OPIC claims become the responsibility of the host country's government, making the claim paid to MidAmerican effectively Indonesian government debt

[13]"Chavez Takes Over Foreign-Controlled Oil Projects in Venezuela," Simon Romero, *New York Times* online edition, May 2, 2007.
[14]"U.S. Oil Giants' Exit Boosts Chavez Only Short-Term," Reuters News, June 28, 2007.

to the U.S. government. From then on, the U.S. government started to pressure the Indonesian government to pay. Successors to Suharto continued to claim that MidAmerican had cut a corrupt deal involving members of the Suharto family. The prospect of reduced foreign investment and strained relations with the United States finally made the Indonesian government capitulate. By mid-2001, the Indonesian government agreed to pay OPIC most, if not all, of the original claim.

14.5 SUMMARY

This chapter discusses how MNCs can measure and manage political and country risk. Its main points are the following.

1. Country risk refers to the potentially adverse impact of a country's economic and political environment on an MNC's cash flows. Political risk is a special case of country risk in which a government or political action negatively affects a company's cash flow. Country risk and political risk are also closely associated with the ability and willingness of a government to repay its foreign debt holders. The risk of nonpayment is often referred to as sovereign risk.

2. Political risk factors include the risk of expropriation, contract repudiation, currency controls that prevent the conversion of local currencies to foreign currencies, and laws that prevent MNCs from transferring their earnings out of the host country. Corruption, civil strife, and war are also factors.

3. Country risk analysis became prevalent after the Debt Crisis began in early 1982. Many developing countries had borrowed heavily from commercial banks in developed countries, using floating-rate dollar debt. When both interest rates and the value of the dollar shot up, many could no longer service the debts. Mexico was the first country to ask for a debt rescheduling in 1982, but many other countries followed.

4. It soon became clear that many countries suffered from debt overhang: They failed to attract new investment as most of the benefits were feared to accrue to the creditors.

5. Many countries attempted to reduce their debt burdens by using operations such as debt–equity swaps and debt buybacks. Some fear that these operations merely provided windfall gains for the creditors.

6. The 1989 Brady Plan finally resolved the Debt Crisis by providing for some form of debt relief—

securitizing the debt in the form of Brady bonds and stimulating economic reforms.

7. To take political risk into account in capital budgeting, we must forecast the effects it will have on expected cash flows. However, we need not adjust the discount rate for political risk because most global companies operate in open, integrated markets. From this perspective, political risk is diversifiable and does not require a discount rate adjustment—only a cash flow adjustment.

8. Only rarely will adjusting the discount rate instead of a company's cash flows yield the same result as a cash flow analysis.

9. Organizations such as Euromoney, Institutional Investor, Economist Intelligence Unit, and Political Risk Services Group produce country risk ratings for most countries in the world.

10. Both quantitative and qualitative information obtained from experts are used to evaluate country and political risks.

11. The ICRG system contains many subcomponents that can be used to tailor a risk measure to the particular situation a multinational corporation faces.

12. While country risk ratings provide very useful information, it is difficult to translate the information into political risk probabilities. Country risk spreads can be more easily converted into political risk probabilities, but they are not available for most countries. Moreover, care must be taken with respect to collateralized cash flows and maturity effects.

13. Most political risk analysis ignores the fact that currency crises and political risk events often occur simultaneously.

14. In capital budgeting, MNCs should not only take into account political risk; they should also take other actions to mitigate the chances of being affected by political risk events. Examples include relying on unique supplies or technologies, doing

business with local lenders and workers, and having good working relationships with local and national governments.

15. MNCs can purchase political risk insurance from either private-sector or public-sector insurers.

16. Public-sector insurers, such as OPIC in the United States and the World Bank's MIGA, are important players in the political insurance market. Some believe that they play a special role because their presence is a deterrent to rogue government actions. In addition, public-sector insurers of large developed countries can put political pressure on foreign governments to pay claims made against them.

17. Insurance is typically available for currency inconvertibility, expropriation, and war and political violence. It is not typically possible to insure all the expected cash flows from an investment.

18. Project financing is a method of financing that is specific to a particular project, typically industrial in nature, in which the providers of the funds are repaid primarily from the cash flows generated by the project.

QUESTIONS

1. Describe the differences between country risk and political risk. What is sovereign risk?
2. What economic variables would give some indication of the country risk present in a particular country?
3. Suppose an MNC is considering investing in Bolivia. Will an overall assessment of Bolivia's country risk suffice to understand the political risk present in the investment?
4. What are three political risk factors?
5. When, where, and why did the Debt Crisis start?
6. What is debt overhang?
7. What is a debt buyback? Why was a program of debt buybacks not sufficient to resolve the Debt Crisis?
8. What were the main characteristics of the Brady Plan?
9. Why should the discount rate not be adjusted for political risk?
10. What are some examples of organizations that provide country risk ratings?
11. How can we use current quantitative information to predict future political events, such as expropriation?

12. Suppose a multinational corporation is particularly worried about ethnic warfare in a few countries in which it is considering investing. Do country risk ratings have information on this particular risk?
13. Can Brazil issue a bond denominated in dollars at the same terms (that is, at the same yield) as the U.S. government? Why or why not?
14. What stops governments from defaulting on loans or bonds held by foreigners?
15. What is a Brady bond?
16. Should the "stripped" yield on a Brady bond typically be higher or lower than the regular yield? Explain.
17. How is a political risk probability related to a country spread?
18. What are Cetes? What are Tesobonos?
19. What are the three main types of political risk covered by political risk insurance?
20. What are some organizations or firms that provide political risk insurance?
21. How is it possible to embed political risk insurance in a capital budgeting analysis?
22. What is project finance?

PROBLEMS

1. In February 1994, Argentina's currency board was in place, and 1 peso was exchangeable into 1 dollar. The following interest rates were available:

U.S. LIBOR 90 days: 3.25%
Peso 90-day deposits: 8.99%
Dollar interest rate in Argentina, 90-day deposits: 7.10%

The latter two rates were offered by Argentine banks. What risk does the difference between the 7.10% dollar interest and 3.25% LIBOR reflect? What risk does the difference between the rate on 90-day pesos and 90-day dollar deposits by Argentine banks reflect?

2. Consider the numbers in the previous question. Assume that if the peso were to depreciate, investors

figure it will depreciate by 25%. Also, assume that if the Argentine bank were to default on its dollar obligations, it would pay nothing to investors. Compute the probability that the peso will devalue and the probability that there will be a default.

3. Consider a 10-year Brady bond issued by Brazil. The coupon payment is 6.50%, and the par value has been collateralized by a U.S. Treasury bond. The current price of the bond is $98 (per $100 in par value). Compute the (blended) yield-to-maturity for the bond. What is the stripped yield? Assume that the spot rates on the dollar are the ones reported in Exhibit 14.8.

4. Right at the height of the Mexican peso crisis in January 1995, the default probabilities on U.S. dollar-denominated emerging-market bonds were quite high. A British investment bank, assuming that these bonds would pay 15 cents on the dollar upon default, calculated a 61% chance of default on Venezuelan bonds. Consider a bond with 5 years left to maturity, paying a coupon of 12%. The par value is 80% collateralized by American Treasury bonds. Assume that the U.S. interest rate is 5% for all maturities. What is the price of a bond with $100 par?

5. Badwella United Company (BUC) is worried that its banana plantation in El Salvador will be expropriated during the next 2 years. However, BUC, through an agreement with El Salvador's central bank, knows that compensation of $100 million will be paid if the plantation is expropriated. If the expropriation does not occur, the plantation will be worth $400 million 2 years from now. A wealthy El Salvadoran has just offered $160 million for the plantation. BUC would have used a discount rate of 23% to discount the cash flows from its Honduran operations if the threat of expropriation were not present. Evaluate whether

BUC should sell the plantation now for $160 million. (Hint: Set up a diagram.)

6. You are the chief financial officer of Clad Metal, a U.S. multinational with operations throughout the world. Your capital budgeting department has presented a proposal to you for a 5-year ore-extraction project in Mexico. The expected year-end net dollar cash flows are as follows:

Year	Net Cash Flow
1	$100,000
2	200,000
3	250,000
4	250,000
5	250,000

The initial required investment in plant and equipment is $500,000, and the cost of capital is 16%.

a. What is the present value of the project? Should the project be undertaken?

b. You notice that the proposal does not include any analysis of political risk, but you are concerned about potential expropriation of the investment. You therefore decide to call a meeting to discuss political risk. Who would you invite to this meeting? What information or data would you need? How would you arrive at a political risk probability estimate?

c. Assume that, at the end of the meeting, you decide that the probability of expropriation is between 5% and 7%. Also assume that there is no compensation in the case of expropriation. Would you approve the project?

d. Given the possibility of expropriation, might you want to reconsider converting Mexican peso expected cash flows at forward rates?

BIBLIOGRAPHY

Ahearne, Alan G., William L. Griever, and Francis E. Warnock, 2004, "Information Costs and Home Bias: An Analysis of US Holdings of Foreign Equities" *Journal of International Economics* 62, pp. 313–336.

Bekaert, Geert, Claude Erb, Campbell R. Harvey, and Tadas Viskanta, 1998, "What Matters for Emerging Equity Market Investments?" *Emerging Markets Quarterly* pp. 17–46.

Bekaert, Geert, Campbell R. Harvey, and Christian Lundblad, 2005, "Does Financial Liberalization Spur Growth?" *Journal of Financial Economics* 77, pp. 3–55.

Bray, John, 2004, "MIGA's Experience in Conflict-Affected Countries. The Case of Bosnia and Herzegovina," *Social-Development Papers*, No. 13, Washington, DC: The World Bank.

Bulow, Jeremy, and Kenneth Rogoff, 1991, "Sovereign Debt Repurchases: No Cure for Overhang," *Quarterly Journal of Economics* 106, pp. 1219–1235.

Bulow, Jeremy, and Kenneth Rogoff, 1988, "The Buyback Boondoggle," *Brookings Papers on Economic Activity* 2, pp. 675–698.

Carrieri, Francesca, Vihang R. Errunza, and Sergei Sarkissian, 2004, "Industry Risk and Market Integration," *Management Science* 50, pp. 207–221.

Chari, Anusha, and Peter B. Henry, 2004, "Risk Sharing and Asset Prices: Evidence from a Natural Experiment," *Journal of Finance* 59, pp. 1295–1324.

Copeland, Tom, Tim Koller, and Jack Murrin, 2000, *Valuation*, New York: Wiley.

Damodaran, Aswath, 2003, "Country Risk and Company Exposure: Theory and Practice," *Journal of Applied Finance* 13, 63–76.

DePalma, Anthony, 2000, "Mexico Is Ordered to Pay a U.S. Company $16.7 Million," *New York Times,* August 31, p. C4.

Djankov, Simeon, Rafael La Porta, Florencio Lopez-de-Silanes, and Andrei Shleifer, 2003, "Courts," *The Quarterly Journal of Economics* 118, 453–517.

Domowitz, Ian, Jack Glen, and Anath Madhavan, 1998, "Country and Currency Risk Premia in an Emerging Market," *The Journal of Financial and Quantitative Analysis* 33, 189–216.

Durbin, Erik, and David Ng, 2005, "The Sovereign Ceiling and Emerging Market Corporate Bond Spreads," *Journal of International Money and Finance* 24, pp. 631–649.

Erb, Claude, Campbell R. Harvey, and Tadas Viskanta, 1995, "Country Risk and Global Equity Selection," *Journal of Portfolio Management* 21, 74–83.

Erb, Claude, Campbell R. Harvey, and Tadas Viskanta, 1996, "Expected Returns and Volatility in 135 Countries," *Journal of Portfolio Management*, 46–58.

Esty, Ben C., 1999, "Petrozuata: A Case Study on the Effectual Use of Project Finance," *Journal of Applied Corporate Finance* 12, 26–42.

Ferreira, Miguel A, and Paulo M. Gama, 2005, "Have World, Country, and Industry Risks Changed over Time? An Investigation of the Volatility of Developed Stock Markets," *Journal of Financial and Quantitative Analysis* 40, pp. 195–222.

Froot, Kenneth. 1995, "Futures on the Mexican Peso," Harvard Business School Case N9-296-004.

Godfrey, Stephen, and Ramon Espinosa, 1996, "A Practical Approach to Calculating Costs of Equity for Investments in Emerging Markets," *Journal of Applied Corporate Finance*, 9.

Howell, Llewellyn D., ed., 2001, *The Handbook of Country and Political Risk Analysis*, 3rd ed., PRS Group.

Krugman, Paul, and Maurice Obstfeld, 2003, *International Economics*, 6th ed., New York: Addison-Wesley.

Lapper, Richard, 1995, "Conversion Deals are Back in Fashion – Debt-Equity Programmes," *Financial Times,* February 6, p. 26.

Lessard, Donald R., 1996, "Incorporating Country Risk in the Valuation of Offshore Projects," *Journal of Applied Corporate Finance*, pp. 52–63.

Mariscal, Jorge O., and Rafaelina M. Lee, 1993, *The Valuation of Mexican Stocks: An Extension of the Capital Asset Pricing Model to Emerging Markets*, New York: Goldman Sachs Investment Research.

Mishkin, Frederic S., 1997, *Understanding Financial Crises: A Developing Country Perspective*, Washington, DC: The International Bank for Reconstruction and Development, The World Bank.

Moran, Theodore H., 1998, *Managing International Political Risk*, Malden, MA: Blackwell Publishers.

Moran, Theodore H., 2003, "On the Reauthorization of OPIC," Testimony to the Committee on International Relations, U.S. House of Representatives.

Patro, Dilip K., and John K. Wald, 2005, "Firm Characteristics and the Impact of Emerging Market Liberalizations," *Journal of Banking & Finance* 29, pp. 1671–1695.

PRS Group, *International Country Risk Guide*, East Syracuse, New York: The PRS Group, Inc.

Romero, Simon, "Chavez Takes Over Foreign-Controlled Oil Projects in Venezuela," Simon Romero, *New York Times* online edition, May 2, 2007.

Reuters News, "U.S. Oil Giants' Exit Boosts Chavez Only Short-Term," June 28, 2007.

Rowland, Patrick F., and Linda L. Tesar, 2004, "Multinationals and the Gains from International Diversification," *Review of Economic Dynamics* 7, pp. 789–826.

Schuman, Michael, 2001, "Indonesia to Pay Reduced Claim to U.S. in Long-Disputed Overseas Insurance Case," *Wall Street Journal*, May 11.

Scoffield, Heather, 1999, "Mexico Fights Metalclad in Cross-Border Conflict," *The Globe and Mail*, December 21, p. B15.

Scoffield, Heather, 2000, "NAFTA Ruling Raises Environmental Questions; Mexico Ordered to Pay California-based Metalclad $16.7-million After Municipality Blocks Plans for a Hazardous Waste Dump," *The Globe and Mail*, September 1, p. B5.

Shapiro, Alan C., 2002, *Multinational Financial Management*, 7th ed, Upper Saddle River, NJ: Prentice Hall.

Ul Hague, Nadeem, Donald J. Mathieson, Nelson C. Mark, Manmohan Kumar, and Peter Hole, 2002, "The

Economic Content of Indicators of Developing Country Creditworthiness," International Monetary Fund working paper.

Unal, Haluk, Asli Demirgüc-Kunt, and Kwok-wai Leung, 1993, "The Brady Plan, 1989 Mexican Debt-Reduction Agreement and Bank Stock Returns in United States and Japan," *Journal of Money, Credit, and Banking* 25, pp. 410–429.

United States Department of State, 2006, "Nambia; OPIC Approves $25 Million to Finance Diamond Production," July 14, 2006, *Africa News,* p. 1.

West, Gerald T., and Keith Martin, 2001, "Political Risk Investment Insurance: The Renaissance Revisited," in Theodore H. Moran, ed. *International Political Risk Management: Exploring New Frontiers*, Washington, DC: The World Bank, pp. 207–230.

Zenner, Marc, 2002, "A Practical Approach to the International Valuation and Capital Allocation Puzzle," Salomon Smith Barney research report.

Chapter 15

International Capital Budgeting

*C*apital budgeting is the process by which corporations decide how to allocate funds for investment projects. Whether the decisions involve Caterpillar retooling its road-grader production facility or Pfizer buying an overseas pharmaceutical production facility, managers have to decide whether spending money today is going to make their corporation sufficiently more profitable in the future to warrant the expenditures today.

This chapter examines one methodology that allows corporations to make investment decisions and determine the valuations of international projects. When considering the value of a project done by a foreign subsidiary, we use a multistep approach that begins with the discounted cash flows to the subsidiary and then makes the adjustments necessary to determine whether the project is worthwhile from the parent corporation's point of view. This approach is called **adjusted net present value (ANPV)**. The first sections of this chapter introduce the rationale for why the ANPV approach provides a correct approach to international valuation. Later parts of the chapter develop an extended case involving International Wood Products, Inc., that applies the ANPV approach. International Wood Products has seen a substantial increase in its exports to Europe, so the company is trying to decide whether to locate a subsidiary in Spain to provide products directly to its European customers.

15.1 AN OVERVIEW OF ADJUSTED NET PRESENT VALUE

This section provides an overview of capital budgeting with adjusted net present value (ANPV) analysis. This is not the only way to do capital budgeting. Chapter 16 compares alternative methods, such as the weighted average cost of capital (WACC) method and the flow-to-equity (FTE) method. Although each method can be correctly applied to answer the same capital budgeting question, some methods are easier to apply in different situations than others. It is our view that the ANPV approach lends itself to international applications most easily.

The basic principal of capital budgeting is that all projects with positive ANPVs should be accepted by the corporation. For mutually exclusive projects, the one with the highest ANPV should be undertaken. Modern financial theory develops the ANPV of a project in several steps, as discussed in the following sections.

Step 1: Discount the Cash Flows of the All-Equity Firm

The first step in deriving an ANPV for a project is to calculate the net present value (NPV) of the project's cash flows under the hypothetical scenario in which the project is financed entirely with equity. Any benefits or costs associated with how the project is financed are valued at a later stage. Thus, in the first step, we are unconcerned about the amount of debt issued to finance the project. The effects of the project on the firm's eventual capital structure or the debt–equity ratio that will be in place after the project is up and running are considered in later stages. At this point, we are only concerned that the value of the cash coming into the firm from the perspective of the firm's shareholders is greater than the value of the cash going out of the firm.

The project's all-equity NPV is the sum of all discounted expected future revenues minus the sum of current and discounted expected future costs. The revenues and costs must be measured on an incremental, after-tax, cash flow basis. Clearly, all cash flows should be measured in the same currency, and the discount rate must be appropriate for the currency of denomination of the cash flows.[1] The discount rates that are used for the all-equity NPV of the project should reflect both the time value of the money in which the forecasts are made and any risk premium that the firm's equity holders would demand. As we argued in Chapter 13, a risk premium arises when the return on the project covaries with the return on a well-diversified international portfolio, in which case the cash flows from the project contain non-diversifiable risk.

Example 15.1   The Vincenzo Uno Project

Suppose that an Italian company, Vincenzo Uno, has a project with the following expected cash flow characteristics:

Annual cash inflows	€1,000,000
Annual cash costs	−600,000
Operating income	400,000
Corporate tax (.34 tax rate)	−136,000
After-tax profits	€264,000

If the discount rate for this project is 20%, the present value of these perpetual expected profits is as follows:[2]

$$\frac{264{,}000}{1.20} + \frac{264{,}000}{1.20^2} + \frac{264{,}000}{1.20^3} + \frac{264{,}000}{1.20^4} + \ldots = \frac{264{,}000}{0.20} = 1{,}320{,}000$$

Suppose that the initial investment required to generate these cash flows is €1,350,000. Then, the NPV of this project to Vincenzo Uno is negative:

$$€1{,}320{,}000 - €1{,}350{,}000 = -€30{,}000$$

Because the project has a negative NPV to the all-equity firm, it would not be undertaken unless there were additional benefits available that have not yet been considered. Later examples in this chapter will explore what such benefits might be.

Step 2: Add the Value of the Financial Side Effects

The second part of an ANPV analysis adds the **net present value of financial side effects (NPVF)** that arise from accepting the project. Generally, these effects arise from the following:

---

[1]Chapter 13 examines the choice of the discount rate for a project. Here we take the discount rate as given. Chapter 16 explores issues related to the currency of denomination of the forecasts.
[2]Perpetuity formulas are discussed in the appendix to this chapter.

- The costs of issuing securities
- Taxes or tax deductions associated with the type of financing instrument used (including the tax deductibility of the interest paid on the debt)
- The costs of financial distress
- Subsidized financing from governments

These financial side effects are discussed in more detail later in the chapter.

Step 3: Value the Growth Options

The third part of an ANPV analysis adds the present value of any **growth options (GO)** that arise from doing the project. The classic example of a growth option is the ability to do a sequel to a movie. After assessing the profitability of the first movie in a potential series, studio executives decide if it's worthwhile to make a sequel. Part of the benefit of doing the original movie comes in the form of an option to do the sequel only if the original is successful. These investment options are valuable and should be taken into account when deciding whether to do the first movie.

Although growth options can be considered as part of the all-equity cash flows in step 1 of the ANPV, we break them out separately for two reasons. First, the value of growth options is often difficult to quantify, and second, they are always positive and hence add value to the project. If the ANPV of the project is positive, without adding the value associated with growth options, the ANPV will only be *more* positive after considering the options.

In summary, the adjusted net present value (ANPV) of a project is the net present value (NPV) of the cash flows of a hypothetical, all-equity project, plus the net present value of financing side-effects (NPVF), plus the present value of any growth options (GO) that the project offers:

$$\text{ANPV} = \text{NPV} + \text{NPVF} + \text{GO} \tag{15.1}$$

Next, we examine the cash flows associated with each of these items in more detail.

15.2 DERIVING THE NPV OF FREE CASH FLOW

The first part of an ANPV analysis requires that we determine the discounted expected value of the future **free cash flows (FCF)** of the project.[3] Free cash flow at time t, FCF(t), is the profit that is available for distribution to those who have supplied capital to the firm. The corporation uses FCF to provide returns on the investments that various classes of investors have made in the firm.

FCF of a project is defined to be the after-tax, incremental operating earnings from the project plus any non-cash accounting charges, such as **depreciation**, minus investments that the firm must make because of this project. These investments are of two types: increases in the firm's capital expenditures and increases in the firm's net working capital. **Capital expenditures** relate to the firm's property, plant, and equipment. The firm's **net working capital** is the amount of inventory and cash that the firm must have on hand to run its business. Both of these investments are discussed in more detail shortly.

The firm's managers are responsible for deciding what to do with the firm's FCF. If the firm is all-equity financed, FCF can be used in three ways: The FCF can be paid out to stockholders as a dividend, it can be used to repurchase shares, or it can be retained in the firm. If the managers choose to retain the FCF, they can plan to pay the future value of today's FCF to shareholders as a **liquidating dividend**. A liquidating dividend is the value of final cash that

---

[3]This section provides only a limited overview of the link between accounting concepts and the determination of free cash flow. See Tom Copeland, Tim Koller, and Jack Murrin (2000) for a reconciliation of the accounting statements of a corporation and the determinants of the corporation's free cash flow.

the owners of a firm receive when it goes out of business. Alternatively, the managers can use the accumulated free cash flow to finance future projects.

As long as the firm earns an appropriate rate of return on its retained free cash flow, the firm need not pay out the free cash flow to the shareholders. But if the management of the firm chooses not to pay out the free cash flow, it develops excess cash, called **financial slack**. The problem with financial slack is that it can lead to sloppy management and high agency costs. **Agency costs** arise when managers do not have an incentive to act in the interests of shareholders. With too much financial slack, managers might be tempted to spend the extra money on perks for themselves, such as larger offices or company jets. Financial slack can also reduce managers' incentives to find ways to make the company operate more cost-effectively. If the firm has issued debt, the FCF can be used to pay the interest and principal on the debt.[4] Remember, though, that the first part of an ANPV analysis ignores debt and its associated interest payments. (As we have said, the side effects of debt financing will be introduced later in the chapter.)

Incremental Profits

Before we discuss the components of free cash flow in detail, we remind you that free cash flows must represent the **incremental profits** of the project. When we make an investment, we are interested in how much new cash is going to come into the firm in return. Focusing on incremental cash flows is important because changing the way an international corporation operates can cannibalize some of the firm's existing business. For example, consider the analysis that the German car manufacturer BMW used when it decided to build a manufacturing facility in the Greenville-Spartanburg area of South Carolina in the United States. The investment was worthwhile only if the discounted expected profits from producing and selling cars in the United States were larger than both the cost of constructing the plant there and the possible lost profits on export sales from Germany to the United States. If BMW had been able to sell the cars that it was formerly exporting from Germany to the United States in some other country, all the production from the company's new U.S. plant would have been considered incremental. In this case, the discounted expected profitability of the proposed U.S. plant was the only factor influencing the decision.

Because it is often difficult to forecast how much free cash flow a firm will have and then discount it, we will consider each step in detail. At this point we consider all flows to be denominated in the currency of the country in which the firm has its primary operations. Thus, foreign currency cash flows must be converted into domestic currency cash flows. This, in turn, involves forecasting exchange rates. The steps needed to forecast free cash flow are summarized in Exhibit 15.1.

Exhibit 15.1 Deriving Free Cash Flow

Step 1.	Subtract costs from revenues:
	Revenue − Costs = Earnings before interest and taxes (EBIT)
Step 2.	Subtract taxes on earnings:
	EBIT − Taxes on EBIT = Net operating profit less adjusted taxes (NOPLAT)
Step 3.	Add back non-cash costs:
	NOPLAT + Accounting depreciation = Gross cash flow (GFC)
Step 4.	Subtract investments made to increase future profitability:
	Gross cash flow − Change in net working capital (ΔNWC) − Capital expenditures (CAPX) = Free cash flow (FCF)

---

[4]See Michael Jensen (1986) for a discussion of the use of debt in mergers and acquisitions. Jensen argues that debt disciplines the management by providing incentives to find efficiencies in generating operating cash flow that allows the debt to be repaid.

Revenues

Forecasts of future revenues depend on the economic environment of the corporation. For example, the demand for a firm's product depends on the company's pricing and advertising policies, on the competitive nature of the industry in which it operates, and on macroeconomic factors in the countries where the company's sales occur. Future exchange rates will affect the value of the firm's future revenues. Exporters will be helped by depreciation of the home currency.

Costs

The costs of operating a project include the costs of the raw materials and labor costs. These costs are measured as the costs of goods sold (CGS). The managerial expenses, advertising, and other fixed costs of the project must also be subtracted. These are measured by the selling and general administrative expenses (SGA) of running the business. The final cost that must be subtracted is the accounting cost, measured by depreciation expense. Each of these costs is subtracted from revenues when calculating earnings.

If a firm imports raw materials or intermediate goods and parts, its costs will depend on exchange rates. A depreciation of the home currency will drive up the cost of imports. Forecasting future costs involves understanding how wages and the prices of inputs will evolve in the economy in which the firm is manufacturing and how much it will cost to distribute the product around the world. It also involves understanding how the productivity-enhancing investments the firm makes will affect its future costs.

Earnings Before Interest and Taxes (EBIT)

The pretax operating income that a firm would have if it had no debt is its **earnings before interest and taxes (EBIT)**:

$$\text{EBIT} = \text{Revenue} - \text{Cost of goods sold (CGS)} - \text{Selling and general administrative expenses (SGA)} - \text{Accounting depreciation}$$

An important point to remember is that interest expense is not deducted from EBIT because we are valuing the project, or possibly the whole firm, as if it has no debt in its capital structure. Because interest expense is a cost in most countries' accounting systems, however, we have to be careful to construct EBIT correctly from the firm's accounting statements. For example, in the United States, this means adding the interest deducted on the firm's income statement back into total income to derive EBIT.

Net Operating Profit Less Adjusted Taxes (NOPLAT)

After EBIT is calculated, we must subtract the cash value of taxes that would actually be paid on EBIT to find an after-tax value of net operating profit. **Net operating profit less adjusted taxes (NOPLAT)** equals EBIT minus the taxes that would be paid on EBIT:

$$\text{NOPLAT} = \text{EBIT} - \text{Taxes on EBIT}$$

In practice, calculating the taxes on EBIT from actual income statements involves adding back the taxes the firm did not have to pay because it deducted interest expenses, subtracting any taxes on interest income that the firm earned, and subtracting any taxes incurred on non-operating income. (The value of "tax shields" arising from the ability to deduct interest payments on debt is discussed in Section 15.3.)

Gross Cash Flow

After NOPLAT is derived, free cash flow is only a few short steps away. The first step involves adjusting for depreciation. Because depreciation is an accounting expense, but not an actual cash flow, we must add depreciation to NOPLAT to generate **gross cash flows**:

$$\text{Gross cash flow (GCF)} = \text{NOPLAT} + \text{Accounting depreciation}$$

Free Cash Flow

The second step in going from net operating profits to free cash flow involves subtracting two types of investments that corporations make in their future profitability. The first investments that must be subtracted from NOPLAT to obtain free cash flow are capital expenditures (CAPX). Capital expenditures are the firm's purchases of additional property, plant, or equipment that are required to do the project.

CAPX is typically large in the initial stages of the project. Eventually, the planned capital expenditures in future years will merely be whatever is necessary to maintain the plant and equipment by replacing what is wearing out. We refer to this wearing out of the physical plant and equipment as *economic depreciation*. In many presentations of valuations, it is often assumed for the later stages of a project that CAPX equals depreciation. One must be careful, though, because there may be a big difference between accounting depreciation, which is related to the book value of the firm, and the actual economic depreciation that future CAPX is supposed to represent. For example, if CAPX is replacing the existing plant and equipment as it wears out, and if there is inflation, the nominal value of CAPX will have to exceed the depreciation recorded on the firm's books because it will cost more to replace the real plant and equipment in the future than it cost to purchase it originally.

The second type of investment that must be subtracted from NOPLAT to obtain FCF is changes in net working capital (NWC).[5] If the project involves expected additions to NWC, these investments must be subtracted from the expected net operating profit of the project.

We have now made all the necessary adjustments to NOPLAT to derive free cash flow:

$$\text{FCF} = \text{GCF} - \text{CAPX} - \Delta\text{NWC}$$

Discounting Free Cash Flows

It is usually the case that the sum of the present discounted value of a project's expected future free cash flows is the primary source of the project's value. Therefore, after we have forecast free cash flow into the indefinite future, we must discount these forecasts to find the project's net present value. Let the discount rate that is appropriate for the riskiness of the all-equity future cash flows be denoted r. Then, if the initial capital expenditures associated with the project are included in the initial year's free cash flow, the NPV of the project, on an all-equity basis, is

$$\text{NPV}(t) = \sum_{k=0}^{\infty} \frac{E_t[\text{FCF}(t + k)]}{(1 + r)^k} \tag{15.2}$$

Although the discount rate in Equation (15.2) is assumed to be constant, in general, the discount rate is not required to be the same for each period in the future. The appropriate discount rate for each future period, $t + k$, can be different. In this case, we can denote the rate that is appropriate for discounting expected time, $t + k$, cash flows to time t as $r(t,k)$. Different discount rates can reflect differences in the time value of money for different periods in the future. The importance of this adjustment to Equation (15.2) will be demonstrated in the Consolidated Machine Tool Company capital budgeting case that is considered in detail in Chapter 16.

---

[5]Management of net working capital is reviewed in Chapter 19, where we more formally discuss the idea that increases in net working capital are investments that a firm is making in its future profitability.

Calculating the Terminal Value of a Project

The summation of discounted expected free cash flows in Equation (15.2) goes into the indefinite future. This is because we typically think of the equity of a firm as being infinitely lived. There are several ways that the summation of an infinite number of terms is handled in practice because we cannot input an infinite number of future values into a spreadsheet. One straightforward way to handle the problem is to truncate the forecasts after extending the horizon of the forecasts out sufficiently far, say 75 years. The importance of future cash flows beyond that time is basically zero. Let's see why. Suppose, for example, that the discount rate is 15%; consider the value today of $1 of cash flow that will be earned 75 years in the future:

$$\frac{1}{(1 + 0.15)^{75}} = 0.000028$$

Receiving $1 in 75 years is like having twenty-eight–millionths of a dollar today. Of course, explicitly forecasting 75 years into the future also involves a lot of terms. In addition, it is usually the case that our ability to forecast is limited. After developing explicit forecasts for a few years in the future, we are forced to assume that the free cash flow that the project is expected to generate will settle down, either to a constant value or to growth at some constant rate. The growth rate may be the expected rate of inflation. This will allow us to forecast the terminal value using perpetuity formulas. That is, after the explicit forecasting period, we can calculate a terminal value for the project that represents the discounted present value of all expected future free cash flows in the years extending into the indefinite future beyond the explicit forecast period.

Suppose that we develop explicit forecasts for 10 years into the future. Let the final explicit forecast of free cash flow at time t for 10 years in the future be denoted $E_t[\text{FCF}(t + 10)]$. If we assume that the firm is able to make investments that will allow its free cash flow to grow at a constant rate into the indefinite future, we can use perpetuity formulas to calculate the **terminal value** in year 10. Let's assume that future free cash flows will grow at the rate g, and let the discount rate for these perpetual cash flows be r.[6] The starting value in year 11 is higher than the expected free cash flows in year 10 by $(1+g)$. From the perpetuity formula for a growing cash flow, we know that

$$\text{Terminal value in year 10} = \frac{E_t[\text{FCF}(t + 10)](1 + g)}{(r - g)}$$

After calculating the terminal value in year 10, that quantity can then be discounted to year 0 by multiplying by the appropriate discount factor, which is $1/(1 + r)^{10}$:

$$\text{Terminal value in year 0} = \frac{\text{Terminal value in year 10}}{(1 + r)^{10}}$$

The growth rate of g should primarily reflect the expected rate of inflation in the currency of the forecasts because, eventually, the project's real capacity will be met, and new real investments will have to be made. If there is a forecast of real growth, it would be under the assumption that the firm will be able to maintain its market share and its profitability as the world economy grows. Then, if the forecast of real growth rate is 2%, and if forecast of inflation is 4%, we would forecast that free cash flow would grow at 6.08%, because

$$(1 + 2\%) \times (1 + 4\%) = (1 + 6.08\%)$$

But we must be careful about the assumptions on capital expenditures that support such an assumption. If no new capital expenditures are planned and CAPX is just offsetting depreciation, the physical plant and equipment will not be capable of growing indefinitely. If no new CAPX is planned, it makes more sense to limit the assumed growth to the rate of inflation.

---

[6]The appendix to this chapter provides a derivation of the perpetuity formula used in deriving the terminal value.

Another way of determining the terminal value involves understanding when the firm's return on investment is expected to settle down to the competitive level predicted by the required rate of return that investors demand on capital employed by the firm. This approach to terminal values is discussed in Chapter 16.

15.3 FINANCIAL SIDE EFFECTS

The NPV of a project's free cash flow is usually not the only source of a project's value. There are usually significant side effects that arise from the financing of the project that add value to or subtract value from the project. These financial side effects arise from the costs of issuing securities to finance the project, from the tax deductions that certain types of financing provide, from the costs of financial distress associated with issuing debt, and from the subsidized financing that governments offer to entice corporations to locate in particular countries or regions. We discuss each of these issues in turn.

The Costs of Issuing Securities

When a corporation does not have enough resources from its current and previously generated free cash flows to finance a new project, it must turn to outside investors for additional resources. This process is costly for a number of reasons.

The investment bankers who handle the issuing of securities either to the public or to private investors are financial intermediaries, and they must be compensated for the use of their scarce resources. This compensation includes a monetary fee, but it also usually includes an **underwriting discount**, or spread. The underwriting discount between what the corporation receives from issuing the securities and what the public pays for the securities is often a large part of the compensation of the investment bank that underwrites the issue.

Inmoo Lee, Scott Lockhead, Jay Ritter, and Quanshui Zhao (1996) investigated these costs as a function of the amount raised for initial public offerings (IPOs) of equity. They found that the percentage costs decrease as the amount of money raised increases, indicating that some economies of scale are achieved. Nonetheless, the costs are still large. According to the researchers, the flat expenses charged by underwriters averaged 3.69% of the amount raised, and gross spreads averaged 7.31% across the 1,767 IPOs studied.

Tax Shields for Certain Securities

When a firm issues debt, the interest paid on the debt is deductible for tax purposes because the government views it as a legitimate cost of doing business. The value of the ability to deduct interest payments for tax purposes is often called an **interest tax shield**. Thus, debt financing reduces a firm's income taxes, and issuing debt increases the value of the corporation, at least for small amounts of debt.

To find the value of the interest tax shield, consider the following scenario. Suppose that the required rate of return on a one-period loan of principal D is r_D, which is the market interest rate on the loan. Let the corporate income tax rate be τ. Then, suppose the corporation borrows D in the first period, and it repays $(1 + r_D)D$ in the second period. Because the interest payment is deductible, the corporation also gets a tax deduction of $\tau r_D D$ in the second period. The present value of these flows using the market interest rate as the discount rate is

$$D - \frac{(1 + r_D)D}{(1 + r_D)} + \frac{\tau r_D D}{(1 + r_D)} = \frac{\tau r_D D}{(1 + r_D)} \qquad (15.3)$$

Equation (15.3) demonstrates that the value of a loan at market interest rates is 0 in the absence of tax deductions or subsidies from the government. When interest is deductible, there is a valuable interest tax shield. If there were only benefits associated with issuing debt, the corporation would be entirely debt financed. Something else must be going on. We will examine the costs of debt later in this chapter, but first, we consider how adding debt to the capital structure of Vincenzo Uno's project changes its desirability.

Example 15.2 Vincenzo Uno's Tax Shield

Let's return to Example 15.1 and examine what happens if Vincenzo Uno can issue some debt to finance the project. Suppose the company is able to issue €500,000 of debt at an interest rate of 8% per annum. Further assume that Vincenzo Uno will allow this debt to be outstanding for the indefinite future. The tax shield of $\tau r_D D$ derived in Equation (15.3) now occurs in every period into perpetuity. Hence, the discounted present value of the perpetual tax shield is

$$\frac{\tau r_D D}{(1 + r_D)} + \frac{\tau r_D D}{(1 + r_D)^2} + \frac{\tau r_D D}{(1 + r_D)^3} + \cdots = \tau D$$

With a corporate tax rate of 34%, the value of the tax shield is

$$0.34 \times €500,000 = €170,000$$

Because the net present value, assuming all-equity financing, was −€30,000, the value of the project is now positive, and Vincenzo Uno should do it by issuing both debt and equity.

The Proper Discount Rate

The basic principle of ANPV analysis is that expected values of future cash flows should be discounted at the appropriate discount rate that reflects the riskiness of the cash flows. In Equation (15.3), we violated this procedure by discounting the promised cash flows with the actual market interest rate. We can reconcile the two approaches in the following way. Suppose that δ is the probability of default on the debt, and if the company defaults, it will pay nothing to its creditors. Then the expected payment is the probability-weighted average of the two possible payments:

$$(1 - \delta) \times (1 + r_D)D + \delta \times 0 = (1 - \delta)(1 + r_D)D$$

and the expected tax deduction for interest expense is

$$(1 - \delta) \times \tau r_D D + \delta \times 0 = (1 - \delta)\tau r_D D$$

Suppose that the events that will cause the firm to default are idiosyncratic to the firm. Then the appropriate discount rate for the expected debt cash flows is the risk-free interest rate, r_F. Thus, to find the value of a debt, the expected future values should be discounted at the risk-free rate. The value of a one-period debt is therefore

$$D - \frac{(1 - \delta)(1 + r_D)D}{(1 + r_F)} + \frac{(1 - \delta)\tau r_D D}{(1 + r_F)} \tag{15.4}$$

The expression in Equation (15.4) reduces to the expression in Equation (15.3) when we recognize that the market interest rate is set to reflect the probability of default:

$$(1 - \delta) \times (1 + r_D) + \delta \times 0 = (1 + r_F) \tag{15.5}$$

Substituting from Equation (15.5) into Equation (15.4) gives Equation (15.3).

Costs of Financial Distress

You might think that interest tax shields suggest that a firm should be financed completely with debt because the bigger the debt, the larger is the tax shield. This cannot be right because we do not observe firms acting this way. This section examines why firms limit their leverage. There are costs that offset the benefits of the interest tax shields; they are called the **costs of financial distress**.

The Direct Costs of Financial Distress

A firm is in financial distress if it is having difficulty meeting its commitments to its bond-holders. A firm defaults on its debts when it is unable or unwilling to make the required interest or principal payments on its debts. A bankruptcy proceeding may result, with the assets of the firm being formally transferred from the stockholders to the bondholders. Bankruptcy is costly because the legal, consulting, and accounting fees associated with the process eat away at the value of the company. Academic studies of the direct costs of financial distress find that they are typically around 3% of the market value of the firm.[7]

The Indirect Costs of Financial Distress

The indirect costs of financial distress refer to the loss of the firm's value that occurs because people believe the company may fail. For example, some potential customers will not want to do business with the firm for fear of lack of after-sales service. Suppliers will also be less willing to deal with the firm and may be unwilling to extend it credit, demanding that it pay cash for its purchases. This adversely affects the ability of the firm to manage its cash flow and increases the firm's required investments in its net working capital. Other indirect costs of financial distress can be seen on the managerial side of the business. It will be more difficult to compensate the firm's managers competitively, so they might not perform as well. Or they might spend much of their time looking for other jobs. The firm will also have trouble attracting and retaining a high-quality, skilled labor force. These indirect costs of financial distress are, of course, much more amorphous and therefore difficult to measure than direct costs.

The Equilibrium Amount of Debt

We know that a firm will issue debt up to the point at which the marginal benefit of the debt from the interest tax shield is equal to the marginal costs of financial distress. This is demonstrated in Exhibit 15.2. The marginal benefit of the debt is constant and is given by the tax shield. The marginal cost of debt is increasing. Initially, these costs are low, but eventually they escalate. To find the total benefits and total costs of issuing debt, we need to evaluate the areas under the marginal benefit and marginal cost curves.

Exhibit 15.2 shows that the marginal cost of financial distress is essentially 0 when the firm first begins to take on debt, but it increases quickly as the firm issues more debt. If the marginal cost of financial distress increases quickly as the firm approaches its optimal capital structure, the total cost of financial distress, which is the area under the marginal cost curve, will be minimal and can essentially be ignored in discounting the cash flows. The value of issuing debt is then just the interest tax shield. Of course, it is always better to attempt to value

---

[7]Some classic articles on the costs of bankruptcy include Michele White (1983) and Edward Altman (1984). For a recent discussion of the issues see Avner Kalay, Rajeev Singhal, and Elizabeth Tashjian (2007).

Exhibit 15.2 The Benefits and Costs of Debt

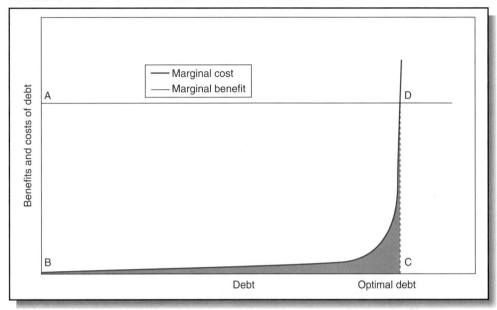

Note: The rectangle ABCD is the total benefit of the debt. The shaded area under the marginal cost curve is the total cost of the debt.

the costs of financial distress by understanding how issuing debt adversely affects the ability of the firm to operate in world markets

Subsidized Financing

When a manufacturing company decides to build a plant in a foreign country, it is often able to get regions of the country, or even entire countries, to compete for the jobs that will be brought to the area. The governments and municipalities of these countries and regions will often offer subsidies to the corporation in the form of lower corporate taxes for a number of years. Alternatively, the subsidies might consist of loans made at below-market interest rates.

Interest subsidies add value to a project. The appropriate discount rate for an interest subsidy is simply the market's required rate of return on the debt of the corporation. Why? Because the corporation is just as likely to default on a subsidized loan from the government as it is on a normal loan at market interest rates. Let's derive an analytical representation of the value of a subsidized loan. Suppose that the government lets a corporation borrow a principal of D for one period at a subsidized interest rate of $r_S < r_D$, which, as before, is the market's required rate of return on the corporation's debt. The corporation borrows D in the first period, and it repays $(1 + r_S)D$ in the second period. Because the actual interest payment is deductible, the corporation also gets a tax deduction of $\tau\, r_S\, D$ in the second period. The present value of the cash flows of the subsidized debt at the market's required rate of return on the corporation's debt is therefore

$$D - \frac{(1 + r_S)D}{(1 + r_D)} + \frac{\tau\, r_S\, D}{(1 + r_D)} = \frac{(r_D - r_S)D}{(1 + r_D)} + \frac{\tau\, r_S\, D}{(1 + r_D)} \tag{15.6}$$

Equation (15.6) demonstrates that the value of a loan at a subsidized, below-market, interest rate is the present value of the interest subsidy, which is the difference between the interest paid on a market loan and the interest on the subsidized loan, plus the present value of the actual interest tax shield. In both cases, the present value is taken at the market's required rate of return on the debt.

15.4 GROWTH OPTIONS

A **growth option** arises when a firm undertakes a project and obtains an option to do another project in the future. The option to do the second project adds value to the first project. A growth option might include a firm's ability to sell a successful domestic product in the international marketplace. Growth options are specific examples of **real options** that also include the ability of a firm to shut down a plant or a mine until operating conditions improve or to delay an important operating decision until more information can be gathered. Real options are valuable.

A good example of how real options add value to investment decisions was a 1989 decision by Procter & Gamble (P&G) to purchase the privately held Brazilian company Phebo. At the time, Phebo was the 13th-largest Brazilian cleaning and personal care products company (see Procter & Gamble, 1991). In doing the valuation of Phebo, P&G used Phebo's projected future free cash flows for Phebo's products, but under P&G management. P&G's discounted cash flow analysis indicated that a price of $91 million was appropriate for Phebo. That said, P&G also recognized that there was significant option value from owning and operating Phebo. The idea was that P&G would learn about operating in Brazil and would be able to expand its presence in Brazil if the Phebo acquisition went well and the Brazilian economy improved.[8]

Example 15.3 Vincenzo Uno's Abandonment Option

Let's return to the example of the Italian company Vincenzo Uno, which we first discussed in Example 15.1. Suppose Vincenzo Uno forecasts that it will either generate €1,250,000 or €750,000 in sales in its first year of operation and that either of the sales levels is as likely as the other. After the first year, though, the managers of the company will know for sure which of the two sales levels will be reached, and these sales levels will persist into the indefinite future. Also, assume that the managers have an option to abandon the project if first-year sales come in only at €750,000. Finally, assume that the scrap value of the plant and equipment will be €700,000.

What should Vincenzo Uno do, given the two different sales scenarios? We summarize the situation with the following table that indicates cash flows in year 1 and in all future years if the project is abandoned in the bad state:

	Year 1		Future Years	
	Good State	**Bad State**	**Good State**	**Bad State**
Annual cash inflows	€1,250,000	€750,000	€1,250,000	0
Annual cash costs	−600,000	−600,000	−600,000	0
Operating income	650,000	150,000	650,000	0
Corporate tax (.34 tax rate)	−221,000	−51,000	−221,000	0
Unlevered free cash flow	€429,000	€99,000	€429,000	0

Thus, in 1 year, the project will have two values. In the good state, the project will be worth that year's free cash flow plus the value of the perpetuity from continuing in the good state, or

$$€429,000 + €429,000/0.20 = €2,574,000$$

---

[8]An additional source of value to the project arose from the fact that part of the investment was able to be done with a debt-equity swap. P&G purchased Brazilian government dollar-denominated debt in the secondary market that was trading at a discount, presented the debt to the Brazilian government, and received in value more cruzeiros than could have been obtained by purchasing cruzeiros at the market exchange rate.

On the other hand, in the bad state, the project will be abandoned and will be worth that year's free cash flow plus the scrap value of the machinery, or

$$€99,000 + €700,000 = €799,000$$

Because these valuations are equally likely, the discounted expected value of the project is

$$[0.5\,(€2,574,000) + 0.5\,(€799,000)] / 1.20 = €1,405,417$$

Because this is more than the cost of the project, even without debt, Vincenzo Uno would undertake the project.

Notice that in the first year, the value of doing the project in the bad state in perpetuity is the discounted value of receiving €99,000 in all future periods, or

$$€99,000/0.2 = €495,000$$

Thus, the abandonment option increases the value of the project in year 1 in the bad state by €700,000 − €495,000 = €205,000. Because there is a 50% chance of this happening, the first-year value of the project increases by

$$[0.5\,(€205,000)] / 1.20 = €85,417$$

This is the difference between the initial value of the project with the abandonment option, which is €1,405,417, and the initial value of the project without the abandonment option, which is €1,320,000, as in Example 15.1.

Problems with the Discounted Cash Flow Approach

The previous section shows that management's real options are important when doing project valuation. The problem with discounted cash flow analysis is that it usually ignores these options. As a result, projects tend to be undervalued. This problem exists whenever a manager can take a discretionary action in the future that affects the cash flows of a project. The ANPV approach adds in the value of real options as a separate valuation term.

Within an international context, perhaps the most important option involves the decision to enter a foreign market. Many factors need to be considered, such as changing costs and prices, changing real exchange rates, and the timing of the market entry. Similarly, the decision to exit the foreign market involves costs and depends on the real exchange rate. One important aspect of market entry is the competition: Does the competition also have the option of entering the same market? There is often a first-mover advantage related to establishing a product in a new market. In such a situation, the value of a firm's option to wait to enter can get competed away (see Steven Grenadier, 2002). Option pricing can help value projects, given these situations.

POINT–COUNTERPOINT
Valuing a Project Using Discounted Cash Flows Versus a Ratio Analysis

Freedy is poring over the income statement of German firm Bayer, trying to develop a spreadsheet model of the discounted free cash flows of the company. His fingers are flying, and the computer is churning. He has a meeting with Ante in a few minutes, and he is trying to justify an investment by the Handel Brothers Trust Fund in the ADR of Bayer, which is listed on the

NYSE. Ante asked him to find three or four undervalued equities that would make good investments. For Freedy, an undervalued equity means that the stock price is less than the present discounted value of the firm's free cash flow plus any adjustments for debt and growth options. He knows Ante doesn't necessarily do valuations this way.

Suddenly, Ante bursts into the room, sees Freedy's spreadsheets, and shouts, "What are you doing? I only wanted some sensible **ratio analysis**. That discounted free cash flow analysis never works. The valuations always depend on bogus assumptions about the terminal value. On Wall Street, they just check the **price–earnings (P/E) ratio**, and they buy low P/E stocks and sell high P/E stocks. You'll never make an investment if you stick to that discounted cash flow stuff."

Freedy, feeling a bit overwhelmed by his brother's tirade, meekly responds, "Well, I'm a value investor. When I invest, I want to see future profits discounted at some sensible required rate of return and know that I'm not paying too much for a stock. Think about all the people who got burned investing in the dot-coms in 2000. The managers of those firms would explain to investors that they had 'good ratios' of stock prices to future earnings, but nobody at those firms even had a plan for becoming profitable. It was all a bubble. Ratio analysis is simply stupid."

As Ante is clenching his fist, in walks Suttle Trooth. As usual, Suttle quickly sees the argument boiling to a head and asks, "What's all the fuss about?"

Both brothers talk at once, and Suttle realizes what's up. He says, "Well, I like doing a discounted cash flow analysis in lots of situations, and I like using a ratio analysis in others. Let's try to think about the relationship between them. We know that in a rational world, the stock price reflects the discounted expected payoffs to the stockholders. In fact, we know that higher P/E ratios are produced either by faster growth or lower required rates of return on the equity.

"A discounted cash flow analysis is a scientific tool," says Suttle, "but you've got to have the right forecasts to go into the tool. Otherwise, you'll get a garbage-in, garbage-out result. You've really got to understand the sources of a firm's profitability. Does a firm's production process give it a cost advantage that is sustainable? Are there barriers to entry in the market that significantly affect the firm's competitive situation? Have its marketing campaigns generated loyal customers? Is its accounting accurate and an honest reflection of reality? What do we think of the quality of the firm's management team? These are some of the forces that determine profitability, both now and in the future.

"Lots of times," continues Suttle, "analysts become comfortable with the nature of an industry and realize that the firms in that industry are all trading at prices around a certain multiple of some measure of current or projected future earnings. The analysts can then make their trades based on P/E ratios, and they can be fairly sure that in the short run, they're in the right ballpark. But ratio analysis is just a quick, summary statistic. It's still necessary to do the due diligence of free cash flow analysis to really value a company."

The brothers looked at each other and smiled. Suttle was on target once again.

15.5 PARENT VERSUS SUBSIDIARY CASH FLOWS

There are often substantial differences between the cash flows from a project that accrue directly to the foreign subsidiary and the cash flows that can ultimately be paid to the parent. Consequently, we must be clear about whose ANPV we are trying to evaluate. The fundamental point of the free cash flow analysis in the previous section is that we are trying to determine the net present value of the cash that is available for distribution to the ultimate shareholders of the corporation. It therefore follows that the parent's perspective is the most relevant for our analysis. If tax regulations and foreign exchange controls severely limit the amount of funds that can be transferred from the foreign subsidiary to the parent, the project is less valuable than if it were being done by an independent company that owned the project inside the country.

Of course, the parent's free cash flows from a project undertaken by a foreign subsidiary can also substantially exceed the subsidiary's free cash flow because of **royalty payments**, **licensing agreements**, and **overhead management fees**. Subsidiaries must pay these costs to the parent corporation. Hence, the subsidiary's income is reduced by these costs, but the parent's income is enhanced.

In addition, if the parent is selling any intermediate goods to the subsidiary, part of the subsidiary's cost of goods sold includes the amount of profit that is included in the transfer pricing of the intermediate goods. Clearly, this profit enhances the value of the project from the parent company shareholder's perspective.

Although the parent's perspective is ultimately what we want to value, it is often easiest to do international capital budgeting with a three-step approach. We begin with the subsidiary's viewpoint of free cash flow and then consider how the cash flows change when the parent's viewpoint is taken into account. Finally, we adjust for financial side effects and growth options. We now consider these three steps in detail.

A Three-Step Approach to Determining the Value of a Foreign Subsidiary

The first step in deriving the value to the parent corporation of a foreign subsidiary involves conducting the NPV cash flow analysis on the foreign subsidiary as if it were an independent, all-equity firm. We can think of this analysis as the value that an independent company would place on the foreign project if it were licensed to use the technology of the parent corporation, and we consider the royalty payments, licensing fees, and other overhead management fees that the subsidiary must pay the parent as costs.

Second, we consider the cash flow implications from the parent's perspective. Several issues are important at this point. We begin with the dividends that the subsidiary will pay to the parent, but we must take account of withholding taxes that will be paid on these dividends. Foreign governments usually tax the repatriation of profits. These taxes can significantly reduce the value of the free cash flow that accrues to the parent relative to what accrues to the subsidiary. From the parent's perspective, though, the after-tax values of the royalty payments, licensing fees, and management fees that the subsidiary pays the parent are profits that increase the parent's valuation of the foreign subsidiary. We must also include any profits on sales of intermediate goods from the parent to the foreign subsidiary. Finally, we must watch for **cannibalization of exports** to the market served by the subsidiary. These lost exports could be from the parent or from another one of its foreign subsidiaries in a different country. If no market can be found for the goods that were formerly being exported to a country, the lost profits on these exports must be considered to be a cost of accepting the project.

In the third step, we must adjust the value of the project for the net present value of financing side effects and possible growth options. Often, there will be loans and subsidies that must be valued. Opportunities for additional growth in the future will also typically be present. These three steps are now demonstrated in an extensive case analysis.

15.6 THE CASE OF INTERNATIONAL WOOD PRODUCTS

International Wood Products, Inc. (IWPI), is considering whether to build a Spanish manufacturing facility that would serve its European market. IWPI is a U.S.-based corporation that manufactures wooden tables and chairs, primarily using oak, maple, and pine. The stylishly designed furniture, with its beautifully finished natural woods, has found its way into better European homes, and the company forecasts that demand for its furniture in Europe is likely to increase significantly over the next 10 years. IWPI is currently serving its European customers with exports from its New Hampshire manufacturing plant. Because the demand for the company's products in Europe has been growing at 10% per year for the past 5 years, the New Hampshire plant is now operating at 100% of planned capacity. Hence, this is an appropriate time for IWPI to consider establishing a new production facility in Europe.

Although Spain is not centrally located in Europe, the availability of skilled Spanish craftworkers at relatively low wages makes locating in Spain desirable. In addition, the Spanish government is offering a 10-year loan of €4 million at an attractive interest rate of 5% per annum. The interest payments on the loan would be due annually at the end of the year, and the repayment of principal would be a final balloon payment at the end of year 10.

IWPI-Spain's Free Cash Flows

Initial Investments

IWPI's managers have discovered a manufacturing facility outside of Madrid, Spain, that can be acquired for €27.2 million. They estimate that the total cost of equipping the plant with the necessary machines would be €48 million. An initial investment in cash and inventory would require another €3.2 million. Hence, the total initial expenditure on the project is

$$(€27.2 + €48 + €3.2) \text{ million} = €78.4 \text{ million}$$

At the spot exchange rate of €1.04/$, the total initial dollar investment in the proposed project is therefore

$$€78.4 \text{ million} / (€1.04/\$) = \$75.4 \text{ million}$$

After the acquisition, IWPI managers estimate that the plant could be running at partial capacity within 2 months. Hiring and training the Spanish workforce would not be difficult, but given IWPI's high quality standards and the many designs that are in the IWPI catalog, it seems reasonable to expect less than full production during the first year of operation. Consequently, IWPI forecasts that only one-half of the first year's European demand could be met by the Spanish facility.

Forecasting Total Revenue

Exhibit 15.3 presents forecasts for the next 10 years of expected sales revenue from IWPI-Spain. Line 1 indicates that growth in European demand is expected to be 10% in the first year; to increase to 12% by the third year, as new showrooms are opened throughout Europe; and then to decline to 1% by year 10, as the market becomes saturated. Line 2 translates these forecasts of future growth into forecasts of unit sales. Because the current European demand for IWPI's furniture is 40,000 units, 10% growth in year 1 implies that European sales are expected to be 44,000 units. One-half of this, or 22,000 units, will be produced in Spain. Thereafter, IWPI plans to satisfy the entire European demand with product from the Spanish plant. Hence, the 2nd-year forecast is $44,000 \times 1.11 = 48,840$. By the 10th year, the Spanish plant is forecast to be producing slightly more than 76,000 units. The Madrid facility is sufficiently large that this growth can be accommodated without a major expansion of plant and equipment.

The current price of a typical unit of IWPI furniture is $2,307.69, which in euro terms at the current exchange rate is

$$(€1.04/\$) \times \$2,307.69 = €2,400$$

Exhibit 15.3 Revenue Forecasts for IWPI-Spain

	\multicolumn{10}{c}{Year in the Future}									
	1	**2**	**3**	**4**	**5**	**6**	**7**	**8**	**9**	**10**
1. Real growth rates of unit sales	10%	11%	12%	10%	8%	6%	4%	3%	2%	1%
2. Unit sales	22,000	48,840	54,701	60,171	64,985	68,884	71,639	73,788	75,264	76,017
3. Euro inflation rates	8%	7%	6%	6%	6%	6%	6%	6%	6%	6%
4. Euro price per unit	2,592	2,773	2,940	3,116	3,303	3,501	3,711	3,934	4,170	4,420
5. Total euro revenue (1,000,000's) (Line 2) × (Line 4)	57.02	135.45	160.81	187.51	214.66	241.19	265.89	290.30	313.87	336.03

Sales in the parts of Europe that do not use the euro will be priced in local currencies, but the retail prices will be dictated by the euro price. This retail price is expected to increase at the euro rate of inflation. The forecasts of the euro rate of inflation in Line 3 of Exhibit 15.3 indicate that IWPI expects the euro rate of inflation to be 8% next year, 7% in year 2, and 6% thereafter into the indefinite future. At these rates of inflation, the retail price of a unit of furniture is expected to increase from €2,592 = €2,400 × 1.08 next year to €4,420 in 10 years.

Line 5 of Exhibit 15.3 multiplies the expected euro price per unit in Line 4 by the expected number of units that will be sold in Line 2 to provide forecasts of total euro revenue. Total revenue forecasts increase from €57.02 million = 22,000 units × (€2,592 per unit) in the first year to €336.03 million 10 years from now.

Forecasting Net Working Capital, Capital Expenditures, and Depreciation

Exhibit 15.4 presents forecasts of investments that IWPI-Spain must make to maintain its productivity and satisfy the demand for its products. These investments are presented now because they will determine how much accounting depreciation is available. Accounting depreciation is a cost of doing business, but it is not a cash outflow. Accounting depreciation is derived in Exhibit 15.4.

Because the required stock of net working capital is expected to be 8.5% of total revenue, Line 1 presents the total revenue forecasts from Line 5 of Exhibit 15.3. The required stocks of net working capital for each year are then presented in Line 2 of Exhibit 15.4. The initial stock of net working capital in year 0 is €3.20 million. This expenditure represents the initial cash and inventory that the firm must have on hand to conduct its business. Because total revenue is forecast to grow, the required stock of net working capital is forecast to grow

Exhibit 15.4 Forecasts of Additions to Net Working Capital and Capital Expenditures for IWPI-Spain

		\multicolumn{10}{c}{Year in the Future}									
	0	**1**	**2**	**3**	**4**	**5**	**6**	**7**	**8**	**9**	**10**
1. Total revenue (Exhibit 15.3, Line 5)		57.02	135.45	160.81	187.51	214.66	241.19	265.89	290.30	313.87	336.03
2. Stock of NWC (year 0 given, then 8.5% of Line 1)	3.20	4.85	11.51	13.67	15.94	18.25	20.50	22.60	24.68	26.68	28.56
3. Addition to NWC (Line 2 year i – Line 2 year (i–1))		1.65	6.67	2.16	2.27	2.31	2.26	2.10	2.07	2.00	1.88
4. Capital expenditures	75.20	4.06	4.35	4.61	4.88	5.18	5.49	5.81	6.16	6.53	6.93
5. Depreciation (20-year straight line)		3.76	3.78	3.80	3.84	3.90	3.96	4.04	4.12	4.23	4.34

Notes: All numbers are in millions of euros. Capital expenditures are the nominal spending necessary to keep the real capital stock constant.

proportionately. The additions to net working capital are presented in Line 3 of Exhibit 15.4. For example, the first year's total revenue is forecast to be €57.02 million, and 8.5% of this value is €4.85 million. Because the initial stock of net working capital is €3.20 million, an investment of

$$€4.85 \text{ million} - €3.20 \text{ million} = €1.65 \text{ million}$$

is required in year 1. The other figures in Line 3 of Exhibit 15.4 are derived analogously.

Line 4 of Exhibit 15.4 presents the forecasts of capital expenditures (CAPX). IWPI management assumes that nominal capital expenditures in any year will be whatever is necessary to keep the real plant and equipment constant from year to year. Here we assume that economic depreciation requires that 5% of the physical capital stock be replaced each year. Thus, the amount of nominal euros that must be spent to keep the real capital stock constant from year to year will increase over time because of inflation.

The Spanish tax authorities require that accounting depreciation be linear over 20 years. Therefore, one-twentieth of the value of the capital can be deducted as accounting depreciation in each year for tax purposes. Hence, even in this case, in which the economic life of the plant and equipment is similar to the period over which accounting depreciation can be deducted, economic depreciation and the corresponding CAPX will differ from accounting depreciation because of inflation.

To see this, recall that in the initial year, IWPI invested

$$€75.20 = €78.40 \text{ (total investment)} - €3.20 \text{ (initial NWC)}$$

in the physical capital stock of its foreign subsidiary. The initial book value of the project is therefore €75.2 million, which is the initial cost of the plant, €27.2 million, and the equipment, €48 million. For the first year, because 5% of the physical capital stock will need to be replaced, and because the rate of inflation is forecast to be 8%, CAPX in year 1 will be

$$€4.06 \text{ million} = 0.05 \times 1.08 \times €75.20$$

In later years, CAPX grows with the euro rate of inflation, $\pi(t+k,€)$, because purchasing the same 5% of the real plant and equipment gets progressively more expensive:

$$\text{CAPX}(t+k) = \text{CAPX}(t+k-1) \times (1 + \pi(t+k,€)$$

Line 5 of Exhibit 15.4 presents the forecasts of accounting depreciation, which are presented here only because they are related to forecasts of capital expenditures (CAPX) and because we need them as costs of doing business. Because the Spanish tax authorities require that accounting depreciation be done on a straight-line basis over the useful life of the investment, which is taken to be 20 years in this case, one-twentieth (or 5%) of the book value of the project, which is

$$€3.76 \text{ million} = 0.05 \times €75.2 \text{ million}$$

can be deducted as an expense in the first year. This depreciation expense is also deducted from revenue in each of the next 20 years. Remember, also, that each year the book value of the project would decline by this amount if there were no capital expenditures. But if the firm makes capital expenditures to offset the economic depreciation of the plant and equipment, this CAPX increases the book value of the project. Because depreciation is an accounting concept, it will not correspond exactly to economic depreciation. The value for accounting depreciation in year $t+k$ is the previous year's accounting depreciation plus 5% (one-twentieth) of the change in the book value of the company, which is the amount by which capital expenditures exceed depreciation:

$$\text{Depreciation}(t+k) = \text{Depreciation}(t+k-1) + 0.05 \times [\text{CAPX}(t+k-1) \\ - \text{Depreciation}(t+k-1)]$$

Forecasting Total Costs

Exhibit 15.5 forecasts the total costs for IWPI-Spain, which include variable costs and fixed costs. Variable cost per unit has three components. Labor costs in Line 1.a begin at €779 and are estimated to increase each year at the euro rate of inflation, as given in Line 3 of Exhibit 15.3. Materials sourced in Europe, presented in Line 1.b, are forecast to cost €629 per unit in the first year. Materials sourced from the parent company, IWPI-U.S., are presented in Line 1.c. These intermediate parts are forecast to cost €584 per unit in the first year. The euro prices of both materials sourced in Europe and materials sourced in the United States are forecast to increase each year at the euro rate of inflation. This is consistent with the dollar prices of the parts being expected to increase at the dollar rate of inflation and the euro/dollar exchange rate being expected to satisfy relative purchasing power parity (which we discussed in Chapter 8).

Total variable cost in Line 2 represents the estimated number of units sold in a particular year (Line 2 of Exhibit 15.3) multiplied by the sum of the per-unit variable labor costs and the two material costs. Total variable cost is forecast to increase from €43.82 million in the first year to €258.24 million 10 years from now.

The next part of Exhibit 15.5 forecasts the costs associated with the royalty agreement and the overhead allocation agreement between IWPI-U.S. and IWPI-Spain. Line 3 calculates the royalty fee that will be paid by IWPI-Spain to its parent as 5% of total revenue, which is presented in Line 5 of Exhibit 15.3. Line 4 of Exhibit 15.5 calculates the overhead allocation fee as 2% of total revenue. This fee is paid to the parent corporation for accounting and other managerial assistance. Because these fees are a constant percentage of total revenue, they will grow at the same rate as total revenue, which, in turn, is growing both because of real growth in the number units sold and because of euro inflation.

The fixed costs and direct overhead expenses of running the Spanish plant are presented in Line 5 of Exhibit 15.5. These begin at €1.59 million and increase each year at the euro rate of inflation. Depreciation, calculated in Exhibit 15.4, is the last cost, and for completeness it is included again as Line 6 of Exhibit 15.5.

Total cost in Line 7 of Exhibit 15.5 is the sum of total variable cost in Line 2, the royalty fee in Line 3, the overhead allocation fee in Line 4, the overhead expenses in Line 5, and

Exhibit 15.5   Cost Forecasts for IWPI-Spain

	Year in the Future									
	1	**2**	**3**	**4**	**5**	**6**	**7**	**8**	**9**	**10**
1. Variable cost per unit										
a. Labor	779	834	884	937	993	1,053	1,116	1,183	1,254	1,329
b. Materials sourced in Europe	629	673	713	756	801	849	900	954	1,012	1,072
c. Parts purchased from IWPI-U.S.	584	625	662	702	744	789	836	886	940	996
2. Total variable cost (Lines 1.a + 1.b + 1.c) × (Exhibit 15.1, Line 2)	43.82	104.10	123.59	144.10	164.97	185.36	204.34	223.10	241.21	258.24
3. Royalty fees @ 5% of total revenue (0.05 × Exhibit 15.1, Line 5)	2.85	6.77	8.04	9.38	10.73	12.06	13.29	14.51	15.69	16.80
4. Overhead allocation @ 2% of total revenue (0.02 × Exhibit 15.1, Line 5)	1.14	2.71	3.22	3.75	4.29	4.82	5.32	5.81	6.28	6.72
5. Overhead expenses	1.59	1.70	1.81	1.91	2.03	2.15	2.28	2.42	2.56	2.72
6. Depreciation (Exhibit 15.4, Line 5)	3.76	3.78	3.80	3.84	3.90	3.96	4.04	4.12	4.23	4.34
7. Total cost (Lines 2 + 3 + 4 + 5 + 6)	53.17	119.06	140.45	162.99	185.92	208.35	229.27	249.96	269.97	288.82

Note: All numbers except the per-unit values in Line 1 are in millions of euros.

Exhibit 15.6 Forecasts of After-Tax Profit for IWPI-Spain

	Year in the Future									
	1	2	3	4	5	6	7	8	9	10
1. Total revenue (Exhibit 15.3, Line 5)	57.02	135.45	160.81	187.51	214.66	241.19	265.89	290.30	313.87	336.03
2. Total cost (Exhibit 15.5, Line 7)	53.17	119.06	140.45	162.99	185.92	208.35	229.27	249.96	269.97	288.82
3. Earnings before tax (EBIT) (Line 1 – Line 2)	3.86	16.39	20.36	24.52	28.74	32.84	36.62	40.34	43.90	47.21
4. Corporate income tax @ 35% (0.35 × Line 3)	1.35	5.74	7.13	8.58	10.06	11.49	12.82	14.12	15.36	16.52
5. Earnings after tax (NOPLAT) (Line 3 – Line 4)	2.51	10.66	13.23	15.94	18.68	21.34	23.80	26.22	28.53	30.68

Note: All numbers are in millions of euros.

depreciation in Line 6. Total costs are forecast to increase from €53.17 million in the first year to €288.82 million 10 years from now.

Forecasting Net Operating Profit Less Adjusted Taxes (NOPLAT)

Exhibit 15.6 forecasts net operating profit less adjusted taxes (NOPLAT). Line 1 reproduces the forecasts of total revenues from Line 5 of Exhibit 15.3. Line 2 reproduces the forecasts of total costs from Line 7 of Exhibit 15.5. The difference between these two lines is earnings before interest and taxes (EBIT), which is presented in Line 3. The appropriate Spanish corporate income tax rate is 35%. Hence, corporate taxes are found as 35% of EBIT in Line 4. Line 5 presents the calculation of after-tax earnings, which are the forecasts of NOPLAT. The forecasts of net operating profit less adjusted taxes of IWPI-Spain start at €2.51 million in the first year and increase to €30.68 million 10 years from now.

Forecasting IWPI-Spain's Free Cash Flow

Exhibit 15.7 presents the forecasts of IWPI-Spain's free cash flow. The first line presents after-tax earnings (NOPLAT), derived in Line 5 of Exhibit 15.6. To NOPLAT we must add the accounting depreciation that was subtracted as a cost in Line 6 of Exhibit 15.5 because accounting depreciation is not a cash flow. The firm's investments, the change in its net working capital and its capital expenditures, from Lines 3 and 4 of Exhibit 15.6 are then subtracted. The results in Line 5 of Exhibit 15.7 are the firm's forecasts of free cash flows for each year in the future. The initial free cash flow is negative and represents the initial cost of the project. Forecasts of free cash flow start at €0.56 million in year 1 and grow to €30.68 million in year 10.

The Net Present Value of IWPI-Spain

After the forecasts of free cash flow are derived, they must be discounted to the present. The discount rate for this project is taken to be 20% per annum. The discount rate reflects a 10.65% nominal interest rate on 10-year Spanish government bonds (which is the risk-free euro interest rate), a beta for the project of 1.1, and an 8.5% equity risk premium:

$$20\% = 10.65\% + (1.1 \times 8.5\%)$$

The discount factor for year k in the future is therefore $1/(1 + 0.20)^k$, and these values are given in Line 6 of Exhibit 15.7. Multiplying these discount factors by the forecasts of free cash flow in Line 5 gives the present values of the free cash flows in Line 7. The sum of these present values plus the terminal value provides the net present value of the project.

Exhibit 15.7 Net Present Value of Project Free Cash Flows for IWPI-Spain

	0	1	2	3	4	5	6	7	8	9	10
					Year in the Future						
1. Earnings after tax (NOPLAT) (Exhibit 15.6, Line 5)		2.51	10.66	13.23	15.94	18.68	21.34	23.80	26.22	28.53	30.68
2. Depreciation (Exhibit 15.4, Line 5)		3.76	3.78	3.80	3.84	3.90	3.96	4.04	4.12	4.23	4.34
3. Change in NWC (Exhibit 15.4, Line 3)	3.20	1.65	6.67	2.16	2.27	2.31	2.26	2.10	2.07	2.00	1.88
4. Capital expenditures (CAPX) (Exhibit 15.4, Line 4)	75.20	4.06	4.35	4.61	4.88	5.18	5.49	5.81	6.16	6.53	6.93
5. Free cash flow (FCF) (Lines 1 + 2 − 3 − 4)	−78.40	0.56	3.42	10.28	12.63	15.09	17.56	19.93	22.11	24.22	26.22
6. Discount factors (@ 20% per annum)	1.00	0.83	0.69	0.58	0.48	0.40	0.33	0.28	0.23	0.19	0.16
7. Present value of FCF (Line 5 × Line 6)	−78.40	0.47	2.38	5.95	6.09	6.07	5.88	5.56	5.14	4.69	4.23
8. Terminal value	32.06										
9. NPV of the project (sum of Line 7 + Line 8)	0.11										

Notes: All numbers except the discount factors are in millions of euros. The terminal value is the discounted value of free cash flow from years 11 to infinity, calculated as a perpetuity growing at the euro rate of inflation of 6%.

Deriving the Terminal Value

The terminal value in Line 8 of Exhibit 15.7 represents the discounted present value of all expected future free cash flows in years 11 and beyond into the indefinite future. The year 0 value of the terminal value is calculated to be €32.06 million. This terminal value is calculated in two steps. First, the terminal value of free cash flow in year 10 is taken to be a perpetuity that is growing at the long-run euro rate of inflation of 6%. The perpetuity must be discounted at 20%, and its starting value in year 11 will be 6% higher than the expected value of the free cash flow in year 10. That is, the terminal value in year 10 is

$$\frac{(€26.22 \text{ million}) \times (1 + 0.06)}{(0.20 - 0.06)} = €198.52 \text{ million}$$

Second, the terminal value in year 10 is discounted to year 0 by dividing by $(1 + 0.20)^{10}$:

$$\text{Terminal value in year 0} = \frac{€198.52 \text{ million}}{(1 + 0.20)^{10}} = €32.06 \text{ million}$$

Notice that IWPI managers forecast a 6% growth rate of free cash flow into the indefinite future, which is the expected euro rate of inflation. This reflects IWPI's assessment that the real demand for its products will be met by the existing Spanish plant and equipment. However, no more than 76,000 units can be produced with this plant and equipment. Thus, free cash flow cannot grow faster than 6% without additional investments being made. We will discuss possible other investments later because IWPI will have growth options.

The last line of Exhibit 15.7 adds the present values of the free cash flows in Line 7 and the terminal value in Line 8 to obtain a net present value of the project that is marginally positive, at €0.11 million. This is the value that an independent all-equity Spanish company that was licensed by IWPI would place on the cash flows coming from IWPI-Spain.

The Parent Company's Perspective

This section considers how the value of a project changes when we take the perspective of the U.S. parent corporation. We first need to adjust for differences in taxes because the U.S. parent will owe U.S. taxes on the dividends it receives, but the parent will also receive some tax credits. More importantly, though, many items that were costs to the subsidiary will provide profit to the parent. This additional profit will substantially enhance the value of the project to the parent. Throughout this section, we will continue to present the analysis in euros, although we note that U.S. taxes must be paid in dollars.

Forecasting the Dividends Received by IWPI-U.S.

We assume that IWPI-Spain will pay all of its free cash flow to its parent company, IWPI-U.S., as a dividend in the year in which the free cash flow arises. The actual amount that IWPI-U.S. receives depends on both Spanish and U.S. tax laws. Exhibit 15.8 demonstrates that IWPI-U.S. will initially receive 10% less than what is paid by IWPI-Spain because the Spanish government imposes a 10% withholding tax on dividends paid by subsidiaries to their parent corporations.

Calculating the U.S. Foreign Tax Credit

Under U.S. tax law, IWPI-U.S. is able to claim a foreign tax credit for the withholding tax that is paid on the international dividends it receives. IWPI-U.S. also receives a tax credit for part or all of the Spanish income tax paid by IWPI-Spain. The proportion of tax credit is determined by the deemed-paid credit, which is discussed shortly. These tax benefits are offset by the income tax liability that IWPI-U.S. incurs to the U.S. tax authorities, who tax the dividends received by IWPI-U.S. from its Spanish subsidiary. Exhibit 15.9 presents the calculations associated with the U.S. foreign tax credit, and Exhibit 15.10 derives the potential U.S. tax liability.

Exhibit 15.8   Dividends Received by IWPI-U.S.

	Year in the Future									
	1	**2**	**3**	**4**	**5**	**6**	**7**	**8**	**9**	**10**
1. Dividend paid to IWPI-U.S. (Exhibit 15.7, Line 5)	0.56	3.42	10.28	12.63	15.09	17.56	19.93	22.11	24.22	26.22
2. Spanish withholding taxes @ 10% (0.10 × Line 1)	0.06	0.34	1.03	1.26	1.51	1.76	1.99	2.21	2.42	2.62
3. After-tax dividend rec'd by IWPI-U.S. (Line 1−Line 2)	0.50	3.08	9.25	11.37	13.58	15.81	17.93	19.89	21.80	23.59

Note: All numbers are in millions of euros.

Exhibit 15.9   Calculation of Foreign Tax Credit for IWPI-U.S.

	Year in the Future									
	1	**2**	**3**	**4**	**5**	**6**	**7**	**8**	**9**	**10**
1. Net income to IWPI-Spain (Exhibit 15.6, Line 5)	2.51	10.66	13.23	15.94	18.68	21.34	23.80	26.22	28.53	30.68
2. Dividend paid by IWPI-Spain (Exhibit 15.8, Line 1)	0.56	3.42	10.28	12.63	15.09	17.56	19.93	22.11	24.22	26.22
3. Income tax paid by IWPI-Spain (Exhibit 15.6, Line 4)	1.35	5.74	7.13	8.58	10.06	11.49	12.82	14.12	15.36	16.52
4. Deemed-paid credit to IWPI-U.S. for income taxes paid by IWPI-Spain ((Line 2/Line 1) × Line 3)	0.30	1.84	5.53	6.80	8.13	9.46	10.73	11.90	13.04	14.12
5. Withholding tax paid (Exhibit 15.8, Line 2)	0.06	0.34	1.03	1.26	1.51	1.76	1.99	2.21	2.42	2.62
6. Total foreign tax credit (Line 4 × Line 5)	0.36	2.18	6.56	8.06	9.64	11.21	12.72	14.11	15.46	16.74

Note: All numbers are in millions of euros.

Exhibit 15.10 Calculation of U.S. Tax Liability of IWPI-U.S.

	Year in the Future									
	1	2	3	4	5	6	7	8	9	10
1. Grossed-up foreign dividend received (Exhibit 15.8, Line 3 + Exhibit 15.9, Line 6)	0.86	5.26	15.81	19.43	23.22	27.02	30.65	34.01	37.26	40.33
2. Tentative U.S. tax liability @ 34% (0.34 × Line 1)	0.29	1.79	5.38	6.61	7.89	9.19	10.42	11.56	12.67	13.71
3. Available foreign tax credit (Exhibit 15.9, Line 6)	0.36	2.18	6.56	8.06	9.64	11.21	12.72	14.11	15.46	16.74
4. Net U.S. tax owed (Line 2 – Line 3, if Line 2 > Line 3)	0.00	0.00	0.00	0.00	0.00	0.00	0.00	0.00	0.00	0.00
5. Excess Foreign tax credit (Line 3 – Line 2, if Line 2 < Line 3)	0.06	0.39	1.19	1.46	1.74	2.03	2.30	2.55	2.79	3.02

Note: All numbers are in millions of euros.

The most important and complicated part of Exhibit 15.9 is the calculation of the deemed-paid credit in Line 4. If the ratio of the dividend paid by IWPI-Spain to the after-tax income of the subsidiary is less than 1, only a fraction of the income tax paid by IWPI-Spain is allowed as a credit against U.S. taxes owed by IWPI-U.S. For example, Line 1 of Exhibit 15.9 shows that the forecast of after-tax income (NOPLAT) of IWPI-Spain in year 1 is €2.51 million. Because of the investments in the change in net working capital and CAPX that IWPI-Spain plans to make in that year, IWPI-Spain will not pay its full after-tax income as a dividend. Line 2 of Exhibit 15.9 records that the forecast of IWPI-Spain's free cash flow is only €0.56 million, and this amount will be paid to the parent as a dividend. Consequently, even though IWPI-Spain is expected to pay €1.35 million in Spanish income taxes, only €0.30 million is allowed currently as a U.S. foreign tax credit because this is the same proportion of the income tax as the income paid by IWPI-Spain to its parent as a dividend:

$$\frac{€0.56 \text{ million}}{€2.51 \text{ million}} \times €1.35 \text{ million} = €0.30 \text{ million}$$

The reason that only €0.30 million of the Spanish tax of €1.35 million is allowed as a foreign tax credit is that the U.S. government recognizes that only that fraction of the income earned by the foreign subsidiary was paid to the parent. The values of these deemed-paid credits are calculated for each year in Line 4 of Exhibit 15.9. The sum of the deemed-paid credit (Line 4) and the dividend withholding tax paid (Line 5) gives the foreign tax credit in Line 6 of Exhibit 15.9.

Calculating the U.S. Income Tax Liability for IWPI-U.S.

Exhibit 15.10 calculates whether IWPI-U.S. will owe additional U.S. income tax on the dividends it receives from IWPI-Spain or whether there will be excess foreign tax credits that can be used to offset the U.S. income tax IWPI-U.S. owes on the income it earns either on this project or on other foreign projects. The analysis begins in Line 1, where we calculate the **grossed-up dividend**, which is the sum of the actual dividend received (Exhibit 15.8, Line 3) plus the foreign tax credit (Exhibit 15.9, Line 6). In year 1, the dividend received after paying the Spanish withholding tax is €0.50 million. The foreign tax credit in year 1 is €0.36 million. Hence, for U.S. tax purposes, the grossed-up dividend is (€0.50 million + €0.36 million) = €0.86 million. Because the U.S. corporate income tax rate is 34%, the U.S. corporate income tax on this amount would be

$$0.34 \times €0.86 \text{ million} = €0.29 \text{ million}$$

Expected values for future years are presented in Line 2 of Exhibit 15.10. If the tentative U.S. tax liability is less than the available foreign tax credit, which was calculated in Exhibit 15.9 and presented in Line 3 of Exhibit 15.10, then no additional U.S. tax is owed. This analysis is evaluated in Line 4. Line 5 of Exhibit 15.10 subtracts the U.S. tax liability from the available foreign tax credit to calculate the excess foreign tax credit. These excess foreign tax credits can be used by IWPI-U.S. to offset U.S. income taxes owed on the foreign income generated from other foreign projects.

Calculating the Net Present Value of After-Tax Dividends Received by IWPI-U.S.

Now, we can calculate the after-tax value of the dividends received by IWPI-U.S. Exhibit 15.11 demonstrates that the present value of after-tax dividends received by IWPI-U.S. is €70.66 million. This is less than the €78.4 million calculated in Exhibit 15.7 as the total year 0 cost of the project. The Spanish withholding tax basically reduces the free cash flow from the project by 10%, and this reduces the value of the project to the parent corporation. If dividends were the only source of value, the project would have a negative net present value and would not be undertaken; but there are additional sources of value from the project to the parent. IWPI-U.S. receives royalty fees and overhead allocation fees that add additional profit and value to the project. The forecasts and valuations of these profits are calculated in Exhibit 15.12.

Forecasting the Royalty and Overhead Allocation Fees

The royalty fee in Line 1 of Exhibit 15.12 is forecast to be 5% of total revenue, which was calculated in Exhibit 15.3. The Spanish government extracts a 10% withholding tax on royalty payments, which is presented in Line 2, in recognition of the fact that the royalty payment is income to the parent, just like a dividend is. The overhead allocation fee in Line 3 of Exhibit 15.12 is also a cost to the subsidiary and a profit to the parent. It is forecast to be 2% of total revenue, and the Spanish government extracts a 14% withholding tax on such payments, as is calculated in Line 4. Line 5 of Exhibit 15.12 calculates the sum of the royalty and overhead fees and subtracts the two withholding taxes. This results in the income forecasts for IWPI-U.S. The tentative U.S. corporate tax liability of 34% is calculated in Line 6, based on the gross of foreign tax royalties and fees received, and Line 7 presents the excess foreign tax credit that is available from Exhibit 15.10. The net U.S. tax owed is calculated in Line 8. IWPI receives a tax credit for the two withholding taxes and can use the excess foreign tax credit from its dividends.

Exhibit 15.11 Net Present Value of After-Tax Dividends for IWPI-U.S.

	Year in the Future										
	0	1	2	3	4	5	6	7	8	9	10
1. After-tax value of dividends to IWPI-U.S. (Exhibit 15.8, Line 3 – Exhibit 15.10, Line 4)		0.50	3.08	9.25	11.37	13.58	15.81	17.93	19.89	21.80	23.59
2. Discount factors (@ 20% per annum)	1.00	0.83	0.69	0.58	0.48	0.40	0.33	0.28	0.23	0.19	0.16
3. Present value of after-tax dividends (Line 1 × Line 2)		0.42	2.14	5.35	5.48	5.46	5.29	5.00	4.63	4.22	3.81
4. Terminal value of dividends	28.85										
5. NPV of after-tax dividends (Sum of Line 3 + Line 4)	70.66										

Notes: All numbers except the discount factors are in millions of euros. The terminal value is the discounted value of dividends from years 11 to infinity, calculated as a perpetuity growing at the euro rate of inflation of 6%.

Exhibit 15.12 Net Present Value of After-Tax Royalty and Overhead Allocation Fees Received by IWPI-U.S.

					Year in the Future						
	0	1	2	3	4	5	6	7	8	9	10
1. Royalty fee @ 5% of total revenue (Exhibit 15.5, Line 3)		2.85	6.77	8.04	9.38	10.73	12.06	13.29	14.51	15.69	16.80
2. Spanish withholding tax @ 10% (0.10 × Line 1)		0.29	0.68	0.80	0.94	1.07	1.21	1.33	1.45	1.57	1.68
3. Overhead fee @ 2% of total revenue (Exhibit 15.5, Line 4)		1.14	2.71	3.22	3.75	4.29	4.82	5.32	5.81	6.28	6.72
4. Spanish withholding taxes @ 14% (0.14 × Line 3)		0.16	0.38	0.45	0.53	0.60	0.68	0.74	0.81	0.88	0.94
5. After-tax fees received by IWPI-U.S. (Line 1 – Line 2 + Line 3 – Line 4)		3.55	8.43	10.00	11.66	13.35	15.00	16.54	18.06	19.52	20.90
6. Tentative U.S. tax liability @ 34% 0.34 × (Line 1 + Line 3)		1.36	3.22	3.83	4.46	5.11	5.74	6.33	6.91	7.47	8.00
7. Excess foreign tax credit from dividends (Exhibit 15.10, Line 5)		0.06	0.39	1.19	1.46	1.74	2.03	2.30	2.55	2.79	3.02
8. Net U.S. tax owed (Line 6 – Line 2 – Line 4 – Line 7)		0.85	1.77	1.39	1.54	1.69	1.83	1.96	2.09	2.23	2.35
9. After-tax value of fees to IWPI-U.S. (Line 5 – Line 8)		2.70	6.65	8.62	10.12	11.66	13.17	14.58	15.96	17.30	18.55
10. Discount factors (@20% per annum)		0.83	0.69	0.58	0.48	0.40	0.33	0.28	0.23	0.19	0.16
11. Present value of after-tax fees (Line 8 × Line 9)		2.25	4.62	4.99	4.88	4.69	4.41	4.07	3.71	3.35	3.00
12. Terminal value of fees	22.68										
13. NPV of after-tax fees (Sum of Line 11 + Line 12)	62.64										

Notes: All numbers except the discount factors are in millions of euros. The terminal value is the discounted value of fees from years 11 to infinity, calculated as a perpetuity growing at the euro rate of inflation of 6%.

For example, in year 2, IWPI-U.S. receives €8.43 million of after-withholding-tax fees, based on €9.48 of gross income. This gross income generates a tentative U.S. tax liability of €3.22 million. But IWPI-U.S. paid withholding taxes of €0.68 million on the royalty and €0.38 million on the overhead, for which it receives foreign tax credits. IWPI-U.S. can also use the €0.39 million of excess foreign tax credits associated with the income tax on its dividends, calculated in Exhibit 15.10, to offset U.S. tax owed. The net result is a tax liability of

$$€3.22 \text{ million} - €0.68 \text{ million} - €0.38 \text{ million} - €0.39 \text{ million} = €1.77 \text{ million}$$

Subtracting the actual U.S. tax liability in Line 8 of Exhibit 15.12 from the after-tax fees received in Line 5 gives the after-tax value of the fees to IWPI-U.S. shown in Line 9. These profits are also discounted at 20% per annum, and the discount factors are again presented in Line 10. Multiplying the expected values in Line 9 by the discount factors in Line 10 gives the present values of the fees in Line 11. The terminal value of the fees for years 11 to the indefinite future discounted to year 0 is calculated just like the terminal value of the free cash flow was calculated in Exhibit 15.7:

$$€22.68 \text{ million} = \frac{€18.55 \text{ million} \times 1.06}{(0.20 - 0.06) \times (1.20)^{10}}$$

The net present value of the fees, which is the sum of the discounted values in Line 11 and the terminal value in Line 12, is €62.64 million.

Forecasting the Profits Earned from Intermediate Goods

Because IWPI-U.S. will sell intermediate goods to IWPI-Spain, there is an additional source of profit in the project for IWPI-U.S. from these exports. Exhibit 15.13 calculates the net present value of the profits on the exports of IWPI-U.S. to IWPI-Spain. Export revenue is calculated in Line 3 as the product of the euro price of exported parts per unit in Line 2 multiplied by the unit sales forecast in Line 1. The profit margin on these export sales is known to be 16%, and this is calculated in Line 4. U.S. corporate income tax on this profit is 34% in Line 5, and the after-tax profits are presented in Line 6. After discounting these expected euro cash flows at 20% and calculating the terminal value as in Exhibit 15.7, the net present value of the profits on export sales is €27.60 million.[9]

Valuing the Financial Side Effects

The next aspect of the parent's valuation of IWPI-Spain involves valuing the financial side effects associated with the project. The Spanish government is offering a subsidized loan, which provides value to the project, and the actual interest payments provide a valuable interest tax shield. Let's begin with the valuation of the tax shield.

Exhibit 15.13   Net Present Value of After-tax Profit on Intermediate Goods Sold by IWPI-U.S. to IWPI-Spain

					Year in the Future						
	0	1	2	3	4	5	6	7	8	9	10
1. Unit sales (Exhibit 15.3, Line 2)		22,000	48,840	54,701	60,171	64,985	68,884	71,639	73,788	75,264	76,017
2. Per-unit price of exported parts (Exhibit 15.5, Line 1.c)		584	625	662	702	744	789	836	886	940	996
3. Export revenue of IWPI-U.S. (Line 1 × Line 2)		12.85	30.52	36.23	42.25	48.36	54.34	59.91	65.41	70.72	75.71
4. Before-tax profit @ 16% margin (0.16 × Line 3)		2.06	4.88	5.80	6.76	7.74	8.69	9.59	10.46	11.31	12.11
5. U.S. corporate tax @ 34% (0.34 × Line 4)		0.70	1.66	1.97	2.30	2.63	2.96	3.26	3.56	3.85	4.12
6. After-tax profit (Line 4 − Line 5)		1.36	3.22	3.83	4.46	5.11	5.74	6.33	6.91	7.47	7.99
7. Discount factors (@ 20% per annum)		0.83	0.69	0.58	0.48	0.40	0.33	0.28	0.23	0.19	0.16
8. Present value of after-tax profits (Line 6 × Line 7)		1.13	2.24	2.21	2.15	2.05	1.92	1.77	1.61	1.45	1.29
9. Terminal value of profits	9.78										
10. NPV of after-tax profits (Sum of Line 8 + Line 9)	27.60										

Notes: All numbers except Lines 1 and 2 and the discount factors are in millions of euros. The terminal value is the discounted value of profits from years 11 to infinity, calculated as a perpetuity growing at the euro rate of inflation of 6%.

---

[9]The terminal value at time 0 of the export sales in years 11 and beyond is $\dfrac{€7.99 \text{ million} \times 1.06}{(0.20 - 0.06) \times (1.20)^{10}} =$ €9.78 million.

Interest Tax Shields

The interest rate on the Spanish government loan is 5% per annum, the principal on the loan is €4 million, and the maturity of the loan is 10 years. Hence, for the next 10 years, IWPI-Spain will make annual interest payments of

$$0.05 \times \text{€4 million} = \text{€0.2 million}$$

These interest payments are valuable because they are tax deductible. Consequently, they increase the value of the project each year by the Spanish tax rate multiplied by the interest payment:

$$0.35 \times \text{€0.2 million} = \text{€0.07 million}$$

If IWPI-Spain is certain that it will make these payments, the payments should be discounted at the Spanish government risk-free interest rate. In a more likely scenario, though, the interest payments would not be risk free because there would be a probability of IWPI-Spain failing and being forced into bankruptcy. If there is a bankruptcy probability, the firm's debt will not be risk free, and the firm will not expect to make the full value of the interest payments.

Suppose that IWPI-U.S. knows from its investment bankers that if it were to issue bonds, it would be able to borrow euros at an interest rate that is 250 basis points above the government risk-free rate of 10.65%. Thus, IWPI-Spain's euro-denominated market interest rate is

$$10.65\% + 2.50\% = 13.15\%$$

The increase in the required interest rate above the government interest rate reflects the market's assessment of possible default by IWPI on its debt.

If the risk of an IWPI default on a loan from the Spanish government is the same as the risk of default on a market loan, then 13.15% is the appropriate rate to discount the interest tax shields. These flows are discounted in Exhibit 15.14, where the net present value of the interest tax shields is found to be €0.38 million. This calculation probably overstates the value of the debt to the corporation because it assumes that the costs of financial distress are 0.

The valuation of interest tax shields in Exhibit 15.14, though, also assumes that IWPI does not plan to add any debt to its capital structure in future years. If IWPI plans to issue additional debt to finance the project, or if it plans to have IWPI-Spain issue additional bonds, after the Spanish government's debt is repaid, there would be additional interest tax shields to value.

Interest Subsidies

In this section, we value the interest subsidy provided by the Spanish government loan. If IWPI had to borrow €4 million at its market interest rate of 13.15% per annum, it would pay

$$0.1315 \times \text{€4 million} = \text{€0.53 million}$$

Exhibit 15.14   Net Present Value of Interest Tax Shields

		Year in the Future									
	0	**1**	**2**	**3**	**4**	**5**	**6**	**7**	**8**	**9**	**10**
1. Tax rate × interest paid		0.07	0.07	0.07	0.07	0.07	0.07	0.07	0.07	0.07	0.07
2. Discount factors (@13.15% per annum)		0.88	0.78	0.69	0.61	0.54	0.48	0.42	0.37	0.33	0.29
3. Present value of interest tax shields (Line 1 × Line 2)		0.06	0.05	0.05	0.04	0.04	0.03	0.03	0.03	0.02	0.02
4. NPV of interest tax shields (Sum of values in Line 3)	0.38										

Note: All numbers except the discount factors are in millions of euros.

in interest payments each year. Because it is borrowing from the Spanish government at 5% per annum, IWPI's actual interest payment is only €0.2 million. Each year, there is an interest savings of

$$€0.53 \text{ million} - €0.2 \text{ million} = €0.33 \text{ million}$$

Exhibit 15.15 provides the valuation of this subsidy. Once again, it is appropriate to discount the interest saving at the firm's market interest rate of 13.15%. The net present value of the interest subsidy is €1.76 million.

The Full ANPV of IWPI-Spain

In Line 5 of Exhibit 15.7, the initial cost of the IWPI-Spain project is €78.4 million. This is the sum of the initial capital expenditures for plant and equipment and the initial investment in cash and inventory. Line 5 of Exhibit 15.11 calculates that the net present value of the after-tax dividends that will be returned to IWPI-U.S. from IWPI-Spain is €70.66 million. Hence, if these dividends were the only source of value to IWPI-U.S., the project would not be viable. But there are additional sources of value.

Line 13 of Exhibit 15.12 calculates the net present value of after-tax royalty and overhead fees as €62.64 million. Line 10 of Exhibit 15.13 calculates the net present value of after-tax profits on the sale of intermediate export goods as €27.60 million. The value of the interest tax shield on the loan from the Spanish government is €0.38 million, and the value of the interest subsidy is €1.76 million. Upon adding together all the costs and benefits of the project, we find

$$
\begin{aligned}
\text{ANPV of IWPI-Spain} = {}& -€78.40 \text{ million in initial costs} \\
& + €70.66 \text{ million from dividends} \\
& + €62.64 \text{ million from royalties and fees} \\
& + €27.60 \text{ million from exports} \\
& + €0.38 \text{ million from the interest tax shield} \\
& + €1.76 \text{ million from the interest subsidy} \\
= {}& €84.64 \text{ million}
\end{aligned}
$$

At the current exchange rate of €1.04/$, the dollar value to IWPI-U.S. of setting up a Spanish subsidiary is

$$(€84.64 \text{ million})/(€1.04/\$) = \$81.38 \text{ million}$$

Exhibit 15.15   Net Present Value of Interest Subsidy

		Year in the Future									
	0	**1**	**2**	**3**	**4**	**5**	**6**	**7**	**8**	**9**	**10**
1. Interest subsidy		0.33	0.33	0.33	0.33	0.33	0.33	0.33	0.33	0.33	0.33
2. Discount factors (@13.15% per annum)		0.88	0.78	0.69	0.61	0.54	0.48	0.42	0.37	0.33	0.29
3. Present value of interest subsidy (Line 1 × Line 2)		0.29	0.25	0.23	0.20	0.18	0.16	0.14	0.12	0.11	0.09
4. NPV of interest subsidy (Sum of values in Line 3)	1.76										

Note: All numbers except the discount factors are in millions of euros.

The initial cost of the project is

$$(\text{€}78.40 \text{ million})/(\text{€}1.04/\$) = \$75.39 \text{ million}$$

Thus, by investing \$75.39 million of its shareholders' wealth, IWPI-U.S. is purchasing a series of uncertain, risky cash flows worth

$$\$75.39 \text{ million} + \$81.38 \text{ million} = \$156.77 \text{ million}$$

This is a good managerial decision unless the opportunity cost of lost export sales is too large.

The Cannibalization of Export Sales

There is one final part of the valuation of IWPI-Spain that involves the possibility that IWPI-U.S. may not have another market for the 40,000 units it is currently exporting to Europe. If it does not have another market, the lost profit on these exports to Europe must be valued as a cost of creating the Spanish manufacturing facility.

Exhibit 15.16 presents the net present value of the after-tax profit on sales of 40,000 units between the current year and the indefinite future. The number of units exported is held constant in Line 1, except in year 1, because it is assumed that IWPI-U.S. is currently exporting its maximum capacity from the New Hampshire manufacturing facility and will not be able to accommodate the growth in European demand. Lost sales in the first year are 18,000 units because the Spanish facility will produce 22,000 units, and total European demand is 44,000. Hence, IWPI-U.S. can export 22,000 units to Europe and will lose only $40,000 - 22,000 = 18,000$ units.

Prices per unit are given in Line 2, and they correspond to the euro prices forecast in Exhibit 15.3, Line 4. Export revenue is given in Line 3. It is the product of the euro price per unit multiplied by the number of units exported. Line 4 presents the profit on these export sales, which is assumed to be a margin of 16%, the same profit margin as on the intermediate

Exhibit 15.16 Net Present Value of After-tax Profit on Lost Export Sales by IWPI-U.S.

					Year in the Future						
	0	**1**	**2**	**3**	**4**	**5**	**6**	**7**	**8**	**9**	**10**
1. Unit export sales		18,000	40,000	40,000	40,000	40,000	40,000	40,000	40,000	40,000	40,000
2. Price per unit (Exhibit 15.3, Line 4)		2,592	2,773	2,940	3,116	3,303	3,501	3,711	3,934	4,170	4,420
3. Export revenue (Line 1 × Line 2)		46.66	110.94	117.59	124.65	132.13	140.06	148.46	157.37	166.81	176.82
4. Before-tax profit @ 16% margin (0.16 × Line 3)		7.46	17.75	18.82	19.94	21.14	22.41	23.75	25.18	26.69	28.29
5. U.S. corporate tax @ 34% (0.34 × Line 4)		2.54	6.04	6.40	6.78	7.19	7.62	8.08	8.56	9.07	9.62
6. After-tax profit (Line 4 – Line 5)		4.93	11.72	12.42	13.16	13.95	14.79	15.68	16.62	17.62	18.67
7. Discount factors (@ 20% per annum)		0.83	0.69	0.58	0.48	0.40	0.33	0.28	0.23	0.19	0.16
8. Present value of after-tax profits (Line 6 × Line 7)		4.11	8.14	7.19	6.35	5.61	4.95	4.38	3.86	3.41	3.02
9. Terminal value of profits	22.83										
10. NPV of after-tax profits (Sum of Line 8 + Line 9)	73.84										

Note: All numbers except Lines 1 and 2 and the discount factors are in millions of euros. The Terminal Value is the discounted value of profits from years 11 to infinity calculated as a perpetuity growing at the euro rate of inflation of 6%.

good exports. Line 5 calculates the IWPI-U.S. corporate income tax liability as 34% of the profits in Line 4. After-tax profits are reported in Line 6. Because these are forecasts of risky euro cash flows, it is again appropriate to discount them at 20% per annum. The discount factors are presented in Line 7.

Multiplying the discount factor by the after-tax profit provides the present values of each of the cash flows in Line 8. Line 9 presents the year 0 value of the terminal value, which is calculated as a perpetuity growing, in this case at 6%, the euro rate of inflation, and discounted at 20%.[10] The sum of the cash flows in Line 8 and the terminal value of lost profits from year 11 to the indefinite future in Line 9 is the net present value of the after-tax profits from lost export sales. In Line 10, we see that the year 0 value of the after-tax profits on all lost sales is €73.84 million.

Because the ANPV of the project without lost export sales was €84.64 million, even if IWPI-U.S. does not have another market for its current exports, it should still establish IWPI-Spain. The value added for shareholders, though, falls to

$$(€84.64 \text{ million} - €73.84 \text{ million}) = €10.80 \text{ million}$$

This is still a very valuable project.

15.7 SUMMARY

In this chapter we develop the Adjusted Net Present Value approach to capital budgeting, and we apply the ANPV approach to value a foreign subsidiary. The important points in the chapter are the following:

1. Capital budgeting is the process by which corporations decide how to allocate funds for investment projects. The basic principal of capital budgeting is that all projects with a positive adjusted net present value (ANPV) should be accepted by the corporation.

2. The first part of an ANPV calculates the net present value (NPV) of the project's cash flows under the scenario in which the project is financed entirely with equity. Any benefits or costs associated with being able to issue debt against the cash flows of the project are valued at a later stage. The project's NPV is the discounted sum of all its expected future revenues minus the discounted sum of its current and expected future costs. The discount rate should reflect the riskiness of the project's free cash flows.

3. The second part of an ANPV analysis adds the net present value of financial side effects (NPVF) that arise from accepting the project. The NPVF arises from the direct costs of issuing securities, from taxes or tax deductions because of the type of financing instrument used, from the costs of financial distress, and from subsidized financing provided by governments.

4. The third part of an ANPV analysis adds in the present value of any growth options that arise from doing the project.

5. Free cash flow is the profit available for distribution to a firm's shareholders. Free cash flow is defined as the after-tax operating earnings of the corporation, plus any non-cash accounting charges, minus investments that the firm must make. These investments involve increases in the firm's net working capital and in its property, plant, and equipment.

6. The pretax operating income that a firm would have if it had no debt is often referred to as EBIT (operating earnings before interest and taxes):

$$\text{EBIT} = \text{Revenue} - \text{Costs of goods sold} \\ - \text{Selling and general administrative} \\ \text{expense} - \text{Depreciation}$$

7. Net operating profit less adjusted taxes (NOPLAT) equals EBIT minus taxes on EBIT.

---

[10]The terminal value at time 0 of the after-tax profits on export sales in years 11 and beyond is taken to be a perpetuity growing at 6% discounted at 20%: $\dfrac{€18.67 \text{ million} \times 1.06}{(0.20 - 0.06) \times (1.20)^{10}} = €22.83 \text{ million}$.

8. The terminal value of a project represents the discounted present value of all expected future free cash flows in the years extending into the indefinite future beyond the explicit forecast horizon of the project. A terminal value can be calculated using perpetuity formulas.

9. If a corporation does not have enough free cash flow to finance a project, it must turn to outside investors for additional resources. The costs of raising funds must be subtracted from the value of the project.

10. When a firm issues debt, the interest payments on the debt are often deductible for tax purposes because the government views the interest as a cost of doing business. Thus, debt financing reduces a corporation's income taxes and increases the value of the corporation. The value of the ability to deduct interest payments for tax purposes is called an interest tax shield.

11. The costs of financial distress refer to the loss of firm value that occurs because the firm may experience bankruptcy. These costs include direct costs due to bankruptcy and indirect costs due to the loss of customers who choose not to purchase the firm's products, problems with suppliers who have no long-term interest in the firm, the inability of the firm to hire and retain high-quality managers and skilled workers, and the poor investment decisions managers may make when the firm faces possible bankruptcy in the future.

12. The value of a subsidized loan is the difference between the interest payments on a loan of the same size at market interest rates and the interest payments on the subsidized loan discounted to the present by the market's required rate of return on the debt.

13. If, when a firm undertakes a project, it obtains an option to do another project in future, the option value of the second project adds value to the first project. In international finance, an important example of such a growth option is the decision to enter a foreign market to sell a firm's products.

14. Because there can be a substantial difference between the cash flows from a project that accrue to the foreign subsidiary versus the cash flows that can ultimately be paid to the parent company, a three-step approach to international capital budgeting is appropriate. The first step involves doing an NPV all-equity cash flow analysis on the foreign subsidiary as if it were an independent all-equity firm, recognizing that the royalty payments, licensing fees, and management fees that the subsidiary must pay the parent are costs to the subsidiary. The second step involves looking at the subsidiary's forecast cash from the parent's perspective, including the withholding taxes on the dividends repatriated to the parent, and then adding back the after-tax value of royalty payments, licensing fees, and management fees paid by the subsidiary, along with any profits on the sale of intermediate goods to the subsidiary. The third step involves adjusting the value of the project for the net present value of the project's financial side effects and growth options.

15. The cannibalization of exports to the market that will be served by the subsidiary can substantially reduce the value of establishing the subsidiary. These lost exports could be from the parent or from another foreign subsidiary in a different country.

QUESTIONS

1. Can an investment project of a foreign subsidiary that has a positive net present value when evaluated as a stand-alone firm ever be rejected by the parent corporation? Assume that the parent accepts all projects with positive adjusted net present values.

2. How do licensing agreements, royalties, and overhead allocation fees affect the value of a foreign project?

3. Why does an adjusted net present value analysis treat the present value of financial side effects as a separate item? Isn't interest expense a legitimate cost of doing business?

4. What is meant by the net present value of the financial side effects of a project?

5. Why is it costly to issue securities?

6. What is an interest tax shield? How do you calculate its value?

7. What is an interest subsidy? How do you calculate its value?

8. What are growth options? Provide an example of one in an international context.

9. What is the difference between EBIT and NOPLAT?

10. Why is it important to understand and manage net working capital?

11. What does CAPX mean, and why is it a firm's engine of growth?

12. Why is it sometimes assumed that CAPX equals depreciation in the later stages of a project?

13. What is the terminal value of a project? How is it calculated?
14. What is meant by the cannibalization of an export market?
15. What are the primary sources of value to IWPI-U.S. in establishing a Spanish subsidiary?
16. Why are the profits on exports of intermediate goods by IWPI-U.S. to IWPI-Spain included as part of the value of the project?
17. What risks are present in the IWPI-Spain project? How do they affect the value of the project?

PROBLEMS

1. What percentage of the adjusted net present value of the IWPI-Spain project arises from cash flows that will occur more than 10 years in the future?
2. How sensitive is the value of IWPI-Spain to the assumed discount rate of 20%? What happens to the value of the project if the rate is 22% instead?
3. What would be the terminal values of the profits from IWPI-Spain if they were expected to grow in real terms at 1% rather than 0%?
4. How much does the value of IWPI-Spain, viewed as a stand-alone firm, change if the royalty fee is increased by 1% and the overhead allocation fee is reduced by 1%? What is the change in value to IWPI-U.S.? What is the source of this change in value?
5. **Valuing Metallwerke's Contract with Safe Air, Inc.**
   Consider the discounted expected value of the 10-year contract that Metallwerke may sign with Safe Air in Chapter 9. In the initial year of the deal, Metallwerke sells an air tank to Safe Air for $400. It costs €696 to produce an air tank. The current exchange rate is €2/$. Assume that 15,000 air tanks will be sold the first year. Make the following other assumptions in your valuation:
   a. The demand for air tanks is expected to grow at 5% for the second year, 4% for the third and fourth years, and 3% for the remaining life of the contract.
   b. Euro-denominated costs are expected to increase at the euro rate of inflation of 2%.
   c. The base dollar price of the air tank will be increased at the U.S. rate of inflation plus one-half of any real depreciation of the dollar relative to the euro, but the base dollar price will be reduced by one-half of any appreciation of the dollar relative to the euro. The U.S. rate of inflation is expected to be 4%.
   d. The dollar is currently not expected to strengthen or weaken in real terms relative to the euro.
   e. The German corporate income tax rate is 50%.
   f. The appropriate euro discount rate for the project is 17%.
   g. Metallwerke typically establishes an account receivable for its customers. At any given time, the stock of the account receivable is expected to equal 10% of a given year's revenue.
   h. Accepting the Safe Air project will not require any major capital expenditures by Metallwerke.
   Can you determine the value of the contract to Metallwerke?

6. **Deli-Delights Inc.**
   Deli-Delights Inc. is a U.S. company that is considering expanding its operations into Japan. The company supplies processed foods to storefront delicatessens in large cities. This requires Deli-Delights to have a centralized production and warehousing facility in each of these cities. Deli-Delights has located a possible site for a Japanese subsidiary in Tokyo. The cost to purchase and equip the facility is ¥765,000,000. Perform an ANPV analysis to determine whether this is a good investment, under the following assumptions:
   a. The average per-unit sales price will initially be ¥400.
   b. First-year sales will be 15 million units, and physical sales will then grow at 10% per annum for the next 3 years, 5% per annum for the 3 years after that, and then stabilize at 3% per annum for the indefinite future.
   c. First-year variable costs of production will be ¥225 per unit of labor and $1.75 per unit of imported semi-finished goods. Administrative costs will be ¥300 million.
   d. Depreciation will be taken on a straight-line basis over 20 years.
   e. Retail prices, labor costs, and administrative expenses are expected to rise at the Japanese yen rate of inflation, which is forecast to be 1%. Dollar prices of semi-finished goods are expected to rise at the U.S. dollar rate of inflation, which is expected to be 4%.

f. The yen/dollar exchange rate is currently ¥85/$, and the yen is expected to appreciate at a rate justified by the expected inflation differential between the yen and dollar rates of inflation.

g. There will be a 4% royalty paid by the Japanese subsidiary to its U.S. parent.

h. The Japanese corporate income tax rate is 37.5%, and there is a 10% withholding tax on dividends and royalty payments.

i. The yen-denominated equity discount rate for the project is 13%.

j. Net working capital will average 6% of total sales revenue.

k. Capital expenditures will offset depreciation.

l. All of the Japanese subsidiary's free cash flow will be paid to the parent as dividends.

m. The corporate income tax rate for the United States is 34%.

n. Deli-Delights Inc. has sufficient other foreign income that will allow it to fully utilize any excess foreign tax credits generated by its Japanese subsidiary.

o. Deli-Delights Inc. does not plan to issue any debt associated with this project.

BIBLIOGRAPHY

Altman, Edward. I., 1984, "A Further Empirical Investigation of the Bankruptcy Cost Question," *Journal of Finance*, pp. 1067–1089.

Brennan, Michael, and Eduardo Schwartz, 1985, "Evaluating Natural Resource Investments," *Journal of Business* 58, pp. 135–157.

Copeland, Tom, Tim Koller, and Jack Murrin, 2000, *Valuation: Measuring and Managing the Value of Companies*, 3rd ed., New York: John Wiley & Sons.

Economist Intelligence Unit, 1993, *The Global Tax Handbook*, London: The Economist Intelligence Unit.

Grenadier, Steven, 2002, "Option Exercise Games: An Application to the Equilibrium Investment Strategies of Firms," *Review of Financial Studies* 15, pp. 691–721.

Jensen, Michael C., 1986, "Agency Costs of Free Cash Flow, Corporate Finance and Takeovers," *American Economic Review* 76, pp. 323-329.

Kalay, Avner, Rajeev Singhal, and Elizabeth Tashjian, 2007, "Is Chapter 11 Costly?" *Journal of Financial Economics* 84, pp. 772–796.

Kester, W. Carl, and Julia Morley, 1992, "Note on Cross-Border Valuation," in W. Carl Kester and Timothy A. Leuhrman, eds., *Case Problems in International Finance*, New York: McGraw-Hill, pp. 49–73.

Kester, W. Carl, March–April 1984, "Today's Options for Tomorrow's Growth," *Harvard Business Revie,* March-April, pp. 153–160.

Kulatilaka, Nalin, and Alan J. Marcus, 1992, "Project Evaluation Under Uncertainty: When Does DCF Fail?" *Journal of Applied Corporate Finance* 5, pp. 92–100.

Lee, Inmoo, Scott Lockhead, Jay Ritter, and Quanshui Zhao, 1996, "The Costs of Raising Capital," *Journal of Financial Research* 1.

Lessard, Donald R., 1985, "Evaluating Foreign Projects: An Adjusted Present Value Approach," in Donald R. Lessard, ed., *International Financial Management*, New York: Wiley.

Myers, Stewart C., 1984, "Finance Theory and Finance Strategy," *Interfaces* 14, pp. 126–137.

Procter & Gamble, 1991. "Procter & Gamble in Brazil," Procter & Gamble case.

Siegel, Daniel, James Smith, and James Paddock, 1987, "Valuing Offshore Oil Properties with Option Pricing Models," *Midland Corporate Finance Journal* 5, 22–30.

White, Michelle J., 1983, "Bankruptcy Costs and the New Bankruptcy Code," *Journal of Finance*, pp. 477–488.

Appendix

Deriving the Value of a Perpetuity

This appendix shows the perpetuity formulas that can be used to calculate the terminal value of a sequence of growing free cash flows. Recall that a perpetuity is an infinite sum. Suppose that the growth rate is g so that each cash flow forecast is g higher than the previous value, that each cash flow is discounted at r, and that we are deriving a terminal value for year 10. Thus, based on the forecast of free cash flow in year 10, which we denote $E_t[FCF(t + 10)]$, we have

Terminal value in year 10 = PV of cash flow in year 11

$$+ \text{ PV of cash flow in year 12}$$
$$+ \text{ PV of cash flow in year 13}$$

$$= \frac{E_t[FCF(t + 10)](1 + g)}{(1 + r)}$$

$$+ \frac{E_t[FCF(t + 10)](1 + g)^2}{(1 + r)^2}$$

$$+ \frac{E_t[FCF(t + 10)](1 + g)^3}{(1 + r)^3} + \ldots$$

To evaluate this infinite sum, define $\lambda = [(1 + g)/(1 + r)]$, and move the common term, $E_t[FCF(t + 10)][(1 + g)/(1 + r)]$, outside the brackets. Then, we have

Terminal value in year 10

$$= \frac{E_t[\text{FCF}(t + 10)](1 + g)}{(1 + r)}[1 + \lambda + \lambda^2 + \ldots]$$

Clearly, for this infinite sum to be a finite number, it must be the case that $\lambda < 1$, which requires that $g < r$. Thus, the growth rate of expected future free cash flows must be less than the discount rate. To evaluate the infinite sum, define the term

$$\text{Sum} = [1 + \lambda + \lambda^2 + \lambda^3 + \ldots]$$

Then, $\lambda\text{Sum} = [\lambda + \lambda^2 + \lambda^3 + \ldots]$, and Sum $-\lambda\text{Sum} = 1$. Therefore, $\text{Sum}(1 - \lambda) = 1$, and Sum $= \frac{1}{(1 - \lambda)}$. After substituting for the infinite sum and for λ, we have

$$\text{Terminal value in year 10} = \frac{E_t[FCF(t + 10)](1 + g)}{(r - g)}$$

Example 15.1 is a simple perpetuity with a constant cash flow every year into the indefinite future discounted at a constant rate. In this special case, the formula tells us to set $g = 0$, $r = 0.20$, and $E_t[FCF(t + 10)] = 264{,}000$ to get $1{,}320{,}000 = 264{,}000 / 0.20$.

Chapter 16

Additional Topics in International Capital Budgeting

*T*his chapter discusses several important topics that extend and complement the basic international capital budgeting analysis presented in Chapter 15. In that chapter, we developed a framework for international capital budgeting using adjusted net present value (ANPV) analysis. In this chapter, we consider two alternative approaches. First, we discuss how to value a project using the weighted average cost of capital (WACC) approach to capital budgeting. Then we examine the flow-to-equity (FTE) approach to capital budgeting, which is a third way of valuing projects. We discuss situations in which firms might prefer to use WACC or FTE, we explore the limitations of the different approaches, and we determine when a WACC or an FTE analysis is equivalent to an ANPV analysis.

International capital budgeting can be done in two basic ways: either by forecasting future foreign currency cash flows and then discounting them with a foreign currency discount rate or by converting the foreign currency cash flows into forecasts denominated in the domestic currency and then discounting them with a domestic currency discount rate. The two values should be the same when expressed in a common currency. However, that doesn't always happen in practice unless the two methods are used with the same implicit assumptions. The chapter then considers a case in which a U.S. parent company must evaluate a request from its Australian subsidiary to renovate its plant and equipment. We use this case to demonstrate how easy it is to get different values with the two methods for discounting foreign currency cash flows and what assumptions are required to ensure that the methods are equivalent.

The chapter next returns to the issue of deriving sensible terminal values for a project or firm. We examine what happens if we assume that competition drives the return on investment equal to the cost of capital.

We also examine how to value tax shields and subsidies on a firm's foreign currency loans, and we analyze a case in which a firm must choose between several different subsidized borrowing opportunities denominated in different currencies. The chapter discusses how the presence of outstanding debt can lead to conflicts of interest between the company's bondholders and stockholders. Finally, we briefly note that international differences in accounting standards must be taken into account when valuing corporations in different countries.

Chapter 15 reviewed some of the basic principles of international capital budgeting and project evaluation. We emphasized the importance of estimating the correct cash flows. We also advocated using the ANPV approach to value foreign projects.

The ANPV Approach

In the ANPV analysis, we first find the value of the unlevered, or all-equity, firm or project (which in this chapter we refer to as V_U) by discounting the expected value of the free cash flows. The discount rate was the appropriate risk-adjusted required rate of return on the assets of the firm, r_A, or the rate of return on the assets associated with the project. Then, we explored sources of additional value from the net present value of financial side effects and from the value of growth options. Adding these various sources of value gives the value of the levered firm or project (which we call V_L).

Two Valuation Alternatives to ANPV

The two alternative approaches to capital budgeting are the **weighted average cost of capital (WACC)** approach and the **flow-to-equity (FTE)** approach. When properly used, the three approaches are equivalent. We introduced the ANPV approach first because we like the way it identifies the economic sources of value. Nevertheless, the WACC approach is probably the most widely used approach, and there are some times when the FTE approach is most easily calculated. Hence, it is important to understand all three approaches, as well as their limitations.

The WACC approach to capital budgeting involves forecasting the all-equity free cash flows and then finding the value of the levered firm by discounting the all-equity free cash flows at an appropriate WACC. This is denoted r_{WACC}, and it is the weighted sum of the after-tax required rate of return on the firm's debt, r_D, and the required rate of return on the firm's equity, r_E. The market value of the equity is then found by subtracting the market value of the debt from the value of the levered firm.

The FTE approach finds the value of the equity directly by discounting the forecasts of the flows to equity holders at the appropriate risk-adjusted required rate of return on the equity, r_E. Then the value of the levered firm can be found by adding the value of the debt to the value of the equity.

The WACC Approach to Capital Budgeting

The WACC approach is a one-step method that works well for projects that have stable debt–equity ratios. An important point to remember about WACC is that if it is used for international projects, the weights should be specific to the international project and not to the overall firm. Unfortunately, some firms mistakenly use the same weighted average cost of capital (r_{WACC}) as the discount rate in all their capital budgeting decisions. To understand the logical foundations of WACC and its potential pitfalls, let's examine the derivation of r_{WACC} and how it can be used to value a firm.

The WACC Without Taxes

Consider the value of a firm that has assets that are expected to yield cash flows of Y per year in perpetuity. If the riskiness of these cash flows dictates that they be discounted at r_A, we know from our ANPV analysis of Chapter 15 that the value of the unlevered firm is

$$V_U = \frac{Y}{(1 + r_A)} + \frac{Y}{(1 + r_A)^2} + \frac{Y}{(1 + r_A)^3} + \frac{Y}{(1 + r_A)^4} + \ldots = \frac{Y}{r_A} \qquad \textbf{(16.1)}$$

If the firm has no debt, the value of the equity, E, must be equal to the value of the unlevered firm, V_U.

Now, suppose that the firm issues some debt. The seminal insight provided by Nobel Prize winners Franco Modigliani and Merton Miller (1958, 1961) in this regard is that in the absence of taxes, the presence of debt cannot change the value of the firm. Hence, without taxes, the value of the levered firm, V_L, equals the value of the unlevered firm. In other words, issuing debt does not create wealth—it merely transfers cash flows from the stockholders to the bondholders. If D represents the market value of the firm's debt, and if E_L represents the market value of the firm's levered equity, then because all of the firm's cash flows must go to either the debt holders or the stockholders, we know that the value of the debt plus the value of the equity must be the value of the firm:

$$V_L = D + E_L \qquad \textbf{(16.2)}$$

We also know that the income of the firm must be paid to either the debt holders or the stockholders.[1] Thus, for a firm with income of Y, we have

$$Y = r_A V_L = r_D D + r_E E_L \qquad \textbf{(16.3)}$$

Let the fraction of the value of the firm that is financed by debt be D/V_L, and let the fraction of the value of the firm that is financed with equity be E_L/V_L. Then, if we divide Equation (16.3) by the value of the levered firm, V_L, we find that the return on the assets of the firm must be split into a proportion that goes to the debt holders and a proportion that goes to the stockholders:

$$r_A = \frac{D}{V_L} r_D + \frac{E_L}{V_L} r_E \qquad \textbf{(16.4)}$$

Equation (16.4) indicates that the return on the firm's assets is a weighted average of the return on the firm's debt and the return on the firm's equity. The weights reflect the percentages of the valuation of the firm that are financed with debt and equity. Essentially, investors view the firm as a portfolio of assets, with the return on the assets of the firm as the overall portfolio return and the debt and equity as the individual investments. Without taxes, the weighted average cost of capital, r_{WACC}, is the same as the rate of return on the assets of the firm, r_A.

As the firm changes its leverage, the rate of return on its assets remains constant. Because stockholders get paid only after the bondholders are paid, changing the firm's leverage changes the required rate of return on the equity. We can understand this relation by solving Equation (16.4) for r_E:

$$r_E = \frac{V_L}{E_L} r_A - \frac{D}{E_L} r_D = \frac{E_L + D}{E_L} r_A - \frac{D}{E_L} r_D = r_A + \frac{D}{E_L} [r_A - r_D] \qquad \textbf{(16.5)}$$

Equation (16.5) indicates that the higher the leverage ratio, D/E_L, the higher the required rate of return on the firm's equity. This makes sense because as the firm issues more debt, less of the firm's cash flow is available to pay the stockholders, which makes their position more risky.

The WACC with Taxes

When interest payments can be deducted from a firm's taxes, the firm must only make the after-tax interest payments on its debts. In this situation, as we saw in Chapter 15, issuing debt adds value to the firm. Let the corporate tax rate be τ, and let r_D be the market interest rate on

---

[1]We are discussing payouts of the firm's income as if the firm pays all free cash flow immediately. If a firm retains earnings over and above its investments in capital expenditures and the change in net working capital, the firm must invest those earnings appropriately, or it will destroy value.

the firm's debt. Then, because interest payments are tax deductible to the corporation, the after-tax required rate of return on the firm's debt is $(1 - \tau)r_D$. We will also let Y represent the after-tax cash flow of the firm, in which case the value of the unlevered firm is unchanged.

Assume that the firm issues an amount of debt to finance the project equal to D and assume that this debt will be perpetually outstanding. Then, from our ANPV analysis in Chapter 15, the present value of the interest tax shield is the discounted sum of the perpetual interest deduction,

$$\frac{\tau r_D D}{(1 + r_D)} + \frac{\tau r_D D}{(1 + r_D)^2} + \frac{\tau r_D D}{(1 + r_D)^3} + \ldots = \frac{\tau r_D D}{r_D} = \tau D \tag{16.6}$$

The ANPV of the levered firm is the value of the unlevered firm plus the value of the interest tax shield:

$$V_L = V_U + \tau D \tag{16.7}$$

Now, as before, the cash flows of the firm must be split between the debt holders and the stockholders, but only the after-tax interest is required to be paid:

$$Y = r_D(1 - \tau)D + r_E E_L \tag{16.8}$$

The weighted average cost of capital, r_{WACC}, is defined as the discount rate that sets the value of the levered firm equal to the discounted present value of the expected, after-tax, all-equity cash flows. For a firm that has a perpetual expected after-tax income of Y, we have

$$V_L = \frac{Y}{r_{WACC}} \tag{16.9}$$

If we solve Equation (16.9) for $Y = r_{WACC}V_L$ and then substitute this result for Y in Equation (16.8), and finally divide by V_L, we find the value of the WACC:

$$r_{WACC} = \frac{D}{V_L}(1 - \tau)r_D + \frac{E_L}{V_L}r_E \tag{16.10}$$

Equation (16.10) states that the firm's WACC is the weighted sum of the after-tax required rate of return on the firm's debt and the required rate of return on the firm's equity.

Why r_{WACC} Must Be Less Than r_A

Notice that the weighted average cost of capital, r_{WACC}, is necessarily less than the rate of return on a firm's assets, r_A, because the value of the levered firm, $V_L = Y/r_{WACC}$, is larger than the value of the unlevered firm, $V_U = Y/r_A$. This insight is important in capital budgeting because in both the ANPV and WACC analyses, the all-equity cash flows are in the numerator. The value of financial side effects is added separately in an ANPV analysis, whereas the WACC analysis includes them in one step.

Why Use WACC?

To understand the intuition for using r_{WACC} as the discount rate for a firm's expected all-equity free cash flows in capital budgeting analyses, consider an example. Suppose a firm has a potential project that provides an expected constant infinite stream of income in each future period. Let the expected value of the annual after-tax cash flow from the project be Y, and let the funds needed to undertake this investment project be I. Now, suppose that the fraction D/V_L of the financing for the project will be done with debt, and the fraction E_L/V_L of the financing for the project will be done with equity.

Some of the income from the project must first be paid to the bondholders to provide the required rate of return on the firm's debt, but the firm only loses the after-tax value of the interest payments because interest is tax deductible:

$$\text{Income paid to bondholders} = r_D(1 - \tau) \times (\text{Value of debt in the project})$$
$$= r_D(1 - \tau) \times (D/V_L)I$$

The rest of the income from the project is paid to the stockholders and provides the return on the firm's equity.[2] If this income is just what the stockholders expected to receive and is equal to their risk-adjusted required rate of return, then

$$\text{Income paid to stockholders} = r_E \times (\text{Value of equity in the project}) = r_E \times (E_L/V_L)I$$

From the perspective of the firm, adding the income paid to the bondholders and the income paid to the stockholders exhausts the income from the project:

$$\text{Income from project} = [r_D(1 - \tau)(D/V_L) + r_E(E_L/V_L)]I = r_{\text{WACC}}\, I \qquad \textbf{(16.11)}$$

Now, recognize that a project is a zero net present value investment if the income from the project, Y, just equals the weighted average of the required returns to the firm's bondholders and stockholders, $r_{\text{WACC}}\, I$. If $Y = r_{\text{WACC}}\, I$, the net present value of the project when discounted at r_{WACC} is 0,

$$\text{NPV} = \frac{Y}{r_{\text{WACC}}} - I = 0$$

If the rate of return on the project provides more expected income than $(r_{\text{WACC}}\, I)$, the project's rate of return is larger than r_{WACC}, and the project is positive NPV. If the project's rate of return is smaller than r_{WACC}, the project is not a positive NPV project and should not be done.

Example 16.1   WACC Valuation of Teikiko Printing Co.

Suppose that the Teikiko Printing Co. is considering an investment of ¥20 billion in a modernization project. Assume that the company's stockholders require a 20% rate of return, that the company's bondholders require a 7% rate of return, that the Japanese corporate tax rate is 35%, and that 45% of the project will be financed by debt and 55% will be financed with equity.

The previous analysis has equipped us to answer two questions:

- What is Teikiko Printing's WACC?
- What perpetual annual income must the project generate if the project is to be viable, in the sense of being at least a zero net present value investment?

From Equation (16.10), we find that Teikiko Printing's WACC is

$$r_{\text{WACC}} = [0.45 \times (1 - 0.35) \times 0.07] + [0.55 \times 0.20] = 0.1305$$

or 13.05%.

---

[2]We are intentionally ignoring the possibility of reinvestment of earnings in the firm. This makes no difference as long as the reinvested earnings are invested in zero NPV projects.

From Equation (16.7), we see that if Teikiko Printing is going to be able to provide the required compensation to its bondholders and its stockholders, the annual income from the project must be

$$0.1305 \times ¥20 \text{ billion} = ¥2.61 \text{ billion}$$

In this case, the project has a zero net present value because the value of the project, which is the perpetual income divided by the WACC, is equal to the cost of the project:

$$\frac{¥2.61 \text{ billion}}{0.1305} = ¥20 \text{ billion}$$

Only if Teikiko's project is expected to generate at least ¥2.61 billion per year should Teikiko invest in it.

Deriving r_A from r_D and r_E

One of the reasons that people like the WACC approach to capital budgeting is that it uses the rates of return on traded securities, the debt and equity shares of the firm. In contrast, the ANPV analysis requires using the rate of return on the firm's underlying assets. In order to derive the required rate of return on the firm's assets, we begin by equating the two values of the levered firm in Equations (16.2) and (16.7):

$$E_L + D = V_L = V_U + \tau D \tag{16.12}$$

The value of the equity plus the value of the debt must equal the value of the levered firm, which is the value of the unlevered firm plus the interest tax shield. By rearranging Equation (16.12), we find

$$V_U = E_L + [(1 - \tau)D] \tag{16.13}$$

Because $Y = r_A V_U$ and because the income must be distributed to the bondholders and the stockholders as in Equation (16.8), we can use Equation (16.13) to derive

$$r_A\{E_L + [(1 - \tau)D]\} = [r_D(1 - \tau)D] + [r_E E_L] \tag{16.14}$$

By solving Equation (16.14) for r_A, we find

$$r_A = \frac{D}{[E_L + (1 - \tau)D]}(1 - \tau)r_D + \frac{E_L}{[E_L + (1 - \tau)D]}r_E \tag{16.15}$$

Once again, the return on the assets of the firm can be thought of as a weighted average of the return on the firm's debt and the return on the firm's equity. The denominator of the weights is the value of the unlevered firm. The weight on the after-tax cost of debt is the ratio of debt to the unlevered-firm value, and the weight on the required rate of return on equity is the ratio of the market value of equity to the unlevered-firm value. If the firm has accurate estimates of the required rate of return on its levered equity, r_E, and the required rate of return on its debt, r_D, then Equation (16.15) provides the required rate of return on the assets in the ANPV analysis.

Equation (16.15) can also be solved for r_E to get

$$r_E = r_A + \frac{(1 - \tau)D}{E_L}(r_A - r_D) \tag{16.16}$$

Because $r_A > r_D$, Equation (16.16) indicates how leverage increases the required rate of return on the equity of the firm above the required rate of return on the assets of the firm in the presence of an interest deduction for corporate income tax.

Example 16.2 ANPV Valuation of Teikiko Printing

In Example 16.1 we found that the WACC for Teikiko Printing Co. was 13.05% when the required rate of return on its debt was 7% and the required rate of return on its equity was 20%. The WACC analysis told us that the project was zero NPV. Hence, the value of the project was equal to the cost of the project, or ¥20 billion. Now, let's use an ANPV analysis to check our logic.

Because the value of the debt is 45% of the value of the project, the outstanding debt is

$$0.45 \times ¥20 \text{ billion} = ¥9 \text{ billion}$$

and the value of the equity is

$$¥20 \text{ billion} - ¥9 \text{ billion} = ¥11 \text{ billion}$$

From Equation (16.16), we can calculate the required rate of return on the project's assets as if it were an all-equity firm:

$$r_A = \frac{¥9}{¥11 + [(1 - 0.35)¥9]}(1 - 0.35)0.07 + \frac{¥11}{¥11 + [(1 - 0.35)¥9]}0.20$$
$$= 0.1549$$

or 15.49%. Now, we can do an ANPV analysis of the project to check that the value of the levered project is ¥20 billion. Recall from Example 16.1 that the annual after-tax income from Teikiko Printing's project is ¥2.61 billion. Then, from Equation (16.7), the adjusted net present value of the project is the sum of the discounted value of the perpetual income discounted at the rate of return on assets plus the value of the interest tax shield:

$$\frac{¥2.61 \text{ billion}}{0.1549} + (0.35 \times ¥9 \text{ billion}) = ¥20 \text{ billion}$$

Because this is the cost of the project, the project has a zero ANPV. Notice that the ANPV analysis and the WACC analysis give the same answer.

Pros and Cons of Using WACC

The derivation of r_{WACC} presupposes that the project will perpetually provide the expected level of cash flows. It also assumes that the firm continuously monitors the value of its debt and adjusts the debt to keep the ratio of debt to total firm value, D/V_L, constant (see James Miles and John Ezzel 1980). However, using a constant r_{WACC} in some situations is incorrect and leads to valuation mistakes. For example, you should not use a constant r_{WACC} if the project's leverage is changing, which is often the case in leveraged buyouts, for example.[3] Equation (16.16) indicates that changing leverage changes the required return on the

---

[3]In a leveraged buyout (LBO), a firm is converted from a publicly traded corporation into a private corporation. The purchasers of the outstanding equity often use large amounts of debt, which they plan on paying down over time.

firm's equity, which in turn changes the WACC. In situations of changing leverage, it is better to assume that the rate of return on the firm's assets is constant rather than the return on the WACC.

In the ANPV analysis in Chapter 15, we clearly stated that the discount rate is a project-specific concept. Similarly, in international capital budgeting using a WACC analysis, the cost of capital should be specific to the international project. Using the same WACC for all projects is particularly troublesome for international capital budgeting applications in which foreign currency cash flows are converted into domestic currency and then discounted with a domestic currency discount rate. The nature of cash flow uncertainty when operating in a foreign country, along with the uncertainty of foreign exchange rate changes, can alter the riskiness of the cash flows. As a result, the riskiness of foreign cash flows can be different from the riskiness of domestic cash flows, even if the two projects are similar.

The Flow-to-Equity Method of Capital Budgeting

The third approach to capital budgeting is the flow-to-equity (FTE) method. This approach to capital budgeting is based on the fact that the equity value of a firm is the present discounted value of the expected cash flows to stockholders, discounted at the required rate of return on the equity, r_E. In our analysis, we treated Y as the value of the perpetual after-tax cash flow to the all-equity firm. If the firm has perpetual debt of D, the stockholders do not receive Y each period. The stockholders must first pay the interest on the debt, but they can deduct the interest payments and pay less in taxes. Thus, the stockholders can expect to receive $Y - (1 - \tau)r_D D$ each period.

The value of the levered equity in the firm must therefore be the value of expecting to receive $Y - (1 - \tau)r_D D$ each period, discounted at the required rate of return on the equity:

$$E_L = \frac{Y - (1 - \tau)r_D D}{(1 + r_E)^1} + \frac{Y - (1 - \tau)r_D D}{(1 + r_E)^2} + \frac{Y - (1 - \tau)r_D D}{(1 + r_E)^3} + \cdots$$

$$= \frac{Y - (1 - \tau)r_D D}{r_E} \tag{16.17}$$

The Equivalence of FTE to Other Approaches

For the firm with perpetual cash flows that we've been discussing in this chapter, it is straightforward to demonstrate that the FTE approach to capital budgeting is equivalent to the WACC approach. If it is, then $E_L + D = V_L = Y/r_{WACC}$. Let's assume that this is true and confirm that we can produce the same WACC. We begin by rearranging Equation (16.17) by multiplying both sides by r_E and moving the debt terms to the other side:

$$Y = r_E E_L + (1 - \tau)\, r_D\, D \tag{16.18}$$

Dividing on both sides of Equation (16.18) by the value of the levered firm, V_L, we find

$$\frac{Y}{V_L} = \frac{r_E E_L + (1 - \tau)r_D\, D}{V_L} = r_{WACC} \tag{16.19}$$

Thus, by assuming that the levered firm value is the same in the two cases, we have demonstrated that we produce the same value of r_{WACC}. Thus, the equity value derived from the FTE method is consistent with the equity value found in the WACC analysis.

Example 16.3 Flow-to-Equity Valuation of Teikiko Printing Co.

Let's find the equity value of the Teikiko Printing Co. from the previous examples, using the flow-to-equity method of valuation. As a reminder, we previously found that the project was zero net present value and cost ¥20 billion. We also calculated that the expected annual after-tax income to the all-equity firm was ¥2.61 billion. The firm is going to issue ¥9 billion of debt at an interest rate of 7%, and the required rate of return on the firm's levered equity is 20%. If the debt is ¥9 billion, then the equity should be ¥11 billion. With this information, what is the value of the levered equity from the FTE approach?

Because the corporate tax rate is 35%, the expected annual after-tax income to the stockholders of the firm is

$$\text{¥2.61 billion} - (1 - 0.35) \times .07 \times \text{¥9 billion} = \text{¥2.20 billion}$$

This income is expected to be paid in every future period into perpetuity. We find the discounted present value of the cash flows to stockholders by dividing by the required rate of return on the equity:

$$\frac{\text{¥2.20 billion}}{0.20} = \text{¥11 billion}$$

Thus, the FTE approach to capital budgeting tells us that the equity of the Teikiko Printing Co. is worth ¥11 billion. This is the amount of money that the stockholders would have to contribute to the project because they can borrow ¥9 billion. Because the cost of the project to the stockholders is equal to the value of the project to the stockholders, the project has a zero net present value.

The Pros and Cons of Alternative Capital Budgeting Methods

In Chapter 15 and the first part of this chapter, we have presented three methods for doing capital budgeting: the adjusted net present value (ANPV), the weighted average cost of capital (WACC), and the flow-to-equity (FTE) methods. If used appropriately, the three methods give the same present value of a project.

We stressed the ANPV approach because it categorizes the sources of value and thus lets a manager make an informed decision about the economic profitability of a project versus other sources of value coming from financing and growth. The ANPV approach also provides a great way to discuss risk management and the desirability of hedging foreign exchange risk, which we do in Chapter 17. In addition, the ANPV approach works well for international projects, such as the project being considered by International Wood Products, Inc. (discussed in Chapter 15), in which the firm knows the level of debt. It is also straightforward to value subsidized financing, which is often missed in a WACC analysis. Sometimes, though, the other approaches are easier to use.

The ANPV approach assumes that the manager knows the level of debt in future periods. If, instead, managers are planning to keep the debt–equity ratio constant, as is assumed in the WACC approach, then calculating an ANPV is problematic because the amount of debt depends on the amount of equity and vice versa. Conversely, if the level of debt is going to be changing over time because the firm has subsidized debt that will not be replaced, for example, then the leveraged equity required rate of return, r_E, will be changing, even if the risk-adjusted rate of return on the assets of the firm, r_A, is constant. With changing future values of r_E, both WACC and FTE are difficult to apply. ANPV works best in such situations. Because each of the three methods works well in different situations, it is important to have them all in your toolkit.

16.2 FORECASTING CASH FLOWS OF FOREIGN PROJECTS

The Choice of Currency

Generally, a significant part of the revenue earned by international projects is denominated in foreign currencies because the products produced by the projects are often sold in several countries around the world. Multinational corporations also typically have costs that are denominated in foreign currencies because they source raw materials and intermediate goods in a global market.

Because an international project's cash flows are denominated in different currencies, the first decision in an international valuation is whether to do the valuation using forecasts denominated in a foreign currency or in the domestic currency. Later in the chapter, an extended case demonstrates how international capital budgeting can be done in either currency. We also examine what it takes for the two approaches to result in the same domestic currency value.

Forecasting Cash Flows in the Foreign Currency

As discussed in Chapter 15, we can use a straightforward approach to find the value of a foreign project by forecasting the future foreign currency cash flows and discounting them to the present, using an appropriate foreign currency discount rate. The current value of the foreign project in domestic currency is then determined by multiplying the present value denominated in the foreign currency by the current spot exchange rate between the two currencies. One problem with this approach is that it is sometimes difficult to determine the appropriate foreign currency discount rate.

Forecasting Cash Flows in Domestic Currency

The second way to determine the value of a foreign project is to forecast the foreign currency value of the cash flows and then multiply them by the corresponding forecasts of future exchange rates. The result is a measure of the expected future domestic currency value of the foreign cash flows. Then, using an appropriate domestic currency discount rate to take the present values gives the current value of the foreign project in domestic currency.

Reconciling the Two Methods for Discounting Foreign Cash Flows

To see the equivalence of the two methods for discounting foreign cash flows, let $X(t+k)$ be the foreign currency cash flow at time $t+k$, which is k years in the future, and let $S(t+k)$ be the exchange rate of domestic currency per unit of foreign currency at time $t+k$. Then, $E_t[X(t+k)]$ is the forecast, or expected value of the future foreign currency cash flow, and $E_t[S(t+k)]$ is the forecast, or expected value, of the future exchange rate. Let $r(\text{FC},k)$ and $r(\text{DC},k)$ be the appropriate risk-adjusted discount rates in the foreign currency and domestic currency, respectively, that are used to discount the expected cash flows generated in year $t+k$ back to year t.

Present Value in Domestic Currency from Forecasts of Foreign Currency

Using the first method for discounting foreign cash flows, we first calculate the foreign currency denominated present value of the future cash flow, which is $\dfrac{E_t[X(t+k)]}{[1+r(\text{FC},k)]^k}$. We can convert this into domestic currency by multiplying by $S(t)$. Hence, the domestic currency denominated present value of the future foreign currency cash flow is $\dfrac{S(t)E_t[X(t+k)]}{[1+r(\text{FC},k)]^k}$.

Present Value in Domestic Currency from Forecasts of Domestic Currency

The second method for discounting foreign cash flows is based on using a domestic currency forecast of the future foreign currency cash flows and then applying a home currency discount rate. You can think of this as directly forecasting the product of the exchange rate and the foreign currency cash flow, $E_t[S(t+k)X(t+k)]$, and then using a home currency discount rate. As a practical matter, no one does this. Instead, we first calculate the foreign currency forecasts and then multiply by the forecasts of the exchange rate, $E_t[S(t+k)]E_t[X(t+k)]$, to get the domestic currency value of the future cash flows. We then take the present value using the domestic currency discount rate, $r(\text{DC},k)$. Thus, the domestic currency denominated present value of the future foreign currency cash flow using the second method is $\dfrac{E_t[S(t+k)]E_t[X(t+k)]}{[1+r(\text{DC},k)]^k}$.[4]

Equating the Two Methods of Forecasting

Equating the two methods of discounting the value of future foreign currency cash flows gives

$$\frac{S(t)E_t[X(t+k)]}{[1 + r(\text{FC},k)]^k} = \frac{E_t[S(t+k)]E_t[X(t+k)]}{[1 + r(\text{DC},k)]^k} \tag{16.20}$$

Simplifying Equation (16.20) by dividing both sides by the expected foreign currency cash flow and the current exchange rate and multiplying both sides by 1 plus the discount factors raised to the k power gives

$$[1 + r(\text{DC},k)]^k = [1 + r(\text{FC},k)]^k \frac{E_t[S(t+k)]}{S(t)} \tag{16.21}$$

Equation (16.21) indicates that the two approaches are the same when the discount rates satisfy a parity condition exactly like uncovered interest rate parity, which is discussed in Chapter 7.

It is important to notice that the discount rates will usually be different for different time periods. We know that unless the term structures of interest rates in the two currencies are flat, the expected rate of appreciation will be different for different periods. Therefore, if the discount rate is constant in one currency, it cannot be constant in the other.

The next section examines the valuation of a foreign project using the two methods. We consider an international capital budgeting case in which expected changes in real exchange rates play a role in the valuation of a foreign project.

---

[4]If you are forecasting the product of the exchange rate and the foreign currency cash flow, the domestic currency discount rate is slightly different unless the exchange rate and the foreign currency cash flow are uncorrelated.

16.3 CASE STUDY: CMTC'S AUSTRALIAN PROJECT

It was early Friday evening in St. Louis, Missouri, and Donna Elichalt was still staring at her computer screen. Donna had recently been promoted from financial analyst to assistant treasurer for international operations of the Consolidated Machine Tool Company (CMTC). CMTC was founded in St. Louis in 1972 and had grown rapidly through a series of acquisitions. It now had international manufacturing operations in seven countries and sold its machine tools in 39 countries.

Elichalt had been looking forward to spending the weekend away from the office, but CMTC's chief financial officer had scheduled a capital budgeting meeting for Monday. Now, it was beginning to look as though she would be at the office all night, trying to decide whether to recommend approving a capital budgeting request from CMTC's Australian subsidiary. The project was the largest request that she had analyzed to date in her career with the company.

The Australian Investment Proposal

CMTC's Australian plant manager, Rod Wickens, had recently submitted a proposal to spend 41.1 million Australian dollars to reengineer his plant with new robotics and other computerized machinery. At the current exchange rate of AUD1.42/USD, the request was for USD28.94 million. Such an expenditure would severely cut into the free cash flow of the Australian subsidiary and would eliminate any possibility of a dividend from Australia this year.

In his proposal, Wickens indicated that the investment in new equipment promised significant cost savings in the future. He also argued that the project's cost would be partially offset by the sale of old equipment for AUD11.83 million.

Elichalt had met Wickens on several occasions, and while she thought Wickens probably ran a tight ship on the production lines, she wasn't sure that he really understood the importance of a proper discounted expected cash flow analysis of investment projects. Wickens usually wanted to do any project that lowered his future costs, especially if the payback on the project was within 5 years. He often justified this attitude with statements such as "CMTC can't be profitable if our costs are higher than our competitors' costs."

The Australian plant was not CMTC's oldest plant, but it was one of its first international operations. Elichalt also knew that CMTC's upper management planned to close the Australian plant in 10 years, when it would expand CMTC's operations in China. Chinese labor costs were less than one-tenth of Australian labor costs, and the Australian plant was now exporting over one-fourth of its output to China. As China's demand for machine tools grew, Elichalt knew that more and more of the Australian plant's output would be exported there. Elichalt consequently knew that only 10 years of expected cash flows from the Australian plant would need to be considered in any discounted cash flow analysis.

Details of the Project

In his memorandum outlining the proposed reengineering of the plant, Wickens indicated that the current Australian dollar costs of production were running at AUD45.38 million per year. He argued that Australian dollar costs of production would probably increase at the Australian rate of inflation for the next 5 years. He also noted that costs were likely to increase 1% faster than the Australian rate of inflation for the remaining life of the plant due to the increased cost of maintaining old equipment. On the other hand, Wickens argued that after the reengineering of the plant, manufacturing costs could be expected to be just 90% of the old costs in the first year, 85% in the second year, and 80% in the remaining years of the plant's existence. Although Elichalt knew that production costs at the Australian plant were high relative to other locations in the Pacific Rim, she wondered if such expected cost savings could justify the large initial expenditure associated with the project.

Because Wickens had not provided any explicit future cash flows projections, Elichalt knew that her first job was to forecast the after-tax Australian dollar cash flows of the project. She then needed to discount these expected cash flows to the present, using an appropriate discount factor. She wasn't sure whether to discount the expected cash flows in Australian dollars or to first convert the expected cash flows into U.S. dollars. If she wanted to discount the cash flows in U.S. dollars, she would need forecasts of future exchange rates, whereas if she discounted them in Australian dollars, she would just have to get the Australian dollar discount rate right.

Gathering the Economic Data

To begin her analysis, Elichalt had placed a call to the economic forecasting group at Golder Sax, an investment bank, to get some interest rate data and some forecasts of inflation rates for Australia and the United States. Elichalt's contact at Golder Sax easily provided both U.S. dollar interest rates and Australian dollar interest rates, and this information is in Exhibit 16.1.

The economic analyst indicated that the term structures of interest rates referred to the spot interest rates in each currency. The term structures represent the pure discount bond yields in the respective currencies.[5] Exhibit 16.2 presents a graph of the two term structures of interest rates.

The analyst indicated that the year-by-year forecasts of Australian dollar inflation and U.S. dollar inflation included in Exhibit 16.1 were generated by Golder Sax's proprietary econometric forecasting model. The analyst assured Elichalt that these inflation forecasts were quite close to the consensus forecasts of most business economists.

Expected 1-Year Real Interest Rates

The Golder Sax analyst included year-by-year expected real interest rates for each currency. These real interest rates are calculated from the known market-determined nominal interest rates for different maturities and the forecasts of future inflation rates to reflect the expected real return on a one-period investment that begins a number of periods in the future.

The Golder Sax analyst included a derivation of the 1-year real interest rates, $r^e(t,k)$, $k = 1 \ldots 10$, that are expected to prevail k years in the future. Let $i(t,k)$ be the k-year spot nominal interest rate at time t for payoffs k years in the future and let $\pi^e(t,k)$ be the

Exhibit 16.1   Information on Australian and U.S. Interest Rates and Inflation Rates

Year	Term Structure of Interest Rates		Expected Inflation Rates		Expected Real Interest Rates	
	USD	AUD	USD	AUD	USD	AUD
1	3.02	18.72	2.00	12.00	1.00	6.00
2	3.58	17.91	2.60	11.00	1.50	5.50
3	4.02	17.10	3.10	10.00	1.75	5.00
4	4.40	16.36	3.50	9.25	2.00	4.50
5	4.76	15.65	3.90	8.50	2.20	4.00
6	5.08	15.02	4.20	7.85	2.40	3.80
7	5.37	14.49	4.40	7.45	2.60	3.60
8	5.64	14.03	4.60	7.25	2.80	3.40
9	5.89	13.64	4.80	7.10	3.00	3.20
10	6.11	13.29	5.00	7.00	3.00	3.00

Notes: The term structures of interest rates are the spot rates appropriate for discounting a known future cash flow k years in the future. The expected inflation rates represent analysts' forecasts. The expected real interest rates are derived in Equation (16.24).

---

[5]Chapter 6 explains the term structure of spot interest rates and the relationship between bond prices and pure discount bond yields.

Exhibit 16.2   The Term Structure of U.S. and Australian Interest Rates

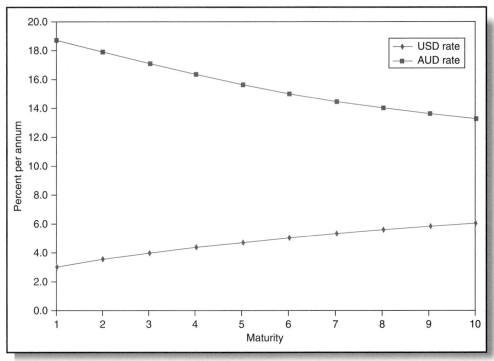

expected 1-year rates of inflation at time t for year $t+k$. One unit of currency borrowed for k years generates a liability of $[1 + i(t,k)]^k$ that must be paid in the future at time $t+k$. The one unit of borrowed currency is invested in the $(k - 1)$-year bond to get a payoff of $[1 + i(t,k - 1)]^{k-1}$ at time $t+k - 1$. When that payoff is received, the proceeds from investing in the $(k - 1)$-year bond are invested at the 1-year interest rate, $i(t+k - 1,1)$, that will be known at the end of year $t + k - 1$ and will pay off at the end of year $t+k$. Because the strategy requires no investment today, the expected return must equal the expected cost, ignoring risk premiums. Thus,

$$\{1 + E_t[i(t+k-1,1)]\} \, [1 + i(t,k-1)]^{k-1} = [1 + i(t,k)]^k \qquad (16.22)$$

Now, remember that the Fisher equation implies that 1 plus the expected nominal interest rate can be broken into 1 plus the expected real interest rate multiplied by 1 plus the expected rate of inflation, or

$$\{1 + E_t[i(t+k-1,1)]\} = [1 + r^e(t,k)][1 + \pi^e(t,k)]\} \qquad (16.23)$$

Substituting from Equation (16.23) into Equation (16.22) and solving for $[1 + r^e(t,k)]$ gives

$$[1 + r^e(t,k)] = \frac{[1 + i(t,k)]^k}{[1 + i(t,k-1)]^{k-1}[1 + \pi^e(t,k)]} \qquad (16.24)$$

These real interest rates will later be linked to the expected real depreciation of the Australian dollar.

Book Value and Depreciation

To begin the task of constructing expected cash flows, Elichalt checked with CMTC's accounting department and determined that the book value of the Australian plant's existing equipment was AUD10.5 million. Hence, the sale of the old equipment would generate some taxable income. Accounting had also informed Elichalt that for depreciation purposes, the remaining life of the old equipment was 5 years and that straight-line depreciation was being used. The new equipment would be depreciated on a straight-line basis over the course of 10 years. Finally, the accounting group had suggested that a 40% tax rate was the appropriate rate to apply to the Australian dollar cash flows. Armed with this information, Elichalt knew that she could generate appropriate forecasts of Australian dollar cash flows. Only the choice of a discount rate remained to be settled.

Discounted Cash Flows

As she reached for her well-thumbed copy of Bekaert and Hodrick's *International Financial Management*, Elichalt thought she remembered that they advocated using equity discount rates that reflect both the spot nominal interest rates for each period and the riskiness of the individual project's equity cash flows. Elichalt knew that historically the Australian dollar profits of the Australian subsidiary, when converted into U.S. dollars, were quite similar to the dollar equity returns of other CMTC plants. Hence, she knew that an equity risk premium of 8% seemed appropriate in U.S. dollars when discounting expected U.S. dollar cash flows from the Australian subsidiary.

But Elichalt also knew that Wickens would want to see an analysis done in Australian dollars. This raised the question of whether it mattered if the analysis were done in U.S. dollars or in Australian dollars. Elichalt didn't relish a clash with Wickens or the CFO on Monday.

Case Solution

Elichalt's solution proceeds in several logical steps. First, Exhibit 16.3 presents the Australian dollar after-tax cash flows forecast for the current year and the next 10 years. The units in Exhibit 16.3 are the millions of nominal Australian dollars generated in the particular year listed in Column 1. Each of the columns will be explained. Then, Exhibit 16.4 presents forecasts of expected Australian dollar–U.S. dollar exchange rates that are used in Exhibit 16.5 to derive the expected dollar cash flows from the project. These are discounted using U.S. dollar equity discount rates. Exhibit 16.6 then demonstrates how the analysis can be done directly in Australian dollars.

The Initial Outlay for the Project

The initial outlay for the project of AUD41.1 million enters negatively in Column 2 of Exhibit 16.3 as a year 0 value because it is the project's cost. This cost represents the resources that the firm must invest today for the new equipment if the firm is to achieve the projected future cost saving.

Exhibit 16.3 Cash Flows in Millions of Expected Australian Dollars

Year	Outlay	After-Tax Salvage Value	Old Production Costs	New Production Costs	Cost Saving	After-Tax Cost Saving	Depreciation Tax Shields Old	Depreciation Tax Shields New	Total AUD Cash Flow
0	−41.10	11.30	45.38						−29.80
1			50.82	45.74	5.08	3.05	−0.84	1.64	3.85
2			56.41	47.95	8.46	5.08	−0.84	1.64	5.88
3			62.05	49.64	12.41	7.45	−0.84	1.64	8.25
4			67.79	54.23	13.56	8.13	−0.84	1.64	8.94
5			73.55	58.84	14.71	8.83	−0.84	1.64	9.63
6			80.06	64.05	16.01	9.61		1.64	11.25
7			86.83	69.46	17.37	10.42		1.64	12.06
8			93.99	75.19	18.80	11.28		1.64	12.92
9			101.60	81.28	20.32	12.19		1.64	13.84
10			109.73	87.79	21.95	13.17		1.64	14.81

The After-Tax Salvage Value of the Old Equipment

The old equipment can be sold for AUD11.83 million, which provides an immediate year 0 benefit to the project. Because the market price of the old equipment is greater than its AUD10.5 million book value, CMTC generates taxable income from the sale of the old equipment, and the after-tax benefit of the sale is listed in Column 3. The firm achieves a year 0 benefit of the sale price of the old equipment minus the income tax rate multiplied by the difference between the sale price and the book value of the old equipment:

$$\text{AUD11.83 million} - 0.40 \times (\text{AUD11.83 million} - \text{AUD10.5 million})$$
$$= \text{AUD11.30 million}$$

The After-Tax Cost Savings of the Project

Column 4 of Exhibit 16.3 shows forecasts of the plant's old costs. As Wickens indicated, the old costs are expected to increase at the Australian dollar rate of inflation for years 1 through 5, and then at a rate that is 1 percentage point higher than the rate of inflation in years 6 through 10. Thus, if $\pi^e(t,k,\text{AUD})$ is the forecast at time t of the annual Australian dollar rate of inflation that will occur k years in the future, the old costs in year $t + k$ are expected to be

$$\text{Old costs in } k \text{ years} = [1 + \pi^e(t,k,\text{AUD})] \times [\text{Old costs in } (k-1) \text{ years}], k = 1,\dots,5$$
$$\text{Old costs in } k \text{ years} = [1 + \pi^e(t,k,\text{AUD}) + 1\%] \times [\text{Old costs in } (k-1) \text{ years}],$$
$$k = 6,\dots,10$$

For example, because the costs in year 0 are AUD45.38 million and the expected Australian dollar rate of inflation in year 1 is 12%, the first-year costs are expected to be

$$\text{AUD45.38 million} \times 1.12 = \text{AUD50.82 million}$$

Column 5 of Exhibit 16.3 shows the forecast of new costs. These were generated according to the percentage savings that Wickens had predicted over the next 10 years. Thus,

$$\text{New costs in year } 1 = 0.90 \times (\text{Old costs in year } 1)$$
$$\text{New costs in year } 2 = 0.85 \times (\text{Old costs in year } 2)$$
$$\text{New Costs in year } k = 0.80 \times (\text{Old costs in year } k), k = 3,\dots,10$$

Column 6 of Exhibit 16.3 shows the expected cost savings, which are the differences between the old costs forecast for year k and the new costs forecast for year k. Notice that the benefit of this investment project is almost entirely due to the cost savings. It is assumed that the new equipment will produce machine tools that are identical to the old machines that CMTC would have sold but that the new equipment will do so more cheaply. CMTC forecasts that it will sell exactly as many machine tools in the future if the investment is made, but each machine tool it sells will generate more profit because it will be produced at lower cost. Of course, because CMTC will be more profitable, it will have to pay income tax on the additional profit. Hence, the after-tax value of the cost savings, listed in Column 7 of Exhibit 16.3, provides the primary benefit of the project. The expected after-tax cost savings in year k is 1 minus the tax rate of 40% multiplied by the expected cost savings in year k.

Depreciation Tax Shields

The depreciation of equipment is an accounting cost that reduces the before-tax income of the firm. If the firm generates a before-tax cash flow of Y and takes depreciation of Dep, the before-tax income of the firm is $(Y - \text{Dep})$. If the corporate tax rate is τ, the firm pays $\tau(Y - \text{Dep})$ of tax, and its after-tax income is $(1 - \tau)(Y - \text{Dep})$. Because depreciation is not a cash flow, we must add Dep to the after-tax income to get the after-tax cash flow of the firm:

$$(1 - \tau)(Y - \text{Dep}) + \text{Dep} = (1 - \tau)Y + \tau\text{Dep}$$

The after-tax cash flow is 1 minus the tax rate multiplied by the pretax cash flow plus the tax rate multiplied by the amount of depreciation. Consequently, depreciation provides a tax benefit to the project, which is often called the depreciation tax shield. The depreciation tax shield equals the tax rate multiplied by the amount of depreciation. Column 8 of Exhibit 16.3 recognizes that when the old equipment is sold, CMTC will lose the remaining 5 years of depreciation tax shields associated with the old equipment. With the straight-line method of depreciation, the lost depreciation expense in years 1 through 5 would be one-fifth (20%) of the book value of the equipment, which is AUD10.5 million. Hence, the firm will lose a depreciation tax shield of

$$(0.40) \times (0.20) \times (\text{AUD10.5 million}) = \text{AUD0.84 million}$$

in each year of the first 5 years of the project.

Because the firm is purchasing new equipment, it will generate new depreciation tax shields, which are given in Column 9 of Exhibit 16.3. The new depreciation tax shield recognizes that the life of the equipment is 10 years. Hence, 10% of the value of the purchase will be deducted in each of the next 10 years, and the tax rate multiplied by this value provides the new depreciation tax shield:

$$(0.40) \times (0.10) \times (\text{AUD41.1 million}) = \text{AUD1.64 million}$$

The Total Expected After-Tax Cash Flows in Australian Dollars

The expected total after-tax cash flows of the project in millions of Australian dollars are given in Column 10 of Exhibit 16.3. The year 0 value is the sum of the initial outlay in Column 2 and the after-tax salvage value of the old equipment in Column 3. The year 1 through year 10 cash flows are the sums of the after-tax cost savings in Column 7 and the depreciation tax shields in Columns 8 and 9. To determine whether or not the project is acceptable, we must take the present value of these cash flows, either in Australian dollars or in U.S. dollars after converting them to expected U.S. dollars.

Notice that the equipment is assumed to be fully depreciated and of zero economic value after the end of the 10-year forecast period. If this were not the case, some terminal value or residual salvage value of the equipment would be available as an additional benefit of the project.

Forecast Future Spot Rates

It is straightforward to construct the expected future spot exchange rates from the current spot rate and the term structures of spot interest rates in each currency that are supplied in Exhibit 16.1. Let $S(t)$ denote the current spot exchange rate of Australian dollars per U.S. dollar, which is AUD1.42/\$. Let $i(t,k,\text{AUD})$ denote the nominal Australian dollar, k-year spot interest rate at time t. For example, the 5-year Australian dollar interest rate is 15.65% in Exhibit 16.1. Let $i(t,k,\$)$ denote the nominal U.S. dollar k-year spot interest rate at time t and notice that the 5-year U.S. dollar interest rate is 4.76% in Exhibit 16.1. Then, from interest rate parity, a k-year forward rate of Australian dollars per U.S. dollars that was quoted at time t for delivery in year $t + k$ would have to satisfy

$$F(t,k) = S(t) \times \frac{[1 + i(t,k,\text{AUD})]^k}{[1 + i(t,k,\$)]^k} \tag{16.25}$$

Exhibit 16.4 Forecasted Australian Dollar–U.S. Dollar Exchange Rates from Interest Rate Parity

Year	Forecasts of AUD/USD	Percentage Nominal Appreciation of the U.S. Dollar
0	1.4200	
1	1.6364	15.24
2	1.8401	12.45
3	2.0260	10.10
4	2.1910	8.14
5	2.3283	6.27
6	2.4428	4.92
7	2.5387	3.92
8	2.6182	3.13
9	2.6808	2.39
10	2.7319	1.90

Substituting the current spot rate and the 5-year interest rates into Equation (16.25), we find an implicit forward rate at time t for year $t + 5$ of

$$(\text{AUD}1.42/\$) \times \frac{(1.1565)^5}{(1.0476)^5} = \text{AUD}2.3283/\$$$

Because Australian dollar nominal interest rates are substantially higher than U.S. dollar nominal interest rates, the U.S. dollar is at a large premium in the forward market.

In the absence of information that would indicate the presence of a risk premium in the forward foreign exchange market, Equation (16.25) can be used to generate expected future spot exchange rates. That is, we can assume that the implicit forward rates are unbiased predictors of future spot rates:

$$F(t,k) = E_t[S(t+k)] \tag{16.26}$$

Expected future spot exchange rates that are constructed in this way from Equations (16.25) and (16.26) using the data of Exhibit 16.1 are presented in Column 2 of Exhibit 16.4. The third column expresses the annualized expected rates of appreciation of the U.S. dollar relative to the Australian dollar implicit in these forecasts. These will be used in a later analysis.

If it is also assumed that the future spot exchange rates and the Australian dollar cash flows from the project are independent, the expected after-tax Australian dollar cash flows of the project, $E_t[X(t+k,\text{AUD})]$, can be converted into expected U.S. dollar cash flows by dividing by the forecast of the exchange rate in year $t+k$ from Exhibit 16.4:

$$\text{Expected value at time } t \text{ of U.S. dollars in year } t+k = \frac{E_t[X(t+k,\text{AUD})]}{E_t[S(t+k)]} \tag{16.27}$$

For example, the forecast for year 1 of the Australian dollar after-tax cash flow from Exhibit 16.3 is AUD3.85 million, and the forecast of the Australian dollar–U.S. dollar exchange rate for year 1 from Exhibit 16.4 is AUD1.6364/USD. Hence, the forecast of U.S. dollar value of the Australian dollar cash flows in year 1 is

$$\frac{\text{AUD}3.85 \text{ million}}{\text{AUD}1.6364/\text{USD}} = \text{USD}2.35 \text{ million}$$

The present value of the expected U.S. dollar cash flows calculated in Equation (16.27) is found by discounting them at U.S. dollar equity discount rates, $r_E(t,k,\$)$:

Present value at time t of expected U.S. dollars in year $t+k$

$$= \frac{E_t[X(t+k,\text{AUD})]/E_t[S(t+k)]}{[1 + r_E(t,k,\$)]^k} \qquad (16.28)$$

The U.S. Dollar Discount Rates

The choice of appropriate U.S. dollar discount rates for the expected U.S. dollar cash flows involves two considerations. First, from the spot interest rates, we know that the time value of the U.S. dollar is not constant. Thus, the dollar equity discount rates should also reflect this fact. The second consideration is that the projected U.S. dollar cash flows are not risk free. Because the realized profits from the Australian subsidiary are equity cash flows, it is appropriate to discount the expected cash flows with discount rates that reflect the riskiness of the equity. We are told in the case that Elichalt thinks that an 8% U.S. dollar equity risk premium is appropriate. Consequently, the appropriate U.S. dollar equity discount rates are the U.S. dollar nominal risk-free interest rates plus 8%:

$$r_E(t,k,\$) = i(t,k,\$) + 8\%$$

These dollar equity discount rates are presented in Column 3 of Exhibit 16.5.

The Net Present Value of the Project in U.S. Dollars

The present values corresponding to Equation (16.28) are presented in Column 4 of Exhibit 16.5. When the sum of these present values is taken, the net present value of the project is $0.42 million. Because the project is positive NPV, it should be accepted.

How Incorrect Discounting Leads to Problems

Often in actual capital budgeting analyses, a single discount rate is used for all the future cash flows. If a 10-year project is being analyzed, the 10-year discount rate is used for all years. Sometimes this is an innocuous assumption, if the term structure of interest rates is reasonably flat, but it is not innocuous in this case. If each of the 10 years of expected U.S. dollar cash flows is discounted by the 10-year U.S. dollar equity discount factor, which is 14.11%, the project does not have a positive NPV. Exhibit 16.5 indicates that this value is $-$0.47 million.

Exhibit 16.5 The Net Present Value of CMTC's Proposed Project, in Millions of U.S. Dollars

Year	USD Cash Flow	USD Equity Discount Rates	Year 0 Values
0	−20.99		−20.99
1	2.35	11.02	2.12
2	3.20	11.58	2.57
3	4.07	12.02	2.90
4	4.08	12.40	2.56
5	4.14	12.76	2.27
6	4.61	13.08	2.20
7	4.75	13.37	1.97
8	4.94	13.64	1.78
9	5.16	13.89	1.60
10	5.42	14.11	1.45

USD NPV @ Variable rates = 0.42
USD NPV @ 14.11% = −0.47

The reason that the value of the project is negative when this incorrect method is used is that the term structure of U.S. interest rates is upward sloping. An upward-sloping term structure of spot interest rates indicates that expected future U.S. dollar short-term nominal interest rates are higher than current short-term interest rates. Hence, longer-term expected U.S. dollar cash flows require higher discount rates than nearer-term cash flows. If the expected dollar profits from the early years of the project are discounted by the high dollar rate of return that is appropriate only for discounting cash flows in year 10, the present value of the project is penalized needlessly.

The Net Present Value of the Project in Australian Dollars

The previous analysis derives the net present value of the project in U.S. dollars by discounting the expected U.S. dollar cash flows with U.S. dollar equity discount rates. It is also possible to derive a U.S. dollar NPV for the project by first discounting the expected Australian dollar cash flows with appropriate Australian dollar equity discount rates, $r_E(t,k,\text{AUD})$:

$$\text{Present value at time } t \text{ of expected AUD in year } t + k$$
$$= \frac{E_t[X(t+k,\text{AUD})]}{[1 + r_E(t,k,\text{AUD})]^k} \tag{16.29}$$

The U.S. dollar NPV of the project can subsequently be found by dividing the NPV in Australian dollars by the current spot rate of Australian dollars per U.S. dollar:

$$\text{U.S. dollar present value at time } t \text{ of expected AUD in year } t + k$$
$$= \frac{E_t[X(t+k,\text{AUD})]}{[1 + r_E(t,k,\text{AUD})]^k} \times \left(\frac{1}{S(t,\text{AUD}/\$)}\right) \tag{16.30}$$

If the two methods of deriving a U.S. dollar NPV are to provide the same value, the expression in Equation (16.28) must equal the expression in Equation (16.30) from which we find the following equality:

$$\frac{E_t[X(t+k,\text{AUD})]}{[1 + r_E(t,k,\text{AUD})]^k} \times \left(\frac{1}{S(t,\text{AUD}/\$)}\right) = \frac{E_t[X(t+k,\text{AUD})]/E_t[S(t+k,\text{AUD}/\$)]}{[1 + r_E(t,k,\$)]^k} \tag{16.31}$$

The relation between the Australian dollar discount rate and the U.S. dollar discount rate in Equation (16.31) can then be written as

$$[1 + r_E(t,k,\text{AUD})]^k = [1 + r_E(t,k,\$)]^k \times \frac{E_t[S(t+k,\text{AUD}/\$)]}{S(t,\text{AUD}/\$)} \tag{16.32}$$

By solving Equation (16.31) for the Australian dollar discount rate, we find

$$r_E(t,k,\text{AUD}) = [1 + r_E(t,k,\$)] \times \left(\frac{E_t[S(t+k,\text{AUD}/\$)]}{S(t,\text{AUD}/\$)}\right)^{1/k} - 1 \tag{16.33}$$

From the derivation of the expected rates of appreciation of the U.S. dollar relative to the Australian dollar in Exhibit 16.1, we know that we can calculate

$$\frac{E_t[S(t+k,\text{AUD}/\$)]}{S(t,\text{AUD}/\$)} = \frac{[1 + i(t,k,\text{AUD})]^k}{[1 + i(t,k,\$)]^k} \tag{16.34}$$

Exhibit 16.6 The Net Present Value of CMTC's Proposed Project, in Millions of Australian Dollars

Year	AUD Cash Flow	AUD Equity Discount Rates	Year 0 Values
0	−29.80		−29.80
1	3.85	27.94	3.01
2	5.88	27.02	3.65
3	8.25	26.11	4.11
4	8.94	25.28	3.63
5	9.63	24.48	3.22
6	11.25	23.78	3.13
7	12.06	23.18	2.80
8	12.92	22.67	2.52
9	13.84	22.22	2.27
10	14.81	21.83	2.06

AUD NPV @ Variable rates = 0.60
Corresponding USD NPV = 0.42

AUD NPV @ 21.83% = 3.06
Corresponding USD NPV = 2.15

We can substitute these market-determined forecasts in Equation (16.34) into Equation (16.33). Alternatively, we could use proprietary forecasts of expected rates of appreciation of the U.S. dollar relative to the Australian dollar, but we should have a reason why our proprietary forecasts differ from the market forecasts. In either case, we generate the necessary Australian dollar discount rates.

Notice that the expected rate of appreciation of the U.S. dollar relative to the Australian dollar over the next k years, when expressed at an annual rate as in Equation (16.33) by taking the $(1/k)$-th power of the ratio of the expected future spot rate to the current spot rate, is just the ratio of 1 plus the spot nominal interest rate on the Australian dollar for k years in the future to 1 plus the spot nominal interest rate on the U.S. dollar for k years in the future:

$$\left(\frac{E_t[S(t+k,\text{AUD}/\$)]}{S(t,\text{AUD}/\$)}\right)^{1/k} = \frac{[1 + i(t,k,\text{AUD})]}{[1 + i(t,k,\$)]} \tag{16.35}$$

By substituting from Equation (16.35) into Equation (16.33), we find

$$r_E(t,k,\text{AUD}) = [1 + r_E(t,k,\$)] \times \frac{[1 + i(t,k,\text{AUD})]}{[1 + i(t,k,\$)]} - 1 \tag{16.36}$$

The values of the Australian dollar equity rate of return that satisfy Equation (16.36) are given in Column 2 of Exhibit 16.6.

When the expected Australian dollar cash flows are discounted at these required equity rates of return, the NPV of the project is AUD0.60 million. Dividing the Australian dollar NPV by the current exchange rate of AUD1.42/$ gives the U.S. dollar NPV of $0.42 million. Notice that this is the same value we found by discounting the expected U.S. dollar cash flows at the U.S. dollar required rate of return.

An Incorrect Approach—Again

We demonstrated that if the expected U.S. dollar cash flows are discounted at the common discount rate associated with the 10-year maturity, the project would have a negative U.S. dollar NPV. This occurred because using a common discount rate ignores expected changes in U.S. dollar interest rates, which in this case are expected to increase over time.

Analogously, we get the wrong present value for the project if each of the 10 years of expected Australian dollar cash flows is incorrectly discounted by the common 10-year Australian dollar discount rate, which is 21.83%. If we discount with this common rate, the project has an even larger positive NPV in Australian dollars. Exhibit 16.6 indicates that this value is AUD3.06 million, which is $2.15 million when converted at the current exchange rate.

The reason the value of the project is higher when this incorrect method is used is that the term structure of Australian dollar interest rates is downward sloping. A downward-sloping term structure indicates that future short-term nominal Australian dollar interest rates are expected to be lower than current short-term interest rates. Hence, longer-term Australian dollar cash flows should be discounted at lower discount rates, and nearer-term Australian dollar cash flows should be discounted at higher rates. If the expected Australian dollar profits from the early years of the project are discounted by the low Australian dollar rate of return that is appropriate only for year 10 cash flows, the value of the project appears to be more favorable than it actually is.

The Expected Real Appreciation of the U.S. Dollar

The nominal interest rates for the two currencies imply that the U.S. dollar is expected to appreciate relative to the Australian dollar in nominal terms, as demonstrated in Exhibit 16.4. Given the expected rates of inflation from Exhibit 16.1, we can also determine that the U.S. dollar is expected to appreciate relative to the Australian dollar in real terms. This is demonstrated in Exhibit 16.7. Knowing that the Australian dollar is expected to weaken in real terms is important because it implies that the forecast U.S. dollar cash flows from the project that might be generated from an assumption of relative purchasing power parity would seriously overvalue the project.

Using purchasing power parity to forecast foreign currency cash flows is appropriate only if relative purchasing power parity is expected to hold in all future periods. If one of the currencies is strong in real terms and is expected to depreciate, as is the Australian dollar in this case, then PPP forecasts will be invalid.

Recall that the expected rate of real appreciation of the U.S. dollar relative to the Australian dollar is defined as the percentage change in the real exchange rate. The real exchange rate in this situation is the nominal exchange rate of AUD/USD multiplied by the U.S. price level divided by the Australian price level:

$$RS(t) = \frac{S(t)P(t,\$)}{P(t,\text{AUD})}$$

Exhibit 16.7 The Forecasted Real Appreciation of the U.S. Dollar

Year	Percentage per Year	Real Appreciation of the U.S. Dollar Compounded
1	4.95	4.95
2	3.94	9.09
3	3.19	12.57
4	2.45	15.33
5	1.76	17.36
6	1.37	18.97
7	0.97	20.13
8	0.58	20.83
9	0.19	21.06
10	0.00	21.06

Let the percentage change in the real exchange rate be $rs(t+1)$, and let the actual rates of inflation be $\pi(t+1,\$)$ and $\pi(t+1,\text{AUD})$. Then

$$rs(t + 1) = \frac{[S(t+1)P(t+1,\$)/P(t+1,\text{AUD})]}{[S(t)P(t,\$)/P(t,\text{AUD})]} - 1$$

$$= \frac{[1 + s(t+1)][1 + \pi(t+1,\$)]}{[1 + \pi(t+1,\text{AUD})]} - 1$$

To generate expected rates of real appreciation, we can substitute expected values for actual values, using the expected rates of nominal appreciation derived in Exhibit 16.4 and the expected U.S. dollar and Australian dollar rates of inflation in Exhibit 16.1.

The calculations in Exhibit 16.7 indicate that the U.S. dollar is expected to strengthen in real terms by 4.95% in the first year. The expected rate of real appreciation subsequently declines until it reaches 0.19% in year 9 and 0% in year 10. Exhibit 16.7 also shows the compound, or cumulative, expected percentage change in the real exchange rate. Given the nominal interest rates and the expected rates of inflation associated with two currencies, the financial markets are predicting that the U.S. dollar will strengthen in real terms relative to the Australian dollar by 21.1% over the next 10 years. If the valuation of the project did not allow for this real appreciation of the U.S. dollar, the value of the project would be severely overstated.

Chapter 9 notes that changes in real exchange rates often substantively affect the profitability of foreign operations. There is nothing in the present case that captures this important aspect of forecasting. This does not mean that the effect is unimportant. We merely left it out to simplify the discussion.

16.4 TERMINAL VALUE WHEN ROI EQUALS r_{WACC}

Terminal Value with Perpetual Growth

This section presents an alternative way to determine the terminal value of a project. In Chapter 15, we argue that capital budgeting valuations should consider the rate at which a firm will grow in the long run and should discount the firm's free cash flow at the firm's cost of capital. From the perpetuity formula for a cash flow growing at rate g, discounted rate r, we argue that if we have explicit forecasts for a 10-year horizon, then

$$\text{Terminal value in year 10} = \frac{\text{FCF}(t + 11)}{(r\% - g\%)} \tag{16.37}$$

where FCF $(t + 11)$ is the expected value at time t of free cash flow in year $t + 11$. Notice that if we are doing a WACC analysis, we set $r = r_{\text{WACC}}$, whereas if we are doing an ANPV analysis, we set $r = r_A$, and we handle the tax shields of perpetual debt separately.

Although calculating the terminal value in such a way is perfectly correct, it requires an understanding of the growth rate of the firm for the indefinite future. One assumption is that the only growth will be due to inflation because any real growth would require ongoing investment by the firm. In such a situation, people often assume that the firm's capital expenditures are just equal to depreciation.

Equilibrium Rate of Return on Investment

An alternative way of deriving terminal values involves developing explicit forecasts up to the point at which you think the firm's return on investment (ROI) equals its weighted average cost of capital, r_{WACC}. This is a sensible condition because if the firm is earning a return on its investments that is larger than its cost of capital, either the firm should expand or, more likely, competitors will notice the above-average returns and will enter the industry, thereby driving down the rate of return on invested capital.

The Return on Investment

The **return on investment (ROI)** is the change in a firm's future operating profit, which is its increase in gross cash flow, divided by its investment. In the notation in Chapter 15, gross cash flow, GCF, is the firm's net operating profit less adjusted taxes (NOPLAT) plus accounting depreciation. The investments of the firm, INVEST, are its capital expenditures, CAPX, and its change in net working capital, ΔNWC, or INVEST = CAPX + ΔNWC. Thus,

$$\text{ROI}(t+1) = \frac{\text{GCF}(t+1) - \text{GCF}(t)}{\text{INVEST}(t)} \tag{16.38}$$

Because free cash flow is the difference between gross cash flows and investments, we can write

$$\text{FCF}(t) = \text{GCF}(t) - \text{INVEST}(t) = \text{GCF}(t) \times \left[1 - \frac{\text{INVEST}(t)}{\text{GCF}(t)}\right] \tag{16.39}$$

The Importance of the Plowback Ratio

In Equation (16.39), the ratio of investment to gross cash flows is called the *reinvestment ratio*, or the **plowback ratio**, which we denote PB(t). The plowback ratio is the fraction of operating profits that management chooses to reinvest in the firm.

If we multiply both sides of Equation (16.38) by INVEST(t) and divide both sides by GCF(t), we find

$$\text{ROI}(t+1) \times \frac{\text{INVEST}(t)}{\text{GCF}(t)} = \frac{\text{GCF}(t+1) - \text{GCF}(t)}{\text{GCF}(t)} \tag{16.40}$$

The left-hand side of Equation (16.40) is the return on investment multiplied by the plowback ratio, and the right-hand side is the rate of growth of the gross cash flow:

$$\text{ROI}\,(t+1)\,\text{PB}(t) = g$$

This makes perfect sense. A firm's income grows faster the higher the rate of return on its investments and the more of its previous income the firm chooses not to pay out to its shareholders.

The Terminal Value Calculation

If we substitute for FCF $(t+1)$ in Equation (16.37) using Equation (16.39), we find

$$\text{Terminal value in year 10} = \frac{\text{GCF}(t+11) \times [1 - \text{PB}(t+11)]}{r - g} \tag{16.41}$$

From Equation (16.40), $[1 - \text{PB}(t+11)] = [1 - g/\text{ROI}(t+11)] = [\text{ROI}(t+11) - g]/\text{ROI}(t+11)$. A key insight is that if a firm has exhausted all its positive NPV projects, then the firm's return on investment will just equal its cost of capital. Thus, we should set ROI = r, and by substituting into the expression for terminal value in Equation (16.41), we find

$$\text{Terminal value in year 10} = \frac{\text{GCF}(t+11)\left(\dfrac{r-g}{r}\right)}{(r-g)} = \frac{\text{GCF}(t+11)}{r} \tag{16.42}$$

This expression looks like a no-growth perpetuity, but gross cash flow is actually growing at rate g.

Example 16.4 Conundrum Corporation's Terminal Value

Assume that the Conundrum Corporation has a weighted average cost of capital of 15%. It also reinvests 40% of its gross cash flow in new projects. What is Conundrum's growth rate if the new investment projects are zero NPV?

Because ROI = r in this case, we use Equation (16.40) to find Conundrum's growth rate:

$$g = r \times \text{PB} = 15\% \times 40\% = 6\%$$

If the final year of our 10-year forecast for Conundrum's gross cash flow is $40 million, what is the terminal value of Conundrum in year $t + 10$?

We can find the terminal value in two ways. We know that the last forecast of Conundrum's free cash flow will be 60% of $40 million because 40% of GCF is reinvested. Thus, $\text{FCF}(t + 10) = 0.60 \times \$40$ million $= \$24$ million. Free cash flow in year $t + 11$ will be 6% higher because the firm is growing at 6%, or $\text{FCF}(t + 11) = \$24$ million $\times 1.06 = \$25.44$ million. Equation (16.37) indicates that we find the terminal value by taking the perpetuity value of $25.44 million growing at 6% and discounted at 15%. Thus,

$$\text{Terminal value in year } t + 10 = \frac{\$25.44 \text{ million}}{0.15 - 0.06} = \$282.67 \text{ million}$$

Alternatively, we can calculate the terminal value using Equation (16.42). In year $t + 11$, GCF will be 6% higher than year $t + 10$'s $40 million, or $42.4 million. Thus,

$$\text{Terminal value in year } t + 10 = \frac{\$42.4 \text{ million}}{0.15} = \$282.67 \text{ million}$$

POINT–COUNTERPOINT

Does Faster Growth Lead to More Value?

It's springtime, and the Handel brothers are watching their cousin Courtney, Suttle's little sister, play soccer for her U-14 travel team. Out of the blue, Ante says, "You know, Freedy, I think we've got to invest more of our equity portfolio in growth companies. Faster growth leads to higher rates of return, and higher rates of return mean we'll retire earlier."

Freedy is a little taken aback because his mind was on the soccer game, and Courtney is on a breakaway, but he manages to reply, "Ante, you just don't get it, do you? Only if the managers of the firm are creating value by investing in positive NPV projects that weren't anticipated by the market can there be higher-than-normal, risk-adjusted rates of return."

After Courtney scores a goal, Ante argues, "Well, in Bekaert and Hodrick's book, faster growth translates into higher terminal values because you're dividing the last forecast of free cash flow by $r - g$. A larger g makes the denominator smaller, and that makes the terminal value bigger, so faster growth leads to more value. That's my story, and I'm stickin' to it!"

Just then, the referee blows the whistle to signal half-time. Suttle looks over and asks if the brothers saw Courtney's goal. "She split the two defenders and put quite a move on the goalie, don't you think? There was no stopping that shot." Both brothers shrug their shoulders and frown, and Suttle knows that an argument is brewing. "Okay, what are you two arguing about now?" he asks. After a recap of the argument, Suttle says, "I think we need pencil and paper for this one. Let's sit down after the game, and we'll work through a couple of examples."

After the game, Ante, Freedy, and Suttle are gathered around the kitchen table. "Let's revisit the part in Bekaert and Hodrick's book in which they discuss growth and terminal values. I think it is Example 16.4," says Suttle, who then shows the brothers that growth depends on the plowback ratio multiplied by the return on investment.

"So, I'm right!" exclaims Ante. "If a firm invests more, it grows faster."

Freedy, red in the face, argues, "But it isn't worth any more if the investment is just earning the cost of capital."

At this point, Suttle says, "Ante, you're right that a higher plowback ratio leads to more growth, and Freedy, you're wrong that the firm won't be worth more. But, Ante, you're wrong, too. The increase in firm value will only be worth the amount that is invested, if Freedy is correct, and the firm is only earning its WACC. Let's assume that Conundrum Corporation changes its plowback ratio from 40% to 50. Equation (16.40) indicates that the firm's growth rate will increase from 6% to 7.5% $= 50\% \times 15\%$. The additional investment in year $t + 10$ is \$4 million $= 10\% \times \$40\%$ million. Thus, free cash flow in year $t + 10$ falls from \$24 million to \$20 million. The terminal value calculation is now done by recognizing that free cash flow will be growing at 7.5% and will be discounted at 15%:

$$\text{Terminal value in year } t + 10 = \frac{\$20 \text{ million} \times 1.075}{0.15 - 0.075} = \$286.67 \text{ million.}$$

"Notice that this is \$4 million higher than before," says Suttle, "which is the amount of the investment."

Suttle continues, "To do the alternative terminal value calculation in Equation (16.42), recognize that in year $t + 11$ gross cash flow will be 7.5% higher than year $t + 10$'s \$40 million, or \$43 million. Thus, Terminal value in year $t + 10 = \dfrac{\$43 \text{ million}}{0.15} = \$286.67 \text{ million.}$"

After Suttle presents his analysis, he says, "Growth does lead to increases in value. But only if the return on investment is larger than the WACC does the firm's value increase by more than the amount of the investment."

16.5 TAX SHIELDS ON FOREIGN CURRENCY BORROWING

When a corporation borrows foreign currency, it gets an interest deduction just as if it borrows in the home currency. But when the loan is repaid, the corporation may experience either a capital gain (if the home currency strengthens in value relative to the foreign currency) or capital loss (if the home currency weakens relative to the foreign currency). The capital gains are treated as income to the firm and are subject to tax. The capital losses are deductible for tax purposes and provide additional tax shields. This section first explores the theory associated with these capital gains and losses. It then analyzes the borrowing possibilities of Banana Computers.

The Tax Implications of Borrowing in a Foreign Currency

Suppose a U.S. corporation borrows a certain amount of foreign currency at time t for 1 year. Let the foreign currency principal be denoted $D(FC)$, and let the foreign currency interest rate be $i(FC)$. Then, if the exchange rate, $S(t)$, is dollars per foreign currency, the dollar value of the principal on the loan is $S(t) \times D(FC)$. In 1 year, the firm will repay the foreign currency principal plus interest, and it will be able to deduct the dollar value of the actual interest paid. A weakening of the dollar increases the amount of interest paid, and a strengthening of the dollar decreases the amount of interest paid. Thus, the actual interest deduction at time $t + 1$ will be $S(t+1) \times i(FC) \times D(FC)$.

Changes in the exchange rate will also affect the dollar value of the repayment of the foreign currency principal, which is $S(t+1) \times D(FC)$ dollars. If the dollar has strengthened versus the foreign currency when it is time to repay the principal, $S(t + 1) < S(t)$, in which case the corporation will repay fewer dollars of principal than it borrowed. The difference between the dollar amount borrowed and the dollar amount repaid, $[S(t) - S(t + 1)] \times D(\text{FC})$, is the corporation's capital gain. Because capital gains are income to the firm, the firm will have to pay income tax on this capital gain.

Conversely, if the dollar has weakened versus the foreign currency when it is time to repay the principal, $S(t + 1) > S(t)$. The corporation must repay $S(t + 1) \times D(\text{FC})$ dollars, which is more dollars than it borrowed. The difference between the dollar amount repaid and the dollar amount borrowed, $[S(t + 1) - S(t)] \times D(\text{FC})$, is the firm's capital loss. The firm will be able to deduct that loss from its income, which allows the firm to pay less income tax.

Because interest rates differ across countries, there are expected changes in exchange rates, and consequently, there are expected capital gains and losses when borrowing foreign currencies. The expected taxes on capital gains or expected deductions for capital losses are necessary to prevent the firm from having an incentive to borrow in high interest rate currencies to get larger interest tax shields. Because high interest rate currencies are expected to depreciate relative to the home currency, the borrower would expect to have a capital gain on the repayment of principal. The tax on the capital gain offsets the higher interest tax shield and prevents the existence of a tax incentive to borrow in high interest rate currencies.

The next section presents an analysis of a case in which Banana Computers is confronted with alternative foreign currency borrowing opportunities. Banana uses an ANPV analysis to find the best one.

Foreign Currency Borrowing by Banana Computers

If a corporation has two mutually exclusive projects, ANPV analysis dictates that the firm should accept the project with the largest ANPV. One situation in which this type of analysis arises is when an importer is buying goods with subsidized financing provided either by the exporter or by the exporter's government. If the imported goods are really the same from country to country, the importer's problem is just to find the best financing. An ANPV analysis of the financing takes account of the interest tax shields as well as any capital gain taxes or capital loss subsidies that arise from changes in exchange rates. This section provides a concrete demonstration of these effects.

Banana's Borrowing Possibilities

Suppose Banana Computers, a U.S. company, wants to buy some computer hard drives from either a German manufacturer or a Japanese manufacturer. From Banana's perspective, the hard drives are the same, but the financing is different. The German company has arranged for Banana to borrow EUR300 million for 8 years at an annual interest rate of 3.5%. This rate is below the 8-year, risk-free euro interest rate of 5%. The Japanese manufacturer has also arranged for Banana to borrow JPY36,000 million for 8 years at an even lower interest rate of 1.5%. The 8-year, risk-free yen interest rate is 2.5%. At the current exchange rate of JPY120/EUR, the principals on the loans are identical because

$$(\text{JPY120/EUR}) \times \text{EUR300 million} = \text{JPY36,000 million}$$

Both exporters require that the loan be repaid in equal annual installments. Amortization is the process of repaying the principal on a long-term debt over time. Because interest is paid only on the outstanding principal, amortizing a loan with equal annual payments means that the borrower pays more interest in the earlier years of the life of the loan and more principal in the later years of the life of the loan.[6]

---

[6]In Microsoft Excel, the command PMT(*rate, nper, pv, fv, type*) returns the value of an annual payment associated with borrowing an amount, *pv*, at an interest rate, *rate*, for *nper* years with future value *fv*. *type* indicates whether the payments are at the beginning or the end of the year. The commands IPMT and PPMT provide the breakdown of the payment into interest and principal.

If the hard drives are identical, which foreign loan should Banana take? Alternatively, should Banana borrow in dollars at its market rate of 6% when the risk-free dollar interest rate is 4%? At the spot exchange rate of USD1.0909/EUR, the dollar principal would be

$$(\text{USD1.0909/EUR}) \times \text{EUR300 million} = \text{USD327.27 million}$$

Exhibits 16.8 through 16.10 present the ANPV cash flow analyses associated with the dollar loan, the euro loan, and the yen loan, respectively.

The Dollar Loan

The dollar loan is the most straightforward and is the benchmark to which the other loans can be compared. Exhibit 16.8 indicates that eight annual payments of USD52.70 million are required to repay the USD327.27 million principal at an interest rate of 6%. Because interest is paid only on the outstanding balance, the first interest payment is

$$0.06 \times \text{USD327.27 million} = \text{USD19.64 million}$$

By year 8, only USD49.72 million of principal is outstanding, so the last interest payment is

$$0.06 \times \text{USD49.72 million} = \text{USD2.98 million}$$

The ANPV analysis values the expected after-tax dollar cash flows that are received or paid in each year. In the first year, Banana receives the $327.27 million as the principal of the loan. In future years, the cash outflow is the sum of the interest paid and the principal repaid minus the interest tax shield. With a corporate tax rate of 34%, the deductibility of interest paid provides an interest tax shield in the first year equal to

$$0.34 \times \text{USD19.64 million} = \text{USD6.68 million}$$

The amount by which the present value of the future after-tax payments associated with the loan is less than the value of the principal borrowed is the ANPV of the loan. These debt cash flows should be discounted at Banana's market-debt interest rate of 6%. Exhibit 16.8 indicates that the ability to borrow USD327.27 million at 6% is worth USD26.42 million.

The Euro Loan

Exhibit 16.9 presents the analysis of the euro loan. We see that eight annual payments of EUR43.64 million are required to amortize the EUR300 million principal at an interest rate of 3.5%. Because interest is paid on the outstanding balance, the first interest payment is

Exhibit 16.8 The Value of a Dollar Loan

				Years in the Future					
	0	**1**	**2**	**3**	**4**	**5**	**6**	**7**	**8**
Dollar payments on the USD327.27 million loan									
Interest @ 6%		19.64	17.65	15.55	13.32	10.96	8.45	5.80	2.98
Principal		33.07	35.05	37.15	39.38	41.76	44.25	46.91	49.72
Total		52.70	52.70	52.70	52.70	52.70	52.70	52.70	52.70
Expected dollar cash flows associated with the USD loan									
Interest		−19.64	−17.65	−15.55	−13.32	−10.96	−8.45	−5.80	−2.98
Principal	327.27	−33.07	−35.05	−37.15	−39.38	−41.75	−44.25	−46.91	−49.72
Interest tax shield		6.68	6.00	5.29	4.53	3.73	2.87	1.97	1.01
Dollar cash flows	327.27	−46.03	−46.70	−47.42	−48.17	−48.98	−49.83	−50.73	−51.69
NPV of dollar cash flows @ 6%	26.42								

Notes: All cash flows are in millions of dollars and are rounded to two decimal places. Inflows are positive, and outflows are negative.

Exhibit 16.9 The Value of a Subsidized Euro Loan

	0	1	2	3	4	5	6	7	8
					Years in the Future				
Euro payments on the EUR300 million loan									
Interest @ 3.5%		10.50	9.34	8.14	6.90	5.61	4.28	2.90	1.48
Principal		33.14	34.30	35.50	36.75	38.03	39.36	40.74	42.17
Total		43.64	43.64	43.64	43.64	43.64	43.64	43.64	43.64
Expected USD/EUR from interest rate parity with $i(\text{USD}) = 4\%$ and $i(\text{EUR}) = 5\%$									
Exchange rate	1.0909	1.0805	1.0702	1.0600	1.0499	1.0399	1.0300	1.0202	1.0105
Expected dollar cash flows associated with the euro loan									
Interest		−11.35	−10.00	−8.63	−7.24	−5.83	−4.41	−2.96	−1.49
Principal	327.27	−35.81	−36.71	−37.63	−38.58	−39.55	−40.55	−41.56	−42.61
Interest tax shield		3.86	3.40	2.93	2.46	1.98	1.50	1.01	0.51
Capital gains subsidy or tax		−0.12	−0.24	−0.37	−0.51	−0.66	−0.81	−0.98	−1.15
Dollar cash flows	327.27	−43.42	−43.55	−43.70	−43.87	−44.06	−44.27	−44.50	−44.75
NPV of dollar cash flows @ 6%	54.31								

Note: All cash flows are in millions and are rounded to two decimal places. In the top panel, the currency is the euro, in the bottom panel it is the dollar.

$$0.035 \times \text{EUR300 million} = \text{EUR10.50 million}$$

By year 8, only EUR42.17 million of principal is outstanding, so the final interest payment is

$$0.035 \times \text{EUR42.17 million} = \text{EUR1.48 million}$$

The Yen Loan

Exhibit 16.10 presents the analysis of the yen loan. Here, eight annual payments of JPY4,809.02 million are required to amortize the JPY36,000 million principal at an interest rate of 1.5%. The first interest payment is

$$0.015 \times \text{JPY36,000 million} = \text{JPY540 million}$$

In year 8, the outstanding principal is JPY4,737.96 million, so the final interest payment is

$$0.015 \times \text{JPY4,737.96 million} = \text{JPY71.07 million}$$

Comparing the Foreign Currency Loans

Because Banana Computers is a U.S. company, it can compare the values of the two subsidized deals by converting the expected future foreign currency cash flows into expected future dollars, using expected future exchange rates. Exhibits 16.9 and 16.10 use uncovered interest rate parity, calculated using the risk-free interest rates, to generate forecasts of future exchange rates. It is assumed that the term structures of interest rates are flat in each of the currencies. In Exhibit 16.9, the spot exchange rate of dollars per euro is USD1.0909/EUR, and the forecast of the exchange rate k years in the future is

$$E_t[S(t+k)] = (\text{USD1.0909/EUR}) \times [1.04/1.05]^k$$

Because the dollar interest rate is less than the euro interest rate, the dollar is expected to appreciate relative to the euro. The expected dollar appreciation implies that capital gains are expected on the repayment of the euro principal. The capital gain arises because it takes fewer dollars to repay the euro principal on the loan, which increases the income of Banana Computers. The associated capital gains taxes reduce the value of the deal.

Exhibit 16.10 The Value of a Subsidized Yen Loan

	Years in the Future								
	0	**1**	**2**	**3**	**4**	**5**	**6**	**7**	**8**
Yen payments on the JPY36,000 million loan									
Interest @ 1.5%		540.00	475.96	410.97	345.00	278.04	210.07	141.09	71.07
Principal		4,269.02	4,333.06	4,398.06	4,464.03	4,530.99	4,598.95	4,667.94	4,737.96
Total		4,809.02	4,809.02	4,809.02	4,809.02	4,809.02	4,809.02	4,809.02	4,809.02
Expected JPY/USD from interest rate parity with $i(\text{USD}) = 4\%$ and $i(\text{JPY}) = 2.5\%$									
Exchange rate	110.00	108.41	106.85	105.31	103.79	102.29	100.82	99.36	97.93
Expected dollar cash flows associated with the yen loan									
Interest		−4.98	−4.45	−3.90	−3.32	−2.72	−2.08	−1.42	−0.73
Principal	327.27	−39.38	−40.55	−41.76	−43.01	−44.29	−45.62	−46.98	−48.38
Interest tax shield		1.69	1.51	1.33	1.13	0.92	0.71	0.48	0.25
Capital gains subsidy or tax		0.19	0.39	0.61	0.83	1.06	1.29	1.54	1.80
Dollar cash flows	327.27	−42.47	−43.10	−43.73	−44.38	−45.03	−45.70	−46.37	−47.05
NPV of dollar cash flows @ 6%	50.75								

Notes: All cash flows are in millions and are rounded to two decimal places. In the top panel, the currency is the yen, in the bottom panel it is the dollar.

In Exhibit 16.10, the spot exchange rate of yen per dollar is JPY110/USD, and the forecast of the exchange rate k years in the future is

$$E_t[S(t+k)] = (\text{JPY110/USD}) \times [1.025/1.04]^k$$

Because the yen interest rate is less than the dollar interest rate, the dollar is expected to weaken relative to the yen. Hence, Banana Computers expects to have to pay more dollars to repay the yen principal than the amount of dollars it borrows after the conversion of the yen principal at the current exchange rate. Banana therefore expects to take capital losses on the repayment of the yen principal. Because these expected capital losses are tax deductible, they enhance the value of the deal.

With a U.S. corporate tax rate of 34%, the interest tax shield is 34% of the expected dollar interest paid on either the euro loan or the yen loan, just as in the case of a dollar loan. For example, in year 1, interest on the euro loan is €10.50 million, and the expected spot rate is $1.0805/€. The expected dollar interest is therefore $1.0805/€ × €10.5 million = $11.35 million. The interest tax shield is 0.34 × $11.35 million = $3.86 million. In the case of the euro loan, the capital gains tax is 34% of the difference between the dollar value of the principal borrowed and the dollar value of the principal repaid. For example, the principal repaid in year 1 is €33.14 million, and the expected capital gains tax is 0.34 × €33.14 × $\left(\dfrac{\$1.0909}{€} - \dfrac{\$1.0805}{€} \right) = \$0.12$ million. For the yen loan, the tax deductibility of the capital loss provides a subsidy of 34% of the difference between the dollar value of the principal repaid and the dollar value of the principal borrowed.

As in the case of the dollar loan, the ANPV analysis takes the present value of the expected after-tax dollar cash flows that are received or paid in each year using the discount rate of 6% because the future expected dollar cash flows have the same risk characteristics as dollar debt. In the first year, Banana receives the $327.27 million as the principal of the loan. For foreign currency loans, the dollar cash outflow in future years is the sum of the interest paid and principal repaid, minus the interest tax shield and plus any capital gains tax or minus any capital-loss subsidy. The amount by which the present value of the future payments is less than the value of the principal borrowed is the ANPV of the loan.

Exhibit 16.9 indicates that the ANPV of the euro loan is $54.31 million, whereas Exhibit 16.8 indicates that the ANPV of the yen loan is $50.75 million. Both of these dominate the dollar loan because they are subsidized. Because only one loan can be taken, Banana should take the euro loan. By taking the euro loan, Banana adds $54.31 million to the value of the corporation.

16.6 CONFLICTS BETWEEN BONDHOLDERS AND STOCKHOLDERS

Whenever a firm issues debt, potential conflicts of interest arise between the bondholders and the stockholders. These conflicts are one of the difficult-to-quantify aspects of the costs of financial distress. Rather than attempt to quantify the nature of these costs, we merely examine how they arise in an international context. You should remember that the managers of a firm are assumed to be acting in the interests of the shareholders—that is, maximizing shareholder value. This is the natural perspective because the shareholders are the ultimate owners of the firm, and the managers report to the board of directors, who represent the shareholders.

The Incentive to Take Risks

The first conflict between bondholders and stockholders arises because the managers of a firm that is near bankruptcy, who are acting in the interests of the stockholders, have an incentive to invest in very risky projects. The projects might even be ones that may have a negative net present value.

To understand these incentives, consider a U.S. firm that is trying to choose between two mutually exclusive international investment projects. The variance of the return on one project is low, whereas the variance of the return on the other is high. For ease of exposition, assume that there are only two possible states of the world that will affect the projects: Either the foreign currency will appreciate and the dollar will depreciate, implying that the projects will be successful, or the foreign currency will depreciate as the dollar appreciates, and the projects will provide poor returns. Assume that each of the two possible states of the world has a 50% possibility. To simplify the arguments, we ignore discounting throughout.

The Low-Variance Project

If the firm accepts the low-variance project, the value of the firm, its equity, and its bonds in the different states of the world can be summarized as follows:

LOW-VARIANCE PROJECT				
	Probability	Value of Firm	Value of Equity	Value of Bonds
Foreign currency depreciation	0.5	$500	0	$500
Foreign currency appreciation	0.5	$600	$100	$500

If the firm accepts the low-variance project, the expected value of the firm is

$$0.5 \times \$500 + 0.5 \times \$600 = \$550$$

The cash flows from the project are sufficient to cover the firm's outstanding debt in either state of the world, so the debt is riskless. In other words, because the firm always generates enough cash to repay the debt, the debt is worth its face value of $500 whether the dollar appreciates or depreciates. The equity, on the other hand, will be worthless if the dollar strengthens because the firm generates only enough funds to repay the bondholders. However, the equity will be worth $100 if the dollar weakens. The expected value of equity is therefore

$$0.5 \times \$0 + 0.5 \times \$100 = \$50$$

The High-Variance Project

If the firm takes the high-variance project, the cash flows of the firm and its balance sheet can be described as follows:

HIGH-VARIANCE PROJECT				
	Probability	Value of Firm	Value of Equity	Value of Bonds
Foreign currency depreciation	0.5	$400	0	$400
Foreign currency appreciation	0.5	$650	$150	$500

If the firm undertakes the high-variance project, the expected value of the firm is

$$0.5 \times \$400 + 0.5 \times \$650 = \$525$$

If the dollar strengthens, though, the cash flows from the project will be insufficient to cover the firm's $500 outstanding debt, and the value of the debt will be $400. If the dollar depreciates, the full value of the debt can be repaid, and it will be worth $500. The expected value of debt is therefore

$$0.5 \times \$400 + 0.5 \times \$500 = \$450$$

On the other hand, equity will again be worthless if the dollar strengthens, but equity will be worth $150 if the dollar weakens. The expected value of equity is therefore

$$0.5 \times \$0 + 0.5 \times \$150 = \$75$$

Clearly, because the two projects are mutually exclusive, if the firm's managers act in the interest of the stockholders, they will undertake the inferior, high-variance project because it maximizes the value of the firm's equity. The key insight is that because the firm is currently levered, the stockholders get the gain when the dollar weakens, but the stockholders do not experience the loss in value when the dollar strengthens. By taking the high-variance project, the managers of the firm transfer $25 of value from the bondholders to the stockholders. Notice, though, the managers also destroy an additional $25 of firm value. By accepting the wrong project from the perspective of the firm as a whole, the managers are said to have engaged in **asset substitution**.

The Underinvestment Problem

If a firm is near bankruptcy, managers who act in the interest of stockholders often do not have an incentive to make investments that would increase the overall value of the firm because too much of the increase in the firm's value is captured by the existing bondholders. This is known as **underinvestment**. To understand this scenario, examine the following situations.

A Firm Without a New Project

Suppose that a firm has outstanding bonds with a face value of $500, and its cash flows without a new project will be as follows:

FIRM WITHOUT A NEW PROJECT				
	Probability	Value of Firm	Value of Equity	Value of Bonds
Dollar appreciation	0.5	$400	0	$400
Dollar depreciation	0.5	$600	$100	$500

The expected value of the firm's assets is

$$0.5 \times \$400 + 0.5 \times \$600 = \$500$$

Because the firm does not have enough to repay the bonds in the bad state of the world, the expected value of the firm's bonds is

$$0.5 \times \$400 + 0.5 \times \$500 = \$450$$

As the residual claimants to the firm's cash flows, the expected value of the equity is

$$0.5 \times \$0 + 0.5 \times \$100 = \$50$$

A Firm with a New Project

Now suppose that the managers of this firm have an opportunity to invest in a project that costs $100 of equity. Suppose that the cash flows of the firm with the new project would be as follows:

FIRM WITH A NEW PROJECT				
	Probability	Value of Firm	Value of Equity	Value of Bonds
Dollar appreciation	0.5	$500	0	$500
Dollar depreciation	0.5	$760	$260	$500

If the firm accepts the project, the expected value of the firm increases by $130, to

$$0.5 \times \$500 + 0.5 \times \$760 = \$630$$

Because the firm now has enough resources to repay the bonds, the expected value of the firm's bonds is $500:

$$0.5 \times \$500 + 0.5 \times \$500 = \$500$$

The stockholders remain the residual claimants to the firm's cash flows, and the expected value of the equity of the firm is

$$0.5 \times \$0 + 0.5 \times \$260 = \$130$$

What has been accomplished by investing the additional $100 of shareholders' equity? First, the value of the firm has increased by $130. Consequently, this is a positive NPV project for the firm as a whole. But will the stockholders want the managers to invest in this project? The answer is no.

Earlier, we determined that the value of equity without an investment in the new project is $50. With the new project, equity value rises to $130. Hence, from the stockholders' perspective, they invest $100, but they see their equity value increase by only $80. The problem is, of course, that the existing bondholders of the firm are reaping a substantial benefit from the new project. Their bonds increase in value by $50, from $450 to $500.

In this situation, as in the previous section, managers who are acting in the interests of stockholders and are maximizing shareholder value do not make a correct investment decision. If the manager does not take this investment project, this is a true cost of financial distress because the project is positive NPV for the firm as a whole.

Underinvestment in Emerging Market Crises

Economists think that the problems associated with underinvestment partially explain the prolonged nature of the Debt Crisis in the 1980s. The governments of emerging-market countries with large outstanding foreign debts could not credibly commit not to tax the positive returns to investments made in their countries. Thus, because managers of firms perceived that too much of the return on investment would be captured by the governments to repay the foreign loans, no one wanted to invest in these countries. Without investments, the countries could not grow and could not generate enough tax revenues to allow the governments to repay the foreign debts. Debt forgiveness, in the form of the Brady Plan, helped to overcome the problems and allowed growth to resume.

Other Managerial Problems Caused by Financial Distress

The previous section demonstrates that stockholders might not want to contribute new equity to a project that has a positive NPV if too much of the benefit of the new project will go to existing bondholders. A natural counterpart to this idea is that stockholders would like to see cash distributed from the firm when it is near financial distress. Of course, when cash is distributed from the firm, the market value of the firm's stock will fall, but it will fall less than the value of any cash dividends because bondholders will suffer some of the loss, as well.

The managers of a firm that is close to financial distress also have an incentive to misrepresent the financial condition of the firm to keep creditors at bay. The firm may be forced to cut its capital expenditures by doing less maintenance than is desirable, and its research and development expenditures may be slashed. Such actions buy time for the current managers, but they may destroy the value of the firm's assets.

16.7 INTERNATIONAL DIFFERENCES IN ACCOUNTING STANDARDS

Historically, international valuations were often complicated because accounting standards differed significantly across countries. Nevertheless, there is good news to report on this front. Beginning in 2005, the major countries of Europe and Asia began to require international financial reporting standards (IFRS), which were developed by the International Accounting Standards Board.[7] Most countries are now under pressure to adopt either IFRS or U.S. generally accepted accounting principles (GAAP) to provide investors and analysts with transparent financial statements that can be easily compared across countries. Tim Koller, Marc Goedhart, and David Wessels (2005) also note that the principles underlying IFRS and U.S. GAAP are quickly converging. The U.S. Securities and Exchange Commission (SEC) has set a target date of 2009 for accepting financial statements of its foreign registrants that comply with IFRS.

Before jumping for joy and thinking that comparisons across countries will be easy in the future, it is important to think about some issues raised by Ray Ball (2005), who argues, "All accounting accruals (versus simply counting cash) involve judgments about future cash flows. Consequently, there is much leeway in implementing accounting rules. . . . Achieving uniformity in accounting standards seems easy in comparison with achieving uniformity in actual reporting behavior" (p. 27).

Ball notes that while many countries use the metric system, the weight of the butcher's thumb on the scale differs across countries and is constrained by the eye of the customer, the butcher's concern for reputation, and the monitoring mechanisms of state and private systems. So too will it be with international accounting. The roles of auditors, regulators, courts, boards, analysts, rating agencies, the press, and others who use financial information in overseeing the financial reporting of corporations differ across countries and over time in a specific country. Hence, it is unlikely that uniformity in accounting rules will be followed quickly by uniformity in accounting practice.

---

[7] For a discussion of the key differences between U.S. GAAP and IFRS, see Chapter 21 of Tim Koller, Marc Goedhart, and David Wessels (2005).

16.8 SUMMARY

This chapter examines advanced international capital budgeting. The main points in the chapter are as follows:

1. The weighted average cost of capital, r_{WACC}, is defined as the weighted sum of the after-tax required rate of return on the firm's debt and the required rate of return on the firm's equity, where the weights represent the percentage of the firm's value financed with debt versus equity. Discounting all-equity free cash flows at r_{WACC} provides a correct valuation only when the riskiness of the cash flows and the ability of the project to support debt are the same as those of the overall corporation.

2. The flow-to-equity (FTE) approach discounts the after-tax free cash flows to stockholders at the required rate of return on the equity to derive the value of a project.

3. The ANPV method works well when a firm knows the level of its debt in future periods. If the ratio of debt to value is more likely to be constant, the WACC approach or FTE approach may be easier to use.

4. The domestic currency value of a foreign project can be found in either of two ways. You can discount the expected foreign currency cash flows with an appropriate foreign currency discount rate and then convert them into domestic currency using the current spot exchange rate, or you can forecast future exchange rates and multiply them by the expected value of the future foreign currency cash flows and then discount them using a domestic currency discount rate.

5. The CMTC case demonstrates that expected rates of real appreciation between currencies must be taken into account in international valuations. Furthermore, it may be necessary to use different discount rates for different future horizons.

6. The terminal value of a project can be calculated by assuming that the rate of return on an investment will fall, because of competition, to the weighted average cost of capital.

7. When determining the tax shields associated with borrowing foreign currency, you must take into account the expected capital gains or losses that might occur due to the expected appreciation or depreciation of the domestic currency relative to the foreign currency.

8. The presence of debt can give rise to conflicts between a firm's stockholders and bondholders. These conflicts can cause the firm's managers to engage in asset substitution or underinvestment. Asset substitution occurs when the managers invest in projects that are more risky than bondholders expected. Underinvestment occurs when managers refuse to take on low-risk projects that would increase the firm's value because too much of the value from the project accrues to the bondholders.

9. Differences in accounting conventions across countries must be taken into account when doing international capital budgeting.

QUESTIONS

1. Why should the required rate of return for a capital budgeting problem be project specific? Doesn't the firm just have to satisfy an overall cost-of-capital requirement?

2. What is the conceptual foundation of the flow-to-equity approach to capital budgeting?

3. What is the weighted average cost of capital?

4. Should a firm ever accept a project that has a negative NPV when discounted at the weighted average cost of capital?

5. Can you do capital budgeting for a foreign project using a domestic currency discount rate? Explain your answer.

6. Why might it be important to use period-specific discount rates when doing capital budgeting?

7. Why is it necessary to consider real currency appreciation and depreciation forecasts when doing an international capital budgeting analysis?

8. What is the rate of return on invested capital? How is it calculated?

9. If you borrow a foreign currency, what interest deduction would you receive on your taxes?

10. If you borrow a foreign currency, are there any capital gains taxes to worry about?

11. Why might a manager accept a high-variance, low-value project instead of a low-variance, high-value project?

12. Why would a manager not accept a positive net present value project?

PROBLEMS

1. Suppose that the required rate of return on a firm's debt is 8%, the corporate tax rate is 34%, and the required rate of return on the firm's equity is 15%. If the firm finances its projects with 40% debt, what is the firm's WACC?

2. Suppose that UK Motors Ltd. is considering an investment of £30 million to develop a new factory. Assume that the company's stockholders require a 22% rate of return, that the company's bondholders require a 9% rate of return, that the UK corporate tax rate is 40%, that 35% of the project will be financed by debt, and that 65% of the project will be financed with equity. What must be the annual income from the project if it is to be a zero net present value investment?

3. If the risk-free rate is 5%, the equity beta is 1.4, the equity risk premium is 5.5%, the corporate tax rate is 34%, and the debt–equity ratio is 0.5, what is the expected rate of return on the assets of the firm that is predicted by the CAPM?

4. Suppose that a firm's corporate headquarters thinks that the appropriate dollar rate of return on investments in Japan is thought to be 18% per annum. If the dollar is expected to weaken relative to the yen by 4% per annum, what is the Japanese yen required rate of return on the expected yen cash flows?

5. Which is a better deal: borrowing at 1% in yen when the risk-free yen interest rate is 3% and the firm's market-debt rate is 4% or borrowing in euros at 3% when the risk-free euro interest rate is 5% and the firm's market-debt rate is 6%? Assume that uncovered interest rate parity holds and that the corporate tax rate is 34%.

6. Consider a firm that owes $700 to its bondholders facing the following two mutually exclusive projects:

Project A

	Probability	Value of Firm
Dollar appreciation	0.5	$700
Dollar depreciation	0.5	$800

Project B

	Probability	Value of Firm
Dollar appreciation	0.5	$650
Dollar depreciation	0.5	$830

If the managers are operating in the interest of the stockholders, which project will the firm take? Why?

7. Suppose that a firm has $700 of bonds outstanding, and its cash flows without a new project will be as follows:

Firm Without a New Project

	Probability	Value of Firm
Dollar appreciation	0.5	$600
Dollar depreciation	0.5	$800

Suppose that the cash flows of the firm with a new project that costs $60 would be as follows:

Firm with a New Project

	Probability	Value of Firm
Dollar appreciation	0.5	$700
Dollar depreciation	0.5	$840

If the managers are acting in the interests of the shareholders, will they accept this project? Why or why not?

BIBLIOGRAPHY

Ball, Ray, September 5, 2005, "International Financial Reporting Standards (IFRS): Pros and Cons for Investors," PD Leake Lecture. Institute of Chartered Accountants in England & Wales, London, UK.

Koller, Tim, Marc Goedhart, and David Wessels, 2005, *Valuation: Measuring and Managing the Value of Companies*, 4th ed., New York: Wiley.

Miles, James A., and John R. Ezzell, 1980, "The Weighted Average Cost of Capital, Perfect Capital Markets and Project Life," *Journal of Financial and Quantitative Analysis* 15, pp. 719–730.

Modigliani, Franco, and Merton Miller, 1958, "The Cost of Capital, Corporation Finance, and the Theory of Investment," *American Economic Review* pp. 261–297.

Modigliani, Franco, and Merton Miller, 1961, "Dividend Policy, Growth, and the Valuation of Shares," *Journal of Business,* pp. 411–433.

Ross, Stephen A., and Michael M. Walsh, 1983, "A Simple Approach to Pricing Risky Assets with Uncertain Exchange Rates," *Research in International Business and Finance* 3, pp. 39–54.

Chapter 17

Risk Management and the Foreign Currency Hedging Decision

*F*irms hedge foreign exchange risk by using instruments such as forward and futures foreign exchange contracts, interest rate and currency swaps, and foreign currency options and by choosing to denominate assets and liabilities in foreign currencies. This chapter examines why a firm would want to use these financial instruments to hedge foreign exchange risk.

We first explore why hedging would be desirable in an entrepreneurial venture. Here, simply reducing the variance of profits is the motive for a risk-averse entrepreneur. However, in a modern, publicly held corporation, the benefits of hedging are less clear. Indeed, the logic of Franco Modigliani and Merton Miller (1958, 1961) implies that investors can always undo any hedging a corporation does. Nevertheless, there are modern arguments for and against hedging, and we know that the assumptions of Modigliani and Miller probably do not hold for most situations. To set the stage, we first review the Modigliani–Miller arguments that imply the irrelevance of hedging. We also examine three arguments against hedging: that hedging is costly, that hedging is impossible for equity-like cash flows, and that hedging increases the costs of financial distress by exposing bondholders to a possible bait and switch.

After discussing these arguments, we place the hedging decision within the context of the adjusted net present value (ANPV) models of Chapters 15 and 16. Hedging is valuable because it can reduce the future taxes that a firm expects to pay, lower the costs of financial distress, and improve the investment decisions the firm will face in the future. When there is asymmetric information between the managers of a firm and its shareholders, hedging may also affect the ability of shareholders to evaluate the quality of the management.

The chapter then explores the logic behind Merck's decision to hedge its foreign exchange risk with foreign currency options. A number of empirical studies and surveys have sought to determine why firms actually hedge, and we review the literature before providing a summary of the chapter.

17.1 TO HEDGE OR NOT TO HEDGE

This section examines the desirability of **hedging** foreign exchange risk in two situations: in an entrepreneurial venture and in a modern publicly held corporation. Hedging foreign exchange risk is one type of **risk management**. Generally, risk management is the use of **derivative securities** to take positions in financial markets that offset the underlying sources of risks that arise in a company's normal course of business. Derivative securities, or *derivatives* for short, are discussed in more detail in Chapter 20; they include financial contracts such as forwards, futures, swaps, and options whose value depends on the value of an underlying asset price. Taking positions in derivatives that increase in value when the firm would take a loss or decrease in value when the firm would experience a gain reduces the variance of the firm's profits.

Hedging in an Entrepreneurial Venture

One persistent theme of this book is that future foreign exchange rates are uncertain. The volatility of foreign exchange rates implies that firms choosing not to hedge foreign exchange risk will experience more volatility in their cash flows than firms choosing to hedge foreign exchange risks. This volatility makes it harder to predict the profitability of firms, in the sense that the forecast errors are bigger.

While reducing the volatility of future cash flows might seem like a good reason to hedge, the volatility of foreign exchange rates provides a necessary but not a sufficient condition for a modern corporation to hedge foreign exchange risk. To understand why this is so, we must understand what the goals of management are and how these goals are affected by hedging.

The first time students encounter discussions of hedging, they are often surprised that reducing uncertainty is not a sufficient condition for hedging. One reason for this opinion may be that students tend to think of themselves as individual entrepreneurs facing the foreign exchange risks, and they react to the situation as risk-averse individuals. It turns out that in this case, their intuition is actually right.

Reducing the uncertainty of a firm's future cash flows does provide an appropriate motivation for hedging foreign exchange risk if the firm is privately owned and the owner-managers of the firm are risk averse. Someone who is risk averse wants to increase his or her wealth without a lot of volatility in his or her portfolio. That is, the person prefers his or her cash inflows to have a higher mean and a lower variance. Likewise, an entrepreneurial firm's hedging is useful because the profits it earns are a significant part of the entrepreneur's wealth. Unlike regular investors, entrepreneurs are unable to diversify away such risks through transactions in their own portfolios. Hence, if forward rates are unbiased predictors of future spot rates, **risk-averse entrepreneurs** will choose to hedge their future foreign currency cash flows because doing so will reduce the variance of the flows without changing their expected values in the domestic currency. Therefore, reducing the variance of future profits would increase the entrepreneur's expected utility.[1]

Hedging in a Modern Corporation

When we consider a large, publicly held corporation, simply reducing the uncertainty of future cash flows by hedging becomes problematic. To understand why, let's review the sources of value of a corporation.

The adjusted net present value (ANPV) approach to corporate valuation developed in Chapter 15 starts with the present value of expected after-tax cash flows discounted at the rate that would be appropriate if the firm were an all-equity firm. Next, the ANPV approach adds the present values of any tax shields and any interest subsidies. Then, the present value of any financial distress–related costs due to debt is subtracted. Finally, the ANPV approach adds the

---

[1]Chapter 7 indicates that the issue of whether forward rates are unbiased predictors of future spot rates is still unresolved. If the forward rate is a biased predictor, but the bias is due to an equilibrium risk premium, investors in forward contracts experience either an expected profit or loss, depending on the position in the contract. In either case, the expected value of the profit or loss provides compensation for the riskiness of the position. If the bias in the forward contract is due to market inefficiency, the entrepreneur would possibly face a nontrivial trade-off between a reduced variance of profits and a reduced expected value of profits.

present value of any growth opportunities that the firm may have. In summary, Chapter 15 argues that

$$ANPV = \text{Present value of future after-tax cash flows for the all equity firm}$$
$$+ \text{Present value of future interest tax shields}$$
$$+ \text{Present value of interest subsidies}$$
$$- \text{Present value of the costs of financial distress due to debt}$$
$$+ \text{Present value of the firm's growth opportunities}$$

To derive the equity value of the firm, we must subtract the market value of debt from the ANPV of the firm's overall value:

$$\text{Equity value of the firm} = ANPV - \text{Market value of the firm's debt}$$

If the goal of a corporation's management is to maximize shareholder value, we should be able to address how hedging and other risk management activities increase the equity value of the firm. If hedging increases the equity value of the firm, it must affect one or more of the terms in the adjusted present value of the firm, or it must decrease the market value of the debt. Later on in this chapter, we will examine how each of the ANPV terms can be affected by hedging.

The Hedging-Is-Irrelevant Logic of Modigliani and Miller

In this section, we review the logic of the **Modigliani–Miller proposition** regarding the valuation of cash flows from a corporation. Modigliani and Miller argued that a corporation's financial policies, such as issuing debt, hedging foreign exchange risk, and other purely financial risk management activities, do not change the value of the firm's assets unless these financial transactions lower the firm's taxes, affect its investment decisions, or can be done more cheaply than individual investors' transactions can be done.

The reason that reducing the uncertainty of future cash flows, per se, does not lead to a rationale for hedging is that it may not change investors' perceptions of the firm's systematic risk. We know from modern portfolio theory that the required rate of return on the equity cash flows of a corporation does not depend on the standard deviation of the firm's cash flows but only on the systematic risk associated with those cash flows. The fact that a firm's cash flows are uncertain is a necessary but not a sufficient condition for discounting the cash flows at a discount rate higher than the risk-free interest rate. Hence, unlike in the case of an entrepreneurial firm, if hedging merely reduces the unsystematic risk of the corporation's cash flows while leaving unchanged both the systematic risk and the expected value of the cash flows, hedging will not have any effect on the firm's value. Investors will still discount the same expected cash flows at the same required rate of return that is appropriate for the firm's systematic risk.[2]

Modigliani and Miller also argued that, if individuals have the same investment opportunities as firms, investors can "undo" the financial transactions of corporations. In other words, individuals can adjust the leverage of their portfolios to the levels they want. They can also buy and sell foreign exchange forward contracts or option contracts to match their desired hedging levels—regardless of the firm's preferred hedging level. Notice in each of these situations that transaction costs and taxes must be the same for both the corporation and the individual.

Because major corporations can command better foreign exchange rate terms than the typical individual investor—that is, they transact at smaller bid–ask spreads—there is a rationale

---

[2]Essentially, the value of the hedged firm equals the value of the unhedged firm plus the value of any forward contracts. If the forward rate is an unbiased predictor of the future spot rate, the forward contracts have zero value when initiated. If the forward rate is biased, but the bias is due to an equilibrium risk premium, the forward contracts have value, and hedging changes the firm's expected cash flows. But hedging also changes the firm's systematic risk such that the expected value of the hedged firm is unchanged.

for corporations to hedge *for* investors. But we could easily argue that major institutional investors, such as the mutual fund investment companies Fidelity and Vanguard, who invest on behalf of individual investors, can deal in the foreign exchange market on terms comparable to those of a major corporation. As a result, we should look for reasons other than transaction costs as to why a firm might want to hedge.

17.2 ARGUMENTS AGAINST HEDGING

First, though, we take up three arguments against hedging. The first argument is that hedging is costly. The second argument against hedging is that most foreign exchange risk is equity related. Equity risk is long term in nature and effectively impossible to hedge away. The third argument is that hedging can create bad incentives. Let's look at each of these arguments in turn.

Hedging Is Costly

One frequently encountered argument against hedging is that it is costly, so firms should avoid doing it. Often, people who make this argument have in mind an incorrect notion of the cost of hedging. They argue that if the firm is selling foreign currency in the forward market, a forward discount on the foreign currency is a cost of hedging because the domestic currency forward price of foreign currency is less than the spot price. Conversely, a forward premium is viewed as providing a benefit or profit from hedging when the firm is selling foreign currency forward. In contrast, a forward premium is thought to increase the costs of the firm if it is buying foreign currency in the forward market.

This argument was first discussed in Chapter 3, where we note that the argument is incorrect because it reflects an irrelevant accounting perspective on the nature of costs rather than an appropriate economic perspective. We know that the forward rate differs from the current spot rate because of differences in interest rates (the time values of the two monies). The foreign currency cash flow is occurring in the future, not today. This makes the current spot rate irrelevant when it comes to valuing the future foreign currency cash flow unless the cash flow is first discounted to the present. If the forward rate of domestic currency per foreign currency is less than the current spot rate, the foreign interest rate is greater than the domestic interest rate. Any future foreign currency cash flows cannot be valued using the current spot rate, then, because that amount of foreign currency is not available for conversion into domestic currency at the spot rate.

A True Hedging Cost: The Bid–Ask Spread

Bid–ask spreads are typically larger in the forward market than in the spot market. Thus, one of the true costs of hedging is that the costs of transacting in the forward market typically exceed the costs of transacting in the spot market. This incremental cost is small for near-term transactions. In near-term transactions, the difference is only a few hundredths of a percent of the current spot rate. But the bid–ask spread widens as one contracts more distantly in the future. In this sense, the cost of forward hedging increases with the maturity of the contract.

The Employee Cost

An additional cost of hedging is that a firm must use employees to determine the types and sizes of various hedging instruments. These employees must then be monitored to prevent them from engaging in speculative behavior. Their compensation also must not be based on the profitability of their transactions alone. Otherwise, they will be motivated to speculate, and they will take off hedges that become profitable so that they can book accounting profits. Of course, this will expose the underlying risk that was being hedged. The following example illustrates how this works.

Example 17.1 Incorrectly Booking Profit on a Hedge

Suppose that a firm will receive 5,000,000 Swiss francs in 1 year. Let the 1-year forward rate be CHF1.50/USD. Suppose the treasurer of the firm makes a forward contract to sell CHF5,000,000 such that the firm will receive

$$\frac{CHF5,000,000}{CHF1.50/USD} = USD3,333,333.33$$

in 1 year. Now let 6 months pass and suppose that the 6-month forward rate is CHF1.70/USD. The value of the firm's underlying Swiss franc asset has fallen from USD3,333,333.33 to

$$\frac{CHF5,000,000}{CHF1.70/USD} = USD2,941,176.47$$

for a loss of USD392,156.86. Remember, though, that the firm is hedged because it sold the CHF5,000,000 forward, and the forward contract to sell CHF5,000,000 at CHF1.50/USD has increased in value by USD392,156.86.

If the treasurer of the company were trying to maximize profit on the contracts he makes, he could enter the 6-month forward market, say, by purchasing CHF5,000,000 to offset the firm's existing forward contract that has 6 months left to maturity. The dollar profit on this transaction would equal the fall in the forward rate of dollars per Swiss franc multiplied by the contractual amount of Swiss francs:

$$\left[\frac{1}{CHF1.5/USD} - \frac{1}{CHF1.7/USD} \right] \times CHF5,000,000 = USD392,156.86$$

Because this is a hedging situation, we know that the dollar value of the CHF5,000,000 account receivable has fallen in value by this same amount. If the firm's cost accountants decide that the treasurer should receive a profit of USD392,156.86, the loss on the receivable must be booked somewhere. If the sales division is allocated the corresponding loss, some serious incentive problems will arise in terms of getting the treasurer to hedge correctly.

Instead of hedging, the treasurer will begin to speculate. Taking off the hedge by buying CHF5,000,000 in the 6-month forward market would lock in the "profit" for the treasurer, but it would expose the firm's original, underlying Swiss franc asset to the risk that the Swiss franc might weaken even more. It is unlikely that the treasurer of a corporation has the ability to make profitable calls about the direction of exchange rates. If he or she does, the person should be working for an investment bank or hedge fund, where this ability can be leveraged and where investors are hoping for superior performance.

Now, let's examine the second argument against hedging.

Hedging Equity Risk Is Difficult, if Not Impossible

People sometimes argue that it is effectively impossible for a corporation to hedge the change in the value of its equity with a change in the exchange rate because the value of equity is the present discounted value of an infinite series of cash flows. To understand this argument, let's consider an example.

The Weehawken Widget Project

Consider the situation of Weehawken Widget Works, Inc. Weehawken Widget is a U.S. firm that has the opportunity to invest in a UK project. If the company spends $1,900 today, it gets a project that will return a random amount of pounds per year. Weehawken will receive either £125 or £75 of free cash flow for every year from next year into the infinite future. (Later, we treat each pound as £1 million to make the argument more forceful, but for now, let's just keep things simple.) Each of the possible pound cash flows is equally likely. Hence, the expected value of the cash flow each year is

$$0.5 \times £75 + 0.5 \times £125 = £100$$

If the appropriate pound discount rate for these cash flows is 10% per annum, the present value of the project is a perpetuity of £100, discounted at 10%:

$$\frac{£100}{1.1} + \frac{£100}{1.1^2} + \frac{£100}{1.1^3} + \ldots = \frac{£100}{0.1} = £1,000$$

If the current spot exchange rate is $2/£, the dollar present value of the project is

$$(\$2/£) \times £1,000 = \$2,000$$

To find the net present value of the project, we must subtract its cost, which is $1,900. Hence, if Weehawken's investors pay $1,900 today, they obtain a project with a discounted expected value of $2,000. Accepting the project causes the value of Weehawken to increase by $100.

Changes in the Project's Value over Time

Now, let's see how the value of the project changes over time. Suppose, for simplicity, that the exchange rate in each year can either increase or decrease by $0.20/£ with equal probability. Then, next year, the exchange rate will be either $2.20/£ or $1.80/£. If forward rates are unbiased forecasts of future spot rates, the current forward rates for all maturities will be $2.00/£. Let's assume that the dollar discount rate for these cash flows is also 10% and that the discount rates do not change over time. These assumptions are simplistic, but they allow us to easily make the necessary calculations. Finally, let's also assume that the realization of the project cash flow is independent of the realization of the exchange rate.

Exhibit 17.1 provides the four possible values for the project in 1 year, where by the value of the project we mean the payoff on the project in the first year, plus the ongoing value of the project, plus any gains or losses from hedging. For example, if the exchange rate turns out to be $2.20/£ and the project returns £125, the value of the project at time $t+1$ is

$$\overset{\text{Term A}}{[(\$2.20/£) \times £125]} + \overset{\text{Term B}}{[(\$2.20/£) \times £1,000]} = \$2,475$$

Term A represents the dollar value of the time $t+1$ pound cash flow, and Term B is the dollar value of the infinite stream of future expected pound cash flows that still has a present value of £1,000. In general, if $S(t+1,\$/£)$ is the dollar–pound exchange rate and $CF(t+1,£)$ is the pound cash flow at time $t+1$, the dollar value of the unhedged project at time $t+1$ is

$$[S(t+1,\$/£) \times CF(t+1,£)] + [S(t+1,\$/£) \times £1,000]$$

Exhibit 17.1   The Value of Weehawken's Project with Unhedged Cash Flows

		Possible Future Exchange Rates	
		$2.20/£	**$1.80/£**
Possible pound returns	£125	$2,475	$2,025
	£75	$2,365	$1,935

Exhibit 17.2 The Value of Weehawken's Project with 1-Year Hedged Cash Flows

		Possible Future Exchange Rates	
		$2.20/£	**$1.80/£**
Possible pound returns	£125	$2,455	$2,045
	£75	$2,345	$1,955

The Project's Value with 1 Year of Hedged Cash Flows

Now, let's consider the value of the project if Weehawken hedges 1 year of pound cash flows. Because the 1-year forward rate at time t is the expected value of the future spot rate, or $2.00/£, and because Weehawken hedges by selling the expected value of next year's cash flow, £100, in the 1-year forward market, the possible values of the project, including the time $t+1$ cash flow, are given in Exhibit 17.2. The values in Exhibit 17.2 are found just as they were in Exhibit 17.1. If the exchange rate turns out to be $2.20/£ and the project returns £125, the value of the project at time $t+1$ is

$$\underset{\text{Term C}}{[(\$2.00/£) \times £100]} + \underset{\text{Term D}}{[(\$2.20/£) \times £25]} + \underset{\text{Term B}}{[(\$2.20/£) \times £1,000]} = \$2,455$$

Term C represents the dollar value of the forward sale of pounds. Term D is the dollar value of the extra pound return that was not sold forward and that must therefore be sold in the spot market. Term B is, once again, the dollar value of the infinite stream of future expected pound cash flows that has a present value of £1,000. If the project returns only £75, Weehawken will have to purchase £25 in the spot market to deliver on the forward contract. In general, the value of the project at time $t+1$ with 1 year of hedged cash flows is

$$[(\$2.00/£) \times £100] + S(t+1,\$/£)] \times [CF(t+1,£) - £100] + [S(t+1,\$/£) \times £1,000]$$

By rearranging this expression, we see that it is the dollar value of the underlying unhedged pound asset plus the dollar return on a forward contract to sell £100 at $2.00/£:

$$[S(t+1,\$/£) \times CF(t+1,£)] + [S(t+1,\$/£) \times £1,000]$$
$$+ [(\$2.00/£) - S(t+1,\$/£)] \times £100$$

By comparing the entries in Exhibit 17.1 with those in Exhibit 17.2, we see that the forward hedge has transferred $20 of cash flow from the good state of the world, in which the pound strengthens, to the bad state of the world, in which the pound weakens. This $20 represents the difference between the forward rate and the future exchange rate multiplied by the expected cash flow, which is sold forward.

The Project's Value with 2 Years of Hedged Cash Flows

Now, suppose that Weehawken hedges by selling the first and second years of expected future pound revenue in the forward market, and under our assumptions, the 2-year forward rate at time t is also $2.00/£. The possible values of the project at time $t+1$, including the time $t+1$ cash flow, are given in Exhibit 17.3. If the exchange rate turns out to be $2.20/£ and the project returns £125, the value of the project at time $t+1$ is

$$\underset{\text{Term C}}{[(\$2.00/£) \times £100]} + \underset{\text{Term D}}{[(\$2.20/£) \times £25]} + \underset{\text{Term E}}{\left[\frac{(\$2.00/£) \times £100}{1.1}\right]} + \underset{\text{Term F}}{\left[\frac{(\$2.20/£) \times £1,000}{1.1}\right]}$$
$$= \$2,436.82$$

Exhibit 17.3 The Value of Weehawken's Project with 2-Year Hedged Cash Flows

		Possible Future Exchange Rates	
		$2.20/£	**$1.80/£**
Possible pound returns	£125	$2,436.82	$2,063.18
	£75	$2,326.82	$1,973.18

Terms C and D are again the dollar value of the 1-year forward contract and the dollar value of the extra pounds that must be sold in the spot market. Term E is the present value of the payment on the 2-year forward contract that has 1 year remaining, and Term F is the dollar value of the unhedged £100 perpetuity whose first cash flow begins 2 years from now. As noted earlier the dollar discount rate is assumed to be a constant 10%. By making the 2-year forward contract, Weehawken transfers an additional ($20/1.1) = $18.18 from the good state, in which the pound strengthens, to the bad state, in which the pound weakens. The $18.18 represents the present value of the profit on a forward contract that could be locked in at time $t+1$ because the 1-year forward rate at that time would equal the spot rate of $2.20/£ because the two interest rates are assumed to be equal to each other.[3]

The Project's Value with an Infinite Sequence of Hedged Cash Flows

Say that Weehawken makes an infinite sequence of forward contracts at time t—that is, if it contracts to sell £100 in every year from time $t+1$ to the infinite future at the assumed forward rates of $2.00/£. The fully hedged values of the project at time $t+1$ are given in Exhibit 17.4. If the exchange rate turns out to be $2.20/£, and the project returns £125, the dollar value of the fully hedged project at time $t+1$ is

$$
\overbrace{[(\$2.00/£) \times £100]}^{\text{Term C}} + \overbrace{[(\$2.20/£) \times £25]}^{\text{Term D}} + \overbrace{\left[\frac{(\$2.00/£) \times £100}{1.1}\right]}^{\text{Term E}}
$$

$$
+ \overbrace{\left[\frac{(\$2.00/£) \times £100}{1.1^2}\right]}^{\text{Term G}} + \overbrace{\left[\frac{(\$2.00/£) \times £100}{1.1^3}\right]}^{\text{Term H}} + \ldots = \$2,255
$$

Terms C and D are, once again, the value of the 1-year forward contract and the value of the extra pounds that must be sold in the spot market. Term E represents the dollar value of the 2-year forward contract that has 1 year remaining, as we just demonstrated. Term G and H represent the present value in dollars of previously made forward contracts to sell £100 that now have 2 and 3 years remaining to maturity, and so on, into the indefinite future.

Of course, an infinite number of forward-contract maturities are not available to the firm in the real world. Also, the bid–ask spreads in the forward market start to widen with maturities beyond a few years. Hence, Weehawken would not be able to sell pounds forward at $2/£ for all maturities because the transaction costs would cause the rates to be lower and lower for future maturities. Consequently, it is possible to mitigate the fluctuations in the value of the pound revenue stream due to foreign exchange rates, but it is not possible to eliminate them completely.

---

[3]Because £100 was sold forward at time t for each of 2 years, at $t+1$ the present value of the profit or loss on the forward contract that could be locked in by buying £100 in the 1 year forward market is

$$
£100 \times \left[\frac{F(t,2) - F(t+1,1)}{(1 + i(t+1,1))}\right] = £100 \times \left[\frac{(\$2.00/£) - (\$2.20/£)}{1.1}\right] = -\$18.18
$$

Exhibit 17.4 The Value of Weehawken's Project with Infinitely Hedged Cash Flows

		Possible Future Exchange Rates	
		$2.20/£	**$1.80/£**
Possible pound returns	£125	$2,255	$2,245
	£75	$2,145	$2,155

The Project's Value with an Equity Hedge

An alternative way to hedge this situation would be for Weehawken to do a sequence of 1-year forward contracts in which it sells £1,100 forward, which is the expected future value of the equity in 1 year. The possible returns on the project at time $t + 1$ in this case are actually the same as those in Exhibit 17.4, but they are calculated differently. The dollar value of the project at time $t + 1$ would be

$$\underset{\text{Term I}}{[(\$2.00/£) \times £1,100]} - \underset{\text{Term J}}{\{S(t+1,\$/£) \times [£1,100 - CF(t+1,£)]\}} + \underset{\text{Term K}}{[S(t+1,\$/£) \times £1,100]}$$

Term I is the dollar value of the forward sale of £1,100. Term J subtracts the realization of the pound cash flow at time $t + 1$ from the £1,100 that was sold forward to determine a net amount of pounds that must be purchased in the spot market to deliver the pounds that were sold forward. Weehawken would have only the return on the project at time $t + 1$ as a pound cash flow and would have to purchase the rest in the spot market. Term K is the dollar value of the £100 into perpetuity that Weehawken still expects to receive. By rearranging terms and canceling, we can rewrite the value of the pound perpetuity as

$$(\$2.00/£) \times £1,100 + S(t+1,\$/£) \times [CF(t+1,£) - £100]$$

which is the same value as the sequence of infinite forward contracts. For example, when the spot exchange rate at time $t+1$ is $2.20/£ and the cash flow is £125, we find the value to be $2,255, as before. The problem with this approach to hedging is that Weehawken must sell in the 1-year forward market more than 10 times the amount of pounds that it expects to receive in the next period. Then, after 1 year, it must enter the spot market and purchase a large amount of pounds to deliver on the forward contract.

In order to see the problem with this strategy more clearly, remember that the additional value to the firm from this project is only $100, which is the original $2,000 of projected cash flows minus the $1,900 initial cost. To put the issue in better perspective, think of each pound as representing 1 million pounds, with the value of the project representing the firm's entire value. Then, Weehawken would have an initial equity value of $2 billion. Initial investors would have invested $1.9 billion, and the firm's positive NPV project would increase its value to $2 billion. It is questionable whether a bank would allow a firm with an equity value of $2 billion to make a 1-year forward sale of £1.1 billion or a 1-year purchase of $2.2 billion. It is in this sense that the firm would have difficulty fully hedging the cash flows.

Reality Is More Complicated

The equity cash flows we have just examined are quite simple, fluctuating between only two values, year in and year out, and the firm confidently forecasts that this pattern will persist forever. Neither the dollar discount rate nor the pound discount rate fluctuates in the example, and the exchange rate is a simple process with an expected value that depends on the realization of the exchange rate.[4] In a more realistic equity project, the pattern of cash flows would

---

[4]We specified only the first year of the time series process for the exchange rate with plus or minus $0.20 increments. Obviously, the increments to this process cannot be constant because the exchange rate cannot be negative, but the expected value can depend on the current realization.

involve forecasts of growth and the possibility of total loss. The real profitability of the foreign project also would probably be related to the real exchange rate. In the simple example, however, Weehawken's nominal pound cash flows were simply being converted into dollars by the nominal exchange rate.

As you can see, the world is much more complicated and more uncertain than the Weehawken example indicates. Nevertheless, Weehawken's situation provides an important intuition: Because much of the value of a firm's equity is due to its cash flows in the relatively far distant future, Weehawken cannot fully hedge even simple equity cash flows.

Hedging Can Create Bad Incentives

Of course, as investors in firms, we must be aware of how changes in hedging policies can be used to the advantage of one class of stakeholders and the disadvantage of others. Chapter 16 describes how equity shareholders prefer projects with high variances to projects with low variances, especially when the firm is near financial distress. One way that a firm can increase the variance of its cash flows is to stop a hedging program that is already in place. For example, if a firm has foreign currency revenues and is having difficulty meeting its fixed obligations, it can leave the foreign currency cash flows unhedged and hope for a strengthening of the foreign currency. In such a situation, any weakening of the foreign currency when the firm is unhedged simply creates additional losses, most of which are borne by the firm's bondholders.

Of course, even though a firm is actively engaged in a financial hedging program, the financial officers who are in charge of the hedging program must be supervised to prevent them from speculating with the firm's money. Such a temptation would surely grow as the firm gets closer to financial distress.[5] After all, what better way is there to come up with the principal on a bond issue than to try to make some money in the "casinos" of foreign exchange futures and options markets? The CFO of a firm facing financial distress might think exactly this way.

In light of the arguments mentioned, some managers say that the firm simply should not try to hedge. But there are other arguments that support hedging. It is to those that we now turn.

17.3 ARGUMENTS FOR HEDGING

This section examines how hedging can enhance the value of a firm by affecting the various terms in an ANPV analysis. We begin by demonstrating that hedging can increase the after-tax value of a firm's cash flows under certain conditions.

Hedging Can Reduce the Firm's Expected Taxes

Hedging can increase the value of a firm by reducing its expected future income taxes. One way that expected income taxes can be decreased is by making sure that the firm does not experience losses. When a firm is unprofitable, it owes no current tax, but it does not get an immediate refund from the government. Instead, the firm generates a **tax-loss carry-forward** that allows it to offset the losses that were incurred against future income. Thus, the firm pays less tax in the future. But, a tax-loss carry-forward is an accounting convention that only allows a firm to offset $1 of future income against $1 of loss incurred today. Because the economic value of $1 of income in the future is worth less than $1 of income

---

[5]An interesting example of this phenomenon is provided by Stephen Ross, Randolph Westerfield, Jeffrey Jaffee, and Bradford Jordan (2007), p. 458, who relate the following story. When Federal Express encountered severe financial difficulty a few years after its inception, Frederick Smith, the founder, is reputed to have taken $20,000 of corporate funds to gamble in Las Vegas. He apparently won enough money to save the firm from bankruptcy. Had he lost, the firm would have gone bankrupt, and the creditors of the firm would have received $20,000 less.

Exhibit 17.5 A Convex Income Tax

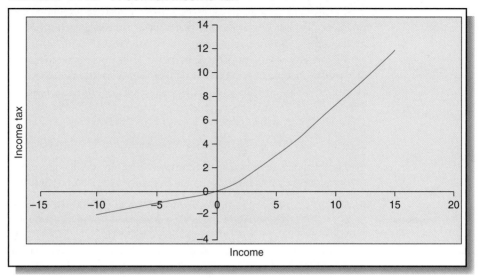

today, due to the time value of money, having $1 of future tax-loss carry-forward is not as valuable as avoiding $1 of tax today. Hence, there is a reason for avoiding losses today.

Tax-loss carry-forwards also usually have a statutory time limit. They cannot be extended beyond a certain date in the future. Any unused tax-loss carry-forwards simply expire if the firm is unable to generate sufficient taxable income by the expiration date. The fact that tax-loss carry-forwards can expire unused provides another reason for avoiding losses today. Consequently, if hedging can help a firm avoid losses, then it is valuable. Avoiding financial losses also increases the probability that a firm's tax shields from depreciation and interest payments can be fully utilized in the future.

Finally, hedging reduces expected future taxes if the tax code is convex. A **convex tax code** imposes a larger tax rate on higher incomes and a smaller tax rate on lower incomes. Exhibit 17.5 provides a hypothetical convex tax code.

Although the corporate tax rates in many countries are a flat percentage of income, if the firm loses money, and those losses are not refunded immediately at the same rate as the rate for positive income, the tax function is effectively convex. Example 17.3, which appears a little later in the chapter, demonstrates this principal.

In the presence of a convex tax code, a firm prefers to pay tax on its expected income with certainty rather than to determine its expected tax by taking the probability weighted average of the taxes on possible incomes in the uncertain future states of the world. Because hedging allows the firm to shift income across different states of the world, hedging reduces expected taxes and increases the firm's value.

Some examples will help to clarify this discussion.

Example 17.2 Starpower's Swiss Project with Non-convex Taxes

Assume that a U.S. firm, Starpower, has a project that provides a Swiss franc revenue of CHF40,000,000 in 1 year. Starpower's project costs $19,000,000, and we assume this amount is paid in 1 year. Although the dollar cost of the project will be paid with certainty and the Swiss franc revenue from the project will be received with certainty, the dollar revenue from the project is uncertain because the future spot exchange rate is uncertain. Let's assume that there are only two possible future spot exchange rates. Either the spot rate in 1 year will be $0.55/CHF with 50% probability, or it will be $0.45/CHF, also with 50% probability. If Starpower is unhedged, it will experience a positive income of $3,000,000 with 50% probability because

$$[(\$0.55/CHF) \times CHF40,000,000] - \$19,000,000 = \$3,000,000$$

or Starpower will experience a loss of $1,000,000 because

$$[(\$0.45/CHF) \times CHF40,000,000] - \$19,000,000 = -\$1,000,000$$

The expected dollar value of Starpower's before-tax income on the unhedged project is therefore the probability weighted average of the two possibilities:

$$[0.5 \times \$3,000,000] + [0.5 \times (-\$1,000,000)] = \$1,000,000$$

Suppose that the tax rate is 35% and that the government also will immediately subsidize 35% of all losses. That is, the government refunds $35\% \times \$1,000,000 = \$350,000$ to the firm in the event of a loss. The expected value of Starpower's after-tax income on the unhedged project is the probability weighted average of the after-tax cash flows:

$$[0.5 \times \$3,000,000 \times (1 - 0.35)] + [0.5 \times (-\$1,000,000) \times (1 - 0.35)]$$
$$= \$650,000$$

Suppose that Starpower has the opportunity to hedge its CHF cash flow by selling the CHF40,000,000 revenue in the forward market at the 1-year forward rate of $0.50/CHF. Note that this forward rate is also the expected future spot rate because

$$[0.5 \times (\$0.55/CHF)] + [0.5 \times (\$0.45/CHF)] = \$0.50/CHF$$

If Starpower fully hedges, it will receive

$$(\$0.50/CHF) \times CHF40,000,000 = \$20,000,000$$

of dollar revenue no matter what the future exchange rate turns out to be. Hence, Starpower will have a sure income of

$$\$20,000,000 - \$19,000,000 = \$1,000,000$$

Consequently, Starpower's after-tax income will be

$$\$1,000,000 \times (1 - 0.35) = \$650,000$$

Notice, in this example, that although hedging allows the firm to reduce the variance of its income while keeping its expected income the same, hedging provides no after-tax gain. Starpower's expected after-tax income is the same whether the firm hedges or not. This situation occurs because the tax treatment of losses is identical to the tax treatment of gains. The tax schedule is linear, not convex.

Example 17.3 Starpower's Swiss Project with Convex Taxes

Consider the same project as in Example 17.2, but now suppose that Starpower can claim only a 25% refund on its losses. We will continue to assume that the firm is taxed at a 35% rate on its positive income. With these new tax rates, the expected value of the after-tax income on the unhedged project falls to

$$[0.5 \times \$3,000,000 \times (1 - 0.35)] + [0.5 \times (-\$1,000,000) \times (1 - 0.25)]$$
$$= \$600,000$$

The firm's expected tax bill is the difference between the expected before-tax income of $1,000,000 and the expected after-tax income of $600,000, or

$$\$1,000,000 - \$600,000 = \$400,000$$

Equivalently, the firm's expected tax bill is the probability weighted average of taxes that will be paid in the good state (35% of $3 million) minus subsidies that will be received in the bad state (25% of $1 million):

$$[0.5 \times \$1,050,000] - [0.5 \times \$250,000] = \$400,000$$

When Starpower has the ability to hedge, it takes no losses in this example, and its after-tax income is unchanged from the previous example. We calculated that Starpower's after-tax income was $650,000, which implies that the firm expects to pay taxes of only

$$\$1,000,000 - \$650,000 = \$350,000$$

if it hedges versus the $400,000 in taxes it expects to pay if it does not hedge. By reducing its expected income tax payment, Starpower has increased its expected after-tax value by $50,000.

What happens to the expected tax saving if we increase the volatility of Starpower's income while leaving the expected value of its income the same? It will turn out that the expected tax savings from hedging increases. Next, we show how this is so.

Example 17.4   Starpower's Swiss Project with a Larger Variance

Let the possible values of the future exchange rate be $0.60/CHF and $0.40/CHF, which are again equally probable. The forward rate will remain at $0.50/CHF. The dollar income from Starpower's project will now be either

$$[(\$0.60/\text{CHF}) \times \text{CHF}40,000,000] - \$19,000,000 = \$5,000,000$$

or

$$[(\$0.40/\text{CHF}) \times \text{CHF}40,000,000] - \$19,000,000 = -\$3,000,000$$

where each event again has a probability of 50%. The expected value of Starpower's before-tax income remains $1,000,000 because

$$[0.5 \times \$5,000,000] + [0.5 \times (-\$3,000,000)] = \$1,000,000$$

The expected value of the after-tax income on the project if Starpower does not hedge is now

$$[0.5 \times \$5,000,000 \times (1 - 0.35)] - [0.5 \times (\$3,000,000) \times (1 - 0.25)]$$
$$= \$500,000$$

Consequently, Starpower expects to pay

$$\$1,000,000 - \$500,000 = \$500,000$$

of tax if it does not hedge.

Now, consider what happens if Starpower hedges. Suppose that the firm sells CHF40,000,000 forward. Then, Starpower's expected income is still $1,000,000, and its expected after-tax income remains $650,000. The firm expects to pay only $350,000 of tax instead of the $500,000 of expected tax if it does not hedge. Starpower now saves $150,000 of expected tax payments when the possible returns on the project are $5,000,000 and −$3,000,000 versus the $50,000 of expected tax saving when the possible returns on the project were $3,000,000 and −$1,000,000. Hence, we see that the more volatile Starpower's income, the greater the expected tax saving from hedging.

The tax benefit of hedging also increases if the convexity of the tax rates is greater. In our two-state example, greater convexity amounts to a greater difference between the tax rate on positive income and the refund rate on losses.

Example 17.5 Starpower's Swiss Project with a More Convex Tax Schedule

Suppose in Example 17.3 that positive income is taxed at a rate of 45% instead of 35%, whereas losses are again refunded at the 25% rate. Then, if Starpower does not hedge, its expected after-tax income is

$$[0.5 \times (\$5,000,000) \times (1 - 0.45)] + [0.5 \times (-\$3,000,000) \times (1 - 0.25)] = \$250,000$$

Hence, the firm now expects to pay tax of

$$\$1,000,000 - \$250,000 = \$750,000$$

If Starpower hedges by selling CHF40,000,000 forward at $0.50/$, it will again pay taxes on the $1,000,000 of sure income, giving it an after-tax income of

$$\$1,000,000 \times (1 - 0.45) = \$550,000$$

When Starpower hedges, however, it expects to pay $450,000 of tax instead of the expected tax of $750,000 when it does not hedge. Starpower therefore saves $300,000 of expected tax payments.

Unfortunately, the tax benefits of hedging decrease if more of the pretax income of the firm is in the non-convex region of the tax code.

Example 17.6 Starpower's Swiss Project with Greater Profitability

Let's continue with our two-state examples and keep the spread between the two possible exchange rates the same as in Example 17.5, but now let's make Starpower more profitable by increasing the exchange rates to $0.65/CHF and $0.45/CHF. If the forward rate equals the expected future spot rate, the forward rate now increases to

$$[0.5 \times (\$0.65/\text{CHF})] + [0.5 \times (\$0.45/\text{CHF})] = \$0.55/\text{CHF}$$

Now, if Starpower does not hedge, its pretax income in the good state is

$$[(\$0.65/\text{CHF}) \times \text{CHF}40,000,000] - \$19,000,000 = \$26,000,000 - \$19,000,000$$
$$= \$7,000,000$$

In the bad state, Starpower takes a loss because its income is

$$[(\$0.45/CHF) \times CHF40{,}000{,}000] - \$19{,}000{,}000 = \$18{,}000{,}000 - \$19{,}000{,}000$$
$$= -\$1{,}000{,}000$$

Starpower's expected after-tax income if it does not hedge is

$$[0.5 \times (\$7{,}000{,}000) \times (1 - 0.45)] + [0.5 \times (-\$1{,}000{,}000) \times (1 - 0.25)]$$
$$= \$1{,}550{,}000$$

If the firm hedges by selling CHF40,000,000 forward at the forward rate of $0.55/CHF, its after-tax income is

$$\{[(\$0.55/CHF) \times CHF40{,}000{,}000] - \$19{,}000{,}000\} \times (1 - 0.45)$$

$$= \$3{,}000{,}000 \times (1 - 0.45) = \$1{,}650{,}000$$

If Starpower does not hedge, it now expects to pay tax of

$$\$3{,}000{,}000 - \$1{,}550{,}000 = \$1{,}450{,}000$$

If Starpower hedges, it will pay tax of

$$\$3{,}000{,}000 - \$1{,}650{,}000 = \$1{,}350{,}000$$

Starpower therefore saves $100,000 of expected tax payments when more of its income is in the non-convex region of the tax code with revenues of $26 million or $18 million compared to the $300,000 of expected tax payments that it saved by hedging when its possible future revenues were $24 million or $16 million.

General Principles

Examples 17.2 through 17.6 illustrate some general principles. First, risk management or hedging has definite tax benefits when there is convexity to the tax code. Progressive tax rates on positive income are one source of convexity in tax codes. Most countries, though, do not have progressive corporate income taxes on positive income. The same percentage tax rate is applied to all positive income and to losses. But other factors in tax codes, such as tax-loss carry-forwards, alternative minimum taxes, and investment tax credits, do impart convexity to tax schedules in their treatment of losses and their encouragement to undertake certain transactions.

The general principles revealed by the examples are that the tax benefits of hedging are larger in the following situations:

- When the tax code is more convex, or progressive
- When a firm's pretax income is more volatile
- When more of a firm's income occurs in the convex region of the tax code

Hedging Can Lower the Costs of Financial Distress

Hedging can increase the value of a firm by reducing the expected costs of financial distress (see Clifford Smith and René Stulz, 1985). Chapter 15 explains that the costs of financial distress are the losses of value that a firm experiences because it may experience bankruptcy in the future. These costs are distinct from the losses of value experienced by a firm that trigger an actual default or a declaration of bankruptcy. As explained in Chapter 15, the costs of financial distress include the direct costs of bankruptcy, such as the legal and administrative expenses. But they also include indirect costs, such as a firm's inability to make binding commitments to its customers, suppliers, workers, and managers and vice versa. In addition, the managers of a firm may be led to act selfishly in the interest of stockholders at the expense of bondholders. Hedging reduces the probability that a firm will encounter financial distress and thus mitigates these problems.

Hedging Can Improve the Firm's Future Investment Decisions

Chapter 16 describes how firms that are near financial distress can be led to reject a positive NPV project because too much of the return on the project accrues to the bondholders and not enough to the shareholders. If hedging avoids the fall in firm value that would place the firm in a state in which it would make such a poor investment decision, then hedging improves the firm's future investment decisions.

More generally, a model by Kenneth Froot, David Scharfstein, and Jeremy Stein (1993) argues that imperfections in capital markets provide a strong rationale for hedging. Whenever externally generated funds for investment projects are more costly to the firm than internally generated funds from retained earnings, hedging increases the firm's value by providing it with a reliable, less volatile stream of internally generated profits, which it can use to finance its research and development and capital expenditures. Hedging effectively provides a source of cash flow that allows a firm to exercise its investment opportunities and its growth options at the point in time when it is optimal to invest.

The Basic Logic of the Argument

Suppose that a firm does not hedge. Then, variability in cash flow from assets in place will be reflected in variability in free cash flow to equity holders. Now, remember that free cash flow to equity cannot be negative. If free cash flow to equity were to begin to be negative, the firm would either have to raise cash externally, or it would have to cut back on the firm's investment policy. Because variability in investment or research and development is generally undesirable, the firm would normally use external capital markets to finance investment, when the firm has insufficient internally generated cash. However, in imperfect capital markets, the marginal cost of raising external funds may increase with the amount of funds raised. In that case, the firm will find it optimal to cut back on investments and research and development when internally generated cash flow is low. If the firm hedges, it can avoid the shortfall in internally generated cash and avoid the drop in investment.

Asymmetric Information Is the Problem

The managers of a firm usually know more about the firm's future prospects than investors do. This asymmetric information consequently makes it difficult and sometimes impossible for financial markets to price new offerings of debt or equity being used by a firm. This uncertainty leads investors to demand a premium for financing new projects, and the premium may increase with the amount of funds the company is trying to raise. As a result, the cost of raising externally generated funds is high, and firms prefer to finance their investment projects from internally generated funds.

A corporation in an industry that relies heavily on internally generated funds for its investment projects should definitely consider instituting a hedging program. This appears to be Merck's rationale for hedging, as we will see later in the chapter.

Hedging Can Change the Assessment of a Firm's Managers

Another argument for financial hedging that relies on asymmetric information between the managers of the firm and its shareholders has been offered by Peter DeMarzo and Darrell Duffie (1995). Shareholders must gauge the quality of the managers based on their observations of the firm's profitability and earnings, as disclosed in its accounting data. From this perspective, hedging makes good sense at first glance. Hedging reduces the amount of "noise" in earnings data that is not due to actions of the managers. In other words, hedging increases the informational content of a firm's profits about a manager's ability. DeMarzo and Duffie demonstrate that in this situation, the accounting treatment of hedging and the optimal hedging policy are intimately linked. Because managers are better able to gauge the different financial risks the company faces, they have an incentive to hedge these risks to reduce the variability of the firm's earnings and, with that, the variability of their own income stream, which will be linked to the firm's earnings. A manager does not want to face an unexpected currency depreciation that adversely affects the firm's profits.

The disclosure of information, though, will make shareholders better able to gauge the true ability of a manager. Shareholders can then make the managers' compensation more sensitive to the firm's performance. To avoid this additional variability in their income, managers may chose not to hedge. If the additional informational content of hedged earnings is sufficiently high, the shareholders may optimally decide not to disclose the firm's hedging activities, to give managers an incentive to hedge.

POINT–COUNTERPOINT
Asymmetric Information and the Pecking Order

Ante, Freedy, and Suttle are visiting Berlin, strolling by the Brandenburg Gate, discussing the fall of the Berlin Wall and the collapse of communism in 1989. Freedy says, "Isn't capitalism great? Look at all the new buildings in what used to be East Germany."

Ante replies, "The buildings are cool, and the architecture is fantastic, but capitalism would be a lot better if we could just stop managers from ripping off investors. I don't know why anybody buys equity."

Freedy says, "What's the big deal, Ante? Equity markets are efficient. Any information that is out there pretty quickly finds its way into market prices."

Ante, getting hot under the collar, blurts, "Well, if that's true, why do Bekaert and Hodrick argue that asymmetric information is a big deal in risk management? If managers know more than investors when it comes to risk management, they also know more than investors when it comes to issuing equity. The managers would issue equity when it is overvalued, and they would buy back equity when it is undervalued. Markets are stupid!"

At this point, Suttle sees that the brothers are about to really get into it, so he feels it necessary to intervene. "Hey, you guys need to understand something," says Suttle. "Markets can't know everything. Indeed, there is good reason to think that managers know more than the shareholders about the prospects of the firm. Some pretty good economists have figured out the implications of these ideas for corporate finance."

"For example," says Suttle, "Stephen Ross (1977) developed one of the first models of corporate finance to rely on asymmetric information. In the Ross model, managers know the prospects of the firm better than the financial markets. Without a signal from the managers, investors will view all firms as the same. To signal a firm's good prospects, the managers of the good firm must do something that is costly and cannot be mimicked by the managers of the firms with poorer prospects. Managers can signal the prospects of the firm to the capital markets by choosing an appropriate level of debt. Thus, Ross argues that the firms with good prospects signal this information by taking on more debt than firms with bad prospects. This action is an effective signal because bankruptcy is costly. A high-debt firm that has good prospects is less likely to incur the bankruptcy costs than a similarly levered firm with poorer prospects."

Freedy and Ante smile at how loquacious Suttle can be. Ante pipes up, "That's fine for debt, but I was talking about equity."

Suttle replies, "Well, Stewart Myers wrote two important papers extending this asymmetric information intuition to the decision to issue equity. It is called the **'pecking order' theory of**

financing,[6] and it states that investments should be financed with the least information-sensitive source of funds. Myers argues that managers are better informed about the prospects of their firm than the capital markets, but the capital markets understand this. Managers consequently will not want to issue equity to finance a project when they think the firm is undervalued by capital markets. In fact, they will try to issue equity when it's overvalued. Because capital markets understand this logic, capital markets will view issuing equity as a very bad signal.

"The pecking order for financing investments is the result. Internally generated cash is used first because no explanation has to be given to the capital markets about why or how it is being used. Debt is the next source of finance because the cash flows paid to the debt holders are fixed and insensitive to future cash flows of the firm. Firms without enough internally generated funds but good future prospects can do this. Resorting to equity to finance investment projects is the least preferred method because it is such a bad signal. Consequently, only firms with insufficient internally generated funds and no ability to issue debt will rely on issuing equity."

Freedy and Ante grab Suttle and say, "Come on. We've had enough of this asymmetric information economics. Let's go get a good German bratwurst. We're hungry!"

17.4 MERCK'S HEDGING RATIONALE

Only a few firms have actually written down why they chose to institute a hedging program and to explain the logic of their analysis. This section describes Merck's decision to use foreign currency options to hedge its foreign currency revenue.[7]

At the time that Merck decided to institute a hedging policy in 1988, it had sales of $6.6 billion in a pharmaceutical industry with total sales of roughly $103.7 billion. No one firm in the industry commanded more than a 5% share of total market sales. Approximately 50% of Merck's revenue came from foreign sales of its drugs. Merck had approximately 70 subsidiaries around the world that imported semi-finished product and were responsible for finishing, marketing, and distributing final product in the countries in which they were incorporated. The competitive nature of the business dictated that final sale prices were usually denominated in local currencies. In addition, many of the local prices were regulated. Therefore, if a local currency weakened relative to the dollar, Merck had limited ability to increase the local price of its products.

The dividends repatriated from Merck's foreign subsidiaries formed a substantial fraction of its earnings and profits. It was from these internally generated funds that Merck usually financed its research and development and its capital expenditures.

Merck's decision to hedge came in the mid-1980s, following a rough patch when the dollar strengthened. The dollar appreciation really hurt Merck; the company developed a sales index that measured the strength of the dollar relative to a basket of currencies weighted by the revenue it produced in that currency. The index declined from a base level of 100 in 1978 to 60 in 1984. During that time, Merck experienced a cumulative loss of revenue of approximately $900 million. In response, Merck cut back on its research and development and investment projects.

However, after reviewing the performance of the firm during this period, Merck's managers decided that this was a flawed decision. One important aspect of the competitive nature of the industry is its emphasis on the development of new drugs. By decreasing its research and development, Merck risked becoming uncompetitive in the global marketplace.

---

[6]See Stewart Myers (1984) and Stewart Myers and Nicolais Majluf (1984).

[7]Merck's decision is described in detail in Judy Lewent and John Kearney (1990). At the time of the analysis, Ms. Lewent was Merck's vice president and treasurer, and in 2006, she was executive vice president and chief financial officer. The following section summarizes their argument.

Developing Natural Operating Hedges

The first line of defense Merck considered using was an **operating currency hedge**. That is, Merck considered shifting the company's operations across countries to provide a better balance between the costs and revenues denominated in different currencies. Unfortunately, because Merck wanted to continue to conduct most of its research and development in the United States as well as keep its corporate headquarters there, this option was not really feasible.

Merck's Five-Step Procedure

Merck developed a five-step procedure to help decide whether to hedge with financial contracts and what types of financial hedges to choose. The five steps were as follows:

1. Develop forecasts of the distribution of future exchange rates to determine the probability of adverse movements in exchange rates.
2. Assess the impact of exchange rate changes on the firm's 5-year strategic plan.
3. Decide whether to hedge the firm's exchange rate exposure.
4. Select the appropriate hedging instruments.
5. Simulate alternative hedging programs to determine those most cost-effective, given the risk tolerance of Merck's managers.

We next consider the factors that enter into each of these steps.

Step 1: Develop Forecasts of the Distribution of Future Exchange Rates to Determine the Probability of Adverse Movements Related to Them

Merck considered four main factors in determining the probability of future changes in exchange rates: economic fundamentals, government interference in the setting of exchange rates, past exchange rates, and professional forecasts. Lewent and Kearney (1990) note that the economic fundamentals include variables such as the trade balance deficit, international capital flows, and government budget deficits, which are used to define an "equilibrium" exchange rate, but they are not specific about the equilibrium model. Merck's model also recognizes that central bankers often set explicit or implicit target zones for currency prices, which they stand ready to defend with intervention. In addition, Lewent and Kearney note that the Merck model is "mean reverting" in the sense that when there have been several large movements of the exchange rate in the same direction, the probability of future movements in that direction is reduced. The idea is that such a large movement in the nominal exchange rate would most surely be associated with a large movement in the real exchange rate. Such a large change in the real exchange rate would create forces in the trade balance that would limit the likelihood of an additional change in the same direction. The fourth factor affecting Merck's assessment of future exchange rates involved obtaining the opinions of various professional forecasting services. The staffs of the world's major investment and commercial banks routinely supply forecasts of future exchange rates. In Merck's case, external forecasters were split almost evenly on the outlook for the dollar, although none were predicting that the dollar would strengthen in the way that it did in the early 1980s.

Step 2: Assess the Impact of Exchange Rate Changes on the Firm's 5-Year Strategic Plan

Merck's second step involved assessing the impact of adverse changes in exchange rates on the firm's strategic plan. This involved examining cash flow and earnings projections for 5 years into the future under various exchange rate scenarios. These forecasts had to incorporate the effects that past profitability would have on the firm's future investment decisions.

Step 3: Decide Whether to Hedge the Firm's Exchange Rate Exposure

Examining the cash flow projections in the previous step gave Merck an idea about the likelihood that it would encounter adverse circumstances and how these situations would affect the firm's future investment decisions. For example, if a firm's net operating profits are forecast to be sufficiently high, this will give it enough cash to continue to finance its R&D activities in order to remain competitive. Then there is little reason to hedge. However, for the sake of illustration, let's assume that this is not the case and that in some scenarios, exchange rate movements are forecast to adversely affect the firm's operating profits so that they fall below the level needed to finance its desired capital expenditures. How, then, will the firm finance its investment projects?

One way the firm can finance its investment projects is to turn to the external capital markets for financing. But can the firm successfully raise the funds that it needs at reasonable required rates of return in those states of the world? Remember, the firm will be going to the financial markets when it is unprofitable. As a result, participants in the financial markets might not think that the unprofitability is strictly due to adverse fluctuations in exchange rates. What happens if the market decides that other reasons, such as poor managerial decisions, are to blame? In such a case, the firm's managers will find it difficult to pursue the projects they believe will keep the firm competitive. Hedging would prevent this from happening.

Merck came to the conclusion that it should hedge against exchange rate volatility because a large proportion (typically 50% or more) of the company's earnings are generated overseas, and the volatility of the cash flows potentially adversely affects the firm's ability to execute its strategic plan—namely invest in R&D. In addition, the pharmaceutical industry has a very long planning horizon, one that reflects the complexity of the research involved as well as the lengthy process of product registration. It often takes more than 10 years between the discovery of a product and its market launch. Success in the industry generally requires a continuous, long-term commitment to a steadily increasing level of research funding. In this regard, it made sense for Merck to hedge.

Step 4: Select the Appropriate Hedging Instrument

The available financial hedging instruments are forward and futures contracts, foreign currency debts, currency swaps, and currency options. Forward foreign exchange contracts, futures contracts, foreign currency debt, and currency swaps "fix" the value of domestic currency that will be received in the future in return for a *given* amount of foreign currency delivered. In other words, the amount of the domestic currency received cannot be increased or decreased. In contrast, put options provide insurance against a strengthening of the dollar against the foreign currency because they give the firm the right, but not the obligation, to sell foreign currency at a contractual price. (We discuss put options in Chapter 20.) The firm can either exercise this right or, if the exchange rate in the market is better, it can experience higher dollar payoffs by ignoring its option. Of course, the firm must pay the option premium for this privilege. Merck decided that it was unwilling to forgo the potential gains if the dollar weakened, so options were the company's preferred hedging vehicle.

Step 5: Simulate Alternative Hedging Programs to Determine Those Most Cost-effective, Given the Risk Tolerance of Merck's Managers

After deciding that options were the most advantageous hedging vehicle, the issue of how exactly to implement a hedging plan with a 5-year horizon remained to be determined. Several questions had to be addressed when making such a decision, including the following: What term of the hedge is appropriate? Should it be multiyear or year-by-year? What strike prices (contractual exchange rates) should the put options have?

Merck considered "out-of-the-money" options as a means of reducing costs. An out-of-the-money option means that the strike price, which is the contractual exchange rate in the option, is fewer dollars per foreign currency than the current exchange rate.

What percentage of income should be covered? In other words, can the firm afford partially to "self-insure" its risks—that is, to leave part of the exposure unhedged, thereby reducing current expenditures to implement the hedge? Merck used a privately developed Monte Carlo simulation model. A Monte Carlo simulation model generates alternative cash flow scenarios and exchange rates. The simulation determined that (1) Merck should hedge for several years, using long-term options, (2) there was no gain to be had by using far-out-of-the-money options, and (3) Merck should partially self-insure.

Merck's strategy worked well throughout the 1990s, as its profitability remained high and its stock price went from $12.40 in the beginning of 1990 to $90.50 a share in terms of current prices (that is, adjusted for stock splits) in December 2000. As the general market fell in the early 2000s, Merck's stock price fell also. Then, unfortunately, one of Merck's most important pain-relief drugs, Vioxx, had to be taken off the market in 2004, when it was reported that Vioxx caused heart attacks. Although Merck vowed to fight all the subsequent lawsuits, its stock price suffered when the firm lost in court. By June 2006, the stock price had fallen to $36.43 per share. By June 2007, the price was back to $50.44 per share.

17.5 HEDGING TRENDS

Accountants treat many hedges as off–balance sheet items. Because only balance sheets and income statements tend to get reported, gathering information about hedge activity and trends must be done some other way. Some scholars have used survey data, and others have directly read the footnotes of annual reports and other regulatory filings.

Information from Surveys

Deane Nance, Clifford Smith, and Charles Smithson (1993) were among the first to use surveys to attempt to determine the characteristics of firms that actively hedge versus those that do not. Their findings provide some support for the framework developed in this chapter.

In particular, Nance, Smith, and Smithson find that firms with large R&D expenditures are active hedgers. This may be because it is more difficult for high-R&D firms to raise external financing either because their principal assets are intangible and cannot be used as collateral or because there is more asymmetric information about the quality of their new projects. There is also some evidence that more highly levered firms (ones with larger debt–equity ratios) hedge more. Firms that are highly levered do not want to encounter financial distress, so they actively manage their risks to prevent it.

One interesting finding is that firms with higher dividend payouts are also more likely to hedge. Apparently, these firms have a substantial amount of free cash flow and are not constrained in a traditional sense. Yet managers may view a dividend policy as a commitment to the firm's shareholders that cannot be violated. Hedging allows the firm both to maintain its dividend policy and to fund its future investments.

The Wharton/CIBC Survey
A Wharton/CIBC Survey, conducted by Gordon Bodnar, Greg Hayt, and Richard Marston (1998), obtained responses from 399 non-financial firms on their use of derivatives and their risk management practices. Bodnar, Hayt, and Marston found that 83% of large firms and only 12% of small firms used derivatives to hedge. The fact that the larger firms in the study tended to hedge and the smaller ones tended not to hedge is consistent with the argument that the cost of hedging contains a fixed cost. Only when a firm is sufficiently large to overcome the fixed costs of hedging does the firm institute a hedging policy.

The foreign exchange exposure of the firms in the study varied widely. Some 40% of the firms with foreign exchange exposure reported that their foreign currency revenues constituted at least 20% or more of their total revenues. Almost 40% of firms reported that their foreign currency expenses were 20% or more of their total expenses. On the other hand, 60% of the firms reported that their total foreign currency revenues and expenses were effectively balanced. It is possible that these firms were naturally operationally hedged.

The Wharton/CIBC survey does not explicitly explore the reasons for hedging, but it nonetheless offers some insights. The results indicate that firms employed only partial hedges and did not hedge very far into the future. In fact, Bodnar, Hayt, and Marston found that firms with a significant amount of regularly recurring foreign exchange exposure tended to hedge only a small fraction of their exposure. Most of the firms used short-term hedges; the vast majority of the hedges matured in 90 days or less. One potential explanation for this phenomenon is that the transaction costs of longer-term hedges are higher.

Finally, the Wharton/CIBC survey finds that some firms use derivatives more for speculative purposes than for hedging. In fact, Bodnar, Hayt, and Marston find that a little under one-third of firms using derivatives reported that their market view of exchange rates leads them to do so at least occasionally. Bengt Pramborg (2005) finds similar evidence for firms in Korea and Sweden.

Empirical Analysis of Why Firms Hedge

Christopher Géczy, Bernadette Minton, and Catherine Schrand (1997) examined the footnotes of firms' annual reports and their periodic reports to the Securities and Exchange Commission for 372 non-financial Fortune 500 firms in 1990 to determine their use of currency derivatives. Approximately 41% of these firms used currency swaps, forwards, futures, options, or combinations of these derivative instruments. The econometric analysis indicates that firms with greater growth opportunities are more likely to use currency derivatives for hedging purposes. This finding is consistent with the notion that firms use derivatives to reduce the volatility of their cash flow to avoid being in a situation in which they might otherwise be precluded from investing in one of their growth opportunities.

Géczy, Minton, and Schrand also found an important difference between firms that had foreign currency exposures because they had foreign operations and firms that had foreign operations and also had foreign debt. R&D expenses were high among the group of firms that did not have foreign currency debt, but R&D expenses were no longer a significant determinant of the use of currency derivatives for the firms with debt. This suggests that issuing debt in a foreign currency can serve the same function as hedging.

In another study, George Allayannis and Eli Ofek (2001) find that the level of firms' foreign sales and trade are the only determinants of the amount of currency hedging that firms do.

While the aforementioned studies explore why and how much firms hedge, George Allayannis and James Weston (2001) attempt to quantify whether firms that use foreign currency derivatives have an increased market value compared to firms that do not use derivatives. Allayannis and Weston find evidence consistent with the hypothesis that hedging increases a firm's value by a little under 5%. This conclusion must be considered with some caution because it assumes that some managers are smart and increase the value of their firms while others are not acting in the best interests of the firm's owners. The alternative hypothesis is that the econometrician has failed to hold constant all the aspects that make the firms different.

To Hedge or Not to Hedge: Understanding Your Competitors

Unfortunately, no clear-cut economic model exists to explain why different firms in different industries and countries hedge or don't hedge. That said, when choosing a hedging policy for your firm, it pays to keep an eye on what your competition is doing. You should ask yourself if there is any gain to be had by deviating from the accepted industry practice. If you do not hedge and everyone else does, what will happen to you in the bad and good states of the world?

Similarly, if everyone else is not hedging, is there a gain to be had by being the first in your industry to hedge? When would the gains arise? Would you have a competitive advantage in that state of the world if you were more profitable?

It is also important to understand the nature of your competition. Is your competition domestic or foreign? How will changes in real exchange rates affect your ability to compete? Hedging cannot change the fact that changes in real exchange rates will change the competitive position of firms in different countries, but hedging can mitigate some of the losses that a firm would otherwise suffer.

17.6 SUMMARY

This chapter examines risk management and hedging of foreign exchange risk. The main points in the chapter are as follows:

1. Hedging foreign exchange risk reduces the uncertainty of a firm's future cash flows. This makes sense for entrepreneurial firms run by risk-averse owner-managers who are unable to diversify their risks as regular investors can.

2. Modigliani and Miller argue that a corporation's financial policies, such as hedging foreign exchange risk, will not change the value of a firm unless they affect the firm's taxes, affect its investment decisions, or introduce costs savings relative to an individual's transaction costs. Thus, for large, publicly held corporations, hedging is valuable if it either increases the discounted present value of expected after-tax cash flows, increases the present value of financial tax shields, reduces the present value of any costs of financial distress, or improves the present value of the firm's future growth options.

3. Hedging is costly because the firm must allocate time and effort to making the hedging decision and because transaction costs in the forward market exceed transaction costs in the spot market. The forward discount on a foreign currency, if the firm is selling foreign currency forward, and the option premium on a foreign currency option are not legitimate costs of hedging.

4. Hedging the foreign exchange risk of an equity position is difficult because much of equity value depends on the indefinite future. Also, equity values are affected by real foreign exchange risk, but most hedges are nominal.

5. Hedging foreign exchange risk reduces a firm's expected future taxes if the corporate tax code is convex. A convex tax code imposes larger tax rates on higher incomes and smaller tax rates on lower incomes. Although the corporate tax rates in most countries are flat, if the government doesn't immediately refund the losses a firm experiences at the same rate as it taxes its income, the tax code is effectively convex.

6. The tax benefits of hedging are larger the more convex or progressive the tax code is, the more volatile a firm's pretax income is, and the more a firm's income occurs in the convex region of the tax code.

7. Hedging is valuable because it can reduce the future taxes that a firm expects to pay, lower the costs of financial distress, and improve the investment decisions that the firm will face in the future.

8. Under asymmetric information, hedging affects the ability of shareholders to assess the quality of management. If the profits and losses from financial hedges are pooled with the profits and losses of the firm's projects, managers will be motivated to hedge so as to reduce the variability of their earnings. If their hedging activities are disclosed, though, managers may choose to hedge less because hedging would make it easier for shareholders to disentangle the real contribution of the managers to the firm's earnings and thus could exacerbate the sensitivity of managerial compensation to earnings.

9. Surveys and empirical research generally support the idea that managers hedge foreign currency risks to ensure that their firms will have a sufficient amount of cash flow to fund important projects.

QUESTIONS

1. Why would an entrepreneur find it desirable to hedge his or her foreign exchange risk?

2. Explain Modigliani and Miller's argument that hedging is irrelevant. What are the most likely

violations of Modigliani and Miller's assumptions in actual markets?

3. Suppose that after joining the treasury department of a large corporation, you find out that it avoids hedging because the cost of hedging comes out of the treasury department's budget. What argument could you make to the CFO to get the firm interested in letting you be the firm's hedging guru?

4. Your CFO thinks that the value of your firm fluctuates enormously with the yen–dollar exchange rate, but he does not want to hedge because he thinks it is an impossible risk to hedge. Can you convince him otherwise?

5. What does it mean for a tax code to be convex? If a country's corporate tax rate is flat, does it make sense for a firm to hedge?

6. If the tax code is convex and the forward rate equals the expected future spot rate, why would a firm prefer to pay taxes on the hedged value of a foreign currency cash flow rather than wait to pay the taxes on the realized foreign currency cash flow?

7. Why is the gain in a firm's value greater when more of its future foreign currency income is in the low tax region of the tax code?

8. Why would the managers of a firm take a foreign project with a lower domestic currency NPV and a higher return variance rather than a foreign project with a higher domestic currency NPV but a lower return variance?

9. Why would a firm ever forgo a positive NPV project? How can hedging help prevent this situation from arising?

10. Suppose the cash flows from financial hedging are pooled with the cash flows from a firm's operations and that the shareholders cannot ascertain the ultimate sources of profits and losses. Would the managers of the firm want to hedge or to speculate in the forward foreign exchange market?

11. Why is an internally generated cash flow of such importance to Merck? Can't Merck use the financial markets as a source of funds?

12. True or false: The cost or benefit of hedging foreign exchange risk when a firm is selling the foreign currency forward is accurately measured by the forward discount or premium on the foreign currency.

PROBLEMS

1. Chapeau Rouge has a Swiss project that will return either CHF300 million or CHF250 million per year of free cash flow indefinitely. Each of the possible CHF cash flows is equally likely. Chapeau Rouge's CHF discount rate for these cash flows is 13% per annum, the cost of the project is €1,100 million, and the current exchange rate is CHF1.67/EUR. Should Chapeau Rouge accept the project? Suppose that Chapeau Rouge has a €400 million line of credit with its bank. Will Chapeau Rouge have trouble hedging the CHF cash flows?

2. Fleur de France has a project that will provide £20 million in revenue in 1 year. The project has a euro cost of €30 million that will be paid in 1 year. The cost of the project is certain, but the future spot exchange rate is not. Assume that there are only two possible future spot exchange rates. Either the spot rate in 1 year will be €1.54/£ with 55% probability, or it will be €1.48/£ with 45% probability. Assume that the French tax rate on positive income is 45%, that a firm's losses are immediately refunded at a rate of 35%, and that the forward rate of euros per pound equals the expected future spot rate.

a. If Fleur de France chooses not to hedge its foreign exchange risk, what is the expected value of its after-tax income on the unhedged project?

b. If Fleur de France chooses to hedge its foreign exchange risk, what is the expected value of its after-tax income on the hedged project?

c. How much does Fleur de France gain by hedging?

3. How would your answer to problem 2 change if instead of allowing refunds at 35%, the refund rate were only 25%?

4. How would your answer to problem 2 change if the possible exchange rates in the future were €1.56/£ and €1.46/£?

5. Assume that U.S. Machine Tool has $50 million of debt outstanding that will mature next year. It currently has cash flows that fluctuate with the dollar–pound exchange rate. Over the next year, the possible exchange rates are $1.50/£ and $1.90/£, and each exchange rate is equally likely. The company thinks that it will generate $30 million of cash flow from its U.S. operations, and its expected pound cash flow is £12 million.

a. If U.S. Machine Tool does not hedge its foreign exchange risk, what will be the current market value of its debt and equity, assuming, for simplicity, that the appropriate discount rates are 0?

b. Suppose that U.S. Machine Tool has access to forward contracts at a price of $1.70/£. What is the value of the firm's debt and equity if it hedges its foreign exchange risk? Would the shareholders want the management to hedge?

c. Suppose U.S. Machine Tool could invest $1 million today in a project that returns £1-

million next period. Is this a good project for the firm?

d. Suppose that U.S. Machine Tool is unhedged, that its managers are trying to maximize the value of the firm's equity, and that the $1 million must be raised from current shareholders. Will the managers accept the project?

e. If U.S. Machine Tool hedges its foreign exchange risk, would the firm accept the project?

BIBLIOGRAPHY

Abuaf, Niso, 1991, "The Nature and Management of Foreign Exchange Risk," in Robert W. Kolb, ed., *The International Finance Reader*, Miami: Kolb.

Allayannis, George, and Eli Ofek, 2001, "Exchange Rate Exposure, Hedging, and the Use of Foreign Currency Derivatives," *Journal of International Money and Finance* 20, pp. 273–296.

Allayannis, George, and James P. Weston, 2001, "The Use of Foreign Currency Derivatives and Firm Market Value," *Review of Financial Studies* 14, pp. 243–276.

Bodnar, Gordon, Greg S. Hayt, and Richard C. Marston, 1998, "1998 Wharton Survey of Financial Risk Management by U.S. Non-financial Firms," *Financial Management* 27, pp. 70-91.

DeMarzo, Peter M., and Darrell Duffie, 1991, "Corporate Financial Hedging with Proprietary Information," *Journal of Economic Theory* 45, pp. 353–369.

DeMarzo, Peter M., and Darrell Duffie, 1995, "Corporate Incentives for Hedging and Hedge Accounting," *Review of Financial Studies* 8, pp. 743–771.

Froot, Kenneth A., David S. Scharfstein, and Jeremy C. Stein, 1993, "Risk Management: Coordinating Corporate Investment and Financing Policies," *Journal of Finance* 48, pp. 1629–1658.

Géczy, Christopher, Bernadette A. Minton, and Catherine Schrand, 1997, "Why Firms Use Currency Derivatives," *Journal of Finance* 52, pp. 1323–1354.

Hekman, Christine R., Fall 1986, "Don't Blame Currency Values for Strategic Errors: Protecting Competitive Position by Correctly Assessing Foreign Exchange Exposure," *Midland Corporate Finance Journal*, pp. 45–55

Lessard, Donald R., Winter 1990, "Global Competition and Corporate Finance in the 1990s," *Journal of Applied Corporate Finance,* pp. 59–72.

Lewent, Judy C., and A. John Kearney, Winter 1990, "Identifying, Measuring, and Hedging Currency Risk at Merck," *Journal of Applied Corporate Finance,* pp. 19–28.

Maloney, Peter J., Winter 1990, "Managing Currency Exposure: The Case of Western Mining," *Journal of Applied Corporate Finance,* pp. 29–34.

Modigliani, Franco, and Merton Miller, 1958, "The Cost of Capital, Corporation Finance, and the Theory of Investment," *American Economic Review,* pp. 261–297.

Modigliani, Franco, and Merton Miller, 1961, "Dividend Policy, Growth, and the Valuation of Shares," *Journal of Business,* pp. 411–433.

Myers, Stewart, 1984, "The Capital Structure Puzzle," *Journal of Finance* 39, pp. 575–592.

Myers, Stewart, and Nicolais Majluf, 1984, "Corporate Financing and Investment Decisions When Firms Have Information that Investors Do Not Have," *Journal of Financial Economics* 13, pp. 187–221.

Nance, Deana R., Clifford W. Smith, and Charles W. Smithson, 1993, "On the Determinants of Corporate Hedging," *Journal of Finance* 48, 267–284.

Pramborg, Bengt, 2005, "Foreign Exchange Risk Management by Swedish and Korean Non-financial Firms: A Comparative Survey," *Pacific Basin Finance Journal* 13, 343–366.

Rawls, S. Waite, and Charles W. Smithson, 1990, "Strategic Risk Management," *Journal of Applied Corporate Finance* 1, pp. 6–18.

Ross, Stephen A., 1977, "The Determination of Financial Structure: The Incentive Signaling Approach," *Bell Journal of Economics* 8, pp. 23–40.

Ross, Stephen A., Randolph W. Westerfield, Jeffrey F. Jaffee, and Bradford D. Jordan, 2007, *Corporate Finance: Core Principles and Applications*, 3rd ed., New York: McGraw-Hill Irwin.

Smith, Clifford W., Charles W. Smithson, and D. Sykes Wilford, 1990, *Managing Financial Risk*, New York: Harper & Row.

Smith, Clifford W., and René Stulz, 1985, "The Determinants of Firm's Hedging Policies." *Journal of Financial and Quantitative Analysis* 20, pp. 391–405.

Stulz, René, 1984, "Optimal Hedging Policies," *Journal of Financial and Quantitative Analysis* 19, pp. 127–140.

Stulz, René, 1990, "Managerial Discretion and Optimal Financing Policies," *Journal of Financial Economics* 26, 3–27.

Chapter 18

Financing International Trade

*I*nternational trade has been conducted for over 2,000 years. A host of institutional arrangements, some of them quite elaborate, have developed over the years to facilitate such activity. Major international banks, in particular, are key players in bringing together importers and exporters. This chapter introduces and describes these institutional relationships.

The chapter first introduces the fundamental problems of international trades. Then it examines the important documents that control the ownership and insurance of goods that are being shipped internationally. Commercial banks require these documents when they provide financing to importers and exporters. We then look at alternative payment methods and a variety of ways in which exports can be financed. Governments often have special export–import banks that provide subsidized financing and insurance to promote international trade. Finally, we consider countertrade and the host of ways goods can be traded more or less directly for other goods.

18.1 THE FUNDAMENTAL PROBLEM WITH INTERNATIONAL TRADE

Shipping goods across a country as large as the United States poses many complex logistical and financial problems. Shipping goods across international borders creates a host of additional complications.

Exhibit 18.1 describes the fundamental situation: An importer in Canada, Jean Claude Richot Men's Apparel, Inc., would like to buy some sweaters from a Scottish exporter of wool sweaters, Albemarle's Scottish Sweaters. Because it takes time to ship the sweaters internationally, the sweaters cannot be delivered from the Scottish exporter to the Canadian importer immediately after an agreement is reached to purchase the goods. Either the Canadian importer or the Scottish exporter must own the sweaters during the time they are being shipped. Consequently, either the exporter or the importer must engage in some method of financing because the goods cannot be sold immediately after production.

When the shipment and sale of goods occur within a single country, there is a common jurisdiction and system of courts that adjudicates contractual disputes between buyers and sellers. When goods are shipped across borders, though, additional legal complexities arise. One such complexity relates to collecting on delinquent accounts. Differences in languages, cultures, accounting standards, and other information issues make it quite difficult, in some cases, to assess who is a good credit risk and who is not. The International Chamber of

Exhibit 18.1   An Example of the Fundamental Problem in International Trade

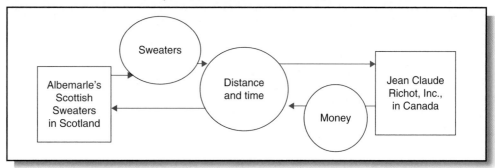

Commerce, which we discuss in the following box, attempts to overcome some of these problems.

Of course, just as any producer must obtain financing during the production process, exporters must also obtain financing from someone while they are manufacturing the goods. They can finance their production in a number of ways: from retained earnings, with bank loans, by issuing securities, or by obtaining advanced payments from importers.

Techniques for handling these international financing issues and credit transactions differ across countries and industries and have evolved over time.[1] Firms within the same industry can use a variety of methods, depending on the competitive pressures specific to the individual firm. For example, established exporters who are the international leaders of their industry are in a better position to demand more stringent payment terms from importers than other exporters. A single firm might also use different strategies, depending on its customer. For example, the policy that an exporting firm finds appropriate when dealing with an importer located in a developed country will probably not be appropriate for importers located in a developing country. This chapter explores alternative ways that firms deal with such financing and credit issues to establish overall credit policies. Before discussing these issues, however, we cover the documents that banks and other intermediaries use to control the ownership of the goods, the insurance, and the billing processes.

The International Chamber of Commerce

The **International Chamber of Commerce (ICC)**, based in Paris, was founded in 1919 with the goals of promoting international trade and investment, opening international markets for goods and services, and facilitating the free flow of capital between countries. The original members of the ICC were private companies in Belgium, Britain, France, Italy, and the United States. Membership has expanded dramatically, and today, the ICC is a world business organization with thousands of member companies and associations in more than 130 countries.

The activities of the ICC include setting rules and standards for international trade, arbitration and other forms of dispute resolution, and business self-regulation; making the political case for open trade and the market economy system; fighting corruption; and combating

---

[1]Avner Greif (1993) describes how some eleventh-century traders known as the Maghribi developed an institutional coalition to overcome the problems inherent in international trade. The Maghribi were Jewish traders who were operating in the Muslim western Mediterranean. Greif notes, "Agents provided merchants with many trade-related services, including loading and unloading ships; paying the customs, bribes and transportation fees; storing the goods; transferring the goods to market; and deciding when, how, and to whom to sell the goods, at what price, and at which credit terms" (p. 528).

commercial crime. Each year the ICC International Court of Arbitration hears an increasing number of cases. Since 1999, the court has received more than 500 new cases per year. The disputed amounts range from $30,000 to $40 million, and the cases come from around the world. The disputes are quite varied; examples include differences over the supply of steel pipes, the opening of investment accounts, the liquidation of a bank, the interpretation of a shareholders' agreement, the insurance for a film, and the construction of a shopping center.

One of the ICC's most important activities is setting standards for commercial contracts. This includes establishing the meaning of acronyms used internationally. The acronyms indicate who pays the costs of shipping, insurance, and import duties. For example, ICC Publication No. 460, titled *INCOTERMS*, groups these terms into four different categories. The *E* terms, as in *EXW* for "ex works," indicate the goods are available to the buyer at the seller's premises. The *F* terms, such as *FAS* for "free alongside ship" and *FOB* for "free on board," indicate that the price quoted by the seller includes delivery of the goods to a carrier appointed by the buyer. The *C* terms, including *CFR* for "cost and freight," and *CIF* for "cost, insurance, and freight," imply that the exporter's quoted price includes the cost of transportation to the named port of destination for CFR and that the cost of insurance is also included in the price, in addition to the transportation charges for CIF. The *D* terms, such as *DDU* for "delivered duty unpaid," and *DDP* for "delivered duty paid," imply that the exporter's quoted price includes the cost of transportation to the premises of the importer with either import duties paid, for DDP, or unpaid, for DDU.

The ICC's Uniform Customs and Practice for Documentary Credits (UCP 500) consists of a set of rules banks use to finance billions of dollars of world trade annually. The ICC is also leading the charge to establish standards for e-commerce. For example, a supplement to UCP 500, called the eUCP, was added in 2002 to create standards for electronic international trade documents. In addition, the ICC's codes on advertising and marketing influence both national legislation and the rules adopted by professional associations.

18.2 INTERNATIONAL TRADE DOCUMENTS

This section examines several of the important documents of international trade. International banks require many of these documents when financing international trade. The documents include bills of lading, which come in various types; commercial invoices; packing lists; insurance certificates; consular invoices; and certificates of analysis. Exhibit 18.2 provides a summary of the documents and their definitions.

Exhibit 18.2   Documents of International Trade

bill of lading A contract issued to an exporter or a shipper of goods by the company that will transport the goods from the place of shipment to the destination.

commercial invoice A detailed description of merchandise being sold, including the unit prices of the items and the number of items that are being shipped as well as the financial terms of the sale, including the amount due from the buyer and any charges to the buyer arising from insurance and shipping.

packing list A description of merchandise to be exported, including the containers in which the goods are packed, the contents of each container, and the total number of containers.

insurance Documents indicating that the owner of goods will be compensated in the event that the goods are damaged, destroyed, or stolen when being transported internationally.

consular invoice A document that must be filled out by an exporter in consultation with the consulate of the importing country that is located in the exporting country; it provides information to customs officials in the importing country, with the goal of preventing false declarations of the value of the merchandise.

certificate of analysis A document which assures an importer and possibly government officials that a shipment meets certain standards of purity, weight, sanitation, or other measurable characteristics.

Bills of Lading

A **bill of lading (B/L)** is a contract issued to an exporter of goods by the shipping company (also called a *common carrier*) that will transport the goods to their destination. The bill of lading serves several purposes, but most importantly, it documents that the exporter's goods have been received by the carrier.

The bill of lading contains the contractual terms between the carrier and the shipper (exporter). It describes the kind and quantity of goods being shipped, who the shipper (also called the *consignor*) is, who the importer (also called the *consignee*) is, the ports of loading and discharge, the carrying vessel, and the cost of the shipping. A **negotiable bill of lading** is the most common form. It can be used to transfer title or ownership of goods between different parties.

In our example, Albemarle's Scottish Sweaters receives a bill of lading from its shipping company. If Jean Claude Richot, Inc., had already paid for the sweaters, a negotiable B/L would indicate that Jean Claude Richot, Inc., should receive the sweaters upon their arrival in Canada.

Straight Bill of Lading

In its simplest form, a **straight bill of lading** states that a carrier has received merchandise from a shipper (a consignor) and will deliver the merchandise to a designated party (the consignee). A straight bill of lading is not title to the goods and is consequently not required for the consignee to obtain delivery of the merchandise. Because it is not a title to the merchandise, a straight bill of lading is not negotiable and cannot be used to transfer title of the goods to a third party. Consequently, it cannot serve as collateral with a commercial bank and is used only when no export or import financing is desired. A straight bill of lading is used when goods have been paid for in advance, when the exporter is financing the shipment and retaining title to the goods, or when the shipment is between affiliated parties of the same corporation.

Order Bill of Lading

If the transfer of title to goods is desired, or if some form of third-party financing is desired, an **order bill of lading** is used. Because most export transactions do involve financing, the order bill of lading is the most common form of B/L. An order bill of lading consigns the goods to a party named in the contract. This is usually the exporter because the exporter wants to retain title to the goods until payment from the importer has been received. The exporter can endorse the order bill of lading on the reverse side to transfer title of the goods to a specific party designated in the endorsement. At the destination, the carrier of the goods delivers the goods only to the party bearing the endorsed order bill of lading, who surrenders it to the carrier.

Having an order bill of lading is tantamount to having the title to the goods. This means that the goods can be used as collateral for bank loans. Banks are willing to lend to the party bearing an endorsed order bill of lading. In addition, the goods are usually fully insured. An order bill of lading is also required with a documentary credit or for discounting drafts, as we will see later in the chapter. Discounting is simply the taking of the present value of the payment promised in the draft.

On-board vs. Received-for-Shipment Bills of Lading

Bills of lading have several unique characteristics. An **on-board bill of lading** indicates that goods have been placed on a particular vessel for shipment. This is the type of bill of lading that is usually used in a documentary credit. An alternative form is a **received-for-shipment bill of lading**, which indicates only that the merchandise is at the dock awaiting transport. A received-for-shipment bill of lading is not an acceptable document in a bank financing unless it has been explicitly authorized in a documentary credit. A received-for-shipment bill of lading is issued by the carrier upon receipt of the merchandise. It is easily converted into an on-board bill of lading when it is stamped appropriately with the name of the vessel, dated, and signed or initialed by an authorized representative of the carrier. The reason a received-for-shipment bill of lading is not acceptable in bank financing is that no one knows for sure when the goods will be shipped.

Clean vs. Foul Bills of Lading

A bill of lading contains information on the status of the merchandise in question when the merchandise is received by the carrier. A **clean bill of lading** indicates that the carrier believes the merchandise was received in good condition. This evaluation is based only on an external visual inspection of the merchandise. The carrier is not responsible for conducting a formal evaluation of the condition of the merchandise. In contrast, a **foul bill of lading** indicates that the carrier's initial inspection of the merchandise uncovered some damage that occurred before the goods were received by the carrier for shipment. Foul bills of lading are typically not negotiable because no one knows the extent of the damage to the merchandise.

Commercial Invoices

A **commercial invoice** is issued by an exporter and given to an importer. A commercial invoice contains a detailed description of the merchandise in question, including the unit prices of the items and the number of items that are being shipped. The invoice also specifies the financial terms of the sale, including the amount due from the importer and any charges to the importer arising from insurance and shipping.

In the example that we have been following, the total number of sweaters of all types might be 7,500, and if each sweater costs $200, the total invoice would be for $1,500,000. Notice that in this case, the U.S. dollar is used as the currency of invoice even though neither party to the transaction is in the United States. Alternatively, the transaction could be denominated in British pounds, the currency of the exporter, or in Canadian dollars, the currency of the importer.

Packing Lists

Because goods shipped internationally are often prepackaged in a container, the shipper must include a **packing list**. This list contains a description of the merchandise to be exported, including the containers in which the goods are packed, the contents of each container, and the total number of containers. In our example, the packing list would contain a description of the numbers and types of sweaters.

Insurance

Merchandise that is shipped internationally is invariably insured. The insurance documents must be signed by an authorized representative of the insurance company, its agents, or its underwriters. (An insurance broker's signature is unacceptable.) The insurance must either be issued in the name of the consignee or in the name of the exporter, who can then endorse the policy to the consignee. The value of the insurance must be expressed in the same currency as the currency of the invoice. Otherwise, there would be transaction foreign exchange risk.

Open Insurance Policies

Firms that do a substantial amount of exporting can purchase insurance policies that are described as "open," or "floating." Such a policy automatically covers all the exports of a firm, which eliminates the necessity of arranging coverage for each individual export order. In such cases, the evidence of insurance is an insurance certificate that the insurance company supplies. The entry of information on the insurance certificate should conform exactly to the information describing the merchandise on the bill of lading, the commercial invoice, and, if it is required, the consular invoice, which we discuss next.

Consular Invoice

Imports into many countries require a **consular invoice**. This document must be filled out by the exporter in consultation with the local consulate of the importing country located in the exporting country. A consular invoice provides information to customs officials in the importing country, with the goal of preventing false declarations of the value of the merchandise. Failing to fill out such forms correctly can lead to fines and substantial delays in the clearing of goods through customs. A consular invoice is sometimes combined with a **certificate of origin** of the goods, which indicates the source of the goods.

Certificates of Analysis

A **certificate of analysis** is sometimes required to assure an importer that a shipment meets certain standards of purity, weight, sanitation, or other measurable characteristics. These documents may be required by the health or other officials of the importing country, especially when it comes to food and drug imports. Certificates of analysis may be issued by private organizations or by governments.

18.3 Methods of Payment

Ideally, an exporter wants to be paid when the importer orders the goods, especially if they are being made to order. Prepayment helps finance the production of the goods and assures the exporter of his profit. Moreover, if the exporter must finance the production of a highly customized good, the exporter will usually demand that the importer bear some of the cost. Importers, on the other hand, prefer to pay as late as possible. If an importer can pay the exporter after being paid by the final buyer of the product, the exporter essentially finances the importer's inventory until it is sold.

This section examines the different methods available for an importer to pay an exporter. We begin the discussion with cash in advance, which is the most straightforward method and the one that is the least risky from the exporter's perspective. Then, we continue with documentary credits, documentary collections, and open accounts, which are increasingly risky methods of payment from the exporter's point of view.

Cash in Advance

Cash-in-advance transactions, of course, require the importer to pay the exporter before the goods are shipped. Hence, the exporter does not have to finance the goods during their shipment because the payment for them has already been received. From the exporter's perspective, cash in advance is obviously the least risky policy. The importer must finance the purchase of the goods, incurs the cost of shipping them, and bears the risk of their being damaged in transit.

Cash in advance is used primarily with high credit-risk trading partners and in countries in which political risks are large. If a credit-rating agency, such as Dun & Bradstreet, has given a foreign firm a low credit rating, or if a credit insurance agency has removed the foreign firm from its list of eligible firms, the exporter may demand cash in advance. Also, if the exporter thinks the importer may have difficulty securing foreign currency because the importer's foreign exchange market may be closed by the country's government during the time of shipment, the exporter may demand cash in advance. If the importer is unable to get trade finance, negotiations between the exporter and the importer might break down.

Because few importers are willing to pay for goods in advance, international banks developed a method of securing payment that substitutes the bank's credit risk for the importer's credit risk. This method is the documentary credit.

Documentary Credits

Documentary credits (D/Cs) are designed to solve the problems caused by the fact that importers and exporters want to pay and be paid at different times.[2] Documentary credits also provide a way for exporters to finance the production of their goods. With a documentary

Exhibit 18.3   A Documentary Credit

Irrevocable   Est. 1847
Documentary Credit

Bank of Quebec
860 Rene-Levesque Blvd W
Montreal, PQ H3B4A5 CA

International Division   Commercial D/C Department   www.boq.com

Documentary Credit No.: 0087349824   Amount: USD1,500,000   Date: July 3, 2008
This number must be mentioned
on all drafts and correspondence.

. Albemarle's Scottish Sweaters   . Bank of Edinburgh
. Edinburgh, Scotland   . Edinburgh, Scotland
.   .

Dear Madame or Sir:

   By order of   Jean Claude Richot Men's Apparel, Inc.

and for the account of   SAME

we hereby authorize you to draw on   Ourselves

up to an aggregate amount of   One Million, Five Hundred Thousand, U.S. Dollars

Available by your drafts at   Ourselves, but not before October 3, 2008

Accompanied by
Signed invoice in triplicate
Packing list in triplicate
Full set of clean ocean bills of lading, made out to order of shipper, blank endorsed, marked freight prepaid and notify: Jean Claude Richot Men's Apparel, Inc., Montreal, dated on board not later than July 30, 2008.
Insurance policy/certificate in triplicate for 110% of invoice value, covering all risks.

Covering: Shipment of sweaters, as per buyer's order no. 86354011, dated June 15, 2008, from Edinburgh, Scotland port C.I.F. to Montreal, Quebec, CANADA.
Partial Shipments not permitted.
Transshipment is not permitted.
Documents must be presented within 7 days after the board date of the bills of lading, but in any event not later than August 7, 2008.

Drafts must be drawn and negotiated not later than August 3, 2008
All drafts drawn under this credit must bear its date and number and the amounts must be endorsed on the reverse side of this Documentary Credit by the negotiating bank. We hereby agree with the drawers, endorsers, and bona fide holders of all drafts drawn under and in compliance with the terms of this credit, that such drafts will be duly honored upon presentation to the drawee. This credit is subject to the uniform customs and practice for documentary credits (International Chamber of Commerce Publication No. 500)

                                              Francois Montblanc
                                              Commercial Credit Officer
                                              Bank of Quebec

---

[2]In the United States, a documentary credit is often referred to as a letter of credit (L/C).

Exhibit 18.4 An Example of a Time Draft

not before October 3, 2008	July 3, 2008 Montreal, Quebec, Canada
INDICATE ABOVE WHETHER PAYABLE ON DEMAND, ARRIVAL, OR OTHER TIME LIMIT	DATE AND LOCATION

PAY TO THE ORDER OF   ALBEMARLE'S SCOTTISH SWEATERS   USD 1,500,000

ONE MILLION, FIVE HUNDRED THOUSAND UNITED STATES DOLLARS

JEAN CLAUDE RICHOT'S IMPORTED MEN'S APPAREL, INC.

VALUE RECEIVED AND CHARGE TO ACCOUNT OF

TO   Bank of Quebec

860 Rene-Levesque Blvd W, Montreal, PQ, H3B4A5 CA

No.   D/C No. 0087349824

Robert Rochambeau, Treasurer
Jean Claude Richot, Inc.

---

credit, at least one commercial bank stands between the importer and the exporter. The exporter must assess the credit risk of this international bank, not the credit risk of the importer. Because the involvement of commercial banks in the transaction is extensive, using a documentary credit is the most expensive of the methods of payment.

Exhibit 18.3 presents an example of a documentary credit associated with the transaction between an importer, Jean Claude Richot Men's Apparel, Inc., and an exporter, Albemarle's Scottish Sweaters, written by the importer's bank, Bank of Quebec.

Drafts

A D/C is created when an importer asks its commercial bank to write a letter to an exporter on behalf of the importer. In the D/C, the importer's bank indicates that it will honor a draft drawn on itself if the exporter satisfies certain conditions set forth in the D/C. The draft is a written order by the bank to pay the exporter and may be either a **sight draft** or a **time draft**.

Exhibit 18.4 presents an example of a time draft. The time draft indicates that the Bank of Quebec will pay $1,500,000 to Albemarle Scottish Sweaters 3 months after the date the D/C was written, at which time the draft can be presented to the bank. The account of Jean Claude Richot, Inc., will be charged for the payment. If the draft is a sight draft, the bank is obligated to pay the draft any time it is presented, as long as the documents associated with the D/C are in order.

If a bank accepts a time draft, the draft becomes a **banker's acceptance (B/A)**. The creation of these instruments is discussed in more detail in a later section, but the basics are that the bank stamps and signs the time draft as accepted, indicating that the bank agrees to pay the face value of the draft at maturity.

Once the documentary credit is established, it becomes a financial document that substitutes the credit of the bank for the credit of the importer. The conditions that the exporter must satisfy in order to be paid include providing formal documentary evidence that the goods have been shipped, that the freight has been paid, and that the goods have been insured.

Advantages of Documentary Credits to Exporters

Documentary credits offer a number of advantages to exporters:

1. The most important advantage of a D/C is that it substitutes the creditworthiness of the bank for the credit risk of the importing firm. The exporter therefore must only be concerned with the credit risk of the bank that issues the D/C. If the exporter satisfies the requirements of the D/C, the exporter will be paid by the bank.
2. Establishing a documentary credit enhances the probability that the exporter will not experience delays in payment due to the imposition of foreign exchange controls or other political risks. Countries are well aware of the importance of international trade. As a result, governments generally permit banks to honor existing documentary credits.

Failing to do so severely damages a country's reputation and its ability to borrow in international financial markets in the future.

3. A D/C reduces the uncertainty of a transaction by clearly establishing the acts that the exporter must carry out in order to receive payment.

4. Because a D/C is a legally binding document between a bank and an exporter, the exporter is protected if the importer desires to cancel the contract during the production processes. This is especially important if the goods are being made to order.

5. A D/C makes it easy for an exporter to receive early payment because a time draft can be accepted by the bank, which creates a banker's acceptance. These are discussed in detail later in this section, but basically, the bank agrees to pay the exporter a discounted value of the draft immediately.

Advantages of Documentary Credits to Importers

Documentary credits also have advantages from the importer's perspective:

1. The foremost advantage for an importer is that a D/C clearly indicates a time frame by which the goods must be shipped. The importer knows that the exporter must ship the goods by a certain date and must provide certain documents to the bank if the exporter wants to be paid. The importer is thus assured of having the goods when they are needed for the importer's production process or for resale in the importer's market.

2. Another advantage of a D/C from the importer's perspective is that an importer's bank assumes responsibility for checking the documents provided by an exporter. Hence, if the exporter does not properly ship the goods, the bank will not pay the exporter, and the importer is protected from having to pay for goods that are not valuable. Eventually, if the importer takes possession of the goods and it is discovered that there is a problem with the shipment that should have been caught by examining the shipping documents, the bank is responsible for this oversight.

3. The fact that a D/C substitutes the bank's credit standing for the importer's credit standing means that the importer may be able to command better payment terms. One of the terms may be that the deal actually gets done; many exporters will refuse to export without either cash in advance or a D/C.

4. If some form of prepayment is required by an exporter, an importer is better off depositing money in an escrow account at its domestic bank than with a foreign company. If the exporter encounters some difficulty that limits its ability to follow through on its contractual commitments, the importer can recover its deposit from a local bank more easily than it could from the foreign exporter.

Attributes of Documentary Credits

A documentary credit can be either revocable or irrevocable. A **revocable D/C** is a means of arranging payment, but it provides no guarantee of payment. The importer reserves the right to revoke the D/C at any time prior to the presentation of the draft by the exporter to the bank. A revocable D/C establishes that the importer has a working business relationship with a reputable bank. It also establishes that the transaction is one that is legitimately eligible for scarce foreign exchange if there is a crisis in the importer's country. Hence, it is useful for transactions between related affiliates of a multinational corporation to assure that exchange controls do not disrupt the importing process. It is less expensive than an irrevocable D/C.

Most documentary credits between unrelated parties are irrevocable. An **irrevocable D/C** cannot be revoked unless all parties, including the exporter, agree to the revocation. International transactions between parties not well known to each other are typically conducted with irrevocable documentary credits. Otherwise, much of the benefit of substituting the credit of the bank for the credit of the importer would be lost. Once an irrevocable documentary credit has been received, the exporter is assured that it will be paid by the importer's bank if it performs certain tasks by certain dates in the future.

A documentary credit can also be confirmed or unconfirmed. A **confirmed documentary credit** is one in which a second commercial bank agrees to honor the draft presented by the exporter. Typically, the bank that issues the documentary credit is from the country of the importer. Two issues arise from the perspective of the exporter. First, although the issuing bank may be a reputable international bank, it is still subject to the legal jurisdiction of the importing country and may not be well known to the exporter. Second, the exporter might ultimately want to present the draft to a bank in the exporting country. By having a bank in the exporting country confirm the D/C, the exporter obtains a guarantee that a domestic bank that the exporter trusts will accept the responsibility for paying the draft. Of course, the second bank will demand some additional compensation for the confirmation of the documentary credit, and this increases the transaction costs of the confirmed documentary credit.

In summary, the three primary types of documentary credits, in decreasing order of security to the exporter, are (1) an irrevocable, confirmed D/C; (2) an irrevocable, unconfirmed D/C; and (3) a revocable D/C. Choosing among these three and who pays for the increased cost of the deal depends on the bargaining strength of the importer and the exporter. Making the deal more secure for the exporter makes the deal more expensive because banks charge additional fees. This added expense must be paid for either by the importer, who agrees to a higher cost, or by the exporter, who accepts a lower price. Of course, if the exporter demands the most stringent terms and forces the importer to pay the transaction costs, the exporter risks losing business to lower-cost exporters willing to take greater risks.

Summary of the Creation and Use of a D/C and a B/A

As we have seen, international trade can be handled in a number of different ways. This section provides a summary diagram of some complex transactions—the creation and use of a documentary credit with the discounting of a draft to create a banker's acceptance. Exhibit 18.5 provides a general diagram of the transactions involved:

1. The importer orders goods from the exporter and asks whether the exporter is willing to ship the goods under a documentary credit containing a time draft.
2. The exporter and importer agree to ship the goods under a documentary credit. The two parties negotiate the price of the goods and the other aspects related to how the goods will be shipped.
3. The importer applies for a documentary credit to its commercial bank, designated in Exhibit 18.5 as "Bank IMP." The D/C is issued, with the exporter named as the beneficiary, and the D/C specifies the information associated with the deal.
4. Bank IMP issues the documentary credit, with the exporter named as the beneficiary. The D/C is sent to an advising bank, "Bank EXP," in the exporter's country.
5. Bank EXP advises the exporter that the documentary credit has arrived. If the exporter so desires, Bank EXP confirms the documentary credit for a fee and adds its guarantee to Bank IMP's guarantee.
6. The exporter ships the goods to the importer using a common carrier.
7. The exporter presents a time draft, with a maturity of, say, 90 days in the future, to Bank EXP. The draft is drawn on Bank IMP, as specified in the documentary credit from Bank IMP. The exporter also presents the documents required by the D/C, including the order bill of lading. The exporter endorses the order bill of lading "in blank" so that the title of the goods passes to the holder of the endorsed bill of lading, which is Bank EXP at this point in the transaction.
8. Bank EXP presents the draft and the export documents to Bank IMP, which accepts the draft and takes possession of the documents. A banker's acceptance, B/A, with a maturity of 90 days is created.
9. Either Bank IMP returns the accepted draft to Bank EXP, or Bank EXP could ask for the discounted cash value of the B/A, in which case Bank IMP would deduct a

Exhibit 18.5 Exporting with a Documentary Credit (D/C) and a Banker's Acceptance (B/A)

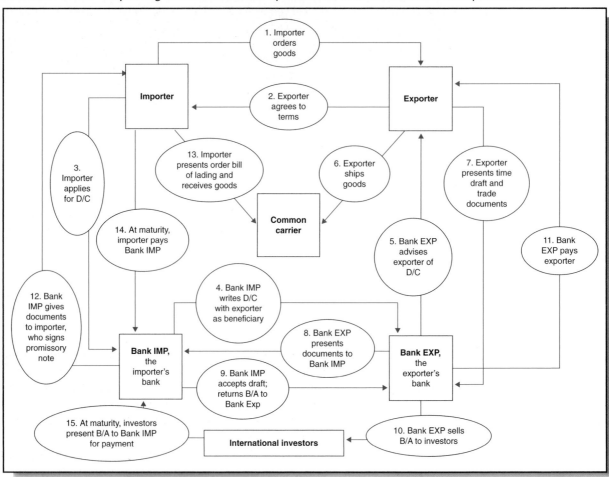

discounting fee. The interest rate in the B/A market is used to take the present value in the discounting process.

10. Assuming that Bank EXP receives the B/A, it now either gives the B/A to the exporter or pays the exporter. In the latter case, Bank EXP can either hold the B/A in its own portfolio or sell the B/A to an investor in the international financial markets.

11. Normally, the exporter receives the discounted cash value for the B/A less any bank charge for a discounting fee rather than wait for 90 days to receive a cash payment.

12. Bank IMP informs the importer that the documents have arrived. The importer either signs a promissory note or follows through with some mutually agreed-upon plan for paying Bank IMP, at which point Bank IMP releases the documents, including the order bill of lading, to the importer. Often, the maturity of the promissory note is the same as the maturity of the B/A, which is 90 days in this case.

13. When the goods arrive, the importer collects them from the common carrier, using the order bill of lading.

14. At the maturity of the promissory note, the importer pays Bank IMP.

15. At the maturity of the B/A, Bank IMP pays the holder of the matured banker's acceptance. The investor receives the face value of the B/A. The holder may present the B/A directly to Bank IMP, or it may have Bank EXP collect the amount through its normal banking relationships with Bank IMP.

Documentary Collections

Firms can avoid directly assessing the creditworthiness of their trading partners by using a **documentary collection**. With a documentary collection, the exporter retains control of the goods until the importer has paid or is legally bound to pay for them, and the exporter gets banks involved in the collection process, although the degree of responsibility banks bear for assuring payment to the exporter in a documentary collection is not as high as with a confirmed documentary credit. Documentary collections are also less expensive than documentary credits.

When conducting an export transaction through documentary collection, the exporter uses a remitting bank as its agent to collect the payment from the importer. The exporter ships the merchandise to the importer, but the exporter retains title to the goods. The exporter next presents the shipping documents to the remitting bank. These shipping documents, which we discussed earlier in the chapter, include the bill of lading, the commercial invoice, the packing list, the insurance certificates, and consular invoices. The exporter also submits a draft or bill of exchange to the remitting bank that is drawn on the importer. The remitting bank (the agent of the exporter) sends the documents, the draft, and the instructions to a bank in the importer's country. This bank is called the collecting, or presenting, bank. The collecting bank could be a branch of the remitting bank in the foreign country, or it could be a separate bank in the foreign country that does business with the remitting bank. The collecting, or presenting, bank notifies the importer that the documents are available and that they may be obtained when the importer complies with the terms of the documentary collection.

The exporter will have instructed its remitting bank that the payment should be collected from the importer in one of two ways, either as a **documents against payment (D/P) collection** or as a **documents against acceptance (D/A) collection**. Under a D/P collection, the importer must pay the amount of the sight draft to the collecting bank before the documents are released. When the funds are received, they are transmitted to the remitting bank for payment to the exporter. The exporter consequently does not give up control of the merchandise until payment is received by the collecting bank.

Under a D/A collection, the exporter extends credit to the importer in the following way. The collecting bank presents a time draft to the importer, who must sign it, date it, and write *accepted* across it. The shipping documents are then released to the importer. By accepting the draft, the importer acknowledges his legal obligation to pay the face amount of the draft at maturity, which is usually 30, 60, or 90 days after the date of the acceptance. An accepted draft is known as a **trade acceptance**. It can be retained by the collecting bank on behalf of the exporter for presentation to the importer at maturity, or it may be returned to the exporter. At maturity, the draft is presented by the collecting bank to the importer, who must pay the face amount. The funds are then transmitted to the remitting bank for payment to the exporter.

With a D/A collection, the exporter gives up title to the goods in exchange for the legally binding commitment of the importer to pay the trade acceptance. Hence, it is important for the exporter to understand the creditworthiness of the importer.

Advantages of Documentary Collections

From an exporter's perspective, the documents against acceptance collection create a negotiable trade acceptance, which is an enforceable debt instrument. Not only is the importer legally bound to pay, but the exporter can sell the trade acceptance in the short-term money market to obtain financing. Of course, the sale of a trade acceptance is done at a discount that reflects both the time value of the money in which the acceptance is denominated and the money market's perception of the default risk of the importer.

Exporters often find that they are paid more promptly when using documentary collections rather than just invoicing the importers because importers are more responsive to their local banking communities than to the invoices of the exporter. The documentary collection does add the expenses of the remitting and collecting banks to the process, but these transaction costs are lower than the expenses involved in establishing a documentary credit.

Disadvantages of Documentary Collections

The chief disadvantage of a D/A collection arises because the banks are only acting as the agents of the exporter and are not obligated to pay, as they are with a documentary credit. The exporter consequently must bear the importer's default risk.

How might the deal break down? One way is if the importer refuses to take ownership of the shipment after inspecting the shipping documents. The importer consequently refuses to pay the sight or time draft. Or it might happen if, from the viewpoint of the importer, there is a document discrepancy. Documents are rejected by importers for a variety of reasons. The invoice price may not be the price that the importer agreed to in the sales contract. The goods may have been shipped late or incorrectly packaged. Sometimes, importers will use documentary discrepancies that are otherwise superficial as a reason to refuse shipment when they have changed their minds about the deal because their business has slowed down. In such a circumstance, if the exporter is not able to reconcile the issue with the importer, the exporter is forced either to warehouse the goods until another buyer is located in the foreign country or the exporter must pay to have the goods reshipped. Sometimes, even though the exporter has a trade acceptance that is signed by the importer, getting paid by the importer entails a lengthy and costly legal battle in the courts of the importing country.

Finally, because the exporter is extending credit to the importer, the exporter must bear the political risk of the importer's country. Situations can arise, having nothing to do with the importer, that prevent the exporter from being able to repatriate funds at the maturity of the trade credit. For example, the government of the importing country might impose delays or prohibit the payment of foreign exchange to foreign corporations. Delays can also arise when foreign exchange is rationed by a country's central bank, and the importer or the collecting bank must wait in the queue for its turn to buy convertible currencies.

Sales on Open Account

Demanding cash in advance poses the least risk to the exporter, but it imposes the most financial burden on the importer. At the other extreme, export firms allow **sales on open account**, which poses the most risk to the exporter. Under an open-account arrangement, the exporter establishes an account for the importer, who is allowed to order goods, which are either produced to order or shipped from inventory at the instruction of the importer. The payment for the goods is based on an invoiced amount, but there is no particular date in the future when the payment must be made. In other words, the exporter extends trade credit on certain terms to the importer. There is typically a discount offered from the invoiced amount if payment is made within a certain number of days. In contrast, the invoice indicates that overdue payments carry additional interest and financial service charges. The terms of such accounts must be negotiated and are subject to the competitive pressures of the industry in which the firms operate.

Open accounts are used primarily between related affiliates of the same multinational corporation, but they also arise when exporting and importing firms have long-standing relationships with one another or when the credit rating of the importer is high. Open accounts offer importers more flexibility with regard to their financing, which can enhance an exporter's sales, and transaction costs are lower because banks are not involved in the process.

The open account method of payment is risky to the exporter, though, because an unpaid invoice is the only evidence of an importer's indebtedness to an exporter. If an importer fails to pay, the exporting firm must use the importing country's courts to attempt to enforce payment. It is possible that a court in the importing country might decide that an unpaid open account invoice is not an enforceable debt instrument. In that case, the exporter will have no rights in a bankruptcy proceeding against an insolvent importer.

An exporter is also exposed to political risks of foreign exchange controls that may prevent a solvent importer from fulfilling its promise to pay. Before granting an open account to an importer, it is therefore prudent for the exporter to monitor the macroeconomic and political developments in the country of the importer. The exporter wants to avoid, for example, blocked funds. Blocked funds arise when the currency of a country is completely inconvertible into the currencies of other countries. We will discuss this further in Chapter 19.

International Financing on the Internet

Usually, successful electronic trading requires an element of standardization, which is somewhat lacking in international trade because no two deals are ever the same. But the entrepreneurial spirit and the lure of the World Wide Web are powerful driving forces. Two companies are trying to create an Internet marketplace for the international trade transactions markets. The first company is iTradeFinance (www.itradefinance.com), which seeks to create an independent, secure, Internet-accessible meeting place for participants in the global trade and trade finance marketplace. The iTradeFinance website allows financial providers, such as commercial banks, investment banks, insurance companies, hedge funds, and other investors, to offer trade-based financing for importers and exporters. The second company is TradeCard (www.tradecard.com), which electronically connects trading partners and routes and stores their trade documentation from purchase orders to electronic invoices. By 2006, TradeCard had participated in over $260 billion of transactions.

18.4 FINANCING EXPORTS

Now that we have seen how payments can be arranged between importers and exporters, let's examine how exporters can obtain financing while they are awaiting payment from importers. Exhibit 18.6 lists the six methods that we will study. The most straightforward way that an exporter can arrange credit is to obtain a bank line of credit. Surveys indicate that this is the most popular financing method among U.S. exporters. The next most popular method is the discounting of a banker's acceptance. Other techniques include setting up a buyer credit, organizing a receivables purchase, arranging limited-recourse financing, and export factoring. We will address each of these methods in turn.

Bank Line of Credit

Often, exporters finance their accounts receivable from importers with a bank line of credit. The terms of this type of loan agreement allow the borrower to draw up to a prespecified maximum amount during a given time period at a stated interest rate. The line of credit is generally renewable, usually annually. Although the exporter's normal revenue stream is thought to be the primary source of repayment of interest and principal associated with the line of credit,

Exhibit 18.6 Methods of Export Financing

1. Bank line of credit
2. Discounting of a banker's acceptance
3. Buyer credit
4. Receivables purchase
5. Limited-recourse financing—forfaiting
6. Export factoring

banks may require that the exporter designate assets to serve as collateral. The bank may also require that the exporter purchase insurance, in which the bank is the beneficiary, covering the value of the exports.

Banker's Acceptances

In Section 18.3 we saw how the use of a time draft in a documentary credit creates the opportunity for the creation of a banker's acceptance. The bank stamps and signs the draft as accepted, indicating that it will pay the face value of the draft at maturity. The accepted draft can then be discounted either by the issuing bank or in the money market. Given the current and historical importance of this method of export financing, let's examine the creation, use, and pricing of a banker's acceptance in more detail.

There are two types of banker's acceptances. As we have seen, a documentary acceptance is created by the use of a time draft in a documentary credit. A **clean acceptance** is created under a separate credit agreement, without an underlying documentary credit between the exporter and the bank. The bank agrees to accept a certain number of time drafts for various amounts that are submitted by the exporter. The bank then immediately discounts the drafts to provide financing for the exporter. At maturity, the exporter repays the face amount of the draft to the bank.

Using a banker's acceptance to finance exports involves two associated costs. One is the acceptance commission charged by the bank, and the other is the discount due to the time value of money. Typical acceptance commissions for medium-sized companies range between 0.75% and 2% of the face value of the draft. The cost tends to be lower for larger firms, but it can also be higher. When setting the commission rate, which is negotiable, the bank takes into account the creditworthiness of the company, any country risk factors that affect the exporter's business, and the bank's competitive position. Whether the exporter or the importer bears the cost of the acceptance commission depends on their respective competitive strengths in negotiating the overall deal.

Eligible vs. Ineligible Banker's Acceptances

In the United States, the Federal Reserve regulates the market for banker's acceptances. A distinction is drawn between eligible and ineligible banker's acceptances. If a bank sells an **eligible banker's acceptance**, it does not have to maintain reserves against the proceeds of the sale. On the other hand, if the bank sells an **ineligible banker's acceptance**, the bank must keep the proceeds of the sale on reserve with the Federal Reserve in a non-interest-bearing account. Clearly, if banks want to use the proceeds of the B/A for future lending, they must sell an eligible B/A.

The eligibility requirements for banker's acceptances are as follows:

1. The tenor, or maturity, of the B/A must not be greater than 180 days, although it is possible to seek an exception.
2. The acceptance must be created within 30 days of the date of shipment of the export goods.
3. The transaction must be between two separate legal entities either within the United States, between a U.S. firm and a foreign firm, or between two foreign firms.
4. The eligible B/A cannot be renewed at maturity unless a legitimate delay occurs in the transaction that is being financed.
5. During the transaction, only one B/A is allowed to be outstanding, although the importer and the exporter can finance the transaction, just not for an overlapping interval of time.
6. The B/A cannot be drawn without recourse to the second party in the transaction. In other words, if the bank that accepts the B/A defaults, the holder of the B/A must have

recourse to the drawer of the B/A (that is, the party ultimately responsible for paying the bank).

7. The B/A must not be used to finance trade with any country for which trade is prohibited by the U.S. Department of the Treasury.

Buyer Credit

When expensive capital equipment is being purchased, an exporter sometimes arranges for a financial institution or a syndicate of financial institutions to grant credit to the importer in what is known as a **buyer credit**. By arranging the credit for the importer, the exporter is ultimately paid cash up front, and the financial intermediaries bear most of the default risk of the importer.

Setting up a typical buyer credit involves several steps. First, the exporter and the importer must agree to a commercial contract for which the importer can pay a down payment of 10% to 20% of the face value of the invoice. Then, the exporter must agree to provide part of the financing to the importer, which allows the bank to establish an analogous agreement with the importer in a commercial contract. The exporter must insure the goods with an export credit insurer and assign the insurance policy to the bank. After delivery of the goods, the bank either purchases the signed promissory notes of the importer from the exporter or grants a direct loan to the importer. In either case, the exporter receives its cash right then. Notice that the buyer credit is a contract between the bank and the importer, so there can be no recourse against the exporter by the bank if the importer defaults. Consequently, the credit of the exporter is unaffected by the transaction.

Buyer credits are much longer-term contracts than banker's acceptances. The maturity can be from 4 to 12 years, and the interest rate in the contract typically floats with a spread over LIBOR. The spread reflects the riskiness of the importer and the bank's competitive position, including its potential to win other business associated with the deal. Other costs of a buyer credit include an arrangement fee and a commitment fee of 0.25% to 0.75% annually on the unused portion of the loan.

Selling Accounts Receivable

If an exporter wants to raise cash, it can sell drafts or invoices related to its accounts receivable to a financial intermediary. The sale could be on a recourse or non-recourse basis. In the United States, it is usually done with recourse to the exporter. That is, the exporter remains financially liable for the payments that the importer is scheduled to make should the importer default in the future. Typically, the accounts receivable must also be insured. European customs are somewhat different. In these markets, a method of export finance developed to allow financing without recourse to the exporter.

Limited-Recourse Financing: Forfaiting

In limited-recourse financing, the financial intermediary purchases the promissory notes of the importer from the exporter at a discount. The term **forfaiting** is often used interchangeably with the term *note purchase* to describe this financing technique.[3] The forfaiter must assess and ultimately bear all the commercial and political risks of the project. Typically, the forfaiter removes the commercial risk by requiring the guarantee of the importer's government or its bank (which may be government owned).

---

[3]The expression derives from the French phrase *forfait et sans garanties*, which means that the legal right of recourse (to the exporter) has been forfeited, or surrendered.

Exporters often use limited-recourse financing, or forfaiting, to finance medium-term projects for importing countries that have substantial commercial and political risk. In such a financing, the exporter receives cash, and the financial intermediary bears the risks without recourse to the exporter unless the exporter fails to fulfill its contractual commitments or commits fraud. If the exporter fulfills its contractual terms, it does not have to worry about getting paid.

Forfaiting describes the practices of European banks and their subsidiaries in various countries such as Germany, Switzerland, Austria, and the United Kingdom. Banks in these countries were requested to finance capital goods exports to eastern European countries and needed to develop expertise in assessing the risks of delayed payments. Although the techniques were developed to deal with eastern European countries when they were state controlled, they can be applied more broadly.

The Mechanics of Forfaiting

Let's examine several stages of a typical forfaiting transaction.

First, the exporter and the importer agree on a commercial transaction that covers a fixed interval of time. The exporter agrees to ship various amounts of goods to the importer at various points in time in return for periodic payments made against the progress of the project.

Second, the exporter and the forfaiter negotiate financing in which the forfaiter discounts the payments promised by the importer at a fixed discount rate. The exporter receives the discounted amount when the promissory notes of the importer are delivered to the forfaiter. The forfaiter charges the exporter an additional standby fee of 0.1% or 0.125% per month between the time that a commitment is made to the exporter and the time that the exporter delivers the notes. The forfaiter must arrange to have the funds available when the exporter presents the notes, which might require the forfaiter to borrow and deposit the funds in the short-term money market.

Third, the importer signs a sequence of promissory notes obligating it to pay the exporter certain sums, usually every 6 or 12 months, contingent upon the exporter performing certain functions related to the project. The notes are usually guaranteed by the importer's government or the importer's bank. In Europe, this irrevocable guarantee is referred to as an **aval**. With this guarantee, all subsequent holders of the note will view the importer's government or its bank as the primary obligor to the note.

Fourth, the importer delivers the notes to the exporter. The exporter then endorses the notes "without recourse" and sells them to the forfaiter at the agreed-upon discount.

Fifth, the forfaiter endorses the notes and sells them in the money market. Investors know that the notes are the liabilities of both the importer's bank and the forfaiting institution, but it is the latter whose credit risk is of most concern.

The final step involves investors presenting the notes to the importer or its bank at maturity. If both of these default on the scheduled payments, the investor turns to the forfaiter for payment because the forfaiter provides a guarantee with its endorsement.

Essentially, the forfaiting institution provides two services to the exporter: country risk assessment and financial intermediation in the money market. In its role as country risk assessor, the forfaiter must price the default risks of different countries. In its role as a financial intermediary, the forfaiter packages discounted notes in various maturities for sale to the money market. Because the forfaiter guarantees the notes it sells, the success of the forfaiter ultimately depends on its ability to price the default risks of countries.

Export Factoring

A technique for financing exports that is closely related to forfaiting is export factoring. An **export factor** is a company that performs credit risk investigations and collects funds from the accounts receivable of other firms. In international trade, factors provide both these services to exporters. They may also provide financing of exporters' accounts receivable.

An example is the International Factors Group (IF-Group) of companies. When dealing with the International Factors Group of companies, one IF-Group member acts as the export factor, which deals with the seller's country; the second member of the IF-Group, the import factor, handles credit risk cover and collection in the buyer's country. *Credit risk cover* is the amount that the factor accepts as a risk that an individual buyer may be financially unable to pay.

Factors perform several services for exporters. The primary service is credit investigation. During the negotiations between an exporter and a foreign importer, the exporter provides information to the factor about the potential importer and the nature of the deal under negotiation. The factor uses its network of local affiliates in various countries, which are usually in partnership with local banks, to perform a credit check on the importer. The factor may also be asked to provide a guarantee to the exporter, which stipulates that if the importer defaults, the factor pays the bill.

Factors give two types of credit approvals: order approvals and revolving credit lines. With an order approval, the factor provides the approval for a specific shipment by the exporter to an importer. With a revolving credit line, the exporter obtains advance approval for what is anticipated to be the maximum shipment to an importer for a given period of time. If the factor buys the receivables of the exporter at a discount, it is the responsibility of the factor to collect payment from the importer. The factor's local affiliate adheres to the standard collection practices in the particular countries involved.

If an exporter is small, a factor can also perform various accounting functions for the exporter. These include providing a monthly statement of cash flows, including all sales to the factor, commissions paid, and other debits and credits. The factor also provides statements of the credit lines outstanding for various importers, notices of disputes with any importers over specific invoices, and reports on outstanding risk exposures classified by importer and whether the factor guarantees the invoice.

Methods of Payment

Factors pay exporters in a variety of ways. One is on a collection basis. Under this arrangement, the exporter gets paid when the factor receives funds from the importer. Exporters also get paid by factors when the importer is declared insolvent or when a specific political event in the contract occurs that prevents the importer from paying.

The exporter may also receive payment on an average collection basis, which reflects the past experience of the factor collecting from an importer. The factor calculates the average number of days that a particular exporter's customers have taken to pay and remits payment to the exporter in the following month, based on that average experience. For example, if an importer pays earlier or later than average, the exporter receives interest from or pays interest to the factor.

Funds can also be remitted on a maturity basis. Under this method, the factor calculates the weighted-average maturity date of all invoices maturing in a particular month, adds a specified number of collection days, and pays the sum of that month's invoices on that date. For example, suppose Invoice A for $50,000 is due on September 1, Invoice B for $25,000 is due on September 30, and 10 days are added for collection. Then, the exporter would receive $75,000 on September 21 because the weighted average of the payments times is

$$(50/75) \times (1 \text{ day}) + (25/75) \times (30 \text{ days}) + 10 \text{ days} = 20.67 \text{ days}$$

Past-due interest is charged to the exporter for any receivable outstanding at the end of the month.

An exporter can arrange for financing either through the factor handling the servicing of the exports or from another financial intermediary, such as a commercial bank. Factors structure their lines of credit somewhat differently than do commercial banks. Factors agree with exporters on a percentage of exports that will be advanced to the exporter, in contrast to the set credit limit established by a commercial bank. The percentage advanced from factors to exporters varies between 70% and 90%, depending on the financial characteristics of the exporter. Exporters like this arrangement because it gives them additional capital to exploit additional growth opportunities without having to recontract with a financial intermediary. Exporters pay for this growth option, however, because factors charge slightly higher interest rates than banks.

In addition, exporters and factors can involve a second financial intermediary in a **tripartite arrangement**. Under a tripartite arrangement, the factor services the exporter, which assigns any credit balances due from the factor to a financial intermediary that provides funds to the exporter.

Government Sources of Export Financing and Credit Insurance

The governments of countries that have substantial export sectors have developed specialized financial intermediaries to provide export finance, insurance, and possibly subsidies to their exporters. A case in point is the China Export and Credit Insurance Corp., or **Sinosure**, which was established in 2002. Within just 1 year of its formation, Sinosure was involved in $5.5 billion of trade, representing 3% of the total trade of China.

Export subsidies serve several purposes: They provide credit to exporters or their customers when the private market fails to do so, they offer loans to exporters at below-market interest rates, and they provide insurance or guarantees at below-market prices. Ultimately, the subsidies are paid for by the taxpayers of the country. Governments justify these subsidies by claiming that they are designed to promote employment and to keep their exporters technologically competitive, especially in light of the subsidies that other countries offer their exporters.

Ex-Im Bank

The Export–Import Bank of the United States, commonly called **Ex-Im Bank**, is an independent U.S. government corporation involved in financing and facilitating U.S. exports. It was established in 1934 to stimulate the foreign trade of the United States, primarily with the Soviet Union. Ex-Im Bank was rechartered in 1945 by an act of Congress that broadened its mission to allow Ex-Im Bank to offer a variety of guarantees and financing for short-term (180 days or less), medium-term (181 days to 5 years), and long-term (more than 5 years) export transactions. The 1945 act explicitly states that Ex-Im Bank should supplement and not compete with private capital and that its loans should be for specific purposes and offer reasonable assurances of repayment.

Ex-Im Bank does not try to compete with private-sector lenders. Rather, it provides export financing products that private-sector lenders do not offer. For example, Ex-Im Bank assumes credit risks and country risks that the private sector is unwilling to accept. It also provides working capital guarantees that help exporters with their financing prior to their shipping products abroad. In addition, it provides export credit insurance and offers loan guarantees and direct loans to importers of U.S. products.

The majority of Ex-Im Bank's resources are devoted to long-term financing. Its two major programs involve direct loans and financial guarantees. These programs facilitate the export of construction projects, such as power plants, and the production of other long-term capital goods, such as commercial aircraft and locomotives. Ex-Im Bank's medium-term programs primarily benefit the exporters of agriculture, construction, general aviation, mining, and refining equipment; its short-term programs primarily benefit producers of small manufactured goods, such as consumer goods and replacement parts.

Ex-Im Bank operates under a number of political and economic constraints. Its long-term loans are made directly to foreign borrowers wanting to purchase long-lived U.S. exports.

The maturity of the credit cannot be longer than the economic life of the export good. The loans are denominated in dollars, and principal and interest must be repaid in dollars. Repayment typically occurs semi-annually, with the first payment due after delivery of the goods or start-up of the project.

Ex-Im Bank typically deals in amounts of $5 million or more, and all Ex-Im Bank loans are required to have "reasonable assurance of repayment." Ex-Im Bank consequently may require a foreign borrower to obtain an unconditional guarantee from its government or an internationally respected bank. Ex-Im Bank also requires a borrower to demonstrate that its project is technically feasible.

PEFCO

Ex-Im Bank often works in cooperation with the **Private Export Funding Corporation (PEFCO)**, which is a private corporation whose mission is to make dollar loans to foreign purchasers of U.S. exports. PEFCO was created in 1971 by a consortium of private banks, an investment bank, and several large industrial firms. PEFCO acts either as a direct lender or as a secondary market buyer of export loans originated by lenders. Its programs cover short-term, medium-term, and long-term export finance. To be eligible for financing by PEFCO, loans must be protected against nonpayment under an appropriate guarantee or insurance policy issued by Ex-Im Bank or by a guarantee issued by the U.S. Small Business Administration. Because PEFCO loans are insured by Ex-Im Bank, and because the attorney general of the United States has ruled that Ex-Im Bank's liabilities are general obligations of the United States backed by the full faith and credit of the federal government, PEFCO can borrow at interest rates close to U.S. Treasury rates. However, PEFCO's rates are set higher than those on U.S. Treasury bonds to reflect both the cost of PEFCO's funds and a margin for risk.

For example, with typical PEFCO financing, an importer of, say, U.S. airplanes, borrows from a commercial bank at short-term maturities, from Ex-Im Bank at long-term maturities, and from PEFCO at medium-term maturities.

Export Credit Insurance

Although exporters who offer more favorable credit terms to importers are more likely to win business, exporters and their banks want to be repaid. Thus, if the commercial or political risk of a deal is too large, the private credit market may not finance the deal.

Because the extension of credit to importers is often an important part of a deal, governments have stepped in to provide insurance to cover export financing. The insurance protects an exporter or an exporter's bank against losses due to commercial and political risks. Of course, here, again, it is ultimately the taxpayers of the exporter's country who are subsidizing the export market.

In the United States, the **Financial Credit Insurance Association (FCIA)** is an unincorporated association of private marine, property, and casualty insurance companies that joined together with Ex-Im Bank to provide export credit insurance. However, during the Debt Crisis of the early 1980s, many private insurers withdrew from the FCIA. This basically left the FCIA as an agency of Ex-Im Bank. Indeed, in 1983, Ex-Im Bank assumed full responsibility for all commercial and political risks insured by the FCIA.

The FCIA offers a variety of different types of insurance policies to protect exporters against commercial and political risks. The two basic types of insurance policies are the multibuyer policy and the single-buyer policy. A multibuyer policy covers all of the insured's exports for a given period of time. The coverage of losses due to commercial risks ranges between 90% and 95%, and the coverage of losses due to political risks ranges between 95% and 100%. The insurance premium depends on a number of factors, such as the countries to which the exporter is shipping, the exporter's previous experience with export sales, the length of time for which credit is being extended, and the amount of the risk that is covered.

POINT–COUNTERPOINT

On Bicycles and Countertrade

Ante and Freedy are in Vienna, Austria, visiting Helga, whom they are told is the daughter of their mother's uncle's second cousin. Helga had realized that with the collapse of the former Soviet Union, the central European and eastern European regions would see a big increase in international trade. Along with German and English, Helga had learned Polish and Russian, which allowed her to move pretty comfortably around the region as a consultant, setting up trading operations for corporations in these emerging markets.

Helga wanted some advice from Ante and Freedy: "I've gotten a call from a Ukrainian bicycle manufacturer that wants to import some gears from the Italian company Campagnolo. I called Campagnolo, and they said they don't export to such companies unless the importer gets a documentary credit from a major international bank. I checked with the Ukrainians, and they said the banks they deal with charge too much for a D/C. They feel ripped off. Do you have any suggestions?"

Ante said, "Yeah, let them pay cash in advance. That'll make Campagnolo happy."

Freedy seized the moment to squash his brother. "Oh sure, these Ukrainians have mountains of hard currency sitting around, waiting to be paid to their shareholders, so the bicycle company will just dip into its massive stockpile of cash and buy the gears. Silly me!"

Ante felt embarrassed when he realized how impractical his suggestion was, but he tried again, "Okay, cash in advance is impractical, and a D/C is too expensive. Maybe the Italians will accept a documentary collection."

Helga interjected, "I've already been down that route with Campagnolo's CFO, and he said no dice. He thinks the credit risk is too high. I think these Ukrainian bikes are really high quality. There has got to be another way to do this deal."

Of course, Suttle Trooth was traveling with his cousins, and he had been listening in. Suttle offered the following insight: "Helga, there is always another way. Why don't you contact a major importer of bicycles here in Vienna or up in Berlin, and get them to take a look at the Ukrainian bikes? Then, if they like the quality, they can contract with the Ukrainians to buy the bicycles, but part of the contract will be to pay Campagnolo for the gears that will be exported to the Ukraine. In fact, a major bicycle distributor probably even has an open account with Campagnolo. Gears will go to the Ukraine, bikes will go to Berlin, and Campagnolo will increase its accounts receivable from the Berlin bike distributor. It's easy." Helga was impressed with Suttle's assessment of the situation. She asked, "Does that transaction have a name?"

Suttle replied, "Yes, it's a form of countertrade."

18.5 COUNTERTRADE

Countertrade emerged in the 1960s as a way to facilitate East–West trade, and its complexity continues to evolve to this day. Countertrade makes it possible for exporters and importers to exchange goods and services without necessarily having to use money as a medium of exchange. Countertrade does not describe one particular type of international transaction, however, but a related set of activities that encompasses various types of barter. It can occur between two or more parties, involve one or more contracts, and use money or not.

The United Nations estimates that at least 25% of all international trade involves some form of countertrade. The **Global Offset and Countertrade Association (GOCA)** holds annual conferences and supports a website (http://www.globaloffset.org/) devoted to the

Exhibit 18.7 Types of Countertrade

Trades Without Money	Trades Involving Money or Credit
Barter	Buybacks
Clearing arrangements	Counterpurchases
Switch trading	Offsets

practice. Some representative member companies of the GOCA include Boeing, Dell, General Dynamics, Embraer, General Electric, Lucent Technologies, Motorola, and Raytheon.

One quintessential example of an early countertrade involved PepsiCo, which began operating in the Soviet Union in 1974. PepsiCo agreed to license several Soviet-owned bottling plants and to supply them with cola concentrate. In return for its concentrate, PepsiCo agreed to become the exclusive importer to the United States of the Soviet Union's Stolichnaya vodka.

Exhibit 18.7 lists the specific types of countertrade, of which there are two broad categories (see Grant Hammond, 1990). Within each category are three subcategories. The first category contains transactions that are designed to avoid the use of money. These include barter, clearing arrangements, and switch trading. The second category of transactions uses money or credit and is designed to impose commitments on the exporter. These transactions include buybacks, counterpurchases, and offsets. We will examine each of the six types of countertrade in turn.

Transactions Without Money

Barter

International barter involves the transfer of goods or services from a party in one country to a party in another country in return for some other good or service. Trade is balanced in the sense that the value of what is being exported equals the value of what is being imported. Although money is not involved, money may be the numeraire that determines the values of the goods. However, the difficulty in valuing various goods and the disagreements that can ensue about their equivalence have led to the decline of barter as an instrument of international trade.

Clearing Arrangements

Clearing arrangements allow barter to be conducted on credit. Under a clearing arrangement, each of the two parties to a transaction agrees to import a certain value of goods and services from the other. A clearing account is established, and the values of the imports and exports are debited and credited over time as the shipments are made. If the contract has a specified end date, the two parties can settle any nonzero, residual balance with a final shipment of goods or a money payment at the end of the specified period.

Switch Trading

Switch trading involves a third party, a switch trader, who facilitates the eventual clearing of an imbalance of trade between two partners to a bilateral clearing arrangement. Often, governments are involved in the creation of a clearing arrangement. If one of the countries generates an imbalance of trade, and no hard currency is available to offset the imbalance, it may be sold at a discount to a switch trader, who uses the account to purchase goods in the country that has run the trade balance deficit. The switch trader then resells the goods on world markets.

For example, Brazil and Romania might agree to exchange Brazilian coffee for Romanian fertilizer during the coming year, with the intention of balancing trade by year end. If the value of Romania's coffee imports exceeds the value of its fertilizer exports, a switch trader could purchase the clearing balance from Brazil with hard currency. The switch trader would then have the right to purchase other Romanian goods with the clearing balance, and these goods would be exported to the world market.

Some critics of switch trading note that there is no guarantee that Romania would not be dumping its manufactured goods, where *dumping* is defined as selling goods internationally for less than they cost to produce. If dumping is occurring, though, it is being done indirectly by a third party, the switch trader, and not directly by the manufacturer. Other critics note that by failing to establish a foreign distribution network, countries such as Romania, in our example, never learn how to make their products more attractive to foreign buyers.

Countertrade Involving Money or Credit

Buybacks

A **buyback** involves an agreement in which an exporter of physical capital agrees to accept payment in the form of the output of a plant that the exporter helps to construct and equip in a foreign country. There are three varieties of buybacks. In one, the exporter receives products directly from the factory that was constructed, and these products may be similar to what the exporter also produces. The exporter must be aware that the increased supply of the foreign product could drive down its world price, with adverse consequences on the exporter's other markets. This is what PepsiCo realized would happen with its deal in the Soviet Union if it accepted cola produced in the Soviet Union. Hence, the company bought back vodka instead. In another variety of buyback, the exporter receives resultant products that are unrelated to the exporter's industry. Here the problem is that the exporter has less ability to assess the value of the products and no marketing network. In a third type of buyback, the exporter receives a mix of resultant products and other products of the country.

A famous example of a buyback is the agreement by several western European countries to supply the Soviet Union with the pipe, compressors, controls, and other equipment necessary to build a natural gas pipeline from the Soviet Union to western Europe. The payment for the pipeline was natural gas delivered through the pipeline to western Europe over the course of several years.

Counterpurchases

A **counterpurchase** is similar to a buyback, except the exporter purchases totally non-resultant products from the importer. For example, in 1983, Rockwell, a U.S.-based company, won a bidding contest to supply an $8 million printing press to Zimbabwe by offering a 100% counterpurchase. Rockwell agreed to buy $8 million of ferrochrome and nickel from Zimbabwe and export the minerals out of the country. The agreement to purchase the minerals was linked explicitly to the sales agreement in which Zimbabwe agreed to pay cash to Rockwell for the printing press.

Offsets

An **offset** is a requirement of an importing country that the price of its imports be offset in some way by the exporter. Offsets are common in contracts for weapons and contracts for other large expenditures, such as power-generating facilities. The exporter agrees to purchase goods in the importer's country, to increase its imports from that country, to transfer technology to the country, or to conduct additional direct foreign investment in the country in return for setting up the facility. For example, in 1984, General Dynamics entered into an agreement to sell 160 fighter jets to Turkey. This $4.2 billion contract contained offsets requiring General Dynamics to enter into co-production in Turkey, to transfer technology to Turkey, and to export miscellaneous Turkish products as well as electronic and military components produced in Turkey.

The set of issues involved in various forms of countertrade has expanded to the point where some people now prefer to talk in terms of **compensatory trade**, or "mandated reciprocity." For example, the website for the Beijing Investment Guide (http://www.chinavista .com/beijing/invest/invest-types.html) describes compensatory trade in the following way:

> Compensatory trade enterprises are ones in which overseas partners provide equipment and technology and are bound to purchase a certain quantity of the finished products for exportation. Purchase of the equipment and technology can be made on the installment plan. Agreed upon negotiation by both parties of the compensatory trade enterprises, the loans for purchasing and importing the equipment and technology can be paid back in kind with other products as well as the finished equipment and technology as approved of when forming the compensatory trade enterprises.

Clearly, this is countertrade, and as such, parties involved in these complex international trade deals must understand that they may be entering into a long-term deal that will involve many future rounds of not only trade but additional negotiations.

18.6 SUMMARY

This chapter examines some of the institutional details related to how international trade is conducted and financed. The main points in the chapter are as follows:

1. The shipping documents of international trade include bills of lading, commercial invoices, packing lists, insurance certificates, consular invoices, and certificates of analysis.

2. A straight bill of lading instructs a common carrier to deliver merchandise to a designated party, known as the consignee. An order bill of lading transfers the title of goods. An on-board bill of lading indicates that goods have been placed on a particular vessel for shipment, whereas a received-for-shipment bill of lading indicates only that the merchandise is at the dock awaiting transport. A clean bill of lading indicates that a carrier believes the merchandise in question was received in good condition, whereas a foul bill of lading indicates that a carrier's initial inspection of the merchandise in question uncovered some damage before the merchandise was received for shipment.

3. Exporters issue to importers commercial invoices that provide a description of the merchandise, including the unit prices of the items, the number of items shipped, and the financial terms of the sale, including the amount due from the buyer and any

charges to the buyer arising from insurance and shipping. A packing list indicates how the specific goods are stored in various containers.

4. A firm that does a substantial amount of exporting can purchase open, or floating, insurance policies that automatically cover all of the firm's exports. This eliminates the need for the exporter to arrange insurance coverage for each order.

5. A consular invoice, filled out by an exporter in consultation with the consulate of the importing country, provides information to customs officials that prevents false declarations of the value of the merchandise.

6. Certificates of analysis are sometimes required by documentary credits to assure an importer that a shipment meets certain standards of purity, weight, sanitation, or other measurable characteristics.

7. The different methods of payment available for an importer include cash in advance, open account, documentary collections, and documentary credits.

8. Cash in advance requires an importer to pay an exporter before the goods in question are shipped. The importer must finance the purchase of the goods and must bear the risk that the goods will not be exactly what is ordered.

9. An open account arrangement allows an importer to order goods and pay an invoiced amount at some

time in the future. The exporter extends trade credit to the importer, which finances the importer's purchase.

10. A documentary is an instrument that allows an exporter to retain control of the goods until the importer has paid for them or is legally bound to pay for them and that involves a bank in the collection process.

11. With a documentary credit, also called a letter of credit, banks stand between the importer and the exporter, and the exporter must assess the credit risk of the international banks. Because the involvement of banks in the transaction is extensive, the documentary credit is the most expensive of the methods of payment, but a confirmed irrevocable documentary credit is also the safest for the exporter.

12. A banker's acceptance is a document, tradable in financial markets, that is created when a bank stamps and signs a time draft indicating that the bank will pay the face value of a draft at maturity.

13. Exporters can obtain financing through a bank line of credit, through the discounting of a banker's acceptance, by setting up a buyer credit, by arranging a receivables purchase, from limited-recourse financing, and through export factoring.

14. Major exporting countries have export–import banks which offer a variety of programs that subsidize the exports of their countries. The subsidies include providing credit either directly to an exporter or its customers when the private market fails to do so, loans at below-market interest rates, and credit insurance or guarantees at below-market prices.

15. Countertrade refers to various trade agreements that involve contractual links between exports of a good or service and imports of a good or service. The various forms of countertrade include barter, clearing arrangements, switch trading, buybacks, counterpurchases, and offsets.

QUESTIONS

1. What is the fundamental financing problem in international trade?
2. What is a bill of lading?
3. What is the difference between a straight bill of lading and an order bill of lading?
4. What is the difference between a clean bill of lading and a foul bill of lading?
5. What are the purposes of a commercial invoice and a packing list?
6. What do the INCOTERM acronyms FOB, FAS, CFR, and CIF mean?
7. How can an exporter insure against the loss of value of goods while they are being shipped internationally?
8. Why might a country require an exporter to acquire a consular invoice in order to clear the customs of an importing country?
9. Why would a certificate of analysis be important for shipping goods internationally?
10. What are four different methods by which an importer can pay an exporter? List them in increasing order of risk to the exporter.
11. True or false: In a documentary collection, the remitting bank is the agent of the importer.
12. What is the difference between a documents against payment collection and a documents against acceptance collection?

13. How is a trade acceptance created? Whose liability is it? Can it be sold in the international money market?
14. What is meant by a document discrepancy? How might one arise? How can it be resolved?
15. How is a documentary credit created?
16. What are the advantages of a documentary credit to an exporter and an importer?
17. What is a confirmed documentary credit? Why would an exporter demand a confirmed, irrevocable documentary credit?
18. What are the costs of using a documentary credit?
19. What is the most straightforward way for an exporter to finance its accounts receivable?
20. What is a banker's acceptance? How is one created? Whose liability is it?
21. What is the difference between an eligible and an ineligible banker's acceptance, and what are the eligibility requirements?
22. How is a buyer credit arranged?
23. What is forfaiting? How does it work? Why did it arise?
24. What is export factoring? What services does a factor perform for an exporter?
25. What are the differences between receiving payment on a collection basis, on an average collection basis, and on a maturity basis?

26. How does an export–import bank work? Who ultimately pays for the services of an export–import bank?
27. What are the major programs of the U.S. Ex-Im Bank?
28. What are the six different types of countertrade? Describe them.
29. How would a clearing arrangement work between the Ukraine and Lithuania, whereby the Ukraine exports grain and Lithuania exports shoes?
30. There are major natural resource deposits in the People's Republic of China (PRC). How might a buyback arrangement work in which the PRC purchases earthmoving equipment from the Japanese firm Komatsu?
31. The Indonesian government is concerned that it may contribute to the country's balance-of-trade deficit if it follows through with plans to import a large order of trucks from Germany that will be used to develop Indonesian timber resources. How might the Indonesian government use a counterpurchase to its advantage?

BIBLIOGRAPHY

Celi, Louis J., and I. James Czechowicz, 1985, *Export Financing: A Handbook of Sources and Techniques*, Morristown, NJ: Financial Executives Research Foundation.

Financing Foreign Operations, New York: Business International Corporation, various issues.

Greif, Avner, 1993, "Contract Enforceability and Economic Institutions in Early Trade: The Maghribi Traders' Coalition," *American Economic Review* 83, pp. 525–548.

Hammond, Grant T., 1990, *Countertrade, Offsets, and Barter in International Political Economy*, London: Pinter.

Hennart, Jean-Francois, Second Quarter 1990, "Some Empirical Dimensions of Countertrade," *Journal of International Business Studies*, pp. 243–270.

International Chamber of Commerce, 2001, *INCOTERMS 2000*, ICC Publication No. 560.

Lecraw, Donald J., Spring 1989, "The Management of Countertrade: Factors Influencing Success," *Journal of International Business Studies*, pp. 41–59.

Marin, Delia, and Monika Schnitzer, 1995, "Tying Trade Flows: A Theory of Countertrade with Evidence," *American Economic Review* 85, pp. 1047–1064.

Ripley, Andy, 1996, *Forfait Finance of Exporters*, New York: International Thompson Business Press.

Schaffer, Matt, 1990, "Countertrade as an Export Strategy," *Journal of Business Strategy* May/June, reprinted in Linda Catlin and Thomas White, eds., *International Business: Cultural Sourcebook and Case Studies*, Cincinnati, OH: South-Western Publishing Co., 1994.

Chapter 19

Managing Net Working Capital

*T*his chapter discusses the management of short-term assets and liabilities within a multinational corporation. The assets consist of cash, marketable securities, inventories, and accounts receivable. The liabilities consist of short-term debt and accounts payable. We begin by discussing net working capital, an investment that a firm must manage well to ensure its future profitability. The next topic is international cash management, which is followed by a discussion about how a foreign affiliate transfers funds to its parent corporation.

When related affiliates buy goods and services from each other, the prices charged are called *transfer prices*. The chapter explores how different transfer pricing policies can shift a firm's income and income tax burdens around the world and how governments attempt to regulate these shifts. The effect of transfer pricing policies on managerial incentives is also considered.

The chapter also addresses techniques for mitigating the problems associated with blocked funds. The last part of the chapter discusses the management of a firm's accounts receivable and its inventories in an international environment.

19.1 THE PURPOSE OF NET WORKING CAPITAL

Every corporation maintains a stock of current assets and current liabilities to buffer the inflows and outflows of cash generated by the firm's business. **Working capital**, or current assets, is the collection of cash, marketable securities, accounts receivable, and inventories held by a firm at any point in time. By subtracting the value of a firm's current liabilities, which are the corporation's short-term debts and its accounts payable, from its stock of working capital, we arrive at its **net working capital**:

$$\text{Net working capital} = \text{Cash} + \text{Marketable securities} + \text{Accounts receivable}$$
$$+ \text{Inventories} - \text{Short-term debt} - \text{Accounts payable}$$

To the extent that a firm can be managed with a smaller stock of net working capital, cash can be paid to shareholders. Thus, one goal of management is to run a corporation efficiently in order to minimize the need for net working capital.

Increases in net working capital are investments that a firm makes to produce cash in the future. This is perhaps most easily understood when you think about inventories.

Inventories as Assets

The stock of a firm's inventory includes raw materials, goods that represent work-in-progress, and finished goods. Raw materials and work-in-progress are necessary because all goods take some time to produce. Finished goods inventories are necessary because demand is stochastic, and orders are placed randomly by customers.

Firms typically find that costs of production are lower if production is smoothed over time. If a firm tries to match its production to its demand, the firm will have to pay its workers overtime wages and ask its suppliers to expedite shipments when demand is high, both of which increase costs. If a firm does not meet orders, it will incur backlog costs because frustrated customers will be less likely to do business with the firm in the future. Hence, stockpiling inventory can help minimize the cost of production and prevent the loss of future sales, both of which increase profitability. Thus, increasing a firm's inventory is as much of an investment as if the firm were purchasing a new machine to enhance its production and future profits. Of course, as with all other investments, management must decide on the appropriate level of inventories to allow the right rate of return to the capital that is invested in the inventories. We address this issue later in the chapter.

Other Current Assets

Increases in cash, marketable securities, and accounts receivable should also be viewed as investments the firm is making in the operation of its business. For example, suppose Reagon Optical Products sells some contact lenses to a pharmacy on credit. This increases Reagon's accounts receivable because the value of the sale, which increases accounts receivable, is worth more than the decrease in Reagon's inventory. Hence, Reagon's net working capital increases. However, the actual revenue from the sale will not be collected until the future, which means that Reagon is making an investment. For example, Reagon could have induced its customer to pay today by lowering the price of the contact lenses. The fact that the transaction takes place on credit indicates that Reagon's long-run profitability is enhanced by selling the contact lenses at the higher price and financing the sale with an extension of credit to the buyer.

Short-Term Liabilities

Consider a corporation's short-term liabilities. Accounts payable and other short-term borrowings are ways of generating resources and conserving cash. If a firm needs some additional raw materials, and it uses internally generated cash to buy them, no additional funds are needed from investors outside the firm. Hence, there is no change in net working capital because the value of the raw materials, or additional inventory, is equal to the value of the cash paid for them.

In contrast, if a firm takes out a short-term bank loan to purchase inventory, it does not have to tap the long-term debt market or the equity market. Again, however, the firm's net working capital will not change because the increase in its inventory of raw materials matches the increase in its short-term liabilities.

Another way a company can obtain goods for its inventory without using the assets of the firm is to buy on trade credit from its suppliers. This action generates an account payable. Once again, inventories rise, but the firm's *net* working capital has not changed because the increase in working capital is offset by a corresponding increase in the firm's short-term liabilities.

Of course, as noted earlier, firms try to hold enough net working capital to smooth out the production–sales cycle. This implies that there is an optimal amount of net working capital a firm should have on hand. For example, having excessive cash or short-term assets is costly if the investments earn a lower rate of return than shareholders could earn. Also, excessive cash can lead to severe agency problems between the shareholders and the managers, which is also very costly. Now that we've explored the importance of managing net working capital, let's look at how to manage net working capital in an international context.

19.2 INTERNATIONAL CASH MANAGEMENT

The goals of an international money manager of a multinational corporation are (1) to establish control over the cash resources of the organization, (2) to invest excess short-term funds in an optimal way, and (3) to obtain short-term financing at the lowest cost. Establishing control over the cash resources of an organization necessitates creating a reporting system that provides timely and accurate information. When the information is available, the international cash manager can try to improve upon the cash disbursements to and collections from its foreign affiliates. By synchronizing the flows of funds, the international cash manager can lower the cost of moving funds among them. These goals are no different than those of a purely domestic cash manager who transfers money from one account to another (or from one subsidiary to another) so that the firm has an optimal amount of working capital. However, there are constraints on international cash management that domestic managers do not face.

Constraints on International Cash Management

An international cash manager of a multinational corporation often encounters constraints that do not arise in a purely domestic corporation. These constraints include government restrictions on the transfers of funds, taxes that depend on the type of fund transfer, transaction costs in the foreign exchange market, and problems maintaining the liquidity of all foreign affiliates.

We first discussed blocked funds in Chapter 18. **Blocked funds** arise when the government of a foreign country makes the nation's currency completely inconvertible. Foreign exchange controls that impose unattractive foreign exchange rates can also constrain a firm. Host countries also impose taxes on the repatriation of funds from a foreign affiliate to its parent. These taxes often differ, depending on whether the transfer of funds consists of dividends, service fees, or royalty payments. Such taxes can have a constraining effect on a firm's international cash management as well.

Of course, transaction costs are incurred whenever funds are converted from one currency into another. These transaction costs include the fees charged by banks as well as the bid–ask spread that banks use to generate profits, the loss of interest that occurs during the time that funds are withdrawn from one bank and are deposited in another bank, and other transaction fees, such as cable charges. Chapter 2 notes that these transaction costs are quite small for transactions involving the major currencies of the world. Even if transaction costs are a small percentage, too frequent movement back and forth between currencies unnecessarily increases transaction costs. Also, for minor currencies, the transaction costs are larger. The final constraint on an international cash manager is the need to ensure that each of the firm's foreign affiliates maintains an adequate amount of cash to make it liquid enough to function efficiently.

Cash Management with a Centralized Pool

As explained earlier, corporations hold cash balances and short-term marketable securities because the outflows of funds on a day-to-day basis do not perfectly match the inflows of funds. Economists have long noted that short-term cash and liquid assets satisfy the needs of firms that arise from both the transactions and precautionary demands for money. The **transactions demand for money** arises because a firm realizes that it has some expenditure that will be incurred in the near future. The **precautionary demand for money** arises because a firm may need to purchase something due to an unanticipated change in its environment.

Just as an inventory of finished goods buffers the production process and lowers costs, an inventory of cash provides a buffer that lowers the costs of doing business due to the mismatch between inflows and outflows of funds. Of course, holding cash balances and short-term, highly marketable securities has costs. The rates of return on these assets are lower than the rates of return on longer-term assets precisely because these assets are liquid. Holding cash provides flexibility, but the cost of this flexibility is the forgone interest that could have been earned on longer-term, less liquid assets had they been held.

For a multinational corporation with affiliates in several countries, centralizing the management of the short-term cash balances of its affiliates can provide a significant amount of savings. Transaction costs that the organization incurs as a result of moving cash around the world can be reduced, and the overall amount of cash needed by the organization can be minimized. The savings in transaction costs arise from utilizing a multilateral netting system. The savings in the overall level of cash balances arise from exploiting the stochastic nature of the precautionary demand for money by centralizing the holdings of cash. We now consider these issues in detail.

Short-Term Cash Planning

To illustrate how an information system would be set up to help manage a centralized pool of cash for a firm, consider an MNC that has European affiliates operating in Great Britain, Denmark, the Netherlands, and Spain. Exhibit 19.1 presents a daily cash report for each of the

Exhibit 19.1 Daily Cash Reports of an MNC's European Affiliates (in thousands of euros)

Date: October 21, 2009

British Affiliate

Current Cash Position: +200

Five-Day Forecasts

Day	Receive	Pay	Net
+1	200	100	100
+2	150	500	−350
+3	100	150	−50
+4	200	100	100
+5	150	100	50
Net for period			−150

Date: October 21, 2009

Danish Affiliate

Current Cash Position: −100

Five-Day Forecasts

Day	Receive	Pay	Net
+1	300	200	100
+2	400	400	0
+3	600	250	350
+4	100	300	−200
+5	200	300	−100
Net for period			150

Date: October 21, 2009

Dutch Affiliate

Current Cash Position: +250

Five-Day Forecasts

Day	Receive	Pay	Net
+1	450	700	−250
+2	400	100	300
+3	200	700	−500
+4	450	200	250
+5	400	300	100
Net for period			−100

Date: October 21, 2009

Spanish Affiliate

Current Cash Position: +150

Five-Day Forecasts

Day	Receive	Pay	Net
+1	600	100	500
+2	500	100	400
+3	400	100	300
+4	200	700	−500
+5	100	200	−100
Net for period			600

Note: The cash flows for each of the affiliates are converted into euros at current exchange rates.

Exhibit 19.2 Consolidated Daily Cash Reports of an MNC's European Affiliates (in thousands of euros)

	Daily Cash Balances, October 21, 2009		
	Closing Balance	Minimum-Desired Balance	Surplus (Deficit) Cash Balance
British	200	100	100
Danish	−100	200	−300
Dutch	250	300	−50
Spanish	150	250	−100
European total			−350

Notes: The "closing balance" is taken from Exhibit 19.1. The "minimum-desired balance" is typically set by the parent company in consultation with the management of the local affiliate. The "surplus (deficit) cash balance" represents the difference between the "closing balance" and the "minimum-desired balance."

European affiliates, as it might be transmitted to the company's central cash pool located, say, in Geneva, Switzerland. At the close of business each day, the local treasurer of each affiliate would wire, fax, or e-mail the information to the central office in Geneva. The reports are denominated in a single currency—in this case, the euro. The reports indicate that the British affiliate has €200,000 on hand. This is the amount that the British affiliate could spend immediately without drawing on its short-term line of credit from a bank. The Danish affiliate has borrowed €100,000, either from the central pool or from a bank. The Dutch affiliate has an end-of-day cash balance of €250,000, and the Spanish affiliate has a cash balance of €150,000.

Exhibit 19.2 relates the existing cash balances of each European affiliate to its previously agreed-upon, desired cash position. The desired cash balance is the minimum amount of cash the affiliate needs on a daily basis. Exhibit 19.2 also calculates the overall cash surplus or deficit of the entire company.

From Exhibit 19.2, we learn that the British affiliate's current cash balance of €200,000 represents an excess of €100,000 over its minimum desired cash balance. The Danish affiliate's desired cash balance is €200,000, and it is €300,000 below this level because it previously borrowed €100,000. Although the Dutch affiliate has €250,000 in cash on hand, it requires €300,000. Hence, it is €50,000 below its desired cash balance. Finally, the Spanish affiliate's cash balance of €150,000 places it €100,000 below its desired balance. Overall, across the four European affiliates, there is a deficit of €350,000.

Managing Surpluses and Deficits

Once the information in Exhibits 19.1 and 19.2 is collected, the central office must decide how to invest any surpluses and how to cover any deficits. Excess cash can be invested in a variety of short-term money market instruments, and short-term borrowing can be done through banks or in the commercial paper market. In either case, the firm faces several choices. Most important are the currency of denomination and the maturity of the investment or the debt. The appropriate choice will depend on the interest rates in the different currencies, the expectations of the financial manager about the rates of appreciation and depreciation of one currency relative to another, the amount of foreign exchange risk that the organization is willing to bear, and the manager's forecasts of future short-term cash needs of the different affiliates.

For example, suppose the central office thought that a weakening of the Danish krone relative to the euro was imminent. If nominal interest differentials (the Danish krone rate minus the euro rate) did not adequately reflect the expected depreciation of the krone, the central office could instruct the Danish affiliate to borrow additional kroner by drawing on its line of credit. An alternative way of discussing this situation recognizes that the minimum desired balance expressed in Exhibit 19.2 should be adjusted downward in light of the interest rates and the expectations of depreciation. Having the Danish affiliate borrow kroner provides funds to be invested. These extra kroner would be invested in the euro and other currencies that were expected to strengthen relative to the krone.

Forecasts of Cash Flows

Exhibit 19.1 provides information on the forecasted cash receipts and cash disbursements each affiliate expects to have over the following 5 days. The managers of each affiliate generate daily 5-day rolling forecasts of their cash flow needs and share this information with the central office. These 5-day forecasts help the central office improve profitability in at least three ways.

First, the forecasts can be checked for accuracy. The more accurate the forecasts, the better the firm can manage its resources. Hence, helping the affiliates to improve their forecasts should improve the operating cash needs of each affiliate by reducing its precautionary cash balances.

Second, the 5-day forecasts allow the central office to assess the short-term needs of each affiliate in light of the transaction costs related to exchanging different currencies and the interest rates and possible changes in exchange rates that may occur. For example, Exhibit 19.1 shows that the British affiliate is currently sitting on a lot of cash and is forecasting an inflow on day 1, but it has a large payment due on day 3. On net, over the 5 days, it expects to have to borrow. Given the costs of converting between pounds and euros and the losses possible due to adverse currency movements, it probably does not make sense to have the British affiliate transfer funds out of the country.

The third use of the 5-day forecasts is to generate overall forecasts of the net cash flows of the European affiliates. This will provide the central office with information that can be used to assess the maturity and currency of denomination of investments and short-term borrowing. For example, Exhibit 19.3 aggregates the information from Exhibit 19.1 and demonstrates that the four European affiliates are forecasting positive cash flows for the next 3 days, but the cash flow forecasts are negative on days 4 and 5. Hence, this is not an appropriate time to place surplus funds in an investment with a 1-week maturity. Instead, the short-term surpluses should be invested in overnight interest-bearing accounts in anticipation of the need for funds later in the week.

Multilateral Netting Systems

Coordinating the worldwide production and distribution of the many products produced in tandem by the firm's affiliates makes for a large volume of transactions and a heavy flow of funds between them. Of course, the greater the flow of funds, the larger the transaction costs. Although the transaction costs differ with the particular country, it is estimated that they vary between 0.25% and 1.5% of the amount of funds transferred. Thus, there is an incentive for the MNC to avoid fund transfers between affiliates.

The firm can save money on these transactions by using a **multilateral netting system**. Under a multilateral netting system, payments and receipts made among affiliates are

Exhibit 19.3 Consolidated 5-Day Cash Forecasts of an MNC's European Affiliates (in thousands of euros)

	British	Danish	Dutch	Spanish	Total
Day 1	100	100	−250	500	450
Day 2	−350	0	300	400	350
Day 3	−50	350	−500	300	100
Day 4	100	−200	250	−500	−350
Day 5	50	−100	100	−100	−50
5-day total	−150	150	−100	600	500

Notes: The forecasts are taken from Exhibit 19.1. The 5-day total is the sum of the individual forecasts.

recorded over an interval of time such as a month, but the actual transfers of funds between affiliates in different countries only involve net amounts that take into account what is mutually owed between different affiliates. Consider the following example of **bilateral netting**, with netting between two affiliates rather than multiple affiliates.

Example 19.1   Bilateral Netting

Suppose the British affiliate of a firm owes €3,000,000 to the Danish affiliate, and the Danish affiliate owes €4,000,000 to the British affiliate. Under bilateral netting, the Danish affiliate would send €1,000,000 to the British affiliate, and each would cancel its outstanding debts on the other party.

Thus, rather than having the affiliates of the MNC purchase the gross amount of foreign currency to pay off their debts to one another, which is €7,000,000 in this example, only €1,000,000 changes hands, and therefore only €1,000,000 has to be purchased. If transaction costs are 0.4%, bilateral netting saves

$$0.004 \times €6,000,000 = €24,000$$

in this example.

Clearly, bilateral netting is useful only to the extent that affiliates engage in purchases from each other. Multilateral netting extends the concept of bilateral netting to several affiliated parties with commensurate cost savings. Exhibit 19.4 presents a typical month's cumulative cash flows before any multilateral netting for the European affiliates of a multinational corporation.

Exhibit 19.4   The Cash Flows of an MNC's Affiliates Before Multilateral Netting (in thousands of euros)

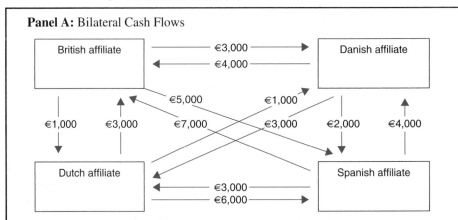

Panel A: Bilateral Cash Flows

Panel B: Intracompany Payments Matrix (in thousands of euros)

Receiving Affiliate	Paying Affiliate				Total Receipts	Net Receipts (Payments)
	British	**Dutch**	**Spanish**	**Danish**		
British	—	3,000	7,000	4,000	14,000	5,000
Dutch	1,000	—	3,000	3,000	7,000	(3,000)
Spanish	5,000	6,000	—	2,000	13,000	(1,000)
Danish	3,000	1,000	4,000	—	8,000	(1,000)
Total payments	9,000	10,000	14,000	9,000	42,000	—

Exhibit 19.5 Cash Flows After Multilateral Netting (in thousands of euros)

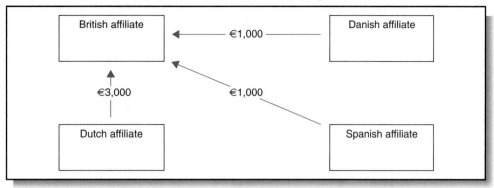

Without multilateral netting, each of the affiliates would make three payments, and each would accept three receipts. For example, the Spanish affiliate owes €4,000,000 to the Danish affiliate, €7,000,000 to the British affiliate, and €3,000,000 to the Dutch affiliate. In turn, the Spanish affiliate has booked receivables of €2,000,000 from the Danish affiliate and is owed €5,000,000 from the British affiliate and €6,000,000 from the Dutch affiliate. If the Spanish affiliate made all these payments and accepted all the receipts, there would be €14,000,000 of payments and €13,000,000 of receipts. By examining the intracompany payment matrix in Exhibit 19.4, we see that the British affiliate has a net receipt of €5,000,000, whereas the other three European affiliates have net payments. The Dutch affiliate owes a net amount of €3,000,000, and the Danish and Spanish affiliates owe a net amount of €1,000,000. Transaction costs are minimized by having each of the European affiliates make just one net payment to the British affiliate. This is summarized in Exhibit 19.5.

Notice in Exhibit 19.4 that there would be €42,000,000 of total transactions between the four affiliates if all affiliates made all their gross payments. If transaction costs in the foreign exchange market average 0.4%, total transaction costs in this example, without multilateral netting, would be

$$0.004 \times €42,000,000 = €168,400$$

However, with the multilateral netting shown in Exhibit 19.5, the total payment between the affiliates is reduced to €5,000,000, which generates transaction costs of only

$$0.004 \times €5,000,000 = €20,000$$

This is a significant savings for the company. In addition, many MNCs facilitate the process of multilateral netting by establishing a foreign subsidiary to serve as a netting center in a country with minimal foreign exchange controls. It is also possible to outsource the netting (and other cash management services) to a bank or other third party. Not surprisingly, Internet-based netting services have also appeared recently.

Using a Centralized Cash Management System to Reduce Precautionary Cash Demands

A benefit of centralizing cash holdings that the MNC in our example can exploit involves the precautionary demand for money that arises from the uncertain timing of future cash inflows and outflows. We can describe this uncertainty of the demand for future cash with a probability distribution. For example, suppose the cash demands of an affiliate are normally distributed. Then, we know that if the affiliate holds cash balances that exceed the mean of the probability distribution by 2 standard deviations, there is slightly less than a 2.5% probability that the affiliate's demand for cash will exceed its available cash.

Exhibit 19.6 European Affiliates' Demands for Cash

	Mean Demand for Cash	One Standard Deviation	Total Demand for Cash
British	€1,000,000	€750,000	€2,500,000
Danish	€2,000,000	€900,000	€3,800,000
Dutch	€1,500,000	€850,000	€3,200,000
Spanish	€2,500,000	€1,150,000	€4,800,000
Total	€7,000,000		€14,300,000

Notes: The first two columns list the affiliates' mean demands for cash and their standard deviations. For example, the British affiliate expects to use €1,000,000 in the coming month, but it may need as much as €1,000,000 + 2 × €750,000 = €2,500,000 to cover unexpected contingencies with 97.5% probability. The third column reports the sum of the mean and 2 standard deviations.

As an example, suppose that there are four European affiliates of the MNC, as in the multilateral netting example: the British, Danish, Dutch, and Spanish affiliates. If each of the affiliates describes its precautionary demand for cash with a probability distribution, the overall organization can reduce the total demand for cash while still satisfying the demands of each affiliate by exploiting the fact that the demands for cash from the different affiliates will not be perfectly correlated in the future.

To be concrete, suppose that if each affiliate were to operate independently, each would desire to hold cash balances equal to its mean demand for cash plus 2 standard deviations of the distribution of cash required. Exhibit 19.6 presents a hypothetical summary of these positions. The total demand for cash of each affiliate equals its mean demand, or what it expects to pay in the near term, plus cash balances equal to 2 standard deviations of its possible future expenditures. For example, the Spanish affiliate forecasts that it expects to spend €2,500,000, but it needs an additional 2 × €1,150,000 = €2,300,000 to be 97.5% sure that it will not be caught short of cash in the future. Consequently, the Spanish affiliate's total demand for cash is €4,800,000. The sum of the total demands for cash of the four European affiliates is €14,300,000.

Now, suppose that we centralize the cash balances at corporate headquarters or at a regional cash management office. What level of cash balances must the central office hold to be sure both that it can meet the expected demands of its affiliates and that it will meet contingent demands for cash 97.5% of the time? To answer this question, recognize that the central office is concerned with the sum of the demands for cash from the four affiliates. Because each demand for cash is normally distributed, the demand for cash of the central office will also be normally distributed. The mean demand for cash will therefore be the sum of the mean demands of the four affiliates:

$$€1,000,000 + €2,000,000 + €1,500,000 + €2,500,000 = €7,000,000$$

The savings in cash balances arise if the precautionary demands for money are less than perfectly correlated with each other. If the precautionary demands for cash are completely uncorrelated, we know that the variance of the sum of four random variables is the sum of their variances. Hence, the standard deviation of the demand for money of the central office is the square root of the sum of the four variances:

$$[(€750,000)^2 + (€900,000)^2 + (€850,000)^2 + (€1,150,000)^2]^{0.5} = €1,848,648$$

If the central office wants to be 97.5% sure of meeting the aggregate demand for cash of the four affiliates, it must hold

$$€7,000,000 + (2 × €1,848,648) = €10,697,296$$

Consequently, the central office can hold

$$€14,300,000 - €10,697,296 = €3,602,704$$

less cash than the sum necessary if each of the affiliates forms its demand for cash independently. If the individual affiliates' precautionary demands for cash are positively correlated, the cash saving will be commensurately less than €3.6 million; but, if the individual affiliates' precautionary demands for cash are negatively correlated, the cash savings will be more than €3.6 million.

19.3 CASH TRANSFERS FROM AFFILIATES TO PARENTS

The primary cash transfers from the foreign affiliates of a multinational corporation to the parent headquarters are made in the form of dividends, royalties, management fees, and payments related to the sale of goods and their transfer prices. Government officials in host countries are often reluctant to see the profits of a multinational corporation leave their country. They prefer to see the free cash flows of foreign affiliates reinvested in the host country rather than paid as dividends to the shareholders of the MNC. On the other hand, host country governments also recognize that a direct investment by a multinational corporation brings with it valuable technology, capital, managerial skills, and jobs. Payments made by foreign affiliates to their parents in the form of royalties for patents and fees for services are usually recognized as legitimate business expenses of the foreign affiliate and hence reduce corporate income taxes.

Host country governments also apply different tax rates to different types of income being repatriated. Of course, it is the after-tax value of the affiliates' income that is most important to the parent corporation. Minimizing these taxes therefore requires some advance planning by the parent before it establishes an affiliate.

International Dividend Cash Flows

Dividend payments make up the bulk of international cash flows transferred from foreign affiliates to their parent corporations. For U.S. parent corporations, dividends typically represent more than 50% of all remittances. The primary determinants of a firm's dividend policy for a foreign affiliate include the profitability of the affiliate, its investment opportunities, taxes in the host country and the home country, and foreign exchange and political risks.

If a foreign affiliate is profitable, it will be generating cash that could be paid to the parent as a dividend, whereas if it is unprofitable, it will be unable to pay dividends without accessing capital markets to fund these payments. If the investment opportunities of the foreign affiliate are good, the foreign affiliate's earnings should be reinvested because the overall firm wants to undertake as many positive net present value projects as possible. If the foreign affiliate is generating a substantial amount of free cash flow, the parent may want to institute a dividend policy for the subsidiary. A dividend policy requires the corporation to declare a quarterly or annual dividend equal to a certain percentage of its foreign earnings.

Tax Planning

Host country governments tax the income of foreign affiliates directly and withhold additional taxes on the repatriation of dividends. **Tax planning** is the process of minimizing the firm's taxes by choosing when to repatriate funds. The firm should shift its dividends into the future if the firm thinks that the withholding tax on the dividends is going to be reduced. Of course, the firm must be able to reinvest the funds to generate a reasonable expected rate of return if it is going to shift the profits into the future. In addition, the parent corporation often receives a tax credit for the foreign taxes it has paid on its dividends. The tax credit is worth more to the firm if the firm is profitable and paying taxes to the home country. Otherwise, the foreign tax credit would be worthless.

Dealing with Political Risk

The political environments of foreign affiliates can change significantly from year to year. Consequently, it is often advantageous for a multinational corporation to have an established dividend policy that it can easily defend if government officials of the host country question it. Without such a policy or a history of dividend payments, an MNC may have difficulty explaining the reason for any given year's dividend payment.

For example, if the host country is having difficulty financing its balance of payments, it may appear to the government that the MNC's dividend payment is actually an attempt by the company to export capital from the country in a time of crisis. Even if a government blocks the dividends and no transfers can be made, many firms find it to their advantage to at least declare a dividend in order to establish its validity in case the government later relaxes its foreign exchange restrictions.

Some corporations also set a "common" dividend repatriation rate for all their foreign affiliates in different countries. This approach establishes that the shareholders of the parent corporation demand a certain share of the earnings of all of the corporation's foreign subsidiaries and are not merely trying to take capital out of one particular country.

Dealing with Foreign Exchange Risk

If a parent corporation thinks that a depreciation of a foreign currency is imminent, it can try to accelerate the payment of dividends from its foreign affiliate. Conversely, if it is likely that the foreign currency will strengthen, the foreign affiliate can try to delay the dividends. This is part of the normal cycle of speculative activity in which a multinational corporation can engage. The idea of leading and lagging payments is discussed later in the chapter.

Other Factors Affecting Dividend Policy

Of course, if a foreign affiliate is a joint venture with a foreign partner, the dividend policy must be decided in consultation with the corporation's foreign partner. The costs related to negotiating a dividend payout year in and year out will tend to lead to stability in the dividend policy. Firms tend to change their dividend policies only when all parties involved perceive that there has been a permanent change in earnings.

International Royalty and Management-Fee Cash Flows

As discussed in Chapter 15, royalties are payments made to the owners of a technology, a patent, or a trademark for the use of the technology or the right to manufacture under the patent or trademark. Royalty payments are pure profits in the sense that the firm receiving them performs no current services and incurs no current costs to receive the payment. Thus, royalties can be a substantial source of income for a firm that is receiving them.

For example, when Tokyo Disneyland was constructed in 1983, the Walt Disney Company licensed the Disney name with its associated characters and fantasy rides to an unrelated Japanese corporation. The Japanese corporation agreed to pay the Walt Disney Company a yen-denominated royalty associated with the revenues of Tokyo Disneyland. During fiscal year 1984, the yen royalty payments were approximately ¥8 billion, which was more than $32 million at the prevailing exchange rate of ¥248/$. Although this cash flow represented a small part of Disney's 1984 revenues of $1.66 billion, it was a large fraction of Disney's 1984 net income of $97.8 million.[1]

Parent corporations also assess fees for the services they provide to their affiliates, including management and technical consulting services and fees to recover overhead costs

---

[1]The numbers in this example are taken from Carl Kester and William Allen (1987). The case explores the foreign exchange risk associated with Disney's yen-denominated royalty payments and the swap that was designed to mitigate the foreign exchange risk. See Chapter 21 for a discussion of swaps.

associated with day-to-day operations the parent performs for the foreign affiliate. These costs include the foreign affiliate's share of the research and development of the organization, its share of legal and accounting costs for the entire enterprise, its share of the salaries of the general corporate management, and other costs, such as general corporate advertising and public relations. Often, the fees associated with the parent's overhead are based on the affiliate's sales. In other circumstances, the overhead charges are based on a pro rata sharing of all the MNC's fixed costs.

Repatriation in a Joint Venture

Designing a repatriation schedule in a joint venture is especially important because it establishes the rules by which future payments can be made and curtails the problems associated with negotiating between foreign partners whose future interests might not be aligned. Because the foreign corporation often supplies technological and design expertise as well as capital to the company in the host country, it is compensated with a royalty or fee for the technology. Remember from Chapter 15 that the royalty and fee are costs of the joint venture but they provide profits to the foreign company. In light of this fact, the division of profits in the joint enterprise may give a somewhat smaller share of net income to the foreign company than would be dictated by the percentage of capital that it invested to create the joint venture.

Tax Advantages of Royalties and Fees

Royalties and fees often have income tax advantages over dividends. This is because most countries withhold taxes on dividends but not necessarily on royalties and fees. Consequently, when an affiliate pays a dividend to its parent, it does so after paying local income taxes and the withholding tax on the dividend. Under U.S. tax law, the parent obtains tax credits both for the local income tax paid and for the withholding tax paid. However, if the foreign affiliate's combined tax rate is greater than the parent's tax rate, some of the tax credit may be lost.

In contrast, royalties and fees are paid out of pretax income, and if there is a withholding tax, the tax rate is often lower than the rate levied on dividends. Of course, the royalties and fees received by the parent are income, so the parent must pay income taxes on them to the home country.

Transfer Pricing and Cash Flows

Transfer prices are the prices a firm charges its affiliates when selling goods and services to them. These prices are set internally within a firm and thus are not directly determined by market forces. As a result, it is often difficult to determine whether a particular transfer price is close to what would be set in a competitive market. This is especially true of semi-finished manufactured goods for which there is literally no alternative market. Because a higher transfer price shifts income and tax payments from the affiliate that is paying the price to the affiliate that is receiving the price, transfer pricing is a politically contentious issue. Governments often argue that multinational corporations use transfer pricing to avoid paying income taxes, withholding taxes, and tariffs. Governments consequently establish rules and regulations that specify whether a transfer price is appropriate.

Shifting Income and Tax Burdens Between Countries

Let's examine how a multinational corporation could use transfer prices to avoid an income tax. Consider Exhibit 19.7, which shows how a low transfer price (shown in Panel A) affects a company's taxes on net income versus a high transfer price (shown in Panel B). The manufacturing affiliate is located in the home country, where the corporate income tax rate is 30%, and the distribution affiliate is located in a foreign country, where the corporate income tax rate is 60%.

Exhibit 19.7   Effects of High and Low Transfer Prices on Net Income

Panel A: Low-Transfer-Price Policy

	Manufacturing Affiliate (30% tax rate)	Distribution Affiliate (60% tax rate)	Consolidated Company
Sales	$2,200	$3,200*	$3,200*
Less cost of goods sold	1,500*	2,200	1,500*
Less operating expenses	200*	100*	300*
Taxable income	$ 500	$ 900	$1,400*
Less income taxes	150	540	690
Net income	$ 350	$ 360	$ 710

Panel B: High-Transfer-Price Policy

	Manufacturing Affiliate (30% tax rate)	Distribution Affiliate (60% tax rate)	Consolidated Company
Sales	$2,600	$3,200*	$3,200*
Less cost of goods sold	1,500*	2,600	1,500*
Less operating expenses	200*	100*	300*
Taxable income	$ 900	$ 500	$1,400*
Less income taxes	270	300	570
Net income	$ 630	$ 200	$ 830

Note: The numbers marked with an asterisk are the true revenues and costs and do not change with different transfer prices. All other numbers change with different transfer prices.

From the perspective of the company as a whole, it costs $1,800 to produce and sell the good. The analysis is conducted on a per good sold basis. The original cost of goods sold that is incurred by the manufacturing affiliate is $1,500, and the operating expenses are $200 for the manufacturing affiliate and $100 for the distribution affiliate. The good can ultimately be sold for $3,200. Let's assume just for a moment that these numbers cannot be changed by different transfer policies. Hence, there is $3,200 − $1,800 = $1,400 of taxable income for the consolidated company. The transfer price determines what share of this income accrues to the manufacturing affiliate and what share accrues to the distribution affiliate.

The Effect of a Low Transfer Price

Now let's look at what happens when the transfer price is low. In Panel A of Exhibit 19.7, the manufacturing affiliate charges a low transfer price of $2,200. Its cost of goods sold is $1,500, and its operating expenses are $200, so its taxable income is $500. Because the manufacturing affiliate has an income tax rate of 30%, its after-tax net income is $350. The distribution affiliate must pay $2,200 for the goods, and it has expenses of $100. The distribution affiliate can sell the goods for $3,200. Therefore, it has before-tax income of $900. Because it pays income tax at the 60% rate, its net income is 40% × $900 = $360. In this situation, the consolidated company has a taxable income of $1,400, on which it pays income tax of $690, which works out to be a tax rate of 49.3%. That leaves a net income of $710 for the consolidated company.[2]

The Effect of a High Transfer Price

Now, consider what happens if a manufacturing affiliate charges a high transfer price of $2,600, as in Panel B of Figure 19.7. The manufacturing affiliate now has taxable income of $900, and it pays income tax of $270. Consequently, its net income is $630. The distribution

---

[2]A more complete analysis of this issue would examine the ultimate effect of different transfer pricing policies on the ultimate cash flows of the parent corporation. Such an analysis would involve consideration of the dividends that are actually paid to the parent and the foreign tax credits that the parent can use to offset tax owed to the home country tax authority, as in Chapter 15.

affiliate pays $2,600 for the goods, which reduces its taxable income to $500. Its income tax is now $300, which reduces its net income to $200. The consolidated company now pays income tax of $570 on the same taxable income of $1,400, which implies a 40.7% tax rate. The net income of the consolidated company therefore increases to $830. By shifting $400 of income from the regime with the tax rate of 60% to the regime with the tax rate of 30%, the company saves 30% × $400 = $120. This represents an increase in income from $710 to $830.

There is one other effect of the change in transfer pricing policy. Notice that the increase in the transfer price shifted income from the distribution affiliate to the manufacturing affiliate. This obviously would still be the case if the tax rates in the two countries were the same. However, the net income of the consolidated company would not change when moving from a low transfer price to a high transfer price. This shift in income can affect managerial incentives as we explain below.

To see the shift in income, let the tax rate be 30% in both countries. The income tax of the distribution affiliate would fall to $270 under the low-transfer-price policy, which would cause its net income to increase to $630. The net income of the consolidated company would be $980, which is 70% of $1,400. Increasing the transfer price to $2,600 would again cause the taxable income of the distribution affiliate to fall to $500, but with a 30% tax rate, its net income would increase to $350. The net income of the manufacturing affiliate would be $630, and the net income of the consolidated company would be $980. The increase in the transfer price effectively shifts funds from the distribution affiliate to the manufacturing affiliate.

Exhibit 19.7 demonstrates that a high-transfer-price policy can transfer income from high-tax to low-tax countries, which increases the overall income of the MNC. It also demonstrates how a change in transfer price policy can shift funds between countries.

Transfer Pricing Regulations

The governmental authorities that are responsible for taxes are aware of the incentives that multinational corporations face to manipulate transfer prices to avoid taxes. Economists have even been able to demonstrate that the effects are in the data.[3]

Tax regulations and court cases in each country have established a body of law for determining whether a transfer price is appropriate. In the United States, the Internal Revenue Service (IRS) specifies that an appropriate transfer price is one that reflects an "arm's-length price"—that is, one that would be observed in a sale of the good or the service to an unrelated customer.[4] The IRS recognizes five methods that can be used to establish an arm's-length price. The methods are presented here, in decreasing order of general acceptance to tax authorities:

1. The comparable uncontrolled price method
2. The resale price method
3. The cost-plus method
4. The comparable-profits method
5. Other acceptable methods

The OECD also recommends these methods for its member countries.

---

[3]See Eric Bartelsman and Roel Beetsma (2003) for empirical evidence that much of a unilateral increase in corporate taxes in OECD countries is lost because of decreases in reported income. The empirical work in Kimberly Clausing (2003) also indicates that after controlling for other variables that affect trade prices, a lower country corporate tax rate is associated with lower U.S. intrafirm trade export prices to that country and higher import prices from that country, which is consistent with shifting income to the low-tax country. Similar results for Hong Kong are reported by Robert Feenstra and Gordon Hanson (2004).

[4]Section 482 of the U.S. Internal Revenue Code contains provisions that regulate transfer pricing in the United States. Under this law, the IRS can reallocate gross income, deductions, credits, and allowances between related corporations to prevent tax evasion or to more accurately reflect the income of the different parties. As with other aspects of the tax code, if the IRS restates income, the burden of proof is on the taxpayer to demonstrate that the actions of the IRS are arbitrary or unreasonable.

The most accurate evidence of an arm's-length price is to demonstrate that the transfer price is equivalent to a comparable uncontrolled price. Uncontrolled prices are straightforward to determine if the good or service that is being transferred between related affiliates is also being sold by the multinational corporation to an unrelated corporation or if two unrelated corporations trade a similar good or service. However, in practice, it is often difficult to document two transactions that are identical in all features. This problem is particularly difficult when goods are made to order.

The resale price approach to establishing an arm's-length price starts with the retail price to the corporation's customers, subtracts an appropriate profit for the distribution unit, and uses the net price as the allowable selling price for the manufacturing unit. However, if the distributor is adding a great deal of value to the ultimate sale of the product, either by physically performing alterations to the product or in terms of the distribution services it provides, it is difficult to determine the appropriate profit markup the distributor should be paid. Hence, this method is often used when the distributor does not add a substantial amount of value to the product.

The cost-plus method of setting an arm's-length price begins with the costs of the manufacturing unit. An appropriate markup for the profit of that unit is added to the manufacturing costs to arrive at the transfer price that should be paid by the distribution unit. Of course, determining a manufacturer's costs is no minor matter. For example, correctly allocating the manufacturer's fixed costs across the various products it produces is paramount if this method is to be used. Whenever possible, the gross markup is based on a comparable uncontrolled sale.

The comparable-profits method involves comparing the profitability of businesses engaging in similar activities to the profitability of the organization doing the transfer pricing. This method can be used in combination with one of the other methods. It works well unless the organization setting the transfer price is trading valuable intangible products, such as computer software. In this case, the corporation likely bore a significant amount of risk to develop the product and therefore deserves to earn a premium on it.

Other methods can be used when none of the other four is appropriate. The conditions for the application of such an alternative method basically require that the firm supply supporting documents that make the case why none of the other methods applies and why the approach chosen is reasonable. An alternative method is often adopted in conjunction with one of the other four if products that are not routinely traded and difficult to value are being transferred.

Although both the government of the importing country and the government of the exporting country can readily observe transfer prices, it is far more difficult to observe the actual costs of the exporting affiliate. Hence, if the political forces that are currently executing the laws of a country want to allow additional funds to flow to foreign investors, they can allow relatively high transfer pricing policies and still remain within the letter of the law that governs their country. Such a policy partially undoes the detrimental effects that high withholding taxes on dividends have on the incentives for foreigners to invest in the country. Allowing high transfer prices may therefore have the beneficial effect of encouraging additional inflows of capital for direct investment within the country.

How Transfer Prices Affect Managers' Incentives

The managers of a firm with multiple profit centers must evaluate the respective profitability of the different divisions. Transfer prices that do not reflect the true costs of the transactions between the centers can, of course, make it appear that some centers are more profitable than others, even when they aren't. Although the same problem arises in purely domestic firms, international taxes and the need to provide affiliates with enough working capital exacerbates the problem when it comes to MNCs.

If the central managers of an MNC use transfer prices to shift funds between affiliates for either tax or working capital reasons, they should modify the performance evaluation of each affiliate to reflect these facts. For example, if the managers of a distribution affiliate are required to buy manufactured products at a high transfer price, the profit margin for the affiliate will be low. In contrast, the profit margin of the manufacturing affiliate that sold the products to the distribution affiliate will be high. Unless this is understood, the managers of the distribution affiliate might focus excessively on cost-reducing activities, whereas the managers of the manufacturing affiliate might focus too little on cost-reducing activities.

Using Transfer Prices to Offset Tariffs

Just as a transfer pricing policy can be used to lower the incidence of income taxes in a country, it can also be used to offset the effects of tariffs. Tariffs, also called import duties, are taxes that are levied on the value of imported goods. Most tariffs consist of **ad valorem duties**, which increase the price of imported products by a certain percentage, depending on the size of the tariff. To lower the incidence of these taxes, a multinational corporation might attempt to set a low transfer price. Of course, this increases the gross income of the purchasing foreign affiliate, which exposes it to additional income taxes.

The effects of alternative transfer price policies in the presence of a tariff are demonstrated in Exhibit 19.8. The basic numbers in Exhibit 19.8 are the same as those in Exhibit 19.7, but now the distribution affiliate must pay a 10% ad valorem tariff to its host government. Thus, an increase in the transfer price from $2,200 to $2,600 increases the tariff paid from $220 to $260. Because the tariff is deductible, though, the taxable income of the distribution affiliate falls from $680 to $240 rather than from $900 to $500, and its net income falls from $272 to $96. Notice that while a low transfer price lowers the tariff paid, the consolidated company is still better off with a high-transfer-price policy because the income tax saving is greater than the increase in the tariff that has to be paid: Total income increases by $104, from $622 to $726. The basic increase of $120 in income in Exhibit 19.7 is now decreased by the $40 of additional tariff, $260 versus $220, but the tariff makes the distribution affiliate less profitable, which increases the overall income of the company by $24 = 0.60 × $40 through tax savings. Thus, $104 = $120 − $40 + $24.

Exhibit 19.8   High and Low Transfer Prices in the Presence of Tariffs

Panel A: Low-Transfer-Price Policy

	Manufacturing Affiliate (30% tax rate)	Distribution Affiliate (60% tax rate)	Consolidated Company
Sales	$2,200	$3,200*	$3,200*
Less import tariff (10%)		220	220
Less cost of goods sold	1,500*	2,200	1,500*
Less operating expenses	200*	100*	300*
Taxable income	$ 500	$ 680	$1,180
Less income taxes	150	408	558
Net income	$ 350	$ 272	$ 622

Panel B: High-Transfer-Price Policy

	Manufacturing Affiliate (30% tax rate)	Distribution Affiliate (60% tax rate)	Consolidated Company
Sales	$2,600	$3,200	$3,200*
Less import tariff (10%)		260	260
Less cost of goods sold	1,500*	2,600	1,500*
Less operating expenses	200*	100*	300*
Taxable income	$ 900	$ 240	$1,140
Less income taxes	270	144	414
Net income	$ 630	$ 96	$ 726

Notes: The basic numbers are the same as in Exhibit 19.7, except that the distribution affiliate now faces a 10% tariff on its imports. The numbers marked with an asterisk are the true revenues and costs and do not change with different transfer prices. All other numbers change with different transfer prices.

A General Transfer Pricing Policy with Tariffs

Now, let's determine a general policy on transfer pricing in the presence of tariffs. Let t be the tariff rate in the distribution country, let t_m be the income tax rate on the manufacturing affiliate, and let t_d be the income tax rate on the distribution affiliate. First, notice that each dollar increase in the transfer price increases the manufacturing affiliate's net-of-tax profit by $1 - t_m$ dollars per unit sold. Second, a dollar of cost to the distribution affiliate is increased by $1 + t$ because of the tariff. The overall increase in the cost to the distribution affiliate reduces its profitability because it keeps $1 - t_d$ of its income. Thus, each dollar increase in transfer price decreases the distribution affiliate's net-of-tax profit by $(1 + t) \times (1 - t_d)$ dollars per unit sold. Therefore, a high-transfer-price policy is optimal for the consolidated company as long as 1 minus the tax rate on the manufacturing affiliate, $1 - t_m$, is larger than 1 plus the tariff rate times 1 minus the tax rate on the distribution affiliate, $(1 + t) \times (1 - t_d)$. Algebraically, if

$$(1 - t_m) > (1 + t) \times (1 - t_d)$$

a high-transfer-price policy is desirable from the perspective of the consolidated company because it increases the consolidated income. If

$$(1 - t_m) < (1 + t) \times (1 - t_d)$$

then a low-transfer-price policy maximizes the income of the consolidated company.

Example 19.2 Transfer Pricing with Tariffs

In Exhibit 19.8, we have $t_m = 30\%$, $t = 10\%$, and $t_d = 60\%$. Thus,

$$(1 - t_m) = 70\% > (1 + t) \times (1 - t_d) = 1.1 \times 40\% = 44\%$$

Hence, the high-transfer-price policy is optimal. By increasing the price $400, the company saves

$$[(1 - 0.7) - (1.1)(1 - 0.6)] \times \$400 = \$104$$

Exhibit 19.8 indicates that the net income of the consolidated company increases by

$$\$726 - \$622 = \$104$$

Of course, in setting its transfer pricing policy, an MNC must be aware that it risks being charged with tax evasion if its transfer prices do not meet the arm's-length test. Clearly, ethical considerations matter in the setting of transfer prices. A firm must also be aware that possible future tax penalties, litigation, and bad publicity are the potential costs of setting transfer prices too aggressively.

Using Transfer Pricing to Deal with Foreign Exchange Quotas

Some countries set quotas on the amount of foreign exchange available for importing goods into the country. This makes the value of a unit of foreign exchange to a foreign affiliate in that country higher than the stated market price. However, the MNC can partially correct the economic distortion by lowering the transfer price. In this situation, a low transfer price allows the foreign subsidiary to import a greater quantity of goods into the country for a given amount of foreign currency. Conversely, high transfer prices can be used to access blocked funds, as we will discuss shortly.

Transfer Pricing in Joint Ventures

When a multinational corporation enters into a joint venture with a local corporation rather than setting up a wholly owned foreign subsidiary, the MNC is less likely to be able to utilize transfer pricing to its advantage. Like governments, joint-venture partners are likely to question manipulated transfer prices. For example, as we saw in Exhibit 19.7, a high transfer price charged to a joint-venture company will adversely affect the income it earns. This can lead to conflicts between the two firms and jeopardize their venture. Because joint ventures are often expensive to set up, this is usually not a good strategy.

Strategies for Dealing with Blocked Funds

In a fixed exchange rate system, the international reserves of the country may become inadequate to meet market demands. If the government decides to maintain a fixed exchange rate when market forces would otherwise force a devaluation, the government must ration access to foreign exchange.

A multinational corporation operating in such a country experiences the rationing of foreign exchange along with anyone else holding the local currency who wants to buy foreign currency. This gives rise to the problem of blocked funds. For a multinational corporation, though, the problems caused by blocked funds can be severe. For example, an MNC's foreign affiliate operating inside the country might need to acquire foreign currency to purchase imported raw materials or semi-finished goods integral to its production process. Without these goods, the affiliate might have to slow down its production or shut down entirely. The foreign affiliate is also likely to be prohibited from making royalty and fee payments, except possibly at very unattractive foreign exchange rates. It is also quite likely that the parent will be unable to repatriate the affiliate's profits as dividends.

Because of these pitfalls, before investing in a foreign affiliate, a parent company should analyze the factors that might trigger a situation in which blocked funds would occur and how such a situation would affect the affiliate's profitability. The parent should also develop a contingency plan for how its foreign affiliate will operate within the country if such a problem develops.

Fronting Loans

One technique that a multinational corporation can use to increase the probability that its foreign affiliate will be able to transfer funds out of the country is to finance the foreign affiliate with a **fronting loan**. A fronting loan is a parent-to-affiliate loan that uses a large international bank as a financial intermediary. Rather than have the parent corporation make a loan directly to its foreign affiliate, the parent instead makes a deposit with an international bank. The bank, in turn, makes a loan to the foreign affiliate that is equivalent to 100% of the deposited funds. From the bank's perspective, a fronting loan is risk free because the loan is fully collateralized by the deposit of the parent. The bank willingly participates for a small fee, earned in the form of a spread between the deposit rate that is paid to the parent and the rate that is charged to the foreign affiliate.

What is the purpose of involving an international bank in the transaction? The primary reason involves trying to avoid the adverse impact of a blocked-funds situation. When a country rations foreign exchange, it often allows businesses to make some payments but not others. Interest and principal payments on intracompany loans from the foreign affiliate of an MNC operating in the country to its parent are generally given a lower priority by the government than interest and principal payments from the same foreign affiliate to an international bank in a neutral country. Although halting the payments made to large MNCs does have costs, the perceived costs are smaller than those incurred when a country stops allowing payments to be made to major international banks.

International banks can refuse to finance a country's international trade or can hamper the government's ability to borrow funds, whereas MNCs can do little more than threaten not to invest in the country in the future. Fronting loans can also give an MNC a tax advantage. If the local government allows the foreign affiliate to take a tax deduction for interest paid on a bank loan but does not allow a tax deduction for interest paid on an intracompany loan, the use of a fronting loan creates a valuable tax shield.

For example, suppose a parent corporation wants to invest $1,000,000 in its foreign manufacturing affiliate. To simplify the analysis, let the parent make a transfer using a wholly owned financial affiliate that operates in a tax haven with no income tax. Suppose the financial affiliate charges a 7% interest rate on an intracompany loan to the manufacturing affiliate. If the manufacturing affiliate cannot deduct the interest, its after-tax cost of the loan is $70,000 per year, which of course yields an equal amount of income for the financial affiliate.

Now consider what would happen if the parent fronted a loan by transferring $1,000,000 from the financial affiliate to its foreign manufacturing affiliate. The financial affiliate would make a deposit of $1,000,000 to an international bank that would agree to pay 7% interest on the deposit. The bank, in turn, would make a loan to the foreign manufacturing affiliate, charging perhaps 8% interest. Let the income tax rate for the foreign manufacturing affiliate be 50%, and let the interest cost of the bank loan be deductible. Now, the foreign manufacturing affiliate owes $80,000 of interest to the bank, but the after-tax cost of this payment is only $40,000 because the interest payment is tax deductible. The bank gets $10,000 of income for its role as an intermediary. Once again, the financial affiliate is left with $70,000 of income, but the foreign manufacturing affiliate has to pay only $40,000 of after-tax income to achieve the transfer of $70,000 out of the country to the parent.

Reinvesting Working Capital Locally

When a government shuts off access to the foreign exchange market, it is trying to prevent capital from leaving the country. Governments also often place restrictions on nominal interest rates that can be offered in money markets. In such a situation, the yields on short-term money market instruments may produce negative real returns. When this happens, an MNC needs to try to uncover local investment opportunities to help it at least break even. The minimum goal of investing the profits of the local affiliate should be to maintain the real value of the existing principal. Toward this end, the local managers should be given the power to invest in any zero net present value investments. Because the local managers cannot be expected to be able to pick winners in the local economy, given the dire straits that it is in, any market-determined, zero net present value investment should be an acceptable investment from the parent corporation's point of view.

It is possible, however, that the firm may be able to invest in other products in the country that offer market-determined expected rates of return. These investments include commercial bonds and the equities of other firms. Also, an investment in a long-term nominal asset, such as a corporate bond, may put a great deal of the firm's principal at risk if inflation accelerates unexpectedly.

If none of these investments appear to be attractive, the firm can engage in additional direct investment in the country. For example, the firm could, say, purchase local real estate, either land or buildings. Although real assets, such as these, are less liquid than short-term money market investments, they tend to maintain their value when inflation is severe. The firm can also pursue other real investments, including commodities, either for export or to add to its existing inventory, or it might construct additional facilities. Another way for a multinational corporation to use its working capital is to have a local affiliate contract with other firms operating in the country to supply goods or to perform services for the parent or its other affiliates. For example, an architectural firm in a country with blocked funds could be hired to design a factory slated to be built by the parent.

Altering the Terms of Trade

Another tactic MNCs can use to get around the inconvertibility problem was illustrated by the Radisson Hotel chain in 1990, when it began building hotels in the former Soviet Union. Radisson began its foray into the former Soviet Union by first building a hotel in Moscow that accepted only convertible currencies. Then it added others that accepted rubles. Similarly, when McDonald's opened its first two restaurants in Moscow, one accepted rubles, but the other accepted only dollars. Both cases demonstrate how the two firms tried to overcome potential problems related to blocked funds. Although Radisson and McDonald's weren't already doing business in the former Soviet Union, such a strategy could have worked for a multinational that was.

Finally, when a firm knows that it is going to be operating in a country whose money is not fully convertible, it may be able to set up a trading operation to export unrelated products from that country. That is, the firm may be able to use a countertrade strategy.

19.4 MANAGING ACCOUNTS RECEIVABLE

A critical source of a multinational corporation's working capital is its accounts receivable. Any firm that decides to issue trade credit must therefore perform five tasks within the firm or hire an outside firm to do so.[5] First, the credit risk of the customer must be assessed. Second, the terms of the credit must be determined. These terms include the length of time between the sale and the payment and any interest penalties for late payments. Third, the receivable must be financed between the production and receipt of funds from the sale. Fourth, the receivable must be collected. Fifth, the firm must bear the risk that the companies to which it extends credit will default.

Like purely domestic companies, MNCs commonly extend credit to their customers. However, the problems related to managing the company's accounts receivable are more complex for the MNC. In addition to the five tasks just mentioned, the MNC also must decide the currency of denomination of its accounts receivable. We look at this issue next.

Currency of Denomination

When doing business in foreign countries, an MNC must decide whether the sales should continue to be denominated in the domestic currency, in the currency of the foreign customer, or possibly in a third currency. Often, MNCs are advised to price their exports in hard currencies (ones that are likely to appreciate) and to denominate their imports in soft currencies (ones that are likely to depreciate). Does this advice make sense? If the two parties to a transaction agree on the distribution of future exchange rates and face the same cost of hedging, the advice is irrelevant. The currency of denomination of the sales contract then does not matter to the parties because there is a foreign currency price for the product that both parties agree is equal to the domestic currency price of the product. Let's look at an example to see why this is true.

---

[5]See Shehzad Mian and Clifford Smith (1992) for a discussion of the economics of whether these five tasks should be done within the firm or contracted outside the firm. Alternative policies include doing everything within the firm, financing the receivables with secured debt, establishing a captive financial subsidiary, using a credit information firm, using a credit collection agency, using a credit insurance company, and using non-recourse factoring or recourse factoring.

Suppose Boeing, a U.S. firm, enters into a contract to sell several of its airplanes to British Airways. If the contract is denominated in dollars, British Airways will have to pay $100,000,000 in 1 year when the planes are delivered. With the deal denominated in dollars, British Airways is also confronted with the risk that the dollar will strengthen relative to the pound. Suppose that the spot exchange rate and the 1-year forward rate are as follows:

$$\text{Spot rate} = \$1.65/\pounds$$
$$\text{1-year forward rate} = \$1.60/\pounds$$

If British Airways does not want to bear the risk that the dollar will strengthen relative to the pound, it can contract to buy dollars forward with pounds at the forward rate of $1.60/£. In this case, British Airways converts its $100,000,000 account payable into a pound-denominated account payable of

$$\$100,000,000/(\$1.60/\pounds) = \pounds62,500,000$$

Notice that if Boeing were to denominate the deal in pounds, with payment again in 1 year, British Airways would be indifferent between paying £62,500,000 and hedging the $100,000,000 payment. Analogously, if Boeing decided to denominate the deal in pounds and chose not to bear the transaction foreign exchange risk, it would generate $100,000,000 in 1 year by charging £62,500,000 for the planes and selling that amount of pounds forward for dollars.

Example 19.3 demonstrates the important point that the currency of invoice really does not matter if the two parties have the same hedging opportunities and view exchange risk symmetrically. In negotiating a deal, though, it is often the case that the two parties do not have equal access to hedging opportunities. Also, in many circumstances, there are no well-developed forward markets. Money market hedges might not be available either because of the difficulty of securing loans in the foreign currency.

When hedging is impossible, one of the parties will be forced to bear the foreign exchange risk. Once again, though, if the two parties agree on the distribution of future exchange rates, and if the cost to each of the parties of bearing the risk is the same, there will be a foreign currency price that each party agrees is equivalent to the proposed domestic currency price.

If the parties disagree about the nature of the distribution of future exchange rates, or if the perceived cost to the parties of bearing the risk is not the same, the two parties will disagree about the foreign currency price that is equivalent to the possible domestic currency price. The next example demonstrates this point.

Suppose that Boeing is selling airplanes to a new Thai company, Bangkok Airways. Boeing must choose whether to denominate the contract in U.S. dollars or Thai baht. Suppose that the spot exchange rate is THB25/$ and that there is no forward market.

Suppose there is a possibility that the baht will be devalued relative to the dollar during the next year. If Boeing prices in dollars, it will charge $100,000,000, and it will expect payment in 1 year. In this case, Bangkok Airways has two choices. It can buy dollars today and invest them for 1 year if it wants to hedge, or it can bear the exchange risk that the Thai baht will weaken relative to the dollar. In this case, we will assume that it is financially infeasible for Bangkok Airways to buy dollars today because it cannot borrow the requisite amount of dollars or baht.

In order to analyze the values that the two parties will attribute to the price quotes in the two different currencies, we must understand the distribution of future spot exchange rates that each party perceives. To summarize Bangkok Airways's and Boeing's probability distributions of future exchange rates in a simple way, assume that both parties think either the baht will remain at THB25/$ or the baht will be devalued. Suppose Bangkok Airways thinks there is a 50% probability the exchange rate will increase to THB40/$. Then, Bangkok Airways's expected future spot rate is

$$[0.5 \times (THB25/\$)] + [0.5 \times (THB40/\$)] = THB32.5/\$$$

Suppose Boeing also thinks that the exchange rate may increase to THB40/$, but Boeing believes there is a 55% probability of a devaluation. Hence, Boeing's expected future spot rate is

$$[0.45 \times (THB25/\$)] + [0.55 \times (THB40/\$)] = THB33.25/\$$$

When Boeing quotes a price of $100,000,000, Bangkok Airways expects to pay

$$(THB32.5/\$) \times \$100,000,000 = THB3,250,000,000$$

If Boeing quotes a price denominated in baht that is equivalent in expected value (from its perspective) to $100,000,000 in one year, it will quote

$$(THB33.25/\$) \times \$100,000,000 = THB3,325,000,000$$

Notice, in this example, that Bangkok Airways would prefer to be invoiced in dollars because the expected value (from its perspective) of the $100,000,000 when converted into baht is less than the sure baht payment that it would have to make if it were invoiced in baht.[6] If Bangkok Airways accepts the dollar-denominated payment, it will pay either THB2,500,000,000 if there is no devaluation or THB4,000,000,000 if there is a devaluation.

Examples 19.3 and 19.4 indicate that the decision about the currency in which to invoice cannot be made in isolation of the perceived probability distributions of future exchange rates, the opportunities that the parties have to hedge their foreign exchange risk, the determination of a local currency price for the product, and the riskiness of cash flows denominated in

---

[6]Notice that Bangkok Airways must compare a sure payment of baht in the future to an expected payment of baht in the future. To determine the baht cost today, it must take present values. Notice that Bangkok Airways will take the present value of a sure baht payment with the risk-free interest rate and the present value of an expected baht payment with an appropriate rate that reflects the systematic risk of the uncertain payment. If there is no systematic risk of the devaluation, the two payments can be compared with the baht risk-free rate. Analogously, Boeing would quote a baht price equal to the $100,000,000 times the expected value of the baht–dollar exchange rate only if the systematic risk of a devaluation of the baht relative to the dollar were zero.

different currencies. If, in Example 19.4, Boeing were to place a probability on the devaluation that was lower than 50%, say 40%, its expected future spot rate would be

$$[0.6 \times (THB25/\$)] + [0.4 \times (THB40/\$)] = THB31/\$$$

Then, Boeing would quote

$$(THB31/\$) \times \$100,000,000 = THB3,100,000,000$$

as the baht price for its planes. Bangkok Airways would happily agree to be invoiced for THB3,100,000,000 rather than for $100,000,000, and Boeing would be left with the foreign exchange risk. Notice that if the true probability of devaluation were actually 50%, Boeing would have mispriced the deal.

Leading and Lagging Payments

MNCs make use of leading and lagging payments to manage the net working capital needs of their foreign affiliates. A **leading payment** is a payment made earlier than usual; a **lagging payment** is a delayed payment. By shortening and lengthening the payment cycle between related affiliates, an MNC can affect the liquidity of its affiliates around the world.

For example, suppose the British affiliate of an MNC typically sells $2 million worth of goods each month to the German affiliate of the MNC. When the sale takes place, the British affiliate extends an account receivable to the German affiliate, which books an account payable. If the average period over which credit is extended is 60 days, the German affiliate is, on average, obtaining $4 million worth of financing from the British affiliate. That is, at any given point in time, the average account receivable of the British affiliate from the German affiliate is 2 months' worth of shipments, or $4 million. If the terms of the credit are extended to 90 days, the British affiliate provides an additional $2 million of financing to the German affiliate. Net working capital is increased at the British affiliate, and it is reduced at the German affiliate. If, on the other hand, the terms of the credit are reduced to 30 days, the British affiliate's net working capital is reduced from $4 million to $2 million, and the German firm's net working capital is increased by the same amount.

What are the determinants of leading and lagging? First, and foremost, the MNC must understand the relevant opportunity costs associated with the net working capital of each of its affiliates. This interest rate must be based on a common currency, such as the dollar, and it should be calculated on an after-tax basis. Funds should then be moved from affiliates that have a low opportunity cost of net working capital to affiliates that have a high opportunity cost of net working capital.

Of course, short-term borrowing and lending rates differ. Usually, the interest rate at which an affiliate can borrow in the short-term money market is substantially above the interest rate at which it can lend. If all borrowing rates are above all lending rates, the movement of funds through leading and lagging is simple. Funds should be moved from affiliates that are lending to the short-term money market to affiliates that are borrowing from short-term money markets. This is done by allowing the affiliates that are borrowing to lag their payments to the affiliates that are lending and by having the affiliates that are lending accelerate their payments to the affiliates that are borrowing.

The problem is only slightly more complicated if all the affiliates have surplus funds. Then, the affiliate with the best investment opportunity should receive accelerated payments from the other affiliates. In contrast, if all the affiliates have deficits of funds and are therefore borrowing, the MNC should attempt to borrow as much as possible through the affiliate that has the lowest borrowing cost.

The following example provides a numeric illustration of this issue.

Example 19.5 Different Borrowing and Lending Rates for Different Affiliates

Suppose the dollar borrowing and lending rates for a U.S. parent and its British affiliate for 90-day periods are as follows:

	Borrowing Rate (in percent per annum)	Lending Rate (in percent per annum)
U.S. parent	8.0	7.0
British affiliate	8.2	6.9

At the margin, both the U.S. parent and its British affiliate can have either positive short-term funds that they want to invest or short-term borrowing requirements. Consequently, four situations must be considered. In each of these four situations, we can determine which direction funds should flow and the return to the MNC of transferring $1 million:

1. **The U.S. parent has surplus funds, and the British affiliate must borrow:** If the U.S. parent were to invest funds, it can earn only 7%, whereas the British affiliate must borrow at 8.2%. Clearly, funds should flow from the U.S. parent to the British affiliate in this case. For each $1 million transferred for 90 days, the corporation saves

$$\$1,000,000 \times (8.2 - 7)/100 \times (90/360) = \$3,000$$

2. **The U.S. parent must borrow, and the British affiliate has surplus funds:** If the U.S. parent must borrow funds, it does so at 8.0%, whereas the British affiliate can earn only 6.9% on its lending. Clearly, funds should flow from the British affiliate to the U.S. parent in this situation: For each $1 million transferred for 90 days, the corporation saves

$$\$1,000,000 \times (8.0 - 6.9)/100 \times (90/360) = \$2,750$$

3. **The U.S. parent has surplus funds, and the British affiliate has surplus funds:** Because both the U.S. parent and the British affiliate have funds to invest, we merely compare what they can earn. The U.S. parent can earn 7%, whereas the British affiliate can only earn 6.9%. Clearly, funds should flow from the British affiliate to the U.S. parent. For each $1 million transferred for 90 days, the corporation earns

$$\$1,000,000 \times (7 - 6.9)/100 \times (90/360) = \$250$$

4. **The U.S. parent must borrow, and the British affiliate must borrow:** Because both the U.S. parent and the British affiliate are required to borrow, we merely compare their respective borrowing rates. The U.S. parent borrows at 8.0%, whereas the British affiliate borrows at 8.2%. Clearly, funds should flow from the U.S. parent to the British affiliate. For each $1 million transferred over 90 days, the corporation saves

$$\$1,000,000 \times (8.2 - 8.0)/100 \times (90/360) = \$500$$

Of course, governments are aware of the incentives that multinational corporations have to engage in leading and lagging of payments. Consequently, they regulate the credit terms that can be extended across borders.

Credit Terms

An MNC can extend credit not only to its affiliates but to its independent customers as well. How does an MNC decide on the terms of payments for its independent customers?

Fundamentally, the optimal policy involves increasing the term of an account receivable and reducing the interest charge until the marginal benefit of the affiliate's increased sales equals the marginal costs imposed by the five tasks involved in managing accounts receivable (mentioned at the outset of our discussion). The better the credit terms an MNC offers, the more sales it is likely to make. The problem for a firm is to be sure that today's sale on credit is actually contributing positive cash flow to the organization. Quoting easier credit terms can attract undesirable buyers who are slow to pay or who default on their payments.

Credit assessment is costly, so the longer the term of the credit, the more extensive should be the investigation of the creditworthiness of the customer. Collecting what is owed is also costly, as is financing the accounts receivable. There is also an opportunity cost associated with letting resources sit in the firm's accounts receivable. After all, this is money that could be used to finance other productive projects if it could be collected. Finally, the larger a firm's accounts receivable, the more default risk the firm faces.

An exception to this occurs if an MNC has a lower cost of capital than its local customers. In this case, the MNC can increase its profits by extending relatively long credit terms to its customers and charging them financing fees. If the MNC can finance the inventory of its customers at a cheaper rate than the customer would be charged by local banks, it makes sense for the MNC to do the financing. Of course, the MNC must address the question of the default risk of its customers. The higher interest rate or limited borrowing capacity of a local customer might simply reflect that there is a high default risk associated with doing business with the customer.

However, a multinational corporation that is a manufacturer may have an advantage over a bank if the collateral used to secure the loan is worth more to the manufacturer than it is to a neutral third party (or bank). If the credit in the account receivable is not repaid, the manufacturer should be able to repossess the merchandise and possibly resell it on more favorable terms than a bank or another financial intermediary could. The manufacturer might also have better information about the default risk of its customers than a bank has.

19.5 INVENTORY MANAGEMENT

As explained earlier, inventories are held to smooth the production process and to make sure that goods are available for customers when their orders arrive. But inventory is costly for a firm to hold because the stocks of inventories are the firm's assets, and they must be financed. If the firm's cost of capital is 15% and the firm is holding $100,000,000 of inventory, its annual financing cost is $15,000,000. The inventories also must be stored in a safe place, which requires warehouses and personnel to manage the storage. The firm is also exposed to losses in the event that the inventory is stolen or destroyed as a result of a fire or another natural disaster, or if it becomes obsolete. Of course, the firm can purchase insurance to guard against these risks, but there is a direct cost of doing so. Finally, inventories can lose value if the market prices of the goods fall. Commodities such as raw materials used in manufacturing are especially vulnerable to price drops.

So how does a firm decide how much inventory to hold? Optimal inventory theory, discussed next, can help a firm formulate a policy.

Optimal Inventory Theory

Optimal inventory theory states that a firm's level of inventory should be increased until the marginal benefit arising from its reduced production costs and increased sales revenue equals the marginal cost of storing and financing the inventories. Although the inventory management problems multinational firms face are similar to those faced by purely domestic firms, the volatility of prices and exchange rates makes determining an optimal policy even more challenging for an MNC.

Devaluation or Depreciation Risk

Managers of foreign subsidiaries are often confronted with the risk of devaluation or depreciation of the local currency. This risk raises the question of whether additional inventory from foreign suppliers should be purchased prior to a devaluation of the local currency relative to the foreign currency. A naïve answer to this question would appear to be "yes." After all, the local currency price of the inventory will rise after the devaluation. But let's examine this issue in more detail to gain insight about the balancing of marginal costs and marginal benefits.

Consider a two-period model in which a German subsidiary of a U.S. firm buys some imported goods today to place in inventory, and the subsidiary sells the goods in Germany in the next period. The German firm can borrow in euros to buy the goods, which are priced in dollars, and the company incurs a euro-denominated storage cost that increases with the amount of goods stored. Because the parent corporation is a U.S. firm, the objective of the German subsidiary is to maximize its dollar profit in the second period. Assume that the markets for both the imported goods and the final goods are competitive, so the firm cannot influence the prices of these goods by the amounts that it buys or sells.

To facilitate the analysis, let the dollar-euro exchange rate at time t be $S(t,\$/€)$, let $P(t,\$)$ be the dollar price of the imported good at time t, let $P(t,€)$ be the euro retail price of the good at time t, let $i(t,€)$ be the euro interest rate that will be paid at time $t+1$, and let $C(t+1,€)$ be the euro-denominated marginal storage cost that is increasing in the amount of inventory. Let's build up the equilibrium condition in steps.

The expected dollar revenue from selling a unit of the good next period is

$$E_t[S(t+1,\$/€) \times P(t+1,€)]$$

The expected marginal cost from buying the good on credit and storing the good for one period has two parts. The euro cost of the good at time t is $P(t,\$)/S(t,\$/€)$. This amount must be borrowed and repaid with interest at time $t+1$. Hence, the dollar value of the euro interest plus principal at time $t+1$ is

$$S(t+1,\$/€) \times P(t,\$) \times (1 + i(t,€))/S(t,\$/€)$$

The firm must also pay the dollar value of the marginal storage cost, $S(t+1,\$/€) \times C(t+1,€)$.

The equilibrium condition that determines the optimal inventory of goods imported into Germany requires that the expected marginal dollar revenues at time $t+1$ equal the expected dollar marginal costs:

$$E_t[S(t+1,\$/€) \times P(t+1,€)] = E_t[S(t+1,\$/€) \times P(t,\$)$$
$$\times (1+i(t,€))/S(t,\$/€)] + E_t[S(t+1,\$/€) \times C(t+1,€)] \qquad \textbf{(19.1)}$$

Consider the implications of Equation (19.1). On the revenue side, the important point is whether the local-currency prices in the retail market, $P(t+1,€)$, will increase to keep pace with any depreciation of the local currency as $S(t+1,\$/€)$ falls with a depreciation of the euro. If retail prices are expected to increase faster than the rate of depreciation, this force would motivate managers to purchase a larger amount of inventory, other things being equal. If, on the other hand, a depreciation of the euro will be accompanied by a price freeze, the expected increase in the retail price is less than the expected rate of depreciation of the local currency. This would motivate managers to purchase a smaller amount of inventory.

Now let's look at how a possible depreciation of the euro would affect the firm's marginal costs. If local interest rates fail to increase sufficiently to reflect the expected depreciation, the firm's marginal costs will be lower, and larger inventories should be purchased. On the other hand, if interest rates are higher than warranted by the expected depreciation, the firm's inventory carrying costs will be high, and smaller inventories should be purchased.

Finally, consider the second term on the right-hand side of Equation (19.1). If marginal costs are expected to be low, possibly because the firm's warehousing costs are fixed in nominal terms, this would cause the firm to choose larger inventories. In contrast, if the firm's workers are likely to strike after the depreciation, which would increase costs, smaller inventories are optimal.

In summary, the prospects of a depreciation of a local currency are insufficient in and of themselves to warrant an increase in inventories. Only by balancing the anticipated marginal benefits and anticipated marginal costs of holding the inventory can we arrive at the optimal stock. What will happen to future retail prices and whether nominal interest rates will accurately and rationally reflect the probabilities of devaluation are equally as important as the fact that the local currency is expected to depreciate.

POINT–COUNTERPOINT

Planning for a Dinjonasian Devaluation

Ante, Freedy, and Suttle are again in Chappaqua, New York, visiting their Uncle Fred, the importer–exporter. Uncle Fred is explaining that last year, he set up a textile manufacturing plant in Tajarka, Dinjonasia. The plant produces really cheap v-neck cotton t-shirts that are the rage in California. Uncle Fred is trying to figure out how to respond to a request from his Dinjonasian plant manager, Mr. Ibrahim.

"This e-mail from Ibrahim has me puzzled," says Uncle Fred. "He thinks the Dinjonasian rupiah (DJR) is going to crater versus the dollar sometime within the next year, and I agree. The latest figures show the stock of international reserves of Bank Dinjonasia at \$32 billion, and they're losing over \$4 billion per month intervening in support of the rupiah. At that rate of loss, they've got less than 8 months to figure out what to do before a devaluation of the rupiah is forced upon them. Ibrahim is worried that I'll fire him when the plant is less profitable after the devaluation. Last year, he made a profit of DJR8,100,000,000, which sounds impressive, but it only converted to USD900,000 at the fixed exchange rate of DJR9,000/USD. If the rate goes to DJR12,000/USD, as the media are anticipating, he'll only produce profit of

$$\frac{DJR8,100,000,000}{(DJR12,000/USD)} = \$675,000.$$

Uncle Fred continues, "Ibrahim wants to speculate to protect the dollar value of his budget. The stumbling block to this plan is that the Dinjonasian government has frozen forward trading in the rupiah—basically outlawing the forward market. I understand that he could sell rupiah forward for dollars and make a killing after the rupiah crashes, but if he can't do that, what can he do? I'm obviously not going to fire him for something that is out of his control."

"Well, he should be worried about his job if all that he can think of is forward contracts," shouts Ante. "There are lots of other ways to speculate against the rupiah."

"Name one," comes the cry from Freedy. "You're asleep in international finance most times I look."

Ante thinks for a second and responds, "Well, you could always have Ibrahim buy some extra inventory. Doesn't he get his cotton from Egypt? The dollar value of the cotton is set on world markets, and if he buys cotton before the devaluation, its rupiah value will increase with the devaluation."

Uncle Fred interjects, "Ante, that's a good suggestion, but what if the price of cotton falls in a few months? I've heard the Egyptians think there will be a huge harvest, and the price of cotton has consequently been trending downward for the past 2 weeks. I think cotton prices are going to fall 20% to 30% in the next 6 months. We could find ourselves with some really high-priced cotton on the books, which wouldn't look so good either. I think I'll just tell Ibrahim not to worry."

"Wait a minute," says Freedy. "Can't Uncle Fred do some leading and lagging of payments? It seems to me that he should maximize his dollar assets. That means lengthening out the Dinjonasian plant's accounts receivable that are denominated in dollars and shortening the plant's accounts payable. Uncle Fred should delay paying Ibrahim for the shirts, and Ibrahim should accelerate the payment of management fees and royalties to Uncle Fred. What would happen if everybody did that?"

Suttle interjects, "Freedy, you're right on the mark. Even though Bank Dinjonasia has tried to prevent speculation in the capital markets, all commercial firms will have an incentive to accelerate their purchases of dollars with rupiah and to delay their sales of dollars for rupiah. If you're going to buy dollars for some legitimate international trade purpose, you'd rather do it at DJR9,000/USD than at DJR12,000/USD. Similarly, if you can delay converting out of dollars into rupiah until after the devaluation, you'll get the capital gain. Of course, there may be a run on the reserves of Bank Dinjonasia, even with all the capital market controls in place. Leading and lagging international payments can have a first-order effect on the flow of international reserves, much to the displeasure of central bankers."

Ante and Freedy nod approvingly, but Uncle Fred shakes his head and interjects, "Suttle, don't you have to worry about interest rates in these strategies?"

Suttle smiles and says, "You certainly do, Uncle Fred!"

19.6 SUMMARY

This chapter explores issues related to managing a multinational corporation's net working capital. The main points in the chapter are as follows:

1. Net working capital is the difference between a firm's current assets of cash, marketable securities, accounts receivable, and inventories and its current liabilities. The change in the stock of net working capital is an investment in its future profitability.

2. The goals of an international money manager of a multinational corporation are to establish control over the cash resources of the organization, to invest excess short-term funds in an optimal way, and to obtain short-term financing at the lowest cost.

3. Managing cash from a centralized pool of resources can reduce a firm's costs by minimizing its transaction costs and by optimizing the currency of denomination and the maturity of any of its investments or borrowing.

4. A multilateral netting system reduces transaction costs between the affiliates of a multinational corporation by eliminating gross transfers and substituting net transfers that take account of what is owed among them.

5. The precautionary demand for money arises because a firm cannot perfectly match its current production to its current sales. A centralized cash management system can improve a multinational corporation's cash flows by exploiting the fact that the demands for cash by different affiliates are less than perfectly correlated.

6. The primary cash transfers that foreign affiliates make to their parent corporations are dividends. Other cash transfers to the parent include royalties, fees, and payments related to transfer prices. The parent should plan how it will repatriate the profits it earns from its affiliates and how it will minimize the taxes owed on the profits.

7. Transfer prices are the prices that a firm charges its affiliates when selling goods and services to them. Because transfer prices are set internally within a firm rather than by market forces, it is often difficult to determine whether a particular transfer price is close to what would be set in a competitive market.

8. Higher transfer prices shift income and tax burdens from distribution affiliates to manufacturing affiliates. Lower transfer prices shift income and tax

burdens from manufacturing affiliates to distribution affiliates.

9. In the United States, the Internal Revenue Service (IRS) specifies that an appropriate transfer price is one that reflects an arm's-length price—that is, the price a seller would charge to an unrelated buyer.

10. Prior to investing in a foreign affiliate, a parent company should analyze the factors that might trigger a situation in which blocked funds would occur and how such a situation would affect the affiliate's profitability. The parent should also develop a contingency plan for how the affiliate would operate within the country if such a problem developed.

11. A fronting loan is a parent-to-affiliate loan that uses a large international bank as a financial intermediary. Such a loan helps an MNC avoid the adverse effects of potential blocked-funds situations. The loan can also result in valuable tax shields that benefit both the affiliate and its parent.

12. A critical source of a multinational corporation's working capital is its accounts receivable. A firm that issues credit must assess the credit risk of its customers and determine the terms of the credit, including the length of time credit will be extended, interest penalties for late payments, and the currency in which it will be denominated. The firm must also finance its accounts receivable and bear the risk associated with them and the costs of collecting them. The appropriate terms of credit balance the marginal benefits the firm receives from the increased sales it makes on credit with the marginal costs it incurs performing the aforementioned tasks.

13. The appropriate currency of denomination of accounts receivable cannot be determined without understanding the perceived distributions of future exchange rates of each party, the opportunities that the parties have to hedge their foreign exchange risk, the determination of a local currency price for the product, and the riskiness of the cash flows denominated in different currencies.

14. Leading and lagging the payments made between its affiliates allows an MNC to affect the liquidity of the affiliates and to speculate on changes in exchange rates.

15. Stocks of inventories, consisting of raw materials, work-in-progress, and finished goods, are held to smooth production and to make sure that goods are available for customers when orders arrive. The benefits of holding inventories arise from better production planning and a reputation for reliability in supplying products. These benefits must be balanced at the margin against the storage, insurance, and financing costs inherent in holding inventories.

QUESTIONS

1. What is net working capital? Why should it be considered an investment that a firm must make to increase its future profitability?

2. What distinguishes international cash management from purely domestic cash management? In particular, what constraints arise in the international environment?

3. Why is it important for a foreign affiliate to have a well-defined dividend policy for repatriating profits to its parent corporation?

4. What is the difference between a royalty and a fee?

5. What are the determinants of leading and lagging payments between related international affiliates?

6. What principles determine the appropriateness of transfer prices under U.S. regulations?

7. How can transfer pricing be used to shift income around the world?

8. How can transfer pricing be used to avoid tariffs?

9. What are blocked funds? How can a corporation structure its foreign affiliates to mitigate problems with blocked funds?

10. What is a fronting loan? How does its structure potentially create value for a multinational corporation?

11. Why is the threat of devaluation an insufficient reason for a firm to build up its stocks of inventories?

12. What are the five tasks involved in issuing trade credit?

13. What is wrong with the rule that firms should invoice their customers in hard currencies?

14. Why does it make sense for a multinational corporation to allow its foreign customers to pay on credit if there is rationing in the foreign credit market?

1. Euroshipping Corporation maintains separate production and distribution facilities in Sweden, France, Spain, and Italy. The corporate headquarters is in France. As a consultant to the treasurer of Euroshipping, you have been asked to estimate how much money the firm could save by creating a centralized cash management pool. Currently, each affiliate maintains precautionary cash balances equal to 3 standard deviations above its expected demand for cash.

Affiliate	Mean Demand for Money	1 Standard Deviation
Swedish	€25,000,000	€7,000,000
French	€50,000,000	€13,000,000
Italian	€35,500,000	€10,000,000
Spanish	€20,000,000	€6,000,000

By how much could Euroshipping reduce its overall demand for cash if it were to create a centralized cash pool for the four affiliates? (Assume that the cash needs are normally distributed and are independent of each other.)

2. Euroshipping is also considering developing a multilateral netting system.
   a. Given the cumulative monthly payments in the following payments matrix, derive the minimum transfers that could be made.

Euroshipping Intracompany Payments Matrix (millions of euros)

Receiving Affiliate	Paying Affiliate			
	Swedish	French	Italian	Spanish
Swedish	—	16	14	18
French	19	—	12	15
Italian	22	7	—	11
Spanish	9	15	3	—

   b. If the transaction costs on these fund transfers are 0.45%, how much would the company save by switching to a multilateral netting system?

3. Suppose the euro borrowing and lending rates for a German parent and its Spanish affiliate for a 90-day period are as follows:

	Borrowing Rate (in percent per annum)	Lending Rate (in percent per annum)
German parent	9.3	8.1
Spanish affiliate	9.6	7.9

In each of the following cases, determine the direction funds should flow and the return to the MNC of transferring EUR1,000,000:
   a. The German parent has positive funds; the Spanish affiliate has negative funds.
   b. The German parent has negative funds; the Spanish affiliate has positive funds.
   c. The German parent has positive funds; the Spanish affiliate has positive funds.
   d. The German parent has negative funds; the Spanish affiliate has negative funds.

4. Consider a situation in which a manufacturing affiliate is selling to a distribution affiliate. The relevant tax information, operating expenses, and cost of goods sold are given in the following table. Fill out the entries in the table and determine how the overall income of the consolidated company would change if it were to increase the transfer price by $500:

	Manufacturing Affiliate (35% tax rate)	Distribution Affiliate (55% tax rate)	Consolidated Company
Sales	$4,500	$5,700	
Less cost of goods sold	2,600		
Less operating expenses	1,000	450	
Taxable income			
Less income taxes			
Net income			

5. If a manufacturing affiliate faces a 55% income tax rate, and its distribution affiliate faces a 40% income tax rate and a 15% import tariff, should transfer prices be high or low?

6. Caterpillar is selling earthmoving equipment to an Indonesian construction company. Caterpillar must choose whether to denominate the contract in U.S. dollars or in Indonesian rupiah. Suppose that the spot exchange rate is IDR9150/$ and that there is no

forward market. Suppose, too, that there is a possibility that the rupiah will be devalued relative to the dollar during the next year. If Caterpillar prices the contract in dollars, it will charge $15,000,000 and will expect to be paid in 1 year. It is also willing to discuss pricing the machines in rupiah. The Indonesian firm thinks that there is a 60% chance the exchange rate will remain the same and a 40% chance it will increase to IDR9,300/$. Caterpillar thinks that there is a 65% probability of the exchange rate remaining the same and a 35% probability that it will increase to ID9,450/$. How should the deal be priced, and who will bear the risk of devaluation of the rupiah?

BIBLIOGRAPHY

Al-Eryani, Mohammad F., Alam Pervaiz, and Syed H. Akhter, 1990, "Transfer Pricing Determinants of U.S. Multinationals," *Journal of International Business Studies*, pp. 409–425.

Anvari, M., 1986, "Efficient Scheduling of Cross-Border Cash Transfers," *Financial Management*, pp. 40–49.

Barrett, M. Edgar, 1977, "Case of the Tangled Transfer Price," *Harvard Business Review*, pp. 20–36, 176–178.

Bartelsman, Eric J., and Roel Beetsma, 2003, "Why Pay More? Corporate Tax Avoidance through Transfer Pricing in OECD Countries," *Journal of Public Economics* 87, 2225–2252.

Brennan, Michael, Vojislav Maksimovic, and Josef Zechner, 1988, "Vendor Financing," *Journal of Finance* 43, pp.1127–1141.

Clausing, Kimberly. A., 2003, "Tax-Motivated Transfer Pricing and US Intrafirm Trade Prices," *Journal of Public Economics* 87, pp. 2207–2223.

Emery, Gary W., 1984, "A Pure Financial Explanation of Trade Credit," *Journal of Financial and Quantitative Analysis* 19, pp. 271–285.

Feenstra, Robert C., and Gordon H. Hanson, 2004, "Intermediaries in Entrepot Trade: Hong Kong Re-Exports of Chinese Goods," *Journal of Economics and Management* 13, 3–35.

Grubert, Harry, Timothy Goodspeed, and Deborah Swenson, 1993, "Explaining the Low Taxable Income of Foreign-Controlled Companies in the United States," in Alberto Giovannini, R. Glenn Hubbard, and Joel Slemrod, eds., *Studies in International Taxation*, Chicago: University of Chicago Press.

Kester, W. Carl, and William B. Allen, 1987, "The Walt Disney Co.'s Yen Financing," Harrvard Business School Case No. 9-287-058.

Laster, David S., and Robert N. McCauley, 1994, "Making Sense of the Profits of Foreign Firms in the United States," *Federal Reserve Bank of New York Quarterly Review* 19, pp. 44–75.

Mian, Shehzad L., and Clifford W. Smith, 1992, "Accounts Receivable Management Policy: Theory and Evidence," *Journal of Finance* 47, pp. 169–200.

Schwartz, Robert A., and David F. Whitcomb, 1979, "The Trade Credit Decision," in J. Bicksler, ed., *Handbook of Financial Economics*, Amsterdam: North-Holland Publishing Co.

Chapter 20

Foreign Currency Futures and Options

*T*his chapter considers foreign currency futures and options and demonstrates how they can be used for hedging or speculative purposes. Because the profits and losses earned on futures and option contracts, as well as those earned on forward contracts, depend on how the spot exchange rate evolves over time, all these instruments are considered **derivative securities**. Derivative securities are securities whose values depend on the values of other, more basic underlying variables—in this case, the spot exchange rate.

As with other instruments in the foreign exchange market, much of the trade in futures contracts and options is conducted by banks. Commercial and investment banks deal aggressively in foreign currency options in order to meet the demands of their corporate and institutional customers, who use them to hedge their foreign exchange risks. In addition to banks, hedge funds and other investors trade foreign currency futures and options purely for speculative purposes—that is, strictly in order to earn a profit.

This chapter begins by introducing the institutional detail of the foreign currency futures market. It then discusses the differences between forward contracts and futures contracts and hedging with futures. Section 20.3 presents the basics of foreign currency options, and Section 20.4 discusses options and risk management. Section 20.5 examines some exotic options.

20.1 THE BASICS OF FUTURES CONTRACTS

Futures Versus Forwards

Foreign currency futures contracts, or futures contracts for short, allow individuals and firms to buy and sell specific amounts of foreign currency at an agreed-upon price determined on a given future day. Although this sounds very similar to the forward contracts discussed in Chapter 3, there are a number of important differences between forward contracts and futures contracts.

Exchange Trading
The first major difference between foreign currency futures contracts and forward contracts is that futures contracts are traded on an exchange, whereas forward contracts are made by banks and their clients. Examples of futures exchanges include the International Monetary Market (IMM), which is a subdivision of the Chicago Mercantile Exchange

(CME); Euronext.liffe, the derivatives arm of the New York Stock Exchange (NYSE) Euronext; and the Tokyo Financial Exchange (TFX). With exchange trading, futures contracts are standardized by the exchange, whereas the terms of forward contracts are negotiable.

In addition, with exchange trading, orders for futures contracts must be placed during the exchange's trading hours, and pricing occurs in the "pit" by floor traders or on an electronic trading platform where demand is matched to supply. In contrast to forward contracts, where dealers quote bid and ask prices at which they are willing either to buy or sell a foreign currency, for each party that buys a futures contract, there is a party that sells the contract at the same price. The price of a futures contract with specific terms changes continuously, as orders are matched on the floor or by computer.

Standardized Amounts

The futures exchanges standardize the amounts of currencies that one contract represents. Thus, futures contracts cannot be tailored to a corporation's specific needs as can forward contracts. But the standardized amounts are relatively small compared to a typical forward contract, and if larger positions are desired, one merely purchases more contracts. Standardization with small contract sizes makes the contracts easy to trade, which contributes to market liquidity. Some examples of the current contract sizes on the IMM for currencies versus the dollar are JPY12,500,000, EUR125,000, CAD100,000, GBP62,500, CHF125,000, AUD100,000, and MXN500,000. Other dollar-based contracts are also traded, ranging from the Swedish krona to the New Zealand dollar to a number of emerging market currencies, including the Brazilian real and the Russian ruble. Cross-rate products, such as GBP/EUR or JPY/EUR, are also traded.

Fixed Maturities

In the forward market, a client can request any future maturity date, and active daily trading occurs in contracts with maturities of 30, 60, 90, 180, or 360 days. The standardization of contracts by the futures exchanges means that only a few maturity dates are traded. For example, IMM contracts mature on the third Wednesday of March, June, September, and December. These dates are fixed, and hence the time to maturity shrinks as trading moves from 1 day to the next, until trading begins in a new maturity. Typically, only three or four contracts are actively traded at any given time because longer-term contracts lose liquidity. Consistent with the delivery procedures on spot foreign exchange contracts, trading in futures contracts stops at the end of the trading day, 2 business days before the maturity day of the contract.

Credit Risk

Another major difference between forward contracts and futures contracts concerns credit risk. This issue is perhaps the chief reason for the existence of futures markets. In the forward market, the two parties to a forward contract must directly assess the credit risk of their counterparty. As the box on the origins of the IMM indicates, banks are willing to trade with large corporations, hedge funds, and institutional investors, but they typically don't trade forward contracts with individual investors or small firms with bad credit risk.

The futures market is very different. In the futures markets, a retail client buys a futures contract from a futures brokerage firm, which in the United States must register with the **Commodity Futures Trading Commission (CFTC)** as a **futures commission merchant (FCM)**. Legally, FCMs serve as the principals for the trades of their retail customers. Consequently, FCMs must meet minimum capital requirements set by the exchanges and fiduciary requirements set by the CFTC. In addition, if an FCM wants to trade on the IMM, it must become a **clearing member** of the CME. In years past, clearing memberships used to be tradable, and the prices at which they traded were indications of how profitable futures trading on the exchange was expected to be. In 2000, the CME became a for-profit stock

The Origins of the IMM

Although the CME began trading agricultural futures contracts as early as the late 1800s, the first foreign currency futures contract was not traded until 1972. It was done via the IMM, which is a subdivision of the CME. The IMM was the brainchild of Nobel Laureate Milton Friedman of the University of Chicago and Leo Melamed, the head of the CME, which was a world center for trading commodity futures. In the late 1960s, Friedman became convinced that the Bretton Woods system of fixed exchange rates was doomed. He predicted that the dollar would devalue relative to various European currencies, including the Deutsche mark, after the breakup.

Friedman wanted to profit from the situation, which he correctly foresaw, but he was frustrated by his attempts to purchase Deutsche mark–denominated forward contracts at a bank because he had no "legitimate" business purpose for doing so—aside from speculating, which banks frowned upon. Consequently, he approached Melamed about having the CME develop futures contracts for foreign currencies in which the average citizen could "vote with his dollars" on the government policies being discussed in Washington and other capitals around the world. Melamed liked the idea, and by 1972, foreign currency futures contracts were approved for trading by the CFTC, and the IMM was born. Unfortunately for Friedman, the breakdown of Bretton Woods and the devaluation of the dollar occurred in August 1971, when President Richard M. Nixon withdrew the commitment of the United States to redeem dollars for gold—before Friedman could place his bet.

corporation, and its shares now trade on the NYSE. To obtain trading rights, an FCM must buy a certain amount of B-shares of CME stock and meet all CME membership requirements.

When a trade takes place on the exchange, the **clearinghouse** of the exchange, which is an agency or a separate corporation of the futures exchange, acts as a buyer to every clearing member seller and a seller to every clearing member buyer. The clearinghouse imposes margin requirements and conducts the daily settlement process known as marking to market that mitigates credit concerns. These margin requirements are then passed on to the individual customers by the futures brokers.

Margins

When someone enters a forward contract, no money changes hands, and the only cash flow is at the maturity of the contract. Assessing credit risk is thus very important. When a futures contract is purchased or sold, credit risk is handled differently—by margin accounts and marking to market. When a futures contract is purchased or sold, the investor must deposit some assets into a **margin account** to fulfill the **initial margin** requirement and ensure that any future losses on the contract will be covered.

Clearing members of the CME clearinghouse can accept margin payments in the form of cash, U.S. government obligations, securities listed on the NYSE or the American Stock Exchange (valued at 70% of their market prices), gold warehouse receipts (valued at 70% of the afternoon price of gold on the London Stock Exchange), or letters of credit of at least the amount required for the initial margin. It is important to realize that depositing assets in a margin account is not a payment for the futures contract. The investor still owns the assets that are in the margin account and can receive interest on monies deposited in the account.

As the futures prices change, one party to the contract experiences profits, and the other party experiences losses. The daily profits and losses are deposited to and subtracted from the margin accounts of the respective parties. This is the **marking to market** process that we will examine in detail shortly.

Initial margins on the IMM are in the range of $1,500 to $2,000 per contract (see www.futuresview.com/margins1.htm), whereas typical **maintenance margins** are in the range of $1,000 to $1,500. The maintenance margin is the minimum amount that must be kept in the account to guard against severe fluctuations in the futures prices and the losses that would be incurred by one of the parties. When the value of the margin account reaches the maintenance margin, there is a **margin call**, at which point the account must be brought back up to its initial value.

Because margins are intended to control risk, their magnitude depends on the size of the contract and the variability of the currencies involved. With the dollar values of the contracts being fairly similar, the greater volatility of the Mexican peso versus the U.S. dollar compared to the volatility of the Canadian dollar versus the U.S. dollar should naturally lead to a larger initial margin for the peso. The data from futuresview (for March 23, 2007) list the margin for the peso at $1,875 whereas the margin for the Canadian dollar was only $1,148.

Of course, the initial margin payments must eventually reach the CME's clearinghouse. This happens through a pyramid structure. The clearinghouse, which sits at the top of the pyramid, collects the margins from clearing member FCMs, which collect the margins from non-clearing member FCMs, which collect them from their customers and execute their trades through FCM clearing members.

Marking to Market

The system of margin accounts coupled with a process of daily marking to market ensures that retail and corporate users of these contracts present little credit risk to the FCMs and thus to the clearinghouse of the exchange. To better understand the process, let's examine marking to market, using a euro futures contract. Let's assume that each contract represents €125,000.

Suppose it is September, and you buy a December euro futures contract. Buying the contract means that you "go long in December euro," and it means that you will profit if the euro appreciates relative to the dollar. Conversely, you will take losses if the euro depreciates. You place your order to buy with your broker, and the order is executed on the futures exchange at a price at which another trader is willing to sell the identical contract. This trader could be selling for his own account, or he could be executing an order on behalf of someone who has placed an order to "short" the December euro contract.

Consider how the contractual profits and losses evolve over time and how this affects your margin account. Exhibit 20.1 provides a 7-day example. Suppose that your trade was filled on September 16, at the end of trading, and the **settle price**, or final futures trading price, for that day for the December contract was $1.3321/€. When you purchase the December euro contract, you must place the initial margin, which is assumed to be $2,000, into your margin account. The individual who sold the euro contract to you must also place $2,000 into his or her margin account. We assume that the maintenance margin is $1,500. In other words, if the value of your margin account drops by more than $500 because of losses on your futures position, you will be required to bring the account's balance back up to the initial $2,000.

Suppose that on September 17, the dollar price of the December euro futures contract falls by $0.0006/€, to $1.3315/€. This is the new daily settle price of the contract, and it affects the balance in your margin account. Because you are long in the euro contract, and the

Exhibit 20.1 An Example of Marking to Market in the Futures Market

Day	Futures Price ($/€)	Change in Futures Price ($/€)	Gain or Loss	Cumulative Gain or Loss	Margin Account
t	1.3321	0	0		$2,000.00
$t+1$	1.3315	−$0.0006	−$75.00	−$75.00	$1,925.00
$t+2$	1.3304	−$0.0011	−$137.50	−$212.50	$1,787.50
$t+3$	1.3288	−$0.0016	−$200.00	−$412.50	$1,587.50
$t+4$	1.3264	−$0.0024	−$300.00	−$712.50	$2,000.00
$t+5$	1.3296	+$0.0032	+$400.00	−$312.50	$2,400.00
$t+6$	1.3301	+$0.0005	+$62.50	−$250.00	$2,462.50

Notes: The futures price column lists the daily settle prices in the futures market. The contract size for the euro contract is assumed to be €125,000. The initial margin is $2,000, and the maintenance margin is $1,500. The gain or loss is the change in the futures price ($/€) multiplied by the size of the contract. The cumulative gain or loss is the sum of the daily gain or loss.

futures price of the euro fell, money is taken out of your margin account. Conversely, the person who sold the December futures contract—that is, the one who shorted the euro—gains money. How much will be taken from your margin account to be placed in the margin account of the individual who sold the euro short? The answer is the change in the settle price times the contract size:

$$(\$0.0006/€) \times €125{,}000 = \$75$$

This process continues every day, until the maturity date of the contract. Exhibit 20.1 indicates that if the euro futures price falls to $1.3264/€ by day $t+4$, you will have a cumulative loss of $712.50. Because this cumulative loss makes the value of your margin account less than the maintenance margin of $1,500, you will receive a margin call from your broker, notifying you that you have to increase your margin account back to the initial margin of $2,000. Exhibit 20.1 also indicates that funds will be credited to your margin account if the December futures price increases as it does on days $t+5$ and $t+6$. These funds could either be left in your account, as in Exhibit 20.1, or they could be withdrawn to leave the margin account at the value of the initial margin ($2,000).

On the last trading day of the futures contract, 2 business days remain before delivery. Arbitrage guarantees that the futures price at the maturity of the contract will be equal to the spot exchange rate on that day because both the futures price and the spot price are ways of purchasing euros with dollars for delivery in 2 business days. Hence, if on the Monday before the third Wednesday of December, the spot price is $1.3421/€, the futures price will have risen by

$$\$1.3421/€ - \$1.3321/€ = \$0.0100/€$$

You will have had an inflow of profit equal to

$$(\$0.0100/€) \times €125{,}000 = \$1{,}250$$

Of course, because you received the $1,250 in increments, it will actually be worth something slightly more than this amount because you will have received interest on your profits.

The marking-to-market process means that entering a futures contract can be thought of as a sequence of bets on the direction of the change in the price of the contract rather than a direct future purchase of foreign currency. This is an accurate description because all gains and losses are settled every day. Each day, you face the decision of sticking with your long or short position, which is called your **open interest**, or ending the bet by taking the reverse position. If you are long one contract and you sell one contract for the same maturity, the clearinghouse simply nets your position to zero. This is the way most futures contracts are closed out.

The Pricing of Futures Contracts

Because forward and futures contracts both allow you to buy or sell foreign currency at a particular future time at an exchange rate known today, you might think that the two prices should be the same. However, because forward contracts entail no cash flows until maturity, whereas futures contracts are marked to market, the two prices can, in theory, be slightly different.

The Payoff on a Forward Contract
Let's illustrate the payoff patterns for forward and futures contracts in symbols. Let $F(t)$ be the forward price of the foreign currency at time t. Then, the payoff per unit of foreign currency at maturity, time T, depends on the future spot rate, $S(T)$. If you purchase the foreign currency forward, the payoff equals

$$S(T) - F(t)$$

You win if $S(T) > F(t)$, and you lose if $S(T) < F(t)$.

The Payoff on a Futures Contract

Suppose you buy a foreign currency futures contract at time t at the futures price, $f(t)$, and you hold the contract until maturity, the same time T as the maturity of the forward contract. Because the payoff dribbles in over time due to marking to market, the per-unit payoff is

$$
\begin{array}{ll}
\text{Day } t+1: & f(t+1) - f(t) \\
\text{Day } t+2: & f(t+2) - f(t+1) \\
\text{Day } t+3: & f(t+3) - f(t+2) \\
& \quad\vdots \\
\text{Day } T: & f(T) - f(T-1)
\end{array}
$$

If we ignore the time value of money and add up all the cash flows, the aggregate payoff is

$$
[f(t+1) - f(t)] + [f(t+2) - f(t+1)] + [f(t+3) - f(t+2)] + \ldots \\
+ [f(T) - f(T-1)] = f(T) - f(t)
$$

because the intermediate futures prices cancel out. Because arbitrage drives the futures price at maturity, $f(T)$, to equality with the spot rate on that day, $S(T)$, the payoff on the futures contract is essentially the same as the payoff on the forward contract.

Why Futures Can Differ from Forwards

The payoffs of futures contracts and forward contracts are only "essentially the same" because a slight difference in payoffs arises when we do not ignore the interest that is earned on future profits or that must be paid on future losses. Technically, if the path of short-term interest rates could be foreseen—that is, if there were no random elements in the change in future short-term interest rates—there would be an arbitrage possibility if the forward exchange rate were different from the futures price because you would know how you could invest the profits or borrow to finance your losses. However, future interest rates are not known with certainty, so forward prices and futures prices can be different, in theory. In practice, though, the price differentials are minimal, and they appear to be within the transaction costs of the forward market. Therefore, we argue that futures prices are "essentially the same" as forward prices, and we don't explore further how futures contracts are valued.

Wall Street Journal *Futures Quotes*

Now that you understand how futures markets work, let's examine Exhibit 20.2, which shows an example of the IMM futures market listing that appears daily in the *Wall Street Journal*. The information reports trading from December 1, 2004, and the first trade, which is the **open price** on that day, for a December euro contract was $1.3286/€.

During the day, trades occurred at prices as high as $1.3338/€ and as low as $1.3276/€. At the end of the trading day, the settle price was $1.3321/€. The settle price often represents the last trading price. But if that price is stale (in the sense of being relatively early in the day), it is established through the consensus of the traders in the pit who are given the responsibility by the IMM for setting this price. Because of this institutional feature, the settle price can actually be higher than the daily high price or lower than the daily low price at which trades were made. The column labeled "CHG" in Exhibit 20.2 indicates that the new settle price is $0.0029/€ higher that the previous day's settle price.

The next two columns indicate that the lifetime high and low for this contract since it began trading are $1.3338/€ and $1.0735/€, respectively. The final column represents the open interest that is outstanding, which is 225,736. The open interest is the number of pairs of contracts bought and sold that have not yet been closed out. Notice that the largest open interest is in the contract closest to maturity. This is typically true until the contract enters the maturity month, in which case activity switches to the next-closest contract. Finally, the

Exhibit 20.2 Futures Quotes (*Wall Street Journal*, December 2, 2004)

Currency Futures

	OPEN	HIGH	LOW	SETTLE	CHG	LIFETIME HIGH	LIFETIME LOW	OPEN INT
Japanese Yen (CME)–¥12,500,000; $ per ¥100								
Dec	.9714	.9752	.9713	.9743	.0022	.9795	.8800	193,872
Mr05	.9805	.9811	.9775	.9804	.0022	.9850	.8873	2,954
Est. vol. 15,189; vol. Tue 36,917; open int. 296,960, +2,589.								
Canadian Dollar (CME)–CAD 100,000; $ per CAD								
Dec	8421	8467	8386	8445	.0016	8530	6940	95,667
Mr05	8420	8463	8382	8442	.0016	8526	7150	7,074
June	8442	8451		8445	.0016	8495	7150	2,066
Sept	8447	8447	8435	8452	.0016	8490	7160	732
Dec	8445	8445	8415	8461	.0016	8515	7480	353
Est. vol. 27,913; vol. Tue 30,936; open int. 105,893, +222.								
British Pound (CME)–£62,500; $ per £								
Dec	1.9075	1.9320	1.9075	1.9315	.0225	1.9320	1.6850	84,963
Est. vol. 30,973; vol. Tue 34,608; open int. 88,044, +60.								
Swiss Franc (CME)–CHF 125,000; $ per CHF								
Dec	.8775	.8812	.8735	.8767	–.0015	.8833	.7264	73,241
Est. vol. 22,083; vol. Tue 16,875; open int. 75,035, +795.								

	OPEN	HIGH	LOW	SETTLE	CHG	LIFETIME HIGH	LIFETIME LOW	OPEN INT
Australian Dollar (CME)–AUD 100,000; $ per AUD								
Dec	.7723	.7783	.7688	.7749	.0028	.7938	.6150	69,742
Mr05	.7674	.7731	.7630	.7694	.0028	.7879	.6400	3,067
Est. vol. 12,357; vol. Tue 24,014; open int. 73,359, +54.								
Mexican Peso (CME)–MXN 500,000; $ per MXN								
Dec	.08900	.08955	.08872	.08947	.00072	.08955	.08270	90,439
Mr05	.08790	.08825	.08717	.08810	.00072	.08825	.08200	5,346
June	.08637	.08685	.08635	.08667	.00072	.08685	.08160	536
Est. vol. 14,803; vol. Tue 10,984; open int. 96,439, +3,024.								
Euro/US Dollar (CME)–€ 125,000; $ per €								
Dec	1.3286	1.3338	1.3276	1.3321	.0029	1.3338	1.0735	225,736
Mr05	1.3301	1.3345	1.3287	1.3331	.0029	1.3345	1.1363	6,793
June	1.3320	1.3352	1.3317	1.3352	.0029	1.3352	1.1750	441
Est. vol. 108,109; vol. Tue 114,578; open int. 233,254, –1,340.								
Euro/US Dollar (NYBOT)–€ 200,000; $ per €								
Dec	...	...	...	1.3324	.0030	1.3318	1.2037	696
Est. vol. 304; vol. Tue 472; open int. 696, +95.								
Euro/Japanese Yen (NYBOT)–€ 100,000; ¥ per €								
Dec	136.73	136.94	136.73	136.69	–.04	138.02	131.37	9,110
Est. vol. 1,731; vol. Tue 853; open int. 11,604, +276.								
Euro/British Pound (NYBOT)–€ 100,000; £ per €								
Dec	.6931	.6931	.6903	.6897	–.0065	.7043	.6824	14,217
Est. vol. 2,994; vol. Tue 3,586; open int. 14,276, –541.								

newspaper reports that about 108,109 euro contracts were traded on this day. This represents total volume of

$$€125,000 \text{ per contract} \times 108,109 \text{ contracts} = €13.26 \text{ billion}$$

A Futures Contract on the Mexican Peso

In addition to trading futures contracts on the major currencies of the world, the IMM now trades quite a few contracts on emerging-market currencies. The first of these to be established was for the Mexican peso, which began trading in April 1995.

At that time, trading futures contracts for the Mexican peso was quite a courageous move. Mexico had just witnessed a severe currency crisis, and Larry Summers, the U.S. Secretary of the Treasury, argued that introducing Mexican peso futures would be a bad idea because it would be easier for currency speculators to bet against the Mexican peso. Moreover, when plans for the contract were unfolding, it became clear that the usual delivery procedures of the CME were incompatible with the capital controls in place in Mexico.

In addition, the CME wanted to involve the Mexican government in the process of establishing the contract. Fortunately, the Mexican minister of finance at the time, Guillermo Ortiz, a Stanford-trained economist, thought that the introduction of a CME Mexican peso futures contract fit in well with his plans to restore confidence in the Mexican government and the economy and to move policy toward more of a market orientation. Ortiz argued that an effective futures contract would be hugely beneficial to international trade between the United States and Mexico because it would facilitate hedging, and he did not feel it would generate excessive exchange rate volatility. In fact, Ortiz decided to lift the Mexican capital controls, making it possible for the CME to employ its usual delivery procedures for the Mexican peso contract when it launched in April 1995.

This turned out to be a good decision in facilitating the success of the contract because actual delivery of currency was used more often than is the case with major currencies. That is, many of the users of the contracts turned out to be exporters and importers who desired the actual delivery of the currencies.

For the CME, this was the beginning of an Emerging Markets division that now has contracts listed not only on the Mexican peso but also on the Brazilian real, the Russian ruble, three eastern European currencies (the Czech koruna, the Hungarian forint, and the Polish zloty, both relative to the dollar and relative to the euro), the Chinese renminbi, the Korean won, the Israeli shekel, and the South African rand.

20.2 HEDGING TRANSACTION RISK WITH FUTURES

This section examines how futures contracts can be used to hedge exposures to transaction exchange risk. It does so in the context of an extended example.

Hedging at Nancy Foods

Suppose it is the middle of February, and Nancy Foods, an American firm, has just contracted to sell frozen quiches to Kühlerkuchen, a German firm. Nancy Foods will receive €250,000 in the middle of March and is considering hedging the exposure with futures contracts.

The Hedging Decision

First, because the contract size on the IMM is €125,000, Nancy Foods will use two contracts. Second, Nancy Foods has to determine whether it wants to buy or sell the futures contracts. Because it has a €250,000 account receivable, which is a euro asset, Nancy Foods will lose money if the euro weakens relative to the dollar because the euro receivable will then purchase fewer dollars. The company will gain if the euro strengthens relative to the dollar. Consequently, to hedge its exposure, Nancy Foods must enter into futures contracts that provide profits when the euro weakens and losses when the euro strengthens. That is, Nancy Foods hedges by acquiring a euro liability whose value is equivalent to the value of the underlying receivable.

If Nancy Foods sells two euro futures contracts, it establishes a price today of $/€ at which it will sell euros for dollars. The company will gain on the futures position if the euro depreciates because it will then be able to buy euros at a lower dollar price in the spot market and sell euros at the higher contractual futures price. The company will lose on the futures contract if the euro strengthens because the dollar price of the euro will rise in the spot market, and Nancy Foods will have to buy euros high and sell them low.

Notice that if the maturity date of the receivable is the third Wednesday in March, the maturity of the euro asset from the underlying receivable and the euro liability represented by Nancy Foods's sale of the futures contracts are matched exactly. Hence, the company will be effectively hedged.

A Numeric Example

To be concrete, let's assume that the following exchange rates are observed:

	Spot Rate	Futures Rate (March contract)
February	$1.24/€	$1.23/€
March	$1.35/€	$1.35/€

The March futures rate coincides with the spot rate because both are for the third Wednesday in March.

Suppose that the 30-day euro interest rate is 3% per annum, and the receivable will be paid in 30 days. Then, the present value of the €250,000 is

$$\frac{€250{,}000}{\left(1 + 0.03 \times \dfrac{30}{360}\right)} = €249{,}377$$

At the time of the contract in February, the value of the euro receivable is therefore

$$€249{,}377 \times \text{spot rate} = €249{,}377 \times \$1.24/€ = \$309{,}227$$

However, Nancy Foods is exposed to euro depreciation because it receives the euros only 1 month from now, in March. Consequently, to hedge against a depreciation of the euro, the company goes short two futures contracts, at the futures rate of $1.23/€. What are the final cash flows?

First, when Nancy Foods sells the euro receivables in the spot market in March, the cash flow is

$$€250{,}000 \times \$1.35/€ = \$337{,}500$$

Second, the futures contract will have lost money because Nancy Foods established a short position in the futures market, and the euro appreciated versus the dollar. The cash flow on the futures contract is the change in the futures price multiplied by the contractual amount:

$$[(\$1.23/€) - (\$1.35/€)] \times €250{,}000 = -\$30{,}000$$

Combining the cash flow from the euro receivables with the loss on the futures contracts yields a total cash flow of

$$\$337{,}500 - \$30{,}000 = \$307{,}500$$

The effective exchange rate at which Nancy Foods sells the euro receivables is

$$\$307,500 / €250,000 = \$1.23/€$$

Thus, by transacting in the futures market, Nancy Foods effectively locks in the original futures price.

Potential Problems with a Futures Hedge

There are two obvious problems associated with using futures contracts to hedge transactions exposures. First, futures contracts are sold only in standardized sizes (€125,000 in our example). Hence, if you need to hedge an amount that is not a multiple of the standard size, some of your risk cannot be covered. A second problem is caused by the relatively low number of delivery dates. If the maturity of your foreign currency asset or liability does not match a settlement date in the futures market, the relationship between the spot exchange rate at the time the transaction takes place and the futures price of the foreign exchange is somewhat uncertain.

Basis Risk

To provide a perfect hedge, the price of the futures contract should move one-for-one with the spot exchange rate. Then, being long in the foreign currency from an underlying transaction can be hedged by going short in the corresponding futures contract. If this is not the case, the hedge is said to suffer **basis risk**. The basis is the difference between the spot price at time t, $S(t)$, and the futures price at time t, $f(t,T)$, for maturity date at time T:

$$\text{Basis} = \text{Spot price} - \text{Futures price} = S(t) - f(t,T)$$

Mostly, we will be talking about a single maturity, so we will omit the T indicator.

To see how the basis affects the quality of a hedge, let's ignore the time value of money because the maturity is short and consider the portfolio value, $V(t)$, of being long one unit of foreign currency and short one futures contract for a unit of the foreign currency:

$$V(t) = S(t) - f(t)$$

This is identical to the basis! Why is this portfolio important in hedging? Intuitively, it reflects the joint value of a receivable (a future currency asset) and the futures position set up to hedge it (a foreign currency liability).

Let's make this very concrete by tabulating how such values would move over time in Exhibit 20.3. Initially, the value of the receivable per unit of foreign currency is worth $S(t)$, the value of the spot exchange rate. The problem is that you can only sell the receivable at time T at the as-of-yet unknown exchange rate $S(T)$. The uncertain change in value $S(T) - S(t)$ represents your transaction exchange risk. Column 2 in Exhibit 20.3 shows how the value of the

Exhibit 20.3 Hedging a Receivable with Futures

Time	Value of Receivable	Cumulative Value of Futures Hedge (short position)	Hedged Position
t	$S(t)$	0	$S(t)$
$t+1$	$S(t+1)$	$f(t) - f(t+1)$	$f(t) + [S(t+1) - f(t+1)]$
$t+2$	$S(t+2)$	$[(f(t+1) - f(t+2)] + [f(t) - f(t+1)]$ $= f(t) - f(t+2)$	$f(t) + [S(t+2) - f(t+2)]$
$\vdots$		$\vdots$	$\vdots$
T	$S(T)$	$f(t) - f(T)$	$f(t) + [S(T) - f(T)]$

Note: The hedged position reflects the sum of the previous two columns.

receivable moves with the spot rate. When you hedge a foreign currency asset using the futures market, you sell the foreign currency futures. Initially, the futures contract has no value, but on day 2, the cash flows start coming in (or leaving) your margin account. We record the cumulative cash flows in the third column. The fourth column reflects the value of the hedged position: the receivable plus the cash flows earned or lost in the futures market. It is easy to see that the hedged position equals the futures rate at which you entered the contract plus the basis. Consequently, to make sure you really lock in the future rate, the basis at maturity must be zero.

Suppose we hold the contract until maturity. In that case, the futures rate converges to the spot rate; that is, the basis is zero at maturity. Then, Exhibit 20.3 shows that the hedged position is worth $f(t)$; you effectively sell the receivable at the futures rate. If the maturities of the receivable and the futures contract do not coincide, the basis will not equal zero when the futures contract is closed, and there will be basis risk. Note that the value of the hedged position has changed as follows between time t and time T:

$$ f(t) + [S(T) - f(T)] - S(t) = [S(T) - f(T)] - [S(t) - f(t)] = V(T) - V(t) $$

Hence, the change in value in the hedged position is the change in portfolio value of the long–short portfolio we set up before. It also equals the change in basis between time t and T. If the basis is zero at maturity, this change in value is perfectly known at time t. Although basis risk is typically much smaller than the risk associated with an uncovered position, a substantial amount of risk may nevertheless remain. Risk managers often use quantitative techniques to figure out the best way to mitigate basis risk, but these techniques are beyond the scope of this book.

Example 20.1   A Euro Receivable and Basis Risk

Let's return to the situation in which Nancy Foods is contracting to sell quiches in Germany, thereby generating a €250,000 receivable. This time, assume that the contract is made in January, and payment is scheduled for early March. Now, the delivery date for the quiches does not coincide with the maturity date of the futures contract, and Nancy Foods consequently faces basis risk. We assume that the following exchange rates are observed:

	Spot Rate	Futures Rate (March contract)
January	$1.21/€	$1.22/€
March	$1.33/€	$1.325/€

At the time of the contract, the value of the euro receivable appears to be

€250,000 × Spot rate = €250,000 × $1.21/€ = $302,500

However, Nancy Foods receives the euros only a little less than 2 months from now, in March. Consequently, to protect itself from euro depreciation, Nancy Foods sells two futures contracts at the futures rate of $1.22/€. What are the final cash flows now?

First, Nancy Foods sells the euro receivables in the spot market, receiving

€250,000 × $1.33/€ = $332,500

Second, the futures contract will have lost money because the euro appreciated, and Nancy Foods established a short position in the futures market. The total cash flow will have been:

[($1.22/€) − ($1.325/€)] × €250,000 = −$26,250

So, ultimately, the euro receivables plus the loss on the futures contract yields

$332,500 − $26,250 = $306,250

The effective exchange rate at which Nancy Foods sold the euro receivables is

$$\$306{,}250/€250{,}000 = \$1.225/€$$

This does not equal the futures rate of $\$1.22/€$ because of basis risk. The difference of $\$0.005/€$ with the futures rate exactly reflects the basis (Spot rate − Futures rate = $\$1.33/€ - \$1.325/€$) at the time that the futures contract was closed out and the receivable sold for dollars in the spot market. In this case, basis risk had a positive effect on Nancy Foods's cash flow. That is, we have, as in Exhibit 20.3,

$$\text{Effective rate} = \text{Futures rate} + \text{Basis}$$
$$\$1.225/€ = \$1.22/€ + [\$1.33/€ - \$1.325/€]$$

After the fact, we see that Nancy Foods would have been better off not hedging at all because the euro actually appreciated, and the company had a euro receivable. If Nancy Foods wanted to hedge completely, though, the futures market works pretty well—even in the presence of basis risk.

In Section 20.3, we will look at how options allow companies to hedge while retaining some benefit from advantageous exchange rate movements. But first, we need to see how the Handel brothers are doing.

POINT-COUNTERPOINT

On Good Beer and Korunas

The Handel family reunion on Uncle Fred's estate in Chappaqua, New York, brought Ante, Freedy, and Suttle together again with their flamboyant uncle who's in the export–import business. Uncle Fred was keen to get his nephews' insights on the international financial issues he faced. After dinner, he insisted that they all meet at the bar in his den because he had something to show them.

Uncle Fred poured a particularly clear lager from a funky-looking bottle and roared, "Here my friends, drink this!"

"What beer is this?" Ante inquired, "This tastes wonderful!"

"Well, my friends, this is Pilsner Kozquell, an authentic Czech lager," their uncle explained. "It is brewed under strict purity laws—only hops, yeast, malt, and water can be used. The result is very different from that chemically, carbon dioxide–infused, scrub water they make as beer in America! And guess what? This wonderful beer may soon be available in America at reasonable prices, as I am hoping to start importing the stuff! I have bid for the import license with the Czech brewery, and if everything goes well, the first shipment should arrive in 6 months."

"That's wonderful news, Uncle!" exclaimed Freedy.

"Well, there are problems," sighed their uncle. "I'm not sure I'm going to win the bid, and the brewery will take a month to decide. Moreover, they insist on being paid in Czech korunas. I've got a potentially huge koruna liability 6 months from now, and I am worried about the currency risk. I was kind of hoping you guys could help me out. What can I do to hedge this risk? At current exchange rates, my margins are not that great, and I cannot afford to pay many more dollars for the beer. On top of all that, the dollar has been weakening, and my bank is not willing to do a koruna forward contract with me. They say I've maxed out my credit limit."

"Ha," said Ante, "I would not hedge! The Czech Republic is now a member of the European Union, and it may soon adopt the euro as its currency. Because it is an emerging market, it likely still has tons of inflationary pressure, and I suspect its currency will depreciate tremendously in the run-up to adopting the euro. If that happens, your liability will be melting away in dollar terms if the dollar stays even with the euro."

"No way, Uncle! Don't take that risk!" Freedy interjected. "If the koruna moves with the euro versus the dollar, the opposite may happen. Also, the koruna might appreciate against both currencies, as people hoard it in anticipation of joining the euro monetary system. With the weak dollar, your koruna exposure is very risky now! I would use the futures market to hedge. The IMM has introduced futures contracts on the koruna, so you can go long in koruna futures. If the koruna appreciates, the payment for the shipment is going to cost you more dollars, but the futures position will gain money, too, offsetting the loss on the payable."

"That sounds interesting," Uncle Fred mused. "But, Suttle, tell me what you think."

Suttle reluctantly put down his glass of Pilsner Kozquell and said, "I think there is indeed a chance the koruna will depreciate as Ante claims, but I've heard that the Czech economy is doing very well, and the currency has been stable. In fact, the Czech central bank has competently adopted a modern monetary policy, and the inflation rate there has recently run at a lower rate than in the European Union. Hence, the risk of koruna appreciation versus the euro is real. The risk of euro appreciation versus the dollar is also very real. With such risks and low profit margins, some form of hedge is probably a good idea. However, it depends on your point of view. How sure are you that you will win the contract? If you hedge with a long koruna futures position and don't get the contract, you'll take losses if the koruna weakens. I think you need to look into options. Because you need to buy koruna, why not buy a koruna call option? You pay a bit of a premium, but you are hedged, and you still profit from a lower dollar payment in case the koruna depreciates. If you don't get the contract, the most you can lose is the option premium, and these options also trade at the IMM."

Ante gasped: "Options? Gee, I've got to study this for our international finance exam. They're so complicated!" Uncle Fred just smiled and poured another Pilsner Kozquell lager. He knew what to do.

20.3 BASICS OF FOREIGN CURRENCY OPTION CONTRACTS

A **foreign currency option contract** gives the buyer of an option the right, but not the obligation, to trade a specific amount of foreign currency for domestic currency at a specific exchange rate. Foreign currency options are traded both by money center banks and on organized exchanges. The Philadelphia Stock Exchange (PHLX) began trading foreign currency options in 1982, and it was once the most active market in the world for this type of trading. PHLX has now lost much of its trading volume in foreign currency options to other venues, especially the over-the-counter markets.

Basic Option Terminology

The two fundamental types of options are calls and puts. A **foreign currency call option** gives the buyer of the option the right, but not the obligation, to buy a specific amount of foreign currency with domestic currency at an exchange rate stated in the contract. A **foreign currency put option** gives the buyer of the option the right, but not the obligation, to sell a specific amount of foreign currency for domestic currency at an exchange rate stated in the contract. Because the buyer of the option purchases from the seller the right to transact, the buyer must pay the seller the value of the option, which is the option's price. Market participants also refer to the option price as an **option premium**. The seller of the option is also referred to as the *writer* of the option.

European vs. American Options

Like foreign currency futures, a foreign currency option has an expiration date, or maturity date. If the buyer of an option decides to engage in the transaction at the time specified in the option contract, she is said to have "exercised" her option. If the buyer has not exercised her option by the expiration date, the option becomes worthless. An option that can be exercised only at maturity is called a **European option**. An option that can be exercised at the discretion of the buyer at any time between the purchase date and the maturity date is called an **American option**. If an American option is exercised prior to maturity, the person is said to have engaged in **early exercise**.[1]

Strike Prices and Intrinsic Value

The exchange rate in an option contract is called the option's **strike price**, or **exercise price**. In the options markets, investors commonly compare a contract's strike price with the current spot exchange rate. If some revenue could be earned by exercising the option immediately, even though the option holder might not want to exercise it, the option is said to be "in the money." If no revenue could be earned by exercising the option immediately, the option is said to be "out of the money." An "at-the-money" option has a strike price equal to the current exchange rate. If an option is traded on an exchange, the option transaction can also be terminated by reversing the original transaction, as in the futures markets. That is, the buyer of the option can simply sell the contract on the exchange.

The immediate revenue from exercising an option is called the option's **intrinsic value**. Let K be the strike price, and let S be the current spot rate, both in domestic currency per unit of foreign currency. Then, the intrinsic value per unit of a foreign currency option can be represented as

$$\text{Call option: } \max[S - K, 0]$$
$$\text{Put option: } \max[K - S, 0]$$

Here, max denotes the operation that takes the maximum of the two numbers between square brackets. For example, when the spot rate is smaller than the stock price ($S < K$), the call option is not worth exercising immediately, so its intrinsic value is 0.

Now that we have examined the terminology of options, let's look at some concrete examples.

Example 20.2   A Euro Call Option Against Dollars

A euro call option against dollars gives the buyer the right, but not the obligation, to purchase a certain amount of euros, such as €1 million, with dollars at a particular exchange rate, such as $1.20/€. If the spot exchange rate of dollars per euro in the future is greater than the exercise price of $1.20/€, the buyer of the option will exercise the right to purchase euros at the lower contractual price. When exercising the option, the buyer pays the seller of the option

$$(\$1.20/€) \times €1,000,000 = \$1,200,000$$

and the seller delivers the €1,000,000. The buyer of the option can then sell the euros in the spot market for dollars at whatever spot rate, $S(\$/€)$, prevails at that time, generating dollar revenue of

$$S(\$/€) \times €1,000,000$$

Hence, the net dollar revenue generated for the buyer of the option is equal to the difference between the current spot price and the exercise price multiplied by the contractual

---

[1]Note that the terminology describing when options can be exercised—that is, European vs. American— has nothing to do with where the options are traded or how the exchange rates are quoted. The terminology only describes the inability (European) or ability (American) of the buyer to exercise the option prior to maturity.

amount. If the spot rate is \$1.25/€, the net dollar revenue from exercising the euro call option on €1,000,000 is

$$[(\$1.25/€) - (\$1.20/€)] \times €1,000,000 = \$50,000$$

Note that this is the intrinsic value of the option at the time of exercise, $\max[S - K, 0]$, multiplied by the contract size. Remember that the \$50,000 is purely the revenue from exercising the option. It is not the profit to the purchaser of the option because it does not subtract the cost of the option position.

Notice also that the right to buy €1,000,000 with dollars at the exchange rate of \$1.20/€ is equivalent to the right to sell \$1,200,000 for €1,000,000. This option is described as a dollar put option against the euro with contractual amount of \$1,200,000 and a strike price of

$$€1,000,000/\$1,200,000 = 1/(\$1.20/€) = €0.8333/\$$$

These options are the same; they are just described differently.

Also, note that the buyer of the option could accept a payment of \$50,000 from the seller of the option to close out the position rather than take delivery of the €1,000,000 and resell the euros in the spot market. Many option contracts are closed in this way.

Example 20.3   A Yen Put Option Against the Pound

A Japanese yen put against the British pound in a European contract gives the buyer of the option the right, but not the obligation, to sell a certain amount of yen, say ¥100,000,000, for British pounds to the seller of the option at the maturity of the contract. The sale takes place at the contractual exchange rate of pounds per 100 yen, say £0.6494/¥100. If the spot exchange rate of pounds per 100 yen at the exercise date in the future is less than the strike price, the buyer of the option will exercise the right to sell the ¥100,000,000 for pounds at the higher contractual price. When exercising the option, the buyer delivers ¥100,000,000 to the seller of the option, who must pay

$$(£0.6494/¥100) \times ¥100,000,000 = £649,400$$

Suppose that the spot exchange rate at maturity is £0.6000/¥100 yen, which is less than the strike price. Then, the buyer of the option can purchase ¥100,000,000 in the spot foreign exchange market for £600,000 and sell the yen to the person who wrote the put contract. By exercising the option, the buyer of the yen put generates pound revenue equal to the difference between the exercise price of £0.6494/¥100 and the current spot price of £0.6000/¥100 multiplied by ¥100,000,000:

$$[(£0.6494/¥100) - (£0.6000/¥100)] \times ¥100,000,000 = £49,400$$

This corresponds to the intrinsic value of the contract at maturity multiplied by the contract size—that is, Revenue = $\max[K - S, 0] \times$ Contract size. Once again, this is purely the revenue from the option contract; it is not the profit to the purchaser of the option because it does not subtract the original cost of the put option.

Notice, also, that the right to sell ¥100,000,000 for British pounds at the exchange rate of £0.6494/¥100 is equivalent to the right to buy £649,400 with yen at the exchange rate of

$$¥100,000,000/£649,400 = 1/(£0.6494/¥100) = ¥153.99/£$$

This latter option is a British pound call option against the Japanese yen.

Options Trading

Most options are traded by banks, either in the interbank market or as over-the-counter (OTC) transactions with the bank's clients. That is, transactions are done in a dealer network and are not listed on any centralized exchange. Typical OTC options use the European exercise convention. In the OTC market, though, a reasonable request by a corporate customer for any type of option with a particular strike price, maturity date, or other characteristic will be met with a price quoted by a bank. OTC options are also typically written for much larger amounts than exchange-traded options, and a much broader range of currencies is covered.

The cash flows generated by exercise of an OTC option are handled either by exchange of the relevant currency amounts 2 business days after the notification of exercise or, often, by cash settlement. In the latter case, the writer of the option compensates the buyer of the option for the revenue that the option generates when the option ends up in the money.

As with forward contracts, there is a considerable amount of counterparty risk that concerns both bank traders and corporate treasurers. Banks manage their counterparty risks by establishing maximum exposure limits to particular clients, and corporate treasurers must be aware of the risks of dealing with particular banks.

Currency Options on the Philadelphia Stock Exchange

The PHLX primarily trades options on spot currencies versus the U.S. dollar. The contracts are traded in different amounts: AUD50,000, GBP31,250, CAD50,000, EUR62,500, JPY6,250,000, and CHF62,500. The expiration months are March, June, September, and December plus the 2 nearest future months. The last trading day is the Friday before the third Wednesday of the expiring month because the contracts settle on the third Wednesday of the expiration month. Most options are of the American-exercise type, but some European-exercise contracts trade as well. The option quotes are all in U.S. cents per unit (of the foreign currency), except for the yen, where premiums are expressed in 1/100 cent per yen. The PHLX partially owns the Options Clearing Corporation, which serves as the official clearinghouse for options trades on the PHLX. The Options Clearing Corporation also clears options trades for other exchanges, such as the Chicago Board Options Exchange. Because trading volume on the PHLX has dwindled somewhat in recent years, we provide only one example of a quote.

Example 20.4   A Pound Call Option Against Dollars

On December 6, 2004, a British pound call option with a strike price of "194" was quoted for 1.15 cents per pound. Because the strike price is expressed in cents per pound, we can convert it to dollars per pound, or $1.94/£, and a similar transformation of the option price gives $0.0115/£. For a contract size of £31,250, this option would have cost

$$(\$0.015/£) \times £31,250 = \$359.38$$

If the buyer had chosen to exercise the option, the cost of purchasing the £31,250 would have been the strike price multiplied by the contract amount, or

$$(\$1.94/£) \times £31,250 = \$60,625$$

Notice that the option premium (the cost of the option) represents less than 1% of the value of the underlying purchase:

$$(\$359.38/\$60,625) \times 100 = 0.59\%$$

Currency Options on the Chicago Mercantile Exchange

On the CME, the buyer of an option is entitled to the right to buy (for a call) or to sell (for a put) the corresponding CME currency futures contract. Consequently, the contract sizes and expiration months follow those of the IMM futures contracts. Trading closes on the Friday immediately preceding the third Wednesday of the contract month. Exhibit 20.4 contains examples of options quotes from the *Wall Street Journal*.

Wall Street Journal *Options Quotes*

In Exhibit 20.4, the first line associated with the option contract identifies the currency, the contract size, and the units in which option premiums are expressed. For example, the British pound contract size is £62,500, and prices of the options are quoted in U.S. cents per pound. The option prices for most other currencies are also quoted in cents per unit. The exception is the Japanese yen, where the units are cents per 100 yen. The quotations for the strike prices are unusual, and the user should be aware of current futures prices to ensure a correct interpretation of the units. Most currencies, such as the euro, are quoted in 1/100 cent per unit,

Exhibit 20.4 Options on Futures Quotes (*Wall Street Journal*, December 2, 2004)

Currency

Japanese Yen (CME)
12,500,000 yen; cents per 100 yen

Price	Dec (Calls)	Jan (Calls)	Feb (Calls)	Dec (Puts)	Jan (Puts)	Feb (Puts)
9650	1.07	2.11	...	0.14	0.57	...
9700	0.70	1.77	2.12	0.27	0.73	1.08
9750	0.42	1.49	...	0.49	0.95	...
9800	0.22	1.25	...	0.79	1.21	...
9850	0.13	...	1.43	...	...	...
9900	0.08	0.85	1.25	1.65	...	...

Est vol 744 Tu 269 calls 194 puts
Op int Tues 29,896 calls 18,548 puts

Canadian Dollar (CME)
100,000 Can.$, cents per Can.$

Price	Dec (Calls)	Jan (Calls)	Feb (Calls)	Dec (Puts)	Jan (Puts)	Feb (Puts)
8350	1.00	1.52	...	0.05	0.60	...
8400	0.57	1.21	1.51	0.12	0.79	1.09
8450	0.26	0.96	...	0.31	...	...
8500	0.12	0.75	...	0.67	...	...

STRIKE	CALLS-SETTLE		PUTS-SETTLE		
8550	0.05	...	...	1.10	...	...
8600	0.02	0.43	...	...	...	...

Est vol 898 Tu 296 calls 513 puts
Op int Tues 9,404 calls 13,799 puts

British Pound (CME)
62,500 pounds; cents per pound

Price	Dec (Calls)	Jan (Calls)	Feb (Calls)	Dec (Puts)	Jan (Puts)	Feb (Puts)
1910	2.31	2.76	...	0.16	1.71	...
1920	1.53	2.25	...	0.38	2.20	...
1930	0.85	1.80	2.60	0.70	2.75	...
1940	0.44	1.43	2.20	...	...	...
1950	0.20	1.12	...	...	...	...
1960	0.10	0.86	1.56	...	...	...

Est vol 1,991 Tu 1,683 calls 817 puts
Op int Tues 5,937 calls 4,177 puts

Swiss Franc (CME)
125,000 francs; cents per franc

Price	Dec (Calls)	Jan (Calls)	Feb (Calls)	Dec (Puts)	Jan (Puts)	Feb (Puts)
8650	1.27	2.14	...	0.10	0.60	...
8700	0.86	1.80	...	0.19	0.76	...
8750	0.50	1.50	...	0.33	0.96	...
8800	0.29	1.23	...	0.62	1.19	...
8850	0.16	1.01	...	...	...	...
8900	0.09	0.82	...	...	...	...

Est vol 192 Tu 156 calls 15 puts
Op int Tues 3,297 calls 1,796 puts

Euro Fx (CME)
125,000 euros; cents per euro

Price	Dec (Calls)	Jan (Calls)	Feb (Calls)	Dec (Puts)	Jan (Puts)	Feb (Puts)
13200	1.35	2.35	...	0.14	1.04	...
13250	0.96	2.05	...	0.25	1.24	1.82
13300	0.63	1.77	2.38	0.42	1.46	2.07
13350	0.38	1.52	...	...	...	...
13400	0.25	1.30	1.92	1.04	1.99	...
13450	0.14	...	...	...	...	...

Est vol 8,358 Tu 10,635 calls 5,884 puts
Op int Tues 62,337 calls 56,857 puts

Note: © 2004 Reuters.

as the first euro strike price is 13,200, which corresponds to an exchange rate of $1.32/€. But the strike prices for the pound are quoted in 1/10 cent per pound, as 1,910 corresponds to an exchange rate of $1.91/£, and the strike prices for the yen are in 1/1,000 cent per yen, as 9,650 corresponds to an exchange rate of $0.009650/¥.

Each row related to a contract price provides the strike price in the first column followed by three columns of call prices and three columns of put prices. The three columns refer to different expiration months. The December contract is linked to the December futures contract. The January and February options are called *serial options*, and the underlying futures contract is the March 2005 contract. When the February contract expires, April and May serial contracts will be introduced on the June 2005 futures contract. To check your understanding of the information provided in Exhibit 20.4, let's consider the purchase of a yen put option contract because the units are a little tricky.

Example 20.5   A Yen Put Option Against Dollars

Consider a Japanese yen put option contract with a strike price of 9,800 ($0.009800/¥) and a maturity of December, which costs 0.79 U.S. cents per 100 yen. If we want to express the strike price in dollars per yen, we must first divide by 100 to convert from cents per 100 yen to cents per yen, and then we must divide by 100 again to convert from cents per yen to dollars per yen. Hence, the cost of the option goes from 0.79/100 cents per yen to 0.0079 cents per yen, or $0.000079/¥. Consequently, the buyer of the contract would pay

$$(\$0.000079/¥) \times ¥12,500,000 = \$987.50$$

to the seller of the contract at the initiation of the deal. Because the contract is an American-style option, the buyer of the contract would have the right, but not the obligation, to sell ¥12,500,000, or one futures contract, at the strike price of $0.0098/¥ in the futures markets, and the seller would be obligated to purchase the yen futures contract at that price at any time before the December maturity.

Exchange-Listed Currency Warrants

Longer-maturity foreign currency options, called **currency warrants**, are sometimes issued by major corporations and are actively traded on exchanges such as the American Stock Exchange, the London Stock Exchange, and the Australian Stock Exchange. Currency warrants are typically American-style option contracts. Corporate issuers include AT&T Credit Corp., Ford Motor Credit Co., Goldman Sachs, General Electric Credit Corp., the Macquarie Bank Ltd., the Student Loan Marketing Corp. (Sallie Mae), and Xerox Credit Corp. Maturities often exceed 1 year.

Currency warrants allow retail investors and small corporations that are too small to participate in the OTC markets to purchase long-term currency options. In most cases, the original issuer should not be viewed as bearing the implied currency risk. Instead, the issuer is probably hedging in the bank-dominated OTC market. The issuers are effectively buying a foreign exchange option at a wholesale price and selling the option to the public at a retail price. A currency warrant is generally cash settled, with the payoff clearly explained in the prospectus. Let's look at an example.

Example 20.6   Goldman Sachs Put Warrant

Consider a pound put warrant against the euro issued by Goldman Sachs with a maturity date of June 6, 2005, that traded on the London Stock Exchange. The warrant was characterized by a strike price of €1.45/£ and a multiplier of £10. The payoff to the put warrant was specified as

$$\max\left[0, \frac{\text{Strike price} - \text{Spot rate}}{\text{Spot rate}} \right] \times \text{Multiplier}$$

For example, suppose the spot exchange rate was €1.40/£ at maturity. Then, the settlement value for one warrant would have been

$$\frac{(€1.45/£) - (€1.40/£)}{(€1.40/£)} \times £10 = £0.3571$$

Note that, as is true with exchange-traded options, an investor can close out his position at any point by selling the warrant back into the market.

20.4 THE USE OF OPTIONS IN RISK MANAGEMENT

Now that you understand the basics of foreign currency options, we can examine how they can be used to manage foreign exchange risk. The classic use of a foreign currency option contract as a hedging device arises in a bidding situation.

A Bidding Situation at Bagwell Construction

Suppose that Bagwell Construction, a U.S. company, wants to bid on the construction of a new office building in Tokyo. The Japanese developer has instructed all interested parties to submit their yen-denominated bids by June 30. Because the bids are complex contracts involving many more parameters than just the overall yen price of the contract, it will take the Japanese developer a month to evaluate the bids, and the winner will not be announced until July 31.

Bagwell management has determined that it can do the construction in Tokyo for $80,000,000, which will be paid out more or less evenly over the course of a year. If the firm gets the contract, it will receive yen revenue from the Japanese developer in five equal installments. There will be an initial yen payment on July 31, followed by four quarterly installments.

The Transaction Risk

By bidding a fixed amount of yen to do this project, Bagwell Construction incurs transaction foreign exchange risk. If Bagwell gets the project and the yen weakens relative to the dollar, the contractual yen revenue will purchase fewer dollars in the future. Notice that as soon as Bagwell bids on the contract, it acquires a transaction exposure. If the firm does nothing to hedge its contingent yen asset exposure during the time that the contracts are being evaluated and the yen weakens relative to the dollar, Bagwell's entire dollar profit could be eliminated before it even begins construction. If its strategy is to get the contract and then hedge, it could be too late.

The Problem with a Forward Hedge

Can Bagwell Construction hedge this risk with a forward contract? If Bagwell sells yen forward, it acquires an uncontingent yen liability. No matter what happens in 30 days, Bagwell will have to sell a specific amount of yen to the bank. Everything will be fine if Bagwell gets the contract. But what would happen if Bagwell sells yen forward and then fails to win the construction contract?

If the company does not get the construction job, it will still have to buy yen to fulfill the uncontingent commitment of the forward contract. If the yen strengthens such that the dollar price of yen in the spot market is higher than the contractual forward price, Bagwell will lose money because it will cost more dollars in the spot market to buy the yen to be delivered on the forward contact than the amount of dollars that the company will receive from the bank. Hence, if the yen strengthens versus the dollar, Bagwell will lose money.

The Options Solution

Foreign exchange options provide a much better solution to Bagwell's problem of hedging in June prior to the resolution of the contract because options provide the purchaser with a contingent claim. How would an option contract work, and which option should be used?

Because Bagwell ultimately wants to sell the yen it will be paid if it gets the contract, the company should hedge by buying a yen put against the dollar. The yen put gives the buyer the right, but not the obligation, to sell yen for dollars at the strike price. Then, if Bagwell gets the contract and the yen has weakened relative to the dollar, the loss of value on the construction contract is offset by a gain in the value of the yen put. The company can sell yen from the construction contract at the exercise price, which is higher than the dollar price of yen in the spot market.

If Bagwell does not win the contract, the value of the yen put is the maximum that the firm can lose. But if at the maturity of the option, the yen has weakened relative to the dollar, the right to sell yen at a high dollar price will be valuable. Bagwell will consequently be able to recoup some of the premium that was initially paid for the option. Purchasing the option thus provides insurance against transaction risk.

Using Options to Hedge Transaction Risk

We now turn to the use of options in managing transaction exchange risk. While forwards and futures can be used, options allow the firm to hedge while retaining some of the upside potential from favorable exchange rate changes. Our next example considers an exporting situation.

Example 20.7 Exporting Pharmaceutical Products from the United States to the United Kingdom

Suppose it is Thursday, September 16. Pfimerc, an exporter of pharmaceutical products from the United States to the United Kingdom, has an account receivable of £500,000 due on Wednesday, October 20. The following data are available:

Spot rate (U.S. cents per British pound): 153.22
34-day forward rate (U.S. cents per British pound): 152.92
U.S. dollar 34-day interest rate: 3.75% p.a.
British pound 34-day interest rate: 6.65% p.a.
Option data for October contracts in ¢/£:

Strike	Call Prices	Put Prices
150.0	4.14	1.22
152.5	2.70	2.28
155.0	1.50	3.57

How might Pfimerc hedge this transaction using foreign currency options?

The first thing to determine is the type of option that provides an effective hedge. Because Pfimerc will be receiving British pounds, the transaction risk is that the pound will weaken relative to the dollar. If the company does nothing to hedge, it could experience a large loss when it sells the £500,000 in the spot market on October 18. The option that provides a hedge is the one that gives Pfimerc the right, but not the obligation, to sell pounds at a contractual strike price of dollars per pound. This is a pound put option.

Because Pfimerc knows the date on which it wants to sell pounds and the amount of pounds it wants to sell, the appropriate hedge would be a European put option with 34 days until maturity. Let's work with the October pound put option with a strike price of 152.5¢/£. The cost per unit of this contract is 2.28¢/£ or $0.0228/£.

Because the pound contract size is £31,250, Pfimerc must buy 16 contracts $(16 \times £31,250 = £500,000)$ to hedge the pound receivable. Hence, as the buyer of the contracts, it must pay today

$$16 \times £31,250 \times (\$0.0228/£) = \$11,400$$

If, at maturity in October, the dollar value of the pound falls below the strike price of $1.5250/£, Pfimerc will exercise the option to sell £500,000 at that price. Consequently, the minimum October revenue that Pfimerc will receive is

$$£500,000 \times \$1.5250/£ = \$762,500, \text{ if } S(t+32) \leq \$1.5250/£$$

When the future spot rate exceeds the strike price, the company will sell its pounds in the future spot market, and its revenue will be

$$£500,000 \times S(t+32) > \$762,500, \text{ if } S(t+32) > \$1.5250/£$$

Whether Pfimerc exercises the option or not, if it hedges with put options, it must subtract the October value of the cost of the puts that was paid in September from its October revenue to get a net revenue figure. This opportunity cost of purchasing the option is therefore

$$[\$11,400 \times (1 + i(\$))] = [\$11,400 \times (1.0035)] = \$11,439.90$$

where the interest factor is $(3.75/100)(34/360) = 0.0035$. Hence, the minimum net revenue that Pfimerc receives in October if it hedges with puts is

$$\$762,500 - \$11,439.90 = \$751,060.10$$

On a cents-per-pound basis, the October cost of the put option is

$$(2.28¢/£) \times (1.0035) = 2.29¢/£$$

Exhibit 20.5 summarizes the transaction risk exposure related to various strategies for selling British pounds. The horizontal axis shows the possible realizations of the future spot exchange rates expressed in U.S. cents per pound. The vertical axis measures the net revenues Pfimerc will receive (also in cents per pound) when it follows a particular strategy for selling pounds for dollars. The three different lines represent its net revenues as functions of the realizations of the future exchange rate.

The 45-degree line represents the unhedged strategy. If Pfimerc chooses not to hedge and must sell pounds for dollars in the future spot market, its revenue will increase one for one with pound appreciation. But its revenue will also be lower one for one with any pound depreciation. Pfimerc's risk of loss is therefore unlimited.

The horizontal line in Exhibit 20.5 represents the strategy of hedging with a forward contract. If Pfimerc sells pounds forward at $1.5292/£, its October revenue is

$$(\$1.5292/£) \times £500,000 = \$764,600$$

Exhibit 20.5 Hedging Pound Revenues

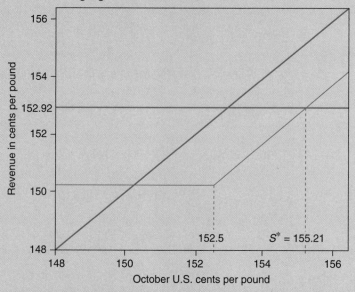

Notes: The horizontal axis presents different possible future exchange rates. The vertical axis represents the revenue in cents per pound from three different strategies. The horizontal line reflects the revenue implied by a forward contract, which is not dependent on the future exchange rate. The upward-sloping line is the 45-degree line and represents the unhedged strategy: The revenue equals the future exchange rate. The "hockey stick" line represents the payoff from hedging the receivable with a put option.

On a cents-per-pound basis, Pfimerc's revenue will be the same (equal to the forward rate of 152.92¢/£) no matter what spot exchange rate is realized in the future.

The kinked line (shaped like a hockey stick) in Exhibit 20.5 represents the net revenue from the strategy of buying the 152.5 October pound put. The minimum net revenue is

$$152.50¢/£ - 2.29¢/£ = 150.21¢/£$$

This occurs when Pfimerc exercises its put contracts—that is, when the future spot rate is less than or equal to 152.50¢/£. Notice that the option hedge provides a floor on Pfimerc's revenue, while allowing it to participate in any strengthening of the pound relative to the dollar.

Notice also that the net revenue from the option hedge is below the net revenue from the forward hedge when the exchange rate in the future is below a certain exchange rate, denoted $S^*(¢/£)$ in Exhibit 20.5. If the future spot rate is greater than S^*, the net revenue from the option hedge exceeds the revenue from the forward hedge. This is an example of no-free-lunch economics. If the option hedge puts a floor on your net revenue, but it allows you to participate in a possible strengthening of the pound, which increases your net revenue, the floor must be below the forward rate. Otherwise, the option strategy would strictly dominate the forward strategy.

We can determine the value of $S^*(¢/£)$ by equating the two net revenues on a cents-per-pound basis. The net revenue from the option hedge is $S^*(¢/£) - 2.29¢/£$, and the revenue from the forward hedge is 152.92¢/£. Therefore, we find that S^* is

$$S^*(¢/£) - 2.29¢/£ = 152.92¢/£$$
$$S^*(¢/£) = 155.21¢/£$$

Because the current spot rate is 153.22¢/£, the pound must strengthen relative to the dollar by 1.30%—that is, to 155.21¢/£—before the hedging with puts provides a higher net revenue than the forward hedge.

So should Pfimerc use the option strategy or the forward hedge strategy? To decide, the company must calculate the probability that the exchange rate in the future will exceed $S^*(¢/£)$. We will discuss how this question is answered later in the chapter.

Example 20.8 Importing Watches to the United States from Switzerland

Consider the case of an importer who must pay in the exporter's currency. Here, the importer will use call options on the exporter's currency to hedge.

Suppose it is Thursday, September 16, and Orlodge, an importer of Swiss watches to the United States, has an account payable of CHF750,000 due on Wednesday, December 15. The following data are available:

Spot rate: 71.42¢/CHF
90-day forward rate: 71.14¢/CHF
U.S. dollar 90-day interest rate: 3.75% p.a.
Swiss franc 90-day interest rate: 5.33% p.a.
Option data for December contracts (¢/CHF):

Strike	Call	Put
70	2.55	1.42
72	1.55	2.40

How might you hedge this transaction using foreign currency options?

Orlodge must first determine the type of option that provides a hedge. Because Orlodge will be paying Swiss francs in 90 days, the transaction risk is that the Swiss franc will strengthen versus the dollar, which increases the cost of the CHF750,000. To hedge, Orlodge should buy the option that gives it the right, but not the obligation, to buy Swiss francs at a strike price of dollars per Swiss franc. This is a Swiss franc call option.

Because Orlodge knows the date on which it wants to buy Swiss francs and the amount of Swiss francs it wants to buy, the appropriate hedge is a European call option with 90 days until maturity. Let's work with the December Swiss franc call option with a strike price of 72¢/CHF. The cost per unit of this contract is 1.55¢/CHF, or $0.0155/CHF.

Because the Swiss franc option size is CHF62,500, Orlodge must buy 12 contracts (12 × CHF62,500 = CHF750,000). Hence, as the buyer of the contracts, Orlodge must pay today

$$12 \times CHF62,500 \times \$0.0155/CHF = \$11,625$$

If, at maturity in December, the dollar value of the Swiss franc is greater than or equal to the strike price of $0.7200/CHF, Orlodge will exercise its option to buy CHF750,000 at that price. Consequently, Orlodge's maximum payment is

$$CHF750,000 \times \$0.7200/CHF = \$540,000, \text{ if } S(t+88) \geq (\$0.7200/CHF)$$

At all exchange rates less than \$0.7200/CHF, Orlodge will buy its francs in the spot market, and its cost will be

$$CHF750{,}000 \times S(t{+}88) < \$540{,}000, \text{ if } S(t{+}88) < (\$0.7200/CHF)$$

Whether Orlodge exercises its option or not, though, if it hedges with call options, it must add the December value of the September cost of the call options to the December cost of the Swiss francs to get a total cost figure. This opportunity cost is

$$\$11{,}625 \times [1 + i(\$)] = \$11{,}625 \times (1.0094) = \$11{,}734.28$$

where the interest factor is $(3.75/100)(90/360) = 0.0094$. Hence, Orlodge's maximum December total if it hedges with call options is

$$\$540{,}000 + \$11{,}734.28 = \$551{,}734.28$$

In terms of cents per Swiss franc, the December cost of the call option is

$$(1.55¢/CHF) \times (1.0094) = 1.56¢/CHF$$

Exhibit 20.6 has cents per Swiss franc on the horizontal axis and the cost in cents per Swiss franc on the vertical axis. The different lines now represent the cost in cents per Swiss franc of different strategies, depending on the realization of the future exchange rates. As before, the 45-degree line represents the unhedged strategy.

Exhibit 20.6 Hedging Swiss Franc Costs

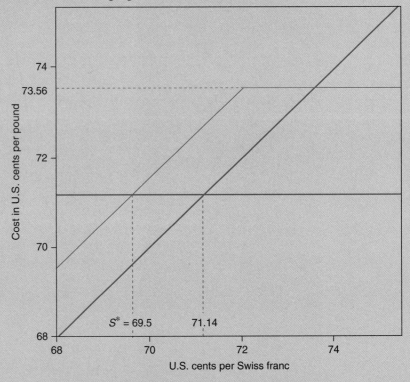

Notes: The horizontal axis presents different possible future exchange rates. The vertical axis represents the costs in cents per Swiss franc from three different strategies. The horizontal line reflects the cost implied by a forward contract, which is not dependent on the future exchange rate. The upward-sloping line is the 45-degree line and represents the unhedged strategy: The cost equals the future exchange rate. The inverted "hockey stick" line represents the cost from hedging the payable with a call option.

If Orlodge chooses not to hedge, it must buy its Swiss francs with dollars in the future spot market. Its cost will increase one for one with any strengthening of the Swiss franc versus the dollar, but its cost will also be lower, one for one, with any weakening of the Swiss franc. Its risk of loss is therefore unlimited.

The horizontal line in Exhibit 20.6 represents hedging with a forward contract. If Orlodge buys Swiss francs forward at $0.7114/CHF, its December cost is

$$\$0.7114/\text{CHF} \times \text{CHF750,000} = \$533,550$$

On a cents-per-franc basis, Orlodge's cost will be 71.14¢/CHF no matter what spot exchange rate is realized in the future.

The kinked line (shaped like an inverted hockey stick) in Exhibit 20.6 represents the total cost of hedging with the 72 December Swiss franc call options. The maximum total cost is

$$72.00¢/\text{CHF} + 1.56¢/\text{CHF} = 73.56¢/\text{CHF}$$

This cost arises when Orlodge exercises its call options—that is, when the future spot rate in December is greater than or equal to 72.00¢/CHF.

Notice that the option hedge provides a ceiling on Orlodge's costs, while allowing it to participate in any strengthening of the dollar relative to the Swiss franc, which can reduce the company's costs. Notice also that the total cost from the option hedge is above the total cost from the forward hedge whenever the exchange rate in the future is above $S^*(¢/\text{CHF})$. If the future spot rate is less than S^*, the total cost from the option hedge is less than the cost from the forward hedge. This is another example of no-free-lunch economics: If the call option hedge puts a ceiling on your total cost, but it allows you to participate in a possible strengthening of the dollar that can reduce your costs, the ceiling must be above the forward rate.

We can determine the value of S^* by equating the total costs of the two hedges on a cents-per-franc basis. The total cost from the option hedge is $[S^*(¢/\text{CHF}) + 1.56¢/\text{CHF}]$, and the cost from the forward hedge is 71.14¢/CHF. Therefore,

$$S^*(¢/\text{CHF}) + 1.56¢/\text{CHF} = 71.14¢/\text{CHF}$$

or

$$S^*(¢/\text{CHF}) = 69.58¢/\text{CHF}$$

Because the current spot rate is 71.42¢/CHF, the Swiss franc must weaken by 2.58% relative to the dollar, to 69.58¢/CHF, before the call option contract provides a lower cost than the forward hedge.

As Orlodge considers different strategies for dealing with the Swiss franc payable, including alternative option strategies or the forward hedge, the firm should attempt to calculate the probability that the future spot rate will be less than $S^*(¢/\text{CHF})$. We will discuss this in the next section, which compares option hedges to the purchase of insurance.

Hedging with Options as Buying Insurance

In the two previous examples, option strategies hedge transaction exchange risks. Here, we consider how hedging with options is analogous to purchasing insurance. Before we do so, we summarize more generally how to hedge foreign currency receivables and payables with forward, futures, and option contracts. Exhibit 20.7 gives an overview of this discussion. It also includes some speculative option strategies that we will discuss later.

Exhibit 20.7 Hedging and Speculating Strategies

	Underlying Transaction	
	Foreign Currency Receivable	**Foreign Currency Payable**
Forward hedge (or futures hedge)	Sell forward (Go short)	Buy forward (Go long)
Option hedge	Buy a put Establishes a revenue floor of $K - (1 + i)P$	Buy a call Establishes a cost ceiling of $K + (1 + i)C$
Option speculation	Sell a call Imposes a revenue ceiling of $K + (1 + i)C$ but allows unlimited risk	Sell a put Imposes a liability floor of $K - (1 + i)P$ but allows unlimited risk

Notes: K is the strike price, C is the call option premium, P is the put option premium, and i is the appropriate de-annualized interest rate factor.

Hedging Foreign Currency Risk with Forwards and Options

Exporters who price in foreign currency generate foreign currency revenues. The appropriate forward hedge in this case is to sell the foreign currency receivable in the forward market. The appropriate option hedge is to buy a foreign currency put contract. The put contract gives you the right, but not the obligation, to sell the foreign currency revenue at the strike price of domestic currency per foreign currency, which establishes a floor on your net revenue equal to the strike price minus the future value of the option premium.

If you buy a put option, you are not contractually committed to sell the foreign currency that you will receive through that option. You retain the right to sell the foreign currency in the spot market if the domestic currency value of the foreign currency exceeds the strike price. This allows your net revenue to exceed the floor established by the put option and to increase as the foreign currency strengthens. If the foreign currency strengthens sufficiently, your net domestic currency revenue from the option hedge can substantially exceed the revenue from the forward hedge. Nevertheless, because some money is paid up front, the net revenue from the option hedge remains less than the revenue that would have been generated if the option contract had not been purchased. Of course, this can only be known *ex post*—that is, after the realization of future uncertain exchange rates. But, of course, the strategy must be chosen first.

Importers often generate foreign currency costs. The appropriate forward hedge in this case is to buy the foreign currency needed to pay the liability in the forward market. The appropriate option hedge is to buy a **foreign currency call option** contract. This gives you the right, but not the obligation, to buy the foreign currency at the strike price, which places a ceiling on your total costs. The ceiling on your costs is the strike price plus the future value of the option premium.

When you buy a call option, you retain the right to buy foreign currency in the spot market if the domestic currency value of the foreign currency is less than the strike price. This allows your costs to fall below the ceiling, and there is some amount of strengthening of the domestic currency that is required before the cost from the option strategy is less than the cost from the forward hedge. If the domestic currency strengthens a lot, the costs from the option hedge can be substantially less than the costs from the forward hedge. But your total costs can never be less than the costs that would have been generated if the option contract had not been purchased. Of course, again, this can only be known *ex post*, and, unfortunately, you must choose your strategy first.

Options as Insurance Contracts

How are the examples just discussed like insurance policies? Consider the purchase of fire insurance for a home. A homeowner pays annual premiums for insurance that provides a certain amount of coverage in the event of a fire. The quality of the coverage can be varied.

The more of the home's value that the homeowner wants to protect, the more costly is the fire insurance. Expensive insurance completely replaces the home if it is destroyed by fire, and less expensive policies pay some fraction of the loss.

Clearly, the homeowner puts a ceiling on his possible losses by purchasing fire insurance. If there is a fire, the homeowner can repair the home, and the insurance company pays some part of the bill. But, suppose the homeowner lives in the home for 10 years, and no fires occur. *Ex post*, the homeowner will not have needed fire insurance, but he will have paid 10 years of insurance premiums. The homeowner will also have captured the appreciation in the home's value. Nevertheless, the homeowner will not be as well off as he would have been without purchasing the insurance. Of course, this does not mean that purchasing the insurance was a bad idea. It just means that the homeowner did not need the insurance when he lived in the home.

With foreign currency transaction exposures, purchasing the right type of option is like purchasing an insurance policy. Take Example 20.7, in which Pfimerc has a British pound receivable. A weakening of the pound is like a fire because it destroys part of the value of Pfimerc's pound asset. By contracting in advance with an option, some of the value is replaced. That is, if Pfimerc purchases a put option, it places a floor on the dollar value of its pound receivable, even if the pound depreciates. If, on the other hand, the pound strengthens, that is like an appreciation of the value of the home without a fire. Pfimerc ignores the put option, which gives it the right to sell pounds at a low dollar price, and it sells the pounds in the spot market instead. If no fire occurs, the insurance policy that protected the home's value is irrelevant.

Changing the Quality of the Insurance Policy

Can we carry the fire insurance analogy further? If a homeowner can purchase different qualities of fire insurance at different prices, is there a range of insurance quality when it comes to hedging foreign exchange risk?

Let's first consider hedging a foreign currency receivable with a put option. High-quality insurance in this context means that the floor we create on our domestic currency revenue is as high as possible. As we discussed, the floor is first of all directly related to the strike price of the put option. The higher the strike price of the option, the less the foreign currency must depreciate before we can exercise the option and cut our losses. Just as insurance that covers more losses is more expensive, put options with higher strike prices are more expensive. We discuss valuation issues in more detail in the next section.

Similarly, high-quality insurance in the context of a foreign currency liability means that we would like to make the ceiling on our cost of the foreign currency as low as possible. This can be accomplished by buying call options with lower strike prices. Again, there is a trade-off because these options will be more expensive. To fully understand this, let's work through a numeric example.

Example 20.9   Purchasing Better, but More Expensive, Insurance

In Example 20.8, Orlodge was importing Swiss watches, and we worked with a December Swiss franc European call option with a strike price of 72¢ per Swiss franc. The cost to hedge the Swiss franc liability was 1.55¢/CHF. Alternatively, we could choose a December call option with a strike price of 70¢/CHF that costs 2.55¢/CHF. This more expensive "insurance" should provide a lower ceiling on the total Swiss franc cost. The trade-off will be that the exchange rate, $S^*(¢/CHF)$, at which Orlodge has the same cost as the forward hedge will now be lower. Hence, the probability of having lower costs than the forward hedge will be lower because Orlodge gets lower costs only if the exchange rate in the future is less than this new S^*.

Exhibit 20.8 Alternative Option Hedges

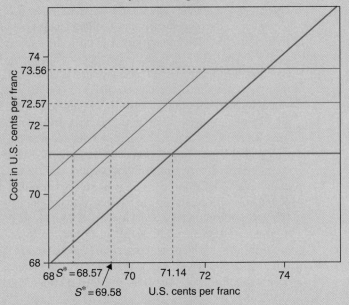

Notes: The horizontal axis represents the future exchange rate in cents per Swiss franc. The vertical axis represents the cost in cents per Swiss franc of various strategies for dealing with a Swiss franc liability. The horizontal line shows that a forward hedge locks in a cost per Swiss franc of 71.14 cents. The 45-degree line represents the unhedged strategy, and the two inverted "hockey stick" lines represent the *ex post* costs of two option strategies, struck at different strike prices.

Exhibit 20.8 presents the cost diagrams for the two option strategies with strike prices of 70¢/CHF and 72¢/CHF. The initial cost of the insurance from the call option with the lower strike price is

$$CHF750,500 \times (\$0.0255/CHF) = \$19,125$$

compared to the \$11,625 in Example 20.8. At maturity in December, if the dollar value of the Swiss franc is greater than or equal to the strike price of \$0.70/CHF, Orlodge will exercise its option to buy CHF750,000 at that price. Consequently, the maximum that Orlodge will pay in December is

$$CHF750,000 \times \$0.70/CHF = \$525,000, \text{ if } S(t+88) = \$0.70/CHF$$

At all exchange rates less than \$0.70/CHF, Orlodge will buy Swiss francs in the spot market, and its cost will be

$$CHF750,000 \times S(t+88) < \$525,000, \text{ if } S(t+88) < \$0.70/CHF$$

Of course, Orlodge must add the December value of the cost of the call options that was paid in September to the December cost of the Swiss francs to get a total cost figure. This opportunity cost is

$$[\$19,125 \times 1.0094] = \$19,304.78$$

where the interest factor is $(3.75/100)(90/360) = 0.0094$. Hence, the maximum total cost that Orlodge will pay in December if it hedges with call options is

$$\$525,000 + \$19,304.78 = \$544,304.78$$

In Example 20.8, the corresponding figure is $551,734.28. Hence, Orlodge has improved the quality of its insurance because its total cost is now lower in the bad states of the world in which the dollar weakens relative to the Swiss franc.

On a cents-per-franc basis, the December cost of the call option with a strike price of 70¢/CHF is

$$2.55¢/CHF \times 1.0094 = 2.57¢/CHF$$

Hence, the total cost of the liability per unit of foreign currency is, at most,

$$70¢/CHF + 2.57¢/CHF = 72.57¢/CHF$$

We can again determine the value of $S^*(¢/CHF)$ that equates the cost of the option hedge to the cost of the forward hedge. The total cost from the option hedge is $S^*(¢/CHF) + 2.57¢/CHF$, and the cost from the forward hedge is 71.14¢/CHF. Therefore,

$$S^*(¢/CHF) + 2.57¢/CHF = 71.14¢/CHF$$

in which case we find

$$S^*(¢/CHF) = 68.57¢/CHF$$

This is less than the S^* of 69.58¢/CHF in Example 20.8. With more expensive insurance, more strengthening of the dollar relative to the Swiss franc must occur before Orlodge's cost is lower than the cost of the forward hedge. Because the current spot rate is 71.42¢/CHF, the Swiss franc must weaken by 3.99%, to 68.57¢/CHF, before the call option contract with a strike price of 70¢/CHF provides a lower total cost than the forward hedge.

Speculating with Options

Examples 20.7 and 20.8 discuss hedging transaction exchange risk with options. Choosing the right strategy in these examples is tantamount to purchasing insurance. Example 20.7 places a floor on the firm's foreign currency revenues, and Example 20.8 places a ceiling on the firm's foreign currency costs. Sometimes, firms think that this insurance is too expensive. If it is, a firm can profit from a speculative strategy. But the firm must understand that speculating does not protect the firm's revenues from potential losses or its costs from potential increases due to exchange rate changes.

If option insurance seems too costly, rather than purchase insurance, you can use the option markets to sell insurance. If purchasing a put provides insurance when you have a foreign currency receivable, then selling a call allows you to sell the foreign currency, either to the purchaser of the call option or in the spot market, and your revenue is enhanced by the option premium. Of course, you are now selling insurance to someone who may want to exercise his or her option.

Similarly, if purchasing a call seems too expensive when hedging a foreign currency liability, you might want to write a put. The put obligates you to buy the foreign currency at the strike price when the put buyer exercises that option to sell foreign currency to you. Once again, though, the option premium provides you with revenue that lowers the effective cost of your foreign currency liability.

Speculating on Foreign Currency Receivables

Let's illustrate these speculative strategies with the foreign currency receivable in Example 20.7. Suppose Pfimerc is scheduled to receive £500,000 in 34 days. The pound put option provides the hedge: It gives Pfimerc the right, but not the obligation, to sell pounds at a contractual strike price of dollars per pound. But suppose this put option seems expensive. Would a different option strategy allow Pfimerc to sell pounds for dollars and have the potential to generate more dollar revenue?

Pfimerc could achieve this objective by selling someone the right, but not the obligation, to buy pounds from it in exchange for dollars. This option describes a pound call option against the dollar. Because Pfimerc knows the date on which it wants to sell pounds and the amount of pounds it wants to sell, it could sell someone a European pound call option against the dollar with 34 days until maturity. When Pfimerc sells the pound call option, it generates dollar revenue in September, and this revenue enhances its dollar return in the future.

This strategy is speculative, though, because Pfimerc loses protection against downside risk. If the pound weakens substantially relative to the dollar, the purchaser of the pound call option from Pfimerc will find it to be worthless. Pfimerc will be forced to sell its pounds in the spot market precisely when the dollar value of those pounds is low. Also, its ability to participate in a strengthening of the pound versus the dollar is limited.

Suppose that at maturity the dollar–pound spot rate is above the exercise price of the call option contract. The purchaser of Pfimerc's call option will consequently want to buy pounds at the exercise price. Pfimerc will therefore have to sell the pounds at the exercise price. The company will then miss participating in any further strengthening of the pound relative to the dollar. Nevertheless, Pfimerc does take in revenue for selling the call options, and if options are expensive, this revenue can be substantial.

Example 20.10   Speculating on British Pound Receivables

To see how speculating receivables works with actual data, let's examine the options on British pounds we used before. The October British pound call option with a strike price of 155¢/£ costs 1.50¢/£, or $0.015/£. Now consider the October value of the revenue Pfimerc gets from selling the call option in September. The buyer of the call options will have paid

$$£500,000 \times \$0.0150/£ = \$7,500$$

to Pfimerc in September. If, at the maturity in October, the dollar value of the pound is above the strike price of $1.55/£, Pfimerc will have to sell £500,000 to the option buyer, who will want to exercise the option to buy pounds at the strike price. Pfimerc's maximum revenue in October will therefore be

$$£500,000 \times \$1.55/£ = \$775,000, \text{ if } S(t+32) > \$1.55/£$$

At all exchange rates less than or equal to $1.55/£, the option Pfimerc sold will be worthless, so Pfimerc will sell its pounds in the spot market instead. Its revenue in October will then be

$$£500,000 \times S(t+32) = \$775,000, \text{ if } S(t+32) = \$1.55/£$$

In both cases, though, Pfimerc can add the October value of the September revenue from the option sale to get net revenue. This additional revenue is

$$\$7,500 \times (1 + i(\$)) = \$7,500 \times 1.0035 = \$7,526.25$$

where the interest factor is $(3.75/100)(34/360) = 0.0035$. Hence, the maximum net revenue that Pfimerc receives in October if it sells the call option is

$$\$775,000 + \$7,526.25 = \$782,526.25$$

On a cents-per-pound basis, the additional October revenue is

$$1.50¢/£ \times 1.0035 = 1.51¢/£$$

This is the amount of extra revenue on a cents-per-pound basis that Pfimerc can use to offset any weakening of the pound. To find the future spot exchange rate, $S^*(¢/£)$, at which Pfimerc has the same revenue as the forward rate, we must equate the revenue from the two strategies:

$$S^*(¢/£) + 1.51¢/£ = 152.92¢/£$$
$$S^*(¢/£) = 151.41¢/£$$

Because the current spot exchange rate is $153.22¢/£$, the pound would have to weaken by 1.18% over the next 34 days before this strategy generated lower revenue than the forward hedge. Exhibit 20.9 illustrates the revenue payoff for this speculative strategy.

Notice that there is a range of values of future spot rates over which this speculative strategy has the highest net revenue. On a cents-per-pound basis, maximum revenue from selling the option equals the strike price of $155¢/£$ plus the $1.51¢/£$. Consequently, the spot exchange rate in the future must be

$$155¢/£ + 1.51¢/£ = 156.51¢/£$$

before the unhedged strategy provides more revenue *ex post* than the speculative option strategy. This requires an appreciation of the pound of 2.15% over the course of 34 days. If you think that the volatility of the exchange rate is not very large, the probability of it reaching this value may not be very large.

Exhibit 20.9 Speculating with Pound Revenue

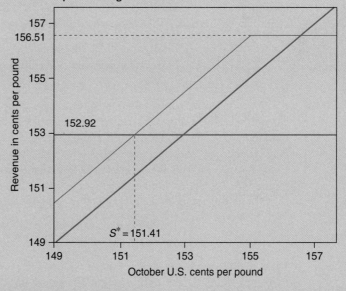

Notes: The horizontal axis represents the future exchange rate in cents per pound. The vertical axis represents the revenue in cents per pound of various strategies for selling a pound asset. The horizontal line shows that a forward hedge locks in revenue of 152.92 cents. The 45-degree line represents the unhedged strategy, and the inverted "hockey stick" line represents the *ex post* revenue from the strategy of selling a call option with a strike price of 155.

Speculating on Foreign Currency Liabilities

Exhibit 20.7 summarizes how the speculative strategies work. In the case of a foreign currency liability, you must buy foreign currency. Selling someone a **foreign currency put option** forces you to buy the foreign currency at the strike price when the buyer of the option finds it advantageous to sell foreign currency to you—that is, when the exchange rate of domestic currency per foreign currency is lower than the strike price. If the exchange rate ends up higher than the strike price, the option expires worthless, and you must buy the foreign currency in the spot market, exactly when it is relatively expensive. However, whatever happens, writing the option yields revenue, and this strategy may be advantageous when the exchange rate is not anticipated to move very far from its current value.

Options Valuation

We saw that the buyer of an option pays a premium to the seller of the option. How expensive is this type of contract? The purpose of this section is to give you an intuitive idea about how options are valued.

The actual formal valuation of options is beyond the scope of this book because it is quite mathematically complex. The first formal option pricing model was written in the early 1970s by the economists Fischer Black and Myron Scholes (1973). Their paper revolutionized the financial industry, and it was no surprise when Scholes and Robert Merton, who wrote similarly seminal articles on option pricing, earned a Nobel Prize for their efforts in 1997. Unfortunately, Fischer Black died in 1995 and was therefore ineligible to receive the prize. In 1983, Mark Garman and Stephen Kolhagen extended the Black–Scholes option pricing formula to value foreign currency options.

The Intrinsic Value of an Option

When we introduced option terminology, we briefly explained the intrinsic value of an option. Recall that the intrinsic value of an American option is the return, or revenue, generated from the immediate exercise of the option. Intrinsic value is another way of describing whether an option is in the money, at the money, or out of the money. So, if K is the strike price of a euro call option against the dollar, and S is the current spot exchange rate, both expressed in \$/€, then

$$\text{Intrinsic value of the euro call} = S - K, \text{ if } S > K$$
$$\text{Intrinsic value of the euro call} = 0, \text{ if } S \leq K$$

Because the buyer of the call option must pay the seller of the option for the right to exercise it, the option's price (or its value) must be at least as great as the intrinsic value of the option. The intrinsic value of a call is positive if the strike price is below the current spot exchange rate because the buyer of the option could exercise the right to buy pounds at K and then sell euros in the spot market for the higher price S. If the strike price is higher than the spot rate, immediately exercising the option would result in a loss of money, so the intrinsic value of the option is 0. The option is out of the money.

For an American-style euro put option, we have the following relationships:

$$\text{Intrinsic value of the euro put} = K - S, \text{ if } S < K$$
$$\text{Intrinsic value of the euro put} = 0, \text{ if } S \geq K$$

Once again, because the buyer of the put option must pay the seller of the option for the right to exercise it, the option's price (or its value) must be at least as great as the intrinsic value of the option. The intrinsic value of a put is positive if the put's strike price is greater than the current exchange rate because the buyer of the option could exercise her right to sell euros at K, having bought euros in the spot market for the lower price S. If the strike price is lower than the spot rate, immediately exercising the option would result in a loss of money. Therefore, the option's intrinsic value is 0. The option is out of the money.

The Time Value of an Option

The **time value** of an option is the current price or value of the option minus its intrinsic value:

$$\text{Time value of an option} = \text{Option price} - \text{Intrinsic value}$$

To understand what creates time value, think about a European call option—that is, an option that can only be exercised at maturity. To be concrete, let's think of a euro call option against dollars with a maturity of 90 days.

When we introduced forward contracts in Chapter 3, we discussed the probability distribution of future spot exchange rates. Based on our information today, we do not know exactly what the exchange rate of dollars per euros will be in 90 days. Hence, we express our ignorance with a probability distribution, as in Exhibit 20.10. To derive Exhibit 20.10, we must think of the possible states of the world that can lead to euro depreciation and euro appreciation versus the dollar, and we must weigh these different events with their probabilities. When we have done this for all possible events, we have a probability distribution of future possible spot exchange rates of dollars per euro. Exhibit 20.10 indicates that the expected value of the dollar–euro rate is $1.25/€ and that values between $1.30/€ and $1.40/€ are fairly likely, while values less than $1.05/€ and greater than $1.45/€ are possible but unlikely to happen.

A European call option will be valuable to the buyer of the option at maturity only if the spot exchange rate of dollars per euro in the future is greater than the exercise price of the option. Only then are dollars generated by exercising the option to buy euros at the strike price, K, and then selling the euros in the spot market. The dollar revenue is therefore $S(t+90) - K$, if this is positive, and it is 0 otherwise. Hence, we can write that for a European option, the euro call option price at time t, $C(t)$, is

$$C(t) = \text{Value at time } t \text{ of } \max[0, S(t+90) - K]$$

To determine the value of an option, we must take the present value of the option payoff at the maturity of the contract. This turns out to be a fairly nontrivial problem. At this point, it is sufficient to simply understand the intuition of what gives options value.

Exhibit 20.10 Probability Distribution of Future USD/EUR

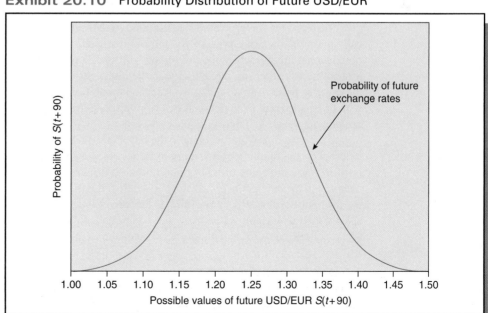

Exhibit 20.11 Probabilities of Exercising Alternative Options

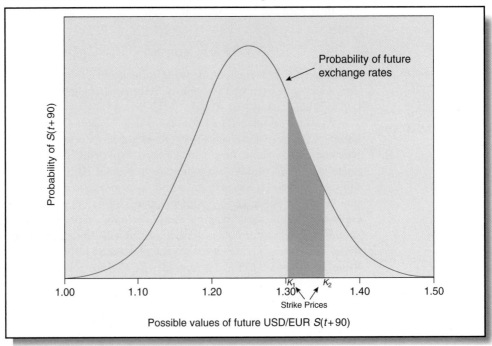

Increasing the Exercise Price

If we hold constant the maturity date of an option and increase its exercise price, what happens to the value of the call option? From the previous discussion, we know that holding constant the maturity date implies that the distribution of possible future exchange rates is the same for the two options. Hence, it should be apparent that increasing the exercise price of a euro call must decrease the value of a call option because it removes possible states of the world over which the contract provides revenue when the strike price is lower. This is demonstrated in Exhibit 20.11 in which two strike prices, K_1 and K_2, are labeled.

The region of the probability distribution to the right of K_1 gives the probability that the call option with a strike price of K_1 will be exercised. The shaded region contains the additional probability for which the call option with strike price K_1 will be exercised relative to the probability of exercising the option with the higher strike price of K_2. So, when we increase the exercise price from K_1 to K_2, we lose the probability of generating the revenue associated with the shaded region, which makes the option with the strike price K_2 less valuable than the option with the strike price K_1.

A put option provides revenue to the buyer at expiration only if the spot rate in the future is less than the option's exercise price. Hence, increasing the exercise price of a put option must increase the value of a put option because it increases the possible states of the world over which the contract is profitable. We see this in Exhibit 20.11. The probability of exercising the option with a strike price of K_2 is the area of the probability distribution below K_2. The shaded area of Exhibit 20.11 gives the additional probability of exercising an option with strike price K_2 versus one with strike price equal to K_1.

An Increase in the Variance

How does increasing the variance of future exchange rates affect an option's value? Exhibit 20.12 compares two probability distributions—one with a small variance, associated with tranquil periods, and one with a larger variance, associated with turbulent periods.

Exhibit 20.12 Different Probability Distributions of Future USD/EUR

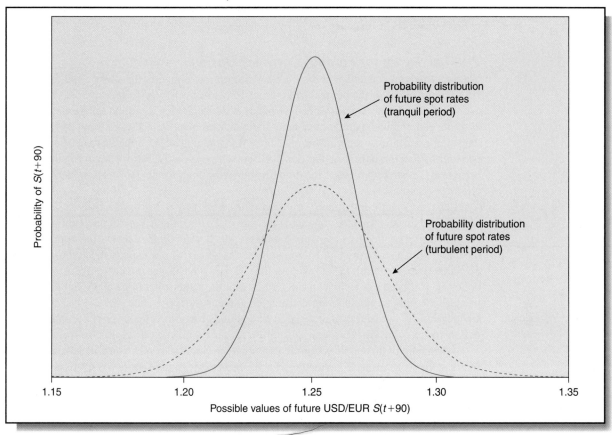

To understand how an increase in variance affects option prices, suppose we place the strike price of a call option at the conditional mean of the two probability distributions in Exhibit 20.12—that is, we choose $K = \$1.25/€$. The increase in the variance of the possible future exchange rate clearly increases the possible range of future exchange rates. But, because the conditional mean is still $\$1.25/€$, the probability that the option will finish in the money is still one-half because one-half of the probability distribution remains above the strike price. However, if the option does finish in the money, the distribution with the larger variance yields possibly larger payoffs, and the option will cost more. A symmetrical argument can be applied to a put option. (Can you explain how?) Therefore, an increase in the variance of future possible exchange rates increases both call and put option values.

Increasing the Time to Expiration

How does increasing the time to expiration affect an option's value? Here, it is important to distinguish clearly between American-style and European-style options. For American options, the effect is unambiguous: Increasing the time to maturity always increases an option's value because it increases the uncertainty of the spot exchange rate at maturity. When this effect is combined with the fact that the holder of a 6-month option can always treat the option as a 3-month option, we clearly see that the additional 3 months of maturity cannot hurt the payoff to the holder of the option as long as the holder of the option can exercise it early.

For European options, the situation is not so simple. Although the effect of an increase in time to maturity is technically ambiguous, in most situations, the effect of the increased uncertainty of the spot exchange rate at maturity dominates, and option prices increase.

Nevertheless, this is not always true because it is possible for a European option that is currently in the money to lose value as time evolves. You would like to be able to exercise the option to lock in the revenue now, but you cannot do so prior to maturity.

Put–Call Parity for Foreign Currency Options

The fact that you can hedge and speculate with options suggests that there should be a link between the prices of the put and call options for a given strike price and the forward foreign exchange rate. Because money changes hands at the beginning of option transactions as well as at the end, the interest rate must enter the relationship as well. **Put–call parity** is the fundamental no arbitrage relationship that links the common strike price of domestic currency per unit of foreign currency, the domestic currency prices of European-style put and call options at that strike price, and the domestic currency interest rate. How can we derive this no arbitrage relationship?

Let's work with dollar–euro exchange rates. One way to unconditionally sell euros for dollars is to make a forward contract at the rate of F. A synthetic way to unconditionally sell euros in the future involves two option transactions. If you purchase a euro put option against the dollar with a strike price of K, you will exercise the option whenever the dollar–euro spot exchange rate at maturity, $S(T)$, is less than K. Let your dollar cost of purchasing the put option be P. If you sell or write a call option with the same strike price of K, you give someone else the right to purchase euros from you at that strike price. She will exercise her option whenever $S(T)$ is greater than or equal to K. You will charge the purchaser of the call option C dollars today.

When both of these option transactions are done simultaneously, you will sell euros in the future at the strike price, K, no matter what happens to the future spot rate. That is, at maturity, you will unconditionally sell euros for dollars at the strike price, K, but your dollar revenue will be enhanced by the future value of the difference between the revenue from selling the call option and the cost of buying the put option, which is $(C - P)[1 + i(\$)]$. Therefore, the two option transactions create a **synthetic forward contract**, and absence of arbitrage requires that the forward exchange rate must be equal to the strike price adjusted for the future values of the revenue from selling the call minus the cost of purchasing the put. That is, put–call parity requires

$$F = K + (C - P)[1 + i(\$)]$$

If you can purchase euros in the forward market at F dollars per euro, and this price is less than the dollar price at which you can synthetically sell euros forward through the two option transactions just described, you can obviously make money. Such an arbitrage transaction is called a **conversion**.

What if the market's forward price is higher than the synthetic forward price? In this case, traders do what is called a **reversal**: They create a synthetic forward purchase of euros and contract to sell euros in the forward market. The synthetic purchase of euros can be done by buying a euro call option with strike price K, which generates a cost of C today; selling a put option with the same strike price, which brings in revenue of P today; and investing or borrowing the difference. The future profit on a reversal is therefore

$$F - K - (C - P)[1 + i(\$)]$$

When neither conversions nor reversals are profitable, the market prices satisfy put–call parity.

Of course, as with interest rate parity, put–call parity will not be an exact equality because it is difficult to do the required transactions simultaneously. Also, we would need to be explicit about the bid and ask prices in the various markets. Once again, though, transaction costs are quite small, and actual option prices are usually close to those implied by put–call parity.

An Alternative Representation of Put–Call Parity

From interest rate parity (described in Chapter 6), we know that the forward rate, again in dollars per euro, is equal to the spot rate adjusted by the ratio of 1 plus the interest rates in the two currencies:

$$F = S \times \frac{1 + i(\$)}{1 + i(€)}$$

After substituting from this expression for the forward rate into the put–call parity equation and rearranging terms, we can express put–call parity in a different way:

$$P - C = \frac{K}{1 + i(\$)} - \frac{S}{1 + i(€)}$$

This equation states that the difference between the current dollar price of a put and the current dollar price of a call with the same exercise price and the same maturity must be equal to the common exercise price divided by 1 plus the dollar interest rate minus the current spot rate divided by 1 plus the euro interest rate. Once we have priced call options, the prices of put options can be found directly from put–call parity.

Example 20.11 Putting Numbers to Put-Call Parity

To illustrate how put–call parity works, let's consider the exchange rates and options that Orlodge was facing in Example 20.8. We'll use the options with a strike price of 70¢/CHF. Note that the call option costs 2.55¢/CHF, which is more than the 1.42¢/CHF cost of the put option. We should expect the call option to cost more than the put because the call option is in the money, whereas the put option is not (the current exchange rate is 71.42¢/CHF). Put–call parity states that one can sell the Swiss franc forward at a predetermined rate in two ways: through a forward contract or through buying a put and writing a call. Recall from Example 20.8 that the forward rate is 71.14¢/CHF. The option strategy yields an effective rate of the strike price plus the net cost or revenue of the two option transactions, adjusted for the time value of money. That is, the synthetic forward rate obtained by buying a put and writing a call is

$$70¢/CHF + (2.55¢/CHF - 1.42¢/CHF) \times \left(1 + 0.0375 \times \frac{90}{360}\right) = 71.14¢/CHF$$

This is the same as the forward rate. Hence, put–call parity holds in these quotes. You can verify that it also holds for options with a 72¢/CHF strike price.

20.5 COMBINATIONS OF OPTIONS AND EXOTIC OPTIONS

Corporations and institutional investors are increasingly using options and other derivative instruments to manage their exchange rate and interest rate risks.[2] Hedge funds and other institutional investors also often want to invest in instruments that allow them to express their

---

[2]See the discussion of current risk management practices in Chapter 17.

views about various risks and rewards in currency markets. Consequently, investment banks now design products specifically for the tastes of their clients. Often, such products represent combinations of basic put and call options that lower the cost of managing a particular risk. Options with different payoff patterns and features than the basic options discussed in this chapter are mostly referred to as **exotic options**. Some of the more standard exotic options are discussed briefly in this section.

First, though, a word of caution for the purchasers of these options. How can banks offer exotic options that seem like good deals to clients? Banks will hedge an exotic option position by doing the opposite transaction with some other counterparty or by creating synthetic options by trading the underlying assets to offset their risk. Of course, because you can't get something for nothing, purchasers of exotic options should be aware that the ability of the bank to offer such a contract indicates that the purchaser's distribution of future spot rates is probably somewhat different from the market's implied distribution of future spot rates. For example, in terms of Exhibit 20.12, if option prices seem expensive to you, it may be because the market is pricing options from a distribution with a wider conditional variance than you are using. Of course, your personal distribution of future exchange rates may differ in other ways from the market's distribution, and you may be right. But, you should be careful not to delude yourself into thinking that you are getting a good deal; you need to understand the distribution implied by market prices and the implied payoffs on your contract.

Range Forwards and Cylinder Options

Corporate treasurers often argue that option strategies are expensive. They dislike incurring the up-front cost of option premiums. They also encounter difficulty explaining their hedging expenses to their superiors, especially when the insurance they purchase seems to have been unnecessary after the fact. If they think the purchase of an option is expensive because the implied volatility is too high, they nevertheless might shy away from writing the opposite option because they would still be exposed to the underlying risk of large losses.

Some market participants dislike up-front costs but still want some of the hedging features provided by option strategies. Financial institutions have proposed several solutions that retain some of the hedging features of options but reduce the upfront costs. One solution, designed in 1985 by the investment bank Salomon Brothers, is a range forward contract. A **range forward contract** allows a company to specify a range of future spot rates over which the firm can sell or buy foreign currency at the future spot rate. When the future spot rate falls outside the range, the firm sells or buys the currency at the limits of the range. For example, if the firm is selling foreign currency, it enters into a contract to sell the currency for dollars within a particular range. This creates a floor on the firm's dollar revenue in case the foreign currency weakens. However, it also creates a ceiling on the firm's dollar revenue in case the foreign currency strengthens. If the firm's treasurer thinks that the foreign currency is unlikely to strengthen, or at least not strengthen very much, she will not believe she is sacrificing any upside potential.

At exchange rates in between the limits of the range forward contract, the firm simply sells its foreign currency at the spot rate in the future. Although the firm gets some upside potential, the firm doesn't need to pay money up front for the range forward contract. Range forward contracts were quickly modified by Citibank and other financial institutions, which developed cylinder options. **Cylinder options** allow buyers to specify a desired trading range and either pay money or possibly receive money up front for entering into the contracts.

Synthesizing Cylinder Options
How can we use our knowledge of call and put options to construct synthetic cylinder options and range forward contracts when we are selling foreign currency in the future? Consider a slight modification to our derivation of put–call parity. Here, we express all exchange rates in dollars per pound, just to be concrete.

Suppose you must buy pounds in the future to pay for some British goods. It is possible to construct cylinder options or a range forward contract that allows you to buy pounds in the future at the spot rate over a particular range but places a ceiling on your costs to provide you with insurance. Unfortunately, you must also agree to have a floor on your costs that prevents you from participating fully in dollar appreciation. The ceiling on your costs is established by purchasing a call option, and the floor is established by selling a put option at a lower strike price.

Let the strike price of the put option that is sold be K_p, and let the strike price of the call option that is purchased be K_c, with $K_p < K_c$. Then, depending on the realization of the future spot rate, you will buy pounds in the following way:

If $S \le K_p$, you buy pounds at K_p because the put you wrote is exercised.
If $K_p < S < K_c$, you buy pounds at S with no exercise of options.
If $S \ge K_c$, you buy pounds at K_c by exercising your call.

In all cases, the firm has an expense equal to the future value of the call premium, $C(K_c)$, that it purchased, and it has revenue equal to the future value of the put premium, $P(K_p)$, that it sold. Hence, its net revenue is augmented by

$$[P(K_p) - C(K_c)] \times [1 + i(\$)]$$

This additional revenue can be adjusted by changing the strike prices on the options to be either positive, negative, or zero. Because the range forward contract requires no cash flows other than the purchase of the pounds, the strike prices must be set such that $P(K_p) = C(K_c)$. The firm might propose the ceiling on its trading range, which establishes the strike price of the call, and the investment bank then sets the floor of the trading range to correspond to the strike price of a put option with the same value as the call option.

Example 20.12   A Cylinder Option Contract

Let's work with some data to create a synthetic cylinder option for a situation in which you have an inflow of foreign currency. As in Example 20.7, suppose it is September, and Pfimerc has a £500,000 account receivable due in October. The following data are available:

Spot rate (U.S. cents per British pound): 153.22
34-day forward rate (U.S. cents per British pound): 152.92
U.S. dollar 34-day interest rate: 3.75% p.a.
British pound 34-day interest rate: 6.65% p.a.
Option data for October contracts in cents per pound (¢/£):

Strike	Call Prices	Put Prices
150.0	4.14	1.22
152.5	2.70	2.28
155.0	1.50	3.57

In Example 20.7, Pfimerc bought the October put option with a strike price of 152.5¢/£ at a cost of 2.28¢/£. This established a floor on their revenue. Now, suppose that Pfimerc wants to guarantee itself the right to exchange the £500,000 in the range between $1.50/£ to $1.55/£. Pfimerc could purchase the 150 October put option for 1.22¢/£ and sell the 155 call option for 1.50¢/£. The net revenue from the two option contracts would be $1.50¢/£ - 1.22¢/£ = 0.28¢/£$, or $0.0028/£. The future value of this net revenue using the interest rate calculated in Example 20.7 is

$$£500,000 \times \$0.0028/£ \times 1.0035 = \$1,404.90$$

With these two transactions, Pfimerc's dollar revenue would range from

$$(£500,000 \times \$1.50/£) + \$1,404.90 = \$751,404.90$$

if $S(\$/£) = \$1.50/£$ to

$$(£500,000 \times \$1.55/£) + \$1,404.90 = \$776,404.90$$

if $S(\$/£) = \$1.55/£$. This range of revenues can be compared to the forward contract. If Pfimerc sell pounds forward at $1.5292/£, its October revenue is

$$\$1.5292/£ \times £500,000 = \$764,600$$

Other Exotic Options

Average-Rate Options

An **average-rate option**, which is sometimes called an Asian option, is one of the most common exotic options. The payoff on an average-rate call option on one unit of foreign currency with a strike price of K is $\max[0, \overline{S} - K]$, where $\overline{S}$ defines the average exchange rate between the initiation of the contract and the expiration date. To calculate the average exchange rate, the counterparties to the option contract must agree on a source for the data and a way of computing the average. They must decide on a time interval for the observations entering the average, which could be daily, weekly, or monthly, and they must decide whether the average is an arithmetic or geometric average.[3] At the maturity of an average-rate option, the seller of the option settles the contract by delivering the option payoff to the buyer. Because an average of future exchange rates is less volatile than the future spot rate at maturity, average-rate options are less expensive than standard European options.

Barrier Options

A **barrier option** is like a traditional option, with an additional requirement that either activates the option or extinguishes it if the exchange rate passes through a prespecified barrier exchange rate. For example, suppose the current exchange rate is $1.50/£. A 1-year, up-and-out European put option on the pound with a strike price of $1.45/£ and a barrier of $1.53/£ specifies that the holder of the option has the right, but not the obligation, to sell pounds for dollars at $1.45/£ in 1 year unless the exchange rate crosses the barrier of $1.53/£ prior to the maturity of the option. If the exchange rate crosses the barrier, the option is worthless. Such an option is desirable for people who have pound receivables because they may think that the put option hedge is not necessary if the pound strengthens during the life of the contract.

Barrier options can be either calls or puts, and there are four essential varieties. In addition to the up-and-out option described earlier, there are up-and-in, down-and-out, and down-and-in options. Each of these options specifies a barrier that either activates the option, in the cases of the up-and-in and down-and-in options, or that extinguishes the option if the barrier is crossed, in the cases of the up-and-out and down-and-out options.

---

[3]If there are n observations, the arithmetic average is $(1/n)\sum_{i=1}^{n}S_i$, and the geometric average is $(\prod_{i=1}^{n}S_i)^{1/n}$, where $\sum$ denotes the summation operator and $\prod$ denotes the product operator.

Lookback Options

Suppose you want to assure yourself today that in 1 year, you will have bought foreign exchange at the minimum dollar value that occurs during the coming year. You can actually do this by purchasing a **lookback option**. For example, let S_{min} be the minimum exchange rate (in dollars per foreign currency) realized during the year, and let $S(T)$ be the exchange rate in 1 year. The payoff on the lookback call option is

$$\max[0, S(T) - S_{min}]$$

Because the minimum exchange rate may occur on the last day, $S(T)$ is at least as big as S_{min}, and the payoff can be written as $S(T) - S_{min}$. A lookback put option can be defined analogously. It allows you to sell foreign currency at the highest exchange rate of dollars per foreign currency that is realized during the life of the option. Of course, when you transact with a lookback option, you are transacting at the prices that are the most favorable to you. Hence, lookback options are more expensive than traditional call and put options.

Digital Options

The two basic **digital options**, or binary options, are cash-or-nothing and asset-or-nothing options. They can be European or American; they can be structured as a call or a put; and they are mostly cash settled. A European cash-or-nothing digital option pays off a fixed amount of money when it expires in the money and nothing otherwise. For example, suppose you buy a digital call option on the dollar/euro exchange rate with a strike price of $1.35/€ and a principal of $1,000,000. If, at expiration, the exchange rate is higher than $1.35/€, you obtain the $1,000,000; if not, the payoff is 0. The American equivalent of this digital option pays off $1,000,000 if the exchange rate reaches the $1.35/€ level any time before expiration. Obviously, such options are issued only at strike prices that are out of the money. If the payout is specified in euros (for example, €1,000,000), the option is really an asset-or-nothing option because the dollar amount represented by the euro payoff, $S(T) \times €1,000,000$, is uncertain from the perspective of the U.S. investor.

Binary options are interesting because they are useful building blocks in the creation of complex payoff patterns. For example, an option that pays off a very large amount when the exchange rate is within a certain range (a sort of lottery payoff) can be constructed by buying and selling digital call options with different strike prices.

20.6 SUMMARY

The purpose of this chapter is to develop an understanding of futures markets and foreign exchange options markets and the use of futures and options in hedging transaction exchange risks. The main points in the chapter are as follows:

1. Foreign currency futures are standardized contracts that allow one to buy or sell specific amounts of foreign currency at a price determined today, with delivery on a given day in the future. The contracts are traded on organized exchanges.
2. The clearinghouse of an exchange is the counterparty to all transactions. To guarantee that the terms of the contracts will be met, buyers and sellers must maintain margin accounts.

3. Marking to market is the process by which the clearinghouse of an exchange debits and credits the losses and profits that arise from the daily changes in futures prices to the margin accounts.
4. Futures contracts are rarely held until delivery and are closed out by simply reversing the original transaction.
5. Futures contracts are used to hedge transaction exchange risks in a fashion similar to forward contracts. To hedge a foreign currency receivable, one must go short in that foreign currency futures contract. To hedge a foreign currency payable, one goes long in the foreign currency futures contract.
6. If the maturity of a futures contract does not coincide with the maturity of the receivable or payable to be hedged, there is basis risk.

7. Foreign currency call options give the buyer of an option the right, but not the obligation, to buy a specific amount of foreign currency at the strike price, which is an exchange rate stated in the contract. Foreign currency put options give the buyer of an option the right to sell foreign currency.

8. Foreign currency options are primarily traded in the over-the-counter interbank market, but they are also traded on exchanges.

9. Option payoffs are functions of the future spot rate. The payoff on a call option is either 0 or the difference between the spot rate and the strike price, $\max[0, S(T) - K]$; for a put option, the payoff is $\max[0, K - S(T)]$.

10. The classic use of option contracts as hedges arises in bidding situations.

11. Transaction exchange risks can be hedged with an option that gives you the right, but not the obligation, to do the transaction that gives rise to the risk.

12. Purchasing foreign currency options in hedging situations is like purchasing insurance, and varying the strike price varies the quality of the insurance.

13. Increasing the strike price of a foreign currency call (put) option decreases (increases) the option's value because it removes (adds) possible states of the world over which the contract provides revenue.

14. An increase in the variance of possible future exchange rates increases the possible range of future exchange rates for any given date in the future that increases the value of both call and put options.

15. Option prices are mostly positively related to time to maturity because an increase in time to maturity primarily increases the conditional variance of the distribution of future exchange rates.

16. Put-call parity is a no arbitrage relationship between the prices of European put and call options, the forward exchange rate, and the domestic interest rate.

17. Average-rate call options have a payoff that is the maximum of the average future exchange rate minus the strike price of the option. This is only one example of a complex payoff that can be earned by exercising various exotic options.

QUESTIONS

1. How does a futures contract differ from a forward contract?

2. What effects does "marking to market" have on futures contracts?

3. What are the differences between foreign currency option contracts and forward contracts for foreign currency?

4. What are you buying if you purchase a U.S. dollar European put option against the Mexican peso with a strike price of MXN10.0/$ and a maturity of July? (Assume that it is May and the spot rate is MXN10.5/$.)

5. What are you buying if you purchase a Swiss franc American call option against the U.S. dollar with a strike price of CHF1.30/$ and a maturity of January? (Assume that it is November and the spot rate is CHF1.35/$.)

6. What is the intrinsic value of a foreign currency call option? What is the intrinsic value of a foreign currency put option?

7. What does it mean for an American option to be "in the money"?

8. Why do American option values typically exceed their intrinsic values?

9. Suppose you go long in a foreign currency futures contract. Under what circumstances is your cumulative payoff equal to that of buying the currency forward?

10. What is basis risk?

11. Your CEO routinely approves changes in the fire insurance policies of your firm to protect the value of its buildings and manufacturing equipment. Nevertheless, he argues that the firm should not buy foreign currency options because, he says, "We don't speculate in FX markets!" How could you convince him that his positions are mutually inconsistent?

12. Why do options provide insurance against foreign exchange risks in bidding situations? Why can't you hedge with a forward contract in a bidding situation?

13. Suppose that you have a foreign currency receivable (payable). What option strategy places a floor (ceiling) on your domestic currency revenue (cost)?

14. Describe qualitatively how changing the strike price of the option provides either more or less expensive insurance.

15. Why does an increase in the strike price of an option decrease the value of a call option and increase the value of a put option?

16. Why does an increase in the volatility of foreign exchange rates increase the value of foreign currency options?
17. How does increasing time to maturity affect foreign currency option value?
18. What is the payoff on an average-rate pound call option against the dollar?

19. Suppose the current spot rate is $1.29/€. What is your payoff if you purchase a down-and-in put option on the euro with a strike price of $1.31/€, a barrier of $1.25/€, and a maturity of 2 months? When would someone want to do this?

PROBLEMS

1. If you sold a Swiss franc futures contract at time t and the exchange rate has evolved as shown here, what would your cash flows have been?

Day	Futures Price $/CHF	Change in Futures Price	Gain or Loss	Cumulative Gain or Loss	Margin Account
t	0.7335				
$t + 1$	0.7391				
$t + 2$	0.7388				
$t + 3$	0.7352				
$t + 4$	0.7297				

2. Given the following information, how much would you have paid on September 16 to purchase a British pound call option contract with a strike price of 155 and a maturity of October?

Data for September 16

	Calls	Puts
50,000 Australian Dollar Options (cents per unit)		
64 Oct	—	0.48
65 Oct	—	0.90
67 Oct	0.22	—
31,250 British Pounds (cents per unit)		
152½ Dec	—	4.10
155 Oct	1.50	3.62
155 Nov	2.35	—

3. Using the data in problem 2, how much would you have paid to purchase an Australian dollar put option contract with a strike price of 65 and an October maturity?
4. Suppose that you buy a €1,000,000 call option against dollars with a strike price of $1.2750/€. Describe this option as the right to sell a specific amount of dollars for euros at a particular exchange rate of euros per dollar. Explain why this latter option is a dollar put option against the euro.
5. Assume that today is March 7, and, as the newest hire for Goldman Sachs, you must advise a client on the costs and benefits of hedging a transaction with options. Your client (a small U.S. exporting firm) is scheduled to receive a payment of €6,250,000 on April 20, 44 days in the future. Assume that your client can borrow and lend at a 6% p.a. U.S. interest rate.
   a. Describe the nature of your client's transaction exchange risk.
   b. Use the appropriate American option with an April maturity and a strike price of 129¢/€ to determine the dollar cost today of hedging the transaction with an option strategy. The cost of the call option is 3.93¢/€, and the cost of the put option is 1.58¢/€.
   c. What is the minimum dollar revenue your client will receive in April? Remember to take account of the opportunity cost of doing the option hedge.
   d. Determine the value of the spot rate ($/€) in April that would make your client indifferent *ex post* to having done the option transaction or a forward hedge. The forward rate for delivery on April 20 is $1.30/€.
6. Assume that today is September 12. You have been asked to help a British client who is scheduled to pay €1,500,000 on December 12, 91 days in the future. Assume that your client can borrow and lend pounds at 5% p.a.
   a. Describe the nature of your client's transaction exchange risk.
   b. What is the option cost for a December maturity and a strike price of £0.72/€ to hedge the transaction? The option premiums per 100 euros are £1.70 for calls and £2.40 for puts.
   c. What is the minimum pound cost your client will experience in December?
   d. Determine the value of the spot rate (£/€) in December that makes your client indifferent *ex post* to having done the option transaction or a forward hedge if the forward rate for delivery on December 11 is £0.70/€.
7. Assume that today is June 11. Your firm is scheduled to pay £500,000 on August 15, 65 days in the

future. The current spot is $1.75/£, and the 65-day forward rate is $1.73/£. You can borrow and lend dollars at 7% p.a. Suppose you think options are overpriced because you think the dollar will be in a tight trading range in the near future. You have been thinking about selling an option as a way to reduce the dollar cost of your pound payable.

   a. If an August pound option with a strike price of 175¢/£ costs 4.5¢/£ per pound for the call and 4¢/£ for the put, what is the minimum effective exchange rate in August that you will pay? Over what range of future exchange rates will this price be achieved?

   b. How much must the pound appreciate before your speculative option strategy ends up costing you more than the forward rate?

8. Upon arriving for work Monday, you observe a violation of put–call parity. In particular, the synthetic forward price of dollars per yen is above the current forward rate. How would you capitalize on this information?

9. On April 28, 1995, the Paine Webber Group introduced a new type of security on the NYSE: *U.S. dollar increase warrants on the yen*. At exercise, each warrant entitled the holder to an amount of U.S. dollars calculated as

$$\text{Greater of (i) 0 and (ii) \$100}$$
$$- \left[\$100 \times (¥83.65/\$/\text{Spot rate}) \right]$$

The "spot rate" in the formula refers to the yen/dollar rate on any day during the exercise period, which extended until April 28, 1996. The 1-year forward rate on April 28 was ¥79.72/$, and the spot rate was ¥83.65/$.

   a. What view on the future yen/dollar rate do investors in this security hold?

   b. This security was issued at a price of $5.50. To see whether the security is fairly priced, which option prices would you want to examine?

BIBLIOGRAPHY

Bates, David, and Roger Craine, 1999, "Valuing the Futures Market Clearinghouse's Default Exposure During the 1987 Crash," *Journal of Money, Credit and Banking* 31, pp. 248–272.

Black, Fischer, and Myron Scholes, 1973, "The Pricing of Options and Corporate Liabilities," *Journal of Political Economy* 81, pp. 637–659.

Bodnar, Gordon, Gregory S. Hayt, and Richard C. Marston, 1998, "Wharton Survey of Financial Risk Management by U.S. Non-Financial Firms," *Financial Management* 27, pp. 70–91.

Cornell, Bradford, and Marc R. Reiganum, December 1981, "Forward and Futures Prices," *Journal of Finance* pp. 1035–1045.

Cox, John C., Jonathan E. Ingersoll, and Stephen A. Ross, 1981, "The Relation Between Forward Prices and Futures Prices," *Journal of Financial Economics* 9, pp. 321–346.

Cox, John C., and Mark Rubinstein, 1985, *Option Markets*, Upper Saddle River, NJ: Prentice Hall.

Day, Theodore E., and Craig M. Lewis, 2004, "Margin Adequacy and Standards: An Analysis of the Crude Oil Futures Market," *Journal of Business* 77, pp. 101–136.

DeRosa, David F., 1992, *Options on Foreign Exchange*, Chicago: Probus Publishing Company.

Garman, Mark B., and Steven W. Kolhagen, 1983, "Foreign Currency Option Values," *Journal of International Money and Finance* 2, pp. 231–237.

Hull, John, 1991, *Introduction to Futures and Options Markets*, Upper Saddle River, NJ: Prentice Hall.

Karmel, Roberta S., 2000, "Turning Seats into Shares: Implications of Demutualization for the Regulation of Stock and Futures Exchanges," working paper.

Modest, David, 1989, "Currency Forwards and Futures" in Boris Antl, ed., *Management of Foreign Exchange Risk: Volume 1*, London: Euromoney Publications, pp. 285–300.

Muelbroek, Lisa, 1992, "A Comparison of Forward and Futures Prices of an Interest Rate–Sensitive Financial Asset, *Journal of Finance* 47, pp. 381–396.

Chapter 21

Interest Rate and Foreign Currency Swaps

*T*his chapter examines interest rate and currency swaps, which are additional instruments for your risk management toolkit. We have previously discussed a number of ways of managing a firm's currency risks using derivative securities, including forward contracts in Chapter 3 and futures and options in Chapter 20. The maturities for these instruments are somewhat limited, whereas the maturities in the swap markets extend to 30 years. We have also noted that exchange rate exposures can be thought of as arising from a general mismatch between assets and liabilities denominated in different currencies. We will see how interest rate swaps allow firms to change the nature of their liabilities for a given currency from fixed to floating interest rates or from floating to fixed interest rates. Currency swaps can be used to change the currency of denomination of a firm's liabilities. Changes such as these can be desirable as the nature of a firm's business changes. Swaps also allow firms to seek out low-cost financing without sacrificing their preferred type of debt.

Section 21.1 introduces the basic ideas associated with swaps and discusses the impressive size of the swap market. Section 21.2 provides a detailed analysis of the cash flows of interest rate swaps, and Section 21.3 provides a detailed analysis of the cash flows of currency swaps. The chapter concludes with a discussion of back-to-back and parallel loans. Although these contracts are much less important than swaps, they were the precursors of the currency swap market, and they remain a part of the toolkit of an international financial manager, especially in creatively dealing with situations involving borrowing by subsidiaries in emerging markets.

21.1 INTRODUCTION TO SWAPS

Swaps are agreements between two counterparties to exchange a sequence of cash flows. In the modern swap market, over-the-counter dealers at major banks quote bid–ask spreads at which they are willing to do either side of a swap. The cash flows of interest rate and currency swaps are structured like the cash flows of standard bonds, and the maturities extend from 1 year to 30 years and even more. Many international financial managers now actively use swaps to manage their companies' interest rate and currency risks and for speculative purposes.

The World Bank–IBM Swap

In 1981, the World Bank and IBM engaged in one of the first currency swaps. The World Bank had substantial outstanding debt denominated in dollars as well as in Deutsche marks and Swiss francs. It considered its liabilities to be unbalanced and wanted to reduce its dollar debt and increase its Deutsche mark and Swiss franc debt. Although it could have issued additional debt in the European currencies and retired its dollar debt, the World Bank was near its official borrowing limit in the European currencies. Meanwhile, IBM had outstanding debts denominated in Deutsche marks and Swiss francs, but the company wanted the debt denominated in dollars. Why? Because much of IBM's revenues were generated in dollars, and the firm was worried that the dollar would soon depreciate, making it relatively more difficult for IBM to repay its Deutsche mark– and Swiss franc–denominated debt.

It occurred to smart financial advisors that the World Bank and IBM could both benefit by swapping their debts. The result was that the World Bank agreed to take over IBM's Deutsche mark and Swiss franc debt service in return for IBM taking over the World Bank's dollar debt service. Since then, the swap market has grown tremendously, and interest rate and currency swaps have become indispensable risk management tools for multinational corporations.

The nature of the contract between swap counterparties is usually based on the best practices suggested by the **International Swap and Derivatives Association (ISDA)**. The ISDA is a trade organization that was chartered in 1985 and now represents more than 725 member institutions from 50 countries. Its members include most of the world's major financial institutions that deal in privately negotiated derivatives, as well as their clients who rely on over-the-counter derivatives to manage the financial market risks inherent in their core economic activities. The most important ISDA document is the ISDA Master Agreement Protocol, which controls the legal aspects of swap cash flows, such as how swaps are closed out in the event of default.

Currency Swaps Versus Interest Rate Swaps

A **currency swap** allows a multinational corporation to change the currency of denomination of its debts, as the World Bank and IBM did. Exhibit 21.1 presents the basic idea of a currency swap. Counterparty A is paying interest and principal on a dollar amount to Counterparty B. Counterparty B, in turn, is paying interest and principal on a yen amount to Counterparty A. At the beginning of the swap, the dollar principal is equal to the yen principal. These principals

Exhibit 21.1 Foreign Currency Swap Diagram

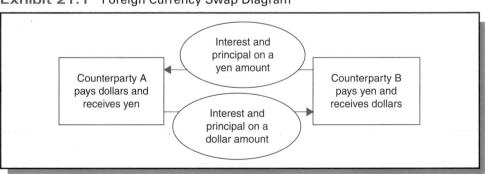

Exhibit 21.2 Interest Rate Swap Diagram

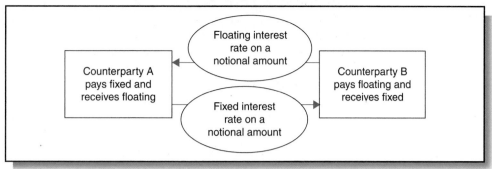

will again be exchanged at the end of the currency swap, but if the exchange rate has changed, the values of the principals will no longer be equal at the end of the swap.

Because swap cash flows are like bonds, MNCs can use them to change the type of interest payments on their debts. An **interest rate swap** allows an MNC to change the nature of its debt from a fixed interest rate to a floating interest rate or from a floating interest rate to a fixed interest rate. Exhibit 21.2 provides a basic interest rate swap diagram. Counterparty A is paying a fixed amount of interest on a **notional principal** to Counterparty B, and Counterparty A is receiving floating interest rate cash flows on the same notional amount from Counterparty B. The term *notional* indicates the basic principal amount on which the cash flows of the interest rate swap depend. Unlike a currency swap, no exchange of principal is necessary because the principal is an equal amount of the same currency.

The Size of the Swap Markets

The growth in the use of swaps since their introduction in the early 1980s has been truly phenomenal. Exhibit 21.3 presents data on the interest rate and currency swaps outstanding in 2001 and 2004. The data are from the triennial survey of central banks conducted by the Bank for International Settlements. Notice that the notional amount of interest rate swaps on the books of corporations and banks around the world in 2004 was $137 *trillion* dollars, whereas in 2001, the notional value of aggregate interest rate swaps was $57 trillion. This represents a growth rate of over 33% per year. These figures are adjusted for the obvious double-counting problem that arises because each contract is counted on the books of two counterparties. The notional value of currency swaps is significantly smaller than the notional value of interest rate swaps, but it was still an incredibly large $7.9 trillion in June 2004.

In thinking about these notional values, it is important to understand that, like forward contracts, interest rate swaps and currency swaps begin life as zero net present value contracts.

Exhibit 21.3 The Size and Growth of Interest Rate and Currency Swap Markets (Amounts outstanding in billions of U.S. dollars)

	Notional Amounts		Gross Market Values	
	June 2001	June 2004	June 2001	June 2004
Interest rate swaps	57,220	132,277	1,531	3,978
Currency swaps	4,302	7,939	339	506

Note: Data are taken from the Bank for International Settlements, *Central Bank Survey of Foreign Exchange and Derivatives Market Activity,* December 2004. Copyright © 2004 Bank for International Settlements. All rights reserved. Reprinted by permission.

That is, swaps have no market value initially because the present value of the cash flows that are to be paid by one of the counterparties is exactly equal to the present value of the cash flows that are to be paid by the other counterparty. Subsequently, though, changes in interest rates and especially exchange rates imply that one of the counterparties to the swap experiences a profit and the other experiences an equivalent loss.

Exhibit 21.3 also shows that the gross market value of the outstanding interest rate swaps in 2004 was 3.0% of the notional value, or $3.978 trillion, whereas the market value of outstanding currency swaps was 6.4% of notional value, or $506 billion. These are the market values of the debts that are owed between counterparties at that time.

As you can see from Exhibit 21.3, interest rate and particularly currency swaps can become quite valuable. Of course, value created on one side of a swap is a loss when viewed from the other side. So, swaps can be the source of large trading losses, especially when they are being used for speculative purposes. Consequently, counterparty risk of swaps can be substantial, and the same marking-to-market techniques that are used in the futures market have become common in the swap market to mitigate these risks. Some observers of the markets, though, argue that the growth rate of the swap market has been too fast and that the magnitudes outstanding in the swap markets are a financial catastrophe waiting to happen.

It is difficult to know whether the market can police itself effectively or whether a large default by a leading hedge fund, as in the 1998 collapse of Long Term Capital Management (LTCM), could lead to significant losses for major commercial and investment banks around the world. LTCM lost $1.6 billion on trades in the swap markets, and it lost more than $4 billion in total, causing the Federal Reserve Bank of New York to organize a $3.6 billion bailout of LTCM counterparties to prevent a crisis (see Lowenstein, 2000). Only by understanding the structure of the swap market will you begin to have an informed opinion on this issue.

21.2 INTEREST RATE SWAPS

Interest rate swaps allow corporations to manage their interest rate risk or to speculate on the direction of interest rates. In this section, we first discuss the cash flows associated with interest rate swaps. Then we discuss why a corporation might prefer floating-rate debt to fixed-rate debt or vice versa, which is related to the issue of the choice of debt contracts in Chapter 11. We then discuss why interest rate swaps would be used in a world where many different debt contracts are available. We begin with an example of an interest rate swap between Jocko Sports and Banco Coloro.

Example 21.1   A 5-year Interest Rate Swap

Suppose Jocko Sports is paying the floating-rate side of a dollar interest rate swap and receiving fixed interest rate payments from Banco Coloro. Let the notional principal on the 5-year swap be $25 million, and let the fixed interest rate be 8%. Because Banco Coloro pays the fixed interest rate side of the swap, it would owe 10 semiannual payments of

$$0.5 \times 0.08 \times \$25 \text{ million} = \$1 \text{ million}$$

These payments would be fixed for 5 years. In return, Jocko Sports would pay Banco Coloro semiannual interest payments on $25 million at the London Interbank Offered Rate (LIBOR), as indicated in Exhibit 21.4.

Exhibit 21.4   The Cash Flows of an Interest Rate Swap

	Banco Coloro		Jocko Sports	
Time Period	Pays the Fixed Rate	Receives the Floating Rate	Receives the Fixed Rate	Pays the Floating Rate
Year 0.5	($1 m)	LIBOR × $25 m	$1 m	(LIBOR × $25 m)
Year 1.0	($1 m)	LIBOR × $25 m	$1 m	(LIBOR × $25 m)
Year 1.5	($1 m)	LIBOR × $25 m	$1 m	(LIBOR × $25 m)
Year 2.0	($1 m)	LIBOR × $25 m	$1 m	(LIBOR × $25 m)
Year 2.5	($1 m)	LIBOR × $25 m	$1 m	(LIBOR × $25 m)
Year 3.0	($1 m)	LIBOR × $25 m	$1 m	(LIBOR × $25 m)
Year 3.5	($1 m)	LIBOR × $25 m	$1 m	(LIBOR × $25 m)
Year 4.0	($1 m)	LIBOR × $25 m	$1 m	(LIBOR × $25 m)
Year 4.5	($1 m)	LIBOR × $25 m	$1 m	(LIBOR × $25 m)
Year 5.0	($1 m)	LIBOR × $25 m	$1 m	(LIBOR × $25 m)

Note: The fixed interest rate is 8% per annum, and the notional principal is $25,000,000. Hence, the fixed rate payment is $0.5 \times 0.08 \times \$25,000,000 = \$1,000,000$. The parentheses indicate negative cash flows.

Exhibit 21.4 indicates what each counterparty to the swap would be expected to pay and what each would expect to receive. However, only a net interest payment is actually transferred between the two parties because the currency is the same. That is, the party with the higher interest rate pays the net interest payment to the party with the lower interest rate. Suppose the current 6-month LIBOR is 10% p.a. What cash flow payments are made?

Because Jocko Sports is paying the LIBOR rate of 10% and receiving the fixed rate of 8%, Jocko Sports must pay the de-annualized 2% net interest rate payment on the $25 million, which amounts to

$$0.5 \times 0.02 \times \$25 \text{ million} = \$250,000$$

Interest Rate Risk

Fixed vs. Floating-Rate Debt

Many corporations have revenue cash flows that are pro-cyclical, which means their revenues are high during booms and low during recessions. Short-term interest rates are also pro-cyclical. That is, short-term interest rates tend to rise during expansions in the business cycle and fall during recessions. A corporation whose sales are pro-cyclical can afford to borrow continually in the short-term money market. The corporation does not mind making high interest rate payments during a boom because its revenues are high, too. During recessions, the corporation likes its interest costs to be low because its revenues are relatively lower as well. But if the corporation borrows at long-term fixed rates, its fixed interest costs are a higher percentage of its cash flows during contractions in business cycles than during expansions. This cyclical pattern increases the corporation's risk of default.

One danger of borrowing short-term, though, is that the lender may refuse to renew the loan agreement when the circumstances of the corporation change for the worse. Hence, there is a corporate demand for long-term contracts that have floating-rate payments.

Banks are happy to provide long-term contracts with floating interest rates. Although banks' liabilities are mostly short term, and the interest rates they pay on their deposits fluctuate, the banks' deposit bases are often quite stable. This allows banks to enter into relatively long-term contracts to receive floating interest rate cash flows. In addition, many investors prefer the certainty of long-term, fixed interest rate debt. Some borrowers, such as corporations with stable revenues can afford to make fixed-rate payments during both booms and recessions. Thus, there are demands and supplies for all types of interest rate contracts, and all types of interest rate contracts exist.

Changed Circumstances

Although a company might have rationally determined that a long-run, fixed-rate debt was the right type of loan to take out when a debt was initially issued, over time, the firm's circumstances might change. For example, suppose the company subsequently forecasts that its cash flows are likely to deteriorate at a time when short-term interest rates are low. In this case, the firm can perhaps stave off its difficult financial situation by swapping out of its fixed-rate debt and into a short-term debt with a lower interest rate.

Alternatively, consider a firm that typically borrows with floating-rate debt because its cash flows are cyclical. After the firm acquires another company, the combined firm's cash flows might, become much less cyclical. This would prompt the company's managers to swap from floating-rate debt to fixed-rate debt.

Views on the Future

While we have stressed the risk management role of derivative contracts, it is no secret that the treasury departments of major corporations often place bets on the direction of interest rates, currencies, and other financial variables. When managers view future short-term interest rates as unusually low, they may try to lower the company's interest costs by converting its existing fixed-rate debt into floating-rate debt. Alternatively, if they forecast that interest rates are going to rise, they may want to swap out of floating-rate debt and into fixed-rate debt.

Minimizing the Cost of Debt

As indicated in Chapter 11, corporations can fund their projects in a number of ways: via bank loans, floating-rate debt, Eurobonds, and so forth. When a company's financing needs are large, shaving a few basis points off the cost of the debt can mean millions of dollars in cost savings. Hence, a large corporation figures out what kind of debt it ultimately wants, it determines the cheapest way to raise the funds, and it uses the swap market to convert the actual debt into the desired debt.

Research is beginning to find support for this view. For example, Haitao Li and Connie Mao (2003) find that certain firms with low credit ratings or none at all are relegated by the markets to borrowing from banks that make floating-rate loans because the banks do not want to risk lending to these firms at fixed rates. Nevertheless, these firms can then enter into interest rate swaps as fixed-rate payers to eliminate their exposure to interest rate risk. By doing so, the lowly rated firms are able to borrow the amount of money they want at the rates they want.

Manipulating Earnings

Another use of swaps that has been discussed in the literature involves their use by management to manipulate earnings. Michael Faulkender (2006) presents some empirical evidence that swap activity is partially driven by the desire of managers to manipulate the earnings of firms so as to meet their earnings forecasts and keep their pay high.

The Nature of Interest Rate Swap Contracts

Major commercial and investment banks serve as market makers for interest rate swaps by quoting bid–offer rates for various maturities at which they are willing to swap fixed interest rate debts for floating interest rate debts or floating interest rate debts for fixed interest rate debts. By convention, the quotes in the dollar interest rate swap market usually use 6-month LIBOR as the base rate of the floating-rate side of the transaction. The bank's bid interest rate is the fixed rate that the bank is willing to pay over a given maturity in return for receiving semiannual payments corresponding to 6-month LIBOR. The bank's higher offer, or ask, interest rate is the fixed rate that the bank will receive from a counterparty over a given maturity if the bank is to pay 6-month LIBOR to that counterparty.

In the case of the U.S. dollar, the bank's fixed bid and offer interest rates are often quoted in terms of a **swap spread**—that is, a number of basis points that are added to the yield to maturity on a U.S. government bond corresponding to that maturity.[1] The swap spread reflects differences in credit quality of the private sector relative to the U.S. Treasury and the liquidity differences in the markets.

Notional Principal

As noted earlier in this chapter, the actual interest payments in an interest rate swap are based on what is called a notional principal. The notional principal is the amount of the outstanding debts. In an interest rate swap, the underlying currency is the same for the two parties of the transaction. Hence, there is no exchange of principal at the beginning or end of the transaction because these amounts are identical and simply cancel one another out.

Bid–Ask Prices for Interest Rate Swaps

Assume that at the 5-year maturity, the market sets the price of U.S. Treasury bonds to have a yield to maturity of 8.66% p.a. Consider the following indicative bid–ask quotes on an interest rate swap. The bank structures the bid side of its swap as the yield on Treasury bonds plus a swap spread of 55 basis points. Thus, the bank is willing to pay fixed-rate interest payments to a high-quality corporate customer at

$$8.66\% + 0.55\% = 9.21\%$$

In return, the bank receives a floating-rate payment from the corporation equal to 6-month LIBOR. The bank structures the offer side of its swap as the yield on Treasury bonds plus 60 basis points. The bank is willing to receive fixed interest rate payments from a high-quality corporation for the next 5 years at

$$8.66\% + 0.60\% = 9.26\%$$

In return, the bank is willing to pay interest to the corporation at 6-month LIBOR.

The Profitability of Interest Rate Swaps

To the extent that a bank successfully matches the aggregate amount of interest rate swaps for a given maturity in which it must make fixed interest rate payments with the aggregate notional amount on which it receives fixed interest rate payments from its counterparties, the bank will earn the bid–ask spread on that aggregate amount. For example, if the bank has an outstanding notional principal of $100 billion from both sides of these transactions, the bank generates $50 million in revenue per year from the five-basis-point spread between the bid and offer rates because

$$0.0005 \times \$100 \text{ billion} = \$50 \text{ million}$$

Notice, though, that if there is a mismatch between the aggregate notional amounts on which the bank is paying the fixed rate versus receiving the fixed rate, the bank is exposed to interest rate risk.

---

[1]Francis In, Rob Brown, and Victor Feng (2003) report that the average swap spreads for daily data from 1998 to 2001 for the 5-year and 10-year U.S. dollar contracts were 56 and 64 basis points, respectively.

Interest Rate Risk

Suppose that at a particular maturity, the value of the Second National Bank of Chicago's contracts to pay LIBOR is larger than the value of Second Chicago's contracts to receive LIBOR. Second Chicago is consequently exposed to interest rate risk because an increase in LIBOR will cause losses. If short-term interest rates rise in the future, Second Chicago will be required to pay interest at a higher rate while continuing to receive contractual long-term interest payments that are fixed. Conversely, if Second Chicago enters into more contracts in which it is paying the fixed rate than in which it is receiving the fixed rate, the bank will experience losses if LIBOR falls. If short-term interest rates fall, Second Chicago must continue to pay interest at the contractually fixed high interest rate while receiving short-term interest payments that are falling.

Dealing with Credit Risks: Requiring Collateral and Marking to Market

Of course, the bid–offer rates quoted by banks typically only indicate prices at which the bank is willing to transact with other banks or counterparties with AAA credit risk ratings. Most corporate customers pose a substantial amount of default risk. Consequently, even though interest rate swaps carry the right of offset in that the bank can stop making its side of the payments if the corporation defaults on its side of the transaction, the bank will widen its bid–offer spread in dealing with less creditworthy corporate or institutional customers.

Alternatively, the bank may ask for a credit enhancement in the form of collateral, which is what the International Swaps and Derivatives Association now recommends. The amount of collateral is equal to the mark-to-market value of the swap contract.[2] The increased use of collateral is evidenced in the 2006 ISDA Margin Survey, which reported that 109,733 collateral agreements were in place in 2006—up from 70,892 in 2005 and up from only 12,000 in 2000.

The Bank's Credit Risk

A similar problem arises from the corporate perspective. Most corporate customers are not in the business of assessing the credit risks of banks. They therefore want their banking counterparties to have excellent credit ratings. Many commercial banks and investment banks have responded to this demand by establishing subsidiaries that conduct swap transactions and providing those subsidiaries with enough capital to become AAA rated.

21.3 FOREIGN CURRENCY SWAPS

A currency swap is essentially an agreement between two parties to exchange the cash flows of two long-term bonds denominated in different currencies. The parties exchange initial principal amounts in the two currencies that are equivalent in value when evaluated at the spot exchange rate. Simultaneously, the parties agree to pay interest on the currency they initially receive, to receive interest on the currency they initially pay, and to reverse the exchange of principal amounts at a fixed future date.

The principal amount of one of the currencies is determined by negotiation between the two parties, and the corresponding principal amount of the other currency in the swap is set by the prevailing spot exchange rate. For example, suppose one of the parties wants to exchange

---

[2]Michael Johannes and Suresh Sundaresan (2007) explore the effect that collateral enhancement has on the pricing of interest rate swap contracts.

$10 million with its counterparty for euros, and the spot exchange rate is $1.25/€. Then, the euro amount in the swap corresponding to the $10 million is

$$\$10 \text{ million}/(\$1.25/€) = €8 \text{ million}$$

Currency swaps usually involve both parties exchanging the interest and principal payments. If only a net interest payment from one counterparty to the other is desired, in the beginning, the counterparty that initially receives the high interest rate currency will owe funds to the counterparty that is initially receiving the low interest rate currency. Usually, the interest payments are made semiannually. As the exchange rate changes, though, the value of the fixed interest payments in the different currencies change, and the net amount paid in the currency swap evolves.

Example 21.2 Michaelone's Currency Swap with Margon Stonely

Suppose that the Italian company Michaelone is the party that pays €8 million and receives $10 million initially, as we were discussing, and the investment bank Margon Stonely is the counterparty that initially pays $10 million and receives €8 million. Then, in future periods, Michaelone will owe dollar interest to Margon Stonely on the $10 million, and Margon Stonely will owe euro interest on the €8 million to Michaelone.

Suppose the maturity of the swap is 5 years, and the interest rates for that maturity are 4% on dollars and 6% on euros. Exhibit 21.5 describes the cash flows, with the interest rates, the exchange rate, and the principal amounts given here. Twice per year for 5 years, Margon Stonely, the initial receiver of euros, would owe Michaelone semi-annual euro payments of

$$0.5 \times 0.06 \times €8 \text{ million} = €240,000$$

Exhibit 21.5 The Cash Flows of a Currency Swap

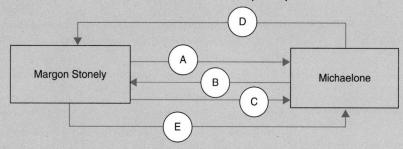

Notes: The currency swap diagram summarizes the transactions and various cash flows:

A. Margon Stonely gives $10 million to Michaelone. The U.S. dollar interest rate is 4%. Michaelone will owe semiannual interest payments of $0.5 \times 0.04 \times \$10$ million $= \$200,000$.

B. Michaelone gives Margon Stonely €8 million in exchange for the $10 million in A. The exchange rate is $1.25/€. The euro interest rate is 6%. Margon Stonely will owe semiannual interest payments of $0.5 \times 0.06 \times €8$ million $= €240,000$.

C. A semiannual net interest payment of €240,000 − [$200,000/S(t+k,$/€)] is made from Margon Stonely to Michaelone as long as the spot exchange rate $S(t+k,\$/€) > \$0.8333/€$. If the exchange rate falls below this value, the net payment flows from Michaelone to Margon Stonely.

D. In the final period, Michaelone must repay the $10 million to Margon Stonely.

E. In the final period, Margon Stonely must repay the €8 million to Michaelone.

Michaelone, the initial receiver of dollars, would owe semiannual dollar payments to Margon Stonely of

$$0.5 \times 0.04 \times \$10 \text{ million} = \$200,000$$

If the exchange rate did not move from the original value of $1.25/€ by the time an interest payment was due, the euro value of the $200,000 would be €160,000 = $200,000/($1.25/€). Because this is fewer euros than Michaelone is to receive from Margon Stonely, if only a net interest payment is being made, Margon Stonely would be required to pay Michaelone the net interest payment of

$$€240,000 - €160,000 = €80,000$$

More realistically, though, the actual net interest payment made by Margon Stonely to Michaelone would depend on the evolution of the exchange rate. At a future payment date $t+k$, the net interest payment would be the €240,000 owed minus the euro value of $200,000:

$$€240,000 - \$200,000/S(t+k, \$/€)$$

Notice that if the dollar strengthened relative to the euro to an exchange rate that is smaller than $0.8333/€ = $200,000/€240,000, the euro value of the $200,000 would be greater than €240,000. Consequently, a net dollar payment would have to be made from Michaelone to Margon Stonely. For example, at the exchange rate of $0.75/€, Michaelone would owe Margon Stonely

$$\$200,000 - (\$0.75/€) \times €240,000 = \$20,000$$

Although currency swaps were originally special contracts, they have now become standardized products of financial intermediaries. The next section explains how modern currency swaps are quoted and traded.

The Mechanics of Modern Currency Swaps

As the market for U.S. dollar interest rate swaps and currency swaps grew and participants searched for ways to standardize these contracts, financial intermediaries began to quote bid–offer rates for fixed foreign currency interest rates at which they were willing to swap versus paying or receiving floating interest rate payments given by the 6-month dollar LIBOR. Consider the following quotations on 5-year fixed interest rate and currency swaps that might be offered by the Commercial Credit Bank:

U.S. dollars: 5.25% bid and 5.35% offered against 6-month dollar LIBOR
British pounds: 8.00% bid and 8.10% offered against 6-month dollar LIBOR

Notice that the first of these quotations for the U.S. dollar is just an interest rate swap. The second quote involves a transformation of both the currency and the interest rate. Commercial Credit is willing to pay to its counterparty either the fixed interest rate of 5.25% in U.S. dollars or 8.00% in pounds against receiving 6-month dollar LIBOR from its counterparty. Commercial Credit is also willing to receive from its counterparty the fixed interest rates of 5.35% in dollars or 8.10% in pounds against paying 6-month dollar LIBOR to its counterparty. Because Commercial Credit is willing to participate on either side of these transactions versus 6-month dollar LIBOR, one can easily structure a currency swap between fixed-rate pounds and fixed-rate U.S. dollars.

The following example demonstrates how a currency swap could be structured with these quoted rates. Exhibit 21.6 also illustrates the process.

Exhibit 21.6   The Cash Flows for Floyds from a Currency Swap

Time Period	Part 1		Part 2	
	Floyds Pays the $ Fixed Rate	Floyds Receives the $ Floating Rate	Floyds Pays the $ Floating Rate	Floyds Receives the £ Fixed Rate
Year 0			$360,000,000	(£200,000,000)
Year 0.5	($9,630,000)	LIBOR × $360 m	(LIBOR × $360 m)	£8,000,000
Year 1.0	($9,630,000)	LIBOR × $360 m	(LIBOR × $360 m)	£8,000,000
Year 1.5	($9,630,000)	LIBOR × $360 m	(LIBOR × $360 m)	£8,000,000
Year 2.0	($9,630,000)	LIBOR × $360 m	(LIBOR × $360 m)	£8,000,000
Year 2.5	($9,630,000)	LIBOR × $360 m	(LIBOR × $360 m)	£8,000,000
Year 3.0	($9,630,000)	LIBOR × $360 m	(LIBOR × $360 m)	£8,000,000
Year 3.5	($9,630,000)	LIBOR × $360 m	(LIBOR × $360 m)	£8,000,000
Year 4.0	($9,630,000)	LIBOR × $360 m	(LIBOR × $360 m)	£8,000,000
Year 4.5	($9,630,000)	LIBOR × $360 m	(LIBOR × $360 m)	£8,000,000
Year 5.0	($9,630,000)	LIBOR × $360 m	($360,000,000 + LIBOR × $360 m)	£200,000,000 + £8,000,000

Notes: The interest rate at which Commercial Credit receives fixed dollar payments is 5.35% p.a., and $(0.5) \times (0.0535) \times \$360$ million $= \$9.63$ million. The interest rate at which Commercial Credit makes fixed pound payments is 8.00% p.a., and $(0.5) \times (0.08) \times £200$ million $= £8$ million.

Example 21.3   Floyds' Currency Swap with Commercial Credit Bank

Suppose a large insurer such as Floyds has outstanding pound debt and wants to swap into fixed-rate dollar debt because its U.S. business has grown. Let the principal amount be £200 million, which corresponds to $360 million at a spot exchange rate of $1.8/£. Because Floyds wants to pay dollar interest to Commercial Credit Bank, Floyds will swap at an interest rate of 5.35%, the offer rate quoted by the bank when it receives dollars in return for paying interest at the 6-month LIBOR. This part of the transaction is an interest rate swap. The cash flows are represented in Part 1 of Exhibit 21.6. Because the fixed-rate payments are made semiannually, the dollar interest payments are

$$0.5 \times 0.0535 \times \$360 \text{ million} = \$9.63 \text{ million}$$

In the other part of the transaction, Floyds wants to receive pound interest payments from Commercial Credit. The bank is willing to do this at 8.00%, its bid rate, in return for receiving floating-rate dollar payments from Floyds. The cash flows for the second part of the transaction are under Part 2 of Exhibit 21.6. Because the fixed-rate pound payments are received semiannually, the pound interest receipts are

$$0.5 \times 0.08 \times £200 \text{ million} = £8 \text{ million}$$

Because this part of the transaction involves a change of currencies, the principal amounts are exchanged both at the beginning of the swap and in the reverse direction at the end of the 5 years. Hence, in the final period, Floyds must pay the $360 million principal in addition to its final dollar interest payment, and it will receive £200 million plus its final pound interest receipt from Commercial Credit. Notice that the dollar LIBOR receipts in Part 1 are equal to the dollar LIBOR payments in Part 2. Hence, Floyds has swapped out of fixed pound debt payments into fixed dollar debt payments. Floyds can then use the pound principal and interest received from Commercial Credit to pay the bondholders of its pound-denominated debt.

In Example 21.3, Floyds is content to transact at the quoted rates provided by Commercial Credit. But because the cash flows on a corporation's debt will typically not exactly equal the cash flows from the swap quoted by the financial intermediary, some residual foreign exchange risk can be present.

Later in this chapter, we will consider an extended example that shows how the cash flows of a swap can be adjusted to eliminate the exchange rate risk. First, though, we examine how a currency swap would have been done in the 1980s when financial intermediaries first arranged deals that allowed firms to issue bonds in one currency and then swap the cash flows with a firm that had issued bonds in a different currency. This first part of the example introduces the important concept of comparative advantage in borrowing.

Comparative Borrowing Advantages in Matched Currency Swaps

The Goodweek-Bridgerock Situation

Consider two tire companies, Goodweek and Bridgerock, which both want to issue 5-year, fixed-rate debt. Suppose Goodweek wants to raise approximately $200 million, and Bridgerock wants to raise €100 million, which is equal to $200 million at the current exchange rate of $2/€. Exhibit 21.7 shows the possible bond issues that the two firms are considering.

Investment bankers are quoting dollar interest rates of 8.5% for Goodweek and 9.5% for Bridgerock, with one annual interest payment. Both companies would have to pay a 1.875% fee to the banks for their help in issuing the bonds. Hence, if $200 million of bonds were issued at par, the proceeds to the two firms would be

$$(1 - 0.01875) \times \$200 \text{ million} = \$196,250,000$$

The coupon payments for Goodweek would be

$$0.085 \times \$200 \text{ million} = \$17,000,000$$

per year. Bridgerock would make coupon payments of

$$0.095 \times \$200 \text{ million} = \$19,000,000$$

per year.

The all-in cost (AIC) of a debt issue (see Chapter 11) is the internal rate of return on the company's cash flows given by the net proceeds to the firm in year 0 as an inflow and given

Exhibit 21.7 Possible Bond Issues for Goodweek and Bridgerock

Goodweek Bridgerock	Dollar Bond Issues 200 million @ 8.5% with 1.875% fee 200 million @ 9.5% with 1.875% fee		Euro Bond Issues 100 million @ 13.5% with 2.25% fee 100 million @ 13.75% with 2.25% fee	
Year	Goodweek's Cash Flows	Bridgerock's Cash Flows	Goodweek's Cash Flows	Bridgerock's Cash Flows
0	196.25	196.25	97.75	97.75
1	−17.00	−19.00	−13.50	−13.75
2	−17.00	−19.00	−13.50	−13.75
3	−17.00	−19.00	−13.50	−13.75
4	−17.00	−19.00	−13.50	−13.75
5	−217.00	−219.00	−113.50	−113.75
All-in cost	8.98%	9.99%	14.16%	14.41%

Note: Yearly cash flows are in millions of dollars or euros.

the coupon interest payments made in years 1 through 5 and the final return of principal in year 5 as outflows. If Goodweek does the dollar debt issue, its AIC is 8.98%. If Bridgerock does the dollar debt issue, its AIC is 9.99%.

It is also possible for the two firms to issue euro-denominated debt, in which case the size of the issue must be €100 million in order to raise $200 million. Investment bankers are quoting euro interest rates of 13.5% for Goodweek and 13.75% for Bridgerock. In both cases, there would be a 2.25% fee, and the proceeds of the issue to either firm would be

$$(1 - 0.0225) \times €100,000,000 = €97,750,000$$

or $195,500,000 at the current exchange rate of $2/€. The coupon payments for Goodweek would be

$$0.135 \times €100,000,000 = €13,500,000$$

per year. Bridgerock would make coupon payments of

$$0.1375 \times €100,000,000 = €13,750,000$$

per year. Exhibit 21.7 indicates that if Goodweek does the euro debt issue, its AIC is 14.16%. If Bridgerock does its euro debt issue, its AIC is 14.41%.

How should the firms choose the currency of denomination of their bonds? We need to consider their hedging motives as well as the direct AICs of the different debts. Suppose Goodweek would like to have euro debt because it has positive euro cash flows from the sales of its products in Europe. The euro debt would provide a partial hedge to the revenue stream from Goodweek's European sales. Suppose, analogously, that Bridgerock would like to have dollar debt because it has positive dollar cash flows from the sales of its products in the United States. Given the firms' hedging motives, each firm could issue the bonds denominated in its preferred currency. In this case, Goodweek would issue euro bonds, and Bridgerock would issue U.S. dollar bonds. But, as we will demonstrate, this is inefficient given the quoted all-in costs.

Absolute vs. Comparative Advantage

With the bond yields quoted in Exhibit 21.7, Goodweek has an **absolute borrowing advantage** in both currencies because its all-in costs are lower in both currencies, but Bridgerock has a comparative borrowing advantage when it comes to issuing euro debt. This implies that Goodweek has a comparative borrowing advantage in issuing U.S. dollar debt.

What does it mean for Bridgerock to have a **comparative borrowing advantage** in issuing euro debt? Because neither firm is borrowing at the risk-free rate, investors have demanded a default premium, which is built into the quoted rates and the all-in costs. If the firms borrow dollars, Bridgerock must pay 9.99%, an additional 101 basis points compared to 8.98% for Goodweek. If the two firms borrow in euros, Bridgerock must pay only an additional 25 basis points—14.41% for Bridgerock versus 14.16% for Goodweek. Because euro interest rates are higher than dollar interest rates, the euro is at a discount relative to the dollar. Consequently, a euro basis point in the future is actually worth less than a dollar basis point in the future. If the relative borrowing costs in the two currencies were the same for the two companies, the number of euro basis points corresponding to 101 dollar basis points would have to be higher, not lower, than 101.

The euro debt of Bridgerock is being priced by the market more favorably than its dollar debt, and this means Bridgerock has a comparative advantage borrowing in euros, and Goodweek has a comparative advantage borrowing in dollars. Later on, we will discuss the possible sources of these comparative advantages. For now, let's examine whether there is an opportunity for each firm to issue debt in the currency in which it has a comparatively cheaper borrowing cost and then to benefit by doing a currency swap. Bridgerock will consequently issue euro debt, and Goodweek will issue dollar debt. Then, we will see if it is possible for a financial intermediary to match up the two parties, allow each company to make the other's interest and principal payments, and produce all-in costs for each company that are below their direct borrowing costs in their preferred currencies. In the end, Goodweek will have its desired euro debt, and Bridgerock will have its desired dollar debt.

Using a Financial Intermediary in a Currency Swap

Can an investment bank such as Bank Carribus do the Goodweek–Bridgerock currency swap and still make money? The answer is yes because currency swaps were originally handled this way until the mid-1980s. Financial intermediaries would know of two counterparties that could benefit by swapping the interest and principal payments on bonds denominated in different currencies. The financial intermediary would arrange the swap, act as counterparty for both firms, and walk away with a handsome profit.

Exhibits 21.8 and 21.9 demonstrate how the cash flows for a currency swap could be structured for Goodweek, Bridgerock, and Bank Carribus. Exhibit 21.8 presents the actual cash flows, and Exhibit 21.9 provides a summary diagram of the cash flows and the all-in costs. The currency swap begins with each firm issuing bonds denominated in the currency in which it has a comparative borrowing advantage: Goodweek issues a dollar-denominated bond to investors, and Bridgerock issues a euro-denominated bond to investors.

Bank Carribus wants each firm to make the interest and principal payments associated with the bond issue of the other company in return for receiving cash flows that are equivalent to the interest and principal payments that each firm owes its bondholders. What must be determined is how much money will change hands initially, at the beginning of the swap. This initial transfer will determine the all-in costs of the swap to each company.

If it participates in the currency swap, Goodweek receives dollar interest and principal from Bank Carribus that exactly match the cash flows that Goodweek owes its bondholders. In return, Goodweek pays Bank Carribus the sequence of euro cash flows associated with Bridgerock's bond issue. Bank Carribus then gives these euro cash flows to Bridgerock, and Bridgerock makes the dollar interest and principal payments to Bank Carribus that are equivalent to the cash flows associated with Goodweek's dollar debt.

The challenge for Bank Carribus is to make the swapping of these cash flows attractive to both counterparties. It can do this by quoting an all-in cost to Goodweek for the euro cash flows the firm will pay to Bank Carribus that is less than 14.16%, Goodweek's direct all-in cost. It must also quote an all-in cost to Bridgerock for the dollar cash flows that Bridgerock will pay Bank Carribus that is less than Bridgerock's direct borrowing cost of 9.99%.

Exhibit 21.8 Swaps with Bank Carribus as the Financial Intermediary

Year	Goodweek's Cash Flows			Bridgerock's Cash Flows			Bank Carribus's Cash Flows	
	$ Bond Issue	Swap with Bank Carribus		€ Bond Issue	Swap with Bank Carribus		Net	
		Dollar	Euro		Dollar	Euro	Dollar	Euro
0	196.25	−196.25	99.83	97.75	191.57	−97.75	4.68	−2.08
1	−17.00	17.00	−13.75	−13.75	−17.00	13.75	0.00	0.00
2	−17.00	17.00	−13.75	−13.75	−17.00	13.75	0.00	0.00
3	−17.00	17.00	−13.75	−13.75	−17.00	13.75	0.00	0.00
4	−17.00	17.00	−13.75	−13.75	−17.00	13.75	0.00	0.00
5	−217.00	217.00	−113.75	−113.75	−217.00	113.75	0.00	0.00
AIC	8.98%	8.98%	13.80%	14.41%	9.60%	14.41%		
					Bank Carribus's net dollar profit		0.5206	

Note: All cash flows are in millions of dollars or euros.

Exhibit 21.9 Intermediated Currency Swap Diagram

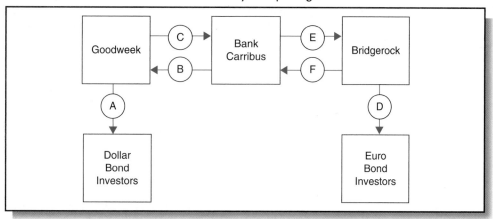

Notes: The currency swap diagram summarizes the rates of return and the various cash flows:

A. Goodweek issues $200 million of bonds to investors with 8.5% coupons. After fees of 1.875%, the all-in cost is 8.98%.

B. Goodweek gives the net proceeds of the bond issue, $196.25 million, to Bank Carribus in exchange for €99.83 million, which is the present value at 13.80% of the € cash flows given in C. Goodweek receives from Bank Carribus the dollar interest and principal payments that it owes to bondholders in A.

C. Goodweek makes the euro payments to Bank Carribus of the interest and principal associated with the bond issue of Bridgerock in D that has an AIC of 13.80%.

D. Bridgerock issues €100 million of bonds with 13.75% coupons. After fees of 2.25%, the company's AIC is 14.41%.

E. Bridgerock gives the net proceeds of the debt, €97.75 million, to Bank Carribus in exchange for $191.57 million, which is the present value at 9.60% of the dollar cash flows given in F. Bridgerock receives from Bank Carribus the euro interest and principal payments that it owes to bondholders in D.

F. Bridgerock makes payments to Bank Carribus of the dollar payments of interest and principal with an AIC of 9.60% associated with the bond issue of Goodweek in A.

These interest rates are the opportunity costs of the respective firms of borrowing directly in their desired currencies.

Exhibit 21.8 is structured with quotes from Bank Carribus of 13.80% in euros for Goodweek and 9.60% in dollars for Bridgerock. The euro interest rate of 13.80% is used to discount the sequence of euro cash flows that Goodweek will make to Bank Carribus. In exchange for the $196,250,000 raised in the bond issue, Goodweek gets the present value of the euro cash flows discounted at 13.80%, which is €99,827,517.60. Similarly, the dollar interest rate of 9.60% is used to discount the sequence of cash flows that Bridgerock will make to Bank Carribus. In exchange for the €97,750,000 raised in its bond issue, Bridgerock gets the present value of the dollar cash flows discounted at 9.60%, which is $191,574,344.

How much does Bank Carribus make in the deal? At the initiation of the deal, Bank Carribus has a net dollar cash inflow of

$$\$196,250,000 - \$191,574,344 = \$4,675,656$$

and a net euro cash outflow of

$$€99,827,517.60 - €97,750,000 = €2,077,517.60$$

At the current spot exchange rate of $2/€, the dollar value of the euro outflow is

$$(\$2/€) \times €2,077,517.60 = \$4,155,035.20$$

Hence, Bank Carribus makes a net dollar profit of

$$\$4,675,656 - \$4,155,035.20 = \$520,620.80$$

Bank Carribus's initial euro cash flow must be negative because it must induce Goodweek to make the euro interest and principal payments associated with the Bridgerock bonds. At Bridgerock's borrowing cost of 14.41%, the net proceeds of the euro bond issue are equal in present value to the euro cash flows that Goodweek will pay to Bank Carribus. But Bank Carribus cannot give Goodweek only the net euro proceeds of Bridgerock's bond issue because that would imply an all-in cost for Goodweek of 14.41%. Because Goodweek can borrow directly in euros at an interest rate of 14.16%, Bank Carribus must offer Goodweek more euros up front than Bank Carribus will receive from Bridgerock's bond issue.

Bank Carribus has an initial positive dollar cash flow because it can keep some of the dollar proceeds of Goodweek's bond issue, which raises the internal rate of return on the cash flows, while offering a dollar AIC to Bridgerock that is lower than Bridgerock's opportunity cost. The reason Bank Carribus has a positive net cash flow is that the currency swap exploits the comparative borrowing ability of each firm, which allows each of the participants, including the financial intermediary, to gain.

Bank Carribus also bears the credit risk of each counterparty, and it must be compensated for bearing this risk. If either Goodweek or Bridgerock stops making its payments to Bank Carribus, Bank Carribus can stop making payments to that firm. Depending on how interest rates and exchange rates have evolved, one of the parties will owe the other a net payment. But Bank Carribus must continue to serve as the financial intermediary for the other side of the deal.

The Sources of the Gains from a Swap

In the preceding example, Goodweek is clearly considered a better credit risk than Bridgerock in both the dollar and euro bond markets. The top panel in Exhibit 21.10 repeats the AICs for the different bond issues. The differences between the AICs Goodweek faces and the rates Bridgerock faces represents a credit spread (recall the discussion in Chapter 11). The reason Bank Carribus managed to lower the AIC for both Goodweek and Bridgerock with a swap is that it exploited the differential credit spread for the two firms in the dollar versus the euro market.

In the dollar market, Bridgerock faces a spread of 101 basis points over Goodweek's cost of funding; in the euro market, the spread is only 25 basis points. However, as indicated earlier, absolute spreads in different currencies are not strictly comparable because, in this case, a euro basis point is worth less than a dollar basis point because the euro is trading at a discount.

Exhibit 21.10 The Gains from Swapping

	Funding Costs in Different Currencies	
	Dollar	**Euro**
	Before the Swap	
Goodweek	8.98%	14.16%
Bridgerock	9.99%	14.41%
Absolute spread	101 bp	25 bp
Multiplicative spread	93 bp	22 bp
	After the Swap	
Goodweek	8.98%	13.80%
Bridgerock	9.60%	14.41%
Absolute spread	62 bp	61 bp
Multiplicative spread	57 bp	54 bp

Notes: AICs are reported for loans in dollars and euros before and after the swap. The absolute spread is the difference between the AIC of Bridgerock and the AIC of Goodweek. The multiplicative spread (mcsp) solves

$$(1 + AIC_{Goodweek})(1 + mcsp) = (1 + AIC_{Bridgerock})$$

In Chapter 11, we introduced the concept of a multiplicative spread, and the computation is repeated in the notes to Exhibit 21.10. We argued that arbitrage should keep multiplicative spreads in line across countries. In Exhibit 21.10, we show that there is a large difference in the two multiplicative spreads, and it is this difference of 71 basis points that is exploited in the swap.

First, Bridgerock brings its dollar AIC down from 9.99% to 9.60%, lowering its multiplicative spread in the dollar market relative to Goodweek to 57 basis points, which lowers the multiplicative spread by 36 basis points (93 bp – 57 bp). Second, Goodweek lowers its AIC in euros to 13.80%, which increases the multiplicative spread relative to Bridgerock's AIC by 32 basis points (54 bp – 22 bp). The sum of these two "gains" is 68 basis points. This leaves 3 basis points on the table, which constitutes the intermediary fee for Bank Carribus, and the spreads are now almost fully equalized in the two currencies. To see that Bank Carribus is making only a small fee, consider that the bank's profit of $520,620.80 is 0.26% of the $200 million swapped.

POINT–COUNTERPOINT
More on Comparative Advantage

Ante, Freedy, and Suttle were visiting their cousin Reid, who is a high school debater. Reid had just opined on the virtues of international trade and why outsourcing is no big deal. At a break in the tournament, Ante said, "I thought comparative advantage was an international trade concept, but Bekaert and Hodrick argue that it motivates currency swaps."

Freedy replied, "Well, I remember comparative advantage from international trade, but I'm not really clear on how it works. I sort of remember that international trade is motivated by differences in technology that provide countries with opportunities for specialization and that specialization is supposed to make everybody better off. That always seemed a little like magic to me, but the logic made me a firm believer in free trade. So, if comparative advantage works in trade, why not in currency swaps?"

As usual, Ante was the denser of the two. "I get it that if it takes 4 hours for me to clean the house and 2 hours to cook dinner, while it takes you 3 hours to clean the house and 3 hours to cook dinner, we're better off with you cleaning the house and me making dinner. That is just comparative common sense. But, if it takes you 5 hours to clean the house and 5 hours to make dinner, which it does by the way, then you're just less productive than I am, and I should just make everything for myself."

Freedy, trying to stay cool, replied, "Well, I don't think you're more productive than I am, but suppose you're right. How would trade work?"

At this point, Suttle Trooth figured he'd better get involved. He said, "Let's take your productivity figures and see who should do what. It takes Ante twice as long to clean the house as it does to make dinner (4 hours vs. 2 hours), but Freedy can make dinners just as fast as he cleans houses (5 hours vs. 5 hours). If you both have 20 hours that you can work each week, Ante can clean 5 houses (20 hours / 4 hours per house), or make 10 dinners (20 hours / 2 hours per dinner), or split his time between the two activities. Freedy, on the other hand, can clean 4 houses (20 hours / 5 hours per house), or make 4 dinners (20 hours / 5 hours per dinner), or split his time between the two activities."

Suttle continued, "Because Ante's dinner cost of clean houses is 2 (4 hours per clean house / 2 hours per dinner), whereas Freedy's dinner cost of clean houses is 1 (5 hours per clean house / 5 hours per dinner), Freedy is comparatively, or relatively, more efficient at cleaning houses than Ante. Comparative advantage dictates that Freedy should produce 4 clean houses in his 20 hours but he would sell house cleaning services to Ante in return for dinners. Ante would, in turn, specialize in making dinners but would sell some dinners to

Freedy for clean houses. For example, you two might agree that 1 cleaning of the house should cost 1.5 dinners. Freedy could sell Ante 2 house cleanings for 3 dinners:

$$3 \text{ dinners} = 2 \text{ house cleanings} \times 1.5 \text{ dinners per house cleaning}$$

"After trading, Freedy would have 2 clean houses and 3 dinners, which would have cost him 25 hours (2 clean houses × 5 hours per clean house + 3 dinners × 5 hours per dinner) to make if he had done it himself, but he worked only 20 hours. Ante would have 2 clean houses and 7 dinners, which would have cost him 22 hours (2 clean houses × 4 hours per clean house + 7 dinners × 2 hours per dinner) to make if he had done it himself, but he also only worked 20 hours."

"Therefore," concluded Suttle, "you're both better off by specializing in the production of the good that you are relatively efficient at producing and then engaging in trade. The secret is to produce the good in which you have a comparative advantage. Alternatively, you can remember that you should sell the good that is relatively inexpensive for you to produce. Trade is ultimately related to what the differences in relative prices would be if there were no trade. Does this help you understand swaps any better?"

Both brothers decided that spending a little more time thinking about the interest rates in the Goodweek–Bridgerock case might be useful.

Swapping Bond Proceeds and Coupon Rates with Quoted Swap Rates

We noted earlier that swaps have become like financial commodities, with financial intermediaries quoting bid and offer rates on swaps for large amounts. Exhibit 21.11 demonstrates how currency swaps are done with a financial intermediary using quoted swap rates.

We will continue to illustrate the issues with Bank Carribus acting as the financial intermediary for Goodweek and Bridgerock. Now, though, each firm will deal individually with Bank Carribus, starting from the bank's quoted swap rates. The end result will be that Bank Carribus will again have a positive net present value for the two transactions because it will systematically make payments in currencies at lower interest rates than the payments it receives from firms.

This example has aspects that are both more complex and simpler than the typical swap. The example is more complex because we will require the financial intermediary to make the payments on actual bonds. Standard "plain-vanilla" swaps simply pay the quoted swap rates on an even notional amount, but no attempt is made to match the cash flows of an underlying bond issue. If the financial intermediary is required to match the cash flows of a bond, as we are doing in this case, the swap is considered to be "off market," and the additional cash flows required to match the bond payments must be valued somehow. Because the additional payments happen at different times in the future, the interest rates used for different periods may differ, depending on the time period at which the payments are made. The simplification we will use in the example is that the interest rates are the same at all maturities.[3]

Suppose that Bank Carribus offers the following quotations on 5-year fixed interest rate and currency swaps for annual cash flows:

U.S. dollars: 8.25% bid and 8.35% offered against the 1-year dollar LIBOR
Euros: 13.00% bid and 13.10% offered against the 1-year dollar LIBOR

Let's explore how the swaps would be done.

---

[3]The financial intermediary would use the appropriate zero-coupon interest rates for different maturities to value the future cash flows. In general, zero-coupon interest rates for different maturities are not the same. In the swap market, traders derive zero-coupon interest rates from the swap rates, and it is this term structure, or "swap curve," that they use to value cash flows.

Exhibit 21.11 Swaps as Individual Transactions at Quoted Rates

GOODWEEK'S DOLLAR BOND ISSUE AND CASH FLOWS IN THE SWAP INTO EUROS WITH BANK CARRIBUS

Year	Dollar Bond Issue	Swap Receipts (+) and Payments (−) with Bank Carribus			Extra Dollar Interest	Extra Euro Interest	Effective Euro Cash Flows
		Notional $	Dollars	Notional €			
0	196.25	−200.00	−196.25	100.00			98.13
1	−17.00	16.50	17.00	−13.10	0.50	0.28	−13.38
2	−17.00	16.50	17.00	−13.10	0.50	0.28	−13.38
3	−17.00	16.50	17.00	−13.10	0.50	0.28	−13.38
4	−17.00	16.50	17.00	−13.10	0.50	0.28	−13.38
5	−217.00	216.50	217.00	−113.10	0.50	0.28	−113.38
AIC	8.98%	8.25%	8.98%	13.10%			13.93%

BRIDGEROCK'S EURO BOND ISSUE AND SWAP INTO DOLLARS WITH BANK CARRIBUS

Year	Euro Bond Issue	Swap Receipts (+) and Payments (−) with Bank Carribus			Extra Euro Interest	Extra Dollar Interest	Effective Dollar Cash Flows
		Notional €	Euros	Notional $			
0	97.75	−100.00	−97.75	200.00			195.50
1	−13.75	13.00	13.75	−16.70	0.75	1.33	−18.03
2	−13.75	13.00	13.75	−16.70	0.75	1.33	−18.03
3	−13.75	13.00	13.75	−16.70	0.75	1.33	−18.03
4	−13.75	13.00	13.75	−16.70	0.75	1.33	−18.03
5	−113.75	113.00	113.75	−216.70	0.75	1.33	−218.03
AIC	14.41%	13.00%	14.41%	8.35%			9.60%

BANK CARRIBUS'S CASH FLOWS

Year	Receipts (+) from Goodweek Payments (−) to Goodweek		Receipts (+) from Bridgerock Payments (−) to Bridgerock		Dollars	Euros
	Dollars	Euros	Dollars	Euros		
0	196.25	−98.13	−195.50	97.75	0.75	−0.38
1	−17.00	13.38	18.03	−13.75	1.03	−0.37
2	−17.00	13.38	18.03	−13.75	1.03	−0.37
3	−17.00	13.38	18.03	−13.75	1.03	−0.37
4	−17.00	13.38	18.03	−13.75	1.03	−0.37
5	−217.00	113.38	218.03	−113.75	1.03	−0.37
AIC	8.98%	13.93%	9.60%	14.41%		

				Present Value @	8.35%	13.00%
					4.84	−1.67
				Value in Dollars	1.50	

Note: All cash flows are in millions of dollars or euros.

The Transactions of Goodweek

Consider how Goodweek might interact with Bank Carribus in a currency swap based on quoted swap rates. Goodweek issues the dollar bond, but it wants euro debt. Goodweek therefore asks Bank Carribus to make the interest and principal payments on its dollar bond issue. In return, Goodweek will make euro-denominated payments to Bank Carribus. If Bank Carribus is using the quoted swap rates, Bank Carribus is willing to make fixed dollar payments to Goodweek at an interest rate of 8.25%. For $200 million principal, Bank Carribus would expect to pay interest of

$$0.0825 \times \$200 \text{ million} = \$16.50 \text{ million}$$

Because the quoted interest rate at which Bank Carribus is willing to receive euro payments is 13.10%, and because the euro principal that is equivalent to $200 million is €100 million, the notional cash flows for Goodweek involve interest of

$$13.10\% \times €100 \text{ million} = €13.10 \text{ million}$$

However, this plain-vanilla swap does not suit Goodweek for two reasons. First, Goodweek does not have $200 million to exchange because it raised only $196.25 million in bond proceeds. Second, Goodweek must pay $17 million in annual interest to its bondholders, and Goodweek would like to receive that much from Bank Carribus.

Consequently, the actual swap will require two adjustments. First, in exchange for the $196.25 million proceeds of the bond issue, Bank Carribus will give Goodweek the equivalent value in euros at the exchange rate of $2/€:

$$\$196.25 \text{ million}/(\$2/€) = €98.13 \text{ million}$$

Second, Goodweek would like to have Bank Carribus pay it the full dollar interest on its bonds, which is more dollar interest than Bank Carribus is quoting on the swap, in exchange for which Goodweek will pay extra euro interest to Bank Carribus. This requires a **basis point adjustment** on the swap

Deriving the Basis Point Adjustment

The extra dollar interest that Bank Carribus must pay to Goodweek is $0.50 million for each of the next 5 years. The present value of this amount at 8.25% is $1.98 million.[4] In order to find the extra euro interest that Goodweek must pay each year, we convert the present value of the extra dollar interest into euros at the spot exchange rate. Thus, we get a euro principal of

$$\$1.98 \text{ million}/(\$2/€) = €0.99 \text{ million}$$

We now want to find the value of the annual euro payment that is equivalent to this euro principal, using the euro interest rate of 13.10%. It turns out that the present value of five payments of €0.28 million when discounted at 13.10% is equivalent to €0.99 million. Hence, the euro discounted present value of five payments of €0.28 million at 13.10% is equivalent to five payments of $0.50 million discounted at 8.25% when the exchange rate is $2/€. This extra euro interest is added to the €13.10 million of notional interest, and Goodweek will owe interest of €13.38 million. This provides Goodweek with an all-in cost of 13.93%, which is less than its direct euro borrowing cost of 14.16%.

The Transactions of Bridgerock

The transactions of Bridgerock's swap with Bank Carribus would be structured in an analogous way. Bridgerock wants dollar debt, but it issues a euro bond. Bridgerock asks Bank Carribus to make the interest and principal payments on its euro bond issue in return for letting the company make dollar-denominated interest and principal payments to the bank.

Because Bank Carribus is using the quoted interest rates we discussed, Bank Carribus would be willing to make fixed euro payments to Bridgerock at an interest rate of 13.00%. For €100 million principal, Bank Carribus would expect to pay interest of

$$0.13 \times €100 \text{ million} = €13 \text{ million}$$

Because the quoted interest rate at which Bank Carribus is willing to receive dollar payments is 8.35%, and because the dollar principal that is equivalent to €100 million is $200 million, the notional cash flows for Bridgerock involve interest of

$$8.35\% \times \$200 \text{ million} = \$16.70 \text{ million}$$

---

[4]The assumption of a flat term structure of interest rates is important in taking this present value with the 5-year rate as this cash flow pattern is quite different from a standard 5-year bond.

However, this plain-vanilla swap does not suit Bridgerock for two reasons. First, Bridgerock does not have €100 million to exchange because it raised only €97.75 million in bond proceeds. Second, Bridgerock must pay €13.75 million in annual interest to its bondholders, and Bridgerock would like to receive that much from Bank Carribus.

Consequently, the actual swap will require two adjustments: a change in the initial principals and a basis point adjustment. First, in exchange for the €97.75 million proceeds of the bond issue, Bank Carribus will give Bridgerock the equivalent value in dollars, at the exchange rate of $2/€:

$$€97.75 \text{ million} \times (\$2/€) = \$195.50 \text{ million}$$

Second, Bridgerock will require Bank Carribus to pay extra euro interest, in exchange for which Bridgerock will pay extra dollar interest to Bank Carribus. The extra euro interest that Bank Carribus must pay to Bridgerock is €0.75 million for each of the next 5 years. The present value of this amount at 13% is €2.64 million. In order to find the extra dollar interest that Bridgerock must pay each year, we convert the present value of the extra euro interest to dollars at the spot exchange rate. Thus, we get a dollar principal of

$$€2.64 \text{ million} \times (\$2/€) = \$5.28 \text{ million}$$

We now want to find the value of five annual dollar payments that is equivalent to this dollar principal, using the dollar interest rate of 8.35%. It turns out that the present value of five payments of $1.33 million when discounted at 8.35% is equivalent to $5.28 million. Hence, the dollar discounted present value of five payments of $1.33 million at 8.35% is equivalent to five payments of €0.75 million discounted at 13% when the exchange rate is $2/€. This extra dollar interest is added to the $16.70 million of notional interest, and we find that Bridgerock will owe interest of $18.03 million. This provides Bridgerock with an all-in cost of 9.60%, which is less than its direct dollar borrowing cost of 9.99%.

The Transactions of Bank Carribus

The last part of Exhibit 21.11 provides the actual dollar and euro cash flows for Bank Carribus from engaging in the two swaps. At the beginning of the currency swap, Bank Carribus exchanges principal amounts that are equivalent at the spot exchange rate. The net inflow of dollars to Bank Carribus is $0.75 million, which is equivalent to its net outflow of euros, €0.38 million.

In years 1 through 5, Bank Carribus makes interest payments in dollars to Goodweek of $17 million and receives dollar interest payments from Bridgerock of $18.03 million, giving it a net dollar inflow of $1.03 million. Bank Carribus also makes interest payments in euros to Bridgerock of €13.75 million and receives euro interest payments from Goodweek of €13.38 million, giving it a net euro outflow of €0.37 million. In the fifth year, the exchange of principals occurs with each firm, but Bank Carribus has no net cash flows of either dollars or euros because the principal amounts are equal.

Because Bank Carribus is not attempting to perfectly match the future cash flows of two counterparties, it bears some risk from these two transactions due to possible fluctuations in interest rates and exchange rates. Without knowing Bank Carribus's overall portfolio of cash flows, though, we cannot know whether Bank Carribus is taking on additional risk. Because Bank Carribus is making a market in these transactions, it is only concerned about the net exposure it generates from all the transactions it makes.

Because Bank Carribus now experiences dollar and euro cash flows in all 5 years instead of just in the present, we must take the present values of the future cash flows to determine how much net revenue Bank Carribus has generated in the two transactions. The present value of the dollar cash inflow can be taken at the swap rate of 8.35%, because this is the swap rate at which the bank receives dollars. The dollar present value is $4.84 million. The euro cash outflow from Bank Carribus is discounted at 13%, which is the rate at which Bank Carribus pays euros. The euro present value is €1.67 million. The net of these two cash flows in dollars is

$$\$4.84 \text{ million} - [(\$2/€) \times €1.67 \text{ million}] = \$1.50 \text{ million}$$

Currency Swaps as a Package of Forward Contracts

In the 5-year swap just described, Goodweek contracts to pay euros in return for receiving dollars at various dates in the future. Bridgerock is paying dollars in return for receiving euros at various contractual dates in the future. These transactions are analogous to long-term forward contracts. Goodweek's transactions define bid prices of dollar per euro from Bank Carribus's perspective, and Bridgerock's transactions define ask prices of dollars per euro, again from the perspective of the financial intermediary.

Notice, though, that the structure of the 5-year swap has four exchanges of currencies at the same implicit forward exchange rate and a fifth exchange at a different rate. That is, the exchanges of the five interest payments are done at the same implicit forward rate, and the final return of principal is done at the original spot rate. When interest rates differ across currencies, the implicit forward rates in the swap are very different from the long-term forward rates that we have calculated in earlier chapters using the spot exchange rate and the term structures of spot interest rates. To understand the difference and to get an idea why the long-term swap market exits, let's examine how Goodweek and Bridgerock might go about hedging their transactions in the forward market.

Euro Bond Issues with Forward Hedging

Rather than doing currency swaps, both Goodweek and Bridgerock could exploit their comparative advantages in borrowing and achieve the desired currencies of denomination for their liabilities by issuing bonds in their comparatively low-cost currencies and using long-term forward contracts to hedge the bond payments. In this scenario, Goodweek issues dollar bonds and contracts to buy dollars with euros in the long-term forward market to cover the dollar interest and principal payments owed to its bondholders. Goodweek would offset its outstanding dollar liability with the forward-market contracts of a financial intermediary, like Bank Carribus, which promises to deliver dollars to Goodweek in return for the company making euro payments to the bank. Analogously, Bridgerock would issue euro bonds and contract to sell dollars forward for euros in the long-term forward market to cover its euro interest and principal payments. Bridgerock matches its euro liabilities with a sequence of euro assets that Bank Carribus delivers to the company in return for the company making dollar payments to the bank.

If the currency swap is to be preferred by both Goodweek and Bridgerock, the transaction costs in the long-term forward market must exceed those in the currency swap market. Exhibit 21.12 presents a set of forward bid and ask exchange rates such that this is indeed the case. The midpoints of the bid and ask forward rates for year k in the future are determined from covered interest rate parity using the midpoints of the dollar and euro swap rates:

$$(\$2/€) \times (1.0830/1.1305)^k$$

This is the right computation because the term structure of interest rates is assumed to be flat. The higher euro interest rate results in a substantial forward dollar discount on the euro. The forward market transaction costs are given by the percentage bid–ask spreads in the % Spread column, and they increase with maturity.

In Exhibit 21.12, Goodweek issues the dollar bond and converts the $196.25 million proceeds into €98.12 million at Bank Carribus's ask rate of $2.0002/€ in the spot market. We use the ask rate because Goodweek is selling dollars to Bank Carribus for euros. In years 1 through 5, Goodweek buys dollars from Bank Carribus with euros, which gives Goodweek euro liabilities. These transactions are done at Bank Carribus's bid rates of dollars per euro.

Exhibit 21.12 Bond Issues Hedged in the Forward Market

		Dollars/Euro			Goodweek's Dollar Bond Hedged into Euro		Bridgerock's Euro Bond Hedged into Dollars	
Year	Bid	Midpoint	Ask	% Spread	Dollars	Euros	Euros	Dollars
0	1.9998	2.0000	2.0002	0.02	196.25	98.12	97.75	195.48
1	1.9143	1.9160	1.9176	0.17	−17.00	−8.88	−13.75	−26.37
2	1.8316	1.8355	1.8393	0.42	−17.00	−9.28	−13.75	−25.29
3	1.7516	1.7583	1.7651	0.77	−17.00	−9.71	−13.75	−24.27
4	1.6742	1.6845	1.6947	1.22	−17.00	−10.15	−13.75	−23.30
5	1.5990	1.6137	1.6284	1.82	−217.00	−135.71	−113.75	−185.23
				All-in costs	8.98%	13.96%	14.41%	9.79%

Notes: Midpoint forward prices are $(\$2/€) \times (1.0830/1.1305)^k$, where k is the number of years in the future. Cash flows are in millions of dollars or euros. The % spread is $100 \times (\text{Ask} − \text{Bid})/[(\text{Ask} + \text{Bid})/2]$.

We use the bid rates because Goodweek is contracting to buy dollars forward from Bank Carribus with euros. For example, Goodweek's first-year euro payment is

$$€8.88 \text{ million} = \$17 \text{ million}/(\$1.9143/€)$$

Goodweek's resulting euro all-in cost for these transactions is 13.96%. This is slightly higher than the all-in cost of 13.93% achieved in the currency swap, so Goodweek would prefer the currency swap.

To use the forward market hedge, Bridgerock would issue the euro bond and convert the €97.75 million proceeds into $195.48 million at Bank Carribus's bid rate of $1.9998/€ in the spot market. In years 1 through 5, Bridgerock would contract to buy euros from Bank Carribus with dollars, which gives Bridgerock dollar liabilities. These transactions would be done at Bank Carribus's forward ask rates of dollars per euro. Bridgerock's resulting dollar all-in cost for its euro bond issue hedged into dollars in the forward market is 9.79%, which is higher than the 9.60% achieved in the currency swap. Hence, Bridgerock would prefer the currency swap as well.

The Value of a Currency Swap

As explained earlier, currency swaps begin life as zero net present value contracts. Over time, though, as interest rates and exchange rates change, the currency swap develops a positive value to one of the counterparties, with a corresponding negative value to the other participant. Consider the perspective of Goodweek. It owes euro interest and principal to Bank Carribus and is receiving dollar interest and principal from Bank Carribus. Essentially, the currency swap gives Goodweek an asset in the form of a dollar bond with a principal of $200 million and coupons of 8.50% because it is receiving $17 million of interest; it gives Goodweek a liability in the form of a euro bond with a principal of €100 million and coupons of 13.38% because it is paying €13.38 million of interest.

Let $B(t, \$200 \text{ m}, 8.50\%)$ and $B(t, €100 \text{ m}, 13.38\%)$ represent the market prices of these dollar and euro bonds at some time, t, in the future, and let $S(t, \$/€)$ be the spot exchange rate. Then, the dollar market value of the currency swap, from Goodweek's perspective, is

$$B(t, \$200 \text{ m}, 8.50\%) − [B(t, €100 \text{ m}, 13.38\%) \times S(t, \$/€)]$$

The market value of the swap is affected by three things. It rises if the dollar strengthens relative to the euro because the dollar value of Goodweek's euro liability falls. The swap also increases in value if dollar interest rates fall or if the euro interest rates rise because these interest rate changes directly affect the present values of the fixed cash flows in the swap.

Exhibit 21.13 Valuing a Swap to Close Out the Position

	BRIDGEROCK'S EURO BOND ISSUE AND SWAP INTO DOLLARS WITH BANK CARRIBUS		
		Swap Receipts (+) and Payments (−) with Bank Carribus	
Year	**Euros**	**Dollars**	
2	13.75	−18.03	
3	13.75	−18.03	
4	13.75	−18.03	
5	113.75	−218.03	
	105.32	−206.72	
	PV @ 12%	PV @ 8%	
Euro value of the Swap at USD2.25/EUR		13.44	

Notes: The euros Bridgerock is to receive are discounted at 12%, the dollars Bridgerock is to pay are discounted at 8%, and the spot exchange rate is USD2.25/EUR.

Bridgerock's perspective is the opposite of Goodweek's. Bridgerock owes dollar interest and principal, and it is receiving euro interest and principal. The currency swap consequently gives Bridgerock an asset in the form of a euro bond with principal of €100 million and coupons of 13.75% because Bridgerock receives €13.75 million of interest; the swap gives Bridgerock a liability in the form of a dollar bond with principal of $200 million and coupons of 9.015% because it pays interest of $18.03 million. If $B(t, \$200 \text{ m}, 9.015\%)$ and $B(t, €100 \text{ m}, 13.75\%)$ represent the market prices of these dollar and euro bonds at some future time, t, the euro market value of the currency swap, from Bridgerock's perspective, is

$$B(t, €100 \text{ m}, 13.75\%) - [B(t, \$200 \text{ m}, 9.015\%)/S(t, \$/€)]$$

This euro market value rises if the dollar weakens relative to the euro, if dollar interest rates rise, or if euro interest rates fall.

If either firm wants to exit the swap early, the market value of the swap determines which firm receives money. Exhibit 21.13 determines the market value of Bridgerock's swap if it decides to close out the swap after 1 year, with 4 years of interest and the final principal payment remaining. The spot exchange rate is $2.25/€, the dollar interest rate for 4-year bonds is 8%, and the euro interest rate for 4-year bonds is 12%. At these prices, the euro cash flows that Bridgerock is scheduled to receive have a present value of €105.32 million, which is greater than the face value because the euro interest rate has fallen. The dollar present value of what Bridgerock is required to pay has increased to $206.72 million because the dollar interest rate has also fallen. The net euro value of these cash flows at the spot rate is

$$€105.32 \text{ million} - [\$206.72 \text{ million}/(\$2.25/€)] = €13.44 \text{ million}$$

If Bridgerock wanted to close out the swap, Bank Carribus would pay Bridgerock €13.44 million. Of course, Bridgerock would still owe its euro bondholders.

Note that the changes in valuation that we have discussed ignore the issue of credit risk, which is critical in advanced valuation methodologies, as exemplified by the analysis of Darrell Duffie and Kenneth Singleton (1997).

The Rationale for Currency Swaps

A currency swap is a low-transaction-cost instrument for changing the currency of denomination of debt financing. This by itself does not explain why the currency swap market has grown so rapidly. The growth of the currency swap market reflects and has contributed to the increased integration of the world's international financial system. No longer are corporations tied to the financial markets of their country of residence. They can issue bonds in any currency and swap into their desired currency at the lowest all-in cost.

In the early days of the currency swap market, swaps were often driven by regulatory restraints and tax arbitrage opportunities. Chapter 11 notes the famous Exxon and RJR cases in which these companies substantially lowered their costs of funding by exploiting certain regulatory restrictions on Japanese institutional investors. Swaps played an integral role in making those deals work.

Differences in the way credit risks are analyzed across countries and the associated differences in spreads over risk-free rates also continue to provide an opportunity for lowering the cost of debt using swaps. When one party has a comparative borrowing advantage over another, it makes sense for the parties to issue debt in their least expensive currencies and to enter into a swap if the debts are not in the currencies of denomination that they prefer. These comparative advantages arise because institutional differences across countries lead to debt pricing that is slightly different, depending on the ultimate holder of the debt and its currency of denomination. Some of these pricing differences are due to the different ways credit risks are analyzed around the world. Essentially, these differences amount to a market inefficiency that can be exploited for profit. The result is that some companies can more easily issue debt in some currencies than in other currencies.

Regulations on the types of debt instruments that institutions can hold and accounting and tax differences across countries also have contributed to the growth of the swap market by providing demands for certain types of bonds that borrowers might not otherwise want to issue. Financial intermediaries who understand these demands and know borrowers who can supply the debts are then in a position to do a swap that results in lower borrowing costs for the issuer and a profit for the financial intermediary.

Why Swaps and Not Forwards?

Although we explained how long-dated forward contracts can be used to convert bonds issued in one currency into bonds denominated in a preferred currency, this method of financing is not widely used because long-dated forward markets are relatively illiquid. The bid–ask spreads of long-dated outright forward contracts begin to widen beyond a maturity of 1 year.

Banks also like swaps because the associated cash flows are just like those of bonds, and they can easily hedge the swaps in the bond markets later. In other words, if the swap book has too many dollars coming into the bank at the 5-year maturity, the bank can simply sell a 5-year bond from its portfolio to balance that risk.

Because the cash flows of forward contracts are not like the cash flows of bonds, banks find it difficult to offset their exposures in long-term outright forward contracts with other business transactions. They consequently try to make the offsetting trade directly in the forward market with a different financial intermediary, which only pushes the problem onto someone else. If it is expensive for a bank to hedge a long-term forward contract, the costs will ultimately be pushed onto the demanders of the contracts, making them more expensive and therefore less popular.

21.4 PARALLEL LOANS AND BACK-TO-BACK LOANS

Currency swaps are a comparatively new method of international financial contracting. These swaps are actually modern counterparts of parallel loans and back-to-back loans, which are still used but are much less important than currency swaps. Parallel loans originated as a means of securing low-cost funding for foreign subsidiaries and to circumvent various government regulations, such as currency controls. Another motivation of these contracts was the desire to avoid taxation on intracompany multinational transactions.

Parallel Loans

Exhibit 21.14 provides a diagram of a **parallel loan**. Two corporations with headquarters in two different countries, each having a subsidiary in the other corporation's country, enter into an agreement. For example, a U.S. parent corporation, say, Stars and Stripes Inc., might have a subsidiary in Indonesia, and an Indonesian corporation, say, Java Cava Inc., might have a subsidiary in the United States. Each subsidiary would like to borrow in the currency of the country in which it is operating. In this case, the Stars and Stripes subsidiary operating in Indonesia wants to borrow rupiah, and the Java Cava subsidiary operating in the United States wants to borrow dollars.

The funding needs of the subsidiaries could be met in several ways. The most direct way is for each subsidiary to simply borrow the currency it needs. But if a subsidiary is not well known in the foreign money market, it could be assessed a high default risk premium on the loan, which would make the loan very expensive. A second way for the subsidiaries to raise funds would be for the parent of each subsidiary to borrow the currency the subsidiary needs and to make an intracompany loan. Because parent corporations are usually better credit risks, this is less costly, but the interest payments that the subsidiary makes to the parent may be subject to withholding taxes. This leads to additional expenses of borrowing.

Exhibit 21.14 Parallel Loan Diagram

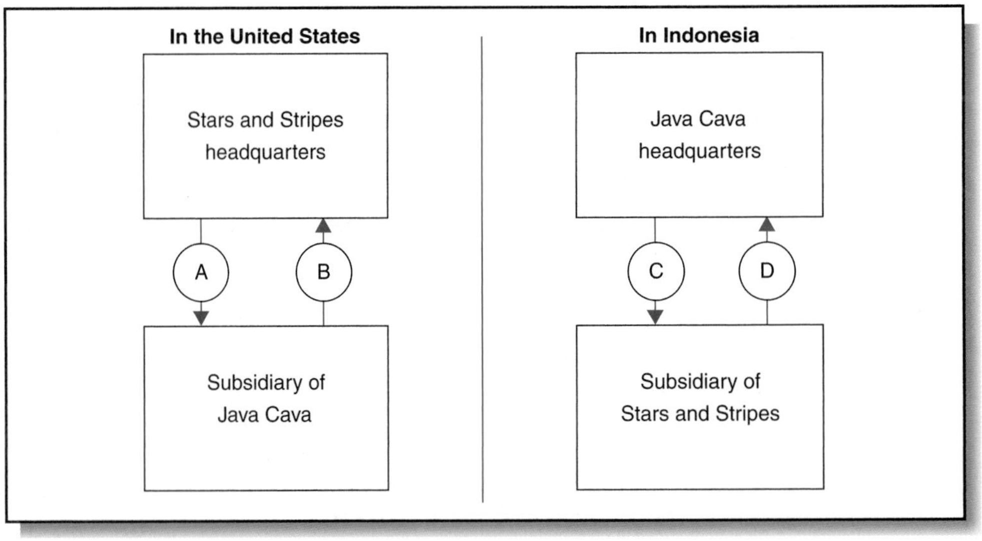

Notes: The parallel loan diagram summarizes the transactions and various cash flows:

- A. The Stars and Stripes headquarters lends USD1 million to the U.S. subsidiary of the Indonesian MNC, Java Cava.
- B. The U.S. subsidiary of Java Cava pays the Stars and Stripes headquarters interest and principal in dollars on the USD1 million loan.
- C. The Java Cava headquarters lends IDR10,000 million to the Indonesian subsidiary of Stars and Stripes. This is equivalent to the USD1 million in A at the spot exchange rate of IDR10,000/USD.
- D. The Indonesian subsidiary of Stars and Stripes pays the Java Cava headquarters interest and principal in euros on the IDR10,000 million loan.

A parallel loan avoids these extra expenses. In our example, the Stars and Stripes parent corporation makes a dollar loan to the Java Cava subsidiary operating in the United States, and the Java Cava parent corporation simultaneously makes a rupiah loan of equivalent value to the Stars and Stripes subsidiary operating in Indonesia. Because the loans are between entities operating in the same country, problems with the inconvertibility of currencies, exchange controls, and withholding taxes are avoided.

Exhibit 21.14 shows a parallel loan whereby the Stars and Stripes subsidiary operating in Indonesia borrows IDR10,000 million and the Java Cava subsidiary in the United States borrows $1 million. These amounts are equivalent if the exchange rate is IDR10,000/USD. Thus, the Java Cava parent gives IDR10,000 million to the Stars and Stripes subsidiary operating in Indonesia, and the Stars and Stripes parent gives $1 million to the Java Cava subsidiary operating in the United States. The parent corporations can raise the funds in any number of ways, including internally generated funds, issuing debt, or issuing equity. The two important features of the arrangement are that the initial values of the two simultaneous loans are equivalent (although they are denominated in different currencies) and that the interest rates on the loans are acceptable to the two counterparties. Usually, the interest rates are set at fixed rates corresponding to commercial rates prevailing on the respective currencies. But if the default risks of the two subsidiaries are quite different, one or both of the parent corporations may have to supply a credit guarantee.

The two loans are separate contractual obligations of the respective parties. This means that interest and principal repayment on one of the parallel loans must be continued even if the other subsidiary defaults on a payment. For example, if the Stars and Stripes subsidiary defaults on its rupiah loan that is owed to the Java Cava parent, the Java Cava subsidiary must continue to pay dollar interest and principal to the Stars and Stripes parent. Parallel loans do not contain a "right of offset," which, in this example, would allow the Java Cava subsidiary to stop payments on the dollar loan if the Stars and Stripes subsidiary defaults on the euro loan.

In many parallel loans, the interest payments are made at the same intervals in time, the maturity of the loans is the same, and the principal is repaid only at the end of the loan in a "bullet" payment rather than being amortized over the life of the loan. Because parallel loans are negotiated between the two parties to the agreement, it is possible to deviate from these usual features. For example, if one of the subsidiaries wants a variable interest rate or floating-rate debt, it might be feasible to structure one side of the loan agreement to have an interest rate that is a fixed premium over a short-term reference rate, such as the 6-month LIBOR. Transactions that involve amortization of principal are also possible, although they are relatively rare.

Topping-up Clauses

Many parallel loans include **topping-up clauses** that require additional advances or repayments of principal under specified conditions. These clauses are triggered by movements in the exchange rate between the two currencies over the life of the loan. Usually these clauses are triggered only when the exchange rate crosses a preset barrier rather than by each and every movement in the exchange rate.

Consider how this might work in our example. Suppose in our previous example that the initial exchange rate is IDR10,000/USD and that 1 year later, the rupiah has weakened relative to the dollar to IDR11,000/USD. A topping-up clause might require the Java Cava parent to advance the Stars and Stripes subsidiary an additional IDR1,000 million if the exchange rate rises above IDR11,000/USD for a period of more than 30 days. This makes the ratio of the principals outstanding on the two loans equal to

$$(\text{IDR10,000 million} + \text{IDR1,000 million})/\text{USD1 million} = \text{IDR11,000/USD}$$

which corresponds to a new exchange rate. In contrast, if the dollar weakens to IDR9,000/USD, the Stars and Stripes subsidiary might be required to repay IDR1,000 million to Java Cava. Once again, the ratio of the outstanding principals on the two loans:

$$(\text{IDR10,000 million} - \text{IDR1,000 million})/\text{USD1 million} = \text{IDR9,000/USD}$$

is equal to the new spot exchange rate.

Back-to-Back Loans

Back-to-back loans are similar in structure to parallel loans, with two key differences: (1) They involve simultaneous loans between multinational parent corporations (vs. subsidiaries) in two different countries, and (2) they contain the right of offset. In terms of the corporations in our example, a back-to-back loan involves the U.S. headquarters of Stars and Stripes making a dollar loan to the Indonesian headquarters of Java Cava. Simultaneously, the Indonesian headquarters of Java Cava would make a rupiah loan of equivalent value to the headquarters of Stars and Stripes. Unlike with parallel loans, the parent corporations would then make intercompany loans to their subsidiaries. A back-to-back loan involves only a single loan document and contains a provision for the right of offset. The **right of offset** clause stipulates that if one party defaults on a payment, the other party can withhold corresponding payments of equal value. Because the exchange control regulations of many countries explicitly prohibit rights of offset, parallel loans are more common than back-to-back loans.

Exhibit 21.15 provides a diagram of a back-to-back loan, using our example of the U.S. multinational corporation Stars and Stripes and the Indonesian multinational corporation

Exhibit 21.15 Back-to-Back Loan Diagram

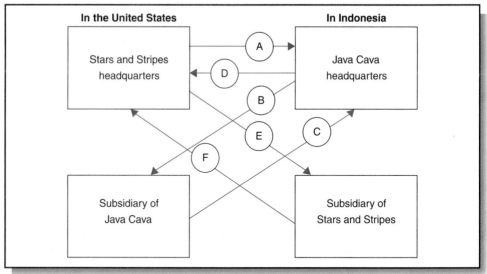

Notes: The back-to-back loan diagram summarizes the transactions and various cash flows:
  A. Stars and Stripes headquarters lends USD1 million to Java Cava headquarters.
  B. Java Cava headquarters lends USD1 million to its U.S. subsidiary.
  C. Java Cava's U.S. subsidiary pays its headquarters USD interest and principal on the USD1 million loan, which is used to service the loan in A.
  D. Java Cava headquarters lends IDR10,000 million to Stars and Stripes headquarters. This is equivalent to the USD1 million in A at the spot exchange rate of IDR10,000/USD.
  E. Stars and Stripes headquarters lends IDR10,000 million to its Indonesian subsidiary.
  F. The Stars and Stripes Indonesian subsidiary pays its headquarters IDR interest and principal on the IDR10,000 million loan, which is used to service the loan in D.

Java Cava. Because these transactions involve cross-border intercompany loans, there is a possibility that withholding taxes will be applied. However, the terms of the back-to-back loan can sometimes be altered to protect the parties against withholding taxes.

21.5 SUMMARY

This chapter examines interest rate and currency swaps. The major points of the chapter are as follows:

1. The cash flows of swaps are structured like the cash flows of bonds. Banks act as market makers in interest rate and currency swap markets. The outstanding volume of swaps is in the trillions of dollars.
2. Interest rate swaps allow a corporation or an institution to convert from fixed-rate debt to floating-rate debt or from floating-rate debt to fixed-rate debt, using a bank as an intermediary. No principal payments are made. The actual cash flows associated with interest rate swaps are based on the notional principal, which is the conceptual amount of the outstanding debt.
3. In a currency swap, the counterparties exchange principal amounts in two different currencies, and they agree to pay and receive interest on those currencies, as well as reverse the initial exchange of principal amounts at a fixed date in the future. The amount of one of the currencies to be swapped is determined by negotiation, and the corresponding amount of the other currency in the swap is set by the prevailing spot exchange rate.
4. Currency swaps can be used to exploit a company's comparative advantage in borrowing. Differences in the way credit risks are analyzed around the world

affect the pricing of debts in different countries. These differences allow corporations to exploit borrowing opportunities in certain currencies and then swap into their preferred currencies of denomination.
5. Swap market transaction costs are lower than transaction costs in the long-term forward market because the structure of swaps allows banks to easily trade in the bond markets to hedge their exposures.
6. The following is an example of a parallel loan: A U.S. parent corporation makes a dollar loan to the subsidiary of an Indonesian corporation operating in the United States, and the Indonesian parent corporation simultaneously makes a euro loan of equivalent value to the subsidiary of the U.S. corporation operating in Indonesia. The structure of a parallel loan satisfies the financing needs of both subsidiaries and avoids any problems with international inconvertibility of currencies or international taxes.
7. In a back-to-back loan, two multinational parent corporations in different countries lend one another money in different currencies and then subsequently lend the currencies to their foreign subsidiaries. A back-to-back loan involves only a single loan document and contains a provision for right of offset not present in parallel loans.

QUESTIONS

1. How does an interest rate swap work? In particular, what is the notional principal?
2. What is a currency swap? Describe the structure of and rationale for its cash flows.
3. Banks quote interest rate and currency swaps using the 6-month LIBOR as a basis for both transactions. How can a bank make money if it does not speculate on movements in either interest rates or exchange rates?
4. What is the all-in cost of a bond issue?
5. What is a comparative advantage in borrowing, and how could it arise?

6. What is basis point adjustment? Why is it not appropriate simply to add the basis point differential associated with the first currency to the quoted swap rate that the firm will pay?
7. Discuss the sense in which a 5-year currency swap is a sequence of long-term forward contracts. How do the implicit forward exchange rates in a currency swap differ from the long-term forward exchange rates for those maturities?
8. What are the determinants of the value of a currency swap as time evolves? Is it possible to close out a swap before it has reached maturity?

9. How does a parallel loan work? What motivated the financial markets to develop such contracts?

10. What is a topping-up clause in a parallel loan? Why might such a clause be included in the loan agreements?

11. How does a back-to-back loan work? What motivated the financial markets to develop such loans?

PROBLEMS

1. General Motors wants to swap out of $15,000,000 of fixed interest rate debt and into floating interest rate debt for 3 years. Suppose the fixed interest rate is 8.625% and the floating rate is dollar LIBOR. What semiannual interest payments will GM receive, and what will GM pay in return?

2. Searle, Inc., is a U.S. firm with considerable euro assets. It is considering entering into a currency swap involving $10 million of its dollar debt for an equivalent amount of euro debt. Suppose the maturity of the swap is 8 years, and the interest rate on Searle's outstanding 8-year dollar debt is 11%. The interest rate on the euro debt is 9%. The current spot exchange rate is $1.35/€. How could a swap be structured?

3. At the 7-year maturity, the market sets the price of U.S. Treasury bonds to have a yield to maturity of 7.95% p.a. The Second Bank of Chicago states that it will make fixed interest rate payments on dollars at the yield on Treasury bonds plus 55 basis points in exchange for receiving dollar LIBOR, and it will receive fixed interest rate payments on dollars at the yield on Treasury bonds plus 60 basis points in exchange for paying dollar LIBOR. If you enter into an interest rate swap of $10 million with Second Chicago, what will be your cash flows if you are paying the fixed rate and receiving the floating rate?

4. The swap desk at UBS is quoting the following rates on 5-year swaps versus 6-month dollar LIBOR:

U.S. dollars: 8.75% bid and 8.85% offered
Swiss francs: 5.25% bid and 5.35% offered

You would like to swap out of Swiss franc debt with a principal of CHF25,000,000 and into fixed-rate dollar debt. At what rates will UBS handle the transaction? If the current exchange rate is CHF1.3/$, what would the cash flows be?

5. Suppose that Viacom can issue $100,000,000 of dollar debt at an all-in cost of 9.42%, whereas Gaz de France can issue $100,000,000 of dollar debt at an all-in cost of 10.11%. Suppose that the exchange rate is $1.35/€. If Viacom issues euro-denominated bonds equivalent to $100,000,000, its all-in cost will be 8.27%, whereas if Gaz de France issues such bonds, its all-in cost will be 9.17%. Which firm has a comparative advantage when borrowing euros? Why?

6. Suppose in problem 5 that because of currency risk, Viacom would prefer to have dollar debt, and Gaz de France would prefer to have euro debt. How could an investment bank structure a currency swap that would allow each of the firms to issue bonds denominated in the currency in which the firm has a comparative advantage while respecting the firms' preferences about currency risks?

7. Suppose Sony has an opportunity to issue $100,000,000 of 5-year dollar bonds. Nomura and Goldman Sachs will handle the bond issue for a fee of 1.875%. The investment banks have told Sony that the bonds will be priced at par if they carry a coupon of 8.5%. As the swap trader for Tokyo Big Bank, you have been quoting the following rates on 5-year swaps:

U.S. dollars: 8.00% bid and 8.10% offered against the 6-month dollar LIBOR
Japanese yen: 4.50% bid and 4.60% offered against the 6-month dollar LIBOR

Sony would like to do the dollar bond issue, but it prefers to have fixed-rate yen debt. If Tokyo Big gets the proceeds of the dollar bond issue, giving Sony an equivalent amount of yen, and Tokyo Big agrees to make the dollar interest payments associated with Sony's dollar bonds, what yen interest payments should Tokyo Big charge Sony? What is Sony's all-in cost in yen? The current spot exchange rate is ¥98.50/$.

8. Assume that 1 year has passed since you entered into the transaction described in problem 4. Assume that the new spot exchange rate is CHF1.45/$ and that Union Bank of Switzerland is now quoting the following interest rates on 4-year swaps:

U.S. dollars: 7.50% bid and 7.60% offered against the 6-month dollar LIBOR
Swiss francs: 6.75% bid and 6.85% offered against the 6-month dollar LIBOR

If you close out the swap transaction of problem 4, what net dollar cash flow will you experience? Explain why this is the correct amount. You can assume that the term structures of interest rates in both currencies are flat.

9. Suppose you are the CFO of the Singapore subsidiary of an Australian multinational that would like to borrow 25,000,000 Singapore dollars for plant expansion. The current exchange rate is SGD1.5/AUD. If you were to borrow funds directly, you anticipate that your long-term interest rate in Singapore dollars would be 13%. Your Australian parent can borrow Australian dollars at 11%. Rather than borrow Singapore dollars directly, your investment banker has suggested that you consider a parallel loan with a Singapore multinational that has an Australian subsidiary. The investment banker has found a Singapore shipping firm whose Australian subsidiary is thinking of doing an Australian dollar bond issue at 12.5%. The shipping firm can borrow Singapore dollars at 10%. Is there a possibility for a parallel loan? What would be its structure?

10. How would a back-to-back loan be structured in problem 9? What advantages or disadvantages would it have?

BIBLIOGRAPHY

Apedjinou, Kodjo M., 2004, "What Drives Interest Rate Swap Spreads," Columbia Business School working paper.

Bank for International Settlements (BIS), 2004, *Central Bank Survey of Foreign Exchange and Derivatives Market Activity*, Basel, Switzerland: BIS.

Das, Satyajit, 1989, "Currency Swaps," in Boris Antl, ed., *Management of Currency Risk*, London: Euromoney Publications PLC.

Duffie, Darrell, and Kenneth Singleton, 1997, "An Econometric Model of the Term Structure of Interest Rate Swap Yields," *Journal of Finance* 52, pp. 1287–1323.

Fabozzi, Frank J., 1993, *Bond Markets, Analysis and Strategies*, 2nd ed., Upper Saddle River, NJ: Prentice Hall.

Faulkender, Michael, 2006, "Why Are Firms Using Interest Rate Swaps to Time the Yield Curve?" manuscript, Olin School of Business, Washington University, St. Louis.

In, Francis, Rob Brown, and Victor Feng, 2003, "Modeling Volatility and Changes in the Swap Spread," *International Review of Financial Analysis* 12, pp. 545–561.

International Swaps and Derivatives Association (ISDA), 1999, *ISDA 1999 Collateral Review*. New York: ISDA.

International Swaps and Derivatives Association (ISDA), 2002, *ISDA 2002 Master Agreement Protocol*. New York: ISDA.

International Swaps and Derivatives Association (ISDA), 2006, *ISDA 2006 Margin Survey*. New York: ISDA.

Johannes, Michael, and Suresh Sundaresan, 2007, "Pricing Collateralized Swaps" *Journal of Finance* 62, pp. 383–410.

Li, Haitao, and Connie X. Mao, 2003, "Corporate Use of Interest Rate Swaps: Theory and Evidence," *Journal of Banking and Finance* 27, pp. 1511–1538.

Lowenstein, Roger, 2000, *When Genius Failed: The Rise and Fall of Long-Term Capital Management*, New York: Random House.

GLOSSARY

absolute borrowing advantage   A situation in which one corporation's all-in costs are lower in each of two currencies than another corporation's all-in costs.

absolute purchasing power parity   The idea that the exchange rate should adjust to equate the internal and external purchasing powers of a money in which case the exchange rate, quoted as domestic currency per foreign currency, should equal the ratio between the domestic and foreign price levels.

ad valorem duties   Tariffs that are quoted as a certain percentage of the export price.

ADR (American depositary receipt)   A stock certificate traded in the U.S. representing a specific number of shares in a company listed in a foreign stock exchange that are held in custody by a U.S. depositary bank that issues the ADR.

affiliate bank   A bank partly owned but not controlled by a foreign parent bank.

agency costs   The costs that the owners of a firm incur because of the separation of ownership and control.

AIC (all-in cost)   The discount rate or internal rate of return that equates the present value of all the future interest and principal payments to the net proceeds (face value minus fees) received by the issuer.

American option   An option that can be exercised at the discretion of the buyer any time between the purchase date and the maturity date.

American quote   The dollar price of a foreign currency—that is, the amount of dollars it takes to purchase one unit of the foreign currency.

ANPV (adjusted net present value)   A capital budgeting technique that derives the value of a firm or project in steps, first deriving the present value of the all-equity free cash flows and then adding the present value of financial side effects and growth options.

appreciation   In discussing changes in exchange rates, the strengthening or increase in value of one currency relative to another.

APT (arbitrage pricing theory)   An asset pricing model based on the idea that a number of economy-wide factors systematically affect the returns on a large number of securities and hence drive their expected returns.

arbitrage   The process of earning riskless profits by simultaneously buying and selling equivalent assets or commodities.

ASEAN (Association of Southeast Asian Nations)   A regional economic and political organization that is designed to promote trade and investment in its member countries, Brunei Darussalam, Cambodia, Indonesia, Laos, Malaysia, Myanmar, Philippines, Singapore, Thailand, and Vietnam.

ask rate   The price (exchange rate) at which a dealer is willing to sell one currency in return for another currency. Also called the offer price.

asset securitization   The packaging of assets or obligations into securities for sale to third parties.

asset substitution   A situation in which managers, acting in the interests of shareholders, accept a high-variance project that may lower overall firm value but that increases shareholder value.

aval   An irrevocable guarantee of the debts of an importer, usually guaranteed by the importer's government or its bank.

average-rate option   An option contract in which the payoff depends on the difference between the strike price and the average exchange rate, calculated from the initiation of the contract to the expiration date.

B/A (banker's acceptance)   A document, tradable in financial markets, that is created when a bank stamps and signs a time draft indicating that the bank will pay the face value of a draft at maturity.

back-to-back loan   An agreement that is similar in structure to a parallel loan but in which the loans are made between the multinational parent corporations, which then lend to their subsidiaries in two different countries, and containing the right of offset.

Baker Plan   A 1985 plan that constituted a second phase of the handling of the developing country Debt Crisis. It relied heavily on countries agreeing to change their economic policies following guidelines set by the IMF in exchange for a modest amount of new loans extended to developing countries by private commercial banks and the World Bank.

balance-sheet hedge   The practice of denominating debt in a currency in which a firm has revenues.

banker's bourse   A stock market where banks are the major, and sometimes only, securities traders.

barrier option   A traditional option with an additional requirement that either activates the option or extinguishes it if the exchange rate passes through a prespecified barrier exchange rate.

Basel Accord   An agreement between G10 countries that sets capital requirements for internationally active banks.

basis point adjustment   The process of changing the interest rate on the side of a currency swap the client is paying away from the bank's quoted rate when the client wants to receive interest cash flows from the bank at something other than the bank's quoted rate.

basis risk   The risk arising from differences between the current spot price and the futures price and the fact that the maturity of what is being hedged may not be the maturity of the futures contract.

basket of currencies A composite currency composed of various units of other currencies.

beta The systematic risk of an individual asset in the capital asset pricing model (CAPM), which is measured as the covariance of the rate of return on the security with the rate of return on the market portfolio divided by the variance of the rate of return on the market portfolio.

bid rate The price (exchange rate) at which a dealer is willing to buy one currency in return for another currency.

bid–ask spread The difference between the ask rate and the bid rate. The spread constitutes a source of profits for market makers.

bilateral netting system A payment system between two parties who agree to transfer only the net amounts that are owed to each other.

BIS (Bank for International Settlements) An international organization based in Basle, Switzerland, that promotes international monetary and financial stability and serves as a bank for the world's central banks.

BIT (bilateral investment treaty) An agreement between two countries who promise mutual respect for, and protection of, investments in each other's territory, with the purpose of encouraging international capital investment.

B/L (bill of lading) A contract issued to an exporter by a shipping company that will transport the exporter's goods to their destination.

blocked funds A problem encountered by multinational corporations when government restrictions in a host country prevent the transfer of foreign currency out of that country.

BOP (balance of payments) A summary of the value of the transactions between a country's residents, businesses, and government with the rest of the world for a specific period of time, such as a month, a quarter, or a year.

Brady bonds Bonds issued by countries in response to the Brady Plan in which the principal and some initial interest payments are collateralized.

Brady Plan A comprehensive plan to resolve the developing countries Debt Crisis developed in 1989 by then U.S. Treasury Secretary Nicholas Brady. This plan put pressure on banks to offer some form of debt relief to developing countries. It also called for an expansion in secondary market transactions aimed at debt reduction.

Bretton Woods agreement An accord signed by 44 Allied nations toward the end of World War II. Ratified in 1944, it established regulations and regulatory bodies for an international monetary system, based on a target zone relative to the dollar, which itself was fixed relative to gold at $35 per ounce. The system collapsed in 1971.

buyback An agreement in which an exporter of physical capital agrees to accept payment, in the form of the output of a plant, which the exporter helps to construct in a foreign country.

buyer credit An international finance method used when expensive capital equipment is imported in which the exporter arranges for a financial institution to grant credit to the importer to enable payment to the exporter.

CAL (capital allocation line) A description of the feasible tradeoffs between expected return and standard deviation that arise when allocating capital between a risk-free asset and a single risky asset.

call option *See* foreign currency call option.

cannibalization of exports The possible loss of export revenue when a foreign market is served by direct foreign investment and the former exports to that market are unable to be sold elsewhere.

capital account A major account of the balance of payments that records the purchases and sales of foreign assets by domestic residents as well as the purchases and sales of domestic assets by foreign residents.

capital controls A set of regulations that restrict the flow of capital into and out of a country.

capital expenditures The investments in plant and equipment that a firm makes in expectation of future profitability.

capital flight An outflow of capital from a country, typically associated with a prospective devaluation of the currency or other actions by the country's government that would result in a loss of wealth for investors in that country.

capital inflow Purchases by foreign residents of the assets of a country, such as its stocks, bonds, or real estate, or the sale of foreign assets by domestic residents.

capital outflow Purchases by domestic residents of the assets of a foreign country, such as its stocks, bonds, or real estate, or the sale of domestic assets by foreign residents.

CAPM (capital asset pricing model) A model in which an asset's risk premium, its expected return in excess of the risk free rate, is determined by its beta with respect to the market portfolio times the risk premium on the market portfolio.

carry trade Investment in a high-yield currency while borrowing in a low-yield currency (or buying the high-yield currency in the forward market relative to the low-yield currency).

centralized debt denomination A situation in which an MNC borrows in the company's domestic currency.

certificate of analysis A document that attests to some measurable characteristics of a shipment.

certificate of origin A document that indicates the source of a shipment of merchandise.

CFTC (Commodity Futures Trading Commission) The government organization that regulates the U.S. futures industry.

CHIPS (Clearing House Interbank Payments System) An electronic payment system that transfers funds and settles transactions in U.S. dollars.

clean acceptance An export finance method in which a bank agrees to accept a certain number and amount of time drafts submitted by the exporter. The bank immediately discounts the drafts to provide financing for the exporter, and the exporter repays the face amount of the draft to the bank at maturity.

clean bill of lading A shipping contract which indicates that the carrier believes the merchandise was received in good condition, based on visual inspection.

clearing arrangements International barter conducted with the extension of credit from one party to the other.

clearinghouse An agency or a separate corporation of a futures exchange that acts as a buyer to every clearing member seller and a seller to every clearing member buyer. The clearinghouse also settles trading accounts, collects and maintains margin monies, regulates delivery, and reports trading data.

clearing member A member of an exchange clearinghouse, usually held by a company, which is responsible for the financial commitments of the customers that clear their trades through this firm.

closed-end fund An investment fund that trades on a stock exchange at a price that may differ from the net asset value of the assets of the managed portfolio.

commercial invoice A document given by an exporter to an importer that contains a detailed description of the merchandise in question, including unit prices, the number of items, and the financial terms of the sale.

comparative advantage The idea that international trade makes everyone better off when countries specialize in the production of goods that they produce relatively most efficiently.

comparative borrowing advantage A situation in which one corporation's ratio of all-in costs for borrowing in two currencies is lower than another corporation's ratio of all-in costs.

compensatory trade A type of complex countertrade.

compound interest Interest that is earned on interest from previous periods.

conditional expectation The probability weighted average of future events, such as possible future exchange rates, which is also the mean of a conditional probability distribution for that variable. Also called the conditional mean.

conditional mean *See* conditional expectation.

conditional probability distribution A description of possible future events and their respective probabilities of occurrence that is based on an information set at a point in time.

conditional standard deviation The square root of the variance of a conditional probability distribution of a particular variable; like the rate of currency appreciation. Often called the conditional volatility when applied to a financial return.

conditional volatility *See* conditional standard deviation.

confirmed D/C A documentary credit in which, in addition to the bank that issues the documentary credit, a second commercial bank that is usually well known to the exporter agrees to honor the draft presented by the exporter.

consular invoice A document filled out by an exporter in consultation with the local consulate of the importing country that provides information to customs officials in the importing country, with the goal of preventing false declarations of the value of the merchandise.

conversion The process of buying a foreign currency in the forward market and selling it forward with a synthetic forward contract constructed with options.

convertible bond A corporate bond that is convertible into a fixed number of equity shares of the corporation prior to maturity.

convex tax code A tax system that imposes a larger tax rate on higher incomes and a smaller tax rate on lower incomes, also called a progressive system of taxation.

corporate governance The legal and financial structure that controls the relationship between a company's shareholders and its management.

correlation A number between −1 and 1 that indicates how closely related are the random variations in two variables.

correspondent bank A bank that performs services as a proxy for financial institutions that lack an onsite presence in a particular country.

costs of financial distress The loss of firm value from the direct costs of bankruptcy associated with legal, consulting, and accounting fees and the indirect losses associated with the possibility that the firm may go into bankruptcy.

counterpurchase A trading activity that is similar to a buyback, except the exporter agrees to purchase goods that are not produced by the importer.

countertrade A variety of international trade activities in which exporters and importers exchange goods and services without necessarily having to use money as a medium of exchange.

country credit spread The difference between the yield on a bond issued by a developing country in an international currency and the government bond yield of the country that issues the international currency. This spread reflects sovereign risk.

country fund A closed-end fund that invests in the securities of one particular country.

country risk The risk that a country's political environment as well as its economic and financial environment may adversely affect a company's cash flows.

country risk premium The additional yield above the risk free rate demanded by investors in government bonds to protect them against political risk.

country risk rating Assessments of various political and economic events that could adversely affect companies operating in a country, which are produced by a number of specialized organizations.

covariance The probability weighted average of the product of the deviations of two random variables from their means, which measures how the two random variables move together, or covary with each other.

covered interest rate arbitrage An arbitrage that exploits deviations from covered interest rate parity.

covered interest rate parity A no-arbitrage relationship between spot and forward exchange rates and the two nominal interest rates associated with these currencies.

crawling peg system A target zone system wherein the bands are reset over time, typically in response to movements in inflation.

credit rating A rating that is provided by a credit-rating firm and that indicates the creditworthiness of a corporate or government borrower.

credit spread The difference between the borrowing cost of a corporate borrower and the borrowing cost of the government on a security with similar maturity.

credit transaction In balance of payments accounting, any transaction that results in a receipt of funds from foreigners; in other words, any transaction that gives rise to a conceptual inflow or source of foreign currency.

cross-currency settlement risk The risk that a financial institution will fail to deliver currency on one side of a foreign exchange transaction, even though the financial institution has received the other currency from its counterparty to the transaction. Also called Herstatt risk.

cross-holding The practice of one firm owning shares in another firm.

cross-listing The practice of listing shares on an exchange outside the country in which the company is headquartered.

cross-rate An exchange rate between two currencies not involving the U.S. dollar.

currency board An exchange rate system in which the monetary base of the domestic currency is 100% backed by a foreign reserve currency and is fully convertible into the reserve currency at a fixed rate and on demand.

currency swap An agreement between two counterparties to exchange principals denominated in two currencies of equivalent value at the spot exchange rate and then to have one party pay interest and principal on the currency it received and the other party to pay interest and principal on the currency it received.

currency warrants Longer-maturity foreign currency options that are sometimes issued by major corporations and are actively traded on exchanges.

current account A major account of the balance of payments that records transactions in goods and services, transactions associated with the income flows from assets, and unilateral transfers.

cylinder option A contract that allows the buyer to specify a desired trading range in the future so that if the future spot rate falls outside of the range, the buyer transacts at the limits of the range. Unlike the range forward contract, the trading range is set to allow the buyer either to pay money or possibly to receive money up front for entering into the contract.

D/A (documents against acceptance) collection A method of international trade in which an exporter extends credit to an importer, which acknowledges its legal obligation to pay the face amount of a draft at maturity, by having the collecting bank present a time draft to the importer who must sign it, date it, and write *accepted* across it before the shipping documents are released to the importer.

D/C (documentary credit) A method of international trade in which commercial banks stand between an importer and an exporter to assure the exporter of payment after fulfilling certain requirements. In the United States, also known as a letter of credit (L/C).

debit transaction In balance of payments accounting, any transaction that results in a payment to foreigners; in other words, any transaction that gives rise to a conceptual outflow or use of foreign currency.

debt buyback A situation in which a country buys back its own outstanding loans at a discount.

Debt Crisis A 1980s economic and financial crisis that occurred in a large number of developing countries after many defaulted on their loan payments to international banks and that took a full decade to be resolved.

debt–equity swap A situation in which an MNC buys the debt of a country from an original creditor at a discount, presents the debt to the debtor government, receives local currency equal to the face value of the debt, and then uses the local currency to make an equity investment in that country.

decentralized debt denomination A situation in which an MNC borrows in the currencies in which its revenues are received.

deficit In balance of payments accounting, the idea that debits on a particular account are greater than credits on that account.

deflation The rate of change of the price level when prices are falling.

demand curve A function that indicates the quantity demanded by consumers, given the relative price of a product.

demutualization The process of converting stock exchanges from nonprofit, member-owned organizations to for-profit, investor-owned, and typically publicly traded companies.

density function The mathematical formula that describes a probability distribution.

depreciation (accounting) Accounting deductions for corporate income tax associated with previous capital expenditures on plant and equipment.

depreciation In discussing changes in exchange rates, a weakening or decrease in the value of one currency relative to another.

derivative securities Financial contracts, such as forwards, futures, options, and swaps, whose values depend on the values of underlying asset prices, such as exchange rates, interest rates, or stock prices.

devaluation A change in a fixed exchange rate that increases the domestic currency price of foreign currency and thus decreases the value of the domestic currency.

devaluation premium The part of the interest rate on a particular currency that reflects its expected depreciation relative to another currency.

digital options Contracts that pay off an amount of cash or the value of an asset when a certain condition is met—for example, when the spot rate is lower than the strike price.

direct quote An exchange rate quote expressed as an amount of domestic currency per unit of foreign currency.

dirty float currency system   A floating exchange rate system in which a central bank nonetheless intervenes in the foreign exchange market, buying and selling its currency to affect to affect its foreign exchange value.

discount rates   Expected rates of return that are used to take present values.

documentary collection   A method of international trade, with some bank involvement, in which an exporter retains control of goods until an importer has paid or is legally bound to pay.

dollarization   The phenomenon in which use of a foreign currency drives out the domestic currency as a means of payment and as a savings vehicle.

domestic bonds   Bonds that are issued and traded within the internal market of a single country and are denominated in the currency of that country.

domestic CAPM   An application of the CAPM which assumes that the assets of a country are held only by investors who reside in that country so that the market portfolio is a local market index.

D/P (documents against payment) collection   A method of international trade in which an importer must pay the amount of a sight draft to the collecting bank before the trade documents are released.

DR (depositary receipt)   A stock certificate that represents a specific number of shares in a company listed in a foreign stock exchange that are held in custody by a depositary bank that issues the DR.

dragon bond   A Eurobond targeted at the Asian market (outside Japan) with Asian syndication.

dual-currency bond   A straight, fixed-rate bond issued in one currency, say yen, which pays coupon interest in that same currency, but the promised repayment of principal at maturity is denominated in another currency, say U.S. dollars.

early exercise   The exercise of an American option prior to maturity.

EBIT (earnings before interest and taxes)   Revenue minus cost of goods sold minus selling and general administrative expense and minus accounting depreciation.

economic exposure   *See* real exchange risk.

ECU (European Currency Unit)   A historical currency basket in the European Monetary System composed of specific amounts of 12 different European currencies.

Edge Act bank   A federally chartered subsidiary of a U.S. bank that is physically located in the United States but is allowed to engage in a full range of international banking activities. This bank can accept deposits from foreign customers, finance international trade, transfer international funds, and even own equity in U.S. corporations.

EEC (European Economic Community)   An agreement, created by the Treaty of Rome in 1957, between six countries (Belgium, West Germany, Luxembourg, France, Italy, and the Netherlands) to remove trade barriers between themselves and to form a "common market."

efficient frontier   The set of risky portfolios that maximize the expected return on the portfolio for each level of portfolio variance.

elasticity   The percentage change in the quantity demanded with a percentage change in the relative price of a product but defined to be a positive number.

eligible B/A   A banker's acceptance that meets the requirements of the Federal Reserve and consequently does not require the bank to hold reserves against the B/A.

emerging markets   In equity trading, the stock markets of developing countries, or more generally, the countries themselves.

EMS (European Monetary System)   A target zone system created in 1979 for currencies of European Union countries to prevent large currency fluctuations relative to one another, which was replaced by a monetary union in 1999.

equity market liberalization   A policy reform that allows foreign investment in the local stock market and allows local investors to invest abroad.

equity risk premium   In general, the expected return on an equity in excess of the risk free return, and specifically, the expected excess return on the market portfolio.

ETF (exchange-traded fund)   An investment fund that trades on an exchange but whose price is kept close to the value of the underlying portfolio through arbitrage activities by a few institutional investors.

EU (European Union)   An intergovernmental union of 27 European countries that was established in 1992 by the Maastricht Treaty to promote economic and political integration.

eurobank   A bank that operates in the Eurocurrency market, making short-term loans and extending eurocredits to other financial institutions, corporations, sovereign governments, and international organizations.

eurobond   An international bond that is denominated in one or more currencies but that is traded in external markets outside the borders of the countries issuing the currencies.

eurocredit   A long-term loan granted by a syndicate of banks to a bank, a corporation, a government, or an international organization; typically issued at a spread above LIBOR.

euro-equity market   A market for issuing shares in multiple foreign markets, sometimes simultaneously with distribution in the domestic market.

euro-MTNs (euro-medium-term notes)   Notes that are similar to euronotes but whose maturity is longer—between 9 months and 10 years.

euronotes   Short-term, negotiable promissory notes distributed for a borrower by an international bank over a specified period (5 to 7 years). They are more flexible than floating-rate notes and usually cheaper than syndicated loans.

European option   An option that can be exercised only at maturity.

European quote   An exchange rate quote expressed as the amount of foreign currency needed to buy 1 dollar.

eurozone   The group of countries that use the euro as their currency.

exchange controls   Government regulations that interfere with the buying and selling of foreign exchange (for example, taxes or quotas on foreign exchange transactions).

exchange rate   The relative price of two currencies, such as the Japanese yen price of the U.S. dollar, the U.S. dollar price of the British pound, or the Mexican peso price of the euro.

exchange rate pass-through   The amount that a given change in the exchange rate changes the prices of products.

exercise price   *See* strike price.

Ex-Im Bank   The Export–Import Bank of the United States, an independent U.S. government corporation involved in financing and facilitating U.S. exports.

exotic options   Options with different payoff patterns and features than the basic call and put options.

expectations hypothesis   Theory of the term structure that holds that long-term interest rates are an appropriate weighted average of the current short-term rate and expected future short-term rates.

expected value   The probability weighted average of future events.

export factor   A company that performs credit risk investigations for exporters and collects funds from an exporter's accounts receivable while possibly providing financing to the exporter.

exports   Sales of domestic goods and services to foreign residents.

expropriation   The act of a government seizing property without compensating the owners for it—in particular by turning private companies into state-owned companies.

external currency market   The interbank market for deposits and loans that are denominated in currencies that are not the currency of the country in which the bank is operating.

external equity market   *See* euro-equity market.

external purchasing power (of a currency)   The amount of goods and services that can be purchased with the domestic currency in a foreign country.

Fama-French three-factor model   An asset pricing factor model in which the factors are the excess return on the market portfolio, the excess return on a portfolio long in small stocks and short in big stocks, and the excess return on a portfolio long in high book-to-market stocks (value stocks) and short in low book-to-market stocks (growth stocks).

FCF (free cash flows)   The cash that can be returned to investors, which is gross cash flow minus investments in plant and equipment and working capital.

FCM (futures commission merchant)   An individual or organization that accepts orders to buy or sell futures contracts or options on futures and accepts money or other assets from customers to support such orders.

Fedwire   A real-time gross settlement system operated by the Federal Reserve System of the United States that instantly moves dollar balances between financial institutions.

Financial Credit Insurance Association (FCIA)   An unincorporated association of U.S. private marine, property, and casualty insurance companies that provides export credit insurance in connection with the U.S. Ex-Im Bank.

financial disintermediation   The process whereby corporate borrowing happens via a tradable security issued in the public market, rather than a non-tradable loan provided by financial intermediaries.

financial slack   The presence of excess cash that is not needed to efficiently run a firm.

fixed currency   *See* pegged currency.

fixed-rate debt   Debt for which the interest amount is fixed over time.

floating currency   An exchange rate system in which the relative values of currencies are determined by market forces, without government interventions or restrictions.

floating-rate debt   Debt for which the interest rate varies through time, according to variation in a reference rate, which is often LIBOR.

forecast error   The difference between the actual realization of a random variable (like the future spot exchange rate) and the forecast of that random variable.

foreign bonds   Bonds issued in a domestic market by a foreign borrower, denominated in the domestic currency, marketed to domestic residents, and regulated by the domestic authorities.

foreign branch of a bank   A bank that is legally a part of its parent bank but operates like a local bank. A foreign branch allows the parent bank to offer its domestic, foreign, and international customers direct, seamless service in a foreign country.

foreign currency call option   A contract that gives the buyer of the option the right, but not the obligation, to buy a specific amount of foreign currency with domestic currency at an exchange rate stated in the contract.

foreign currency futures contracts   Contracts, traded on futures exchanges and not over-the-counter, that are similar to forward contracts and that allow one to bet on the direction of change of an exchange rate and effectively buy or sell foreign currency at an agreed-upon price, determined on a given future day.

foreign currency put option   A contract that gives the buyer of the option the right, but not the obligation, to sell a specific amount of foreign currency with domestic currency at an exchange rate stated in the contract.

foreign exchange brokers   Financial intermediaries in the foreign exchange market who do not put their own money at risk but who receive a brokerage fee for matching buyers and sellers of currencies.

foreign exchange dealers   Traders of currencies at commercial banks, investment banks, and brokerage firms in the major financial cities around the world.

foreign exchange market   An over-the-counter market where currencies are traded.

foreign exchange reserves   The foreign currency assets held by a central bank.

forfaiting   The sale of an exporter's accounts receivable without recourse to the exporter.

forward contract   An agreement between two parties to exchange specific amounts of two currencies at a future time at a quoted forward exchange rate.

forward foreign exchange market   The over-the-counter market for the exchange of currencies at a future time at contractual prices (forward rates) agreed today. Also called the forward market.

forward market investment   A long or short position in the forward market to be closed out at the future spot rate.

forward market return   The return on a forward market investment that represents the difference between the future spot rate and the forward rate for a long contract or the negative of that for a short contract.

forward premium or discount   The difference between the forward and spot exchange rates expressed as a percentage of the spot rate. A premium specifies a positive value, and a discount specifies a negative value.

forward rate   An exchange rate in a forward contract that is quoted today for exchange of currencies at a future time.

forward rate bias   The difference between the expected future spot rate and the corresponding forward rate.

forward settlement date   The date the exchange of currencies occurs in a forward foreign exchange contract. Also called the forward value date.

forward value date   *See* forward settlement date.

foul bill of lading   A shipping contract which indicates that the carrier received the merchandise in a damaged condition, based on visual inspection.

frequency distribution   A histogram with observations in each interval expressed as fractions of the total number of observations.

frontier markets   The young stock markets of the least developed countries.

fronting loan   A parent-to-affiliate loan that uses a large international bank as a financial intermediary.

FTE (flow to equity)   A capital budgeting approach that finds equity value by directly discounting expected cash flows to equity holders with an appropriate risk-adjusted rate.

full-service bank   *See* universal bank.

future value   The value of an investment in the future, found by multiplying the current value by 1 plus the interest rate.

GATT (General Agreement on Tariffs and Trade)   A multilateral agreement, signed in 1947, that was designed to provide an international forum to encourage free trade between member states by regulating and reducing tariffs on traded goods and by providing a common mechanism for resolving trade disputes. It was superseded in 1995 by the World Trade Organization (WTO).

GDP (gross domestic product)   The market value of all final goods and services produced within a country in a given period of time.

GDR (global depositary receipt)   A depositary receipt that trades across multiple markets and can settle in the currency of each market.

global bond   A bond issued simultaneously in a domestic market and in the Eurobond market.

global minimum-variance portfolio   The portfolio of assets with the least variance among all possible portfolios.

Global Offset and Countertrade Association (GOCA)   An industry trade association that holds annual conferences and supports a website (www.globaloffset.org) devoted to the practice of countertrade.

globalization   The process of increasing global connectivity and integration between countries, corporations, and individuals within these nations and organizations in their economic, political, and social activities.

GNI (gross national income)   The total income of an economy equal to gross domestic product plus the foreign income accruing to domestic residents minus the income from the domestic market accruing to nonresidents plus unilateral transfers from foreigners.

GO (growth option)   The option to do an additional project if the first project is successful. Its presence adds value to the first project.

gold standard   An exchange rate system in which a currency is pegged to a specified amount of gold and can be exchanged for gold at the central bank.

government budget surplus   The difference between taxes and total government expenditures (including spending on goods and services, transfer payments, and interest on government debt). Also known as national government saving.

gross cash flows   Net operating profit less adjusted taxes plus accounting depreciation.

grossed-up dividend   The value of dividends received from a foreign subsidiary plus the tax credit for taxes paid to foreign governments.

GRS (global registered share)   An ordinary share of a company that trades and transfers freely across national borders.

hedging   The act of using financial markets, especially derivative securities, to reduce or eliminate risks arising from underlying business transactions.

Herstatt risk   *See* cross-currency settlement risk.

histogram   A method of determining the likelihoods of the occurrences of a random variable by grouping observations into intervals of equal length and recording the number of observations in each interval.

home bias   The phenomenon that investors of countries are not very well internationally diversified but instead own portfolios concentrated in the securities of their home markets.

IBF (international banking facility)   A separate set of asset and liability accounts, used to record international transactions, that is segregated on the parent bank's books and is not a unique physical or legal entity.

ICC (International Chamber of Commerce)   A world business organization based in Paris that has thousands of member companies and associations in more than

130 countries, whose activities include setting rules and standards for international trade and arbitration and other forms of dispute resolution.

ICSID (International Center for the Settlement of Investment Disputes) An organization within the World Bank that administers legal disputes filed as claims under bilateral investment treaties.

idiosyncratic risk The part of the uncertainty of a return that is not systematic. *See also* systematic risk.

import competitor A domestic company that competes for business in the domestic market with foreign competitors.

imports Purchases of foreign goods and services by domestic residents.

incremental profits The additional cash that comes into a firm as a result of making an investment.

index funds Open-end funds that passively track stock indices, such as the S&P 500, without trying to outperform them.

indexing formula A clause in a contract that requires changes in prices based on the realization of certain contingencies such as the amount of inflation or depreciation of a currency.

indirect quote An exchange rate quote expressed as an amount of foreign currency per unit of domestic currency.

ineligible B/A A banker's acceptance that does not meet the requirements of the Federal Reserve, which consequently requires that the bank hold reserves against the B/A.

inflation A general increase in monetary prices of goods and services in an economy measured as the rate of change of the price level.

information set The collection of all information used to predict the future value of an economic variable.

initial margin The initial amount of wealth that must be placed in a margin account, as determined by the futures exchange.

integrated market A market where securities are priced in the global capital market.

interbank forex market The wholesale part of the foreign exchange market where major banks trade.

interest rate swap An agreement in which two counterparties agree to exchange fixed interest payments for floating interest rate payments on the same notional principal.

interest subsidy The firm value created by the ability of a firm to borrow at an interest rate below the firm's market-determined interest rate.

interest tax shield The firm value created by the tax deductibility of interest on debts.

internal purchasing power (of a currency) The amount of goods and services that can be purchased with the domestic currency in the domestic country.

international barter International trade in which the transfer of goods or services from a party in one country is made directly to a party in another country in return for some other good or service of equal value.

international bonds Bonds traded outside the country of the issuer.

intertemporal budget constraint The idea that the present value of expenditures must be balanced by the present value of revenue.

international CAPM A version of the CAPM that takes exchange rate risk into account.

international investment income account The account on the balance of payments that is associated with flows of investment income.

intertemporal budget constraint The idea that the present value of expenditures must be balanced by the present value of income.

intrinsic value The immediate revenue generated from exercising an option.

investment barriers Direct or indirect investment restrictions that limit or prevent foreign investors from investing in a country.

investment trust The UK version of a closed-end fund.

irrevocable D/C A documentary credit that cannot be revoked unless all parties, including the exporter, agree to the revocation.

ISDA (International Swap and Derivatives Association) A derivatives trade organization, whose members include most of the world's major financial institutions, which sets standards for derivative transactions.

joint venture An organizational form in which two or more independent firms form and jointly control a different entity, which is created to pursue a specific objective.

lagging payment A payment delayed beyond what is usual.

lag operation An exporter's method of profiting from international trade by collecting payment after a rise in the value of a foreign currency (for example, by lengthening the maturity of trade credits).

law of one price The idea that the price of a commodity in a particular currency should be the same throughout the world.

leading payment A payment made earlier than usual.

lead operation An importer's method of profiting from international trade by prepaying for goods before a fall in the value of the local currency.

Level I ADR An ADR that trades over the counter in New York—in what is called pink sheet trading—and is not listed on a major U.S. stock exchange.

Level II ADR An ADR that trades on the NYSE, NASDAQ, or the AMEX and hence must satisfy the exchange's listing requirements.

Level III ADR An ADR that trades on one of the major exchanges in the United States and is also issued to raise capital in the United States.

LIBOR (London Interbank Offer Rate) The external currency interest rate in London, which is the most important reference rate in international loan agreements.

licensing agreements Fees paid to a firm for the use of a technology, copyright, or patent.

limit order book A listing of investors' desired buy and sell orders that are awaiting execution at specific prices and will be executed if prices rise or fall sufficiently.

liquidating dividend   The final payment to shareholders when a firm goes out of business.

liquidity   The property of a market in which buyers and sellers are easily matched, making the transaction costs of trading low.

lookback option   An option in which the payoff depends on the difference between the spot rate at maturity and the minimum spot rate during the life of the option.

MacPPP   The idea that the exchange rate quoted as domestic currency per foreign currency should equal the ratio between the domestic currency and foreign currency prices of McDonald's Big Macs.

maintenance margin   The minimum value that a margin account can have before an investor gets a margin call and must bring the margin account back to the initial margin.

margin account   Deposits of cash and other assets from which losses on futures contracts are deducted and to which profits are added.

marginal cost   The cost of producing the last unit of output.

marginal revenue   The revenue from selling the last unit of output.

margin call   A notification to an investor that his or her margin account is below the maintenance margin.

market impact   The effect of a large trade on the price of a security.

market maker (in the forex market)   A trader who stands ready to buy and sell particular currencies.

market portfolio   The portfolio that contains all securities in proportions equal to their market values as percentages of the total market value.

market risk   The exposure of a return to fluctuations in the return on the market portfolio, which cannot be diversified away.

market risk premium   The expected excess return on the market portfolio.

market variance   The variance of the return on the market portfolio.

marking to market   The process of crediting and debiting daily profits and losses on futures accounts to margin accounts.

mean   The expected value of a probability distribution of a random variable, which is the probability weighted average of future events.

mean standard deviation frontier   The locus of the portfolios in expected return–standard deviation space that have the minimum standard deviation for each expected return. Also known as the minimum-variance frontier.

mean-variance preferences   The idea that an investor's preferences depend positively on the expected return of the investor's portfolio and negatively on the portfolio's variance.

median   The value of a random variable for which 50% of the values will be greater and 50% will be less.

menu costs   Costs of changing prices that are a source of sticky prices.

merchandise trade balance   The value of exports of goods minus imports of goods on a country's balance of payments.

merchant bank   A bank that performs both traditional commercial banking and investment banking functions.

MIGA (Multilateral Investment Guarantee Agency)   Part of the World Bank Group established in 1988 to promote development by facilitating investment in emerging and transitioning economies (for instance, by providing political risk insurance).

minimum-variance frontier   *See* mean standard deviation frontier.

MNC (multinational corporation)   A company engaged in producing and selling goods or services in more than one country.

Modigliani–Miller proposition   A proposition which states that a corporation's financial policies, such as issuing debt, hedging foreign exchange risk, and other purely financial risk management activities do not change the value of the firm's assets unless these financial transactions lower the firm's taxes, affect its investment decisions, or can be done more cheaply than individual investors' transactions can be done.

monetary base   The sum of a central bank's liabilities (that is, currency in circulation plus total reserves of banks at the central bank).

monetary union   A system in which several countries use a common currency by official agreement, with monetary policy administered by one central bank.

money market hedge   The process of acquiring foreign currency liabilities or assets in the money markets to offset underlying exposures to foreign currency receivables or payables.

monopolist   The sole seller of a good.

multilateral netting system   A payment system in which only the net amounts of what is mutually owed are transferred.

MVE (mean-variance-efficient) portfolio   The one portfolio on the efficient frontier that maximizes the Sharpe ratio and hence is the optimal risky portfolio for all investors with mean-variance preferences.

NAFTA (North America Free Trade Agreement)   A free trade agreement between Canada, the United States, and Mexico.

national government saving   *See* government budget surplus.

nationalization   A government take over of a private company.

negotiable bill of lading   The most common shipping contract, which can be used to transfer title or ownership of goods between parties.

net exporter   A firm that has more exports than imports and benefits from a real depreciation of the home currency.

net foreign assets   *See* net international investment position.

net foreign income   Income that accrues to domestic residents from ownership of foreign assets and from working abroad minus the income that accrues to foreign workers who are employed domestically and to foreign owners of domestic assets.

net importer   A firm that has more imports than exports and benefits from a real appreciation of the home currency.

net international investment position   The difference between the value of a country's ownership of foreign assets and the value of foreign ownership of the country's assets at a given point in time. Also known as net foreign assets.

net private saving   The difference between private saving and the private sector's expenditures on investment goods.

net working capital   The value of short-term assets minus short-term liabilities necessary to run a firm.

nominal price   The amount of money that is paid for a good or service.

NIPA (National Income and Product Accounts)   Government statements of the sources of income and the value of final production for a country.

non-sterilized intervention   The buying or selling of foreign exchange by a central bank in the currency markets, which affects the money supply because the central bank does not use offsetting open market operations.

nonsystematic variance   The part of the variance of a return that can be diversified away. Also called idiosyncratic risk.

NOPLAT (net operating profit less adjusted taxes)   Earnings before interest and taxes (EBIT) minus taxes on EBIT.

normal distribution   A probability distribution characterized by a symmetrical bell-shaped curve that is completely described by its mean and variance.

notional principal   The conceptual principal amount that controls the cash flows of an interest rate swap.

NPVF (net present value of financial side effects)   The firm value created by the ability to issue debt, including the value of interest tax shields and the value of interest subsidies but minus the costs of financial distress.

null hypothesis   A hypothesis that is tested using data and a test statistic.

OECD (Organization for Economic Cooperation and Development)   A group of 30 relatively rich countries that examines, devises, and coordinates policies to foster employment, rising standards of living, and financial stability.

offer price   See ask rate.

official international reserves   Assets of the central bank that are not denominated in the domestic currency, that is, the sum of foreign exchange reserves, gold reserves, and IMF-related reserve assets.

official reserves account   See official settlements account.

official settlements account   The account of the balance of payments that records changes in the official reserves of a country's central bank. Also known as official reserves account.

offset   The requirement of an importing country that the effective cost of its imports be offset in some way by the exporter, who must contract to purchase items from the importing country; common in large expenditure contracts for weapon systems and power-generating facilities.

offshore banking center   A center that primarily services the borrowing and lending needs of foreigners. Transactions are typically initiated outside the banking center whose location is in a country with low or zero taxation, moderate or light financial regulation, banking secrecy, and anonymity of transactions.

OLS (ordinary least squares)   A statistical methodology that estimates the relationship between a dependent variable and one or more independent variables by minimizing the sum of squared residuals.

on-board bill of lading   A shipping contract which indicates that goods have been placed on a particular vessel for shipment.

open-end fund   An investment fund that grows in size with new investments and shrinks with redemptions.

open interest   The total number of contracts outstanding for a particular derivative contract.

open market operation   The purchase or sale of government bonds by the central bank, which is done to affect the money supply.

open price   The first price at which a transaction is completed on an exchange.

operating currency hedge   The process of shifting a company's operations across countries to provide a better balance between the costs and revenues denominated in different currencies.

operating exposure   See real exchange risk.

OPIC (Overseas Private Investment Company)   The U.S. government's political risk insurance company.

optimal portfolio   A portfolio that maximizes the utility function of an investor.

optimum currency area   A collection of countries for which a monetary union is optimal in that it balances the microeconomic benefits of perfect exchange rate certainty against the costs of macroeconomic adjustment problems.

option premium   The price the buyer of an option must pay to the seller or writer of the option.

order bill of lading   A shipping contract that legally consigns goods to a party named in the contract.

order-driven trading system   A trading system in which orders are batched together and then auctioned off at an equilibrium market price.

outright forward contract   A forward contract that contains only one transaction to buy or sell foreign currency.

outsourcing   The shifting of non-strategic functions, such as payroll, information technology, maintenance, facilities management, and logistics, to specialist firms, sometimes in other countries, to reduce costs.

overhead management fees   Fees paid by a subsidiary to a parent corporation for managerial activities such as accounting.

overvalued currency   A currency with larger external purchasing power than internal purchasing power.

packing list   A description of merchandise to be exported, including the contents of each container and the total number of containers.

parallel loan   A situation in which two corporations have headquarters in two different countries and each makes a loan of equivalent value to the subsidiary of the other company that operates in its country.

P/E (price–earnings) ratio   The ratio of stock price to earnings per share.

"pecking order" theory of financing   A theory of how firms finance their investments with the least information-sensitive sources of funds: first using internally generated cash, then using debt, and finally using equity.

PEFCO (Private Export Funding Corporation)   A private corporation whose mission is to make dollar loans to foreign purchasers of U.S. exports.

pegged currency   A currency whose value relative to other currencies is set by the government; a currency in a fixed exchange rate system. Also known as a fixed currency.

peso problem   A phenomenon that arises when rational investors anticipated events that did not occur during the sample or at least did not occur with the frequency the investors expected.

pink sheet trading   Over-the-counter trading of Level I ADRs in New York.

pip   Trader jargon for the fourth decimal point in a currency quote.

plowback ratio   The fraction of operating profits that management chooses to reinvest in a firm.

political risk   The possibility of a government adversely affecting the return to a foreign investment or the cash flows of a multinational corporation (for example, by imposing exchange controls, taxes on foreign investments, or by outright expropriation).

political risk insurance   Insurance against political risk provided by private firms, governments, and international organizations.

PPP (purchasing power parity)   A simple theory of the determination of exchange rates in which the exchange rate adjusts to equate the internal and external purchasing powers of a currency.

precautionary demand for money   Money balances held because of the uncertain timing of future cash inflows and outflows.

present value   The current value of an expected future payment, which requires discounting of the expected future payments at an appropriate risk adjusted discount factor.

price index   The ratio of the price level at a particular time to the price level in a base year multiplied by 100.

price-driven trading system   A trading system in which market makers stand ready to buy at their bid prices and sell at their ask prices.

price level   The price of a consumption bundle of goods and services.

pricing to market   A situation in which a firm charges different prices for the same good in different markets.

primary market   A market in which corporations raise funds by issuing securities (equities or bonds).

private bourse   A stock market that is privately owned and operated by a corporation founded for the purpose of trading securities.

private placement bonds   Bonds that are not sold to the market at large but that are placed privately with sophisticated, well-endowed investors such as pension funds, life insurance companies, or university endowments.

private saving   The difference between the disposable income and consumption of the private sector.

probability distribution   A description of possible future events associated with a random variable and their respective probabilities of occurrence.

project finance   Financing of a particular industrial project in which the providers of the funds receive a return on their investment primarily from the cash flows generated by the project.

public bourse   A stock market where the government appoints brokers, typically ensuring them a monopoly over all stock market transactions.

purchasing power   The amount of goods and services that can be purchased with an amount of money.

pure discount bond   A bond that promises a single face value payment at the maturity of the bond.

put–call parity   The fundamental no-arbitrage relationship that links the forward rate to the spot rate, the prices of European put and call options at a common strike price, and the domestic currency interest rate.

put option   *See* foreign currency put option.

RADR (Rule 144 ADR)   A capital-raising ADR in which the securities are privately placed with qualified institutional investors, such as pension funds and insurance companies.

range forward contract   A contract that allows a company to specify a range of future spot rates over which the firm can transact in foreign currency at the future spot rate without any other cash flow. If the future spot rate falls outside of the range, the firm transacts at the limits of the range.

ratio analysis   The use of financial ratios in the valuation of firms.

rational expectations   Expectations of investors that do not involve systematic mistakes or systematically biased forecasts.

real appreciation   An increase in the real exchange rate of the denominator currency.

real depreciation   A decrease in the real exchange rate of the denominator currency.

real exchange rate   A nominal exchange rate that is adjusted by the ratio of the price levels in the two countries.

real exchange risk   A change in the profitability of a firm due to changes in real exchange rates. Also known as economic exposure and operating exposure.

real option   The ability of management to strategically alter the future cash flows from a project in response to realizations of certain contingencies.

real profitability   The purchasing power of nominal profits.

received-for-shipment bill of lading   A shipping contract which indicates only that the merchandise is at the dock awaiting transport.

regression analysis   A statistical methodology that tries to find the best fit between a dependent (or explained) variable (denoted y) and an independent (or explanatory) variable (denoted x). Most popular is the linear regression model, where $y = a + bx + e$, and e is the non-explained part, or residual.

REIT (real estate investment trust)   A corporation that invests in real estate and reduces or eliminates corporate income taxes because it is required to distribute a large majority of its income to investors who pay tax on the income they receive.

relative price   The nominal price of a specific good divided by the price level, which consequently has units of general goods per specific good.

relative purchasing power parity   The idea that the rate of change of the exchange rate should offset the difference in the rates of inflation between two countries.

representative office   A small service facility staffed by parent bank personnel that is designed to assist clients of the parent bank in their dealings with the bank's correspondents or with information about local business practices and credit evaluation of the MNC's foreign customers.

required reserves   The amount of a bank's deposit liabilities that it is required to hold as assets at the central bank.

revaluation   A change in a fixed exchange rate that increases the value of the domestic currency relative to foreign currency.

reversal   The process of selling a foreign currency in the forward market and buying it forward with a synthetic forward contract.

revocable D/C   A documentary credit that arranges payment without guaranteeing payment and which indicates that the importer has a working business relationship with a reputable bank.

Ricardian equivalence   The idea that the timing of taxes is irrelevant because individuals will increase their saving in response to a reduction in current taxation because they know that they will be taxed more in the future to pay the interest and principal on the government's debt.

right of offset   A clause in swap agreements and back-to-back loans which stipulates that if one party defaults on a payment, the other party can withhold corresponding payments.

risk-averse entrepreneurs   Individuals who start a company and have a substantial amount of their wealth invested in the non-diversified assets of the company and who therefore desire to lower the variability of the company's cash flows.

risk management   The use of derivative securities to take positions in financial markets that offset the underlying sources of risks that arise in a company's normal course of business.

risk premium   The expected return on an asset in excess of the return on a risk-free asset.

ROI (return on investment)   The change in a firm's future operating profit divided by its current investment.

royalty payments   Fees paid to the owner of intellectual property rights for the right to use a copyright, a patent, a trademark, an industrial design, or procedural knowledge.

Rule 144A   Enacted in 1990 to allow institutional investors in the US to invest in private placement issues that do not necessarily meet the information disclosure requirements of publicly traded issues.

sales on open account   An international trade method in which an exporter establishes an account for an importer, who is allowed to order goods with payment based on an invoiced amount.

sample mean   The average of the realizations of a random variable.

sample variance   The average of the squared deviations of a random variable from the sample mean.

secondary market   A market in which securities are sold by and transferred from one investor or speculator to another, in contrast to the primary market in which firms sell securities to investors to raise capital.

securitization   The packaging of designated pools of loans or receivables into a new financial instrument that can be sold to investors.

segmented market   A security market where local investors, not global investors, price securities.

seigniorage   The real resources the central bank obtains through the creation of base money.

sensitivity analysis   Use of alternative scenarios other than the expected value to determine how the discounted present value of a firm or project changes with important variables that drive firm value.

settle price   The last traded futures price, unless that price is stale, in which case appointed traders in the pit establish the value of the futures price by consensus.

shelf registration   A process through which an issuer in the U.S. can preregister a securities issue and then shelve the securities for later sale when financing is needed.

sight draft   A document indicating that an importer's bank will pay a certain amount to an exporter when the exporter presents the document to the bank after the exporter fulfills its contractual obligations.

Sinosure   The China Export and Credit Insurance Corp., which is a specialized financial intermediary established to help facilitate Chinese exports.

sovereign borrower   A government borrower in international debt markets.

sovereign risk   The risk that a government may default on its bond payments.

speculating   The act of intentionally taking positions in financial markets that are exposed to potential losses in the hope of making profits.

spot interest rate   The interest rate on a deposit when there are no intervening cash flows between the time the deposit is made and the maturity of the deposit.

spot market   The market for the immediate exchange of currencies.

standard deviation   The square root of the variance, also called the volatility of a financial variable.

standard normal random variable   A normal random variable with mean 0 and standard deviation 1.

statistical discrepancy   A technical term for the balancing item in the balance of payments to make credit and debit items sum to zero, which is also called errors and omissions.

sterilized intervention   An intervention in the foreign exchange market that is offset by an open market transaction in the domestic bond market that restores the monetary base to its original size.

sticky prices   The idea that prices of goods and services are slow to adjust compared to asset prices like exchange rates.

straight bill of lading   A bill of lading which is not title to the goods but indicates that a carrier has received merchandise from a shipper and will deliver the merchandise to a designated party.

strategic alliance   An agreement between legally distinct entities to share the costs and benefits of what is hoped to be a beneficial activity.

strike price   The exchange rate in an option contract at which the buyer can transact. Also called the exercise price.

subsidiary bank   A bank that is at least partly owned by a foreign parent bank but that is incorporated in the country in which it is located.

surplus   In balance of payments accounting, the idea that credits on a particular account are greater than debits on that account.

swap   An agreement between two parties to exchange a sequence of cash flows.

swap points   Basis points that must be added to or subtracted from spot exchange rates to obtain outright forward rates.

swap spread   An amount of basis points added to the yield to maturity on a government bond corresponding to that maturity to get the fixed interest rate of an interest rate swap.

SWIFT (Society of Worldwide Interbank Financial Telecommunications)   A computer network in which member banks throughout the world send and receive messages pertaining to foreign exchange transactions, payment confirmations, documentation of international trade, transactions in securities, and other financial matters.

switch trading   The entry of a third party who facilitates the eventual clearing of a trade imbalance between two partners to a bilateral clearing arrangement.

syndicate   A group of banks that take different roles in the debt-arranging process for a single borrower.

synthetic forward   A forward contract manufactured using a spot contract and borrowing and lending, or using put and call options with the same strike price to create an uncontingent purchase or sale of foreign currency at maturity.

systematic risk   The part of the uncertainty of an asset's return that gives rise to risk premiums because it creates a covariance of the return with the return on the market portfolio and thus cannot be diversified away.

TARGET (Trans-European Automated Real-time Gross settlement Express Transfer system)   An electronic payment system that transfers funds and settles transactions in euros.

target zone system   An exchange rate system in which the exchange rate can fluctuate within a fixed band of values.

tax planning   The process of minimizing tax by choosing when to repatriate funds.

tax-loss carry-forward   A tax benefit that allows current business losses to be used to reduce tax liability in future years.

terminal value   The value of a firm attributable to the future beyond an explicit forecasting period.

term structure of interest rates   The relationship between the maturities of different zero-coupon bonds and their corresponding (spot) interest rates.

time draft   A document which indicates that an importer's bank will pay a certain amount to an exporter at a future point in time, after the exporter fulfills its contractual obligations.

time value   The difference between the current price of an option and its intrinsic value.

topping-up clauses   Requirements in debt contracts that additional advances or repayments of principal occur under specified conditions, usually triggered by an exchange rate crossing a preset barrier.

trade acceptance   A draft signed "accepted" by the importer in a documents against acceptance collection.

trade account   An account on the BOP that collects all items on the current account, excluding those associated with flows of investment income.

trade balance   The difference between credits and debits on the trade account.

trade-weighted real exchange rate   An average of all the bilateral real exchange rates of a country using the relative amount of trade between countries as weights.

trading costs   Costs of buying a security, which include a brokerage commission, the bid-ask spread and, potentially, market impact.

transaction demand for money   Money balances held because a firm or an individual predicts having some expenditures that will be incurred in the near future.

transaction exchange risk   The possibility of loss in a business transaction due to adverse fluctuations in exchange rates.

transfer prices   The prices set within a firm when buying or selling goods and services between related entities of the firm.

transfers   Monetary transactions between residents of a country and foreigners, such as gifts and grants, which do not involve purchases or sales of goods, services, or assets.

triangular arbitrage   An arbitrage process involving three currencies that keeps cross-rates (such as euros per British pound) in line with dollar exchange rates.

tripartite arrangement   A contractual arrangement under which an export factor services an exporter, who assigns any credit balances due from the factor to a financial intermediary that provides funds to the exporter.

turnover The total volume of trade done on an exchange during a particular period (for example, 1 year) divided by the exchange's total market capitalization.

two-fund separation The property that the minimum-variance frontier can be spanned (or generated) by any two portfolios on the minimum-variance frontier.

unbiased forecast A forecast for which the average forecast error is zero.

unbiasedness hypothesis The proposition that the forward rate equals the expected future spot rate corresponding to the maturity of the forward rate.

uncovered foreign money market investment An investment in a foreign money market in which the currency exposure is not hedged.

uncovered interest rate parity A theory which holds that the expected rate of return on an unhedged investment of domestic currency in the foreign money market equals the domestic interest rate.

UNCTAD (United Nations Conference on Trade and Development) A permanent intergovernmental body that was established in 1963 as part of the United Nations General Assembly to deal with issues related to international trade, investment, and development.

underinvestment A situation in which managers, acting in the interests of shareholders, do not make investments that would increase the overall value of the firm because too much of the increase in the firm's value is captured by the bondholders.

undervalued currency A currency with smaller external purchasing power than internal purchasing power.

underwriting discount A form of payment to investment banks that issue securities equaling the difference between the value that investors pay for the securities and the value that the firm receives.

universal bank A bank that provides a wide, comprehensive array of services, including securities activities.

utility function A function that mathematically links the consumption of units of real goods to a level of satisfaction.

VAR (value at risk) A measure of the loss that a given portfolio position can experience with a specified probability over a given length of time.

variance The probability weighted average of the squared deviations of a random variable from its mean.

vehicle currency A currency that is actively used in many international financial transactions around the world.

volatility *See* standard deviation.

volatility clustering A property of many financial variables, such as rates of appreciation of currencies and stock returns, in which periods of high or low variance persist over time.

WACC (weighted average cost of capital) A capital budgeting approach that finds the value of the levered firm by discounting forecasts of the all-equity free cash flows with a weighted average of the required rates of return to the firm's debt and equity.

warrant A certificate that grants the bondholder the right to purchase a certain amount of common stock of the company at a specified price. Bonds with warrants are similar to convertible bonds, as both give the investor an equity option, but a warrant is detachable and can trade separately from a bond.

working capital The collection of cash, marketable securities, accounts receivable, and inventories held by a firm at any point in time to facilitate its business.

world CAPM The CAPM that uses a large internationally well-diversified portfolio of securities as the market portfolio.

WTO (World Trade Organization) An international organization based in Geneva, Switzerland, that establishes rules for how international trade is conducted and resolves disputes among its 150 member states.

yield curve The relationship between the maturities of coupon-paying bonds and the yields to maturity on those bonds.

yield to maturity The single common discount rate that equates the present value of a sequence of coupon payments and the final, face-value payment to the current price of the bond.

zero coupon bond *See* pure discount bond.

INDEX

Boldface page number indicates glossary term.

A

Abel, Andrew B., 132
ABN AMRO, 15, 18, 383, 398
Absolute borrowing advantage, **763**–764
Absolute purchasing power parity, **263**–265,
    280–282
Abuaf, Niso, 649
Accounting standards, 440, 441, 449, 622
Accounts receivable, 665, 695–700. *See also*
    Receivables
Ad valorem duties, **691**
Adjusted net present value (ANPV), **555**–584
    in cash flow analysis, 557–562, 574–575
        (*See also* Cash flows)
    discount rates in, 563–564, 607–608
    dividends in, 576, 577–578
    financial side effects in, 562–565
    growth options in, 566–567
    hedging affected by, 627
    in loan analysis, 615–619
    perpetuity formulas, 561, 587–588
    pros and cons of, 597–598
    steps in calculating, 555–557, 590
    in subsidiary analysis (*see* Subsidiaries)
    weighted average cost of capital versus, 595
Adler, Michael, 481n, 503
AEGON, 383
Affiliate banks, 398, **399**
African Development Bank, 20
Agency costs, **558**
Aggarwal, Reena, 455
Ahearne, Alan G., 503, 552
Aitken, Brian J., 27n, 28n, 34
Akhter, Syed H., 706
Al-Eryani, Mohammad F., 706
Alcalá, Francisco, 2n, 34
Alexander, Gordon, 455
Ali, Muhammad, 199n
Aliber, Robert, 212
All-in-cost (AIC) principle, **409**–413
Allayannis, George, 646, 649
Allen, Bill, 251
Allen, Franklin, 15, 34
Allen, Helen, 343, 377
Allen, William B., 686n, 706
Altman, E.I., 564n, 587
AMB, 7
Amegbeto, Koffi, 160n, 176
American Depositary Receipts (ADRs),
    440–442, 450, 488, 490–491.
    See also Cross-listing
American International Group (AIG), 543
American options, 719–**720**
American quote, **44**
American Stock Exchange, 709
Amihud, Yakov, 445, 455
Amiti, Mary, 34
Ammer, John, 56, 65

Andersen, Torben G., 95, 96
Ang, Andrew, 385n, 421, 466, 496, 499, 503
AngloGold, 448–449
AngloGold Ashanti, 449
Anti-globalization, 26–28
Antl, Boris, 750
Antonveneta, 18
Anvari, M., 706
Apedjinou, Kodjo M., 781
Appreciation, **61**–64, 70, 289–291, 299
Arbitrage, **36**
    goods market, 264–265 (*See also*
        Purchasing power parity (PPP))
    interest rate parity and, 180, 185–188,
        190–196
    triangular, 46–51
Arbitrage pricing theory (APT), **497**–498
Arcelor, 1
ARCH model, 93n
Arm's-length price, 689–690
Arndt, Sven W., 333
Arthur Andersen, 12
Ashanti Goldfields Corporation, 448–449
Asian Development Bank (ADB), 20, 389,
    391, 543
Ask rates, **51**. *See also* Bid-ask spreads
Asset market approach, 346–347
Asset securitization, **402**
Asset substitution, **620**
Assets
    in balance of payments, 112–113
    on central bank balance sheet, 145–147
    current, 676, 677 (*See also* Net working
        capital (NWC))
    defined, 103
Association of Southeast Asian Nations
    (ASEAN), **3**, 168
Asymmetric economic shocks, 173
Asymmetric information, 640, 641–642
AT&T Credit Corp., 724
Auer, Peter, 34
Australian Stock Exchange, 430
Autoregressive process, **352**
Aval, **666**
Average-rate options, **746**

B

Bacchetta, Philippe, 132
Back-to-back loans, **778**–779. *See also*
    Currency swaps; Swaps
Baele, Lieven, 503
Baidu.com, 443
Baillie, Richard, 96, 251
Baker, H. Kent, 455
Baker, James, 513
Baker Plan, **513**
Balance of payments (BOP), **102**–133
    account transactions in

capital, 102–103, 107–108
    current, 102–103, 104–107
    official reserves, 108–109
    correcting problems with, 19
    examples, 104–107
    financial openness affecting, 24–25
    Point-Counterpoint, 126–128
    purchasing power parity and, 282
    surpluses and deficits in, 109–118
        capital and financial accounts,
            111–113, 115
        current account, 109–111, 113–114
        effects of, 118–122
        official settlements account, 115–116
        savings and spending link to, 122–126,
            128–129
        worldwide statistics, 116–118
Balance-sheet hedge, **381**–382
Ball, Ray, 622, 624
Banca D'Italia, 15
Banca Nazionale del Lavoro, 15
Banca Popolare Italiana (BPI), 15
Banco Bilbao Vizcaya Argentario, 15
Bangkok International Banking
    Facilities, 400
Bank for International Settlements (BIS), **21**
    bond market definitions, 391
    forward contract survey, 82
    on international investment position, 121
    on offshore banking centers, 399
    on trade volume risk, 59
    trading volume of, 38
Bank holidays, 198n
Bank line of credit, 663–664
Bank Negara, 198
Bank of America, 525
Bank of Credit and Commerce International
    (BCCI), 399
Bank of New York, 440, 443
Bank of Tokyo, 415
Banker's acceptance (B/A), **657**, 659–660,
    664–665
Banker's bourses, **427**
Bankhaus Herstatt, 58
Banking. *See* Central banks; International
    banking
Bansal, Ravi, 239n, 251
Barclays Global Investors (BGI), 18,
    364, 398
Barings Bank, 8
Barrett, M. Edgar, 706
Barrier options, **746**
Barro, Robert J., 132
Bartelsman, E. J., 689n, 706
Barter, international, 671
Base money, 145
Basel Accord, 385, **402**–403, 407
Basel Committee on Banking Supervision,
    21, 402, 406
Basel II framework, 21, 402–403